THE OXFORD
SCHOOL
DICTIONARY

COMPILED BY

DOROTHY C. MACKENZIE

THIRD EDITION

REVISED BY

JOAN PUSEY

OXFORD UNIVERSITY PRESS

Oxford University Press, Walton Street, Oxford OX2 6DP

OXFORD LONDON GLASGOW
NEW YORK TORONTO MELBOURNE WELLINGTON
KUALA LUMPUR SINGAPORE JAKARTA HONG KONG TOKYO
DELHI BOMBAY CALCUTTA MADRAS KARACHI
NAIROBI DAR ES SALAAM CAPE TOWN

© *Oxford University Press 1974*

First edition 1957
Second edition 1960
Third edition 1974
Reprinted 1974 (with corrections), 1975
1976 (with corrections), 1976 (twice)
Eleventh impression 1979

Filmset by computer
Printed in Hong Kong by Dai Nippon Printing Co. (H.K.) Ltd.

CONTENTS

PREFACE

THIS completely revised edition has been type-set by computer in order to simplify the incorporation of up-to-date material in future impressions. Although the scope of the dictionary has been extended, its purpose remains unchanged: it is designed as a school dictionary for English-speaking pupils between the ages of 11 and 16.

The entire text of the previous edition has been scrutinized and revised in the light of the latest available information, and a special effort has been made to provide definitions which are clear and straightforward. The vocabulary has been considerably enlarged by the addition of new words, senses, and phrases which reflect the present times, including the more common scientific and technical terms. Some obsolete and archaic words and expressions have been dropped, whereas others of literary or historical significance have been retained or added.

Because of the space taken up by the increased vocabulary, it has not been possible to include etymologies. It is hoped that such information, when it is needed, will be readily obtainable by reference to a larger dictionary (e.g., the *Concise Oxford Dictionary* or the *Pocket Oxford Dictionary*) in the classroom.

New features of this edition include an appendix of adjectives relating to some proper nouns, rules for the spelling of regular inflected forms of words, an expanded guide to pronunciation, and a section entitled *Notes on the Use of the Dictionary* which follows this preface and to which the reader's attention is especially drawn.

While making this revision, the Editor has had the advantage of working in the *Oxford English Dictionary* rooms at the Clarendon Press, with full use of the reference library and the quotation files built up by the Editor of *A Supplement to the Oxford English Dictionary*, Mr. R. W. Burchfield, and his colleagues. She is grateful to him and to members of the O.E.D. Department for help of various kinds. She would also like to express her thanks to the many members of the teaching profession who gave advice and help in the planning of this edition, and to Miss Joyce Hawkins who read the proofs and made a large number of useful suggestions.

E. J. P.

November 1973

iv

NOTES ON THE USE OF THE DICTIONARY

1. **Dictionary entries.** Words defined are arranged in alphabetical order. The word at the beginning of each entry, the **headword**, is printed in **bold** type. Compounds of this, and words derived from it (derivatives), are often included in the same entry and are also printed in **bold** type. A definition is given for each of these unless the meaning can easily be worked out from that given for the headword, e.g.

> **bas′kėt** (bah-), *n.* container of plaited or woven osier, cane, etc. **basket-ball,** team game played, usu. indoors, with large inflated ball and basket-like goals. **bas′kėtful,** *n.* (pl. *-fuls*).

Words with the same spelling but with different and unconnected meanings are given separate entries and numbered, e.g.

> **peer**[1], *v. i.* look closely (*at, into*).

> **peer**[2], *n.* person's equal in rank or merit; duke, earl, marquis, viscount, or baron.

Words which can be spelt in more than one way are given as follows:

> **wag′on, wagg′on** (either spelling is correct). **quartet(te)′** (the word can be spelt either 'quartet' or 'quartette'). Sometimes part of a compound is bracketed, e.g. **reverse (gear).** This means that the gear can be called either 'reverse' or 'reverse gear'.

Phrases are usually entered under the headword and are printed in *italic* type (or '*italics*'), e.g.

> **hand,** *n.* extremity of human arm beyond wrist or of limb of monkey, etc. . . . *at hand,* near. *in hand,* available; receiving attention; under control. *to hand,* within reach, accessible.

2. **Pronunciation.** For a full explanation of the method used to show how words are pronounced, see PRONUNCIATION, p. x.

3. **Parts of speech.** These are given after the headword and before the definition. They are also given after derivatives, but are not usually given after compounds or phrases. They are printed in *italic* type, and abbreviated, e.g. *n., v., a., adv.,* etc. (see ABBREVIATIONS USED IN THE DICTIONARY, p. viii).

If a word can act as more than one part of speech, the abbreviation is given before the meaning or set of meanings to which it applies, e.g.

> **fīle**[3], *n.* row of persons, etc., one behind the other. *v. i.* march or walk in file.

v

Sometimes in a short entry the two are put together, e.g.

chuck′le, *n.* & *v. i.* (make) suppressed sound expressing mirth, exultation, etc.

4. Inflexion. Inflected forms of words are given when they are irregular or difficult. They are printed in *italic* type and in brackets after the part of speech, e.g. **drive,** *v.* (p. t. *drōve*; p. p. *driven*); **wife,** *n.* (pl. *wives*). See INFLEXION, p. vii.

5. Definitions. These are printed in ordinary ('roman') type. Different meanings are usually separated by a semi-colon, e.g.

chest, *n.* large strong box; coffer; upper front part of body.

Brackets are used in some definitions to save space by avoiding repetition. For example the word 'maize' can mean either the seed of a cereal plant or the plant itself. The two are put together thus:

maize, *n.* (edible seed of) American cereal plant.

Words which always or very frequently occur with the headword to form a phrase are printed in *italic* type, e.g.

amount′, *v. i.* add up *to*; be equivalent *to*.

rèbel′, *v. i.* (p. t. *rebelled*), act as rebel (*against*).

In the latter example '*against*' is bracketed because the verb 'rebel' can also be used without it.

Some words or senses have a usage or subject 'label' in brackets, e.g. (*archaic*), (*informal*), (Chem.), (Mus.), (Hist.). The abbreviations used in this way are given in ABBREVIATIONS USED IN THE DICTIONARY (see p. viii), and the words thus used are defined in their alphabetical places in the dictionary.

6. Foreign words and phrases. Some foreign words are used in English but are still felt to be 'foreign'. In entries for these, the language from which they come is shown at the end of the entry, e.g.

carte blanche (kart blahnsh), full power to act according to one's judgement. (French)

in memor′iam, in memory of. (Latin)

7. Hyphens. When a compound word that is normally hyphened falls partly in one line and partly in the next, the hyphen is printed at the line-end and repeated at the beginning of the next line. When a word which normally contains no hyphen has to be divided (e.g. 'repetition' in paragraph 5 above, and 'judgement' in paragraph 6) the hyphen is not repeated at the beginning of the next line.

8. Appendices. These are printed at the end of the book. APPENDIX I: *Prefixes and Suffixes*; APPENDIX II: *Adjectives relating to some Geographical and other Proper Nouns*; APPENDIX III: *Some Abbreviations in General Use*.

INFLEXION

A WORD is 'inflected' when it is changed, for example by the addition of a suffix to a noun, verb, or adjective, to form another word, especially of one of the kinds mentioned below. In the following rules for the spelling of regular inflected forms of words, the terms used are:

sibilants = s, x, z, sh, or ch (except where pronounced k or *ch*)
-o words = words ending in -o but not -oo (e.g. *potato*, but not *moo*)
-e words = words ending in silent (or 'mute') -e
-y words = words ending in -y not preceded by a vowel (e.g. *cry, deny, puppy*, but not *play, donkey*)

RULES:

1. **Plural of nouns.** Words ending in a sibilant add -es (*guesses, boxes, churches*); -y words change -y into -ies (*cries, puppies*); the plural of -o words is always given, thus: **phō′tō,** *n.* (pl. *photos*); **potā′tō,** *n.* (pl. *potatoes*); other nouns add -s (*books, pages, plates, days, births, zoos*).

2. **Possessive of nouns.** Singular nouns, and plural nouns that do not end in -s, take apostrophe s (*man's, baby's, James's; men's, geese's*); plural nouns ending in -s take an apostrophe only (*boys', girls'*).

3. **Comparative and superlative of adjectives and adverbs.** Monosyllables, and some words of two syllables (e.g. those ending in -y), add -er and -est (*colder, soonest*), -e words dropping the -e (*abler, purest*), and -y words changing -y into -ier, -iest (*drier, funniest*); in other cases *more* and *most* are used (*more beautiful, most comfortable*). Monosyllables double a final single consonant (except -x and -w) if preceded by a single vowel (*dimmer, hottest*).

4. **Third person singular present of verbs.** -o words and words ending in sibilants add -es (*goes, pushes*); -y words change -y into -ies (*cries, hurries*); other words add -s (*sings, writes, plays, coos*).

5. **Past tense and past participle of verbs.** -e words add -d (*amused*); -y words change -y into -ied (*carried*); other verbs add -ed (*corrected, finished, played, visited*); if the final consonant is doubled, it is stated in the dictionary, thus: **rub,** *v.* (p. t. *rubbed*); **admit′,** *v.* (p. t. *admitted*); **trav′el,** *v.* (p. t. *travelled*).

6. **Present participle of verbs.** All verbs add -ing (*fishing, going, saying, crying, visĭting*), -e words dropping the -e (*dancing*); monosyllables double a final single consonant (except -w or -x) if preceded by a single vowel (*getting, shedding, cramming*); if the final consonant of other verbs is doubled in the past tense, it is doubled also in the present participle (*admitting, travelling*).

7. **Addition of suffixes** (see APPENDIX I). -y words of more than one syllable change y into i when adding -able to form adjectives (*variable*); -er to form nouns denoting agent (*carrier*); -less to form adjectives (*penniless*); -ly to form adverbs (*happily*); -ness to form nouns (*cowardliness*).

Exceptions to the above rules are given in the dictionary, thus: **loaf**, *n.* (pl. *loaves*); **far**, *a.* (*farther, farthest*); **tāke**, *v.* (p. t. *took*; p. p. *taken*); **permit'** *v.* (p. t. *permitted*). In the last example the past participle is not given separately because it is identical in form to the past tense.
Regular forms are given where there might be doubt or confusion.

ABBREVIATIONS USED IN THE DICTIONARY

For a list of *Abbreviations in General Use* see APPENDIX III

(Some of the abbreviations that follow may appear in either roman or *italic* type)

a., aa., adjective(s)
abs., absolute
abbrev., abbreviation
adj., adjective, adjectival
adjj., adjectives
adv., advv., adverb(s)
Afr., African
Amer., American
Anglo-Ind., Anglo-Indian
approx., approximate(ly)
Archit., architecture
Arith., arithmetic
Astron., astronomy
attrib., attributive(ly)
Austral., Australian
aux., auxiliary

Bibl., biblical

Biol., biology
Bot., botany

c., circa (L.), about
c., century
cent., cents., century, centuries
Ch., Church
Chem., chemistry
comb., combination, combining
compar., comparative
cond., conditional
conj., conjunction
contempt., contemptuous(ly)
cu., cubic
cwt., hundredweight

d., *denarius, denarii* (L.), (old) penny, pence

E., east(ern)
E. Afr., East African
e.g. *exempli gratia* (L.), for example
E. Ind., East Indian
Electr., electricity
esp., especially
etc., etcetera
excl., exclamation
expr., expressing

fem., feminine
Feud., feudal
fig., figurative(ly)
Footb., football

ABBREVIATIONS USED IN THE DICTIONARY

ft., foot, feet

G.B., Great Britain
Geog., geography
Geol., geology
Geom., geometry
Gk., Greek
Gk. myth., Greek mythology
Gram., grammar
Gt., Great

Herald., heraldry
Hist., historical(ly), history

i., intransitive
i.e., *id est* (L.), that is
imper., imperative
impers., impersonal
in., inch(es)
ind., indicative
inf., infinitive
int., interjection
interrog., interrogative(ly)
Ir., Irish

L., Latin
£, pound(s) sterling
lb., pound(s) (in weight)

Math., mathematics
Mech., mechanics
Med., medicine
Mil., military
Mus., music
Myth., mythology

N., north(ern)
n., noun
N. Amer., North American
Naut., nautical
N.B., *nota bene* (L.), note well.
NE., north-east
neg., negative
n. fem., noun feminine
nn., nouns
north., northern
n. pl., noun plural

N.T., New Testament
NW., north-west
N.Z., New Zealand

obj., objective
obs., obsolete
opp. (as) opposed to, opposite
orig., originally
O.T., Old Testament
oz., ounce(s)

P., proprietary term (see p. xii)
p., page, participle, (new) penny or pence
part., participle
pass., passive
pers., person(al)
Photog., photography
phr., phrr., phrase(s)
Phys., physics
Physiol., physiology
pl., plural
Poet., poetic
poss., possessive
p. p., past participle
pr., pronounced
pred. a., predicative adjective
pref., prefix
prep., preposition
pres., present
pres. ind., present indicative
pres. p., present participle
pron., pronoun
Psychol., psychology
p. t., past tense

R.A.F., Royal Air Force
R.C. (Ch.), Roman Catholic (Church)
refl., reflexive
rel., relative
Rom., Roman
Rom. myth., Roman mythology

S., south(ern)
s., singular, shilling(s)
S. Afr., South African
S. Amer., South American
Sc., Scots, Scottish
SE., south-east
sent., sentence
sing., singular
Sp., Spanish
Sp. Amer., Spanish American
sq., square
subj., subjective
suf., suffix
superl., superlative
Surg., surgery
SW., south-west

t., transitive
Theatr., theatrical
Theol., theology
trans., transitive
Trig., trigonometry

U.K., United Kingdom
Univ., university
U.S., United States (of America)
U.S.A., United States of America
usu., usually

v., verb (transitive and intransitive)
v. aux., verb auxiliary
v. i., verb intransitive
v. refl., verb reflexive
v. t., verb transitive
vv., verbs

W., west(ern)
W. Afr., West African
W. Ind., West Indian

yd., yds., yard(s)

Zool., zoology

PRONUNCIATION

THE pronunciation indicated represents the standard speech of southern England. It is shown by marks on the headwords or derivatives, or given in brackets immediately after these, e.g. **cōld, laugh** (lahf).

Words of two or more syllables are usually pronounced with one syllable accented more heavily than the rest of the word. This is shown by the **stress mark '** placed after the stressed syllable, e.g. **bī'nary, partic'ūlar.** It is not usually given for hyphened compounds, in which the regular usage is for the first word to be stressed, e.g. **knee-cap.**

The sounds represented are as follows:

Vowels

a	as in cat		er	as in per'son
ā	as in plāte		ēr	as in hēre
ah	as in shah		eu	as in feud
ai	as in pain		ew	as in new
air	as in fair		i	as in ill
ar	as in cart		ī	as in sīde
ār	as in cāre		ie	as in thief
au	as in haul		ir	as in bird
aw	as in law		īr	as in hīre
ay	as in say		o	as in hot
e	as in let		ō	as in pōst

but final **e** when unmarked is silent (or 'mute'), i.e. not pronounced, thus **āpe** is pronounced āp. Where final e is pronounced, it is marked, e.g. as in **re'cipė.** Where e is silent in the headword, it is silent also (unless marked) in compounds and derivatives placed in the same entry, e.g. **shāme, shāme'fāced, shāme'ful, shāme'less.**

			oa	as in boat
			oi	as in coin
			oo	as in book
			ōō	as in rōōm
			oor	as in moor
			or	as in port
			ou	as in found
			ow	as in how
			oy	as in boy
			u	as in cup
ē	as in hē		ū	as in dū'ty
ė	as in bėgin', nā'kėd, pock'ėt		ur	as in burn
ea	as in beat		ūr	as in pūre
ear	as in fear		y	as in happ'y
ee	as in bee			(see also consonant y)
eer	as in cheer		ȳ	as in crȳ
ei	as in cei'ling		ȳr	as in tȳre

Unmarked vowels which occur in unstressed syllables often represent vague or indistinct sounds, e.g. the **a** in **absurd'**; the **o** in **hill'ock**; the **u** in **cheer'ful.**

PRONUNCIATION

Consonants

b as in **bat**

c as in **cat**
but **c** before **e, i,** or **y,** is 'soft' and
= s, as in **īce, scent, cit′y, ī′cy.**

ch as in **chin**

ch as in **loch** (-*ch*)

d as in **dog**

dg as in **hedge**

dh as in **that** (dh-)

dj as in **adj′ĕctive**

f as in **fat**

g as in **gō**
but **g** before **e, i,** or **y,** is 'soft' and
= j, as in **āge, gī′ant, or′gy.** Pronunciation is given for all exceptions
to this rule, e.g., **get** (g-), **bĕgin′** (-g-).

h as in **hat**

j as in **jam**

k as in **king**

l as in **lot**

m as in **mē**

n as in **nō**
but **n** before **k,** 'hard' **c, q,** or **x**
= ng, as in **sink**
and **ñ** indicates French nasalization of

the preceding vowel as in **fiancé**
(fiahn′sā)

ng as in **sing**

ngg as in **fing′er** (-ngg-)

p as in **pen**

ph as in **phō′tō**

qu as in **queen**

r as in **road**

rh as in **rhȳme**

s as in **sit**

sh as in **shop**

t as in **top**

tch as in **catch**

th as in **thin**

v as in **van**

w as in **wish**

wh is pronounced w *or* hw
as in **when, whȳ,** etc., *except* where
pronunciation is given in brackets,
e.g. **who** (hoō)

x as in **fox**

y as in **yard**
(see also vowels y, **ȳ**)

z as in **zoō**

zh as in **divi′sion** (-zhn)

The following word-endings are pronounced as here shown:

-ace = -is, as in **pref′ace**

-age = -ij, as in **vill′age**

-al, -el preceded by **t, d,** or **n** = -l, as in
den′tal, funn′el

-en, -ent preceded by **t, d** = -n, -nt, as in
fatt′en, stū′dent

-ey = i, as in **donk′ey**

-le after consonant(s) = -l, as in **ax′le,
buck′le, kett′le**

-ous = -us, as in **fūr′ious**

-sm = -zm, as in **bap′tism**

-tion = -shn, as in **ac′tion, nā′tion**

-ture = -cher, as in **nā′ture**
or -tūr, as in **ca′ricatūre**
Some common words ending in **-ture**
can be pronounced either -cher *or*
-tūr.

PROPRIETARY TERMS

THIS dictionary includes some words which are or are asserted to be proprietary names or trade marks. Their inclusion does not imply that they have acquired for legal purposes either a non-proprietary or general significance or any other judgement concerning their legal status. In cases where the editor has some evidence that the word is used as a proprietary name or trade mark this is indicated by the symbol **P**, but no judgement concerning the legal status of such words is made or implied thereby.

xii

A

A1 (ā wun), *a.* (of ship) first-class; (*informal*) excellent, perfect.

a, an[1], *a.* (*indefinite article*: *a* before consonant; *an* before vowel sound or silent *h*, e.g. *an hour*) one; any; per, each.

a-[1], *pref.* on, in, at; up; of, from.

a-[2], **an-**[1], *pref.* (*a-* before consonant; *an-* before vowel or *h*), not, without.

a-[3], *pref.*: see **ad-**.

ab-, abs-, a-[4], *pref.* (*ab-* in most cases; *abs-* before *c, q, t*; *a-* before *v*), away, off.

aback', *adv. taken aback*, surprised, disconcerted.

ab'acus, *n.* (pl. *abacī* or *abacuses*), calculating frame with balls or beads sliding on wires.

aban'don, *v.t.* give up; desert. *n.* careless freedom of manner. **aban'doned**, *a.* forsaken; given up to bad ways. **aban'donment**, *n.*

abāse', *v.t.* degrade; humble; humiliate. **abāse'ment**, *n.*

abash', *v.t.* cause to feel embarrassed or confused. **abashed'**, *a.*

abāte', *v.* make or become less. **abāte'ment**, *n.*

abattoir (ab'atwar), *n.* slaughter-house.

abb'ess, *n.* woman superior of community of nuns.

abb'ey, *n.* community of monks or nuns; monastic buildings; church of an abbey.

abb'ot, *n.* superior of community of monks.

abbrē'viāte, *v.t.* shorten. **abbrēviā'tion**, *n.* short form, esp. of a word.

A B C (ābēsē), alphabet; rudiments (*of* subject); alphabetical railway timetable.

ab'dicāte, *v.* give up (an office); renounce the throne. **abdicā'tion**, *n.*

ab'domen (*or* abdō'men), *n.* front part of body below diaphragm, belly; hinder part of insect's body. **abdom'inal**, *a.*

abduct', *v.t.* kidnap; carry off (person) illegally. **abduc'tion, abduc'tor**, *nn.*

abeam', *adv.* on line at right angles to ship's length.

aberrā'tion, *n.* mental or moral slip or error; deviation from type; distortion. **abe'rrant**, *a.*

abet', *v.t.* (p.t. *abetted*), help or encourage, esp. in wrongdoing. **abett'er**, *n.* **abett'or**, *n.* (Law).

abey'ance (-bā-), *n.* state of suspension or temporary disuse.

abhor', *v.t.* (p.t. *abhorred*), regard with disgust and hatred, detest. **abho'rrence**, *n.* **abho'rrent**, *a.*

abide', *v.* (p.t. & p.p. *abōde*), remain, stay (*archaic*, Poet.); tolerate. *abide by*, keep (promise, etc.). **abī'ding**, *a.* permanent, lasting.

abil'ity, *n.* power or capacity (*to* do); cleverness, talent.

ab'ject, *a.* degraded; wretched; contemptible. **ab'jectness**, *n.*

abjure' (-joor), *v.t.* renounce on oath. **abjurā'tion**, *n.*

ab'lative, *a. & n.* (Gram.) (case) expressing source, agent, cause, etc.

ab'laut (-owt), *n.* vowel-change in related words, as in *sing, sang, sung*.

ablāze' *adv. & a.* on fire; glittering.

ā'ble, *a.* (*abler, ablest*), having the means or ability (*to* do); clever, competent. *able-bodied*, physically fit, robust. **ā'bly**, *adv.*

ablu'tion (-loo-), *n.* ceremonial or (pl.) ordinary washing of hands or body.

abnēgā'tion, *n.* denial; renunciation.

abnor'mal, *a.* different from what is normal, usual, or expected. **abnor'mally**, *adv.* **abnormal'ity**, *n.*

aboard' (-ord), *adv. & prep.* on board.

abōde'[1], *n.* dwelling-place, home.

abōde[2], *p.t. & p.p.* of **abide**.

abol'ish, *v.t.* do away with, put an end to. **aboli'tion**, *n.* abolishing.

A-bomb (ā-), *abbrev.* atomic bomb.

abom'inable, *a.* detestable, disgusting. *abominable snowman*, see **yeti**. **abom'ināte**, *v.t.* loathe. **abominā'tion**, *n.* (act or object deserving) disgust and hatred.

abori'ginal, *a.* existing in a country from the beginning. *n.* earliest inhabitant. **abori'ginēs** (-z), *n.pl.* aboriginal inhabitants (*also in sing.*, **abori'ginė**).

abort', *v.* (cause to) miscarry; remain undeveloped; come to nothing; (U.S.) terminate (e.g. mission of spacecraft) in emergency.

abor'tion, *n.* expulsion of foetus from womb before it is capable of surviving; operation, etc., causing this; failure (of plan, etc.).

abor'tive, *a.* coming to nothing; unsuccessful.

abound', *v.i.* be plentiful; be rich *in*, teem *with*.

about', *adv. & prep.* all round; somewhere round; here and there; astir; approximately; facing round; in connection with, concerning. *about to* (do), on the point of (doing).

above' (-uv), *adv.* higher up, overhead; in

addition to. *prep.* over; higher than; more than. **above-board**, *pred. a. & adv.* open(ly), fair(ly).

abracadab'ra, *n.* spell; gibberish.

abrăde', *v.t.* scrape off, wear away, injure (skin, etc.), by rubbing. **abrā'sion** (-zhn), *n.* **abrā'sive**, *a. & n.* (substance) capable of rubbing or grinding down.

abreast' (-est), *adv.* side by side (in advancing). *abreast of*, not behind (times, etc.).

abridge', *v.t.* condense, shorten. **abridge'-ment**, *n.*

abroad' (-awd), *adv.* out of one's country; widely, in different directions.

ab'rogăte, *v.t.* repeal; cancel. **abrogā'tion**, *n.*

abrupt', *a.* sudden; hasty; steep. **abrupt'-ness**, *n.*

abs-, *pref.*: see **ab-**.

ab'scess (-ses), *n.* collection of pus in any part of the body.

abscond', *v.i.* go away secretly; flee from the law.

ab'sence, *n.* being absent or away; lack.

ab'sent, *a.* not present; lacking. **absent'**, *v. refl.* stay away. **absent-minded**, preoccupied, not paying attention. **ab'sently**, *adv.* absent-mindedly.

absentee', *n.* person not present, esp. not at work. **absentee landlord**, one living away from his property. **absentee'ism**, *n.* (esp.) habitual absence from work without good reason.

ab'sinth(e), *n.* wormwood; liqueur flavoured with wormwood or other herbs.

ab'solūte (*or* -ŏŏt), *a.* complete, entire; not limited; despotic; (Gram., of form of word) standing independently. **ab'solutely**, *adv.*

absolu'tion (-ŏŏ- *or* -ŭ-), *n.* absolving; forgiveness of sins, esp. through a religious act.

absolve', *v.t.* set free (from sin, etc.); declare not guilty.

absorb', *v.t.* drink in; suck in; hold the attention of. **absorbed'**, *a.* deeply interested. **absor'bent**, *n. & a.* (substance) that absorbs (moisture, etc.).

absorp'tion, *n.* absorbing, being absorbed; deep interest.

abstain', *v.i.* hold oneself back, esp. from drinking alcohol; refrain from using vote. **abstain'er**, *n.*

abstē'mioùs, *a.* sparing or moderate in consuming food, drink, etc.

absten'tion, *n.* refraining, holding back; not using one's vote.

ab'stinence, *n.* refraining from food, drink, pleasure, etc. **ab'stinent**, *a.*

ab'stract, *a.* not concrete; ideal, theoretical; (of noun) expressing a quality. *n.* summary. **abstract'**, *v.t.* remove; steal; summarize. **abstrac'ted**, *a.* absent-minded. **abstrac'-tion**, *n.* taking away; absent-mindedness.

abstruse' (-ŏŏs), *a.* hard to understand; profound.

absurd', *a.* unreasonable, ridiculous. **ab-**

sur'dity, *n.*

abun'dance, *n.* plenty, more than enough. **abun'dant**, *a.* plentiful.

abūse' (-z), *v.t.* misuse; revile. **abūse'** (-s), *n.* misuse; unjust or corrupt practice; insolent language. **abū'sive** (-s-), *a.* insulting. **abū'-siveness**, *n.*

abut', *v.* (p.t. *abutted*), border (*on*); end *on*, lean *against*. **abut'ment**, *n.* (Archit.) masonry supporting end of arch, etc.

abys'mal (-z-), *a.* bottomless; (fig.) extreme.

abyss', *n.* bottomless chasm; deep gorge.

ac-, *pref.*: see **ad-**.

acā'cia (-sha), *n.* genus of leguminous trees and shrubs.

academ'ic, *a.* scholarly; theoretical, logical, not practical. **academ'ical**, *a.* of a college or university. **academi'cian** (-shn), *n.* member of an academy (esp. Royal Academy of Arts).

acad'emy, *n.* place of study or special training; society for art, literature, etc.

accēde' (aks-), *v.i.* agree (*to*). *accede to*, enter upon (office or dignity), come to (throne).

acceleran'dō (aks-), (as musical direction, abbrev. *accel.*) gradually faster.

accel'erăte (aks-), *v.* increase speed (of). **accelerā'tion**, *n.* **accel'erător**, *n.* thing that increases speed, esp. device opening throttle of motor car, etc.; apparatus for giving high speed to electrons, etc.

ac'cent (aks-), *n.* stress on a syllable; mark indicating vowel quality, stress, etc.; particular way of pronouncing; rhythmical stress. **accent'**, *v.t.* mark with accent(s); emphasize. **accen'tūăte**, *v.t.* emphasize. **accentūā'tion**, *n.*

accept' (aks-), *v.* receive (something offered); answer affirmatively; agree to; believe. **accept'able**, *a.* welcome. **accept'ance**, *n.* accepting or being accepted.

ac'cess (aks-), *n.* approach, admittance; attack (of illness, anger, etc.).

access'ible (aks-), *a.* that can be reached. **accessibil'ity**, *n.*

accession (akse'shn), *n.* acceding (esp. to throne); thing added.

access'ory (aks-), *a.* additional. *n.* helper in (esp. criminal) act; accessory thing, accompaniment; (pl.) useful additions to car, bicycle, woman's dress, etc.

ac'cidence (aks-), *n.* part of grammar dealing with inflexions.

ac'cident (aks-), *n.* unexpected happening; unintentional act; mishap, disaster; **acci-den'tal**, *a.*

acclaim', *v.t.* welcome loudly; hail. *n.* shout of applause; **acclamā'tion**, *n.*

accli'matize, *v.t.* accustom to a new climate. **acclīmatīzā'tion**, *n.*

accliv'ity, *n.* upward slope.

acc'olăde, *n.* ceremony of conferring knighthood.

accomm'odăte, *v.t.* adapt; oblige; find lodg-

ing for. **accomm'odäting,** *a.* obliging.
accommodä'tion, *n.* lodging; adjustment.
accom'paniment (akum-), *n.* accompanying thing; (Mus.) part supporting solo instrument, voice, etc. **accom'panist,** *n.* performer of accompaniment.
accom'pany (-um-), *v.t.* go with; (Mus.) support by playing accompaniment.
accom'plice (-um-), *n.* partner in crime.
accom'plish (-um-), *v.t.* perform, carry out, succeed in doing. **accom'plishment,** *n.* achievement; (pl.) skill in music, art, etc.
accord', *v.* agree, be consistent, *with*); grant. *n.* agreement; harmony; consent. *of one's own accord,* voluntarily. **accor'dance,** *n.* agreement, conformity.
accor'ding, *adv.* (with *as*) in proportion as; (with *to*) in a manner consistent with; as stated by. **accor'dingly,** *adv.* in accordance with what preceded; therefore.
accor'dion, *n.* portable musical instrument with bellows, keys, and metal reeds.
accost', *v.t.* approach and speak to.
account', *v.* consider, regard as. *account for,* give reckoning for, explain. *n.* reckoning; statement of money received and paid, with balance; explanation; narration. *on account of,* because of. *take account of, take into account,* take into consideration.
accoun'table, *a.* responsible; explicable. **accountabil'ity,** *n.*
accoun'tant, *n.* keeper or inspector of accounts. **accoun'tancy,** *n.* profession, duties, of an accountant.
accout'rements (-ōōt-), *n.pl.* equipment, trappings.
accred'it, *v.t.* send out with credentials (as ambassador, etc.). **accred'itĕd,** *a.* officially recognized.
accrē'tion, *n.* growth, esp. by external addition.
accrue' (-ōō), *v.i.* come as natural increase or result.
accū'mulāte, *v.* pile up; grow numerous, continue to increase. **accūmulā'tion,** *n.* **accū'mulative,** *a.*
accū'mulātor, *n.* rechargeable electric battery.
acc'ūrate, *a.* exact, correct. **acc'ūracy,** *n.*
accurs'ĕd, *a.* under a curse; detestable.
accūsā'tion (-z-), *n.* accusing or being accused; charge of doing wrong.
accū'sative (-z-), *a. & n.* (Gram.) (case) indicating object of action, etc.
accūse' (-z-) *v.t.* charge with wrong or unlawful act; blame. **accū'ser,** *n.*
accus'tom, *v.t.* make (person, etc.) used (*to* or *to doing* something). **accus'tomed** (-md), *a.* usual.
āce, *n.* the 'one' on playing-cards; expert airman; champion. *within an ace of* (victory, death, etc.), very close to.
acerb'ity, *n.* sourness; bitterness of speech, manner, or temper.

a'cétāte, *n.* salt of acetic acid, esp. cellulose acetate, used for textile fibre, etc.
acē'tic, *a.* of vinegar, sour. **acetic acid,** acid contained in vinegar.
acet'ylēne, *n.* colourless gas that burns with very bright flame.
ache (āk), *v.i. & n.* (suffer) continuous or prolonged pain or longing.
achieve', *v.t.* accomplish; reach successfully. **achieve'ment,** *n.*
Achilles heel (akil'ēz), vulnerable part. **Achilles tendon,** tendon connecting calf muscles to bone of heel.
a'cid, *a.* sour; of acid(s). *n.* sour substance; (Chem.) compound, usu. sour and corrosive, containing hydrogen which may be replaced by a metal to form a salt. **acid test,** (esp.) severe or conclusive test. **acid'ity,** *n.*
acid'ūlātĕd, *a.* made slightly sour. **acid'ūlous,** *a.* slightly acid.
acknowl'edge (aknol-), *v.t.* admit the truth of; show recognition of; announce receipt of; express appreciation of. **acknowl'edgement,** *n.*
ac'mĕ, *n.* highest point; perfection.
ac'nĕ, *n.* skin eruption with pimples esp. on face.
ac'olyte, *n.* attendant, assistant.
ac'onite, *n.* plant with poisonous root.
ā'corn, *n.* fruit of oak, oval nut growing in shallow woody cup.
acotylĕd'on, *n.* plant with no distinct cotyledons, as fern, moss, etc.
acous'tic (-ōō-), *a.* of hearing; of sound.
acous'tics, *n.* science of sound; properties of room, etc., in respect of audibility of sounds. **acous'tical,** *a.*
acquaint', *v.t.* make aware or familiar; inform. *be acquainted with,* have personal knowledge of. **acquain'tance,** *n.* being acquainted; person one knows slightly but not intimately.
acquiesce (akwēes'), *v.i.* agree, esp. silently or without protest. **acquies'cence,** *n.* **acquies'cent,** *a.*
acquire', *v.t.* gain, get, come to have. **acquired',** *a.* gained, not inherited or innate.
acquisi'tion (-z-), *n.* act of gaining; thing gained; useful addition. **acquis'itive,** *a.* eager to acquire.
acquit', *v.t.* (p.t. *acquitted*), declare not guilty. *acquit oneself,* play one's part. **acquitt'al,** *n.* deliverance from charge by verdict of 'not guilty'.
acre (ā'ker), *n.* measure of area (4,840 sq. yds., 4,047 sq. m.); (pl.) lands, fields. **acreage** (-rij), *n.* number of acres, extent of land.
ac'rid, *a.* sharp, biting. **acrid'ity,** *n.*
ac'rimony, *n.* bitterness of temper or manner. **acrimō'nious,** *a.*
ac'robat, *n.* performer of spectacular gymnastic feats. **acrobat'ic,** *a.* **acrobat'ics,** *n. pl.* acrobatic feats.
ac'ronym, *n.* word formed from initial letters

of other words (e.g. *Ernie, Nato*).

acrop′olis, *n.* upper fortified part of Gk. city, esp. *the Acropolis* at Athens.

across′, *prep.* & *adv.* from side to side of; crosswise; to or on the other side of.

acros′tic, *n.* poem, etc., in which first (and last) letters of lines form word(s).

act, *n.* deed; law passed by legislative body; division of play; item in variety or circus programme. *v.* play a part; perform; behave.

actin′ic, *a.* (of ray, light) capable of causing photo-chemical changes.

ac′tion, *n.* doing, working, exertion of energy; deed; style of movement; mechanism of instrument, etc.; lawsuit; battle. **ac′- tionable,** *a.* giving grounds for a lawsuit.

ac′tivăte, *v.t.* make active; make radioactive.

ac′tive, *a.* working, acting, operative; energetic. *active voice,* (Gram., opp. *passive*) form of verb used when subject is doer of the action of the verb. **activ′ity,** *n.* being active or lively; sphere or kind of occupation.

ac′tor, *n.* dramatic performer. **ac′tress,** *n. fem.*

ac′tŭal, *a.* existing, real; present, current. **actŭal′ity,** *n.* reality. **ac′tŭally,** *adv.*

ac′tŭary, *n.* insurance expert who calculates risks and premiums. **actŭār′ial,** *a.*

ac′tŭăte, *v.t.* cause to act; motivate.

acū′ity, *n.* sharpness; acuteness.

acū′men (*or* ak′-), *n.* sharpness of mind; keen insight; shrewdness.

acūte′, *a.* sharp, keen; penetrating; (of illness) coming sharply to a crisis, not chronic; (of angle) less than a right angle. *acute accent,* the accent (′). **acūte′ness,** *n.*

ad-, *pref.* (becoming *ac-* before *c, af-* before *f, ag-* before *g, al-* before *l, an-* before *n, ap-* before *p, ar-* before *r, as-* before *s, at-* before *t;* contracted to *a-* before *sc, sp, st*), to, towards.

ad′age, *n.* proverb; old saying.

adagio (adah′jyō), *adv.*, *a.* & *n.* (pl. *adagios*), (Mus.) (movement or passage) in slow time.

Ad′am, *n.* the first man. **Adam's apple,** projection of thyroid cartilage in neck.

ad′amant, *n.* extremely hard substance, *a.* unyielding. **adaman′tine,** *a.*

adapt′, *v.t.* make suitable; modify, alter. **adap′table,** *a.* (esp.) able to adapt oneself to new circumstances, etc. **adaptabil′ity, adaptă′tion,** *nn.* **adap′ter, adap′tor,** *nn.*

add, *v.* join (thing *to* another) as increase or supplement. *add together, up,* find sum of, amount *to.*

adden′dum, *n.* (pl. *addenda*), thing to be added, esp. at end of book.

add′er, *n.* small venomous snake.

add′ict, *n.* one who is addicted, esp. to a dangerous drug, alcohol, etc. (*drug addict,* etc.); enthusiastic devotee of a sport or pastime (*television addict,* etc.). **addic′ted,** *a.* (with *to*) having formed and become dependent upon a harmful habit, esp. drug-taking;

enthusiastically devoted *to* a sport or pastime. **addic′tion,** *n.* **addic′tive,** *a.* (of drug) causing addiction.

addi′tion, *n.* adding; thing added. *in addition,* as added thing(s)(*to*). **addi′tional,** *a.* added, extra.

add′le, *v.t.* make rotten. **add′led,** *a.* (of egg) rotten; (fig.) muddled, crazy.

address′, *v.t.* speak to; write person's address on (envelope, etc.). *address oneself to,* (start to) work at (task, etc.). *n.* speech; particulars of where person lives or where firm, etc., is situated. **addressee′,** *n.* person to whom letter, etc., is addressed.

ad′enoids, *n.pl.* enlarged lymphoid tissue at back of nose. **adènoi′dal,** *a.*

ad′ept (*or* adept′), *a.* highly skilled. **ad′ept,** *n.* skilled person, expert.

ad′equate, *a.* sufficient, having the qualities needed. **ad′equacy,** *n.*

adhēre′ (-h-), *v.i.* stick fast (*to*); give support or allegiance *to.* **adhēr′ence,** *n.* **adhēr′ent,** *n.* & *a.* **adhē′sion** (-zhn), *n.* adhering. **adhē′sive,** *a.* sticking, sticky. *n.* adhesive substance. **adhesive tape,** sticky cellulose tape for sealing, etc.; sticking-plaster.

ad hoc, arranged for this purpose. (Latin)

adieu (adū′), *int.* & *n.* (pl. *adieus* or *adieux,* pr. -dŭ), good-bye.

ad infini′tum, for ever. (Latin)

ad′ipōse, *a.* fatty.

adjā′cent, *a.* lying near *to*; adjoining.

adjèc′tive, *n.* descriptive word added to noun. **adjèctī′val,** *a.*

adjoin′, *v.t.* be next to (and touching).

adjourn (ajern′), *v.* break off till another time; suspend; move together elsewhere. **adjourn′ment,** *n.*

adjudge′, *v.t.* pronounce or award judicially; be of the opinion.

adjud′icate (ajōō-) *v.* give judgement or decision on; act as judge. **adjudicā′tion, adju′dicātor,** *nn.*

adj′unct, *n.* non-essential but useful addition or extra.

adjure (ajoor′), *v.t.* request earnestly. **adjurā′tion,** *n.*

adjust′, *v.t.* put in order, arrange; adapt (*to*). **adjust′able,** *a.* **adjust′ment,** *n.*

adj′utant (-oo-), *n.* army officer assisting superior officer.

ad lib, ad lib′itum, to desired extent or amount. (Latin). **ad-lib′,** *v.* (p.t. *ad-libbed*), (Theatr., etc., *informal*) improvise (words, etc.).

admin′ister, *v.* manage (affairs, etc.); apply; dispense, give. **administrā′tion,** *n.* administering; management (esp. of public affairs); Government. **admin′istrative,** *a.* **admin′- istrātor,** *n.*

ad′mirable, *a.* worthy of admiration; excellent.

ad′miral, *n.* naval officer of high rank in command of fleet or squadron; ship carrying admiral. **Ad'miralty,** *n.* (Hist.) British department of State superintending navy.

admīre', *v.t.* regard with pleasure and wonder; approve warmly of. **admirā'tion,** n.

admīr'er, *n.* one who admires; suitor.

admiss'ible, *a.* that may be admitted or allowed.

admi'ssion (-shn), *n.* admitting; (fee for) being admitted.

admit', *v.* (p.t. *admitted*), let in; accept as true; confess. **admit of,** leave room for (excuse, etc.). **admitt'ance,** *n.* **admitt'edly,** *adv.*

admix', *v.t.* add as ingredient; mix with. **admix'ture,** *n.*

admon'ish, *v.t.* warn; reprove gently; exhort. **admon'ishment,** *n.*

admoni'tion, *n.* admonishing; warning; reproof. **admon'itory,** *a.*

ado' (-ōō), *n.* fuss; difficulty.

adō'bè, *n.* sun-dried brick.

adoles'cent, *a.* & *n.* (person) between childhood and manhood or womanhood. **adoles'-cence,** *n.*

Adō'nis, *n.* (Gk.Myth.) beautiful youth loved by Venus; handsome youth.

adopt', *v.t.* take into relationship, esp. as one's own child; take and use (idea, etc.); take up, choose; accept. **adop'tion,** *n.*

ador'able, *a.* lovable, delightful.

adorā'tion, *n.* worship; love.

adore', *v.t.* regard with deep respect and affection; worship; like very much.

adorn', *v.t.* add beauty or ornament(s) to. **adorn'ment,** *n.*

adrē'nal (gland), either of pair of glands above the kidneys. **adren'alin,** *n.* hormone secreted by adrenal glands.

adrift', *adv.* drifting; at mercy of wind or tide, or of circumstances.

adroit', *a.* skilful, clever, dextrous.

ad'ūlăte, *v.t.* flatter servilely or excessively. **adūlā'tion,** *n.* **a'dūlătory,** *a.*

ad'ult (*or* adult'), *a.* fully grown, mature. *n.* adult person, animal, or plant.

adul'terăte, *v.t.* debase by mixing with inferior ingredients. **adulterā'tion,** *n.*

adul'tery, *n.* voluntary sexual intercourse of married person with person other than own wife or husband. **adul'terer,** *n.* man guilty of adultery. **adul'teress,** *n.fem.* **adul'terous,** *a.*

ad'umbrăte, *v.t.* indicate faintly; foreshadow. **adumbrā'tion,** *n.*

advance' (-vah-), *v.* move or put forward; help on; lend; make progress; (of price) rise. *n.* going forward; progress; rise in price; loan. *in advance,* ahead, beforehand. **advanced',** *a.* ahead of times; far on in progress. **advance'ment,** *n.*

advan'tage (-vah-), *n.* better position; superiority; gain; favourable circumstance. *take advantage of,* use (circumstance) profitably; exploit (person). **advantā'geous** (-jus), *a.* profitable, favourable.

ad'vent, *n.* coming, esp. important one. **Ad'-vent,** *n.* coming of Christ; season including four Sundays immediately preceding Christmas.

adventi'tious (-shus), *a.* accidental, chance.

adven'ture (-cher), *n.* daring enterprise; exciting experience. *v.* risk; venture. **adven'-turer,** *n.* one who seeks adventures; one who lives by his wits. **adven'turess,** *n.fem.*

adven'turous, *a.* enterprising; daring; eager for adventure.

ad'verb, *n.* word qualifying or modifying a verb, an adjective, or another adverb. **adver'bial,** *a.*

ad'versary, *n.* enemy; opponent. **ad'verse,** *a.* hostile; unfavourable. **adver'sity,** *n.* trouble; misfortune.

ad'vertīse (-z), *v.* make generally or publicly known; proclaim merits of, esp. to encourage sales. **adver'tisement,** *n.*

advice', *n.* opinion given as to action; information, notice.

advī'sable (-z-), *a.* expedient, prudent. **advīsabil'ty,** *n.*

advīse' (-z), *v.* give advice to; notify. **advī'-ser,** *n.* (esp.) person habitually consulted.

advīsed' (-zd), *a.* considered, deliberate. **advī'sèdly,** *adv.*

advī'sory (-z-), *a.* giving advice.

ad'vocacy, *n.* pleading in support of.

ad'vocate, *n.* one who pleads for another; supporter (of policy, etc.). **ad'vocăte,** *v.t.* speak for; support.

adze, *n.* axe-like tool with arched blade at right angles to handle.

ae'gis (ē-), *n.* shield, protection (esp. in phr. *under the aegis of*).

Aeo'lian, aeo'lian (ēō-), *a.* of Aeolus, mythical god of winds; of, caused by, carried by, the wind. **Aeolian harp,** instrument producing musical sounds when wind blows over the strings.

ae'on (ē-), **ē'on,** *n.* immense period of time.

ā'erate (*or* āī'-), *v.t.* expose to action of air; pass air through (a liquid); charge with carbon dioxide. **aerā'tion,** *n.*

aer'ial (āī-), *a.* existing, moving, happening, in the air; of or like air; imaginary. *n.* wire(s) or rod(s) used in transmitting or receiving radio waves.

aer'ie, aer'y (āī- *or* ēī-), *n.* eyrie.

aero- (āī-), air-, of aircraft. **aerobat'ics,** *n. pl.* feats of expert and spectacular flying. **aer'-odrōme,** *n.* airfield. **aerodÿnam'ics,** *n.* dynamics of solid bodies in motion in air. **aer'ofoil,** *n.* any of the lift-producing surfaces of an aircraft. **aer'olite, aer'olith,** *nn.* meteorite. **aeronau'tical,** *a.* of aeronautics. **aeronau'tics,** *n.* science, art, or practice of flying. **aer'oplăne,** *n.* heavier-than-air powered flying machine with wings. **aer'-osol,** *n.* suspension of very small particles in air or gas; device for producing fine spray. **aer'ospăce,** *n.* region of earth's atmosphere and the space beyond it.

aes'thēte (ēs- *or* es-), *n.* professed lover of beauty. **aesthet'ic,** *a.* of the appreciation of beauty; having, showing, good taste (in art, etc.). **aesthet'icism, aesthet'ics,** *nn.*

aetiol'ogy (ē-), *n.* the assigning of a cause or reason; (Med.) science of the causes of disease.

af-, *pref.*: see **ad-.**

afar', *adv.* at a distance.

aff'able, *a.* easy to talk to; courteous. **affabil'ity,** *n.*

affair', *n.* business, concern; happening; love affair; (pl.) business of any kind.

affect'¹, *v.t.* move, touch, (in mind or feelings); produce effect on; (of disease) attack.

affect'², *v.t.* pretend to have or feel; pretend (*to* do). **affectā'tion,** *n.* artificiality of manner; pretentious display. **affect'ĕd,** *a.* full of affectation.

affec'tion, *n.* kindly feeling, love, (*for, towards*); disease. **affec'tionate,** *a.* loving.

affidā'vit, *n.* written statement confirmed by oath.

affil'iāte, *v.t.* adopt, attach *to,* connect *with*; become affiliated; fix paternity of (illegitimate child) for maintenance. **affiliā'tion,** *n.*

affin'ity, *n.* relationship; resemblance; attraction; (Chem.) tendency of certain substances to react on each other.

affirm', *v.* state as fact; make affirmation. **affirmā'tion,** *n.* (esp.) declaration by one who conscientiously declines oath. **affir'mative,** *a.* affirming, expressing assent. *n.* affirmative answer, yes.

affix', *v.t.* fasten, append, attach. **aff'ix,** *n.* thing affixed; prefix or suffix.

afflict', *v.t.* distress with bodily or mental suffering. **afflic'tion,** *n.*

aff'luence, (-loo-) *n.* wealth, abundance. **aff'luent,** *a.* rich. *n.* tributary stream.

afford', *v.t.* spare the time or money for; yield; supply.

affo'rĕst, *v.t.* convert into forest; plant with trees. **afforèstā'tion,** *n.*

affray', *n.* brawl, riot.

affront' (-unt), *v.t.* insult openly; cause offence to. *n.* open insult.

afield', *adv.* away from home; to or at a distance (esp. in phr. *far afield*).

aflāme', *adv.* in flames; glowing.

afloat', *adv.* floating; at sea.

afoot', *adv.* on foot; in progress.

afore-, *pref.* before, previously. **afore'said,** *a.* previously mentioned. **afore'thought,** *a.* thought out beforehand, premeditated.

afraid', *a.* frightened, feeling fear or dread; sorry to say.

afresh', *adv.* with fresh start; again.

Af'rican, *a. & n.* (native) of Africa.

Afrikaans' (-ahns), *n.* form of Dutch spoken in S. Africa.

aft (ah-), *adv.* in, near, or towards stern of ship or tail of aircraft.

af'ter (ah-), *adv.* behind, later. *prep.* behind, later than; in pursuit of; according to; in imitation of. *conj.* at or during a time later than. *a.* later, following. **af'terbirth,** placenta.

af'ter-care, care or attention after hospital treatment, etc.

af'terdamp (ah-), *n.* poisonous gases left in mine after explosion of firedamp.

af'terglow (ah-; -ō), *n.* glow after sunset.

af'termath (ah-), *n.* consequence, outcome; second mowing (of grass, etc.).

afternoon' (ah-), *n.* time between noon and evening.

af'terthought (ah-; -awt), *n.* idea that occurs to one later.

af'terwards (ah-; -z), *adv.* later, subsequently.

ag-, *pref.*: see **ad-.**

again', *adv.* a second time, another time, once more; further, besides.

against', *prep.* in opposition to; in contrast to; in anticipation of; into collision with; in contact with, supported by.

agāpe', *adv. & pred. a.* gaping.

ā'gar(-ā'gar), *n.* gelatinous substance obtained from kinds of seaweed.

ag'ate, *n.* a hard semi-precious stone.

āge, *n.* length of life or existence; great geological or historical period; (*informal,* esp. pl.) long time. *come of age,* reach *age of majority,*18 (formerly 21) years. *v.* (pres. part. *āg(e)ing*), grow old; cause to grow old. **āged,** *a.* of the age of. **ā'gĕd,** *a.* old. **āge'less,** *a.* not becoming old or outdated.

ā'gency, *n.* business or office of agent; action; means.

agen'da, *n.* (list of) things to be done or considered at a meeting.

ā'gent, *n.* person acting for another in business, politics, etc.; person or thing producing an effect.

agglom'erāte, *v.* collect, heap up, into a mass. **agglomerā'tion,** *n.*

aggran'dīze (*or* ag'-), *v.t.* increase power, rank, etc., of. **aggran'dizement,** *n.*

agg'ravāte, *v.t.* increase the seriousness of; (*informal*) annoy. **aggravā'tion,** *n.*

agg'règate, *n.*ˏtotal; assemblage, collection. *a.* collective; *v.* (-gāt), collect together; total.

aggre'ssion (-shn), *n.* beginning of quarrel; unprovoked attack. **aggress'ive,** *a.* **aggress'or,** *n.*

aggrieved' (-vd), *a.* hurt in one's feelings; having a grievance.

aghast' (-gah-), *a.* amazed and horrified.

a'gīle, *a.* nimble, active. **agil'ity,** *n.*

a'gitāte, *v.* shake about; disturb; excite; stir up (public) disquiet and unrest. **agitā'tion,** *a'gitātor,** *nn.*

agnos'tic, *n.* one who holds that nothing is known of the existence of a God. *a.* of or holding this theory. **agnos'ticism** (-isizm), *n.*

agō', *adv.* past, gone by; since.

agog', *adv. & pred. a.* eager(ly), excited(ly).

ag'onĭze, v. suffer agony; make desperate efforts. **ag'onizing,** a. causing agony.

ag'ony, n. intense bodily or mental suffering.

agoraphŏb'ia, n. unreasoning dread of open spaces.

agrār'ian, a. relating to cultivated land or land ownership.

agree', v.i. (p.t. agreed; pres. p. agreeing), consent (to); be in accord, harmonize in opinion, etc., (with).

agree'able, a. pleasing; well disposed.

agree'ment, n. agreeing; mutual understanding; legal contract.

ag'riculture (-cher), n. cultivation of the soil. **agricul'tural,** a. **agricul'turalist,** n.

aground', adv. & pred.a. (of ship) on the bottom in shallow water.

ǎ'gŭe, n. malarial fever with hot and cold stages; shivering fit.

ah, int. expressing joy, sorrow, surprise, etc.

ahead (a-hed'), adv. in advance; forward.

ahoy (a-hoi'), int. (Naut.) hailing shout.

aid, v. help, promote. n. help; thing that helps, e.g. hearing aid, visual aid, etc.

aide, n. aide-de-camp; assistant. **aide--de-camp** (ād'dikahṅ), n. (pl. aides--de-camp, pr. same), officer assisting higher--ranking officer, esp. general.

ail, v. trouble; be ill. **ail'ment,** n.

ail'eron, n. flap on trailing edge of aircraft--wing controlling lifting and banking.

aim, v. direct (at); point (gun, etc.); have as purpose. n. aiming; thing aimed at; purpose. **aim'less,** a. having no purpose.

air, n. mixture of gases, chiefly oxygen and nitrogen, enveloping the earth; atmosphere; melody; appearance; (pl.) affected manners. by air, by aircraft. on the air, (being) broadcast by radio. v.t. expose to air; ventilate; dry off; show off; make known.

air'borne, a. (of troops) carried by air; (of aircraft) in the air.

air'-conditioning, n. control of temperature and moisture of air in room, etc.

air'craft (-ah-), n. aeroplanes, airships, etc.; any one of these. **aircraft-carrier,** ship that carries and acts as base for aircraft. **air'-craftman,** man of lowest rank in R.A.F.

Aire'dāle (te'rrier) (ārd-), large brown rough--coated terrier.

air'field, n. area of land where aircraft are accommodated and maintained and may take off or land.

air' force, branch of armed forces using aircraft in fighting.

air'-gun, n. gun worked by compressed air.

air' hŏstess, stewardess in aircraft.

air'ing, n. exposure to fresh air or (of clothes, etc.) to warm air.

air'less, a. stuffy; still; calm.

air' letter, air mail letter written on folding form of special design.

air'-lift, n. transportation of supplies, etc., by air to area otherwise inaccessible.

air' līne, air transport system or company. **air'-līner,** large passenger aircraft.

air'-lock, n. (bubble of air causing) stoppage of flow in pipe, etc.; air-tight compartment between pressurized chamber and outer air.

air' mail, mail carried by aircraft.

air'man, n. (pl. -men), pilot or member of crew of aircraft.

air'port, n. airfield for aircraft carrying passengers, goods, etc.

air' rald, an attack by aircraft.

air'-screw (-ōō), n. propeller of aircraft, etc.

air'ship, n. dirigible motor-driven cigar--shaped passenger-carrying balloon.

air' spăce, air as medium for flying, esp. area above a country and subject to its jurisdiction.

air'strip, n. strip of land cleared for taking off and landing of aircraft.

air'-tight (-tīt), a. not allowing air to enter or escape.

air'way, n. ventilating shaft for mine; regular route of aircraft; air line.

air'worthy (-werdhi), a. (of aircraft) fit to fly.

air'y, a. well-ventilated; light, unsubstantial; sprightly; flippant. **air'ily,** adv.

aisle (īl), n. division of church, esp. parallel to nave and choir; passage between rows of pews or seats.

ajar', adv. (of door, etc.) slightly open.

akim'bŏ, adv. (of the arms) with hands on hips and elbows out.

akin', a. related; similar.

al-, pref.: see **ad-.**

al'abaster (-bah-), n. translucent, esp. white, gypsum rock. a. of alabaster; white and smooth like alabaster.

à la carte, (of meals, etc.) ordered by separate items, from the menu. (French)

alack', int. (archaic) expressing sorrow.

alac'rity, n. quick and eager readiness.

à la mŏde, in the fashion, fashionable. (French)

alarm', n. (apparatus giving) warning sound or signal; frightened anticipation of danger. v.t. arouse to sense of danger; frighten. **al-ar'mist,** n. & a. (person) encouraging fears, esp. needless ones.

alas', int. expressing grief, pity, concern.

alb, n. priest's long white vestment.

al'batross, n. very large oceanic bird of the petrel family.

albē'it (awl-), conj. although.

albi'nŏ (-bē-), n. (pl. albinos), person or animal (almost) without natural colouring--matter in hair, skin, or eyes. **al'binism,** n.

al'bum, n. blank book for photographs, stamps, autographs, etc.

al'bŭmen, n. white of egg.

al'bŭmin, n. soluble protein occurring in white of egg, milk, blood serum, and animal and plant tissues. **albŭ'minoid, albŭ'-minous,** aa.

al'chemy (-k-), n. medieval chemistry, esp.

attempt to change baser metals into gold. **al'chemist,** *n.*

al'cohol, *n.* inflammable intoxicating liquid formed by fermentation of sugars and present in wine, etc.; any compound analagous to this in chemical structure; alcoholic drink. **alcohol'ic,** *a.* of or containing alcohol. *n.* person suffering from alcoholism. **al'coholism,** *n.* addiction to drinking of alcohol; illness resulting from this.

al'cŏve, *n.* recess in room, garden, etc.

al'der (awl-), *n.* tree related to birch.

al'derman (awl-), *n.* (pl. *-men*), (Hist.) senior councillor, elected by councillors.

āle, *n.* liquor made from malt, beer.

alert', *a.* watchful; lively. *n.* warning of danger, attack, etc. *on the alert,* wide awake and watchful.

Alexan'drĭne, *a.* & *n.* (verse) of six iambic feet.

alfal'fa, *n.* lucerne.

alfres'cō, *adv.* out of doors. *a.* outdoor.

al'gae (-jē), *n.pl.* (sing. *alga*), group of primitive plants including seaweeds.

al'gĕbra, *n.* branch of mathematics in which letters are used to represent quantities. **algĕbrā'ic(al),** *aa.*

ā'lias, *adv.* otherwise called. *n.* (pl. *aliases*), assumed name.

al'ibĭ, *n.* (pl. *alibĭs*), plea of being elsewhere; (*informal*) excuse.

ā'liĕn, *a.* foreign; opposed (*to*). *n.* foreigner, esp. one who is not naturalized.

ā'liĕnāte, *v.t.* turn away (friendship, etc.); transfer ownership of; estrange; divert. **āliĕnā'tion,** *n.*

alight'¹ (-īt), *v.i.* get down from (horse, bus, etc.); descend and settle.

alight'² (-īt) *a.* on fire, lighted up.

align' (-īn), *v.* place or form in line; bring into line. **align'ment,** *n.*

alike', *pred.a.* similar; like one another. *adv.* in the same way.

alimen'tary, *a.* concerned with feeding. **alimentary canal,** channel in the body through which food passes in process of digestion.

al'imony, *n.* allowance paid to wife or former wife after legal separation or divorce.

alīve', *a.* living; active, brisk. *alive to,* aware of. *alive with,* swarming with.

al'kali, *n.* (pl. *alkalĭs*), (chem.) compound dissolving in water to form solution that neutralizes acids. **al'kalĭne,** *a.*

al'kaloid, *n.* (Chem.) any nitrogenous base of vegetable origin.

all (awl) *a.* the whole amount or quantity of. *pron.* the whole number; everyone. *n.* everything; everyone. *adv.* wholly, completely. *all over,* in every part of; at an end. *all right,* satisfactory, well, safe; (as answer to suggestion) 'yes, I consent'. *all-round,* good at many games, etc. *all the same,* in spite of that. **All Hallows,** All Saints' Day. **All Saints' Day,** 1st November. **All Souls' Day,** 2nd November.

Allah (al'a), *n.* Muslim name of God.

allay', *v.t.* make (pain, fears, excitement) less.

allege' (-ej), *v.t.* state as fact, esp. without proof. **allĕgā'tion,** *n.*

allĕ'giance (-jns), *n.* duty of subject to sovereign or government; loyalty.

all'ĕgory, *n.* story or description in which there is a deeper meaning underlying the subject. **allĕgo'ric(al),** *aa.*

allĕgrett'ō, *adv.,* *a.* & *n.* (pl. *allegrettos*), (Mus.) (movement or passage) in moderately quick time. **alle'grŏ** (-lā-), *adv.,a.* & *n.* (pl. *allegros*), (Mus.) (movement or passage) in quick lively time.

allēlu'ia (-lōōya), *int.* & *n.* cry or song of praise to God.

all'ergy, *n.* condition of reacting acutely to certain foods, pollens, drugs, etc. **aller'gic,** *a.* of, having, allergy. *allergic to,* sensitive to; (fig.) repelled by.

allē'viāte, *v.t.* relieve; lessen; make lighter. **allēviā'tion,** *n.* **allē'viatory,** *a.*

all'ey, *n.* narrow street; walk, avenue; enclosure for skittles.

alli'ance, *n.* union, esp. of States (by treaty), or families (by marriage); relationship.

all'igātor, *n.* reptile of SE. United States, related to crocodile.

alliterā'tion, *n.* commencement of two or more closely connected words with the same letter. **allit'erative,** *a.*

all'ocāte, *v.t.* set apart for special purpose or person(s); assign. **allocā'tion,** *n.*

allot', *v.t.* (p.t. *allotted*), distribute by lot or with authority; assign. **allot'ment,** *n.* share; small plot of land let for cultivation.

allow', *v.* permit; admit; give (periodical sum); deduct, give a rebate of. *allow for,* take into consideration. **allow'able,** *a.* **allow'ance,** *n.* fixed sum allowed; deduction, discount.

all'oy (*or* aloi'), *n.* mixture of two or more metals. **alloy',** *v.t.* mix two or more metals to form alloy; (fig.) debase.

all'spīce (awl-), *n.* (spice obtained from) dried unripe berry of W. Indian tree.

allūde' (*or* -lōōd), *v.i.* refer indirectly or briefly to.

allūre', *v.t.* attract, charm, entice. **allūre'ment,** *n.*

allu'sion (-lōōzhn *or* -lūzhn), *n.* indirect or brief reference. **allu'sive,** *a.*

allŭv'ial (*or* -lōō-), *a.* of sand, silt, etc., deposited by river or flood. *n.* alluvial soil.

allŭv'ium (*or* -lōō-), *n.* (pl. *alluvia, alluviums*), deposit of sand, silt, etc., left by flowing water, esp. in river valleys and deltas.

ally', *v.t.* join or unite for a special purpose. *allied to,* connected with. **all'ȳ** *n.* (pl. *allies,* pr. -līz), person, State, etc., in alliance with another.

al'manac (awl-), *n.* calendar with astronomical and other information.

almighty (awlmīt'i), *a.* all-powerful. *The Almighty*, God.

alm'ond (ahm-), *n.* (kernel of stone-fruit of) tree related to peach.

alm'oner (ahm-), *n.* official distributor of alms; former name for social worker at hospital.

al'mōst (awl-), *adv.* very nearly.

alms (ahmz), *n.* charitable relief of the poor; donation. **alms-house(s)**, charitable foundation for housing aged and needy persons, often in cottages in row or square.

al'ōe, *n.* plant with a bitter juice.

aloft', *adv.* & *pred.a.* high up; upward. (Naut.) in(to) upper part of rigging.

alōne', *a.* not with others, solitary. *adv.* only, exclusively. *let* or *leave alone*, not interfere with.

along', *prep.* through (any part of) the length of. *adv.* onward; in company or conjunction *with*. **along'sīde**, *adv.* & *prep.* close to side of.

aloōf', *adv.* & *pred.a.* away, apart; at a distance (*from*). *stand aloof*, take no part in, show no sympathy with.

aloud', *adv.* in normal voice, not silently or in a whisper; loudly.

alp, *n.* high, esp. snow-capped, mountain.

alpac'a, *n.* kind of llama with fine long wool; its wool; material made from this.

al'penstock, *n.* staff with iron point, used in mountain climbing.

al'pha, *n.* first letter of Greek alphabet.

al'phabet, *n.* letters used in a language. **alphabet'ical**, *a.* in the order of the alphabet.

al'pīne, *a.* of *the Alps* (in Europe), or other high mountains.

already (awlred'i), *adv.* by this (that) time; thus early; previously.

Alsā'tian (-shn), *n.* large strong intelligent dog, the German sheep-dog.

al'sō (awl-), *adv.* besides, as well, too.

al'tar (awl- *or* ol-), *n.* table for offerings to a deity; Communion table. **al'tarpiece**, painting or sculpture above back of altar.

al'ter (awl- *or* ol-), *v.* make or become different; change. **alterā'tion**, *n.*

al'tercāte (awl- *or* ol-), *v.i.* quarrel, argue angrily. **altercā'tion**, *n.*

alter'nate (awl- *or* ol-), *a.* (of things of two kinds) coming each after one of the other kind. **alter'nately**, *adv.* **al'ternāte**, *v.* arrange in alternate order; succeed each other by turns. *alternating current*, (Electr.) current which reverses its direction at regular intervals. **alternā'tion**, *n.* **alter'native**, *a.* offering either of two things; available in place of another (thing). *n.* choice between two (or more) things. **alter'natively**, *adv.*

although (awldhō'), *conj.* though.

al'timēter, *n.* instrument used, esp. in aircraft, to measure altitude.

al'titūde, *n.* vertical height; height above sea-level; (pl.) high regions.

al'tō, *n.* (pl. *altos*), (musical part for, singer having,) male voice higher than tenor (also called *countertenor*), or lowest female voice (usu. called *contralto*).

altogether (awltoogedh'er), *adv.* entirely; on the whole.

al'truism (-oo-izm), *n.* unselfish consideration for the welfare of others. **al'truist**, *n.* **altruis'tic**, *a.*

al'um, *n.* sulphate of aluminium used in medicine and in industry.

alūmin'ium, *n.* a very light, .silvery-white metal.

always (awl'wāz), *adv.* at all times, on all occasions; continually.

am, 1st pers. sing. pres. of **be**.

amal'gam, *n.* alloy of mercury; mixture, combination.

amal'gamāte, *v.* mix; unite, combine. **amalgamā'tion**, *n.*

amanūen'sis, *n.* (pl. *amanūensēs*), person who writes from dictation; literary assistant.

am'aranth, *n.* (Poet.) imaginary unfading flower; purple colour. **amaran'thīne**, *a.*

amaryll'is, *n.* flowering plant resembling lily.

amass', *v.t.* pile up; accumulate (esp. wealth).

am'ateur (-tūr), *n.* one who takes keen interest in or practises art, music, sport, etc., as pastime, not professionally. **amateur'ish**, *a.* not expert.

am'atory, *a.* of lovers or love-making.

amāze', *v.t.* fill with great surprise or wonder. **amā'zing**, *a.* **amāze'ment**, *n.*

Am'azon, *n.* fabulous female warrior. **amazō'nian**, *a.*

amb-, *pref.*: see **ambi-**.

ambass'ador, *n.* minister sent to foreign country as representative of his State or on a mission. **ambassador'ial**, *a.* **ambass'-adress**, *n.fem.*

am'ber, *n.* yellow fossil resin.

am'bergris (-ēs), *n.* wax-like substance from sperm-whale, used in perfumes.

ambi-, amb-, *pref.* (*ambi-* before consonant, *amb-* before vowel), both, on both sides.

ambidex'trous, *a.* able to use either hand with equal ease and skill.

am'biènt, *a.* surrounding.

ambig'ūous, *a.* having more than one possible meaning; doubtful, uncertain. **ambigū'ity**, *n.*

am'bit, *n.* bounds; extent.

ambi'tion, *n.* strong desire to be successful or famous, or to do something; object of such desire. **ambi'tious** (-shus), *a.* full of or showing ambition.

ambi'valent, *a.* having either or both of two contrary or similar values or meanings; having contradictory feelings (as love and hatred) towards same person or thing. **ambi'valence**, *n.*

am'ble, *v. i.* walk or ride at an easy pace. *n.* easy pace.

ambro'sia (-z- *or* -zhya), *n.* (Gk. myth.) food of the gods. **ambro'sial**, *a.*

am'bulance, *n.* vehicle for injured, ill, or wounded persons.

am'bulatory, *a.* of or for walking. *n.* covered place for walking, esp. in apse of church.

ambuscâde', *n.* & *v.* ambush.

am'bush (-oosh), *n.* troops, etc. concealed in a wood, etc., for surprise attack; their hiding--place. *v. t.* attack from ambush.

amê'liorâte, *v.* make or become better. **amê-liorâ'tion**, *n.*

a'men' (ah- *or* â-), *int.* (used at end of prayer, etc.) may it be so, it is truly so.

amê'nable, *a.* docile; responsive (*to*).

amend', *v. t.* improve, correct; make improvements in, alter in detail. **amend'ment**, *n.*

amends' (-z), *n. make amends*, compensate, make up, (*for*).

amê'nity, *n.* pleasantness; (pl.) pleasant or convenient features of place, etc.

Ame'rican, *a.* of America or the United States. *n.* (esp.) citizen of the U.S.

am'ethyst, *n.* precious stone of purple or violet colour.

â'miable, *a.* feeling and inspiring friendliness. **âmiabil'ity**, *n.* **â'miably**, *adv.*

am'icable, *a.* friendly. **amicabil'ity**, *n.* **am'icably**, *adv.*

amid', **amidst'**, *prep.* in the middle of, among. **amid'ships**, *adv.* (Naut.) in middle of ship.

amiss', *adv.* & *pred. a.* wrong(ly); bad(ly).

am'ity, *n.* friendship.

ammo'nia, *n.* a colourless gas with pungent smell; solution of this gas in water. **ammo'-niac, ammoni'acal, ammô'niâtéd**, *aa.*

amm'onîte, *n.* flat coiled fossil shell of extinct mollusc.

ammûni'tion, *n.* supply of cartridges, etc. for guns, etc.

amnê'sia (-z-), *n.* loss of memory.

am'nesty, *n.* general pardon, esp. for offences against State.

amoe'ba (-mê-), *n.* (pl. *amoebae, amoebas*), primitive microscopic animal constantly changing shape.

amok' (-uk), **amuck'**, *adv. run amok*, run about in murderous frenzy; get out of control.

among', **amongst'** (-mu-), *prep.* in the midst of; in the number of; between.

âmo'ral, *a.* neither moral nor immoral; outside the scope of morality.

am'orous, *a.* of or showing love; inclined to make love.

amor'phous, *a.* having no definite shape or form.

amount', *v. i.* add up *to*; be equivalent *to*. *n.* total; quantity.

amp, *n.* ampere. **am'pêre**, *n.* unit of amount of flow in electric current.

amphi-, amph-, *pref.* (*amph-* before vowel), both, on both sides.

amphib'ian, *n.* & *a.* (animal) able to live both on land and in water; (aircraft, tank, etc.) able to operate on both land and water.

amphib'ious, *a.* living both on land and water; amphibian.

am'phithêatre (-ter), *n.* oval or circular building with tiers of seats surrounding central space; semicircular gallery in theatre.

am'phora, *n.* (pl. *amphorae, amphoras*), Greek or Roman two-handled jar.

am'ple, *a.* spacious; abundant; quite enough. **am'ply**, *adv.*

am'plify, *v.* expand, enlarge; (Electr., Radio) increase strength of (current, signals, etc.). **amplificâ'tion**, *n.* **am'plifîer**, *n.* (esp.) apparatus for increasing loudness of sounds.

am'plitûde, *n.* breadth; abundance.

am'poule (-ōol), *n.* small sealed (glass) vessel holding solution for injection.

am'pûtâte, *v. t.* cut off (limb, etc.), esp. surgically. **ampûtâ'tion**, *n.*

amuck: see **amok.**

am'ûlèt, *n.* thing worn as charm against evil.

amûse' (-z), *v. t.* make time pass pleasantly for; make (person) laugh or smile. **amûse'-ment**, *n.* **amû'sing**, *a.*

an¹, *a.*: see **a.**

an², *conj.* (*archaic*) if.

an-¹, *pref.*: see **a-².**

an-², *pref.*: see **ad-.**

ana-, an-³, *pref.* (*ana-* before consonant, *an-* before vowel), up, back, again.

anach'ronism (-k-), *n.* error in dating something; introduction into narrative, etc., of person, thing, or event belonging to a later period. **anachronis'tic**, *a.*

anae'mia, (-nê-), *n.* deficiency in quantity or quality of red cells and haemoglobin in the blood. **anae'mic**, *a.* suffering from anaemia; (fig.) lacking vigour.

anaesthesia (anesthê'zia), *n.* loss of sensation in part of body, or in whole body with loss of consciousness. **anaesthet'ic**, *a.* & *n.* (drug, etc.) that produces anaesthesia; *n. pl.* branch of medicine concerned with anaesthetic drugs, etc. **anaes'thêtist** (anês-), *n.* expert in administering anaesthetics. **anaes'thêtize** (anês-), *v. t.* administer anaesthetic to; render insensible.

an'agram, *n.* word or phrase formed by rearranging the letters of another.

analgê'sia (-z-), *n.* absence of pain. **analgê'-sic**, *a.* & *n.* (drug) relieving pain.

anal'ogous, *a.* similar; parallel; comparable.

an'alogue (-og), *n.* analogous thing.

anal'ogy, *n.* partial likeness to, or agreement with, another thing; reasoning from parallel cases.

an'alÿse (-z), *v. t.* examine in detail by separating into component parts; (Chem.) find the elements of (a compound); (Gram.) break up (sentence) into its grammatical parts. **anal'-**

ysis, *n.* (pl. *analysēs*), process of analysing; statement of the result of this; psycho--analysis. **an′alyst,** *n.* one skilled in analysis; psycho-analyst. **analyt′ic, analyt′ical,** *aa.* of or using analysis.

an′apaest (-pēst), *n.* metrical foot of two short (or unstressed) syllables followed by one long (or stressed) syllable. **anapaes′tic,** *a.*

an′archism (-k-), *n.* theory that government and laws are undesirable and unnecessary. **an′archist,** *n.* **anarchis′tic,** *a.*

an′archy (-k-), *n.* absence of government or control; disorder, confusion. **anar′chic(al),** *aa.* lawless.

anastigmat′ic, *a.* (of lens) with astigmatism corrected.

anath′ēma, *n.* curse; accursed or detested person or thing. **anath′ēmatīze,** *v. t.*

anat′omy, *n.* science of the structure of animals and plants; dissection; structure of an organism. **anatom′ical,** *a.* **anat′omist,** *n.* one skilled in anatomy.

an′cestor, *n.* any of those from whom one's father or mother is descended; forefather. **ances′tral,** *a.* belonging to or inherited from ancestors. **an′cestry,** *n.* (line of) ancestors.

anch′or (-ngk-), *n.* heavy iron instrument, with hooks, for mooring ship to bottom of sea, etc. *v.* secure (ship) with anchor; cast anchor; come to anchor; fix firmly. **anch′-orage** *n.* place where ships may lie at anchor; refuge.

anch′orīte (-ngk-), *n.* hermit.

an′chovy (*or* anchō′-), *n.* small fish with strong flavour.

ān′cient (-shnt), *a.* of times long past; very old; *the ancients,* civilized nations of antiquity.

ancill′ary, *a.* serving or supporting something of greater importance.

and, *conj.* (used to connect words, clauses, and sentences), together with; as well as; in addition to.

andan′tè, *adv., a.,* & *n.* (Mus.) (movement or passage) in moderately slow time.

an′diron (-īīn), *n.* one of pair of iron bars for supporting burning logs in fireplace.

an′ecdōte, *n.* brief account of interesting or amusing incident or event.

anèmom′ēter, *n.* instrument for measuring speed of wind.

anem′onè, *n.* cultivated or (*wood anemone*) woodland flower; sea anemone.

an′eroid (**barom′ēter**), barometer that measures air-pressure by its action on flexible lid of box nearly exhausted of air.

anew′, *adv.* again, esp. in new or different way.

ān′gel (-j-), *n.* attendant and messenger of God; (fig.) kind or lovely person. **angel′ic** (-j-), *a.*

angel′ica (-j-), *n.* (candied root of) aromatic plant.

an′gèlus (-j-), *n.* Roman Catholic prayer said at morning, noon, and sunset, at sound of bell; bell for this.

ang′er (-ngg-), *n.* strong feeling of displeasure; rage. *v. t.* rouse anger in.

angī′na (**pec′toris**) (-j-), *n.* painful spasm of chest due to over-exertion when heart is diseased.

angle¹ (ang′gl), *n.* space between two lines or planes that meet; inclination of two lines to each other; corner; (fig.) point of view. **an′gled** (-ld) *a.* having angle(s).

angle² (ang′gl), *v. i.* fish with line, hook, and bait; (fig.) try to gain by hints, etc. **ang′ler,** *n.*

Angle (ang′gl), *n.* member of Germanic tribe that settled in Britain in fifth c. A.D.

Ang′lican (angg-), *a.* & *n.* (member) of reformed Church of England or other Church in communion with, and recognizing leadership of, see of Canterbury. **Ang′licanism,** *n.*

Ang′licism (angg-), *n.* English idiom. **ang′licize,** *v. t.* make English.

Anglō- (angg-), *pref.* English. **Ang′lō--In′dian,** *a.* & *n.* (person) of British birth living or having lived in India; (vocabulary) adopted into English from language(s) of India; Eurasian. **Ang′lō-Sax′on,** *a.* & *n.* English (person, language) before Norman Conquest; (person) of English descent.

angor′a, *n.* fabric made from hair of Angora goat, mohair; yarn made from hair of Angora rabbit and sheep's wool. *Angora cat, goat, rabbit,* varieties with long silky hair.

ang′ry (angg-), *a.* feeling or showing anger; (of wound, cut, etc.) inflamed. **ang′rily,** *adv.*

ang′uish (anggw-), *n.* severe bodily or mental pain or suffering.

ang′ūlar (angg-), *a.* having angles; sharp--cornered; measured by angle. **angūla′rity,** *n.*

anhȳ′drous, *a.* (Chem.) without water.

an′ilīne, *n.* chemical compound used in manufacture of dyes, drugs, etc.

animadvert′, *v. t.* criticize unfavourably; blame. **animadver′sion,** *n.*

an′imal, *n.* living being, able to feel and move about; animal other than man. *a.* of or like animals; physical (as opp. spiritual); sensual. **animal′cūle,** *n.* microscopic animal.

an′imate, *a.* living, not inanimate. **an′imāte,** *v. t.* give life to; enliven; inspire. **animated cartoon,** film, usu. comic, made by photographing a series of drawings. **animā′tion,** *n.* (esp.) liveliness, vivacity.

animos′ity, *n.* enmity; hatred.

an′ise (-nis), *n.* plant with aromatic seeds. **an′iseed,** *n.* seed of anise.

ank′le, *n.* joint connecting foot with leg; slender part of leg below calf. **ank′lèt,** *n.* ornament worn round ankle.

ann′als (-z), *n. pl.* narrative of events year by year; historical records. **ann′alist,** *n.* writer of annals.

anneal', v.t. toughen (metal, glass) by cooling very slowly after heating.

annex', v.t. take possession of (territory, etc.); add, append. **annexā'tion**, n.

ann'ex(e), n. additional building.

anni'hilāte (-nī-i-), v.t. destroy completely. **annihilā'tion**, n.

anniver'sary, n. yearly return of the date of an event; celebration of this.

Ann'ō Dom'inī, phr. in the year of the Lord, since the birth of Jesus Christ (abbrev. A.D., e.g. A.D. 1900, etc.). (Latin)

ann'ōtāte, v. add notes to; make notes on. **annōtā'tion, ann'ōtātor**, nn.

announce', v.t. proclaim; make known; give notice of. **announce'ment**, n.

announ'cer, n. (esp.) official at broadcasting station who announces programme, reads news bulletin, etc.

annoy', v.t. make rather angry; irritate; molest. **annoy'ance**, n. irritation; vexation.

ann'ūal, a. yearly; reckoned by year. n. plant living only one year or less; yearly periodical. **ann'ūally**, adv.

annū'ity, n. fixed sum of money paid to person yearly during lifetime; form of insurance to provide such payment. **annū'itant**, n. one who receives an annuity.

annul', v.t. (p.t. annulled), cancel; put an end to. **annul'ment**, n.

ann'ūlar, a. ring-shaped.

Annunciā'tion, n. announcement of angel Gabriel to Virgin Mary that she was to be mother of Jesus Christ.

an'ōde, n. (Electr.) positive electrode, from which current flows.

an'odȳne, a. & n. (drug, etc.) able to lessen pain; (anything) mentally soothing.

anoint', v.t. apply oil or ointment to, esp. as religious ceremony.

anom'alous, a. irregular; abnormal.

anom'aly, n. irregularity; exceptional condition or circumstance.

anon', adv. (archaic) soon, presently.

anon., abbrev. anonymous.

anon'ymous, a. of unknown or undisclosed name or authorship. **anonym'ity**, n.

an'orak, n. weather-proof jacket with hood attached.

anoth'er (-udh-), a. an additional; a different. pron. another one.

an'serīne, a. of geese.

answer (ahn'ser), v. speak, write, act, etc. in reply (to); be responsible (for); correspond to; fulfil (purpose, etc.). n. something said, written or done in return; reply; solution to (problem, riddle, etc.). **an'swerable**, a. responsible.

ant, n. small hard-working social insect. **ant--eater**, any of various mammals feeding on ants. **ant-hill**, mound over ants' nest.

ant-, pref.: see **anti-**.

antag'onism, n. active opposition; hostility. **antag'onist**, n. opponent. **antagonis'tic**, a.

antag'onīze, v.t. arouse hostility in.

antarc'tic, a. of the South Polar regions.

antē-, pref. before.

antēcē'dent, a. previous. n. preceding thing or circumstances; (Gram.) noun, etc., to which following adverb or pronoun refers; (pl.) person's past history.

an'tēchámber, n. room leading into a larger room or hall.

an'tēdāte, v.t. affix or assign earlier than true date to; precede in time.

antēdilūv'ian, (or -lōō-), a. before the Flood; very old-fashioned.

an'tēlōpe, n. animal resembling deer.

an'tē merid'iem, between midnight and noon (abbrev. a.m., e.g. 7 a.m., etc.). (Latin)

antēnā'tal, a. before birth.

antenn'a, n. (pl. antennae), one of pair of feelers on head of insect, crustacean, etc.; (Radio) aerial.

antēr'ior, a. more to the front; prior to.

an'tēroöm, n. room leading into another; sitting-room in officers' mess.

an'them, n. sacred composition, usu. sung by church choir; song of praise or gladness.

an'ther, n. (Bot.) part of stamen containing pollen.

anthol'ogy, n. collection of chosen poems or prose passages. **anthol'ogist**, n.

an'thracīte, n. very hard variety of coal, burning with hot smokeless flame.

an'thrax, n. acute infectious disease of sheep, cattle, etc., that can be transmitted to man by infected wool, etc.

an'thropoid, a. resembling man. n. (also anthropoid ape) one of the furred tailless arboreal mammals, of the order of primates, most nearly related to man (chimpanzee, gibbon, gorilla, orang-utan).

anthropol'ogy, n. science of man; study of man as an animal and of human societies. **anthropolo'gical**, a. **anthropol'ogist**, n.

anti-, ant-, pref. (anti- before consonant or in hyphenated word; ant- before vowel), against, opposed to.

anti-air'craft (-ah-), a. (of gun, etc.) for defence against enemy aircraft.

antibīot'ic, a. & n. (substance) produced by a micro-organism and destroying or preventing growth of other micro-organisms (e.g. bacteria).

an'tibody, n. substance formed in the blood to counteract infection.

an'tic, n. (often pl.) absurd movement, trick, etc., intended to amuse.

anti'cipāte, v.t. look forward to; expect; foresee and satisfy (a need) in advance; use in advance. **anticipā'tion**, n. **anticipā'tory**, a.

anticli'max, n. lame ending to anything promising a climax. **anticlimac'tic**, a.

anti-clock'wīse (-z), adv. & a. in direction opposite to that taken by hands of clock.

anticȳ'clōne, n. atmospheric system in which

barometric pressure in the centre is high, generally associated with fine weather.

an'tidôte, *n.* drug, etc., that counteracts a poison; (fig.) something that counteracts an evil.

an'ti-freeze, *n.* chemical added to water to lower its freezing point.

an'tigėn, *n.* substance that stimulates production of antibodies.

antihis'tamine, *n.* synthetic drug used esp. in treatment of certain allergic conditions (e.g. hay-fever).

antimacass'ar, *n.* protective covering for back of chair, etc.

an'timony, *n.* brittle bluish-white metal.

antip'athy, *n.* strong and settled dislike.

antip'odês (-z), *n.pl.* region of the earth diametrically opposite, esp. to Europe. **antipodê'an,** *a.* & *n.*

antiquâr'ian, *a.* connected with the study of antiquities. *n.* antiquary. **an'tiquary,** *n.* student or collector of antiquities.

an'tiquâtèd, *a.* out of date.

antique' (-têk), *a.* dating from ancient or former times; old-fashioned. *n.* interesting, usu. valuable, object of former times, esp. work of art or piece of furniture.

anti'quity, *n.* ancientness; ancient times, esp. period of ancient Greek and Roman civilizations; (pl.) ancient buildings or objects.

antirrhi'num (-rī-), *n.* snapdragon.

antiscorbū'tic, *a.* & *n.* (medicine, etc.) preventing or curing scurvy.

anti-sėmit'ic, *a.* hostile to Jews. **antisem'itism,** *n.*

antisep'tic, *a.* & *n.* (substance) destroying or preventing growth of the bacteria that cause disease and decay.

antisô'cial (-shl), *a.* opposed to organized society; hostile to normal social practices.

antith'ėsis, *n.* (pl. *antithesės*) contrast of ideas; direct opposite.

antitox'in, *n.* serum, etc., that counteracts the toxin of a disease.

ant'ler, *n.* one of pair of bony outgrowths, often branched, on head of deer.

an'tonym, *n.* word exactly contrary in meaning to another.

an'trum, *n.* (pl. *antra*), cavity in the body, esp. one in the upper jaw-bone.

ā'nus, *n.* lower and external opening of alimentary canal.

an'vil, *n.* block, usu. of iron, on which smith hammers metal into shape.

anxī'ėty (angz-), *n.* feeling of dread and uncertainty about the future; worry; eager desire.

anxious (angk'shus), *a.* feeling anxiety; eager.

any (en'i), *a.* & *pron.* one, some, every, no matter which. *adv.* at all. *in any case*, whatever may happen. **an'ybody,** *n.* & *pron.* any person. **an'yhow,** *adv.* in any way; in any case; in a careless manner. **an'yone** (-wun), *n.* & *pron.* anybody. **an'ything,** *n.*

any thing. **an'yway,** *adv.* in any way; in any case. **an'ywhere,** *adv.* in or to any place.

An'zac, *n.* & *a.* (member) of Austral. and N.Z. Army Corps in war of 1914-18. **Anzac Day,** 25th April, day of remembrance in Australia and New Zealand.

âor'ta *n.* great artery issuing from left ventricle of heart. **âor'tic,** *a.*

ap-¹, *pref.*: see **ad-**.

ap-², *pref.*: see **apo-**.

apâce', *adv.* speedily, swiftly.

Apach'ė, *n.* (member of) Indian tribe of SW. U.S.A. **apache'** (-ahsh), *n.* Parisian street ruffian.

ap'anage, app'anage, *n.* natural accompaniment or attribute; perquisite.

apart', *adv.* distant; aside; separate(ly); into pieces. *apart from*, besides, without considering or including.

apart'heid (-t-hāt), *n.* (South African) policy of keeping people of different races apart; (racial) segregation. (Afrikaans)

apart'ment, *n.* a room in a house; (pl.) set of rooms; (U.S., sing.) flat.

ap'athy, *n.* absence of feeling or interest; indifference. **apathet'ic,** *a.* showing or having apathy.

âpe, *n.* anthropoid ape; monkey. *v.t.* imitate, mimic.

apēr'iėnt, *a.* & *n.* (medicine) causing action of the bowels; laxative.

ape'ritif, apéritif (ape'ritéf), *n.* alcoholic drink taken before meal as appetizer.

ap'erture, *n.* opening, gap; space through which light passes in camera, etc.

ā'pex, *n.* (pl. *apexes* or *apicės*), tip; summit; peak; vertex.

aphā'sia (-z-), *n.* loss of ability to use or to understand speech.

ā'phid, *n.* (pl. *aphids*), aphis.

ā'phis, *n.* (pl. *aphidēs*) very small insect, infesting leaves and young shoots of plants; greenfly, plant-louse.

aph'orism, *n.* short pithy truth or maxim.

ā'piary, *n.* place where bees are kept. **ā'piarist,** *n.* bee-keeper.

apiece', *adv.* for, to, or by each one.

ā'pish, *a.* of or like an ape.

aplomb' (-m), *n.* confidence, self-possession.

apo-, *pref.* (*ap-* before vowel or *h*), off, from, away; separate.

apoc'alypse, *n.* revelation (esp. of knowledge from God). **Apoc'alypse,** 'Revelation of St. John' in Bible. **apocalyp'tic(al),** *aa.*

Apoc'rypha, *n.* Old Testament books not accepted as genuinely inspired. **apoc'ryphal,** *a.* of doubtful authenticity.

ap'ogee, *n.* point in orbit of moon, etc., farthest from earth; highest point; climax.

Apoll'ō, *n.* (Gk. myth.) god of music and poetry; the sun-god (*Phoebus Apollo*).

apologet'ic, *a.* regretfully acknowledging fault or failure; of the nature of an apology.

apol'ogīze, *v.i.* make an apology.

apol'ogy, *n.* statement expressing regret for offence; excuse; explanation, vindication.

ap'oplexy, *n.* sudden loss of power to think, feel, or move, caused by blockage or rupture of artery in brain. **apoplec'tic,** *a.*

apos'tasy, *n.* abandonment of one's religion, political party, or principles. **apos'tate,** *n.* & *a.* (person) guilty of apostasy.

Apos'tle (-sl), *n.* any of the twelve sent forth by Christ to preach the Gospel; (*apostle*), leader of mission or reform. **apostol'ic,** *a.* of the Apostles; of the Pope as successor of St. Peter.

apos'trophe, *n.* sign (') of omitted letter(s) or of possessive case; exclamatory address to person or thing. **apos'trophize,** *v.t.* address.

apoth'ecary, *n.* (*archaic*) dispensing chemist.

apotheō'sis, *n.* (pl. *apotheosēs*), deification; transformation; deified ideal.

appal' (-awl), *v.t.* (p.t. *appalled*), dismay, terrify, shock deeply. **appall'ing,** *a.* shocking, horrifying.

appanage: see **apanage.**

apparā'tus, *n.* (pl. *apparātuses*), equipment, an appliance, for doing something, esp. scientific experiment.

appa'rel, *v.t.* (p.t. *apparelled*), dress, attire. *n.* dress, clothing.

appa'rent (*or* -ār-), *a.* clear to sight or mind; seeming. *heir apparent:* see **heir. appa'rently,** *adv.*

appari'tion, *n.* appearance, esp. of a startling kind; ghost.

appeal', *v.* apply to higher court for alteration of lower court's decision; make earnest request; be attractive. *n.* act or quality of appealing. **appea'ling,** *a.* moving; attractive.

appear', *v.i.*, become visible; present oneself; seem; (of book, etc.) be published. **appear'ance,** *n.* appearing; seeming; look, aspect; (pl.) outward show.

appease' (-z), *v.t.* soothe, calm; pacify by satisfying demands. **appease'ment,** *n.*

appell'ant, *a.* concerned with appeals. *n.* one who appeals to higher court. **appellā'tion,** *n.* title, name.

append', *v.t.* attach as adjunct; add as appendix. **appen'dage,** *n.* thing attached; addition.

appendici'tis, *n.* inflammation of the vermiform appendix.

appen'dix, *n.* (pl. *appendicēs*), subsidiary addition, esp. at end of book. (**vermiform**) **appendix,** small blind tube extending from beginning of large intestine.

appertain', *v.i.* belong, be appropriate, be relevant, *to.*

app'etīte, *n.* desire or inclination (*for* food, pleasure, etc.); enjoyment of food. **app'etīzer,** *n.* something taken to increase appetite for a meal. **app'etīzing,** *a.* exciting the appetite.

applaud', *v.* express approval, esp. by hand-clapping; praise.

applause' (-z), *n.* approval loudly expressed, esp. by hand-clapping.

app'le, *n.* (tree bearing) round firm fleshy edible fruit. *upset one's apple cart,* upset one's plans. *apple of one's eye,* cherished person or object. *in apple-pie order,* extremely neat and tidy.

appli'ance, *n.* applying; instrument or apparatus for a particular use; fire-engine.

app'licable, *a* that may be applied; appropriate, suitable. **applicabil'ity,** *n.*

app'licant, *n.* one who applies (for something, esp. office or position).

applicā'tion, *n.* applying; request; effort, attention.

applied' (-līd), *a.* put to practical use.

appliqué (aplē'kā), *n.* ornamental cut-out material applied to another material.

apply', *v.* put close *to,* put in contact; put into use; be relevant (*to*); make request or application (*for* help, post, etc., *to*). *apply oneself to,* attend closely to.

appoint', *v.t.* choose and name (person to fill office, etc.); fix (time, etc.). *well appointed,* well equipped. **appoint'ment,** *n.* act of appointing; agreement to meet at particular time; office assigned; (pl.) equipment.

appor'tion, *v.t.* assign as share; divide and share out. **appor'tionment,** *n.*

app'osite (-z-), *a.* (of remark, etc.) fitting, to the point.

apposi'tion (-z-), *n.* (Gram.) placing of word, etc., syntactically parallel with another. *in apposition,* so placed, in same case, etc.

appraise' (-z), *v.t.* fix price of; estimate value of. **apprai'sal,** *n.*

appre'ciable (-sha-), *a.* enough to be noticed or felt; perceptible.

appre'ciāte (-shi-), *v.* think highly of; be grateful for; perceive rightly; rise in value. **apprecia'tion,** *n.* **appre'ciative,** *a.* (esp.) showing gratitude or enjoyment.

apprehend', *v.t.* arrest by legal authority; understand; fear.

apprehen'sion (-shn), *n.* anxious fear, dread; understanding; arrest. **apprehen'sive,** *a.* afraid, uneasy in mind.

appren'tice, *n.* one learning craft from employer whom he is legally bound to serve for a specified period. *v.t.* bind as apprentice. **appren'ticeship,** *n.*

apprise' (-z), *v.t.* inform.

approach', *v.* come near to; make request or proposals to. *n.* (way of) approaching; way towards. **approach'able,** *a.* accessible; friendly.

approbā'tion, *n.* approval; good opinion.

appro'priate, *a.* suitable, fitting. **appro'priate,** *v.t.* take and use as one's own; devote to special purpose. **appropria'tion,** *n.*

appro'val (-rōō-), *n.* approving. *on approval* (abbrev. *on appro*), (of goods) that may be returned if not satisfactory.

approve' (-ōōv), *v.* agree to, sanction; pronounce good, have favourable opinion *of*.

approx′imate, *a*. reasonably or nearly correct; very near. **approx′imāte,** *v*. bring or come near (*to*). **approximā′tion,** *n*.

appur′tėnance, *n*. adjunct; accessory; (pl.) apparatus, gear.

ā′pricot, *n*. (tree bearing) orange-pink stone-fruit.

A′pril (ā-), *n*. fourth month of year. **April fool,** person hoaxed on *April Fools' Day*, 1st April.

ā′pron, *n*. garment worn in front of body to protect clothes; (Theatr., also *apron stage*) strip of stage in front of curtain; hard-surfaced area on airfield for aircraft on ground.

apropos′ (-pō), *adv. & pred. a*. to the point or purpose. *apropos of*, concerning, with reference to.

apse, *n*. semicircular domed or vaulted recess esp. at end of church. **ap′sidal,** *a*.

apt, *a*. suitable; quick-witted. *apt to*, inclined to, likely to. **apt′ly,** *adv*. **apt′ness,** *n*.

ap′teryx, *n*. kiwi.

ap′titūde, *n*. natural ability, talent.

a′qualung, *n*. portable breathing-apparatus for underwater swimming.

aquamarine′ (-ēn), *n*. bluish-green transparent precious stone; colour of this.

aquarelle′, *n*. painting in transparent water-colours.

aquār′ium, *n*. tank, usu. glass-sided, for aquatic plants or animals; place with such tanks.

Aquār′ius, *n*. the Water-carrier, constellation and eleventh sign of the zodiac.

aquat′ic, *a*. (of plant or animal) growing or living in or near water; (of sport) taking place on or in water.

a′quatint, *n*. (print produced by) method of engraving on copper.

a′quėduct, *n*. artificial channel for water, esp. elevated structure of masonry across valley, etc.

ā′quėous, *a*. of, like, in, water; watery; (Geol.) produced by action of water.

a′quiline, *a*. of or like an eagle; (of nose) curved like eagle's beak.

ar-, *pref.*: see **ad-**.

A′rab, *n*. person of Arabia or Arabian descent; Arab breed of horse. *a*. Arabian.

arabesque′ (-sk), *n*. design of fancifully twisted scrolls, leaves, etc.; (Mus.) ornate passage or piece; a pose in ballet dancing.

Arā′bian, *a*. of Arabia or the Arabs. *n*. Arab.

A′rabic, *n. & a*. (language) of the Arabs. **Arabic numerals,** those (1,2,3, etc.) in common use in all western countries.

a′rable, *n. & a*. (land) fit for ploughing.

arach′nid (-k-), *n*. (Zool.) member of class comprising spiders, etc.

Aramā′ic (a-), *n. & a*. (of) Semitic language formerly spoken in and around Syria.

ar′biter, *n*. person with entire control *of*;

arbitrator.

arbit′rament, *n*. decision of an arbitrator.

ar′bitrary, *a*. based on opinion only, not on reason; despotic. **ar′bitrarily,** *adv*.

ar′bitrāte, *v*. act as arbitrator; settle (dispute). **arbitrā′tion,** *n*. **ar′bitrātor,** *n*. impartial person appointed to settle a dispute; umpire.

arbor′ėal, *a*. of or living in trees.

arborē′tum, *n*. garden for cultivation and exhibition of rare trees.

ar′bour (-ber), *n*. shady nook or archway of trees or climbing plants.

arc, *n*. part of circumference of circle; (Electr.) luminous discharge produced by flow of electric current between two electrodes. **arc-lamp, arc-light,** brilliant light produced by means of electric arc.

arcāde′, *n*. covered walk; row of arches.

arcāne′, *a*. secret, mysterious.

arch[1], *n*. curved structure used to carry weight of roof, wall, bridge, etc., or as ornament or gateway; curve. *v*. furnish with arch; form (into) arch. **arch′way,** *n*. arched passage or entrance.

arch[2], *a*. playfully mischievous.

arch-, *pref*. chief, principal.

archaeol′ogy (-ki-), *n*. study of antiquities or of prehistoric remains. **archaeolo′gical,** *a*. **archaeol′ogist,** *n*.

archā′ic (-k-), *a*. antiquated; (of word or phrase) no longer in common use. **ar′-chāism,** *n*. (esp.) archaic word or phrase.

arch′ångel (-k-; -j-), *n*. angel of highest rank.

archbish′op, *n*. chief bishop.

archdea′con, *n*. Church dignitary next below bishop.

arch′dūke, *n*. (Hist.) son of Emperor of Austria.

ar′cher, *n*. one who shoots with bow and arrows. **ar′chery,** *n*. (art of) shooting with bow and arrows.

ar′chėtype (-k-), *n*. original model.

arch′fiend′, *n*. Satan.

archipel′agō (-k-), *n*. (pl. *archipelagos*), sea with many islands; group of islands.

ar′chitect (-k-), *n*. professional designer of buildings, etc.

ar′chitecture (-k-), *n*. science of building; style of building. **architec′tural,** *a*.

ar′chives (-kīvz), *n.pl*. (place for keeping) public records and other historical documents. **ar′chivist,** *n*. person in charge of archives.

arc′tic, *a*. of the North Polar regions; (fig.) very cold.

ar′dent, *a*. eager, zealous, passionate; burning. **ar′dency,** *n*.

ar′dour (-der), *n*. enthusiasm; warmth.

ar′dŭous, *a*. difficult; laborious; strenuous.

are, *pres. ind. pl*. of **be**.

ār′ėa, *n*. extent of surface; amount of surface within given limits; region; sunk yard before basement of house.

arē′na, *n*. central part of amphitheatre or of

stadium; scene of conflict or action.

ar′gil, *n.* (potter's) clay. **argillā′ceous** (--shus), *a.* of or like clay.

ar′gosy, *n.* (Hist., Poet.) large, esp. richly laden, merchant ship.

ar′got (-ō). *n.* slang used by particular class or group, esp. thieves.

ar′gūe, *v.* maintain or prove by reasoning; debate, discuss; dispute.

ar′gūment, *n.* arguing; reason put forward; summary of book. **argūmen′tative**, *a.* fond of arguing.

Ar′gus, *n.* (Gk. myth.) fabulous person with a hundred eyes. **argus-eyed**, *a.* vigilant.

a′ria (ah-), *n.* song for solo voice in opera or oratorio.

a′rid, *a.* dry, parched. **arid′ity**, *n.*

Aries (ār′iēz), *n.* the Ram, constellation and first sign of the zodiac.

aright′ (-īt), *adv.* rightly.

arīse′ (-z), *v.i.* (p.t. *arōse*, p.p. *arisen*), come into being; come up for consideration; result from; (*archaic*) get up.

aristoc′racy, *n.* the nobility; (country with) government by persons of highest social rank. **a′ristocrat**, *n.* member of the nobility. **aristocrat′ic**, *a.* of the aristocracy; having distinguished bearing and manners.

arith′mētic, *n.* science of numbers; reckoning by numbers. **arithmet′ical**, *a.* **arithmēti′cian** (-shn), *n.*

ark, *n.* covered floating vessel in which Noah, his family, and animals were saved from the Flood.

arm[1], *n.* either of two upper limbs of human body, from shoulder to hand; sleeve; branch; armlike thing. **arm′chair**, chair with supports for arms. **arm′ful** (pl. *armfuls*), as much as arm(s) can hold. **arm′pit**, hollow under arm at shoulder.

arm[2], *n.* particular kind of weapon; (pl.) weapons; (pl., Heraldry) pictorial design used by (noble) family, city, university, etc. *v.* equip with weapons; prepare for war; provide, furnish, *with.*

arma′da (-mah-), *n.* fleet of warships. (*Spanish*) *Armada*, fleet sent by Spain against England in 1588.

armadill′ō, *n.* (pl. *armadillos*), S. Amer. burrowing mammal with body encased in bony plates.

Armagedd′on (-g-), *n.* battle at end of world, described in the biblical book Revelation.

ar′mament, *n.* (usu. pl.) military forces and their equipment; (usu. pl.) weapons; arming for war.

ar′mature, *n.* keeper of magnet; (Electr.) current-carrying part of dynamo or electric motor; moving part of electric bell, buzzer, etc.

ar′mistice, *n.* agreement to stop fighting and negotiate peace terms; short truce. **Armistice Day**, 11th November, anniversary of armistice ending war of 1914-18. See also **Remembrance Sunday.**

arm′let, *n.* band worn round arm or sleeve.

armor′ial, *a.* of heraldic arms. **armorial bearings**, arms, coat of arms.

ar′mour (-mer), *n.* defensive covering formerly worn in battle; steel plates protecting ship, train, car, etc.; armoured vehicles. **ar′moured** (-merd), *a.* furnished with armour, equipped with armoured vehicles. **ar′mourer**, *n.* maker of arms; official in charge of arms. **ar′moury**, *n.* place where arms are kept.

ar′my, *n.* organized body of persons armed for fighting on land; vast number; organized body of people.

arō′ma, *n.* distinctive fragrance of a spice, plant, etc.; agreeable smell. **aromat′ic**, *a.*

arose, *p.t.* of **arise**.

around′, *adv. & prep.* on every side (of); in every direction; all round; round; about.

arouse (-z), *v.t.* stir up, move to action; awaken.

arpe′ggio (-ejiō), *n.* (pl. *arpeggios*), (Mus.) striking of notes of chord in quick succession; chord so struck.

arraign′ (-rān), *v.t.* call before lawcourt and charge; find fault with. **arraign′ment**, *n.*

arrānge′ (-nj), *v.* put in order; settle; form plans; (Mus.) adapt (composition) for different instrument(s). **arrange′ment**, *n.*

a′rrant, *a.* downright, notorious.

a′rras, *n.* (hangings of) tapestry.

array′, *v.t.* dress, esp. showily; assemble and arrange (forces). *n.* dress; military order; imposing show.

arrears′ (-z), *n.pl.* outstanding debts; work, etc., in which one is behindhand. *in arrears*, behindhand.

arrest′, *v.t.* seize by legal authority; stop; catch (person's attention, etc.). *n.* legal seizure; stopping. **arres′ting**, *a.* (fig.) striking.

arri′val, *n.* coming to one's destination; person, thing, that has arrived.

arrive′, *v.i.* come to destination or end of journey; establish one's position. *arrive at*, reach.

a′rrogant, *a.* overbearingly conceited, haughty. **a′rrogantly**, *adv.* **a′rrogance**, *n.*

a′rrogāte, *v.t.* claim unduly.

a′rrow (-ō), *n.* pointed missile shot from bow; direction-sign shaped like arrow or arrow-head. **arrow-head**, pointed end of arrow, often wedge-shaped.

a′rrowroot, *n.* nutritious starch obtained from a W. Indian plant and used as food, esp. for invalids.

ar′senal, *n.* place for manufacture or storage of weapons and ammunition.

ar′senic, *n.* a chemical element; a violently poisonous compound of this. **arsen′ical**, *a.*

ar′son, *n.* wilful setting on fire of building(s) or other property.

art[1], (*archaic*) 2nd pers. sing. pres. of **be**.

art[2], *n.* skill, esp. applied to design, representation, and imaginative creation; human skill (as opp. to nature); cunning; subject requiring skill and practice; (pl.) (esp.) subjects other than the sciences. **fine arts,** painting, sculpture, music, etc.

ar'tĕfact, ar'tifact, *n.* object made by man.

artēr'ial, *a.* of, in, like, an artery. **arterial road,** important main road.

ar'tery, *n.* one of the tubular vessels conveying blood from the heart to all parts of the body; important channel of communication and supply.

artĕ'sian well (-z-), deep well in which water rises to surface in continuous flow.

art'ful, *a.* skilful in using available methods to achieve purpose; cunning.

arthrī'tis, *n.* inflammation of joint. **arthrit'ic,** *a.*

ar'thropod, *n.* animal with jointed limbs and hard jointed external skeleton (e.g. insect, spider, crab, etc.).

Arthūr'ian, *a.* of, concerning, legends of King Arthur and his knights.

ar'tichōke, *n.* (*Jerusalem*) *artichoke*, sunflower-like plant with edible tuber. *globe artichoke*, thistle-like plant of which parts of young flower-heads are edible.

ar'ticle, *n.* piece of writing published in newspaper, magazine, etc.; clause in agreement, treaty, etc.; (particular) thing; (Gram.) *definite article*, the; *indefinite article*, a, an. *v.t.* bind by articles of apprenticeship.

artic'ūlar, *a.* of the joints.

artic'ūlate, *a.* (of speech) clear and distinct; able to express oneself in speech; having joints. **artic'ūlāte,** *v.* speak distinctly; express clearly; connect by joints. **articulated lorry,** one with trailer joined flexibly to driver's cab. **articūlā'tion,** *n.*

ar'tifice, *n.* device; cunning; skill. **artif'icer,** *n.* craftsman.

artifi'cial (-shl), *a.* not natural, not real; made by the art of man. **artificial respiration,** any of various methods of restoring suspended natural breathing. **artificial'ity** (-shia-), *n.*

artill'ery, *n.* large guns; cannon; branch of army that uses these.

artisan' (-z-), *n.* skilled workman; craftsman.

ar'tist, *n.* one who practises one of the fine arts, esp. painting; highly gifted practiser of any art. **artis'tic,** *a.* **ar'tistry,** *n.*

artiste' (-tēst), *n.* professional singer, dancer, etc.

art'less, *a.* natural, simple; without guile. **art'lessness,** *n.*

ăr'um li'ly, plant with showy white spathe.

as (az) *adv.* in same degree; similarly; like; in the character of. *conj.* while, when; since, seeing that.

as-, *pref.*: see **ad-**.

asbes'tos (az-), *n.* fibrous mineral used in manufacture of incombustible fabric and building material.

ascend', *v.* go or come up; rise; mount; climb.

ascend the throne, become king or queen.

ascen'dancy, ascen'dency, *n.* control; powerful influence.

ascen'dant, ascen'dent, *a.* & *n.* rising. *in the ascendant,* rising in power and influence; predominant.

ascen'sion (-shn), *n.* ascent, esp. of Christ to heaven. **Ascension Day,** sixth Thursday after Easter, when this is commemorated.

ascent', *n.* ascending; upward path or slope.

ascertain', *v.t.* find out. **ascertain'able,** *a.*

ascet'ic, *a.* severely abstinent; austere. *n.* one who is severe in self-discipline. **ascet'icism,** *n.*

ascor'bic a'cid, vitamin C, the antiscorbutic vitamin, occurring in citrous fruits and green vegetables.

ascrībe', *v.t.* consider as belonging *to* (person, cause).

as'dic (az-), *n.* sonar.

ăsep'sis, *n.* absence of sepsis or of harmful bacteria; aseptic method in surgery. **ăsep'tic,** *a.* preventing septic infection by securing absence of bacteria; sterilized.

ăsex'ūal, *a.* without sex; (Biol., of reproduction) by other than sexual means.

ash¹, *n.* (wood of) forest tree.

ash², *n.* powdery residue left after substance is burned; (pl.) remains of human body after cremation. **ash-tray,** receptacle for tobacco--ash, etc. **Ash Wednesday,** first day of Lent.

ashāmed' (-md), *a.* abashed or upset by feeling of shame.

ash'en, *a.* of ash wood; of the colour of ashes; deathly pale.

ash'lar, *n.* square hewn stone(s); masonry of this.

ashore', *adv.* to or on shore.

ash'y, *a.* of or like ashes; pale.

Asian (ā'shn), **Asiat'ic** (āshi-), *nn.* & *aa.* (native) of Asia.

aside', *adv.* to or on one side; away, apart. *aside from,* (U.S.) apart from. *n.* words spoken aside by actor, supposed not to be heard by others on stage.

as'inine, *a.* of asses; stupid.

ask (ah-), *v.* put a question to; make a request (for); invite, demand. *ask after someone,* inquire about his health.

askance', *adv.* sideways. *look askance at,* view suspiciously.

askew', *adv.* obliquely., crookedly.

aslant' (-ahnt), *adv.* obliquely. *prep.* slantingly across.

asleep', *adv.* & *pred. a.* in a state of sleep; (of limbs) benumbed.

asp, *n.* small venomous snake.

aspa'ragus, *n.* plant cultivated for its tender edible shoots.

as'pect, *n.* way thing presents itself to sight or mind; direction in which building, etc., faces, side facing in stated direction.

as'pen, *n.* kind of poplar with quivering leaves.

aspe′rity, *n.* roughness; harshness (of temper, etc.); bitter cold (of weather).

asper′sion (-shn), *n.* slander. *cast aspersions on*, attack reputation of.

as′phalt, *n.* bituminous substance occurring naturally or derived from petroleum; mixture of this with sand, etc., used for surfacing flat roofs, pavements, etc. *v.t.* surface with asphalt.

asphyx′ia, *n.* suffocation. **asphyx′iăte**, *v.t.* suffocate. **asphyxiă′tion**, *n.* .

as′pic, *n.* savoury jelly, usu. containing cooked meat, fish, eggs, etc.

aspidis′tra, *n.* plant with broad pointed leaves, grown indoors as pot-plant.

as′pirant (*or* aspīr′-), *n.* one who aspires.

as′pirate, *n.* sound of *h*; sound with an *h* in it. **as′pirăte**, *v.t.* pronounce with *h*.

aspiră′tion, *n.* aspiring; ambition; aspirating.

aspīre′, *v.i.* have earnest desire or ambition (*to*, *after*).

as′pirin, *n.* drug, usu. in tablet form, taken to relieve pain and reduce fever.

ass, *n.* long-eared quadruped related to horse but smaller, donkey; (*slang*) stupid person.

assagai: see **assegai**.

assail′, *v.t.* attack, assault. **assail′able**, *a.* open to attack. **assail′ant**, *n.*

assass′in, *n.* one hired to kill another treacherously; murderer. **assass′inăte**, *v.t.* kill by treacherous violence. **assassină′tion**, *n.*

assault′, *n.* armed attack on fortress, etc., by sudden rush; unlawful attack on person. *v.t.* make assault on.

assay′, *n.* testing of alloy or ore to determine proportion of a given metal; testing of gold and silver for fineness. *v.t.* test purity of; (*archaic*) attempt.

ass′ĕgai, ass′agai (-gī), *n.* slender spear used as missile by S. Afr. peoples.

assem′blage, *n.* collection; concourse of people.

assem′ble, *v.* bring or come together; fit together parts of (machine, etc.).

assem′bly, *n.* gathering of people, esp. for a common purpose; putting together. **assembly line**, sequence of machines, workers, etc., for assembly of product.

assent′, *v.i.* agree (*to*); express agreement; say yes. *n.* agreement; formal consent.

assert′, *v.t.* declare positively; maintain claim to. *assert oneself*, insist on one's rights. **asser′tion**, *n.* **asser′tive**, *a.* positive, dogmatic.

assess′, *v.t.* fix amount of (tax, damages, etc.); estimate value of (property, etc.), esp. for taxation. **assess′ment**, *n.* **assess′or**, *n.* one who assesses property, income, taxes, etc.; adviser to judge or magistrate.

ass′et, *n.* (pl.) all the available property of person or company; (sing.) item of this in balance-sheet; (sing.) any possession or useful quality.

assev′erăte, *v.t.* solemnly declare. **asseveră′-tion**, *n.*

assidū′ity, *n.* constant and careful attention. **assi′dŭous**, *a.* persevering, diligent.

assign′ (-īn), *v.t.* give to person as his share or duty; transfer formally; appoint; ascribe.

assigna′tion (-gn-), *n.* appointment of time and place (esp. for a private meeting).

assign′ment (-īn-), *n.* task allotted; legal transference.

assim′ilăte, *v.* absorb, be absorbed, into the system; make or become like. **assimilă′tion**, *n.*

assist′, *v.* help. **assis′tance**, *n.* help.

assis′tant, *n.* helper; subordinate worker, esp. serving customers.

assīze′, *n.* (usu. pl.) periodical sessions held (until 1971) by judges on circuit in counties of England and Wales.

assō′ciăte (*or* -shi-), *v.* join or connect; connect in idea. *associate with*, be often in the company of. **assō′ciate** (-shiat), *n.* partner, companion; subordinate member of association. *a.* allied.

assōciă′tion (*or* -shi-), *n.* organized body of persons; fellowship; connection of ideas. **Association football**, kind of football played with round ball which may be handled only by goalkeeper when it is in play.

ass′onance, *n.* resemblance of sound between two syllables; rhyme depending on similarity of vowel-sounds only. **ass′onant**, *a.*

assor′tĕd, *a.* of different sorts put together; matched, suited. **assort′ment**, *n.* assorted set of goods; mixture.

assuage′ (-swāj), *v.t.* soothe; allay. **assuāge′ment**, *n.*

assūme′, *v.t.* take as true; take upon oneself; simulate.

assump′tion, *n.* assuming; thing assumed.

assur′ance (ashoor-), *n.* positive statement; self-confidence; (life) insurance.

assure (ashoor′), *v.t.* tell confidently; convince; make certain. **assur′ĕdly**, *adv.* certainly.

as′ter, *n.* composite plant with showy flowers.

as′terisk, *n.* star (*) as mark of reference.

astern′, *adv.* (Naut.) in, at, towards, stern; behind, backwards.

as′teroid, *n.* any of numerous small planets between orbits of Mars and Jupiter.

asth′ma (asm-), *n.* disease marked by difficulty in breathing. **asthmat′ic**, *a.* of, suffering from, asthma. *n.* person suffering from asthma.

astig′matism, *n.* defect in eye or lens preventing proper focusing.

astir′, *adv.* & *pred. a.* in motion; out of bed.

aston′ish, *v.t.* amaze; surprise. **aston′ishing**, *a.* very surprising. **aston′ishment**, *n.*

astound′, *v.t.* shock with surprise.

astrakhan′ (-kan), *n.* (cloth imitating) Persian lamb, a soft tightly-curled fur.

as′tral, *a.* of or connected with stars.

astray′, *adv.* & *pred. a.* out of the right way;

in, into, error or wrongdoing.

astride', *adv.*, *pred. a.*, & *prep.* with one leg on each side of; with legs wide apart.

astrin'gent (-j-), *a.* contracting or drawing together organic tissues; (fig.) severe. *n.* astringent substance. **astrin'gency**, *n.*

astrol'ogy, *n.* study of supposed influence of stars on human affairs. **astrol'oger**, *n.* **astrolo'gical**, *a.*

as'tronaut, *n.* traveller in space. **astronau'tics**, *n.* science of navigation in space. **astronau'tic(al)**, *aa.*

astron'omy, *n.* science of the heavenly bodies. **astron'omer**, *n.* student of, expert in, astronomy. **astronom'ic(al)** *aa.* of or concerned with astronomy; very big, immense.

astrophys'ics (-fiz-), *n.* branch of astronomy dealing with the physical and chemical properties of the heavenly bodies.

astūte', *a.* shrewd, crafty.

asun'der, *adv.* apart; in pieces.

asy'lum, *n.* (place of) refuge or shelter; (*formerly*) mental hospital.

asymm'etry (*or* ā-), *n.* absence of symmetry. **asymmet'rical**, *a.*

at, *prep.* expressing position or time of day; indicating direction, occupation, rate, degree, value, cost. *at all*, in any way, of any kind.

at-, pref.: see **ad-**.

at'avism, *n.* resemblance to remote ancestors rather than to parents. **atavis'tic**, *a.*

ate, p.t. of **eat**.

ā'theism, *n.* disbelief in the existence of God. **ā'theist**, *n.* **ātheis'tic**, *a.*

athirst', *pred. a.* (*archaic*) thirsty; eager (*for*).

ath'lēte, *n.* one who competes or excels in sport(s), esp. running, jumping, etc.

athlet'ic, *a.* of athletes; physically powerful. **athlet'ics**, *n. pl.* physical exercises; sports, esp. running, jumping, etc.

athwart' (-ort), *adv.* & *prep.* across; from side to side of.

at'las, *a.* book of maps.

at'mosphere, *n.* mixture of gases surrounding the earth or any heavenly body; mental or moral environment; air. **atmosphe'ric**, *a.* *atmospheric pressure*, pressure of weight of column of air above given point. **atmosphe'rics**, *n. pl.* electrical discharges in the atmosphere interfering with radio reception.

atoll' (*or* at'-), *n.* coral reef or series of coral reefs surrounding a lagoon.

at'om, *n.* (Phys.) smallest particle of an element that can exist alone or in combination with other particles, consisting of a positively charged nucleus round which negatively charged electrons orbit; very small thing. **atom bomb**, atomic bomb. **atom'ic**, *a.* of atom(s). **atomic bomb**, bomb deriving destructive power from partial conversion of atomic energy. **atomic energy**, energy released by fission of heavy atomic nuclei or

by fusing of light atomic nuclei. **atomic pile**, nuclear reactor (see **reactor**).

at'omize, *v.t.* reduce (liquid) to fine spray; damage or destroy with atomic weapon. **at'omizer**, *n.* device for spraying liquid.

ātō'nal, *a.* (Mus.) composed without observance of a key. **ātōnal'ity**, *n.*

atōne', *v.i.* make amends (*for* sin, wrong done); expiate. **atōne'ment**, *n.*

ā'trium, *n.* (pl. *atria*), either of two upper cavities of the heart that receive blood from the veins.

atrō'cious (-shus), *a.* excessively cruel or wicked; very bad. **atro'city**, *n.* atrocious act; (*informal*) hideous object.

at'rophy, *n.* wasting away for lack of nourishment or use. *v.* cause or suffer atrophy.

attach', *v.* fasten, join; connect; bind by love or affection; attribute *to*; seize by legal authority. **attach'ment**, *n.*

attaché (atash'ā), *n.* junior official attached to staff of embassy. **attaché case**, small rectangular case for carrying documents etc.

attack', *v.t.* fall upon with (esp. armed) force; assault; criticize adversely in speech or writing; act destructively on. *n.* act of attacking; assault; onset or period of illness, etc.

attain', *v.* reach, gain, accomplish; arrive at. **attain'able**, *a.* **attain'ment**, *n.* attaining; (esp., pl.) personal accomplishments.

attempt', *v.t.* try; try to accomplish or master. *n.* attempting; endeavour.

attend', *v.* be present at; accompany as attendant; look after (as doctor or nurse). *attend to*, give one's mind or energies to; wait upon, serve (customer, etc.). **atten'dance**, *n.* being present; the persons present. **atten'dant**, *a.* accompanying. *n.* employee; servant.

atten'tion, *n.* act of applying one's mind to something; care, consideration; drill position in which one stands straight and still; (pl.) kind and polite acts; courtship. **atten'tive**, *a.* heedful, observant; polite.

atten'ūate, *v.t.* make thin or slender; weaken; dilute. **atten'ūation**, *n.*

attest', *v.t.* certify validity of; be or give proof of. **attes'ted**, *a.* (of cattle) certified free from disease. **attestā'tion**, *n.*

att'ic, *n.* (room in) storey immediately under roof.

attīre', *v.t.* & *n.* dress, array.

att'itūde, *n.* posture of body; settled opinion or way of thinking.

attor'ney (-ter-), *n.* one authorized (by *letter or power of attorney*) to act for another in business or legal matters; (U.S.) lawyer.

attract', *v.t.* draw towards oneself or itself; arouse interest or pleasure in. **attrac'tion**, *n.* act or power of attracting; thing that attracts. **attrac'tive**, *a.* charming, good-looking, pleasing.

attrib'ūte, *v.t.* (with *to*) consider to be result or author of; ascribe as belonging or appropriate to. **att'ribūte**, *n.* characteristic quality;

object regarded as appropriate to person or office. **attrib'ūtive,** *a.* (Gram., of adjective or noun, opp. *predicative*) qualifying.

attri'tion, *n.* friction, abrasion; wearing out.

attūne', *v. t.* bring into harmony or agreement; adapt.

au'burn, *a.* (usu. of hair) reddish brown.

auc'tion, *n.* sale in which articles are sold to maker of highest bid. *v. t.* sell by auction. **auctioneer',** *n.* one who conducts auction.

audā'cious (-shus), *a.* daring; bold; impudent. **auda'city,** *n.*

au'dible, *a.* that can be heard. **audibil'ity,** *n.*

au'diènce, *n.* assembly of listeners or spectators; persons. within hearing; formal interview.

audio-, *pref.* of sound or hearing. **audio-frē'quency,** *n.* frequency of normally audible sound-waves. **audio-vis'ūal** (-z- *or* -zh-), *a.* directed at both hearing and sight.

au'dit, *n.* official examination of accounts. *v. t.* examine (accounts) officially.

audi'tion, *n.* trial hearing of actor, singer, etc. *v. t.* give audition to.

au'ditor, *n.* one who audits accounts; hearer, listener.

auditor'ium, *n.* part of building occupied by audience.

au'ditory, *a.* of or concerned with hearing.

au'ger (-'g-), *n.* tool, larger than gimlet, for boring holes in wood.

aught (awt), *n.* (*archaic*) anything.

augment', *v.* increase in size, number, or amount. **augmentā'tion,** *n.*

au'gur, *n.* religious official of ancient Rome who observed omens to discover whether gods approved a proposed plan of action. *v.* foretell; be a sign or warning of. **au'gūry,** *n.* prediction; omen.

august', *a.* majestic, venerable, impressive.

Au'gust, *n.* eighth month of year.

auk, *n.* any of various northern sea-birds, including puffin, guillemot, and extinct flightless *great auk.*

aunt (ahnt), *n.* father's or mother's sister or sister-in-law. **Aunt Sally,** game of throwing balls at wooden head.

au pair (ō pār), (foreigner) performing domestic, etc., duties in return for hospitality, opportunity to learn language, etc. (French)

au'ra, *n.* subtle atmosphere surrounding and thought to come from person or thing.

au'ral, *a.* of the ear or the sense of hearing.

au'rèōle, *n.* halo.

au revoir (ō rivwar'), (goodbye) till we meet again. (French)

au'ricle, *n.* outer part of ear; small appendage to atrium of heart. **auric'ūlar,** *a.* of the ear.

aurif'erous, *a.* yielding gold.

Auror'a, *n.* Roman goddess of dawn. **aurora boreā'lis,** streamers or bands of coloured light sometimes seen above horizon in northern latitudes (*northern lights*); **aurora austrā'lis,** similar phenomenon seen in southern latitudes.

aus'pice, *n.* omen; (pl.) patronage. *under the auspices of,* helped and encouraged by. **auspi'cious** (-shus), *a.* favourable; promising.

austēre', *a.* morally strict; stern; severely simple, without ornament or comfort. **auste'rity,** *n.*

Austrā'lian, *a. & n.* (native, inhabitant) of Australia.

aut-, *pref.*: see **auto-.**

au'tarchy (-k-), *n.* absolute sovereignty.

au'tarky, *n.* self-sufficiency (esp. of a State in its economic affairs).

authen'tic, *a.* of undisputed origin, genuine; reliable. **authen'tically,** *adv.* **authen'ticāte,** *v. t.* establish the truth or authorship of. **authenticā'tion,** *n.* **authenti'city,** *n.* genuineness; quality of being authentic.

au'thor, *n.* writer of book, etc; originator. **au'thoress,** *n. fem.* **au'thorship,** *n.*

authoritār'ian (-o-ri-), *a. & n.* (person) favouring obedience to authority as opposed to individual liberty. **authoritār'ianism,** *n.*

autho'ritative, *a.* having authority.

autho'rity, *n.* power or right to enforce obedience; person or official body having authority; (book, etc., referred to for) conclusive opinion or statement; expert.

au'thorize, *v. t.* sanction; empower; justify. **Authorized Version** (of Bible), English translation of 1611. **authorizā'tion,** *n.*

au'tism, *n.* (Med.) condition of morbid self-absorption and inability to communicate or form relationships with others. **autis'tic,** *a.*

auto-, aut-, *pref.* (*auto-* before consonant or in hyphenated word; *aut-* before vowel), self-; by one's or its own agency.

autobiog'raphy, *n.* (writing of) person's own life story. **autobiog'rapher,** *n.* **autobiograph'ic(al),** *aa.*

autoc'racy, *n.* government by ruler with unlimited power. **aut'ocrat,** *n.* ruler with unlimited power; overbearing person. **autocrat'ic,** *a.*

au'tograph (-ahf), *n.* one's own handwriting, esp. signature. *v. t.* write one's name on or in, sign.

automat'ic, *a.* acting of itself; mechanically self-operating; (of actions) unconscious, involuntary. *n.* automatic pistol. **automatic pilot,** device in aircraft for maintaining set course and height. **automat'ically,** *adv.*

automā'tion, *n.* automatic control of manufacture of product through successive stages.

autom'aton, *n.* (pl. *automatons, automata*), piece of mechanism with concealed motive power and lifelike actions; machine-like person.

au'tomobile (-ēl), *n.* (chiefly U.S.) motor car.

auton'omous, *a.* self-governing. **auton'omy,** *n.* (right of) self-government.

autop'sy (*or* aw'-), *n.* post-mortem examination.

au'tumn (-m), *n.* third season of year,

between summer and winter. **autum'nal**, *a*.

auxil'iary (-gz-), *a*. helpful; supplementary; subsidiary; (of verb) serving to form tenses, moods, or voices of other verbs. *n*. assistant; auxiliary verb.

avail', *v*. be of use or assistance (to); help, benefit. *avail oneself of*, make use of. *n*. use, advantage.

avail'able, *a*. capable of being used; ready for one's use; obtainable. **availabil'ity**, *n*.

av'alanche (-lahnsh), *n*. great mass of snow, ice, rock, etc., loosened and sliding swiftly down mountain.

av'arice, *n*. excessive desire for getting and hoarding wealth. **avari'cious** (-shus), *a*. greedy, miserly.

Ave Maria (ah'vā marē'a), (*Hail Mary*), devotional recitation and prayer to Virgin Mary. (Latin).

avenge' (-nj), *v. t*. take vengenance for; inflict retributive punishment on behalf of.

av'ĕnŭe, *n*. roadway, approach to house, bordered by trees; way of approach; wide street.

aver', *v. t*. (p.t. *averred*), assert; affirm.

av'erage, *n*. arithmetical mean, the result of adding several quantities together and dividing total by number of quantities; ordinary or usual standard or rate. *a*. estimated by average; of ordinary standard. *v. t*. estimate the average of; amount to as an average.

averse', *a*. opposed (*to*); unwilling. **aver'sion** (-shn), *n*. dislike or antipathy; object of dislike.

avert', *v. t*. turn away; ward off.

ā'viary, *n*. large cage or building in which birds are kept.

āviā'tion, *n*. (science of) flying in powered aircraft. **ā'viātor**, *n*.

av'id, *a*. eager, greedy. **avid'ity**, *n*.

avoca'do (-kah-), *n*. (pl. *avocados*), succulent pear-shaped tropical fruit.

avoca'tion, *n*. minor occupation, hobby.

avoid', *v. t*. keep away from; refrain from; evade. **avoi'dance**, *n*.

avoirdupois (averdŭpoiz'), *n*. system of weights with ounces, etc., as units.

avow', *v. t*. admit; declare openly; confess. **avow'al**, *n*. **avow'ĕdly**, *adv*.

avunc'ŭlar, *a*. of or like an uncle.

await' (a-w-), *v. t*. wait for.

awāke' (a-w-), *v*. (p.t. *awōke*, p.p. *awāked* or *awōken*), cease to sleep; become active, be aroused *to*; rouse from sleep, *pred. a*. not asleep; watchful. *awake to*, aware of. **awā'ken**, *v*. awake, arouse (*to*).

award' (a-word), *v. t*. give or grant (by official decision). *n*. judicial decision; thing awarded.

awāre' (a-w-), *pred. a*. conscious, not ignorant (*of*). **awāre'ness**, *n*.

awash' (a-wo-), *pred. a*. level with or washed over by the waves.

away' (a-w-), *adv*. to or at a distance; continuously; to nothing.

awe, *n*. reverence mingled with fear. *v. t*. inspire with awe. **awe'some**, *a*. terrible, dread. **awe'struck**, *a*. overwhelmed by awe.

aweigh (a-wā'), *adv*. (Naut., of anchor) just raised from bottom.

aw'ful, *a*. solemnly impressive; (*informal*) very bad, very great. **aw'fully**, *adv*. (esp., *informal*) very (much).

awhile' (a-w-), *adv*. for a short time.

awk'ward, *a*. ill-adapted for use; hard to deal with; clumsy. **awk'wardness**, *n*.

awl, *n*. small tool for making holes.

awn, *n*. bristly end of grain-sheath of barley, oats, etc.

aw'ning, *n*. roof-like covering of canvas, etc.

awoke, *p. t*. of **awake**.

awry (a-rī'), *adv*. crookedly; amiss.

axe, *n*. chopping-tool, usu. of iron with steel edge and wooden handle. *v. t*. cut down (also fig.); eliminate, dismiss.

ax'iom, *n*. self-evident truth; established principle. **axiomat'ic**, *a*.

ax'is, *n*. (pl. *axēs*), line round which a body rotates; line dividing regular figure symmetrically.

ax'le, *n*. rod on or with which wheel or pair of wheels revolves; axle-tree. **axle-tree**, *n*. bar connecting pair of wheels on vehicle.

ay, aye[1] (ī), *int*. yes. *n*. (pl. *ayes*), answer or vote in the affirmative.

ayah (ī'a), *n*. (in India, etc.) children's nurse.

aye[2] (ā), *adv*. (*archaic*) always.

azā'lĕa, *n*. shrubby flowering plant.

a'zūre (*or* azh-), *n*. sky blue; (Poet.) blue unclouded sky. *a*. sky-blue.

B

baa (bah), *n. & v. i*. (p.t. *baaed*), bleat.

Bā'al, *n*. (pl. *Baalim*), Phoenician and Canaanite god; false god.

babb'le, *v*. talk indistinctly, foolishly, or excessively; (of stream) make low continuous sound. *n*. idle talk; prattle.

bābe, *n.* baby.

bā'bel, *n.* scene of confusion; noisy assembly.

baboōn', *n.* large monkey with dog-like snout.

bā'by, *n.* very young child; childish person. **bā'byhood,** *n.* **bā'byish,** *a.*

bā'by-sitter, *n.* person employed to remain with child(ren) while parents are out.

bacc'arat (-rah), *n.* gambling card-game.

bacch'anal (-ka-), *a.* of Bacchus (Greek god of wine) or his rites. **bacchanā'lia,** *n.pl.* drunken revelry.

bach'elor, *n.* unmarried man; one who has taken first university degree (*Bachelor of Arts*, etc.).

bacill'us, *n.* (pl. *bacilli*), rod-shaped bacterium, esp. one causing disease.

back, *n.* surface of human body adjacent to spine; corresponding part of animal's body; part of thing(s) situated behind, away from front; rear; (player in) defending position in some team-games. *a.* situated behind; remote; belonging to past period. *adv.* to the rear; in(to) earlier or remote position. *v.* put or be a back or background to; support with money or argument; bet on; cause to move, go, backwards. *back out of,* withdraw from. *back up,* support. **back benches,** seats in House of Commons occupied by members **(back-benchers)** not entitled to sit in front benches (see **front benches).**

back'bīte, *v.t.* speak ill of, slander. **back'-bīter,** *n.*

back'bōne, *n.* spine, main support; firmness of character.

back'cloth, *n.* painted cloth at back of scene or stage.

back'er, *n.* supporter; one who backs (horse, etc.).

back'fīre', *n.* (noise caused by) too early explosion of gas in an engine. **backfīre',** *v.i.* produce backfire.

backgamm'on, *n.* game for two played on double board with draughts and dice.

back'ground, *n.* back part of scene; obscure or less prominent position; person's social surroundings, education, etc.

back'hand, back'handed, *aa.* delivered with back of hand or with back of hand turned in direction of stroke; (of handwriting) sloping to left; sarcastic or ambiguous. **backhan'-der,** *n.* backhand blow.

back'lash, *n.* sudden violent backward movement; slack or play between parts of mechanism, etc.

back'log, *n.* arrears of work, etc.

back'slīde, *v.i.* fall back into sin, error, etc. **back'slī'der,** *n.*

backstāge', *adv.* (Theatr.) behind the scenes.

back'stitch, *v.* sew with stitches overlapping on wrong side. *n.* stitch made thus.

back'ward(s), *adv.* back foremost; reverse way. **back'ward,** *a.* directed backwards; slow in learning.

back'water (-waw-), *n.* still water beside stream and fed by its flow; place or condition where there is no progress.

back'woods (-z), *n.pl.* remote forest-land. **back'woodsman,** *n.* (pl. -*men*), settler in this.

bā'con, *n.* cured back and sides of pig.

bacteria: see **bacterium.**

bactēriol'ogy, *n.* study of bacteria, esp. as branch of medicine. **bactēriolo'gical,** *a.* **bactēriol'ogist,** *n.*

bactēr'ium, *n.* (pl. *bacteria*), microscopic single-celled organism occurring in large numbers, some types causing decay and disease.

bad, *a.* (*worse, worst*), worthless; defective; unfavourable; disagreeable; wicked; decayed; harmful, painful; ill, in pain.

bad, bade, *p.t.* of **bid.**

badge, *n.* thing worn as mark of office, membership, etc.

badg'er, *n.* nocturnal, dark-furred, burrowing mammal. *v.t.* worry, pester.

bad'inage (-ahzh), *n.* banter.

bad'ly, *adv.* unsuccessfully; incorrectly; to a serious extent.

bad'minton, *n.* game somewhat resembling lawn-tennis, played with shuttlecock.

baff'le, *v.t.* perplex, frustrate, foil. **baff'ling,** *a.* bewildering.

bag, *n.* container made of cloth, leather, paper, etc., with opening usu. at top; all game a sportsman has shot. *v.* (p.t. *bagged*), put in bag; bulge; hang loosely. **bagg'y** (-g-), *a.* hanging loosely.

bagatelle', *n.* mere trifle; game played with (cues and) balls on board with semicircular end.

bagg'age, *n.* portable equipment of army; luggage.

bag'pipe(s), *n.* musical instrument with wind-bag held under arm. **bag'piper,** *n.*

bail[1], *n.* security for accused person's appearance for trial; person who becomes surety. *v.t.* **bail** (*out*), become bail for and secure temporary liberation of.

bail[2], *n.* (Cricket) either of the cross-pieces over the stumps.

bail[3], **bāle**[3], *v.* **bail** (*out*), throw water out of boat, etc., with pail, etc. *bale out,* (of airman) make emergency descent from aircraft by parachute.

bai'ley, *n.* (Hist.) open space enclosed by fortification.

Bai'ley bridge, emergency bridge designed for rapid construction from prefabricated parts.

bai'lie, *n.* a magistrate in a Scottish burgh.

bai'liff, *n.* sheriff's officer; landowner's agent or manager.

bairn, *n.* (Sc.) child.

bait, *v.t.* worry (animal) by setting dogs at it; torment (person) by jeers; put bait on or in (fish-hook, trap, etc.). *n.* food to entice prey; temptation, allurement.

baize, *n.* coarse, usu. green, woollen stuff used for covering tables, etc.

bāke, *v.* cook by dry heat; harden by heat; be or become baked. **bāking-powder,** powder used to make cakes, etc., rise.

bā′kĕlīte, *n.* brand of plastic material. **P.**

bā′ker, *n.* professional maker of bread, cakes, etc. *baker's dozen,* thirteen. **bā′kery,** *n.* place for, trade of, baking bread, etc.

Balacla′va (hel′met) (-klahva), woollen cap covering head and neck.

balalai′ka (-līka), *n.* Russian guitar-like instrument with triangular body.

bal′ance, *n.* apparatus for weighing; steady position; excess of assets over liabilities and vice versa; remainder. *v.* weigh; bring or come into a steady position; equalize (the two sides of) an account. **bal′ance-sheet,** statement of assets and liabilities.

bal′cony, *n.* outside balustraded platform with access from upper-floor window; (Theatr.) set of tiered seats usu. above circle.

bald (bawld), *a.* wholly or partly without hair on scalp; without fur, feathers, etc.; bare; meagre, dull. **bal′ding,** *a.* going bald.

baldachin, baldaquin (bawl′dakin; *or* bal′-), *n.* canopy over altar, throne, etc.

bal′derdash (bawl-), *n.* jumble of words, nonsense.

bal′dric (bawl-), *n.* belt for sword, bugle, etc., worn over shoulder.

bāle[1], *n.* (*archaic*) evil, destruction, woe. **bāle′ful,** *a.* evil, harmful.

bāle[2], *n.* large bundle or package of merchandise, *v.t.* make up into bales.

bale[3]: see **bail**[3].

baleen′, *n.* whalebone.

balk, baulk (bawk), *n.* roughly squared timber beam; stumbling-block. *v.* hinder; discourage; jib, shy.

ball[1] (bawl), *n.* solid or hollow sphere, esp. one used in a game; rounded mass of anything; missile for cannon, rifle, etc. **ball-bearing,** bearing in which revolving parts turn on small steel balls. **ball-point (pen),** pen with small ball-bearing as writing-point.

ball[2] (bawl), *n.* social gathering for dancing. **ball′room,** *n.*

ball′ad, *n.* simple song; narrative poem in short stanzas. **ball′adry,** *n.* ballad poetry.

ball′ast, *n.* heavy material carried in ship's hold, balloon, etc., for stability. *v.t.* supply with ballast.

ballerin′a (-ēna), *n.* female solo ballet-dancer.

ball′et (-lā), *n.* stage entertainment telling story or expressing idea in dancing and mime.

ballis′tic, *a.* of projectiles. **ballistic missile,** guided missile, with powered ascent and free fall. **ballis′tics,** *n.* science of projectiles.

balloon′, *n.* large air-tight bag inflated with gas lighter than air or with hot air, sometimes with basket slung beneath for passengers, etc.; small rubber bag inflated with air or gas as toy.

ball′ot, *n.* secret voting; ball or paper used in ballot; drawing of lots. *v.i.* vote by ballot; draw lots.

ballyhoo′, *n.* noisy or vulgar or misleading publicity.

balm (bahm), *n.* fragrant oil or resin from various trees; ointment; soothing influence; tree yielding balm. **balm′y,** *a.* of or like balm; mild, fragrant, soothing; barmy.

balmo′ral, *n.* round Scottish cap.

bal′sa (bawl- *or* bol-), *n.* tropical American tree. *balsa* (*wood*), its extremely light wood.

bal′sam (bawl- *or* bol-), *n.* balm; tree yielding balm; a flowering plant.

bal′uster, *n.* short pillar; post supporting handrail of staircase; (pl.) posts and handrail.

balustrāde′, *n.* row of balusters with rail as parapet to balcony, etc.

bamboo′, *n.* tropical giant grass with hollow jointed stem that becomes woody.

bamboo′zle, *v.t.* hoax, mystify.

ban, *v.t.* (p.t. *banned*), forbid. *n.* formal order that forbids something.

banal′ (-ahl; *or* bā′nal), *a.* commonplace. **banal′ity,** *n.*

bana′na (-nahna), *n.* tropical fruit-tree; its finger-shaped fruit.

band, *n.* flat strip of thin material; hoop of iron, rubber, etc.; stripe of colour, etc.; belt connecting wheels; body of musicians; group of persons. *v.* form into league; put band on.

ban′dage, *n.* strip of material for binding up wound, etc. *v.t.* tie up with bandage.

bandann′a, *n.* large coloured handkerchief with white or yellow spots.

band′box, *n.* cardboard box for hats.

ban′deau (-dō), *n.* (pl. *bandeaux*, pr. -dōz), woman's hair-band.

ban′dit, *n.* outlaw; brigand.

bandoleer′, bandolier′ (-ēr), *n.* belt with loops for cartridges, worn over shoulder.

band′stand, *n.* (roofed) platform for band.

ban′dy, *v.t.* throw or pass to and fro; exchange. *n.* old form of hockey. *a.* (of legs) wide apart at the knees.

bāne, *n.* cause of ruin or trouble; (*archaic*) poison. **bāne′ful,** *a.*

bang[1], *v.* strike or shut noisily; make sound as of blow or explosion; treat roughly. *n.* loud noise; sharp blow. *adv.* with a bang.

bang[2], *n.* hair cut straight across forehead.

bang′le (-nggl), *n.* rigid bracelet or anklet.

ban′ish, *v.t.* compel (person) to leave his country; send or drive away. **ban′ishment,** *n.*

ban′ister, *n.* post supporting handrail of staircase; (pl.) posts and handrail.

ban'jō, *n.* (pl. *banjos*), guitar-like instrument with circular body.

bank[1], *n.* raised shelf of ground; slope; ground at edge of river; mass (of clouds). *v.* confine within banks; build up outer edge of (road, etc., at bend); (of aircraft, esp. when turning) fly with one side higher.

bank[2], *n.* establishment for keeping, paying out, lending, and exchanging money; (Med.) reserve supply (of blood, etc.). *v.* deposit money at bank. *bank on*, rely on. **bank holiday**, day when banks are closed by law, kept as public holiday. **bank'nôte**, piece of paper money issued by a bank. **bank'er**, *n.* partner, director, etc., of a bank.

bank'rupt, *a.* unable to pay debts. *n.* person unable to pay his debts. *v.t.* make bankrupt. **bank'ruptcy**, *n.*

bann'er, *n.* piece of cloth, cardboard, etc., bearing announcement or slogan, carried on pole(s) in procession, etc.; flag.

bann'ock, *n.* (Sc.) flat round cake of oatmeal.

banns (-z), *n.pl.* notice of intended marriage, read on three Sundays in church.

ban'quet, *n.* feast; dinner with speeches. *v.* regale; take part in banquet.

ban'shee', *n.* (Gaelic folklore) spirit whose wail is an omen of death.

ban'tam, *n.* small kind of fowl, of which the cock is a fighter.

ban'ter, *n.* humorous ridicule. *v.* make good-humoured fun of; jest.

Ban'tu (-tōō), *n.* (pl. same), large group of African negroid races; their languages.

ban'yan, *n.* banyan (*tree*), Indian fig whose branches root themselves over a large area.

bā'obab, *n.* African tree having extremely thick trunk and woody fruit with edible pulp.

bap, *n.* soft flattish bread roll.

bap'tism, *n.* religious rite of immersion in, or sprinkling with, water to denote admission to the Christian Church. **baptis'mal** (-z-), *a.*

Bap'tist, *n.* one of a sect objecting to infant baptism and practising immersion.

baptize', *v.t.* give baptism to; christen; give a name to.

bar, *n.* piece of rigid material, long in proportion to its thickness; broad line, band; barrier; strip of silver across medal-ribbon as extra distinction; (Mus., usu. *bar-line*), vertical line dividing piece into sections of equal time-value; (Mus.) such section; (room containing) counter at which refreshments are served; barristers, their profession. *v.t.* (p.t. *barred*), fasten with bars; keep in or out thus; obstruct, prevent.

barb, *n.* backward-curved point of arrow, fish-hook, etc. *v.t.* furnish with barb.

barbā'rian, *a.* uncivilized, uncultured. *n.* such a person.

barba'ric, *a.* cruel, uncultured; of barbarians.

bar'barism, *n.* uncivilized or uncultured state; uncultured expression.

barba'rity, *n.* savage cruelty.

bar'barous, *a.* uncivilized; savage.

bar'bēcūe, *n.* fireplace or framework for broiling or roasting, esp. in open air; meat, etc., cooked on barbecue; outdoor social gathering where barbecue is served. *v.t.* cook on barbecue. **barbecue sauce**, highly seasoned sauce of vinegar, spices, etc.

barbed wīre (-bd), wire for fences, with short pointed wires twisted in at intervals.

bar'ber, *n.* one who cuts hair and shaves beards, men's hairdresser.

bar'bican, *n.* outer defence to city or castle, esp. double tower over gate.

bar'carôle, **bar'carolle**, *n.* gondolier's song; imitation of this.

bard, *n.* Celtic minstrel; poet. **bar'dic**, *a.*

bāre, *a.* unclothed, uncovered; unadorned; scanty; mere. *v.t.* uncover; expose. **bāre'-back**, on unsaddled horse. **bāre'fāced**, shameless, impudent. **bāre'foot**, with bare feet.

bāre'ly (-ārl-), *adv.* scarcely, hardly; only just.

bar'gain (-gin), *n.* agreement about buying or selling or exchanging something; thing acquired cheap or by bargaining. *v.i.* haggle; stipulate. *bargain for*, be prepared for, expect.

barge, *n.* flat-bottomed cargo boat; ornamental vessel. *v.i.* lurch or bump heavily (into, against). **bargee'**, *n.* man in charge of barge.

ba'ritône, *a.* between tenor and bass. *n.* baritone voice or singer.

bār'ium, *n.* white metallic element.

bark[1], *n.* outer sheath of tree trunk and branches. *v.t.* strip tree of bark; scrape (shins, etc.).

bark[2], **barque** (-k), *n.* three-masted vessel; (Poet.) boat.

bark[3], *v.* (of dog, fox, etc.) utter sharp explosive cry; speak angrily; cough. *n.* such a sound.

bar'ley, *n.* cereal plant; its grain. **barley-sugar**, sweet made of boiled sugar.

barm, *n.* froth on fermenting malt liquor, yeast.

bar'maid, **bar'man**, *nn.* attendant at refreshment bar.

bar'my, *a.* (*slang*) crazy; silly.

barn, *n.* roofed building for storing grain, hay, etc.

bar'nacle, *n.* Arctic goose; hard-shelled sea-animal clinging to rocks, ships' bottoms, etc.

barn'-dance (-dah-), *n.* kind of country dance.

barn'storm, *v.i.* travel from place to place giving theatrical performances, holding political meetings, etc. **barn'stormer**, *n.*

barom'ēter, *n.* instrument measuring atmospheric pressure and used to forecast weather. **baromet'ric(al)** (ba-ro-), *aa.*

ba'ron, *n.* nobleman of lowest rank in British peerage; (Hist.) great noble. **ba'roness**, *n.*

baron's wife; female baron in her own right.

ba′ronet, *n*. member of lowest hereditary titled order. **ba′ronetcy**, *n*. rank of a baronet.

barŏ′nial, *a*. of or befitting a baron.

ba′rony, *n*. baron's rank or domain.

barŏque′ (-k; *or* -ok), *a*. grotesque, whimsical. *n*. ornate style of architecture, etc.

barouche′ (-ōōsh), *n*. four-wheeled horse--drawn carriage for four occupants.

barque: see **bark²**.

ba′rrack, *n*. (usu. pl.) permanent building in which soldiers are lodged. *v.t.* hoot at, jeer at.

ba′rrage (-rahzh), *n*. dam across river, etc.; obstacle to enemy, esp. concentrated gunfire.

ba′rrel, *n*. cylindrical bulging wooden vessel; metal tube of a gun. *v.t.* (*p.t. barrelled*), put in barrels.

ba′rrel-organ, *n*. musical instrument worked mechanically by a revolving cylinder turned by a handle.

ba′rren, *a*. not bearing, unable to bear, (children, fruit, etc.); unprofitable. **ba′rrenness** (-n-n-), *n*.

barricáde′ (ba-ri-), *n*. barrier; hastily erected rampart across street, etc. *v.t.* block or defend with a barricade.

ba′rrier, *n*. structure of rails, etc., barring advance or preventing access; obstacle that prevents communication, success, etc.

ba′rrister, *n*. lawyer having right to practise as advocate in the higher courts.

ba′rrow¹ (-ō), *n*. ancient burial-mound.

ba′rrow² (-ō), *n*. two-wheeled hand-cart.

bar′ter, *v*. exchange (goods, rights, etc.). *n*. trade by exchange.

basalt (bas′awlt *or* basawlt′; *or* -olt), *n*. dark rock of volcanic origin. **basal′tic**, *a*.

bāse¹, *a*. morally low, mean, selfish; debased. **bāse′ly**, *adv*. **bāse′ness**, *n*.

bāse², *n*. foundation; principle; starting-point; depot or headquarters of armed force, expedition, etc.; (Math.) starting-number for system of numeration or logarithms; (Chem.) substance that combines with an acid to form a salt. *v.t.* found or rest (on). **bāse′less**, *a*. groundless, unfounded.

bāse′ball (-sb-), *n*. (ball used in) U.S. national field-game between teams of nine players.

bāse′ment (-sm-), *n*. lowest part of building; storey below ground level.

bash, *v.t.* strike so as to dent or smash (*in*). *n*. heavy blow.

bash′ful, *a*. shy; sheepish. **bash′fully**, *adv*.

bā′sic, *a*. of, at, forming, the base; fundamental. **bā′sically**, *adv*.

bas′il (-z-), *n*. aromatic herb.

basil′ica (-z-), *n*. oblong hall with apse at one end and two colonnades; Christian church so built.

bas′ilisk (baz-), *n*. fabulous reptile blasting by its breath or glance, cockatrice.

bā′sin, *n*. open vessel, usu. circular or oval, for holding water, etc.; hollow depression; dock with flood-gates; landlocked harbour; region drained by river.

bā′sis, *n*. (pl. *bāsēs*), base; foundation; main ingredient or principle.

bask (bah-), *v.i.* enjoy warmth and light.

bas′kẹt (bah-), *n*. container of plaited or woven osier, cane, etc. **basket-ball,** team game played, usu. indoors, with large inflated ball and basket-like goals. **bas′-kẹtful,** *n*. (pl. *-fuls*).

bas-rẹlief′, *n*. carving or sculpture projecting only slightly from background.

bass¹, *n*. sea-fish spawning in estuaries.

bass², *a*. deep-sounding; of lowest part in music. *n*. bass voice or singer or part.

bassōōn′, *n*. bass wood-wind instrument of oboe family.

bas′tard, *n. & a.* (person) born of parents not married to each other. **bas′tardy,** *n*.

bāste¹, *v.t.* sew together with long loose stitches, tack.

bāste², *v.t.* moisten roasting meat with fat; thrash, cudgel.

bastinā′dŏ, *n*. (pl. *-s* or *bastinadoes*), caning on soles of feet. *v.t.* cane thus.

bas′tion, *n*. projecting part of fortification, often five-sided.

bat¹, *n*. flying mammal resembling mouse, active in twilight and at night.

bat², *n*. wooden implement for striking ball, esp. in cricket, baseball, etc. *v.i.* (*p.t. batted*), use bat, have innings. **bat′sman,** *n*. (pl. *-men*), player with bat in cricket, etc.

bat³, *v.t.* (*p.t. batted*), (*informal*) blink. *not bat an eyelid,* (fig.) show no emotion.

batch, *n*. loaves baked at one time; group or collection or set.

bāte, *v*. abate; restrain (breath).

bath (-ah-), *n*. washing of the body, esp. by immersion in water; (also *bath-tub*) vessel for bathing in; exposure of (part of) body to sun, steam, etc.; (pl., pr. -dhz) building for bathing in, swimming-bath. *v*. wash in bath. **bath′rōōm,** *n*.

Bath chair (bah-), invalid's wheeled chair.

bāthe (-dh), *v*. immerse in water, etc.; take bath or bathe. *n*. immersion in water esp. of sea, river, etc. **bathing-costume, -drawers, -dress, -suit,** *nn*. garment for bathing or swimming in. **bathing-machine,** *n*. small hut on wheels, formerly used by sea-bathers for changing in. **bā′ther,** *n*.

bā′thos, *n*. fall from sublime to ridiculous; anticlimax.

bath′yscaphe, bath′ysphēre, *nn*. strongly built vessels for deep-sea exploration and observation.

bat′man, *n*. (pl. *batmen*), army officer's servant.

bat′on, *n*. staff as symbol of office; policeman's truncheon; conductor's stick for beating time; short stick passed from one runner to another in relay race.

battal′ion, *n*. large body of men in battle

array; part of a regiment.

batt'en[1], *n.* strip of wood, esp. one used to secure tarpaulin over hatchway. *v.t.* fasten (*down*) with battens.

batt'en[2], *v.i.* feed *on*; grow fat (*on*).

batt'er, *v.* strike repeatedly; knock about. *n.* mixture of flour and eggs beaten up with liquid for cooking.

batt'ering-ram, *n.* (Hist.) heavy beam with iron end used for breaching walls.

batt'ery, *n.* (Law) hitting or touching menacingly a person or his clothes, etc.; set of guns with men and vehicles; platform for guns; apparatus for generating and storing electricity.

batt'le, *n.* combat, esp. between organized forces. *v.i.* struggle (*with* or *against*).

batt'le-axe, *n.* medieval weapon.

batt'ledore (-ld-), *n.* bat or small racket for striking shuttlecock.

batt'ledress (-ld-), *n.* army, etc., uniform of belted blouse and trousers.

batt'lement (-lm-), *n.* (usu. pl.) indented parapet; this and roof.

batt'leship (-lsh-), *n.* warship of most heavily armed and armoured class.

bau'ble, *n.* showy trinket.

baulk: see **balk.**

baux'ite, *n.* ore of aluminium.

baw'dy, *a. & n.* humorously indecent (talk).

bawl, *v.* shout or cry loudly.

bay[1], *n.* kind of laurel.

bay[2], *n.* part of sea filling wide-mouthed opening of land.

bay[3], *n.* recess; projecting window space. **bay window,** window filling bay.

bay[4], *n.* bark of large dog. *at bay,* (of hunted animal) surrounded by dogs and unable to escape; (fig.) in a desperate position. *keep at bay,* ward off. *v.* (of large dog) bark (at).

bay[5], *a. & n.* reddish brown (horse).

bay'onet, *n.* stabbing blade attached to rifle. *v.t.* stab with bayonet.

bazaar' (-zar), *n.* oriental market; sale of goods to raise funds, esp. for charity.

bazoo'ka, *n.* weapon firing anti-tank rockets.

be (bē, bi), *v.i.* (pres. ind. *am, is,* pr. iz, pl. *are*; p.t. *was,* pr. woz, pl. *were,* pr. wer; pp. *been*), exist, occur; remain, continue; have specified state or quality. *v.aux.* (see **auxiliary**).

be-, *pref.* adding idea of *all over, around,* to transitive verbs; intensifying meaning of transitive verbs; making intransitive verbs transitive.

beach, *n.* sandy or pebbly shore of sea, lake, etc. *v.t.* run (boat, etc.) ashore.

beach'comber (-kōmer), *n.* loafer on beaches and wharves who lives by collecting and selling jetsam, etc., esp. white man in islands of S. Pacific.

bea'con, *n.* light placed on pole, etc., as warning of danger; signal-fire on hill.

bead, *n.* small ball, cylinder, etc., pierced for threading with others, used for ornament; (pl.) rosary; drop of liquid.

bea'ding, *n.* moulding like row of beads.

bea'dle, *n.* (Hist.) parish officer appointed to keep order in church.

bea'dy, *a.* (of eyes) small and bright.

bea'gle, *n.* small hound for hunting hares, followed on foot.

beak, *n.* horny projecting jaws of bird; aquiline nose; prow of warship; spout.

bea'ker, *n.* large drinking-cup; straight-sided glass vessel for scientific experiments.

beam, *n.* long piece of squared timber; bar of balance; ray of light, etc.; directed radio wave(s); radio signal used to guide aircraft; any of cross-timbers of ship; breadth of hull at widest point. *v.* emit light; shine; smile radiantly; direct by radio wave.

bean, *n.* plant with kidney-shaped seeds in long pods; seed of this or of coffee and other plants. **bean-feast,** festive meal or outing; merry time. **bea'no,** *n.* (*slang*) bean-feast.

bear[1] (bār), *n.* large thick-furred quadruped; surly person. **bear-garden,** scene of tumult. **bear'skin,** Guards' tall furry cap.

bear[2] (bār), *v.* (p.t. *bore*; p.p. *borne*), carry; endure, tolerate; give birth to (p.p. *born* in passive); produce, yield. **bear'able,** *a.* endurable.

beard, *n.* hair of lower part of man's face; tuft on chin of animal; awn of grasses. *v.* oppose openly, defy. **beard'ed,** *a.* having a beard.

bear'er (bār-), *n.* bringer of letter, etc.; presenter of cheque; one who helps to carry (coffin, stretcher); (in India, etc.) male servant.

bear'ing (bār-), *n.* behaviour, aspect; device on a coat of arms; direction; (pl.) relative position; part of machine supporting a moving part.

beast, *n.* animal; quadruped; cruel or disgusting person. **beast'ly,** *a.* abominable; disgusting; (*informal*) unpleasant, annoying.

beat[1], *v.* (p.t. *beat;* p.p. *beaten*), strike repeatedly; whip (eggs, cream, etc.) to a froth; defeat; mark (time) with hand or baton.

beat[2], *n.* stroke on drum; movement of conductor's baton; rhythm; set walk or round of policeman, etc.

beat[3], **beat'nik,** *nn.* person rebelliously unconventional in dress, ideas, and way of life.

bea'ter, *n.* man employed to rouse game.

bē'atific, *a.* blissful; making blessed. **bēat'ify,** *v.t.* make supremely happy; (R.C. Ch.) pronounce to be Blessed (as step towards canonization). **bēatificā'tion,** *n.*

bēat'itūde, *n.* blessedness; (pl.) Christ's sermon on blessedness (Matt. 5: 3-11).

beau (bō), *n.* (pl.-*s* or *beaux,* pr. bōz), (*archaic*) dandy; suitor.

beau'tèous (bū-), *a.* (Poet.) beautiful.

beau'tiful (bū-), *a.* having beauty; excellent.

beau'tify (bū-), *v.t.* make beautiful.

beau'ty (bū-), *n.* physical, moral, or artistic harmony which inspires admiration; beautiful woman or thing. **beauty-spot,** small patch stuck on woman's face to heighten its beauty; place with beautiful scenery.

bea'ver[1], *n.* amphibious soft-furred rodent that builds lodges and dams; its fur.

bea'ver[2], *n.* lower face-guard of helmet.

becalmed' (-kahmd), *a.* (of sailing-ship) motionless because of lack of wind.

became, *p.t.* of **become.**

because' (-koz), *adv.* by reason (of). *conj.* for the reason that, since.

beck[1], *n.* significant nod or gesture.

beck[2], *n.* (north.) brook, mountain stream.

beck'on, *v.* summon by gesture, esp. of hand; make silent signal to.

become' (-kum), *v.* (p.t. *became;* p.p. *become*), come to be; begin to be; suit, look well on. **becom'ing,** *a.* suitable, befitting; looking well on. **becom'ingly,** *adv.*

bed, *n.* thing to sleep or rest on, esp. framework with mattress; animal's resting-place; garden plot; bottom of sea, river, etc. *v.t.* (p.t. *bedded*), provide bed for; plant in a bed. **bed-clothes,** sheets, blankets, etc. **bed--fellow,** sharer of bed. **bed-pan,** invalid's chamber-pot. **bed'ridden,** confined to bed by illness or weakness. **bed'room,** room to sleep in. **bed'side,** place or position by (esp. invalid's) bed. **bed'spread,** cover lying over bed-clothes. **bed'stead,** framework of bed. **bed'time,** hour for going to bed.

bedd'ing, *n.* mattress and bed-clothes; litter for cattle.

bedeck', *v.t.* adorn.

bedev'il, *v.t.* (p.t. *bedevilled*), torment; confuse. **bedev'ilment,** *n.*

bedew', *v.t.* sprinkle (as) with dew.

bediz'en (*or* -iz-), *v.t.* decorate or dress gaudily.

bed'lam, *n.* madhouse; scene of uproar.

Bed'ouin, Bed'uin (-oo-in), *n.* (pl. same), Arab of the desert.

bedragg'le, *v.t.* wet (dress, etc.) by trailing it. **bedragg'led,** *a.* wet, untidy, dishevelled.

bed'rock, *n.* solid rock below soil; (fig.) bottom, foundation.

bee, *n.* winged, stinging, social insect producing wax and honey; meeting for combined work or amusement (*sewing-bee, spelling--bee*). **bee'hive,** artificial home for bees. **bee-line,** straight line between two places. **bees'wax** (-z-), wax secreted by bees.

beech, *n.* smooth-barked tree; its wood. **beech'mast** (-mahst), *n.* beech nuts collectively. **beech'en,** *a.* of beech or beechwood.

beef, *n.* flesh of ox, bull, or cow used as food; **beef'eater,** *n.* one of the Yeomen of the Guard. **beef-tea,** stewed beef juice. **beef'y,** *a.* solid, muscular.

Beel'zebub, the Devil.

been, *p.p.* of **be.**

beer, *n.* alcoholic liquor made from fermented malt flavoured with hops. **beer'y,** *a.*

beet, *n.* plant with sweet edible root. **beet'-root,** root of beet. **beet-sugar,** sugar made from beet.

bee'tle[1], *n.* heavy-headed tool for crushing, ramming, driving wedges, etc.

bee'tle[2], *n.* insect with hard wing-cases in place of front wings.

bee'tle[3], *v.i.* overhang. **beetle-browed,** *a.* with shaggy or projecting eyebrows.

befall' (-awl), *v.* (p.t. *befell,* p.p. *befallen*), happen, happen to.

befit', *v.t.* (p.t. *befitted*), be suited to. **befitt'-ing,** *a.*

befog', *v.t.* (p.t. *befogged*), envelop in fog; (fig.) obscure.

before', *adv.* ahead; in front; previously; already. *prep.* in front of; in the presence of; earlier than. *conj.* sooner than; rather than. *before Christ,* (usu. abbrev. *B.C.* and appended to dates, e.g. *55 B.C.*) reckoned backwards from birth of Jesus Christ.

before'hand (-for-h-), *adv.* in readiness; before the time.

befriend' (-frend), *v.t.* act as a friend to; help.

beg, *v.* (p.t. *begged*), ask for (food, money, clothes, etc.); live by begging; ask earnestly. *beg the question,* assume the very fact one is trying to prove.

began, *p.t.* of **begin.**

beget' (-g-), *v.t.* (p.t. *begot,* p.p. *begotten;* pres. p. *begetting*), give existence to (as father); be the cause of.

begg'ar, *n.* person who begs or lives by begging; poor person. *v.t.* reduce to poverty. **begg'arly,** *a.* poor; mean. **begg'ary,** *n.* extreme poverty.

begin' (-g-), *v.* (p.t. *began;* p.p. *begun;* pres. p. *beginning*), set about; make a start with; come into being. **begin'ner,** *n.* learner. **begin'ning,** *n.* time or place at which thing begins; origin, source.

begone', *int.* away with you!

bego'nia, *n.* plant with brightly coloured flowers which have no petals.

begot, begotten, *p.t. & p.p.* of **beget.**

begrime', *v.t.* make grimy.

begrudge', *v.t.* envy (person) the possession of; be unwilling to give or allow.

beguile' (-gīl), *v.t.* delude, cheat; amuse; cause (time, etc.) to pass easily.

begun, *p.p.* of **begin.**

behalf' (-ahf), *n. on behalf of,* in the interest of; as representative of.

behave', *v.i. & refl.* conduct oneself, act; show good manners.

beha'viour (-yer), *n.* manners, conduct, way of behaving.

behead' (-hed), *v.t.* cut off the head of; execute thus.

beheld, *p.t. & p.p.* of **behold.**

behem'oth (*or* bē'i-), *n.* enormous creature.

behest', *n.* command.

behind', *adv. & prep.* in or to the rear (of);

hidden (by); late (with); in support of. *n.* buttocks. **běhind'hand,** *a.* & *adv.* behind time; too late.

běhōld', *v.t.* (p.t. *beheld*), see; take notice, observe.

běhōl'den, *a.* under obligation (to).

běhōve', *v.t. impers.* be the duty of; befit.

beige (bāzh), *n.* the colour of wool left undyed and unbleached, yellowish or brownish grey. *a.* of this colour.

bē'ing, *n.* existence; living person.

bělā'bour (-ber), *v.t.* beat hard.

bělā'ted, *a.* (too) late.

bělay', *v.t.* (p.t. *belayed*), coil (rope) round fixed projection to secure it.

belch, *v.* emit wind noisily from stomach through mouth; (of volcano, gun, etc.) send out (fire, smoke, etc.). *n.* belching.

bělea'guer (-ger), *v.t.* besiege.

bel'emnīte, *n.* tapering sharp-pointed fossil bone of extinct cuttlefish.

bel'fry, *n.* bell tower; part of church tower in which bells hang.

bělie', *v.t.* (pres.p. *belying*), fail to justify (expectations, etc.); give false notion of.

bělief', *n.* trust, confidence; acceptance as true or existing; what one believes.

bělieve', *v.* accept as true; have faith in; trust word of. **běliev'able,** *a.* **běliev'er,** *n.* one who believes, esp. in a religion.

Beli'sha bea'con (bilēsha), yellow (flashing) globe on post at zebra crossing.

bělitt'le, *v.t.* cause to seem unimportant or of small value; disparage.

bell, *n.* cup-shaped metal instrument which makes a ringing sound when struck by tongue hung within or by a hammer activated by a spring or by electricity; bell-shaped object. *v.t.* provide with bell. **bell-bottomed,** (of trousers) widening from below knees to bottom of legs. **bell-buoy,** bell with bell rung by movement of the sea. **bell'man,** town crier. **bell-ringer,** one who rings changes, etc., on church bells. **bell-ringing,** art of ringing church bells. **bell-wether,** leading sheep of flock, with bell on neck.

belladonn'a, *n.* poisonous plant, the deadly nightshade; drug prepared from this.

belle, *n.* handsome woman; reigning beauty.

belles lettres (bel letr), studies and writings of a purely literary kind. (French)

bell'icōse, *a.* inclined to fight.

belli'gerent, *a.* waging regular war; engaged in conflict; aggressive. *n.* nation, party, or person engaged in conflict. **belli'gerency,** *n.*

bell'ow (-ō), *v.* roar like a bull; shout with pain or anger. *n.* bellowing sound.

bell'ows (-ōz), *n.pl.* instrument or machine producing strong current of air for blowing a fire or for sounding organ, harmonium, etc.

bell'y, *n.* abdomen, stomach; cavity or bulging part of anything. *v.* swell out.

bělong', *v.i.* (with *to*) be the property of; be proper *to* or connected *with*; be rightly placed

or classified.

bělong'ings (-z), *n.pl.* one's property.

bělov'ed, *a.* (-uv'id) & *p.p.* (-uvd'), dearly loved. *n.* (-uv'id), beloved person.

bělow (-ō), *adv.* at or to a lower level; in a lower position or rank. *prep.* lower than; unworthy of, beneath.

belt, *n.* strip of leather, etc., worn round waist, etc.; endless strap connecting wheels in machinery; any (wide) strip or band; zone or district. *v.t.* put belt round; thrash.

bel'vedēre, *n.* raised turret or summer-house to view scenery from.

běmoan', *v.t.* lament.

běmūse' (-z), *v.t.* stupefy.

bench, *n.* long seat of wood, stone, etc.; judge's or magistrate's seat; court of law; carpenter's table.

bend, *v.* (p.t. *bent*), make or become curved or crooked; lean over from upright position, bow, stoop; submit, force to submit. *n.* bent part of a thing; curve.

bene-, *pref.* well.

běneath', *adv.* & *prep.* below, under.

běnēdic'tion, *n.* blessing. **běnēdic'tory,** *a.*

běnēfac'tion, *n.* doing good; gift for charitable purpose. **ben'ēfactor,** *n.* one who has given friendly help; patron, donor. **ben'ēfactress,** *n.fem.*

ben'ēfice, *n.* livelihood of priest in charge of parish, (church) living.

běnef'icent, *a.* doing good. **běnef'icence,** *n.* active kindness.

běnēfi'cial (-shl), *a.* advantageous, helpful.

běnēfi'ciary (-sha-), *n.* receiver of benefits, esp. money or property under a will; holder of a benefice.

ben'ēfit, *n.* advantage; profit; good; allowance, etc., to which person is entitled. *v.* do good to; receive benefit.

běnev'olent, *a.* doing good; kindly; generous. **běnev'olence,** *n.*

běnīght'ed (-nīt-), *a.* overtaken by night; intellectually and morally ignorant.

běnign' (-nīn), *a.* kindly; favourable; (of disease, etc.) mild, not malignant. **běnig'nant,** *a.* kind, kindly, gracious. **běnig'nancy, běnig'nity,** *nn.*

ben'ison (-zn), *n.* blessing.

bent[1], *n.* rush-like stiff-stemmed grass.

bent[2], *n.* mental inclination; aptitude.

bent[3], *p.t.* & *p.p.* of **bend.**

běnumb' (-m), *v.t.* make numb or torpid; paralyse (mind, etc.).

ben'zēne, *n.* volatile hydrocarbon got from coal-tar.

ben'zine (-zēn), *n.* mixture of liquid hydrocarbons got from mineral oils and used as solvent, for dry-cleaning, etc.

běqueath' (-dh), *v.t.* leave by will.

běquest', *n.* thing bequeathed.

běrāte', *v.t.* scold.

běreave', *v.t.* rob, dispossess *of* (p.p. usu. *bereft*); deprive, esp. by death (pp.

bereaved). **bereave'ment**, *n.* loss by death.

be'ret (-rā), *n.* round flat cap.

berg, *n.* iceberg; (S.Afr.) mountain.

be'ribe'ri, *n.* tropical disease caused by vitamin deficiency.

be'rry, *n.* any small round or oval juicy fruit without a stone. **be'rried** (-id), *a.* having berries.

berserk', *a.* frenziedly or insanely violent, (esp. in phr. *go berserk*).

berth, *n.* ship's place at wharf or anchor; space for ship; sleeping-place in train, ship, etc.; post, appointment. *v.t.* moor (ship) in berth.

be'ryl, *n.* pale-green precious stone; mineral species including emerald.

beseech', *v.t.* (p.t. *besought*, pr.' -sawt), ask earnestly for; entreat.

beset', *v.t.* (p.t. *beset*), hem in; attack. *besetting sin*, sin that most frequently tempts one.

beside', *prep.* at the side of; close to; compared with; wide of. *beside oneself*, at the end of one's self-control.

besides' (-dz), *prep.* in addition (to); otherwise than. *adv.* also; moreover.

besiege', *v.t.* surround (town, etc.) with armed forces in order to capture it; pester (with requests, etc.).

besmirch', *v.t.* make dirty, discolour.

be'som (-z-; *or* bi'-), *n.* broom made of bundle of twigs.

besott'ed, *a.* infatuated, obsessed; stupefied, esp. by drink or drugs.

besought, *p.t. & p.p.* of **beseech.**

bespang'le (-anggl), *v.t.* cover (as) with spangles.

bespatt'er, *v.t.* spatter all over.

bespeak', *v.t.* (p.t. *bespōke*, p.p. *bespōke* or *bespōken*), engage beforehand; order (goods); be evidence of.

best, *a.* (superl. of *good*), of the most excellent kind. *adv.* (superl. of *well*), in the best way. *v.t.* defeat, outwit. **best man**, bridegroom's supporter at wedding. **best-seller**, (author of) book with very large sale.

bes'tial, *a.* of or like a beast; cruel; barbarous. **bestial'ity**, *n.*

bestir', *v. refl.* (p.t. *bestirred*), exert, rouse (*oneself*).

bestow' (-ō), *v.t.* confer as gift; put, place. **bestow'al**, *n.*

bestrew' (-rōo), *v.t.* (p.p. *bestrewed* or *bestrewn*), strew, scatter about.

bestride', *v.t.* (p.t. *bestrōde*, p.p. *bestridden*), sit astride on; stand astride over.

bet, *v.* (p.t. & p.p. *bet*), risk one's money, etc., against another's on result of an event. *n.* money, etc., so risked.

be'ta, *n.* second letter of Greek alphabet.

betāke', *v. refl.* (p.t. *betook*, p.p. *betāken*), *betake oneself to*, go to, apply oneself to.

be'tel, *n.* leaf chewed in some eastern countries with slices of betel-nut. **betel-nut**, seed of a kind of palm.

bête noire (bāt nwar), thing or person one dislikes intensely. (French)

beth'el, *n.* nonconformist chapel.

bethink', *v. refl.* (p.t. & p.p. *bethought*, pr. -thawt), reflect, stop to think.

betide', *v.* (only in 3rd pers. sing. pres. subjunctive), happen; happen to.

betimes' (-mz), *adv.* in good time.

betō'ken, *v.t.* be a sign of.

betook, *p.t.* of **betake**.

betray', *v.t.* give up or reveal treacherously; be disloyal to; reveal involuntarily. **betray'al**, *n.*

betrōth' (-dh), *v.t.* bind with promise to marry. **betrō'thal**, *n.* **betrōthed'** (-dhd), *a. & n.*

bett'er, *a.* (compar. of *good*) of more excellent kind; recovering, having recovered (health). *adv.* (compar. of *well*) in a better way. *n.* better thing or person; superiority or mastery. *v.* improve; surpass. **bett'erment**, *n.* improvement.

between', *prep.* in or into space or interval; in shares among; to and from. *choose between*, choose one or other of. *adv.* in or into intermediate place or time.

betwixt', *prep.* (*archaic* or Poet.) between.

bev'el, *n.* edge or surface sloping from the horizontal or vertical; tool for making bevels. *v.* give bevel to; slant.

bev'erage, *n.* any kind of drink.

bev'y, *n.* a company or gathering.

bewail', *v.t.* wail over, mourn for.

bewāre', *v.* (only in imper. & inf.) be cautious (*of*), be on one's guard.

bewil'der, *v.t.* confuse, puzzle. **bewil'dering**, *a.* **bewil'derment**, *n.*

bewitch', *v.t.* put a magic spell on; delight. **bewitch'ing**, *a.*

bey (bā), *n.* (Hist.) Turkish governor.

beyond', *adv.* at or to the further side; further on. *prep.* at or to the further side of; later than; more than; except. *n.* life after death, the unknown.

bez'el, *n.* sloped edge of chisel, etc.; groove for watch-glass, etc.

bēzique' (-ēk), *n.* card-game for two.

bī-, *pref.* twice; having two; occurring or appearing once in every two.

biann'ūal, *a.* occurring twice a year.

bi'as, *n.* inclination, leaning; prejudice; (in game of bowls) curved course of bowl due to its shape. *on the bias*, (Dressmaking) diagonally across fabric. *v.* (p.t. *bīased* or *bīassed*), give bias to; prejudice.

bib¹, *n.* cloth placed under child's chin to protect clothing; top of apron or overalls.

bib², *v.* (p.t. *bibbed*), (*archaic*) tipple.

Bī'ble, *n.* sacred writings of the Christian faith; sacred book. **bib'lical**, *a.* of the Bible.

bibliog'raphy, *n.* history of books; list of books of any author, subject, etc. **bibliog'rapher**, *n.* **bibliograph'ic(al)**, *aa.*

bib'liophīle, *n.* book-lover.

bib′ūlous, *a.* addicted to alcoholic drink.

bicarb′onate, *n.* salt of carbonic acid in which metal replaces only one hydrogen atom. **bicarbonate (of soda),** sodium bicarbonate, used in cookery, medicine, etc.

bicentē′nary, *a.* & *n.* (of) the 200th anniversary or its celebration.

bī′ceps, *n.* muscle with double head or attachment, esp. that at front of upper arm.

bick′er, *v. i.* quarrel, squabble.

bīcus′pid, *a.* & *n.* two-cusped (tooth).

bī′cycle, *n.* two-wheeled pedal-driven vehicle. *v. i.* ride on bicycle.

bid, *v.* (p.t. *bad, bade, bid;* p.p. *bidden, bid*), command (p.t. *bad*); invite (p.t. *bade*); offer (price), make bid at bridge (p.t. *bid*). *n.* offer of price; (Bridge) statement of number of tricks one hopes to make. **bidd′able,** *a.* obedient. **bidd′ing,** *n.* command; offers at auction; bids at bridge.

bīde, *v. bide one's time,* await one's opportunity.

bidet (bē′dā), *n.* low basin which can be sat on for washing lower parts of body.

bienn′ial, *a.* occurring every two years; lasting two years. *n.* plant that lives two years and flowers in second year.

bier (bēr), *n.* movable stand on which coffin is placed.

bifō′cal, *a.* (of spectacle lenses) with two parts, for distant and near vision. **bifō′cals** (-z), *n. pl.* bifocal spectacles.

bī′furcāte, *v.* divide into two branches; fork. **bīfurcā′tion,** *n.*

big, *a.* (*bigger, biggest*), large; grown up; important; boastful. **big′wig,** *n.* (*informal*) important person.

big′amy, *n.* second marriage while first is still valid. **big′amist,** *n.* **big′amous,** *a.*

bight (bīt), *n.* loop of rope; curve, recess, of coast, river, etc.

big′ot, *n.* person who holds obstinately or unreasonably to a creed or opinion. **big′oted,** *a.* **big′otry,** *n.*

bīke, *n.* & *v. i.* (*informal*) bicycle.

bikī′ni (-kē-), *n.* woman's scanty two-piece bathing-suit.

bīlat′eral, *a.* of, on, with, two sides; between two parties.

bil′berry, *n.* dwarf shrub of heaths, etc.; its deep-blue edible fruit; whortleberry.

bīle, *n.* bitter fluid secreted by the liver to aid digestion; anger, peevishness.

bilge, *n.* nearly horizontal part of ship's bottom; (also *bilge-water*) foul water that collects in bilge; (*slang*) nonsense, rot.

bīling′ual (-nggwal), *a.* in or speaking two languages.

bil′ious, *a.* caused by, affected by, disorder of the bile.

bilk, *v. t.* avoid payment of (creditor, bill); cheat, esp. by running away.

bill¹, *n.* bird's beak; narrow promontory. *v. i.* (of doves) stroke bill with bill. *bill and coo,* exchange caresses.

bill², *n.* draft of proposed Act of Parliament; note of charges for goods, work done, etc.; poster. *v. t.* announce on poster. **bill-poster, bill-sticker,** man who pastes up posters, etc.

bill′abong, *n.* (Austral.) branch of river forming backwater or stagnant pool.

bill′et *n.* place where soldier, etc., is lodged. *v. t.* quarter (soldiers, etc., on town, etc.). **billètee′,** *n.* person billeted.

billet-doux (bēlădoo′, *or* bili-), *n.* (pl. *billets-doux,* pr. same), love-letter. (French)

bill′-hook, *n.* implement for pruning.

bill′iards (-lyerdz), *n.* game played with cues and balls on cloth-covered table (*billiard-ball, -cue, -table*).

bill′ingsgate (-z-), *n.* abusive language (as spoken in *Billingsgate* fish-market in 17th c.).

bill′ion, *n.* a million millions; (U.S. and Canada) a thousand millions.

bill′ow (-ō), *n.* great wave. *v. i.* rise or move in billows. **bill′owy,** *a.*

bill′y, bill′y-can, *n.* tin can with (lid and) wire handle used as kettle, etc., in camping.

bill′y-goat, *n.* male goat.

bin, *n.* container for corn, coal, bread, etc.; receptacle for rubbish.

bī′nary, *a.* of two, dual; (Math., of scale, system) with two, not ten, as base of notation. **binary digit,** one of two digits (0 *and* 1) in a binary system of notation.

bīnd, *v.* (p.t. & p.p. *bound*), tie, fasten, attach; fasten or hold together; edge with tape, etc.; impose obligation on; fasten (sheets of book) into cover. **bīn′der,** *n.* bookbinder; sheaf-binding machine. **bīn′ding,** *a.* obligatory (*on*). *n.* book-cover; braid, etc., for binding raw edges of fabric.

bīnd′weed, *n.* convolvulus.

bīne, *n.* flexible shoot; stem of climbing plant, esp. the hop.

bing′ō (-ngg-), *n.* popular gambling game, a form of lotto.

binn′acle, *n.* box on deck holding ship's compass.

binoc′ūlar, *a.* for both eyes. **binoc′ūlars** (-z), *n. pl.* optical instrument for both eyes, making distant objects appear nearer.

binō′mial, *a.* & *n.* (algebraic expression) consisting of two terms joined by + or −.

bīo-, *pref.* life.

bīochem′istry (-ke-), *n.* the chemistry of living organisms.

bīog′raphy, *n.* written life of a person. **biog′rapher,** *n.* **biograph′ical,** *a.*

bīol′ogy, *n.* science of life, dealing with morphology, physiology, behaviour, origin, and distribution of animals and plants. **bīolo′gical,** *a.* **biol′ogist,** *n.*

bīophy′sics (-z-), *n.* science dealing with mechanical and electrical properties of living organisms.

bī′ped, *a.* & *n.* two-footed (animal).

bī'plāne, *n.* aeroplane with two pairs of wings, one above the other.

birch, *n.* smooth-barked tree; (also *birch-rod*) bundle of twigs used for flogging. *v.t.* flog with birch.

bird, *n.* vertebrate animal with feathers and wings. *bird of passage,* migrant; sojourner. *bird of prey,* bird that kills and feeds on small birds, mice, etc. *birds of a feather,* people of like character. **bird-lime,** sticky substance spread on · trees to catch birds. **bird--watching,** study of birds in their natural surroundings.

bird's'-eye (-zī), *n.* plant with small bright flowers, esp. speedwell. *bird's-eye view,* view of town, etc., as seen from above.

bīr'ō, *n.* (pl. *biros*), ball-point pen. **P.**

birth, *n.* emergence of child or animal from body of mother; process of producing young; beginning; origin, descent. *give birth to,* (of mother) produce (young) from body. **birth--control,** prevention of unwanted pregnancy, contraception. **birth'day,** anniversary of one's birth. **birth-mark,** mark on body from birth. **birth-place,** place where one was born. **birth-rate,** yearly number of births per thousand of population. **birth-right,** rights, privileges, etc., to which person is entitled as member of his family, citizen of his country, etc.

bis'cuit (-kit), *n.* kind of crisp dry cake or bread, usu. small, flat, and thin.

bīsect', *v.t.* divide in two (usu. equal) parts. **bīsec'tion,** *n.* **bīsec'tor,** *n.* bisecting line.

bish'op, *n.* clergyman of high rank who is governor of a diocese; a chessman. **bish'-opric,** *n.* office or diocese of bishop.

bis'muth (-z-), *n.* reddish-white brittle metallic element.

bī'son, *n.* wild ox with massive shaggy head and humped shoulders.

bit¹, *n.* small piece or amount; cutting-part of tool, etc.; part of key engaging with levers of lock; metal bar of bridle, put into horse's mouth.

bit², *n.* binary digit.

bitch, *n.* female of dog, fox, or wolf.

bīte, *v.* (p.t. *bit*; p.p. *bitten*), seize, cut into or off, with the teeth; penetrate; grip. *n.* act of biting; wound made by biting; taking of bait by fish; grip. **bī'ting,** *a.* cutting, severe.

bitt'er, *a.* very sour, harsh, in taste; hard to bear; biting, harsh. **bitt'erly,** *adv.* **bitt'-erness,** *n.*

bitt'ern, *n.* long-legged wading bird.

bit'ümen, *n.* mineral pitch; any natural (esp. solid) hydrocarbon. **bitü'minous,** *a.*

bī'valve, *n.* & *a.* (shellfish) with double hinged shell.

biv'ouac (-voo-ak), *n.* temporary encampment without tents. *v.i.* camp out in this way.

bizarre' (-zar), *a.* fantastic, incongruous; very strange.

blab, *v.* (p.t. *blabbed*), talk indiscreetly; reveal (secrets).

black, *a.* of the darkest colour; opposite to white; dark-skinned; dismal; angry; wicked. *n.* black colour; black speck; mourner's clothes; Negro. *v.t.* make black; polish with blacking. *black out,* darken (windows, etc.) so that no light is visible from outside or from the air.

black'amoor, *n.* Negro; dark-skinned person.

black'ball (-awl), *v.t.* exclude candidate from club, etc. (by placing black ball in ballot--box).

black-bee'tle, *n.* cockroach.

black'berry, *n.* berry, black when ripe, the fruit of the bramble.

black'bird, *n.* European song-bird.

black'board (-bord), *n.* board for chalking on in class-room, etc.

black box, (esp.) apparatus on an aircraft recording details of its flight.

black'cock, *n.* male of black grouse.

black coff'ee, coffee without milk.

black com'ëdy, violent or gruesome theme treated as comedy.

black'en, *v.* make or grow black; speak evil of.

blackguard (blag'ard), *n.* scoundrel. *v.t.* abuse in strong terms.

black'ing, *n.* paste or liquid for blacking boots.

black'lead' (-led), *v.t.* & *n.* (polish with) graphite.

black'leg, *n.* person who continues to work while fellow workers are on strike.

black list, list of persons under suspicion or considered undesirable. **black'list,** *v.t.* enter on black list.

black ma'gic, evil magic.

black'mail, *n.* (attempt at) extortion of money by threats, esp. by threatening to disclose discreditable secret. *v.t.* extort money from (a person) thus.

black mar'kèt, unlawful trading in scarce or rationed goods.

black'out, *n.* period of darkening of windows, etc.; material for this; sudden temporary loss of vision or consciousness.

black sheep, good-for-nothing person.

black'smith, *n.* smith working in iron, esp. one who repairs tools and shoes horses.

black'thorn, *n.* shrub bearing white flowers and dark-purple fruit (*sloes*).

bladd'er, *n.* bag-like organ in the body, esp. that in which urine collects; round or oval inflated thing.

blāde, *n.* flat narrow leaf of grass and cereals; flattened part of oar, bat, spade, etc.; cutting part of knife, etc.; flat bone, esp. shoulder--blade; gay, dashing fellow.

blāme, *v.t.* find fault with; fix blame on. *n.* responsibility for bad result. **blāme'able,** *a.* **blāme'less,** *a.* innocent. **blāme'worthy** (-werdhi), *a.* deserving blame.

blanch (-ah-), *v.* make white; grow pale.

blancmange (blamonzh'), *n.* opaque jelly made with cornflour, etc., and milk.

bland, *a.* gentle, polite; mild, soothing. **bland'ly,** *adv.* **bland'ness,** *n.*

blan'dishment, *n.* (usu. pl.) flattering words or actions.

blank, *a.* not written or printed on; without interest or expression; empty. *n.* emptiness; space left to be filled up; blank ticket in sweepstake. **blank cartridge,** cartridge with explosive charge but without a ball. **blank verse,** unrhymed verse. **blank'ly,** *adv.* without expression.

blank'et, *n.* large, usu. woollen, covering used on beds, to cover horse in stable, etc. *a.* covering, inclusive. *v.t.* cover (as) with blanket.

blare, *v.* make sound of trumpet; trumpet forth. *n.* blaring sound.

blar'ney, *n.* persuasive talk. *v.* persuade by flattery.

blasé (-ahz'ā), *a.* bored, indifferent, because used to pleasure, luxury, etc.

blaspheme', *v.* speak irreverently about God and sacred things; treat with irreverence, revile. **blas'phemous,** *a.* **blas'phemy,** *n.*

blast (-ah-), *n.* strong gust; blowing or sound of wind instrument; current in blast-furnace; destructive wave of compressed air spreading outwards from explosion. *v.t.* blow up with explosive; blight, shrivel. **blast-furnace,** furnace into which draught of compressed hot air is driven. **blast off,** (of rocket or spacecraft) take off. **blast-off,** *n.*

bla'tant, *a.* very obvious; noisy, clamorous.

blather: see **blether.**

blaze¹, *n.* bright flame or fire or light; violent outburst of passion. *v.i.* flame; burn with excitement, etc.

blaze², *n.* mark chipped on bark of tree to indicate route; white marking on face of horse. *v.t.* mark (tree, path) with blaze(s).

blaze³, *v.t.* proclaim (*abroad, forth*).

bla'zer, *n.* unlined (coloured) jacket worn with sports clothes or as part of school uniform.

bla'zon, *n.* (detailed description of) coat of arms. *v.t.* describe or paint (arms) heraldically; proclaim.

bleach, *v.* whiten in sunlight or by chemical process. *n.* bleaching substance.

bleak, *a.* bare; exposed; cold; dreary.

blear, *a.* dim, watery. **blear-eyed,** having blear eyes. *v.t.* dim (eyes); blur. **blear'y,** *a.*

bleat, *v.i.* (of sheep, goat, etc.) utter cry; speak, complain, feebly. *n.* cry of sheep, goat, etc.; similar cry; (feeble) complaint.

bleed, *v.t.* (p.t. & p.p. *bled*), lose blood; draw blood surgically from; (of plant) lose sap.

bleep, *n.* & *v.i.* (emit) high-pitched intermittent sound, esp. as signal.

blem'ish, *v.t.* spoil beauty or perfection of; mar. *n.* flaw, defect, stain.

blench, *v.i.* flinch, quail.

blend, *v.* (p.p. *blended*, also *blent*), mix together; mix so as to become one; mingle harmoniously. *n.* mixture.

bless, *v.t.* (p.t. & p.p. *blessed*, usu. pr. blest, or *blest*), consecrate; worship, adore; invoke God's favour on; make happy. **bless'ed,** **blest,** *aa.* consecrated; revered; fortunate; in paradise. **bless'ing,** *n.* declaration, invocation, or bestowal of divine favour; grace before or after meal; thing one is thankful for.

bleth'er, blath'er (-dh-), *v.i.* talk nonsense. *n.* such talk.

blew, *p.t.* of **blow.**

blight (-īt), *n.* (insect or fungus causing) plant disease; (fig.) withering influence. *v.t.* affect with blight; spoil, frustrate. **blight'er,** *n.* (*slang*) annoying person; fellow.

blind, *a.* without sight; lacking understanding or insight; reckless; secret; closed at one end. *v.t.* deprive of sight; make mentally blind. *n.* obstruction to sight or light; screen for window; something designed to mislead. **blind alley,** alley closed at one end, not leading anywhere (often fig.). **blind'fold,** (*a.*) with eyes bandaged; (*v.t.*) cover eyes (of person) with bandage. **blind-man's-buff,** game in which blindfold player tries to catch others. **blind'ly,** *adv.* without seeing; recklessly. **blind'ness,** *n.* state of being blind; folly.

blink, *v.* shut eyelids momentarily and involuntarily; cast sudden or momentary light; ignore or shirk (facts). *n.* blinking movement; momentary gleam.

blink'ers (-z), *n.pl.* eye-screens on bridle preventing horse from seeing sideways.

bliss, *n.* heavenly joy; perfect happiness. **bliss'ful,** *a.* **bliss'fully,** *adv.*

blis'ter, *n.* small bubble on skin filled with watery fluid; similar swelling on plant, metal, painted surface, etc. *v.* raise blister on; develop blister(s).

blithe (-dh), *a.* gay, joyous. **blithe'ly,** *adv.*

blitz, *n.* sudden violent attack, esp. from the air.

blizz'ard, *n.* severe snowstorm with violent wind.

bloa'ted, *a.* swollen, inflated.

bloa'ter, *n.* herring cured by salting and smoking.

blob, *n.* drop of liquid; small round mass or spot.

bloc, *n.* combination of parties to form government, or of groups, nations, etc. to further a particular interest.

block, *n.* large solid piece of wood or stone; (Hist.) piece of wood on which the condemned were beheaded; mould, shape; piece of wood, etc., engraved for printing; obstruction; buildings surrounded by (usu. four) streets; large number or quantity. **block capitals, letters,** (writing with) detached (capital) letters. *v.t.* obstruct; shape (hat) on block.

blockade', *n.* blocking of place, harbour, etc.

by hostile forces to prevent people and supplies from entering or leaving. *v.t.* block thus.

block′age, *n.* obstruction.

block′head (-hed), *n.* stupid person.

block′house, *n.* detached fort; timber building with loopholes.

blond, blonde, *a. & n.* fair-skinned and fair-haired (person).

blood (blud), *n.* red liquid circulating in the veins and arteries of vertebrates; bloodshed; race; relationship. **blood-curdling,** horrific. **blood donor,** giver of blood for transfusion. **blood group,** any of four main groups into which blood may be divided on basis of compatibility for transfusion. **blood-heat,** normal temperature. **blood′hound,** large dog able to track person by scent. **blood-poisoning,** illness resulting from presence of harmful bacteria in the blood. **blood-pressure,** pressure of blood against walls of arteries. **blood′shed,** spilling of blood; slaughter. **blood′shot,** (of eye) tinged with blood. **blood′thirsty,** eager for bloodshed. **blood-vessel,** tube (vein or artery) through which blood circulates in the body.

blood′less (blud-), *a.* without blood or bloodshed.

bloody (blud′i), *a.* smeared with blood; involving bloodshed; cruel.

bloom, *n.* flower; prime; freshness. *v.i.* bear blooms; be in flower; flourish.

bloom′ers (-z), *n.pl.* women's knickerbockers.

bloss′om, *n.* flower; mass of flowers on tree. *v.i.* open into flower.

blot, *n.* spot of ink, etc.; blemish; disgraceful act. *v.t.* (p.t. *blotted*), make blot on; stain; dry with blotting-paper. *blot out,* make blot over, hide from view. **blott′er,** *n.* pad of blotting-paper. **blott′ing-paper,** absorbent paper for drying wet ink quickly.

blotch, *n.* inflamed patch on skin; dab of ink, etc. **blotched** (-cht), **blot′chy,** *aa.*

blouse (-owz), *n.* woman's loose-fitting garment for upper part of body; upper part of battledress.

blow[1] (-ō), *v.* (p.t. *blew* pr. blōō; p.p. *blown*), move as wind does; puff; send out current of air from mouth; work or sound by blowing; direct air current at; (of fly) deposit eggs on; (of electric fuse) melt when overloaded; clear (nose) by breathing out sharply through it. *blow up,* inflate; shatter or be shattered by explosion. *n.* blowing; puff of fresh air. **blow′fly,** fly which deposits its eggs in dead flesh, bluebottle. **blow-lamp,** portable apparatus for directing intensely hot flame on limited area. **blow-pipe,** tube for increasing heat of flame by blowing air into it; tube for propelling darts or arrows by blowing. **blow′y,** *a.* windy.

blow[2] (-ō), *n.* hard stroke with hammer, fist, etc.; disaster, shock.

blowzed (-zd), **blow′zy,** *aa.* red-faced; coarse-looking; dishevelled.

blubb′er, *n.* whale fat. *a.* swollen. *v.* weep noisily; sob out (words).

bludg′eon (-ujn), *n.* heavy stick. *v.t.* strike heavily or repeatedly (as) with bludgeon.

blue (blōō), *a.* coloured like sky or deep sea on a clear day. *n.* blue colour; blue powder used in laundering; sky, sea; (award to) athlete, etc., representing Oxford or Cambridge University; (pl.) the dumps; (pl.) melancholy music of Amer. Negro origin. *v.t.* make blue. **blue′bell,** wild hyacinth; (Sc.) harebell. **blue′bottle,** blowfly. **blue-gum,** variety of eucalyptus. **blue′jacket,** seaman in Navy. **Blue Peter,** blue flag with central white square hoisted before sailing. **blue′print,** photographic print of plan, etc., with white lines on blue ground; detailed plan. **blue ribbon,** ribbon of the Garter; highest honour or distinction. **blue-stocking,** woman having or affecting literary tastes and learning. **blue tit,** titmouse with blue crown and blue and yellow feathers.

bluff[1], *a.* having broad precipitous front; blunt, frank, hearty. *n.* bluff headland.

bluff[2], *v.* make pretence of strength to gain advantage, etc.; deceive. *n.* bluffing.

blu′ish (blōō-), *a.* tending towards blue.

blun′der, *n.* stupid or careless mistake. *v.i.* move blindly; make gross mistake.

blun′derbuss, *n.* ancient large-bored gun firing many bullets.

blunt, *a.* not sharp; without edge or point; plain-spoken, callous. *v.t.* make blunt. **blunt′ness,** *n.*

blur, *n.* smear; dimness. *v.* (p.t. *blurred*), smear; make or become indistinct.

blurb, *n.* publisher's praise of book on jacket, etc.

blurt, *v.t.* (usu. with *out*) utter abruptly or tactlessly.

blush, *v.i.* be or become red (as) with shame, etc. *n.* blushing; rosy glow.

blus′ter, *v.i.* (of wind, waves) rage; talk overbearingly. *n.* blustering; self-assertive talk. **blus′tery,** *a.* windy.

bō′a, *n.* large snake which kills by crushing (also *boa constrictor*); woman's fur or feather throat-wrap.

boar (bor), *n.* male pig; wild pig.

board (bord), *n.* thin plank; flat piece of wood, cardboard, etc., used for special purpose; thick stiff paper used in bookbinding, etc.; daily meals; table; councillors, committee; (pl.) the stage. *on board,* on ship, aircraft, train, etc. *v.* cover with boards; provide with, receive, meals at fixed rate; get on or into (ship, aircraft, etc.). **boarding-house,** house in which persons board and lodge. **boarding-school,** school in which pupils live during term. **board′er,** *n.* one who is lodged and fed at a fixed rate; boy or girl at boarding-school. **boar′ding,** *n.* erection of boards.

boast, *n.* statement praising oneself; thing one is proud of. *v.* brag; praise oneself; possess as a thing to be proud of. **boast'ful,** *a.*

boat, *n.* small open vessel for travelling on water; (small) ship; boat-shaped receptacle. *v.i.* go in a boat. **boat-hook,** long pole with hook and spike. **boat-house,** shed for boats. **boat-race,** rowing contest.

boa'ter, *n.* hard flat straw hat.

boat'man, man who hires out (and rows, sails, etc.) boats.

boatswain (bō'sn), *n.* senior seaman supervising work of other seamen and in charge of ship's boats, rigging, etc.

bob, *n.* weight on pendulum, etc.; bobbed hair; horse's docked tail; curtsy. *v.* (p.t. *bobbed*), move up and down; cut (hair) to hang short of shoulders.

bobb'in, *n.* cylinder for holding thread or yarn; spool, reel.

bob'-sled, bob'-sleigh (-slā), *nn.* long sled with steering mechanism; (either of) two short sleds coupled together.

bob'tail, *n.* (dog or horse with) docked tail. *rag, tag, and bobtail,* the rabble.

bōde, *v.* portend; foretell.

bod'ice, *n.* upper part of woman's dress down to waist; woman's undergarment for upper part of body.

bod'ily, *a.* of the body. *adv.* in the body, in person; as a whole.

bod'kin, *n.* blunt thick needle for drawing elastic, etc., through hem; (Hist.) dagger.

bod'y, *n.* material frame of man or animal; corpse; trunk; main part of a structure; person; aggregate of persons or things, collection; piece of matter; solidity, substance. **bod'yguard,** escort, retinue; personal guard. **body politic,** the State.

Bō'er, *n.* S. African of Dutch descent.

boff'in, *n.* (*slang*) person engaged in (esp. technical) research.

bog, *n.* wet spongy ground, too soft to bear weight on its surface. *v.t.* (p.t. *bogged*), trap or submerge in bog. **bogg'y** (-g-), *a.*

bō'gey (-gi), *n.* number of strokes a good golfer is reckoned to need for hole or for course.

bogg'le, *v.i.* start with fright; hesitate, demur, *at.*

bō'gie (-gi), *n.* undercarriage pivoted below end of locomotive, etc.

bō'gus, *a.* sham.

bō'gy, (-gi), *n.* the devil; goblin; bugbear.

Bohē'mian, *a.* socially unconventional; of free and easy habits. *n.* Bohemian person, esp. artist or writer.

boil¹, *n.* painful inflamed suppurating swelling on skin.

boil², *v.* (of liquid) reach or be at temperature at which change into gas occurs; bubble up; bring (liquid, etc.) to the boil; cook by boiling. *n.* boiling heat. **boiled sweet,** sweet

made of boiled sugar. **boiling-point,** temperature at which liquid boils.

boi'ler, *n.* vessel for boiling, esp. for making steam in engine; tank in which water is heated for domestic use.

bois'terous, *a.* violent, rough; noisily cheerful.

bōld, *a.* courageous, confident, enterprising; impudent, immodest; vigorous, clear. **bold(-face, -faced),** (of printing-type) thick. **bōld'ly,** *adv.* **bōld'ness,** *n.*

bōle, *n.* trunk of a tree.

boler'ō (-ār-), *n.* (pl. *boleros*), (music for) lively Spanish dance; (pr. bol'erō), jacket reaching barely to waist.

boll'ard, *n.* post on ship or quay for securing rope; short thick post in street, etc.

Bol'shèvik, *n.* member of Russian revolutionary party that seized power in 1917; revolutionary. **Bol'shèvism** (-zm), *n.* **Bol'shèvist,** *n. & a.*

bōl'ster, *n.* long stuffed pillow. *v.t.* (usu. *bolster up*) support with bolster, prop up.

bōlt¹, *n.* door-fastening of sliding bar and staple; metal pin with head, usu. secured with nut; roll of cloth; short heavy arrow of crossbow; discharge of lightning; running away. *v.* dart off, run away; gulp down unchewed; fasten with bolt. *bolt upright,* erect.

bōlt², *v.t.* sift (esp. flour).

bomb (-m), *n.* case filled with explosive, gas, etc., dropped from aircraft, fired from gun, thrown, or deposited, and exploded by impact or time mechanism. *v.* attack with or throw bombs. **bomb-proof,** giving protection against exploding bombs. **bomb'shell,** sudden shocking event, etc. **bomb'er** (-mer), *n.* aircraft, soldier, using bombs.

bombard', *v.t.* attack with gunfire; assail with abuse; subject to impact of electrons, etc. **bombard'ment,** *n.*

bombardier' (-ēr; *or* bumb-), *n.* artillery non-commissioned officer below sergeant; bomb-aimer in aircraft.

bom'bast, *n.* pompous talk. **bombas'tic,** *a.*

bō'na fī'dè, *a. & adv.* genuine(ly), sincere(ly). **bō'na fī'dēs** (-z), *n.* honest intention, sincerity. (Latin)

bon'bon, *n.* sweet.

bond¹, *n.* that which binds or unites; binding agreement; document binding government, company, etc., to pay or repay money (with interest); (pl.) fetters, chains. *v.t.* place (goods) in bond. *in bond,* in bonded warehouse. **bonded warehouse,** place where importer's dutiable goods are stored until customs duty is paid.

bond², *a.* (*archaic*) in serfdom or slavery. **bond'maid, bond'man, bond'servant, bond'slave, bonds'man,** serf or slave.

bon'dage, *n.* serfdom or slavery; confinement, constraint.

bōne, *n.* any of the separate parts of a verte-

brate skeleton; substance of which these consist; (pl.) skeleton, mortal remains. *v.t.* remove the bones from. **bone-dry**, quite dry. **bone′setter**, one who sets broken or dislocated bones but who is not a qualified doctor.
bon′fīre, *n.* large open-air fire.
bon′homie (-nomē), *n.* geniality.
bonn′et, *n.* woman's or baby's (brimless) outdoor head-dress with strings; (Sc.) man's cap; hinged cover over engine of motor vehicle.
bonn′y, *a.* pleasant-looking, healthy-looking.
bō′nus, *n.* something extra, esp. addition to dividends or wages.
bō′ny, *a.* of or like or abounding in bones; big-boned.
boo, *int.*, *n.* (pl. *boos*), & *v.* (make) sound of disapproval or contempt, hoot.
boo′by, *n.* silly or awkward fellow. **booby prize**, prize for last or lowest competitor. **booby trap**, thing(s) balanced on top of door to fall on head of first comer; apparently harmless object designed to explode when disturbed.
book, *n.* number of sheets of paper, printed, written on, or blank, fastened together in cover; literary composition that would fill book; main division of literary work, or of the Bible; (pl.) account-books. *v.t.* enter in book or list; secure (seat, etc.) in advance.
book′binder, *n.* one who binds books. **book′binding**, *n.*
book′-cāse, *n.* stand with shelves for books.
book′ing-clerk (-ark), *n.* clerk who sells tickets at railway station, etc. **book′ing-office**, *n.* place where tickets are sold.
book′ish, *a.* fond of reading; studious.
book′-keeper, *n.* one who keeps business accounts. **book′-keeping**, *n.*
book′let, *n.* small book, usu. in paper cover.
book′mäker, *n.* person whose business is taking bets on horse-races.
book′seller, *n.* one who sells books. **book′-selling**, *n.*
book′stall (-awl), *n.* kiosk where books, newspapers, etc., are sold.
book′worm (-werm), *n.* larva of various insects which destroys books; great reader.
boom¹ *n.* spar stretching foot of sail and attached at one end to mast; floating timber barrier across harbour mouth or river.
boom², *n.* deep resonant sound; sudden increase in activity in commerce, etc. *v.* send forth, utter with, boom; increase greatly and rapidly in prosperity, popularity, etc.
boo′merang, *n.* Australian missile of curved wood that can be so thrown as to return to thrower; (fig.) argument or proposal that recoils on its author. *v.i.* recoil thus.
boon¹, *n.* request; favour; blessing.
boon², *a.* convivial (obs. except in phr. *boon companion*).
boor, *n.* peasant; ill-mannered fellow. **boor′-ish**, *a.* **boor′ishness**, *n.*

boost, *v.t.* shove, hoist (*up*); produce increase or improvement in; raise (voltage, pressure, etc.). *n.* boosting. **boos′ter**, *n.* (esp.) first stage in multi-stage rocket.
boot¹, *n.* *to boot*, as well. *v.i. impers.* (*archaic*) be of advantage, avail. **boot′less¹**, *a.* unavailing.
boot², *n.* outer foot-covering of leather, etc., reaching above ankle; luggage receptacle in car, coach, etc. *v.t.* kick. **boot-jack**, appliance for pulling boots off. **boot′lace**, cord, etc., for lacing boots. **boot-tree**, shaped block inserted in boot to preserve shape. **boo′tĕd**, *a.* wearing boots. **bootee′**, *n.* infant's knitted boot; woman's lined boot. **boot′less²**, *a.* without boots.
booth (-dh), *n.* covered stall at market; tent at fair.
boot′leg, *a.* (esp. of alcoholic liquor) illegal, smuggled. *v.t.* trade illegally in liquor. **boot′legger** (-g-), **boot′legging** (-g-), *nn.*
boots, *n.* hotel servant who carries luggage, cleans shoes, etc.
boo′ty, *n.* plunder; spoils; prize.
booze, *v.i.* (*informal*) drink alcohol continuously or in large quantities. *n.* drinking-bout; drink. **booz′y**, *a.* given to drinking; fuddled.
bora′cic, *a.* boric.
bor′ax, *n.* salt of boric acid.
bor′der, *n.* side, edge; boundary, frontier; distinct edging round anything. *v.* to be or put a border to; adjoin; resemble closely.
bor′derer, *n.* one who dwells on or near the border of England and Scotland. **bor′-derland**, area on either side of frontier or border. **bor′derline**, *n.* boundary between areas. *a.* near the line of division between different groups, etc.
bore¹, *p.t.* of **bear²**.
bore², *v.* make deep hole in, esp. with drill. *n.* hollow of gun-barrel, calibre of gun. **bore-(hole)**, small deep hole made to find water, oil, etc.
bore³, *n.* tiresome person. *v.t.* weary by tedious talk or dullness. **bore′dom**, *n.*
bore⁴, *n.* tide-wave with precipitous front moving up some estuaries.
bor′ēal, *a.* of the north wind or the north.
bor′ic, *a.* of boron. **boric acid**, mild antiseptic used in form of ointment, etc.
born, *p.p.* of **bear²**, chiefly in *be born*, come into existence by birth. *a.* destined (*to be*).
borne, *p.p.* of **bear²**.
bor′on, *n.* non-metallic solid element.
borough (bu′ra), *n.* town with municipal corporation; town electing Member(s) of Parliament.
bo′rrow (-ō), *v.* get temporary use of (something to be returned); appropriate. **bo′-rrōwer**, *n.*
Bor′stal (Institū′tion), institution to which young offenders may be sent for reformative training.
bor′zoi, *n.* Russian wolf-hound.

bosom (boo'zm), *n.* breast; enclosure formed by breast and arms; midst; heart, thoughts. **bosom friend,** intimate friend.

boss¹, *n.* round knob or stud.

boss², *n.* master, manager, person in authority. *v. t.* control. **boss'y,** *a.* domineering.

bot'any, *n.* scientific study of plants. **botan'ic(al),** *aa.* **bot'anist,** *n.* **bot'anize,** *v. i.* study plants, esp. by seeking them where they grow.

botch, *v. t.* patch, mend, clumsily; bungle. *n.* botched work; bungled task.

both, *a.* the pair of. *pron.* the two together. *adv. both.. and..,* not only.. but also..

both'er (-dh-), *v.* be troublesome to; take trouble. *n.* worry, fuss. *int.* of annoyance. **botherā'tion,** *n.* & *int.* (*informal*) bother. **both'ersome,** *a.* annoying, troublesome.

bott'le, *n.* narrow-necked usu. glass container for liquids. *v. t.* put into bottle(s). *bottle up,* restrain (feelings, etc.). **bottle-green,** dark green. **bottle-neck,** narrow stretch or restricted outlet of road, etc; anything obstructing even flow of production, etc.

bott'om, *n.* lowest part of anything; buttocks; ground under water of sea, etc.; base. *a.* lowest, last. *v. t.* touch bottom of (sea, etc.). **bott'omless,** *a.* unfathomable.

boudoir (boo'dwahr), *n.* lady's private room.

bough (bow), *n.* large branch of tree.

bought, *p. t.* & *p. p.* of **buy.**

boul'der (bōl-), *n.* large water-worn stone; large weather-worn piece of rock.

boulevard (bool'var), *n.* broad tree-lined street.

bounce, *v.* (of ball, etc.) spring back after striking ground, etc.; move violently or noisily; swagger; hustle or bluff. *n.* rebound; swagger, assurance. **boun'cing,** *a.* big and hearty.

bound¹, *n.* (usu. pl.) encircling boundary, limit. *v. t.* be boundary of. *out of bounds,* outside permitted area.

bound², *v. i.* (of ball, etc.) recoil from wall or ground; spring, leap. *n.* recoil of ball, etc.; leap forward or upward.

bound³, *a.* ready to start or having started (*for*).

bound⁴, *p. t.* & *p. p.* of **bind.**

boun'dary, *n.* limiting line; (Cricket) hit to or over limit of field, runs scored for this.

bound'less, *a.* without limits.

boun'tèous, boun'tiful, *aa.* showing bounty, generous, lavish.

boun'ty, *n.* generosity in giving; gift; gratuity; subsidy.

bouquet (bookā'), *n.* bunch of flowers; perfume of wine; bunch of herbs for flavouring.

bourgeois (boor'zhwah), *n.* & *a.* (person) of the middle class.

bout, *n.* spell or turn of work, illness, drinking, etc.; round, contest.

boutique (boo'tēk), *n.* small shop, esp. one selling clothes or articles of the latest fashion.

bō'vine, *a.* of oxen; dull, slow.

bow¹ (bō), *n.* piece of wood curved by tight string, for shooting arrows; wooden rod with horsehair stretched from end to end, for playing violin, etc.; slip-knot with one loop or two; ribbon, etc., so tied. **bow-legged,** bandy. **bow-window,** curved bay window.

bow² (bow) *v.* bend the head or body in sign of submission or reverence; cause to bend; incline one's head in salutation or assent. *n.* bowing of head or body.

bow³ (bow), *n.* (often pl.) fore-end of boat or ship.

bowd'lerīze, *v. t.* remove objectionable words, etc. from (book).

bow'el, *n.* (usu. pl.) intestine; (pl.) entrails, tender feelings, inside.

bow'er, *n.* arbour; (Poet.) boudoir.

bowie-knife (bō'i-nīf), *n.* knife with long blade, double-edged at point.

bowl¹ (bōl), *n.* basin, esp. for drink or food; bowl-shaped part of anything.

bowl² (bōl), *n.* wooden ball shaped to make it run curved course; ball used in skittles; (pl.) game played on green with bowls. *v.* play bowls; roll; go along at smart even pace; (Cricket) deliver ball to batsman; dismiss (batsman) by knocking off bails in bowling. **bowl'er¹,** *n.* person bowling at cricket; player at bowls.

bowl'er² (bō-), *n.* hard felt hat with round crown and narrow brim.

bow'line (bōl-), *n.* knot used in making fixed loop at end of rope.

bowl'ing-alley (bōl-), *n.* enclosure for game of skittles.

bowl'ing-green (bōl-), *n.* ground for playing bowls.

bow'man (bō-), *n.* (pl. *bowmen*), archer.

bow'sprit (bō-), *n.* spar running forward from ship's bow.

box¹, *n.* small evergreen shrub. **box(wood),** wood of this.

box², *n.* container, usu. with lid, rectangular, and for solids; separate compartment in a theatre, stable, etc. *v. t.* put in a box. **box-office,** office for booking seats for theatre, etc.

box³, *n.* slap *on the ear*(*s*) *v.* slap (person's *ears*); fight with fists, usu. in padded gloves. **box'er,** *n.* one who boxes; pugilist; smooth-coated dog of bulldog type. **box'ing,** *n.* act or sport of fighting with fists. **boxing-gloves,** padded gloves used in boxing.

Box'ing Day, first weekday after Christmas when Christmas boxes are traditionally given.

boy, *n.* male child or youth, son; male native servant. **Boy Scout,** see **scout. boy'hood,** *n.* time of being a boy. **boy'ish,** *a.* of or like boys; high-spirited.

boy'cott, *v. t.* refuse all contact or dealings with (person, goods, etc.) as punishment or

for purpose of coercion. *n.* such treatment.
bra (-ah), *n.* brassière.
brace, *v.t.* strengthen or tighten; invigorate.
n. thing that braces or connects; wire device
for straightening teeth; pair; (pl.) straps worn
over shoulders to support trousers.
brace'let (-sl-), *n.* ornamental band, chain,
etc., for arm or wrist.
brack'en, *n.* fern abundant on heaths.
brack'et, *n.* projection from wall serving as
support; wooden or metal angular support;
one of pair of marks ( ) used for enclosing
word(s), figure(s), etc. *v.t.* enclose in brackets; couple names, etc., together.
brack'ish, *a.* (of water) slightly salt.
bract, *n.* (Bot.) modified leaf below calyx.
brad'awl, *n.* small boring tool.
brae (-ā), *n.* (Sc.) hill side, steep bank.
brag, *v.* (p.t. *bragged*), talk boastfully, boast.
n. boastful talk.
bragg'art, *n.* person given to boasting.
Brah'ma, *n.* supreme Hindu deity.
Brah'min, *n.* member of Hindu priestly caste.
braid, *n.* plaited tress of hair; silk or thread or
wire woven into a band. *v.t.* plait, interweave; trim with braid.
braille (-āl), *n.* system of writing or printing
for the blind with raised characters.
brain, *n.* mass of nervous tissue contained in
skull, controlling processes of sensation,
intellectual activity, and memory; (often pl.)
intellectual ability. *v.t.* dash out the brains
of. **brain-washing**, process of forcing person
to give up established ideas and accept new
ones. **brain-wave**, bright idea. **brain'y**, *a.*
clever.
braise (-z), *v.t.* cook meat slowly with vegetables, herbs, etc.
brake[1], *n.* thicket, brushwood.
brake[2], *n.* apparatus for checking motion of a
wheel or vehicle. *v.* apply brake; check with
brake. **brake-van**, railway carriage from
which train's brakes can be worked.
brake[3], *n.* large wagonette.
bram'ble, *n.* rough prickly shrub, esp. the
blackberry bush; (Sc.) blackberry.
bram'bling, *n.* mountain finch.
bran, *n.* inner husks of grain separated from
flour after grinding.
branch (-ah-), *n.* limb growing from stem or
bough of tree; lateral extension or subdivision of something. *v.i.* put *out* branches;
divide, diverge, *off, out*, etc., in new path.
brand, *n.* piece of burning or smouldering
wood, torch; (mark left by) iron stamp used
red-hot; stigma; sword (Poet.); goods of particular make or trade-mark. *v.t.* stamp with
brand; impress on memory; mark with disgrace. **bran'ded**, *a.* sold under particular
name or trade-mark. **brand-new**, *a.* per-
fectly new.
bran'dish, *v.t.* wave about, flourish.
bran'dy, *n.* strong spirit distilled from wine or
grapes. **brandy-snap**, crisp sticky rolled up

wafer flavoured with ginger (and brandy).
brash, *a.* impudent; hasty, rash.
brass (-ahs), *n.* yellow alloy of copper with
zinc; memorial tablet of inscribed brass;
brass wind instruments; (fig.) impudence. *a.*
made of brass.
brassard', *n.* armlet (with badge).
brass'ière (-yār), *n.* woman's undergarment
supporting breasts.
brass'y (-ah-), *a.* like brass in colour, sound,
or taste; brazen.
brat, *n.* (*contemptuous*) child.
brava'dō (-vah-), *n.* show of courage;
pretended boldness.
brave, *a.* ready to face and steady in enduring
danger and pain; splendid, spectacular. *n.*
Red Indian warrior. *v.t.* face, go into, meet,
without showing fear. **bra'very**, *n.* brave
conduct; splendour, finery.
bra'vō (-ah-), *int. & n.* (pl. *bravos*), cry of
approval.
brawl, *n.* noisy quarrel. *v.i.* quarrel in a noisy
and vulgar way; (of stream) flow noisily.
brawn, *n.* muscle; cold dish made with meat
of pig's head. **braw'ny**, *a.* strong, muscular.
bray, *n.* ass's cry; loud harsh jarring sound. *v.*
emit bray; utter harshly.
brāze, *v.t.* solder with alloy of brass and zinc.
bra'zen, *a.* made of brass; like brass; shameless. *v.t.* carry off impudently (esp. in phr.
brazen it out).
bra'zier (*or* -zher), *n.* basket-like iron framework for holding charcoal or coal fire.
brazil', *n.* (now usu. **brazil-wood**), hard
brownish-red wood of various tropical trees.
brazil-nut, large three-sided nut of Brazilian
tree.
breach, *n.* breaking of rule, duty, promise,
etc.; quarrel; opening, gap. *v.t.* make a gap
in (wall, etc.).
bread (-ed), *n.* flour moistened and kneaded
into dough, formed into loaves, and baked;
necessary food, livelihood. **bread'winner**,
person who supports a family.
breadth (-ed-), *n.* broadness, distance from
side to side; liberality of mind, toleration.
break (-āk), *v.* (p.t. *brōke*; p.p. *brōken*),
divide or split or separate otherwise than by
cutting; destroy; tame; fall to pieces; make or
become bankrupt; act contrary to (law, promise, etc.). *break down*, fail or collapse,
itemize, analyse. *break even*, emerge with
neither gain nor loss. *break in(to)*, get in(to)
by force. *break out*, escape; appear, start,
suddenly. *break through*, (esp.) surmount
obstacle or barrier. *break up*, become feeble,
dismiss, disperse, break small. *n.* breaking;
broken place; breach, gap; pause in work,
etc. **break'able**, *a.* that can be broken. *n.*
(pl.) things easily broken. **break'age**, *n.*
breaking; (pl.) broken articles, loss by breaking.
break'down (-āk-), *n.* collapse; failure in
health or function; analysis (of statistics,

etc.).

break'er (-āk-), *n.* heavy ocean-wave breaking on coast or over reef.

break'fast (brek-), *n.* first meal of the day. *v. i.* take breakfast.

break'neck (-āk-), *a.* headlong, dangerous.

breakthrough (brāk'thrōō), *n.* breaking through; major advance in scientific knowledge, etc.

break'water (-ākwaw-), *n.* pier or mole erected to form or protect harbour; groyne.

bream, *n.* freshwater or sea fish.

breast (-est), *n.* either of the milk-secreting organs of a woman; upper front part of human body, corresponding part in animals; seat of affections. *v. t.* face; struggle with (waves, etc.). **breast'bone,** bone connecting ribs in front. **breast'plate,** piece of armour for the breast.

breath (-eth), *n.* air drawn in and expelled by the lungs; breathing, one respiration; slight movement of air; whisper.

breathalyser (breth'alīzer), *n.* device for measuring amount of alcohol in the breath.

breathe (-ēdh), *v.* draw breath into and send it out of the lungs; live; inhale or exhale or instil; speak or utter softly. **brea'ther,** *n.* short pause for rest. **brea'thing,** *n.* **breathing space,** time to breathe, pause.

breath'less (-eth-), *a.* panting; unstirred by wind; holding one's breath. **breath'lessly,** *adv.* pantingly, in suspense.

bred, *p. t. & p. p.* of **breed.**

breech, *n.* back part of gun or gun-barrel.

breeches (brich'iz), *n. pl.* short trousers fastened below the knee. **breeches buoy,** lifebuoy fitted with canvas breeches and slung on rope, for saving life at sea.

breed, *v.* (p.t. & p.p. *bred*), produce offspring; keep (cattle, etc.) for purpose of producing young, esp. by mating selected animals; train; give rise to. *n.* race, strain; family with hereditary qualities. **bree'ding,** *n.* training, good manners.

breeze, *n.* gentle wind. **bree'zy,** *a.* pleasantly windy; lively, irresponsible.

Bren'-gun, *n.* light magazine-fed automatic rifle.

breth'ren (-dh-), *archaic* pl. of **brother.**

brēve, *n.* (Mus.) the longest note, now rarely used, equal to two semibreves.

brē'viary (*or* bre-), *n.* book containing R.C. Divine Office for each day.

brev'ity, *n.* conciseness, shortness.

brew (-ōō), *v.* make beer, etc., by fermenting malt; make (tea, punch, etc.); plot, concoct. *n.* amount brewed at one time; liquor brewed. **brew'er,** *n.* one who brews beer. **brew'ery,** *n.* building in which beer is brewed.

briar: see **brier.**

brībe, *n.* reward given or offered to procure (esp. dishonest or illegal) service. *v. t.* persuade by bribe(s). **brī'bery,** *n.*

bric'-à-brac, *n.* artistic or old-fashioned odds and ends of china, furniture, etc.

brick, *n.* building-material of baked clay in oblong blocks; brick-shaped block; toy building-block; (*slang*) generous or loyal person. *v. t.* block *up* with brick. **brick'bat,** piece of brick, esp. as missile. **brick-kiln,** place for baking bricks. **brick'layer,** workman who lays bricks in building. **brick'work** (-erk), *n.* (part of) structure of bricks.

brī'dal, *a.* of bride or wedding.

bride, *n.* woman on her wedding day and shortly before and after it. **bride'grōōm,** man on his wedding day. **brīdes'maid** (-dz-), unmarried woman attending bride at wedding.

bridge[1], *n.* structure carrying road, railway, etc., across river, ravine, etc.; (Naut.) platform amidships for officer in charge; upper bony part of nose; prop under strings of violin, etc. *v. t.* make bridge over; span as with bridge. **bridge-head,** (Mil.) position held on enemy's side of water-barrier; any position established in face of enemy.

bridge[2], *n.* card-game developed from whist.

brī'dle, *n.* head-stall, bit, and reins by which a horse is controlled. *v.* put bridle on; control; draw up one's head in anger, etc. **brī'dle-path,** path fit for riders but not for vehicles.

brief, *a.* of short duration; concise. *n.* (Law) solicitor's summary for guidance of barrister; (pl.) very short knickers. *v. t.* instruct by brief, employ, (barrister); give instructions, necessary information, etc., to. **brief'ing,** *n.* **brief-case,** flat case of leather, etc., for carrying papers, etc. **brief'less,** *a.* (of barrister) without clients.

brī'er[1], **brī'ar**[1], *n.* prickly shrub; wild rose, esp. sweet-brier with fragrant leaves and flowers.

brī'er[2], **brī'ar**[2], *n.* heath whose root is used for pipe-bowls; brier pipe.

brig, *n.* two-masted square-rigged sailing vessel.

brigāde', *n.* military sub-unit of a division; organized band of workers, etc.

brigadier' (-ēr), *n.* brigade-commander.

brig'and, *n.* member of a robber gang. **brig'andage,** *n.* robbery, pillage.

brig'antine (-ēn) *n.* two-masted vessel with square-rigged foremast and fore-and-aft rigged mainmast.

bright (-īt), *a.* shining; brilliant; cheerful; quick-witted. **bright'ly,** *adv.*

bright'en (-īt-), *v.* make or become bright.

brill, *n.* flat-fish related to turbot.

brill'iant (-lya-), *a.* bright, sparkling; highly talented; distinguished. *n.* diamond of finest quality. **brill'iance,** *n.*

brill'iantine (-yantēn) *n.* cosmetic for keeping hair smooth and glossy.

brim, *n.* edge of cup, hollow, etc.; projecting edge of hat. *v.* (p.t. *brimmed*), fill or be full to the brim. **brim'ful**, *a.*

brim'stone, *n.* sulphur; (Bibl.) fuel of hell--fire.

brin'dled (-dld), *a.* brownish with streaks of other colour.

brine, *n.* strongly salted water for pickling; salt water, the sea.

bring, *v.t.* (p.t. *brought* pr.-awt), cause to come; come with or convey in any way; cause, result in. **bring about**, cause to happen. **bring forth**, give birth to. **bring off**, succeed in. **bring round**, restore to consciousness. **bring up**, tend and educate, rear.

brink, *n.* edge of precipice, etc.; verge.

bri'ny, *a.* of the sea, salt. *n.* (Poet.) the sea.

briquette' (-ket), *n.* block of compressed coal--dust.

brisk, *a.* active, lively, quick.

brisk'et, *n.* breast of animals, esp. as joint of meat.

bris'ling (*or* -z-), *n.* young sprat or herring.

bri'stle (-sl), *n.* short stiff hair, esp. of hog's back and sides. *v.i.* (of hair, etc.) stand up; show temper; be thickly set (*with* difficulties, etc.). **bri'stly** (-sli), *a.*

Brit'ain (-tn), *n.* (also *Great Britain*), England, Wales, and Scotland.

Britann'ia (-ya), *n.* Britain personified.

Britann'ic, *a.* of Britain.

Brit'ish, *a.* of Great Britain or the British Commonwealth; of the ancient Britons.

Brit'on, *n.* native of Gt. Britain; (also *ancient Briton*) inhabitant of S. part of island at time of Roman invasion.

britt'le, *a.* hard but easily broken; fragile.

broach, *n.* tapered boring tool. *v.t.* pierce or begin drawing from (cask); start using; bring up for discussion.

broad (-awd), *a.* wide, extensive; comprehensive, tolerant; full, clear; (of humour or speech) coarse; (of accent or dialect) marked, strong. *n.* broad part.

broadcast (brawd'kahst), *v.* (p.t. *broadcast*), sow (seed) by scattering freely, not in rows; spread (information, etc.) widely; transmit (news, music, etc.) to public by radio or television; perform, etc., for such transmission. *a.* & *adv.* (sown, transmitted) by broadcasting. *n.* act of broadcasting, broadcast programme, etc.

broad'cloth (-awd-), fine quality woollen cloth; cotton fabric resembling poplin.

broad'en (-awd-), *v.* make or become broader.

broad'loom (-awd-), *a.* (of carpet) woven in broad widths.

broad'sheet (-awd-), *n.* large sheet of paper printed on one side only.

broad'side (-awd-), *n.* ship's side; all guns on one side; simultaneous firing of these.

broadsword (brawd'sord), *n.* sword with broad straight blade.

brocade', *n.* fabric woven with raised pattern.

brocc'oli, *n.* hardy variety of cauliflower.

bro'chure (-sh-) *n.* booklet, pamphlet.

brock, *n.* badger.

brogue (-g), *n.* strong shoe for country wear; marked local, esp. Irish, accent.

broil, *v.* cook on (gridiron over) fire; grill; make or be very hot. **broi'ler**, *n.* (esp.) young chicken suitable for broiling.

broke, *p.t.* of **break.**

bro'ken, *p.p.* of **break.** *a.* in pieces, shattered; despairing; imperfect, incomplete; interrupted. **bro̅ken-hearted**, crushed by grief. **bro'kenly**, *adv.* by jerks, with breaks.

bro'ker, *n.* middleman; stockbroker. **bro'kerage**, *n.* broker's fees or commission.

bro'mide (-īd), *n.* compound of bromine with another element.

bro'mine (-ēn), *n.* (Chem.) liquid non--metallic element.

bronch'ial (-ngk-), *a.* of the two main divisions of the windpipe and their branches.

bronchi'tis (-ngk-), *n.* inflammation of the bronchial mucous membrane.

bron'co, *n.* (pl. *broncos*), wild or half-tamed horse of western N. America.

brontosaur'us, *n.* gigantic prehistoric reptile of dinosaur family.

bronze, *n.* brown alloy of copper and tin; its colour; work of art made of bronze. *a.* made of, coloured like, bronze. *v.* give bronze-like surface to; make or grow brown, tan.

brooch (bro̅ch), *n.* ornament with hinged pin and catch, worn on garment.

brood, *n.* birds or other animals produced at one hatch or birth. *v.i.* sit on eggs; meditate deeply, fret *over.* **brood-mare**, mare kept for breeding. **broo'dy**, *a.* (of hen) wanting to sit on eggs.

brook[1], *v.t.* put up with, tolerate.

brook[2], *n.* small stream. **brook'let**, *n.*

broom, *n.* yellow-flowered shrub; long--handled sweeping-brush. **broom'stick**, *n.* broom-handle.

broth, *n.* thin soup made from liquid in which meat or poultry has been boiled.

broth'el, *n.* house of prostitutes.

broth'er (-udh-), *n.* son of the same parents as another person; companion, equal; (with pl. *brethren*) member of religious order, fellow member of church, order, trade union, etc. **brother-in-law**, one's wife's or husband's brother; one's sister's husband. **broth'erhood**, *n.* fellowship; association of men for mutual help, etc. **broth'erly**, *a.* of or like a brother; affectionate. **broth'erliness**, *n.*

brougham (broo'am), *n.* one-horse four--wheeled closed carriage.

brought, *p.t.* & *p.p.* of **bring.**

brow, *n.* forehead; (usu. pl.) eyebrow; edge of cliff, etc.; top of hill in a road. **brow'beat**, *v.t.* harass; bully.

brown, *a.* colour produced by mixing red, yellow and black pigments; dark, dark--skinned. *n.* brown colour or pigment. *v.* make or grow brown. **brown study**, deep thought, reverie.

brow'nie, *n.* shaggy goblin fabled to do household work secretly; (*Brownie*), junior Guide.

browse (-z-), *v.* feed on leaves and young shoots; read (parts of book or books) for enjoyment.

Bru'in (-ōō-), *n.* name for bear in folk-tales.

bruise (-ōōz), *n.* injury caused by blow or pressure discolouring skin. *v.* pound, batter; inflict bruise(s) on; show effects of blow.

bruit (-ōōt), *v.t.* spread (report) *about, abroad.*

brunette' (-ōō-), *a.* & *n.* dark-haired and dark-skinned (woman).

brunt, *n.* stress of shock or attack.

brush, *n.* cleaning or hairdressing or painting implement of bristles, hair, etc., set in holder; (act of) brushing; fox's tail; skirmish. *v.* use brush on; touch lightly in passing. **brush'wood,** *n.* undergrowth, thicket.

brusque (-oosk *or* -usk), *a.* blunt, offhand.

Bruss'els sprouts, edible buds of kind of cabbage.

bru'tal (-ōō-), *a.* as of brutes; rude, coarse, cruel. **brutal'ity,** *n.* **bru'talize,** *v.t.* make brutal.

brute (-ōōt), *a.* not gifted with reason. *n.* animal other than man; large or frightening beast; coarse and cruel person. **bru'tish,** *a.*

brў'ony, *n.* climbing hedge plant.

bubb'le, *n.* globe or half-globe of liquid or glass enclosing air or gas; unpractical scheme. *v.i.* send up, rise in, make the sound of, bubbles. **bubb'ly,** *a.* full of bubbles. *n.* (*slang*) champagne.

bŭbon'ic, *a.* characterized by inflamed swellings of glands, esp. in groin or armpit. **bubonic plague,** highly infectious, often fatal, epidemic disease.

buccaneer', *n.* pirate adventurer. **buccaneer'ing,** *a.* piratical. *n.* roving like a pirate.

buck[1], *n.* male of deer, antelope, etc., hare, or rabbit.

buck[2], *v.* (of horse) leap vertically from gound with back arched; throw (rider) *off* thus.

buck[3], *v.* (*slang*) (with *up*) hurry; become or make more cheerful or vigorous.

buck'ét[1], *n.* vessel with handle, for carrying or holding water, etc.; scoop for hoisting, dredging, etc. **buck'étful,** *n.* (pl. *bucketfuls*).

buck'ét[2], *v.* ride (horse) hard; make jerky or bumpy progress.

buck'le, *n.* clasp with hinged tongue used for straps, belts, etc. *v.* fasten, or put *on,* with buckle; give way under pressure; *buckle to,* set to work vigorously. *buckle up,* crumple up.

buck'ler, *n.* small round shield; (fig.) protector or protection.

buck'ram, *n.* coarse linen or cotton fabric stiffened with paste, etc.

buck'shot, *n.* large coarse shot.

buck'skin, *n.* soft leather made from skin of deer, goat, etc.; (pl.) breeches of this.

buck'wheat *n.* cereal plant.

bŭcol'ic, *a.* of shepherds, of country life.

bud, *n.* small knob from which branch or leaf-cluster or flower develops; flower or leaf not fully open. *v.* (p.t. *budded*), put forth buds, sprout as buds; begin to grow or develop; graft bud on to another plant. *nip in the bud,* destroy at early stage.

Buddhism (bood'izm), *n.* religion founded by Buddha (6th - 5th c. B.C.). **Budd'hist,** *n.*

budd'leia (-lēa), *n.* shrub with fragrant lilac or yellow flowers.

budge, *v.* move in slightest degree, stir.

budg'erigar, *n.* Australian love-bird, the grass parakeet, often kept as cage-bird.

budg'ét, *n.* Chancellor of the Exchequer's annual estimate of revenue and expenditure; private person's similar estimate; amount of money required or available. *v.i. budget for,* allow or arrange for in a budget.

buff, *n.* strong velvety dull-yellow leather; colour of this. *a.* of this colour. *v.t.* polish with buff or soft pad.

buff'alō, *n.* (pl. *buffaloes*), kind of ox.

buff'er, *n.* (often pl.) apparatus for deadening or taking the shock of a collision, esp. on railway locomotive, truck, etc., or at termination of railway lines. **buffer state,** neutral State between two possible belligerents.

buff'ét[1], *n.* blow given with hand; blow dealt by wave, etc., or by fortune. *v.t.* deal blows to, knock about.

buffet[2] (boo'fā), *n.* refreshment bar; sideboard or table from which food and drink are served.

buffoon', *n.* person who makes himself ridiculous to raise laughter, joker. **buffoon'ery,** *n.*

bug, *n.* small blood-sucking insect infesting beds; (*informal*) any insect, infection, microbe; (*slang*) concealed microphone. *v.t.* (p.t. *bugged*), (*slang*) equip with alarm system or hidden microphone.

bug'bear (-bār), *n.* object of (needless) dread; imaginary terror.

bugg'y (-g-), *n.* light horse-drawn vehicle.

bū'gle[1], *n.* small trumpet-like brass instrument without valves. *v.* sound (call on) bugle. **bū'gler,** *n.*

bū'gle[2], *n.* tube-shaped glass bead sewn on dress, etc., for ornament.

build (bild), *v.* (p.t. *built,* pr. bilt), construct by putting parts together; base hopes *on.* *build up,* establish, make bigger or stronger. *built-in,* (of furniture, etc.) constructed as fixture. *built-up,* (of area, etc.) covered with buildings. **build,** *n.* make, style of construction; proportions of human body.

buil'der (bil-), *n.* (esp.) contractor for building houses. **buil'ding,** *n.* house or other structure with roof and walls.

bulb, *n.* nearly spherical base of stem enclosing modified shoot in such plants as lily, onion, tulip, etc.; roundish swelling in tube, etc.; glass container of electric light filament.

bul'bous, *a.* of, having, growing from, bulb(s); bulb-shaped.

bulbul (bool'bool), *n.* song-bird of Asia and Africa.

bulge, *n.* irregular swelling-out of surface or line; (temporary) increase in numbers or volume. *v.i.* form or show bulge.

bulk, *n.* cargo; quantity, volume, esp. when large. *the bulk of,* the mass or greater part of. *v.i.* *bulk large,* appear large or important.

bulk'head, upright partition in ship's hull between cabins or watertight compartments.

bul'ky, *a.* large, unwieldy.

bull[1] (bool-), *n.* order or edict from the Pope.

bull[2] (boo-), *n.* uncastrated male ox; male of elephant, whale, and other large animals. **bull'dog,** powerful and courageous large-headed smooth-haired dog. **bull'fight,** (esp. Spanish) sport and spectacle of fight between men, horsemen and a bull. **bull'finch,** fine-plumaged song-bird. **bull-ring,** arena for bullfight. **bull's-eye,** centre of target; spherical, usu. peppermint, boiled sweet.

bull'dōze (boo-), *v.* clear with bulldozer; (*informal*) make *way* forcibly; intimidate. **bull'dōzer,** *n.* powerful tractor with broad steel blade in front, used for clearing or levelling ground, etc.

bull'et (boo-), *n.* spherical or conical missile for rifle, pistol, etc. **bullet-proof,** impenetrable to bullets.

bull'etin (boo-), *n.* short official statement of news, invalid's condition, etc.

bull'ion (boo-), *n.* gold or silver, in bulk or bars, before coining or manufacture.

bull'ock (boo-), *n.* castrated male ox:

bull'y[1] (boo-), *n.* person who uses strength or power to coerce others by fear. *v.t.* act the bully towards, persecute.

bull'y[2] (boo-), *n.* *bully(-beef),* tinned beef.

bull'y[3] (boo-), *n.* (Hockey) procedure for putting ball in play. *v.i.* put ball in play by a bully; (also *bully off*) start play thus.

bul'rush (boo-), *n.* kind of tall reed.

bul'wark (boo-), *n.* rampart, earthwork, etc.; person or principle that protects; ship's side above deck.

bum'ble-bee, *n.* large loud-humming bee.

bum'boat, *n.* boat plying with fresh provisions to ships at anchor in harbour, etc.

bump, *n.* dull-sounding blow, collision; knock, swelling caused by it; jolt of vehicle; (variation of air-pressure causing) jolt of aircraft in flight. *v.* strike or come bump against; jolt. *adv.* with a bump, suddenly, violently.

bum'per, *n.* brimming glass; record harvest score, etc.; fender at front or rear of motor vehicle, to take first shock of collision.

bump'kin, *n.* country lout.

bump'tious (-shus), *a.* self-assertive; conceited.

bum'py, *a.* full of bumps, causing jolts.

bun, *n.* small soft round (currant) cake; small coil of hair at back of head.

bunch, *n.* cluster of things growing or fastened together; lot, collection. *v.* make into bunch or bunches; gather in folds; come or cling together. **bun'chy,** *a.*

bun'dle, *n.* odds and ends tied up in cloth, etc.; sticks, etc., bound up together. *v.* tie in a bundle; throw confusedly *in*(*to*) receptacle; go or send abruptly *away, out,* etc.

bung, *n.* stopper, esp. large cork plugging hole in cask. *v.t.* stop with bung; stop *up.* **bung-hole,** hole through which cask is filled.

bung'alow (-nggalō), *n.* one-storeyed house.

bungle (bung'gl), *v.* go awkwardly to work; mismanage, fail to accomplish. *n.* piece of bungling.

bun'ion (-yon), *n.* inflamed swelling on foot esp. at side of first joint of big toe.

bunk, *n.* sleeping-berth, bed, esp. one of two or more in tiers.

bun'ker, *n.* large bin or compartment for storing fuel, etc.; pit or hollow as hazard on golf-course; reinforced concrete shelter.

bun'kum, *n.* insincere talk; nonsense.

Bun'sen bur'ner, gas burner for burning mixed air and gas, giving very hot flame.

bun'ting[1], *n.* any of various small birds.

bun'ting[2], *n.* (worsted or cotton fabric used for making) flags.

buoy (boi), *n.* anchored float marking navigable channel or indicating submerged reef(s), etc.; lifebuoy. *v.t.* mark with buoy(s). *buoy up,* keep afloat, sustain, uplift.

buoy'ancy (boi-), *n.* ability or tendency to float; recuperative power, resilience. **buoy'ant,** *a.* apt to float, light; cheerful.

bur, burr[2], *n.* clinging hooked fruit or flower-head; plant producing burs.

bur'den, *n.* load, task, weight of grief, obligatory expense; ship's tonnage; refrain of song, theme. *v.t.* load, encumber, lie heavy on. **bur'densome,** *a.* oppressive, wearying.

bur'dock, *n.* plant with prickly flower-heads and dock-like leaves.

bureau (būr'ō), *n.* (pl. *bureaux,* pr. -z), writing-desk; office, esp. of Government department.

bureau'cracy (būrok-), *n.* government by officials; centralization; officialism. **būr'eaucrat** (-ō-), *n.* **būreaucrat'ic,** *a.*

burgee', *n.* small swallow-tailed pennant flown on yacht.

bur'geon (-jn), *v.i.* bud, shoot.

bur'gess, *n.* freeman of borough, citizen.

burgh (bu'ra), *n.* Scottish borough.

burg'her (-ger), *n.* (*archaic*) citizen, esp. of foreign town.

burg'lar, *n.* person entering building illegally with intent to steal, etc. **burg'lary,** *n.* **bur'gle,** *v.* rob thus.

burg'omaster (-ah-), *n.* mayor of Dutch or Flemish town.

bur'gundy, *n.* (usu. red) wine of Burgundy in France.

bu'rial (be-), *n.* burying, esp. of dead body; funeral.

bur'lap, *n.* coarse canvas, sacking.

burlesque' (-sk), *a.* imitating mockingly for the purpose of amusing. *n.* parody of literary or dramatic work, etc. *v.t.* imitate in an amusing way, caricature, travesty.

bur'ly, *a.* of large sturdy build.

burn¹, *n.* (Sc.) brook.

burn², *v.* (p.t. & p.p. **burnt** or **burned**), consume or be consumed by fire; blaze or smoulder; feel intense heat or emotion; injure or mark by burning. *n.* sore or mark made by burning.

bur'ner, *n.* part of lamp, gas-stove, etc., that shapes the flame.

bur'nish, *v.* polish by rubbing; take a polish.

burnt, *p.t.* & *p.p.* of **burn.**

burr¹, *n.* whirring sound; rough sounding of letter *r*, esp. rough uvular trill.

burr²: see **bur.**

bu'rrow (-ō), *n.* hole in earth dug out by animals as dwelling. *v.* make or live in burrow; excavate.

bur'sar, *n.* treasurer of college, etc.; holder of bursary. **bur'sary,** *n.* bursar's office; grant made to student at college, etc.

burst, *v.* fly violently asunder or give way suddenly; explode; rush, move, speak, be spoken, suddenly or violently. *n.* explosion, outbreak; spurt. **bur'sting,** *a.* full to overflowing; able to contain with difficulty.

bury (be'ri), *v.t.* place in, commit to, earth or tomb or sea, (with funeral rites); hide, forget.

bus, *n.* (pl. *buses*), passenger-carrying vehicle plying on fixed route or in service of hotel, etc. *v.* (p.t. *bus(s)ed*), go, transport, by bus. **bus'man,** bus driver. **bus-stop,** fixed stopping place for buses.

bus'by (-z-), *n.* tall fur cap of hussars, etc.

bush (-oo-), *n.* shrub; (Austral., S. Afr., etc.) woodland, uncultivated district. **Bush'man,** member or language of S. Afr. aboriginal race; (*bushman*) dweller or traveller in Australian bush. **bush-ränger,** Australian brigand living in bush. **bush-telegraph,** rapid spreading of information, rumour, etc. **bushed** (-sht), *a.* lost in the bush.

bush'el (-oo-), *n.* measure of capacity (8 gallons) for corn, fruit, etc.

bush'y (-oo-), *a.* growing thickly.

business (biz'nis), *n.* occupation, trade, profession; work; commercial transactions; firm. **business-like,** systematic, practical, prompt. **business man,** man engaged in commerce.

bus'ker, *n.* wandering musician, etc.; street performer.

bus'kin, *n.* thick-soled boot lending height to ancient-Athenian tragic actor.

bust, *n.* sculpture of head, shoulders, and chest; upper front part of woman's body, bosom.

bus'tard, *n.* large swift-running bird.

bu'stle¹ (-sl), *v.* make show of activity, hurry about; make (others) hurry. *n.* excited activity.

bu'stle² (-sl), *n.* (Hist.) pad or framework puffing out top of woman's skirt at the back.

busy (biz'i), *a.* working earnestly, fully occupied; meddlesome. *v.t.* occupy, keep busy. **bus'ybody,** meddlesome person, mischief-maker.

but, *conj.* nevertheless, yet, still. *adv.* only. *prep.* except, apart from.

butch'er (-oo-), *n.* slaughterer of animals for food; dealer in meat; merciless or brutal slayer. *v.t.* slaughter people wantonly or cruelly. **butch'ery,** *n.* butcher's trade; needless or cruel slaughter.

but'ler, *n.* head manservant, in charge of wine-cellar, plate, etc.

butt¹, *n.* large cask; barrel.

butt², *n.* thicker end of tool, weapon, etc.

butt³, *n.* mound behind target; grouse-shooter's stand screened by low turf or stone wall; (pl.) shooting-range; (sing.) person frequently ridiculed.

butt⁴, *v.* push or strike with head; meet end to end. **butt in,** (*informal*) force oneself into (conversation, company); interrupt. *n.* (violent) push or blow with head or horns.

butt'er, *n.* fatty food-substance made from cream by churning. *v.t.* spread, cook, etc., with butter. *butter-fingers,* -*fingered,* (person) apt to let things fall or slip.

butt'ercup, *n.* yellow-flowered ranunculus.

butt'erfly, *n.* insect with large wings often of brilliant colours; gay person, idler.

butt'ermilk, *n.* liquid left after butter-making.

butt'erscotch, *n.* kind of toffee.

butt'erwort (-wert), *n.* purple-flowered bog-plant.

butt'ery, *n.* place in college, etc., where provisions are kept.

butt'ock, *n.* either of the two rounded parts of the body on which person sits; (pl.) rump.

butt'on, *n.* disc or knob sewn to garment for fastening or for ornament; small knob; flower-bud; (pl.) page-boy with many-buttoned coat. *v.* fasten with button(s). **button-hole,** *n.* hole or slit through which button is passed; flower(s) to be worn in button-hole. *v.t.* seize or detain (unwilling listener). **button-hook,** hook for fastening buttons.

butt'ress, *n.* support built against a wall, etc.; buttress-like projection of hill. *v.t.* support or strengthen.

bux'om, *a.* plump and comely.

buy (bī), *v.t.* (p.t. *bought* pr. -awt), obtain by paying a price; gain, win over, by bribery.

buy'er (bī-), *n.* one who buys; one who selects and buys stock for (department of) shop, etc.

buzz, *n.* sound made by bee, etc., when flying, by many people talking, by machinery in rapid motion, etc. *v.* make buzz; (of aircraft) warn, annoy, by flying close to. *buzz off,* (*slang*) go away.

buzz′ard, *n.* kind of hawk.

buzz′er, *n.* electric buzzing-machine for sending signals; steam-whistle.

bȳ, *adv.* near; aside, in reserve; past. *prep.* near to, beside; past; through the action or means of; not later than; in accordance with. *by oneself,* alone. *by way of,* see **way. by and by,** (*adv.*) before long; (*n.*) the future. **by the by, by the way,** incidentally.

bȳe, *n.* (Cricket) run made from ball that passes batsman and wicket-keeper; (in tournament) position of person or team left without opponent after heats are drawn.

bȳ′-election, *n.* election to fill vacancy caused by death or resignation.

bȳ′gone, *a.* past, departed. **bȳ′gones** (-nz), *n. pl.* past, past offences.

bȳ′-law, bȳe′-law, *n.* regulation made by local authority, etc.

bȳ′-pass (-ahs), *n.* road providing alternative route for through traffic, esp. round town, etc.

bȳ′-play, *n.* action, usu. dumb show, of minor characters on the stage.

bȳ′-product, *n.* substance, etc., produced incidentally in the making of something else.

bȳre, *n.* cow-house.

bȳ′road, *n.* side-road.

bȳ′stander, *n.* spectator.

bȳ′-way, *n.* secluded road; less commonly known department of subject.

bȳ′word (-werd), *n.* person, place, or thing notorious for something; familiar saying.

Byzan′tine, *a.* of Byzantium or Constantinople; of the architectural style of the Eastern Roman Empire (with domes, etc.).

C

C,c, as Roman numeral, 100.

cab, *n.* taxi; shelter for crew of locomotive or driver of lorry, etc.; (chiefly Hist.) horse-drawn vehicle plying for hire.

cabal′, *n.* (small group of persons engaged in) private intrigue.

cab′aret (-rā), *n.* entertainment provided in restaurant, etc., while guests are at table.

cabb′age, *n.* green vegetable with round head or 'heart' of unexpanded leaves.

cā′ber, *n.* trunk of pine- or fir-tree used in Scottish sport of *tossing the caber.*

cab′in, *n.* small roughly made dwelling; hut; private or public room on ship. **cab′in-boy,** boy waiting on ship's officers or passengers.

cab′inet, *n.* piece of furniture with drawers, shelves, or compartments; (*Cabinet*), body of ministers attending councils with Prime Minister. **cab′inet-maker,** skilled maker of fine furniture.

cā′ble, *n.* anchor chain; strong thick rope, esp. of wire; insulated submarine or underground line containing telegraph, telephone, or electric wires; cablegram. *v.* send (message) by cable. **ca′blegram,** telegraph message sent by submarine cable. **cable railway,** (esp. mountain) railway worked by endless cable. **ca′bleway,** cable railway; transport system of cars suspended from overhead cable.

cabōōse′, *n.* cook-room or kitchen on ship's deck.

cabriolet′ (-lā), *n.* light two-wheeled one-horse carriage.

cacā′ō, *n.* tropical Amer. tree; its seed from which cocoa and chocolate are made.

cache (-sh), *n.* hidden store of provisions, etc. *v. t.* store in cache.

cachet (ka′shā), *n.* distinguishing mark; evidence of authenticity; prestige.

cack′le, *n.* clucking of hen, calling of geese; foolish talk; loud silly laughter. *v.* make cackling sound; utter or express with cackle.

cacoph′ony, *n.* ugly sound, esp. of words or music. **cacoph′onous,** *a.*

cac′tus, *n.* (pl. *cactī,* or *cactuses*), any of various succulent plants with thick fleshy stem, spines, and usu. no leaves.

cad, *n.* ill-mannered person; person who behaves dishonourably. **cadd′ish,** *a.*

cadav′erous, *a.* corpse-like; deathly pale.

cadd′ie, cadd′y¹, *n.* golfer's attendant carrying clubs, etc. *v. i.* act as caddie.

cadd′y², *n.* small box for holding tea.

cā′dence, *n.* rhythm; rise and fall of voice in speaking; (Mus.) progression of notes or chords closing movement or phrase.

caden′za, *n.* (Mus.) florid passage for solo instrument in concerto.

cadet′, *n.* student in naval, military or air force college; schoolboy or student receiving military, etc., training.

cadge, *v.* get by begging; beg. **cadg′er,** *n.*

cad′mium, *n.* soft bluish-white metal.

Caesaŕ'ĕan, Caesaŕ'ian (sēz-), *a.* of Julius Caesar or the Caesars. **Caesarean operation, section,** delivery of child by cutting walls of abdomen.

caesuŕ'a (siz-), *n.* point of natural pause near middle of verse line.

café (kaf'ā), *n.* tea-room; restaurant.

cafetēr'ia, *n.* self-service restaurant.

caff'eine (-ēn), *n.* vegetable alkaloid occurring in coffee and tea plants.

cāge, *n.* prison of wire or with bars, esp. for birds or animals; open framework; lift in mineshaft. *v.t.* place or keep in cage.

cairn, *n.* pyramid of rough stones.

cairn'gorm, *n.* yellow or brown form of rock crystal used as gem-stone.

caiss'on (*or* kasōōn'), *n.* (esp.) watertight chamber used in laying foundations under water.

cait'iff, *n.* (*archaic*) coward or rascal.

cajōle', *v.t.* persuade by flattery, promises, etc. **cajōl'ery,** *n.*

cāke, *n.* baked sweetened mixture of flour, butter, eggs, dried fruit, etc., often in flattish round shape; flattish compact mass. *v.* form into a compact mass, harden.

cal'abash, *n.* drinking or cooking vessel made from gourd or from hard shelled fruit of **calabash (tree)** of tropical America.

calam'ity, *n.* serious disaster or misfortune. **calam'itous,** *a.* causing or marked by calamity.

calcaŕ'ĕous, *a.* containing calcium carbonate or limestone.

calc'ifȳ, *v.* harden by deposit of calcium salts. **calcificā'tion,** *n.*

cal'cine, *v.* reduce or be reduced to quicklime or powder by burning or roasting. **calcinā'tion,** *n.*

cal'cium, *n.* soft silver-white metallic element, the basis of lime.

cal'cŭlāte, *v.* reckon with numbers; ascertain by exact reckoning. **cal'cŭlāted,** *a.* intentional, prearranged. **calcŭlā'tion, cal'cŭlātor,** *nn.*

cal'cŭlus, *n.* (pl. *calculī*), (Math.) particular method of calculation.

Calèdōn'ian, *a.* & *n.* (native) of ancient Scotland.

cal'endar, *n.* list of months, weeks, days, festivals, etc., of a particular year; register or list; system fixing year's beginning, length, divisions, etc.

calf[1] (kahf), *n.* (pl. *calves*), young of cow or of elephant, whale, etc. *calf love*, romantic affection between young boy and girl.

calf[2] (kahf), *n.* (pl. *calves*), fleshy back part of leg below knee.

cal'ibre (-ber), *n.* internal diameter of gun or tube; quality of mind or character.

cal'icō, *n.* (pl. *calicoes*), plain (esp. white) cotton cloth.

cal'iph (*or* kā-), *n.* (Hist.) title of ruler in Muslim countries.

call (kawl), *v.* speak in loud tone; utter characteristic note; summon; pay brief visit; name, describe as; read *over* (list of persons). *call for,* demand, need; go and fetch. *call off,* cancel, abandon (project). *call up,* (esp.) summon to serve in armed forces. *n.* shout, bird's cry, signal on bugle, etc.; summons; demand, need; short visit; (summons to) telephone conversation. **call-box,** public telephone kiosk. **call'er**[1] (kawl-), *n.* visitor; one making telephone call.

call'er[2] (kal-), *a.* (Sc.) fresh.

callig'raphy, *n.* beautiful handwriting; handwriting as an art. **callig'rapher,** *n.*

call'ing (kaw-), *n.* profession, occupation.

call'iper, *n.* (*pl.*) compasses for measuring diameter of convex bodies, cavities, etc.; (*sing.*) support for weak or injured leg.

callisthen'ics, *n.pl.* exercises to develop strength and grace.

callos'ity, *n.* area of thickened and hardened skin caused by friction or pressure.

call'ous, *a.* hardened; unfeeling, unsympathetic. *n.* callosity. **call'ousness,** *n.*

call'ow (-ō), *a.* unfledged; inexperienced.

call'us, *n.* a callosity.

calm (kahm), *a.* still, tranquil; windless; not agitated. *v.* make or become calm. *n.* stillness, tranquillity. **calm'ness,** *n.* calm condition.

cal'orie, *n.* unit of heat; unit for measuring heat- or energy-producing capacity of food. **calo'ric,** *a.* of heat. **calorif'ic,** *a.* heat--producing.

calorim'ēter, *n.* heat-measuring apparatus.

calum'niāte, *v.t.* slander; utter calumny about. **calum'niātor,** *n.* **calumniā'tion,** *n.*

cal'umny, *n.* slander; false charge. **calum'nious,** *a.*

Cal'vary, *n.* place, representation, of the crucifixion of Christ.

calve (kahv), *v.i.* give birth to calf.

Cal'vinism, *n.* religious doctrine of John Calvin (1509-64), and his followers. **Cal'vinist,** *n.* **Calvinis'tic,** *a.*

calyp'sō, *n.* (pl. *calypsos*) West Indian song, usu. improvised and topical.

cā'lyx (*or* -a-), *n.* (pl. *calycēs,* or *calyxes*), whorl of leaves (called *sepals*) forming outer case of flower-bud.

camara'derie (-ahd-), *n.* friendliness, mutual trust, of comrades.

cam'ber, *n.* slightly arched form of deck, road, etc. *v.t.* construct with camber.

Cam'brian, *a.* of Wales. *n.* Welshman.

cam'bric, *n.* fine white linen or cotton fabric.

came, *p.t.* of **come.**

cam'el, *n.* large ruminant mammal with one hump (*Arabian camel*) or two humps (*Bactrian camel*), much used in desert countries for riding and carrying goods.

camē'llia (*or* -e-), *n.* (rose-like flower of) evergreen shrub.

cam'ĕō, *n.* (pl. *cameos*), onyx or similar stone

carved in relief.

cam'era, *n.* apparatus for taking photographs.

cam'eraman, man who operates film or television camera. *in camera*: see **in camera.**

cam'isōle, *n.* under-bodice.

cam'omīle, *n.* aromatic herb.

cam'ouflage (-ooflahzh), *n.* disguising, disguise, of guns, ships, buildings, etc., by means of paint, netting, boughs, etc.; disguise, concealment. *v.t.* hide by camouflage.

camp, *n.* place where troops, etc., are lodged in tents, huts, etc.; temporary quarters of explorers, holiday-makers, gipsies, etc.; (persons) camping out; (remains of) ancient entrenched and fortified site. *v.* encamp, be in camp. *camp out,* sleep in tent or in the open. **camp bed,** portable folding bed. **camp-follower,** non-military follower of army.

campaign' (-ān), *n.* series of military operations; organized course of action. *v.i.* take part in, go on, a campaign.

campanil'ē (-nē-), *n.* bell-tower, esp. when detached from main building.

campanol'ogy, *n.* science and art of bell--founding and bell-ringing.

campan'ūla, *n.* any of various plants with bell-shaped flowers.

cam'phor, *n.* whitish crystalline aromatic bitter substance. **cam'phorāte,** *v.t.* treat with camphor.

cam'pion, *n.* wild flowering plant.

camp'us, *n.* grounds of university or college.

can[1], *n.* metal vessel for liquids; tinplate container in which food, etc., is sealed for preserving. *v.t.* (p.t. *canned*), preserve (food, etc.) in can.

can[2], *v. aux.* (neg. *cannot, can't,* pr. kahnt; past & cond. *could,* pr. kood), be able to; have the right to; be permitted to.

Canā'dian, *a. & n.* (native, inhabitant) of Canada. **Canā'dian canoe,** open canoe with single-bladed paddle(s).

canal', *n.* artificial watercourse; tube, esp. in animal body, for passage of food, air, etc.

can'alīze, *v.t.* convert (river) into canal by straightening course, etc.; give desired direction to.

canar'y, *n.* yellow-feathered song-bird, commonly kept in cage. *a.* bright yellow.

canas'ta, *n.* card-game resembling rummy.

can'can, *n.* high-kicking dance.

can'cel, *v.* (p.t. *cancelled*), cross out; withdraw (order); call off (plan, etc.); neutralize; (Math.) strike out (same factor) from two sides of (equation, etc.). *cancel out,* neutralize or balance each other. **cancellā'tion,** *n.*

can'cer, *n.* (disease caused by) malignant growth; (fig.) evil. **can'cerous,** *a.*

Can'cer, *n.* the Crab, constellation and fourth sign of the zodiac. *Tropic of Cancer,* northern tropic.

candē'la, *n.* unit of luminous intensity.

candēla'brum (-lah-), *n.* (pl. *candelabra*),

large branched candlestick.

can'did, *a.* frank; sincere; outspoken.

can'didāte, *n.* one who seeks or is nominated for some office or honour; one who takes an examination. **can'didature,** *n.*

candied: see **candy.**

can'dle, *n.* cylinder of wax or tallow formed round wick, burned to give light. **can'-dlepower,** illuminating power of electric lamp, etc., measured in candelas. **can'-dlestick,** stand for holding candle. **can'-dlewick,** (thick soft cotton yarn used for) raised, usu. tufted, embroidery.

Can'dlemas (-lm-), *n.* feast of Purification of Virgin Mary, 2nd February.

can'dour (-der), *n.* candidness.

can'dy, *n.* sugar crystallized by repeated boiling and evaporation; (U.S.) sweet(s). *v.* make or become candy; preserve fruit, etc. by coating with sugar. **can'died,** *a.* preserved or coated with sugar; sugared.

can'dytuft, *n.* plant with white, pink, or purple flowers in flat clusters.

cāne, *n.* stem of reeds and giant grasses or of slender palms, used as walking-stick, rod for punishment, for making chairs, etc.; stem of raspberry, etc. *v.t.* beat with cane; weave cane into (chair, etc.). **cane-sugar,** sugar obtained from sugar-cane.

ca'nine, *a.* of or as of dog(s). **canine tooth,** any of four pointed teeth between incisors and molars.

can'ister, *n.* small container for tea, etc.

can'ker, *n.* any of various diseases (of human mouth, horse's hoof, bark of trees and shrubs); (fig.) corrupting influence. *v.t.* corrupt; infect or consume with canker.

cann'abis, *a.* preparation of hemp, smoked as narcotic.

cann'ibal, *n.* person who eats human flesh; animal that eats its own species. **cann'-ibalism,** *n.* **cannibalis'tic,** *a.* **cann'ibalize,** *v.t.* take parts from (machine) as spares for others.

cann'on, *n.* mounted gun firing projectile larger than bullet (pl. usu. *cannon*); (Billiards) hitting of two balls successively by player's ball. *v.i.* make cannon at billiards; run or strike (obliquely) *against, into,* etc. **cann'on-ball,** (Hist.) solid metal ball fired from cannon. **cannonāde',** *n.* continous gunfire. *v.* fire continuously, bombard.

cannot: see **can**[2].

cann'y, *a.* shrewd, quiet, cautious.

canoe' (-noo), *n.* light boat propelled by paddle(s). *v.i.* (pres.p. *canoeing*), go in canoe. **canoe'ist,** *n.*

can'on[1], *n.* Church decree; principle, rule; list of Bible books accepted by Church; (Mus.) composition in which melody is imitated by different parts successively. **can'on law,** ecclesiastical law.

can'on[2], *n.* member of cathedral chapter. **can'onry,** *n.*

cañon: see **canyon.**

canon'ical, *a.* appointed by canon law; of (member of) cathedral chapter; authoritative or accepted. **canon'icals,** *n.pl.* appointed dress of clergy.

can'onīze, *v.t.* admit formally to list of saints. **canonīzā'tion,** *n.*

can'opy, *n.* covering hung or held over throne, bed, person, etc.; roof-like covering. *v.t.* supply or be canopy to.

cant¹, *n.* slanting surface; tilted position; slanting push or jerk. *v.* push or jerk or hold out of level; tilt, slant; bevel.

cant², *n.* thieves' slang; jargon of class, sect, etc.; insincere pious talk; hypocrisy. *v.i.* use such talk.

can't: see **can².**

Cantabri'gian, *a. & n.* (member) of Cambridge University (abbrev. *Cantab.*).

can'taloup (-ōōp), *n.* variety of melon.

cantank'erous, *a.* quarrelsome.

canta'ta (-tahta), *n.* choral composition.

canteen¹, *n.* restaurant in factory or office--building; provision shop in camp or barracks; soldier's mess-tin or water-bottle; case of table cutlery.

can'ter, *n.* easy gallop. *v.* go, make go, at a canter.

Can'terbury bell, kind of campanula.

can'ticle, *n.* biblical hymn used in church services.

can'tilēver, *n.* bracket projecting from wall to support balcony, etc. **cantilever bridge,** bridge in which great cantilevers run out from the piers and are connected by girders.

can'tō, *n.* (pl. *cantōs*), division of long poem.

can'ton (*or* kanton'), *n.* State of Swiss Federation.

canton'ment (-ōōn-), *n.* living quarters of troops.

can'vas, *n.* strong coarse cloth of hemp or flax for sails, tents, oil-paintings, etc.

can'vass, *v.* ask for votes or orders; try to ascertain views of. *n.* canvassing.

can'yon, cañon (kan'yon), *n.* deep gorge cut by river.

cap, *n.* soft brimless outdoor head-covering, often with peak; woman's (indoor) head--dress (Hist.); cap worn as sign of inclusion in team, its wearer; cap-like covering. *v.t.* (p.t. *capped*), put or confer cap on, cover (as) with cap; surpass.

cā'pable, *a.* able, competent. *capable of,* having the power or fitness for. **cāpabil'ity,** *n.*

capā'cious (-shus), *a.* roomy.

capa'citance, *n.* (Electr.) ability of apparatus to store electric charge.

capa'citor, *n.* (Electr.) device for obtaining (esp. specified) capacitance.

capa'city, *n.* ability to contain; cubic content; mental power; capability; position, character.

capa'rison, *n.* ornamental covering for horse. *v.t.* put caparison upon.

cāpe¹, *n.* short cloak.

cāpe², *n.* headland, promontory.

cā'per¹, *n.* prickly shrub; (pl.) its pickled flower-buds, used in sauces, etc.

cā'per², *v.i.* leap about playfully. *n.* playful leap, frisky movement. *cut a caper,* dance or act fantastically.

capercai'llie, capercai'lzie (-lyi), *n.* largest bird of grouse kind.

capill'ary, *a.* of or like hair. *n.* tube of hair--like diameter, esp. very small slender blood--vessel.

cap'ital, *a* involving loss of life; punishable by death; fatal; chief; excellent; (of letter) large, as used at beginning of sentence, etc. *n.* chief town of country, etc; capital letter; head of cornice of pillar; money with which business, etc., is started; accumulated wealth; money invested or loaned.

cap'italism, *n.* economic system with ownership and control of capital in private hands.

cap'italist, *n.* owner of (esp. large amount of) capital.

cap'italīze, *v.t.* use as capital; realize present value of. **capitalīzā'tion,** *n.*

capitā'tion, *n.* tax, fee, charge, of same sum for each person.

capit'ūlāte, *v.i.* surrender on stated conditions; yield. **capitūlā'tion,** *n.*

cā'pon, *n.* castrated cock.

caprice' (-ēs), *n.* sudden change of mind or conduct; whim, fancy. **capri'cious** (-shus), *a.* guided by whim, inconstant.

Cap'ricorn, *n.* the Goat, constellation and tenth sign of the zodiac. *Tropic of Capricorn,* southern tropic.

cap'sicum, *n.* any of various plants with hot--tasting capsules and seeds; fruit of these.

capsize', *v.* overturn, esp. on water.

cap'stan, *n.* revolving barrel for winding in cable, etc.

cap'sūle, *n.* plant's seed-case; (Med.) small gelatine case enclosing drug, etc.; compartment, usu. detachable, of rocket or spacecraft.

cap'tain (-tin), *n.* chief, leader; naval or military officer; master of merchant ship; leader of side in games. *v.t.* lead (team,etc.). **cap'taincy,** *n.* position of captain.

cap'tion, *n.* heading, title; wording on cartoon, cinema screen, etc.

cap'tious (-shus), *a.* fond of finding fault; carping.

cap'tivāte, *v.t.* fascinate, charm. **captivā'tion,** *n.*

cap'tive, *a.* taken prisoner; kept in confinement. *n.* captive person or animal. **captiv'ity,** *n.*

cap'tor, *n.* one who takes captive.

cap'ture, *n.* seizing, taking possession of; taking of fortress, etc. *v.t.* take prisoner; seize.

car, *n.* wheeled vehicle; motor car, tram-car; part of airship, etc., for passengers.

carafe' (-ahf), *n.* glass bottle for the table, for

holding water or wine.

ca'ramel, *n.* brown substance obtained by heating sugar or syrup and used for colouring and flavouring; soft toffee.

ca'rapāce, *n.* upper body-shell of tortoise, turtle, or crustacean.

ca'rat, *n.* meaure of weight of gems or of fineness of gold.

ca'ravan (*or* -van'), *n.* van fitted out as dwelling, drawn by horse or motor vehicle; company travelling together for safety, esp. in desert country.

caravan'serai (-rī), *n.* Eastern inn with large courtyard, where caravans stay overnight.

ca'raway, *n.* plant with small aromatic fruits (*caraway-seeds*) used in cakes, etc.

car'bine, *n.* short rifle.

carbohȳ'drāte, *n.* any of various compounds of carbon, hydrogen, and oxygen, including sugars, starches, and cellulose.

carbol'ic (acid), a disinfectant and antiseptic.

car'bon, *n.* non-metallic element found as diamond, graphite, charcoal, etc.; carbon rod used in arc-lamp. **carbon dioxide**, a colourless odourless gas. **carbon monoxide**, a poisonous colourless odourless gas. **carbon paper**, thin paper coated with carbon, etc., used for taking copies of letters, etc. **carbonā'ceous** (-shus), *a.* containing carbon. **car'bonate**, *n.* salt of carbonic acid. **carbon'ic**, *a.* of carbon. **carbonic acid**, compound of carbon dioxide and water.

carbonif'erous, *a.* coal-producing.

car'bonīze, *v.t.* convert into carbon; reduce to charcoal or coke by burning.

car'boy, *n.* large round wicker-covered glass bottle.

car'buncle, *n.* garnet cut in round knob shape; inflamed swelling under the skin.

carbūrett'or, carbūrett'er, *n.* apparatus mixing air with petrol vapour for combustion in motor engines.

car'cass, *n.* dead body of beast; framework or skeleton.

card[1], *n.* toothed instrument, wire brush, etc., for combing wool, etc. *v.t.* comb with card.

card[2], *n.* (piece of) thick paper or thin pasteboard; ticket of admission, invitation, etc.; one of 52 pieces of pasteboard making pack for playing games. **card'board**, pasteboard for making boxes, etc. **card index**, index with each item on separate card. **card--sharper**, professional swindler at card--games.

car'diac, *a.* of the heart.

car'digan, *n.* knitted jacket.

car'dinal, *a.* fundamental, chief; deep scarlet. *n.* (R.C.Ch.) one of dignitaries forming pope's council and electing new pope; cardinal colour or number. **cardinal numbers**, one, two, three, etc. **cardinal points**, North, South, East, West.

cāre, *n.* anxiety, concern; charge, protection; task; serious attention. *v.i.* feel concern or interest or affection.

careen', *v.* turn (ship) on one side for repair; heel over.

career', *n.* swift course; course or progress through life; way of making one's living. *v.i.* go swiftly or wildly. **career'ist**, *n.* person intent chiefly on personal advancement.

cāre'free (-ārf-), *a.* free from anxiety.

cāre'ful (-ārf-), *a.* painstaking, cautious; concerned for. **cāre'fully**, *adv.*

cāre'less (-ārl-), *a.* unconcerned, thoughtless, inaccurate.

caress', *n.* loving or affectionate touch, kiss. *v.t.* touch lovingly.

ca'rĕt, *n.* mark (∧) used to show place of omission in writing or print.

cāre'tāker (-ārt-), *n.* person employed to take charge of house in owner's absence, or of school, etc. *a.* (only) temporarily in control.

cāre'worn (-ārw-), *a.* worn by anxiety and trouble.

car'gŏ, *n.* (pl. *cargoes*), goods carried in ship or aircraft.

ca'ribou (-bōō), *n.* (pl. same, or *caribous*) N. Amer. reindeer.

ca'ricatūre, *n.* grotesque or ludicrous representation of person, etc. *v.t.* make or give a caricature of. **caricatūr'ist**, *n.* person.

cār'iēs (-z), *n.* decay (of tooth or bone).

ca'rillon (-lyon), *n.* set of bells on which tunes can be played.

car'mine, *n.* vivid crimson pigment and colour. *a.* of this colour.

car'nage, *n.* great slaughter.

car'nal, *a.* sensual; sexual; worldly. **carnal'ity**, *n.*

carnā'tion[1], *a. & n.* (of) light rosy pink.

carnā'tion[2], *n.* garden plant with white, pink, or red sweet-smelling flowers.

carnelian: see **cornelian**.

car'nival, *n.* festive days before Lent; riotous revelry.

car'nivore, *n.* animal that feeds on other animals. **carniv'orous**, *a.*

ca'rol, *n.* joyous song, esp. Christmas hymn. *v.i.* (p.t. *carolled*), sing joyfully.

carouse' (-z), *v.i.* take part in drinking-bout. **carouse', carous'al** (-z-), *nn.*

carp[1], *n.* freshwater fish, often bred in ponds.

carp[2], *v.i.* find fault; complain.

car'penter, *n.* craftsman in (esp. rough, solid) woodwork. **car'pentry**, *n.*

car'pĕt, *n.* thick fabric for covering floor, etc. *v.t.* cover with carpet. **carpet-bag,** travelling bag (originally made of carpet).

ca'rriage (-rij), *n.* conveying of goods, etc., cost of this; manner of carrying oneself; horse-drawn wheeled vehicle for persons; vehicle for passengers in railway train, coach; moving part of machine shifting other part(s). **ca'rriageway,** (part of) road intended for vehicles.

ca'rrier, *n.* person or company conveying goods for payment; part of bicycle, etc., for carrying luggage, etc.; person or animal conveying germs of disease. **carrier-pigeon,** homing pigeon used for carrying messages.

ca′rrion, *n.* dead and decaying flesh.

ca′rrot, *n.* plant with orange-red root used as vegetable.

ca′rry, *v.* move (thing, person, etc.) from one place to another by hand, in vehicle, etc., convey, transport; support; be bearer of; succeed in establishing, passing, etc. *carry on,* conduct, continue. *carry out,* execute (plan, work, etc.).

cart, *n.* strong two- or four-wheeled, usu. horse-drawn, vehicle. *v.* carry in cart, use cart. **cart-horse,** horse of heavy build. **cart′wheel,** wheel of cart; sideways somersault with arms and legs extended. **cart′-wright** (-rīt), maker of carts. **car′tage,** *n.* (cost of) carting. **car′ter,** *n.*

carte blanche (kart blahnsh), full power to act according to one's judgement. (French)

cartel′, *n.* manufacturers' union to control prices, etc.

car′tilage, *n.* firm elastic skeletal or connective tissue in vertebrates; gristle.

cartog′raphy, *n.* map-drawing. **cartog′-rapher,** *n.* **cartograph′ic(al),** *aa.*

car′ton, *n.* light box or case.

cartōn′, *n.* sketch; humorous topical illustration; animated cartoon; strip cartoon. **cartōn′ist,** *n.*

cart′ridge, *n.* case containing explosive charge, or explosive charge with bullet or shot. **cart′ridge paper,** thick rough paper for drawing, etc.

carve, *v.* cut, make by cutting; hew, sculpture; adorn with cut figures, etc.; cut up meat at or for table; subdivide. **car′ver,** *n.* (esp.) knife, (pl.) knife and fork, for carving meat. **car′ving,** *n.* carved work or figure or design.

cascāde′, *n.* waterfall; one section of large broken waterfall. *v. i.* fall in or like cascade.

cāse[1], *n.* instance or example of thing's occurring; supposed or actual situation; plight or condition; (Law) suit or cause; (Gram.) (relation expressed by) inflected form of noun, etc. *in case,* in the event (*of*). *in any case,* in any event, anyhow.

cāse[2], *n.* box, bag, sheath, etc., designed to hold something. *v.t.* enclose in case. **case-harden,** *v.t.* harden surface of; render callous.

cās′ein, *n.* main protein of milk, forming basis of cheese.

cāse′ment, (-sm-), *n.* hinged (part of) window.

cash, *n.* money in the form of coins or bank-notes. *v.t.* give or obtain cash for (cheque, etc.). **cash register,** till recording amounts put in.

cashier[1] (-ēr′), *n.* person who receives or pays out money in bank or other business firm.

cashier[2] (-ēr′), *v.t.* dismiss (esp. commissioned officer) with dishonour and disgrace.

cash′mēre, *n.* (fabric of) fine soft wool from goats of Kashmir, etc.

cā′sing, *n.* enclosing material, framework.

casī′nō (-sē-), *n.* (pl. *casinos*), public building for gambling, etc.

cask (-ah-), *n.* barrel for liquids.

cas′kĕt (kah-), *n.* small box for valuables.

cassā′va (-sah-), *n.* tropical plant; starch or flour obtained from its roots.

cass′erōle, *n.* covered vessel in which food is both cooked and served.

cassette′, *n.* container of electromagnetic tape for insertion into **cassette-(tape-)recorder.**

cass′ock, *n.* long, usu. black, garment worn by clergymen, etc.

cass′owary (-o-w-), *n.* large flightless bird related to emu.

cast (kah-), *v.* (p.t. *cast*), throw; throw off, lose; give (vote); form (molten metal, clay, etc.) in mould; assign part to (actor, etc.). *cast down,* depress. *cast off,* abandon. *n.* throw of missile, fishing line, etc.; mould for casting metal, clay, etc., thing cast in it; set of actors in play, etc.; slight squint; type, quality. **cast iron,** unpurified iron, smelted and cast. **cast-iron,** *a.* of cast iron; hard, rigid, unshakeable.

cas′tanet (*or* -et′), *n.* one of pair of small concave wooden or ivory shells held in hand and clicked in time with dancing.

cast′away (kah-), *n.* shipwrecked person.

caste (kahst), *n.* one of Hindu hereditary social classes; system of dividing people into such classes; exclusive class elsewhere.

cas′tellāted, *a.* having battlements.

caster: see **castor.**

cas′tigāte, *v.t.* punish or rebuke severely. **castigā′tion,** *n.*

cast′ing (kah-), *n.* (esp.) piece of metal, etc., cast in mould. *a.* (of vote) deciding issue when votes on each side are equal.

castle (kah′sl), *n.* large fortified building; mansion that was formerly fortified; piece in chess (usu. called *rook*).

cas′tor, cas′ter (kah-), *n.* small swivelled wheel fixed under leg or corner of piece of furniture; vessel with perforated top for sprinkling sugar, etc. **castor sugar, caster sugar,** very finely granulated white sugar.

cas′tor oil (kah-), vegetable oil used as purgative and lubricant.

castrāte′, *v.t.* remove testicles of, geld. **castrā′tion,** *n.*

ca′sual (-zhoo- *or* -zū-), *a.* due to chance; not regular; careless, unconcerned; informal.

ca′sualty (-zhoo- *or* -zū-) *n.* person killed, wounded or injured; accident, mishap. **casualty department, ward,** hospital department for treatment of accidental injuries.

ca′suist (-zū- *or* -zhoo-), *n.* theologian, etc., who studies and resolves cases of conscience, etc.; sophist, quibbler. **casuis′-tic(al),** *aa.* **ca′suistry,** *n.*

cat, *n.* small furry domesticated carnivorous

quadruped; any feline animal; (*slang*) spiteful woman. **cat-o'-nine tails,** whip with nine knotted lashes. **cat's cradle,** child's game with string. **cat's-eye,** reflector stud on road, etc. **cat's-paw,** person used as tool by another. **cat'walk,** narrow footway along bridge, over engine-room, etc. **catt'ish,** *a.* catlike; catty. **catt'y,** *a.* spiteful.

cata-, cat-, cath-, *pref.* (*cata-* before consonant; *cat-* before vowel; *cath-* combining with *h*), down; wrongly, mis-; against; thoroughly.

cat'aclysm, *n.* deluge, violent upheaval, **cataclys'mic** (-z-), *a.*

cat'acomb (-m; *or* -ōōm), *n.* underground gallery with recesses for tombs.

cat'afalque (-k), *n.* platform for coffin of distinguished person before or during funeral.

cat'alepsy, *n.* trance or seizure with loss of sensation and consciousness. **catalep'tic,** *a.*

cat'alogue (-g), *n.* complete list in alphabetical or other systematic order. *v.t.* make catalogue of; enter in catalogue.

catal'ysis, *n.* (pl. *catalysēs*), facilitation of a chemical reaction by an added substance which is not itself changed in the reaction. **cat'alȳse** (-z), *v.t.* **catalyt'ic,** *a.*

cat'alyst, *n.* substance causing catalysis.

catamaran', *n.* boat with twin hulls.

cat'apult, *n.* contrivance of forked stick and elastic for shooting small stones, etc.; engine for hurling stones, etc. (Hist.); gear for launching aircraft from deck of carrier. *v.t.* launch by catapult.

cat'aract, *n.* large precipitous waterfall; disease causing clouding of lens of eye.

catarrh' (-ar), *n.* inflammation of mucous membrane, esp. of nose, etc. **catarrh'al,** *a.*

catas'trophė, *n.* great disaster; sudden upheaval. **catastroph'ic,** *a.*

catch, *v.* (p.t. *caught,* pr. kawt), capture, get hold of, seize; hold; be infected with; become entangled; grasp; surprise, detect, trick. *catch sight of,* get glimpse or view of. *catch up,* draw level with. *n.* act of catching; fastening or holding device; thing or person caught or worth catching; question designed to trick; (Mus.) round. **catch'word,** word placed at corner of page, etc., to attract attention; phrase temporarily popular. **catch'ing,** *a.* (esp.) infectious; captivating. **catch'ment area,** whole area from which water flows into river, reservoir, etc. **catch'y,** *a.* (of tune, etc.) easily learned and remembered.

cat'echism (-k-), *n.* form of (esp. religious) instruction by question and answer; series of questions. **cat'echist** (-k-), *n.*

cat'echize (-k-), *v.t.* instruct by question and answer; question or interrogate.

catėgo'rical, *a.* unconditional, absolute, explicit.

cat'ėgory, *n.* class, rank, or order of ideas or things.

catė'nary, *n.* & *a.* (like) curve formed by hanging chain.

cā'ter, *v.i.* procure and supply food; provide amusement, etc., *for.* **cā'terer,** *n.*

cat'erpillar, *n.* larva of butterfly or moth; endless articulated steel band with treads passing round wheels of vehicle to be used on rough ground (**P**).

cat'erwaul, *v.i.* scream like cats.

cat'gut, *n.* material made from intestines of sheep, etc., used for strings of violins, tennis rackets, etc., and for surgical sutures.

cathar'sis, *n.* purging; purification or release of emotion. **cathar'tic,** *a.*

cathē'dral, *n.* principal church of diocese, with bishop's throne.

Cath'erine-wheel, *n.* rotating firework.

cath'ōde, *n.* (Electr.) negative electrode, to which current flows.

cath'olic, *a.* universal; of wide sympathies; (*Catholic*), including all Christians: (esp.) of the Roman Catholic Church. *n.* member of Catholic, esp. R.C., Church. **cathol'icism,** *n.* adherence to Catholic Church.

cat'kin, *n.* hanging flower spike of willow, hazel, etc.

cat'mint, *n.* a scented plant.

catt'le, *n.pl.* oxen (cows, bulls, bullocks). **cattle grid,** system of bars laid at road level to prevent passage of cattle, etc., but to allow passage of traffic.

Caucā'sian (-z-), *a.* & *n.* (member) of white--skinned race of mankind.

cauc'us, *n.* local political party committee.

cau'date, *a.* having a tail.

caught, *p.t.* & *p.p.* of **catch.**

caul, *n.* membrane occasionally found covering child's head at birth.

caul'dron, *n.* large boiling-vessel.

caul'iflower (kol-), *n.* kind of cabbage with large edible flower-head.

caulk (-awk), *v.t.* stop up seams of (ship) with oakum and pitch.

cause (-z), *n.* what produces an effect; ground or reason for action; case of one party in lawsuit; side in a struggle, etc.; subject of interest. *v.t.* be the cause of; make happen. **cause'less,** *a.* without cause.

cause'way (-zw-), *n.* raised road across water or low or wet place; raised footway at side of road.

caus'tic, *a.* that burns or corrodes; sarcastic, biting. *n.* caustic substance.

caut'erize, *v.t.* sear with hot iron or caustic substance, esp. surgically. **cauterizā'tion,** *n.*

cau'tion, *n.* avoidance of rashness; attention to safety; warning. *v.t.* warn, admonish. **cau'tionary,** *a.* conveying warning.

cau'tious (-shus), *a.* having or showing caution.

cavalcāde', *n.* company of riders; procession.

cavalier' (-ēr), *n.* horseman; gallant; lady's escort; 17th-century royalist. *a.* off-hand, haughty.

cav'alry, *n.* horse-soldiers, mounted troops.

cave, *n.* large natural underground hollow, usu. with horizontal entrance. *v. cave in,* fall in, give way to pressure, submit. **cave--dweller, caveman,** (pl. *-men*), person, esp. prehistoric man, living in cave.

cā'vēat (*or* ka-), *n.* (Law) notice to suspend proceedings.

cav'ern, *n.* (large) cave. **cav'ernous,** *a.* full of caverns; huge or deep as a cavern.

cav'iare, *n.* salted roe of sturgeon.

cav'il, *v.i.* (p.t. *cavilled*), raise unfounded objection. *n.* frivolous objection.

cav'ity, *n.* empty space within solid body.

cavort', *v.i.* prance.

caw, *n.* cry of crow, rook, etc. *v.i.* utter caw.

cayenne (pepper) (kā-en'), hot red pepper made from seeds of kinds of capsicum.

cease, *v.* come or bring to an end. *cease from,* stop (doing, etc.). **cease-fire,** (Mil.) order or signal to stop firing. **cease'less,** *a.* unceasing, continual.

cē'dar, *n.* (fragrant fine-grained wood of) evergreen coniferous tree.

cēde, *v.t.* give up; surrender (territory).

cedill'a, *n.* mark placed under c (ç) to indicate that it is pronounced as *s.*

cei'ling, *n.* under-surface of top of room, etc.; maximum altitude of aircraft, etc.; upper limit of prices, etc.

cel'andīne, *n.* yellow-flowered spring plant.

cel'ēbrant, *n.* priest officiating, esp. at Eucharist.

cel'ēbrāte, *v.* solemnly perform (rite, etc.); keep festival or commemorate event; extol; make famous. **cel'ēbrāted,** *a.* famous. **celēbra'tion,** *n.*

cēleb'rity, *n.* fame; celebrated person.

cēle'rity, *n.* swiftness; promptness.

cel'ery, *n.* plant of which blanched stems are used as salad and vegetable.

celēs'tial, *a.* of the sky; heavenly, divine. **celestial sphere,** imaginary sphere with earth as centre, on which heavenly bodies appear to lie.

cel'ibacy, *n.* unmarried state. **cel'ibate,** *a.* & *n.* unmarried (person); (person) bound or resolved not to marry.

cell, *n.* small room (for one person) in monastery or prison; hermit's one-roomed dwelling; (Biol.) unit of structure of living matter, usu. containing nucleus; (Electr.) unit of a battery.

cell'ar, *n.* underground room for storage, etc.; wine-cellar.

cell'ō, 'cell'ō (ch-), *n.* (pl. *cellos*), violoncello. **cell'ist** (ch-), *n.* violoncellist.

cell'ophāne, *n.* glossy transparent material used as wrapping, etc. **P.**

cell'ūlar, *a.* of or having or consisting of cells; porous, of open texture.

cell'ūloid, *n.* solid inflammable substance used for making films, etc.

cell'ūlōse, *n.* carbohydrate forming chief constituent of cell walls of plants; compounds of this used in rayon, plastics, paints, etc.

Cel'sius, *a.* (of scale, thermometer) centigrade.

Celt (k- *or* s-), *n.* member of one of ancient peoples of W. Europe or of peoples speaking languages related to those of ancient Gauls. **Cel'tic,** *a.* & *n.* (language) of the Celts.

cement', *n.* mixture of lime and clay setting like stone; plastic material for filling tooth cavity; adhesive substance. *v.t.* apply cement to; unite firmly.

cem'ētery, *n.* burial-ground other than churchyard.

cen'otaph (-ahf), *n.* monument to person(s) whose remains are elsewhere.

cen'ser, *n.* vessel in which incense is burnt.

cen'sor, *n.* official who examines films, books, letters, etc., to suppress what is obscene or seditious or unacceptable to military or other authorities. *v.t.* act as censor of. **cen'sorship,** *n.*

censor'ious, *a.* severely critical; fault-finding.

cen'sure (-sher), *n.* expression of disapproval or blame. *v.t.* criticize unfavourably, reprove.

cen'sus, *n.* official numbering of the population, with various statistics.

cent, *n.* hundredth of dollar, etc. *per cent,* for, in, to, every hundred.

cen'taur (-tor), *n.* (Gk. myth.) creature with man's head, trunk, and arms on horse's body and legs.

centēnār'ian, *n.* & *a.* (person) aged 100 years or more.

cente'nary, *a.* of a hundred years. *n.* hundredth anniversary.

centenn'ial, *a.* of, having lived or lasted, a hundred years. *n.* centenary.

centi-, *pref.* hundred; one hundredth.

cen'tigrāde, *a.* having 100 degrees; (of scale, thermometer) that has 0° for freezing-point and 100° for boiling-point of water.

cen'tigram, cen'tilitre (-ēter), **cen'timĕtre** (-ter), *nn.* hundredth part of gram, litre, metre.

cen'tipēde, *n.* small wingless crawling animal with many pairs of legs.

cen'tral, *a.* of, in, at, from, containing, the centre; leading, principal. **central heating,** heating of building by conveying hot water, steam, or air through pipes, etc., from central source. **cen'trally,** *adv.*

cen'tralīze, *v.* come together at centre; concentrate (administrative powers) in one centre, bring (State, etc.) under this system. **centralīzā'tion,** *n.*

cen'tre (-ter), *n.* middle point or part; point of concentration or dispersal. *a.* at or of the centre. *v.* place in, bring to, be at, have as, centre. **cen'treboard,** (sailing-boat with) board for lowering through keel.

centri'fūgal (*or* -fū'-), *a.* moving or tending to move away from a centre.

centri'pĕtal, *a.* moving or tending to move towards a centre.

cen'tuple, *a.* hundredfold. *v.t.* multiply by a hundred.

centūr'ion, *n.* commander of a century in ancient Roman army.

cen'tūry, *n.* a hundred years; (Rom. hist.) company in army; a hundred, esp. 100 runs at cricket.

cèphal'ic, *a.* of or in the head.

ceph'alopod, *n.* mollusc with tentacles attached to its head.

ceram'ic, *a.* of (the art of) pottery. **ceram'ics,** *n.* ceramic art.

Cer'berus, *n.* (Gk. myth.) three-headed dog guarding Hades.

cēr'ĕal, *a.* of edible grain. *n.* any of various plants cultivated for seed as (esp.) human food; food, esp. breakfast dish, made from cereal.

ce'rèbral, *a.* of the brain. *cerebral palsy,* see **palsy.**

cerèbrā'tion (se-r-), *n.* the working of the brain.

cerèmō'nial (se-r-), *a.* with or of ceremony, formal. *n.* system of rites or ceremonies.

cerèmō'nious (se-r-), *a.* fond of, marked by, ceremony; punctilious.

ce'rèmony, *n.* religious rite; piece of formal procedure; polite observance; formal behaviour.

cerise' (-ēz *or* -ēs), *n. & a.* light clear red, cherry-red.

cer'tain (-tin), *a.* settled; sure to happen; unfailing; sure; some. **cer'tainly,** *adv.* surely; with certainty; admittedly. **cer'tainty,** *n.* undoubted fact; absolute conviction.

certif'icate, *n.* document formally attesting a fact. **certif'icāte,** *v.t.* furnish with certificate.

cer'tifȳ, *v.t.* attest formally; declare officially.

cer'titūde, *n.* feeling of certainty.

ceru'lèan (-ōō-), *a.* sky-blue.

cer'vical (*or* -vī'-), *a.* of neck; of the cervix.

cer'vix, *n.* neck; neck-like structure, esp. neck of womb.

cessā'tion, *n.* ceasing; pause.

ce'ssion (-shn), *n.* ceding, giving up.

cess'pit, cess'pōol, *nn.* well or pit dug to receive house-drainage.

chāfe, *v.* rub (skin, etc.) to restore warmth; make or become sore by rubbing; irritate; fret.

chaff (-ahf), *n.* separated grain husks; chopped hay and straw; good-humoured teasing or joking. *v.* tease, jest.

chaff'er, *v.i.* haggle, bargain. *n.* bargaining.

chaff'inch, *n.* common small bird.

chag'rin (sh-; *or* shagrēn'), *n.* humiliating disappointment. *v.t.* vex, mortify.

chain, *n.* series of links passing one through another; connected series (*of* facts, events, mountains, etc.); measuring-line, its length, 66 ft.; (pl.) fetters. *v.t.* secure with chain. **chain-armour,** armour of metal rings linked together. **chain-gang,** convicts chained together at work, etc. **chain-mail,** chain--armour. **chain(reaction,** (Chem.) self--maintaining, esp. nuclear, reaction. **chain--store,** one of series of shops owned by one firm and selling same goods.

chair, *n.* seat for one, usu. movable and with support for back; seat of authority; professorship; seat, office, of person presiding at meeting, etc. *v.t.* install in chair; carry aloft (as) in chair. **chair'man,** person who presides over meeting, committee, etc.

chaise (shāz), *n.* light horse-drawn carriage formerly used for travelling or pleasure.

chalced'ony (k-), *n.* semi-precious variety of quartz.

chalet (shal'ā), *n.* Swiss hut or house of wood with overhanging roof; house built in this style; small dwelling for holiday-makers.

chal'ice, *n.* wine-cup used at Eucharist; (Poet.) goblet.

chalk (-awk), *n.* white soft limestone; stick of white or coloured substance used for writing or drawing. *v.t.* rub, draw, or write with chalk. **chalk'y,** *a.*

chall'enge (-nj), *n.* demand (by sentry, etc.) to stop and give name, password, etc.; objection (to juryman, etc.); invitation to contest. *v.t.* give, send, be, a challenge to; dispute; invite to a contest.

châm'ber, *n.* room, esp. bedroom; (pl.) set of rooms; enclosed space, cavity. **chamber--pot,** vessel used in bedroom for urine, etc.

châm'berlain (-lin), *n.* officer managing royal household; steward.

châm'bermaid, *n.* housemaid at hotel.

chamē'lèon (ka-), *n.* small lizard with power of changing colour of skin to that of its surroundings.

chamois (sham'wah), *n.* small mountain antelope; (pr. sham'i) soft leather made from skin of sheep, goat, etc.

champ, *v.* munch (fodder) noisily; bite hard upon (bit).

champagne (shampān'), *n.* a sparkling white wine.

cham'pion, *n.* person who fights for another or for a cause; person, animal, etc., that has defeated all competitors. *v.t.* maintain the cause of. **cham'pionship,** *n.*

chance (-ah-), *n.* way things happen; accident; possibility; opportunity. *a.* accidental. *v.* happen; risk.

chan'cel (-ah-), *n.* (railed off) part of church near altar.

chan'cellery (-ah-), *n.* position or offices of a chancellor.

chan'cellor (-ah-), *n.* State or law official; titular head of a university.

chan'cery (-ah-), *n.* division of the High Court of Justice; office attached to embassy.

chan'cy (-ah-), *a.* risky.

chandelier' (sh-; -ēr), *n.* branched hanging support for lights.

chand'ler (-ah-), *n.* dealer in candles, oil, paint, groceries, etc. **chand'lery,** *n.*

chānge (-nj), *n.* variation, alteration; substitution of one for another; money in small coins; (*pl.*) different orders in which peal of bells can be rung. *v.* make or become different; exchange; give or get money change; change one's clothes. **change-over,** (*esp.*) alteration from one working system to another. **chānge'able,** *a.* likely to change; often changing. **chāngeabil'ity,** *n.* **chānge'less,** *a.*

chānge'ling (-njl-), child substituted for another, esp. elf-child supposedly thus left by fairies.

chann'el, *n.* bed in which water runs; passage for liquid; groove; means or agency; narrow piece of water connecting two seas. *v. t.* (p.t. *channelled*), form channel(s) in; groove.

chant (-ah-), *n.* music to which unmetrical psalms are sung; measured monotonous song; sing-song intoning. *v.* sing; sing a chant; intone.

chan'ter (-ah-), *n.* melody pipe of bagpipe.

chan'ticleer, *n.* (Poet.) domestic cock.

chanty: see **shanty**[2].

chā'os (k-), *n.* formless void which was thought to precede the Creation; great confusion. **chāot'ic,** *a.* utterly without order.

chap[1], *n.* crack, esp. in skin, caused by frost, wind, etc. *v.* (p.t. *chapped*), (cause to) develop chaps.

chap[2], **chop**[2], *n.* (usu. pl.) jaws, cheeks.

chap[3], *n.* (*informal*) man, boy; fellow.

chap'book, *n.* (Hist.) cheap small pamphlet of tales, ballads, etc.

chap'el, *n.* place of worship, esp. one attached to institution or private house; small part of church with an altar; Non-conformists' place of worship.

chap'erŏn (sh-), *n.* lady in charge of girl on social occasions. *v. t.* act as chaperon to.

chap'lain (-lin), *n.* priest, clergyman, of institution or attached to armed forces, etc. **chap'laincy,** *a.*

chap'lĕt, *n.* wreath or circlet for head; string of beads; one-third of rosary.

chap'man, *n.* (pl. *-men*), (Hist.) pedlar.

chap'ter, *n.* division of a book; (meeting, assembly, of) clergy of cathedral under dean, or members of monastic order. **chap'ter--house,** room in which chapter meets.

char[1], *v.* (p.t. *charred*), scorch or blacken with fire; burn to charcoal.

char[2], *v. i.* (p.t. *charred*), act as charwoman.

charabanc (sha'rabang), *n.* (chiefly Hist.) motor coach, esp. with long seats facing forward.

cha'racter (k-), *n.* (of person community, etc.) mental or moral nature; moral strength; reputation; distinctive mark; letter; sign; person in novel, play, etc.

characteris'tic (ka-), *a.* typical, distinctive. *n.* distinctive quality or mark.

cha'racterize (k-), *v. t.* show the character of; be a characteristic of. **characterīzā'tion,** *n.*

charade (sha-rahd'), *n.* (usu. pl.) game of guessing word, etc., from acted clue(s).

char'coal, *n.* black porous residue of partly burnt wood, etc.; form of carbon.

charge, *n.* load; filling of explosive; (accumulation of) electrical energy; (Herald.) bearing; price demanded; task; guardianship; thing or person entrusted to the care of another; accusation; attack. *in charge,* having charge or care (*of*), in(to) custody of police. *v.* supply with charge of explosive or electricity; fill (*with*); entrust *with*; solemnly urge; accuse; demand as price of; attack at gallop or run. **charge'able,** *a.*

chargé d'affaires, (shar'zhā dafā̆r') (pl. *chargés d'affaires,* pr. as sing.) deputy ambassador. (French)

char'ger[1], *n.* cavalry officer's horse.

char'ger[2], *n.* (*archaic*) large flat dish.

cha'riot, *n.* horse-drawn car used in ancient warfare and racing; stately vehicle.

charioteer', *n.* driver of chariot.

charisma (ka-riz'ma), *n.* divine gift or talent; capacity for inspiring followers with devotion and enthusiasm. **charismat'ic,** *a.*

cha'ritable, *a.* generous in giving alms; lenient in judging others.

cha'rity, *n.* Christian good feeling; kindness; lenience in judging others; alms-giving; institution, foundation, etc., for benefit of poor or needy persons.

charl'atan (sh-), *n.* one who makes false claims to knowledge or skill; quack.

charl'ock, *n.* field mustard.

charm, *n.* word(s), act, or object supposed to have magical power; thing worn to avert evil; trinket on bracelet, etc.; attractiveness. *v. t.* bewitch; delight. **char'ming,** *a.* (esp.) very pleasing, delightful.

char'nel-house, *n.* place containing corpses or bones.

chart, *n.* map, esp. for sea or air navigation or showing weather conditions, etc.; sheet of information arranged in tables or diagrams. *v. t.* make chart of.

char'ter, *n.* document granting rights, esp. from ruler or government to borough, city, university, etc.; privilege, admitted right. *v. t.* grant charter to; license; hire (aircraft, ship, vehicle, etc.).

char'tered (-erd), *a.* having charter; privileged; licensed; (of aircraft, ship, etc.) hired for particular purpose.

Char'tism, *n.* working-class reform movement of 1837-48. **Char'tist,** *n.*

char'woman (-woo-), *n.* (pl. *-women*), woman paid by the hour or day for doing housework.

chā̆r'y, *a.* cautious, careful, sparing, (*of*).

chāse[1], *v. t.* emboss or engrave (metal).

chāse[2], *v. t.* try to overtake, pursue. *n.* hunting; pursuit.

chasm (kazm), *n.* deep cleft, gulf, fissure; wide difference.

chassis (shas'i), *n.* (pl. same), base-frame of carriage, motor-car, etc.

chaste, *a.* refraining from having (esp. unlawful or immoral) sexual intercourse, pure, virgin; restrained, pure in taste or style. **chas'tity**, *n.*

chasten (-sn), *v.t.* discipline by suffering; refine; subdue.

chastise' (-z), *v.t.* punish; beat. **chastise'ment**, *n.*

chastity: see chaste.

chat, *v.i.* (p.t. *chatted*), talk in easy familiar way. *n.* such talk. **chatt'y**, *a.* talkative; of the nature of a chat.

château (shat'ō), *n.* (pl. *châteaux*, pr. -ōz), French castle or mansion.

chat'elaine (sh-), *n.* chain(s) holding keys, etc., formerly worn hanging from woman's belt; mistress of castle or large house.

chatt'el, *n.* movable possession. *goods and chattels*, personal property.

chatt'er, *v.i.* talk quickly, incessantly, trivially or indiscreetly; (of teeth) rattle together. *n.* sound of chattering; incessant trivial talk. **chatt'erbox**, talkative person, esp. child.

chatty: see chat.

chauffeur (shō'fer), *n.* professional driver of private or hired motor-car.

chau'vinism (shōv-), *n.* exaggerated patriotism; fervent support for a cause. **chau'vinist**, *n.* **chauvinis'tic**, *a.*

cheap, *a.* costing little, inexpensive; easily got; worthless; held in low esteem.

cheap'en, *v.* make or become cheap.

cheat, *v.* act in dishonest way to gain advantage or profit; deceive. *n.* one who cheats; dishonest trick.

check¹, *n.* sudden halt or pause, stoppage; rebuff; restraint; control to secure accuracy, etc.; (Chess) position of king when exposed to attack. *v.* stop suddenly; restrain; test accuracy of; (Chess) subject (opponent or his king) to check. *check in, out,* record arrival at, departure from, (hotel, etc.). **check-out**, desk at which payment is made in self-service shop.

check², *n.* (fabric with) pattern of crossed lines forming squares. **checked** (-kt), *a.*

check'mate, *n.* final defeat at chess or in any enterprise. *v.t.* defeat at chess; frustrate.

cheek, *n.* side of face below the eye; impudent speech; effrontery. **cheek'y**, *a.* impudent.

cheep, *v.i. & n.* (utter) chick's shrill note.

cheer, *n.* shout of encouragement or applause; frame of mind; (*archaic*) food. *v.* urge on; applaud; comfort, gladden. *cheer up,* comfort, be comforted. **cheer'ful**, *a.* contented, happy; pleasant; willing. **cheer'less**, *a.* gloomy, dreary. **cheer'y**, *a.* lively, genial.

cheese (-z), *n.* food made by pressing curds; shaped portion or ball of this. **cheese'-paring**, *a.* stingy. *n.* stinginess.

chee'tah, *n.* swift-running feline animal of Africa and SW. Asia.

chef (sh-), *n.* male head cook.

chef-d'oeuvre (shāder'vr), *n.* (pl. *chefs-d'oeuvre*, pr. as sing.) masterpiece. (French)

chem'ical (k-), *a.* of or made by chemistry. *n.* substance obtained by or used in chemical process.

chemise (shimēz'), *n.* woman's shirt-like undergarment; chemise-like dress.

chem'ist (k-), *n.* person skilled in chemistry; (also *pharmaceutical chemist*), dealer in medicinal drugs.

chem'istry (k-), *n.* science of elements and their laws of combination and behaviour.

chenille (shinēl'), *n.* (fabric with weft of) velvety yarn.

cheque (chek), *n.* written order to banker to pay sum of money.

chequer (chek'er), *n.* (often pl.) patterns made of squares, esp. of alternating colours. *v.t.* mark with squares; vary. **che'quered** (-kerd), *a.* (esp., fig.) marked by contrast or diversity.

che'rish, *v.t.* tend lovingly; keep in one's heart.

cheroot' (sh-), *n.* cigar with both ends open.

che'rry, *n.* small round stone-fruit, tree bearing it, wood of this.

che'rub, *n.* (pl. *cherubs, cherubim*), angelic being; beautiful child. **cheru'bic** (-ōo-), *a.*

chess, *n.* game for two players with 32 pieces (*chessmen*) on chequered board with 64 squares (*chess-board*).

chest, *n.* large strong box; coffer; upper front part of body. *chest of drawers,* piece of furniture with set of drawers in frame.

ches'terfield, *n.* kind of sofa.

chest'nut, *n.* tree or its glossy brown seed (see **horse-chestnut, sweet chestnut**); bright reddish brown; horse so coloured; stale anecdote. *a.* chestnut-coloured.

chêval'-glass (sh-;-ahs), *n.* tall mirror swung on uprights.

chevalier' (sh-;-ēr), *n.* member of certain orders of knighthood, etc.

chev'iot (*or* chē-), *n.* cloth made from wool of sheep of Cheviot Hills.

chev'ron (sh-), *n.* inverted V-shaped bar in heraldry (∧); V-shaped bar (inverted or not) on sleeve of uniform indicating rank, etc.

chew (-ōo), *v.* work about between teeth; grind to pulp or indent by repeated biting. *chew the cud,* (of cattle, etc.) bring back half-digested food into mouth for further chewing. **chewing-gum,** preparation of gum(s) for prolonged chewing.

chiaroscuro (kyaroskoor'ō), *n.* light and shade effects in painting or nature; use of contrast in literature, etc.

chic (shēk), *a.* stylish, elegant.

chicân'ery (sh-), *n.* legal trickery; underhand dealing; sophistry.

chick, *n.* newly hatched bird, esp. chicken.

chick'weed, small weed.

chick'en, *n.* young domestic fowl; its flesh as food; youthful person. **chick'en-hearted,** *a.* cowardly. **chick'enpox,** *n.* infectious disease with rash of small blisters.

chic'ory, *n.* (salad plant with) root ground and used with or instead of coffee.

chide, *v.* (p.t. *chid*; p.p. *chidden* or *chid*), rebuke, scold.

chief, *n.* leader or ruler; head of tribe or clan. *a.* first in importance or influence; prominent, leading.

chief'ly, *adv.* above all; mainly.

chief'tain (-tn), *n.* leader or ruler; head of clan or tribe or robber-band.

chiff'-chaff, *n.* bird of warbler kind.

chiff'on (sh-), *n.* transparent silky fabric.

chiffonier' (sh-;-ēr), *n.* low sideboard.

chignon (shē'nyawn), *n.* coil or roll of hair worn at back of head.

chil'blain, *n.* inflamed itching swelling, esp. on hand or foot, caused by exposure to cold.

child, *n.* (pl. *children*), young human being; son or daughter. **child'bed,** (*archaic*) childbirth. **child'birth,** giving birth to child. **child'hood,** *n.* time from birth to puberty. **child'ish,** *a.* of or like a child. **child'like,** *a.* innocent, frank, simple.

chil'i, *n.* (pl. *chilies*), hot-tasting red dried pod of kinds of capsicum.

chill, *n.* sensation of cold; slight illness with shivering and fever; coldness of air, etc. *a.* lacking warmth. *v.* make or become cold; depress.

chill'y, *a.* rather cold; cold-mannered. **chill'iness,** *n.*

chime, *n.* set of attuned bells; series of sounds made by this. *v.* make (bell) sound; ring chimes (on); show (hour) by chiming; be in agreement.

chimēr'a (kī- *or* ki-), *n.* bogy; fanciful idea. **chime'rical,** *a.* imaginary.

chim'ney, *n.* (pl. *chimneys*), structure for carrying off smoke or steam; glass tube protecting lamp-flame; narrow cleft by which cliff may be climbed. **chim'ney-piece,** mantelpiece. **chim'ney-pot,** pipe at top of chimney. **chim'ney-sweep,** man who sweeps soot from chimneys.

chimpanzee', *n.* dark-furred arboreal African ape, bearing closest resemblance to man of all anthropoids.

chin, *n.* front of lower jaw.

chi'na, *n.* (articles made of) hard fine porcelain. *a.* of china. **china-clay,** kaolin.

chine, *n.* backbone of animal; hill-ridge.

Chinēse' (-z), *a.* of China. *n.* (pl. same) native or language of China. **Chinese lantern,** collapsible lantern of coloured paper. **Chinese white,** zinc oxide as pigment.

chink¹, *n.* sound as of glasses or coins striking together. *v.* (cause to) make chink.

chink², *n.* narrow opening, esp. one that lets light, air, etc., through.

chintz, *n.* colour-printed glazed cotton cloth.

chip, *v.* (p.t. *chipped*), cut or break (*off*) at surface or edge; cut into small pieces. *n.* thin piece cut off; chipped place; counter in gambling game; (pl.) small stick-shaped pieces of potato fried.

chip'munk, *n.* N. Amer. striped squirrel-like rodent.

chipola'ta (-lah-), *n.* small thin sausage.

Chipp'endāle, *n.* & *a.* (furniture) in style of 18th-c. London cabinet-maker.

chirop'odist (ki-), *n.* expert in treatment of minor ailments of the feet. **chirop'ody,** *n.* work, profession, of chiropodist.

chirp, *n.* short sharp thin sound (as) of bird or insect. *v.i.* make this noise; talk merrily. **chir'py,** *a.* cheerful.

chi'rrup, *n.* & *v.i.* (make) series of chirps.

chis'el (-zl), *n.* edged tool for cutting. *v.t.* (p.t. *chiselled*), cut, shape, with chisel; (*slang*) defraud, cheat.

chit¹, *n.* young child; small woman.

chit², *n.* written note.

chit'-chat, *n.* small talk; gossip.

chiv'alry (sh-), *n.* medieval knightly system; inclination to help or defend weaker party; courage and courtesy. **chiv'alrous,** *a.*

chive, *n.* culinary herb related to onion.

chiv'y, *v.t.* (*informal*) chase, harry.

chlor'ide (kl-), *n.* compound of chlorine.

chlorine (klor'ēn), *n.* non-metallic element, a yellowish-green gas, used in bleaching, disinfecting, etc. **chlor'ināte,** *v.t.* treat, sterilize (water, etc.), with chlorine.

chlo'roform (kl-), *n.* heavy volatile liquid whose inhaled vapour produces unconsciousness. *v.t.* render unconscious with this.

chlo'rophyll (kl-), *n.* colouring matter of green parts of plants.

chock, *n.* block of wood; wedge. *v.t.* make fast, wedge, with chocks. **chock-a-block,** jammed together; crammed *with.* **chock-full,** crammed, stuffed.

choc'olate, *n.* paste, slab, etc., of roasted, ground, and sweetened cacao-seed; drink made of this; (pl.) sweets made with it; dark brown colour. *a.* chocolate coloured.

choice, *n.* choosing; preference; variety to choose from; thing chosen. *a.* of picked quality; exquisite.

choir (kwīr), *n.* group of persons trained to sing together, esp. to lead singing in church; choral society; chancel.

chōke, *v.* stop breath of, suffocate; suffer temporary stoppage of breath; block up wholly or partly. *n.* valve for partially closing air-inlet of petrol engine.

chol'er (ko-), *n.* anger. **chol'eric,** *a.* angry; irritable.

chol'era (ko-), *n.* severe infectious epidemic disease.

chōose (-z), *v.* (p.t. *chōse*; p.p. *chōsen*), take by preference from two or more; decide *between* (one and another); decide (*to*).

chōōs'(e)y, *a.* (*informal*) cautious in choosing; fastidious.

chop¹, *v.* (p.t. *chopped*), cut by striking with axe or edge-tool; cut thus into small pieces. *n.* chopping blow; small thick slice of meat, usu. including rib. **chopp'er,** *n.* large-bladed short axe. **chopp'y,** *a.* (of the sea) breaking in short irregular waves.

chop²: see **chap².**

chop³, *v.i.* chop and change, alter, change, esp. repeatedly or frequently.

chop'sticks, *n.pl.* pair of small sticks held in one hand and used by Chinese in eating.

chor'al (k-), *a.* of, for, sung by, choir or chorus. **choral society,** group of singers meeting regularly to practise choral music.

chorale (korahl'), *n.* (metrical hymn set to) simple tune.

chord¹ (k-), *n.* (Poet.) string of harp, etc.; (Math.) straight line joining ends of arc.

chord², (k-), *n.* (Mus.) combination of notes sounded together.

chore, *n.* odd job; dull tedious job; (pl.) daily light work of house, etc.

choreog'raphy (ko-), *n.* arrangement of the dancing in a ballet. **choreog'rapher,** *n.* **choreograph'ic,** *a.*

cho'rister (ko-), *n.* member of choir; choir-boy.

chor'tle, *n.* & *v.i.* (give a) joyful chuckle.

chor'us (k-), *n.* band of singers and dancers in ancient Greek play; band of singers; choir; thing said or sung by many at once; refrain of song. *v.t.* say or sing in chorus.

chose(n): see **choose.**

chough (chuf), *n.* red-legged crow.

chow, *n.* Chinese breed of dog.

Christ (kr-), *n.* title, now treated as proper name, given to Jesus.

christen (kri'sn), *v.t.* baptize and give name to; name. **chri'stening,** n. ceremony of baptism.

Christendom (kri'sn-), *n.* Christians, Christian countries.

Christian (kris'tyan), *a.* of Christ or his teaching; belonging to the religion of Christ. *n.* one who believes in or professes the religion of Christ. **Christian era,** era counted from supposed year of Christ's birth. **Christian name,** name given at christening. **Christian science,** religion and system by which health and healing are sought by Christian faith and without medical treatment.

Christian'ity (kr-), *n.* Christian faith, quality, or character; the teaching of Christ.

Christmas (kris'mas), *n.* Christmas Day or Christmas-tide. **Christmas box,** small present given at Christmas. **Christmas Day,** festival of Christ's birth, December 25th. **Christmas rose,** white-flowered plant blooming in winter. **Christmas-tide,** season of Christmas.

chromat'ic (k-), *a.* of colour, in colours. (Mus., of scale), proceeding by semitones.

chrōme (k-), *n.* yellow pigment obtained from compounds of chromium.

chrō'mium (k-), *n.* metallic element, used esp. in electroplating and in alloys.

chrō'mosōme (k-), *n.* (Biol.) one of thread-like structures occurring in cell-nucleus and carrying genes.

chron'ic (k-), *a.* constantly present or recurring; habitual; (*informal*) bad, intense.

chron'icle (k-), *n.* register of events in order of time. *v.t.* enter in chronicle; record. **chron'icler,** *n.*

chronolo'gical (k-), *a.* arranged in order of time.

chronol'ogy (k-), *n.* arrangement or table of events with dates.

chronom'eter (k-), *n.* time-measuring instrument, esp. one unaffected by temperature changes.

chrys'alis (k-), *n.* pupa of butterfly, moth, etc.

chrysan'themum (k-), *n.* cultivated composite plant flowering in autumn.

chub, *n.* coarse-fleshed river-fish.

chubb'y, *a.* plump, round-faced.

chuck¹, *v.t.* throw, toss; touch playfully *under the chin.* chuck out, expel. *n.* act of chucking.

chuck², *n.* part of lathe holding work.

chuck'le, *n.* & *v.i.* (make) suppressed sound expressing mirth, exultation, etc.

chug, *n.* & *v.i.* (p.t. *chugged*), (make, progress with) intermittent explosive sound.

chum, *n.* (*informal*) close friend.

chump, *n.* lump of wood; blunt end of loin of lamb; (*slang*) head.

church, *n.* building for Christian worship; (*Church*), organized Christian body with distinguishing principles; Christians collectively; the clerical profession. **church'-war'den,** elected lay representative of parish; long clay pipe. **church'yard,** enclosed ground round church, often used for burial.

churl, *n.* surly ill-mannered person; miser. **chur'lish,** *a.*

churn, *n.* butter-making vessel or machine; large milk-can. *v.* make butter by agitating cream in churn; stir or wash about, seethe.

chute (shōōt), *n.* slide for conveying things to lower level; rapid smooth flow of water over slope.

chut'ney, *n.* (pl. *chutneys*), hot-tasting relish of fruits, chilies, etc.

cica'da (-kah- *or* -kā-), *n.* winged chirping insect.

cic'atrice, *n.* scar of healed wound.

cicerō'nė (*or* chich-), *n.* (pl. *ciceroni,* pr. -nē), guide who explains history, etc., of place.

ci'der, *n.* fermented drink made from apple-juice.

cigar', *n.* roll of tobacco-leaf for smoking. **cigarette',** *n.* cut tobacco rolled in paper for smoking.

cil'ia, *n.pl.* eyelashes; similar fringe on leaf or

insect's wing.

cinch, *n.* saddle-girth used in Mexico, etc.; (*slang*) sure or easy thing, certainty.

cinc'ture, *n.* (Poet.) girdle, belt.

cin'der, *n.* residue of coal, etc., that has ceased to flame.

Cinderell'a, *n.* neglected or despised member of group, etc.

cin'ecamera, *n.* motion-picture camera. **cin'-êfilm,** *n.* film for cinecamera.

cin'êma, *n.* motion-picture theatre. **(the) cinéma,** motion pictures, films; cinematography.

cinêmat'ograph, *n.* (Hist.) cinema camera or projector. **cinématog'raphy,** *n.* art, process, of making and projecting motion pictures. **cinématograph'ic,** *a.*

cineraŕ'ia, *n.* flowering plant with ashy down on leaves.

cin'erary, *a.* of ashes (esp. of urn holding cremated ashes).

cinn'amon, *n.* E. Indian tree; (colour of) its aromatic yellowish-brown inner bark used as spice. *a.* cinnamon-coloured.

Cinque Ports (-nk), certain ports (orig. five) on SE. coast of England.

ci'pher, *n.* arithmetical symbol 0; nonentity; any Arabic numeral; secret way of writing; monogram. *v.* do sums; write in cipher.

cir'ca, *prep.* about (abbrev. *c.*). (Latin)

Cir'cê, *n.* (Gk. myth.) enchantress who turned her victims into swine.

cir'cle, *n.* plane figure enclosed by curved line every point on which is same distance from centre; line enclosing it; roundish enclosure, ring; curved tier of seats in theatre, etc.; set or group or class; period or cycle. *v.* move in circle (round).

cir'clêt, *n.* small circle; circular band as ornament for head, etc.

cir'cuit (-kit), *n.* distance round an area; judge's journey through district to hold courts, such district; (Electr.) course or path of current. **circû'itous,** *a.* roundabout, indirect.

cir'cûlar, *a.* of, in form of, moving in, circle. *n.* letter, etc., sent round in same form to several people. **cir'cûlarize,** *v.t.* send circulars to.

cir'cûlate, *v.* go or send round. **circûla'tion,** *n.* movement of blood from and back to heart; movement from and back to a starting--point; transmission, distribution; number of copies of newspaper, etc., sold.

circum-, *pref.* round, about.

cir'cumcise (-z), *v.t.* cut off foreskin of. **circumci'sion** (-zhn), *n.* religious rite or surgical operation of circumcising.

circum'ference, *n.* line enclosing circle; distance round a thing.

cir'cumflex (accent), *n.* the accent (^).

circumlocu'tion, *n.* use of many words where few would do; roundabout expression.

circumnav'igâte, *v.t.* sail round.

cir'cumscrîbe, *v.t.* draw line round; mark or lay down limits; restrict.

circumscrip'tion, *n.* limitation; inscription round coin, etc.

cir'cumspect, *a.* cautious; taking everything into account. **circumspec'tion,** *n.*

cir'cumstance, *n.* (pl.) all the external conditions surrounding act, event, etc.; (pl.) person's financial position; detail, incident.

circumstan'tial (-shl), *a.* of or dependent on circumstances; (of evidence) based on details which tend to establish disputed point but do not prove it directly; full of detail.

circumvent', *v.t.* get the better of by cunning; outwit.

cir'cus, *n.* arena for outdoor sports; travelling show of riders, acrobats, trained animals, etc.; (circular) space in town where streets converge.

ci'rrus, *n.* (pl. *cirri*), form of cloud with diverging filaments or wisps.

cis'tern, *n.* tank for storing water.

cit'adel, *n.* fortress guarding city.

cite, *v.t.* summon at law; quote in support; mention as example. **citâ'tion,** *n.* summons; reference; mention in official dispatch, recommendation for honour.

cit'izen, *n.* burgess, freeman, or inhabitant of city or town; enfranchised member of a State. **cit'izenship,** *n.* state, status, rights, of a citizen.

cit'ric a'cid, sharp-tasting acid found in juice of lemon, orange, lime, etc.

cit'ron, *n.* fruit like lemon but larger; tree bearing it.

cit'rus, *n.* & *a.* (of) genus which includes lemon, orange, lime, etc. **cit'rous,** *a.*

cit'y, *n.* important town; town created city by charter.

civ'êt, *n.* musky-smelling substance got from the *civet*(-*cat*), a carnivorous quadruped.

civ'ic, *a.* of city or citizenship. **civ'ics,** *n.* study of civic rights and duties.

civ'il, *a.* of (the community of) citizens; non--military; (Law) not criminal; polite. **Civil Service,** all public State departments or services except armed forces. **civil servant,** official employed in Civil Service. **civil war,** war between fellow citizens.

civil'ian, *a.* not in or of the armed forces. *n.* civilian person.

civil'ity, *n.* politeness.

civilizâ'tion, *n.* making or becoming civilized; (esp. advanced) stage of social development.

civ'ilize, *v.t.* bring out of primitive and unenlightened condition; make cultured.

clack, *n.* sharp sound; clatter of tongues. *v.i.* make clack; chatter.

clad, *p.p.* & *a.* clothed.

claim, *v.t.* demand as one's due; assert; call for, need. *n.* demand; right, title (*to*); (Mining, etc.) piece of ground marked out or allotted.

clai′mant, *n.* person making claim, esp. in lawsuit.

clairvoy′ance, *n.* faculty of seeing mentally what is out of sight; second sight. **clairvoy′ant,** *n.* & *a.*

clam, *n.* large edible bivalve shellfish.

clam′ber, *v.i.* climb with help of hands; climb with difficulty.

clamm′y, *a.* moist and sticky.

clam′our (-mer), *n.* shouting; confused noise. *v.i.* shout; make loud demand. **clam′orous,** *a.*

clamp¹, *n.* brace or band of iron, etc.; gripping appliance tightened by screw, etc. *v.t.* strengthen or fasten with clamp.

clamp², *n.* pile (of bricks for burning, or potatoes, etc., under straw and earth for storing).

clan, *n.* social group, esp. of Scottish Highlanders, with a common ancestor; tribe. **clann′ish,** *a.* keeping together in one group.

clandes′tine, *a.* secret; underhand.

clang, *n.* loud resonant metallic sound. *v.i.* make this sound. **clang′our** (-ngger), *n.* continued clanging.

clank, *n.* sound as of heavy chain rattling. *v.* (cause to) make clank.

clans′man (-z-), *n.* (pl. *-men*), member of clan.

clap, *v.* (p.t. *clapped*), strike palms loudly together; flap (wings) audibly; put, place, quickly or with clap. *n.* peal of thunder; sound or act of clapping.

clapp′er, *n.* tongue or striker of bell; rattle for scaring birds.

clap′trap, *n.* language meant to catch applause, nonsense.

cla′rendon, *n.* thick-faced printing-type.

cla′ret, *n.* red wine from Bordeaux.

cla′rify, *v.* make clear; free from impurities; become transparent.

clarinet′ (-a-r-), *n.* wood-wind instrument with single reed. **clarinett′ist,** *n.*

cla′rion, *n.* shrill trumpet; rousing call to action. *a.* loud and clear.

clarionet′ (-a-r-), *n.* clarinet.

cla′rity, *n.* clearness.

clash, *n.* loud sound as of cymbals; collision, conflict; discord of colours, etc. *v.* make clash; disagree (*with*).

clasp (-ah-), *n.* contrivance of two interlocking parts for fastening; embrace, handshake; inscribed bar on medal ribbon. *v.t.* fasten; encircle, grasp; hold closely. **clasp-knife,** folding knife.

class (-ah-), *n.* rank, order of society; set of pupils or students taught together; division according to quality. *v.t.* place in a class. **class′room,** room in school, etc., where class is taught.

class′ic, *a.* of acknowledged excellence; standard; simple and harmonious in style. *n.* classic writer or artist; ancient Greek or Latin writer; any great literary work; (pl.) study of

ancient Greek and Latin. **class′icism,** *n.*

class′ical, *a.* of or based on ancient Greek and Latin authors or art; standard, first-class; in or following restrained style of classical antiquity; (of music, etc.) serious, not popular.

class′ify, *v.t.* arrange in classes. **classifica′tion,** *n.* **class′ificatory,** *a.*

clatt′er, *n.* rattling sound; noisy talk. *v.i.* make a clatter.

clause (-z), *n.* sentence or part of a sentence; single article in treaty or law or contract.

claustropho′bia, *n.* fear of being shut in a room or building; dislike of enclosed places. **claustropho′bic,** *n.* prone to, inducing, claustrophobia.

clave: see **cleave².**

clav′ichord (-k-), *n.* earliest stringed musical instrument with keyboard.

clav′icle, *n.* collar-bone.

claw, *n.* pointed horny nail of beast's or bird's foot; grappling-iron. *v.* scratch or tear or seize with claws or nails.

clay, *n.* stiff tenacious earth used for bricks, pottery, etc. **clay′ey,** *a.*

clay′more, *n.* ancient Scottish two-edged broadsword.

clean, *a.* free from dirt or smoke; freshly washed; free of defilement or disease; neat, clear. *adv.* completely. *v.t.* make clean. *n.* cleaning. **clean′er,** *n.* one who, thing that, cleans. **clean′ly¹,** *adv.* in a clean manner.

clean′ly² (-en-), *a.* habitually clean; attentive to cleanness. **clean′liness,** *n.*

cleanse (-enz), *v.t.* make clean.

clear, *a.* transparent; not clouded; distinct, intelligible; well-defined; unobstructed, open; unhampered. *adv.* clearly; completely. *v.* make or become clear; remove encumbrance, etc., from; show to be innocent; make sum as net gain. *clear off, out,* go away. **clear-cut,** sharply defined. **clear-sighted,** discerning.

clear′ance, *n.* clearing; clear space; room to pass.

clear′ing, *n.* (esp.) piece of land cleared for cultivation.

clear′ly, *adv.* distinctly; undoubtedly.

clear′way, *n.* main road where vehicles may not stop on carriageway.

cleat, *n.* tightening-wedge; projecting piece of wood, etc., to give footing, fasten ropes to, etc.

clea′vage, *n.* split, way of splitting.

cleave¹, *v.* (p.t. *clove* or *cleft*; p.p. *cloven* or *cleft*), split, divide; chop or break apart; make way through.

cleave², *v.i.* (p.t. *cleaved* or archaic *clave*; p.p. *cleaved*), be faithful; stick fast *to.*

clea′ver, *n.* butcher's chopper.

clef, *n.* (Mus.) symbol placed on stave to indicate pitch of notes.

cleft¹, *p.t.* & *p.p.* of **cleave¹.**

cleft², *n.* space or division made by cleavage; fissure, split.

cleg, *n.* horse-fly.

clem'atis, *n.* flowering climbing shrub.

clem'ency, *n.* merciful treatment or feeling.

clem'ent, *a.* mild; showing mercy.

clench, *v.t.* press firmly together, close tightly; grasp firmly.

cler'gy, *n.* (*collective*) persons ordained for service in Christian Church. **cler'gyman,** *n.* (pl. *-men*), member of clergy.

cle'ric, *n.* clergyman.

cle'rical, *a.* of clergy or clergyman; of clerk(s).

clerk (-ark), *n.* person employed to make written entries, file, keep accounts, etc.; officer in charge of records, etc., of corporation, court, etc.

clev'er, *a.* quick in learning and understanding; skilful, talented.

clew (-ōō), *n.* ball of thread; corner of sail.

cliché (klē'shā), *a.* hackneyed or commonplace phrase or expression.

click, *n. & v.i.* (make) slight sharp sound.

cli'ent, *n.* person using services of lawyer or other professional man; customer.

clientele (klēontel'), *n.* clients; customers.

cliff, *n.* steep rock-face, esp. on seashore.

climac'teric, *a.* making a turning-point, critical.

climac'tic, *a.* of, forming, a climax.

cli'mate, *n.* prevailing conditions of temperature, rainfall, etc., of a region. **climat'ic,** *a.*

climax, *n.* highest point; culmination; point of greatest interest or importance.

climb (-m), *v.* ascend, mount; go up. *n.* piece of climbing; place to be climbed. **cli'mber** (-mer), *n.* (esp.) mountaineer; climbing plant.

clime, *n.* (Poet.) region; climate.

clinch, *v.* secure (nail) by hammering point sideways; settle conclusively; (Boxing) grapple at close quarters. *n.* clinching, resulting state or position.

cling, *v.i.* (p.t. & p.p. *clung*), keep hold; stick, hold tightly, *together, to.*

clin'ic, *n.* institution giving medical and other treatment or advice to outpatients, etc.; teaching of medicine at hospital bedside.

clin'ical, *a.* of, at, the sick-bed.

clink, *n.* sharp ringing sound, chink. *v.* (cause to) make this sound.

clink'er, *n.* (piece of) hard mass of fused ash of coal, etc., left in furnace, etc.

clink'er-built (-bilt), *a.* (of boat) with planks overlapping and secured with clinched nails.

clip¹, *n.* appliance for holding things together or for attaching something. *v.t.* (p.t. *clipped*), fasten or attach with clip.

clip², *v.t.* (p.t. *clipped*), cut with shears or scissors; trim thus; cut short. *n.* clipping, shearing; yield of wool. **clipp'er,** *n.* (esp.) instrument for clipping (usu. pl.); swift mover; ship with bow projecting beyond keel. **clipp'ing,** *n.* (esp.) piece clipped off, cutting from newspaper, etc.

clique (-ēk), *n.* exclusive set of associates.

clit'oris, *n.* small erectile female sexual organ.

cloak, *n.* outer garment hanging loosely from shoulders; pretext. *v.t.* cover with a cloak; hide. **cloak'room,** room for leaving outdoor garments, luggage, etc.; lavatory.

cloche (-sh), *n.* bell-shaped glass, transparent frame, for protecting plant(s).

clock¹, *n.* instrument measuring time and indicating it on a dial, etc.; (*informal*) taximeter, speedometer, or mileage recorder. *v.t.* time by clock or stop-watch. *clock in, out*, register time of arrival, departure. **clock'wise,** moving in direction taken by hands of clock. **clock'work,** mechanism like that of clock; regular, mechanical.

clock², *n.* ornamental pattern on sides of stocking or sock.

clod, *n.* lump of earth or clay; lout. **clod-hopper,** bumpkin, lout.

clog, *n.* wooden-soled shoe; log fastened to leg to hinder movement; encumbrance. *v.* (p.t. *clogged*), hamper, hinder; choke *up*; become obstructed.

clois'ter, *n.* covered walk, esp. of convent, college, or cathedral buildings; convent, monastery. *v.t.* shut up (as) in convent. **clois'tered** (-terd), *a.* secluded; having cloister.

clop, *n.* sound of hoofs on road, etc.

close¹, *a.* narrow, confined; stifling; secret; niggardly; dense; near; near together; nearly equal. *adv.* closely. *n.* enclosed place; passage or entry. **close-fisted,** niggardly, mean. **close quarters,** immediate contact; uncomfortable closeness. **close season,** period during which taking of certain kinds of game or fish is illegal. **close-up,** cinema or television shot taken at close range. **close'ly,** *adv.* **close'ness,** *n.*

close² (-z), *v.* shut; declare, be declared, not open; draw near; bring or come to an end. *n.* conclusion, end.

clos'et (-z-), *n.* private or small room; cupboard; water-closet. **clos'eted,** *a.* in private conference, etc.

clo'sure (-zher), *n.* closing, closed state; closing of debate.

clot, *n.* semi-solid lump formed from liquid, esp. blood. *v.* (p.t. *clotted*), form into clots; curdle.

cloth, *n.* (piece of) woven or felted material; table-cover; woollen material for clothes.

clothe (-dh), *v.t.* (p.t. *clothed* or archaic *clad*), provide with clothes; put clothes upon; cover as with clothes.

clothes (-ōdhz *or* -ōz), *n.pl.* things worn to cover the body and limbs; bedclothes.

clo'thier (-dh-), *n.* dealer in cloth and men's clothes.

clo'thing (-dh-), *n.* clothes.

cloud, *n.* visible (mass of) condensed watery vapour floating in the air; mass of smoke, dust, etc.; gloom; suspicion. *v.* overspread or darken with clouds or gloom; become overcast. **cloud'burst,** sudden and violent rainstorm. **cloud'less,** *a.* **cloud'y,** *a.* obscured by clouds; lacking elearness.

clout, *v.t.* (*informal*) hit or rap. *n.* rap or blow; cloth, piece of clothing (Sc. & north.).

clŏve[1], *n.* dried bud of tropical tree, used as spice.

clŏve[2], *n.* one division of bulb of garlic, etc.

clove[3], *p.t.* of **cleave**[1]. **clŏve hitch,** knot used to fasten rope round spar, pole, etc.

cloven, *p.p.* of **cleave**[1]. **clŏ'ven hŏŏf,** divided hoof of ruminants.

clŏ'ver, *n.* trefoil plant used as fodder. **in clover,** in luxury.

clown, *n.* jester in pantomime or circus; person acting like clown; ignorant or ill-bred man. *v.* behave like clown. **clown'ish,** *a.*

cloy, *v.t.* weary by richness or sameness.

club, *n.* heavy stick with one thick end used as weapon; kind of stick used in golf; (premises of) body of persons associated for social or other purposes. *v.* (p.t. *clubbed*), strike with club. *club together,* contribute to common expense.

cluck, *n.* hen's cry. *v.i.* make cluck.

clue (-ōō), *n.* fact, idea, etc., which suggests possible answer to problem, mystery, etc.

clump, *n.* cluster of trees. *v.* tread heavily; plant in a clump.

clum'sy (-z-), *a.* awkward in movement or shape; badly contrived; tactless. **clum'-siness,** *n.*

clung, *p.t. & p.p.* of **cling.**

clus'ter, *n.* number of similar things growing closely together; number of persons, animals, etc., in close group. *v.i.* form cluster.

clutch[1], *v.* seize eagerly; take or keep hold of with hand(s). *n.* tight grasp; device for coupling and uncoupling driving and driven parts of mechanism.

clutch[2], *n.* set of eggs; brood of chickens.

clutt'er, *n.* untidy state. *v.t.* (often with *up*) litter, crowd untidily (*with*).

co-, *pref.* (contracted form of *com-*, used orig. only before vowels, *h*, and *gn*; now used before any letter), joint(ly), mutual(ly); (Math.) of the complement; complement of.

coach, *n.* four-wheeled horse-drawn carriage; long-distance bus; railway carriage, often divided into compartments; tutor or trainer. *v.* train, tutor; travel by coach. **coach'man,** *n.* (pl. *coachmen*), driver of horse carriage.

cŏag'ŭlāte, *v.* change from fluid to solid state; curdle, clot, set. **cŏagŭlā'tion,** *n.*

coal, *n.* black or blackish stratified rock consisting of carbonized plant tissue and used as fuel, etc. *v.* put coal into (ship, etc.); take in coal. **coal'field,** district in which coal is found and mined. **coal-gas,** gas extracted from coal and used as fuel. **coal'mine,** mine from which coal is dug. **coal-scuttle,** portable receptacle for coal. **coal-tar,** thick black liquid obtained in manufacture of coal-gas.

cŏalesce' (-es), *v.i.* come together and form one whole. **cŏales'cence,** *n.*

cŏali'tion, *n.* uniting; temporary union between political parties.

coarse (kors), *a.* not fine in texture; rough; common; vulgar, obscene. **coars'en,** *v.* make or become coarse. **coarse'ness,** *n.*

coast, *n.* land bordering the sea; line of shore. *v.i.* sail along coast; travel downhill on bicycle without pedalling or in car with engine idling. **coast'guard,** man, body of men, employed to watch coast, report wrecks, etc. **coast'line,** line or contour of seashore. **coas'tal,** *a.* **coas'ter,** *n.* (esp.) coasting vessel. **coast'wise,** *adv. & a.* along coast.

coat, *n.* outer garment with sleeves; beast's hair, fur, etc.; layer of paint, etc. *v.t.* cover with a surface layer (of paint, etc.). **coat of arms,** shield bearing heraldic arms. **coat'ee,** *n.* short jacket. **coat'ing,** *n.* cloth for coats; layer of paint, etc.

coax, *v.t.* persuade gently.

cob, *n.* strong short-legged riding-horse; male swan; kind of hazel nut; stalk of maize-ear.

cŏ'balt (-awlt), *n.* a metal; deep blue colouring-matter made from it.

cobb'le, *n.* water-worn rounded stone used for paving; (pl.) paving of cobbles. *v.t.* mend; patch roughly.

cobb'ler, *n.* mender of shoes; clumsy workman.

cŏ'bra, *n.* venomous hooded snake.

cob'web, *n.* spider's network or thread.

cŏ'ca, *n.* (dried leaves of) S.Amer. shrub.

cocaine', *n.* alkaloid obtained from coca and used as local anaesthetic, etc.

coc'cyx (-ks-), *n.* bone ending spinal column.

coch'ineal, *n.* (dried insects yielding) red dye.

cock[1], *n.* male of domestic fowl; any male bird; tap or valve controlling flow of liquid or gas; lever in gun. *v.t.* set in upright or slanting position; set (gun) ready for firing. **cock-crow,** dawn. **cock-a-hoop,** exultant. **cock-eyed,** set aslant. **cock-fighting,** setting cocks to fight as sport. **cock of the walk,** dominating person in any company.

cock[2], *n.* small conical heap of hay. *v.t.* put (hay) in cocks.

cockāde' *n.* rosette, etc., worn in hat.

cockatŏō', *n.* crested parrot.

cock'atrice (*or* -ĭ-), *n.* basilisk.

cock'boat, *n.* small ship's-boat.

cock'chāfer, *n.* large brown loud-humming beetle.

cocked hat (-kt), hat with wide brim turned up at sides or front and back.

cock'er, *n.* breed of spaniel.

cock'erel, *n.* young cock.

cock'le[1], *n.* (shell of) edible bivalve shellfish found on sandy coasts. *cockles of the heart,* innermost feelings. **cockle-shell,** shell of cockle; small frail boat.

cock'le[2], *n.* bulge, pucker. *v.* (cause to)

wrinkle or pucker.

cock'ney, *n.* native of London; London English. *a.* of cockneys.

cock'pit, *n.* cock-fighting arena; place of many battles; space for pilot, etc., in aeroplane, driver in racing-car, etc.

cock'roach, *n.* dark-brown beetle-like nocturnal insect infesting kitchens, etc.

cock'sure (-shoor), *a.* quite convinced; dogmatic, confident.

cock'tail, *n.* drink of spirit mixed with wine, fruit juice, sugar, ice, etc.; appetizer.

cock'y, *a.* conceited, pert; cock-a-hoop.

co'co, *n.* (pl. *cocos*), tropical palm bearing coconut. **co'conut,** *n.* seed of coco with edible white lining enclosing whitish liquid (*coconut milk*). *coconut matting*, matting made from fibre of outer husk of coconut.

co'coa (-kō), *n.* powder of crushed cacao seeds; drink made from this.

cocoon', *n.* silky case spun by larva of many insects to protect them in pupa stage, esp. that of silkworm.

cod, *n.* large edible sea-fish. **cod-liver oil,** medicinal oil rich in vitamins.

codd'le, *v.t.* treat as invalid, pamper; cook gently in hot, not boiling, water.

cōde, *n.* systematized collection of laws; set of rules; system of signals; arbitrary symbols used for brevity or secrecy. *v.t.* put into code symbols.

co'dicil, *n.* addition to a will, altering or revoking original contents.

co'dify̆, *v.t.* arrange (laws) into a code or system. **cōdifica'tion,** *n.*

cod'ling, *n.* small cod.

cōedūca'tion, *n.* education of boys and girls together. **cōedūca'tional,** *a.*

cōeffi'cient (-shnt), *n.* (Algebra) number placed before and multiplying known or unknown quantity; (Phys.) number used as measure of some property, etc.

cōerce', *v.t.* force into obedience. **cōer'cive,** *a.* **cōer'cion** (-shn), *n.* force; government by force.

cōē'val, *a. & n.* (person, etc.) of the same age, duration, or epoch.

cōexist' (-gz-), *v.i.* exist together or *with.* **cōexis'tent,** *a.* **cōexis'tence,** *n.*

coff'ee *n.* a shrub; its seeds (*coffee-beans*); drink made from the seeds roasted, ground, and infused in boiling water; pale brown colour.

coff'er, *n.* box, esp. for valuables; (pl.) funds or treasury. **coffer-dam,** caisson.

coff'in, *n.* chest in which body is buried or cremated.

cog, *n.* one of series of projections on wheel, etc., transferring motion by engaging with another series. **cog-wheel,** wheel with cogs.

co'gent, *a.* convincing, forcible. **co'gency,** *n.*

co'gitāte, *v.* think deeply. **cogitā'tion,** *n.*

cog'nāte, *a.* of the same origin; coming from the same root; related to. *n.* cognate word or person.

cogni'tion, *n.* knowing or perceiving; perception, notion. **cog'nitive.** *a.*

cog'nizance, *n.* being aware, notice. **cog'nizant,** *a.* having knowledge, being aware (*of*).

cognō'men, *n.* nickname; surname.

cōhab'it, *v.i.* live together as husband and wife. **cōhabitā'tion,** *n.*

coheir (kōār'), *n.* joint heir. **coheir'ess,** *n. fem.*

cōhēre', *v.i.* stick together; remain united.

cōhēr'ent, *a.* holding together; (of speech, argument, etc.) consistent, easily followed. **cōhēr'ence,** *n.*

cōhē'sion (-zhn), *n.* sticking together; union. **cohēs'ive,** *a.*

cō'hort, *n.* tenth part of Roman legion; band of warriors.

coif, *n.* (Hist.) close-fitting cap.

coiffeur (kwafer'), **coiffeuse'** (-erz), *nn.* male, female, hairdresser. (French)

coiffure (kwaf'ūr), *n.* style of hairdressing.

coil, *v.* wind (rope, etc.) continuously round one point; twist into spiral or circular shape. *n.* coiled length of rope, wire, etc.

coin, *n.* piece of stamped metal money; coined money. *v.t.* make (money) by stamping metal; turn into money; invent, fabricate. **coin-operated,** *a.* set in motion by coin placed in slot.

coi'nage, *n.* (right of) coining; coins; currency; coined word.

cōincide', *v.i.* occur at the same time; agree or be identical *with.*

cōin'cidence, *n.* notable occurrence at the same time of unconnected events. **cōin'cident, cōinciden'tal,** *aa.*

coi'ner, *n.* (esp.) maker of false money.

coir, *n.* fibre of coconut husk.

cō'itus, cōi'tion, *nn.* insertion of penis into vagina and (usu.) ejaculation of semen.

cōke, *n.* solid substance left after gases have been extracted from coal.

col, *n.* dip in summit-line of mountain-chain.

col-, *pref.*: see **com-.**

col'ander (ku-), *n.* perforated vessel used as strainer in cookery.

cōld, *a.* of low temperature, esp. when compared with human body; feeling cold; chilling; without friendliness. *n.* low temperature; inflammation of mucous membrane of nose and throat. *in cold blood*, coolly, deliberately. **cōld'ly,** *adv.* **cōld'ness,** *n.*

col'ic, *n.* severe griping abdominal or intestinal pains.

coli'tis, *n.* inflammation of colon.

collab'orāte, *v.i.* work together (*with*); co-operate treacherously with the enemy. **collaborā'tion,** *n.* **collab'orātor,** *a.*

coll'age (-ahzh), *n.* picture made by sticking pieces of paper, cloth, etc., to a surface.

collapse', *n.* tumbling down or falling to ruin; giving way; breakdown. *v.i.* fall to ruin;

break down. **collap'sible,** *a.* folding.

coll'ar, *n.* part of garment turned back at neck or encircling neck; leather band round animal's neck. *v. t.* seize by the collar, capture.

coll'ar-bône, *n.* bone joining breast-bone and shoulder-blade.

collâte', *v. t.* compare in detail.

collat'eral, *a.* side by side; parallel; subordinate but from same source; contributory; descended from same stock but in different line. *n.* collateral kinsman; collateral security.

collâ'tion, *n.* collating; light meal.

coll'eague (-g), *n.* associate in office, etc.; member of same profession, etc.

coll'ect[1], *n.* short prayer in prayer-book, esp. appointed for particular day.

collect'[2], *v.* bring or come together; accumulate (specimens, pictures, stamps, etc.); gather (contributions, taxes, etc.); gather (one's thoughts). **collec'ted,** *a.* (esp.) cool, calm.

collec'tion, *n.* collecting; collecting of money at church service, etc.; money collected; set of things collected.

collec'tive, *a.* including many; combined. **collective noun,** noun used in singular (often taking plural verb) to denote many individuals.

collec'tor, *n.* one who collects specimens, curiosities, rent, taxes, etc.

coll'ege, *n.* body of teachers and students forming part of a university; similar foundation outside a university; society of persons with special rights and privileges; buildings of college. **collê'giate,** *a.* of, constituted as, a college.

collîde', *v. i.* come into collision.

coll'ie, *n.* Scottish sheep-dog with long hair, pointed nose, and bushy tail.

coll'ier, *n.* coal-miner; coal-ship, member of its crew. **coll'iery,** *n.* coal-mine.

colli'sion (-zhn), *n.* violent encounter of moving bodies; clash of opposed interests, etc.

collô'quial, *a.* belonging to everyday speech; not formal or literary. **collô'quialism,** *n.* colloquial word or idiom.

coll'oquy (pl. *colloquies*), *n.* talk, conversation.

collû'sion (-zhn; *or* -ōō-), *n.* deceitful agreement between seeming opponents. **collusive,** *a.*

cologne' (-ōn), *n.* eau-de-cologne.

cô'lon[1], *n.* greater part of the large intestine. **colon'ic,** *a.*

cô'lon[2], *n.* punctuation mark (:).

colonel (ker'nl), *n.* senior officer of army regiment.

colô'nial, *a.* of colony or colonies. *n.* inhabitant of colony.

col'onist, *n.* settler in or part-founder of colony. **col'onize,** *v.* establish or join a colony. **colonîzâ'tion,** *n.*

colonnâde', *n.* row of columns set at equal intervals, usu. supporting roof, etc.

col'ony, *n.* settlement, settlers, in new territory remaining subject to parent State; persons of one nationality, occupation, etc., forming community in town, etc.; birds, etc., similarly congregated.

Colora'dô bee'tle (-ahd-), small beetle whose larva is destructive to potato plant.

colorâ'tion (ku-), *n.* colouring; arrangement of colours.

coloss'al, *a.* vast, gigantic, huge.

coloss'us, *n.* (pl. *colossi* or *colossuses*), statue of gigantic size; gigantic person or personified power.

col'our (ku'ler), *n.* sensation produced in eye by varying wavelengths of light; any particular hue; pigment; hue of skin of darker, esp. Negro, races; (pl.) flag of regiment or ship. *v.* give colour to; paint or stain or dye; blush. **colour-blind,** unable to distinguish some colours. **col'oured,** *a.* (esp.) Negro, of Negro origin. **col'ourful,** *a.* bright, gay. **col'ouring,** *n.* coloration; artist's use of colour. **colouring matter,** substance which gives colour to something. **col'ourless,** *a.* pale; wanting in character or vividness.

côlt, *n.* young male of horse.

col'umbîne, *n.* cultivated flowering plant.

col'umn (-m), *n.* round pillar, esp. one with base and capital; column-shaped thing; vertical division of page as in newspapers; formation of troops, ships, etc., one behind the other. **col'umnist,** *n.* journalist writing column of general comments.

com-, *pref.* (*com-* before *b*, *p*, *m*; becoming *col-* before *l*, *cor-* before *r*, *con-* before most other consonants; contracted to *co-* before vowels, *h*, and *gn*, see also **co-**), with, together; altogether, completely.

cô'ma, *n.* prolonged complete loss of consciousness caused by illness or injury. **cô'matôse,** *a.* in or like coma.

cômb (-m), *n.* toothed strip of rigid material for disentangling and arranging the hair; thing of similar shape or function, esp. for dressing wool; red fleshy crest of cock, etc.; honeycomb. *v. t.* draw comb through; dress (wool, etc.) with comb; search minutely.

com'bat (*or* ku-), *n.* fight, struggle. *v.* do battle; strive against. **com'batant** *a.* fighting. *n.* fighter. **com'bative,** *a.* wanting to fight, pugnacious.

combe, coomb (kōōm), *n.* deep hollow or valley.

combinâ'tion, *n.* combining; set of things or persons combined; united action; chemical union; (pl.) undergarment for body and legs.

combîne', *v.* join together, unite; enter into chemical union (*with*). **combining form,** special form of word used to form compounds. **com'bîne,** *n.* group of business firms, etc., combined for a purpose. **com'bîne (harvester),** combined reaping and threshing machine.

combus'tible, *a.* capable of burning; easily set

alight. *n.* (pl.) combustible things. **combustibil'ity,** *n.*

combus'tion (-chn), *n.* process of burning; destruction by fire; oxidation.

come (kum), *v. i.* (p.t. *cāme*; p.p. *come*), draw near, advance towards; arrive; occur; become; prove, turn out. **come about,** come in course of events, happen. **come across,** find or meet by chance. **come-back,** retort, return. **come-down,** descent, downfall.

comē'dian, *n.* comic performer; actor in comedy.

comēdienne' (-en), *n.* comic actress.

com'edy, *n.* light, amusing play; branch of drama concerned with comedies.

comely (kum'li), *a.* pleasant to look at. **come'liness,** *n.*

comes'tibles (-lz), *n. pl.* things to eat.

com'ēt, *n.* heavenly body with star-like nucleus and 'tail' of light.

com'fit (kum-), *n.* (*archaic*) a sweet.

com'fort (kum-), *n.* relief in trouble, consolation; being comfortable; (pl.) things that make life pleasant. *v. t.* soothe, console.

com'fortable (kum-), *a.* at ease, free from hardship, pain, and trouble; promoting content. **com'fortably,** *adv.*

com'forter (kum-), *n.* one who comforts; woollen scarf; baby's dummy teat.

com'fortless (kum-), *a.* dreary, cheerless.

com'ic, *a.* of or like comedy; funny; mirth--provoking. *n.* comic actor or person; (children's) periodical consisting largely of pictorial stories. **comic strip,** set of drawings, usu. humorous, forming part of series in newspaper, etc.

com'ical, *a.* laughable; odd, queer. **comical'ity,** *n.*

com'ity, *n.* courtesy. **comity of nations,** friendly recognition by nations of other nations' laws and customs.

comm'a, *n.* punctuation-mark (,).

command' (-ah-), *v.* order; give orders; be in command; hold in check; have control of; look down over. *n.* order given; control, mastery; troops, district, etc., under a commander.

commandant', *n.* commanding officer of depot, particular force, fortress, etc.

commandeer', *v. t.* seize for military use; take arbitrarily.

comman'der (-ah-), *n.* one who commands or has command; naval officer.

comman'ding (-ah-), *a.* in command; impressive; dominant.

command'ment (-ah-), *n.* divine command.

comman'dō (-ah-), *n.* (pl. *commandos*), picked soldier, etc., trained for special missions.

commem'orāte, *v. t.* celebrate in speech or writing or by some ceremony; be a memorial of. **commemorā'tion,** *n.* commemorating; ceremony in memory of an event. **commem'orative,** *a.*

commence', *v.* begin. **commence'ment,** *n.* beginning, start.

commend', *v. t.* praise; speak favourably of; entrust, commit. **commend'able,** *a.* praiseworthy. **commendā'tion,** *n.* praise; act of commending.

commen'surable (-sher-), *a.* measurable by the same standard. **commensurabil'ity,** *n.*

commen'surate (-sher-), *a.* extending over the same space; proportionate.

comm'ent, *n.* explanatory or critical remark. *v. i.* write explanatory notes; make remarks (*upon*).

comm'entary, *n.* explanatory notes on book, etc; series of continuous comments on some public event while it is in progress.

comm'entātor, *n.* speaker of (esp. broadcast) commentary; writer of commentary.

comm'erce, *n.* exchange of merchandise, esp. on a large scale; dealings.

commer'cial (-shl), *a.* of or engaged in commerce; (of radio or television) paid for by revenue from broadcast advertisements. *n.* broadcast advertisement. **commercial traveller,** agent sent out to obtain orders for firm.

comminā'tion, *n.* threatening of divine punishment, cursings. **comm'inatory,** *a.* threatening, denunciatory.

commin'gle (-nggl), *v.* mingle together.

commis'erāte (-z-), *v.* (often with *with*) feel or express pity for. **commiserā'tion,** *n.* pity, compassion. **commis'erative,** *a.*

commissar', *n.* official of Communist party or Soviet government.

commissār'iat, *n.* food and stores department of army; food-supply.

comm'issary, *n.* deputy, delegate; head of commissariat.

commi'ssion (-shn), *n.* act of committing; task entrusted to (person); body of persons appointed to discharge a task; warrant conferring authority on naval, army, or air force officer; percentage on sales, etc. *in commission,* (of ship) manned, armed, and ready for sea. *v. t.* appoint by commission; empower a person to do some service.

commissionaire' (-shun-), *n.* uniformed door--attendant at theatre, hotel, etc.

commi'ssioner (-shun-), *n.* member of a Government board or other commission; representative of supreme authority in district, department, etc.

commit', *v. t.* (p.t. *committed*), entrust; hand over; be guilty of; pledge, involve. **commit'ment,** *n.* engagement that restricts freedom of action.

committ'al, *n.* committing (esp. of person to prison, or body to grave at burial); committing of oneself.

committ'ee, *n.* body of persons appointed for special function by (and usu. out of) larger body.

commōde', *n.* chest of drawers; chamber-pot

enclosed in chair or stool.

commō′dious, a. roomy.

commod′ity, n. useful thing; article of trade.

comm′odore, n. naval officer; courtesy-title for senior captain of ships cruising together, president of yacht club, etc.; senior captain of shipping-line. *Air Commodore*, officer in R.A.F.

comm′on, a. shared by all; of ordinary kind; occurring often; of inferior quality; vulgar; (of noun, etc.) applicable to every individual of class, etc.; (Math.) belonging to two or more quantities. **common law**, unwritten law of England, derived from ancient customs. **common market**, customs union, esp. the *European Economic Community.* **the common people**, ordinary people, below rank of peer. **common sense**, good practical sense in everyday matters. **comm′on**, n. land belonging to community, esp. unenclosed waste land; right over another's land or water. *in common*, in joint use, shared. *in common with*, like.

comm′oner, n. person below rank of peer; person with right of common.

comm′only, adv. usually, frequently.

comm′onplăce, n. trite quotation or everyday saying. a. lacking originality.

comm′ons (-z), n.pl. the common people; food. **(House of) Commons**, lower house of Parliament.

comm′onwealth (-wel-), n. State; group of States. **(British) Commonwealth**, association of Great Britain and certain self-governing nations.

commō′tion, n. noisy confusion.

comm′ūnal, a. of or for the community; for common use; public.

comm′ūne[1], n. smallest administrative division in France, etc.

commūne′[2], v.i. converse intimately *with*.

commū′nicable, a. that may be communicated or imparted.

commū′nicant, n. receiver of Holy Communion; one who gives information.

commū′nicăte, v. impart, transmit, (*to*); have communication (*with*); (of room, etc.) be connected by door, etc., *with*; receive Holy Communion.

commūnică′tion, n. imparting or exchange of information; message, etc., given; connection between places; (pl.) means of communicating.

commū′nicative, a. ready to talk and give information; not reserved.

commū′nion, n. sharing, participation; fellowship. **(Holy) Communion**, (participation in) the Eucharist.

commū′niqué (-kā), n. official announcement or report.

comm′ūnism, n. social system based on common ownership of means of production, distribution, and exchange. **comm′ūnist**, n. & a. **commūnis′tic**, a.

commū′nity, n. body of persons forming political or social unity; body of persons having race, religion, profession, etc., in common. **community centre**, building(s), etc., providing social, recreational, etc., facilities for a neighbourhood.

comm′ūtātor, n. device for altering direction of electrical current.

commūte′, v. exchange, interchange; change (esp. punishment) *to*, *into*, another (less severe); travel regularly, esp. daily, to and from work, etc. **commū′ter**, n.

com′pact[1], n. binding agreement.

compact′[2], a. close, dense; well-knit. v.t. join firmly together; compress, condense. **com′-pact**, n. small flat case for face-powder.

compan′ion, n. one who accompanies another; comrade; mate; thing that matches another; member of lowest grade of order of knighthood. **compan′ionable**, a. sociable. **compan′ionship**, n. fellowship.

compan′ionway, n. staircase from deck to cabin.

com′pany (kum-), n. being with another or others; persons assembled together; guests; body of persons combined for commercial or other purpose; subdivision of infantry battalion; (Naut.) entire crew. *keep company* (*with*), associate (*with*).

com′parable, a. that can be compared (*with*); fit to be compared (*to*).

compa′rative, a. of or involving comparison; (Gram., of adj. or adv.) expressing higher degree of quality, etc., denoted by simple form. n. comparative degree or form.

compāre′, v. liken *to*; estimate similarity of; bear comparison (*with*).

compa′rison, n. comparing; simile. *degrees of comparison*, (Gram.) positive, comparative, and superlative.

compart′ment, n. division; space partitioned off, esp. in railway coach.

com′pass (kum-), n. instrument with magnetized needle which points to magnetic north; *points of the compass*, 32 equidistant points on compass-card with needle's pivot at centre (N., S., E., W., etc.); instrument for describing circles (often pl., also *pair of compasses*); area, extent, range. v.t. go round; surround; bring about.

compa′ssion (-shn), n. pity inclining one to be merciful or helpful. **compa′ssionate**, a. feeling or showing compassion.

compat′ible, a. not contradictory; able to coexist (*with*). **compatibil′ity**, n.

compat′riot, n. fellow-countryman.

compeer′, n. equal, peer; comrade.

compel′, v.t. (p.t. *compelled*), urge irresistibly; bring about by force.

compen′dious, a. brief but comprehensive.

compen′dium, n. (pl. *compendiums* or *compendia*), summary; package of table-games, writing-paper, etc.

com′pensāte, v. counterbalance; give something, esp. money, to make up (*for* loss, injury, etc.). **compensā'tion**, *n.* compensating; something given to compensate (*for*). **com'pensătory**, *a.*

compēte', *v. i.*, strive against others; enter into rivalry (*with*); contend (*for*).

com'pĕtence, *n.* ability; income large enough to live on; means. **com'pĕtency**, *n.* competence.

com'pĕtent, *a.* properly qualified; able.

compĕti'tion, *n.* competing; rivalry; contest. **compet'itive**, *a.* **compet'itor**, *n.*

compīle', *v. t.* collect together (facts, quotations, etc.). **compilā'tion**, *n.*

complā'cency, *n.* self-satisfaction; quiet contentment.

complā'cent, *a.* self-satisfied; contented.

complain', *v. i.* express dissatisfaction or discontent, murmur; state that one is suffering (from illness, etc.); make complaint.

complaint', *n.* statement that one has a grievance or is dissatisfied; formal protest; bodily ailment.

com'plĕment, *n.* that which completes; full number required; (Math.) number of degrees required to make up given angle to 90°. *v. t.* complete; form complement to. **complĕmen'tary**, *a.*

complēte', *a.* having all its parts; finished; thorough. **complēte'ly**, *adv.* wholly; in every way. **complēte'**, *v. t.* finish; make whole or perfect. **complē'tion**, *n.* completing.

com'plex, *a.* consisting of parts; complicated. *n.* complex whole; (Psychol.) group of repressed emotional ideas, etc., influencing person's behaviour.

comple'xion (-kshn), *n.* natural colour and texture of skin, esp. of face; character.

complex'ity, *n.* state of being complex; complicated thing.

complī'ance, *n.* complying; yielding. *in compliance with*, in accordance with. **complī'ant**, *a.*

com'plicāte, *v. t.* make complicated, entangle. **com'plicāted**, *a.* intricate, hard to unravel. **complicā'tion**, *n.* complicated state; complicating circumstance; (Med.) new illness arising during course of disease.

compli'city, *n.* partnership in wrongdoing.

com'pliment, *n.* polite expression of praise; (pl.) formal greetings. *v. t.* pay compliment to (person *on* something). **complimen'tary**, *a.* expressing or conveying compliment; (of tickets, etc.) presented as courtesy.

com'pline, *n.* last service of day (esp. in R.C. Church).

complȳ', *v. i.* act in accordance (*with*).

compō'nent, *a.* going to the making of a whole; constituent. *n.* part.

comport', *v. refl. & i.* behave (oneself); agree or accord *with*.

compōse' (-z), *v. t.* form or constitute; put together in literary or (esp.) musical form; arrange artistically; make tranquil; set up

(type). **compōsed'**, *a.* quiet, calm. **compōs'edly**, *adv.* calmly.

compōs'er (-z-), *n.* one who composes, esp. music.

com'posite (-zit *or* -z̄t), *a.* consisting of various parts or materials; (of plants) with heads made up of many florets, as the daisy.

composi'tion (-z-), *n.* formation, construction; art of composing music; thing composed; essay; compound artificial substance.

compos'itor (-z-), *n.* type-setter.

com'post, *n.* mixture, esp. of decomposed organic matter, used as fertilizer.

compō'sure (-zher), *n.* calmness.

com'pōte, *n.* fruit cooked in syrup.

compound'¹, *v.* mix or combine into a whole; settle by mutual agreement.

com'pound², *a.* made up of two or more parts; not simple; (Chem.) consisting of elements chemically united in fixed proportions. *n.* mixture; compound word; compound substance. **compound interest**, interest reckoned on principal and on accumulations of interest.

com'pound³, *n.* enclosure round building(s), esp. in Eastern countries.

comprehend', *v. t.* grasp mentally, understand; include. **comprehen'sible**, *a.* intelligible. **comprehen'sion** (-shn), *n.* understanding.

comprehen'sive, *a.* including much; of wide scope; (of school) providing all types of secondary education.

compress'¹, *v. t.* squeeze together; force into smaller volume, condense. **compress'ible**, *a.* **compre'ssion** (-shn), **compress'or**, *nn.*

com'press², *n.* pad for compressing artery, etc.; wet bandage.

comprīse' (-z), *v. t.* include; consist of.

com'promīse (-z), *n.* agreement reached by each side giving up part of its claim. *v.* settle (dispute) by mutual concessions; make concessions; bring under suspicion.

compul'sion (-shn), *n.* compelling, being compelled. *under compulsion*, because one is compelled. **compul'sive**, *a.*

compul'sory, *a.* enforced; obligatory.

compunc'tion, *n.* pricking of conscience; feeling of regret.

compūte', *v. t.* calculate, reckon. **compūtā'tion**, *n.*

compū'ter, *n.* electronic apparatus for performing mathematical and logical operations. **compū'terize**, *v. t.* install computer(s) in (office, etc.); operate or solve by computer.

com'rade, *n.* mate or fellow; companion or associate. **com'radeship**, *n.*

con¹, *v. t.* (p.t. *conned*), study, learn.

con², *v. t.* (p.t. *conned*), direct steering of (ship).

con³, *n.* (*slang*) confidence. *v. t.* trick, persuade, (as) by confidence trick.

con⁴: see **pro and con.**

con-, *pref.*: see **com-**.

concatēnā'tion, *n.* series of events, ideas, etc., linked together.

con'cāve, *a.* curved like interior of sphere or circle (opp. **convex**). **concav'ity**, *n.*

conceal', *v.t.* hide or keep secret. **coneal'ment**, *n.*

concēde', *v.t.* admit, allow; grant, yield.

conceit' (-sēt), *n.* over-high opinion of, too much pride in, oneself or one's abilities. **conceit'ĕd**, *a.* full of conceit.

conceive' (-sēv), *v.* become pregnant; form in the mind, imagine; formulate, express. **conceiv'able**, *a.* **conceiv'ably**, *adv.*

con'centrāte, *v.* bring together to one point; focus (attention), keep mind or attention fixed (*on*); increase strength of (solution, etc.), esp. by evaporation. *n.* product of concentration. **concentrā'tion**, *n.* **concentration camp**, camp for detention of political prisoners, etc.

concen'tric, *a.* having a common centre. **concentri'city**, *n.*

con'cept, *n.* idea underlying class of objects; general notion. **concep'tūal**, *a.* of concept or mental conception.

concep'tion, *n.* fertilization of ovum; becoming pregnant; being conceived; thing conceived; idea.

concern', *v.t.* relate to; affect; be relevant to; interest or involve (*oneself*). *n.* thing that concerns one; solicitude, anxiety; business; (pl.) one's affairs. **concerned'** (-nd), *a.* ·involved; troubled. **concern'ing**, *adv.* about.

con'cert¹, *n.* agreement, union; a musical entertainment.

concert'², *v.t.* plan, arrange, together with others. **concert'ĕd**, *a.* agreed upon, done, together.

concerti'na (-tē-), *n.* portable musical instrument with hexagonal bellows, finger-studs, and metal reeds.

concert'ō (-cher- *or* -chār-), *n.* (pl. *concertos*), (Mus.) composition for solo instrument(s) accompanied by orchestra.

conce'ssion, *n.* conceding; thing conceded; monopoly or similar right or privilege. **concessionaire'**, *n.* holder of concession.

conch (*or* -ngk), *n.* (large spiral shell of) marine mollusc. **conchol'ogy** (-ngk-), *n.* study of shells and shellfish.

concil'iāte, *v.t.* appease, win over from hostility; reconcile. **conciliā'tion**, *n.* **concil'iatory**, *a.*

concise', *a.* brief and comprehensive. **concise'ness**, *n.*

con'clāve, *n.* assembly, meeting-place, of cardinals for election of Pope; private or secret assembly.

conclude¹ (-ōōd), *v.* bring or come to an end; reach an opinion; settle.

conclu'sion (-ōōzhn), *n.* ending, close; inference; final opinion. **conclu'sive**, *a.* convincing.

concoct', *v.t.* make up of mixed ingredients; invent (story). **concoc'tion**, *n.*

concom'itant, *a. & n.* accompanying (thing).

con'cord, *n.* agreement; harmony. **concor'dance**, *n.* agreement; index of (chief) words occurring in a book or an author's works. **concor'dant**, *a.* agreeing.

concor'dat, *n.* agreement between church and State.

con'course (-kors), *n.* flocking together; crowd; open space or central hall in large building, railway station, etc.

con'crēte, *a.* having objective reality; not abstract; made of concrete. *n.* (esp.) composition of gravel, cement, etc. *v.* build, pave, etc., with concrete; (*concrēte'*) form into mass, solidify. **concrē'tion**, *n.* forming into mass; solidified mass.

con'cūbine, *n.* woman living with man as his wife but not married to him; (among polygamous peoples) secondary wife. **concū'binage**, *n.*

concū'piscence, *n.* sexual desire, lust. **concū'piscent**, *a.*

concur', *v.i.* (p.t. *concurred*), agree, express agreement, (*with*); happen together. **concu'rrent**, *a.* running together, occurring together; agreeing. **concu'rrence**, *n.*

concu'ssion (-shn), *n.* violent shaking or shock; injury to brain, etc., due to heavy blow, fall, etc.

condemn' (-m), *v.t.* blame; give judgement against; sentence (*to*); pronounce unfit for use. **condemnā'tion**, *n.*

condense', *v.* make denser or briefer; compress; reduce, be reduced, from gas or vapour to liquid. **condensā'tion**, *n.* (liquid formed by) condensing. **conden'ser**, *n.*

condescend', *v.i.* stoop from one's position of dignity or pride; act graciously but in manner that shows one's feeling of superiority. **condescen'ding**, *a.* **condescen'sion** (-shn), *n.*

con'diment, *n.* seasoning (e.g. salt, pepper, etc.) or relish for use with food.

condi'tion, *n.* stipulation; something that must exist or occur if something else is to exist or occur; state; (pl.) circumstances. *v.t.* stipulate; be necessary condition of; bring to desired condition, make physically fit. **condi'tional**, *a.* depending on, containing, a condition; (Gram.) expressing a condition.

condōle', *v.i.* express sympathy (*with* person *on* loss, etc.). **condō'lence**, *n.*

condomin'ium, *n.* joint control of State by two or more others; territory so controlled.

condōne', *v.t.* forgive, overlook (fault, offence). **condonā'tion**, *n.*

condūce', *v.i.* lead or contribute *to*. **condū'cive**, *a.*

con'duct, *n.* behaviour; manner of conducting oneself, business, etc. **conduct'**, *v.* lead, guide; control, manage; behave (*oneself*); (Phys.) transmit (heat, electricity, etc.); **conduc'tion**, *n.* (Phys.) conducting of heat, electricity, etc. **conduc'tive**, *a.* **conductiv'ity**, *n.*

conduc'tor, *n.* director of orchestra or choir; official who collects fares on bus, etc. (fem. **conduc'tress);** thing that conducts (heat, etc.).

con'duit (-dit *or* -dūit; *or* kun-), *n.* channel or pipe; tube protecting electric wires.

cōne, *n.* solid figure tapering from a circular base to a point; dry scaly fruit of pine, fir, etc.; cone-shaped object.

coney: see **cony.**

confab'ūlāte, *v.i.* chat, converse. **confabūlā'tion,** *n.*

confec'tion, *n.* sweet, cake, etc.; prepared dish; article of dress.

confec'tioner, *n.* maker or seller of sweets, cakes, etc. **confec'tionery,** *n.*

confed'eracy, *n.* group of confederated States; league, conspiracy.

confed'erate, *a.* allied. *n.* ally; accomplice. *v.* bring or come into alliance. **confederā'tion,** *n.* permanent union of sovereign States.

confer', *v.* (p.t. *conferred*), meet for discussion; grant, bestow. *confer with,* seek advice from.

con'ference, *n.* (formal meeting for) consultation or discussion.

confer'ment, *n.* bestowing (of honours).

confess', *v.* acknowledge, admit; make formal confession of; (of priest) hear confession of. **confess'ĕdly,** *adv.* as confessed or admitted.

confe'ssion (-shn), *n.* acknowledgement of fact, sin, guilt, etc.; statement of one's principles. **confe'ssional,** *a.* of confession. *n.* enclosed place or stall in which priest hears confession.

confess'or, *n.* priest who hears confession.

confett'i, *n.pl.* bits of coloured paper thrown by wedding guests at bride and bridegroom.

confidant', *n.* (fem. *confidante*), person trusted with another's private affairs.

confide', *v.* impart (secret *to*); entrust *to*; place confidence *in*. **confī'ding,** *a.* trustful, unsuspicious.

con'fidence, *n.* firm trust, sure expectation; imparting of private matter, thing imparted; belief in one's own ability. **confidence trick,** swindle worked by gaining credulous person's trust.

con'fident, *a.* assured; bold; positive.

confiden'tial (-shl), *a.* written, etc., in confidence; entrusted with secrets. **confiden'tially,** *adv.*

configūrā'tion, *n.* shape or outline.

confine'1, *v.t.* keep *within, to,* limits; imprison. *be confined,* (esp.) give birth to child.

con'fine2, *n.* (usu. pl.) boundaries.

confine'ment (-nm-), *n.* being confined; imprisonment; giving birth to child.

confirm', *v.t.* make stronger; corroborate; ratify; administer confirmation to.

confirmā'tion, *n.* corroborating circumstance or statement; rite in which persons confirm vows made for them at baptism.

confirm'ative, confirm'atory, *aa.* strengthening, corroborating.

con'fiscāte, *v.t.* seize private property as penalty or by authority. **confiscā'tion,** *n.*

conflagrā'tion, *n.* great and destructive fire.

con'flict, *n.* fight; collision; clashing (of opposed principles, etc.). **conflict',** *v.i.* be at odds or inconsistent (*with*); struggle.

con'fluent (-floo-), *a.* flowing together, uniting. *n.* stream, etc., flowing into another. **con'fluence,** *n.*

conform', *v.* comply with rules or general custom; adapt, make similar (*to*). **confor'mable,** *a.* adapted or corresponding (*to*). **conformā'tion,** *n.* conforming; structure. **confor'mist,** *n.* one who conforms to usages of Church of England. **confor'mity,** *n.* likeness; compliance.

confound', *v.t.* mix up, confuse; astound; baffle; defeat.

confront' (-unt), *v.t.* bring face to face *with*; face, esp. in hostility. **confrontā'tion,** *n.*

confūse' (-z), *v.t.* throw into disorder; obscure, mix up.

confū'sion (-zhn), *n.* confused state; tumult; discomfiture.

confūte', *v.t.* prove wrong or false. **confūtā'tion,** *n.*

congé (kawn'zhā), *n.* abrupt dismissal. (French)

congeal' (-j-), *v.* become solid by cooling; stiffen, coagulate.

congē'nial (-j-), *a.* suiting one's disposition or tastes; pleasurable *to.* **congēnial'ity,** *n.*

congen'ital (-j-), *a.* belonging to, affecting, person from birth. **congen'itally,** *adv.*

con'ger (eel) (-ngg-), *n.* large sea eel.

conges'ted (-j-), *a.* overcrowded; overcharged with blood.

conges'tion (-jeschn), *n.* overcrowded condition (of population, traffic, etc.); excessive accumulation of blood in a part of the body.

conglom'erate, *a. & n.* (rock) formed of rounded pebbles, etc., sticking together. *v.* (-āt), collect into coherent mass. **conglomerā'tion,** *n.*

congrat'ūlāte, *v.t.* offer expression of pleasure (*on* occasion, event, etc.). **congratūlā'tion,** *n.* congratulating; (pl.) congratulatory expressions. **congrat'ūlātory,** *a.*

cong'rēgāte (-ngg-), *v.* assemble or flock together, meet in a large body.

congrēgā'tion (-ngg-), *n.* assemblage, esp. of persons taking part in religious worship. **congrēgā'tional,** *a.* of congregation. **Congrēgā'tional,** *a.* of Congregationalism. **Congrēgā'tionalism,** *n.* system by which individual churches are self-governing. **Congrēgā'tionalist,** *n.*

cong'ress (-ngg-), *n.* formal meeting of delegates for discussion; *Cong'ress,* national legislative body of U.S.A., etc. **congre'ssional** (-shun-), *a.*

cong'ruence (-nggroo-), **congru'ity** (-ōō-), *nn.* agreement; harmonious relation. **cong'-**

ruent, cong'ruous, aa.

con'ic, a. of cone; cone-shaped. con'ical, a. cone-shaped.

cō'nifer, n. tree bearing cones. conif'erous, a. cone-bearing.

conjec'tural a. depending on conjecture.

conjec'ture n. opinion formed on incomplete evidence; guess. v. make conjecture.

conjoin', v. join together, unite. conjoint' (or con'-), a. conjoined, combined.

con'jugal (-joo-), a. of marriage; of husband and wife.

con'jugate (-joo-), v.t. inflect (verb) in voice, mood, tense, number, and person; join together. conjuga'tion, n. inflection scheme of verbs; class of verbs; joining together.

conjunc'tion, n. union, connection; word used to connect other words, clauses or sentences.

conjuncti'va, n. mucous membrane lining eyelid. conjunctivi'tis, n. inflammation of this.

conjunc'tive, a. serving to join or unite.

conjunc'ture, n. position of affairs at a particular moment.

conjura'tion, n. solemn appeal.

conjure'[1] (-oor), v.t. request earnestly.

conjure[2] (kun'jer), v. produce magical effects; do sleight-of-hand tricks. conjure up, bring before the imagination.

con'jurer, con'juror (kun'jerer), n. skilled performer of conjuring tricks.

con'ker, n. horse-chestnut.

connect', v. join, fasten, or link together. connec'tive, a. serving as connection.

connec'tion, conne'xion, n. being linked together or in communication; connecting part; connecting train, boat, etc.; family relationship.

conn'ing-tower, n. superstructure of submarine, used for navigation, etc., on or near surface.

connive', v.i. connive at, tolerate, disregard, (misbehaviour). conni'vance, n.

connoisseur (koniser'), n. critical judge, esp. of the fine arts.

connōte', v.t. imply; include in its meaning. connota'tion, n.

connū'bial, a. of or relating to marriage.

con'quer (-ngker), v. defeat; overcome; take possession of by force. con'queror, n.

con'quest, n. what is won by conquering; winning of person's affections, person so won.

consanguin'ity (-nggw-), n. kinship.

con'science (-shens), n. moral sense of right and wrong; awareness of moral quality of one's actions and motives. conscience-stricken, overcome with remorse.

conscien'tious (-shi-en'shus), a. obedient to conscience; scrupulous. conscientious objector, person who objects to service in armed forces on grounds of conscience.

con'scious (-shus), a. having physical and mental faculties awake and active; aware, knowing. con'sciously, adv. con'sciousness, n.

con'script, n. one who is compulsorily enrolled in armed forces. conscript', v.t. enrol compulsorily. conscrip'tion, n. compulsory enlistment for service in army, navy, or air force.

con'sēcrate, v.t. set apart as sacred (to); sanctify; devote to (purpose). consēcra'tion, n. consecrating, being consecrated; dedication.

consec'ūtive, a. following continuously.

consen'sus, n. agreement (of opinion, etc.).

consent', v.t. express willingness (to), agree (to). n. voluntary agreement, compliance; permission.

con'sequence, n. that which follows as result or effect of something; importance; influential position.

con'sequent, a. that results; following as consequence.

consequen'tial (-shl), a. following as result or inference; self-important.

con'sequently, adv. as a result; therefore.

conser'vancy, n. commission controlling river, etc.; preservation (of forests, etc.).

conserva'tion, n. preserving, conserving.

conser'vative, a. opposed to change; (of estimate) moderate; (of, belonging to, Conservative Party. n. member of Conservative Party. Conservative Party, English political party believing in maintenance of existing institutions, individual liberty, etc. conser'vatism, n.

conser'vatoire (-twahr), n. public institution in France, etc., for teaching music, etc.

con'servator, n. preserver; custodian.

conser'vatory, n. greenhouse for tender plants; conservatoire.

conserve', v.t. preserve; keep from harm, decay, or loss. n. fruit, etc., preserved in sugar; jam.

consid'er, v. contemplate; think carefully about; reckon with, allow for; be of the opinion; show thoughtfulness for.

consid'erable, a. important; great; much.

consid'erate, a. thoughtful for others.

considera'tion, n. considering; serious thought; fact, thing, regarded as a reason; payment; thoughtfulness for others.

consid'ering, prep. in view of.

consign' (-īn), v.t. commit or hand over; transmit, send. consign'ment, n. consigning; goods sent in one lot. consignee', consign'or, nn. person to whom, by whom, goods are consigned.

consist', v.i. be composed of; be comprised or contained in.

consis'tence, n. degree of denseness, esp. of thick liquids; firmness, solidity. consis'tency, n. consistence; being consistent.

consis'tent, a. not contradictory; constant to same principles.

consōl'able, a. capable of being consoled.

consolā'tion, *n.* consoling; alleviation of grief or disappointment. **consol'atory** (*or* -sōl-), *a.* consoling, comforting.

consōle'[1], *v.t.* comfort, soothe.

con'sōle[2], *n.* bracket supporting cornice; frame containing keyboard, stops, etc., of organ.

consol'idāte, *v.* make or become solid; strengthen; combine into one. **consolidā'tion**, *n.*

consommé (konsom'ā), *n.* clear soup.

con'sonance, *n.* agreement, harmony.

con'sonant, *a.* agreeable *to*; harmonious *with*. *n.* (letter denoting) speech sound other than vowel.

con'sort, *n.* husband or wife, esp. of ruler; partner. **consort'**, *v.i.* associate or keep company (*with*); be in harmony.

conspic'ūous, *a.* striking to the eye; readily seen; outstanding.

conspi'racy, *n.* plot or plotting together for evil purpose. **conspi'rator**, *n.*

conspire', *v.i.* form or take part in conspiracy; agree together.

con'stable (kun-), *n.* officer of police force, esp. (*police constable*) policeman of lowest rank; (Hist.) great officer of royal household. **constab'ūlary**, *a. & n.* (organized body) of police.

con'stancy, *n.* faithfulness; firmness; steadiness.

con'stant, *a.* unchanging; faithful; resolute. *n.* quantity that does not vary. **con'stantly**, *adv.* always; often.

constellā'tion, *n.* fixed stars forming group.

consternā'tion, *n.* dismay; horrified amazement.

con'stipāte, *v.t.* affect with constipation. **constipā'tion**, *n.* difficulty in evacuating the bowels.

constit'ūency, *n.* body of voters who elect representative member (esp. Member of Parliament); place so represented.

constit'ūent, *a.* making part of whole; electing. *n.* part; voter.

con'stitūte, *v.t.* appoint, make into; establish; be essence or components of.

constitū'tion, *n.* constituent parts, essential nature; nature of the body in regard to healthiness, strength, etc.; temperament; form in which State is organized.

constitū'tional, *a.* of or due to one's constitution; in harmony with constitution of State. *n.* walk taken as healthy exercise.

constrain', *v.t.* compel; hinder by force. **constrained'** (-nd), *a.* forced; not natural; embarrassed.

constraint', *n.* compulsion; confinement; repression of natural feelings; embarrassment.

constrict', *v.t.* compress, contract; encircle and squeeze. **constric'tion**, *n.*

construct', *v.t.* fit together; build.

construc'tion, *n.* thing constructed; interpretation. **construc'tional**, *a.*

construc'tive, *a.* of a positive or helpful kind.

construe' (-ōō; *or* kon'-), *v.* translate word for word; interpret; combine grammatically *with*.

con'sul, *n.* State's agent in foreign town; either of two chief magistrates in ancient Roman republic. **con'sular**, *a.* **con'sūlate**, *n.* office or establishment of consul.

consult', *v.* seek information or advice from; confer *with*. **consult'ant**, *a. & n.* (physician, etc.) to whom others refer their patients for advice; (engineer, etc.) giving expert advice. **consultā'tion**, *n.* **consul'tative**, *a.*

consūme', *v.* eat or drink; use up; destroy (by fire, wasting). *be consumed with*, be filled with (envy, curiosity, grief, etc.).

consū'mer, *n.* buyer and user of product or service.

consumm'āte[1], *a.* perfect; complete.

con'summāte[2], *v.t.* complete (esp. marriage by sexual intercourse). **consummā'tion**, *n.*

consump'tion, *n.* consuming; wasting disease, esp. tuberculosis of lungs. **consump'tive**, *a. & n.* (person) affected with tuberculosis.

con'tact, *n.* touch, touching; connection; (state of) being in communication; (esp. useful) acquaintance; (Med.) person who has been exposed to infectious disease. *v.t.* get into contact with (person).

contā'gion (-jn), *n.* communication of disease by direct or indirect contact; corrupting influence. **contā'gious** (-jus), *a.*

contain', *v.t.* have within, hold; include; hold under control. **contai'ner**, *n.* receptacle; large receptacle for transporting goods by road, rail, or sea.

contam'ināte, *v.t.* make dirty or impure; infect. **contaminā'tion**, *n.*

con'templāte, *v.t.* survey steadily with eyes or mind; intend. **contemplā'tion**, *n.* contemplating; meditative state. **contem'plative**, *a.* meditative, thoughtful.

contemporā'nèous, *a.* belonging to, existing at, the same time.

contem'porary, *a.* of these times; equal in age; contemporaneous. *n.* contemporary person.

contempt', *n.* act, mental attitude, of despising; disobedience to lawful authority. **contemp'tible**, *a.* deserving contempt. **contemp'tūous**, *a.* feeling or showing contempt; insolent.

contend', *v.* strive; struggle; compete, argue (*with*); maintain (*that*).

content'[1], *a.* satisfied; pleased, willing. *v.t.* satisfy. *n.* contented state, satisfaction. **conten'ted**, *a.* satisfied, happy. **conten'tedness**, **content'ment**, *nn.*

con'tent[2], *n.* capacity, amount contained; (pl.) what is contained.

conten'tion, *n.* contending; strife; point contended; claim. **conten'tious** (-shus), *a.* quarrelsome; likely to cause contention.

con'test, *n.* competition; dispute; strife. **con-**

test', _v.t._ dispute; contend or compete for. **contes'tant**, _n._

con'text, _n._ what precedes or follows word or passage and helps to fix meaning.

contigū'ity, _n._ contact; nearness. **contig'- ūous**, _a._ touching; next (_to_); neighbouring.

con'tinent[1], _a._ self-restraining; chaste. **con'tinence**, _n._

con'tinent[2], _n._ any of the main land masses of the earth. _the Continent_, the mainland of Europe. **continen'tal**, _a._ of or characteristic of continent or the Continent.

contin'gency (-j-), _n._ contingent event, etc; chance occurrence.

contin'gent (-j-), _a._ of uncertain occurrence; incidental; dependent (_on_); conditional. _n._ body or group contributed to army, larger group, etc.

contin'ūal, _a._ occurring on every occasion; seeming incessant.

contin'ūance, _n._ continuing in existence or operation; duration.

continūā'tion, _n._ going on with or resuming something; thing that continues something else.

contin'ūe, _v._ go on with; take up again; remain in existence. **continū'ity**, _n._ uninterrupted connection or series.

contin'ūō, _n._ (Mus.) bass accompaniment to oratorio, etc.; instrument(s) playing this.

contin'ūous, _a._ unbroken; uninterrupted.

contort', _v.t._ twist or force out of normal shape. **contor'tion**, _n._ **contor'tionist**, _n._ acrobat adopting contorted postures.

con'tour (-oor), _n._ outline of figure, object, coast, etc. **contour (line)**, line drawn on map joining all points at given elevation.

contra-, _pref._ against; (in names of musical instruments) an octave below in pitch.

con'traband, _n._ prohibited trading, smuggling; smuggled goods. _a._ forbidden to be imported or exported.

contracep'tion, _n._ prevention of conception in womb, birth-control. **contracep'tive**, _a._ & _n._ (drug or device) preventing conception.

con'tract[1], _n._ mutual, esp. business, agreement; agreement enforceable by law.

contract'[2], _v._ make contract; incur (disease, debt); draw together; make or become smaller; shorten.

contrac'tion, _n._ contracting; shrinking; shortening of word.

contrac'tor, _n._ one who undertakes contract, esp. in building, etc., or for public body.

contrac'tūal, _a._ of (nature of) contract.

contradict', _v.t._ deny; oppose verbally; be at variance with. **contradic'tion**, _n._ denial; direct opposition; inconsistency. **contradic'tory**, _a._ contradicting; conflicting.

contradistinc'tion, _n._ distinction by opposite qualities.

contral'tō, _n._ (pl. _contraltos_), (singer having) lowest female voice.

contrap'tion, _n._ (_informal_) strange-looking apparatus or contrivance.

contrapun'tal, _a._ of or in counterpoint.

contrarī'ety, _n._ contrariness.

con'trariwise (-z; _or_ kontrār'-), _adv._ on the other hand; in the opposite way.

con'trary, _a._ opposed in nature or tendency or direction; (_contrār'y_), self-willed, perverse. _n. the_ opposite. _adv._ in opposition (_to_).

con'trast (-ah-), _n._ difference between things as shown by direct comparison; thing showing a striking difference to another. **contrast'** (-ah-), _v._ put in, subject to, contrast; show striking difference.

contravēne', _v.t._ break (rule, etc.); conflict with. **contraven'tion**, _n._

contretemps (kawn'tritahn), _n._ unfortunate happening; set-back. (French)

contrib'ūte, _v._ give, pay to a common fund, etc. _contribute to_, have part or share in. **contribū'tion**, _n._ payment to a common fund; thing, help, contributed.

contrib'ūtor, _n._ one who contributes (esp. literary articles). **contrib'ūtory**, _a._ that contributes; contributing.

con'trīte, _a._ deeply penitent. **contri'tion**, _n._ sorrow for sin.

contrī'vance, _n._ contriving; contrived article or appliance.

contrive', _v._ devise, plan, skilfully; bring about, manage.

con'trōl, _n._ power of command; restraint; check; supervision; device or mechanism for controlling. _v.t._ (p.t. _controlled_), have control of; govern; restrain. **contrō'llable**, _a._

controver'sial (-shl), _a._ of, leading to, or enjoying, controversy.

con'troversy (_or_ kontrov'-), _n._ dispute, contention; prolonged argument.

con'trovert (_or_ -vert'), _v.t._ dispute about; deny.

con'tūmacy, _n._ stubborn disobedience. **contūmā'cious**, _a._

con'tūmely, _n._ insulting language or treatment. **contūmēl'ious**, _a._

contūse' (-z), _v.t._ bruise.

contū'sion (-zhn), _n._ bruise.

conun'drum, _n._ riddle, puzzle.

conurbā'tion, _n._ group of towns united by expansion.

convalesce', _v.i._ be convalescent. **convales'cence**, _n._ gradual recovery of health after illness. **convales'cent**, _n._ & _a._ (person) recovering from illness.

convec'tion, _n._ (Phys.) conveyance of heat by (usu. upward) movement of heated substance, as air or water. **convec'tor**, _n._ appliance that warms room by convection.

convēne', _v._ summon; assemble (for a meeting, etc.). **convē'ner**, _n._ (esp.) person appointed to convene meetings of committee, etc.

convē'nience, _n._ that which is convenient or suitable; advantage; useful appliance; (esp. public) lavatory.

convĕ′nĭĕnt, *a.* suitable, fit; well-adapted; within easy reach.

con′vent, *n.* religious community, esp. of women; its building.

conven′ticle, *n.* (Hist.) meeting or meeting-house, esp. of religious dissenters.

conven′tion, *n.* formal assembly; agreement or covenant; accepted custom. **conven′-tional**, *a.* in accordance with social custom. **conventional′ity**, *n.*

converge′, *v. i.* tend to meet in a point; approach nearer together. **conver′gence**, *n.* **conver′gent**, *a.*

conver′sant (*or* kon′-), *a.* well-acquainted *with* (subject).

conversā′tion, *n.* talk, interchange of thought and words. **conversā′tional**, *a.* **conversā′-tionalist**, *n.* good talker.

converse′¹, *v. i.* talk.

con′verse², *a.* opposite, contrary. *n.* converse statement or position. **converse′ly**, *adv.*

conver′sion (-shn), *n.* converting; being converted.

convert′, *v. t.* change (from one form, use, etc., *into, to,* another); cause to turn (*to* faith, opinion, etc.); (Rugby footb.) kick goal from (try). **con′vert**, *n.* person converted, esp. to religious faith.

conver′tible, *a.* that can be converted.

con′vex, *a.* curved like outside of sphere or circle (opp. **concave**). **convex′ity**, *n.*

convey′ (-vā), *v. t.* transport, carry; transmit; impart, communicate (idea, meaning); transfer by deed or legal process.

convey′ance (-vāans), *n.* conveying; means of conveying, vehicle, carriage; document transferring property. **convey′ancing**, *n.* (Law) preparation of documents transferring property.

convey′er, convey′or (-vāer), *n.* person or thing that conveys. **convey′or(-belt)**, endless band running over rollers for conveying objects or material, esp. in factory.

convict′¹, *v. t.* prove or declare guilty.

con′vict², *n.* criminal undergoing prison sentence.

convic′tion, *n.* convicting; verdict of guilty; convincing; firm belief.

convince′, *v. t.* cause to acknowledge truth *of*; bring to a belief.

conviv′ial, *a.* festive; jovial.

convocā′tion, *n.* convoking, calling together; assembly.

convōke′, *v. t.* call together; summon to assemble.

con′volŭte, con′volŭted, *aa.* coiled or spiral. **convolŭ′tion**, *n.* coiled state; one turn of coil or spiral.

convol′vŭlus, *n.* twining plant with trumpet-shaped flowers.

con′voy, *v. t.* escort, esp. ships, with armed force. *n.* an escort; number of ships, etc., under escort.

convulse′, *v. t.* cause violent movements or convulsions. **convul′sion** (-shn), *n.* violent and involuntary contraction of the muscles; upheaval, disturbance; (pl.) fit of laughter. **convul′sive**, *a.*

cō′ny, cō′ney, *n.* (pl. *conies, coneys*), rabbit (now only as shop name of fur).

cōō, *n.* & *v. i.* (make) soft murmuring sound (as) of doves.

cook, *v.* prepare food by the application of heat; undergo cooking. *n.* one who cooks; person employed to cook.

cook′er, *n.* stove or vessel for cooking; fruit, etc., suitable for cooking.

cook′ery, *n.* art and practice of cooking.

cōōl, *a.* moderately cold; calm, self-possessed; lacking zeal or warmth. *v.* make or become cool. **cōōl′ly** (-l-li), *adv.* **cōōl′-ness**, *n.*

cōō′lie, *n.* unskilled labourer or porter in Eastern countries.

coomb: see **combe**.

cōōp, *n.* cage or pen for fowls. *v. t.* put in coop; shut (*up*) in small space.

cō-op′, *n.* (*informal*) co-operative society or store.

cōōp′er, *n.* maker or mender of casks, barrels, etc. *v. t.* repair (casks, etc.). **coop′erage**, *n.* cooper's work(-shop) or charges.

cō-op′erāte, *v. i.* work or act together for a common purpose. **cō-operā′tion**, *n.*

cō-op′erative, *a.* co-operating, willing to co-operate, helpful. *n.* co-operative association or enterprise. **co-operative society**, trading, etc., organization in which profits are shared among members, esp. as dividend on purchases.

cō-opt′, *v. t.* elect (to committee, etc.) by votes of existing members. **co-op′tion**, *n.*

cō-or′dinate, *a.* equal in rank. **cō-or′dinate**, *v. t.* make co-ordinate; bring (parts of system) into proper relation. **cō-ordinā′tion**, *n.*

cōōt, *n.* water-bird with white shield above bill.

cōpe¹, *n.* vestment like long semicircular cloak. *v. t.* provide with cope or coping.

cōpe², *v. i.* contend on even terms or successfully (*with*).

cō′peck, *n.* Russian coin, hundredth part of rouble.

cō′ping, *n.* top course of masonry or brickwork in wall. **coping-stone**, *n.* stone used in coping; finishing touch.

cō′pious, *a.* plentiful; abundant.

copp′er, *n.* metal of reddish-brown colour; bronze coin, penny; washing boiler. *v. t.* cover with copper. **copp′erplāte**, (*n.*) copper plate for engraving or etching; print taken from it; (*a.*) (of writing) flowing, neat, and regular.

copp′ice, copse, *n.* small wood of small trees grown for periodical cutting.

cop′ra, *n.* dried kernels of coconut.

copse: see **coppice**.

cop′ŭla, *n.* (Gram.) verb (esp. part of *to be*)

connecting subject and predicate.

cop′ūlăte, *v. i.* unite in coitus (*with*). **copūlā′tion**, *n.* **cop′ūlatory**, *a.*

cop′y, *n.* reproduction (of writing, picture, etc.); imitation; one example of edition of book, etc.; matter to be set up in type. *v.* make a copy of; imitate; crib. **copy-book**, book of handwriting exercises.

cop′yist, *n.* one who copies or transcribes.

cop′yright (-rīt), *n.* sole right to produce or reproduce literary, musical, etc., work by making copies or by performance, etc. *a.* protected by copyright. *v. t.* secure copyright of.

cŏ′quetry (-kit-), *n.* coquettish behaviour.

coquette′ (-ket), *n.* woman who flirts. *v. i.* flirt (*with*). **coquett′ish**, *a.*

cor-, *pref.*: see **com-**.

co′racle, *n.* wicker boat covered with watertight material.

co′ral, *n.* hard substance secreted by sea creatures of simple structure; piece of coral as ornament, etc. *a.* of, of (red) colour of, coral. **coral island**, one formed by growth of coral.

co′ralline, *a.* of or like coral.

cor anglais (ahṅg′glā), wood-wind instrument resembling oboe but with lower pitch.

cor′bel, *n.* piece of stone or timber jutting out from wall to support weight.

cord, *n.* length of several threads or strands twisted together; measure of cut wood; cord-like structure in animal body. *v. t.* secure with cord. **cor′dage**, *n.* ropes or cords, esp. in rigging of ship. **cor′ded**, *a.* (esp. of fabric) having ribbed appearance.

cor′date, *a.* (Bot.) heart-shaped.

cor′dial, *a.* heartfelt, sincere, warm; stimulating. *n.* stimulating drink. **cordial′ity**, *n.*

cor′dīte, *n.* smokeless explosive.

cor′don, *n.* line or ring of police, etc.; ornamental cord.

cordon bleu (kor′dawṅ bler), (pl. *cordons bleus*, pr. same), first-class cook. (French)

cor′duroy, *n.* ribbed cotton velvet.

core, *n.* heart or innermost part of anything; horny capsule containing seeds of apple, etc. *v. t.* remove the core from.

cō-rèspon′dent, *n.* person proceeded against together with respondent in divorce suit.

cor′gi (-gi), *n.* (pl. *corgis* or *corgwyn*), small short-legged dog of Welsh origin.

cork, *n.* bark of the *cork-oak*; piece of this used as bottle-stopper, float, etc. *a.* made of cork. *v. t.* close (*up*) with or as with cork.

cork′screw (-ōō), *n.* implement for pulling out corks. *v.* twist or (cause to) proceed spirally.

corm, *n.* swollen underground base of stem in crocus, etc.

cor′morant, *n.* large greedy sea-bird.

corn[1], *n.* grain or seed of cereal plant; cereals (esp. wheat) in growth, their seed after threshing; (U.S.) maize. *v. t.* preserve (meat) with salt. **corn′crake**, bird with hoarse

croaking cry. **corn′flour**, fine-ground maize flour. **corn′flower**, blue-flowered plant.

corn[2], *n.* horny tender place with hard centre, esp. on foot.

cor′nèa, *n.* transparent part of covering of eyeball in front of iris.

cornē′lian, carnē′lian, *n.* red or reddish variety of chalcedony.

cor′ner, *n.* angle of room, box, etc.; remote place; buying up of whole of commodity by one person or organization for re-selling. *v. t.* drive into a corner; establish corner in (commodity). **corner-stōne**, one of stones forming external angle of wall; indispensable part.

cor′nèt, *n.* brass wind instrument of trumpet family; conical wafer for holding ice-cream.

cor′nice, *n.* moulding of room wall just below ceiling; overhanging mass of hardened snow on mountain precipice.

cornūcō′pia, *n.* horn of plenty, represented as goat's horn overflowing with flowers, fruit, and corn, as symbol of abundance.

coroll′a, *n.* whorl of petals forming inner envelope of flower.

coroll′ary, *n.* proposition that follows directly from one already proved; natural consequence.

corō′na, *n.* halo of white light round sun, seen in total eclipse.

co′ronach (-*ch*), *n.* Highland dirge.

co′ronary, *a.* resembling, encircling like, crown. **coronary artery**, one supplying blood to heart tissues. **coronary thrombosis**, blocking of coronary artery by blood clot.

coronā′tion (ko-r-), *n.* ceremony of crowning king or queen.

co′roner, *n.* public official holding inquest on corpse to find out cause of death, or on treasure trove to ascertain owner.

co′ronèt, *n.* small crown.

cor′poral[1], *n.* non-commissioned officer of lowest rank, below sergeant.

cor′poral[2], *a.* of the body. **corporal punishment**, beating, whipping.

cor′porate, *a.* of or forming one body of many individuals.

corporā′tion, *n.* body of persons authorized to act as individual; mayor, aldermen, and councillors of borough, etc.

corpor′èal, *a.* having a body; material.

corps (kor), *n.* (pl. same, pr. korz), military force; organized body. **corps de ballet**, body of dancers in ballet (not soloists).

corpse, *n.* dead (usu. human) body.

cor′pūlence, *n.* bulkiness of body. **cor′pūlent**, *a.* fat.

cor′puscle (-sl), *n.* microscopic or minute body, particle. **corpus′cūlar**, *a.*

corral′, *n.* enclosure for cattle, etc. *v. t.* (p.t. *corralled*), put in corral.

correct′, *a.* in accordance with the facts; accurate; right, proper. *v. t.* make or set right (error or fault); reprove; counteract or neutralize. **correct'ly**, *adv.* **correct'ness**, *n.*

correc'tion, *n.* correcting; thing substituted for what is wrong; punishment.

correc'titude, *n.* correct behaviour.

correc'tive, *a. & n.* (thing) serving to correct.

co'rrĕlăte, *v.* have or bring into mutual relation (*with, to*). **corrĕlā'tion**, *n.* mutual relationship. **corre'lative**, *a.*

correspond' (ko-r-), *v.i.* be similar (*to*); be in agreement or harmony (*with*); be analogous (*to*); exchange letters (*with*). **correspon'-dence**, *n.* exchange of letters; letters; agreement, similarity; analogy. **correspon'dent**, *a.* corresponding. *n.* one who writes letter(s) to another or to newspaper, or contributes to newspaper, esp. from abroad.

co'rridor, *n.* long passage from which doors open into rooms or compartments; narrow passage, strip of land, etc.

corrigen'dum (ko-r-), *n.* (pl. *corrigenda*), thing to be corrected, esp. in book.

co'rrigible, *a.* that can be corrected.

corrob'orăte, *v.t.* give support to; confirm. **corroborā'tion**, *n.* **corrob'orative**, *a.*

corrōde', *v.* affect with or suffer corrosion; eat into. **corrō'sion** (-zhn), *n.* wearing away or gradual destruction from surface inwards. **corrō'sive**, *a.* producing corrosion. *n.* corrosive agent.

co'rrugăte (-oo-), *v.* wrinkle; bend into wavy ridges. **corrugā'tion**, *n.*

corrupt', *a.* rotten; depraved, immoral; influenced by bribery. *v.* make corrupt; bribe; rot, decompose. **corrupt'ible**, *a.*

corrup'tion, *n.* corrupting; decay; wickedness.

cor'sair, *n.* privateer; pirate-ship.

cor'sĕt, *n.* close-fitting, usu. stiffened, undergarment for waist and hips.

cors'lĕt, corse'lĕt (-sl-), *n.* (Hist.) piece of armour covering body. **corse'lĕt(te)**, *n.* woman's undergarment combining corset and brassière.

cortège (-āzh'), *n.* (esp. funeral) procession.

cor'tex, *n.* outer covering, esp. outer grey matter of brain; inner bark.

co'ruscăte, *v.i.* sparkle, flash. **coruscā'tion**, *n.*

corvette', *n.* small fast naval escort vessel.

cos[1], *n.* crisp long-leaved lettuce.

cos[2] (-z), *abbrev.* cosine.

cōsē'cant (*or* -se-), *n.* (Trig., abbrev. *cosec*) reciprocal of sine.

cosh, *n.* (*informal*) short heavy stick used as weapon. *v.t.* strike with cosh.

cō'sĭne, *n.* (Trig., abbrev. *cos*) sine of complement of given angle.

cosmet'ic (-z-), *a. & n.* (preparation) designed to beautify complexion, hair, etc.

cos'mic (-z-), *a.* of the cosmos. **cosmic rays**, high energy radiations originating in outer space.

cosmog'raphy (-z-), *n.* description, mapping, of universe or earth. **cosmograph'ic(al)**, *aa.*

cosmol'ogy (-z-), *n.* study or philosophy of the universe. **cosmolo'gical**, *a.*

cos'monaut (-z-), *n.* (esp. Russian) astronaut.

cosmopol'itan (-z-), *a.* of all parts of world; free from national limitations. *n.* cosmopolitan person. **cosmopol'itanism**, *n.*

cos'mos (-z-), *n.* universe as ordered whole; ordered system of ideas, etc.; all stars in existence.

Coss'ack, *n.* one (of descendants) of settlers on Russian frontiers, famous as horsemen.

coss'ĕt, *v.t.* pamper, pet.

cost, *v.t.* (p.t. *cost*), have as price; involve payment or sacrifice of; estimate price of. *n.* what thing costs; (pl.) legal expenses.

cos'ter(monger) (-mungg-), *n.* street-seller of fruit, etc., from barrow.

cos'tive, *a.* constipated.

cost'ly, *a.* of great value; expensive. **cost'-liness**, *n.*

cos'tŭme, *n.* style of dress; historical, national, etc., clothes worn on stage, at fancy-dress ball, etc.; woman's suit. **cos-tŭm'ier**, *n.* maker of, dealer in, costumes.

cō'sy (-z-), *a.* comfortable, snug.

cot[1], *n.* (Poet.) cottage; cote.

cot[2], *n.* child's bed (with sides); light bedstead; (Naut.) bed suspended like hammock.

cot[3], *abbrev.* cotangent.

cōtan'gent (-j-), *n.* (Trig., abbrev. *cot*) reciprocal of tangent.

cōte, *n.* shelter for animals, etc.

cō'terie, *n.* select set or circle of people.

cotill'ion, cotill'on, (-lyon), *n.* ballroom dance with elaborate steps, etc., popular in 19th century.

cott'age, *n.* small house, esp. in the country. **cott'ager**, *n.* one who lives in a cottage.

cott'ar, *n.* Scottish farm-labourer living in cottage on farm.

cott'on, *n.* white downy fibrous covering of seeds of cotton-plant; thread spun, cloth made, from this. **cotton wool**, raw cotton, esp. as prepared for wadding, etc.

cotylē'don, *n.* seed leaf of some plants.

couch, *n.* long piece of furniture for lying or sitting on; sofa. *v.* (of animal) lie ready to spring; express *in* words, etc.

couch'-grass (-ahs; *or* kŏō-), *n.* grass with long creeping underground stems.

couch'ant, *a.* (Herald.) in couching position.

cou'gar (kŏō-), *n.* (U.S.) puma.

cough (kof), *v.* expel air from lungs violently and noisily. *n.* (sound of) coughing.

could, *p.t.* of **can**[2].

coulomb (kŏō'lom), *n.* unit of electric charge.

coul'ter (kōl-), *n.* blade in front of plough-share making vertical cut in soil.

coun'cil, *n.* body of persons elected or appointed to advise and make decisions; local administrative body of town, county, etc.

coun'cillor, *n.* member of a council.

coun'sel, *n.* deliberation, consultation;

advice; barrister. *v. t.* advise.

coun'sellor, *n.* adviser.

count[1], *v.* repeat numerals in order; reckon (*up*); include or be included in reckoning. *count down*, count seconds, etc., backwards to zero as time for launching of spacecraft, etc. **count-down,** *n.* **count**[1], *n.* counting; reckoning; total; each charge in indictment.

count[2], *n.* title of foreign nobility.

coun'tenance, *n.* face; expression of face. *v. t.* sanction; encourage.

coun'ter[1], *n.* small disc, etc., used in scoring at cards, etc.; long table for transaction of business in shop or bank.

coun'ter[2], *a.* opposed; opposite. *adv.* in opposite direction; contrary. *v.* oppose; meet with answering move.

counter-, *pref.* against, opposing; reciprocating; opposite in position or direction; corresponding.

counteract', *v. t.* hinder, defeat, by contrary action.

coun'ter-attack, *v. & n.* attack in reply to enemy's attack.

coun'ter-attrac'tion, *n.* rival attraction.

coun'terbalance, *n.* weight, force, balancing another. *v. t.* act as counterbalance to.

coun'terblast (-ah-), *n.* energetic declaration against something.

coun'tercharge, *n. & v.* (bring) charge against accuser.

coun'ter-claim, *n.* claim set up against another.

coun'ter-clock'wise (-z), *adv. & a.* anti-clockwise.

coun'terfeit (*or* -fit), *a.* made in imitation; not genuine; forged. *n.* counterfeit thing. *v. t.* imitate; forge.

coun'terfoil, *n.* part of cheque, receipt, etc., kept as record.

coun'termand (-ah-), *v. t.* cancel (command). *n.* order issued cancelling previous one.

coun'termarch, *n. & v.* (cause to) march in the contrary direction.

coun'terpane, *n.* bedspread, coverlet, quilt.

coun'terpart, *n.* person or thing exactly like or forming complement to another.

coun'terplot, *n.* plot contrived to defeat another. *v. i.* make counterplot.

coun'terpoint, *n.* (Mus.) melody added as accompaniment to given melody; combination of parts or melodies, each retaining its identity.

coun'terpoise (-z), *n.* counterbalancing weight or force. *v. t.* counterbalance; bring into or keep in equilibrium.

coun'tersign (-īn), *n.* word to be given in answer to sentry's challenge. *v. t.* add confirming signature to.

coun'tersink, *v. t.* (p.t. *countersank*; p.p. *countersunk*), bevel (top of hole) to receive head of screw, etc.; sink (screw, etc.) in such hole.

counter-ten'or, *n.* (musical part for, singer with) male voice of alto range.

coun'tess, *n.* wife, widow, of count or earl; lady ranking with count or earl.

coun'ting-house, *n.* building, room, devoted to book-keeping.

count'less, *a.* too many to count.

coun'trified, (kun-; -īd), rustic, rural.

coun'try (kun-), *n.* territory of nation; land of one's birth or citizenship; region; agricultural, pastoral, etc., districts as opp. to towns. **country dance,** traditional dance, folk--dance. **country gentleman,** gentleman owing house (**country house, country seat**) and land in the country. **coun'tryman,** **coun'trywoman,** man, woman, of one's own or specified country or living in rural parts. **coun'tryside,** any rural district.

coun'ty, *n.* territorial division in the United Kingdom, shire; people, esp. gentry, of county. **county borough,** large borough. **county council,** elected governing body of county.

coup (kōō), *n.* successful stroke or move.

coup d'état (kōō dātah'), violent or illegal change of government. (French)

coupé (kōō'pā), *n.* closed two-seater car; (Hist.) closed carriage for two.

coup'le (ku-), *n.* two, a pair; married or engaged pair. *v.* link or fasten together; unite.

coup'let (ku-), *n.* pair of successive lines of rhyming verse.

coup'ling (ku-), *n.* link connecting railway carriages or parts of machine.

cou'pon (kōō-), *n.* detachable ticket or form entitling holder to something.

cou'rage (ku-), *n.* bravery; fortitude. **courā'geous** (-jus), *a.* brave, fearless.

cou'rier (koo-), *n.* official of travel agency accompanying group of travellers, esp. on Continent; messenger.

course (kors), *n.* onward movement; race or career; a series; line of action; ground on which race is run; one of successive parts of a meal; layer of bricks, stone, etc. in building. *v.* pursue (game); move quickly; (of liquids) run.

court (kort), *n.* space enclosed by walls or buildings; area of ground within walls or marked out for games; sovereign's residence; assembly of judges, magistrates, etc., administering justice; lawcourt; attention paid to attract favour or affection. *v. t.* pay court to; woo, esp. with view to marriage; invite (danger, etc.). **court-card,** playing-card with picture of king, queen, or knave. **court martial,** (trial of offence against military law by) court of officers.

court'eous (ker-), *a.* polite in manner.

courtesan (kortezan'), *n.* (Hist.) refined prostitute.

court'esy (ker-), *n.* polite and considerate behaviour.

court'ier (kor-), *n.* person often in attendance

at royal court.

court′ly (kor-), *a.* polished, refined, in manner; ceremonious. **court′liness,** *n.*

court′ship (kor-), *n.* courting.

court′yard (kor-), *n.* space enclosed by walls or buildings.

cous′in (kuz-), *n.* child of one's uncle or aunt. **cous′inly,** *a.*

côve, *n.* small bay or inlet.

co′ven (ku-), *n.* gathering of witches.

co′vĕnant (ku-), *n.* agreement, bargain; legal contract. *v.* make covenant.

co′vĕnanter (ku-), *n.* (Sc. hist.) adherent of the Covenants of 1638 and 1643.

Cov′entry, *n.* *send person to Coventry,* refuse to speak to or associate with him.

co′ver (ku-), *v.t.* place (one substance or thing) over (another); lie or extend over; conceal or shield; include, comprise; pass over (ground), travel (certain distance), report (event, etc.) for newspaper, etc. *cover up,* cover completely, conceal. *n.* thing that covers; shelter; screen or pretence; covert. **co′verage,** *n.*, area, risk, etc., covered. **co′verlĕt,** *n.* bedspread, counterpane.

co′vert (ku-), *a.* secret, disguised; not open or explicit. *n.* wood or thicket giving cover for game; (pl.) feathers covering bases of wing and tail feathers.

co′vĕt (ku-), *v.t.* long to possess; desire eagerly (esp. what is another's). **co′vĕtous,** *a.*

co′vey (ku-), *n.* brood of partridges, etc.

cow¹, *n.* (pl. *cows,* archaic *kīne*), female ox, esp. of domestic kind kept for milk; female of elephant, whale, seal, etc.

cow², *v.t.* intimidate; dispirit.

cow′ard, *n.* person who shows fear and lacks courage in face of danger, pain, etc. **cow′ardly,** *a.*

cow′ardice, *n.* cowardly conduct.

cow′boy, *n.* man in charge of cattle on ranch.

cow′er, *v.i.* crouch or shrink with fear or with cold.

cowl, *n.* monk's hooded cloak; its hood; hood-shaped top of chimney or shaft.

cow′pox, *n.* virus disease of cattle.

cow′rie, *n.* (marine mollusc with) oval shell having narrow toothed aperture.

cow′slip, *n.* yellow-flowered wild plant growing in pastures.

cox, *n.* coxswain, esp. of racing boat. *v.* act as cox (to).

cox′cômb (-m), *n.* foolish conceited showy person; (Hist.) jester's cap like cock's comb.

coxswain (kok′sn), *n.* boat's helmsman, esp. one in charge of ship's boat.

coy, *a.* (affectedly) modest, shy.

crab¹, *n.* crustacean with ten legs, of which front pair are adapted as pincers. *catch a crab,* in rowing, get oar-blade jammed under water.

crab², crab′-apple, *nn.* (sour harsh fruit of) wild (or similar cultivated) apple-tree.

crabb′ed (-bd), *a.* bad-tempered; (of hand-writing) irregular and hard to read.

crack, *n.* sudden sharp noise; sharp blow; fissure; partial break (with parts still cohering); (*informal*) first-rate. *v.* make sharp noise; break partially; (of voice) suffer change of tone. **cracked** (-kt), *a.* (*informal*) crazy.

crack′er, *n.* kind of firework; thin unsweetened biscuit.

crack′le, *n.* sound of repeated slight cracking. *v.i.* emit crackle.

crack′ling, *n.* cracking sound; crisp skin of roast pork.

cracks′man, *n.* (pl. -*men*), housebreaker, burglar.

crä′dle, *n.* infant's bed, esp. on rockers; place where thing is first tended; framework like a cradle. *v.t.* place in cradle; be the cradle of.

craft (-ah-), *n.* skill; cunning; art, trade; boat, aircraft (pl. *craft*).

crafts′man (-ahf-), *n.* (pl. -*men*), one who practises a craft. **crafts′manship,** *n.*

craft′y (-ah), *a.* cunning, artful.

crag, *n.* steep rugged rock. **cragg′y,** *a.*

crags′man (-z-), *n.* (pl. -*men*), skilled climber of crags.

cram, *v.* (p.t. *crammed*), fill to excess; force (*into*); stuff (*down*); fill mind with facts, etc., for examination. *n.* cramming for examination. **cramm′er,** *n.* one who crams examinees.

cramp¹, *n.* sudden painful contraction of muscles from chill, strain, etc. *v.t.* restrict; enclose too narrowly; affect with cramp. **cramped** (-pt), *a.* (esp., of handwriting) very small or close.

cramp², *n.* & *v.t.* (fasten with) clamp.

cram′pon, *n.* spiked iron plate fixed to boot for climbing, etc., on ice.

cran, *n.* measure (37½ gallons) for fresh herrings.

cran′berry, *n.* (red acid berry of) dwarf shrub.

crāne, *n.* large wading bird; machine for moving heavy weights. *v.* stretch (one's neck).

crane-fly, two-winged long-legged fly. **cranes′bill,** wild geranium.

crā′nium, *n.* (pl. *crania*), bones enclosing the brain; skull. **crā′nial,** *a.*

crank¹, *n.* part of shaft bent at right angles for giving rotary motion or for converting up-and-down to rotary motion and vice versa. *v.t.* start (engine) by turning crank.

crank², *n.* odd or eccentric person. **crank′y,** *a.*

crann′y, *n.* chink; crack; crevice. **crann′ied,** *a.*

crāpe, *n.* thin wrinkled fabric, usu. of black silk, used for mourning.

crash¹, *n.* sudden violent noise; violent fall or collision; sudden downfall or collapse. *v.* move, go, drive, throw, with crash; (cause to) come into violent collision, fall heavily, etc.; fail, esp. financially. **crash-helmet,** protective helmet. **crash-land,** (of aircraft)

land hurriedly, esp. without lowering under-
-carriage.

crash², *n.* coarse linen cloth.

crass, *a.* grossly stupid; without sensibility.

crāte, *n.* openwork case of wood or wicker for
protecting goods during transport.

crā'ter, *n.* mouth of volcano; bowl-shaped
hole.

cravat', *n.* kind of necktie.

crāve, *v.* long for; beg for. **crā'ving**, *n.*
intense longing (*for*).

crā'ven, *a.* & *n.* cowardly (person).

crawl, *v.i.* move on hands and knees; move
slowly; creep abjectly. *n.* crawling; fast
swimming stroke.

cray'fish, craw'fish, *n.* edible freshwater
shell-fish resembling small lobster.

cray'on, *n.* stick or pencil of coloured chalk,
usu. mixed with wax. *v.t.* draw with crayons.

crāze, *v.t.* drive crazy. *n.* mania; temporary
fashion or enthusiasm.

crā'zy, *a.* mad; half-witted; madly eager; (of
building, etc.) unsound, shaky; (of paving,
quilt, etc.) of irregular pieces fitted together.

creak, *n.* harsh grating sound as of unoiled
hinge. *v.i.* make creaking sound.

cream, *n.* fatty part gathering on top of milk;
kind of food containing or resembling cream;
cream-like preparation used for polishing, as
cosmetic, etc; best part of anything;
yellowish-white colour of cream. **cream'ery**,
n. factory preparing, shop selling, dairy produce. **cream'y**, *a.*

crease, *n.* line made by folding; wrinkle;
(Cricket) white line defining position of
bowler or limit of batsman's ground. *v.* make
creases in; develop creases.

crēāte', *v.t.* bring into existence; invest (person) with rank; originate. **crēā'tive**, *a.*

crēā'tion, *n.* creating (esp. of the world); all
created things; invention.

crēā'tor, *n.* one who creates. *the Creator*,
God.

creature (krē'cher), *n.* human being or animal; contemptible person. **creature comforts**, material comforts (food, clothing,
etc.).

crèche (-āsh), *n.* public day-nursery for babies
and young children.

crē'dence, *n.* belief. *letter of credence*, letter
of introduction.

crēden'tials (-shlz), *n.pl.* letter(s) of introduction.

cred'ible, *a.* believable. **credibil'ity**, *n.*

cred'it, *n.* belief, trust; good reputation;
allowing of deferred payment; sum at person's disposal in bank, etc.; sum entered on
credit side of account; (also *credit title*) acknowledgement of authorship, performance,
direction, etc., esp. at beginning or end of
film. *v.t.* believe; carry to credit side of
account. *credit with*, give credit for (also
fig.). **credit transfer**, simple system of
transferring credits from one (bank) account

to another. **cred'itable**, *a.* praiseworthy.

cred'itor, *n.* person or body to whom debt is
owing.

crē'dō, *n.* (pl. *credos*), creed.

cred'ūlous, *a.* too ready to believe. **crēdū'-
lity**, *n.*

creed, *n.* formal summary of Christian beliefs;
set of opinions on any subject.

creek, *n.* inlet on sea-coast; arm of river;
small stream.

creel, *n.* wicker basket for carrying fish.

creep, *v.i.* (p.t. *crept*), crawl with body close
to ground; move slowly or stealthily or
timidly; (of plants) grow along ground, wall,
etc.; (of flesh, skin) prickle with fear, etc. *n.*
(pl.) shrinking horror. **creep'er**, *n.* creeping
or climbing plant. **creep'y** *a.* giving a feeling
of horror.

crēmāte', *v.t.* reduce (esp. corpse) to ashes by
fire. **crēmā'tion**, *n.* **cremator'ium**, *n.* (pl.
crematoriums, crematoria), establishment
for cremation.

cren'ellāted, *a.* having battlements.

Crē'ōle, *n.* descendant of European settlers in
W. Indies, etc.; French-speaking descendant
of early French settlers in Louisiana, etc.;
person of mixed Creole and Negro descent.
a. of or characteristic of Creoles; (of animals, etc.) naturalized in W. Indies, etc.

crē'osōte, *n.* oily antiseptic liquid distilled
from wood-tar.

crêpe (-āp), *n.* textile fabric with wrinkled surface. **crêpe de Chine** (shēn), fine silk crêpe.
crêpe paper, thin crinkled paper. **crêpe rubber**, crude rubber with wrinkled surface.

crept, *p.t.* & *p.p.* of **creep.**

crescen'dō (-sh-), (as musical direction,
abbrev. *cres.*) gradually louder.

cres'cent, *n.* figure of moon in first or last
quarter; representation of this, esp. as symbol of Muslim religion; crescent-shaped
thing, esp. row of houses. *a.* (of moon) wax-
ing; crescent-shaped.

cress, *n.* any of various plants, usu. having
pungent edible leaves.

crest, *n.* tuft or outgrowth on head of animal
or bird; plume or central ridge of helmet; top,
esp. of mountain, wave, etc; heraldic figure
above shield or used separately. *v.t.* serve as
crest to; reach top of.

crest'fallen (-fawl-), *a.* disheartened;
humbled.

cret'in, *n.* person suffering from deformity
and mental retardation caused by thyroid
deficiency. **cret'inism**, *n.* **cret'inous**, *a.*

cret'onne (*or* -on'), *n.* strong colour-printed
cotton cloth.

crèvasse', *n.* deep open crack in glacier.

crev'ice, *n.* narrow opening, fissure, esp. in
rock, building, etc.

crew¹ (-ōō), *n.* body of men engaged in particular piece of work, esp. manning ship, boat,
or aircraft; gang, mob. *v.* act as crew (*for*).

crew cut, (hair) cut very short all over.

crew[2]: see **crow**[1].

crew'el (-ōō-), *n.* thin worsted yarn for embroidery.

crib, *n.* barred rack for fodder; small bed for child; model representing Nativity; translation for (esp. illegitimate) use of students. *v.* (p.t. *cribbed*), use crib; copy unfairly or without acknowledgement.

cribb'age, *n.* card-game with board on which points are scored with pegs.

crick, *n.* painful stiffness of muscles of neck, etc. *v.t.* produce crick in.

crick'et[1], *n.* insect producing shrill noise by rubbing parts of front wings together.

crick'et[2], *n.* open-air team-game with ball, bats, and wickets. **crick'eter**, *n.*

cried, *p.t. & p.p.* of **cry**.

cri'er, *n.* officer who makes public announcements; town crier.

crime, *n.* act punishable by law; wicked act.

crim'inal, *a.* of (nature of) crime: *n.* person guilty of crime. **criminal'ity**, *n.* **crim'inally**, *adv.*

criminol'ogy, *n.* scientific study of crime.

crimp, *v.t.* press into small folds.

crim'son (-z-), *a. & n.* rich deep purplish red (colour). *v.* turn crimson.

cringe (-nj), *v.i.* cower; behave servilely. *n.* act of cringing.

crink'le, *n. & v.* wrinkle. **crink'ly**, *a.*

crin'oline (*or* -ēn), *n.* hooped petticoat formerly worn to expand skirt.

cripp'le, *n.* lame or disabled person. *v.t.* deprive (wholly or partly) of use of limbs.

cri'sis, *n.* (pl. *crisēs*), turning-point; time of acute danger or difficulty.

crisp, *a.* brittle; bracing; brisk; curly. *n.* (pl.) very thin fried slices of potato eaten cold. *v.* make or become crisp.

criss'-cross, *n.* (network of) crossing lines, etc. *a.* crossing, in crossing lines. *adv.* crosswise. *v.t.* mark with criss-cross lines.

criter'ion, *n.* (pl. *criteria*), principle taken as standard in judging something.

crit'ic, *n.* person who attempts or is skilled in criticism; fault-finder.

crit'ical, *a.* fault-finding; skilled in criticism; of or at a crisis; involving suspense.

crit'icism, *n.* judging of merit, esp. of literary or artistic work; critical observation; expression of disapproval.

crit'icīze, *v.* discuss critically; find fault with.

critique' (-tēk), *n.* critical essay.

croak, *n.* sound resembling deep hoarse note of frog or raven. *v.* utter croak; utter dismally.

cro'chet (-shā *or* -shi), *n.* kind of knitting done with hooked needle. *v.* (p.t. *crocheted* pr. -shād), do crochet; make by crochet.

crock, *n.* earthen pot or jar; broken piece of earthenware. **crock'ery**, *n.* earthenware vessels, esp. for domestic use.

croc'odīle, *n.* large amphibious reptile; children walking two and two. **crocodile tears**, hypocritical tears.

cro'cus, *n.* dwarf plant growing from corm and having yellow, purple, or white flowers.

croft, *n.* small piece of arable or pasture close to house; small-holding, esp. in Scottish highlands. **croft'er**, *n.* one who cultivates a croft.

crom'lech (-k), *n.* (in Wales) dolmen; (in France) prehistoric stone circle.

crône, *n.* withered old woman.

cro'ny, *n.* intimate friend.

crook, *n.* (esp. shepherd's) staff with rounded hook at one end; crosier; (*slang*) swindler, criminal. *v.* bend, curve.

crooked, *a.* (pr. krookt), having hook-shaped handle; (pr. krook'id), not straight; bent, twisted; deformed; dishonest.

crōōn, *v. & n.* (hum or sing in) low monotonous tone. **crōōn'er**, *n.* singer who croons.

crop, *n.* pouch in bird's gullet; handle of whip; produce of cultivated (esp. cereal) plants or lands; cutting or wearing of hair short. *v.* (p.t. *cropped*), cut off; (of animal) bite off; gather, reap; cut short; raise crop on, bear crop; turn *up* unexpectedly.

cro'quet (-ki), *n.* game played on lawn with hoops, wooden balls, and mallets.

cro'sier, cro'zier (-z-; *or* -zher), *n.* staff of bishop or abbot, usu. shaped like shepherd's crook.

cross, *n.* stake with transverse bar used by the ancients for crucifixion; representation of this as emblem of Christian religion; trial, affliction; figure of two lines crossing near their centres; cross-shaped thing; decoration for valour; intermixture of breeds. *on the cross*, diagonally. *a.* transverse; reaching from side to side; intersecting; peevish. *be at cross purposes*, misunderstand one another.

cross, *v.* go across (road, sea, etc.); place crosswise; draw line across; make sign of cross on; meet and pass; thwart; cross-breed. *cross off, out*, cancel.

cross'-bar, *n.* transverse bar, esp. fixed between or across uprights.

cross'bill, *n.* bird with mandibles crossing when beak is closed.

cross'bow (-ō), *n.* medieval weapon consisting of bow fixed across wooden stock, with mechanism for shooting bolt.

cross'-breed, *v.* breed from individuals of different species, etc. *n.* breed so produced; cross-bred individual. **cross'-bred**, *a.*

cross-coun'try (kun-), *a.* across fields, not along roads.

cross'-cut, *a.* (of saw) adapted for cutting across grain. *n.* diagonal cut or path.

crosse, *n.* netted crook used in lacrosse.

cross-examinā'tion, *n.* questioning of witness with view to checking or casting doubt on previous evidence. **cross-exam'ine**, *v.t.*

cross-fer'tilize, *v.t.* fertilize (plant) with pollen from another plant.

cross'-fīre, *n.* (Mil.) lines of fire from two or

more positions crossing each other.

cross'-grained (-nd), *a.* (of wood) with grain running across regular grain; (fig.) perverse; ill-tempered.

cross'ing, *n.* point where lines, roads, etc. intersect; place where street, etc., is crossed.

cross'patch, *n.* ill-tempered person.

cross-ques'tion (-chn), *v.t.* question in order to get more information or test accuracy.

cross-ref'erence, *n.* reference from one part of book, etc., to another.

cross'-road, *n.* road that crosses another or connects two; (pl.) place where roads cross each other.

cross'wise (-z), *adv.* across, diagonally; in form of cross.

cross'word (puzzle) (-werd), puzzle in which words crossing vertically and horizontally in chequered pattern are to be filled in from clues.

crotch, *n.* fork, esp. of human body where legs join trunk.

crotch'et, *n.* (Mus.) black-headed note with stem, equal to half minim; whim, fad. **crotch'ety**, *a.* faddy, ill-tempered.

crouch, *v.i.* stoop or stand with knees bent; (of animal) lie close to ground.

croup[1] (-ōō-), *n.* inflammation of larynx and trachea in children, with sharp cough.

croup[2] (-ōō-), *n.* hindquarters, esp. of horse.

croup'ier (-ōō-), *n.* person who rakes in and pays out money at gaming table.

crow[1] (-ō), *v.i.* (p.t. crowed, archaic crew, pr. -ōō), utter cock's cry; (esp. of baby) utter joyful sounds. *n.* cock's cry; baby's crowing.

crow[2] (-ō), *n.* large black glossy-plumaged bird. **crow's-foot**, (pl. -feet), wrinkle at outer corner of eye. **crow's-nest**, barrel, etc., at mast-head for look-out man.

crow'bar (-ō-), *n.* bar of iron used as lever.

crowd, *n.* large number of persons gathered together; large number of things. *v.* collect in crowd; fill, cram (with). *crowd out*, exclude by crowding.

crown, *n.* wreath for the head; monarch's head-covering or circlet; supreme governing power in monarchy; British coin formerly current, worth 5s.; top of head or hat. *v.t.* place crown on; form chief ornament to; be finishing touch to. **Crown Court**, court of justice for criminal cases.

crozier: see crosier.

cru'cial (-ōōshl), *a.* decisive; critical.

cru'cible (-ōō-), *n.* vessel withstanding great heat, and used for fusing metals, etc.

cru'cifix (-ōō-), *n.* image of Christ on the Cross. **crucifi'xion** (-kshn), *n.* crucifying, esp. (*Crucifixion*) of Christ. **cru'cify**, *v.t.* put to death by fastening to a cross; mortify or chasten.

cru'ciform (-ōō-), *a.* cross-shaped.

crude (-ōō-), *a.* in natural or raw state; rough; rude, blunt. **crude'ness, cru'dity**, *nn.*

cru'el (-ōō-), *a.* (crueller, cruellest), callous

to or delighting in others' pain; disposed to inflict suffering; painful, distressing. **cru'elty**, *n.*

cru'et (-ōō-), *n.* small bottle with stopper for use at table, cruet-stand. **cruet-stand**, stand holding cruets, mustard-pot, etc.

cruise (-ōōz), *v.i.* sail about on sea, either for pleasure or, in war, looking for enemy ships; travel at cruising speed. *n.* cruising voyage. **cruising speed**, speed suitable for maintaining for long periods.

cruis'er (-ōōz-), *n.* warship designed for speed; yacht designed for cruising.

crumb (-m), *n.* small fragment, esp. of bread; soft inner part of bread. *v.t.* cover with crumbs; break into crumbs. **crumb'y** (-mi), *a.*

crum'ble, *v.* break or fall into crumbs or fragments. **crum'bly**, *a.*

crum'pet, *n.* flat soft unsweetened cake, eaten toasted and buttered.

crump'le, *v.* crush together into creases; become creased; collapse.

crunch, *n.* sound made by chewing crisp food or treading on gravel. *v.* crush with teeth, esp. noisily; make crunch.

crupp'er, *n.* strap at back of harness looped under horse's tail.

crusâde' (-ōō-), *n.* medieval military expedition made by Christians to regain Holy Land from Muslims; campaign or movement against recognized evil. *v.i.* take part in crusade. **crusâ'der**, *n.*

cruse (-ōōz), *n.* (archaic) earthenware jar.

crush, *v.t.* compress with violence; (be liable to) crumple; overwhelm. *n.* crowded mass (esp. of people).

crust, *n.* hard outer part of bread; similar casing of anything; pastry covering pie; surface of the earth. *v.* form into, become covered with, crust.

crustâ'cean (-āshn), *n. & a.* (animal) of mainly aquatic group, of which many have hard shell and numerous jointed legs.

crus'ty, *a.* having much crust; irritable.

crutch, *n.* staff, usu. with cross-piece fitting under arm, for lame person; crotch.

crux, *n.* crucial point; puzzle.

cry, *n.* loud excited utterance; fit of weeping. *v.* (p.t. cried), utter cry or cries; utter loudly, exclaim; weep. *cry off*, withdraw. **cry'ing**, *a.* (esp., of evil) calling for notice, shameful.

cry'o-, *pref.* freezing. **cry'ogen**, *n.* freezing-mixture. **cryogen'ic**, *a.* of or producing very low temperatures.

crypt, *n.* vault, esp. one below church.

cryp'tic, *a.* secret, mysterious; obscure.

cryp'togram, *n.* anything written in cipher. **cryptograph'ic**, *a.*

crys'tal, *n.* substance solidified in definite geometrical form; transparent quartz (*rock crystal*); very transparent glass; (vessels of) cut glass. *a.* of, like crystal; clear as crystal.

crys'talline, *a.* of, like, clear as, crystal.

crys′tallize, v. form into crystals or (fig.) into definite or permanent state. **crys′tallized,** a. (esp. of fruit) preserved in and usu. coated with sugar. **crystalliza′tion,** n.

crystallog′raphy, n. science of crystal structure. **crystallog′rapher,** n.

cub, n. young of fox, bear, lion, etc. **Cub Scout,** junior Scout.

cubb′y-hôle, n. very small room, cupboard; snug place.

cûbe, n. solid figure contained by six equal squares; product of a number multiplied by its square. v.t. find cube of (number).

cû′bic, a. of three dimensions; involving cube of quantity.

cû′bical, a. cube-shaped.

cû′bicle, n. small compartment or room or partitioned-off space for sleeping, dressing, etc., in.

cû′bism, n. style in art in which objects are presented as geometrical figures. **cû′bist,** n.

cû′bit, n. ancient measure of length (18-22 in.), based on length of forearm.

cuckoo (koo′kōō), n. migratory bird appearing in spring and laying its eggs in nests of other birds; its call.

cuck′old, n. husband of adulterous wife. v.t. make cuckold of.

cû′cumber, n. (creeping plant with) long fleshy fruit eaten as salad, etc.

cud, n. food that ruminant brings back from first stomach and chews at leisure.

cudd′le, v. hug affectionately; nestle together. n. hug, embrace.

cudg′el, n. thick stick used as weapon. v.t. beat with cudgel.

cûe¹, n. actor's words, etc., as signal for speech, action, etc.; signal, hint.

cûe², n. billiard player's long straight rod.

cuff¹, n. (ornamental) band, lace, etc. at bottom of sleeve; (stiffened) wristband of linen, etc. **cuff link,** pair of linked buttons for fastening cuff.

cuff², n. blow with open hand. v.t. strike thus.

cuirass′ (kwi-), n. body armour.

cuisine (kwizēn′), n. style of cooking.

cûl′-de-sac (or koo-), n. (pl. culs-de-sac, pr. same), street, passage, etc., closed at one end, blind alley.

cul′inary, a. of or for cooking.

cull, v.t. pick (flower, etc.); select; pick out and kill (surplus deer, seals, etc.).

cul′minâte, v.i. reach highest point. **culmi-nâ′tion,** n.

culp′able, a. blameworthy, criminal. **culpa-bil′ity,** n.

cul′prit, n. guilty person; accused person.

cult, n. system of religious worship; devotion, homage; fad.

cul′tivâte, v.t. prepare and use (soil) for crops; raise, produce (plant, etc.); improve, develop. **cultivâ′tion,** n. **cul′tivâtor,** n. (esp.) implement for breaking up ground, etc.

cul′ture (-cher), n. cultivating; production; improvement of mind, tastes, etc., by education and training; form or type of civilization. v.t. cultivate. **cul′tural,** a. **cul′tured,** a. (esp.) refined, well-educated.

cul′vert, n. covered channel conveying water across beneath road, railway, etc.

cum′ber, v.t. hamper, hinder; burden. **cum′-bersome, cum′brous,** aa. hampering; unwieldy, clumsy.

cumm′erbund, n. waist-sash.

cû′mulative, a. increasing by successive additions; tending to accumulate.

cû′mulus, n. (pl. cumuli), rounded masses of cloud heaped one on the other.

cû′neiform (-ni-), a. & n. (writing, character) composed of wedge-shaped marks.

cunn′ing, n. skilful deceit; skill, dexterity. a. possessing or displaying cunning.

cup, n. drinking-vessel, with or without handle; ornamental cup or other vessel as prize; cupful. **cup′ful,** n. (pl. cupfuls).

cupboard (kub′erd), n. (usu. shelved) closet or cabinet.

cûpid′ity, n. greed, esp. for money or property.

cû′pola, n. rounded dome forming roof; small dome above roof.

cû′pro-nick′el, n. alloy of copper and nickel used for coins.

cur, n. worthless or snappish dog.

cûrar′ê, n. vegetable poison used by S. American Indians on arrows.

cûr′ate, n. assistant to parish priest. **cûr′acy,** n.

cûr′ative, a. tending to cure. n. curative drug, etc.

cûrâ′tor, n. person in charge, esp. of museum or art gallery.

curb, n. chain fastened to bit and passing under horse's lower jaw, used as check; (fig.) check. v.t. restrain.

curd, n. coagulated substance formed by action of acids on milk. **cur′dy,** a.

cur′dle, v. coagulate, form into curd.

cûre, n. remedy; course of treatment; spiritual charge (of parishioners, etc.). v.t. restore to health, heal; preserve (meat, etc.).

cur′few, n. (under martial law) time after which inhabitants may not be out of doors; (Hist.) ringing of bell at fixed evening hour as signal for fires to be extinguished.

cûr′iô, n. (pl. curios), object prized for its rarity, beauty, etc.

cûrios′ity, n. desire to know; inquisitiveness; strange or rare thing.

cûr′ious, a. eager to learn; inquisitive; strange, surprising.

curl, v. bend round; coil into spiral shape; proceed in curve; play at curling. n. spiral lock of hair; anything spiral or curved inwards. **cur′ly,** a.

cur′lew, n. wading bird with long slender curved bill and characteristic cry.

cur'ling, *n.* game played on ice with large round flattish stones.

curmudg'eon (-jn), *n.* churlish or miserly person.

cu'rrant, *n.* dried fruit of small seedless grape; (small round edible black, red, or white berry of) any of various shrubs.

cu'rrency, *n.* time during which thing is current; prevalence (of words, ideas, etc.); money in actual use in a country.

cu'rrent, *a.* in general circulation or use; (of time) now passing; of the present time. *n.* water, air, etc. moving in a given direction; flow of electrically charged particles; general tendency. **current account**, (at bank) one that may be drawn on by cheque.

curric'ulum, *n.* (pl. *curricula*), course of study.

curric'ulum vi'tae (ve̅'tī), brief account of one's life. (Latin)

cu'rry[1], *n.* dish of meat, etc., cooked with ground hot-tasting spices.

cu'rry[2], *v.t.* rub down (horse). **curry-comb**, rubber brush for horses. **curry favour**, try to please by doing more than is necessary.

curse, *n.* calling down of destruction or punishment; profane oath. *v.* utter curse against, afflict *with*; utter curses. **cur'sèd**, *a.* damnable.

cur'sive, *a.* & *n.* (writing) done without lifting pen between letters.

cur'sory, *a.* hasty, hurried.

curt, *a.* noticeably or rudely brief; abrupt. **curt'ness**, *n.*

curtail', *v.t.* cut down, shorten, reduce. **curtail'ment**, *n.*

cur'tain (-tn), *n.* cloth, etc., hung as screen, esp. at window or between stage and auditorium. *v.t.* provide, shut off, with curtains.

curt'sy, *n.* woman's movement of respect or salutation made by bending knees. *v.i.* make curtsy (*to*).

cur'vature, *n.* curving; curved form.

curve, *n.* line of which no part is straight; curved form or thing. *v.* bend or shape so as to form curve.

curvet', *n.* horse's frisky leap. *v.i.* (p.t. *curvetted*), perform this.

cushion (koo'shn), *n.* bag of cloth, etc., stuffed with soft material; rubber lining of sides of billiard-table. *v.t.* provide with, protect (as) with, cushion(s).

cush'y (koo-), *a.* (*slang*, of job, etc.) easy, comfortable.

cusp, *n.* point of meeting of two curves.

cus'tard, *n.* pudding or sauce made of beaten eggs and milk. **custard powder**, cornflour, etc., as substitute for eggs in custard sauce.

custo̅'dian, *n.* guardian, keeper, esp. of public building, etc.

cus'tody, *n.* care; imprisonment.

cus'tom, *n.* usual practice; established usage; business patronage or support; (pl.) duty levied on imports; department of Civil Service (*the Customs*) dealing with levying of duty.

cus'tomary, *a.* usual.

cus'tomer, *n.* purchaser at shop, etc.; client of bank.

cut, *v.* (p.t. *cut*; pres. p. *cutting*), wound, make incision in, divide, with sharp instrument; detach or shape by cutting; divide pack of cards; refuse to recognize. *cut down*, fell (tree, etc.); reduce (expenses). *cut in*, enter abruptly; interrupt. *cut off*, remove by cutting; interrupt (supplies); exclude (*from*). *cut out*, (esp.) shape by cutting; (of engine, etc.) stop working abruptly. *cut up*, cut in pieces. *n.* act of cutting; sound or mark made by cutting; reduction; way thing is cut; joint or piece of meat, etc. **cut glass**, (vessels of) glass with designs cut into surface. **cut--throat**, (*n.*) murderer; (*a.*) murderous; (of competition, etc.) intensive, merciless.

cutan'eous, *a.* of the skin.

cute, *n.* (*informal*) clever, ingenious.

cu'ticle, *n.* outer skin, epidermis; skin at base of finger-nail or toe-nail.

cut'lass, *n.* (Hist.) sailors' short sword.

cut'ler, *n.* maker of, dealer in, knives, etc.

cut'lery, *n.* knives, scissors, etc.; knives, forks, and spoons used at table.

cut'lêt, *n.* small piece of meat, fish, etc.

cutt'er, *n.* person or thing that cuts; warship's small boat; small boat; small sloop-rigged vessel.

cutt'ing, *n.* excavation of high ground for railway, road, etc.; piece cut from newspaper, etc.; piece cut from plant and planted to form roots of its own.

cutt'lefish (-lf-), *n.* ten-armed marine cephalopod ejecting black fluid when pursued.

cwm (koo̅m), *n.* (in Wales) combe.

cy'anide, *n.* a highly poisonous compound.

cybernet'ics, *n.* study of communication and control in living organisms and machines.

cyc'lamen, *n.* plant with handsome pink, white, or crimson flowers.

cy'cle, *n.* recurrent period (of successive events, etc.); period of a thing's completion; complete set or series; bicycle. *v.i.* move in cycles; ride, travel by, bicycle.

cy'clic, **cy'clical**, *aa.* recurring in cycles; belonging to a cycle.

cy'clist, *n.* rider of bicycle.

cy'clo̅ne, *n.* moving area of low atmospheric pressure with rotating winds; violent destructive form of this. **cyclon'ic**, *a.*

cy'closty̅le, *n.* & *v.t.* (reproduce by) device for making copies of written document from stencil-plate.

cyg'nêt, *n.* young swan.

cyl'inder, *n.* solid or hollow straight-sided body of circular section (i.e. shaped like rolling-pin, tube, etc.). **cylin'drical**, *a.*

cym'bal, *n.* one of pair of concave brass plates struck together to make ringing sound.

cyn'ic, *n.* sarcastic disbeliever in human sincerity or goodness. **cyn′ical**, *a.* incredulous of human goodness; sneering. **cyn′icism** (-sizm), *n.*

cȳn′osure (-shoor; *or* sin-), *n.* centre of attraction or interest.

cȳ′press, *n.* evergreen coniferous tree with dark foliage.

cyst, *n.* bladder or sac containing liquid secretion, morbid matter, etc.

czar (zar), *n.* tsar.

D

D, d, as Roman numeral, 500.

dab[1], *n.* slight blow, pat; brief application of soft thing to surface without rubbing; moisture, colour, etc., so applied. *v.* (p.t. *dabbed*), make dab(s) (*at*); apply by dabbing.

dab[2], *n.* small flat fish.

dabb′le, *v.* wet slightly; splash about; engage in amateur way (*in*).

dab′chick, *n.* small grebe (*little grebe*).

dāce, *n.* (pl. same), small freshwater fish.

dachshund (dahks′-hoont), *n.* small short-legged German breed of dog.

dacoit′, *n.* (Hist.) Indian or Burmese armed robber. **dacoit′y**, *n.* gang robbery.

dac′tyl, *n.* metrical foot of one long (or stressed) syllable followed by two short (or unstressed) syllables. **dactyl′ic**, *a.*

dad, dadd′y, *nn.* (*informal & familiar*) father. **daddy-long-legs**, crane-fly.

dā′dō, *n.* (pl. *dados*), lower part (of different material or colour) of interior wall.

daff′odil, *n.* yellow-flowered bulbous plant.

daft′ (-ah-), *a.* foolish, wild, crazy.

dagg′er (-g-), *n.* short two-edged pointed weapon.

dague′rreotȳpe (-gero-), *n.* (photograph made by) early photographic process.

dahl′ia (dāl-), *n.* composite plant cultivated for its brightly coloured flowers.

dai′ly, *adv.* every day. *a.* done, occurring, published, etc., every day or weekday. *n.* daily newspaper or domestic worker. **daily bread**, necessary food.

dain′ty, *n.* choice morsel, delicacy. *a.* choice; prettily neat; particular. **dain′tily**, *adv.* **dain′tiness**, *n.*

dair′y, *n.* place for keeping, processing, or selling milk, etc. **dairy farm**, farm producing chiefly milk, butter, etc. **dair′ymaid**, woman employed in dairy. **dair′yman** (pl. -*men*), dealer in milk, etc.

dā′is, *n.* low platform.

dai′sy (-z-), *n.* composite field or garden flower. **daisy-chain**, string of field daisies linked together.

dāle, *n.* valley. **dales′man** (-z-), *n.* (pl. -*men*), dweller in dales of north of England.

dall′y, *v.* spend time idly, flirt (*with*); loiter. **dall′iance**, *n.*

Dalmā′tian (-shn), *n.* large white dog with black or brown spots.

dam[1], *n.* barrier checking flow of water. *v.t.* (p.t. *dammed*), confine with dam; block (*up*) or restrain (as) with dam.

dam[2], *n.* mother (usu. of animal).

dam′age, *n.* loss of what is desirable; injury; (pl.) sum of money in compensation for injury or loss. *v.t.* do harm to; injure.

dam′ask, *n.* & *a.* (of) reversible figured woven fabric; (of) blush-red colour of damask rose. **damask rose**, sweet-scented red rose orig. brought from Damascus.

dāme, *n.* lady (*archaic*); title of woman who has received order of knighthood; female character in pantomime, played by male actor.

damn (-m), *v.* doom to eternal torment; censure or condemn; curse. **dam′nable**, *a.* hateful. **damnā′tion**, *n.* damning; eternal punishment in hell.

damp, *n.* moisture; firedamp. *a.* slightly wet; moist. *v.t.* moisten; stifle, dull; depress. **damp course**, layer of slate, etc., in wall to keep damp from rising. **dam′pen**, *v.t.* damp. **dam′per**, *n.* metal plate in flue controlling draught.

dam′sel (-z-), *n.* (*archaic*) young unmarried woman.

dam′son (-z-), *n.* small dark-purple plum; tree bearing it.

dance (-ah-), *v.* move with rhythmic steps, glides, etc., to music; jump about, move in a lively way. *n.* (music for) piece of dancing; dancing-party. **dan′cer**, *n.* one who dances, esp. in public for pay.

dan′dèlion, *n.* yellow-flowered wild plant.

dan′dle, *v.t.* dance (child) on knee or in arms.

dan′druff, *n.* scurf on scalp and among hair.

dan′dy, *n.* man paying excessive attention to smartness in dress, etc., fop.

Dāne, *n.* native of Denmark; (Hist.) Scandinavian invader of England. **great Dane,** large powerful breed of dog.

dān'ger (-j-), *n.* liability or exposure to harm or risk of death; thing that causes peril. **dān'gerous,** *a.*

dangle (dang'gl), *v.* hang loosely; hold or carry (thing) swaying loosely; hold out (hopes, etc.); hover around.

Dā'nish, *a.* & *n.* (language) of Denmark or the Danes.

dank, *a.* unpleasantly damp.

daph'nè, *n.* genus of flowering shrubs.

dapp'er, *a.* neat, smart.

dapp'le, *v.t.* fleck with rounded spots of darker colour or shade. **dapple-grey,** (horse) of grey with darker spots.

dāre, *v.t.* venture; have the courage (to); defy challenge. *I dare say,* it seems to me probable or likely. **dare-devil,** reckless (person). **dār'ing,** *n.* (esp.) adventurous courage. *a.* bold, fearless.

dark, *a.* with little or no light; gloomy; secret; brown-complexioned or dark-haired. *n.* absence of light; nightfall; want of knowledge; dark colour. **dar'ken,** *v.* make or become dark. **dark'ling,** *adv.* & *a.* in the dark. **dark'ness,** *n.* absence of light.

dar'ling, *n.* beloved person; favourite; pet. *a.* beloved, prized.

darn, *v.t.* mend by interweaving yarns across hole. *n.* place so mended.

dar'nel, *n.* grass growing as weed among corn.

dart, *n.* light pointed missile thrown by the hand; (pl.) game in which darts are thrown at target; sudden rapid movement; tapering stitched fold in garment. *v.* (cause to) move suddenly and rapidly.

dash, *v.* shatter *to pieces*; fling, thrust, rush, *away, off,* etc.; bespatter *with*; frustrate, discourage. *n.* rush; showy appearance; horizontal stroke (—); sprinkling. **dash'board,** panel in front of driver of motor car, etc., carrying controls and dials.

dash'ing, *a.* spirited; showy.

das'tard, *n.* brutal coward. **das'tardly,** *a.*

dā'ta, *n.pl.* plural of **datum;** (esp., also with sing. verb) detailed information.

dāte¹, *n.* oblong stone-fruit; tree (*date-palm*) bearing this.

dāte², *n.* (statement of) day or year of writing, happening, etc., of anything; period; duration. *out of date,* obsolete, old-fashioned. *up to date,* in accordance with modern standards, requirements, etc. *v.* mark with date; give a date to; be or become out of date. *date from,* have existence since. **dā'table,** *a.* **dāte'less,** *a.* timeless.

dā'tive, *a.* & *n.* (grammatical case) denoting indirect or remoter object of verb's action.

dā'tum, *n.* (pl. *data*), fixed starting-point of scale, etc.; (in pl., also with sing. verb) thing known or assumed, as basis for reasoning, calculation, inference, etc.

daub, *v.* coat or smear (*with* clay, etc.); smear *on*; paint roughly. *n.* stuff daubed on; rough picture.

daughter (daw'ter), *n.* female child in relation to her parents; female descendant. **daughter--in-law,** son's wife.

daunt, *v.t.* discourage, intimidate. **daunt'-less,** *a.* not to be daunted; intrepid.

dauph'in, *n.* (Hist.) title of eldest son of king of France.

dav'enport, *n.* writing-desk with drawers and hinged front; (U.S.) large sofa.

dav'it, *n.* one of pair of curved uprights at ship's side for suspending or lowering boat.

Dāv'y lamp, miner's safety lamp.

daw'dle, *v.i.* go slowly and lazily; idle.

dawn, *v.i.* begin to grow light; appear faintly. *n.* first light, daybreak; beginning.

day, *n.* time while sun is above horizon; daylight, dawn; period of twenty-four hours (from midnight); time, period (often pl.); specified or appointed day. **day-dream,** (have) idle pleasant thoughts. **day'light,** light of day; dawn. *daylight saving,* putting clocks forward so that darkness falls at a later hour. **day-nursery,** place where young children are cared for during day. **day'spring,** (Poet.) dawn.

dāze, *v.t.* stupefy; bewilder. *n.* dazed state.

dazz'le, *v.t.* confuse sight by excess of light; confound by brilliant display. *n.* bright confusing light.

de-, *pref.* un-, not; down; away; completely.

dea'con, *n.* clergyman below priest; layman dealing with secular affairs of church. **dea'-coness,** *n.* churchwoman appointed to undertake some ministerial duties.

dead (ded), *a.* no longer alive; lifeless; dull; obsolete; not effective; complete; exact. *dead to,* unconscious of, not heeding. *n. the dead,* dead person(s); all who have ever died. *dead of night, winter,* period of intensest darkness, cold. *adv.* profoundly; completely. **dead-alive,** dull, spiritless. **dead-beat,** utterly exhausted. **dead end,** closed end of passage, etc. **dead heat,** race in which winners finish even. **dead letter,** law no longer observed; unclaimed letter at post office. **dead-line,** fixed time limit. **dead'lock,** position from which no progress is possible. **dead-nettle,** non-stinging nettle-like plant. **dead weight,** heavy inert weight. **dead'en,** *v.* deprive of or lose vitality, force, etc.; make insensible to.

dead'ly (ded-), *a.* causing fatal injury or death; intense. **deadly nightshade,** shrub with purple flowers and poisonous black berries.

deaf (def), *a.* wholly or partly without hearing; heedless. **deaf-aid,** hearing-aid. **deaf--mute,** deaf and dumb person.

deaf'en (def-), *v.t.* deprive of hearing by noise.

deal[1], *n.* a great (or *good*) *deal*, a large (or fairly large) amount.

deal[2], *n.* (sawn) fir or pine wood.

deal[3], *v.* (p.t. *dealt*, pr. delt), distribute, give *out*, among several; assign as share; deliver (blow); do business or occupy oneself *with*; be concerned *with*. *n.* dealing, turn to deal; business transaction. *raw deal*, unfair treatment. **deal'er**, *n.* person dealing at cards; trader. **deal'ings**, *n.pl.* conduct; transactions.

dean, *n.* head of cathedral chapter; (usu. *rural dean*) clergyman with authority over group of parishes; fellow of college with disciplinary duties; head of university faculty.

dea'nery, *n.* dean's house or office; group of parishes under rural dean.

dear, *a.* beloved, loved (often merely polite); precious *to*; costing much money, expensive. *n.* beloved or lovable person. *adv.* at high price. *int.* expressing surprise, distress, etc.

dearth (der-), *n.* scarcity and dearness of food; scanty supply *of*.

death (deth), *n.* dying, end of life; being dead; end, destruction. **death duty,** tax levied before property passes to heir(s). **death--mask,** cast taken from dead person's face. **death-rate,** yearly number of deaths per thousand of population. **death's head,** skull as emblem of mortality. **death-trap,** dangerous place, etc. **death-warrant,** order for execution. **death-watch (beetle),** insect which makes sound like watch ticking, the larva of which bores in old wood. **death'less,** *a.* immortal. **death'ly,** *a. & adv.* deadly; like death.

débâcle (dābah'kl), *n.* sudden and complete collapse or downfall. (French)

dēbar[1], *v.t.* (p.t. *debarred*), exclude; prevent.

dēbark', *v.* disembark.

dēbāse', *v.t.* lower in quality, value, or character; depreciate (coin). **dēbāse'ment,** *n.*

dēbāt'able, *a.* that can be disputed or debated.

dēbāte', *v.* dispute about, discuss; engage in (formal) argument or discussion; ponder. *n.* discussion; public argument. **debating society,** society for practice in debating.

dēbauch', *v.t.* lead astray from virtue or morality; corrupt. **dēbauchee'** (*or* -shē), *n.* person given to debauchery. **dēbau'chery,** *n.* indulgence in sensual pleasures.

dēbil'itāte, *v.t.* enfeeble. **dēbil'ity,** *n.* feebleness; weakness.

deb'it, *n.* entry in account of sum owing. *v.t.* enter (sum) *against* or *to*.

debonair', *a.* cheerful, blithe.

dēbouch' (*or* -ōōsh), *v.i.* emerge from wood, etc., into open country.

dē-brief'ing, *n.* interrogation of (pilot, etc.) after completion of mission.

deb'ris (-rē), *n.* scattered fragments, wreckage, drifted accumulation.

debt (det), *n.* what is owed; state of owing something. *in, out of, debt,* owing, not owing, money, etc. **debt'or,** *n.* person in debt.

début (dā'bu *or* -ōō), *n.* first appearance in society or as performer, etc.

débutante (deb'ūtahnt; *or* dā-), *n.* girl making first appearance in society.

deca-, *pref.* ten.

dec'āde, *n.* period of ten years; set or series of ten.

dec'adence, *n.* falling to lower level (in art, literature, etc., esp. after period at high level). **dec'adent,** *a.* in state of decay or decline; belonging to decadent age. *n.* decadent person.

dec'agon, *n.* plane figure with ten sides and angles. **decag'onal,** *a.*

dec'agram, dec'alitre (-lēter), **dec'amètre** (-ter), *nn.* ten grams, litres, metres.

dec'alogue (-og), *n.* the Ten Commandments (in *Exodus* 20).

dēcamp', *v.i.* break up or leave camp; go away secretly.

dēcant', *v.t.* pour off (wine, etc.) gently. **dēcan'ter,** *n.* bottle with stopper, from which decanted wine is served.

dēcap'itāte, *v.t.* behead. **dēcapitā'tion,** *n.*

dec'apod, *n.* ten-footed crustacean.

dēcar'bonīze, *v.t.* (esp.) remove carbon deposit from (engine of car, etc.).

decasyll'able, *n.* metrical line of ten syllables. **decasyllab'ic,** *a.*

dēcath'lon, *n.* athletic contest in which each competitor takes part in ten events.

dēcay', *v.* rot, decompose; decline in power, wealth, etc. *n.* decline, falling off; ruinous state; decomposition.

dēcease', *n.* death. *v.i.* die. **dēceased'** (-st), *a. & n.* dead (person).

dēceit' (-sēt), *n.* deceiving; trick; deceitfulness. **dēceit'ful,** *a.* in the habit of deceiving; intended to deceive.

dēceive' (-sēv), *v.t.* cause to believe what is false; mislead; disappoint.

dē'celerāte, *v.* decrease speed (of).

dē'cency, *n.* being decent, propriety; respectability.

dē'cent, *a.* seemly, not immodest or obscene; respectable; passable; (*informal*) kind.

dēcep'tion, *n.* deceiving or being deceived; trick; sham. **dēcep'tive,** *a.* misleading.

deci-, *pref.* one tenth.

de'cibel, *n.* unit for measuring intensity of sound.

dēcīde', *v.* settle; give judgement; come, bring, to resolution or decision. **dēci'dĕd,** *a.* definite; unquestionable; settled. **dēci'dĕdly,** *adv.* undoubtedly.

dēcid'ūous, *a.* shedding periodically; (of tree or shrub) shedding its leaves annually.

de'cigram, de'cilitre (-lēter), **de'cimètre** (-ter), *nn.* one tenth of gram, litre, metre.

de'cimal, *a.* of tenth parts or number ten; proceeding by tens. *n.* decimal fraction or figure. **decimal currency,** currency in which units are decimal multiples or fractions of each other. **decimal fraction**, one whose denominator is a power of ten, usu. expressed in figures (*decimal figures*) to right of units figure after a dot (*decimal point*). **decimal system**, system of weights and measures with each denomination ten times that immediately below. **de'cimalize**, *v.t.* express as decimal or in decimal system. **decimaliza'tion**, *n.*

de'cimate, *v.t.* kill a tenth or a large proportion of. **decima'tion**, *n.*

deci'pher, *v.t.* find the meaning of (cipher, bad writing, etc.). **deci'pherable**, *a.*

deci'sion (-zhn), *n.* act of deciding; settlement; formal judgement; conclusion reached; firmness. **decis'ive**, *a.* deciding; conclusive; decided.

deck, *n.* floor, usu. of planks, extending from side to side of (part of) ship or boat; floor of bus, etc. *v.t.* array, adorn. **deck-chair**, folding reclining chair. **deck-hand**, ordinary sailor.

declaim', *v.* speak or say impressively or dramatically; make impassioned speech. **declama'tion**, *n.* **declam'atory**, *a.*

declara'tion, *n.* declaring; emphatic or formal statement. **decla'ratory**, *a.*

declare', *v.* proclaim or announce publicly, formally, or explicitly; acknowledge possession of (dutiable goods).

declen'sion, *n.* (Gram.) list of case-forms of noun, adjective, or pronoun; group of these with similar endings.

decline', *v.* show downward tendency; decrease, deteriorate; refuse; (Gram.) give the case-forms of (noun, etc.). *n.* gradual decrease or deterioration; wasting disease.

decliv'ity, *n.* downward slope.

declutch', *v.i.* disengage clutch.

decoc'tion, *n.* extraction, liquid obtained, by boiling.

decode', *v.t.* decipher (coded message).

décolleté (dākol'tā), *a.* (fem. *décolletée*), low--necked; wearing low-necked dress. (French)

decompose' (-z), *v.* separate or resolve into elements; rot. **decomposi'tion**, *n.*

decontam'inate, *v.t.* rid of (esp. radioactive) contamination. **decontamina'tion**, *n.*

decontrol', *v.t.* (p.t. *decontrolled*), release from (esp. Government) control.

décor (dā'kor), *n.* all that makes up appearance of room, stage, etc.

dec'orate, *v.t.* adorn; beautify; paint, paper, etc. (room, etc.); invest with order, medal, etc. **dec'orative**, *a.*

decora'tion, *n.* decorating; medal, etc., conferred and worn as honour; (pl.) flags, etc., put up on festive occasion.

dec'orator, *n.* (esp.) tradesman who paints and papers houses.

dec'orous, *a.* not offending against decency or seemliness.

decor'um, *n.* seemliness, propriety, etiquette.

decoy', *n.* netted pond into which wild duck, etc., may be enticed; bird, etc., used to entice others; enticement, trap. *v.t.* entice; ensnare.

decrease', *v.* make or become less; diminish. *n.* (dē'-), decreasing.

decree', *n.* order given out by authority; judicial decision. *v.t.* order by decree; determine. **decree ni'si**, order for divorce, remaining conditional for a period.

decrep'it, *a.* weak and feeble with age. **decrep'itude**, *n.*

decry', *v.t.* disparage; belittle.

ded'icate, *v.t.* devote or give up (*to* God, special purpose, etc.); inscribe (book, etc.) *to* patron, etc. **dedica'tion**, *n.* **ded'icatory**, *a.*

deduce', *v.t.* arrive at (conclusion, etc.) by reasoning (*from* facts).

deduct', *v.t.* subtract; take away or withhold. **deduc'tion**, *n.* deducting; amount deducted; deducing; thing deduced. **deduc'tive**, *a.*

deed, *n.* thing consciously done; fact, reality; legal document. **deed-poll**, deed made and executed by one party only.

deem, *v.t.* believe, consider, judge.

deep, *a.* going far down or far in; profound; heartfelt; low-pitched. *n.* *the deep*, the sea. *adv.* far down or in. **deep-freeze**, refrigerator kept at very low temperature for rapid freezing and continuous refrigeration of food, etc. **dee'pen**, *v.* make or become deep or deeper.

deer, *n.* (pl. same), hoofed ruminant mammal with deciduous antlers. **deer'skin**, hide of deer. **deer'stalker** (-awk-), cloth cap with peak before and behind.

deface', *v.t.* disfigure; make illegible. **deface'ment**, *n.*

de fac'to (*or* dā), in fact, whether by right or not. (Latin)

defalca'tion, *n.* using of funds for wrong purpose; breach of trust concerning money.

defame', *v.t.* attack good reputation of. **defama'tion**, *n.* **defam'atory**, *a.*

default', *n.* failure to act or appear or pay. *v.i.* fail to meet obligations.

defeat', *v.t.* overcome in battle or other contest; baffle. *n.* lost battle or contest. **defeat'ism**, *n.* tendency to accept defeat as inevitable. **defea'tist**, *n.* & *a.*

de'fecate, *v.i.* discharge faeces from bowels. **defeca'tion**, *n.*

defect', *n.* lack of something essential to completeness or perfection; failing; blemish. *v.i.* desert.

defec'tion, *n.* abandonment of leader or cause.

defec'tive, *a.* incomplete, faulty; wanting, deficient.

defence', *n.* defending from, resistance against, attack; (Mil., pl.) fortifications; defendant's case in lawsuit. **defence'less**, *a.*

defend', *v.* ward off attack made on; keep safe, protect; conduct defence (of) in lawsuit.

defen'dant, *n.* person accused or sued in lawsuit.

dèfen'der, *n.* one who defends.

dèfen'sible, *a.* easily defended; justifiable.

dèfen'sive, *a.* serving for defence; not aggressive. *n.* state or position of defence.

dèfer'¹, *v. t.* (p.t. *deferred*), put off, postpone. **dèfer'ment**, *n.*

dèfer'², *v. i.* (p.t. *deferred*), submit or make concessions *to* (person, etc.).

def'erence, *n.* compliance with advice, etc., of another; respectful conduct. **deferen'tial** (-shl), *a.*

dèfi'ance, *n.* challenge to fight; open disobedience or disregard.

dèfi'ant, *a.* disobedient; rebellious.

dèfi'ciency (-shn-), *n.* lack or shortage; thing wanting. **dèfi'cient** (-shnt), *a.* incomplete; insufficient; wanting *in.*

def'icit, *n.* amount by which sum, esp. of money, is too small; amount by which payments exceed receipts.

dè'file¹, *n.* narrow gorge or pass. **dèfile'**, *v. i.* march in file. **dèfile'ment¹**, *n.*

dèfile'², *v. t.* make dirty, pollute; corrupt. **dèfile'ment²**, *n.*

dèfine¹, *v. t.* mark out (limits, boundary); show clearly; state exact meaning of. **dèfin'able**, *a.* that can be defined.

def'inite, *a.* distinct, precise, determinate. **def'initely**, *adv.*

defini'tion, *n.* statement of precise meaning of word(s); making or being distinct.

dèfin'itive, *a.* decisive; final.

dèflāte', *v. t.* let air out of (tyre, etc.); reduce inflation of (currency). **dèflā'tion**, *n.* **dèflā'tionary**, *a.*

dèflect', *v.* bend or turn aside from straight line. **dèflec'xion** (-kshn), **dèflec'tion**, *n.*

dèfo'rèst, *v. t.* clear of forest. **dèforèstā'tion.** *n.*

dèform', *v. t.* spoil aspect or shape of; disfigure. **dèformed'** (-md), *a.* badly or unnaturally shaped. **dèfor'mity**, *n.* deformed state; malformation.

dèfraud', *v. t.* fraudulently deprive, cheat.

dèfray', *v. t.* provide money for.

dèfrock', *v. t.* unfrock.

dèfrost', *v. t.* remove ice or frost from, thaw.

deft, *a.* dextrous; clever and neat in action.

dèfunct', *a.* dead; obsolete.

dèfȳ, *v. t.* challenge *to* do or prove something; resist openly; present insuperable obstacles to.

dègen'eracy, *n.* degenerate state.

dègen'erate, *a.* having lost qualities proper to race or kind, debased. *n.* degenerate person. *v. i.* (-āt) become degenerate. **dègenerā'tion**, *n.*

degradā'tion, *n.* degrading; disgrace; thing that degrades.

dègrāde', *v. t.* reduce to lower rank; debase. **dègrād'ing**, *a.* dishonouring; humiliating.

dègree', *n.* step or stage in ascending or descending scale or process; stage in intensity or amount; unit by which angles are measured

(symbol °); unit of temperature (symbol °); academic rank given for proficiency in scholarship or as honour.

dēhȳ'drāte, *v.* remove water from, desiccate (esp. foods); lose water. **dēhȳdrā'tion**, *n.*

dē'ifȳ, *v. t.* make a god of. **dēificā'tion**, *n.*

deign (dān), *v. i.* condescend.

dē'ism, *n.* belief in existence of God, but not in divine revelation. **dē'ist**, *n.*

dē'ity, *n.* divine status or nature; god.

dèject', *v. t.* make sad or gloomy. **dèjec'ted**, *a.* **dèjec'tion**, *n.* dejected state.

dē jur'e (joor-; *or* dā yoorā), rightful, by right. (Latin)

dèlay', *v.* put off; hinder. *n.* tardiness; hindrance.

dèlec'table, *a.* delightful.

dēlectā'tion, *n.* enjoyment.

del'egacy, *n.* body of delegates.

del'ègāte, *v. t.* send as representative(s) to council or conference; hand over (authority) to representative(s). **del'egate**, *n.* such representative.

dèlègā'tion, *n.* delegating; delegacy; body of delegates.

dèlēte', *v. t.* cross out, erase (letter, word, etc.). **dèlē'tion**, *n.*

dèlētēr'ious, *a.* harmful.

delf(t), *n.* kind of earthenware originally made at Delft in Holland.

dèlib'erāte, *v.* consider or discuss carefully; **dèlib'erate**, *a.* intentional; fully considered; not hurried. **dèliberā'tion**, *n.* deliberating; being deliberate. **dèlib'erative**, *a.* of or appointed for deliberation or debate.

del'icacy, *n.* delicateness; refined feeling; choice kind of food.

del'icate, *a.* dainty; fastidious; easily harmed; liable to illness; fine, exquisite; sensitive; requiring careful handling.

delicatess'en, *n.* (shop selling) delicacies for table.

dèli'cious (-shus), *a.* very delightful, esp. to taste or smell.

dèlight' (-īt), *v.* please highly; take great pleasure *in. n.* (thing giving) great pleasure. **dèlight'ful**, *a.*

dèlim'it, *v. t.* determine limits or boundary of. **dēlimitā'tion**, *n.*

dèlin'ēāte, *v. t.* portray by drawing or description. **dèlinēā'tion**, *n.* **dèlin'ēātor**, *n.*

dèlin'quency, *n.* being delinquent; neglect of duty; misdeed. **dèlin'quent**, *n.* one who fails in duty or commits offence. *a.* defaulting, guilty.

dèli'rious, *a.* affected with delirium; raving; wildly excited. **dèli'rium**, *n.* disordered state of mind; wildly excited mood.

dèliv'er, *v. t.* rescue, save, set free; transfer or hand over; convey (letters, goods) to addressee or purchaser; aim (blow, ball, attack); utter, pronounce, (speech, etc.); help in birth of. *be delivered of*, give birth to. **dèliv'erer**, *n.*

dĕliv′erance, *n.* rescue; formal speech.

dĕliv′ery, *n.* delivering or being delivered; distribution of letters, etc.; manner of delivering a speech.

dell, *n.* little wooded hollow.

Del′phic, *a.* obscure, ambiguous (like the oracle at Delphi in ancient Greece).

delphin′ium, *n.* genus of flowering plants including larkspur. **delphinium blue,** deep blue.

del′ta, *n.* fourth letter of Greek alphabet, D (written Δ); triangular alluvial tract at mouth of large river. **delta wing,** triangular swept- -back wing of some aircraft.

delude′ (-ōōd *or* -ūd), *v.t.* deceive, mislead.

del′ūge, *n.* great flood, downpour. *v.t.* flood.

dĕlu′sion (-ōōzhn *or* -ūzhn), *n.* false opinion; false belief, esp. as symptom of mental illness. **dĕlu′sive,** *a.* deceptive, raising vain hopes.

dĕ lūxe, *a.* sumptuous; of superior kind.

delve, *v.* dig (*archaic*); make laborious search (*into*).

dem′agogue (-gog), *n.* orator or agitator appealing to passions of mob.

dĕmand′ (-ah-), *n.* request made imperiously; call or need for some article of trade; urgent claim. *v.t.* make demand for.

dĕmarcā′tion, *n.* marking of boundary.

démarche (dā′marsh), *n.* political step or proceeding. (French)

dĕmean′¹, *v.refl.* lower *oneself* in dignity.

dĕmean′², *v.refl.* conduct or bear *oneself* (in specified way). **dĕmean′our,** *n.* bearing.

dĕmen′ted, *a.* beside oneself.

demerār′a, *a.* yellowish-brown raw cane- -sugar.

dĕme′rit, *n.* fault; bad conduct mark.

dĕmesne′ (-ān *or* -ēn), *n.* territory; estate.

demi-, *pref.* half.

dem′igod, *n.* partly divine being; deified man.

dĕmīse′ (-z), *n.* death.

dĕmōb′ilize, *v.t.* disband, release from, armed forces. **dĕmōbiliza′tion,** *n.*

dĕmoc′racy, *n.* government by the people, esp. through elected representatives; State governed in this way. **dem′ocrat,** *n.* one who believes in democracy. **democrat′ic,** *a.* **dĕmoc′ratize,** *v.t.* **dĕmocratizā′tion,** *n.*

dĕmog′raphy, *n.* statistical study of life in human communities. **demograph′ic,** *a.*

dĕmol′ish, *v.t.* pull or throw down (building); destroy. **dĕmoli′tion** (*or* de-), *n.*

dē′mon, *n.* devil or evil spirit. **dĕmon′ic,** *a.* **dĕmonol′ogy,** *n.* study of beliefs about demons.

dĕmō′niac, *a.* possessed by demon; devilish; frenzied. **dĕmoni′acal,** *a.*

dem′onstrable, *a.* that can be shown or proved.

dem′onstrāte, *v.* give or be proof of; establish truth of; make or take part in demonstration. **demonstrā′tion,** *n.* proving or proof; explanation by performance; display of armed force; organized expression of opinion. **dĕmon′strative,** *a.* conclusive; given to, marked by, open expression of feelings; (Gram.) serving to point out or identify. **dem′onstrātor,** *n.* (esp.) science teacher doing practical work with students.

dĕmo′ralize, *v.t.* corrupt morals of; destroy morale of. **dĕmoralizā′tion,** *n.*

dĕmur′, *v.i.* (p.t. *demurred*), raise objections. *n.* raising of objections.

dĕmūre′, *a.* quiet and serious; coy.

den, *n.* wild beasts' lair; small private room.

dĕnār′ius (*or* -ar-), *n.* (pl. *denarii*), ancient- -roman silver coin.

dē′nary, *a.* of ten, decimal.

dēna′tionalize, *v.t.* (esp.) return (nationalized industry, etc.) to private ownership. **dēnationalizā′tion,** *n.*

dendrol′ogy, *n.* study of trees.

dēne, *n.* deep wooded valley.

dĕni′al, *n.* denying or refusing; contradiction.

den′ier, *n.* unit of fineness of silk, nylon, etc., yarn.

den′igrāte, *v.t.* blacken, defame. **denigrā′- tion,** *n.* **den′igrātor,** *n.*

den′im, *n.* twilled cotton fabric.

den′izen, *n.* inhabitant, occupant.

dĕnom′ināte, *v.t.* give name to: call.

dĕnominā′tion, *n.* name, title; class of units in money, etc.; distinctively named Church or sect. **dĕnominā′tional,** *a.* of a Church or sect.

dĕnom′inātor, *n.* number below line in vulgar fraction; divisor.

dĕnotā′tion, *n.* denoting; primary meaning of a word.

dĕnōte′, *v.t.* mark out, be sign of; indicate; signify.

dénouement (dānōō′mahṅ), *n.* final unravelling of plot in play, novel, etc.

dĕnounce′, *v.t.* inform against; speak violently against; give notice of termination of (treaty, etc.).

dense, *a.* closely packed together; crowded together; stupid. **dense′ly** (-sli), *adv.*

den′sity, *n.* closeness of substance; crowded state; stupidity.

dent, *n.* surface hollow or impression made by blow. *v.* mark, become marked, with dent.

den′tal, *a.* of tooth, teeth, or dentistry.

den′tifrice, *n.* paste or powder for cleaning teeth.

den′tist, *n.* person qualified to fill or extract decayed teeth, fit artificial teeth, etc. **den′- tistry,** *n.*

denti′tion, *n.* teething; arrangement of teeth.

den′ture (-cher), *n.* set of artificial teeth.

dēnūdā′tion, *n.* denuding; stripping.

dēnūde′, *v.t.* make naked or bare; strip *of.*

dĕnunciā′tion, *n.* denouncing; accusation. **dĕnun′ciatory,** *a.*

dĕnȳ′, *v.t.* declare untrue or non-existent; refuse; disown. *deny oneself,* be abstinent.

dēō′dorant, *n. & a.* deodorizing (substance).

dĕŏ'dorīze, v. t. rid of smell.

dĕoxyrĭbonŭclē'ic acid, (abbrev. *DNA*), substance present in chromosomes which controls the passing on of hereditary characteristics.

dĕpart', v. go away (from); set out; die; diverge or deviate. **dĕpar'ture** (-cher), n.

dĕpart'ment, n. separate part of a complex whole; branch of administration or business. **department store**, large shop selling great variety of goods. **dĕpartmen'tal**, a.

dĕpend', v. i. be conditional or dependent on; rely, reckon confidently, on. **dĕpend'able**, a. reliable.

dĕpen'dant, n. one who depends on another for maintenance.

dĕpen'dence, n. depending; reliance.

dĕpen'dency, n. something subordinate; State controlled by another.

dĕpen'dent, a. depending; relying; maintained at another's cost. n. dependant.

dĕpict', v. t. represent in picture or in words.

dĕpil'atory, a. & n. (preparation) used to remove hair from face, etc.

dĕplēte', v. t. use up or take away much of (store, etc.). **dĕplē'tion**, n.

dĕplor'able, a. regrettable; shocking.

dĕplore', v. t. regret; grieve over.

dĕploy', v. (of troops, warships, etc.) spread out into line; move strategically. **dĕploy'ment**, n.

dĕpop'ŭlāte, v. t. deprive wholly or partly of inhabitants. **dĕpopŭlā'tion**, n.

dĕport'¹, v. t. remove into exile; send out of the country. **dĕportā'tion**, n.

dĕport'², v. refl. behave or conduct *oneself*. **dĕport'ment**, n. behaviour, bearing.

dĕpōse' (-z), v. remove from office, dethrone; state, testify.

dĕpos'it (-z-), n. sum placed in a bank; sum paid as pledge or part payment; layer of accumulated matter. v. t. lay or set down; entrust for safe keeping; leave as deposit.

dĕposi'tion (-z-), n. deposing; (giving of) sworn evidence.

dĕpos'itor (-z-), n. person who deposits money, etc.

dĕpos'itory (-z-), n. storehouse.

dep'ot (-ō), n. storehouse; (Mil.) place for stores, headquarters; place where buses, etc., are kept.

dĕprāve', v. t. corrupt, esp. in moral character or habits. **dĕprāved'**, a. dissolute. **dĕprav'ity**, n. moral corruption, wickedness.

dep'rĕcāte, v. t. express disapproval or disavowal of; plead against. **dĕprĕcā'tion**, n. **dep'rĕcāting, dep'rĕcatory**, aa.

dĕprē'ciate (-shi-), v. belittle; lower in value. **dĕprecia'tion**, n. fall in value; depreciating. **dĕprē'ciatory**, a. disparaging.

dĕprĕdā'tion, n. plundering; (pl.) ravages. **de'prĕdātor**, n.

dĕpress', v. t. press down, lower; reduce; affect with economic depression; make despondent, deject. **dĕpress'ible**, a.

dĕpre'ssion (-shn), n. part of surface below general level; reduction in vigour or activity, esp. of trade; lowering of barometric pressure, centre of low pressure; (Med.) state of excessive dejection and reduced vitality.

dĕprīve', v. t. dispossess or strip *of*; prevent from use or enjoyment *of*. **dĕprivā'tion**, n. (esp.) keenly felt loss.

depth, n. being deep; measurement from top down, from front to back, or from surface inwards; profundity, intensity; deep or lowest or inmost part.

dĕpŭtā'tion, n. body of persons sent to represent others.

dĕpūte', v. t. commit (task, authority) to another; appoint as substitute.

dep'ūtize, v. i. act as deputy (*for*).

dep'ūty, n. person appointed to act for another or others. a. deputed; vice-.

dĕrail' (*or* dē-), v. t. cause (train) to leave the rails. **dĕrail'ment**, n.

dĕrange' (-j), v. t. throw into confusion. **dĕranged'**, a. insane. **dĕrange'ment**, n.

dĕrāte', v. t. lower or abolish rates on.

de'rĕlict, a. & n. abandoned, ownerless (thing, esp. ship at sea).

dĕrĕlic'tion (de-r-), n. neglect (*of* duty, etc.).

dĕrĕstrict', v. t. remove (specified) restriction(s) from.

dĕrīde', v. t. laugh scornfully at; mock. **dĕri'sion** (-zhn), n. ridicule, mockery. **dĕri'sive, dĕri'sory**, aa. scoffing, mocking.

dĕrivā'tion (de-r-), n. source; formation of a word from its root. **dĕriv'ative**, a. & n. (thing, word, etc.) derived from a source.

dĕrīve', v. obtain or have (*from* a source); have starting-point or origin (*from*); (passive, of words) be formed *from*.

dermatī'tis, n. inflammation of the skin.

dermatol'ogy, n. science of the skin and its diseases. **dermatol'ogist**, n. (esp.) specialist in diseases of the skin.

dĕrog'āte, v. i. detract. **dĕrog'atory**, a. lowering in honour or dignity; disparaging.

de'rrick, n. kind of hoisting-machine, esp. on ship; framework over deep bore-hole, esp. oil-well.

der'vish, n. Muslim friar vowed to poverty.

des'cant, n. (Mus.) melodic independent treble accompaniment to hymn-tune, etc.

dĕscend', v. come or go down; slope downwards; swoop on; be derived or descended *from*. **dĕscen'dant**, n. person or thing descended from another.

dĕscent', n. descending; slope; way down; sudden attack; ancestry.

dĕscrī'bable, a. that can be described.

dĕscrībe', v. t. give description of; mark out, draw, or move in (esp. geometrical figure).

dĕscrip'tion, n. portrait in words; kind, sort. **dĕscrip'tive**, a. serving to describe; characterized by description.

dĕscrý', v. t. succeed in seeing, esp. from a

distance.

des'ecrāte, *v.t.* destroy the sanctity of; profane. **desēcrā'tion,** *n.*

dēseg'rēgāte, *v.t.* end racial segregation in.

dèsert'[1] (-z-), *n.* (usu. pl.) (conduct or qualities deserving) reward or punishment.

dèsert'[2] (-z-), *v.* abandon, depart from, forsake; run away. **dèsert'er,** *n.* (esp.) soldier, etc., who leaves service without permission. **dèser'tion,** *n.*

des'ert[3] (-z-), *a. & n.* uninhabited and barren, esp. waterless (region).

dèserve' (-z-), *v.* be entitled by conduct or qualities to (recompense, good or bad treatment, etc.). **dèserv'ĕdly,** *adv.* **dèser'ving,** *a.* praiseworthy; worthy *of.*

des'iccāte, *v.t.* exhaust of moisture; dry up. **desiccā'tion,** *n.*

dèsign' (-zīn), *n.* plan, purpose; sketch; (art of) evolving general idea, construction, etc.; scheme; pattern. *v.* form or make design(s) for; purpose, intend. **design'er,** *n.*

des'ignāte (-z-), *v.t.* describe as; appoint to office. **des'ignate,** *a.* (placed after noun) appointed to office but not yet installed. **designā'tion,** *n.* name or title.

dèsign'ĕdly (-zīn-), *adv.* intentionally.

dèsign'ing (-zīn-), *a.* crafty, scheming.

dèsir'able (-z-), *a.* worth wishing for; pleasing. **dèsirabil'ity,** *n.*

dèsīre' (-z-), *n.* longing; eagerness to obtain; wish or request; lust. *v.t.* long for, crave, wish; request. **dèsīr'ous,** *a.* wishful, desiring.

dèsist' (-zist), *v.i.* cease (*from*).

desk, *n.* piece of furniture with flat or sloping top for reading, writing, office work, etc.

des'olate, *a.* left alone; uninhabited; dreary, forlorn. **des'olāte,** *v.t.* depopulate, devastate. **desolā'tion,** *n.*

dèspair', *n.* loss or absence of hope; cause of despair. *v.i.* lose or be without hope.

despatch: see **dispatch.**

despera'dō (-ah-), *n.* (pl. *desperadoes*), reckless ruffian.

des'perate, *a.* hopelessly bad; dangerous; reckless. **desperā'tion,** *n.*

des'picable, *a.* contemptible; vile.

dèspīse' (-z), *v.t.* consider oneself superior to; disdain.

dèspīte', *prep.* in spite of.

dèspoil', *v.t.* plunder, rob. **dèspoil'ment, dèspōliā'tion,** *nn.*

dèspond', *v.i.* lose heart or hope, be dejected. **dèspon'dency,** *n.* **dèspon'dent,** *a.*

des'pot, *n.* autocratic ruler; tyrant, oppressor. **dèspot'ic,** *a.* **des'potism,** *n.*

dèssert' (-z-), *n.* course of fruit, nuts, sweetmeats, etc., at end of dinner; (U.S.) sweet course. **dessert-spoon,** one between tablespoon and teaspoon in size.

destinā'tion, *n.* place for which person or thing is bound.

des'tine, *v.t.* foreordain, mark out, set apart (*to, for*).

des'tiny, *n.* what is destined to happen; fate; appointed or ultimate lot.

des'titūte, *a.* lacking the necessaries of life; in absolute poverty. *destitute of*, lacking. **destitū'tion,** *n.*

dèstroy', *v.t.* break up, make useless; kill. **dèstroy'er,** *n.* one that destroys; small fast warship, orig. for attacking torpedo-boats.

dèstruc'tible, *a.* that can be destroyed.

dèstruc'tion, *n.* destroying; ruin.

dèstruc'tive, *a.* causing destruction; (of criticism, etc.) negative, not constructive.

desū'ĕtūde (*or* des'wi-), *n.* state of disuse.

des'ultory, *a.* changing from one subject to another; unmethodical.

dètach', *v.t.* unfasten and remove (*from*); separate. **dètached'** (-cht), *a.* unconcerned; separate. **dètach'ment,** *n.* (esp.) body of troops, etc., separately employed.

dē'tail, *n.* item, small or subordinate particular; dealing with things item by item; (Mil.) small detachment. **dètail',** *v.t.* give particulars of; (Mil.) send off on special duty.

dètain', *v.t.* keep in custody or under restraint; keep back; keep waiting.

dètect', *v.t.* discover; find out. **dètec'tion,** *n.*

dètec'tive, *n.* person, esp. policeman, employed in investigating criminal activities, etc. *a.* of or concerned with detectives or detection.

dèten'tion, *n.* detaining, being detained; confinement.

dèter', *v.t.* (p.t. deterred), discourage, hinder.

dèter'gent, *n. & a.* cleansing (agent).

dètēr'iorāte, *v.* make or grow worse. **dètēriorā'tion,** *n.*

dèter'minant, *n.* decisive factor.

dèter'minate, *a.* limited; of definite scope or nature.

dèterminā'tion, *n.* determining or being determined; settled intention; resoluteness.

dèter'mine, *v.* settle; decide; find out or decide exactly; resolve.

dète'rrent, *a.* serving to deter. *n.* thing that deters, esp. nuclear weapon of a country or alliance intended to prevent attack by another.

dètest', *v.t.* hate or dislike intensely; abhor. **dètest'able,** *a.* **dētestā'tion,** *n.*

dēthrōne', *v.t.* depose (sovereign). **dēthrōne'ment,** *n.*

det'onāte (*or* dē-), *v.* (cause to) explode with loud report. **detonā'tion,** *n.* **det'onātor,** *n.* detonating contrivance.

dètour' (-oor; *or* dā-), *n.* deviation; roundabout way or course.

dètract', *v. detract from*, reduce the credit due to, depreciate (person, his merit). **dètrac'tion,** *n.* **dètrac'tor,** *n.* disparager, belittler.

dētrain', *v.* alight, make (troops) alight, from train.

det'riment, n. harm, damage.

detrimen'tal, a. damaging, harmful.

dêtri'tion, n. wearing away by rubbing.

de trop (di trō), not wanted; in the way; unwelcome. (French)

deuce[1] (dūs), n. the two on dice or playing cards; (Tennis) score of 40 all.

deuce[2] (dūs), n. the devil.

de'vastâte, v.t. lay waste, ravage. **de'-vastâting,** a. (informal) very effective. **devastâ'tion,** n.

dèvel'op, v. unfold, bring or come from latent to active or visible state; (cause to) grow larger, fuller, or to maturity; make usable or profitable, esp. build on (land). **dèvel'oper,** n. (esp.) chemical for developing photographs. **dèvel'opment,** n.

dě'viâte, v.i. turn aside (from); digress. **dèviâ'tion,** n. deviating; turning away from standard, normal position, etc.

dèvice', n. invention, contrivance; scheme, trick; (Herald.) emblem, motto. left to one's own devices, left to amuse oneself.

dev'il, n. personified spirit of evil (the Devil); wicked or cruel person; one who devils for author or barrister. v.i. work without acknowledgement for author or barrister. devil-may-care, happy-go-lucky, reckless. **dev'ilish,** a. monstrously cruel or wicked. **dev'ilment,** n. mischief, wild spirits. **dev'-ilry,** n. black magic; wickedness; reckless daring.

dê'vious, a. winding; indirect.

dèvîse' (-z), v.t. plan, think out, invent.

dèvoid', a. devoid of, empty of, without.

dèvolve', v. throw (task, duty) upon (another); (of duties) be thrown upon (another).

dèvôte', v.t. give up exclusively to. **dèvôt'ed,** a. loving and loyal. **devotee',** n. ardent follower.

dèvô'tion, n. devoutness; strong affection; (pl.) prayers. **dèvô'tional,** a. concerning divine worship.

dèvour' (-ower), v.t. eat up; destroy or consume; take in greedily.

dèvout', a. earnestly religious; reverential.

dew, n. atmospheric vapour condensed in droplets during night; beaded moisture. **dew'drop,** drop of dew. **dew-pond,** shallow pond formerly thought to be entirely fed by atmospheric condensation. **dew'y,** a.

dew'lap, n. fold of loose skin hanging from throat of cattle.

dexte'rity, n. skill; neatness of handling.

dex'trous, a. handling things neatly; skilful.

dho'ti (dō-), n. loin-cloth worn by male Hindus.

dhow (dow), n. Arab sailing-ship.

di-[1], pref. two-, double-.

dia-, di-[2], pref. (di- before vowel), through, thorough(ly), apart, across.

diabê'tês (-z), n. disease characterized by excessive accumulation of glucose in blood. **diabet'ic,** a. of, having, diabetes. n. person having diabetes.

diabol'ic, diabol'ical, aa. of the Devil; atrociously cruel or wicked.

diac'onal, a. of a deacon. **diac'onate,** n. deacon's (term of) office; body of deacons.

di'adem, n. crown or fillet.

diaer'èsis (dī-êr'), n. (pl. diaeresēs), mark (¨) over vowel to show that it is sounded separately (e.g. naïve, pr. nah-ēv').

diagnôse' (-z), v.t. determine nature of (disease). **diagnô'sis,** n. (pl. diagnosēs), identification of disease by means of patient's symptoms, etc. **diagnos'tic,** a.

diag'onal, a. crossing a straight-sided figure from corner to corner. n. line so drawn; any oblique line.

di'agram, n. figure or sketch drawn to explain or illustrate statement, process, etc. **diagrammat'ic,** a.

di'al, n. face of clock or watch; marked face or plate with moving pointer; mechanism of discs for making calls on automatic telephone. v.t. (p.t. dialled), call telephone number by using dial.

di'alect, n. form of speech peculiar to district or class. **dialec'tal,** a.

dialec'tic, n. (usu. pl.) art of arguing; testing truth by discussion.

di'alogue (-og), n. conversation, esp. in play, novel, etc., or as form of literary composition.

diam'êter, n. (length of) straight line passing from side to side through centre of circle, sphere, or other curved body or figure. **diamet'rical,** a. of or along a diameter. **diamet'rically,** adv. directly, entirely.

di'amond, n. very hard and brilliant precious stone; rhombus (or square) placed with diagonals horizontal and vertical.

diapâ'son (-zn), n. (Mus.) either of chief foundation stops of organ; (fig.) swelling burst of harmony.

di'aper, n. fine linen towelling; small towel; baby's napkin.

diaph'anous, a. transparent.

di'aphragm (-am), n. muscular partition between chest and abdomen in mammals; vibrating membrane in acoustic instrument; device for varying aperture of camera lens.

di'arist, n. one who keeps a diary.

diarrhoe'a (-rêa), n. excessive frequency and looseness of bowel-evacuation.

di'ary, n. daily record of events, etc.; book for this or for noting engagements.

diaton'ic, a. (Mus., of scale) proceeding by notes proper to its key without chromatic alteration.

di'atrîbe, n. piece of bitter criticism; abuse, denunciation.

dibb'er, dibb'le, nn. gardener's implement for making holes in ground. **dibb'le,** v.t. put plants in with dibble.

dîce, n.pl. pl. of die[1]. v.i. gamble with dice; cut into small cubes.

dichot'omy (-k-), *n.* division into two.

dick'y, dick'ey, *n.* dicky-bird; false shirt--front; seat at back of vehicle. *a.* (*slang*) unsound, shaky. **dicky-bird,** child's word for small bird.

dicotylē'don, *n.* flowering plant with two cotyledons.

dic'taphōne, *n.* machine recording what is spoken into it. **P.**

dictāte', *v.* say aloud matter to be written down; command firmly. **dic'tāte,** *n.* (usu. pl.) bidding (of conscience, reason, etc.). **dictā'tion,** *n.*

dictā'tor, *n.* absolute ruler; person with supreme authority. **dictator'ial,** *a.* absolute; overbearing, imperious. **dictā'torship,** *n.*

dic'tion, *n.* choice and use of words; manner of speaking, enunciation.

dic'tionary, *n.* book arranged alphabetically containing the words of a language, their meanings, equivalents in other languages, etc.; book of reference with items arranged alphabetically.

dic'tum, *n.* (pl. *dicta*), pronouncement; maxim, saying.

did, *p.t.* of **do.**

didac'tic (*or* dī-), *a.* meant to instruct; having the manner of a teacher.

dīe¹, *n.* (pl. *dīce*, often used as sing.), small cube with faces marked with 1 - 6 spots, used in games of chance; (pl. *dīes*), engraved stamp for impressing design on coin, etc., embossing paper, etc.

dīe², *v.i.* (pres. p. *dỹing*) cease to live; come to an end; fade away. **die-casting,** process of making castings (*die-castings*) from metal mould(s). **die-hard,** one who stubbornly resists change.

diesel (dē'zl), *n.* diesel engine. **diesel engine,** internal-combustion engine in which fuel (*diesel oil*) is ignited by heat generated by air compressed in cylinder(s).

dī'et¹, *n.* congress, esp. as English name for foreign parliament, etc.

dī'et², *n.* kind of food usually eaten (by person, community, animal, etc.); prescribed course or allowance of food. *v.* keep to special diet. **dīetet'ic,** *a.* of diet. **dīetet'ics,** *n.* science of diet. **dīeti'tian, dīeti'cian** (-shn), *n.* expert in dietetics.

dif-, *pref.*: see **dis-.**

diff'er, *v.i.* be unlike; be distinguishable *from*; disagree.

diff'erence, *n.* unlikeness; degree or amount of unlikeness; disagreement.

diff'erent, *a.* of other nature, form, or quality; not the same; unlike.

differen'tial (-shl), *a.* of, showing, depending on, a difference; varying with circumstances; distinctive.

differen'tiāte (-shi-), *v.* constitute the difference between; develop into unlikeness; discriminate. **differentiā'tion,** *n.*

diff'icult, *a.* hard to do, deal with, or understand; troublesome.

diff'iculty, *n.* being difficult to do, understand, etc.; difficult point or situation; obstacle.

diff'idence, *n.* lack of self-confidence; shyness. **diff'ident,** *a.*

diffract', *v.t.* break up (beam of light) into series of dark and light bands. **diffrac'tion,** *n.*

diffūse' (-z), *v.* shed or spread around, disperse; (cause to) intermingle. *a.* (pr.-s) dispersed, not concentrated; wordy, not concise. **diffū'sion** (-zhn), *n.* **diffū'sive,** *a.*

dig, *v.* (p.t. *dug*; pres.p. *digging*), turn up soil with spade, etc.; thrust or plunge *in*, *into*; prod, nudge, poke. *n.* piece of digging; thrust or poke.

digest' (*or* dī-), *v.* prepare (food) in stomach and intestines for use by the body; (of food) undergo digestion; absorb into the mind; summarize. **dī'gest,** *n.* summary. **digest'ible,** *a.*

diges'tion (-schn; *or* dī-), *n.* digesting; power of digesting food. **diges'tive,** *a.* aiding digestion.

digg'er (-g-), *n.* one who digs, esp. for gold.

di'git, *n.* each numeral from 0 to 9; finger or toe. **dig'ital,** *a.*

digitā'lis, *n.* heart stimulant made from dried leaves of foxglove.

dig'nifỹ, *v.t.* give dignity to. **dig'nified** (-īd), *a.* having or showing dignity, stately.

dig'nitary, *n.* holder of high office, esp. in the Church.

dig'nity, *n.* worth, excellence; honourable rank; stateliness.

digress' (*or* di-), *v.i.* turn aside temporarily from the main subject. **digre'ssion** (-shn), *n.* **digress'ive,** *a.*

dīke, dỹke, *n.* channel or ditch; long low wall, embankment. *v.t.* protect with dike(s).

dilapidā'tion, *n.* falling into, being in, state of disrepair or decay. **dilap'idāted,** *a.* in disrepair or decay.

dīlāte', *v.* widen or expand; enlarge. **dīlatā'tion, dīlā'tion,** *nn.*

dil'atory, *a.* slow in doing things; causing delay.

dīlemm'a (*or* di-), *n.* position leaving only a choice between two or more equally unsatisfactory alternatives.

dilèttan'tè, *n.* (pl. *dilettanti*), amateur; one who studies a subject slightly or fitfully. *a.* amateur; desultory.

dil'igence, *n.* persistent application to work. **dil'igent,** *a.* hard-working; showing care and effort.

dill, *n.* herb with seeds used in pickles.

dīlūte' (*or* -ōōt), *v.t.* reduce in strength by addition of water, etc.; thin down, weaken. *a.* diluted. **dīlū'tion,** *n.*

dim, *a.* (*dimmer, dimmest*), not bright or clear; obscure; indistinct. *v.* (p.t. *dimmed*), make or become dim.

dīme, *n.* (U.S.) (coin worth) ten cents.

dimen'sion (-shn; *or* dī-), *n.* any of the measurements length, breadth, or depth; (pl.) size, extent. **dimen'sional,** *a.*

dimin'ish, *v.* make or become less.

diminūen'dō, (as musical direction, abbrev. *dim.*) gradually softer.

diminū'tion, *n.* lessening.

dimin'ūtive, *a.* (of words, etc.) conveying idea of smallness; tiny. *n.* diminutive word (e.g. *droplet, kitchenette*).

dim'ity, *n.* cotton fabric with woven stripes.

dim'ple, *n.* small hollow, esp. in cheek or chin; ripple. *v.* mark with, break into, dimples or ripples.

din, *n.* continuous roar of confused noise. *v.t.* (p.t. *dinned*), utter continuously (fact, advice, *into* person or person's ears).

dine, *v.* take dinner; entertain at dinner. **dī'ner,** *n.* one who dines; dining-car. **dining- -car, -room,** railway coach, room, in which meals are served. **ding-dong,** *adv.* & *n.* (with) sound of bell or alternate strokes of two bells; desperate, neck-and-neck.

ding'hy (-ngi *or* -nggi), *n.* small boat.

dingle (ding'gl), *n.* deep shady dell.

dingo (ding'gō), *n.* (pl. *dingoes*), Australian wild dog.

din'gy (-ji), *a.* dull-coloured; grimy; dirty- -looking. **din'giness,** *n.*

dining: see **dine**.

dinn'er, *n.* chief meal of the day; banquet. **dinner-jacket,** man's short black coat for evening wear.

di'nosaur, *n.* any of various extinct reptiles, some of which were of gigantic size.

dint, *n.* dent. *by dint of,* by force or means of. *v.t.* dent.

dīo'cēsan (-zn), *a.* of diocese. *n.* bishop in relation to diocese.

di'ocese (-sis *or* -sēz), *n.* district under bishop's pastoral care.

diŏx'īde, *n.* oxide with two atoms of oxygen to one of metal, etc.

dip, *v.* (p.t. *dipped*), put or let down temporarily or partially into liquid; go under water and come out quickly; (cause to) go down then up again. *dip* (*into*), read hurriedly. *n.* dipping; downward slope; short bathe; vermin-killing preparation into which sheep are dipped.

diphthēr'ia, *n.* acute infectious disease with inflammation of the throat.

diph'thong, *n.* union of two vowels in one sound.

diplō'ma, *n.* document conferring honour, privilege, or licence, esp. educational institution's certificate.

diplō'macy, *n.* management of international relations; tact.

dip'lomat, *n.* person engaged in diplomacy, esp. accredited to court or seat of government; skilful negotiator. **diplomat'ic,** *a.* of diplomacy; skilled in diplomacy; tactful, artful. **diplō'matist,** *n.* diplomat.

dipp'er, *n.* a diving-bird; ladle.

dipsomā'nia, *n.* excessive craving for alcohol. **dipsomā'niac,** *n.* & *a.*

dīre, *a.* dreadful, terrible. **dīre'ly,** *adv.*

direct' (*or* dī-), *a.* straight; not crooked or devious; frank. *adv.* by direct route; without intermediaries. *v.t.* address (letter, etc., to person etc.); turn (thing, eyes, attention) straight to something; tell the way *to*; command; supervise production of (film, etc.).

direc'tion (*or* dī-), *n.* address of letter, etc.; orders; instructions; course; point to which one moves or looks.

direc'tive (*or* dī-), *a.* giving guidance. *n.* statement for guidance of staff, etc.

direct'ly (*or* dī-), *adv.* at once; very soon; in a direct manner.

direc'tor (*or* dī-), *n.* superintendent, manager; member of board directing affairs of company, etc.; person supervising making of film, etc. **direc'torate,** *n.* board of directors. **direc'torship,** *n.*

direc'tory (*or* dī-), *n.* list of inhabitants of district with their addresses, telephone subscribers with their numbers, etc.

dire'ful (-īrf-), *a.* dire, terrible.

dirge, *n.* song of mourning; lament.

di'rigible, *n.* & *a.* (balloon or airship) that can be steered.

dirk, *n.* kind of dagger.

dirndl (skirt), woman's full gathered skirt with tight waistband.

dirt, *n.* mud, dust, filth; anything worthless or unclean; earth, soil.

dir'ty, *a.* soiled; foul; obscene; mean; (of weather) rough. *v.t.* make or become dirty.

dis-, *pref.* (*dif-* before *f*), asunder, away, apart or between; not, the reverse of.

disabil'ity, *n.* thing that disables or disqualifies.

disā'ble, *v.t.* make incapable of action or use by injury, etc.; cripple. **disā'blement,** *n.*

disabūse' (-z), *v.t.* undeceive.

disaccord', *n.* disagreement.

disadvan'tage (-vah-), *n.* unfavourable condition. **disadvantā'geous** (-jus), *a.*

disaffec'ted, *a.* discontented; unfriendly; disloyal. **disaffec'tion,** *n.*

disagree', *v.i.* differ; fail to agree (*with*); quarrel. **disagree'ment,** *n.*

disagree'able, *a.* unpleasant; ill-tempered.

disallow', *v.t.* reject; prohibit.

disappear', *v.i.* pass from sight; vanish, be lost. **disappear'ance,** *n.*

disappoint', *v.t.* fail to fulfil hopes or expectation. **disappoint'ment,** *n.*

disapprobā'tion, *n.* disapproval.

disapprove' (-ōōv), *v.* have or express unfavourable opinion of. **disappro'val,** *n.*

disarm', *v.* take away weapons from; allay suspicions of, win over; abandon or cut down armaments. **disar'mament,** *n.* reduction of armaments.

disarrange' (-nj), *v.t.* put into disorder. **disarrange'ment,** *n.*

disarray', *n.* disorder, confusion.

disas'ter (-zahs-), *n.* sudden or great misfortune. **disas'trous,** *a.*

disavow', *v.t.* disown; deny knowledge of; repudiate. **disavow'al,** *n.*

disband', *v.* break up; disperse. **disband'ment,** *n.*

disbelieve', *v.* refuse to believe; have no faith in. **disbelief'** (*or* dis'-), *n.*

disburd'en, *v.t.* relieve of burden.

disburse', *v.* pay out; expend money. **disburse'ment,** *n.*

disc, disk, *n.* round flat plate or surface or part; gramophone record. **disc-jockey,** introducer of radio-programme of gramophone records.

discard', *v.* throw out or away; cast aside.

discern', *v.t.* perceive clearly with mind or senses. **discern'ible,** *a.* **discern'ing,** *a.* having quick or true insight. **discern'ment,** *n.*

discharge', *v.* unload; dismiss; release; let flow; send as missile; acquit oneself of (duty, debt); (of river) flow out. *n.* (*or* dis'-) discharging or being discharged.

disci'ple, *n.* one who takes another as his teacher or leader; one of Christ's twelve followers.

disciplina̅r'ian, *n.* maintainer of strict discipline.

dis'ciplinary, *a.* of discipline; promoting discipline.

dis'cipline, *n.* order maintained among persons under control or command; control; chastisement; branch of knowledge. *v.t.* train to obedience and order; chastise.

disclaim', *v.t.* disown, disavow. **disclai'mer,** *n.* disavowal.

disclo̅se' (-z), *v.t.* expose to view; reveal. **disclo̅'sure** (-zher), *n.* disclosing; thing disclosed.

disco'lour (-uler), *v.* spoil the colour of; lose or change colour.

discom'fit (-kum-), *v.t.* defeat; disconcert. **discom'fiture** (-cher), *n.*

discom'fort (-kum-), *n.* uneasiness of body or mind; lack of comfort.

discompo̅se' (-z), *v.t.* disturb composure of; ruffle. **discompo̅'sure** (-zher), *n.*

disconcert', *v.t.* upset; embarrass.

disconnect', *v.t.* sever the connection of or between. **disconnec'ted,** *a.* incoherent, jerky. **disconnec'tion, disconne'xion,** *n.*

discon'solate, *a.* downcast; unhappy; inconsolable.

discontent', *n.* lack of contentment. **discontent'ed,** *a.* dissatisfied, unhappy.

discontin'ūe, *v.t.* cease; not go on with. **discontin'ūance,** *n.* **discontinū'ity,** *n.* **discontin'ūous,** *a.*

dis'cord, *n.* disagreement, strife; harsh noise; lack of harmony. **discor'dance,** *n.* **discor'dant,** *a.*

dis'cothèque (-tek), *n.* club, hall, etc., where dancing is accompanied by recorded music.

dis'count, *n.* deduction from nominal value or price or amount. **discount',** *v.t.* allow for exaggeration; disregard.

discoun'tenance, *v.t.* refuse to approve of; discourage.

discou'rage (-ku-), *v.t.* reduce confidence or spirits of; dissuade. **discou'ragement,** *n.*

dis'course (-kors), *n.* lecture, sermon, treatise; talk, conversation. **discourse',** *v.i.* give discourse; converse.

discour'teous (-ker-), *a.* rude, uncivil. **discour'tesy,** *n.*

disco'ver (-ku-), *v.t.* obtain sight or knowledge of for the first time; find out. **disco'verer,** *n.* **disco'very,** *n.* discovering; thing discovered.

discred'it, *v.t.* refuse to believe; bring dishonour on. *n.* loss of good reputation. **discred'itable,** *a.* bringing discredit, shameful.

discreet', *a.* prudent; cautious in speech or action.

discrep'ancy, *n.* difference; failure to tally. **discrep'ant,** *a.*

discre̅te', *a.* separate, distinct.

discre'tion, *n.* being discreet; sound judgement; freedom to decide or act as one thinks fit. **discre'tionary,** *a.*

discrim'inate, *v.t.* make or see difference (*between*); single out for different treatment. **discrimina'tion,** *n.*

discur'sive, *a.* rambling, digressive.

dis'cus, *n.* heavy disc thrown in athletic contests.

discuss', *v.t.* examine by argument; debate. **discu'ssion** (-shn), *n.*

disdain', *v.t.* treat as unworthy of notice or of oneself; scorn. *n.* contemptuous neglect or dislike. **disdain'ful,** *a.*

disease' (-zēz), *n.* unhealthy condition; (particular) illness or disorder. **diseased',** *a.* affected with disease.

disembark', *v.* put or go ashore. **disembarka'tion,** *n.*

disemba'rrass, *v.t.* rid or relieve *of*; disentangle. **disemba'rrassment,** *n.*

disembod'y, *v.t.* separate, free, from the body.

disembow'el, *v.t.* (p.t. *disembowelled*), remove entrails of; rip up belly of.

disembroil', *v.t.* extricate from confusion or entanglement.

disenchant' (-ah-), *v.t.* free from enchantment or fascination; disillusion. **disenchant'ment,** *n.*

disengage' (-n-g-), *v.* detach; free. **disengaged',** *a.* at leisure; vacant.

disentang'le (-nggl), *v.t.* unravel; extricate. **disentang'lement,** *n.*

disestab'lish, *v.t.* end established status of; (esp.) separate Church from connection with State. **disestab'lishment,** *n.*

disfa̅'vour (-ver), *n.* dislike; disapproval.

disfig'ure (-ger), *v.t.* spoil the beauty or appearance of, deface. **disfig'urement**, *n.*

disfran'chise (-z), *v.t.* deprive of the right of voting. **disfran'chisement**, *n.*

disgorge', *v.* eject; give up; (of river) discharge.

disgrace', *n.* loss of favour, downfall; shame; cause of reproach. *v.t.* dismiss from favour; bring shame upon. **disgrace'ful**, *a.*

disgrunt'led (-ld), *a.* discontented.

disguise' (-gīz), *v.t.* make unrecognizable; pass off *as* something else; cloak or hide. *n.* disguised state; device or garb used to disguise.

disgust', *n.* strong aversion, repugnance; indignation. *v.t.* cause disgust in. **disgus'ting**, *a.*

dish, *n.* shallow flat-bottomed vessel for food; food served in dish or prepared for table; dish-like concavity. *v.t.* put into dish for serving (also *dish up*); make concave or dish--shaped. **dish-cloth**, cloth for washing dishes, etc.

dishabille' (-sabēl), *n.* partly dressed state.

dishar'mony (dis-h-), *n.* lack of harmony, discord.

dishear'ten (dis-har-), *v.t.* make despondent.

dishev'elled (-shevld), *a.* with disordered hair; untidy.

dishon'est (dison-), *a.* not honest; fraudulent; deceitful. **dishon'esty**, *n.*

dishon'our (dison-), *v.t.* treat with indignity; bring dishonour upon. *n.* dishonoured state; loss of good reputation. **dishon'ourable**, *a.* shameful; unprincipled.

disillu'sion (-zhn; *or* -ōozhn), *v.t.* free from illusions; wake to realities. **disillu'sionment**, *n.*

disinclina'tion, *n.* slight unwillingness or dislike. **disincline'**, *v.t.* make unwilling or averse.

disinfect', *v.t.* cleanse of infection, destroy germs of disease in. **disinfec'tant**, *n.* & *a.* (substance) that disinfects. **disinfec'tion**, *n.*

disingen'uous (-j-), *a.* insincere; not frank.

disinhe'rit, *v.t.* deprive of inheritance.

disin'tegrate, *v.* separate into component parts; fall to pieces. **disintegra'tion**, *n.*

disinter', *v.t.* (p.t. *disinterred*), exhume; dig out; unearth.

disin'terested, *a.* not influenced by self--interest, impartial; (*informal*) not interested.

disjoin', *v.t.* separate, disunite.

disjoin'ted, *a.* disconnected; rambling.

disk: see disc.

dislike', *v.t.* not like; have aversion or objection to. *n.* feeling of not liking.

dis'locate, *v.t.* put out of joint; disorganize; disturb. **disloca'tion**, *n.*

dislodge', *v.t.* remove, force to move, from position. **dislodge'ment**, *n.*

disloy'al, *a.* not loyal; betraying trust. **disloy'alty**, *n.*

dis'mal (-z-), *a.* cheerless, gloomy.

disman'tle, *v.t.* strip of equipment or furnishings; take to pieces.

dismast' (-ah-), *v.t.* deprive (ship) of mast(s).

dismay', *n.* consternation; feeling of despair. *v.t.* affect with dismay; reduce to despair.

dismem'ber, *v.t.* tear or cut the limbs from; divide up. **dismem'berment**, *n.*

dismiss', *v.t.* send away; disband; discharge; put out of one's thoughts. **dismiss'al**, *n.*

dismount', *v.* (cause to) alight from horseback, etc.; remove (thing) from its mount.

disobe'dience, *n.* disobeying, rebelliousness. **disobe'dient**, *a.*

disobey' (-bā), *v.* disregard orders; break rules; not obey.

disoblige', *v.t.* disregard convenience or wishes of. **disobli'ging**, *a.*

disor'der, *n.* confusion; tumult, riot; bodily or mental illness. *v.t.* disarrange; upset. **disor'derly**, *a.* untidy; unruly.

disor'ganize, *v.t.* upset working or system of; throw into confusion. **disorganiza'tion**, *n.*

disown' (-ōn) *v.t.* refuse to recognize, repudiate, disclaim.

dispa'rage, *v.t.* speak slightingly of, belittle. **dispa'ragement**, *n.*

dis'parate, *a.* essentially different.

dispa'rity, *n.* inequality; difference.

dispa'ssionate (-shon-), *a.* free from emotion; impartial.

dispatch', **despatch'**, *v.t.* send off; kill; get (business, etc.) done promptly. *n.* sending off; rapidity; official message. **dispatch--rider**, motor-cyclist, etc., carrying military messages.

dispel', *v.t.* (p.t. *dispelled*), drive away; scatter.

dispen'sable, *a.* that can be done without.

dispen'sary, *n.* place where medicine is dispensed.

dispensa'tion, *n.* distributing, dealing out, exemption; ordering or management, esp. by divine providence.

dispense', *v.* distribute, deal out; administer; make up (medicine) from prescription. *dispense with*, do without. **dispen'ser**, *n.* (esp.) person who is trained to dispense medicines; container that dispenses selected quantity at a time.

disperse', *v.* (cause to) go in different directions; scatter. **disper'sal, disper'sion** (-shn), *nn.*

dispi'rit, *v.t.* make despondent, depress.

displace', *v.t.* shift from proper place; oust; remove from office. **displace'ment**, *n.* displacing; amount or weight of liquid displaced by object floating or immersed in it.

display', *v.t.* show; spread out to view. *n.* displaying; exhibition; ostentation.

displease' (-z), *v.t.* offend, annoy; make indignant. **displeas'ure** (-plezher), *n.* anger; disapproval; vexation.

disport', *v.* (*archaic*) frolic; enjoy *oneself*.

dispo'sable (-z-), *a.* that can be got rid of;

available for use.

dispŏ'sal (-z-), *n.* getting rid of; settling, dealing with; sale; control. *at one's disposal*, to be used as one wishes.

dispōse' (-z), *v.* place suitably or in order; bring (person, mind) into certain state; make willing or desirous *to*. *dispose of*, get rid of, finish, kill, sell.

disposi'tion (-zi-), *n.* disposing or arrangement; character, temperament.

dispossess' (-zes), *v.t.* oust or dislodge; deprive (*of*). **disposse'ssion** (-zeshn), *n.*

disprŏof', *n.* refutation, thing that disproves.

dispropor'tion, *n.* lack of proportion. **dispropor'tionate**, *a.* relatively too large or too small.

disprove' (-ōov), *v.t.* prove false or wrong.

dispū'table (*or* dis'-), *a.* that may be questioned or disputed.

dispūtā'tion, *n.* controversial argument; debate. **dispūtā'tious** (-shus), *a.*

dispūte', *v.* hold debate; quarrel; controvert; contend; resist. *n.* controversy, debate; quarrel; difference of opinion.

disqual'ifȳ (-ol-), *v.t.* make unfit or ineligible. **disqualificā'tion**, *n.*

disquī'ĕt, *n.* anxiety, uneasiness. *v.t.* make uneasy. **disquī'ĕtūde**, *n.*

disrĕgard', *v.t.* pay no attention to; ignore. *n.* indifference, neglect.

disrĕpair', *n.* bad condition due to lack of repairs.

disrep'ūtable, *a.* not respectable; having a bad reputation.

disrĕpūte', *n.* bad repute; discredit.

disrĕspect', *n.* lack of respect. **disrĕspect'ful**, *a.* showing disrespect.

disrōbe', *v.* divest of, take off, robe or garment.

disrupt', *v.t.* shatter; separate forcibly; disorganize (communications, etc.). **disrup'tion**, *n.* **disrup'tive**, *a.*

dissatisfac'tion, *n.* discontent.

dissat'isfȳ, *v.t.* fail to satisfy; make discontented.

dissect', *v.t.* cut up (esp. animal body, plant, etc.) to examine and display structure, etc.; examine or criticize. **dissec'tion**, *n.*

dissem'ble, *v.* conceal or disguise; be hypocritical.

dissem'ināte, *v.t.* scatter, spread, disperse, widely. **disseminā'tion**, *n.*

dissen'sion (-shn), *n.* discord arising from difference in opinion.

dissent', *v.t.* differ in opinion, express different opinion (*from*); differ from established or national Church. **dissen'ter**, *n.* (esp.) member of dissenting Church or sect.

dissen'tiĕnt (-shi-), *a.* not agreeing, dissenting. *n.* dissentient person.

dissertā'tion, *n.* discourse or treatise.

disser'vice, *n.* harmful or unhelpful action.

diss'ident, *a.* disagreeing.

dissim'ilar, *a.* unlike. **dissimila'rity**, *n.*

dissim'ūlāte, *v.* be hypocritical; dissemble. **dissimūlā'tion**, *n.*

diss'ipāte, *v.* dispel; disappear; squander or fritter away. **diss'ipāted**, *a.* (esp.) given up to dissipation. **dissipā'tion**, *n.* frivolous and often harmful pleasures; intemperance.

dissō'ciāte (-shi-), *v.t.* cut off from association or society. **dissōciā'tion**, *n.*

dissol'ūble, *a.* that can be dissolved.

diss'olute (-ōot *or* -ŭt), *a.* lax in morals, debauched.

dissolū'tion (-lōo- *or* -lū-), *n.* disintegration; dissolving (of marriage, partnership, etc.); dismissal of assembly, esp. of Parliament before general election.

dissolve' (-z-), *v.* mix with liquid, solid, or gas without chemical action so as to form homogeneous liquid or solution; mix thus *in* liquid; disperse; put an end to.

diss'onant, *a.* discordant; jarring. **diss'onance**, *n.* discord.

dissuade' (-wād), *v.t.* advise to refrain (*from*); persuade against. **dissuā'sion** (-zhn), *n.* **dissuā'sive**, *a.*

dis'taff (-ahf), *n.* cleft stick holding wool or flax for spinning. **distaff side**, female branch of family.

dis'tance, *n.* extent of space between two points; being far off, remoteness; distant behaviour. *v.t.* place, make seem, far off; outdistance.

dis'tant, *a.* at considerable or specified distance; cold in manner.

distāste', *n.* dislike. **distāste'ful**, *a.* disagreeable, offensive.

distem'per[1], *n.* catarrhal disease of dogs; (*archaic*) illness.

distem'per[2], *n.* substance used for painting in colour on plaster. *v.t.* paint with distemper.

distend', *v.* swell out, enlarge, by pressure from within. **disten'sion**, *n.*

distil', *v.* (p.t. *distilled*), subject to, undergo, distillation; make, extract, drive *off*, by distillation.

distillā'tion, *n.* vaporizing and subsequent condensation of substance to purify or decompose it, extract spirit or essence, etc.

distill'er, *n.* (esp.) one who distils alcoholic spirit. **distill'ery**, *n.* establishment for distilling alcoholic spirit.

distinct', *a.* clearly perceptible, definite; separate, different in quality or kind.

distinc'tion, *n.* difference; thing that differentiates; mark of honour; excellence. **distinc'tive**, *a.* distinguishing; characteristic.

disting'uish (-nggw-), *v.* recognize as distinct or different; characterize; perceive; make prominent or eminent. **disting'uished** (-sht), *a.* eminent, famous.

distort', *v.t.* pull or twist out of shape. **distor'tion**, *n.*

distract', *v.t.* divert; draw away attention; bewilder. **distrac'ted**, *a.* beside oneself. **distrac'tion**, *n.* amusement; interruption; confusion, perplexity.

distrain', v.i. (Law) seize goods in satisfaction of debt, etc. **distraint'**, n.

distrait' (-rā), a. (fem. *distraite*, pr. -āt), absent-minded, not attending. (French)

distraught' (-awt), a. distracted; crazed with grief.

distress', n. mental anguish; pressure of want, danger, or fatigue; state of ship, etc., when it requires immediate assistance. v.t. cause severe strain to, exhaust; make anxious or unhappy.

distrib'ūte, v.t. deal out, give each a share of; spread out widely. **distribū'tion**, n. **distrib'-ūtive**, a.

dis'trict, n. region; territory.

distrust', n. lack of trust; suspicion. v.t. have no confidence in. **distrust'ful**, a.

disturb', v.t. break rest or quiet of; worry; disorganize. **distur'bance**, n. disturbing; disturbed state, tumult, disorder.

disū'nion, n. separation; lack of union; dissension.

disūnite', v. separate; divide.

disūse' (-z), v.t. cease to use. **disūse'** (-s), n. state of not being used.

ditch, n. narrow trench for draining off water. v. make or repair ditches.

dith'er (-dh-), v.i. waver; be undecided. n. dithering; tremulous excitement.

ditt'ō, n. (abbrev. *do.*), the same; substitute for repetition of word or phrase.

ditt'y, n. short simple song.

dīurn'al, a. in, of, the day; (Astron.) occupying one day.

divan', n. low couch without back or ends. **divan(-bed)**, low bed without head-board.

dīve, v.i. plunge head foremost into water; move down or out of sight suddenly; descend steeply and fast. n. diving; plunge. **dī'ver**, n. (esp.) one who descends into deep water.

dīve-bomb, (v.t.) bomb from diving aircraft.

dīverge' (or di-), v.i. proceed in different directions from point or each other; deviate. **diver'gence**, n. **diver'gent**, a.

dī'vers (-z), a. various, several.

dīverse' (or di-), a. differing; varied.

dīvers'ifȳ (or di-), v.t. vary; bring variety into.

dīver'sion (or di-), n. diverting; compulsory traffic detour; diverting of attention; recreation, amusement.

dīver'sity (or di-), n. diverseness; variety.

dīvert' (or di-), v.t. turn in another direction; ward off; draw off the attention of; entertain, amuse.

dīvest' (or di-), v.t. unclothe; strip.

dīvīde', v. separate into parts; sunder; cause to disagree; distribute, share; see how many times a quantity contains another. n. watershed; dividing-line. **divi'ders** (-z), n.pl. pair of measuring compasses.

div'idend, n. quantity to be divided by the divisor; sum payable as interest or profit.

divinā'tion, n. divining, esp. by supernatural means; skilful forecast.

divīne', a. of, from, like, God or a god; sacred. n. theologian. v. make out by intuition or guessing; predict.

divī'ner, n. person who seeks to locate underground water or minerals by use of forked stick (*divining-rod*), dowser.

divin'ity, n. divineness; a god; God; theology.

divī'sible (-z-), that can be divided.

divi'sion (-zhn), n. dividing or being divided; part; army unit.

divī'sor (-z-), n. quantity by which another is to be divided.

divorce', n. legal dissolution of marriage; separation between things that should go together. v.t. separate by divorce; sunder. **divorcee'**, n. divorced person.

div'ot, n. (Sc.) turf, sod; (Golf) piece of turf cut out in making stroke.

dīvulge' (or di-), v.t. make known, reveal (secret).

dix'ie, dix'y, n. large iron pot used in camp cooking.

dizz'y, a. giddy, dazed; causing giddiness.

djinn, n. genie.

do (dōō), v.t., i., & aux. (3rd sing. pres. *does*, pr. duz; p.t. *did*; p.p. *done*, pr. dun), perform, effect; deal with, solve; cook (to right degree); make; act or proceed; work at; fare; be suitable, suffice; (*informal*) cheat. *do away with*, put an end to, destroy. *do up*, restore, wrap up, fasten. *do with*, tolerate. *do without*, manage without. **do-it-yourself**, (to be) made, etc., by home handyman. **doer** (dōo'er), n.

dō'cile, a. obedient, teachable, easily managed. **docil'ity**, n.

dock¹, n. tall coarse weed.

dock², v.t. cut short (tail, money, etc.).

dock³, n. basin in harbour or river where ships are (un)loaded and repaired. v. bring (ship), come, into dock; (of two spacecraft) link together in space. **dock'yard**, enclosure for building and repairing ships. **dock'er**, n. labourer in dock.

dock⁴, n. enclosure in court for prisoner on trial.

dock'ĕt, n. label or endorsement on letter, etc., indicating contents, etc.; file; certificate. v.t. enter on, endorse with, docket.

doc'tor, n. holder of highest university degree in any faculty; qualified medical practitioner. v.t. treat medically; adulterate; falsify. **doc'torate**, n. doctor's degree.

doctrinaire', a. theoretical and unpractical.

doc'trine, n. what is taught; religious or political belief or dogma. **doctri'nal** (or doc'tri-), a.

doc'ūment, n. something written or inscribed that gives evidence or information. **docū-ment'** (or dok'-), v.t. provide with, prove or support by, documents. **docūmen'tary**, a. &

n. (esp.) (film, etc.) dealing with real happenings or circumstances.

dodd'er, *v. i.* tremble, totter, esp. with age.

dŏdec'agon, *n.* twelve-sided plane figure.

dodge, *n.* quick movement to evade something; trick. *v.* swerve aside; elude. **dodg'er,** *n.* shifty person.

dŏ'dŏ, *n.* (pl. *dodos*), large extinct flightless bird.

dŏe, *n.* female of fallow deer, reindeer, etc., and of hare or rabbit.

doer, does: see **do.**

doff, *v. t.* take off (hat, etc.)

dog, *n.* carnivorous quadruped, domesticated in great variety of breeds, also found wild; male of this or fox or wolf; mechanical device for gripping or holding. *v. t.* (p.t. *dogged*), follow closely, pursue. **dog-cart,** light two-wheeled horse-drawn carriage. **dog-days,** hot season dated with reference to rising of dog-star. **dog-eared,** (of book) having leaves turned down at corners or crumpled. **dog'fish,** kind of small shark. **dog-leg,** bent like dog's hind leg. **dog-rose,** common wild rose. **dog-star,** Sirius. **dog--tired,** exhausted. **dog-watch,** (Naut.) either of two short or half watches (4-6, 6-8, p.m.).

dŏge (-j), *n.* (Hist.) chief magistrate of Venice or Genoa.

dogg'ĕd (-g-), *a.* tenacious, persistent.

dogg'erel (-g-), *a.* & *n.* irregular and unpoetic (verse).

dog'ma, *n.* (pl. *dogmas*, rarely *dogmata*), principle; system of beliefs. **dogmat'ic,** *a.* put forward as dogma; assertive, arrogant. **dog'matism,** *n.* **dog'matīze,** *v. i.* make dogmatic assertion(s).

doh (dō), *n.* (Mus.) first note of major scale in tonic sol-fa system of notation.

doi'ly, *n.* small ornamental mat placed on plate or under dish, etc.

dol'drums (-z), *n. pl.* equatorial ocean region of calms and light variable winds. *in the doldrums,* becalmed; depressed.

dŏle, *n.* charitable gift, esp. of small amount; (*informal*) unemployment benefit. *v. t.* deal *out* sparingly.

dŏle'ful, *a.* dismal, dreary, sad.

doll, *n.* child's toy representing human figure. *v.* (*informal*) dress *up* finely.

doll'ar, *n.* unit of money of U.S.A., Canada, Australia, and other countries.

doll'y, *n.* child's word for doll; wheeled platform, esp. for television, etc., camera.

dol'men, *n.* prehistoric structure of large flat stone resting on upright stones, forming (part of) burial chamber.

dol'omīte, *n.* (rock of) magnesian limestone.

dol'orous, *a.* painful, sad.

dol'phin, *n.* sea mammal resembling porpoise but with slender pointed snout.

dŏlt, *n.* stupid fellow.

domain', *n.* estate or territory; sphere or scope.

dōme, *n.* rounded vault as roof. **dōmed,** *a.* vaulted; having dome(s).

Domes'day Book (dōomz-), land record of England made in 1086.

domes'tic, *a.* of home, household, or family; of one's own country; tame; fond of home. *n.* household servant.

domes'ticāte, *v. t.* naturalize (plant); accustom (animal) to live near man; attach to home and its duties. **domesticā'tion,** *n.*

domesti'city, *n.* home life; homeliness.

dom'icīle (*or* -il), *n.* place of permanent residence. **dom'icīled,** *a.* having domicile *at* or *in.* **domicil'iary,** *a.* of dwelling-place.

dom'inant, *a.* ruling; most influential; outstanding. *n.* (Mus.) fifth note of any diatonic scale. **dom'inance,** *n.*

dom'ināte, *v.* have commanding influence over; (of place, esp. height) overlook. **dominā'tion,** *n.*

domineer', *v. i.* behave in dominating manner; tyrannize (*over*). **domineer'ing,** *a.*

dom'inie, *n.* (Sc.) schoolmaster.

domin'ion, *n.* sovereignty or lordship; territory of sovereign or government.

dom'inō, *n.* (pl. *dominoes*), hooded cloak worn with half-mask to conceal identity; one of 28 small pieces marked with pips used in game of dominoes.

don[1], *v. t.* (p.t. *donned*), put on.

don[2], *n.* member of teaching staff of college or university; Spanish gentleman.

donāte', *v. t.* make donation of. **donā'tion,** *n.* gift (esp. money given to fund or institution).

done, *p. p.* of **do.**

don'jon, *n.* great tower of castle, keep.

donk'ey, *n.* (pl. *donkeys*), ass.

dō'nor, *n.* giver, bestower.

dŏn't, informal contraction of *do not.*

dŏŏm, *n.* fate, destiny. *v. t.* condemn, sentence. **dŏŏmed** (-md), *a.* (esp.) destined to suffer misfortune or destruction. **dŏŏms'day** (-z-), *n.* Judgement Day.

door (dor), *n.* movable, esp. hinged, barrier for closing entrance to building, room, etc; doorway. *next door,* (in) next house. *out of doors,* in open air. **door'step,** step at threshold of door. **door'way,** opening filled by door, entrance.

dōpe, *n.* thick liquid; narcotic, stupefying drink. *v. t.* treat with dope.

dor'mant, *a.* sleeping; inactive as in sleep.

dor'mer (window), projecting upright window set in sloping roof.

dor'mitory, *n.* sleeping-room with several beds or cubicles.

dor'mouse, *n.* (pl. *dormīce*), small hibernating rodent.

dor'sal, *a.* of or on the back.

dŏs'age, *n.* giving of medicine in doses; amount of dose.

dŏse, *n.* amount of medicine, etc., to be taken at one time. *v. t.* give medicine to.

doss'ier (*or* -syā), *n.* set of documents relating

to person or event.

dost (-u-), (*archaic*) 2 pers. sing. pres. of **do**.

dot, *n*. small spot, point. *v.t.* (p.t. *dotted*), mark with dots; scatter like dots.

dō′tage, *n*. feeble-minded old age. **dō′tard**, *n*. one in his dotage.

dōte, *v.i.* bestow much or too much affection *on*; be feeble-minded because of old age.

doth (-u-), (*archaic*) 3 pers. sing. pres. of **do**.

dott′le, *n*. plug of tobacco left in pipe after smoking.

dou′ble (du-), *a*. consisting of two parts; of twice the amount or intensity; of two kinds; made for two users; deceitful. *adv.* twice the amount; two together. *n.* person or thing mistakable for another; twice the amount; (Mil.) regulation running pace. *v.* make or become double; increase twofold; fold over upon itself; clench (fist); turn sharply. **double--bass**, largest and lowest-pitched instrument of violin family. **double-breasted**, (of garment) having fronts overlapping across breast. **double-cross**, betray (esp. friend). **double-dealing**, deceit by action, etc., contrary to pretended attitude, etc. **double--decker**, (bus, etc.) with two decks. **double--edged**, (esp., of argument, etc.) damaging to user as well as opponent.

doub′lĕt (du-), *n*. close-fitting body-garment worn by men in 14th - 18th centuries; one of two words of same derivation but different form or sense.

doublōōn′ (du-), *n*. (Hist.) Spanish gold coin.

doubt (dowt), *n*. feeling of uncertainty; undecided frame of mind; inclination to disbelieve; uncertain state. *no doubt*, certainly. *v.* be in doubt or uncertainty; question, throw doubt on; mistrust. **doubt′ful**, *a*. feeling or causing doubt; uncertain. **doubt′less**, *adv.* no doubt.

douche (dōōsh), *n*. jet of water applied to the body for cleansing or medicinal purposes.

dough (dō), *n*. flour, etc., kneaded into paste for baking into bread, etc. **dough′nut**, small cake of dough fried in deep fat. **dough′y** (dō′i), *a*. like dough.

dought′y (dowt-), *a*. valiant.

dour (-oor), *a*. (Sc.) stern, obstinate.

douse, *v.t.* extinguish (light); drench.

dove (duv), *n*. pigeon, esp. turtle-dove; symbol of innocence or peace. **dove-cot(e)**, pigeon-house.

dove′tail (duvt-), *n*. joint made with tenon shaped like dove's spread tail fitting into corresponding mortise. *v.* fit together neatly and firmly.

dow′ager, *n*. woman with title or property derived from her late husband.

dow′dy, *a*. lacking smartness, badly dressed. *n.* dowdy woman. **dow′dily**, *adv.* **dow′diness**, *n*.

dow′er, *n*. widow's share for life of husband's estate; dowry; talent. *v.t.* give dowry to; endow *with* talent, etc.

down[1], *n*. open high land; (pl.) chalk uplands of S. England.

down[2], *n*. fine soft short hair or feathers or fluff. **down′y**, *a*. of or like or covered with down.

down[3], *adv.* towards or in lower place or state or number; from earlier to later time; on ground; away from capital or university. *prep.* downwards along or through or into; at lower part of. *a.* directed downwards. *n.* unfavourable change of fortune. *have a down on*, (*informal*) dislike. *down and out*, beaten, destitute. **down′cast**, (of eyes) looking down; dejected. **down′fall**, fall from prosperity, ruin; downpour. **down-hearted**, despondent. **down′hill**, (*a.*) sloping down, declining; (*adv.*) in downward direction. **down′pour**, heavy fall of rain. **down′right**, (*a.*) plain, straightforward, blunt; (*adv.*) thoroughly, quite. **downstairs**, (to, in, of) lower floor of house, etc. **down-stream**, in the direction of the current, lower down river, etc. **down′town**, in(to) business part of town. **down′trodden**, crushed by oppression or tyranny.

down′ward, *a.* & *adv.* **down′wards** (-z), *adv.* towards what is lower.

downy: see **down**[2].

dow′ry, *n*. property woman brings to her husband at marriage.

dowse (*or* -z), *v.i.* use divining-rod in search of water or minerals. **dow′ser**, *n*. diviner. **dow′sing-rod**, *n*. divining-rod.

doxol′ogy, *n*. set form of words praising God.

doyen (dwah′yaň *or* doi′en), *n*. senior member *of* body, esp. of ambassadors.

dōze, *v.i.* be half asleep. *doze off*, fall lightly asleep. *n.* short light sleep.

do′zen (du-), *n*. set of twelve.

drab, *a*. of dull light brown colour; dull; monotonous. *n.* drab colour.

drachm (-am), *n*. unit of weight and unit of fluid measure in *Apothecaries'* system.

drach′ma (-k-), *n.* (pl. *drachmae*, *drachmas*), unit of money of Greece; silver coin of ancient Greece.

draft (-ahft), *n*. (selection of) detachment of troops from larger body; order for drawing money; sketch of work to be done; preliminary version, rough copy. *v.t.* select as draft; prepare preliminary version of (document, speech, etc.). **drafts′man** *n*. (pl. *-men*), one who drafts documents, etc.

drag, *v.* (p.t. *dragged*), pull along with force; trail or go heavily; search bottom of water with nets, etc. *n.* check on progress; kind of harrow or net.

dragg′le, *v.* make wet and dirty by trailing; hang trailing.

drag′oman, *n.* (pl. *-mans*, *-men*), guide, interpreter (in Arabic, Turkish, or Persian).

drag′on, *n.* mythical fire-breathing monster; watchful and stern person.

drag′onflȳ, *n*. insect with long body and two

pairs of wings.

dragŏŏn′, *n.* cavalryman of certain regiments. *v. t.* force into submission.

drain, *v.* draw off (liquid) by pipes, ditches, etc.; dry (land, etc.) thus; drink to the dregs; exhaust; run dry. *n.* channel or pipe carrying off water, sewage, etc. **drain′age,** *n.*

drăke, *n.* male duck.

dram, *n.* avoirdupois weight ($\frac{1}{16}$ oz.); small drink of spirits.

dra′ma (-ah-), *n.* stage-play; dramatic art; play-like series of events. **dramat′ic,** *a.* of drama; theatrical; striking. **dram′atist,** *n.* writer of plays. **dram′atīze,** *v. t.* convert into a play; make a dramatic scene of. **dramatizā′tion,** *n.*

dram′atis persŏn′ae (-nē), characters of drama. (Latin)

drank, *p. t.* of **drink.**

drāpe, *v. t.* cover, hang, adorn, with cloth, etc.; arrange, hang, in graceful folds.

drā′per, *n.* dealer in cloth, linen, etc. **drā′pery,** *n.* draper's wares or trade; clothing or hangings arranged in folds.

dras′tic, *a.* vigorous; violent.

draught (-ahft), *n.* traction; (fish taken at) one drawing of net; one continuous act of drinking; depth of water ship draws; current of air in room, etc.; plan of work to be done; draft; drawing of liquor from cask; (pl.) game for two played on chess-board with 24 discs.

draughts′man (-ahft-), *n.* (pl. *-men*), one who makes drawings or plans; one of pieces in game of draughts; draftsman. **draughts′manship,** *n.* skill in drawing.

draught′y (-ahft-), *a.* with draughts (currents of air) blowing through.

draw¹, *n.* thing that draws custom or attention; drawing of lots; drawn game.

draw², *v.* (p.t. *drew,* pr. -ōō; p.p. *drawn*), pull, drag; attract; deduce, infer; extract; move or come (*near, back,* etc.); entice; make (picture, design, etc.) with pencil, pen, etc.; write out (cheque, etc.); finish (game, battle, etc.) with neither side winning; (of ship) require (stated depth of water) to float; obtain by lot.

draw′back, *n.* disadvantage.

draw′bridge, *n.* bridge across moat, river, etc., hinged for drawing up.

draw′er, *n.* one who draws; receptacle sliding in and out of table, chest, etc.; (pl.) two-legged undergarment.

draw′ing, *n.* delineation with pencil, pen, etc.; sketch.

draw′ing-rŏŏm, *n.* reception room.

drawl, *n.* (esp. lazy or affected) slowness of speech. *v.* speak, say, with drawl.

draw′-well, *n.* well with rope and bucket for drawing water.

dray, *n.* low cart for heavy loads, esp. beer-barrels.

dread (-ed), *v.* anticipate with terror; be in great fear of. *n.* great fear; awe. *a.* dreaded.

dread′ful, *a.* terrible; (*informal*) very bad, great, etc.

dreadnought (dred′nawt), *n.* (Hist.) powerful battleship.

dream, *n.* visions passing through the mind during sleep; indulgence in fancy; day-dream. *v.* (p.t. *dreamt* pr. dremt, or *dreamed*), experience a dream; allow oneself to believe (*that*) or think (*of*); fall into day-dream. **dream′y,** *a.* in the habit of day-dreaming; dream-like.

drear (Poet.), **drear′y,** *aa.* dismal, gloomy.

dredge¹, *n.* apparatus for bringing up oysters, specimens, etc., or for clearing mud, from river or sea bed. *v.* use dredge. **dredg′er¹,** *n.* boat employed in dredging.

dredge², *v. t.* sprinkle *with* flour, etc.; sprinkle (flour, etc.) *over.* **dredg′er²,** *n.* box with holes in lid for sprinkling flour, sugar, etc.

dregs (-z), *n. pl.* sediment, grounds; refuse.

drench, *v. t.* wet all over; soak; force (animal) to take dose of medicine.

dress, *v.* clothe, clothe oneself; put dressing on (wound); cleanse, trim, smooth (hair, wool, etc.). *dress down,* reprimand severely. *dress up,* dress elaborately or in fancy dress. *n.* clothing; woman's or child's outer garment, frock. **dress circle,** lowest circle in theatre, etc. **dress-coat,** man's swallow-tailed coat for formal evening wear. **dress rehearsal,** final rehearsal in costume.

dress′er¹, *n.* (esp.) person who helps actor or actress to dress for stage. **dress′er²,** *n.* kitchen sideboard with shelves for dishes, etc..

dress′ing, *n.* ointment, bandage, etc. applied to wound; manure; sauce. **dressing-gown,** loose garment worn before dressing.

dress′māker, *n.* woman making women's dresses. **dress′māking,** *n.*

dress′y, *a.* fond of, smart in, dress.

drew, *p. t.* of **draw.**

drey (-ā), *n.* squirrel's nest.

dribb′le, *v.* flow or let flow in drops; run at the mouth; (Footb., etc.) work ball forward with repeated touches of feet, etc. *n.* dribbling flow; piece of dribbling.

drib′lėt, *n.* small quantity.

dried, *p. t.* & *p. p.* of **dry.**

drī′er, *n.* thing, person, that dries.

drift, *n.* being driven by current; meaning, purpose; snow, sand, etc., heaped up by wind; matter driven by current. *v.* be carried (as) by current; heap or be heaped into drifts; go aimlessly. **drift-net,** large net for catching herrings, etc. **drift′wood,** wood washed ashore by sea. **drift′er,** *n.* boat used for drift-net fishing.

drill¹, *n.* revolving tool or machine for boring holes; exercise in marching, use of firearms, etc; seed-sowing machine; small furrow. *v.* bore (hole, etc.); train by exact routine; sow in rows.

drill², *n.* strong twilled fabric.

drily: see **dry.**

drink, v. (p.t. *drank*; p.p. *drunk*), swallow liquid; take alcoholic liquor, esp. to excess. *drink in*, listen to with delight. *drink to*, toast. n. liquid for drinking; intoxicating liquor.

drip, v. (p.t. *dripped*), fall or let fall in drops; be so wet as to shed drops. n. dripping liquid.

drip-dry, (of fabric) that may be hung up to dry without wringing, etc., and needs no ironing.

dripp'ing, n. fat that has melted from roasting meat.

drive, v. (p.t. *drōve*; p.p. *driven*), cause to move by force; direct course of (vehicle, animal drawing vehicle, etc.); convey or be conveyed in vehicle; push, send, carry along; strike (ball). n. excursion in vehicle; road, esp. private road to house, etc.; energy.

dri'vel, v.i. (p.t. *drivelled*), talk foolishly. n. silly nonsense.

dri'ver, n. one who drives; a golf-club.

drizz'le, n. & v.i. (fall in) fine dense rain.

drōgue (-g), n. sea-anchor; wind-sock.

drōll, a. amusing; odd. **drō'llery**, n. quaint humour.

drom'edary, n. swift (esp. Arabian one--humped) camel bred for riding.

drōne, n. male or non-worker bee; idler; (continuous single note sounded by) bass-pipe of bagpipe; low monotonous hum. v. make, talk with, utter with, drone.

drōōl, v.i. drivel; slaver.

drōōp, v. incline or hang down; languish, lose heart.

drop, n. round or spherical hanging or falling particle of liquid; small sweet; fall, descent. v. (p.t. *dropped*), fall or shed in drops; let fall; let go; lower; sink to ground. **drop'lĕt**, n. small drop. **dropp'ings**, n.pl. (esp.) dung of beasts or birds.

drop'sy, n. abnormal accumulation of watery fluid in body tissues or cavities. **drop'sical**, a.

drosh'ky, n. Russian horse-drawn carriage.

dross, n. scum from molten metal; impurities; refuse.

drought (-owt), n. continuous dry weather, lack of rain.

drove[1], p.t. of **drive**.

drōve[2], n. moving herd or flock; moving crowd. **drō'ver**, n. driver of or dealer in cattle.

drown, v. die by suffocation in liquid; kill by submersion in liquid; drench or flood; overpower (sound) by greater loudness.

drowse (-z), v.i. be half-asleep. **drow'sy**, a. sleepy.

drub, v.t. (p.t. *drubbed*), thrash, beat. **drubb'ing**, n.

drudge, v.i. toil at distasteful tasks. n. one who drudges. **drudg'ery**, n.

drug, n. substance used in medicine. (*dangerous*) *drug*, narcotic or stimulant drug, esp. one causing addiction. *drug on the market*,

unsaleable commodity. v.t. (p.t. *drugged*), stupefy with drugs; add drug to (drink, etc.).

drugg'ĕt (-g-), n. coarse woven fabric for covering floor or carpet.

drugg'ist (-g-), n. dealer in medicinal drugs.

Dru'id (drōō-), n. priest among Celts of ancient Gaul or Britain.

drum, n. percussion instrument made of hollow cylinder or hemisphere with parchment stretched over end(s); ear-drum; cylindrical object. v. (p.t. *drummed*), play drum; tap or thump continuously. **drum-major**, regimental band-leader. **drum'stick**, stick for beating drum; lower part of leg of cooked fowl. **drumm'er**, n. player of drum.

drunk, p.p. of **drink**. *pred. a.* overcome by strong drink, intoxicated. n. drunken person. **drunk'ard**, n. person often drunk. **drunk'en**, a. drunk.

drupe, n. (-ōō-), stone-fruit.

drȳ, a. without or deficient in moisture; without rain; thirsty; cold, matter-of-fact; uninteresting. v. (p.t. *drīed*), make or become dry. **dry-clean**, clean with spirit, etc., without use of water. **dry rot**, decay in wood caused by fungi. **dry-shod**, without getting feet wet. **dry(-stone) wall**, wall built without mortar. **drī'ly**, adv. **drȳ'ness**, n.

drȳ'ad, n. (Gk. myth.) wood-nymph.

dū'al, a. forming a pair; twofold, double; (of carriageway) with contrary streams of traffic kept separate.

dub, v.t. (p.t. *dubbed*), make (person) knight by touching shoulder with sword; give title or nickname to.

dubb'in(g), n. grease for making leather supple and waterproof.

dŭbi'ĕty, n. feeling of doubt.

dū'bious, a. doubtful; of questionable or suspected character.

dū'cal, a. of, like, a duke.

duc'at, n. gold (or silver) coin formerly current in several European countries.

duch'ess, n. duke's wife or widow. **duch'y**, n. reigning duke's territory.

duck[1], n. common water-bird; female of this; (Cricket, also *duck's egg*) batsman's score of 0. **duckbill**: see **platypus**. **duck'boards**, path of slats laid over wet ground. **duck'weed**, green plant covering still water.

duck[2], v. dive; push under water; bob down to avoid blow, etc.

duck[3], n. strong linen or cotton material; (pl.) trousers of this.

duck'ling, n. young duck.

duct, n. conduit, channel; tube conveying secretions in the body. **duct'less**, a. (of gland) passing its secretions directly into the blood, not through a duct.

dudg'eon (-jn), n. feeling of resentment.

dūe, a. owing, payable; proper, rightful; expected or scheduled. *due to*, caused by. adv. exactly (e.g. *due North*, etc.). n. person's right; (pl.) toll, fee.

dŭ'el, *n.* fight with weapons between two persons; two-sided contest. *v.i.* (p.t. *duelled*), fight duel(s). **dŭ'ellist**, *n.*

dŭenn'a, *n.* governess; chaperon.

dŭet', *n.* musical composition for two voices or two performers.

duff'el, duff'le, *n.* heavy woollen cloth; duffel-coat. **duff'el-bag**, cylindrical canvas bag. **duff'el-coat**, heavy overcoat, usu. with toggle fastenings.

duff'er, *n.* (*informal*) inefficient or stupid person.

dug[1], *n.* animal's udder or teat.

dug[2], *p.t. & p.p.* of **dig.**

dug'-out, *n.* underground shelter esp. for troops in trenches; canoe made by hollowing a tree-trunk.

dŭke, *n.* sovereign prince ruling small State; British peer of highest rank. **dŭke'dom**, *n.* duchy; dignity of duke.

dul'cèt, *a.* melodious, sweet.

dul'cimer, *n.* musical instrument with strings struck by hammers held in hands.

dull, *a.* lacking intelligence; not bright; blunt; tedious. *v.* make or grow dull; lose keenness. **dul'ly** (-l-li), *adv.*

dull'ard, *n.* slow-witted person.

dŭ'ly, *adv.* properly, fitly; sufficiently.

dumb (-m), *a.* unable to speak; silent. **dumb--bell**, short bar with heavy knob at each end, used in pairs for exercising muscles. **dumbfound'** (dumf-), strike dumb with astonishment. **dumb show**, significant gesture(s), acting, without speech.

dum'dum, *n.* (also *dumdum bullet*) soft-nosed bullet expanding on impact.

dumm'y, *n.* sham object; model of human figure. *a.* sham, counterfeit.

dump, *v.t.* deposit (rubbish); throw down; send (surplus goods) to foreign market at low price. *n.* rubbish-heap; (Mil.) temporary depot of munitions, etc.; (pl.) depression, melancholy.

dump'ling, *n.* ball of dough boiled in stew, etc.; (*apple dumpling*) dough baked or boiled with apple inside.

dum'py, *a.* short and stout.

dun[1], *a. & n.* (of) dull greyish brown.

dun[2], *v.t.* (p.t. *dunned*), pester for payment of debt.

dunce, *n.* bad learner; dullard.

dun'derhead (-ed), *n.* stupid person.

dŭne, *n.* mound or ridge of wind-deposited sand, esp. on coast.

dung, *n.* excrement of animals; manure. *v.t.* manure (land). **dung'hill**, *n.* manure-heap.

dungaree' (-ngg-), *n.* coarse Indian calico; (pl.) strong cotton overalls.

dun'geon (-jn), *n.* underground cell for prisoners.

dŭodē'num, *n.* part of small intestine immediately below stomach. **dŭodē'nal**, *a.*

dŭ'ologue (-g), *n.* conversation between two speakers.

dŭpe, *v.t.* deceive and make use of, cheat. *n.* duped person.

dŭ'ple, *a.* (Mus., of time) having two beats in bar.

dŭ'plicate, *a.* double; exactly like thing already existing. *n.* one of two things exactly alike, exact copy. **dŭ'plicāte**, *v.t.* make exact copy or copies of. **dŭplicā'tion**, *n.* duplicating. **dŭ'plicātor**, *n.* apparatus for making copies.

dŭpli'city, *n.* deceitfulness; double-dealing.

dŭr'able, *a.* capable of lasting; resisting wear. **dŭrabil'ity**, *n.*

dŭrā'tion, *n.* continuance in time; time during which thing, action, or state continues.

dŭress' (*or* dūr'-), *n.* forcible restraint; threats or other illegal compulsion.

dŭr'ing, *prep.* throughout or at some point in duration of.

durst, (*archaic*) *p.t.* of **dare.**

dusk, *n.* darker stage of twilight. **dusk'y**, *a.* dim; dark-coloured.

dust, *n.* light fine powder of earth or other solid matter. *v.t.* sprinkle with powder; clear of dust. **dust'bin**, receptacle for rubbish. **dust-jacket**, paper cover of new books. **dust'man**, man employed to remove rubbish from dustbins. **dust'pan**, receptacle into which dust, etc., is swept. **dus'ter**, *n.* cloth for dusting furniture, etc. **dus'ty**, *a.* covered with dust; powdery.

Dutch, *a.* of Holland (*the Netherlands*) or its people or its language. *n.* Dutch language. **Dutch'man, Dutch'woman**, *nn.*

dŭ'tèous, *a.* dutiful, obedient.

dŭ'tiable, *a.* liable to customs duty.

dŭ'tiful, *a.* regular or willing in the performance of duty. **dŭ'tifully**, *adv.*

dŭ'ty, *n.* what one is morally or legally obliged to do; office or function; tax levied on article or transaction.

dwarf (-orf), *n.* person, plant, etc., much below ordinary size; small supernatural being. *a.* undersized, stunted. *v.t.* stunt in growth; make look small. **dwarf'ish**, *a.*

dwell, *v.i.* (p.t. *dwelt*), reside, live; write or speak at length *on.*

dwell'ing, *n.* house, residence.

dwin'dle, *v.i.* waste away; become smaller; lose importance.

dye, *v.* (p.t. *dyed*; pres. part. *dyeing*), colour, tinge, esp. by dipping in liquid; take dye (*well, badly*). *n.* colouring-matter; tinge, hue. **dy'er**, *n.*

dying, *pres. part.* of **die**[2].

dyke: see **dike.**

dynam'ic, *a.* of motive force; potent, forceful. *n.* driving force.

dynam'ics, *n.* branch of mechanics dealing with motion and the action of forces.

dy'namīte, *n.* high explosive of nitroglycerine contained in absorbent substance. *v.t.* blow up with this.

dȳ'namō, *n.* (pl. *dynamos*), machine converting mechanical into electrical energy.
dyn'ast (*or* dī-), *n.* member of a dynasty.
dyn'asty, *n.* line of hereditary rulers. **dynas'tic** (*or* dī-), *a.*

dȳne, *n.* (Phys.) unit of force.
dys-, *pref.* bad.
dys'entery, *n.* disease of the bowels.
dyspep'sia, *n.* indigestion. **dyspep'tic,** *n.* & *a.* (person) subject to indigestion.

E

e-, *pref.*: see **ex-**.
each, *a.* & *pron.* (of two or more) every (one) taken separately. *each other,* one the other, reciprocally.
ea'ger (-g-), *a.* full of keen desire; impatient. **ea'gerness,** *n.*
ea'gle, *n.* large powerful bird of prey, hunting by day. **ea'glėt,** *n.* young eagle.
ear¹, *n.* (esp. external) organ of hearing; sense of hearing; ear-shaped object, as handle, etc. **ear-ache,** pain in internal ear. **ear-drum,** membrane stretched across middle ear. **ear'mark,** (*n.*) owner's mark on ear of sheep, etc.; (*v.t.*) mark (sheep, etc.) thus; assign (fund, etc.) to some definite purpose. **ear'ring,** ornament worn in lobe of ear. **ear'shot,** hearing distance. **ear-trumpet,** trumpet-shaped tube held to ear to aid hearing.
ear², *n.* spike or head of corn, etc., containing flowers or seeds.
earl (erl), *n.* nobleman ranking next below marquis. **earl'dom,** *n.*
ear'ly (er-), *a.* & *adv.* near to the beginning of some portion of time; soon; in advance of others.
earn (ern), *v.t.* obtain as reward of work or merit. **earn'ings** (-z-), *n.pl.* money earned.
ear'nest¹, (er-), *a.* (intensely) serious; zealous. *n.* seriousness. *in earnest,* serious(ly), not joking(ly).
ear'nest² (er-), *n.* money paid as instalment to confirm contract; foretaste.
earth (er-), *n.* the planet we live on; dry land; ground; soil; hole of fox, etc.; (Electr.) wire, etc., as connection with earth. *run to earth,* chase (quarry) to earth; (fig.) find after long search. *v.t.* (Electr.) connect with earth. *earth up,* heap up earth over (roots, etc.). **earth'work,** bank or mound of earth as rampart or fortification. **earth'worm,** worm that lives in the ground.
ear'then (er-), *a.* made of earth or baked clay. **ear'thenwāre,** *n.* baked clay; vessels made of this.
earth'ly (er-), *a.* of the earth, terrestrial. *no earthly use,* (*informal*) no use at all.
earth'quāke (er-), *n.* violent convulsion of earth's surface.

ear'thy (er-), *a.* like, of, earth or soil; grossly material.
ear'wig, *n.* insect with forceps at end of abdomen (formerly thought to creep into the ear).
ease (ēz), *n.* freedom from pain, trouble or constraint; quiet, rest; facility. *v.* relieve from pain, etc.; slacken; lessen or relax gradually.
ea'sel (-z-), *n.* frame to support painting, blackboard, etc.
easily, easiness: see **easy**.
east, *adv., n.,* & *a.* (towards, at, near, blowing from) point of horizon where sun rises; (towards, in) eastern part of world, country, town, etc., or altar-end of church. **east'ward,** *adv., a.,* & *n.* **east'wards,** *adv.*
Eas'ter, *n.* festival of Christ's Resurrection.
eas'terly, *a.* from or to the east.
eas'tern, *a.* of or in the east.
eastward(s): see **east**.
ea'sy (-z-), *a.* not difficult; free from pain or anxiety; comfortable; not ceremonious. *adv.* gently. **easy-going,** not fussy, tolerant, lazy. **ea'sily,** *adv.* without difficulty, comfortably. **ea'siness,** *n.*
eat, *v.* (p.t. *ate,* pr. et; p.p. *eaten*), chew and swallow; destroy, consume. **ea'table,** *a.* fit to be eaten. **ea'tables** (-lz), *n.pl.* articles of food.
eau-de-cologne (ōdekolōn'), *n.* perfume first made at Cologne.
eaves (ēvz), *n.pl.* projecting lower edge of roof. **eaves'drop,** *v.i.* (p.t. *eavesropped*), listen secretly to private conversation. **eaves'dropper,** *n.*
ebb, *n.* flowing back of the tide; decline. *v.i.* flow back; decline.
eb'onite, *n.* vulcanized rubber.
eb'ony, *n.* hard black wood got from various tropical trees. *a.* made of, black as, ebony.
ėbull'iėnt, *a.* exuberant. **ėbull'iėnce,** *n.*
ebulli'tion, *n.* boiling; sudden outburst.
ėccen'tric (-ks-), *a.* odd, whimsical; not concentric; not having its axle, etc., placed centrally; irregular. *n.* eccentric person. **eccentri'city,** *n.* odd habit or behaviour.
ėcclēsias'tic (-zi-), *n.* clergyman. **ėcclēsias'-**

tical, *a.* of church or clergy.

ech′ō (-k-), *n.* (pl. *echoes*), repetition of sound by rebounding of sound waves. *v.* resound with echo; be repeated; repeat, imitate.

éc′lair (ā-; *or* āklār′), *n.* finger-shaped cake filled with cream and iced.

èclec′tic, *a.* adopting ideas, etc., freely from various sources.

èclipse′, *n.* obscuring of light of sun, moon, etc., by another body; loss of brilliance or splendour. *v.t.* intercept light of; outshine, surpass. **èclip′tic**, *a.* of eclipse. *n.* (plane of) sun's apparent orbit.

ec′logue (-og), *n.* pastoral poem.

ècol′ogy, *n.* (branch of biology dealing with) animals and plants in relation to each other and to their environment.

èconom′ic (*or* e-), *a.* of economics; maintained for profit; practical; paying for expenses or costs. **econom′ical**, *a.* thrifty, not wasteful. **econom′ics**, *n.* science of production and distribution of wealth. **ècon′-omist**, *n.* expert in economics.

ècon′omize, *v.* use sparingly; avoid expense.

ècon′omy, *n.* management of affairs and resources of State, business, or household; thriftiness, frugal use.

ec′stasy, *n.* feeling of intense delight, rapture. **ècstat′ic**, *a.* of or in ecstasies.

ècūmen′ical, *a.* of or representing the whole Christian world or Church.

ec′zèma, *n.* skin-disease with itching.

edd′y, *n.* small whirlpool; smoke, etc., moving like this. *v.* move in eddies.

edelweiss (ā′delvīs), *n.* Alpine plant with white flowers.

Ed′en (ē-), *n.* (*garden of*) *Eden*, home of Adam and Eve; delightful place or state.

edge, *n.* cutting side of blade; sharpness; line where two surfaces meet abruptly; rim; boundary, brink. *be on edge*, be excited or irritable. *v.* sharpen; border; move almost imperceptibly. **edge-tool**, cutting-tool. **edge′ways, edge′wise**, *advv.* with edge foremost. **edg′ing**, *n.* border; fringe. **edg′y**, (*informal*) irritable.

ed′ible, *a.* that is suitable for food.

ē′dict, *n.* order, decree, given out by authority.

ed′ifice, *n.* (large and stately) building.

ed′ifȳ, *v.t.* instruct; improve morally. **edifi-cā′tion**, *n.*

ed′it, *v.t.* prepare for publication; act as editor of. **edi′tion**, *n.* form in which literary work is published; copies of book, newspaper, etc., issued at one time. **ed′itor**, *n.* one who edits, esp. one responsible for (section of) newspaper or periodical; publisher's literary manager. **editor′ial**, *a.* of an editor. *n.* newspaper article written by, or under responsibility of, editor.

ed′ūcăte, *v.t.* train (child) intellectually and morally; instruct; train. **ed′ūcable**, *a.* **ed′-ūcător**, *n.*

edūcā′tion, *n.* systematic instruction, schooling, or training. **edūcā′tional**, *a.*

edūcā′tionalist, edūcā′tionist, *nn.* student of, expert in, methods of education.

ed′ūcative, *a.* of education; educating.

éduce′, *v.t.* bring out, develop; infer.

Edwar′dian (edwor-), *a. & n.* (person) of the reign of Edward VII.

eel, *n.* snake-like fish.

e′en (ēn), **e′er** (ār), *advv.* (Poet.) even, ever.

eer′ie, eer′y, *a.* strange; weird.

ef-, *pref.*: see **ex-**.

èfface′, *v.t.* rub or wipe out; eclipse. *efface oneself*, make oneself inconspicuous. **èf-face′ment**, *n.*

èffect′, *n.* result, consequence; impression; efficacy; (pl.) property. *v.t.* bring about, accomplish.

èffec′tive, *a.* successful in working; impressive; actual, existing.

èffec′tŭal, *a.* answering its purpose.

èffec′tŭăte, *v.t.* bring about, accomplish.

èffem′inate, *a.* unmanly, womanish. **èf-fem′inacy**, *n.*

effervesce′, *v.i.* give off bubbles of gas. **effer-ves′cence**, *n.* **efferves′cent**, *a.*

èffète′, *a.* worn out; feeble.

efficā′cious (-shus), *a.* producing desired effect. **eff′icacy**, *n.*

èffi′cient (-shnt), *a.* competent, capable; producing desired result. **èffi′ciency**, *n.*

eff′igy, *n.* image (in wood, stone, etc.); portrait (on coin, etc.).

eff′luènce (-loo-), *n.* flowing out; what flows out. **eff′luènt**, *n.* stream flowing from lake, etc.; outflow from sewage tank, etc.

eff′ort, *n.* exertion, attempt. **eff′ortless**, *a.* (esp.) without effort, easy.

èffront′ery (-un-), *n.* shameless audacity; impudence.

èfful′gence, *n.* lustre, brightness. **èfful′gent**, *a.* bright, radiant.

èffūse′ (-z), *v.t.* pour forth. **èffū′sion** (-zhn), *n.* (literary) outpouring. **èffū′sive** (-s-), *a.* demonstrative, gushing.

ègalitār′ian, *a. & n.* (person) asserting that all men are equal.

egg[1], *n.* more or less spheroid body produced by female of birds, reptiles, insects, fish, etc., containing germ of new individual within shell or membrane; hen's egg, esp. as food; ovum. **egg-cup**, small cup for holding boiled egg. **egg-shell**, shell of bird's egg.

egg[2], *v.t.* *egg on*, encourage, urge.

eg′ō (*or* ē-), *n.* the I, the self; self-esteem. **egōcen′tric**, *a.* self-centred, egoistic.

eg′oism, *n.* systematic selfishness; egotism. **eg′oist**, *n.* **egōis′tic**, *a.*

eg′otism, *n.* practice of talking about oneself; conceit; selfishness. **eg′otist**, *n.* **egotis′-tic(al)**, *aa.*

ègrē′gious (-jus), *a.* gross, flagrant.

ē′gress, *n.* going out; way out.

ē′grĕt, *n.* kind of heron with white plumage.

Egyptian (ijip'shn), *a.* of Egypt. *n.* native of Egypt.

ei'der(-duck) (ī-), *n.* duck of northern regions. **ei'derdown,** *n.* soft breast-feathers of eider-duck; quilt stuffed with eiderdown, feathers, or other soft material.

eight (āt), *n.* & *a.* one more than seven (8, VIII). **eighth** (āt-th), *a.* & *n.* **eight'some,** *a.* (Sc., of reel) for eight persons.

eight'een (āt-), *n.* & *a.* one more than seventeen (18, XVIII). **eighteenth',** *a.* & *n.*

eight'y (āt-), *n.* eight times ten (80, LXXX). **eight'ieth,** *n.* & *a.*

eisteddfod (āstedh'vod), *n.* (in Wales) gathering for competitions in music, poetry, etc.

eith'er (īdh-; *or* ēdh-), *a.* one or other of two. *pron.* each of two. *adv.* & *conj.* introducing first of two alternatives; (with neg. or interrog.) any more than the other.

èjac'ûlăte, *v.* utter suddenly, cry out; eject (fluid) from body. **èjacŭlă'tion,** *n.* **èjac'-ûlatory,** *a.*

èject', *v. t.* throw out; expel; emit. **èjec'tion,** *n.* **èjec'tor,** *n.*

ēke¹, *v. t. eke out,* make (something) suffice, supplement (*with, by*).

ēke², *adv.* (*archaic*) also.

ėlab'orate, *a.* worked out carefully and in detail; highly finished. *v. t.* (-āt), work out in detail; develop. **ėlaborā'tion,** *n.*

ėlapse', *v. i.* (of time) pass.

èlas'tic, *a.* having the power to resume normal shape after expansion or distortion; springy; flexible. *n.* elastic fabric or cord. **èlasti'city,** *n.*

èlāte', *v. t.* raise spirits of, excite. **èlā'tion,** *n.*

el'bow (-ō), *n.* (outer part of) joint between forearm and upper arm; elbow-shaped thing. *v. t.* thrust, jostle. **elbow-room,** space to work or move freely.

el'der¹, *n.* tree with white flowers and black berries. **el'derberry,** *n.* fruit of elder.

el'der², *a.* of greater age; senior. *n.* person of greater age; lay official in Presbyterian Church.

el'derly, *a.* somewhat old; past middle age.

el'dest, *a.* first-born or oldest surviving.

El Dora'dŏ (-ah-), legendary country or city rich in gold.

èlect', *v. t.* choose; choose by vote. *a.* chosen; (following *noun*) elected but not yet in office (e.g. *president elect*).

èlec'tion, *n.* choosing, esp. by vote. **èlec'tioneer',** *v. i.* busy oneself in political elections.

èlec'tor, *n.* person entitled to vote in election. **èlec'toral,** *a.* **èlec'torate,** *n.* body of electors.

èlec'tric, *a.* of, charged with, worked by, electricity. **electric chair,** chair used for executing by electrocution. **èlec'trical,** *a.* relating to, connected with, electricity; electric.

electri'cian (-shn), *n.* person skilled in or dealing with electricity or electrical apparatus.

electri'city, *n.* (study of) form of energy, carried by electrons, etc., that causes attraction and repulsion between charged bodies.

èlec'trifÿ, *v. t.* charge with electricity; convert to electric working; startle, rouse, excite. **èlectrificā'tion,** *n.*

electro-, *pref.* of, by, etc., electricity.

èlec'trocūte, *v. t.* kill by electric current. **èlec'trocū'tion,** *n.*

èlec'trŏde, *n.* conductor by which electricity enters or leaves a substance or a vacuum.

electrol'ysis, *n.* chemical decomposition by action of electric current.

èlec'trolÿte, *n.* (substance that dissolves to give) solution that conducts electricity. **èlec-troly'tic,** *a.*

èlec'tromag'nèt, *n.* magnet consisting of piece of soft iron surrounded by electric coil. **èlec'tromagnet'ic,** *a.* having both electrical and magnetic character or effects. **èlec'-tromag'nètism,** *n.* (study of) magnetic force produced by electricity.

èlec'tron, *n.* indivisible unit of negative electricity and one of the fundamental constituents of matter, rotating about the positive nucleus of every atom. *free electron,* electron not bound within atom. **electron'ic,** *a.* of electrons or electronics. **electron'ics,** *n.* science of control of free electrons; its technological applications.

èlec'troplăte, *v. t.* coat with silver, chromium, etc., by electrolysis. *n.* electroplated ware.

el'ėgance, *n.* grace, refinement. **el'ėgant,** *a.* graceful, tasteful; of refined luxury.

elėgi'ac, *a.* mournful, suited to elegies.

el'ėgy, *n.* song of lamentation, esp. for the dead.

el'ėment, *n.* (Chem.) substance which cannot be decomposed chemically; one of four substances (earth, air, fire, water) formerly supposed to make up all matter; (pl.) forces of nature, the weather; congenial surroundings; component part; resistance wire carrying current in electric heater; (pl.) rudiments of a subject, etc.

elėmen'tal, *a.* of or like the four elements or the powers of nature; essential.

elėmen'tary, *a.* introductory, rudimentary; simple.

el'ėphant, *n.* huge thick-skinned mammal with a trunk and ivory tusks. **elėphant'īne,** *a.* (esp.) huge, unwieldy.

el'ėvăte, *v. t.* lift up; raise.

elėvă'tion, *n.* raising aloft; exaltation, dignity; height above given level; drawing of front, side, etc., of building.

el'ėvâtor, *n.* hoisting-machine; warehouse for storing grain; (U.S.) lift.

elėv'en, *n.* & *a.* one more than ten (11, XI). **elėv'enth,** *a.* & *n.*

elf, *n.* (pl. *elves*), small fairy. **el'fin,** *a.* of elves; elf-like. **el'fish,** *a.*

èli'cit, *v. t.* draw forth (information, truth).

elīde′, *v.t.* omit in pronunciation.

el′igible, *a.* fit or qualified to be chosen; suitable. **eligibi′lity**, *n.*

elim′ināte, *v.t.* remove, get rid of; expel, exclude. **eliminā′tion**, *n.*

eli′sion (-zhn), *n.* suppression of letter (esp. vowel) or syllable in pronouncing.

élite (ālēt′), *n.* choice, best, part (*of*); select group or class. (French)

elix′ir (-ēr), *n.* alchemist's preparation designed to change baser metals into gold or to prolong life indefinitely; sweet solution used in medicines.

elk, *n.* large animal of the deer kind.

ell, *n.* obsolete measure of length (45 in.).

ellipse′, *n.* regular oval, plane figure produced when a cone is cut obliquely by a plane. **ellip′tic(al)**[1], *aa.*

ellip′sis, *n.* (pl. *ellipsēs*), (Gram.) omission of word(s) needed to complete a sentence. **ellip′tic(al)**[2], *aa.*

elm, *n.* large tree with rough bark.

elocū′tion, *n.* art, manner, or style of delivery, pronunciation, etc., in speaking. **elocū′tionary**, *a.*

ē′longāte (-ngg-), *v.t.* lengthen, extend, draw out. **elongā′tion**, *n.*

elōpe′, *v.t.* run away with lover, esp. to be married. **elōpe′ment**, *n.*

el′oquence, *n.* fluent, forcible, and expressive speech. **el′oquent**, *a.*

else, *adv.* besides; instead; otherwise; if not. **else′where**, *adv.* in or to some other place.

elu′cidāte (-loo- *or* -lū-), *v.t.* explain, make clear. **elucidā′tion**, *n.* **elu′cidātory**, *a.*

elude′ (-loo- *or* -lū-), *v.t.* escape by dexterity or stratagem from; evade; baffle. **elu′sive**, *a.*

el′ver, *n.* young eel.

Elys′ium (iliz-), *n.* (Gk. Myth.) abode of the blessed after death. **Elys′ian**, *a.*

em-, *pref.*: see **en-**.

ēmā′ciāte (-shi-), *v.t.* make lean, waste. **ēmāciā′tion** (-si- *or* -shi-), *n.*

em′anāte, *v.i.* come, flow (*from* a source). **emanā′tion**, *n.* emanating; thing that emanates.

ēman′cipāte, *v.t.* free from legal, social, or other restraint; set free (slave). **ēmancipā′tion**, *n.*

ēmas′cūlāte, *v.t.* castrate; weaken; enfeeble. **ēmas′culate**, *a.* castrated; effeminate. **ēmascūlā′tion**, *n.*

ēmbalm′ (-ahm), *v.t.* preserve (corpse) with spices; (fig.) preserve from oblivion; make fragrant. **ēmbalm′ment**, *n.*

ēmbank′, *v.t.* enclose, retain, support, with embankment. **ēmbank′ment**, *n.* mound of earth, stone structure, etc., for confining river, carrying road, etc.

ēmbar′gō, *n.* (pl. *embargoes*), order forbidding ships to enter or leave port; stoppage, prohibition.

ēmbark′, *v.* put or go on board ship; start *on* (enterprise, etc.). **embarkā′tion**, *n.*

ēmba′rrass, *v.t.* cause perplexity, mental discomfort, or anxiety to; encumber, esp. with debt. **ēmba′rrassment**, *n.*

em′bassy, *n.* duty, mission, residence, of ambassador; ambassador and his staff.

ēmbatt′le, *v.t.* set in battle array.

ēmbed′, *v.t.* (p.p. *embedded*), fix in surrounding mass.

ēmbell′ish, *v.t.* beautify, adorn; add fictitious details to (narrative). **ēmbell′ishment**, *n.*

em′ber, *n.* (usu. in pl.), small piece of live fuel in smouldering or dying fire.

ēmbezz′le, *v.t.* take (money, etc.) fraudulently for one's own use. **ēmbezz′lement** (-zlm-), *n.*

ēmbitt′er, *v.t.* arouse bitter feelings in. **ēmbitt′erment**, *n.*

ēmblā′zon, *v.t.* adorn with heraldic figures; portray conspicuously; extol.

em′blēm, *n.* symbol; object, picture, design or sign typifying something. **emblēmat′ic**, *a.*

ēmbod′y, *v.t.* give concrete form to (what is abstract or ideal); incorporate, include, comprise. **ēmbod′iment**, *n.*

ēmbōl′den, *v.t.* make bold, encourage.

ēmboss′, *v.t.* carve or mould in relief.

ēmbrāce′, *v.t.* fold in the arms; enclose; accept, adopt (party, cause, etc.); include. *n.* folding in the arms.

ēmbrā′sure (-zher), *n.* opening in parapet for gun; bevelling of wall at sides of window, etc.

embrocā′tion, *n.* liniment for rubbing limb, etc.

ēmbroi′der, *v.t.* ornament (cloth, etc.) with needlework; work in needlework; enrich with detail. **ēmbroi′dery**, *n.*

ēmbroil′, *v.t.* bring into state of confusion; involve in hostility. **ēmbroil′ment**, *n.*

em′bryō, *n.* (pl. *embryos*), offspring of animal in early stage of development before birth or emergence from egg; rudimentary plant within seed. *in embryo*, in undeveloped stage. **embryon′ic**, *a.*

ēmend′, *v.t.* correct; remove errors from (text of book, etc.). **ēmendā′tion**, *n.*

em′erald, *n.* bright-green precious stone; colour of this.

ēmerge′, *v.i.* come out, come into view (*from*); come to light. **ēmer′gence**, *n.* **ēmer′gent**, *a.* emerging, esp. into nationhood.

ēmer′gency, *n.* situation demanding immediate action.

ēme′ritus, *a.* retired, retaining title after retirement.

em′ery, *n.* crystallized mineral used for polishing metal, etc.

ēmet′ic, *n.* & *a.* (medicine) that causes vomiting.

em′igrant, *a.* emigrating. *n.* person who emigrates.

em′igrāte, *v.i.* leave one's country to settle in another. **emigrā′tion**, *n.*

émigré (em'igrā), *n.* emigrant, esp. refugee from French or Russian Revolution. (French)

em'inence, *n.* recognized superiority; rising ground; cardinal's title of honour.

em'inent, *a,* distinguished, notable. **em'inently**, *adv.* notably, decidedly.

emir' (-ēr), *n.* Arab prince or ruler.

em'issary, *n.* person sent on (esp. odious or underhand) mission.

èmi'ssion (-shn), *n.* emitting; what is emitted.

èmit', *v.t.* (p.t. *emitted*), give or send out (light, heat, sound, opinion, etc.).

èmoll'iènt, *n. & a.* softening or relaxing (substance).

èmol'ūment, *n.* (usu. in pl.), profit from employment; salary.

èmō'tion, *n.* mental sensation (e.g. of love, hate, fear, hope, etc.); vehement or excited mental state, agitation. **èmō'tional**, *a.* of emotion(s); easily moved by emotion.

èmpan'el, *v.t.* (p.t. *empanelled*), enter on panel; enrol.

em'peror, *n.* ruler of an empire.

em'phasis, *n.* (pl. *emphasēs*), stress on word(s) to indicate significance or importance; vigour of expression; importance, prominence. **em'phasize**, *v.t.* lay stress on. **èmphat'ic**, *a.* forcible, strong.

em'pīre, *n.* supreme and wide dominion; extensive territory (esp. group of many States) ruled by emperor or sovereign State.

èmpi'rical, *a.* based or acting on observation and experiment, not on theory. **èmpi'ricism**, **èmpi'ricist**, *nn.*

èmplāce'ment (-sm-), *n.* platform for gun(s).

èmploy', *v.t.* use; use services of; keep occupied. **èmploy'ee**, *n.* person employed for wages. **èmploy'er**, *n.* person who employs others for wages. **èmploy'ment**, *n.* (esp.) regular occupation or business; state of being employed. **employment exchange**, State office helping workers to find employment.

empor'ium, *n.* (pl. *emporiums* or *emporia*), centre of commerce; large shop.

èmpow'er, *v.t.* authorize; enable.

em'press, *n.* wife of emperor; female ruler of empire.

emp'ty (-mt-), *a.* containing nothing; devoid *of;* vacant; meaningless. *n.* emptied box, bottle, etc. *v.* remove contents of; transfer contents of, discharge, *into;* become empty. **emp'tiness**, *n.*

ē'mū, *n.* large flightless fast-running Australian bird with rudimentary wings.

em'ūlāte, *v.t.* try to equal or excel; imitate. **èmūlā'tion**, *n.* **em'ūlative**, *a.* **em'ūlous**, *a.* zealously imitative *of;* moved by spirit of rivalry.

èmul'sifȳ, *v.t.* convert or be converted into emulsion.

èmul'sion (-shn), *n.* suspension of oil in watery liquid.

en-, *pref.* (*em-* before *b, p, m*) in, into, on.

ènā'ble, *v.t.* make able, supply with means (*to* do).

ènact', *v.t.* make into legislative act; decree; play (part). **ènact'ment**, *n.* law enacted.

ènam'el, *n.* glass-like coating on metal; any hard smooth coating; hard, usu. glossy, oil paint. *v.t.* (p.t. *enamelled*), coat with enamel.

ènam'our (-mer), *v.t.* inspire with love; make fond of.

** èncamp'**, *v.* settle in camp; lodge in tents. **èncamp'ment**, *n.*

èncāse', *v.t.* put into case; surround as with case. **èncāse'ment**, *n.*

encèphal'ic, *a.* of the brain.

ènchain', *v.t.* chain up; hold fast.

ènchant' (-ah-), *v.t.* bewitch; delight. **ènchant'er**, *n.* **ènchant'ing**, *a.* **ènchant'ment**, *n.* **ènchant'ress**, *n.fem.*

** èncir'cle**, *v.t.* surround. **èncir'clement**, *n.*

en'clāve, *n.* territory surrounded by foreign dominion.

ènclōse' (-z), *v.t.* put fence, wall, etc., round; shut in; put in (envelope, etc., with letter, etc.). **ènclō'sure** (-zher), *n.* enclosing fence, etc.; enclosed land; thing enclosed.

encō'mium, *n.* (pl. *encomiums*), formal expression of high praise.

** èncom'pass** (-um-), *v.t.* surround.

encore (ongkor'), *int.* again! *n.* repetition of performance or further item given in response. *v.t.* cry encore.

** èncoun'ter**, *v.t.* meet unexpectedly or suddenly (friend, obstacle, danger); meet hostilely. *n.* casual or hostile meeting.

èncou'rage (-ku-), *v.t.* give hope, courage, or confidence to; support. **èncou'ragement**, *n.*

èncroach', *v.i.* intrude *on* others' rights, etc., or beyond natural limits. **èncroach'ment**, *n.*

èncrust', *v.* cover with crust; cover (surface) with ornamental crust.

èncum'ber, *v.t.* hamper; impede; burden with debt. **èncum'brance**, *n.* burden; impediment; mortgage, etc., on property.

èncyc'lical, *a. & n.* (Pope's letter) for wide circulation.

èncy̆clop(a)e'dia (-pē-), *n.* (pl. *encyclop(a)edias*), book or set of books giving information on all branches of knowledge or of one subject. **èncy̆clop(a)e'dic**, *a.*

end, *n.* limit; extreme point or part; conclusion; destruction; death; result; purpose. *end to end,* in line with ends touching. *on end,* in upright position. *v.* bring or come to an end. **end-product,** final product of process of manufacture, etc. **end'ways, end'wise,** *advv.* with end towards spectator or uppermost; end to end.

èndā'nger (-j-), *v.t.* bring into danger.

èndear', *v.t.* make dear. **èndear'ing**, *a.* winning affection. **èndear'ment**, *n.* action or word(s) expressing affection.

èndeav'our (-dever), *v.* try (*to* do); strive. *n.* attempt, effort.

endem'ic, *a. & n.* (disease) regularly found

among (specified) people or in (specified) area, etc.

en'ding, *n.* (esp.) concluding part (of book, etc.); inflexional or formative suffix.

en'dive, *n.* plant with curly leaves eaten as salad.

end'less, *a.* unending; incessant.

en'docrine (*or* -īn), *a.* (of gland) ductless. *n.* ductless gland.

èndorse', *v.t.* write on back of (document); sign name on back of (cheque, etc.); confirm; support. **èndorse'ment**, *n.*

èndow', *v.t.* give, bequeath, permanent income to (institution, etc.); invest *with* ability, qualities, etc. **èndow'ment**, *n.*

èndūe', *v.t.* endow, supply, *with.*

èndūr'ance, *n.* habit or power of enduring.

èndūre', *v.* suffer, undergo, (pain, hardship, etc.); last. **èndūr'able**, *a.*

en'ēma, *n.* (syringe used for) introduction of liquid into rectum.

en'ėmy, *n.* one who hates and wishes or tries to harm another; opposing force or influence; (forces of) nation at war with another. *a.* of or belonging to enemy.

energet'ic, *a.* full of, done with, energy.

en'ergīze, *v.t.* infuse energy into.

en'ergy, *n.* force, vigour; activity; capacity for work.

en'ervāte, *v.t.* weaken; deprive of vigour. **enervā'tion**, *n.*

ènfee'ble, *v.t.* make feeble. **ènfee'blement**, *n.*

ènfōld', *v.t.* wrap; embrace.

ènforce', *v.t.* urge, compel, observance of (law, etc.). **ènforce'able**, *a.* **ènforce'ment**, *n.*

ènfran'chīse (-z), *v.t.* grant the right of voting to; free. **ènfran'chisement**, *n.*

engage', (in-gāj), *v.* bind by contract or promise; pledge oneself; hire; arrange beforehand to occupy; fit, interlock (*with*); take part *in*; employ, occupy; attack, begin fighting. **èngāged'**, *a.* (esp.) occupied; having given promise of marriage (*to*). **èngā'ging**, *a.* winning, attractive. **èngāge'ment**, *n.*

èngen'der (-j-), *v.t.* give rise to.

en'gine (-j-), *n.* complex mechanical contrivance, esp. for converting fuel into mechanical power; locomotive. **engine-driver**, driver of locomotive, esp. on railway.

engineer' (-j-), *n.* one professionally qualified in design, construction, maintenance, etc., of roads, bridges, etc., machines, electrical apparatus, military works, etc. (*civil, mechanical, electrical, military,* etc., *engineer*); one in charge of (esp. ship's) engine(s); (U.S.) engine-driver. *v.* construct, manage, etc., as engineer; contrive, bring about. **engineer'ing**, *n.* science, profession, of engineer.

Eng'lish (ingg-), *a.* of England or the English or their language. *n.* English people or language. **Eng'lishman, Eng'lishwoman**, *nn.*

engraft' (in-grahft), *v.t.* graft in; implant.

engrain' (in-g-), *v.t.* make (dye) sink deeply in.

engrāve' (in-g-), *v.t.* cut on metal plate, etc., for printing; carve, impress deeply (*on* memory, etc.). **èngrāv'ing**, *n.* (esp.) print made from engraved plate.

engrōss' (in-g-), *v.t.* monopolize, absorb, (time or attention).

engulf' (in-g-), *v.t.* swallow up.

ènhance' (-hah-), *v.t.* heighten; intensify.

ènig'ma, *n.* riddle; puzzling person or thing. **enigmat'ic(al)**, *aa.*

ènjoin', *v.t.* command; prescribe.

ènjoy', *v.t.* find pleasure in; have as advantage or benefit. *enjoy oneself,* experience pleasure, be happy. **ènjoy'able**, *a.* **ènjoy'ment**, *n.*

ènlāce', *v.t.* encircle; enfold; entwine.

ènlarge', *v.* make or become larger; speak or write at length *upon.* **ènlarge'ment**, *n.*

ènlight'en (-īt-), *v.t.* instruct; inform; shed light on. **ènlight'ened** (-nd), *a.* (esp.) free from superstition or prejudice. **ènlight'enment**, *n.*

ènlist', *v.* engage, enrol, for military service; secure the support of. **ènlist'ment**, *n.*

ènli'ven, *v.t.* make more lively; cheer.

ènmesh', *v.t.* entangle (as) in net.

en'mity, *n.* hatred, hostility.

ènnō'ble, *v.t.* make (person) a noble; make noble. **ènnō'blement**, *n.*

ennui (on'wē), *n.* boredom.

ènor'mity, *n.* great wickedness; crime.

ènor'mous, *a.* very large. **ènor'mously**, *adv.* **ènor'mousness**, *n.*

ènough' (-nuf), *a., adv.,* & *n.* (in) not less than required quantity, number, or degree (of).

ènounce', *v.t.* pronounce.

enquire: see **inquire.**

ènrāge', *v.t.* make furious.

ènrap'ture, *v.t.* delight intensely.

ènrich', *v.t.* make rich(er). **ènrich'ment**, *n.*

ènrōl', *v.t.* (p.t. *enrolled*), write name on roll, list, or register; enlist; record. **ènrōl'ment**, *n.*

en route (ahn rōōt), *adv.* on the way. (French)

ènsconce', *v.t.* establish safely.

ensemble (ahnsahnbl'), *n.* thing viewed as a whole; (Mus.) (group of musicians taking part in) united performance of instruments or voices.

ènshrine', *v.t.* enclose (as) in shrine; cherish.

en'sign (-sīn *or* -sn), *n.* flag; badge; (Hist.) lowest commissioned officer in infantry.

ènslāve', *v.t.* make a slave of. **ènslāve'ment**, *n.*

ènsnāre', *v.t.* entrap.

ènsūe', *v.* happen later; result (*from*).

ènsure' (-shoor), *v.t.* make safe; make certain; secure.

** èntail'**, *v.t.* settle landed estate on persons successively so that it cannot be bequeathed at pleasure; impose (*on*); necessitate, involve.

en'tail, *n.* entailing; entailed estate.

èntang'le (-nggl), *v.t.* catch in snare, etc.; involve in difficulties; make tangled; complicate. **èntang'lement,** *n.*

entente (ahntahnt'), *n.* friendly understanding between States. (French)

en'ter, *v.* go or come in or into; put (name, fact, etc.) into list, record, etc.; name, name oneself, as competitor *for*.

ènte'ric, *a.* of intestines. **enteric fever,** typhoid. **en'teritis,** *n.* bowel inflammation.

en'terprise (-z), *n.* bold undertaking; readiness to engage in enterprises. **en'terprising,** *a.* full of enterprise.

entertain', *v.t.* receive as guest; amuse; harbour; give consideration to. **entertain'ment,** *n.* hospitality; amusement; public performance.

ènthral' (-awl), *v.t.* (p.t. *enthralled*), enslave, captivate. **ènthral'ment,** *n.*

ènthrône', *v.t.* place (king, bishop, etc.) on throne. **ènthrône'ment,** *n.*

ènthû'siasm (-ziazm), *n.* ardent zeal. **ènthû'siast,** *n.* one who is full of enthusiasm. **ènthûsias'tic,** *a.*

èntice', *v.t.* attract by offer of pleasure or profit. **èntice'ment,** *n.*

èntire', *a.* whole, complete; not broken; of one piece. **èntire'ly,** *adv.* wholly, completely.

èntire'ty (-îrti), *n.* completeness; sum total.

ènti'tle, *v.t.* give (book, etc.) title of; give right or claim *to*.

en'tity, *n.* thing that has real existence.

èntomb' (-ōōm), *v.t.* place in tomb; serve as tomb for. **èntomb'ment,** *n.*

entomol'ogy, *n.* scientific study of insects. **entomolo'gical,** *a.* **entomol'ogist,** *n.*

entourage (ontoorahzh'), *n.* attendant persons; surroundings. (French)

en'trails (-z), *n.pl.* intestines; inner parts.

èntrain', *v.* put or get into train.

en'trance'[1] (-ah-), *v.t.* overpower with strong feeling, esp. of delight, etc.

en'trance'[2], *n.* coming or going in; right of admission; door or passage for entering.

en'trant, *n.* one who enters (profession, *for* competition, etc.).

èntrap', *v.t.* (p.t. *entrapped*), catch (as) in trap.

èntreat', *v.t.* ask earnestly; beg.

èntrea'ty, *n.* earnest request.

entrée (on'trā), *n.* right or privilege of admission; dish served between fish and meat courses.

èntrench', *v.t.* surround or fortify with trench; establish firmly. **èntrench'ment,** *n.*

èntrust', *v.t.* charge *with* (duty, object of care); confide (duty, etc., *to* person, etc.).

en'try, *n.* coming or going in; entrance; item, statement, etc., entered.

entwine', *v.t.* interweave; wreathe.

ènū'mèrâte, *v.t.* count; mention separately. **ènûmèrâ'tion, ènû'mèrâtor,** *nn.*

ènun'ciâte (*or* -shi-), *v.t.* state definitely; proclaim; pronounce. **ènunciâ'tion,** *n.*

ènvel'op, *v.t.* wrap up, cover; surround. **ènvel'opment,** *n.*

en'velôpe (*or* on-), *n.* wrapper, covering, esp. folded (and gummed) cover for letter.

ènven'om, *v.t.* poison.

en'viable, *a.* exciting envy; desirable.

en'vious, *a.* full of envy; feeling envy (*of*).

ènvîr'onment, *n.* surroundings; surrounding objects, circumstances, or influences. **ènvîronmen'tal,** *a.* **ènvîr'ons** (-z; *or* en'vi-), *n.pl.* surrounding districts (*of* town, etc.).

ènvis'age (-z-), *v.t.* face; visualize; contemplate.

en'voy, *n.* diplomatic minister ranking below ambassador; messenger, representative.

en'vy, *n.* resentful or admiring contemplation of another's success, etc.; object of this. *v.t.* feel envy of the.

en'zŷme, *n.* protein produced by living cells and catalysing specific biochemical reactions.

eon: see **aeon.**

ep'aulette (-pol-), *n.* ornamental shoulder--piece of uniform.

èphem'era, *n.* (pl. *ephemerae* or *ephemeras*), insect living only 1-4 days in adult form; short-lived thing. **èphem'eral,** *a.* short--lived, transitory.

epi-, *pref.* upon, at, in addition.

ep'ic, *a. & n.* (poem) narrating heroic deeds of tradition or history.

ep'icûre, *n.* one with refined taste in food and drink. **èpicûre'an,** *a. & n.* (person) devoted to pleasure and luxury.

epidem'ic, *a. & n.* (disease) spreading rapidly through a community for a time.

epider'mis, *n.* outer layer of skin.

epidi'ascôpe, *n.* apparatus for projecting magnified image of opaque or transparent object on to screen.

ep'igram, *n.* short poem with a witty ending; pithy saying. **epigrammat'ic,** *a.*

ep'igraph (-ahf), *n.* inscription on stone, statue, etc. **epigraph'ic,** *a.*

ep'ilepsy, *n.* nervous disorder with recurrent attacks of unconsciousness, mild or severe convulsions, etc. **epilep'tic,** *n. & a.*

ep'ilogue (-g), *n.* concluding part of book, etc.; speech, poem, etc., at end of play.

Epiph'any, *n.* festival (6 Jan.) commemorating the making known of Christ to the Magi.

èpis'copacy, *a.* government of church by bishops; bishops collectively.

èpis'copal, *a.* of or governed by bishops. **èpiscopâl'ian,** *a. & n.* (member) of episcopal church.

ep'isôde, *n.* (description of) one event in a series of events. **episod'ic(al),** *aa.*

èpis'tle (-sl), *n.* letter; poem, etc. in form of letter. **èpis'tolary,** *a.* of or carried on by letters.

ep'itaph (-ahf), *n.* words inscribed on or suitable for a tomb.

ep'ithet, *n.* adjective expressing quality or attribute.

èpit'omè, *n.* summary; thing that represents another in miniature. **èpit'omīze,** *v.t.*

e'poch (-k). *n.* beginning of an era in history, life, etc.; period marked by special events.

e'quable, *a.* uniform, even; not easily disturbed. **equabil'ity,** *n.*

e'qual, *a.* the same in number, size, merit, etc.; adequate; evenly matched. *n.* person, thing, equal to another. *v.t.* (p.t. *equalled*), be equal to. **èqual'ity** (-ol-), *n.* being equal. **e'qualīze,** *v.t.* make equal. **èqualizā'tion,** *n.* **e'qually,** *adv.*

equanim'ity (*or* ē-), *n.* composure, calm.

èquāte', *v.t.* state equality of; treat as equivalent.

èquā'tion, *n.* making equal, balancing; (Math.) statement of equality. **èquā'tional,** *a.*

èquā'tor, *n.* great circle of earth equidistant from poles, or of celestial sphere with plane perpendicular to earth's axis. **equator'ial,** *a.* of or near equator.

equerry (ikwe'ri; *or* ek'-), *n.* officer of British royal household.

èques'trian, *a.* of horse-riding. *n.* rider on horseback. **èquestrienne'** (-en), *n.fem.*

equi-, *pref.* equal(ly).

èquiang'ūlar (-ngg-), *a.* having equal angles.

èquidis'tant, *a.* at equal distance(s).

èquilat'eral, *a.* having all sides equal.

èquilib'rium, *n.* state of balance; balanced state of mind.

e'quine (*or* ē-), *a.* of or like a horse.

èquinoc'tial (-shl; *or* e-), *a.* of, happening at or near, equinox.

e'quinox (*or* e-), *n.* time of year when sun's path crosses equator and day and night are of equal length.

èquip', *v.t.* (p.t. *equipped*), supply with necessary things; provide for journey, etc. **equip'ment,** *n.* outfit, requisites.

è'quipoise (-z; *or* e-), *n.* state of balance; counterpoise.

e'quitable, *a.* fair, just.

equitā'tion, *n.* riding on horseback.

e'quity, *n.* fairness; principles of justice supplementing law; (pl.) stocks and shares not bearing fixed interest.

èquiv'alence, *n.* being equivalent.

èquiv'alent, *a.* equal in value, meaning, etc. *n.* equivalent amount, word, etc.

èquiv'ocal, *a.* of double or doubtful meaning; dubious. **èquiv'ocāte,** *v.i.* use words ambiguously, esp. to conceal truth. **èquivocā'tion,** *n.*

ēr'a, *n.* period of time dating from some particular point; period of history, etc.

èrad'icāte, *v.t.* root out, get rid of. **èradicā'tion,** *n.*

èrāse (-z), *v.t.* rub out, obliterate. **èrās'er,** *n.* preparation of rubber, etc, for rubbing out

writing, etc. **èrā'sure** (-zher), *n.* rubbing out; word, etc., rubbed out.

ere (āῑ), *prep. & conj.* (Poet.) before.

èrect', *a.* upright, vertical. *v.t.* raise, set upright; build. **èrec'tile,** *a.* (esp., of animal tissue) capable of becoming distended and rigid.

èrec'tion, *n.* erecting or being erected; building.

erg, *n.* unit of work or energy.

er'gō, *adv.* therefore. (Latin)

ergonom'ics, *n.* study of efficiency of workers and working arrangements.

E'rin (*or* ēῑ'-), *n.* (Poet.) Ireland.

er'mine, *n.* animal of weasel kind; its white winter fur.

Er'nie, *n.* device for drawing prize-winning numbers of premium bonds (*electronic random number indicator equipment*).

èrōde', *v.t.* destroy gradually; wear away. **èrō'sion** (-zhn), *n.* eroding; wearing away of earth's surface by wind, water, or ice.

èrot'ic, *a.* of, arousing, sexual desire.

err, *v.i.* make mistakes; sin.

e'rrand, *n.* short journey on which person is sent with message, etc.; purpose of journey.

e'rrant, *a.* roaming in search of adventure; wandering; sinning.

èrrat'ic, *a.* irregular; uncertain.

errā'tum (e-r-; *or* -ah-), *n.* (pl. *errata*), error in printing or writing.

errō'nèous (e-r-), *a.* incorrect.

e'rror, *n.* mistake; wrong opinion; transgression.

erst'whīle, *adv. & a.* (*archaic*) former(ly).

èructā'tion, *n.* belching.

e'rudīte (-roo-), *a.* learned. **erudi'tion,** *n.* learning.

èrupt', *v.i.* break out or through. **èrup'tion,** *n.* outbreak of volcanic activity; breaking out of rash, etc. **èrup'tive,** *a.*

es'calāte, *v.* increase or expand by degrees. **escalā'tion,** *n.*

es'calātor, *n.* mechanically operated continuously moving staircase, conveying persons up or down.

escapāde', *n.* act, adventure, in disregard of restraint or rules; prank.

èscāpe', *v.* get free; find way out; elude, avoid. *n.* escaping; leakage; outlet.

èscāpe'ment (-pm-), *n.* mechanism regulating motion of watch, etc.

èscāp'ism, *n.* distraction as relief from realities of life. **èscāp'ist,** *n. & a.*

escarp'ment, *n.* steep bank below rampart; abrupt face of ridge, etc.

eschatol'ogy (esk-), *n.* doctrine of death, judgement, heaven, and hell.

èschew' (-ōō), *v.t.* abstain from, avoid.

es'cort, *n.* body of armed men as guard; person(s) accompanying another for protection or out of courtesy; ship(s), etc., so employed. **èscort',** *v.t.* act as escort to.

èscutch'eon (-chon), *n.* shield with armorial

bearings; key-hole cover.

Es'kimō, a. & n. (pl. *Eskimos*), (native, language) of race inhabiting Arctic coasts of N. America, etc.

esote'ric, a. meant for, intelligible to, only the initiated.

èspal'ier, n. framework for training fruit-tree or shrub.

èspart'ō, n. kind of grass used in paper-making.

èspe'cial (-shl), a. chief; more than ordinary; particular. **èspe'cially**, adv. chiefly; more than in other cases.

Esperan'tō, n. artificial language designed for world use.

es'pionage (-ahzh), n. spying or using spies.

esplanāde', n. level piece of ground, used as promenade or separating fortress from town.

èspous'al (-zl), n. marriage; espousing of cause, etc. **èspouse'** (-z), v.t. marry; support (cause).

espress'ō, n. apparatus for making coffee under pressure; (café, etc., selling) coffee so made.

èspy̆', v.t. catch sight of.

èsquīre', n. (abbrev. *Esq.*) title of courtesy appended to man's name, esp. in addressing letter.

ess'ay, n. piece of writing of moderate length on any subject; attempt. **ess'ayist**, n. essay-writer.

ess'ence, n. true and inmost nature of a thing; indispensable quality; concentrated extract obtained from plant, foodstuff, etc.

èssen'tial (-shl), a. indispensable; necessary. n. indispensable element. **essential oil,** volatile oil giving characteristic odour to plant. **èssen'tially**, adv.

èstab'lish, v.t. set up; settle; place beyond dispute; make (Church) national by law.

èstab'lishment, n. establishing; staff, household; house of business; public institution; established Church; (*the Establishment*), social group with (official or unofficial) authority or influence regarded as having joint interest in resisting change.

èstāte', n. landed property; land developed for housing or industry; person's possessions; status, condition. **estate agent,** one whose business is sale or letting of houses and land. **estate car,** motor car with van-like body and door(s) at back. **estate duty,** death duty.

èsteem', v.t. think highly of; consider. n. favourable opinion, regard.

es'timable, a. worthy of esteem.

es'timate, n. approximate judgement of value, amount, etc.; price quoted for specified work. **es'timāte**, v.t. form an estimate of; fix by estimate at. **estimā'tion**, n. judgement; opinion; esteem.

èstrānge' (-nj), v.t. turn away feelings or affections of. **èstrānge'ment**, n.

es'tŭary, n. tidal mouth of river.

etcet'era (abbrev. *etc.*), and the rest; and so on.

etch, v.t. reproduce (picture, etc.) by engraving metal plate with acid. **etch'ing**, n. (esp.) print made from etched plate.

èter'nal, a. without beginning or end; going on for ever; incessant.

èter'nity, n. being eternal; infinite time; the future life.

ē'ther, n. clear sky, region above clouds; colourless volatile liquid used as anaesthetic and solvent.

èthēr'ēal, a. light, airy; heavenly.

eth'ical, a. of morals or ethics; moral, honourable.

e'thics, n. (as sing.) science of morals, study of principles of human duty; (as pl.) moral principles; rules of conduct.

eth'nic(al), aa. of race.

ethnol'ogy, n. science of races and peoples.

ēthol'ogy, n. study of animal behaviour.

etiology: see **aetiology**.

et'iquette (-ket), n. conventional rules of behaviour; unwritten code of professional conduct.

etymol'ogy, n. (account of) derivation of word from its original form. **etymolo'gical**, a.

eu-, *pref.* well.

eucalyp'tus, n. any of various trees, esp. Australian gum-tree.

Euch'arist (-k-), n. central Christian sacrament of body and blood of Christ, in which bread and wine are partaken of.

Eu'clid, n. geometry of Euclid (Greek mathematician, *c.* 300 B.C.). **Euclid'ēan**, a.

eugen'ics, n. study of production of fine (esp. human) offspring by control of mating. **eugen'ic**, a.

eul'ogīze, v.t. extol, praise highly. **eu'logist**, n. **eulogis'tic**, a.

eul'ogy, n. speech or writing in praise or commendation.

eun'uch (-k), n. castrated male person, esp. one employed in former times in harem or in affairs of State.

euph'ēmism, n. mild expression used in place of harsh or frank one. **euphèmist'ic**, a.

euphō'nium, n. tenor tuba; (in some European countries) bass saxhorn.

euph'ony, n. pleasantness of sounds, esp. in words. **euphō'nious**, a.

euphor'ia, n. sense of well-being.

Eurasian (ūrā'shn), a. of mixed European and Asian parentage; of Europe and Asia. n. Eurasian person.

eurē'ka (ūr-), *int.* I have found it! (Greek)

eurhyth'mics (ūridh-), n. system of expressing musical rhythm in bodily movement.

Europē'an (ūr-), a. & n. (native) of Europe.

euthanā'sia (-z-), n. (bringing about of) gentle and easy death.

èvac'ŭāte, v.t. make empty, clear; withdraw or remove from (place, esp. one considered dangerous). **èvacŭā'tion**, n. **èvacŭee'**, n. person so removed.

èváde′, v.t. escape from, avoid; elude.

èval′ūáte, v.t. find or state amount or value of. **èvalūá′tion**, n.

èvanes′cent, a. quickly fading.

èvangel′ic(al) (-j-), aa. of or according to Gospel teaching; (usu. -ical) of Protestant school of thought maintaining doctrine of salvation by faith.

èvan′gèlism (-j-), n. preaching of the Gospel.

èvan′gèlist (-j-), n. any of the writers (Matthew, Mark, Luke, John) of the four Gospels; preacher of Gospel. **èvangèlis′tic**, a.

èvap′oráte, v. turn into vapour; cause to lose liquid; disappear. **èvaporá′tion**, n.

èvá′sion (-zhn), n. act or means of eluding; excuse. **èvá′sive**, a.

ève, n. evening or day before festival, etc.; time just before event; (Poet.) evening.

Eve (ēv), n. (in Biblical story of the Creation) the first woman.

è′ven¹, n. evening, **è′vensong**, n. service of evening prayer in Church of England. **è′ventíde**, evening.

è′ven², a. level, smooth; equal; equable, calm; divisible by two. v.t. make even. **è′venness** (-n-n-), n.

è′ven³, adv. used to emphasise a statement, comparison, etc.; just, exactly.

ève′ning (-vn-), n. close of day, esp. time from sunset to bedtime.

èvent′, n. occurrence, (esp. important) happening; item, esp. in sports programme; outcome. in the event of, if .. occurs. in any event, whatever happens. **èvent′ful**, a. full of incidents.

èven′tūal, a. likely to happen in certain circumstances; finally resulting. **èventūal′ity**, n. possible event. **èven′tūally**, adv. in the end.

ev′er, adv. at all times; at any time.

ev′ergreen, a. always green and fresh. n. tree, shrub, having green leaves all the year round.

everlas′ting (-ah-), a. lasting for ever; perpetual.

evermore′, adv. for ever; always.

ev′ery (-vr-), a. each; all taken one by one. **ev′erybody**, pron. every person. **ev′eryday**, a. occurring every day; ordinary. **ev′eryone** (-wun), pron. everybody. **ev′erything**, pron. all things; thing of first importance. **ev′erywhere** (-wār), adv. in every place.

èvict′, v.t. expel (person, esp. tenant) by legal process. **èvic′tion**, n.

ev′idence, n. indication, sign; facts giving proof. in evidence, readily seen, conspicuous. v.t. indicate. **ev′ident**, a. obvious, clear. **ev′idently**, adv.

è′vil, a. bad, harmful, wicked. n. evil thing; sin; harm. **evil-doer**, sinner.

èvince′, v.t. show.

èvis′cerate, v.t. disembowel.

èvocá′tion (or e-), n. evoking. **èvoc′ative**, a.

èvōke′, v.t. call forth, produce, (feeling, memory, etc.).

èvolu′tion (-loo- or -lū-), n. evolving; origination of species by development from earlier forms; change of position of troops or ships. **èvolu′tionary**, a.

èvolve′, v. unfold, open out; develop by natural process; produce or modify by evolution.

ewe (ū), n. female sheep.

ew′er, n. pitcher; water-jug.

ex-, pref. (becoming ef- before f; contracted to e- before many consonants), out, forth, without, un-, thoroughly; former(ly).

exa′cerbáte, v.t. aggravate; irritate. **exacerbá′tion**, n.

èxact′ (-gz-), a. precise; accurate. v.t. demand; enforce payment of (fees, etc.). **èxac′tion**, n. exacting; illegal or excessive demand.

èxac′titúde (-gz-), n. exactness.

èxact′ly (-gz-), adv. in an exact manner, just; (as answer or confirmation) quite so.

èxa′ggeráte (-gzaj-), v.t. magnify, enlarge beyond truth; overstate. **èxaggerá′tion**, n.

èxalt′ (-gzawlt; or -olt), v.t. raise in rank, etc.; praise. **exaltá′tion**, n. raising on high; elation; rapturous emotion.

èxaminá′tion (-gz-), n. close inspection; testing of knowledge or ability by questions; formal interrogation of witness, etc.

èxam′ine (-gz-), v. inspect closely, inquire into; test proficiency of (pupils, etc.) by questions; interrogate (witness, etc.). **èxaminee′**, n. person undergoing examination. **èxam′iner**, n.

èxam′ple (-gzah-), n. fact, etc., illustrating general rule; specimen; model, pattern; precedent; warning to others.

èxas′perate (-gz-; or -ahs-), v.t. irritate, make worse. **èxasperá′tion**, n.

ex′cavāte, v.t. hollow out; unearth by digging. **excavá′tion**, n. **ex′cavátor**, n.

èxceed′, v. go beyond; be greater than; surpass. **èxcee′dingly**, adv. very.

èxcel′, v. (p.t. excelled), do better than others; be very good (at).

ex′cellence, n. great merit.

ex′cellency, n. title of ambassadors, governors, etc.

ex′cellent, a. outstandingly good.

èxcept′, v. exclude from general statement, etc. prep. & conj. not including, with exception of, but; (archaic) unless. except for, if it were not for. **èxcept′ing**, a., prep. & conj. except.

èxcep′tion, n. excepting; thing or case excepted; objection. **èxcep′tionable**, a. open to objection.

èxcep′tional, a. forming exception; unusual.

ex′cerpt, n. passage, extract, from book, etc.

èxcess′, n. fact of exceeding; amount by which thing exceeds; intemperance; immoderation; (pl.) outrage. **èxcess′ive**, a. too much; too great; extreme.

èxchánge′ (-nj), n. giving one thing and receiving another in its place; exchanging of money for equivalent in other currency; building where merchants, stockbrokers, etc., assemble to do business; central office where telephone connections are made. *v.* give or take back in exchange.

exche'quer (-ker), *n.* public department charged with receipt and custody of revenue. **Chancellor of the Exchequer,** finance minister in U.K.

ex'cise¹ (-z), *n.* (government office collecting) duty on home-produced goods, various licences, etc.

excise'² (-z), *v.t.* cut out or away. **exci'sion** (-zhn), *n.*

exci'table, *a.* easily excited.

excite', *v.t.* set in motion; stir up; move to strong emotion. **excitā'tion,** *n.* action of exciting. **excī'tedly,** *adv.* **excīte'ment,** *n.* state of being excited.

exclaim', *v.* cry out. **exclamā'tion,** *n.* exclaiming; word(s) exclaimed. **exclamation mark,** punctuation mark (!). **exclam'atory,** *a.*

exclude' (-ōōd), *v.t.* shut out (*from*); leave out, not include; make impossible. **exclu'sion** (-ōōzhn), *n.* excluding, being excluded.

exclus'ive (-lōōs-), *a.* excluding; (of society, etc.) excluding outsiders; not obtainable, not published, etc., elsewhere.

excommū'nicāte, *v.t.* cut off (person) from sacraments or from all communication with Church. **excommūnicā'tion,** *n.*

excor'iāte, *v.t.* remove skin or bark from. **excoriā'tion,** *n.*

ex'crèment, *n.* waste matter discharged form the bowels, dung. **excrêmen'tal,** *a.*

excres'cence, *n.* abnormal outgrowth.

excrēte', *v.t.* separate and expel (waste matter) from the system. **excrē'tion,** *n.*

excru'ciāte (-krōōshi-), *v.t.* pain acutely; torture. **excru'ciāting,** *a.* **excruciā'tion,** *n.*

ex'culpāte, *v.t.* free from blame; clear (*from* accusation, etc.). **exculpā'tion,** *n.*

excur'sion (-shn), *n.* short journey or ramble; pleasure trip. **excur'sionist,** *n.*

excuse' (-z), *v.t.* (attempt to) lessen or remove blame; forgive; grant exemption to. **excūs'able** (-z-), *a.* **excūse'** (-s), *n.* reason given to explain or defend conduct; apology.

ex'ēcrable, *a.* abominable.

ex'ēcrāte, *v.* express or feel abhorrence for; utter curses. **exēcrā'tion,** *n.*

exec'ūtant (-gz-), *n.* performer, esp. of music.

ex'ēcūte, *v.t.* carry out; perform; put to death. **exēcū'tion,** *n.* executing; skill in performing music; capital punishment. **exēcū'tioner,** *n.* one who carries out capital punishment.

exec'ūtive (-gz-), *a.* concerned with the carrying out of laws, policy, etc. *n.* executive branch of government or organization; holder of managerial position in business, etc.

exec'ūtor (-gz-), *n.* person appointed by testator to execute his will. **exec'ūtrix,** *n. fem.*

exem'plary (-gz-), *a.* serving as example; worthy of imitation.

exem'plifȳ (-gz-), *v.t.* give or be an example of. **exemplificā'tion,** *n.*

exempt' (-gz-), *a.* not liable or exposed to (duty, danger, etc.); free *from.* *v.t.* grant immunity or freedom *from.* **exemp'tion,** *n.*

ex'ercise (-z), *n.* use (of faculties, rights, etc.); practice; use of muscles, etc., esp. for health's sake; task. *v.* use; take exercise; give exercise to; perplex.

exert' (-gz-), *v.t.* bring into vigorous action; exercise, apply. **exer'tion,** *n.* exerting; effort.

exeunt: see **exit.**

exhalā'tion, *n.* exhaling; evaporation; what is exhaled.

exhāle', *v.* give off, be given off, in vapour; breathe out. ·

exhaust' (-gzaw-), *v.t.* consume, use up; empty of contents; drain of strength, etc.; tire out. *n.* expulsion or exit of used steam from engine, etc.; gases, etc., expelled. **exhaus'tible,** *a.* **exhaus'tion** (-chn), *n.* (esp.) total loss of strength.

exhaus'tive (-gzaw-), *a.* comprehensive.

exhib'it (-gzi-), *v.t.* display; manifest; show publicly. *n.* thing exhibited. **exhib'itor,** *n.* one who exhibits (at show, etc.).

exhibi'tion (eksi-), *n.* display; public show; sum allowed to student from funds of college, etc. **exhibi'tioner,** *n.* student holding exhibition. **exhibi'tionism,** *n.* tendency to behave so as to attract attention. **exhibi'tionist,** *n.*

exhil'arāte (-gzi-), *v.t.* cheer, enliven, gladden. **exhilarā'tion,** *n.*

exhort' (-gzort), *v.t.* advise earnestly; urge to action. **exhortā'tion,** *n.*

exhūme', *v.t.* dig up after burial. **exhūmā'tion,** *n.*

ex'igence, ex'igency, *nn.* urgent need; emergency. **ex'igent,** *a.* urgent; exacting.

exig'ūous, *a.* scanty, small. **exigū'ity,** *n.*

ex'īle, *n.* penal banishment; long absence from one's country; person in exile. *v.t.* banish.

exist' (-gz-), *v.t.* be; occur, be found; live.

exis'tent (-gz-), *a.* existing, actual.

exis'tence (-gz-), *n.* being, existing; mode of living.

ex'it¹, *n.* way out; departure; death.

ex'it², **ex'ēunt,** (stage directions) (he, etc.) goes, (they) go, off stage. (Latin)

ex'odus, *n.* departure, esp. in considerable numbers; (*Exodus*), second book of Old Testament.

exon'erāte (-gz-), *v.t.* free from blame; release (*from* obligation). **exonerā'tion,** *n.*

exorb'itant (-gz-), *a.* grossly excessive (esp. of price, etc.). **exorb'itance,** *n.*

ex'orcīze, *v.t.* expel (evil spirit) by invocation, etc.; clear (person, place) of evil spirit. **ex'orcism, ex'orcist,** *nn.*

exote'ric, *a.* intelligible to outsiders; ordinary, popular.

exŏt′ic (-gz-), *a.* introduced from abroad; strange, bizarre.

expand′, *v.* spread out; develop; increase; become genial.

expanse′, *n.* wide area or extent of land, space, etc. **expan′sion** (-shn), *n.* expanding, increase.

expan′sive, *a.* able or tending to expand; extensive; genial.

expā′tiate (-shi-), *v. t.* speak or write at length. **expātiā′tion**, *n.*

expat′riāte (*or* -pā-), *v. t.* banish, remove *oneself*, from one's native country. **expat′riate**, *n.* (esp.) person who lives in a foreign country. *a.* expatriated.

expect′, *v. t.* reckon on; anticipate; look for; suppose.

expec′tant, *a.* expecting; expecting to become. **expec′tancy**, *n.*

expectā′tion, *a.* anticipation; what one expects; probability.

expec′torāte, *v.* cough or spit out from lungs or chest; spit. **expectorā′tion**, *n.* **expec′-torant**, *a.* & *n.* (medicine) promoting expectoration.

expē′diĕnt, *a.* suitable, advisable; advantageous (if not just). *n.* contrivance, device. **expē′diĕnce, expē′diĕncy**, *nn.*

ex′pĕdīte, *v. t.* help on, facilitate, progress of; dispatch.

expĕdi′tion, *n.* (men, ships, etc., sent on) journey or voyage for some definite purpose; promptness, dispatch.

expĕdi′tious (-shus), *a.* quick, done quickly.

expel′, *v. t.* (p.t. *expelled*), drive out; eject; turn out from school, etc.

expend′, *v. t.* spend (money, time, care, etc.); use up. **expen′dable**, *a.* (esp.) that can be spared, likely to be sacrificed or destroyed.

expen′diture (-cher), *n.* expending; amount expended.

expense′, *n.* cost, charge; (pl.) outlay in carrying out commission, etc.

expen′sive, *a.* costing much money, dear.

expēr′iĕnce, *n.* knowledge gained by personal observation; event that affects one. *v. t.* meet with, feel, undergo. **expēr′iĕnced**, *a.* (esp.) wise or skilful through experience.

expe′riment, *n.* procedure adopted or action undertaken to make discovery, observation, test, etc. *v. i.* make experiment(s). **experimen′tal**, *a.* of, based on, used in, experiment(s).

ex′pert, *a.* trained by practice, skilful, skilled. *n.* person having special skill or knowledge. **expertise′** (-tēz), *n.* expertness.

ex′piāte, *v. t.* pay penalty of, make amends for (sin). **expiā′tion**, *n.*

expīre′, *v.* breathe out; die; come to an end. **expirā′tion**, *n.*

expīr′y, *n.* end, termination.

explain′, *v. t.* make known; make intelligible; account for. **explanā′tion**, *n.* statement, circumstance, that explains. **explan′atory**, *a.*

serving to explain.

explĕ′tive, *n.* oath.

ex′plicable (*or* iksplik′-), *a.* that can be explained. **ex′plicatory** (*or* iksplik′-), *a.* explanatory.

expli′cit, *a.* expressly stated; definite; outspoken. **expli′citly**, *adv.*

explōde′, *v.* (cause to) burst with a loud noise; discredit (idea, theory, etc.).

ex′ploit, *n.* heroic or spectacular feat. **exploit′**, *v. t.* work (mine, etc.); use for one's own ends. **exploitā′tion**, *n.*

explore′, *v. t.* examine (country, etc.) by going through it; examine thoroughly; inquire into. **explorā′tion**, *n.* **explo′ratory**, *a.*

explō′sion (-zhn), *n.* exploding; (loud noise caused by) sudden and violent bursting; outbreak; sudden violent expansion.

explō′sive, *a.* tending to explode; of or like explosion. *n.* explosive substance.

expō′nent, *n.* person who explains or interprets; type, representative.

export′, *v. t.* send (goods) to another country. **ex′port**, *n.* exported article; (usu. pl.) amount exported. **exportā′tion**, *n.*

expōse′ (-z), *v. t.* leave or place in unprotected position; uncover; lay open (*to* risk, etc.); unmask, show up; subject (film, etc.) to light.

exposi′tion (-z-), *n.* description, explanation.

expos′tūlāte, *v. i.* make (esp. friendly) protest.

expō′sure (-zher), *n.* exposing or being exposed; unmasking; length of time film is exposed.

expound′, *v. t.* set forth in detail; explain, make clear.

express′, *v. t.* represent by symbols, etc., or in language; put into words; reveal, betoken; squeeze out; send by express postal service, train, etc. *a.* definitely stated; done, made, etc., for special purpose; travelling, etc., fast. *n.* fast train, postal service, etc. *adv.* with speed. **express′ible**, *a.* **express′ly**, *adv.* plainly, specially.

expre′ssion (-shn), *n.* (manner or mode of) expressing; word, phrase; look (on face); tone (of voice); expressive quality. **express′-ive**, *a.* serving to express; full of meaning.

exprō′priāte, *v. t.* take away (property); dispossess. **exprōpriā′tion**, *n.*

expul′sion (-shn), *n.* expelling, being expelled.

expunge′ (-nj), *v. t.* erase, strike out.

ex′purgāte, *v. t.* remove objectionable passages from (book, etc.)

ex′quisite (-z-), *a.* of great beauty or delicacy; acute.

ex-ser′vice, *a.* having formerly belonged to (fighting) service. **ex-ser′viceman**, *n.* (pl. -*men*)

extant′ (*or* ex′-), *a.* still existing.

extem′porĕ, *adv.* & *a.* without preparation. **extem′porary**, *a.* **extem′porīze**, *v.* produce, speak, etc., without preparation. **extempori-**

zā'tion, *n.*

extend', *v.* stretch out; reach; accord (*to*); make longer or larger. **exten'dible, exten'sible,** *aa.*

exten'sion (-shn), *n.* extending; enlargement, additional part.

exten'sive, *a.* large; far-reaching.

extent', *n.* degree to which thing is extended; length; area; scope.

exten'ūăte, *v.t.* make (offence, guilt) seem less serious by partial excuse. **extenūā'tion,** *n.*

extēr'ior, *a.* outer, outward. *n.* outward aspect; outer part.

exter'mināte, *v.t.* destroy utterly; root out. **exterminā'tion,** *n.*

exter'nal, *a.* outside; outward. **exter'nals** (-z), *n.pl.* outward aspect; external circumstances; non-essentials.

extinct', *a.* that has died out; (of fire, etc.) extinguished; (of volcano) no longer active.

extinc'tion, *n.* extinguishing; making or becoming extinct; destruction.

exting'uish (-nggw-), *v.t.* cause to stop burning, quench; eclipse; destroy. **exting'uisher,** *n.*

ex'tirpāte, *v.t.* root out; destroy utterly. **extirpā'tion,** *n.*

extōl', *v.t.* (p.t. *extolled*), praise highly.

extort', *v.t.* get by force, threats, etc.

extor'tion, *n.* extorting, esp. of money. **extor'tionate,** *a.* (esp.) exorbitant.

ex'tra, *a.* additional; larger, more, better, than what is usual or agreed. *adv.* more than usually; additionally. *n.* extra thing; thing charged extra.

extra-, *pref.* outside, not within scope of.

extract', *v.t.* take out; draw forth; derive (*from*); obtain (juices, etc.) by pressure, distillation, etc.; copy out, quote. **ex'tract,** *n.* essence; concentrated preparation; passage from book, etc. **extrac'tion,** *n.* extracting; descent.

ex'tradīte, *v.t.* hand over (fugitive accused of crime) to authorities of foreign State where crime was committed. **extradi'tion,** *n.*

extramūr'al, *a.* outside walls of town, etc; (of instruction) organized by university, etc., for persons other than its resident students.

extrā'néous, *a.* of external origin; not natu-rally belonging; foreign.

extraor'dinary (-tror- *or* -tra-or-), *a.* out of usual line of action, etc.; exceptional, surprising; specially employed.

extrasen'sory, *a.* (of perception) made by other means than those of the senses.

extrav'agance, *n.* extravagant expenditure; absurd statement or action. **extrav'agant,** *a.* wild, absurd; exorbitant; profuse, wasteful.

extravert: see **extrovert.**

extrēme', *a.* outermost; utmost; very great; not moderate. *n.* thing at either end, esp. (pl.) things as remote or different as possible; extreme degree, etc. **extrēme'ly,** *adv.* very.

extrem'ity, *n.* extreme point, end; (esp. in pl.) hands and feet; extreme adversity, distress, etc.

ex'tricāte, *v.t.* get (person, thing, *oneself*) free (*from* confinement, difficulty). **extricā'tion,** *n.*

extrin'sic, *a.* not inherent or essential.

ex'trovert, ex'travert, *n.* person with interests directed to things outside self. **extrover'sion** (-shn), *n.*

extrude' (-ōo-), *v.t.* thrust or squeeze out. **extru'sion** (-ōozhn), *n.*

exū'berant (-gz-), *a.* in high spirits, effusive; luxuriant; overflowing. **exū'berance,** *n.*

exūde' (-gz-), *v.* ooze out or give off like sweat. **exūdā'tion,** *n.*

exult' (-gz-), *v.i.* rejoice, triumph (*in, at, over*). **exul'tant,** *a.* **exultā'tion,** *n.*

eye (ī), *n.* organ of sight; iris of this; look; power of seeing; eye-like thing, hole of needle, loop, leaf-bud of potato. *make eyes at,* look amorously at, ogle. *v.t.* (pres. p. *eyeing*), observe, watch closely or suspiciously. **eye'ball,** eye within lids and socket. **eye'brow,** arch of hair over eye. **eye'glass,** lens to assist sight, protect eye, etc. **eye'lash,** one of fringe of hairs on eyelid. **eye'let,** small hole in sail, upper of shoe, etc.; loop-hole. **eye'lid,** movable fold of skin covering eye. **eye'sight,** faculty or power of seeing. **eye'sore,** ugly object. **eye-tooth,** canine tooth under eye. **eye-witness,** one who can describe an event because he saw it happen.

ey'rie (ār- *or* ēr- *or* īr-), *n.* nest of bird (esp. eagle) that builds high.

F

fā'ble, *n.* story not based on fact; short moral tale, esp. about animals. **fā'bled,** *a.* celebrated in fable; legendary.

fab'ric, *n.* woven material; building; framework, structure.

fab'ricāte, *v.t.* invent (fact); forge (document). **fabrică'tion,** *n.*

fab'ūlous, *a.* fabled; (*informal*) marvellous.

façade' (-sahd), *n.* face, esp. principal front, of building; outward appearance.

fâce, *n.* front of head; expression; appearance; surface; front; dial of clock, etc.; effrontery. *v.* meet confidently; be opposite to; look, (Mil.) turn, in some direction; cover part of (garment) with other material, esp. at edge; cover surface of with other material. **face value,** value stated on coin, note, etc.; apparent value. **fâce'less,** *a.* (esp.) unknown, unidentifiable.

fa'cĕt, *n.* one side of a many-sided body, esp. cut gem.

facĕ'tious (-shus), *a.* (intended to be) humorous; fond of jesting.

facia: see **fascia.**

fā'cial (-shl), *a.* of the face.

fa'cile, *a.* easily done or obtained; fluent; superficial; easily led.

facil'itâte, *v.t.* make easy or easier; help forward. **facilitā'tion,** *n.*

facil'ity, *n.* absence of difficulty; readiness of speech; dexterity; (pl.) equipment for doing something (e.g. *washing facilities*).

fā'cing, *n.* material with which garment is faced; surface covering of different material, esp. of stone on wall, etc.

facsim'ilè, *n.* exact copy.

fact, *n.* thing done; thing known to be true; what is true or existent, reality. *in fact,* in reality, really.

fac'tion, *n.* group or party within another; party enthusiasm or strife. **fac'tious** (-shus), *a.*

facti'tious (-shus), *a.* artificial.

fac'titive, *a.* (of verb) expressing idea of making, calling, or thinking to be.

fac'tor, *n.* any of the numbers whose product is the given number; circumstance, fact, influence, contributing to a result; (Sc.) manager of estate.

fac'tory, *n.* building or range of buildings for manufacture of goods.

factō'tum, *n.* man doing all kinds of work or managing employer's affairs.

fac'ultative, *n.* conferring permission, optional.

fac'ulty, *n.* aptitude for particular action; physical or mental power; (teaching staff of) department of learning at university.

fad, *n.* pet notion, craze. **fadd'ist,** *n.* **fadd'y,** *a.*

fāde, *v.* droop, wither; (cause) to lose freshness or colour; disappear gradually; (of sound) grow faint; (of brake) gradually lose power.

faeces (fē'sēz), *n.pl.* waste matter from bowels, excrement. **fae'cal,** *a.*

fag, *v.* (p.t. *fagged*), toil; make or grow weary; (at some schools) do service for

seniors. *n.* drudgery; junior who has to fag.

fagg'ot, *n.* bundle of sticks for fuel; bundle of steel rods. **faggot-stitch,** stitch used in embroidery.

Fahrenheit (fa'renhīt), *a.* (of scale, thermometer) that has 32° for freezing-point and 212° for boiling-point of water.

fail, *v.* not succeed; be missing or insufficient; break down; disappoint; reject or be rejected as candidate; go bankrupt. *n. without fail,* for certain, whatever happens.

fai'ling, *n.* weakness; shortcoming.

fail'ure (-yer), *n.* lack of success; non--performance; bankruptcy; unsuccessful person, thing, or attempt.

fain, *pred. a.* (*archaic*) willing; glad. *adv.* gladly.

faint, *a.* weak; likely to lose consciousness; dim; timid. *v.i. & n.* (suffer) temporary loss of consciousness. **faint-hearted,** *a.* timid, cowardly.

fair[1], *n.* gathering held periodically for sale of goods, livestock, etc., often with shows and amusements; trade exhibition; bazaar. **fair'-ing,** *n.* present bought at fair.

fair[2], *a.* beautiful; blond, not dark; just; passably good; (of weather) fine; (of wind) favourable. *adv.* justly. **fair play,** equal opportunities, just treatment. **fair'ness,** *n.*

fair'ly, *adv.* in fair manner; completely; moderately.

fair'way, *n.* navigable channel; (Golf) area of short grass between tee and green.

fair'y, *n.* small supernatural being supposed to have magical powers. *a.* of fairies; fairy-like. **fair'yland,** home of the fairies. **fairy-tale,** tale about fairies; incredible story; falsehood.

fait accompli (fāt akawn'plē), thing done and past arguing about. (French)

faith, *n.* trust; belief in religious doctrine or divine truth; religion; loyalty, confidence. **faith-healing,** healing by faith, not medical skill.

faith'ful, *a.* loyal, constant; true. **faith'fully,** *adv. yours faithfully,* formula at end of business letter.

faith'less, *a.* (esp.) perfidious, false.

fāke, *v.t.* do *up* or tamper with in order to deceive. *n. & a.* counterfeit, spurious (thing or person).

fakir (fā'ker, *or* fakēr'), *n.* Muslim or Hindu religious ascetic or beggar.

falcon (faw(l)'kn; *or* fol'-), *n.* bird of prey trained to hawk for sport. **falc'oner,** *n.* one who practises falconry. **falc'onry,** *n.* breeding, training, or hunting game-birds with, falcons or hawks.

fall (fawl), *v.i.* (p.t. *fell*, p.p. *fallen*), descend freely, drop, come down; decline; become lower; collapse; sink into sin; perish; lapse; become; occur, happen. *n.* falling; amount that falls; descent, drop; downfall, ruin; (usu. pl.) waterfall; (esp. U.S.) autumn. **fall--out,** (esp.) radioactive dust settling after nuclear explosion.

fallā'cious (-shus), *a.* containing fallacy; misleading. **fall'acy,** *n.* misleading argument; unsound reasoning.

fal'-lal', *n.* piece of finery.

fall'ible, *a.* liable to err or be erroneous. **fallibil'ity,** *n.*

fall'ow (-ō), *a.* ploughed and harrowed but left uncropped for a year; uncultivated. *n.* fallow ground.

fall'ow deer (-ō), medium-sized kind of deer, light fawn, with white spots in summer.

false (fawls *or* fols), *a.* erroneous, deceptive; deceitful, lying; treacherous; not genuine, artificial. *false pretences,* misrepresentations meant to deceive. **false'ness, fal'sity,** *nn.*

false'hood (fawl- *or* fol-) *n.* falseness; lying, lie(s).

falsett'ō (fawl- *or* fol-), *n.* (pl. *falsettos*), man's voice forced above its natural range.

fal'sify (fawl- *or* fol-), *v.t.* alter dishonestly; misrepresent; disappoint. **falsificā'tion,** *n.*

falsity: see **false.**

fal'ter (fawl- *or* fol-), *v.i.* stumble; speak hesitatingly; waver, lose courage.

fāme, *n.* condition of being widely known or much talked about; reputation. **fāmed,** *a.* famous.

famil'iar, *a.* well-known; intimate; common, usual; free in manner. *n.* intimate friend. **familia'rity,** *n.* **famil'iarīze,** *v.t.* make familiar; accustom.

fam'ily, *n.* members of a household, set of parents and children or of relations; person's children; lineage; race; group of objects, languages, etc. **family planning,** use of contraceptive methods to plan spacing and limiting of children born. **family tree,** genealogical tree.

fam'ine, *n.* extreme scarcity of food in district, etc.; starvation.

fam'ish, *v.* reduce, be reduced, to extreme hunger.

fā'mous, *a.* known widely, having fame, celebrated.

fan[1], *n.* instrument, usu. folding and shaped like sector of circle when spread out, waved to create current of air; fan-shaped thing; rotating apparatus giving current of air. *v.t.* (p.t. *fanned*), send current of air on to; spread *out* in fan shape. **fan-belt,** belt driving rotating fan. **fan'light,** semi-circular window over door.

fan[2], *n.* (*slang*) enthusiast, devotee. **fan'mail,** letters from fans.

fanat'ic, *n. & a.* (person) filled with excessive or mistaken enthusiasm, esp. in religion. **fanat'ical,** *a.* **fanat'icism,** *n.*

fan'ciful, *a.* imaginary; whimsical; quaint.

fan'cy, *n.* (power of creating) mental image; something imagined; whim; fondness, liking. *a.* ornamental, not plain; whimsical, extravagant. *v.t.* imagine; like. **fancy dress,** unusual costume, usu. representing fictitious or historical character, etc.

fan'fāre, *n.* flourish of trumpets.

fang, *n.* canine tooth, esp. of dog or wolf; serpent's venom-tooth.

fantā'sia (-z-; *or* -azē'a), *n.* (Mus.) composition in which form is subordinate to fancy; composition based on several familiar tunes.

fantas'tic, *a.* absurdly fanciful; odd, grotesque. **fantas'tically,** *adv.*

fan'tasy, phan'tasy, *n.* imagination; fancy; fantastic idea or design.

far, *adv.* (*farther, farthest, further, furthest*), at or to a great distance; by much. *a.* distant. **far-away,** remote; dreamy. **far-fetched,** forced, unnatural. **far-flung,** *a.* widely extended. **far-sighted,** having foresight.

fa'rad, *n.* (Electr.) unit of capacitance.

farce, *n.* light dramatic work intended only to amuse; absurd or futile proceedings, mockery. **far'cical,** *a.*

fāre, *n.* cost of passenger's conveyance; passenger; food. *v.i.* progress; get on (*well, badly*); be fed.

fārewell' (fār-), *int. & n.* good-bye.

farinā'ceous (-shus), *a.* like flour or meal; starchy.

farm, *n.* tract of land used for cultivation, raising animals, etc.; farm-house. *v.* use land for growing crops, raising animals, etc.; send work *out* to be done by others. **farm-house,** dwelling place attached to farm. **farm'stead,** farm with buildings. **farm'yard,** yard of farm-house. **far'mer,** *n.* one who owns, rents, or manages a farm.

farrago (fa-rah'gō; *or* -rā'gō), *n.* (pl. *farragos*), medley; confused mixture.

fa'rrier, *n.* smith who shoes horses. **fa'rriery,** *n.*

fa'rrow (-ō), *n.* litter of pigs. *v.* (of sow) give birth (to litter of pigs).

far'ther (-dh-), *adv.* more far; (usu. *further*) also, in addition. *a.* more distant or advanced; (usu. *further*) additional, more. **far'thermōst,** *a.* farthest. **far'thest,** *a.* most distant. *adv.* to, at, greatest distance.

far'thing (-dh-), *n.* (Hist.) (coin worth) quarter of a penny.

far'thingāle (-dhingg-), *n.* hooped petticoat worn in 16th and 17th centuries.

fasces (fas'ēz), *n.pl.* (in ancient Rome) bundle of rods with axe in middle, carried before consul.

fā'scia, fā'cia (-sha), *n.* board over shop-front with occupier's name, etc.; dashboard; control panel.

fas'cināte, *v.t.* make (victim) powerless by one's presence or look; charm irresistibly. **fascinā'tion,** *n.*

Fascism (fash'izm), *n.* principles and organization of Italian nationalist anti-Communist dictatorship (1922-43); imitations of this in other countries. **fasc'ist,** *n. & a.*

fa'shion (-shn), *n.* shape, style; way, manner; prevailing style or custom, esp. in dress. *v.t.*

form, shape. **fa'shionable,** *a.* of or in (latest) fashion.

fast¹ (fah-), *v.i.* go without food, esp. as religious observance. *n.* going without food; day, season, of fasting.

fast² (fah-), *a.* quick, rapid; firmly attached; steadfast; (of colour) not fading, etc.; (of person) pleasure-seeking. *adv.* quickly; firmly, tightly.

fasten (fah'sn), *v.* attach, fix; secure by tie or bond; become fast or secure. **fa'stener, fa'stening,** *nn.*

fastid'ious, *a.* not easily pleased; squeamish.

fast'ness (fah-), *n.* (esp.) stronghold.

fat, *a.* (*fatter, fattest*), plump; having much fat; greasy, oily; fertile, abundant. *n.* oily substance in animal bodies; oily substance obtained from seeds, etc. **fat-head,** (*informal*) stupid person.

fā'tal, *a.* causing, ending in, death or disaster. **fā'tally,** *adv.*

fā'talism, *n.* belief that all events are predetermined; submission to all that happens as inevitable. **fā'talist,** *n.* **fātalis'tic,** *a.*

fatal'ity, *n.* death by accident, in war, etc.

fāte, *n.* power looked upon as determining events unalterably; lot, destiny; death, destruction. **fā'ted,** *a.* decreed by fate; doomed. **fāte'ful,** *a.* controlled by fate; decisive, fatal.

fa'ther (fahdh-), *n.* male parent; forefather; priest; head of religious order; oldest member; (pl.) leading men, elders. *v.t.* beget, be the father of; originate. **father-in-law,** wife's or husband's father. **fa'therland,** native country, **fa'therhood,** *n.* **fa'therless, fa'therly,** *aa.*

fath'om (-dh-), *n.* measure of 6 feet, esp. in soundings. *v.t.* sound (depth of water); get to the bottom of. **fath'omless,** *a.* that cannot be fathomed.

fatigue' (-ēg), *n.* weariness from exertion; weary task. *v.t.* tire. **fati'guing** (-ging), *a.*

fatt'en, *v.* make or grow fat.

fatt'y, *a.* of or like fat.

fat'ūous, *a.* silly, purposeless. **fatū'ity,** *n.*

fau'cèt, *n.* tap for barrel, etc.; (U.S.) tap.

fault, *n.* defect, imperfection; responsibility for something wrong; misdeed; (Geol.) break in continuity of strata, etc. *find fault* (*with*), criticize unfavourably; complain (of). **fault'less,** *a.* **faul'ty,** *a.* having fault(s).

faun, *n.* (Rom. myth.) rural deity with pointed ears, horns, and tail.

fau'na, *n.* (pl. *faunas, faunae*), animals of a region or an epoch.

faux pas (fō'pah), indiscreet speech or action, mistake. (French)

fā'vour (-ver), *n.* liking, goodwill, approval; partiality; thing given or worn as mark of favour. *v.t.* treat with kindness; show partiality to; resemble in features.

fā'vourable (-ver-), *a.* giving or showing approval; friendly; promising; helpful.

fā'vourite (-ver-), *a.* & *n.* (person or thing) preferred above others; (person) specially or unduly favoured by superior. *the favourite,* (racing, etc.) competitor thought most likely to win. **fā'vouritism,** *n.*

fawn¹, *n.* deer in first year; light yellowish brown. *a.* fawn-coloured.

fawn², *v.i.* (of dog, etc.) show affection by frisking, licking, tail-wagging, etc.; (of person) behave in a servile manner.

fay, *n.* (Poet.) fairy.

fē'alty, *n.* feudal vassal's obligation of fidelity to his lord.

fear, *n.* emotion caused by impending danger or evil; alarm, dread. *v.* be afraid (of); be anxious; revere (God). **fear'ful,** *a.* terrible; afraid; (*informal*) awful. **fear'less,** *a.* brave. **fear'some,** *a.* (usu. jokingly) frightening.

fea'sible (-z-), *a.* that can be done, practicable; possible. **feasibil'ity,** *n.*

feast, *n.* religious anniversary; sumptuous meal, banquet; anything giving great enjoyment. *v.* entertain or fare sumptuously; regale.

feat, *n.* notable act, esp. of valour; surprising performance.

feath'er (fedh-), *n.* one of fringed outgrowths that cover body of bird; game-birds. *v.* furnish or line or coat with feathers; turn oar so that blade passes through air edgeways. **feather bed,** mattress stuffed with feathers. **feather-weight,** light person or thing. **feath'ery,** *a.* feather-like.

fea'ture (-cher), *n.* part(s) of the face, external appearance (usu. pl.); prominent or characteristic part; prominent article in newspaper, etc; full-length cinema film. *v.* make attraction or special feature of; exhibit as feature; take part (*in*). **fea'tureless,** *a.*

feb'rifūge, *n.* medicine to reduce fever.

Feb'ruary (-roo-), *n.* second month of year.

feck'less, *a.* inefficient, feeble, futile.

fē'cund (*or* fe-), *a.* fertile; fruitful. **fē'cundāte** (*or* fe-), make fruitful; impregnate. **fēcun'dity,** *n.*

fed, *p.t.* & *p.p.* of **feed.** *fed up,* (*slang*) surfeited, disgusted, bored.

fed'eral, *a.* (of States) united, but independent in internal affairs; of central government in federation.

fed'erāte, *v.* unite as federal States or for common object. **fed'erate,** *a.* so united. **federā'tion,** *n.* federating; federated body.

fee, *n.* sum payable to official, professional man, etc., for services; payment, charge; inherited estate. *v.t.* pay fee to; engage for a fee.

fee'ble, *a.* weak; deficient in character or intelligence; wanting in energy or force.

feed, *v.* (p.t. *fed*), supply with food; eat; nourish; keep supplied. *n.* pasturage; fodder; (*informal*) meal. **fee'der,** *n.* (esp.) child's bib; tributary.

feel, *v.* (p.t. *felt*), examine or perceive by touch; be conscious of, be consciously;

experience; be affected by; have pity *for*; have vague or emotional conviction. *n.* sense of touch.

fee′ler, *n.* organ of touch in some animals, antenna; tentative suggestion or hint.

fee′ling, *n.* sense of touch; physical sensation; emotion; consideration for others; conviction or opinion; (pl.) sympathies, susceptibilities. *a.* sympathetic; heart-felt. **fee′lingly**, *adv.*

feet, *pl.* of **foot**.

feign (fān), *v.* pretend; simulate.

feint (fā-) *n.* sham attack, blow, etc., meant to deceive opponent. *v.i.* make feint.

fèli′citāte, *v.t.* congratulate. **fèlicitā′tion**, *n.* (usu. in pl.). **fèli′citous**, *a.* apt, well-chosen, happy. **fèli′city**, *n.* great happiness; pleasing manner of speaking or writing.

fē′line, *a.* of cats or cat family; catlike. *n.* feline animal.

fell[1], *n.* animal's hide or skin with hair; thick matted hair or wool.

fell[2], *n.* mountain, hill, or stretch of high moorland esp. in N. England.

fell[3], *a.* (Poet.) fierce; deadly.

fell[4], *v.t.* strike down; cut down (tree); stitch down (seam).

fell[5], *p.t.* of **fall**.

fell′ah, *n.* (pl. *fellaheen, fellahs*), peasant in an Arab country.

fell′ow (-ō), *n.* comrade, associate; counterpart, equal; graduate member of college with certain privileges; member of some learned societies; (*informal*) man, boy. **fellow-feeling**, sympathy. **fellow-traveller**, person travelling with another; non-communist sympathizer with Communism.

fell′owship (-lō-), *n.* companionship; friendly association; body of associates; status of college fellow.

fel′on, *n.* one who has committed a felony. **fel′ony**, *n.* serious crime, such as murder, manslaughter, arson, etc. **fèlō′nious**, *a.*

felt[1], *n.* fabric made of shrunk and compressed wool, etc. *v.* make into or form felt; mat together.

felt[2], *p.t.* & *p.p.* of **fell**.

fē′māle, *a.* of the sex which bears offspring; (of plants) fruit-bearing; of women; (Mechanics, etc.) adapted to receive corresponding or male part. *n.* female person, animal, or plant.

fem′inine, *a.* of women; womanly; (Gram.) of the gender proper to names of females. **feminin′ity**, *n.*

fem′inism, *n.* advocacy of women's rights. **fem′inist**, *n.*

fē′mur, *n.* thigh-bone. **fem′oral**, *a.*

fen, *n.* low marshy tract of land.

fence, *n.* railing, etc., enclosing field, garden, etc.; receiver of stolen goods. *v.* surround, screen, protect, (as) with fence; practise art of sword-play with foil, etc.; evade skilfully; deal in stolen goods. **fen′cing**, *n.* art of sword-play; (material for) fences.

fend, *v.* ward or keep *off*; provide *for* (oneself, etc.).

fen′der, *n.* thing used to keep something off or lessen shock of impact, esp. mass of rope, etc., hung over vessel's side; frame round hearth to keep in falling coals.

fenn′el, *n.* fragrant yellow-flowered herb used for flavouring.

fer′ment, *n.* leaven or other fermenting agent; agitation, tumult. **ferment′**, *v.* undergo or subject to fermentation; excite, stir up. **fermentā′tion**, *n.* process like that induced by leaven in dough, with effervescence, heat, and change of properties; excitement.

fern, *n.* flowerless plant with feathery fronds.

ferō′cious (-shus), *a.* fierce, cruel. **fero′city**, *n.*

fe′rret, *n.* kind of polecat used in catching rabbits, rats, etc. *v.* hunt with ferrets; rummage or search *about* (*for*), search (*out*).

fe′rric, fe′rrous, *aa.* of or containing iron.

fe′rrule (-ul *or* -ool), *n.* metal ring or cap at end of stick, tube, etc.; rubber cap at end of stick.

fe′rry, *v.* take or go in boat over river, channel, etc.; fly (aircraft, passenger, etc.) from one place to another. *n.* ferrying place or service; boat, etc., for ferrying.

fer′tile, *a.* productive, fruitful. **fertil′ity**, *n.* **fer′tilize**, *v.t.* enrich soil (with manure, etc.); fecundate (individual, organ). **fertilizā′tion**, *n.* fertilizing; fusion of male reproductive cell with female one. **fer′tilizer**, *n.* (esp.) manure; chemical manure.

fer′vent, *a.* hot, glowing; ardent, intense. **fer′vency**, *n.*

fer′vid, *a.* glowing, impassioned.

fer′vour (-ver), *n.* vehemence, passion, zeal.

fes′tal, *a.* of a feast or holiday; gay.

fes′ter, *v.i.* become inflamed and generate pus; rankle; rot. *n.* festering condition.

fes′tival, *n.* festal day; celebration, merry-making; (periodic) series of performances (of music, drama, etc.).

fes′tive, *a.* of feast; joyous.

festiv′ity, *n.* gaiety; festive celebrations; (pl.) festive proceedings.

festoōn′, *n.* hanging chain of flowers, ribbons, etc. *v.t.* adorn with, form into, festoons.

fetch, *v.* go for and bring back; be sold for; draw forth; deal (blow).

fet′ching, *a.* attractive.

fête (fāt), *n.* festival, entertainment; bazaar-like function (esp. to raise funds for charity, etc.). *v.t.* entertain; make much of.

fē′tid (*or* fe-), **foe′tid** (fē-), *a.* stinking.

fē′tish, (*or* fe-), *n.* object supposed to have magical powers and worshipped by primitive peoples; anything irrationally reverenced.

fet′lock, *n.* (tuft of hair growing on) back of horse's leg above hoof.

fett′er, *n.* chain or shackle for feet; (pl.) restraint, captivity. *v.t.* bind (as) with fetters.

fett′le, *n.* condition, trim.

feu (fū), *n.* (Sc. law) land held by perpetual lease at fixed rent.

feud[1] (fūd), *n.* lasting hostility, esp. between two tribes or families.

feud[2] (fūd), *n.* fief.

feu'dal (fū-), *a.* of fief; of, like, feudal system. **feudal system,** system by which vassal held land from lord in return for military service, homage, etc. **feu'dalism,** *n.*

fē'ver, *n.* (illness with) bodily reaction characterized by raised temperature, restlessness, etc.; nervous excitement. **fē'vered** (-verd), *a.* affected by fever; agitated. **fē'verish,** *a.* of, like, having symptoms of, fever; restless, excited.

few, *a.* & *n.* not many. *not a few,* many. *a good few, quite a few,* a considerable number. **few'ness,** *n.*

fey (fā), *a.* (Sc.) fated to die; disordered in mind; possessing or displaying fairylike or unearthly qualities.

fez, *n.* (pl. *fezzes*) red felt brimless hat, formerly national head-dress of Turkish men.

fiancé (fiahn'sā), *n.* (fem. *fiancée*), person to whom one is engaged to be married.

fias'cō, *n.* (pl. *fiascos*), complete failure or breakdown; ignominious result.

fi'at, *n.* authorization; decree.

fib, *n.* trivial lie. *v.i.* (p.t. *fibbed*), tell fib. **fibb'er,** *n.*

fī'bre (-ber), *n.* one of thread-like filaments in animal or vegetable tissue; substance formed of fibres; structure, grain; (fig.) character. **fī'breglass, fī'bre(-)glass,** (any of various materials made or partly made from) fine glass filaments. **fī'brous,** *a.*

fib'ūla, *n.* (pl. *fibulae, fibulas*) bone on outer side of lower leg; (Archaeology) brooch.

fi'chu (-shoo), *n.* woman's small shawl of lace, etc., for shoulders and neck.

fick'le, *a.* not constant, changeable.

fic'tion, *n.* thing invented or imagined; invented narrative, etc.; literature of such narrative, etc., esp. novels. **fic'tional,** *a.*

ficti'tious (-shus), *a.* not genuine; assumed; imaginary.

fidd'le, *n.* violin. *v.* play violin; trifle, potter. **fidd'lestick,** *n.* fiddle-bow. **fidd'lesticks,** *int.* nonsense! **fidd'ler,** *n.* **fidd'ling,** *a.* petty, trifling.

fidel'ity, *n.* faithfulness, loyalty; accuracy.

fid'gėt, *n.* restless state or mood; one who fidgets. *v.i.* move restlessly; make or be uneasy. **fid'gėty,** *a.*

fie, *int.* expressing sense of outraged propriety.

fief, *n.* (Feudal law) land held on condition of homage and service to lord.

field, *n.* (piece of) ground esp. for pasture or tillage or for playing game; tract rich in some natural product, as oil, coal, etc.; scene of battle; expanse of snow, etc.; area or sphere of action, operation, etc.; all competitors or all except favourite. *v.* act as fielder; stop and

return ball. **field-day,** (Mil.) day of exercise in manoeuvres, review; great occasion. **field events,** athletic events other than races. **field-glasses,** binoculars for outdoor use. **Field Marshal,** Army officer of highest rank. **field-sports,** (esp.) hunting, shooting and fishing. **fiel'der, field'sman** (-z-), *nn.* one of side not batting at cricket, etc.; one who fields ball.

fiend, *n.* devil; superhumanly wicked or cruel person. **fien'dish,** *a.*

fierce (fērs), *a.* violent in hostility; raging, vehement; intense. **fierce'ly,** *adv.*

fier'y (fīr-), *a.* flaming; flashing; eager; irritable; spirited.

fife, *n.* small shrill flute. *v.i.* play fife.

fifteen' (*or* fif'-), *a.* & *n.* one more than fourteen (15, XV). **fifteenth',** *a.* & *n.*

fifth, *a.* & *n.* next after fourth. **fifth column,** organized body of persons working for enemy within country at war.

fif'ty, *a.* & *n.* five times ten (50, L). **fif'tiēth,** *a.* & *n.*

fig, *n.* (broad-leaved tree bearing) soft pear-shaped many-seeded fruit; valueless thing.

fight (fīt), *v.* (p.t. *fought,* pr. fawt), contend in battle or single combat or with fists; struggle (*for*), strive. *fight shy of,* avoid, evade. *n.* fighting; battle; boxing-match; strife; conflict. **fight'er,** *n.* (esp.) aircraft designed for aerial combat.

fig'ment, *n.* invented statement; thing that exists only in imagination.

figūrā'tion, *n.* form, shape.

fig'ūrative, *a.* (of words) used not in literal sense but in imaginative way; metaphorical.

fig'ure (-ger), *n.* external form; bodily shape; emblem, type; image; diagram, illustration; character denoting number (0,1,2, etc.). *figure of speech,* words used figuratively; metaphor, hyperbole, etc. *v.* represent in diagram or picture; adorn with design, etc.; imagine; reckon; make appearance. **figure-head,** carved figure over ship's prow; leader in name only.

filagree: see **filigree.**

fil'ament, *n.* slender thread-like body, fibre; fine wire, etc., inside electric bulb or thermionic valve.

fil'bert, *n.* (nut of) cultivated hazel.

filch, *v.t.* steal, pilfer.

file[1], *n.* instrument for abrading or smoothing surfaces. *v.t.* smooth with file. *file away, off,* remove with file.

file[2], *n.* folder, box, drawer, wire, etc., for keeping papers for reference; papers so kept. *v.t.* place on or in file.

file[3], *n.* row of persons, etc., one behind the other. *v.i.* march or walk in file.

fil'ial, *a.* of, due from, son or daughter.

fil'ibuster, *n.* person engaging in unauthorized warfare against foreign State; (chiefly U.S.) hindering, one who hinders, the passing of bills in political assembly by making long speeches, etc. *v. i.* act as filibuster.

fil'igree, fil'agree, *n.* delicate metal openwork of gold or other wire.

fill, *v.* make or become full; occupy all space in; spread through; occupy. *fill in,* complete. *fill up,* fill completely, fill petrol-tank. *n.* as much as will fill or satisfy. **fill'er,** *n.* (esp.) anything used to fill gap, increase bulk, etc. **fill'ing,** *n.* that which fills cavity, etc. **filling-station,** depot for supply of petrol, etc., to motorists.

fill'ĕt, *n.* ribbon, narrow band, worn round head; fleshy boneless piece of meat; strip of fish detached from backbone. *v. t.* bind, encircle, with fillet; divide (fish) into fillets.

fill'ip, *n.* (slight smart stroke made by) sudden release of bent finger from restraint of thumb; stimulus, incentive. *v. t.* give fillip to.

fill'y, *n.* young female of horse.

film, *n.* thin skin, coating, or layer; (piece or roll of) flexible material, coated with light-sensitive emulsion for exposure in camera; motion picture. *v.* cover, become covered (as) with film; take motion picture of. **film-star,** star actor in films. **film-strip,** short length of film with sequence of still pictures. **fil'my,** *a.* gauze-like.

fil'ter, *n.* device for cleaning liquid or gas by passing it through sand, paper, charcoal, etc.; (Photog.) device of glass, etc., for absorbing light of certain colours. *v.* pass through filter; percolate; (of traffic) pass in certain permitted direction when other traffic has to stop.

filth, *n.* loathsome dirt; obscenity. **fil'thy,** *a.*

fil'trāte, *n.* filtered liquor. *v.* filter. **filtrā'tion,** *a.* filtering.

fin, *n.* organ for propelling and steering, projecting from body of fish, etc.; fin-like projection on aircraft, etc.

fi'nal, *a.* at the end, coming last; decisive. *n.* last or deciding heat, match, etc.; (often pl.) last of series of examinations. **fi'nalist,** *n.* competitor in final. **final'ity,** *n.* **fi'nalize,** *v. t.* give final form to. **fi'nally,** *adv.*

fina'lē (-nah-), *n.* last movement of musical composition; close of opera, etc.

finance' (*or* fin-; *or* fī'-), *n.* management of money; (pl.) money resources. *v. t.* furnish with money; find capital for. **finan'cial** (-shl), *a.* **finan'cier,** *n.* one skilled in finance; capitalist.

finch, *n.* any of various small birds.

find, *v. t.* (p.t. *found*), look for and get back; come across, obtain; discover; ascertain; supply. *find out,* discover, detect. *n.* what is found; pleasing discovery. **fin'ding,** *n.* (esp.) verdict of jury.

fine[1], *n.* sum of money fixed as penalty. *v. t.* punish by fine.

fine[2], *a.* of high quality; pure, refined; delicate; thin, in small particles; excellent; handsome, imposing; bright, free from rain;

smart, showy. **fine arts,** see **art**[2]. **fi'nery,** *n.* showy dress or decoration.

finesse', *n.* subtle management; artfulness. *v.* use finesse.

fing'er (-ngg-), *n.* one of five members of hand (or four excluding thumb); finger-like object. *v. t.* touch, turn about, with fingers. **finger-board,** part of neck of stringed instrument where strings are pressed by fingers. **finger-post,** signpost at road turning. **fing'erprint,** impression of finger-tip, esp. as means of identification. **finger-tip,** end of finger. **finger-stall,** cover to protect injured finger. **fing'ering**[1], *n.* proper use of fingers in playing music.

fing'ering[2] (-ngg-), *n.* fine wool for knitting.

fin'ical, fin'icking, fin'icky, *aa.* excessively fastidious or fussy.

fin'ish, *v.* bring or come to an end; perfect, put final touches to. *n.* last stage, decisive result; completed state.

fi'nite, *a.* bounded, limited; (Gram., of verb) limited by number and person.

finn'an (hadd'ock), smoke-cured haddock.

fiord, fjord (fy-), *n.* narrow arm of sea between high cliffs (as in Norway).

fir, *n.* (wood of) any of various evergreen coniferous trees with needles arranged singly on shoots. **fir-cône,** fruit of fir.

fīre, *n.* chemical action accompanied by emission of light and heat; flame, glow; burning fuel; conflagration; fervour, vivacity; discharge of firearms. *on fire,* burning. *under fire,* being shot at. *v.* set fire to; catch fire; bake (pottery, etc.); (cause to) become heated; cause (gun, etc.) to explode; propel from gun. **fire'arm,** gun, pistol, etc. **fire'brand,** piece of burning wood; one who stirs up strife. **fire-break,** area cleared of trees, etc., to stop advance of fire. **fire-brick,** brick that can withstand great heat, used in furnaces, etc. **fire-brigade,** organized body of firemen. **fire'damp,** (miners' name for) explosive mixture of gases formed in coal-mines. **fire'dog,** andiron. **fire-engine,** manned vehicle equipped for putting out fires. **fire-escape,** apparatus for escape from burning building. **fire-extinguisher,** portable metal cylinder, etc., containing chemical for extinguishing fire. **fire'fly,** beetle capable of emitting phosphorescent light. **fire-insurance,** insurance against loss by fire. **fire-irons,** poker, tongs, and shovel. **fire'man,** man employed to put out fires; stoker. **fire'place,** place for fire, esp. recess in room with chimney above. **fire'proof,** proof against fire; incombustible. **fire'side,** space round fireplace; home life. **fire'work,** device giving spectacular effect by use of combustibles, etc.

fīr'ing, *n.* discharging of firearms; fuel.

fir'kin, *n.* small cask.

firm[1], *n.* partnership, company, carrying on business; medical, legal, etc., practice.

firm², *a.* of solid structure; fixed, steady; steadfast, resolute. *v.* solidify; fix firmly.

fir'mament, *n.* vault of the heavens.

first, *a.* earliest in time or order; foremost in position, rank, or importance. *n.* first day (of month); (holder of) place in first class in examination. *adv.* before all or something else; for the first time. **first-aid**, help given to injured, etc., before medical treatment is available. **first-class, first-rate**, of best quality, excellent. **first-fruits**, first products of season; first results of work, etc. **first'ly**, *adv.* (only in enumerating) first.

firth, *n.* arm of sea; estuary.

fis'cal, *a.* of public revenue.

fish, *n.* (pl. *fish, fishes*), vertebrate cold--blooded animal living in water; flesh of fish as food. *v.* try to catch fish; search *for*; draw *out*; seek by indirect means *for*. **fish finger**, small finger-shaped piece of fish for frying. **fish-hook**, barbed hook for catching fish. **fish'monger** (-mungger), dealer in fish. **fish--slice**, cook's flat implement for turning or lifting fish, etc. **fish'wife**, woman selling fish.

fish'erman, *n.* (pl. *-men*), one who lives by fishing; angler.

fish'ery, *n.* business of fishing; fishing ground.

fish'y, *a.* of or like fish; (*slang*) dubious, open to suspicion.

fiss'ile, *a.* tending to split; capable of undergoing nuclear fission.

fi'ssion (-shn), *n.* splitting or dividing into parts; splitting of atomic nucleus. **fi'ssionable**, *a.* capable of undergoing nuclear fission.

fi'ssure (-sher), *n.* narrow opening made by splitting or separation of parts. *v.* split.

fist, *n.* clenched hand. **fis'ticuffs**, *n.pl.* fighting with fists.

fit¹, *n.* sudden attack of epilepsy, hysteria, fainting, etc.; outburst, capricious impulse. *by fits and starts*, spasmodically.

fit², *a.* (*fitter, fittest*), qualified, competent, worthy; proper; in good health or condition. *n.* way thing fits. *v.* (p.t. *fitted*), be of, adjust to, right size and shape; join (*on*, etc.) parts that fit; be in harmony (with); make suitable; supply. **fit'ment**, *n.* piece of fixed furniture. **fitt'er**, *n.* (esp.) mechanic fitting together finished parts of engines, etc. **fitt'ing**, *n.* act of fitting; (usu. pl.) fixture, fitment. *a.* (esp.) becoming, proper.

fit'ful, *a.* acting by fits and starts; spasmodic; intermittent. **fit'fully**, *adv.*

five, *a. & n.* one more than four (5, V). **five'-fōld**, *a. & adv.* **fi'ver**, *n.* (*informal*) £5 note.

fives (-vz), *n.* game in which ball is struck with hands (or bat) against wall of court.

fix, *v.* make firm or stable or permanent; fasten, secure; direct (eyes, etc.) steadily *on*; settle, determine; mend, repair. *n.* dilemma, difficult position; position determined by bearings. **fixā'tion**, *n.* fixing or being fixed.

fix'ative, *n.* preparation for fixing colours, drawings, etc. **fix'ĕdly**, *adv.* intently.

fix'ity, *n.* fixed state; permanence.

fix'ture (-cher), *n.* thing fixed in position; (pl.) articles permanently attached to house, etc.; (date fixed for) match, race, etc.

fizz, *v.i.* hiss, splutter; effervesce. *n.* fizzing sound; effervescence.

fizz'le, *v.i.* hiss or splutter feebly. *fizzle out*, come to lame conclusion. *n.* fizzling sound; fiasco.

fjord: see **fiord**.

flabb'ergast (-gah-), *v.t.* overwhelm with astonishment; astound.

flabb'y, *a.* limp, not firm; feeble.

flac'cid (-ks-), *a.* flabby.

flag¹, *n.* yellow iris growing in moist places.

flag², *n.* flat slab of stone for paving. *v.t.* (p.t. *flagged*), pave with flags. **flag'stone**, *n.* flag.

flag³, *n.* piece of bunting, etc., attached to staff or halyard as standard, ensign, or signal. *v.t.* (p.t. *flagged*), place flag(s) on; mark out with flags; signal to by waving flag, etc. **flag-day**, day on which money is raised for charity by sale of paper flags, etc. **flag'ship**, ship with admiral on board. **flag'staff**, pole on which flag is hung.

flag⁴, *v.i.* (p.t. *flagged*), hang down; droop; lag, lose vigour; (of interest, attention) decline.

flagell'ant (*or* flaj'-), *n. & a.* (one) who whips himself, esp. as religious discipline. **fla'-gellāte**, *v.t.* whip. **flagellā'tion**, *n.*

flageolet' (-jol-), *n.* small wind-instrument resembling recorder.

flag'on, *n.* vessel to hold liquor.

flā'grant, *a.* glaring, scandalous. **flā'grance, flā'grancy**, *nn.*

flail, *n.* hand threshing-implement. *v.* beat (as) with flail.

flair, *n.* instinctive power of discernment; talent.

flāke, *n.* light fleecy tuft or piece, esp. of snow; thin piece peeled off surface; layer. *v.* fall in flakes; take, come, (*off*, etc.), in flakes. **flā'ky**, *a.*

flamboy'ant, *a.* gorgeous, showy.

flāme, *n.* (tongue-like portion of) ignited gas; visible combustion; bright light; (*informal*) sweetheart. *v.i.* emit flames; break out into anger; shine, gleam.

flā'ming, *a.* very hot; vehement.

flaming'ō (-ngg-), *n.* (pl. *flamingoes*), wading-bird with long legs and neck and scarlet wing-feathers.

flamm'able, *a.* easily set on fire. **flamm-abil'ity**, *n.*

flan, *n.* open tart.

flange (-nj), *n.* projecting flat rim or rib.

flank, *n.* side of body between ribs and hip; side of building, mountain, body of troops, etc. *v.t.* guard or strengthen or attack on flank; be posted or situated at side(s) of.

flann'el, *n.* (piece of) soft woollen fabric, usu. without nap; (pl.) (white) flannel trousers. *a.* made of flannel. **flannelette',** *n.* cotton fabric imitating flannel. **flann'elgraph** (-ahf), *n.* sheet of flannel to which cut-out figures, etc., will adhere. **flann'elled** (-ld), *a.* dressed in flannels.

flap, *v.* (p.t. *flapped*), strike with something broad; (cause to) move up and down or from side to side. *n.* light stroke; broad hanging piece attached by one side only.

flare, *v.i.* blaze with bright unsteady flame; (cause to) spread gradually outwards. *flare up*, burst into sudden blaze or anger. *n.* bright unsteady light; unshaded flame in open air, esp. used as signal or guide; outburst of flame; flared shape.

flash, *v.* emit light suddenly or intermittently; break into flame or sparks; appear or occur suddenly. *n.* sudden short blaze or gleam; instant sudden outburst; distinguishing emblem worn esp. on shoulder of uniform. *a.* gaudy, showy; sham. **flash'back,** (Cinema, etc.) scene presenting earlier event(s), interrupting main story of film, etc. **flash'light,** brilliant flash of light for photography indoors, at night, etc.; electric torch. **flash'point,** temperature at which vapour from oil, etc., will ignite; (fig.) point at which something bursts into action. **flash'y,** *a.* gaudy, tawdry.

flask (-ah-), *n.* flat pocket-bottle of metal or glass; narrow-necked bulbous bottle; vacuum flask.

flat[1], *n.* set of rooms, usu. on one floor, forming complete residence. **flat'let,** *n.* small flat, esp. of one room.

flat[2], *a.* horizontal, level; lying full length; smooth, even; not curved or rounded; dull; fixed, unvarying; (Mus.) below pitch. *n.* flat part of anything; stretch of low flat land; (Mus.) note lowered by semitone, sign (♭) indicating this. **flat-fish,** flat-bodied sea-fish swimming on its side and having both eyes on upper side. **flat-footed,** having feet not normally arched. **flat race,** race without hurdles or jumps. **flatt'en,** *v.* make or become flat.

flatt'er, *v.t.* praise too highly; gratify self-esteem of; fawn upon; (of portrait, etc.) exaggerate good points of. **flatt'erer,** *n.* **flatt'ery,** *n.*

flat'ulence, *n.* wind in the stomach or bowels. **flat'ulent,** *a.* causing, troubled by, such wind; inflated, pretentious.

flaunt, *v.* wave proudly; show off; display impudently.

flau'tist, *n.* flute-player.

flā'vour (-ver), *n.* mixed sensation of smell and taste; distinctive taste; characteristic quality. *v.t.* give flavour to; season. **flā'vouring,** *n.*

flaw, *n.* crack, rent; blemish; defect. *v.* crack, damage, mar. **flaw'less,** *a.*

flax, *n.* plant grown for its seeds (*linseed*) and its fibre which is spun into linen. **flax'en,** *a.* of flax; (of hair) very pale yellow.

flay, *v.t.* strip the skin from; peel.

flea, *n.* small wingless jumping insect feeding on human and other blood. **flea-bite,** bite of flea; (fig.) mere trifle.

fleck, *n.* freckle, stain, speck; patch of light or colour. *v.t.* mark with flecks.

fledged (-jd), *a.* (of birds) with fully grown wing feathers; able to fly. **fledg(e)'ling,** young bird just fledged.

flee, *v.* (p.t. *fled*; pres. p. *fleeing*), run away from; take flight; shun.

fleece, *n.* woolly covering, esp. of sheep; wool shorn from sheep. *v.t.* strip, plunder. **flee'cy,** *a.*

fleet[1], *n.* naval force; number of ships or boats under one commander or sailing in company; number of vehicles or aircraft forming group or unit.

fleet[2], *a.* (Poet.) swift, nimble.

flee'ting, *a.* passing quickly.

Flem'ing, *n.* native of Flanders. **Flem'ish,** *n.* & *a.* (language) of Flanders.

flesh, *n.* soft substance, esp. muscular parts, of animal body between skin and bones; meat; pulpy substance of fruit, etc.; plumpness, fat; the body. **flesh and blood,** (material of) body; mankind; human nature; one's near relations. **flesh pots,** luxurious living. **flesh'ly,** *a.* worldly; sensual. **flesh'y,** *a.*

fleur-de-lis (fler'delē'), *n.* (pl. *fleurs-de-lis,* pr. as sing.), heraldic lily; royal arms of France.

flew, *p.t.* of **fly**[2].

flex[1], *v.t.* bend (esp. joint, limb).

flex[2]. *n.* flexible insulated wire for conveying electric current, etc.

flex'ible, *a.* easily bent; pliable; supple. **flexibil'ity,** *n.*

flick, *n.* light blow with whip, duster, etc.; jerk; slight turn of wrist. *v.t.* strike, dash *away* or *off*, with flick.

flick'er, *v.t.* shine or burn unsteadily; vibrate unsteadily. *n.* flickering light or movement.

flier: see **flyer.**

flight (-īt), *n.* act or mode of flying; flock of birds or insects moving together; swift passage of time; series (of stairs); air-force unit; journey in aircraft. **flight-lieutenant,** officer of R.A.F. below squadron-leader. **flight'less,** *a.* (esp., of certain birds) incapable of flying.

flight[2] (-īt), *n.* running away; hasty retreat.

flight'y (-īt-), *a.* fickle; changeable.

flim'sy (-z-), *a.* slight, frail; trivial.·

flinch, *v.i.* draw back, shrink; wince.

fling, *v.* (p.t. *flung*), rush; throw, hurl. *n.* throw, cast; lively dance; spell of indulgence or impulse.

flint, *n.* hard stone found in pebbly lumps; piece of flint used with steel to produce fire;

hard alloy used to produce spark in cigarette-
-lighter, etc. **flin′ty,** *a.*

flip, *n.* fillip, flick. *v.* (p.t. *flipped*), propel,
strike, with flip; make, move with, flick.
flip′side, reverse side (of gramophone
record).

flipp′ant, *a.* treating serious things lightly;
disrespectful. **flipp′ancy,** *n.*

flipp′er, *n.* limb used to swim with by seal,
turtle, penguin, etc.; (underwater) swimmer's footwear resembling this.

flirt, *v.i.* play at courtship (*with*). *n.* woman
who encourages, man who pays, attentions
for amusement. **flirtā′tion,** *n.* **flirtā′tious**
(-shus), *a.*

flit, *v.i.* (p.t. *flitted*), change one's residence;
move, pass, fly, lightly or rapidly.

flitch, *n.* side of bacon.

float, *v.* rest, drift, on surface of liquid; (of
water) support, bear along; set (company,
scheme) going. *n.* thing that floats on surface
of liquid; raft; low-bodied cart. **floa′ting,** *a.*
(esp.) not settled or fixed.

floatation: see flotation.

flock[1], *n.* tuft of wool, cotton, etc.; wool-
-refuse used for stuffing pillows, etc.

flock[2], *n.* large number of people; group of
animals or birds feeding or travelling
together; sheep or goats kept together; congregation. *v.i.* congregate, go in flocks.

flōe, *n.* sheet of floating ice.

flog, *v.t.* (p.t. *flogged*), beat with whip, stick,
etc. **flogg′ing,** *n.*

flood (flud), *n.* overflowing of great quantity
of water over land; downpour; inflow of tide;
(*the Flood*), great deluge recorded in Genesis. *v.* (cause to) overflow; cover or fill with
water. **flood-gate,** gate for letting in or shutting out esp. flood-water.

flood′light (flud′līt), *n.* & *v.t.* (illuminate
with) bright artificial lighting directed on
building, etc. **flood-lighting,** *n.*

floor (-or), *n.* lower surface of interior of
room; storey; level area; part of parliament,
etc., where members sit and speak; right of
speaking. *v.t.* furnish with floor; knock
down; confound; overcome. **floor′ing,** *n.*
material used for making floors.

flop, *v.* (p.t. *flopped*), sway about heavily or
loosely; fall, sit, *down*, heavily or with thud;
(*slang*) fail. *n.* flopping movement or sound;
(*slang*) failure. *adv.* with a flop. **flopp′y,** *a.*

flor′a, *n.* (pl. *floras, florae*), (list of) plants of
a region or an epoch.

flor′al, *a.* of flower(s) or flora(s).

flor′ĕt, *n.* any of small flowers of composite
flower-head.

flo′rid, *n.* much ornamented, flowery; showy;
(of person) ruddy, high-coloured.

flo′rin, *n.* guilder; (Hist.) British two-shilling
piece; (Hist.) name of various gold and other
coins formerly current in Europe.

flo′rist, *n.* one who deals in or grows flowers.

floss, *n.* rough silk enclosing silkworm's

cocoon. **floss′y,** *a.*

flōtā′tion, floatā′tion, *n.* floating; starting of
company or scheme.

flotill′a, *n.* small fleet.

flot′sam, *n.* floating wreckage.

flounce[1], *v.i.* & *n.* (make) abrupt, jerky, or
impatient movement of the body.

flounce[2], *n.* gathered strip with lower edge
hanging, esp. round woman's skirt, etc.

floun′der[1], *n.* small flat-fish.

floun′der[2], *v.i.* struggle and plunge (as in
mud, etc.); proceed in bungling or struggling
fashion.

flour (-ower), *n.* finer part of (esp. wheat)
meal obtained by process of bolting. *v.t.*
sprinkle with flour. **flour′y,** *a.*

flou′rish (flu-), *v.* grow vigorously; thrive;
prosper; wave or throw about. *n.* ornamental
curve in writing; sweeping gesture with
weapon, hand, etc.; (Mus.) florid instrumental passage (esp. for trumpets).

flout, *v.t.* treat with contempt.

flow (-ō), *v.i.* move, glide along, as stream;
circulate; move easily; (of dress, etc.) hang
easily; gush out. *n.* flowing; rise of tide;
plentiful supply.

flow′er, *n.* part of plant (usu. not green) from
which seed or fruit develops; flowering
plant; state of blooming; best part, pick *of.*
v.i. produce flowers. **flow′ered** (-erd), *a.*
ornamented with floral design, etc. **flow′ery,**
a. having many flowers; full of fine phrases.

flown, *p.p.* of **fly**[2].

flu (floō), *n.* (*informal*) influenza.

fluc′tūate, *v.i.* vary, rise and fall; be unstable.
fluctūā′tion, *n.*

flue (floō), *n.* smoke-duct in chimney; channel
for conveying heat.

flu′ĕnt (-oō-), *a.* (of curves, motion, etc.)
graceful, easy; (of speech, style) coming
easily and readily, flowing. **flu′ĕncy,** *n.*

fluff, *n.* light downy stuff separating from
dressed wool; soft down, fur, hair, etc. *v.t.*
make into fluff; shake *out* into fluffy mass.
fluff′y, *a.*

flu′id (floō-), *a.* moving readily, capable of
flowing; not solid or stable. *n.* fluid substance; liquid. **fluid′ity,** *n.*

fluke[1] (floōk), *n.* triangular holding-part of an
anchor.

fluke[2] (floōk), *n.* lucky accidental stroke;
unexpected or undeserved success.

flumm′ox, *v.t.* (*slang*) confound, bewilder.

flunk′ey, *n.* (pl. *flunkeys*), footman; toady.

fluores′cence (floō-), *n.* coloured luminosity
produced in some materials by direct action
of light. **fluores′cent,** *a.*

fluoridā′tion (floō-), *n.* addition of traces of
fluoride to public water-supply to prevent or
reduce tooth-decay. **flu′oride,** *n.* chemical
compound related to common salt.

flu′rry, *n.* nervous hurry, agitation; gust,
squall. *v.t.* agitate, confuse.

flush, *v.* blush; cleanse (drain, etc.) with flow

of water. *n.* glow, blush; (mechanism for) cleansing of drain, etc.; elation; sudden abundance; freshness, vigour. *a.* full; well--supplied; level *with*.

flus′ter, *v.* confuse; make nervous. *n.* agitation; flurry.

flute (flōōt), *n.* reedless wood-wind instrument with mouthpiece at side near upper end; groove in pillar, etc. *v.* play flute; make grooves in.

flutt′er, *v.* flap wings without flying or in short flights; flit, hover; agitate; move irregularly. *n.* fluttering; tremulous excitement; stir.

flu′ty (flōō-), *a.* soft and clear in tone.

flu′vial (flōō-), *a.* of, found in, rivers.

flux, *n.* flowing; inflow of tide; state of continual change.

fly¹, *n.* two-winged insect. **fly′blown,** tainted. **fly′catcher,** bird that catches flies.

fly², *v.* (p.t. *flew*, pr. flōō, p.p. *flown*, pr. flōn), move through air with wings or in aircraft; set or keep (flag) flying; travel swiftly, hasten; flee. *n.* one-horse carriage; flap covering button-holes; flap at entrance of tent; (Theatr., pl.) space over proscenium. **fly′leaf,** blank leaf at beginning or end of book. **fly′-over,** bridge carrying road, etc., over another. **fly′wheel,** heavy-rimmed wheel regulating machinery.

fly′er, fli′er, *n.* one that flees or flies; airman; fast animal, vehicle, etc.

fly′ing, *a.* & *n.* **flying-boat,** kind of seaplane. **flying-bomb,** crewless explosive-filled aircraft. **flying-fish,** fish able to leap into the air. **flying-machine,** heavier-than-air machine that can navigate the air. **flying squad,** police detachment, medical team, etc., organized for rapid movement.

foal, *n.* young of horse, ass, etc. *v.* bear foal.

foam, *n.* mass of bubbles formed on liquid by agitation, fermentation, etc. *v.i.* gather or emit foam. **foam plastic, rubber,** spongy cellular material processed from plastic or latex. **foa′my,** *a.*

fob¹, *n.* (Hist.) small pocket for watch, etc., in waistband of breeches.

fob², *v.t.* (p.t. *fobbed*), palm *off*; put *off with* something inferior.

fo′cal, *a.* of, at, a focus; central.

fo′c′s′le: see **forecastle.**

fo′cus, *n.* (pl. *foci, focuses*), point at which rays of light, etc., meet; point at which object must be situated to give clear image; a central point. *v.* adjust (eye, lens) to get clear image; concentrate (mind, etc.).

fodd′er, *n.* dried food, hay, etc., for cattle. *v.t.* give fodder to.

foe, *n.* enemy; opponent.

foetid: see **fetid.**

foe′tus (fē-), **fe′tus,** *n.* developed embryo in womb. **foe′tal,** *a.*

fog, *n.* thick mist suspended at or near earth's surface. *v.t.* (p.t. *fogged*), envelop (as) in

fog; perplex, bewilder. **fog-horn,** siren for warning ships in fog. **fogg′y,** *a.*

fo′gy, fo′gey (-g-), *n.* (pl. *fogies*), (usu. *old fogy*) person with old-fashioned ideas.

foi′ble, *n.* weak point, fault.

foil¹, *n.* thin sheet or leaf of metal; thing that sets off another by contrast of colour, etc.

foil², *v.t.* baffle, parry, frustrate.

foil³, *n.* blunt-edged sword with button on point, used in fencing.

foist, *v.t.* palm off *on*.

fold¹, *n.* enclosure for sheep; (fig.) church. *v.t.* enclose (sheep) in fold.

fold², *v.* double (flexible thing) over upon itself; clasp; envelop. *n.* hollow between two thicknesses, among hills, etc.; line made by folding. **fol′der,** *n.* cover for holding loose papers, etc.

fo′liage, *n.* leaves (of plant or tree).

fo′lio, *n.* (pl. *folios*), leaf of paper numbered only on front; sheet of paper folded once; large-sized volume.

folk (fōk), *n.* nation, race (*archaic*); (*collective*) people in general; one's relatives. **folk-dance, folk-song,** dance, song, of popular origin. **folk′lore,** (study of) traditional beliefs, tales, etc., of the people.

foll′ow (-ō), *v.* go or come after; pursue; take as guide or master; practise (profession, etc.); be the consequence of; understand. *follow suit,* play card of suit led, do what someone else has done. **foll′ower** (-ōer), *n.* supporter, disciple. **foll′owing,** *n.* supporters. *a.* now to be mentioned. *prep.* after.

foll′y, *n.* foolishness; foolish act, idea, etc.; useless costly structure.

foment′, *v.t.* apply warm or medicated substance to; foster, encourage, (trouble, discontent, etc.). **fōmentā′tion,** *n.*

fond, *a.* tender, loving; doting; foolishly credulous. *fond of,* full of love for, much inclined to. **fond′ness,** *n.*

fond′le, *v.t.* caress.

font, *n.* vessel or basin, usu. of stone, holding water for baptism.

fŏŏd, *n.* substance taken into body through mouth to maintain life; provisions. **food′stuff,** material used as food.

fŏŏl¹, *n.* silly person; simpleton; dupe; (Hist.) jester, clown. *fool's errand,* fruitless errand. *fool's paradise,* happiness unlikely to last. *v.* play the fool; trifle; cheat. **fool′hardy,** foolishly bold; taking needless risks. **fool′proof,** proof against even fool's incompetence. **fŏŏl′ery,** *n.* playing the fool; foolish act. **fŏŏl′ish,** *a.* stupid; unwise; silly.

fŏŏl², *n.* dish of stewed crushed fruit mixed with cream, etc.

fŏŏl′scap, *n.* long folio writing or printing paper.

foot, *n.* (pl. *feet*), termination of leg; infantry; measure of length (12 in.); lower part, base; group of syllables forming rhythmical unit in verse. *on foot,* walking, in motion. *v.t.* add up (account); pay (bill). *foot it*, go on foot. **foot'fall**, sound of footstep. **foot'hold**, support for foot; secure position. **foot'lights**, lights along front of stage. **foot'man**, servant in livery. **foot'note**, note at foot of page. **foot'pad**, unmounted highwayman. **foot'path**, path for pedestrians only. **foot'print**, impression left by foot. **foot'sore**, having sore feet from walking. **foot'step**, tread. **foot'stool**, stool for feet of person sitting.

foot'ball (-awl), *n.* large round or oval inflated ball; any of various team-games played with football. **foot'baller**, *n.*

foot'ing, *n.* foothold; secure position; degree of friendship.

foot'ling, *a.* (*slang*) trivial, silly.

fop, *n.* dandy, vain man. **fopp'ery**, *n.* conduct, etc., of fop. **fopp'ish**, *n.*

for, *prep.* in place of; in defence or favour of; because of; with a view to; in direction of; because of. *conj.* seeing that, since. **forasmuch'** as, (*archaic*) since, because. **for ever**, always, constantly.

for-, *pref.* expressing rejection, exclusion; prohibition; abstention, neglect; intensity.

fo'rage, *n.* food for horses and cattle. *v.* search for food; rummage.

fo'ray, *n.* raid.

forbade, *p.t.* of **forbid**.

for'bear[1] (-bār), *n.* (usu. in pl.) ancestor(s).

forbear'[2] (-bār), *v.* (p.t. **forbore**; p.p. **forborne**), abstain or refrain (from); be patient. **forbear'ance**, *n.* **forbear'ing**, *a.*

forbid', *v.t.* (p.t. **forbade**, pr. -*bad* or -*bād*; p.p. **forbidden**), command not *to* do; not allow; prevent.

forbidd'ing, *a.* uninviting; repellent.

force, *n.* strength, violence, intense effort; power; body of (armed) men; compulsion; (Phys.) (intensity of) influence tending to produce movement. *v.t.* compel; strain, urge; break open by force; drive, propel; hasten maturity of (plant, etc.); produce by effort. **force'able**, *a.*

force'ful (-sf-), *a.* full of force; convincing.

force'meat (-sm-), *n.* (meat) stuffing.

for'ceps, *n.* (pl. same), surgical pincers; (Zool.) organ resembling forceps.

for'cible, *a.* done by, involving use of, force; telling, convincing. **for'cibly**, *adv.*

ford, *n.* shallow place where river, etc., can be crossed. *v.t.* cross (water) at ford; wade through. **for'dable**, *a.*

fore, *adv.* in front. *a.* situated in front. *to the fore*, in front, conspicuous. **fore-and-aft**, at bow and stern; lengthwise. *n.* front part; bow of ship.

fore-, *pref.* before; in front; front part of; anticipatory.

forearm[1] (for'arm), *n.* arm from elbow to wrist.

forearm[2] (forarm'), *v.t.* arm beforehand.

forebode (forbōd'), *v.t.* foreshadow, portend. **forebō'ding**, *n.* presentiment of coming evil;

omen.

forecast (for'kahst,) *v.t.* (p.t. *forecast*), estimate or conjecture beforehand. *n.* estimate of probable events, esp. of coming weather.

forecastle (fok'sl), **fo'c's'le**, *n.* (crew's quarters in) forward part of merchant ship; (Hist.) short raised deck at ship's bow.

foreclose (forklōz'), *v.* bar, prevent; shut out; take away power of redeeming (mortgage). **foreclō'sure** (-zher), *n.*

forecourt (for'kort), *n.* enclosed space in front of building.

forefathers (for'fahdherz), *n.pl.* ancestors.

forefinger (for'fingger), *n.* finger next to thumb.

forefoot (for'foot), *n.* (pl. -*feet*), front foot of animal.

forefront (for'frunt), *n.* very front.

foregoing (for'gō-), *a.* previously mentioned. **foregone** (for'gon), *a.* **foregone conclusion,** easily foreseeable result.

fore'ground (forg-), *n.* part of view nearest observer.

forehand (for'hand), *a.* (Lawn tennis, etc., of stroke) made with palm turned forwards.

forehead (fo'rid, for'hed), *n.* part of face above eyebrows.

fo'reign (-rin), *a.* belonging to another country; not of or in one's own country; alien, strange. **fo'reigner**, *n.*

foreknowledge (fornol'ij), *n.* prior knowledge.

foreland (for'land), *n.* headland, cape.

foreleg (for'leg), *n.* front leg of animal.

forelock (for'lok), *n.* lock of hair just above forehead.

foreman (for'man), *n.* (pl. -*men*), workman superintending others; spokesman of jury.

foremast (for'mahst), *n.* forward lower mast.

foremost (for'mōst), *a.* first, most advanced in position; chief, best. *adv.* first. *first and foremost,* before all else.

forename (for'nām), *n.* first or Christian name.

forenoon (for'nōōn), *n.* part of day before noon.

foren'sic, *a.* of or used in courts of law.

foreordain' (foror-), *v.t.* appoint beforehand.

forerunn'er (for-run-), *n.* one who precedes or heralds another; sign of what is to follow.

foresail (for'sl; *or* -sāl), *n.* principal sail on foremast.

foresee' (fors-), *v.t.* (p.t. *foresaw*, p.p. *foreseen*), see beforehand or in advance.

foreshadow (forshad'ō), *v.t.* be sign or warning of something to come.

foreshore (for'shor), *n.* shore between high and low water marks.

foreshor'ten (forshor-), *v.t.* draw (object) with shortening of lines to give perspective.

foresight (for'sīt), *n.* foreseeing; care in preparing for future needs.

foreskin (for'skin), *n.* loose fold of skin covering end of penis, prepuce.

fo'rèst, *n.* large tract covered chiefly with trees and undergrowth. **fo'rèster**, *n.* officer in charge of forest; one who works in a forest. **fo'rèstry**, *n.* science and art of managing forests.

forestall (forstawl'), *v.t.* be beforehand with in action, and so frustrate (person).

foretaste (for'tāst), *n.* partial enjoyment or suffering in advance.

foretell' (fort-), *v.t.* (p.t. *foretold*), tell of beforehand; predict, prophesy.

forethought (for'thawt), *n.* provident care; deliberate intention.

forewarn (forworn'), *v.t.* warn beforehand.

foreword (for'werd), *n.* preface.

for'feit (-fit), *a.* lost owing to crime or fault. *n.* forfeited thing; fine, penalty. *v.t.* pay or give up as penalty. **for'feiture**, *n.* forfeiting.

forgath'er (-dh-), *v.t.* meet together.

forgave, *p.t.* of **forgive.**

forge[1], *n.* smithy; furnace or hearth for melting or refining metal. *v.* shape by heating in fire and hammering; invent (tale, lie); make imitation with intent to deceive. **for'gery**, *n.* forging or falsifying of document, signature, etc.; forged document, etc.

forge[2], *v.i.* advance with effort (*on, ahead*).

forget' (-g-), *v.* (p.t. *forgot*; p.p. *forgotten*; pres. p. *forgetting*), fail to remember or recall; neglect, overlook. *forget oneself*, act presumptuously, unworthily, etc. **forget'-me-not**, plant with small blue flowers. **forget'ful**, *a.* apt to forget.

forgive' (-g-), *v.t.* (p.t. *forgāve*; p.p. *forgiven*), give up resentment against (offender); remit (debt, etc.). **forgiv'able**, *a.* **forgive'ness**, *n.* **forgiv'ing**, *a.*

forgo', *v.t.* (p.t. *forwent*; p.p. *forgone*), go without; give up.

fork, *n.* pronged implement for digging, etc.; pronged instrument used in eating, cooking, etc.; point where two roads, branches, etc., meet. *v.* form a fork; divide into branches; dig with fork.

forlorn', *a.* forsaken; wretched. **forlorn hope**, enterprise with little chance of success; very faint hope.

form, *n.* shape, arrangement of parts, visible aspect; class in school; set order of words; document with blanks to be filled up; kind, variety; behaviour according to custom; (of horse, athlete, etc.) condition of health and training; bench; hare's lair. *v.* fashion, mould; make; take shape.

for'mal, *a.* conventional; perfunctory; prim, stiff.

formal'ity, *n.* formal act or conduct; primness, precision of manners.

for'malize, *v.t.* make formal; give definite form to.

formā'tion, *n.* forming; thing formed; arrangement, structure.

for'mative, *a.* serving to form; (of suffix, etc.) used in forming words.

for'mer, *a.* of the past, earlier; first-named. *pron. the former*, the first or first-named of two. **for'merly**, *adv.* in former times.

for'mic, *a.* of ants. **formic acid**, acid contained in fluid emitted by ants.

for'midable, *a.* to be dreaded; likely to be difficult to deal with, resist, etc.

form'less, *a.* without distinct or regular form.

for'mūla, *n.* (pl. *formulas, formulae*), set form of words or symbols; recipe; rule, etc., expressed in symbols, etc.

for'mūlary, *a.* & *n.* (collection) of formulas or set forms.

for'mūlāte, *v.t.* express in formula; set forth systematically. **formūlā'tion**, *n.*

fornicā'tion, *n.* voluntary sexual intercourse between man and unmarried woman. **for'nicāte**, *v.i.*

forsāke', *v.t.* (p.t. *forsook*; p.p. *forsāken*), give up; desert, abandon.

forsōōth', *adv.* (*archaic*) indeed.

forswear' (-swār), *v.t.* (p.t. *forswore*; p.p. *forsworn*), renounce; swear falsely; perjure oneself.

fort, *n.* fortified place.

forte[1], *n.* one's strong point.

for'tè[2], *adv.* & *a.* (Mus.) loud(ly).

forth, *adv.* forward(s); into view; out of doors; onwards in time. **forthcom'ing** (-ku-), *a.* approaching; about to appear; ready when needed; friendly, helpful. **forth'right** (-īt), *a.* outspoken. **forthwith'**, *adv.* at once.

fortificā'tion, *n.* (usu. pl.) defensive work(s).

for'tify, *v.t.* strengthen; provide with defensive works; strengthen (wine, etc.) with spirits.

fortiss'imō, *adv.* & *a.* (Mus.) very loud(ly).

for'titūde, *n.* courage in pain or adversity.

fort'night (-nīt), *n.* two weeks. **fort'nightly**, *adv.* & *a.* (happening, appearing) once a fortnight.

fort'ress, *n.* military stronghold.

fortū'itous, *a.* due to chance. **fortū'ity**, *n.*

for'tūnate (*or* -choon-), *a.* lucky, prosperous, auspicious. **for'tunately**, *adv.*

for'tūne (*or* -choon), *n.* chance; luck; prosperity, wealth; large sum of money; coming lot. **for'tune-teller**, foreteller of future.

for'ty, *a.* & *n.* four times ten (40, XL). **for'tieth**, *a.* & *n.*

for'um, *n.* meeting for public discussion; court, tribunal.

for'ward, *a.* in front; towards the front; well-advanced; prompt; presumptuous, pert. *n.* first-line player in some team-games. *adv.* towards future; to front; progressively. *v.t.* help forward; send (letter, etc.) on. **for'wardness**, *n.* pertness. **for'wards** (-z), *adv.* forward.

foss'il, *n.* remains of plant or animal hardened and preserved in earth's crust; antiquated person or thing. *a.* fossilized; antiquated. **foss'ilīze**, *v.* turn into fossil. **fossilīzā'tion**, *n.*

fos'ter, v.t. encourage, harbour (feeling); cherish; bring up (child of others). **foster--child,** child as related to parents who have fostered it. **foster-mother,** woman who brings up child of others (so **foster-father, -daughter, -son, -brother, -sister**).

fought, p.t. & p.p. of **fight.**

foul, a. offensive, disgusting; dirty, soiled; clogged; obscene; unfair; (of weather) wet, rough. n. unfair stroke, etc., in sport; collision, entanglement. v. make or become foul; become entangled; collide with. **foul'ly,** adv. vilely, cruelly.

found¹, v. lay base of; establish; originate; base, build up. **foun'der¹,** n. one who founds insitution, etc. **foun'dress,** n.fem.

found², v.t. melt and mould (metal), fuse (materials for glass); make thus. **foun'der²,** n.

found³, p.t. & p.p. of **find.**

founda'tion, n. founding or establishing; endowed institution; solid ground or base; basis. **foundation-stone,** esp. one laid with ceremony.

founder¹,²: see **found ¹,².**

foun'der³, v.i. (of ship) fill with water and sink; fall down, collapse.

found'ling, n. deserted infant of unknown parents.

foun'dry, n. factory or workshop for founding metal or glass.

fount, n. spring, source, fountain.

foun'tain, n. spring of water; artificial jet of water; source. **fountain pen,** pen containing reservoir of ink.

four (for), a. & n. one more than three (4,IV). *on all fours,* crawling on hands and knees. **four-poster,** bed with four posts supporting canopy. **four'some,** (esp., Golf) game between two pairs; (*informal*) party of four. **four-square,** firmly placed, steady.

four'teen (for-; *or* -ēn'), a. & n. one more than thirteen (14,XIV). **four'teenth,** a. & n.

fourth (forth), a. & n. next after third; quarter, one of four equal parts.

fowl, n. (pl. *fowl, fowls*), bird(s) kept to supply eggs and flesh for food; (game-)bird(s). v.i. shoot or snare wildfowl. **fowling-piece,** light gun. **fowl-pest,** infectious disease of fowls. **fow'ler,** n.

fox, n. quadruped with reddish-brown fur, hunted for sport; crafty person. v.i. (*informal*) deceive, puzzle. **fox'hound,** hound bred to hunt foxes. **fox-hunt, -hunting,** chasing of fox with hounds. **fox-terrier,** short-haired terrier. **fox'trot,** a ballroom dance.

fox'glove (-uv), n. tall plant with spikes of purple or white flowers.

fox'y, a. fox-like; crafty.

foyer (fwah'yā), n. large space in theatre for use in intervals.

frac'tion, n. numerical quantity which is not a whole number; small part or amount.

frac'tional, a. of fraction(s), very small.

frac'tious (-shus), a. peevish, unruly.

frac'ture (-cher), n. breaking or breakage, esp. of bone. v.t. break, crack.

fra'gile, a. easily broken; weak, delicate. **fragil'ity,** n.

frag'ment, n. part broken off; incomplete part, remnant. **frag'mentary,** a. **fragmenta'tion,** n.

fra'grance, n. being fragrant; perfume. **fra'grant,** a. sweet-smelling.

frail, a. fragile; delicate; morally weak. **frail'ty,** n. weakness; foible.

frame, v. shape; construct, contrive, plan; form in the mind; set in frame, serve as frame for; concoct false accusation or contrive evidence against. n. construction; temporary state (*of* mind); skeleton of building, etc.; case, border, enclosing picture, etc.; glazed structure to protect plants. **frame-up,** (*slang*) conspiracy to have innocent person blamed for crime. **frame'work,** basic structure giving shape or support.

franc, n. unit of money of France, Belgium, Switzerland, etc.

fran'chise (-z), n. right to vote, esp. for member of Parliament; citizenship.

frank¹, a. showing clearly thoughts, etc.; open; undisguised.

frank², v.t. stamp (letter) by machine; (Hist.) mark (letter, etc.) to ensure free delivery.

frank'incense, n. aromatic gum resin burnt as incense.

frank'lin, n. (Hist.) landowner of free but not noble birth.

fran'tic, a. wildly excited, beside oneself, with pain, rage, etc.; violent.

frater'nal, a. of brothers, brotherly. **frater'nity,** n. brotherliness; religious body; guild. **frat'ernize,** v.i. make friends with. **fraterniza'tion,** n.

fra'tricide, n. killing, killer, of brother or sister.

fraud, n. criminal deception; dishonest trick. **frau'dulent,** a. deceitful, dishonest. **frau'dulence,** n.

fraught (frawt), a. *fraught with,* involving, threatening, (danger, etc.); full of.

fräulein (froi'līn), n. unmarried German woman; German governess. **Fräulein —,** Miss —. (German)

fray¹, n. fight, noisy quarrel.

fray², v. rub; make or become ragged at edge.

freak, n. absurd or unusual idea or occurrence; monstrosity. **freak, frea'kish,** aa.

freck'le, n. light brown spot on skin. v. spot, become spotted, with freckles. **freck'led,** a.

free, a. (*freer,* pr. frē'er, *freest,* pr. frē'ist), not in bondage to another; having personal rights and liberty of action; (of country) independent, democratic; not in custody or confinement; disengaged, available; (of translation) not literal; lavish, unreserved; unrestricted; not charged for. v.t. (p.t. *freed*;

pres. p. *freeing*), make free; set at liberty, disentangle. **free-hand,** (of drawing) done without ruler, etc. **free-lance,** unattached journalist, etc. **free thinker,** one rejecting authority in religious belief, rationalist. **free trade,** commerce without customs duties. **free-wheel,** (in bicycle) driving-wheel able to revolve while pedals are at rest. **free will,** power of directing one's actions voluntarily.

free′boŏter, *n.* pirate.

free′dom, *n.* condition of being free; independence; undue familiarity; unrestricted use *of*; participation in privileges of citizenship *of* city, etc.

free′hold, *n.* land, etc., owned absolutely; this tenure. *a.* held freehold.

free′man, *n.* (pl.-*men*), holder of freedom *of* city, etc.

free′màson, *n.* member of fraternity having elaborate ritual and secret signs. **free′-màsonry,** *n.*

freeze, *v.* (p.t. *frōze*; p.p. *frōzen*), (cause to) be converted into or covered with ice; be cold enough for water to become ice; become rigid, congeal, chill or be chilled, by frost, cold, or fear; preserve by refrigeration; stabilize (wages, prices). **freezing-point,** temperature at which water freezes. **free′zer,** *n.* deep-freeze; machine for making ice-cream.

freight (frāt), *n.* charge for transport of goods esp. by ship; cargo. **freight′age,** *n.* cost of transporting goods. **freight′er,** *n.* (esp.) cargo ship.

French, *a.* of France or its people or language. *n.* French language. *take French leave,* depart, act, without permission or notice. **French bean,** kind of bean, young green pods of which are cooked whole or sliced. **French horn,** brass wind instrument with tube coiled in circle. **French window,** glazed door or pair of doors, serving as door and window. **French′man, French′woman,** *nn.*

frenet′ic, *a.* frantic, frenzied.

fren′zy, *n.* frantic excitement or fury. **fren′-zied,** *a.* driven to frenzy; frantic.

frē′quency, *n.* frequent occurrence; rate of occurrence; (Phys.) rate of recurrence (of vibration, etc.).

frē′quent[1], *a.* happening often, common; numerous; habitual.

frèquent′[2], *v.t.* go often or habitually to. **frè-quen′ted,** *a.* much resorted to.

fres′cō, *n.* (pl. *frescoes, frescos*), (method of) painting in water-colour on fresh plaster.

fresh, *a.* new; not stale or faded; invigorating; just arrived; refreshing; not salt. *adv.* newly. **fresh′en,** *v.* **fresh′man, fresh′er** (*slang*), *nn.* university student in first year.

fret[1], *n.* ornamental pattern made by straight lines usu. at right angles. *v.t.* (p.t. *fretted*), decorate with carved work. **fret-saw,** very narrow saw stretched in frame, for cutting thin wood in patterns. **fret′work,** wood or

stone cut in patterns.

fret[2], *v.* (p.t. *fretted*), gnaw; wear by rubbing; irritate, worry; grieve. **fret′ful,** *a.* complaining, peevish. **fret′fully,** *adv.*

fret[3], *n.* bar or ridge across finger-board of guitar, etc. *v.t.* provide with frets.

frī′able, *a.* easily crumbled.

frī′ar, *n.* member of certain religious orders. **frī′ary,** *n.* convent of friars.

fric′ative, *n. & a.* (consonant) made by friction of breath through narrow opening (as *t, f, k,* etc.).

fric′tion, *n.* rubbing of one surface against another; chafing; disagreement.

Frī′day, *n.* sixth day of week. **Good Friday,** Friday before Easter, commemorating Crucifixion.

fridge, *n.* (*informal*) refrigerator.

friend (frend), *n.* one attached to another by affection; sympathizer, helper; acquaintance. **Friend,** Quaker. **friend′less,** *a.* without friends. **friend′ly,** *a.* acting as a friend; showing kindness. **friend′liness,** *n.* **friend′-ship,** *n.* being friends; friendly relationship or feeling.

frieze, *n.* ornamental band or strip along wall, usu. at top.

frig′ate, *n.* large escort vessel; (Hist.) large warship.

fright (frīt), *n.* sudden or violent fear; grotesque-looking person.

fright′en (frīt-), *v.t.* throw into fright; drive *away, into,* etc., by fright. **fright′ened** (-nd), *a.* affected with fright *at* or *of.*

fright′ful (frīt-), *a.* dreadful, shocking; ugly; (*slang*) very great or bad, awful. **fright′fully,** *adv.* **fright′fulness,** *n.*

frig′id, *a.* intensely cold; lacking warmth of feeling; (of a woman) sexually unresponsive. **frigid′ity,** *n.*

frill, *n.* strip of material gathered at one edge. **frilled** (-ld), *a.*

fringe (-nj), *n.* edging of loose threads or tassels; front hair cut short over forehead; border, outer edge. *v.t.* adorn with fringe; serve as fringe to.

fripp′ery, *n.* finery; tawdry ornaments.

frisk, *v.i.* caper, gambol. **frisk′y,** *a.* lively, playful.

fritt′er[1], *n.* fried batter often containing slices of fruit, meat, etc.

fritt′er[2], *v.t.* (with *away*) waste (time, etc.).

friv′olous, *a.* trifling; silly, not serious. **frivol′ity,** *n.*

frizz, *v.t.* curl hair tightly. *n.* hair in crisp tight curls. **frizz′y,** *a.*

frizz′le, *v.* fry with sputtering noise.

frō, *adv. to and fro,* backwards and forwards.

frock, *n.* monk's gown, (fig.) priestly office; woman's or child's dress. *frock-coat,* man's long-skirted coat.

frog[1], *n.* small tailless jumping amphibian. **frog′man** (pl. -*men*), underwater swimmer.

frog[2], *n.* elastic horny substance in middle of

sole of horse's foot.

frog³, *n.* ornamental coat-fastening.

frol'ic, *v.i.* (p.t. *frolicked*), gambol, caper about, play pranks. *n.* merrymaking, prank. **frol'icsome**, *a.*

from, *prep.* out of; because of; at a distance; since, ever since.

frond, *n.* leaf-like organ of certain flowerless plants, esp. ferns.

front (frunt), *n.* side or part normally nearer or towards spectator or direction of motion; face; forward position; (Mil.) scene of actual fighting; sea front. *a.* of or at the front. *v.* face, stand opposite to; oppose. **front benches**, seats in House of Commons for members of Government and leaders of Opposition. **fron'tage**, *n.* front of building; land between building and street or water. **fron'tal**, *a.* of or on front. *n.* covering for altar--front; façade.

fron'tier (-un-), *n.* boundary between countries; border of settled or inhabited part of country.

fron'tispiece (-un-), *n.* illustration at beginning of book, etc.

frost, *n.* freezing; frozen dew or vapour. *v.t.* injure with frost; cover (as) with hoar-frost; make (surface of glass, etc.) opaque. *frost--bite*, inflammation of skin, etc., from frost. **fros'ty**, *a.* cold with frost; chilling.

froth, *n.* foam, scum. *v.i.* emit or gather foam. **froth'y**, *a.*

frown, *v.i.* draw eyebrows together, wrinkle brow, esp. in displeasure or concentration of thought. *frown at, on*, express disapproval of. *n.* wrinkled brow; severe or disapproving look.

frow'zy, *a.* fusty; slatternly, dingy.

froze, frozen, *p.t. & p.p.* of **freeze**.

fruc'tify, *v.* bear fruit; make fruitful.

fru'gal (froo-), *a.* thrifty; careful in the use of food, money, etc. **frugal'ity**, *n.*

fruit (froot), *n.* (pl. same or *fruits*), (esp. edible and juicy or pulpy) seed of plant and its surrounding structure; product, result. *v.i.* bear fruit. **fruit machine**, slot-machine for gambling. **fruit'erer**, *n.* dealer in fruit. **fruit'ful**, *a.* fertile; prolific; remunerative. **fruit'less**, *a.* not bearing fruit; useless.

frui'tion (froo-i-), *n.* realization of hopes, etc.

fruit'y, (froot-), *a.* of, like, fruit; rich.

frump, *n.* old-fashioned dowdily-dressed woman. **frum'pish**, *a.*

frustrate', *v.t.* prevent (person) from doing something; prevent fulfilment of (plans, etc.). **frustra'tion**, *n.*

fry¹, *n.* young fishes fresh from spawn. *small fry*, young or insignificant beings.

fry², *v.* cook in hot fat. *n.* fried fish, etc. **fry'ing-pan**, *n.*

fuchsia (fū'sha), *n.* ornamental shrub with drooping flowers.

fudd'le, *v.* make stupid, esp. with alcoholic drink.

fudge, *n.* kind of soft toffee.

fu'el, *n.* material for burning as fire or source of heat or power. *v.* (p.t. *fuelled*), supply fire, engine, etc., with fuel; (of ship, aircraft, etc.) take in fuel.

fug, *n.* stuffy atmosphere. **fugg'y**, *a.*

fu'gitive, *a.* fleeing; fleeting, transient. *n.* one who flees (*from*).

fugue (fūg), *n.* musical composition in which a theme is given by one part and repeated successively by others.

ful'crum, *n.* (pl. *fulcra*), support or pivot of lever.

fulfil' (fool-), *v.t.* (p.t. *fulfilled*), carry out; satisfy; perform, do; finish, complete. **fulfil'ment**, *n.*

ful'gent, *a.* shining.

full¹ (fool), *a.* containing all it will hold; crowded; copious; complete; ample. *adv.* quite, fully. *at full length*, lying stretched out. *in full*, without abridgement. **full age**, age of majority (see **majority**). **full-blown**, (of flower) fully open. **full stop**, punctuation mark (.) at end of sentence. **full-time**, employed for, taking up, the whole working--day, etc.

full² (fool), *v.t.* clean and thicken (cloth). **full'er**, *n.* **fuller's earth**, kind of clay used in fulling.

full'ness (fool-), *n.* being full. *fullness of time*, (Bibl.) proper or destined time.

full'y, *adv.* completely. *fully-fashioned*, (of garment) shaped to fit.

ful'mar (fool-), *n.* sea-bird of petrel family.

ful'minate, *v.* flash like lightning; explode; thunder forth (threats, etc.). **fulmina'tion**, *a.*

ful'some (fool-), *a.* excessive; disgusting by excess.

fum'ble, *v.* grope about; handle or deal with awkwardly. **fum'bler**, *n.*

fume, *n.* strong-smelling smoke, vapour or exhalation (often pl.); fit of anger. *v.* subject to fumes; darken (oak, etc.) thus; show signs of anger or discontent.

fu'migate, *v.t.* subject to fumes; disinfect or purify thus. **fumiga'tion**, *n.*

fun, *n.* sport, amusement; joking. **fun-fair**, (part of) fair devoted to amusements and side-shows.

funam'bulist, *n.* tight-rope walker.

func'tion, *n.* work a thing is designed to do; official duty; formal or important social meeting. *v.i.* fulfil function; act. **func'tional**, *a.* of function(s); shaped, designed, with regard only to function. **func'tionary**, *n.* official.

fund, *n.* permanently available stock; sum of money (esp. for particular purpose); (pl.) stock of money.

fundamen'tal, *a.* serving as base or foundation; essential, primary. *n.* fundamental rule, principle, etc.

fu'neral, *n.* burial or cremation of the dead; funeral procession or service. *a.* of, used at, funeral. **fūnēr′ēal,** *a.* fit for funeral; dismal, dark.

fun′gicīde (-j-), *n.* fungus-destroying substance.

fung′us (-ngg-), *n.* (pl. *fungi,* pr. -jī *or* -gī, *funguses*), flowerless plant lacking chlorophyll and reproducing by spores (e.g. mushroom, toadstool, mould). **fung′ous,** *a.*

fūnic′ūlar, *a.* of, depending on, a rope or cable. **funicular (railway),** railway operating on steep slope and worked by cable and stationary engine.

funk, *n.* (*slang*) fear, panic; coward. *v.* (try to) evade because of fear; be afraid of.

funn′el, *n.* tube with cone-shaped end for conducting liquids into small opening; chimney of steam-engine or ship.

funn′y, *a.* comical, amusing; queer. **funn′ily,** *adv.* **funn′iness,** *n.*

fur, *n.* dressed coat of certain animals used for garments, trimming, etc.; garment of fur (often pl.); short fine hair of some animals; coating, crust. *v.* trim, cover, coat, become coated with, fur. **furry** (fer′i), *a.*

fur′bĕlow (-ō), *n.* flounce; showy trimming.

fur′bish, *v.t.* polish (*up*); renovate.

fūr′ious, *a.* raging, very angry; violent.

furl, *v.* roll up (sail); fold up, close; become furled.

fur′long, *n.* eighth of mile (220 yds.).

fur′lough (-lō), *n.* leave of absence.

fur′nace, *n.* chamber for applying intense heat; closed fireplace for heating water, etc., to warm building; hot place.

fur′nish, *v.t.* supply with furniture; provide (*with*).

fur′niture (-cher), *n.* movable contents of house or room.

fu′rrier, *n.* dealer in, dresser of, furs.

fur′row (-ō), *n.* narrow trench made by plough; rut, groove; wrinkle. *v.t.* make furrows in.

furry: see **fur.**

fur′ther (-dh-), *adv.* to a greater distance; in addition. *a.* more remote; additional. *v.t.* help forward. **fur′therance,** *n.* **fur′-thermore,** *adv.* moreover. **fur′thermost,** *a.* most distant. **fur′thest,** *a.* & *adv.*

fur′tive, *a.* sly; stealthy.

fūr′y, *n.* fierce passion, rage; violence; angry woman.

furze, *n.* gorse, whin.

fūse[1] (-z), *v.* melt with intense heat; blend (as) by melting. *n.* (Electr.) piece of easily--fusible wire in circuit, designed to melt when circuit is overloaded. **fū′sible,** *a.*

fūse[2] (-z), *n.* cord, etc., saturated with combustible matter for igniting explosive. *v.t.* fit fuse to.

fū′selage (-zilij; *or* -ahzh), *n.* body of an aeroplane.

fū′sil (-z-), *n.* obsolete light musket. **fūsilier′** (-ēr), *n.* soldier of some regiments formerly armed with fusil. **fūsillāde′** (-z-). *n.* continuous firing of firearms.

fū′sion (-zhn), *n.* fusing; fused mass; blending of different things into one; energy-releasing union of atomic nuclei to form heavier nucleus.

fuss, *n.* bustle; excessive commotion or concern. *v.* make a fuss; bustle; worry. **fuss′y,** *a.* (in the habit of) making a fuss; excessively ornate.

fūs′tian, *n.* twilled cotton cloth; pompous speech or writing. *a.* made of fustian; bombastic; worthless.

fus′ty, *a.* stale-smelling; mouldy; old--fashioned.

fū′tīle, *a.* useless, worthless, frivolous. **fūtil′-ity,** *n.*

fū′ture (-cher), *a.* about to happen or be or become. *n.* time to come; future condition, events, etc.

fūtūr′ity, *n.* future time, events, etc.

fuzz, *n.* fluff; frizzy hair. **fuzz′y,** *a.*

G

gab′ardine, gab′erdine (-ēn), *n.* twilled cloth, esp. of fine worsted.

gabb′le, *v.* talk rapidly and indistinctly. *n* rapid unintelligible talk.

gā′ble, *n.* triangular part of wall at end of ridged roof.

gad, *v.i.* (p.t. *gadded*), **gad about,** go from place to place, esp. seeking entertainment.

gad′about, *n.* person who gads about.

gad′flÿ, *n.* horse-fly.

gadg′et, *n.* small contrivance or piece of mechanism.

Gael (gāl), *n.* Scottish or Irish Celt. **Gael′ic** (gāl- *or* gal-), *n.* & *a.* (language) of Gaels.

gaff[1], *n.* barbed fishing-spear; stick with iron hook for landing fish.

gaff², *n.* blow the gaff, (*slang*) let out secret.

gaffe, *n.* blunder, faux pas.

gaff'er, *n.* old man (*archaic*); foreman, boss.

gag, *n.* thing thrust into mouth to prevent speech or hold it open; words added by actor in drama. *v.* (p.t. *gagged*), apply gag(s) to, silence; make gags in play.

gag'a (*or* gah'gah), *a.* senile; fatuous.

gâge, *n.* pledge, security; challenge.

gai'ety, *n.* being gay; merrymaking.

gai'ly, *adv.* in gay manner.

gain, *v.* obtain; win; reach; benefit. *n.* increase of wealth, profit; money-making. **gain'ful**, *a.* paying; paid.

gainsay', *v.t.* (p.t. *gainsaid*, pr. -ăd *or* -ed), deny, contradict.

gait, *n.* manner of walking.

gai'ter, *n.* covering of leather, etc., for leg or ankle.

gā'la (*or* gah-), *n.* festive occasion, fête.

galac'tic, *a.* (Astron.) of galaxy.

gal'antine (-ēn), *n.* white meat cut up, boiled, and served cold in jelly.

gal'axy, *n.* luminous band of stars encircling the heavens; brilliant company; (*Galaxy*), Milky Way.

gāle, *n.* strong wind; storm.

gall¹ (gawl), *n.* bile; harshness; rancour

gall² (gawl), *n.* painful swelling, esp. on horse; sore. *v.t.* rub sore; vex, humiliate.

gallant, *a.* (gal'ant) brave; fine, stately; (galant') attentive to women. *n.* (galant') (*archaic*) ladies' man; dandy. **gall'antry**, *n.* bravery; courtliness; polite act or speech.

gall'èon, *n.* (Hist.) Spanish sailing-ship.

gall'ery, *n.* covered walk; raised floor or balcony over part of area of church, etc.; highest balcony in theatre, etc.; corridor; room for showing works of art.

gall'ey, *n.* (pl. *galleys*), low flat vessel usu. rowed by slaves or criminals (Hist.); ancient Greek or Roman warship; large rowing-boat; ship's kitchen; tray for set-up type. **galley proof**, proof on long slip of paper.

Gall'ic, *a.* of Gaul(s); French.

gall'ipot, *n.* small glazed earthen pot.

gallivant', *v.i.* gad about.

gall'on, *n.* measure (four quarts) for liquids, corn, etc.

gall'op, *n.* horse's fastest pace; track or ground for galloping. *v.* go at gallop; make (horse) gallop; read, recite, progress, rapidly.

gall'ows (-ōz), *n.* structure for hanging criminals; any similar structure; punishment of hanging.

galore', *adv.* in plenty.

galosh', **golosh'**, *n.* rubber overshoe.

galvan'ic, *a.* or, produced by, galvanism; (ot smile, etc.) sudden and forced.

gal'vanism, *n.* electricity produced by chemical action. **gal'vanize**, *v.t.* stimulate (as) by electricity, rouse by shock or excitement;

coat iron with zinc.

gam'bit, *n.* kind of opening move in chess; (fig.) any initial move.

gam'ble, *v.i.* play games of chance for money; (fig.) take risks. *n.* gambling; risk, risky undertaking. **gamb'ler**, *n.*

gamboge' (-ōozh), *n.* gum-resin used as yellow pigment.

gam'bol, *n.* & *v.i.* (p.t. *gambolled*), (make) frisky movement, leap.

gāme¹, *n.* pastime; spell of play; sporting contest; jest; animals, birds, etc., hunted for sport or food. *a.* spirited, ready. *v.i.* gamble.

game-bird, bird shot for sport and food.

game-cock, cock of kind bred for fighting.

game'keeper, man employed to breed game, prevent poaching, etc. **gāme'ster** (-ms-), *n.* gambler. **gām'ing**, *n.* gambling (*gam'-ing-house*, *-table*).

gāme², *a.* (of leg, etc.) crippled.

gam'ète, *n.* mature sexual cell.

gamm'a, *n.* third letter of Greek alphabet. **gamma rays**, very short X-rays

gamm'er, *n.* (*archaic*) old woman.

gamm'on, *n.* bottom piece of flitch of bacon including hind leg.

gam'ut, *n.* whole series of recognized notes in music; entire range or scope.

gan'der, *n.* male goose.

gang, *n.* set of workmen, slaves, or prisoners; band of persons acting together, esp. for criminal purposes. **gang'er**, *n.* foreman of gang of workmen.

gang'ling (-ngg-), *a.* loosely built, lanky.

gang'-plank, *n.* plank, usu. with cleats, for walking into or out of boat.

gang'rène (-ngg-), *n.* death of section of body-tissue caused by cutting off of blood supply. **gang'rènous**, *a.*

gang'ster, *n.* member of gang of criminals. **gang'sterism**, *n.*

gang'way, *n.* passage, esp. between rows of seats; bridge from ship's bulwarks to shore.

gann'èt, *n.* large white sea-bird.

gaol (jāl), **jail**, *n.* prison. *v.t.* put in prison. **gaol'bird**, *n.* habitual criminal. **gaol'er**, *n.* man in charge of gaol or prisoners.

gap, *n.* breach in hedge or wall, etc.; unfilled space; interval; wide difference in views, sympathies, etc.

gāpe, *v.i.* open mouth wide; open or be open wide; stare *at*. *n.* yawn; stare.

ga'rage (-ahzh *or* -ij), *n.* building for storage of motor vehicle(s); establishment selling petrol, repairing motor vehicles, etc. *v.t.* put or keep in garage.

garb, *n.* dress of distinctive kind; way one is dressed. *v.t.* dress.

gar'bage, *n.* kitchen waste; rubbish.

gar'ble, *v.t.* distort or confuse (facts, statements, etc.).

gar'den, *n.* piece of ground for growing flowers, fruit, or vegetables; (pl.) pleasure-grounds. *v.* cultivate, work in, garden.

gar'dener, n.

gargan'tŭan, a. gigantic.

gar'gle, v. wash throat with liquid held in mouth and kept in motion by breath. n. liquid so used.

gar'goyle, n. grotesque spout projecting from gutter.

gar'ish, a. excessively bright, gaudy.

gar'land, n. wreath worn as decoration, prize, etc. v. t. adorn with garland.

gar'lic, n. plant with strong-smelling, pungent-tasting bulbs.

gar'ment, n. article of dress.

gar'ner, n. (Poet.) granary. v. t. collect, store up.

gar'net, n. transparent red mineral used as gem.

gar'nish, v. t. decorate, esp. dish of food. n. materials for this.

ga'rret, n. room on top floor, attic.

ga'rrison, n. troops stationed in town. v. t. furnish with, occupy as, garrison.

garrotte' (ga-r-), n. (apparatus for) Spanish method of execution by strangulation. v. t. execute, throttle, thus.

ga'rrulous (-ool-), a. talkative; chattering. **garrul'ity** (-ool-), n.

gar'ter, n. band to keep stocking up; (the Garter), (badge of) highest order of English knighthood.

gas, n. (pl. gases), a fluid state of matter which, unconfined, has no definite shape or volume; coal-gas; nitrous oxide gas as anaesthetic; fire-damp; irritant or poisonous gas used in warfare, etc.; empty talk, boasting. v. kill or injure with gas; talk idly. **gas--fitter,** workman installing or repairing gas--pipes, etc. **gas-holder,** reservoir from which gas is distributed. **gas-mask,** respirator for protection against harmful gases. **gas-meter,** meter registering amount of gas used in house, etc. **ga'sèous** (or gă-), a. of, in form of, gas.

gash, n. long deep cut or wound, cleft. v. t. make gash in.

gas'oline (-ēn), **gas'olēne,** n. (U.S.) petrol (abbrev. gas).

gasom'ēter, n. gas-holder.

gasp (-ah-), v. i. catch breath with open mouth, strain for air or breath; utter with gasps. n. convulsive catching of breath.

gass'y, a. of, full of, like, gas.

gas'tric, a. of the stomach.

gastron'omy, n. art and science of good eating. **gastronom'ical,** a.

gas'tropod, n. mollusc which moves by means of a 'foot' placed ventrally (e.g. snail, limpet).

gāte, n. opening in wall, etc., closable with barrier; barrier closing opening in wall, regulating passage of water, etc.; means of entrance or exit. **gate-crash,** attend social gathering, etc., uninvited. **gate'way,** opening (closed by gate).

gath'er (-dh-), v. bring or come together; collect; pluck; draw together in folds; fester, form pus; draw as conclusion. n. (usu. pl.) gathered part of dress. **gath'ering,** n. assembly; festered swelling.

gauche (gōsh), a. socially awkward, clumsy; tactless. **gauch'erie,** n. gauche behaviour or action. (French)

gau'dy[1], n. grand feast or entertainment, esp. college dinner for old members, etc.

gau'dy[2], a. tastelessly showy.

gauge (gāj), n. standard measure; capacity, extent; instrument for measuring or testing; means of estimating. v. t. measure exactly; measure contents of; estimate.

Gaul, n. inhabitant of ancient Gaul.

gaunt, a. lean, haggard, grim.

gaunt'lèt[1], n. armoured glove thrown down in challenges (Hist.); glove with long, wide wrist.

gaunt'lèt[2], n. run the gauntlet, undergo punishment of passing between two rows of men armed with sticks, etc. (often fig.).

gauze, n. thin transparent fabric of silk, wire, etc. **gau'zy,** a.

gave, p. t. of **give.**

gav'el, n. auctioneer's or chairman's hammer, for calling attention, etc.

gavotte', n. (music for) 18th-century dance in quadruple time.

gawk, n. awkward or shy person. **gaw'ky,** a.

gay, a. light-hearted, mirthful; lively; addicted to social pleasures.

gāze, v. i. look fixedly. n. intent look.

gazē'bō, n. (pl. -s or gazeboes), structure in garden, etc., from which a view may be had.

gazelle', n. small graceful antelope.

gazette', n. newspaper, esp. official journal.

gazetteer', n. geographical dictionary.

gear (gēr), n. apparatus, tackle, tools; set of cog-wheels, etc., connecting motor with its work and usu. allowing change of speed ratio between driving and driven parts (high, low, gear, by which driven part revolves faster, slower). **gear-box,** case enclosing gear--changing mechanism. v. t. put in gear; provide with gear; adjust (to).

geese: see **goose.**

Geiger counter (gī'ger), instrument used for measuring radioactivity.

gei'sha (gā-), n. Japanese professional hostess and entertainer.

gel'atin(e) (or -ēn), n. transparent tasteless substance, used in making jellies, etc. **gèlat'inous,** a.

geld (g-), v. t. castrate. **gel'ding,** n. gelded horse or other animal.

gel'ignite, n. an explosive.

gem, n. precious stone; thing of great beauty or worth; jewel.

Gem'ini (or -nī), n. the Twins, constellation and third sign of the zodiac.

gendarme (zhon'darm), n. soldier employed on police duties, esp. in France.

gen'der, *n.* grammatical classification or one of classes (*masculine, feminine, neuter*) roughly corresponding to the two sexes and sexlessness.

gēne, *n.* (Biol.) unit of heredity in chromosome controlling a particular inherited characteristic of an individual.

gēnèalo'gical, *a.* of genealogy. **genealogical table, tree,** table showing descent from ancestor (in shape of tree with branches).

gēnéal'ogy, *n.* account of descent from ancestor by enumeration of intermediate persons; pedigree; investigation of pedigrees. **gēnéal'ogist,** *n.*

genera: see genus.

gen'eral, *a.* of, affecting, all or nearly all; not special, local, or particular; widespread; usual; vague, indefinite; (of anaesthetic) affecting whole body. *n.* army officer below Field Marshal; commander of army.

generaliss'imō, *n.* (pl. *generalissimos*), commander of combined forces.

general'ity, *n.* general statement; vagueness; majority *of.*

gen'eralize, *v.* draw general conclusion (*from*); bring into general use; speak vaguely. **generalizā'tion,** *n.*

gen'erally, *adv.* in general sense; in most respects; usually.

gen'eralship, *n.* office of general; military skill; tactful management.

gen'erāte, *v.t.* bring into existence. **gen'- erative,** *a.* **gen'erātor,** *n.* apparatus or machine for producing steam, electricity, etc.; dynamo.

generā'tion, *n.* procreation, reproduction; begetting; single step in descent or pedigree; all persons born about same time; period of about 30 years.

gene'ric, *a.* characteristic of genus or class; not specific.

gen'erous, *a.* free in giving; not mean; noble- -minded; abundant. **generos'ity,** *n.*

gen'èsis, *n.* origin; mode of formation; (*Genesis*), first book of Old Testament.

genet'ic, *a.* of genes or genetics.

genet'ics, *n.* scientific study of heredity and variation.

gē'nial, *a.* mild, kindly; cheering; sociable. **gēnial'ity,** *n.*

gē'nie, *n.* (pl. usu. *genii*), sprite or goblin of Arabian tales.

gen'ital, *a.* of animal reproduction. **gen'itals** (-z), *n. pl.* (esp. external) sexual organs.

gen'itive, *a. & n.* (Gram.) (case) indicating source, origin, or possession.

gē'nius, *n.* (pl. *genii*), guardian spirit; (pl. *geniuses*), (person having) unusually great intellectual, creative, or inventive capacity.

genteel', *a.* imitating speech, manners, etc., of upper classes; (*archaic*) polite and well- -bred.

gen'tian (-shian, -shn), *n.* alpine plant with conspicuous, usu. blue, flowers.

gen'tile, *n. & a.* (person) not of Jewish race.

gentil'ity, *n.* being genteel; social superiority; good manners.

gen'tle, *a.* mild, quiet, not rough or severe; well-born; **gen'tlefolk,** people of good family.

gen'tleman (-tlm-), *n.* (pl. -*men*), chivalrous well-bred man; man of good social position. **gen'tlemanly,** *a.* behaving, looking like, befitting, a gentleman.

gen'tleness (-tln-), *n.* kindliness; mildness.

gen'tlewoman (-tlwoo-), *n.* (pl. *gentlewomen,* pr. -wimin), woman of good birth or breeding, lady.

gent'ly, *adv.* mildly; softly; slowly, quietly, tenderly.

gent'ry, *n.* people of good but not of noble birth.

gen'uflect, *v.i.* bend the knee, esp. in worship. **genūfle'xion** (-kshn), *n.*

gen'ūine, *a.* pure-bred; not sham or counterfeit; authentic.

gē'nus, *n.* (pl. *genera*), (Biol.) large group of animals, plants, etc., containing several species; kind.

geo-, *pref.* earth.

gēocen'tric, *a.* considered as viewed from earth's centre; having earth as centre.

gēog'raphy, *n.* science of earth's form, physical features, climate, etc., general features of place. **gēog'rapher,** *n.* **gēograph'ic(al),** *aa.*

gēol'ogy, *n.* science of earth's crust, its strata, and their relations and changes. **gēolo'gical,** *a.* **gēol'ogist,** *n.*

gēom'etry, *n.* science of properties and relations of magnitudes in space, as lines, surfaces, solids. **gēomet'ric(al),** *aa.*

gēophys'ics (-z-), *n.* physics of the earth. **gēophys'ical,** *a.* **gēophys'icist,** *n.*

George Cross (jorj), decoration for gallantry, intended primarily for civilians.

georgette' (jorj-), *n.* thin crêpe of fine twisted yarn (silk, nylon, etc.).

Geor'gian (jor-), *a.* of the time of George I - IV or of George V - VI.

gērā'nium, *n.* kind of wild plant with fruit like crane's bill; cultivated plant with fragrant leaves and showy flowers.

geriat'rics (je-r-), *n.* branch of medicine or of social science dealing with the health of old people. **geriat'ric,** *a.*

germ, *n.* part of organism capable of developing into new one; rudiment, elementary principle; microbe.

Ger'man, *n. & a.* (native, language) of Germany. **German measles,** infectious disease like mild measles.

germāne', *a.* relevant, pertinent, (*to*).

German'ic, *a.* of ancient Teutons or their language; (Hist.) of Germans.

ger'micide, *n.* substance which destroys germs. **germici'dal,** *a.*

ger'minal, *a.* in earliest stage of development.

ger'mināte, v. sprout, bud; cause to shoot, produce. **germinā'tion,** n.

gerontol'ogy (je-r-), n. scientific study of old age and of process of ageing.

ge'rund, n. form of Latin verb constructed as noun; English verbal noun ending in -ing. **gērun'dive,** n. Latin verbal adjective from gerund.

gestic'ūlāte, v. use gestures of arms, etc., with or instead of speech. **gesticūlā'tion,** n. **gestic'ūlative, gestic'ūlatory,** aa.

ges'ture, n. expressive movement of the body, esp. of hands and arms; step or move calculated to evoke response from another.

get (g-), v. (p.t. got; p.p. got, (U.S.) gotten), obtain, earn, gain, win, procure; fetch; learn; experience, suffer; catch or contract; succeed in coming or going to, away, etc., succeed in bringing, placing, etc.; become. **get on,** make progress; be on friendly terms with. **get over,** overcome; recover from. **get through,** (esp.) pass examination, reach or bring to destination. **get up,** (esp.) rise, mount, organize. **get-at-able,** accessible. **get-away,** (esp.) escape.

gew'-gaw (g-), n. gaudy plaything or ornament.

gey'ser (gēz-), n. hot spring; apparatus for heating water.

ghast'ly (gah-), a. horrible, frightful; death-like, wan. **ghast'liness,** n.

gher'kin (ger-), n. young or small cucumber for pickling.

ghett'ō (ge-), n. (pl. ghettos), Jews' quarter in city (Hist.); part of city esp. slum area, occupied by particular racial group(s).

ghost (gō-), n. spirit of dead person spoken of as appearing to the living; shadowy outline, slight trace; (archaic) spirit of life. **ghost--writer,** person doing literary work for which employer takes credit. **ghost'ly,** a. ghostlike; (archaic) spiritual.

ghoul (gool), n. spirit said to prey on corpses. **ghoul'ish,** a. gruesome.

ghyll: see gill².

G.I., abbrev. (U.S.) government (or general) issue. n. enlisted member of a U.S. armed force.

gi'ant, n. being of superhuman size; very tall person, animal, plant, etc. a. very big. **gi'antess,** n. fem.

gibb'er (j-, g-), v.t. chatter unintelligibly. **gibb'erish** (g-, j-), n. meaningless speech.

gibb'ĕt, n. post on which body of executed criminal was exposed; gallows.

gibb'on (g-), n. long-armed anthropoid ape.

gībe, jībe, v. & n. jeer; taunt; scoff.

gib'lets, n.pl. bird's liver, gizzard, etc., removed before cooking.

gidd'y (g-), a. causing, having, the feeling that everything is turning round, dizzy; frivolous. **gidd'iness,** n.

gift (g-), n. thing given or received without payment, present; talent. **gift'ed,** a. talented.

gig (g-), n. light two-wheeled one-horse carriage; light ship's boat; rowing-boat.

gigan'tic, a. huge.

gigg'le (g-), v.i. & n. (utter) foolish or half--suppressed laughter suggestive of uncontrollable amusement.

gi'golō (zh-, j-), n. (pl. gigolos), professional male dancing-partner.

gild (g-), v.t. (p.p. gilded or gilt), cover thinly with gold; tinge with golden colour; give fair appearance to.

gill¹ (g-), n. (usu. in pl.), breathing organ(s) of fish, etc.; flesh below person's ears and jaws.

gill² (g-), **ghyll** (gil), n. deep wooded ravine; narrow mountain torrent.

gill³ (j-) n. quarter-pint measure.

gill'ie (g-), n. man attending sportsman shooting or fishing in Scotland.

gilt (g-), n. gilding. a. thinly covered with gold. **gilt-edged,** (esp. of investments) considered safe.

gim'bals (g- or j-; -z), n.pl. contrivance of rings and pivots for keeping compass, etc., horizontal at sea.

gim'crack, n. worthless ornament. a. flimsy, tawdry.

gim'lĕt (g-), n. small boring-tool.

gimm'ick (g-), n. (slang) device, mannerism, etc., esp. one adopted for the purpose of attracting attention.

gin¹, n. snare, trap; machine separating cotton from seeds. v.t. (p.t. ginned), trap; treat (cotton) in gin.

gin², n. alcoholic spirit distilled from grain and flavoured with juniper, etc.

gin'ger (-j-), n. (tropical plant with) hot spicy root; mettle, spirit; light reddish yellow. v.t. rouse up. **ginger ale, beer, wine,** ginger--flavoured drinks. **gin'gerbread,** cake made with treacle and flavoured with ginger.

gin'gerly (-j-), adv. & a. with or showing extreme care to avoid noise, etc.

gingham (ging'-am), n. plain-woven, often striped or checked, cotton cloth.

gip'sy, gyp'sy, n. member of a wandering race (perhaps originating in India) with dark skin and hair. a. of gipsy or gipsies.

giraffe' (-ahf), n. ruminant quadruped with long neck and legs.

gird (g-), v.t. (p.t. girded or girt), encircle (waist), fasten on (sword, etc.), with belt, etc. gird oneself, gird (up) one's loins, (fig.) prepare for action.

gir'der (g-), n. beam supporting joists; iron or steel beam, lattice, etc., forming span of bridge, etc.

gir'dle¹ (g-), n. cord, belt, used to gird waist; thing that surrounds; corset. v.t. surround with girdle.

gir'dle² (g-), n. (Sc. & north.) round iron plate for cooking scones, cakes, etc., over heat.

girl (g-), n. female child; young unmarried woman; female servant or employee. **Girl**

Guide, see **guide. girl'hood,** *n.* **girl'ish,** *a.*

gir'ō, *n.* simple system of banking and credit transfer.

girt, *p.t.* & *p.p.* of **gird.**

girth (g-), *n.* band round body of horse securing saddle; measurement round more or less cylindrical thing.

gist, *n.* substance or general meaning.

give[1] (g-), *v.* (p.t. *gāve*; p.p. *given*), hand over gratuitously, make a present of; grant; deliver; pledge; devote; present; offer; impart, be source of; collapse, yield, shrink. *give in,* yield. *give off,* emit, send out. *give up,* (esp.) resign, surrender; abandon *oneself to;* do without. *give way,* break, yield; give place, right of way, (*to*). **give'able,** *a.*

give[2] (g-), *n.* yielding to pressure; elasticity. **give-and-take,** mutual concession, exchange of talk.

giv'en (g-), *a.* (esp.) prone, inclined (*to*); stated, fixed, specified. **given name,** Christian name, first name.

gizz'ard (g-), *n.* bird's second stomach for grinding food.

gla'cé (-sā), *a.* sugared, crystallized.

glā'cial (*or* -shl), *a.* of ice, icy.

glā'ciāted (*or* gla-), *a.* marked or polished by the action of ice; covered with glaciers. **glā'ciā'tion,** *n.*

gla'cier (*or* glā-), *n.* slowly moving mass or river of ice in mountain valley.

glad, *a.* pleased; joyful. **gladd'en,** *v.t.* make glad.

glāde, *n.* clear space in forest.

glad'iātor, *n.* trained fighter in ancient Roman shows. **gladiator'ial,** *a.*

gladiō'lus, *n.* (pl. *gladioli*), plant of iris kind with bright flower-spikes.

glad'some, *a.* joyful, blithe.

glad'stone bag, light portmanteau.

glam'our (-er), *n.* enchantment; alluring charm. **glam'orīze,** *v.t.* **glam'orous,** *a.*

glance (-ah-), *v.* give brief or momentary look (*at*); glide *off* object. *n.* brief look; swift sideways movement or impact.

gland, *n.* organ secreting chemical compounds required for particular function of body. **glan'dūlar,** *a.*

glāre, *v.i.* shine disagreeably; look fiercely. *n.* strong light; fierce look. **glār'ing,** *a.* disagreeably bright; conspicuous; (of colour, etc.) crude, gaudy.

glass (-ah-), *n.* substance, usu. transparent, hard, and brittle, made from sand and other ingredients; glass drinking-vessel; looking--glass; lens; telescope, barometer, etc.; (pl.) spectacles, field-glasses. **glass'-blower,** one who fashions glassware by blowing molten glass. **glass-house,** greenhouse. **glass'y,** *a.* like glass; (of eye) fixed, dull.

glāze, *v.* fit with glass or windows; cover (pottery, etc.) with glass-like substance, or (surface) with glossy coating; (of eye) become glassy. *n.* substance used for, surface pro-

duced by, glazing. **glā'zier,** *n.* one whose trade is to glaze windows, etc.

gleam, *n.* soft or fitful light. *v.i.* emit gleam(s).

glean, *v.* gather corn left by reapers; pick up (facts, news, etc.). **glea'ner,** *n.* **glea'nings** (-z), *n.pl.*

glēbe, *n.* land forming part of clergyman's benefice; (Poet.) land, field.

glee, *n.* musical composition for three or more voices; mirth. **glee'ful,** *a.* joyful.

glen, *n.* narrow valley.

glenga'rry (-n-g-), *n.* flat-sided Highland cap, creased from front to back.

glib, *a.* fluent, voluble, plausible.

glide, *v.* pass, move on, smoothly; go stealthily; (of aircraft) fly without engines. *n.* gliding movement. **gli'der,** *n.* engineless aircraft.

glimm'er, *v.i.* shine faintly or fitfully. *n.* feeble light; faint gleam (*of* hope, etc.).

glimpse, *n.* momentary or imperfect view. *v.* catch glimpse of.

glint, *v.i.* & *n.* flash, glitter.

glissade' (-ahd), *n.* & *v.i.* slide down slope of snow or ice.

glis'ten (-sn), *v.i.* shine with twinkling light; sparkle.

glitt'er, *v.i.* & *n.* gleam, sparkle.

gloa'ming, *n.* evening twilight.

gloat, *v.i.* feast eyes or mind greedily, evilly, etc. (*on* or *over*).

glō'bal, *a.* world-wide.

glōbe, *n.* sphere; *the* earth; spherical chart of earth or constellations; (nearly) spherical glass vessel or cover.

glob'ūlar, *a.* globe-shaped; composed of globules.

glob'ūle, *n.* small spherical body, esp. of liquid.

glob'ūlin, *n.* simple protein found in animal and plant tissue.

glōōm, *n.* darkness; melancholy. *v.i.* look or be depressed. **glōō'my,** *a.* dark; dismal; sullen. **glōō'mily,** *adv.*

glor'ia, *n.* doxology beginning 'Glory to the Father'.

glor'ifÿ, *v.t.* make glorious or radiant; praise highly. **glorificā'tion,** *n.*

glor'ious, *a.* possessing or conferring glory; splendid, magnificent.

glor'y, *n.* honourable fame; resplendent majesty, beauty, etc.; halo of saint. *v.i.* exult *in.*

gloss[1], *n.* smooth lustrous surface; deceptively fair appearance. *v.t.* give gloss to. *gloss over,* (fig.) give deceptively favourable appearance to.

gloss[2], *n.* marginal explanation; comment, interpretation. *v.t.* insert glosses in, make or write gloss on; explain away.

gloss'ary, *n.* dictionary of technical or special words, partial dictionary.

gloss'y, *a.* shiny.

glott'is, *n.* opening at upper part of windpipe and between vocal cords. **glott'al,** *a.*

glove (-uv), *n.* hand-covering of leather, cotton, etc. *v.t.* provide with gloves. **glo'ver,** *n.* maker or seller of gloves.

glow (-ō), *v.i.* emit flameless light and heat; burn with bodily heat or emotion; show warm colour. *n.* glowing state; ardour. **glow--worm,** beetle which emits green light from abdomen.

glower, *v.i.* look angrily, (*at*).

glu'cose (gloo-), *n.* kind of sugar found in blood, fruits, etc.

glue (gloo), *n.* substance used for sticking things together. *v.t.* stick with glue. **glue'y** (gloo'i), *a.*

glum, *a.* (*glummer, glummest*), dejected, sullen.

glut, *v.t.* (p.t. *glutted*), feed or indulge to the full, satiate; over-stock. *n.* surfeit; excessive supply.

glu'ten (gloo-), *n.* sticky substance in flour. **glu'tinous,** *a.* sticky, glue-like.

glutt'on, *n.* one who eats excessively; person insatiably eager *for.* **glutt'onous,** *a.* **glutt'-ony,** *n.*

gly'cerine (-ēn), *n.* colourless sweet liquid obtained from oils or fats.

gnarled (narld), *a.* twisted, rough, knobbly.

gnash (n-), *v.* grind (one's teeth).

gnat (n-), *n.* small biting or irritating fly; (Zool.) mosquito.

gnaw (n-), *v.* (p.p. *gnawed*; p.t. *gnawed, gnawn*), bite persistently, wear away thus; (of pain, remorse, etc.) torment, consume.

gnome (nōm), *n.* goblin, dwarf. **gnō'mish,** *a.*

gnō'mon (n-), *n.* rod showing time by its shadow on marked surface of sundial.

gnu (gnoo), *n.* wildebeest.

gō, *v.i.* (p.t. *went*; p.p. *gone*) start, depart; move; pass; walk, travel, proceed; become; (of money) be spent in or on; collapse, give way; extend, reach. **go by,** be guided by, pass. **go on,** continue, happen. **go out,** be extinguished. **go under,** fail, sink, succumb. *n.* (pl. *gōes*), animation; success; turn. **go--ahead,** enterprising. **go-between,** agent between two parties. **go-kart,** (also *kart*) miniature racing-car with skeleton body.

goad, *n.* spiked stick used for urging cattle; thing that incites or torments. *v.t.* urge with goad; drive by annoyance.

goal, *n.* point marking end of race; object of effort; destination; posts between which football, etc., is to be driven, point so won. **goal keeper,** player protecting goal.

goat, *n.* small horned ruminant mammal. **goatee',** *n.* small beard like that of goat. **goat'herd,** *n.* one who tends goats.

gobb'le¹, *v.* eat hurriedly and noisily.

gobb'le², *v.i.* (of turkey-cock) make characteristic sound in throat. **gobb'ler,** *n.* turkey--cock.

gob'lèt, *n.* glass with foot and stem; (*archaic*) bowl-shaped drinking-cup.

gob'lin, *n.* mischievous and ugly spirit or demon.

god, *n.* (*God*) supreme being, creator and ruler of universe; superhuman being worshipped as having divine power; idol. **god'child,** baptized child in relation to godparent. **god'-father, god'mother,** male, female, godparent. **god'fearing,** religious. **god'forsaken,** dismal, forlorn. **god'parent,** person who takes vows on behalf of child at baptism. **god'send,** unexpected welcome event or acquisition. **god'son, god-daughter,** male, female, godchild. **god'less,** *a.* not recognizing God; impious, wicked. **god'like,** *a.* like God or a god. **god'ly,** *a.* pious, devout.

godd'ess, *n.* female deity.

god'head (-hed), *n.* being God or a god; deity; God.

goff'er, goph'er (*or* gō-), *v.t.* make wavy, crimp, with hot irons.

gogg'le, *v.i.* roll eyes about; (of eyes) open widely, protrude. *n.* (pl.) spectacles for protecting eyes from glare, dust, etc. **gogg'le--eyed,** *a.* having prominent or staring eyes.

gō'ing, *n.* (esp.) state of ground for riding, walking, etc. *a.* in action; to be had.

goi'tre (-ter), *n.* enlargement of thyroid gland.

gōld, *n.* precious yellow metal; coins of this; wealth; colour of gold. *a.* of, coloured like, gold. **gold'finch,** bright-coloured song-bird with yellow feathers in wings. **gold'fish,** small golden-red Chinese carp. **gold leaf,** gold beaten into thin sheet. **gold'smith,** smith working in gold.

gō'lden, *a.* of gold, coloured or shining like gold; precious, excellent, important. **golden--rod,** plant with yellow flower-spikes. **golden wedding,** 50th wedding anniversary.

golf, *n.* outdoor game played with clubs (*golf--clubs*) and small hard ball on prepared course (*golf-course, golf-links*). **gol'fer,** *n.*

goll'iwog, *n.* quaint black (male) doll with woolly hair.

golosh: see **galosh.**

gon'dola, *n.* light boat used on canals in Venice; car suspended from airship, etc. **gondol-ier'** (-ēr), *n.* rower of gondola.

gone, *p.p.* of **go.**

gong, *n.* metal disc giving a ringing note when struck.

gonorrhoe'a (-rēa), *n.* a venereal disease.

good, *a.* (*better, best*), having right qualities, adequate; virtuous, morally excellent; worthy; proper; well-behaved; benevolent; agreeable; suitable; considerable. *n.* profit, well-being; (pl.) merchandise, movable property. **good afternoon, evening, morning, night,** salutations at meeting or parting. **good-for-nothing,** worthless (person). **good humour,** cheerful mood, friendliness; **good--humoured,** (*a.*). **good-looking,** handsome. **good-natured,** kindly. **good people,** fairies. **good'ly,** *a.* handsome; of imposing size, etc.

good-bȳe′, *int.* expressing good wishes at parting. *n.* leave-taking, saying good-bye.

good′ness, *n.* virtue; excellence; kindness.

goodwill′, *n.* kindly feeling; established custom or popularity of shop, etc.

good′y, *n.* sweet, bonbon; (*archaic*) old woman. **good′y-goody**, *a.* & *n.* primly or obtrusively virtuous (person).

goo′fy, *a.* (*slang*) silly, stupid.

goose, *n.* (pl. *geese*, pr. **gēs**), web-footed bird between duck and swan in size; simpleton. **goose-flesh**, rough bristling state of skin due to cold or fright. **goose-step**, marching-step with knees kept stiff.

goose′berry (-zb-), *n.* a thorny shrub; its edible berry.

gopher: see **goffer.**

Gor′dian, *a. cut the Gordian knot*, solve problem by force or evasion.

gore[1], *n.* clotted blood.

gore[2], *n.* triangular-shaped piece of cloth in garment, etc. *v.t.* shape with gore.

gore[3], *v.t.* (of horned animals) pierce or wound with horns.

gorge, *n.* narrow opening between hills; contents of stomach. *v.* feed greedily; satiate.

gor′geous (-jus), *a.* richly coloured; splendid, magnificent.

gor′gon, *n.* (Gk. myth.) one of three sisters with snakes for hair, whose looks turned beholder to stone.

gorgonzo′la, *n.* rich Italian cheese.

gorill′a, *n.* large powerful anthropoid ape.

gor′mandīze, *v.t.* eat gluttonously.

gorse, *n.* prickly yellow-flowered shrub; furze, whin.

gor′y, *a.* covered with blood; involving (much) bloodshed.

gos′hawk (-s-h-), *n.* large short-winged hawk.

gos′ling (-z-), *n.* young goose.

Gos′pel, *n.* any of the records of Christ's life by the four evangelists; news of kingdom of God preached by Christ; (*gospel*) thing to be believed, principle one acts upon or preaches.

goss′amer, *n.* filmy substance of small spiders' webs; flimsy thing. *a.* light, flimsy, as gossamer.

goss′ip, *n.* idle, often ill-natured, talk or writing, esp. about persons; idle talker. *v.i.* talk gossip; chatter idly. **goss′ipy**, *a.*

got, *p.t.* & *p.p.* of **get.**

Goth, *n.* one of Germanic invaders of E. and W. Roman Empires in 3rd - 5th cents.; uncivilized person, vandal. **Goth′ic**, *a.* of the Goths; of black-letter type used for printing German; (Archit.) in the pointed-arch style. *n.* Gothic language, architecture, type.

gotten: see **get.**

gouge (gowj), *n.* chisel with concave blade. *v.t.* cut or force (*out*) with or as with gouge.

gou′lash (gōō-), *n.* stew of steak and vegetables seasoned with paprika.

gourd (goord), *n.* (large fleshy fruit of) any of various trailing or climbing plants; dried rind of the fruit used as bottle.

gour′mand (goor-), *n.* lover of good fare; glutton.

gourmet (goor′mā), *n.* connoisseur of table delicacies and wine.

gout (gowt), *n.* disease with painful inflammation of small joints; drop, esp. of blood. **gou′ty**, *a.*

go′vern (gu-), *v.* rule with authority; conduct policy and affairs of State, etc.; control, sway, influence.

go′verness (gu-), *n.* woman teacher, esp. in private household.

go′vernment (gu-), *n.* act, manner, fact, of governing; persons governing State; State as agent; administration or ministry. **government′al**, *a.*

go′vernor (gu-), *n.* ruler; official governing province, town, etc.; one of governing body of institution. **Governor General**, sovereign's representative in non--independent Commonwealth countries.

gown, *n.* woman's dress, esp. formal or elegant; robe of alderman, clergyman, judge, member of university, etc. *v.t.* attire in gown.

grab, *v.* (p.t. *grabbed*), seize suddenly or greedily. *n.* sudden clutch or attempt to seize.

grace, *n.* quality of being attractive or beautiful, esp. in structure or movement; accomplishment, ornament; favour; goodwill; divine kindness and mercy; delay granted; thanksgiving at meals. *with a good* (*bad*) *grace*, (un)willingly. *his, her, your, Grace*, forms for addressing duke, duchess, or archbishop. *v.t.* adorn; honour. **grace′ful**, *a.* full of grace or charm. **grace′fully**, *adv.* **grace′less**, *a.*

grā′cious (-shus), *a.* pleasing; kindly; merciful; condescending.

gradāte′, *v.* (cause to) pass gradually from one shade of colour to another; arrange in gradations.

gradā′tion, *n.* each stage in transition or advance; series of degrees in rank, intensity, etc.; arrangement in grades.

grāde, *n.* degree in rank, merit, etc.; gradient, slope. *make the grade*, succeed. *v.t.* arrange in grades; reduce to easy gradients.

grā′dient, *n.* (amount of) slope in road, railway, etc.

grad′ual, *a.* happening slowly, by degrees; not steep or abrupt. **grad′ually**, *adv.*

grăd′ūăte, *v.* take academic degree; arrange in gradations; mark in degrees or portions. **grad′ūate**, *n.* holder of academic degree. **gradūā′tion**, *n.*

graft[1] (-ah-), *n.* shoot inserted in slit of another stock; piece of transplanted living tissue. *v.t.* insert as graft, insert graft(s). (Surg.) transplant (living tissue).

graft[2], *n.* (practices for securing) dishonest or

unlawful political or business profit or advantage. *v. i.* practise graft.

grail, *n.* (also *holy grail*) legendary platter used by Christ at the Last Supper.

grain, *n.* small hard seed of cereal; corn; wheat; tiny particle; smallest unit in some systems of weight; texture in skin, wood, stone, etc.; arrangement of lines of fibre in wood. *v. t.* paint in imitation of grain of wood.

gram, gramme, *n.* unit of mass or weight in metric system (0·035 oz.).

gramm'alogue (-og), *n.* (Shorthand) word represented by a single sign.

gramm'ar, *n.* study of a language's inflexions or other means of showing relationship between words, rules for employing these; book on grammar. **grammar school**, secondary school with academic curriculum. **grammar'ian**, *n.* expert in grammar. **grammat'ical**, *a.* of, according to rules of, grammar.

gramme: see **gram**.

gram'ophŏne, *n.* apparatus for reproducing sounds recorded on flat discs (*gramophone records*).

gram'pus, *n.* any of various blowing and spouting marine mammals.

gran'ary, *n.* storehouse for grain.

grand, *a.* (in titles) chief, of highest rank; of great importance; splendid; lofty, noble; dignified. *n.* grand piano. **grand'child**, one's child's child. **grand-daughter**, one's child's daughter. **grand'father, grand'mother**, one's parent's father, mother. **grand'father clock**, clock in tall wooden case. **grand'ma, grand'pa**, grandmother, grandfather. **grand piano**, large piano with strings horizontal. **grand'son**, one's child's son. **grand'stand**, principal stand for spectators at races, etc.

grandee', *n.* Spanish or Portuguese nobleman of highest rank.

gran'deur (-dyer), *n.* quality of being grand; majesty, dignity; splendour.

grandil'oquent, *a.* using pompous language. **grandil'oquence**, *n.*

gran'diŏse, *a.* imposing; planned on large scale. **grandios'ity**, *n.*

grânge (-nj), *n.* country-house with farm buildings.

gran'ite, *n.* hard crystalline rock of quartz, mica, etc., used in building.

grann'y, *n.* (*informal*) grandmother; **granny (knot)**, reef-knot crossed the wrong way.

grant (-ah-), *v. t.* consent to give; allow, permit; admit as valid or true. *take for granted*, regard as true or certain to happen. *n.* thing or sum granted.

gran'ūlar, *a.* of or like grains. **gran'ūlāte**, *v.* form into grains; roughen surface of. **granūlā'tion**, *n.* **gran'ūle**, *n.* small grain.

grâpe, *n.* green or purple berry growing in clusters on vine. **grape'fruit**, fruit like large orange, growing in clusters. **grape-shot**, (Hist.) small balls as scattering-charge for cannon. **grape-vine**, (*informal*) channels by which rumours are carried.

graph (*or* -ahf), *n.* diagram showing relation between two variables.

graph'ic, *a.* of drawing, painting, engraving, etc.; vividly descriptive; of writing; of diagrams or graphs.

graph'īte, *n.* soft black form of carbon used in pencils, as lubricant, polish, etc.

grap'nel, *n.* small anchor with several flukes; grappling-iron.

grapp'le, *n.* clutching instrument; grip (as) of wrestler; close contest. *v.* seize, grip; come to close quarters with. **grapp'ling-iron**, iron--clawed instrument thrown to seize and hold (esp., formerly, enemy's ship).

grasp (-ah-) *v.* seize greedily; hold firmly; understand, realize. *n.* fast hold, grip; mental hold, mastery. **gras'ping**, *a.* (esp.) greedy, avaricious.

grass (-ah-), *n.* common low-growing plant, blade-like leaves and stalks of which are eaten by horses, cattle, etc.; grazing; pasture land, lawn. **grass'hopper**, *n.* jumping insect making chirping sound. **grass'land**, land covered with grass. **grass roots**, fundamental level or source. **grass-snake**, harmless common ringed snake. **grass'y**, *a.*

grāte[1], *n.* frame of metal bars holding fuel in fireplace, etc.

grāte[2], *v.* rub to small particles on rough surface; grind, creak; have irritating effect. **grā'ter**, *n.* utensil for grating.

grāte'ful (-tf-), *a.* thankful; feeling or showing gratitude.

grat'ify̆, *v. t.* please, delight; satisfy; indulge. **gratificā'tion**, *n.*

grā'ting, *n.* framework of parallel or crossed metal or wooden bars.

grā'tis (*or* gra-), *adv. & a.* (given, done) without charge, free.

grat'itŭde, *n.* being thankful; appreciation of and desire to return kindness.

gratū'itous, *a.* got or done free; uncalled for. **gratū'ity**, *n.* tip; bounty to soldier, etc.

grāve[1], *n.* hole dug for corpse. *grave clothes*, wrappings of corpse. **grave'stone**, inscribed stone over grave. **grave'yard**, burial ground.

grāve[2], *v. t.* (p.p. **graven, graved**), engrave, carve; (fig.) fix indelibly (*on, in*, mind, etc.). **grā'ven image**, idol.

grāve[3], *a.* serious; dignified, solemn. **grave accent** (grahv), the accent (`).

grav'el, *n.* coarse sand and small stones. *v. t.* (p.t. *gravelled*), lay with gravel.

grav'itāte, *v. i.* move or tend by force of gravity; sink (as) by gravity; be attracted to(*wards*). **gravitā'tion**, *n.*

grav'ity, *n.* solemnity; importance; weight; force by which bodies are attracted towards centre of earth (or other celestial body).

grā'vy, *n.* (sauce made from) juices that exude from meat in cooking.

gray: see **grey.**

gray'ling, *n.* silver-grey freshwater fish.

gräze[1], *v.* touch lightly in passing; abrade (skin etc.) in rubbing past. *n.* grazing; abrasion.

gräze[2], *v.* feed on growing grass; pasture cattle. **grä'zing,** *n.* pasture. **grä'zier** (*or* -zher), *n.* person who feeds cattle for market.

grease, *n.* melted fat of dead animal; fatty or oily matter, esp. as lubricant. *v.t.* smear, lubricate, soil, with grease. **grease-paint,** composition for painting actors' faces. **greas'er,** *n.* (esp. ship's) fireman. **greas'y,** *a.* of, like, smeared with, grease; slimy.

great (grāt), *a.* occupying much space, large, big; considerable in extent or degree; important, pre-eminent; of remarkable ability; (prefixed to terms denoting kinship) one degree farther removed (*great-aunt, great-grandmother, great-nephew,* etc.). **Great Britain:** see **Britain. great'coat,** large overcoat. **great'ly,** *adv.* much. **great'ness,** *n.*

grēbe, *n.* almost tailless diving bird.

Grē'cian (-shn), *a.* Greek.

greed, *n.* excessive desire for food or wealth. **gree'dy,** *a.* gluttonous, avaricious, rapacious. **gree'dily,** *adv.*

Greek, *n.* native of Greece; Greek language. *a.* of Greece or its people.

green, *a.* of colour like grass; unripe; inexperienced; not seasoned or dried. *n.* green colour; grassy common; grass plot for special purpose; (pl.) green vegetables. **green belt,** area of countryside surrounding town, etc., where building is severely restricted. **green finch,** bird with gold and green plumage. **green'fly,** aphis. **green'gage,** roundish green plum. **green'horn,** inexperienced and easily deceived person. **green'house,** building with sides and roof of glass, etc., for delicate plants. **green-room,** room for actors when off stage. **green'stuff,** vegetables. **green'sward,** (Poet.) turf. **green'wood,** woodlands in summer esp. as scene of outlaw life. **green'ish,** *a.* **green'ness,** *n.*

gree'nery, *n.* green foliage.

green'grocer, *n.* one who sells fruit and vegetables. **green'grocery,** *n.*

Greenwich (grin'ij; *or* gren'-). *Greenwich (mean) time* (abbrev. *G.M.T.*), local time of meridian of Greenwich, London, (*prime meridian*).

greet[1], *v.t.* say words of salutation or welcome to; salute, receive (with words, applause, etc.); (of sight, sound, etc.) meet (eye, ear, etc.). **gree'ting,** *n.*

greet[2], *v.i.* (Sc.) weep.

gregār'ious, *a.* living in flocks or communities; fond of company.

grenäde', *n.* small explosive shell thrown by hand (*hand-grenade*), or shot from rifle. **grenadier'** (-ēr), *n.* (Hist.) soldier who threw grenades. **Grenadier Guards,** first regiment of household infantry.

grew, *p.t.* of **grow.**

grey (grā), **gray,** *a.* between black and white in colour, like ashes or lead; clouded, dull. *n.* grey colour; grey horse; cold, sunless light. *v.* make or become grey. **grey'beard,** old man.

grey'hound, *n.* slender swift dog used in coursing hares, etc.

grey'lag, *n.* European wild goose.

grid, *n.* grating; network of lines, railways, electric-power connections, etc.

gridd'le, *n.* girdle[2].

grid'iron (-īrn), *n.* framework of parallel metal bars placed over fire for broiling meat, etc.

grief, *n.* deep or violent sorrow. *come to grief,* meet with disaster, fail.

grie'vance, *n.* real or imagined cause for complaint.

grieve, *v.* give deep sorrow to; feel grief.

grie'vous, *a.* bringing serious trouble or suffering; severe; causing grief.

griff'in, griff'on, gryph'on, *n.* fabulous creature with eagle's head and wings, and lion's body.

grill[1], *n.* barred metal cooking utensil; grilled food; (also *grill-room*) room in restaurant, etc., where food is grilled and served. *v.* cook directly over or under great heat; subject (prisoner, etc.) to severe questioning.

grill[2], **grille,** *n.* grating; latticed screen.

grim, *a.* (*grimmer, grimmest*), stern; severe; ghastly, joyless.

grimäce', *n.* wry face made in disgust or in jest. *v.i.* make grimace.

grimal'kin (-awl-), *n.* old she-cat.

grime, *n.* dirt deeply ingrained. *v.t.* blacken, make dirty. **grī'my,** *a.*

grin, *v.i.* (p.t. *grinned*), show teeth in pain or forced smile; smile broadly. *n.* act of grinning; broad or forced or mirthless smile.

grind, *v.* (p.t. *ground*), crush to small particles; sharpen; study hard; rub gratingly. *n.* hard dull work or task.

grin'der, *n.* thing, person, that grinds; molar tooth.

grind'stone, *n.* (stone used for) revolving disc for grinding, sharpening, etc.

grip, *n.* firm hold, grasp. *v.* (p.t. *gripped*), grasp tightly; take firm hold.

gripe, *v.t.* affect with intermittent spasmodic pain in intestines.

gris'ly (-z-), *a.* causing terror or horror.

grist, *n.* corn for grinding.

gri'stle (-sl), *n.* tough flexible tissues, esp. in meat, cartilage. **gri'stly** (-sli), *a.*

grit, *n.* particles of stone or sand; (*informal*) pluck, endurance. *v.* (p.t. *gritted*), make grating sound; grind or clench (teeth). **gritt'y,** *a.*

grizz'le, *v.i.* (*informal*) whimper, cry fretfully.

grizz'led (-zld), *a.* grey-haired.

grizz'ly, *a.* grey, grey-haired. **grizzly bear,**

large fierce N. American bear.

groan, v. make deep sound expressing pain or grief or disapproval; be oppressed or loaded. n. groaning sound.

groat, n. (Hist.) silver fourpenny piece.

groats, n.pl. hulled (and crushed) grain, esp. oats.

grō'cer, n. dealer in household foods and other stores. **grō'cery**, n.

grog, n. drink of spirits, esp. rum, and water.

grogg'y (-g-), a. tottering; unsteady; shaky.

groin, n. depression between belly and thigh.

grōōm, n. servant who tends horses; bridegroom. v.t. clean, brush, tend, (horse); give smart appearance to. **grooms'man** (-z-), n. (pl. -men), friend attending bridegroom at wedding.

grōōve, n. channel or hollow; routine, rut. v.t. make groove(s) in.

grōpe, v.i. feel about as in the dark (for, after); search blindly. **grope one's way**, find way by feeling, move cautiously.

grōss[1], n. (pl. same), twelve dozen (144).

grōss[2], a. overfed; glaring; total, not net; coarse, indecent. **gross national product,** all goods produced and services provided in a country in one year.

grōtesque' (-sk), n. fantastic style of decorative art. a. distorted; absurd.

grott'ō, n. (pl. grottoes), picturesque cave; structure imitating cave.

ground[1], p.t. & p.p. of **grind.**

ground[2], n. surface of earth; land; bottom of sea, etc.; underlying part, surface; foundation; motive, reason; (pl.) enclosed land attached to house; (pl.) dregs. v. fix in the ground; base, establish; instruct thoroughly; run ashore; keep on ground, prevent (aircraft) from flying. **ground-bait,** bait thrown to bottom to attract fish. **ground floor,** storey on level of outside ground. **ground-nut,** peanut. **ground-rent,** rent paid for ground leased for building. **ground'sheet,** protective waterproof sheet spread on ground. **grounds'man** (-z-), man in charge of cricket ground, etc. **ground staff,** non-flying members of staff of airfield. **ground-swell,** heavy sea due to distant storm. **ground'work,** foundation.

groun'ding, n. (esp.) instruction in elements of subject.

ground'less, a. without reason or foundation.

ground'sel, n. common small weed.

group (-ōō-), n. number of persons or things near or belonging or classed together. v. form or fall into group; classify. **group-captain,** R.A.F. officer above wing commander.

grouse[1], n. (pl. same), game-bird with feathered feet.

grouse[2], v.i. & n. (slang) grumble.

grōve, n. small wood; group of trees.

grov'el, v.i. (p.t. grovelled), lie prone, abase oneself. **grov'eller**, n.

grow (-ō), v. (p.t. grew, pr. -ōō; p.p. grown,

pr. -ōn), develop or exist as living plant; produce by cultivation; increase in size, height, amount, etc.; become gradually. **gro'wer** (-ōer), n. (esp.) person growing produce.

growl, n. guttural sound of anger; rumble; murmur, complaint. v. make growl. **grow'-ler**, n. (esp., archaic) four-wheeled cab.

grown, p.p. of **grow.** **grown-up** (-ō-), n. & a. (person) having reached maturity.

growth (-ōth), n. increase; what has grown or is growing; morbid formation in the body.

groyne, n. structure of wood, etc., built out into sea to check drifting of beach.

grub, v. (p.t. grubbed), dig superficially; dig up by the roots; toil. n. larva of insect; (slang) food. **grubb'y**, a. (esp.) dirty, grimy.

grudge, v.t. be unwilling to give or allow. n. resentment; ill-will.

gru'el (-ōō-), n. liquid food of oatmeal, etc., boiled in milk or water. **gru'elling**, a. exhausting, severe.

grue'some (-ōōs-), a. horrible, grisly.

gruff, a. surly; rough-voiced.

grum'ble, n. complaint, protest; murmur, rumble. v. utter grumble; say grumblingly; complain; murmur. **grum'bler**, n.

grum'py, a. ill-tempered.

grunt, n. low gruff sound such as a pig makes. v.i. utter grunt.

gryphon: see **griffin.**

gua'nō (gwah-), n. droppings of sea-fowl used as fertilizer.

guarantee' (ga-), n. undertaking that certain conditions agreed to in a transaction will be fulfilled; undertaking to be responsible for performance of an obligation; security; guarantor. v.t. be guarantee for; answer for; secure. **guarantor'** n. giver of guarantee. **gua'ranty,** n. guarantee.

guard (gard), n. defensive posture; watch, vigilant state; protector; sentry; official in charge of train; device to prevent injury or accident; soldiers, etc., protecting place or person; (pl.) troops guarding or escorting sovereign. v. protect, defend; take precautions against. **guards'man** (-z-), n. (pl. -men), soldier of the guards.

guar'dian (gar-), n. keeper, protector; person having legal custody of a minor. **guar'-dianship,** n.

gua'va (gwah-), n. (tropical tree with) acid fruit used for jelly, etc.

gudg'eon[1], (-jn), n. small freshwater fish.

gudg'eon[2], (-jn), n. pivot or metal pin.

guel'der rōse (ge-), small tree with balls of white flowers.

guerrill'a (ger-), n. person engaged in irregular war (guerrilla warfare) waged by small bodies acting independently.

guess (ges), v. think likely; hazard opinion about. n. rough estimate, conjecture. **guess'work,** guessing.

guest (gest), n. person entertained at another's house or table, or lodging at hotel, etc.

guffaw', *n.* coarse or boisterous laugh; *v.i.* make guffaw.

gui'dance (gī-), *n.* guiding; direction.

guide (gīd), *n.* one who shows the way; professional conductor of traveller, climber, etc.; adviser; directing principle; (also *guide--book*) book of information about place, etc; (*Guide*), (formerly *Girl Guide*) member of organization parallel to Scouts. *v.t.* act as guide to; lead, direct. **guide-post**, sign-post.

guild, *n.* society for mutual aid or for forwarding common interests, esp. medieval trade- or craft-association. **guild'hall**, meeting--place of medieval guild; town hall.

guil'der (gi-), *n.* Dutch coin.

guile (gīl), *n.* treachery, deceit. **guile'ful**, *a.* **guile'less**, *a.*

guill'emot (gi-), *n.* sea-bird of auk family.

guillotine (gil'otēn), *n.* beheading machine; (in Parliament) method of shortening discussion of bill by fixing times for taking votes. *v.t.* execute on guillotine.

guilt (gi-), *n.* fact of having committed an offence; culpability. **guilt'less**, *a.* innocent.

guil'ty (gi-), *a.* having committed an offence, culpable; conscious of guilt.

guinea (gin'i), *n.* (Hist.) English gold coin; sum of 21s. **guinea-fowl**, bird with white--spotted grey plumage. **guinea-pig**, small S. American tailless rodent, kept as pet or for biological research.

guise (gīz), *n.* external, esp. assumed, appearance; pretence.

guitar' (gi-), *n.* musical instrument with flat back, strings plucked by right hand, and fretted finger-board for left hand.

gulf, *n.* part of sea like a bay but usu. narrower at mouth; deep hollow, chasm; impassable dividing line. **Gulf-stream**, warm oceanic current from Gulf of Mexico.

gull[1], *n.* any of various long-winged sea-birds found mostly near coast.

gull[2], *n. & v.t.* dupe, fool. **gull'ible**, *a.* **gulli-bil'ity**, *n.*

gull'et, *n.* food-passage from mouth to stomach; throat.

gull'y, *n.* water-worn ravine; gutter, drain.

gulp, *v.* swallow hastily or with effort; gasp. *n.* act of gulping; effort to swallow; large mouthful.

gum[1], *n.* firm flesh in which the teeth stand. **gum'boil**, small abscess on gum.

gum[2], *n.* sticky substance obtained from some trees and shrubs, used as glue, etc.; sweet made with gelatine; gum-tree. *v.t.* (p.t. *gummed*), apply gum to; stick with gum. **gum'boot**, rubber boot. **gum-tree**, any tree exuding gum (esp. Australian eucalyptus). **gumm'y**, *a.* sticky.

gump'tion, *n.* (*informal*) practical sense.

gun, *n.* general name for firearms, e.g. cannon, shot-gun, rifle; revolver. **gun'boat**, small warship with heavy guns. **gun--carriage**, wheeled framework for gun. **gun--cotton**, explosive of cotton steeped in nitric and sulphuric acids. **gun'fire**, firing of gun(s). **gun-metal**, alloy of copper and tin or zinc; dark brownish-grey colour. **gun'-powder**, kind of explosive. **gun-running**, smuggling of firearms. **gun'shot**, (*n.*) range of gun; (*a.*) caused by shot from gun(s). **gun'smith**, maker of small firearms.

gunnel: see **gunwale.**

gunn'er, *n.* officer or man of artillery; (Naut.) warrant officer in charge of battery, etc. **gunn'ery**, *n.* management of large guns.

gunn'y, *n.* coarse sacking or sack, usu. of jute fibre.

gunwale (gu'nl), **gunn'el**, *n.* upper edge of ship's or boat's side.

gur'gle, *n.* bubbling sound. *v.i.* make, utter with, gurgle(s).

gush, *n.* sudden or abundant flow; exaggerated or affected enthusiasm. *v.i.* flow with gush; speak or behave with gush.

guss'et, *n.* piece of material inserted to strengthen or enlarge garment, etc.

gust, *n.* sudden violent rush of wind; burst of rain, hail, smoke, etc.; outburst of feeling. **gus'ty**, *a.*

gus'tō, *n.* zest, enjoyment.

gut, *n.* (pl.) bowels or entrails; intestine; catgut; (pl., *slang*) courage. *v.t.* (p.t. *gutted*), remove guts of; remove or destroy internal fittings of (house, etc.).

gutta-per'cha, *n.* rubber-like substance obtained from juice of some Malayan trees.

gutt'er, *n.* shallow trough below eaves, channel at side of street, carrying off water; channel, groove. *v.i.* (of candle) melt away rapidly by becoming channelled on one side. **gutt'ersnipe**, *n.* poor child living mainly in the streets.

gutt'ural, *a.* of or produced in the throat. *n.* guttural sound or letter.

guy[1] (gī), *n.* rope, chain, to steady crane-load, etc., or secure tent, etc. *v.t.* secure with guy(s).

guy[2] (gī), *n.* figure of Guy Fawkes burnt on 5th November; grotesquely dressed person. *v.t.* exhibit in effigy, ridicule by mimicry.

guzz'le, *v.* drink, eat, greedily. **guzz'ler**, *n.*

gȳbe, *v.* (of fore-and-aft sail and boom) swing to other side; make (sail) swing across, change course, thus.

gym, *n.* (*informal*) gymnasium, gymnastics. **gym-slip, -tunic**, girl's short sleeveless garment, worn esp. as school uniform.

gymkha'na (-kah-), *n.* horse- and pony--meeting for competitions, etc.

gymnä'sium (-z-), *n.* (pl. *gymnasiums, gymnasia*), room, etc., fitted up for gymnastics.

gym'nast, *n.* expert in gymnastics.

gymnas'tic, *a.* of gymnastics. **gymnas'tics**, *n.pl.* exercises developing muscles, esp. as done in gymnasium.

gynaecol'ogy (gīni-), *n.* science of diseases of

women. **gynaecolo′gical,** *a.* **gynaecol′ogist,** *n.*

gyp′sum, *n.* mineral from which plaster of Paris is made.

gypsy: see **gipsy.**

gȳrāte′, *v. i.* move in circle or spiral; revolve.

gȳrā′tion, *n.*

gȳr′ō, *n.* gyroscope.

gȳr′oscōpe, *n.* solid rotating wheel mounted in ring, with axis free to turn in any direction, used to maintain equilibrium, constant direction, etc. **gȳroscop′ic,** *a.*

H

hā′bèas cor′pus, (Law) writ requiring person to be brought before judge or into court, to investigate whether he is lawfully imprisoned. (Latin)

hab′erdasher, *n.* dealer in small articles of dress, thread, buttons, etc. **hab′erdashery,** *n.*

hab′it, *n.* settled tendency or practice; dress, esp. of religious order; (also *riding-habit*) woman's riding costume.

hab′itable, *a.* that can be inhabited.

hab′itat, *n.* natural home of plant or animal.

habitā′tion, *n.* inhabiting; dwelling-place.

habit′ūal, *a.* customary; constant, continual **habit′ūally,** *adv.*

habit′ūāte, *v. t.* accustom (*to*). **habitūā′tion,** *n.*

habit′ūé (-ā), *n.* frequent visitor (*of* theatre, restaurant, etc.).

hack¹, *v.* cut roughly, chop, mangle; kick; emit short dry coughs. *n.* gash, wound. **hack-saw,** saw for cutting metal.

hack², *n.* hired horse; horse for ordinary riding; hired, esp. literary, drudge. *v. i.* ride on road at ordinary pace.

hack′le, *n.* steel comb for dressing raw silk, flax, etc.; (pl.) long feathers on neck of domestic cock. *with hackles up,* angry, ready to fight.

hack′ney carriage (-rij), vehicle plying for hire.

hack′neyed (-nid), *a.* made common or trite by repetition.

had, *p. t.* & *p. p.* of **have.**

hadd′ock, *n.* sea-fish of cod family.

Hā′dēs (-z), *n.* (Gk. myth.) the underworld, abode of the spirits of the dead.

haemo-, hemo-, *pref.* blood.

haemoglō′bin (hē-), *n.* oxygen-carrying pigment of red blood-cells of vertebrates.

haemophil′ia (hē-), *n.* hereditary condition in which person's blood will not clot. **haemophil′iac,** *a.* & *n.*

haemorrhage, hemorrhage (hem′orij), *n.* bleeding, esp. profuse.

haemorrhoid, hemorrhoid (hem′oroid), *n.* (usu. in pl.) varicose vein of lower rectum or anus.

haft (hah-), *n.* handle (of knife, etc.).

hag, *n.* ugly old woman.

hagg′ard, *a.* wild-looking (esp. from fatigue, suffering, etc.).

hagg′is (-g-), *n.* minced heart, liver, etc., of sheep boiled in maw with oatmeal, etc.

hagg′le, *v.* dispute, esp. about price or terms.

hagiog′raphy (-gi-), *n.* (writing of) life or lives of saint(s).

ha ha (hah hah), *int.* representing laughter.

ha-ha (hah′hah), *n.* sunk fence bounding park or garden.

hail¹, *n.* pellets of condensed and frozen vapour falling in shower. *v.* pour down as or like hail. **hail′stōne,** *n.* pellet of hail.

hail², *int.* of greeting. *v.* salute; call to; be come *from. n.* hailing.

hair, *n.* any or all of fine filaments growing from skin, esp. of human head; hair-like thing. **hair′breadth** (also *hair's breadth*), very small distance. **hair′dresser,** one who dresses and cuts hair. **hair′line,** (esp.) very thin line. **hair-raising,** full of excitement and terror. **hair′splitting,** making excessively subtle distinctions. **hair′less,** *a.* **hair′y,** *a.*

hāke, *n.* sea-fish of cod family.

hal′berd, *n.* (Hist.) combined spear and battle-axe. **halberdier′** (-ēr), *n.*

hal′cyon, *n.* bird fabled to calm wind and sea; kingfisher. *a.* calm, peaceful.

hāle, *a.* healthy, vigorous.

half (hahf), *n.* (pl. *halves*), one of two (esp. equal) parts into which thing is divided. *a.* amounting to half. *adv.* to extent of half; in part. **half-breed,** (person) of mixed race. **half-brother, -sister,** person related by one parent only. **half-caste,** half-breed. **half-crown,** (Hist.) British coin worth 2s. 6d. **half-hearted,** lacking zeal. **half-mast,** (of flag) lowered to half height of mast as sign of mourning. **half-moon,** (shape of) moon with disc half illuminated; crescent. **half-way,** equidistant from two ends. **half-wit(ted),** imbecile.

halfpenny (hā′pni, *n.* (pl. *halfpence,* pr. hā′pens, *halfpennies*), (coin worth) half a penny.

hal′ibut, *n.* large flat edible sea-fish.

halitō′sis, *n.* (Med.) foul breath.

hall (hawl), *n.* large public room; college dining-room; building for residence of students, etc.; residence of landed proprietor; entrance-passage of house.

hallelujah (-loo′ya), *int. & n.* alleluia.

halliard: see **halyard.**

hall′mark (hawl-), *n.* mark on gold and silver indicating standard of fineness, etc.

hallō′, *int. & n.* (pl. *hallos*), (cry) calling attention or expressing surprise or greeting.

hallōō′, *int. & n.* (cry) inciting dogs to chase, etc. *v.* cry halloo (esp. to dogs); shout.

hall′ow (-ō), *v.t.* make holy; honour as holy. **Hallowe′en,** (-ēn) eve of All Saints′ Day, 31st October.

hallucinā′tion (-lōō-), *n.* illusion; apparent seeing of object not actually present. **hallu′-cinatory,** *a.*

hallu′cinogen (-lōō-), *n.* drug causing hallucinations. **hallucinogen′ic,** *a.*

hal′ma, *n.* game played on board of 256 squares.

hā′lō, *n.* (pl. *haloes*), circle of light round sun, moon, etc.; disc of light round head of sacred figure in painting, etc.

halt[1] (hawlt *or* ho-), *n.* stoppage on march or journey. *v.* come, bring, to a stop.

halt[2] (hawlt *or* ho-), *a.* lame. *v.i.* limp; hesitate. **halt′ing,** *a.* **halt′ingly,** *adv.*

hal′ter (hawl- *or* hol-), *n.* rope or strap with noose or headstall for horses or cattle; rope with noose for hanging person.

halve (hahv), *v.t.* divide into halves; reduce to half.

hal′yard, hall′iard, *n.* rope or tackle for raising and lowering sail, etc.

ham, *n.* back of thigh; thigh and buttock; cured hog′s thigh; (*slang*) radio amateur; (*slang*) inexpert but flamboyant performer. **ham-fisted,** (*slang*) clumsy in using hands.

ham′burger (-ger), *n.* round cake of chopped beef, seasoned and fried.

ham′lêt, *n.* small village, esp. without church.

hamm′er, *n.* instrument for driving nails, beating, breaking, etc.; auctioneer′s mallet. *v.* strike or drive (as) with hammer.

hamm′ock, *n.* bed of canvas or netting suspended by cords at ends.

ham′per(, *n.* wickerwork packing-case.

ham′per), *v.t.* prevent free movement of; hinder.

ham′ster, *n.* small rodent with cheek-pouches for carrying grain.

ham′string, *n.* any of five tendons at back of human knee; tendon at back of hock. *v.t.* (p.t. *hamstrung*), cripple by cutting ham-

string(s).

hand, *n.* extremity of human arm beyond wrist or of limb of monkey, etc.; charge, agency, share (*in* doing); manual worker in factory, etc.; style, esp. of writing; pointer of clock, etc.; 4 in. as measure of horse′s height. *at hand,* near. *in hand,* available; receiving attention; under control. *to hand,* within reach, accessible. *v.t.* deliver or transfer (ås) with hand. *hand over,* give, transfer, with hand or otherwise. **hand′bag,** woman′s bag for carrying purse, etc. **hand′book,** small book giving useful facts or instructions. **hand′cuff,** (pl.) pair of metal rings joined by short chain, for fastening round prisoner′s wrists; (*v.t.*) secure with handcuffs. **hand′maid,** (*archaic*) female servant. **hand′shake,** clasp and shake of person′s hand with one′s own, as greeting, etc. **hand′writing,** (style of) writing by hand.

hand′ful (-ool), *n.* (pl. *handfuls*), enough to fill hand; small number or quantity.

han′dicap, *n.* disadvantage imposed on superior competitor to equalize chances; race, etc., in which handicaps are imposed; disadvantage, disability. *v.t.* (p.t. *handicapped*), impose handicap on; place at disadvantage.

han′dicraft (-ahft), *n.* manual art, trade, or skill.

han′diwork (-werk), *n.* thing done or made by hand or by action of person(s).

handkerchief (hang′kerchif), *n.* square of linen, cotton, silk, etc., used to wipe nose, etc.

han′dle, *n.* part of thing grasped by hand in using or moving it. *v.t.* touch or feel with hand(s); manage, deal with. **han′dlebar(s),** steering bar of bicycle, etc.

hand′some (-ns-), *a.* of fine appearance; generous, considerable.

han′dy, *a.* ready to hand; convenient to handle; clever with one′s hands. **han′dyman,** (pl. *-men*), man able to do all sorts of odd jobs.

hang, *v.* (p.t. *hung*; also *hanged,* as below), (cause to) be supported by hooks, etc., from above; cause to rest on hinges, etc.; attach (wallpaper); droop; depend (upon); (p.t. *hanged*), suspend, be suspended; by neck, esp. as capital punishment. **hang′man,** executioner. **hang′er,** *n.* (esp.) loop, etc., by which a thing hangs. **hang′ings,** *n.pl.* drapery for walls, etc.

hang′ar, *n.* shed for housing aircraft, etc.

hank, *n.* coil or length of yarn, wool, etc.

hank′er, *v.i.* crave, long, *after* or *for.*

hank′y-pank′y, *n.* underhand dealing.

han′som, *n.* (Hist.) two-wheeled cab, with driver seated high at back.

hap, *n.* (*archaic*) chance; luck. *v.i.* happen.

haphaz′ard (-p-h-), *n.* mere chance. *a.* casual. *adv.* casually.

hap′less, *a.* unlucky.

hap'ly, *adv.* (*archaic*) perhaps.

hā''p'orth, *n.* halfpennyworth.

happ'en, *v.i.* come about, occur, esp. by chance. **happ'ening**, *n.*

happ'y, *a.* fortunate; content, glad; apt. **happ'y-go-lucky**, *a.* haphazard, easy-going. **happ'ily**, *adv.* **happ'iness**, *n.*

ha'ra-ki'ri, *n.* Japanese method of suicide by disembowelment with sword.

harangue' (-ang), *n.* speech to assembly; vehement address. *v.* make harangue (to).

ha'rass, *v.t.* worry, trouble; attack repeatedly. **ha'rassment**, *n.*

har'binger (-j-), *n.* forerunner.

har'bour (-ber), *n.* place of shelter for ships; shelter. *v.* come to anchor in harbour; give shelter to; hold in the mind. **har'bourage**, *n.* shelter.

hard, *a.* firm, solid; stern, cruel; severe; harsh, unpleasant to eye or ear; strenuous; difficult to bear or do; (of drug) addictive; (of water) containing salts of calcium, etc., that prevent lathering of soap. *adv.* strenuously; with difficulty. *n.* firm beach or foreshore. **hard'back**, (book) bound in durable cover. **hard-head'ed**, shrewd; business-like. **hard-heart'ed**, unfeeling. **hard lines**, luck, worse fortune than is deserved. **hard up**, short of money. **hard'ware**, ironmongery. **hard-work'ing**, working with diligence. **har'den**, *v.* make or grow hard, callous, or hardy. **hard'ness**, *n.*

har'dihood, *n.* boldness, audacity.

hard'ly, *adv.* with difficulty; barely; harshly.

hard'ship, *n.* hardness of fate or circumstances; severe suffering or privation.

har'dy, *a.* bold; robust; capable of resisting exposure.

hāre, *n.* speedy mammal with long ears, short tail, and divided upper lip. **hare and hounds**, paper-chase. **hare'bell**, slender-stalked pale blue bell-flower. **hare-brained**, rash. **hare-lip**, cleft upper lip.

hār'em (*or* har'ēm), *n.* women's part of Muslim household; its occupants.

ha'ricot (-ō) *n.* (also *haricot bean*) dried ripe seed of French bean.

hark, *v.i.* listen. **hark back**, retrace course; revert (*to* subject).

har'lequin, *n.* (in pantomime) mute character in parti-coloured tights. **harlequināde'**, *n.* part of pantomime.

har'lot, *n.* (*archaic*) prostitute.

harm, *n.* & *v.t.* damage, hurt. **harm'ful**, *a.* that does harm. **harm'less**, *a.* doing no harm.

harmon'ic, *a.* of or relating to harmony.

harmon'ica, *n.* mouth-organ.

harmō'nious, *a.* in concord; tuneful.

harmō'nium, *n.* keyboard musical instrument with bellows and metal reeds.

har'monīze, *v.* bring into, be in, harmony; add notes to (melody) to form chords.

har'mony, *n.* agreement, concord; combina-

tion of notes to form chords; melodious sound.

har'nèss, *n.* equipment of reins, bit, collar, straps etc., for controlling horse, etc., and attaching it to vehicle, etc. *v.t.* put harness on; (fig.) control and use.

harp, *n.* musical instrument, roughly triangular, with strings of graduated lengths played with the fingers. *v.i.* play on harp; dwell tiresomely *on.* **har'pist**, *n.* harp-player.

harpoōn', *n.* spear-like missile for catching whales, etc. *v.t.* strike with harpoon.

harp'sichord (-k-), *n.* keyboard musical instrument with mechanically plucked strings, resembling grand piano in shape.

har'py, *n.* (Gk. & Rom. myth.) monster with woman's face and bird's wings and claws; grasping and cruel woman.

ha'rridan, *n.* haggard or fierce old woman.

ha'rrier, *n.* hound used in hunting hare.

ha'rrow (-ō), *n.* frame with metal teeth or discs for breaking clods, etc. *v.t.* draw harrow over; distress, wound.

ha'rry, *v.t.* harass; lay waste, plunder.

harsh, *a.* severe, unfeeling; rough, esp. to the senses.

hart, *n.* male of (esp. red) deer, esp. after fifth year.

hār'um-scār'um, *a.* & *adv.* reckless(ly).

har'vèst, *n.* season for reaping and storing of grain, etc.; season's yield. *v.t.* reap and gather in. **harvest festival**, service of thanksgiving for harvest. **har'vèster**, *n.* reaper; reaping-machine.

has: see **have.**

hash, *v.t.* cut (cooked meat, etc.) in small pieces. *n.* dish of hashed meat; mess, botch.

hash'ish, *n.* narcotic prepared from hemp.

hasp, *n.* fastening for door, etc., used with staple and pin or with padlock.

hass'ock, *n.* cushion for kneeling on.

hast (*archaic*) 2nd pers. sing. pres. of **have.**

hāste, *n.* urgency or quickness of movement; hurry. *make haste*, be quick.

hā'sten (-sn), *v.* (cause to) proceed or go quickly.

hā'sty, *a.* hurried; rash; quick-tempered. **hā'stily**, *adv.* **hā'stiness**, *n.*

hat, *n.* outdoor head-covering. **hat trick**, (Cricket) taking 3 wickets with 3 successive balls. *v.t.* (p.t. **hatted**), provide with hat.

hatch[1], *v.* (cause to) come forth from egg; incubate; form (plot). *n.* hatching; brood hatched. **hatch'ery**, *n.* place for hatching eggs, esp. of fish.

hatch[2], *n.* lower half of divided door; opening in wall, door, floor, etc.; hatchway, trapdoor over it. **hatch'way**, opening in ship's deck for lowering cargo.

hatch[3], *v.t.* engrave or draw parallel lines on.

hatch'èt, *n.* light short axe.

hāte, *v.t.* dislike strongly.

hāte'ful (-tf-), *a.* arousing hatred.

hā'tred, *n.* active dislike; ill-will.

hatt'er, *n.* one who makes or deals in hats.

haughty (haw'ti), *a.* proud, arrogant.

haul, *v.* pull or drag forcibly; transport; (of wind) shift, veer. *n.* hauling; catch of fish, etc.; amount acquired, booty. haul'age, *n.* (charge for) conveyance of loads. haul'ier, *n.* haulage contractor.

haulm (hawm), *n.* stalks of peas, beans, potatoes, etc.

haunch, *n.* hip and buttock of mammal, including man; leg and loin of deer, etc., as food.

haunt, *v.t.* (of ghosts, etc.) appear repeatedly in; visit frequently. *n.* place frequently visited.

hautboy (hō'boi *or* ō'boi), *n.* old name for oboe.

have, *v.* (3rd sing. pres. *has*, pr. haz; p.t. & p.p. *had*), hold in possession; possess, contain; take, obtain; be obliged *to*; enjoy, suffer. *v.aux.* (see **auxiliary**).

hā'ven, *n.* harbour; refuge.

hav'ersack, *n.* soldier's or traveller's canvas shoulder-bag for provisions.

hav'oc, *n.* devastation, destruction.

haw, *n.* hawthorn berry.

hawk¹, *n.* bird of prey used in falconry. *v.* hunt (game) with hawk or falcon.

hawk², *v.t.* carry (goods) about for sale. haw'ker, *n.* one who hawks goods, esp. from barrow, van, etc.

haw'ser (-z-), *n.* large rope, small cable, often of steel.

haw'thorn, *n.* thorny shrub with white, red, or pink blossom and red berries.

hay, *n.* grass mown and dried for fodder. hay'cock, conical heap of hay. **hay fever**, summer catarrh, etc., caused by pollen, etc. hay'making, cutting and drying grass for hay. hay'rick, hay'stack, regular pile of hay.

haz'ard, *n.* chance; danger, risk. *v.t.* expose to hazard; venture on (guess, etc.). haz'-ardous, *a.* risky.

hāze, *n.* (slight) mist. *v.t.* make hazy.

hā'zel, *n.* bush whose fruit is the hazel-nut; light-brown colour.

hā'zy, *a.* misty; vague.

H-bomb, *abbrev.* hydrogen bomb.

hē, *pron.* subjective case of 3rd personal pron. (pl. *they*; objective *him*, pl. *them*), male person or animal previously referred to. *a.* male. hē-man, masterful or virile man.

head (hed), *n.* upper part of human's, anterior part of animal's, body, containing mouth, sense organs, and brain; seat of intellect or imagination; ruler, chief, principal person; thing like head in form or position; top; division in discourse, etc.; culmination. *v.* lead, direct; be at head or top of; make *for*; strike (football) with head. *head off*, get ahead of (person) so as to turn (him) away. head'-ache, continuous pain in head. head-board,

board at head of bedstead. head-dress, (esp. ornamental) covering for head. head'land, point of high land jutting out into sea. head'-light, powerful light at front of car, etc. head'line, (line at top of page, etc., with) title or summary, esp. of news item. head-mas'ter, headmis'tress, principal master, mistress, of school. head'phone, (Radio, etc.) (usu. pl.) pair of receivers held against ears by head-band; telephone receiver fitting over the head. head'room, overhead space. head'stall, part of bridle or halter fitting round head. head'stone, gravestone. head'way, progress. head wind, wind blowing from directly in front. head'word, word forming a heading, esp. first word, in bold type, of dictionary entry.

head'er (hed-), *n.* (esp.) head-first plunge.

head'ing (hed-), *n.* title, etc., at head of article or page.

head'long (hed-), *a.* & *adv.* reckless(ly), hurried(ly), precipitate(ly).

head'quar'ters (hedkwor-), *n.pl.* centre of operations; commander-in-chief's residence.

heads'man (hedz-), *n.* (pl. *-men*), executioner.

head'strong (hed-), *a.* self-willed.

head'y (hed-), *a.* impetuous; (of wine, etc.) apt to intoxicate.

heal, *v.* restore to health; cure; (of wound, etc.) become sound. hea'ler, *n.*

health (hel-), *n.* soundness of body or mind; condition of body. health'ful, *a.* health-giving; good for the health.

heal'thy (hel-), *a.* having, showing, producing, good health.

heap, *n.* group of things lying one on another. *v.t.* pile in heap; load.

hear, *v.* (p.t. *heard*, pr. herd), perceive with ear; listen, give audience, to; be informed or told; receive message, etc., *from*. hear'say, gossip, rumour. hear'er, *n.* hear'ing, *n.* perception by ear. hear'ing aid, device for improving hearing of partially deaf person.

hear'ken (har-), *v.i.* (*archaic*) listen (*to*).

hearse (hers), *n.* vehicle for conveying coffin at funeral.

heart (hart), *n.* organ which keeps up circulation of blood in the body; centre of emotions or affections; soul, mind; courage; central or vital part. *at heart*, in inmost feelings. *by heart*, in or from memory. heart'beat, pulsation of heart. heart'break, overwhelming distress. heart'breaking, heart'broken, causing, crushed by, great distress. heart'-burn, burning sensation in lower part of chest, caused by indigestion. heart-burning, jealousy, grudge. heart'felt, sincere. heart--rending, distressing. hearts'ease, (esp. wild) pansy. heart'sick, despondent. heart--strings, one's deepest affections.

hear'ten (har-), *v.* encourage, cheer.

hearth (har-), *n.* floor of fireplace.

hear'tily (har-), *adv.* vigorously; very.

heart′less (har-), *a.* unfeeling, pitiless.
hear′ty (har-), *a.* vigorous; genial; sincere; (of meals) large.
heat, *n.* hotness; hot weather; warmth of feeling; anger; oestrus; preliminary contest, winners of which compete in final. *v.* make or become hot; inflame. **heat-wave,** period of very hot weather. **heat′edly,** *adv.* vehemently, angrily.
heath, *n.* flat waste tract of land, esp. covered with shrubs; kind of shrub, esp. ling.
heath′en (-dh-), *a.* not Christian, Jewish, or Muslim. *n.* heathen person; unenlightened person. **heath′enish,** *a.* **heath′endom,** *n.*
hea′ther (hedh-), *n.* (esp.) purple-flowered plant of moors and heaths.
heave, *v.* (p.t. *heaved* or, esp. Naut., *hōve*), lift, raise; utter (sigh) with effort; (Naut.) haul; (*informal*) throw; swell, rise. *heave in sight,* become visible. *heave to,* bring vessel to standstill. *n.* heaving.
heav′en (he-), *n.* abode of God; place of bliss; (pl.) sky. **heav′enly,** *a.* of heaven, divine; of the sky.
heav′y (he-), *a.* of great weight; of great size, amount, force, etc.; abundant; hard to digest; (of ground) difficult to travel over or dig; dull, tedious, oppressive. **heav′ily,** *adv.*
hebdom′adal, *a.* weekly.
Hèbrā′ic, *a.* of Hebrews or Hebrew.
Hē′brew (-rōō), *n.* & *a.* (person, language) of nation descended from Abraham, Isaac, and Jacob; Jew(ish).
heck′le, *v.t.* interrupt or harass speaker (esp. election candidate) with questions.
hec′tāre (*or* -ar), *n.* metric unit of area (10,000 sq. metres; 2·471 acres).
hec′tic, *a.* feverish; (*slang*) exciting, wild.
hecto-, *pref.* hundred. **hec′togram, hec′-tolitre** (-lēter), **hec′tomètre** (-ter), *nn.* 100 grams, litres, metres.
hec′tor, *v.* bluster, bully.
hedge, *n.* fence of bushes or low trees; barrier of turf, stone, etc. *v.* surround with hedge; make or trim hedges; give evasive answer. **hedge′row,** *n.* row of bushes forming hedge. **hedg′er,** *n.* one who makes or trims hedges.
hedge′hog (-j-h-), *n.* small spiny nocturnal insect-eating quadruped.
hē′donism, *n.* doctrine that pleasure is the chief good. **hē′donist,** *n.*
heed, *v.t.* attend to; take notice (of). *n.* care, attention. **heed′ful,** *a.* **heed′less,** *a.*
heel¹, *n.* back part of foot; part of sock, etc., that covers or boot, etc., that supports, heel. *down at heel,* (of person) slovenly, destitute. *v.* furnish with heel. **heel′less** (-l-l-), *a.*
heel², *v.* (of ship, etc.) lean (*over*) to one side; make (ship) heel.
hef′ty, *a.* big, sturdy, stalwart.
heif′er (hef-), *n.* young cow.
heigh (hā), *int.* expressing encouragement or enquiry. **heigh-hō,** *int.* expressing disappointment, boredom, etc.

height (hīt), *n.* measure from base to top; elevation above ground or sea level; high point; top; utmost degree.
heigh′ten (hī-), *v.t.* raise higher; intensify.
hei′nous (hān-), *a.* atrocious.
heir (ār), *n.* person entitled to receive property or rank as legal representative of former owner. **heir apparent,** one whose claim cannot be superseded by birth of nearer heir. **heir presumptive,** one whose claim may be thus superseded. **heir′ess,** *n. fem.*
heir′lōōm (ār-), *n.* piece of property that has been in family for generations.
hel′ical, *a.* spiral.
hel′icopter, *n.* aircraft lifted and propelled by airscrew(s) revolving horizontally.
hēl′io-, *pref.* sun. **hēl′iograph,** *n.* apparatus for signalling by reflecting flashes of sunlight.
hē′liotrōpe (*or* hel-), *n.* plant with small clustered purple flowers; colour or scent of these.
hē′lium, *n.* light non-inflammable gas.
hē′lix (*or* he-), *n.* (pl. *helicēs*), spiral.
hell, *n.* (in some religions) place of punishment after death; place, condition, of suffering or misery. **hell′ish,** *a.*
Hell′ēne, *n.* a Greek, ancient or modern. **Hellē′nic,** *a.*
hellō′, *int.* & *n.* (pl. *hellos*), hallo.
helm, *n.* tiller or wheel for managing rudder; guidance, control. **helms′man** (-z-), *n.* (pl. *-men*), steersman.
hel′mèt, *n.* protective head-cover.
help, *v.t.* act or co-operate so as to ease work of or benefit (person); be of use or service; serve (person) with food; (with *can, cannot,* etc.) avoid, prevent. *n.* act, action, of helping; person, thing, that helps. **help′ful,** *a.* giving help, useful. **hel′ping,** *n.* (esp.) portion of food. **help′less,** *a.* unable to help oneself; without help or power.
help′mate, **help′meet** (*archaic*), *n.* helpful companion, esp. husband or wife.
hel′ter-skel′ter, *adv.* in disordered haste. *n.* spiral slide at fun-fair.
hem, *n.* border of garment, cloth, etc., made by sewing down turned-in edge. *v.t.* (p.t. *hemmed*), sew edge thus. *hem in,* confine, enclose.
hemi-, *pref.* half.
hem′isphēre, *n.* half sphere; half the earth.
hem′lock, *n.* a poisonous plant.
hemo-, *pref.*: see **haemo-.**
hemp, *n.* Asian herbaceous plant; its fibre used for rope, etc.; narcotic drug got from it. **hem′pen,** *a.*
hen, *n.* female of common domestic fowl or of other birds. **hen′bāne,** *n.* a poisonous plant. **hen′pecked** (-kt), *a.* (of husband) domineered over by wife.
hence, *adv.* from here; from now; as result of this. **henceforth′, hencefor′ward,** *advv.* from this time forward.
hench′man, *n.* (pl. *henchmen*), (Hist.) squire,

page; political supporter.

henn′a, *n.* (yellowish-red dye from) Egyptian privet.

hen′ry, *n.* (pl. *henrys*), (Electr.) unit of inductance.

hepta-, *pref.* seven. **hep′tagon,** *n.* plane figure of seven sides. **heptag′onal,** *a.*

her, *pron.* & *a.* objective case of **she**; possessive case of **she**, with absolute form **hers**.

Hēr′a, *n.* (Gk. myth.) wife of Zeus.

he′rald, *n.* officer making State proclamations, organizing processions, regulating use of armorial bearings, etc., and (formerly) carrying messages; forerunner. *v.t.* proclaim the approach of. **heral′dic,** *a.* **he′raldry,** *n.* science of a herald, esp. art of blazoning coats of arms, tracing and recording pedigrees, etc.

herb, *n.* soft-stemmed plant dying after flowering; plant used for food, flavouring, medicine, etc. **herbā′ceous** (-shus), *a.* of or like herbs.

her′bage, *n.* herbs; pasturage.

her′bal, *a.* of herbs. **her′balist,** *n.* dealer in medicinal herbs.

herbār′ium, *n.* (room, case, etc., containing) collection of dried plants.

herbiv′orous, *a.* (of animals) feeding on living plants.

hercū′lēan (*or* -ē′an), *a.* as strong as Hercules; (of task) of great difficulty.

herd, *n.* number of cattle feeding or travelling together; large number of people; herdsman. *v.* go in a herd; tend; drive or crowd. **herds′man** (-z-), *n.* (pl. -*men*), one who looks after herd(s).

hēre, *adv.* in or to this place; at this point. *n.* this place or point. *here and there*, in various places. **hēre′about(s),** *adv.* somewhere near here. **hēreaf′ter,** *adv.* & *n.* (in) the future, (in) the next world. **hēre′bȳ,** *adv.* by this means. **hēre′in,** *adv.* in this book, place, etc. **hēre′inafter,** *adv.* below (in document, etc.). **hēretofore′,** *adv.* formerly. **hēreupon′,** *adv.* after or in consequence of this. **hērewith′,** *adv.* with this.

hered′itary (he-r-), *a.* descending by inheritance; transmitted from one generation to another.

hered′ity (he-r-), *n.* property of organic beings by which offspring inherit characteristics of parents or other ancestors; characteristics, etc., so passed on.

he′resy, *n.* opinion contrary to orthodox Christian belief or to accepted doctrine on any subject. **he′retic,** *n.* person supporting a heresy. **heret′ical,** *a.*

he′ritable, *a.* that can be inherited; capable of inheriting.

he′ritage, *n.* what is or may be inherited; one's portion or lot.

hermaph′rodīte, *n.* & *a.* (person, animal, etc.) with characteristics or organs of both sexes.

hermet′ic, *a.* (of seal, seal..ng) air-tight; (*archaic*) of alchemy. **hermet′ically,** *adv.* so as to be air-tight.

her′mit, *n.* person living in solitude. **her′mitage,** *n.* hermit's dwelling.

her′nia, *n.* (Med.) protrusion of an internal organ through wall of cavity containing it.

hēr′ō, *n.* (pl. *heroes*), man admired for great or noble deeds; person of extreme courage; chief man in poem, play, or story. **herō′ic,** *a.* of, worthy of, having qualities of, a hero; dealing with heroes. **he′rōine,** *n.* female hero. **he′rōism,** *n.* heroic conduct.

he′rōin, *n.* analgesic and hypnotic (addictive) drug prepared from morphine.

he′ron, *n.* long-legged wading bird. **he′ronry,** *n.* place where herons breed.

he′rring, *n.* edible fish of N. Atlantic. **he′rringbōne,** (pattern) of lines etc. set obliquely in alternate rows; (fabric, stitch, etc.) having this pattern.

hers: see **her**.

herself′, *pron.* emphatic and reflexive form of **she**.

hertz, *n.* (pl. same), unit of cyclic frequency.

hes′itant (-z-), *a.* hesitating. **hes′itancy,** *n.*

hes′itāte (-z-), *v.i.* feel or show indecision; be reluctant. **hesitā′tion,** *n.*

hess′ian, *n.* strong coarse cloth.

hetero-, *pref.* other, different.

het′erodox, *a.* not orthodox. **het′erodoxy,** *n.*

heterogē′nēous, *a.* diverse; composed of diverse elements. **heterogenē′ity,** *n.*

heterosex′ūal, *a.* sexually attracted to members of opposite sex. **heterosexūal′ity,** *n.*

heuris′tic (hūr-), *a.* of or concerned with finding out (for oneself).

hew, *v.* (p.t. *hewed*; p.p. *hewed* or *hewn*), chop, cut, with axe, sword, etc.; cut into shape. **hew′er,** *n.*

hexa-, *pref.* six. **hex′agon,** *n.* six-sided plane figure. **hexag′onal,** *a.* **hexahed′ron,** *n.* solid figure having six faces. **hexahed′ral,** *a.* **hexam′ēter,** *n.* line of six metrical feet.

hey (hā), *int.* calling attention or expressing joy, surprise, or question.

hey′day (hā-), *n.* bloom, prime.

hiā′tus, *n.* (pl. *hiatuses*), gap in series, etc.; pause between two vowels.

hī′bernāte, *v.i.* spend winter, (of animals) in torpid state, (of persons) in mild climate; (fig.) remain inactive. **hībernā′tion,** *n.*

hicc′up, hicc′ough (-kup), *n.* involuntary audible spasm of respiratory organs. *v.i.* utter hiccup.

hick′ory, *n.* N. Amer. tree allied to walnut; its wood.

hid, hidden: see **hide²**.

hide¹, *n.* animal's skin, raw or dressed. **hide-bound,** bigoted, rigidly conventional.

hide², *v.* (p.t. *hid*; p.p. *hidden* and *hid*), put or keep out of sight; conceal oneself; keep (fact) secret (*from*); obstruct view of. *n.* place of concealment for observation of wild animals.

hide-out, hiding-place.
hid′eous, *a.* horribly ugly; repulsive.
hi′ding[1], *n.* thrashing, flogging.
hi′ding[2], *n.* (esp.) *in hiding,* hidden. *hiding--place,* place of concealment.
hie, *v.i.* & *refl.* (Poet.) go quickly.
hi′erarchy (-k-), *n.* graded priesthood; any organization or group with grades of authority.
hi′eroglyph, *n.* figure of object standing for word or sound, esp. in ancient Egyptian writing. **hieroglyph′ics,** *n.pl.* hieroglyphs. **hieroglyph′ic,** *a.*
hi-fi, *n.* & *a.* (*informal*) high fidelity.
higg′ledy-pigg′ledy (-gldi), *adv.* & *a.* in utter confusion.
high (hī), *a.* of great or specified upward extent; of exalted rank, position or quality; chief; (of meat, esp. game) slightly tainted; (of sounds) acute in pitch, shrill; great, intense; advanced. *n.* high degree or place or level; area of high barometric pressure. *adv.* far up, aloft; in, to, a high degree. **high′-brow,** intellectual (person). **High Court,** court of justice for civil cases. **high explosive,** powerful and rapidly detonated explosive. **high′falutin(g), high′flown,** absurdly pompous or bombastic. **high fidelity,** (reproduction of, apparatus reproducing, sound) with high degree of fidelity to original. **high--handed,** overbearing. **high light(s),** brightly-lighted part(s) of picture, etc. **high--minded,** of high moral character. **high road,** main road. **high school,** secondary school, esp. one preparing pupils for university. **high seas,** open sea outside territorial waters. **high-spi′rited,** courageous; (of horse) frisky. **high tea,** early evening meal at which tea is served. **high tide, high water,** time, state, of tide when fully in.
high′land (hī-), *a.* of highlands. **high′lander,** *n.* inhabitant of highlands, esp. of Scotland. **high′lands** (-z-), *n.pl.* mountainous or elevated country, esp. (*Highlands*) northern part of Scotland.
high′ly (hī-), *adv.* in a high degree; very; favourably, honourably. **highly strung,** sensitive.
High′ness (hī-), *n.* title of prince, etc.
high′way (hī-), *n.* public road; main route. **high′wayman,** *n.* (pl. *-men*) (Hist.) man, usu. mounted, robbing travellers on highway.
hi′jack, *v.t.* & *n.* (effect) seizure of means of transport, esp. aircraft in flight, by (threat of) violence.
hike, *n.* & *v.i.* walk, tramp. **hi′ker,** *n.*
hilār′ious, *a.* cheerful, merry. **hila′rity,** *n.* merriment.
hill, *n.* small mountain; rising ground, slope. **hill′y,** *a.* **hill′iness,** *n.*
hill′ock, *n.* small hill; mound.
hilt, *n.* handle of sword or dagger. *up to the hilt,* completely.

him, *pron.* objective case of **he. himself′,** *pron.* emphatic and refl. form of **he.**
hind[1], *n.* female of (esp. red) deer.
hind[2], *a.* at back, posterior. **hind′quarter,** leg and loin of beef, etc.; (pl.) rump and hind legs. **hind′sight,** (esp.) perception after event. **hind′er**[1], *a.* hind. **hind′most.** *a.*
hin′der[2], *v.t.* hamper, obstruct, prevent.
hin′drance, *n.* obstruction, obstacle.
Hindu (-dōō), **Hindōō′** (*or* hin′-), *a.* of Hindus or Hinduism. *n.* person who professes Hinduism. **Hin′duism,** *n.* religion of majority of Indian people.
hinge (-nj), *n.* movable joint like that by which door is hung on post. *v.* attach (as) with hinge; turn *on.*
hint, *n.* disguised suggestion; slight indication. *v.* suggest indirectly. *hint at,* give hint of.
hin′terland, *n.* district behind that lying along coast or river-bank.
hip[1], *n.* projection of pelvis and upper part of thigh-bone at side of body.
hip[2], *n.* fruit of wild rose.
hippie: see **hippy.**
hippo-, *pref.* horse.
hipp′odrōme, *n.* (Gk. & Rom. antiquity) course for chariot races, etc.
hippopot′amus, *n.* (pl. *hippopotamuses, hippopotami*), large short-legged thick-skinned African quadruped inhabiting rivers, etc.
hipp′y, hipp′ie, *n.* person rejecting conventional standards and organized society in favour of more natural living.
hire, *n.* payment for use of thing, labour, etc.; hiring, being hired. *v.t.* procure on hire; employ for wages. **hire purchase,** system by which hired thing becomes hirer's property after number of payments. **hire′ling,** *n.* (usu. contemptuous) one who works for hire.
hir′sūte, *a.* hairy, shaggy.
his (-z), *pron.* & *a.* possessive case of **he** (with absolute form the same).
hiss, *n.* sharp sound of *s,* esp. as sign of disapproval, etc. *v.* make hiss; express disapproval thus.
histor′ian, *n.* writer of history.
histo′ric, *a.* noted in history; not fictional or legendary. **histo′rical,** *a.* based on history or the past; belonging to the past.
historiog′raphy, *n.* writing of (official) history. **historiog′rapher,** *n.*
his′tory, *n.* continuous methodical record of important public events; (study of) past events; story.
histrion′ic, *a.* of acting; stagy. **histrion′ics,** *n.pl.* (esp.) dramatically artificial or exaggerated behaviour.
hit, *v.* (p.t. *hit*), strike with blow or missile; direct blow *at;* light *upon,* find. *n.* blow; stroke of sarcasm; success.
hitch, *v.* move with jerk; fasten with loop, etc.; become so fastened; hitch-hike. *n.* jerk; noose, knot; impediment, temporary stop-

page. **hitch-hīke,** v. i. travel by means of lifts in vehicles.

hith′er (-dh-), adv. to this place. **hitherto′** (-ōō), adv. up to now.

hīve, n. beehive; place swarming with busy occupants. v. place, live, store, etc., (as) in hive.

hoar (hor), a. (archaic) hoary. **hoar-frost,** n. white deposit of frozen water vapour or dew.

hoard (hord), n. store (esp. of money or treasure) laid by; amassed stock. v. t. amass and put away, store up.

hoard′ing (hor-), n. temporary board fence round building work, etc., often covered with posters, etc.

hoarse (hors), a. (of voice) rough, husky; having hoarse voice.

hoar′y (hor-), a. white or grey with age.

hoax, v. t. deceive, esp. by way of joke. n. humorous or mischievous deception.

hob, n. flat iron shelf at side of grate. **hob′-nail,** heavy-headed nail for boot-sole.

hobb′le, v. limp; tie horse's legs together to prevent it from straying. n. limping gait.

hobb′ledehoy (-bldi-), n. awkward youth.

hobb′y, n. favourite pursuit outside one's main occupation. **hobb′y-horse,** n. child's toy of horse-headed stick; rocking-horse; horse on merry-go-round; favourite theme, obsession.

hob′goblin, n. mischievous imp; bogy.

hob′-nob, v. i. (p.t. hob-nobbed), converse familiarly (with).

hŏb′ō, n. (pl. -s or hoboes), (U.S.) tramp.

hock[1], n. joint of quadruped's hind leg between true knee and fetlock.

hock[2], n. German white wine from Rhine valley.

hock′ey, n. team-game played with ball and curved sticks between goals; ice hockey.

hŏ′cus-pō′cus, n. deception.

hod, n. open receptacle on staff for carrying bricks, etc.; receptacle for coal. **hod′man,** n. (pl. -men), bricklayer's labourer.

hodge-podge: see **hotch-potch.**

hōe, n. tool for removing weeds, etc. v. (pres. p. hoeing), use hoe; weed (crops), loosen (soil), with hoe.

hog, n. pig, esp. castrated male. v. t. (p.t. hogged), (slang) take all or unfair share of.

hog′manay, n. (Sc.) last day of year; gift of cake, etc., demanded by children on that day.

hogs′head (-z-hed), n. large cask; liquid measure.

hoi polloi′, the masses. (Greek)

hoist, v. t. raise (esp. flag) aloft; raise with tackle, etc. n. elevator, lift.

hoi′ty-toi′ty, a. haughty, petulant.

hōld[1], v. (p.t. held), keep fast; grasp; possess; contain, have room for; observe, celebrate; restrain; not give way; believe; be valid. hold out, offer; persist, endure. hold up, delay; rob with (threat of) violence. n. grasp; means

of holding; (fig.) influence. **hold-all,** portable case for clothes, etc. **hōld′er,** n. possessor for the time; device for holding. **hōld′-ing,** n. land or stocks held.

hōld[2], n. cavity below deck for cargo.

hōle, n. hollow place; gap; burrow; perforation; cavity; (informal) dilemma. v. make holes in; put into hole. hole-and-corner, underhand, secret.

hol′iday, n. day of cessation from work or of recreation; (often pl.) period of this, vacation. **holiday-maker,** person on holiday, esp. away from home.

hō′liness, n. being holy; sanctity. His (Your) Holiness, title of Pope.

holl′and, n. linen fabric, often unbleached.

holl′ow (-ō), a. having hole, cavity, or depression; not solid; (fig.) false, unreal. n. hollow place; valley. v. t. make hollow in. adv. completely.

holl′y, n. evergreen prickly-leaved shrub with red berries.

holl′yhock, n. tall plant with large showy flowers.

holm[1] (hōm), n. islet in river; flat ground by river.

holm[2] (hōm), n. (usu. holm-oak) evergreen oak.

hol′ocaust, n. complete destruction, esp. of large number of persons; sacrifice wholly consumed by fire.

hol′ograph (-ahf), n. document wholly in handwriting of person in whose name it appears.

hōl′pen, (archaic) p.p. of **help.**

hō′lster, n. leather pistol-case.

hō′ly, a. belonging or devoted to God; of high moral or spiritual excellence. **holy day,** religious festival. **Holy Ghost, Holy Spirit,** third person of Trinity. **holy grail,** see **grail. Holy Land,** the former Palestine. **Holy Week,** the week before Easter. **Holy Writ,** the Bible.

hō′lystōne, n. sandstone for scouring.

hom′age, n. (in Feud. law) formal acknowledgement of allegiance; honour, respect.

hōme, n. dwelling-place; one's residence; native land; institution for care of children, old or sick persons, etc. a. of home; made at home. adv. to or at home; to point aimed at. v. i. go home (esp. of pigeons). **home economics,** science of household management. **home′land,** native land. **home-made,** made at home. **home′sick,** unhappy because of absence from home. **home′sickness** (n.). **home′spun,** (cloth) of yarn spun at home. **home′stead,** house with outbuildings; farm. **home′work,** (esp.) school work to be done at home. **hōme′less, hōme′līke,** aa.

hōme′ly (-ml-), a. simple, plain; (U.S.) plain, not good-looking.

hōme′ward (-mw-), a. & adv. (going, leading) towards home. **hōme′wards** (-z), adv. towards home.

hom'icĭde, *n*. killing, killer, of human being. **homici'dal**, *a*.

hom'ily, *n*. sermon, discourse.

hom'inid, *n*. & *a*. (member) of family of primates that includes existing and fossil man.

homo-, *pref*. same.

hŏmoeop'athy (-miop-), *n*. treatment of disease by drugs that in healthy person would produce symptoms of the disease. **hŏ'moeopath**, *n*. **hŏmoeop'athist**, *n*. **hŏmoeopath'ic**, *a*.

homogĕnĕ'ity, *n*. uniformity; sameness. **homogĕ'nĕous**, *a*. of same kind or nature; uniform.

homo'gĕnize, *v.t.* treat (milk) so that fat globules emulsify and cream does not separate.

hom'onym, *n*. word of same form as another but having different meaning.

homosex'ŭal, *a*. sexually attracted only to members of one's own sex. *n*. homosexual person. **homosexŭal'ity**, *n*.

hŏne, *n*. whetstone, esp. for razor. *v.t.* sharpen on hone.

hon'ĕst (on-), *a*. fair and upright; not lying or cheating or stealing. **hon'ĕsty**, *n*. uprightness, truthfulness; plant with purple flowers and flat round semi-transparent fruits.

ho'ney (hu-), *n*. (pl. *honeys*), sweet sticky fluid made by bees from nectar of flowers. **ho'neycomb**, bees' wax structure of hexagonal cells for honey and eggs. **honey-combed**, filled with cavities; undermined. **ho'neydew**, sweet sticky substance secreted by aphides, found on leaves and stems. **ho'neymoon**, (*n*.) holiday of newly married couple. (*v.i.*) spend honeymoon. **ho'neysuckle**, climbing shrub with fragrant flowers; woodbine. **honeyed**, (hu'nid), *a*. sweet, sweet-sounding.

honorar'ium (on-), *n*. (pl. *honorariums, honoraria*), fee for nominally unpaid, esp. professional, services.

hon'orary (on-), *a*. conferred as an honour; unpaid.

honorif'ic, (on-), *a*. & *n*. (expression) implying respect.

honour (on'er), *n*. great respect; high public regard; good reputation; (pl.) civilities to guests, etc.; (pl.) marks of respect, academic distinction, etc. *v.t.* respect highly; confer honour upon; pay (bill) when due.

hon'ourable (oner-), *a*. worthy of, bringing, consistent with, honour; generous, not base; (*Honourable*), official or courtesy title.

hood, *n*. covering for head and neck; (hood-like) garment worn over gown to show university degree; thing like hood in shape or use, esp. waterproof (folding) top of motor car, etc. *v.t.* cover with hood. **hood'wink**, *v.t.* deceive.

hŏof, *n*. (pl. *hooves, hoofs*), horny casing of foot of horse, etc. *v*. strike with hoof. *hoof it*, (*slang*) go on foot. **hŏofed** (-ft), *a*. having hooves.

hook, *n*. bent piece of wire, etc., for catching hold or for hanging things on; curved cutting instrument. *by hook or by crook*, by fair means or foul. *v*. grasp, fasten, with hook; catch with hook. *hook up*, connect or link together (esp. radio, etc., stations). **hook and eye**, small hook and loop as dress-fastener. **hook-up**, (esp.) linking of radio, etc., stations.

hook'ah (-a), *n*. smoking-pipe with long flexible tube and attached vase of water through which smoke is drawn.

hŏo'ligan, *n*. young street rough; member of street gang.

hŏop, *n*. circular band of metal, etc., for binding cask, etc.; circle of wood, iron, etc., trundled by child; iron arch used in croquet. *v.t.* bind with hoops.

hŏop'oe (-ōō), *n*. bird with gay plumage and large crest.

hŏot, *n*. inarticulate shout of disapproval, mockery, etc.; sound of siren, motor-car horn, etc.; characteristic cry of owl. *v*. utter hoot(s); assail with hoots; (cause to) make hoot. **hŏo'ter**, *n*. siren, etc.

hŏo'ver, *n*. kind of vacuum cleaner. *v.t.* clean with vacuum cleaner. **P**.

hop¹, *n*. climbing plant with bitter cones used to flavour beer, etc.; (pl.) ripe cones of this. *v.i.* (p.t. *hopped*), gather hops.

hop², *v*. (p.t. *hopped*), spring on one foot; hop over; (of birds) jump. *n*. hopping; distance travelled by air in one stage. **hop'scotch**, child's game of hopping over lines marked on ground.

hŏpe, *n*. expectation and desire; trust; person, thing, on which hope is based. *v*. expect and desire; feel hope. **hŏpe'ful**, *a*. **hŏpe'less**, *a*.

hopp'er¹, *n*. (esp.) funnel-like device for feeding grain into mill, etc.

hopp'er², *n*. hop-picker.

hop'sack, *n*. woollen dress-fabric woven with threads in pairs.

horde, *n*. large crowd or troop.

horī'zon (ho-r-), *n*. line at which earth and sky appear to meet; limit of mental perception, interest, etc.

horizon'tal (ho-r-), *a*. parallel to plane of horizon; level, flat. *n*. horizontal line, bar, etc.

hor'mōne, *n*. product of living cells carried by the blood to other cells.

horn, *n*. outgrowth, usu. one of pair, often curved and pointed, on head of cattle, etc.; horn-like projection; substance of horns; wind instrument, esp. French horn; device for sounding warning signal. *horn of plenty*, cornucopia. **horn'beam**, tough-wooded hedgerow tree. **horned** (-nd), *a*. having horns.

horn'ĕt, *n*. large insect of wasp family.

horn'pipe, *n*. (music for) lively dance, associated esp. with sailors.

horn′y, *a.* of or like horn; hard.

horol′ogy, *n.* clock-making.

ho′roscope, *n.* astrologer's chart of sky and planets at a given time, supposed to reveal influence of stars on destiny; forecast of such destiny.

ho′rrible, *a.* arousing horror; hideous, shocking; unpleasant. **ho′rribly,** *adv.*

ho′rrid, *a.* horrible; disagreeable.

horrif′ic (ho-r-), *a.* horrifying.

ho′rrify, *v.t.* arouse horror in; shock.

ho′rror, *n.* terrified shuddering; terror; intense dislike or fear; horrifying thing.

hors de combat (ordekawm′bah), disabled, out of the fight. (French)

hors-d'oeuvre (order′vr), *n.* (pl. same, or *hors-d'oeuvres*), extra dish served at beginning of meal.

horse, *n.* quadruped with flowing mane and tail and undivided hoof, used as beast of burden and draught and for riding on; gymnastic vaulting-block; frame for supporting things; cavalry. *on horseback*, mounted on a horse. **horse-box,** closed vehicle for transporting horse(s). **horse-chestnut,** large tree with conical clusters of white or pink flowers; its inedible glossy brown seed. **horse-coper,** horse-dealer. **horse-fly,** large grey (biting) fly troublesome to horses, cattle, etc., and humans. **horse′hair,** hair from mane or tail of horse. **horse′man, horse′woman,** (skilled) rider on horseback. **horse′manship,** skill in riding. **horse′play,** rough or boisterous play. **horse′power,** unit for measuring rate of (mechanical) power. **horse-radish,** plant with pungent root used as condiment. **horse-sense,** (*informal*) strong common sense. **horse′shoe,** narrow iron plate shaped and nailed to horse's hoof; horseshoe-shaped thing. **horse′whip,** (*n.*) whip for horse; (*v.t.*) (p.t. *horsewhipped*), punish (person) with this.

hor′sy, *a.* addicted to horses or horse-racing; affecting dress and language of groom or jockey.

hor′tative, hor′tatory, *aa.* exhorting.

hor′ticulture (-cher), *n.* art of gardening. **horticul′tural,** *a.* **horticul′turist,** *n.*

hosann′a (-z-), *n.* cry of adoration.

hōse (-z), *n.* stockings; (also *hose-pipe*) flexible tube for conveying liquids. *v.* water, wash down, with hose.

hō′sier (-z-), *n.* dealer in hose, men's underwear, etc. **hō′siery,** *n.*

hos′pice, *n.* travellers' house of rest kept by religious order, etc.; home for the destitute or sick.

hos′pitable, *a.* welcoming and friendly to strangers and guests.

hos′pital, *n.* institution for care of sick or injured; (Hist.) charitable institution.

hospital′ity, *n.* friendly and generous reception of guests or strangers.

hōst¹, *n.* large number; (*archaic*) army.

hōst², *n.* one who entertains another; landlord of inn.

Hōst³, *n.* bread consecrated in the Eucharist.

hos′tage, *n.* person handed over as pledge for fulfilment of conditions, or seized to compel satisfaction of demands.

hos′tel, *n.* house of residence for students, etc.

hos′telry, *n.* (*archaic*) inn.

hōs′tess, *n.* woman who entertains guests; mistress of inn.

hos′tile, *a.* of enemy; opposed; unfriendly.

hostil′ity, *n.* enmity; warfare; opposition; (pl.) acts of war.

hot, *a.* (*hotter, hottest*), of high temperature, very warm; ardent; excited; producing sensation of heat on tongue, pungent. *adv.* eagerly, hotly. **hot air,** (*informal*) excited or boastful talk. **hot′bed,** bed of earth heated by fermenting manure; place that promotes growth. **hot dog,** hot sausage sandwiched in bread-roll. **hot′foot,** in great haste. **hot′-head,** hasty person. **hot′house,** heated greenhouse for growing plants out of season, in colder climate, etc. **hot-plate,** (esp.) heated metal plate, portable heater, for cooking, etc. **hot′pot,** dish of stewed meat and vegetables. **hot water,** (esp.) trouble, scrape.

hotch′potch, hodge-podge, *n.* confused collection, jumble, medley.

hôtel′, *n.* building where meals and rooms are provided for travellers, etc.; (large) inn. **hôtel′ier,** *n.* hotel-keeper.

hound, *n.* dog used for hunting. *v.t.* hunt, drive, (as) with hounds; urge *on*.

hour (ower), *n.* twenty-fourth part of a day, 60 minutes; (pl.) fixed habitual time for work, etc. *small hours*, early hours after midnight. **hour-glass,** time-measuring device in which fine sand takes one hour to pass from upper into lower glass bulb through narrow neck.

houri (hoor′i, how′ri), *n.* beautiful young woman of Muslim paradise.

hour′ly (ower-), *adv. & a.* every hour.

house, *n.* (pl. pr. -ziz), building for dwelling in or for specified use; (building of) legislative, etc., assembly; audience in theatre, etc.; business firm; family, dynasty. *v.t.* (-z), provide house(s) for. **house′boat,** boat fitted up for living in. **house′breaker,** person breaking into house with intent to steal, etc.; demolition worker. **house′keeper,** woman managing domestic affairs of house. **house-maid,** maid who does room-cleaning, etc. **house physician, surgeon,** doctor residing in hospital. **house′warming,** party celebrating entry into new house. **house′wife,** mistress of house; (pr. huz′if) case for needles, threads, etc. **housewif′ery,** housekeeping. **house′work,** cleaning, cooking, etc.

house′hold (-s-h-), *n.* all occupants of a house. **household troops,** troops guarding sovereign's person. **household word,** familiar saying or name. **house'hōlder,** *n.* one who occupies house as his own dwelling; head of household.

hous'ing (-z), *n.* (esp.) provision of houses; (protective) covering.

hove: see **heave.**

hov'el, *n.* shed; small mean dwelling.

hov'er, *v.i.* (of bird, etc.) hang in the air; loiter. **hov'ercraft,** vehicle that travels over water or land on cushion of compressed air provided by downward blast.

how, *adv.* in what way; by what means; to what extent. **howev'er,** *adv.* nevertheless; in whatever way; to whatever degree.

how'dah (-a), *n.* seat, usu. with canopy, on elephant's back.

how'itzer, *n.* short cannon firing shell at high angle.

howl, *v.* (of animal) utter long loud doleful cry; (of person) utter long cry of pain, derision, etc. *n.* such cry.

hoy'den, *n.* boisterous girl.

hub, *n.* central part of wheel, from which spokes radiate.

hubb'ub, *n.* confused din (e.g. of many voices); uproar.

huck'aback, *n.* rough-surfaced linen or cotton fabric used for towels, etc.

huck'leberry (-klb-), *n.* low shrub of N. America; its edible dark blue berry.

huck'ster, *n.* hawker. *v.i.* haggle.

hudd'le, *v.* heap, crowd, or nestle closely together. *n.* confused heap, etc.

hūe¹, *n.* colour; tint.

hūe², *n.* **hue and cry,** uproar of pursuit; outcry.

huff, *n.* fit of petulance or offended dignity. **huff'ish, huff'y,** *aa.*

hug, *v.t.* (p.t *hugged*), squeeze tightly in one's arms; keep close to (shore, etc.); cling to. *n.* tight embrace.

hūge, *a.* very large or great. **hūge'ly** (-jli), *adv.* enormously.

hugg'er-mugg'er (-g-), *a.* & *adv.* confused(ly).

Hū'guenot (-genō). *n.* (Hist.) French Protestant in 16th and 17th centuries.

hu'la(-hula) (hōō-), *n.* Hawaiian women's dance.

hulk, *n.* body of dismantled ship; unwieldy vessel. **hulk'ing,** *a.* bulky, clumsy.

hull¹, *n.* outer covering or pod of peas, beans, etc. *v.t.* remove hull of.

hull², *n.* body or frame of ship, etc.

hullabaloo', *n.* uproar.

hullō', *int.* & *n.* (pl. *hullos*), hallo.

hum, *v.* (p.t. *hummed*), sing with closed lips; murmur continously like bee; etc. *n.* humming sound.

hū'man, *a.* of, characteristic of, man or mankind; that is a man or consists of men; not divine or animal or mechanical. *n.* human being. **hū'manly,** *adv.* (esp.) by human means.

hūmāne', *a.* kindly, compassionate.

hū'manism, *n.* system of thought, etc., concerned with human rather than supernatural values, etc. **hū'manist,** *n.*

hūmanitā'rian, *n.* one who devotes himself to welfare of mankind. *a.* benevolent; wishing to do good.

hūman'ity, *n.* human nature; human race; kindness and compassion; (pl., esp.) Greek and Latin classics.

hū'manīze, *v.* make or become human or humane.

hum'ble, *a.* having or showing low estimate of one's own importance; lowly, modest. *v.t.* bring low; make humble.

hum'ble-bee, *n.* bumble-bee.

hum'bug, *n.* sham, deception; impostor. *v.t.* (p.t. *humbugged*), delude, cheat.

hum'drum, *a.* dull, commonplace.

hū'merus, *n.* bone of upper arm.

hū'mid, *a.* damp. **hūmid'ity,** *n.*

hūmil'iāte, *v.t.* cause to feel ashamed; abase. **hūmiliā'tion,** *n.*

hūmil'ity, *n.* humbleness, meekness.

humm'ock, *n.* hillock.

hūmoresque' (-sk), *n.* (Mus.) lively instrumental composition.

hū'morist, *n.* humorous talker or writer.

hū'morous, *a.* full of humour; amusing, funny.

hū'mour (-mer), *n.* mood, state of mind; comicality, humorous imagination. *sense of humour,* faculty of perceiving what is humorous. *v.t.* comply with humour of, indulge.

hump, *n.* rounded lump, esp. on back of camel, etc. **hump'back,** *n.* (person having) back with hump (due to curved spine). **hump'backed** (-kt), *a.*

hū'mus, *n.* vegetable mould.

hunch, *n.* hump; thick piece, hunk; (*slang*) presentiment, intuition. *v.t.* bend, arch, convexly. **hunch'back,** *n.* humpback.

hun'dred, *n.* ten times ten (100, C). **hun'-dredweight** (abbrev. *cwt.*), 112 lb., (U.S.) 100 lb., avoirdupois. **hun'dredfōld,** *a.* & *adv.* **hun'dredth,** *a.* & *n.*

hung, *p.t.* & *p.p.* of **hang.**

hung'er (-ngg-), *n.* discomfort, exhaustion, due to want of food; strong desire. *v.i.* feel hunger; crave *for.* **hunger strike,** refusal to take food.

hung'ry (-ngg-), *a.* feeling or showing hunger; eager.

hunk, *n.* large or clumsy piece, lump.

hunt, *v.* pursue wild animals for food or sport; search *for;* drive *out. n.* hunting; persons hunting with pack.

hun'ter, *n.* one who hunts; horse for hunting. **hun'tress,** *n. fem.*

hunts'man, *n.* (pl.-*men*), hunter; man in charge of pack of hounds.

hur'dle, *n.* portable frame with bars, for temporary fence, etc.; frame to be jumped over in *hurdle-race*; (pl.) hurdle-race. **hur'dler,** *n.* hurdle-maker; hurdle-racer.

hur'dy-gur'dy, *n.* musical instrument played by turning handle; barrel-organ.

hurl, *v. t.* throw violently. *n.* violent throw.

hur'ly-bur'ly, *n.* commotion.

hurrah', hurray' (hu- *or* hoo-), *int.* & *n.* (shout) expressing joy or approval. *v. t.* shout hurrah.

hu'rricāne (*or* -an), *n.* storm with violent wind, esp. W. Indian cyclone.

hu'rry, *n.* excessive haste; eagerness; need for haste. *v.* (cause to) move or act with haste. **hu'rried** (-id), *a.* **hu'rriedly,** *adv.*

hurt, *v. t.* injure, damage, pain; distress, wound. *n.* wound; injury; harm. **hurt'ful,** *a.*

hur'tle, *v. i.* move swiftly, esp. with clattering sound; come with a crash.

hus'band (-z-), *n.* married man, esp. in relation to his wife. *v. t.* manage thriftily. **hus'bandman** (pl. *-men*), farmer. **hus'bandry,** *n.* farming; economy.

hush, *v.* silence; be silent; *hush up*, suppress. *n.* silence. **hush-hush,** (*informal*) very secret.

husk, *n.* dry outer covering of fruit or seed. *v. t.* remove husk from.

hus'ky[1], *a.* dry as husks; hoarse.

hus'ky[2], *n.* Eskimo dog.

hussar' (hooz-), *n.* soldier of light cavalry.

huss'y (*or* -zi), *n.* pert girl; woman of worthless character.

hus'tings (-z), *n.* platform for nomination of candidates for Parliament (Hist.); election proceedings.

hus'tle (-sl), *v.* push roughly; jostle; hurry; bustle. *n.* hustling.

hut, *n.* small roughly built house or shelter; temporary building of wood, etc.

hutch, *n.* box-like pen for rabbits, etc.

hy'acinth, *n.* bulbous plant with spikes of bell-shaped flowers.

hyaena: see **hyena.**

hy'brid, *n.* offspring of two animals or plants of different species, etc.; cross-breed. *a.* cross-bred, mongrel; composed of different elements.

hy'dra, *n.* (Gk. myth.) snake whose many heads grew again when when cut off.

hydrā'ngea (-ja; *or* -an-), *n.* shrub with large clusters of white, blue, or pink flowers.

hy'drant, *n.* water-pipe (esp. in street) with nozzle for hose.

hydrau'lic, *a.* of water (or other liquid conveyed through pipes, etc.; operated by force exerted by moving liquid; (of cement) hardening under water. **hydrau'lics,** *n.* science of conveyance of liquids through pipes, etc., esp. as motive power.

hy'drō, *n.* (*informal*) hydropathic hotel.

hydro-, *pref.* water-; (in Chem. terms) combined with hydrogen. **hydrocar'bon,** *n.* compound of hydrogen and carbon. **hydrochlo'ric a'cid,** solution of hydrogen

chloride in water. **hy'dro-ĕlec'tric,** *a.* using water-power to produce electricity. **hy'drofoil,** *n.* (fast motor-boat, etc., with) device under hull forcing it out of water at speed.

hydrog'raphy, *n.* scientific description of waters of the earth. **hydrom'ēter,** *n.* instrument for finding specific gravity of liquids.

hydrop'athy, *n.* treatment of disease by external and internal application of water. **hydropath'ic,** *a.* **hydrophō'bia,** *n.* aversion to water, esp. as symptom of rabies in man; rabies.

hy'drogĕn, *n.* light colourless odourless gas, combining with oxygen to form water. **hydrogen bomb,** bomb deriving its immensely destructive power from fusion of nuclei of hydrogen atoms. **hydro'gĕnous,** *a.* of or containing hydrogen.

hy'drous, *a.* containing water.

hyĕ'na, hyae'na, *a.* flesh-eating mammal of Africa and Asia, with powerful jaws.

hy'giene (-jĕn), *n.* principles, rules, for healthy living; sanitary science; cleanliness. **hygie'nic,** *a.*

hygrom'ēter, *n.* instrument for measuring humidity of air, etc.

Hy'men[1], *n.* (Gk. & Rom. myth.) god of marriage. **hymēnē'al,** *a.*

hy'men[2], *n.* fold of mucous membrane partially closing vagina of virgin female.

hymn (him), *n.* song of praise to God. *v. t.* praise in hymns.

hym'nal, *a.* of hymns. *n.* hymn-book.

hyper-, *pref.* over, above, excessive.

hyper'bola, *n.* curve produced when cone is cut by plane making larger angle with base than side of cone makes.

hyper'bolĕ, *n.* rhetorical exaggeration. **hyperbol'ical,** *a.*

hypercrit'ical, *a.* too critical.

hyperten'sion (-shn), *n.* abnormally high blood pressure; extreme tension.

hy'phen, *n.* sign (-) used to join or divide words. *v. t.* join, divide, with hyphen. **hy'phenāte,** *v. t.* hyphen.

hypnō'sis, *n.* (pl. *hypnōsēs*), (artificial production of) state like deep sleep in which subject is responsive to suggestion.

hypnot'ic, *a.* of hypnosis. *n.* thing that produces sleep; person under hypnosis.

hyp'notism, *n.* (production of) hypnosis. **hyp'notist,** *n.* **hyp'notīze,** *v. t.* produce hypnosis in.

hypo-, *pref.* below, under.

hypochon'dria (-k-), *n.* excessive, esp. needless, anxiety about one's health. **hypochon'driac,** *a.* of hypochondria. *n.* hypochondriac person.

hypoc'risy, *n.* pretence of being good or virtuous; pretence, sham. **hyp'ocrite,** *n.* one guilty of hypocrisy; one who shams. **hypocrit'ical,** *a.*

hypoder'mic, *a.* introduced beneath the skin. *n.* hypodermic injection or syringe.

hypodermic needle, syringe, used in hypodermic injection.
hypot'enūse (-z), *n.* side opposite right angle of triangle.
hypoth'esis, *n.* (pl. *hypothesēs*), supposition made as basis for reasoning, etc. **hypothet'-**

ical, *a.* of or resting on hypothesis.
hyss'op, *n.* small bushy aromatic herb.
hystēr'ia, *n.* (Med.) disturbance of nervous system; uncontrolled emotion or excitement.
hyste'rical, *a.* **hyste'rics,** *n.pl.* fit of hysteria.

I

I¹, i, as Roman numeral, 1.
I² (ī), *pron.* subjective case of 1st personal pron. (pl. *we*; objective *me*, pl. *us*).
i'amb, *n.*, **iam'bus,** *n.* (pl. *iambuses, iambi*), metrical foot of one short (or unstressed) syllable followed by one long (or stressed) syllable. **iam'bic,** *a.*
i'bex, *n.* (pl. *ibexes*), wild goat.
īce, *n.* frozen water; (with pl.) frozen confection. *v.t.* cover with ice; freeze; cool in ice; cover with icing. **ice'berg,** mass of floating ice at sea. **ice-bound,** (of ship, harbour, etc.) held fast, obstructed, by ice. **ice-box** (esp. U.S.), refrigerator. **ice cream,** frozen cream or custard, flavoured and sweetened. **ice hockey,** form of hockey played on ice-rink with rubber disc (*puck*). **ice-rink,** stretch or sheet of natural or artificial ice for skating, etc.
ichthyol'ogy, (ik-), *n.* study of fishes. **ichthyolo'gical,** *a.* **ichthyol'ogist,** *n.*
i'cicle, *n.* tapering spike of ice hanging from eaves, etc.
īc'ing, *n.* (esp.) coating of sugar, etc., for cake, etc.; formation of ice on wings of aircraft.
i'con, *n.* sacred painting, mosaic, etc.
icon'oclasm, *n.* breaking of images. **icon'oclast,** *n.* breaker of images; one who attacks cherished beliefs. **iconoclas'tic,** *a.*
i'cy, *a.* covered with ice; very cold.
idē'a, *n.* picture in the mind; vague belief, fancy; plan, intention.
idē'al, *a.* perfect; existing only in idea; visionary. *n.* perfect type; actual thing as standard for imitation. **idē'alism,** *n.* idealizing; representation of things in ideal form. **idē'alist,** *n.*
idē'alize, *v.t.* give ideal character to. **idēalizā'tion,** *n.*
iden'tical, *a.* agreeing in all details (*with*); same. **identical twins,** twins from single fertilized ovum, of the same sex and resembling each other closely.

iden'tify, *v.* establish identity of; treat as if identical; associate oneself inseparably *with*. **identificā'tion,** *n.*
iden'tikit, *n.* rough picture of person sought by police, assembled from drawings of facial features indicated by witnesses, etc.
iden'tity, *n.* absolute sameness; being specified person or thing; individuality.
idēol'ogy, *n.* scheme of ideas of political, etc., theory or system; characteristic way of thinking. **idēolo'gical,** *a.*
id'iocy, *n.* mental condition of idiot; extreme imbecility; utter foolishness.
id'iom, *n.* form of expression, phrase, peculiar to a language or dialect. **idiomat'ic,** *a.*
idiosyn'crasy, *n.* opinion, mannerism, etc., peculiar to person. **idiosyncrat'ic,** *a.*
id'iot, *n.* person too deficient in mind to be capable of rational conduct; imbecile; utter fool. **idiot'ic,** *a.*
i'dle, *a.* lazy; unoccupied; (of talk, etc.) frivolous, groundless. *v.* be idle; pass (time) idly; (of engine) run at low speed without doing any work. **i'dleness,** *n.* **i'dler,** *n.* **i'dly,** *adv.*
i'dol, *n.* image as object of worship; false god. **idol'ater,** *n.* worshipper of idols. **idol'atrous,** *a.* **idol'atry,** *n.*
i'dolize, *v.t.* make idol of; venerate or love to excess. **idolizā'tion,** *n.*
i'dyll (*or* ĭ-), *n.* (short poem describing) a picturesque or rustic scene. **idyll'ic,** *a.*
if, *conj.* on the condition or supposition that; whenever; whether.
ig'loō, *n.* Eskimo dome-shaped house built of blocks of snow.
ig'nēous, *a.* of fire; produced by volcanic action.
ignīte', *v.* set fire to; take fire. **igni'tion,** *n.* (esp.) (mechanism for) starting combustion in cylinder of internal-combustion engine.
ignō'ble, *a.* of low birth; mean, base.
ignomin'ious, *a.* shameful; humiliating.
ig'nominy, *n.* dishonour; infamy.

ignorā'mus, *n.* (pl. *ignoramuses*), ignorant person.

ig'norance, *n.* lack of knowledge.

ig'norant, *a.* lacking knowledge; untaught. *ignorant of*, not informed of, unaware of.

ignore', *v.t.* refuse to take notice of.

igua'na (-gwah-), *n.* large S. Amer. tree--lizard.

il-, *pref.*: see **in-**.

ill, *a.* not in good health, sick; evil, harmful; faulty, bad. *n.* evil; harm; (pl.) misfortunes. *adv.* badly, unfavourably; not well, not easily. **ill-advised**, unwise, imprudent. **ill--bred**, rude. **ill-fated**, destined to misfortune. **ill-favoured**, not good-looking. **ill--gotten**, gained by wrongful means. **ill--mannered**, unmannerly. **ill-natured**, bad--tempered. **ill-starred**, ill-fated. **ill-treat**, **ill--use**, treat badly or cruelly. **ill will**, unkind feeling, enmity.

illē'gal, *a.* contrary to law. **illēgal'ity**, *n.*

ille'gible, *a.* not legible, unreadable.

illĕgit'imate (-j-), *a.* not legitimate; born of parents not married to each other. **illĕgit'-imacy**, *n.*

illi'cit, *a.* unlawful, forbidden.

illim'itable, *a.* boundless.

illit'eracy, *n.* inability to read. **illit'erate**, *a.* unable to read; uneducated, unlearned. *n.* illiterate person.

ill'ness, *n.* ill health, sickness; disease.

illo'gical, *a.* not correctly reasoned.

illŭ'minate (*or* -ōō-), *v.t.* light up; throw light on; decorate with lights; decorate (manuscript, etc.) with gold, etc. **illuminā'tion**, *n.* **illu'minative**, *a.*

illŭ'sion (-zhn; *or* -ōō-), *n.* deceptive appearance or belief. **illu'sive**, *a.* **illu'sory**, *a.* deceptive.

ill'ustrate, *v.t.* make clear, esp. by examples or drawings, etc.; adorn with pictures. **illustrā'tion**, *n.* illustrating; example; drawing, etc., in book, etc. **ill'ustrative**, *a.* **ill'-ustrātor**, *n.*

illus'trious, *a.* distinguished, famous.

im-, *pref.*: see **in-**.

im'age, *n.* imitation of object's external form, esp. figure of saint, etc., idol; optical appearance reflected in mirror or refracted through lens, etc.; mental picture, idea. *v.t.* make image of; mirror; picture.

im'agery, *n.* images; statuary; vivid and descriptive figures of speech.

ima'ginable, *a.* that can be imagined.

ima'ginary, *a.* existing only in the imagination; not real.

imaginā'tion, *n.* power of the mind forming images of objects not present to the senses; fancy; creative power of the mind. **ima'-ginative**, *a.*

ima'gine, *v.t.* form mental picture of; suppose, think; fancy.

imā'gŏ, *n.* (pl. -*s* or *imaginēs*), final and perfect stage in metamorphosis of insect.

im'bĕcile (-ēl *or* -ĭl), *a.* mentally weak; stupid. *n.* imbecile person. **imbĕcil'ity**, *n.*

imbībe', *v.t.* drink in; drink; absorb.

imbroglio (imbrō'lyŏ), *n.* confused or complicated situation.

imbūe', *v.t.* saturate, dye; inspire.

im'itable, *a.* that can be imitated.

im'itāte, *v.t.* follow example of; mimic; be like. **imitā'tion**, *n.* **im'itative**, *a.* **im'itātor**, *n.*

immac'ūlate, *a.* pure, spotless; faultless.

imm'anent, *a.* dwelling (in); abiding (in); all--pervading. **imm'anence**, *n.*

immatēr'ial, *a.* not composed of matter; unimportant.

immatūre', *a.* not mature. **immatūr'ity**, *n.*

immea'surable (-mezher-), *a.* not measurable; immense.

immē'diate, *a.* without intervening medium, direct; happening at once. **immē'diately**, *adv.* without delay.

immemor'ial, *a.* ancient beyond memory.

immense', *a.* vast, huge. **immense'ly**, *adv.* vastly; very much.

immen'sity, *n.* vastness; infinity.

immerse', *v.t.* dip, plunge, (*in* liquid); put under water; (fig.) involve deeply, absorb. **immer'sible**, *a.* **immer'sion** (-shn), *n.*

imm'igrant, *n.* & *a.* (person) immigrating.

imm'igrāte, *v.i.* come as settler (*into* country). **immigrā'tion**, *n.*

imm'inent, *a.* impending, soon to happen. **imm'inence**, *n.*

immō'bile, *a.* immovable; motionless. **immo-bil'ity**, *n.*

immod'erate, *a.* excessive; extreme.

immod'est, *a.* indecent, improper; forward, impudent. **immod'esty**, *n.*

imm'olāte, *v.t.* sacrifice; kill as sacrifice. **immolā'tion**, *n.*

immo'ral, *a.* morally wrong or evil; dissolute. **immoral'ity**, *n.*

immor'tal, *a.* undying; famous for all time. *n.* immortal being, esp. (pl.) gods of antiquity. **immortal'ity**, *n.* **immor'talīze**, *v.t.* make immortal.

immō'vable (-mōō-), *a.* not movable; unyielding.

immūne', *a.* having immunity.

immū'nity, *n.* exemption (*from*); living organism's power of resisting and overcoming infection.

imm'ūnīze, *v.t.* make immune (*against* infection). **immūnīzā'tion**, *n.*

immūre', *v.t.* imprison, shut up.

immū'table, *a.* unchangeable. **immūtabil'ity**, *n.*

imp, *n.* child of the Devil; little devil; mischievous child.

impact, *n.* striking, collision; (immediate) effect, influence. **impact'**, *v.t.* drive or wedge together.

impair', *v.t.* damage; weaken. **impair'ment**, *n.* deterioration; injury.

impāle', *v.t.* pierce and transfix with stake, etc. **impāle'ment**, *n.*

impal'pable, *a.* that cannot be perceived by touch; difficult to grasp.

impart', *v.t.* give, give share of; make known (news, etc., *to*).

impar'tial (-shl), *a.* not partial, fair. **impartial'ity** (-shi-), *n.*

impass'able (-pah-), *a.* that cannot be crossed or traversed.

impasse' (-ahs; *or* am-), *n.* deadlock.

impa'ssioned (-shnd), *a.* deeply moved; ardent.

impass'ive, *a.* showing no feeling or emotion. **impass'iveness, impassiv'ity**, *nn.*

impā'tient (-shnt), *a.* not patient; intolerant. **impa'tience** (-shns), *n.*

impeach', *v.t.* accuse, esp. of crime against the State; throw doubt on; discredit. **impeach'ment**, *n.*

impecc'able, *a.* faultless.

impēcū'nious, *a.* having little or no money. **impēcūnios'ity**, *n.*

impēde', *v.t.* retard; hinder.

imped'iment, *n.* hindrance, obstruction; stammer, etc., *in speech.*

impel', *v.t.* (p.t. *impelled*), drive, force; propel.

impend', *v.i.* be about to happen; hang threateningly (*over*).

impen'ētrable, *a.* not penetrable; mysterious. **impenetrabil'ity**, *n.*

impen'itent, *a.* not penitent. **impen'itence**, *n.*

impe'rative, *a.* commanding; urgent; obligatory; (Gram.) expressing command. *n.* (Gram.) imperative mood.

impercep'tible, *a.* which cannot be perceived; very slight or gradual.

imper'fect, *a.* not perfect or complete; faulty; (Gram.) implying action going on but not completed.

imperfec'tion, *n.* faultiness; defect.

impēr'ial, *a.* of empire or large sovereign State; of emperor; majestic. *n.* small pointed beard on chin.

impēr'ialism, *n.* principle or spirit of empire; policy of extending empire and influence. **impēr'ialist**, *n.* **impērialis'tic**, *a.*

impe'ril, *v.t.* (p.t. *imperilled*), endanger.

impēr'ious, *a.* domineering; urgent.

impe'rishable, *a.* that cannot perish.

imper'mēable, *a.* not permeable.

imper'sonal, *a.* not influenced by personal feeling; not referring to particular person; (Gram., of verb) used only in 3rd pers. sing. and having no subject or purely formal one, as English *it.*

imper'sonāte, *v.t.* act the part of; pretend to be (another person). **impersonā'tion**, *n.* **imper'sonātor**, *n.*

imper'tinent, *a.* insolent, saucy; irrelevant. **imper'tinence**, *n.*

impertur'bable, *a.* not excitable; calm. **imperturbabil'ity**, *n.*

imper'vious, *a.* impenetrable; not permeable. *impervious to*, not moved or influenced by (argument, feeling, etc.).

impet'ūous, *a.* moving violently or fast; rash. **impetūos'ity**, *n.*

im'pētus, *n.* moving force; momentum; impulse.

impi'ēty, *n.* lack of piety; ungodliness.

impinge' (-nj), *v.i.* make impact (*on*).

im'pious, *a.* not pious; wicked, profane.

im'pish, *a.* of or like imp.

implac'able, *a.* that cannot be appeased; relentless.

implant' (-ahnt), *v.t.* insert; instil; plant.

im'plēment[1], *n.* instrument or tool for working with.

im'plēment[2], *v.t.* carry out, fulfil. **implēmentā'tion**, *n.*

im'plicāte, *v.t.* involve (person *in* charge, crime, etc.); imply. **implicā'tion**, *n.*

impli'cit, *a.* implied though not expressed; unquestioning.

implore', *v.t.* request earnestly.

implȳ', *v.t.* suggest truth of (something not expressly stated); mean; insinuate, hint.

impolīte', *a.* not polite, rude.

impol'itic, *a.* not politic; not expedient.

impon'derable, *a.* having little or no weight; (fig.) that cannot be estimated. *n.* imponderable thing. **imponderabil'ity**, *n.*

import', *v.t.* bring in (esp. foreign goods) from abroad; imply, mean. **im'port**, *n.* meaning, implication; importance; (usu. in pl.), imported commodity.

impor'tance, *n.* being important; consequence; significance.

impor'tant, *a.* of great influence; having great effect; to be treated seriously; (of person) having position of authority.

impor'tūnate, *a.* making persistent requests; (of affairs) urgent. **importū'nity**, *n.*

impor'tūne (*or* -tūn'), *v.t.* ask, beg, repeatedly and urgently.

impōse' (-z), *v.* lay (tax, duty, etc.) on; inflict (thing, one's company) *on*. *impose* (*up*)*on*, take advantage of (person, his good nature); deceive.

impō'sing (-z-), *a.* impressive, esp. in appearance.

imposi'tion (-z-), *n.* imposing; imposing on; thing imposed.

imposs'ible, *a.* not possible; not easy or convenient. **impossibil'ity**, *n.*

impos'tor, *n.* person pretending to be what he is not; swindler.

impos'ture, *n.* fraudulent deception.

im'potent, *a.* powerless; (of males) lacking sexual power. **im'potence**, *n.*

impound', *v.t.* shut up (cattle) in pound; confiscate.

impov'erish, *v.t.* make poor; exhaust strength of. **impov'erishment**, *n.*

imprac'ticable, *a.* not practicable; (of road) impassable. **impracticabil'ity**, *n.*

imprècā'tion, n. cursing; curse.

impreg'nable, a. that cannot be overcome or taken by force. **impregnabil'ity,** n.

im'pregnāte, v.t. make pregnant; fill, saturate. **impregnā'tion,** n.

impresar'iŏ, n. (pl. *impresarios*), organizer of, esp. musical, entertainments.

impress'¹, v.t. apply (mark, etc.) with pressure; stamp (*on*); enforce (idea, etc.) *on* person; influence; affect strongly. **im'press,** n. mark impressed; (fig.) characteristic mark.

impress'², v.t. force into service.

impre'ssion (-shn), n. impressing, mark impressed; issue, reprint, of book, etc.; effect produced on mind or feelings; vague notion or belief. **impre'ssionable,** a. easily impressed or influenced. **impressionabil'ity,** n.

impre'ssionism (-shn-), n. method of painting or writing so as to give general effect without detail. **impre'ssionist,** n. **impressionis'tic,** a.

impress'ive, a. making deep impression on mind or senses.

imprint', v.t. impress mark on. **im'print,** n. impression, stamp.

impris'on (-z-), v.t. put into prison; confine. **impris'onment,** n.

improb'able, a. not likely to be true or to happen. **improbabil'ity,** n.

impromp'tū, adv. & a. without preparation. n. improvised or extempore performance, composition, etc.

improp'er, a. offending against decency or seemliness; not appropriate; inaccurate, wrong.

impropri'ėty, n. being improper; improper act, remark, etc.

improve' (-ŏŏv), v. make or become better. **improve'ment,** n.

improv'ident, a. not providing for future needs, not thrifty. **improv'idence,** n.

im'provīse (-z), v.t. compose or utter (music, verse) without preparation; provide, organize, quickly and without preparation. **improvisā'tion,** n.

impru'dent (-rŏŏ-), a. rash, indiscreet. **impru'dence,** n.

im'pūdent, a. shamelessly rude; insolently disrespectful. **im'pūdence,** n.

impugn' (-ūn), v.t. express doubt abòut, challenge (statement, action).

im'pulse, n. impelling; moving force; sudden inclination to act without reflection. **impul'sive,** a. apt to be influenced, prompted, by impulse.

impū'nity, n. exemption from punishment. *with impunity*, suffering no injury or punishment as consequence of act.

impūre', a. dirty; unchaste; adulterated. **impūr'ity,** n.

impūte', v.t. attribute, ascribe, (fault, etc., *to*). **impūtā'tion,** n.

in, prep. expressing inclusion or position within limits of space, time, circumstance, etc. adv. expressing position bounded by certain limits, or movement to point enclosed by them; at home; (of player, etc.) having turn or right to play; in fashion or season or office. n. (esp.) *ins and outs*, all the details.

in-¹, pref. (becoming *il-* before *l*, *im-* before *b*, *m*, *p*, and *ir-* before *r*), in, into, on, towards, against.

in-², pref. (becoming *il-* before *l*, *im-* before *b*, *m*, *p*, and *ir-* before *r*), not.

inabil'ity, n. being unable.

inaccess'ible (-aks-), a. that cannot be reached. **inaccessibil'ity,** n.

inacc'ūrate, a. not accurate. **inacc'ūracy,** n.

inac'tion, n. absence of action. **inac'tive,** a. **inactiv'ity,** n.

inad'ėquate, a. not adequate; insufficient. **inad'ėquacy,** n.

inadmiss'ible, a. that cannot be admitted or allowed. **inadmissibil'ity,** n.

inadver'tent, a. negligent; unintentional. **inadver'tence, inadver'tency,** nn.

inā'liėnable, a. that cannot be withdrawn. **ināliėnabil'ity,** n.

ināne', a. empty; silly. **inan'ity,** n.

inan'imate, a. lifeless; not endowed with animal life; dull.

inani'tion, n. exhaustion from lack of nourishment.

inapp'licable, a. not applicable; unsuitable.

inapp'osite (-z-), a. not apposite.

inapprė'ciable (-sha-), a. not appreciable; imperceptible.

inapprō'priate, a. not appropriate.

inapt', a. unsuitable, inappropriate. **inapt'-ness,** n.

inap'titude, n. lack of aptitude.

inartic'ūlate, a. not articulate, indistinct; dumb; not jointed.

inartis'tic, a. not following principles of, unskilled in, art.

inasmuch' (-z-), adv. *inasmuch as*, seeing that.

inatten'tion, n. lack of attention. **inatten'tive,** a.

inau'dible, a. that cannot be heard. **inaudibil'ity,** n.

inau'gūral, a. & n. (ceremony, lecture, etc.) of or at inauguration. **inau'gūrāte,** v.t. admit to, enter upon, with ceremony; begin. **inaugūrā'tion,** n.

inauspi'cious (-shus), a. not of good omen; unlucky.

in'born, a. (of a quality, etc.) existing in person or organism since birth.

in'bred (*or* -ed'), a. inborn; born of closely related parents. **in'-breeding,** n. breeding from closely related individuals.

incal'cūlable, a. too great to be calculated; uncertain. **incalcūlabil'ity,** n.

in cam'era, (Law) in private, not in open court. (Latin)

incandes'cent, a. giving out light when

heated; shining. **incandes'cence,** *n.*
incantā'tion, *n.* spell, charm.
incā'pable, *a.* not capable; disqualified; not able. **incāpabil'ity,** *n.*
incapa'citāte, *v. t.* make incapable or unfit.
incapa'city, *n.* inability; legal disqualification.
incar'cerāte, *v. t.* imprison. **incarcerā'tion,** *n.*
incar'nate, *a.* embodied in flesh, esp. in human form. **incarnā'tion,** *n.*
incau'tious (-shus) *a.* rash.
incen'diary, *a.* of, guilty of, malicious setting on fire of property; (of bomb, etc.) intended to cause fires. *n.* incendiary person or bomb. **incen'diarism,** *n.*
incense'¹, *v. t.* make angry.
in'cense², *n.* gum, spice, giving sweet smell when burned.
incen'tive, *n.* something encouraging or inciting to action; stimulus. *a.* inciting.
incep'tion, *n.* beginning. **incep'tive,** *a.*
incer'titūde, *n.* uncertainty.
incess'ant, *a.* continual; repeated.
in'cest, *n.* sexual intercourse between closely related persons. **inces'tūous,** *a.*
inch, *n.* measure of length, twelfth part of foot; small amount. *v.* move by inches; edge *forward,* etc.
in'cidence, *n.* range or scope of a thing, extent of its influence or effects.
in'cident, *n.* event, occurrence; episode. **inciden'tal,** *a.* casual, not essential. **inciden'tally,** *adv.* (esp.) by the way, parenthetically.
incin'erāte, *v. t.* burn to ashes. **incinerā'tion,** *n.* **incin'erātor,** *n.* (esp.) furnace or container for burning of rubbish.
incip'ient, *a.* beginning.
incīse' (-z), *v. t.* make cut in; engrave. **inci'sion** (-zhn), *n.* **inci'sive** (-s-), *a.* sharp, cutting; acute, clear-cut.
inci'sor (-z-), *n.* any of front teeth between canines.
incīte', *v. t.* urge on, stir up. **incīte'ment,** *n.*
incivil'ity, *n.* rudeness; impolite act, etc.
inclem'ency, *n.* harshness, esp. of weather. **inclem'ent,** *a.* severe, stormy.
inclinā'tion, *n.* slope, slant; tendency; liking; affection.
incline', *v.* lean, cause to lean; bend forward or downward; dispose, be disposed; tend. **in'clīne,** *n.* inclined plane; slope.
include' (-lōōd), *v. t.* reckon in, regard, as part of whole. **inclu'sion** (-zhn), *n.*
inclu'sive (-ōō-), *a.* including, comprehensive; including all charges.
incog'nitō (*or* -nē'tō), *a.* & *adv.* unknown or concealed under false name, etc.
incōhēr'ent, *a.* not coherent; inconsequential. **incōhēr'ence,** *n.*
incombus'tible, *a.* that cannot be burnt or consumed by fire.
in'come (-um), *n.* periodical (esp. annual) receipts from work, investments, etc.
income tax, tax levied on income.
incommen'surable (-sher-), *a.* not commensurable; not comparable.
incommen'surate (-sher-), *a.* out of proportion, inadequate, (*with, to*).
incommōde', *v. t.* trouble, annoy; inconvenience. **incommō'dious,** *a.* too small for comfort; inconvenient.
incom'parable, *a.* matchless.
incompat'ible, *a.* opposed in character, discordant. **incompatibil'ity,** *n.*
incom'pêtent, *a.* not competent; not legally qualified. **incom'pêtence,** *n.*
incomplēte', *a.* not complete, not finished.
incomprêhen'sible, *a.* that cannot be understood. **incomprêhensibil'ity,** *n.*
inconceiv'able (-sēv-), *a.* that cannot be imagined. **inconceivabil'ity,** *n.*
inconclu'sive (-lōō-), *a.* not decisive or convincing.
incong'ruous (-nggroo-), *a.* not in harmony or agreement (*with*); out of place; absurd. **incongru'ity** (-rōō-), *n.*
incon'sèquent, *a.* disconnected; not to the point. **incon'sèquence,** *n.*
inconsèquen'tial (-shl), *a.* inconsequent; of no consequence.
inconsid'erable, *a.* not worth considering; of small size, value, etc.
inconsid'erate, *a.* not considerate of others; thoughtless, rash.
inconsis'tent, *a.* not consistent; self-contradictory. **inconsis'tency,** *n.*
inconsōl'able, *a.* that cannot be comforted.
inconspic'ūous, *a.* not conspicuous.
incon'stant, *a.* fickle, changeable; variable, irregular. **incon'stancy,** *n.*
incontes'table, *a.* that cannot be disputed.
incon'tinent, *a.* lacking self-restraint; unable to control urination or defecation. **incon'tinence,** *n.*
incontrover'tible, *a.* that cannot be controverted.
inconvē'nience, *n.* discomfort, trouble; inconvenient circumstance, etc. *v. t.* cause inconvenience, be troublesome, to. **inconvē'nient,** *a.* awkward; troublesome.
incor'porāte, *v. t.* combine into one substance or whole. **incorporā'tion,** *n.*
incorrect', *a.* inaccurate; untrue; improper.
inco'rrigible, *a.* incurably bad or depraved.
incorrup'tible, *a.* that cannot decay; that cannot be bribed.
increase', *v.* become, make, greater or more numerous; intensify. **in'crease,** *n.* growth, enlargement; increased amount.
incred'ible, *a.* that cannot be believed; surprising. **incredibil'ity,** *n.*
incred'ūlous, *a.* unbelieving, unwilling to believe. **incredū'lity,** *n.*
in'crèment, *n.* (amount of) increase; profit.
incrim'ināte, *v. t.* involve in accusation of crime. **incriminā'tion,** *n.*

incrustā'tion, _n._ encrusting, being encrusted; crust, hard coating.

in'cūbāte, _v._ sit on eggs, brood; hatch (eggs) thus or by artificial warmth. **incūbā'tion,** _n._ incubating; early phase of disease between infection and appearance of symptoms.

in'cūbātor, _n._ apparatus for hatching birds or rearing infants born prematurely.

in'cūbus, _n._ legendary demon supposed to descend on sleeping persons; nightmare; person, thing, oppressing like nightmare.

in'culcāte, _v._ _t._ impress persistently (_upon_, _in_, person, mind). **inculcā'tion,** _n._

in'culpāte, _v._ _t._ accuse, blame; involve in accusation. **inculpā'tion,** _n._

incum'bent, _a._ resting as duty (_up_)_on_. _n._ holder of benefice. **incum'bency,** _n._

incur', _v._ _t._ (p.t. _incurred_), bring upon oneself (debt, blame, etc.).

incūr'able, _a._ & _n._ (person) that cannot be cured. **incūrabil'ity,** _n._

incūr'ious, _a._ indifferent. **incūrios'ity,** _n._

incur'sion (-shn), _n._ invasion; sudden attack.

indebt'ed (-det-), _a._ owing money or gratitude (_to_). **indebt'edness,** _n._

indē'cent, _a._ offending against modesty or propriety, obscene. **indē'cency,** _n._

indēci'pherable, _a._ that cannot be deciphered.

indēci'sion (-zhn), _n._ inability to make up one's mind; hesitation.

indēci'sive, _a._ not decisive; irresolute.

indēcli'nable, _a._ (Gram.) not inflected.

indec'orous, _a._ offending against decency. **indēcor'um,** _n._ lack of decorum.

indeed', _adv._ in truth; really.

indēfat'igable, _a._ tireless.

indēfen'sible, _a._ that cannot be defended or excused.

indēfi'nable, _a._ that cannot be defined.

indef'inite, _a._ vague; unlimited.

indel'ible, _a._ that cannot be deleted or effaced, permanent.

indel'icate, _a._ coarse, not refined; immodest; tactless. **indel'icacy,** _n._

indem'nifȳ, _v._ _t._ secure against loss or legal responsibility; compensate (_for_ loss, etc.). **indemnificā'tion,** _n._

indem'nity, _n._ security against loss; compensation, esp. from defeated belligerent.

indent', _v._ _t._ make notches, dents, or recesses in; make requisition _for_; (Printing) set (beginning of line) further in from margin. **in'dent,** _n._ official requisition order. **indentā'tion,** _n._

inden'ture (-cher), _n._ (also pl.) sealed agreement, esp. binding apprentice to master. _v._ _t._ bind by indenture.

indēpen'dence, _n._ being independent; self-government; independent income.

indēpen'dent, _a._ not dependent on or controlled by other person(s) or thing(s); self-governing. _n._ politician, etc., not belonging to any party.

indēscrī'bable, _a._ too great, beautiful, bad, etc., to be described. **indescrī'bably,** _adv._

indēstruc'tible, _a._ that cannot be destroyed. **indēstructibil'ity,** _n._

indēter'minate, _a._ not fixed; vague; left doubtful.

in'dex, _n._ (pl. _indexes_, _indicēs_), forefinger; pointer on instrument; list of names, subjects, etc., esp. alphabetical list with references. _v._ _t._ provide (book) with index; enter in index.

In'diaman, _n._ (pl. _men_), (Hist.) ship engaged in trade with India.

In'dian, _a._ & _n._ (native) of India; (one of original inhabitants) of America and W. Indies. **Indian corn,** maize. **Indian file,** single file. **Indian ink,** black pigment. **Indian summer,** period of calm fine weather in late summer, esp. in northern U.S.A.

In'dia pā'per, _n._ soft absorbent paper for proofs or engravings; very thin tough opaque printing-paper.

in'diarubb'er, _n._ (esp.) piece of rubber for rubbing out pencil-marks, etc.

in'dicāte, _v._ _t._ point out, make known, show; be sign of. **indicā'tion,** _n._ **in'dicātor,** _n._ thing that points out or gives information.

indic'ative, _a._ giving indications _of_; (Gram., of verbal mood) stating as fact. _n._ indicative mood.

indict' (-dīt), _v._ _t._ accuse, esp. by legal process. **indict'able,** _a._ **indict'ment,** _n._ formal accusation.

indiff'erence, _n._ lack of interest or concern. **indiff'erent,** _a._ not interested, unconcerned; neither good nor bad.

in'digence, _n._ want, poverty. **in'digent,** _a._ needy, poor.

indi'genous, _a._ native; belonging naturally (_to_ soil, etc.).

indiges'tible, _a._ not (easily) digestible. **indiges'tion** (-schn), _n._ difficulty in digesting food.

indig'nant, _a._ moved by anger and scorn or by sense or injury. **indignā'tion,** _n._

indig'nity, _n._ unworthy treatment; insult, slight.

in'digō, _n._ (pl. _indigos_), blue dye obtained from certain plants; colour between blue and violet in spectrum.

indirect', (_or_ -dī-), _a._ not direct; not straight; (of tax) levied on goods and paid by consumer in form of increased price.

indis'cipline, _n._ lack of discipline.

indiscreet', _a._ not discreet; unwise. **indiscre'tion,** _n._ imprudence; rashness; social transgression.

indiscrim'inate, _a._ not discerning; confused; making no distinctions.

indispen'sable, _a._ that cannot be done without; absolutely necessary.

indispōse' (-z), _v._ _t._ make unwilling. **indisposed',** _a._ (esp.) unwell. **indisposi'tion,** _n._ ill-health; disinclination.

indis'pūtable, _a._ that cannot be disputed.

indissol'ūble, *a.* that cannot be dissolved; lasting, stable.

indistinct', *a.* not distinct; confused.

indisting'uishable (-nggw-), *a.* not distinguishable.

indīte', *v.t.* put into words, compose.

individ'ūal, *a.* single; particular; of or for single person or thing; characteristic of particular person, etc. *n.* single member of class, group, etc.; single human being. **individ'-ūalist,** *n.* person who thinks and acts independently. **individūal'ity,** *n.*

indivis'ible (-z-), *a.* not divisible.

indoc'trināte, *v.t.* teach; imbue *with* doctrine, etc. **indoctrinā'tion,** *n.*

in'dolent, *a.* lazy, idle. **in'dolence,** *n.*

indom'itable, *a.* that cannot be subdued or conquered; unyielding.

in'door (-dor) *a.* situated, done, inside a building. **indoors'** (-z), *adv.* in, into a house, etc.

indū'bitable, *a.* beyond doubt.

indūce', *v.t.* persuade; bring about; produce by induction; infer. **indūce'ment,** *n.* (esp.) attraction that leads one on. **indū'cible,** *a.*

induct', *v.t.* install formally.

induc'tance, *n.* (Electr.) coefficient of self--induction.

induc'tion, *n.* inducting; general inference from particular instances; (Med.) inducing (of labour); (Electr.) production of (changes in) current, etc., by proximity of neighbouring circuit, etc. *self-induction,* reaction of current in circuit upon itself. **induc'tive,** *a.*

indulge' (-j), *v.* gratify; give free course to; take one's pleasure freely *in.* **indul'gence,** *n.* indulging; privilege granted; (R.C. Ch.) remission of punishment for sin. **indul'gent,** *a.* (esp.) too lenient or forbearing.

indus'trial, *a.* of industries; engaged in, connected with, industry. **indus'trialism,** *n.* **indus'trialist,** *n.* **indus'trialīze,** *v.t.*

indus'trious, *a.* diligent, hard-working.

in'dustry, *n.* diligence; branch of trade or manufacture; manufacturing.

inē'briāte, *v.t.* make drunk. **inē'briate,** *a.* drunken. *n.* drunkard.

ined'ible, *a.* not fit to be eaten.

ineff'able, *a.* too great to be described in words.

ineffec'tive, *a.* not producing desired effect; inefficient.

ineffec'tūal, *a.* without effect, fruitless.

ineffi'cient (-shnt), *a.* not fully capable; ineffective. **ineffi'ciency,** *n.*

inel'ègant, *a.* not graceful; unpolished. **inel'-ègance,** *n.*

inel'igible, *a.* not eligible, not qualified.

inept', *a.* foolish; clumsy, bungling. **inep'-titūde,** *n.*

inēqual'ity (-ol-), *n.* lack of equality; variableness, unevenness.

ine'quitable, *a.* unfair, unjust.

inėrad'icable, *a.* that cannot be rooted out.

inert', *a.* without power of motion or action; sluggish, slow; (Chem., of gases) chemically inactive. **inert'ness,** *n.*

iner'tia (-sha), *n.* inertness, sloth; (Phys.) property of matter by which it continues in existing state of rest or motion unless acted on by external force.

ines'timable, *a.* too good, too great, etc., to be estimated; invaluable.

inev'itable, *a.* unavoidable; bound to happen or appear. **inevitabil'ity,** *n.*

inèxact' (-gz-), *a.* not exact.

inèxhaus'tible (-gzaw-), *a.* that cannot be exhausted. **inèxhaustibil'ity,** *n.*

inex'orable, *a.* relentless.

inèxpē'dient, *a.* not expedient.

inèxpen'sive, *a.* not expensive, cheap.

inèxpēr'ience, *n.* lack of experience. **inèxpēr'iènced,** *a.*

inex'pert, *a.* unskilful.

inex'plicable (*or* -plik'-), *a.* that cannot be explained or accounted for.

inèxpress'ible, *a.* that cannot be expressed in words.

inèxting'uishable (-nggw-), *a.* that cannot be quenched.

in èxtrē'mis, at the point of death. (Latin)

inex'tricable, *a.* that cannot be solved, unravelled, or escaped from.

infall'ible, *a.* not liable to make mistakes; unfailing, sure. **infallibil'ity,** *n.*

in'famous, *a.* of bad reputation; notoriously vile. **in'famy,** *n.*

in'fancy, *n.* babyhood; minority.

in'fant, *n.* baby; young child; (Law) minor.

infan'ta, *n.* (Hist.) daughter of king of Spain or Portugal.

infan'ticide, *n.* murder of new-born child.

in'fantile, *a.* (as) of infants; childish.

in'fantry, *n.* soldiers who march and manoeuvre on foot.

infat'ūāted, *a.* inspired with unreasonable love or passion. **infatūā'tion,** *n.*

infect', *v.t.* communicate disease to; contaminate; imbue (*with* opinion, etc.).

infec'tion, *n.* infecting or being infected; infectious disease, etc. **infec'tious** (-shus), *a.* communicable by disease-forming micro--organisms, etc., esp. by agency of air, water, etc.; apt to spread.

infer', *v.t.* (p.t. *inferred*), reach conclusion (from facts or reasoning); (of fact or statement) lead to as a conclusion. **in'ference,** *n.* **inferen'tial** (-shl), *a.*

infēr'ior, *a.* lower in rank, etc.; of poor quality. *n.* person of lower rank. **infērio'rity,** *n.*

infer'nal, *a.* of hell; hellish.

infer'nō, *n.* (pl. *infernos*), hell; scene of horror.

infer'tile, *a.* not fertile. **infertil'ity,** *n.*

infest', *v.t.* (of insects, rats, etc.) be present in large numbers, plague. **infestā'tion,** *n.*

in'fidel, *n.* disbeliever in religion. *a.* unbelieving; of infidels.

infidel'ity, *n.* unfaithfulness.

in'filtrâte, *v.t.* introduce or permeate (as) by filtration; penetrate (*into*) gradually. **infiltrâ'tion,** *n.* (esp.) gradual penetration by small groups, etc.

in'finite, *a.* having no limit or end; exceedingly great, vast. **in'finitely,** *a.*

infinites'imal, *a.* extremely small.

infin'itive, *a. & n.* (verb-form) expressing verbal notion in general way, without subject.

infin'itûde, *n.* infinity.

infin'ity, *n.* quality of being infinite; boundless number or extent.

infirm', *a.* physically weak; irresolute. **infir'mity,** *n.*

infir'mary, *n.* hospital.

inflâme', *v.t.* rouse to passion, anger, etc.; aggravate; cause inflammation in.

inflamm'able, *a.* easily set on fire, flammable; easily excited. **inflammabil'ity,** *n.*

inflammâ'tion, *n.* a condition of living tissue characterized by heat, swelling, redness, and usu. pain.

inflamm'atory, *a.* tending to inflame with passion, etc.

inflâte', *v.t.* distend with air or gas; puff up; take action to cause inflation of currency. **inflâ'tion,** *n.* (esp.) fall in value of money due to increase of purchasing power in relation to goods available for purchase.

inflect', *v.t.* (Gram.) change ending or form of (word) to form plural, past tense, comparative, etc.; modulate (voice, etc.). **inflec'tion,** *n.* inflexion.

inflex'ible, *a.* unbendable; unbending; unyielding.

infle'xion (-kshn), *n.* inflecting; inflected form; inflecting suffix, etc.; modulation of voice, etc. **infle'xional,** *a.*

inflict[1], *v.t.* give (blow, etc.); impose; cause to be borne. **inflic'tion,** *n.* (esp.) troublesome, painful, etc., experience.

inflores'cence, *n.* arrangement of flowers, collective flower, of plant.

in'fluence (-loo-), *n.* action exercised by one person or thing over another; (thing or person exercising) moral power; ascendancy. *v.t.* exert influence, have effect, upon. **influen'tial** (-shl), *a.* having great influence.

influen'za (-loo-), *n.* infectious illness with fever and catarrh (abbrev. *flu*).

in'flux, *n.* flowing in.

inform', *v.* tell (person *of* thing, *that*, etc.); instruct. *inform against,* bring evidence or accusation against.

infor'mal, *a.* without formality; (of words, etc.) colloquial, not formal or literary. **informal'ity,** *n.*

infor'mant, *n.* giver of information.

informâ'tion, *n.* telling; what is told; knowledge; news. **infor'mative,** *a.* instructive. **infor'mer,** *n.* one who informs against another.

infra-, *pref.* below. **in'fra-red',** *a.* situated below or beyond red in spectrum.

infra dig. (*abbrev.* of Latin *infra dignitatem*), beneath one's dignity.

infrê'quent, *a.* not frequent. **infrê'quency,** *n.*

infringe' (-nj), *v.t.* break (law, etc.), transgress; violate. **infringe'ment,** *n.*

infûr'iâte, *v.t.* fill with fury, enrage.

infûse' (-z), *v.* pour (*into*); instil (*into*); steep, be steeped, in liquid to extract properties. **infû'sion** (-zhn), *n.* (liquid extract obtained by) infusing; admixture.

ingê'nious (-j-), *a.* showing cleverness of invention or construction. **ingênû'ity,** *n.*

ingen'ûous (-j-), *a.* open, frank; artless.

ingle-nook (ing'gl-), *n.* warm seat within wide old-fashioned fireplace.

inglor'ious (in-g-), *a.* ignominious; not well known.

ing'ot (-ngg-), *n.* mass (usu. oblong) of cast metal, esp. gold, silver, or steel.

ingrained (in'-grând *before noun*, in-grând' *elsewhere*), *a.* deeply rooted.

ingrâtiate (in-grâ'shiât), *v. refl.* *ingratiate oneself,* bring oneself into favour *with.*

ingrat'itûde (in-g-), *n.* lack of gratitude.

ingrê'dient (in-g-), *n.* component part in mixture.

inhab'it, *v.t.* dwell in. **inhab'itant,** *n.*

inhâle', *v.t.* breathe in. **inhalâ'tion,** *n.*

inharmô'nious, *a.* discordant.

inhêr'ent, *a.* existing in; belonging naturally. **inhêr'ently,** *adv.*

inhe'rit, *v.* receive, succeed, as heir; derive from parents or ancestors. **inhe'ritance,** *n.* inheriting; what is inherited. **inhe'ritor,** *n.*

inhib'it, *v.t.* hinder, restrain. **inhibi'tion,** *n.* (esp., Psychol.) blocking of thought or action by emotional resistance.

inhos'pitable, *a.* not hospitable; giving no kindness or shelter.

inhû'man, *a.* brutal, unfeeling, barbarous. **inhuman'ity,** *n.*

inim'ical, *a.* hostile; harmful.

inim'itable, *a.* too good, etc., to be imitated.

ini'quitous, *a.* unjust; wicked.

ini'quity, *n.* wickedness; gross injustice.

ini'tial (-shl), *a.* of, existing or occurring at, the beginning. **ini'tially,** *adv.* **ini'tial,** *n.* (esp.) first letter of name. *v.t.* (p.t. *initialled*), mark, sign, with initials.

ini'tiâte (-shi-), *v.t.* start, set going; (with *into*) instruct in ways of (society, etc.). *n.* (pr. -at), initiated person. **initiâ'tion,** *n.*

ini'tiative (-shya-), *n.* first step; lead; ability to initiate, enterprise.

inject', *v.t.* force (fluid *into*) as by syringe. **injec'tion,** *n.* injecting; fluid, etc., injected.

injudi'cious (-joodishus), *a.* unwise, ill-judged.

injunc'tion, *n.* authoritative order.

in'jure (-jer), *v.t.* do wrong to; hurt, harm, impair. **injur'ious** (-joor-), *a.* wrongful; hurtful. **in'jury,** *n.* wrong, damage, harm.

injus′tice, *n*. unfairness; unjust act.

ink, *n*. coloured (often black or blue-black) fluid for writing or printing. *v.t.* mark (*in*, *over*, etc.) with ink. **ink′pot**, small pot for ink. **ink-well**, inkpot fitted into hole in desk. **ink′y**, *a*.

ink′ling, *n*. hint; slight knowledge or suspicion (*of*).

inlaid, *p.t. & p.p.* of **inlay**.

in′land, *n*. interior of country. *a*. remote from sea or border. *adv*. in, towards, interior.

in-law′, *n*. (*informal*, usu. in pl.) relative by marriage.

inlay′, *v.t.* (p.t. *inlaid*), embed (thing *in* groundwork of another); ornament thus. **in′-lay**, *n*. inlaid ornament.

in′lět, *n*. small arm of the sea.

in lŏc′ō paren′tis, in the place or position of a parent. (Latin)

in′māte, *n*. occupant (*of* house, etc.).

in memor′iam, in memory of. (Latin)

in′mŏst, *a*. most inward.

inn, *n*. public house providing lodging, etc., for travellers. **inn′keeper**, *n*.

innāte′, *a*. inborn.

inn′er, *a*. interior, internal. **inn′ermŏst**, *a*.

inn′ings (-z), *n*. (pl. same), (Cricket, etc.) batsman's or side's turn at batting.

inn′ocent, *a*. sinless; not guilty; simple, guileless; harmless. *n*. innocent person, esp. young child. **inn′ocence**, *n*.

innoc′ūous, *a*. harmless.

inn′ovāte, *v.i.* bring in new ways; make changes. **innovā′tion**, *n*.

innŭen′dō, *n*. (pl. *innuendoes*), hint, allusive remark (usu. depreciatory).

innŭ′merable, *a*. countless.

inoc′ūlāte, *v.t.* introduce attenuated micro-organisms of specified disease into (person, animal) to stimulate production of immunity. **inocūlā′tion**, *n*.

inoffen′sive, *a*. harmless; not objectionable.

inop′erable, *a*. (Med.) that cannot be treated or cured by operation.

inop′erative, *a*. not working or having effect.

inopp′ortūne, *a*. done, coming, at an inappropriate or inconvenient time.

inor′dinate, *a*. excessive.

inorgan′ic, *a*. without organized physical structure; (Chem.) not organic.

in′-pătient (-shnt), *n*. patient who stays in hospital for treatment, etc.

in′put (-oot), *n*. putting in; what is put in.

in′quest (in-kw-), *n*. legal or judicial inquiry, esp. (*coroner's*) inquest into cause of death, or in case of treasure trove.

inquīre′, enquīre′ (in-kw-), *v*. make search (*into*); seek information; ask. **inquīr′y, enquīr′y**, *n*. asking; question; investigation.

inquisi′tion (in-kwiz-), *n*. investigation; official inquiry.

inquis′itive (in-kwiz-), *a*. curious, prying.

inquis′itor (in-kwiz-), *n*. official investigator.

in′road, *n*. raid; (fig., usu. pl.) forcible encroachment.

in′rush, *n*. rushing in.

insalŭ′brious (*or* -ōō-), *a*. unhealthy.

insāne′, *a*. mad; senseless.

insan′itary, *a*. not sanitary.

insan′ity, *n*. madness.

insā′tiable (-sha-), *a*. that cannot be satisfied; greedy. **insatiabil′ity**, *n*. **insā′tiate** (-shyat), *a*. never satisfied.

inscrībe′, *v.t.* write (*in*, *on*); enter on list.

inscrip′tion, *n*. words inscribed on monument, coin, etc.

inscru′table (-ōō-), *a*. entirely mysterious; unfathomable.

in′sect, *n*. small invertebrate animal with segmented body and, usu., six legs and two pairs of wings. **insec′ticide**, *n*. preparation for killing insects. **insectiv′orous**, *a*. insect-eating.

insecūre′, *a*. not secure or safe; not feeling secure. **insecūr′ity**, *n*.

insem′ināte, *v.t.* introduce semen into, fertilize, impregnate. **inseminā′tion**, *n*.

insen′sate, *a*. unfeeling; stupid; mad.

insen′sible, *a*. unconscious; without feeling; imperceptible; unaware. **insen′sibly**, *adv*. **insensibil′ity**, *n*.

insen′sitive, *a*. not sensitive.

insep′arable, *a*. that cannot be separated.

insert′, *v.t.* place or fit or thrust (*in*, *into*); introduce. **in′sert**, *n*. thing (to be) inserted.

inser′tion, *n*. inserting; thing inserted.

in′set, *n*. small diagram, map, etc., within border of page, larger map, etc.; extra page(s) inserted in magazine, etc.

in′shore, *adv. & a*. close to shore.

inside, *n*. (in′sīd′), inner side or part; interior. *a*. (in′-), on, in, coming or derived from, inside. *adv*. (-īd′), on or in or to inside. *prep*. (-īd′), on or to inside of; within.

insid′ious, *a*. treacherous; proceeding secretly or subtly.

in′sight (-īt), *n*. mental perception; deep understanding.

insig′nia, *n.pl*. badges or marks (*of* office, etc.).

insignif′icant, *a*. unimportant; meaningless. **insignif′icance**, *n*.

insincēre′, *a*. not sincere. **insince′rity**, *n*.

insin′ūāte, *v.t.* introduce gradually or subtly; hint. **insinūā′tion**, *n*.

insip′id, *a*. flavourless; dull, lifeless. **insipid′ity**, *n*.

insist′, *v*. dwell emphatically (*on*); maintain positively. *insist* (*up*)*on*, demand urgently or persistently. **insis′tence**, *n*. **insis′tent**, *a*.

in sī′tū (*or* sit′ōō), in its (original) place. (Latin)

in′sōle, *n*. inner sole of shoe; extra sole worn inside shoe for warmth or comfort.

in′solent, *a*. offensively contemptuous; insulting. **in′solence**, *n*.

insol′ūble, *a*. that cannot be dissolved; that cannot be solved. **insolūbil′ity**, *n*.

insol'vent, *a.* unable to pay debts. **insol'-vency**, *n.*

insom'nia, *n.* inability to sleep. **insom'niac**, *n.* person suffering from insomnia.

insomuch', *adv.* to such an extent *that*.

inspect', *v.t.* look carefully into; examine officially. **inspec'tion**, *n.*

inspec'tor, *n.* official who inspects; police officer next below superintendent.

inspira'tion, *n.* creative influence; inspiring principle or person; sudden happy idea.

inspire', *v.t.* infuse (thought, feeling) into; influence, animate, *with* (feeling, idea); be source of ideas to (poet, etc.).

inspi'rit, *v.t.* put life into; encourage.

instabil'ity, *n.* lack of (esp. moral, emotional, etc.) stability.

install' (-awl), *v.t.* place in office with ceremony; put in. **installa'tion**, *n.*

instal'ment (-awl-), *n.* any of several successive parts of sum payable, or of serial story, etc.

in'stance, *n.* example; particular case; request. *v.t.* cite as instance; be an instance of.

in'stant, *a.* urgent; immediate; of the current month (abbrev. *inst.*); that can be prepared or produced immediately. *n.* precise (esp. present) point of time; short time. **in'stantly**, *adv.* at once.

instanta'neous, *a.* occurring, done, etc., in an instant.

instead' (-ed), *adv.* as substitute or alternative; in place *of*.

in'step, *n.* upper part of foot between toes and ankle.

in'stigate, *v.t.* incite (*to*); bring about by persuasion. **instiga'tion**, *n.* **in'stigator**, *n.*

instil', *v.t.* (p.t. *instilled*), introduce (idea, etc., *into* person's mind) gradually.

in'stinct, *n.* inborn tendency to behave in certain way without reasoning or training; intuition, unconscious skill. **instinc'tive**, *a.*

in'stitute, *v.t.* establish, found; set up. *n.* society, organization, for special purpose; its building.

institu'tion, *n.* instituting; established custom; (building of) organization for charitable, etc., purpose. **institu'tional**, *a.*

instruct', *v.t.* give knowledge or information to, teach; direct.

instruc'tion, *n.* teaching; (pl.) directions, orders. **instruc'tional**, *a.*

instruc'tive, *a.* enlightening.

instruc'tor, *n.* **instruc'tress**, *n. fem.* person who instructs.

in'strument (-roo-), *n.* thing used in performing an action; tool, implement, esp. for delicate or scientific work; contrivance for producing musical sounds. **instrument'al**, *a.* serving as means (*in*); performed on musical instruments. **instrumen'talist**, *n.* performer on musical instrument.

insubor'dinate, *a.* disobedient; unruly. **insubordina'tion**, *n.*

insubstan'tial (-shl), *a.* not real; lacking solidity. **insubstantial'ity** (-shi-), *n.*

insuff'erable, *a.* intolerable; unbearably conceited, etc.

insuffi'cient (-shnt), *a.* not enough; inadequate. **insuffi'ciency**, *n.*

in'sular, *a.* of an island; of or like islanders, esp., narrow-minded. **insula'rity**, *n.*

in'sulate, *v.t.* isolate, esp. by non-conductors, to prevent passage of electricity, heat, etc. **insula'tion**, *n.* **in'sulator**, *n.* (esp.) non--conducting substance or device.

in'sulin, *n.* pancreatic hormone used in treatment of diabetes.

in'sult, *n.* scornful abuse; indignity; affront. **insult'**, *v.t.* treat with insult. **insul'ting**, *a.*

insu'perable, *a.* that cannot be surmounted or overcome. **insuperabil'ity**, *n.*

insuppor'table, *a.* unbearable.

insur'ance (-shoor-), *n.* contract to indemnify insured person against loss of or damage to property, etc., or to pay fixed sum(s) on person's death, etc., in return for payment of premium; premium.

insure' (-shoor), *v.* issue, take out, insurance policy.

insur'gent, *a.* in revolt. *n.* rebel.

insurmoun'table, *a.* insuperable.

insurrec'tion, *n.* rising in open resistance to established authority; rebellion.

insuscep'tible, *a.* not susceptible.

intact', *a.* untouched; undamaged; entire.

intan'gible (-j-), *a.* that cannot be touched or mentally grasped.

in'teger, *n.* whole number.

in'tegral, *a.* of or essential to a whole; (Math.) of integer(s). **in'tegrate**, *v.t.* combine (parts) into a whole; end (racial) segregation of. **integra'tion**, *n.*

integ'rity, *n.* wholeness; soundness; uprightness, honesty.

in'tellect, *n.* faculty of knowing and reasoning; power of thought, understanding.

intellec'tual, *a.* of, appealing to, requiring use of, intellect; fond of mental pursuits, highly intelligent. *n.* intellectual person.

intell'igence, *n.* intellect; quickness of understanding; news; secret service. **intelligence quotient** (abbrev. *I.Q.*), ratio of mental age to actual age.

intell'igent, *a.* having high degree of intelligence; clever.

intelligent'sia, *n.* class of intellectuals (esp. in pre-revolutionary Russia).

intell'igible, *a.* that can be understood; clear.

intem'perate, *a.* not temperate; addicted to drinking. **intem'perance**, *n.*

intend', *v.t.* have in mind as fixed object or purpose; design; mean.

intense', *a.* very great or strong; violent; ardent. **intense'ly**, *adv.* **inten'sity**, *n.*

inten'sify, *v.* make or become intense; augment, strengthen.

inten'sive, *a.* concentrated; thorough.

intent', *n.* intention. *to all intents (and purposes)*, practically. *a.* absorbed; eager. *intent on*, with mind and attention directed towards.

inten'tion, *n.* purpose, aim, object. **inten'tional,** *a.* done on purpose. **inten'tionally,** *adv.*

inter', *v.t.* (p.t. *interred*), bury.

inter-, *pref.* among, between; mutual(ly), reciprocal(ly).

interact', *v.t.* act on each other. **interac'tion,** *n.*

interbreed', *v.t.* crossbreed; breed with each other.

intercēde', *v.i.* plead (*for* another); mediate.

intercept', *v.t.* seize, catch, stop, etc., in transit; cut off. **intercep'tion,** *n.*

interce'ssion (-shn), *n.* interceding; prayer on behalf of others.

interchānge' (-nj), *v.t.* put in each other's place; make exchange of; alternate. **in'terchānge,** *n.* reciprocal exchange; alternation. **interchānge'able,** *a.*

in'tercom, *n.* system of internal telephone communication, esp. in aircraft.

intercommū'nicāte, *v.i.* have communication with each other.

intercontinen'tal, *a.* between, connecting, different continents.

in'tercourse (-ors), *n.* social communication, dealings; sexual intercourse.

interdict', *v.t.* prohibit; forbid. **in'terdict,** *n.* official prohibition.

in'terèst, *n.* feeling of concern and curiosity; thing with which one concerns oneself; importance; advantage; money paid for use of loan. *v.t.* arouse interest in. **in'terèsted,** *a.* (esp.) having a private interest in. **in'terèsting,** *a.* arousing interest.

interfēre', *v.i.* come into collision or opposition (*with*); take part (*in*), esp. without having the right to do so. **interfēr'ence,** *n.*

in'terim, *n.* meantime. *a.* temporary.

intēr'ior, *a.* situated within; inland; internal, domestic. *n.* interior part, region, etc.; inside.

interject', *v.t.* say abruptly; break in with remark. **interjec'tion,** *n.* (word or words used as) exclamation.

interlāce', *v.* bind together, cross each other, intricately; interweave.

interlard', *v.t.* intersperse (speech, etc.) *with* (foreign words, etc.).

interlock', *v.* connect, join, etc., by overlapping, etc.; lock together.

interloc'ūtor, *n.* one who takes part in conversation. **interlocū'tion,** *n.*

in'terlōper, *n.* intruder.

in'terlūde (*or* -ōōd), *n.* (music, etc., filling) interval between parts of play, etc.; intervening time.

interma'rriage (-ij), *n.* marriage between members of different families, races, etc.; marriage between near relations. **inter-**

ma'rry, *v.i.*

intermē'diary, *a.* acting between parties; intermediate. *n.* (esp.) mediator.

intermē'diate, *a.* & *n.* (thing) coming *between* in time, place, or order.

inter'ment, *n.* burial.

inter'minable, *a.* endless; tediously long.

interming'le (-nggl), *v.* mix together.

intermi'ssion (-shn), *n.* pause; interval.

intermitt'ent, *a.* stopping for a time; coming or occurring at intervals. **intermitt'ently,** *adv.*

intermix', *v.* mix together. **intermix'ture,** *n.*

intern', *v.t.* confine within certain limits or in camp, etc. **intern'ment,** *n.*

inter'nal, *a.* of or in inside; of inner nature of thing; subjective; of domestic affairs of country. **internal-combustion engine,** engine in which motive power is derived from combustion of fuel inside it.

interna'tional (-shon-), *a.* existing, carried on, between nations. *n.* international contest.

internē'cīne, *a.* mutually destructive.

in'terplay, *n.* action of two things on each other.

In'terpol, *n.* international police organization.

inter'polāte, *v.t.* make (esp. misleading) insertions in; insert or introduce between other things. **interpolā'tion,** *n.*

interpōse' (-z), *v.i.* insert; intervene; make an interruption.

inter'prèt, *v.* explain; translate; bring out meaning of. **interprètā'tion,** *n.* **inter'prèter,** *n.* (esp.) one who translates orally.

interreg'num, *n.* (pl. *interregna*, -*regnums*), interval between successive reigns.

inte'rrogāte, *v.t.* question closely or formally. **interrogā'tion,** *n.* **inte'rrogātor,** *n.*

interrog'ative, *a.* of, used in asking, questions. *n.* interrogative pronoun, etc.

interrog'atory, *a.* of inquiry.

interrupt', *v.t.* break in upon; break continuity of; obstruct view of. **interrup'tion,** *n.*

intersect', *v.* divide by passing or lying across; cross or cut each other. **intersec'tion,** *n.* intersecting; point where lines, etc., cross; (esp. U.S.) cross-roads, road junction.

intersperse', *v.t.* scatter, place here and there (between); diversify *with*.

interstell'ar, *a.* among the stars.

inter'stice, *n.* small intervening space, chink, crevice. **intersti'tial** (-shl), *a.*

intertwīne', *v.* interlace, be interlaced.

in'terval, *n.* intervening time or space; pause; break; (Mus.) difference of pitch between two notes.

intervēne', *v.i.* occur in the meantime; come between; interfere, mediate. **interven'tion,** *n.*

in'terview (-vū), *n.* meeting face to face, esp. for purpose of obtaining statement, assessing qualities of candidate, etc. *v.t.* have interview with.

interweave', *v.t.* (p.t. *interwōve*; p.p. *inter-*

woven), weave together; blend intimately.

intes'tate, *a.* not having made a will. *n.* person who has died intestate. **intes'tacy**, *n.*

intes'tine, *n.* (usu. pl.) lower part of alimentary canal. **intes'tinal** (*or*-īnal), *a.*

in'timate[1], *a.* closely acquainted, familiar; closely personal. *n.* intimate friend. **in'-timacy**, *n.*

in'timate[2], *v.t.* make known, state; imply. **intimā'tion**, *n.*

intim'idāte, *v.t.* inspire with fear, esp. in order to influence conduct. **intimidā'tion**, *n.*

in'to (-too), *prep.* expressing motion or direction to point within, or change, condition, result.

intol'erable, *a.* that cannot be endured.

intol'erance, *n.* lack of tolerance. **intol'erant**, *a.* not tolerant.

intonā'tion, *n.* (esp.) rise and fall of voice in speaking; (Mus.) act of singing or playing in tune.

intône', *v.t.* recite in singing voice.

intox'icant, *a.* & *n.* intoxicating (liquor, etc.).

intox'icāte, *v.t.* make drunk; excite, elate, beyond self-control. **intoxicā'tion**, *n.*

intra-, *pref.* in the inside, within.

intrac'table, *a.* not docile; not easily dealt with. **intractabil'ity**, *n.*

intran'sigent (*or*-z-), *a.* uncompromising.

intran'sitive, *a.* & *n.* (verb) that does not take a direct object.

intravē'nous, *a.* in(to) vein(s).

intrep'id, *a.* fearless; brave. **intrepid'ity**, *n.*

in'tricate, *a.* perplexingly entangled or involved; complicated. **in'tricacy**, *n.*

in'trigue (-ēg; *or* -ēg'), *n.* plot; secret love affair. *v.* (-ēg'), carry on underhand plot; use secret influence; rouse interest or curiosity of.

intrin'sic, *a.* inherent; essential.

intro-, *pref.* to the inside.

introdūce', *v.t.* bring in; bring forward; make (person) known to another; bring into use, draw attention to.

introduc'tion, *n.* introducing; explanatory remarks at beginning of book. **introduc'-tory**, *a.*

introspec'tion, *n.* examination of one's own thoughts or feelings. **introspec'tive**, *a.*

in'trovert, *n.* person concerned chiefly with his own thoughts and feelings (opp. *extrovert*). **introver'sion** (-shn), *n.*

intrude' (-ōōd), *v.* thrust, force, (oneself *into* place, *upon* person); come uninvited. **intru'der**, *n.* **intru'sion** (-zhn), *n.* **intru'sive**, *a.*

intūi'tion, *n.* immediate understanding by the mind without reasoning; immediate insight. **intū'itive**, *a.* of, possessing, perceived by, intuition.

in'undāte, *v.t.* flood; (fig.) overwhelm. **inundā'tion**, *n.*

inūre', *v.t.* habituate, accustom.

invāde', *v.t.* enter into as enemy; encroach on.

in'valid[1], *n.* & *a.* (person) weakened or disabled by illness or injury. *v.t.* (-ēd), remove from active service (usu. *invalid out*); send *home* as invalid.

inval'id[2], *a.* not valid. **inval'idāte**, *v.t.* make invalid. **invalid'ity**, *n.*

inval'ūable, *a.* above price, priceless.

invār'iable, *a.* never changing; constant.

invā'sion (-zhn), *n.* invading; encroachment.

invec'tive, *n.* violent attack in words; abusive speech.

inveigh' (-vā), *v.i.* speak angrily *against*; attack violently in words.

invei'gle (-vā- *or* -vē-), *v.t.* entice, wheedle (*into*).

invent', *v.t.* devise, originate; produce or construct by original thought, etc.; fabricate (false story, etc.). **inven'tion**, *n.* inventing; thing invented; fictitious story, etc. **inven'-tive**, *a.* **inven'tor**, *n.*

in'ventory, *n.* list of goods, furniture, etc. *v.t.* enter in inventory.

inverse' (*or* in'-), *a.* inverted in position, order, or relation. *inverse ratio, proportion*, that between two quantities, one of which increases as other decreases. **inver'sion** (-shn), *n.* turning upside down; reversal of natural order of words.

invert', *v.t.* reverse position, order, relation etc., of. **inverted commas**, punctuation-marks (' ' or " ").

inver'tēbrate, *n.* & *a.* (animal) without a backbone.

invest', *v.* clothe, dress; endue (*with*) qualities, insignia of office, etc.; employ (money *in* stocks, etc.); besiege (town), etc.

inves'tigāte, *v.t.* examine; inquire into. **investigā'tion**, *n.*

inves'titure, *n.* formal investing of person (*with* decoration, etc.) esp. ceremony of conferment of honours by sovereign, etc.

invest'ment, *n.* investing; money invested.

invet'erate, *a.* settled or confirmed in habit, etc.

invid'ious, *a.* giving offence, esp. by injustice, etc.

invi'gilāte, *v.t.* supervise students during examination. **invi'gilātor**, *n.*

invig'orāte, *v.t.* make strong or active.

invin'cible, *a.* unconquerable.

invi'olable, *a.* not to be violated. **inviolabil'ity**, *n.* **invi'olate**, *a.* not violated; unbroken, unprofaned. **invi'olacy**, *n.*

invis'ible (-z-), *a.* that cannot be seen. **invisibil'ity**, *n.*

invīte', *v.t.* request politely to come, *to* do, etc.; ask politely for; attract. **invitā'tion**, *n.* **invī'ting**, *a.* (esp.) attractive, tempting

invocā'tion, *n.* invoking; calling upon (God, etc.) in prayer.

in'voice, *n.* list of goods sent, with prices. *v.t.* make invoice of.

invōke', *v.t.* call on in prayer; appeal to; ask earnestly for.

invol'untary, *a*. done, etc., without exercise of will.

involū'tion (*or* -ōō-), *n*. entanglement; curling inwards; part so curled.

involve', *v.t.* cause (person) to be caught and mixed up *in* trouble, difficulties, etc.; include; have as a necessary consequence. **involved'**, *a*. (esp.) complicated. **involve'-ment**, *n*.

invul'nerable, *a*. that cannot be wounded or hurt. **invulnerabil'ity**, *n*.

in'ward, *a*. situated within; directed towards inside; mental, spiritual. **in'wardly**, *adv.* internally; in mind or spirit. **in'wardness**, *n*. (esp.) inner nature. **inward(s)**, *adv.* towards inside; in mind or soul.

inwrought (inrawt'; before noun, in'-), *a*. decorated; worked in.

ī'odine (-ēn *or* -īn), *n*. non-metallic element; tincture of this as antiseptic.

ī'on, *n*. electrically charged atom or group of atoms; free electron or positron.

ion'osphēre, *n*. region in upper atmosphere, containing ions.

iō'ta, *n*. Greek letter i; jot.

I O U (īōū'), *n*. signed document acknowledging debt.

ip'sō fac'tō, by that very fact; by the fact itself. (Latin)

ir-, *pref.*: see **in-**.

iras'cible (i-), *a*. easily made angry; hot-tempered. **irascibil'ity**, *n*.

īrāte', *a*. angry. **īre**, *n*. (Poet.) anger.

irides'cent (i-), *a*. showing rainbow-like colours. **irides'cence**, *n*.

īr'is, *n*. coloured membrane surrounding pupil of eye; flowering plant with sword-shaped leaves.

Ir'ish (īr-), *a*. of Ireland. *n*. Irish language; Irish people. **Irish stew**, stew of mutton, onions, and potatoes.

irk, *v.t.* trouble, annoy. **irk'some**, *a*. troublesome, tiresome.

iron (īīn), *n*. metal occurring abundantly and much used for tools, etc.; tool, etc., of iron; apparatus with flat under-surface, heated for smoothing cloth, clothes, etc.; golf-club with metal head; (pl.) fetters. *a*. of iron; unyielding. *v.t.* smooth with iron. **iron curtain**, (fig.) barrier to passage of persons and information at limit of Soviet sphere of influence. **iron lung**, rigid case fitted over body of patient for prolonged artificial respiration. **ironmonger**, dealer in iron and other metal goods (*ironmongery*). **iron rations**, emergency rations. **ironstone**, hard iron ore.

īron'ic, īron'ical, *aa*. of, using, said in, irony.

īr'ony, *n*. expression of meaning by use of words normally conveying opposite meaning; apparent perversity of fate or circumstances.

irrā'diāte (i-r-), *v.t.* shine upon; light up; subject to radiation.

irra'tional (i-rashon-), *a*. unreasonable; illog-ical; not endowed with reason.

irrēclaim'able (i-r-), *a*. that cannot be reclaimed or reformed.

irrec'oncīlable (i-r-), *a*. relentlessly opposed; incompatible.

irreco'verable (i-riku-), *a*. that cannot be recovered or remedied.

irrēdee'mable (i-r-), *a*. irreclaimable, hopeless; that cannot be redeemed.

irrēdū'cible (i-r-), *a*. not reducible.

irref'ūtable (i-r-; *or* i-rifū'-), *a*. that cannot be proved false or wrong.

irreg'ūlar (i-r-), *a*. contrary to rule; uneven; varying; (Gram.) not inflected in usual way; (of troops) not in regular service. **irregūla'-rity**, *n*.

irrel'ēvant (i-r-), *a*. not relevant or to the point. **irrel'ēvance, irrel'ēvancy**, *nn*.

irrēli'gion (i-r-; -jn), *n*. hostility or indifference to religion. **irrēli'gious** (-jus), *a*.

irrēmē'diable (i-r-), *a*. that cannot be remedied.

irrep'arable (i-r-), *a*. that cannot be put right or made good.

irrēplāce'able (i-r-; -sabl), *a*. of which the loss cannot be made good.

irrēpress'ible (i-r-), *a*. that cannot be repressed.

irrēproach'able (i-r-), *a*. faultless, blameless.

irrēsis'tible (i-riz-), *a*. too strong, convincing, charming, etc., to be resisted.

irres'olūte (i-rez-; *or* -ōōt), *a*. hesitating; not resolute. **irresolu'tion**, *n*.

irrēspec'tive (i-r-), *irrespective of*, not taking into account, without reference to.

irrēspon'sible (i-r-), *a*. acting, done, without proper sense of responsibility; not responsible for conduct. **irrēsponsibil'ity**, *n*.

irrētrie'vable (i-r-), *a*. lost beyond recovery.

irrev'erent (i-r-), *a*. not reverent; disrespectful. **irrev'erence**, *n*.

irrev'ocable (i-r-), *a*. final and unalterable, that cannot be revoked.

i'rrigāte, *v.t.* supply (land) with water; water (land) by system of artificial channels. **irrigā'tion**, *n*.

i'rritable, *a*. easily annoyed; sensitive to stimuli; inflamed, sore. **irritabil'ity**, *n*.

i'rritant, *n*. & *a*. (substance or agency) causing irritation.

i'rritāte, *v.t.* annoy, make angry; inflame. **irritā'tion**, *n*.

is, 3rd pers. sing. pres. of **be**.

isinglass (ī'zingglahs), *n*. kind of gelatin obtained from sturgeon, etc.

Is'lam (is- *or* iz-; *or* -lahm'), *n*. religion revealed through prophet Muhammad; Muslim world. **Islam'ic**, *a*.

island (ī'l-), *n*. piece of land surrounded by water; isolated thing. **islander** (ī'l-), *n*.

isle (īl), *n*. island. **islĕt** (ī'l-), *n*. small island.

ī'sobar, *n*. line on map, etc., connecting places with same barometric pressure.

ī'solāte, *v.t.* place apart or alone; separate.

i'solable, *a.* isolā'tion, *n.*

īsos'cělēs (-z), *a.* (of triangle) having two sides equal.

i'sotherm, *n.* line on map, etc., connecting places with same temperature.

i'sotōpe, *n.* one of two or more forms of element having same chemical properties but different atomic weight and nuclear properties.

Isrā'ěli (iz-), *a. & n.* (inhabitant) of modern Israel.

Is'rǎělīte (iz-), *n.* Hebrew inhabitant of ancient Israel.

iss'ūe, *n.* outflow; result, outcome; children; question, dispute; issuing; copies of journal, etc., issued at one time. *v.* go or come out, emerge; result; give or send out; publish; supply *with* equipment, etc.

isthmus (is'mus; *or* isth'-), *n.* (pl. *isthmuses*), neck of land.

it, *pron.* subjective and objective cases of 3rd personal pron. (pl. *they*, objective *them*; possessive *its*, pl. *their*), thing, animal, etc., named or in question; as subject of imperso-

nal verb; as subject of verb followed by virtual subject; as indefinite object.

Ital'ian (i-), *a. & n.* (native, language) of Italy.

ital'ic, *a.* (of type) sloping to right (*opp.* roman). ital'ics, *n.pl.* italic-type. ital'icīze, *v.t.* print in italics; emphasize.

itch, *n.* irritation in skin; restless desire. *the itch*, scabies. *v.i.* feel itch; long *for*.

i'tem, *n.* any one of a list of things; piece of news.

it'erāte, *v.t.* repeat. iterā'tion, *n.*

ītin'erant (*or* i-), *a.* travelling from place to place. *n.* itinerant person.

ītin'erary (*or* i-), *n.* route; plan for, record of, journey; guide-book.

its, *pron. & a.* possessive case of **it**.

itself', *pron.* emphatic and refl. form of **it**.

i'vory, *n.* white substance of tusks of elephant, etc. **ivory tower**, (fig., esp. artist's) seclusion from world.

i'vy, *n.* climbing evergreen with shining leaves. i'vied (-id), *a.* overgrown with ivy.

J

jab, *v.t.* (p.t. *jabbed*), poke roughly; stab. *n.* abrupt (stabbing) blow.

jabb'er, *v.* chatter; utter fast and indistinctly. *n.* chatter, gabble.

jabot (zhab'ō), *n.* frill down front of shirt, blouse, etc.

jack, *n.* any of various appliances for turning spit, raising heavy object (esp. motor vehicle) off ground, etc.; small ball aimed at in bowls; knave in cards; ship's flag, esp. showing nationality. *v.t.* hoist (*up*) with jack. jack'boot, large boot reaching above knee. jack-knife, (*n.*) large pocket clasp-knife; (*v.i.*) (esp. of articulated lorry, etc.) double or rise up like blades of jack-knife. jack--of-all-trades, one who can turn his hand to anything. jack'pot, (esp. cumulative) prize in lottery, etc. jack tar, sailor.

jack'al (-awl), *n.* wild animal of dog kind.

jack'anāpes (-ps), *n.* pert fellow.

jack'ass, *n.* male ass; blockhead.

jack'daw, *n.* bird of crow family.

jack'ět, *n.* short coat; outside wrapper of book. *v.t.* cover with jacket.

Jacobē'an, *a.* of reign of James I.

Jac'obin, *n.* (Hist.) member of extreme democratic club formed 1789 in Paris.

Jac'obīte, *n.* supporter of exiled Stuarts.

jāde, *n.* hard translucent light-green, bluish, or whitish stone used for ornaments etc.; carved piece of this; light green.

jā'ded, *a.* worn out, weary.

Ja'ffa (o'range), oval seedless orange.

jag, *n.* sharp projection (e.g. of rock). *v.t.* (p.t. *jagged*), cut, tear, break, unevenly. jagg'ěd, *a.*

jag'ūar, *n.* large Amer. flesh-eating spotted quadruped of cat family.

jail: see gaol.

jam[1], *v.* (p.t. *jammed*), squeeze between two surfaces or bodies; (cause to) become wedged; block (passage); (Radio, etc.) cause interference with (programme, etc.); put (brake) *on* violently. *n.* squeeze; stoppage; crowded mass of things, persons, traffic, etc.

jam[2], *n.* conserve of fruit boiled with sugar.

jamb (jam) *n.* side post, side, of doorway, window, etc.

jamboree', *n.* large rally of Scouts; merry--making, spree.

jangle (jang'gl), *n.* harsh discordant metallic noise. *v.* (cause to) make jangle.

jan'itor, *n.* door-keeper; (U.S.) caretaker of

building.

Jan'ūary, *n.* first month of year.

japan', *n.* hard, usu. black, varnish. *v.t.* (p.t. *japanned*), make black and glossy (as) with japan.

Japanēse' (-z), *a.* & *n.* (native, language) of Japan.

japon'ica, *n.* ornamental plant, the *Japanese quince.*

jar¹, *v.* (p.t. *jarred*), sound discordantly, grate; wrangle. *n.* jarring sound; shock; quarrel. **jarr'ing,** *a.*

jar², *n.* pottery or glass vessel, usu. cylindrical.

jar'gon, *n.* debased or unintelligible language; language peculiar to class, profession, etc.

jas'mine (*or* -z-), *n.* shrub with white or yellow flowers.

jas'per, *n.* red, yellow, or brown opaque quartz.

jaun'dice, *n.* disease marked by yellowness of skin, etc. **jaun'diced,** *a.* affected with jaundice; envious, embittered.

jaunt, *n.* excursion, journey, esp. for pleasure. *v.i.* go for a jaunt.

jaun'ty, *a.* having or showing airy self-satisfaction; sprightly.

jav'elin (-vl-), *n.* light spear for throwing.

jaw, *n.* (esp. lower) bone containing the teeth; (pl.) mouth; (pl.) gripping parts of machine.

jay, *n.* noisy bird of brilliant plumage. **jay-walker,** pedestrian carelessly walking in or across roadway.

jazz, *n.* popular rhythmical music of American Negro origin. *a.* of or in jazz; loud or fantastic. *v.* play, dance to, arrange as, jazz; liven (up). **jazz'y,** *a.*

jeal'ous (jel-), *a.* watchfully tenacious of one's rights, etc.; suspicious, resentful, of rivalry in affections; envious (*of*). **jeal'ousy,** *n.*

jeans (-z), *n.pl.* trousers of heavy twilled cotton fabric.

jeep, *n.* small powerful motor vehicle.

jeer, *v.* scoff derisively (*at*). *n.* taunt.

Jéhō'vah (-a), *n.* O.T. name of God.

jėjune' (-ōōn), *a.* meagre, scanty; unsatisfying to the mind; dull.

jell, *v.i.* (*informal*) set as jelly; take shape.

jell'y, *n.* soft stiffish substance made with gelatin, etc., esp as food; anything of similar consistency. *v.* (cause to) set in or as jelly, congeal. **jelly-fish,** marine animal with jelly-like body and stinging tentacles.

jemm'y, *n.* crowbar used by burglars.

jeop'ardīze (jep-), *v.t.* place in, expose to, danger. **jeop'ardy,** *n.* danger.

jerbō'a, *n.* small African jumping rodent with very long hind legs and tail.

jerėmi'ad (je-r-), *n.* long doleful complaint.

jerk, *n.* sharp sudden pull, throw, twist, etc.; twitch. *v.* pull, thrust, throw, etc., with jerk; move with jerk(s). **jer'ky,** *a.*

jer'kin, *n.* (Hist.) man's close-fitting jacket, often of leather; sleeveless jacket.

je'rry-builder (-bil-), *n.* builder of houses of poor quality with bad materials. **je'rry-building,** *n.* **je'rry-built,** *a.*

jer'sey (-zi), *n.* (pl. *jerseys*), knitted fabric; close-fitting knitted upper garment.

Jerusalem artichoke: see **artichoke.**

jest, *n.* joke; fun; object of mockery. *v.i.* joke, make jests. **jes'ter,** *n.* one who jests; (esp., Hist.) professional entertainer of royal court or noble household.

Jes'ūit (-z-), *n.* & *a.* (member) of Society of Jesus, R.C. priestly order. **Jesūit'ical,** *a.* (Hist.) crafty, casuistical.

Jē'sus (-zuz), Jesus Christ, source of Christian religion, whose life, teaching, etc., are recorded in Gospels of New Testament.

jet¹, *n.* hard black variety of lignite taking brilliant polish. **jet-black,** very black; glossy black.

jet², *n.* stream of gas, liquid, steam, etc., forced out of small opening; spout, nozzle, for emitting jet; jet-propelled aircraft. *v.* (p.t. *jetted*), spurt forth in jets. **jet-propelled,** (of aircraft) deriving thrust from jets of hot gases ejected at rear of engines.

jet'sam, *n.* goods jettisoned; such goods washed ashore.

jett'ison, *v.t.* throw (goods) overboard, esp. to lighten ship, etc., in distress.

jett'y, *n.* landing-pier; breakwater.

Jew (jōō), *n.* person of Hebrew race or religion. **jew's harp,** small musical instrument held between the teeth. **Jew'ess,** *n.fem.* **Jew'ish,** *a.* Jewry (joor'ri), *n.* Jews collectively; Jewish quarter in town, etc.

jew'él (jōō-), *n.* precious stone; ornament with jewels; precious thing. **jew'éller,** *n.* dealer in jewels. **jew'éllery,** *n.*

Jez'ébel, *n.* shameless woman.

jib¹, *n.* (Naut.) small triangular sail in front of foremast.

jib², *v.i.* (p.t. *jibbed*), (of horse, etc.) stop and refuse to go on. *jib at,* show repugnance at, raise objections to.

jibe: see **gibe.**

jiff'(y), *n.* (*informal*) very short time.

jig, *n.* lively dance, music for it. *v.* (p.t. *jigged*), dance jig; move up and down rapidly and jerkily. **jig'saw,** *n.* (U.S.) machine fret-saw. **jig-saw puzzle,** picture, etc., pasted on board and cut in irregular pieces to be fitted together.

jilt, *v.t.* dismiss (lover) after giving encouragement; be faithless to.

jingle (jing'gl), *n.* mixed noise as of shaken keys or small bells; repetition of same or similar sound in words; verse full of jingles. *v.* (cause to) make jingle.

jing'ō (-ngg-), *n.* (pl. *jingoes*), bellicose patriot. **jing'ōism,** *n.* **jing'ōist,** *n.*

jinn, *n.* genie.

jiu-jitsu: see **ju-jitsu.**

job, *n.* (esp. small) piece of work (done for

payment); difficult task; post, employment; what one has to do. *v.* (p.t. *jobbed*), do jobs; buy and sell as broker; handle corruptly. **job lot,** miscellaneous lot. **jobb'ery,** *n.* corrupt dealing. **jobb'ing,** *a.* employed in odd or occasional jobs.

jock'ey, *n.* (pl. *jockeys*), rider in horse-races. *v.t.* manoeuvre *for* advantageous position; trick.

jocōse', *a.* playful; jocular.

joc'ūlar, *a.* humorous, joking. **jocūla'rity,** *n.*

joc'und, *a.* merry, sprightly, cheerful. **jocun'dity,** *n.*

jodhpurs (jod'perz), *n.pl.* riding-breeches reaching to ankle, close-fitting below knee.

jog, *v.* (p.t. *jogged*), shake with push or jerk; nudge; stimulate (memory); walk, trot, at slow pace. *n.* push, nudge; slow walk or trot. **jog'trot,** slow regular trot.

jogg'le, *v.* shake, move (as) by repeated jerks. *n.* slight shake.

John Bull (bool), personification of English nation; typical Englishman.

join, *v.* put together, unite, connect; unite, be united, in friendship, etc.; take part with others (in), become member, etc., (of). *join up,* enlist. *n.* point, line, plane, of junction.

joi'ner, *n.* (esp.) skilled maker of furniture, house fittings, etc., in wood.

joint[1], *n.* place at which two things are joined; structure by which bones fit together; leg, loin, etc., of carcass as used for food. *v.t.* connect by joint(s); divide at joint or into joints.

joint[2], *a.* combined; shared by two or more in common. **joint'ly,** *adv.*

joist, *n.* one of parallel timbers stretched from wall to wall to take ceiling laths or floor boards.

jōke, *n.* thing said or done to arouse laughter. *v.* make jokes. **jō'ker,** *n.* one who jokes; extra card in pack of cards, used in some games.

jollificā'tion, *n.* merrymaking, jollity.

joll'ity, *n.* merrymaking, festivity.

joll'y, *a.* joyful; festive; jovial; (*informal*) pleasant, delightful. *v.t.* (*informal*) talk (person) into good humour.

jōlt, *v.* shake with jerk; move along with jerks. *n.* such jerk; surprise, shock. **jōl'ty,** *a.*

jon'quil, *n.* kind of narcissus with clusters of fragrant flowers.

joss, *n.* Chinese idol. **joss-house,** *n.* Chinese temple. **joss-stick,** *n.* stick of incense.

jo'stle (-sl), *v.* knock or push (*against*, etc.); elbow. *n.* jostling.

jot, *n.* small amount, whit. *v.t.* (p.t. *jotted*), write (*down*) briefly or hastily.

joule (jool), *n.* unit of energy.

jour'nal (jer-), *n.* diary; log-book; daily newspaper; periodical. **journalēse'** (-z), *n.* newspaper-writers' English. **jour'nalism,** *n.* work of journalist. **jour'nalist,** *n.* editor of or writer for newspaper, etc. **journalis'tic,** *a.*

jour'ney (jer-), *n.* (pl. *journeys*), distance travelled; expedition to some distance, round of travel. *v.i.* make journey.

jour'neyman (jer-), *n.* (pl. *-men*), qualified mechanic or artisan working for another.

joust (*or* joo-), *n.* combat with lances between two knights on horseback. *v.i.* engage in joust.

Jōve, *n.* (Rom. myth.) Jupiter.

jō'vial, *a.* full of fun and good humour; merry. **jōvial'ity,** *n.*

jowl, *n.* jaw; lower part of face.

joy, *n.* gladness, delight. *v.i.* rejoice. **joy'-stick,** *n.* (*slang*) control lever of aircraft. **joy'ful, joy'ous,** *aa.* **joy'less,** *a.*

ju'bilant (jōō-), *a.* exultant, showing joy. **jubilā'tion,** *n.*

ju'bilee (jōō-), *n.* anniversary (esp. fiftieth); time of rejoicing.

Ju'das (jōō-), *n.* treacherous person.

judge, *n.* officer appointed to hear and try cases in court of justice; person appointed to decide dispute or contest; person qualified to decide on merits of thing in question. *v.* pass sentence upon; try (case); decide (question); act as judge; form opinion.

judge'ment (-jm), **judg'ment,** *n.* sentence of court of justice, etc.; misfortune as sign of divine displeasure; opinion, estimate; critical faculty; good sense. **Judgement Day,** day of God's trial of souls at end of world.

ju'dicature (jōō-), *n.* administration of justice; body of judges.

judicial (jōōdish'al), *a.* of or by a court of law; of a judge; impartial.

judiciary (jōōdish'ari), *n.* judges collectively.

judicious (jōōdish'us), *a.* sensible, prudent; skilful.

ju'dō (jōō-), *n.* modern development of ju--jitsu.

jug, *n.* deep vessel for liquids with handle and, usu., spout. *v.t.* (p.t. *jugged*), stew (hare, etc.) in jug or jar.

jugg'ernaut (-g-), *n.* cause, belief, institution, to which persons blindly sacrifice themselves or others; huge object, esp. heavy lorry.

jugg'le, *v.* perform feats of dexterity (*with* balls, etc., tossed up); trick. *juggle with,* manipulate deceitfully. **jugg'ler, jugg'lery,** *nn.*

jug'ūlar, *a.* of neck or throat. *n.* one of four great veins of neck.

juice (jōōs), *n.* liquid part of vegetable or fruit; fluid part of animal body or substance. **jui'cy,** *a.* full of juice, succulent.

ju-jitsu, jiu-jitsu (jōōjit'sōō), *n.* Japanese art of wrestling, etc.

jujube (jōō'jōōb), *n.* sweet of gelatin, etc., flavoured with fruit-juice, etc.

juke'-box (jōō-), *n.* coin-operated record--player.

Julÿ' (jōō-), *n.* seventh month of year.

jum'ble, *v.t.* mix (*up*) in confusion. *n.* confused heap, etc.; muddle. **jumble sale,** sale of miscellaneous second-hand goods.

jum'bō, *n.* (pl. *jumbos*), very big person, animal, or thing. **jumbo-size(d),** very big.

jump, *v.* spring from ground, etc.; rise or move with sudden start; move quickly; leap over. *n.* leap; start caused by shock, etc.; sudden rise or transition.

jum'per, *n.* hip-length loose outer garment; upper part of naval rating's uniform; knitted upper garment not opening in front.

jum'py, *a.* nervous.

junc'tion, *n.* joining-point, esp. place where roads, railway lines, etc., meet (and unite or cross).

junc'ture (-cher), *n.* concurrence of events, state of affairs.

June (jōōn), *n.* sixth month of year.

jungle (jung'gl), *n.* land overgrown with tangled vegetation, esp. as home of wild animals; tangled mass.

jun'ior (jōō-), *a.* younger in age; of less standing, of lower position. *n.* junior person.

jun'iper (jōō-), *n.* evergreen shrub with prickly leaves and dark purplish berries.

junk¹, *n.* discarded material, worthless rubbish; (Naut.) old cable, etc. **junk-shop,** (esp.) second-hand dealer's shop.

junk², *n.* flat-bottomed sailing-vessel of China seas.

junk'et, *n.* dish of milk curdled by rennet; feast, outing. *v.i.* feast, go on outing.

Jun'ō (jōō-), *n.* (Rom. myth.) chief goddess, wife of Jupiter. **Junōesque'** (-k), *a.* resembling Juno in stately beauty.

Ju'piter (jōō-), *n.* (Rom. myth.) chief of the gods; largest planet.

jurid'ical (joor-), *a.* of judicial proceedings; legal.

jurisdic'tion (joor-), *n.* administration of justice; (extent or area of) legal or other authority.

jurispru'dence (joorisprōō-), *n.* science, philosophy, of human law.

jur'ist (joor-), *n.* expert in law.

jur'or (joor-), *n.* member of jury.

jury (joor'i), *n.* body of persons sworn to give verdict in court of justice; judges of a competition. **jur'ybox,** *n.* enclosure for jury in court. **jur'yman,** *n.* (pl. *-men*), juror.

just, *a.* upright, fair; correct, due, proper, right. *adv.* exactly; barely; not long before; (*informal*) quite, positively.

jus'tice, *n.* justness, fairness; administration of the law; judge. *Justice of the Peace* (abbrev. J.P.), unpaid lay magistrate.

jus'tify, *v.t.* show justice or rightness of; be adequate reason for; (Printing) adjust (line of type) to fill space neatly. **jus'tifiable,** *a.* **justificā'tion,** *n.*

jut, *v.i.* (p.t. *jutted*). *jut out,* extend outwards, protrude.

jute (jōōt), *n.* fibre from bark of certain plants, used for canvas, cord, etc.

juv'enile (jōō-), *a.* youthful; of, for, young people. *n.* young person. **juvenil'ity,** *n.*

juxtapōse' (-z; *or* juks'-), *v.t.* put side by side. **juxtaposi'tion,** *n.*

K

kail(-yard): see **kale.**

kai'ser (kīz-), *n.* (Hist.) German emperor.

kāle, kail, *n.* hardy winter cabbage. **kail- -yard,** (Sc.) kitchen garden.

kalei'doscōpe (-lī-), *n.* tube in which are seen symmetrical patterns produced by reflections of pieces of coloured glass and varied by moving tube round; (fig.) constantly changing pattern, scene, etc. **kaleidoscop'ic,** *a.*

kangarōō' (-ngg-), *n.* Australian marsupial with strongly developed hindquarters and great leaping power.

kā'olin, *n.* fine white clay used for making porcelain, etc.

kā'pok, *n.* fine silky fibres surrounding seed of *kapok tree,* used to stuff cushions, etc.

kara'tè (-rah-), *n.* Japanese system of

unarmed combat using hands, etc., as weapons.

kart: see **go.**

kay'ak (kī-), *n.* Eskimo canoe of light wood covered with sealskins; canoe resembling this.

kedg'eree, *n.* dish of fish, rice, eggs, etc.

keel, *n.* lowest lengthwise timber on which boat's or ship's framework is built up. *v.* turn (boat, etc.) keel upwards. *keel over,* upset, capsize.

keen¹, *a.* sharp; strong, acute, penetrating; eager, ardent. **keen'ness,** *n.*

keen², *n.* Irish funeral song accompanied with wailing. *v.* utter keen; bewail thus.

keep (p.t. *kept*), *v.* retain possession of;

reserve for future use; protect, have charge of; observe, celebrate; remain in same state; maintain; conduct for profit; have for sale. *n.* maintenance, food; (Hist). strongest tower of castle, etc. **kee'per,** *n.* (esp.) gamekeeper; guard, attendant; bar of soft iron connecting poles of magnet. **kee'ping,** *n.* custody, charge; agreement, harmony.

keep'sâke, *n.* thing treasured for sake of giver.

keg, *n.* small barrel.

kelp, *n.* large kind of seaweed.

kel'pie, *n.* (Sc.) wicked water-spirit, usu. in form of horse.

ken, *n.* range of knowledge or sight. *v.t.* (Sc.) know.

kenn'el, *n.* hut, etc., for shelter of house-dog or hounds. *v.t.* (p.t. *kennelled*), put, keep, in kennel.

kept, *p.t. & p.p.* of **keep.**

kerb, *n.* stone edging to pavement, etc. **kerb'stone,** one of stones forming kerb.

ker'chief (-if), *n.* cloth used as head-covering; (Poet.) handkerchief.

ker'nel, *n.* softer, usu. edible, inner part of nut or fruit-stone; whole seed within husk, etc.; central or essential part.

ke'rosēne, *n.* mixture of liquid hydrocarbons as fuel-oil, etc.; paraffin.

kes'trel, *n.* kind of small hawk.

ketch, *n.* small coastal sailing-vessel.

ketch'up, *n.* sauce made with tomatoes, mushrooms, etc.

kett'le, *n.* metal vessel with spout and handle for boiling water. **kett'ledrum,** *n.* cauldron--shaped drum which can be tuned to produce note of definite pitch.

key (kē), *n.* metal instrument for moving bolt of lock; solution, explanation; code, crib; (Mus.) system of related notes based on keynote; lever pressed by finger in piano, typewriter, etc.; instrument for winding clock, etc. *a.* essential, of vital importance. *v.t.* key up, stimulate, increase nervous tension in. **key'board,** set of keys on piano, etc. **key'-hole,** hole by which key enters lock. **key'-note,** (Mus.) first note of major or minor scale, on which key is based; (fig.) dominant idea, etc. **key signature,** sharp or flat signs at beginning of (section of) composition to indicate key. **key'stone,** central stone of an arch; (fig.) central principle.

kha'ki (kah-), *a.* dull yellowish-brown. *n.* khaki cloth, esp. as used for service uniforms.

khan (kahn), *n.* ruler, official, in Central Asia, Afghanistan, etc.

kibbutz' (-oots), *n.* (pl. *kibbutzim*), communal (esp. agricultural) settlement in modern Israel.

kick, *v.* strike out with foot; strike or move with foot; (of gun) recoil. *n.* kicking; blow with foot; recoil of gun. **kick-off,** (Footb.) kick with which game is started.

kid, *n.* young goat; kid-skin leather; (*slang*) child. *v.* (p.t. *kidded*), give birth to kid; (*slang*) hoax, humbug.

kid'nap, *v.t.* (p.t. *kidnapped*), steal (child); carry off (person) by force and illegally. **kid'napper,** *n.*

kid'ney, *n.* (pl. *kidneys*), either of pair of glandular organs serving to excrete urine. **kidney bean,** French bean.

kill, *v.* put to death, slay; cause death of; destroy; put an end to; consume (time). *n.* killing; animal(s) killed by sportsman. **kill'joy,** depressing person. **kill'ing,** *a.* (esp.) exhausting; (*informal*) overwhelmingly funny.

kiln, *n.* furnace, oven, for making quick-lime, baking bricks, firing pottery, etc.

kil'ō (*or* kē-), *n.* (pl. *kilos*), kilogram.

kilo-, *pref.* 1,000. **kil'ogram(me),** *n.* 1,000 grams, basic unit of mass or weight in metric system. **kil'olitre** (-lēter), *n.* 1,000 litres. **kil'omētre** (-ter), *n.* 1,000 metres. **kil'owatt** (-wot), *n.* 1,000 watts.

kilt, *n.* pleated skirt, usu. of tartan cloth, reaching from waist to knee, esp. as part of Highland dress. **kil'ted,** *a.* wearing a kilt; gathered in vertical pleats.

kimō'nō, *n.* (pl. *kimonos*), long Japanese robe with wide sleeves, worn with sash.

kin, *n.* (*collective*) relatives. **next-of-kin,** nearest relative.

kind[1], *n.* race, natural group, of animals, plants, etc.; class, sort, variety. *in kind,* (of payment) in goods, not money; (of repayment) in same kind as that received.

kind[2], *a.* gentle, benevolent, friendly, considerate. **kīnd'ly**[1], *adv.* in kind manner; please. **kīnd'ness,** *n.*

kin'dergarten, *n.* school or class for very young children.

kin'dle, *v.* set on fire, light; inspire; catch fire; glow. **kind'ling,** *n.* small wood, etc., for lighting fires.

kīnd'ly[2], *a.* kind; sympathetic. **kīnd'liness,** *n.*

kin'drēd, *n.* (*collective*) one's relations. *a.* related by blood; similar.

kīne, *archaic pl.* of **cow.**

kinet'ic (*or* kī-), *a.* of or due to motion.

king, *n.* male sovereign ruler of independent State; piece in chess; playing-card with king on it. **king'cup,** marsh marigold. **king'-fisher,** small bird with brilliant plumage, which dives for fish. **king-pin,** most important person in organization, etc. **king--size(d),** large. **king'ly,** *a.* of or appropriate to king; kinglike, majestic.

king'dom, *n.* State, territory, ruled by a king; domain.

kink, *n.* short twist or curl in wire, rope, hair, etc.; (fig.) mental or moral twist. *v.* form, cause (wire, etc.) to form, kink.

kins'folk (-zfōk), *n.pl.* relations by blood. **kins'man, kins'woman** (-z-), *nn.* (pl. -*men*).

kin'ship, *n.* blood relationship; similarity.

kiosk (kē'osk), *n.* light open structure for sale f newspapers, etc.; structure for public telephone in street, etc.

kipp'er, *v.t.* cure (herring, etc.) by splitting open, salting, drying, and smoking. *n.* kippered fish, esp. herring.

kirk, *n.* (Sc.) church.

kir'tle, *n.* (*archaic*) woman's gown.

kiss, *n.* caress given with lips. *v.* touch with the lips as sign of affection, reverence, etc. *kiss-of-life*, mouth-to-mouth method of artificial respiration.

kit, *n.* equipment, esp. clothing, of soldier, sailor, traveller, etc. **kit-bag**, bag, usu. cylindrical, for carrying kit.

kitch'ën, *n.* room used for cooking. **kitchen garden**, garden for fruit and vegetables. **kitchênette'**, *n.* very small room, alcove, etc., fitted up as kitchen.

kite, *n.* bird of prey of falcon family; light framework covered with paper, etc., flown in wind at end of long string. *fly a kite*, put out statement to test public opinion.

kith, *n.* *kith and kin*, friends and relations; kinsfolk.

kitt'en, *n.* young of cat. *v.i.* give birth to kittens. **kitt'ënish**, *a.*

kitt'iwǎke, *n.* kind of seagull.

kitt'y¹, *n.* pet name for kitten.

kitt'y², *n.* pool in some card-games; joint or accumulated fund.

ki'wi (kē-), *n.* New Zealand flightless bird with undeveloped wings and no tail.

kleptomā'nia, *n.* irresistible tendency to theft in persons not driven to it by need. **kleptomā'niac**, *n.*

knack (n-), *n.* dexterity (acquired through practice) in doing something.

knack'er (n-), *n.* buyer of worn-out horses for slaughter; buyer of old houses, ships, etc. for materials.

knap'sack (n-), *n.* soldier's or traveller's bag, strapped to back.

knap'weed (n-), *n.* weed with purple flowers on globular head.

knǎve (n-), *n.* rogue, scoundrel; lowest court-card of suit. **knǎ'very**, *n.* **knǎ'vish**, *a.*

knead (n-), *v.t.* work up (moist flour, wet clay) into dough or paste; massage.

knee (n-), *n.* joint between thigh and lower leg; part of garment covering this. **knee-cap**, bone in front of knee-joint. **knee-hole**, (of desk, etc.) with space for knees between drawer-pedestals.

kneel (n-), *v.i.* (p.t. *knelt*), fall or rest on knees, esp. in prayer or reverence.

knell (n-), *n.* sound of bell, esp. at funeral or after death; omen of death or extinction.

knelt, *p.t.* & *p.p.* of **kneel**.

knew, *p.t.* of **know**.

knick'erbockers (n-;-z), *n.pl.* loose-fitting breeches gathered in below knee.

knick'ers (n-;-z), *n.pl.* women's two-legged undergarment for lower part of body and (part of) thighs; (*informal*) knickerbockers.

knick'-knack (nik-nak), *n.* light dainty article of furniture, dress, etc.; trinket.

knife (n-), *n.* (pl. *knives*), blade with long sharp edge for cutting, fixed in handle; blade in cutting-machine. *v.t.* (p.t. *knifed*), cut, stab, with knife.

knight (nīt), *n.* person raised to rank below baronetcy; (Hist.) person raised to honourable military rank; piece in chess. *v.t.* make (person) knight. **knight'hood**, rank, dignity, of knight. **knight'ly**, *a.*

knit (n-), *v.* (p.t. *knitted* or *knit*), form (texture, garment) by interlocking successive series of loops of yarn or thread; make, form (wool, etc.) into, knitted fabric; wrinkle (brow); become compact; unite (*together*, *up*). **knitt'ing** (n-), *n.* (esp.) work in process of knitting. **knitting-needle**, **-pin**, slender pointed rod of metal, etc., used in knitting. **knit'wear** (nit'wār), *n.* knitted garments.

knob (n-), *n.* rounded handle of door, drawer, etc.; rounded bulge or mass at end or on surface of thing; small lump of coal, etc.

knob'kerrie (n-), *n.* short knob-headed stick of S. African peoples.

knobb'ly (n-), **knobb'y** (n-), *aa.* (esp.) covered with knobs.

knock (n-), *v.* strike, esp. with hard blow; drive with knock; make knocking noise. *knock about*, treat roughly; wander. *knock down*, strike to ground with blow. *knock out*, make (opponent in boxing) unable to rise or continue; make unconscious. *n.* blow; rap, esp. at door. **knock'er**, *n.* (esp.) metal attachment hinged to door for knocking with.

knöll (n-), *n.* small hill, mound.

knot (n-), *n.* intertwining of parts of one or more strings, etc., to make fastening; tangled mass; hard mass in wood where branch joins trunk; nautical mile per hour as unit of speed; difficulty. *v.* (p.t. *knotted*), tie knot in; form knot(s); entangle. **knott'y**, *a.* full of knots; puzzling.

know (nō), *v.* (p.t. *knew*; p.p. *known*, pr. nōn), be aware (of); be acquainted with; have information (about); recognize. **know-how**, practical knowledge of methods; expertness. **know'ing**, *a.* (esp.) cunning, wide awake. **know'ingly**, *adv.* in knowing manner; consciously, intentionally.

knowl'ëdge (nol-), *n.* knowing; what one knows; all that is or may be known. **knowl'ëdgeable**, *a.* well-informed.

knuck'le (n-), *n.* bone at finger-joint; projection of knee- or ankle-joint of quadruped. *v.* strike, rub, etc., with knuckles. *knuckle under*, give in, submit. **knuck'leduster**, metal instrument to protect knuckles and increase effect of blow.

koa'la (kō-ah-), *n.* (also *koala bear*) Australian tailless arboreal marsupial.

kopp'ie, **kop'je** (-pi), *n.* (S. Afr.) small hill.

Koran' (-ahn; *or* kor'an), *n.* sacred book of

Islam.

kō′sher, *a.* (of food, food-shop, restaurant) fulfilling requirements of Jewish law. *n.* kosher food.

kowtow′, *n.* old Chinese custom of touching ground with forehead as sign of submission or respect. *v.i.* make kowtow; act in servile way (*to*).

kraal (krahl), *n.* S. Afr. hut-village within fence; cattle enclosure.

krem′lin, *n.* citadel of Russian town, esp. Moscow. *the Kremlin,* the Russian Government.

kŭ′dos, *n.* (*slang*) glory, credit.

L

L, l, as Roman numeral, 50.

lab, *n.* (*informal*) laboratory.

lā′bel, *n.* slip attached to object indicating nature, name, destination, etc.; classifying phrase, etc. *v.t.* (p.t. *labelled*), attach label to.

lā′bial, *a.* of lips; (of vocal sound) made by complete or partial closure of lips.

labo′ratory (*or* lab′-), *n.* room or building used for scientific experiments.

labor′ious, *a.* hard-working; involving hard work.

lā′bour (-ber), *n.* exertion of body or mind; task; process of childbirth (esp. contractions of womb); workers; (*Labour*), Labour Party. *v.* exert oneself; work hard; be troubled or impeded; treat at length. **Labour Party,** political party supporting interests of workers. **lā′bourer** (-ber-), *n.* (esp.) man doing unskilled work.

Lab′rador (retriever), breed of retriever with black or golden coat.

labur′num, *n.* small leguminous tree with yellow hanging flowers and poisonous seeds.

lab′yrinth, *n.* network of winding passages; maze; intricate arrangement. **labyrin′thine,** *a.*

lac, *n.* secretion of Indian insect used to make shellac.

lāce, *n.* cord, etc., passed through eyelets in shoes, garment, etc., to draw edges together; fine open-work fabric. *v.t.* fasten, tighten, trim, with lace; flavour (beverage) *with* spirit. **lā′cy,** *a.*

la′cerāte, *v.t.* tear, rend; wound (feelings, etc.). **lacerā′tion,** *n.*

lach′rymal (-k-), *a.* of tears.

lach′rymōse (-k-), *a.* tearful.

lack, *v.* be without, need, (something desirable or necessary). *n.* deficiency, want, need, *of.* **lack-lustre,** (of eye, etc.) dull. **lack′ing,** *a.* needing, deficient (*in*); not available.

lackadai′sical (-z-), *a.* affectedly languid.

lack′ey, *n.* (pl. *lackeys*), (liveried) footman; obsequious person.

lacon′ic, *a.* using, expressed in, few words.

lac′quer (-ker), *n.* hard glossy varnish. *v.t.* coat with lacquer.

lacrosse′, *n.* team-game played with netted crooks (*crosses*) and small ball.

lactā′tion, *n.* secreting and yielding of milk.

lac′tic, *a.* of milk.

lacū′na, *n.* (pl. *lacunas* or *lacunae*), missing portion, blank, gap.

lad, *n.* boy, young fellow.

ladd′er, *n.* set of cross-bars (*rungs*) between two uprights of wood, etc., used as means of ascent; vertical rent in stocking, etc. *v.* (cause to) develop ladder.

lāde, *v.t.* (p.p. *laden*), put cargo on board; ship (goods). **lā′den,** *a.* loaded (*with*); burdened *with.* **lā′ding,** *n.* (esp.) *bill of lading,* receipt to consignor for goods shipped.

lā′dle, *n.* long-handled large-bowled spoon for liquids. *v.t.* transfer with ladle.

lā′dy, *n.* woman of good birth or breeding; (prefixed to name) woman of title; mistress of house; (used courteously) woman. **la′dybird,** small beetle, usu. red with black spots. **Lady-chapel,** chapel in large church, dedicated to Virgin Mary. **Lady Day,** feast of the Annunciation, 25th March. **lady-in-waiting** (pl. *ladies-in-waiting*), lady attending queen, etc. **lady′s maid,** maid in charge of lady's toilet, dress, etc.

lā′dylīke, *a.* behaving like a lady; befitting a lady.

lā′dyship, *n.* (esp.) term used as a substitute for titled lady's name.

lag¹, *v.* (p.t. *lagged*), go too slow; fall behind. *n.* (amount of) retardation or delay. **lagg′ard,** *n.* & *a.* lagging (person).

lag², *v.t.* encase (boiler, etc.) with insulating material. **lagg′ing,** *n.*

lā′ger (beer) (lahg-), light (orig. German)

beer.

lagoon', *n.* shallow salt-water lake parted from sea by sand-bank, coral reef, etc.

laid, *p.t.* & *p.p.* of **lay**⁴.

lain, *p.p.* of **lie**².

lair, *n.* wild beast's lying-place.

laird, *n.* (Sc.) landowner.

laissez-faire (lä'säfār'), *n.* freedom from government interference in industrial, etc., affairs. (French)

lā'ity, *n.* (*collective*) laymen.

lāke¹, *n.* large area of water surrounded by land.

lāke², *n.* pigment or dye (esp. *crimson lake*).

la'ma¹ (lah-), *n.* Tibetan Buddhist monk.

lama²: see **llama**.

lamb (-m), *n.* young sheep, its meat; innocent, weak, or dear person. *v.i.* bring forth lamb. **lambs'wool** (-mz-), fine soft wool of lambs.

lam'bent, *a.* (of flame, etc.) playing about surface; gently brilliant. **lam'bency**, *n.*

lāme, *a.* disabled by injury or defect, esp. in foot or leg; unable to walk evenly; (of story, etc.) unsatisfactory. *v.t.* make lame; disable.

lament', *n.* passionate expression of grief; dirge. *v.* express or feel grief for. **lam'- entable**, *a.* deplorable, regrettable. **lamèn- tā'tion**, *n.*

lam'inated, *a.* (of wood, plastic, etc.) made of succession of layers of material.

Lamm'as, *n.* 1st August, formerly kept as harvest festival.

lamp, *n.* vessel with oil and wick for giving light; other device for giving light. **lamp- -post**, post supporting street-lamp.

lampoon', *n.* virulent satire. *v.t.* write lampoon(s) against.

lam'prey, *n.* (pl. *lampreys*), eel-like sea- -animal with sucker-like mouth.

lance (-ah-), *n.* horseman's long spear (Hist.); similar implement for spearing fish, etc. *v.t.* prick or open with lancet. **lance-corporal,** non-commissioned officer below corporal.

lan'cer (-ah-), *n.* soldier of cavalry regiment; (pl.) kind of square dance.

lan'cet (-ah-), *n.* pointed two-edged surgical knife.

land, *n.* solid part of earth's surface; ground, soil, expanse of country; country, State; (pl.) estates. *v.* disembark, go or put ashore; bring to or reach place, position; bring (aircraft), come, to earth from air; bring (fish) to land. **land'fall,** approach to land, esp. for first time in voyage or flight. **land'lady,** woman keeping inn or lodgings or having tenants. **land'- locked,** almost or quite enclosed by land. **land'lord,** person who rents land or house to another; keeper of inn or lodgings. **land- -lubber,** (Naut.) person ignorant of sea and ships. **land'mark,** conspicuous object; boundary mark; notable event. **land'rail,** corncrake. **land'slide,** landslip; overwhelming majority of votes. **land'slip,** sliding down of mass of land, land fallen, from cliff or mountain side. **land'ward**, *a.* & *adv.* **land'wards** (-z), *adv.*

lan'dau, *n.* four-wheeled horse-drawn carriage with folding top in two parts.

lan'ded, *a.* possessing land; consisting of land.

lan'ding, *n.* coming or bringing to land; landing-place; platform at top of flight of stairs. **landing-place, landing-stage,** place, platform, for landing of passengers and goods from vessels. **landing-strip,** airstrip.

land'scāpe, *n.* piece of inland scenery; picture of inland scenery. **landscape gardening,** art of laying out grounds, parks, etc., to look like natural scenery.

lāne, *n.* narrow road between hedges; narrow street; passage or strip between rows of persons, etc., or marked out for runners in race, streams of traffic, etc.; prescribed route for ships or aircraft.

lang sÿne, (Sc.) (in) the old days.

lang'uage (-nggw-), *n.* words and their use; speech; form of speech used by a people; style; vocabulary; wording.

lang'uid (-nggw-), *a.* lacking vigour; apathetic; slow-moving; faint, weak.

lang'uish (-nggw-), *v.i.* lose strength; droop; pine (*for*).

lang'uor (-ngger), *n.* faintness; listlessness; soft or tender mood. **lang'uorous**, *a.*

lank, *a.* lean and tall; long and limp. **lank'y**, *a.* tall, long.

lan'olin, *n.* fat from sheep's wool used in ointments, etc.

lan'tern, *n.* (portable) transparent case protecting flame of candle, etc.; light- -chamber of lighthouse.

lan'yard, *n.* (Naut.) short cord for fastening or holding something.

lap¹, *v.* (p.t. *lapped*), drink by scooping with the tongue; drink (*up*) greedily; (of waves, etc.) move with lapping sound (*against, on*). *n.* act or sound of lapping.

lap², *n.* front part of skirt held up as receptacle; (part of clothing covering) upper surface of thighs of seated person; one circuit of course in race. *v.* (p.t. *lapped*), enfold, wrap; arrange so as to overlap. **lap-dog,** small pet dog.

lapel', *n.* part of front of coat folded back towards shoulder.

lap'idary, *a.* engraved on stone; (of style) suitable for inscriptions. *n.* cutter, polisher, or engraver of gems.

lap'is laz'ūlī, *n.* (pigment from, colour of,) bright blue semi-precious stone.

lapse, *n.* slip of memory, etc.; slight mistake; backsliding; (of right, etc.) termination through disuse, etc.; elapsing. *v.i.* fall back or away; become void, terminate; elapse.

lap'wing, *n.* kind of plover, pewit.

lar'ceny, *n.* stealing. **lar'cenous**, *a.*

larch, *n.* deciduous coniferous tree; its wood.

lard, *n.* pig fat prepared for cooking, etc. *v.t.* insert strips of bacon in (meat, etc.) before cooking; interlard (speech, etc.). **lar′dy**, *a.*

lar′der, *n.* room or cupboard for storing provisions.

large, *a.* of considerable or relatively great magnitude; of wide range, comprehensive. *at large*, at liberty, free, at full length, in general. **large′ly**, *adv.* (esp.) to a great extent.

largess(e)′, *n.* money, etc., generously or abundantly given.

lar′gō, *adv. & n.* (pl. *largos*), (Mus.) (movement, passage, to be played) slowly and in dignified style.

la′riat, *n.* rope for tethering; lasso.

lark[1], *n.* any of various song-birds (esp. the *skylark*).

lark[2], *n.* bit of fun, frolic. *v.i.* play tricks, frolic *about*.

lark′spur, *n.* delphinium with blue, white, or pink spurred flowers.

lar′va, *n.* (pl. *larvae*), immature insect after leaving egg, grub.

laryn′gēal (-j-), *a.* of the larynx. **laryngī′tis** (-j-), *n.* inflammation of larynx.

la′rynx, *n.* upper part of windpipe, holding vocal cords.

Las′car, *n.* East Indian seaman.

lasciv′ious, *a.* lustful.

lā′ser (-z-), *n.* device producing intense narrow orderly beam of light, optical maser.

lash, *v.* make sudden movement of tail, limb, etc.; beat with thong, etc.; urge as with whip; castigate; tie tightly. *n.* stroke given with whip, etc.; thong forming flexible part of whip; eyelash. **lash′ings** (-z), *n. pl.* (*slang*) plenty.

lass, lass′ie, *nn.* girl.

lass′itūde, *n.* weariness.

lass′ō (*or* -sōō′), *n.* (pl. *lassoes*), rope with running noose, used esp. for catching cattle. *v.t.* catch with lasso.

last[1] (-ah-), *n.* shoemaker's model for shaping shoe, etc., on.

last[2] (-ah-), *a.* after all others; coming at end; most recent; utmost. *adv.* (esp.) on last occasion before present. *n.* last-mentioned person or thing; end. **Last Supper**, last supper of Christ with his disciples, when Eucharist was instituted.

last[3] (-ah-), *v.i.* go on; remain unexhausted or adequate or alive. **las′ting**, *a.* permanent; durable.

last′ly (-ah-), *adv.* finally.

latch, *n.* bar with catch as fastening of gate, etc.; small spring door-lock. *v.t.* fasten with latch.

latch′ĕt, *n.* (*archaic*) thong for fastening shoe.

lāte, *a.* after right time; far on in day or night or period; now dead; that occurred lately. *adv.* after proper time; far on in time. *of late*, recently. **lāt(e)′ish**, *a.* somewhat late. **lāte′ly**, *adv.* not long ago; in recent times.

lā′tent, *a.* concealed; dormant; existing but not developed or manifest.

lat′eral, *a.* of, at, towards, or from side(s).

lā′tex, *n.* milky fluid exuding from some plants, esp. as raw material of rubber.

lath (-ah-), *n.* (pl. pr. lahdhz), thin strip of wood.

lāthe (-dh), *n.* machine for turning wood, metal, etc., while it is being shaped.

lath′er (-dh-), *n.* froth of soap or other detergent and water; frothy sweat of horse. *v.* form lather; cover with lather.

Lat′in, *n.* language of ancient Rome. *a.* of or in Latin; of ancient Rome; of peoples speaking languages descended from Latin.

lat′itūde, *n.* freedom of action or opinion; scope; distance, measured in degrees, that point on earth's surface is N. or S. of equator (0°); (usu. pl.) regions. *line of latitude*, imaginary line connecting places of same latitude.

latrine′ (-ēn), *n.* place for urination or defecation, esp. in camp, barracks, etc.

latt′er, *a.* second-mentioned; belonging to end (of period, etc.). *n.* second-mentioned thing or person. **latter-day**, modern. **latt′erly**, *adv.* of late.

latt′ice, *n.* structure of crossed laths or metal strips as screen, etc. (also *lattice-work*). **latt′iced** (-st), *a.*

laud, *v.t.* praise, extol. **laud′able**, *a.* commendable. **laud′atory**, *a.* giving praise, extolling.

lau′danum, *n.* tincture of opium.

laugh (lahf), *v.* make sounds usual in expressing amusement, exultation, and scorn; utter with laugh. *laugh at*, be amused at; make fun of, ridicule. *n.* sound or act of laughing. **laugh′able**, *a.* amusing, ridiculous. **laughing-gas**, nitrous oxide, used as anaesthetic. **laughing-stock**, object of general derision. **laugh′ter**, *n.* act or sound of laughing.

launch[1], *v.* send forth, hurl; start, send off; set (vessel) afloat. *n.* launching of ship, rocket, etc. **launching pad**, platform from which rocket, etc., is launched.

launch[2], *n.* large mechanically propelled boat.

laun′der, *v.t.* wash and iron (linen, etc.).

launderette′, *n.* establishment where washing-machines and clothes-driers may be used for a fee.

laun′dress, *n.* woman who launders.

laun′dry, *n.* room or establishment for washing clothes, sheets, etc.; clothes, etc., for washing.

laur′ĕate, *a.* wreathed with laurel. **poet laureate**, poet holding position of honour as officer of British Royal Household, and (esp. formerly) writing poems for State occasions.

lau′rel (lo-), *n.* glossy-leaved shrub; (sing. or pl.) wreath of bay-leaves as emblem of victory or poetic merit.

la′va (lah-), *n.* molten rock, etc., which flows

down sides of volcano, becoming solid as it cools.

lav′atory, *n.* water-closet; urinal; room, etc., with wash-basin(s) and water-closet(s).

lāve, *v.t.* (Poet.) wash; wash against.

lav′ender, *n.* a fragrant-flowered shrub; pale purplish colour of its flowers.

lav′ish, *a.* extremely generous, extravagant; (too) abundant. *v.t.* give or spend lavishly.

law, *n.* rule, system of rules, established among community and imposing or prohibiting certain action; rule of action or procedure; legal profession or knowledge; law-courts, litigation; correct statement of invariable sequence of specified conditions and specified phenomenon. *go to law,* have recourse to lawcourt. *lay down the law,* talk authoritatively and dogmatically. **law-abiding,** obedient to law. **law′court,** place where justice is administered. **law′suit,** case, claim, etc., brought to lawcourt.

law′ful, *a.* permitted by law; not illegal.

law′less, *a.* having no laws; disobedient to law; unbridled.

lawn¹, *n.* very fine linen or (now usu.) cotton.

lawn², *n.* close-mown turf in gardens, etc. **lawn tennis,** modification of ancient game of tennis, played with rackets on unwalled hard or grass court.

law′yer, *n.* person practising law as profession; person who has studied law.

lax, *a.* negligent; not strict; vague. **lax′ity,** *n.*

lax′ative, *a. & n.* (medicine) tending to cause evacuation of the bowels.

lay¹, *p.t.* of **lie².**

lay², *n.* narrative poem, minstrel's song.

lay³, *a.* of the people, as distinct from the clergy; non-professional; amateur. **lay brother, sister,** member of religious order employed in manual labour. **lay′man,** *n.* (pl. -*men*), person not in holy orders; person without professional or special knowledge of subject.

lay⁴, *v.t.* (p.t. *laid*), deposit on surface; put down, place; impose, enjoin; cause (dust, ghost, etc.) to subside; prepare (table) for meal; wager; produce (egg). *lay out,* prepare (corpse) for burial; plan arrangement of; spend (money). *lay waste,* see **waste. lay-by,** roadside recess in which vehicle may stop. **lay-out,** (plan or drawing of) arrangement of ground, printed page, etc.

lay′er, *n.* thickness of matter laid over a surface; shoot fastened down to take root. *v.t.* propagate by layers; arrange in layers.

layette′, *n.* clothes, etc., needed for new-born child.

lay fig′ure (-ger), jointed model of human figure used by artists.

layman: see **lay³.**

lāze, *v.* (*informal*) idle.

lā′zy, *a.* unwilling to work; doing little work; idle. **lā′ziness,** *n.*

lea, *n.* (Poet.) tract of open grassland.

lead¹ (lēd), *v.* (p.t. *led*), conduct, guide, esp. by going in front; direct movements of; guide actions or opinions of; guide by persuasion; spend (life, etc.); have first place (in), go or be first; be leader, leading counsel or actor, etc.; (of road, etc.) go *to. n.* leading-place; (player of) chief part; thong, etc., for leading dog.

lead² (led), *n.* heavy soft grey metal; stick of graphite in pencil; bullets; sounding-lead. *v.t.* cover, weight, frame (panes, etc.), with lead. **lead′en** (led-), *a.* (as) of lead; heavy, slow; inert; lead-coloured.

lea′der (lēd-), *n.* one who leads; principal violin-player in orchestra, etc.; leading article. **lea′dership,** *n.*

lea′ding (lēd-), *a.* chief; of most importance; giving guidance. **leading article,** article in newspaper, etc., expressing editor's opinion. **leading lady,** chief actress in play, etc. **leading question,** question so framed as to suggest the answer desired.

leaf, *n.* (pl. *leaves*), expanded organ (usu. green) of plant, springing from stem or branch or from root; foliage; single thickness of folded paper, esp. in book; thin sheet of metal, etc.; hinged or movable part of extending table, etc. **leaf′let,** *n.* small leaf; printed paper, single or folded, for distribution. **lea′fy,** *a.*

league¹ (-g), *n.* (*archaic*) measure of distance, usu. about 3 miles.

league² (-g), *n.* (parties to) agreement for mutual help or association for common interests; group of sports clubs playing matches among themselves. *in league with,* in alliance with. *v.* combine in league.

leak, *n.* flaw in vessel, etc., allowing passage of liquid or gas; liquid or gas escaping through flaw; divulging of (esp. secret) information. *v.* escape, allow escape of, through leak; divulge (secret, etc.). **lea′kage,** *n.* process of leaking. **lea′ky,** *a.* having leak(s).

lean¹, *a.* thin, not plump; meagre, poor; (of meat) not fat. *n.* lean part of meat. **lean′ness,** *n.*

lean², *v.* (p.t. *leant,* pr. lent, or *leaned*), be or put in sloping position; incline (thing, one's body) *against, on,* something for support; incline (*towards*); rely or depend *on.* **lean-to,** shed, etc., with roof leaning against wall of larger building. **lea′ning,** *n.* tendency or inclination.

leap, *v.* (p.t. *leapt,* pr. lept, or *leaped*), & *n.* jump. **leap-frog,** game in which players vault over others bending down. **leap-year,** year with extra day, 29th February, inserted.

learn (lern), *v.* (p.t. *learnt,* or *learned*), get knowledge of, or skill in, by study, experience, or being taught; find out. **learn′ed,** *a.* having or showing much knowledge. **learn′er,** *n.* person learning. **learn′ing,** *n.* knowledge got by study.

lease, *n.* legal contract, by which owner of

land or building (*lessor*) conveys use of it to tenant (*lessee*) for a period, usu. for rent. *v.t.* grant or take on lease.

leash, *n.* thong for holding dogs. *v.t.* put leash on; hold in leash.

least, *a.* smallest. *n.* least amount. *adv.* in least degree.

leath'er (ledh-), *n.* material made by tanning or otherwise dressing hides; article or piece of leather. *v.t.* cover with leather; flog. **leather-jacket**, larva of crane-fly. **leath'-ercloth**, strong fabric coated to resemble leather. **leath'ering**, *n.* flogging. **leath'ern**, *a.* (*archaic*) made of leather. **leath'ery**, *a.* tough like leather.

leave[1], *n.* permission. *leave* (*of absence*), permission to be absent from duty, period for which this lasts. *on leave*, absent thus. *take leave* (*of*), bid farewell (to). **leave-taking**, *n.*

leave[2], *v.* (p.t. *left*), let remain; not consume or deal with; bequeath; go away (from); entrust to another; abandon.

lea'ven (le-), *n.* substance used to make dough ferment and rise; (fig.) spreading and transforming influence. *v.t.* act as leaven upon.

lea'vings (-z), *n. pl.* what is left.

lech'ery, *n.* excessive indulgence of (sexual) lust. **lech'erous**, *a.*

lec'tern, *n.* reading-desk in church.

lec'ture (-cher), *n.* discourse delivered to class or other audience; piece of admonition. *v.* deliver lecture (to); admonish. **lec'turer**, *n.* (esp.) person who teaches at university, etc. **lec'tureship**, *n.*

led, *p.t. & p.p.* of **lead**[1].

ledge, *n.* narrow shelf or projection; rock-ridge below sea-level.

ledg'er, *n.* book in which debtor-and-creditor accounts are kept; horizontal timber in scaffolding. **ledger** (or **leger**) **line(s)**, (Mus.) short line(s) added above or below stave to extend its range.

lee, *n.* shelter given by neighbouring object; side of something away from wind. **lee'way**, drift to leeward; lost time. **leeward** (lū'ard), *a. & adv.* on or towards side away from wind. *n.* leeward direction or region.

leech[1], *n.* (*archaic*) doctor.

leech[2], *n.* small blood-sucking worm living in wet places; person clinging to another (and draining his resources).

leek, *n.* onion-like vegetable.

leer, *n. & v.i.* glance with lascivious or evil expression.

lees (-z), *n. pl.* sediment of wine, etc.; dregs.

leeward, leeway: see **lee.**

left[1], *p.t. & p.p.* of **leave**[2].

left[2], *a.* of or on side of body which has, in most persons, the less easily and skilfully used hand (opp. *right*); having corresponding relation to front of any object. *n.* left side; (Politics) more advanced or radical party, etc. **left-hand**, *a.* of, on, left side. **left--handed**, *a.* using left hand in preference to

right.

leg, *n.* one of limbs on which person or animal walks and stands; support of chair or other piece of furniture.

leg'acy, *n.* thing or sum left by will; something handed down by predecessor.

lē'gal, *a.* of or based on law; appointed or required or permitted by law. **lēgal'ity**, *n.* lawfulness. **lē'galīze**, *v.t.* make lawful; bring into harmony with law.

leg'ate, *n.* papal ambassador.

legatee', *n.* recipient of legacy.

lēgā'tion, *n.* diplomatic minister and his suite; his official residence.

lēga'tō (-ah-), *a. & adv.* (Mus.) smooth(ly) and connected(ly).

le'gend, *n.* traditional story, myth; inscription or motto on coin, etc. **le'gendary**, *a.* famous in legend; existing only in legend.

le'gerdēmain, *n.* juggling, conjuring tricks.

leger line: see **ledger.**

legg'ing (-g-), *n.* (usu. in pl.) covering of leather, etc., for lower leg.

legg'y (-g-), *a.* having disproportionately long legs.

leghorn' (-gorn; or leg'h-), *n.* (hat of) kind of plaited straw; breed of fowls.

le'gible, *a.* easily read, clear. **legibil'ity**, *n.*

lē'gion (-jn), *n.* division of 3,000 - 6,000 men in ancient-roman army; great number. *British Legion*, national association of ex-service men. *Foreign Legion*, body of foreign volunteers in (esp. French) army. **lē'gionary**, *a.* of legion or legions. *n.* soldier of legion.

le'gislāte, *v.i.* make laws. **legislā'tion**, *n.* (enacting of) laws. **le'gislative**, *a.* **le'-gislātor**, *n.* **le'gislature**, *n.* law-making body of a State.

lēgit'imacy, *n.* being legitimate. **lēgit'imate**, *a.* lawful; permitted; born of parents married to each other. **lēgit'imāte**, *v.t.* make legitimate.

lēgū'minous, *a.* bearing seed in pods (as beans, peas, etc.).

leisure (lezh'er), *n.* spare time; freedom from pressing business. **lei'sured**, *a.* having plenty of leisure. **lei'surely**, *a.* deliberate, not hurried. *adv.* without hurry.

leitmotiv (līt'mōtēf), *n.* (Mus.) theme associated throughout a composition with some person, situation, or sentiment. (German)

lemm'ing, *n.* small rodent of arctic regions.

lem'on, *n.* pale-yellow acid fruit; its colour; tree bearing it. **lemonāde'**, *n.* drink made from or flavoured with lemons.

lē'mur, *n.* nocturnal mammal resembling monkey but with pointed muzzle.

lend, *v.t.* (p.t. *lent*), grant temporary use of (thing); let out at interest or for hire; bestow.

length, *n.* measurement from end to end in space or time; long stretch or extent. *at length*, at last. **leng'then**, *v.* make or become longer. **length'ways** (-z), *adv.* **length'wise** (-z), *adv. & a.* (in direction) parallel with thing's length. **leng'thy,** *a.* of unusual length; tedious.

le'nient *a.* not severe, tolerant; mild. **lē'niènce, lē'nièncy,** *nn.*

lens (-z), *n.* (pl. *lenses*), piece of glass, etc., curved on one or both sides, used in spectacles, cameras, etc.; transparent body behind iris of eye.

lent, *p.t.* & *p.p.* of **lend.**

Lent, *n.* (in Christian Church) period of fasting and penitence including forty weekdays before Easter Day. **len'ten,** *a.* of or in Lent.

len'til, *n.* (seed of) leguminous plant grown for food.

Lē'ō, *n.* the Lion, constellation and fifth sign of the Zodiac.

lē'onine, *a.* lion-like; of lions.

leop'ard (lep-), *n.* large carnivore of cat family, with dark-spotted fawn coat, panther.

lē'otard, *n.* close-fitting body-garment worn by dancers, acrobats, etc.

lep'er, *n.* person suffering from leprosy.

lepidop'terous, *a.* of order of insects that includes moths and butterflies.

lep'rosy, *n.* chronic disease affecting skin, nerves, etc. **lep'rous,** *a.*

les'bian (-z-), *a.* (of woman) homosexual. *0.* homosexual woman. **les'bianism,** *n.*

lese-maj'èsty (lēz-), *n.* (Hist.) treason.

less, *a.* smaller; of lower rank or degree; of smaller quantity, not so much (of). *n.* smaller amount or quantity or number. *adv.* to smaller degree or extent or amount. *prep.* minus, not including.

lessee: see **lease.**

less'en, *v.* make or become less.

less'er, *a.* not so great as the other or the rest, smaller.

less'on, *n.* thing to be learnt by pupil; spell of teaching; reading from Bible at morning or evening prayer; warning experience; example.

lessor: see **lease.**

lest, *conj.* in order to avoid or prevent (occurrence); (after *fear, be afraid*) that.

let[1]**,** *v.t.* (p.t. *let*), (*archaic*) hinder, obstruct. *n.* hindrance.

let[2]**,** *v.* (p.t. *let*), allow or enable or cause to; grant use of for rent or hire.

lē'thal, *a.* causing, sufficient or designed to cause, death.

leth'argy, *n.* lack of interest or energy; dull and sluggish state. **lethar'gic,** *a.*

lett'er, *n.* any of symbols of which written words are composed; written message, epistle; literal meaning; (pl.) literature, learning. **letter-box,** official box for posting, private box for delivery of, letters. **letter-card,** folded card with gummed edges, for use as letter. **lett'erpress,** matter printed from type. **lett'ered,** *a.* (esp.) literate, well-read. **lett'ering,** *n.* (esp.) (style of) letters drawn, inscribed, etc.

lett'uce (-tis), *n.* crisp-leaved cultivated plant

much used as salad.

leukae'mia (lūkē-; *or* lōo-), *n.* progressive disease affecting the white blood cells.

Levant', *n.* East Mediterranean region. **Levan'tīne,** *a.*

lev'ee (-vi), *n.* sovereign's reception for men only.

lev'el, *n.* (instrument for giving or testing) horizontal line or plane; social or intellectual standard; plane of rank or authority; flat surface or country. *a.* horizontal; even; in same line or plane (*with*). *v.* (p.t. *levelled*), make level, even, or uniform; destroy completely; take aim *at*. **level crossing,** intersection of road and railway, etc., at same level. **level-headed,** mentally well-balanced. **lev'elled** (-ld), *a.* **lev'eller, lev'elling,** *nn.* **lev'elly** (-l-li), *adv.*

lē'ver, *n.* rigid bar used as mechanical aid to raise heavy weight; prising tool. *v.* use lever; move (as) with lever. **lē'verage,** *n.* power, advantage gained by use, of lever.

lev'erèt, *n.* young hare.

lèvī'athan, *n.* sea monster (Bibl.); huge ship; anything very large of its kind.

lev'ity, *n.* tendency to treat serious matters without respect; frivolity.

lev'y, *n.* collecting of tax or compulsory payment; enrolling of soldiers, etc.; amount collected; number enrolled. *v.t.* raise or impose compulsorily.

lewd (lūd, lōōd), *a.* indecent, lustful.

lexicog'rapher, lexicog'raphy, *nn.* maker, making, of dictionaries.

lex'icon, *n.* dictionary.

liabil'ity, *n.* being liable; (pl.) debts, etc., for which one is liable. **li'able,** *a.* legally bound; subject *to,* answerable *for;* exposed or apt *to.*

liais'on (-zn), *n.* connection, touch, intercommunication (*between, with*).

lia'na (liah-), *n.* tropical climbing plant.

li'ar, *n.* (esp. habitual) teller of lies.

libā'tion (*or* li-), *n.* drink-offering to a god.

li'bel, *n.* (publishing of) written or printed statement damaging to person's reputation; false defamatory statement. *v.t.* (p.t. *libelled*), attack falsely the good name of. **li'bellous,** *a.*

lib'eral, *a.* generous, open-handed; abundant; open-minded, unprejudiced; (of education, etc.) directed towards general enlargement of mind; of Liberal Party. *n.* holder of liberal views; member of Liberal Party. **Liberal Party,** political party favouring individual liberty, democratic reform, etc. **lib'eralism,** *n.* **liberal'ity,** *n.* (esp.) generosity; freedom from prejudice. **lib'erally,** *adv.*

lib'erāte, *v.t.* set at liberty, release. **liberā'tion,** *n.* **lib'erātor,** *n.*

libertār'ian, *n.* & *a.* (person) advocating (extreme) liberty of thought and action.

lib'ertine (*or* -ēn), *n.* man leading immoral and debauched life.

lib'erty, *n.* being free, freedom; right or

power to do as one pleases; piece of presumption.
libid'inous, *a.* lustful, lewd.
Lib'ra, *n.* the Scales, constellation and seventh sign of the Zodiac.
librār'ian, *n.* person in charge of library. **li'-brary,** *n.* collection of books; building or room in which it is kept.
librett'ō, *n.* (pl. *libretti* or *librettos*), text of opera, oratorio, etc.
lice, *pl.* of **louse.**
li'cence, *n.* (document giving) formal permission from constituted authority (to marry, drive motor vehicle, keep dog, carry on trade, etc.); (excessive) liberty of action. **poetic licence,** poet's freedom to disregard rules. **li'cense,** *v.t.* authorize; grant licence to or for; authorize use of (premises), esp. for sale of alcoholic drinks. **licensee',** *n.* holder of licence.
līcen'tiate (-shi-), *n.* holder of certificate from examining body.
licen'tious (-shus), *a.* lascivious, lewd.
li'chen (-k-; *or* lich'-), *n.* plant organism composed of fungus associated with alga growing on rocks, trees, etc.
lick, *v.t.* pass tongue over; take *off* or *up* by licking; (of flame, etc.), play lightly over; (*slang*) thrash, defeat. *n.* act of licking; smart blow.
lic'tor, *n.* ancient-roman official bearing fasces before consul.
lid, *n.* cover for aperture, esp. at top of vessel; eyelid. **lidd'ed,** *a.* having lid(s).
li'dō (lē-), *n.* (pl. *lidos*), public open-air swimming-pool or pleasure-beach.
lie¹, *n.* false statement made intentionally; imposture; false belief. *v.i.* (p.t. *lied*; pres.p. *lȳing*), tell lies; be deceptive.
lie², *v.i.* (p.t. *lay*; p.p. *lain*; pres. p. *lȳing*), be in or assume horizontal position on supporting surface; be at rest on something; be situated, spread out to view, etc.; remain, be. *n.* way thing lies. *lie of the land,* (fig.) state of affairs.
lief, *adv.* (*archaic*) willingly.
liege, *a.* (Hist.) entitled to receive or bound to give feudal service or allegiance. *n.* liege lord; vassal, subject.
lieu (lū), *n. in lieu,* instead (*of*).
lieuten'ant (left-; Navy let-; U.S. lōōt-), *n.* deputy, subordinate commander; naval or military officer.
life, *n.* (pl. *lives*), state of ceaseless change and functional activity peculiar to animals and plants; living state; living things and their movements; energy, liveliness; mode of existence; period from birth to death; events of individual's existence or written story of them. **life-belt,** ring or belt of buoyant material or inflated with air, for keeping person afloat in water. **life-blood,** blood necessary to life; (fig.) vitalizing influence. **life--boat,** boat of special construction for saving

life in storms. **life'buoy** life-belt. **life insur-ance,** contract to pay fixed sum on person's death in return for payment of premium(s). **life-jacket,** appliance in form of jacket for keeping person afloat. **life'time,** duration of person's life. **life'less,** *a.* dead; lacking animation, etc. **life'līke,** *a.* exactly like real person or thing. **life'long,** *a.* continued for life-time.
lift, *v.* raise to higher level; take up, hoist; steal, plagiarize; (of fog, etc.) rise, disperse. *n.* lifting; apparatus for raising or lowering persons or goods from one floor or level to another; ride in vehicle given to walker; lifting power. **lift-off,** take-off of rocket, etc., from launching pad.
lig'ament, *n.* tough fibrous tissue binding bones together.
lig'ature *n.* thing used in tying (esp. blood--vessel, etc., in Surgery).
light¹ (līt), *n.* natural agent that makes things visible; presence or effect of this; source of light; (pl.) traffic lights; means of procuring fire; brightness of eyes or aspect; mental illumination; way thing presents itself to mind. *come, bring, to light,* be revealed, reveal. *a.* having plenty of light, not dark; (of colours) pale, not deep. *v.* (p.t. *lit* or *lighted*), set burning; begin burning; give light to; show way with light; burn; brighten with animation. **light'house,** tower or other structure with beacon light for guiding or warning ships. **light'ship,** anchored ship with beacon light. **light-year,** (Astron.) distance light travels in one year. **light'er¹,** *n.* (esp.) device for producing flame.
light² (līt), *a.* of little weight, not heavy; deficient in weight; easy to lift or digest or do; not clumsy; elegant; trivial, slight, fickle. *adv.* lightly. *v.i.* (p.t. & p.p. *lit* or *lighted*), come by chance (*upon*). **light-fingered,** thievish. **light-headed,** dizzy, delirious. **light-hearted,** cheerful.
light'en¹ (līt-), *v.* make or grow bright; flash; emit lightning.
light'en² (līt-), *v.* make or grow lighter; reduce weight or load of; relieve of care; mitigate.
lighter¹: see **light¹.**
light'er² (līt-), *n.* boat, usu. flat-bottomed, for shifting goods between ship and land.
light'ning (līt-), *n.* visible electric discharge between clouds or between cloud and ground. **lightning-conductor, lightning--rod,** metal rod or wire fixed to building to divert lightning to earth.
lights (līts), *n.pl.* lungs of sheep, pigs, etc., as food, esp. for cats and dogs.
light'some (līt-), *a.* gracefully light, merry.
lig'nīte, *n.* coal, usu. brownish-black, of woody texture.
like, *a.* having same or similar characteristics, appearance, etc.; such as, characteristic of; in promising state or right mood for (esp. in phrr. *look like, feel like*). *prep.* in the manner

of, to the same degree as. *n.* counterpart, equal; like thing or person; (*pl.*) what one likes. *v.t.* find agreeable or satisfactory; feel attracted by; (with *should, would*) wish. **like-minded**, having same tastes, views, etc. **like'able**, *a.*

like'lihood (-kl-), *n.* probability.

like'ly (-kl-), *a.* probable; to be expected *to*; promising, apparently suitable. *adv.* probably.

li'ken, *v.t.* represent as similar *to*.

like'ness (-kn-), *n.* resemblance; portrait.

like'wise (-kwīz), *adv. & conj.* also, moreover, too; (Bibl.) similarly.

li'king, *n.* one's taste; regard, fondness *for*.

li'lac, *n.* shrub with fragrant, usu. pale pinkish-violet, blossoms; colour of these. *a.* lilac-coloured.

Lillipū'tian (-shn), *a.* of diminutive size.

lilt, *v.* sing rhythmically. *n.* (song with) marked rhythm or swing; light, springing step.

lil'y, *n.* any of various bulbous plants with large showy flowers. **lily of the valley**, spring flower with small fragrant white bells.

limb (-m), *n.* leg, arm, or wing; bough of tree; arm of cross.

lim'ber, *a.* flexible; lithe, agile. *v. limber up*, exercise in preparation for athletic, etc., exertion.

lim'bō, *n.* condition of neglect or oblivion; place of forgotten things; (in R.C. theology) abode of souls of just who died before Christ's coming and of unbaptized infants.

lime[1], *n.* white caustic substance got by burning limestone or chalk. *v.t.* treat with lime; catch (bird) with bird-lime. **lime-kiln**, furnace for making lime. **lime'light**, intense white light; (fig.) glare of publicity. **lime'stone**, rock containing much lime.

lime[2], *n.* small round acid citrous fruit.

lime[3], *n.* (also *lime-tree*) ornamental tree.

lim'erick, *n.* humorous or nonsense poem of five lines.

lim'it, *n.* bounding line; terminal point, bound that may not or cannot be passed; restriction. *v.t.* set limits to; serve as limit to; restrict. **limitā'tion**, *n.* limiting rule or circumstance; limited condition, disability. **lim'ited**, *a.* (of quantity) small; (of views, etc.) restricted, narrow. **limited (liability) company**, business firm whose members are liable for its debts only to extent of capital sum they have provided.

lim'ousine (-oozēn), *n.* motor car with closed body and partition behind driver.

limp[1], *v.i.* walk lamely. *n.* limping walk.

limp[2], *a.* not stiff, not springy; without energy.

lim'pet, *n.* shell-fish with low conical shell, adhering tightly to rocks.

lim'pid, *a.* transparently clear. **limpid'ity**, *n.*

linch'pin, *n.* pin passed through axle-end to keep wheel on.

lin'den, *n.* lime-tree.

line[1], *n.* (long) narrow mark on a surface; piece of cord, etc., serving some purpose; (Math.) extent of length without breadth or thickness; wire over which telegraphic, etc., messages travel; row or series of persons or things; series of ships, etc., following same route; single verse of poetry; lineage; direction, course, track; boundary; out!ine; equator; regular regiments, esp. infantry. *in line with*, (fig.) in agreement with. *v.* mark with lines; draw *up* in line(s).

line[2], *v.t.* apply layer of material to inside of; fill (purse, etc.); serve as lining for.

lin'eage, *n.* ancestry, lineal descent. **lin'eal**, *a.* in direct line of descent.

lin'eament, *n.* (usu. pl.) distinctive feature(s) or characteristic(s), esp. of face.

lin'ear, *a.* of or in lines; long and narrow and of uniform breadth.

lin'en, *a.* made of flax. *n.* linen cloth; articles made of this or of cotton; undergarments, sheets, etc.

li'ner, *n.* one of a line of passenger-ships, aircraft, etc.

lines'man (-nz-), *n.* (pl. *-men*), umpire's or referee's assistant at boundary line.

ling[1], *n.* long slender edible sea-fish.

ling[2], *n.* common variety of heather.

ling'er (-ngg-), *v.i.* be slow to depart; wait about, dally; delay; be protracted.

lingerie (lan'zherē), *n.* women's underclothing.

ling'ō (-ngg-), *n.* (pl. *lingoes*), a foreign language; queer way of talking.

ling'ual (-nggw-), *a.* of the tongue; of speech or languages.

lin'guist (-nggw-), *n.* person skilled in (foreign) languages. **linguis'tic**, *a.* of study of languages; of language. **linguist'ics**, *n.* science of language.

lin'iment, *n.* medicinal liquid used in rubbing bruised, sprained, or aching limb, etc.

li'ning, *n.* layer of material applied to inside of garment, box, vessel, etc.; inside layer.

link, *n.* one ring or loop of chain, etc.; thing or person that connects or unites; cuff-link. *v.* connect, join *to, together*, etc.; intertwine.

links, *n.pl.* golf-course.

linn'et, *n.* a common song-bird.

li'nō, *n.* (pl. *linos*), linoleum. **li'nocut**, (print from) design cut on block of linoleum.

linō'leum, *n.* floor-covering of canvas thickly coated with oxidized linseed-oil.

lin'seed, *n.* seed of flax. **linseed-oil**, oil pressed from linseed.

lint, *n.* soft material for dressing wounds, etc.; fluff.

lin'tel, *n.* horizontal timber or stone over door or window.

li'on, *n.* large powerful tawny carnivore of cat family; courageous person; celebrity. **li'oness**, *n. fem.* **li'onize**, *v.t.* treat as celebrity.

lip, *n.* either of fleshy edges of opening of mouth; edge of vessel, cavity, etc. **lip-**

-reading, method (used by deaf people) of understanding speech from lip movements.

lip′stick, stick of cosmetic for colouring lips.

li′quefȳ, v. make or become liquid. **liquefac′tion,** n.

liqueur′ (-kūr or -ker), n. strong sweet alcoholic liquor with aromatic flavouring.

li′quid, a. in fluid state, like water or oil, not solid or gaseous; clear (as water); (of sounds) flowing, clear; (of assets, etc.) easily convertible into cash. n. liquid substance.

li′quidāte, v. pay (debt); wind up affairs of (company, etc.); put an end to, get rid of (often by violent means). **liquidā′tion,** n.

liquid′ity, n. being liquid. **li′quidize,** v.t. cause to become liquid. **li′quidīzer,** n.

li′quor (-ker), n. liquid (usu. fermented or distilled) for drinking; liquid used in or resulting from some process.

li′quorice (-ker-), n. black substance used in medicine and as sweet; plant from whose root it is obtained.

lisle thread (līl thred), fine hard-twisted kind of thread.

lisp, v. use the sound th for s in speaking; say lispingly. n. lisping speech.

liss′om, a. lithe, agile.

list¹, n. roll or catalogue or inventory. v.t. enter in list.

list², n. inclination of ship, etc., to one side; v.i. lean over to one side.

li′sten (-sn), v.i. make effort to hear something, hear with attention; pay attention to. **listen in,** listen to radio transmission; tap telephone communication, etc.

list′less, a. without energy, languid, indifferent.

lists, n.pl. (Hist.) (fences enclosing) tilting ground; (fig.) scene of conflict.

lit, p.t. & p.p. of **light¹,²**.

lit′any, n. series of petitions for use in church services.

lit′eracy, n. quality or state of being literate.

lit′eral, a. of letters of alphabet; exactly corresponding to original; giving words their ordinary sense. **lit′erally,** adv.

lit′erary, a. of or constituting or concerned with literature.

lit′erate, a. able to read and write; having some knowledge of literature. n. literate person.

lit′erature, n. books and other writings valued for form and style; writings of period, country, etc.; books, etc., dealing with a subject; (informal) printed matter.

lithe (-dh), a. supple; easily bent.

lith′ograph (-ahf), v.t. draw or write on stone and print impressions from it. n. such impression. **lithog′rapher,** n. **lithog′raphy,** n. **lithograph′ic,** a.

lit′igant, n. & a. (party) engaged in lawsuit. **lit′igāte,** v. go to law; contest in lawcourt. **litigā′tion,** a.

liti′gious (-jus), a. fond of litigation, contentious.

lit′mus, n. blue colouring turned red by acids and restored to blue by alkalis.

litre (lē′ter), n. unit of capacity in metric system (about 1¾ pints).

litt′er, n. carrying-couch formerly used as carriage; stretcher; bedding for beasts; odds and ends, rubbish, lying about; young born at one birth. v. provide (horse, etc.) with litter; make (place) untidy; (of animals) bear young.

litt′le, a. not great or big or much; small; short; unimportant; paltry or mean. n. some, but not much. adv. to small extent; not at all. **little people,** fairies.

litt′oral, a. of, on, near, the shore. n. region lying along shore.

lit′urgy (-ter-), n. set form of public worship. **litur′gical,** a.

live¹, v. have life; be or continue alive; conduct oneself in specified way; pass or spend; dwell. **live′able,** a.

live², a. that is alive or real or active; not dead or fictitious or exhausted or (of broadcast, etc.) recorded; capable of being exploded; charged with electricity. **live′stock,** domestic animals kept for use or profit. **live wire,** (fig.) forceful and energetic person.

live′lihood (-vl-), n. means of living; sustenance.

live′long (-vl-), a. whole length of.

live′ly (-vl-), a. full of life or energy; gay; lively, realistic. **live′liness,** n.

li′ven, v. brighten (up).

liv′er, n. bodily organ secreting bile and purifying blood; animal's liver as food. **liv′erish,** a. having symptoms of disordered liver.

liv′eried, a. provided with, wearing, livery.

liv′erwort (-wert), n. primitive flowerless plant related to mosses.

liv′ery, n. distinctive clothes worn by members of city company or person's servant. **livery stable,** stable where horses are kept for owner or hired out.

liv′id, a. of bluish leaden colour; (informal) furiously angry.

liv′ing, n. (esp.) livelihood. (church) **living,** benefice. a. (esp.) now alive; (of likeness) exact. **living-room,** room for general day use.

liz′ard, n. reptile related to snakes but having (usu.) four legs.

lla′ma, la′ma (lah-), n. S. Amer. ruminant mammal related to camel, but woolly-haired and without hump.

lō, int. (archaic) look! behold!

load, n. what is carried or borne; amount that cart, etc., can carry; total amount of electric current supplied at given time. v. put load on; put (goods, etc.) aboard or on vehicle, etc.; burden; charge (gun, etc.).

load′stōne, lōde′stōne (-ds-), n. magnetic oxide of iron; piece of it used as magnet; thing that attracts.

loaf[1], *n.* (pl. *loaves*), piece of bread baked alone or as part of a batch. **loaf sugar,** sugar cut into small lumps.

loaf[2], *v. i.* spend time idly; saunter. **loa'fer,** *n.*

loam, *n.* rich fertile soil; clay paste for brick-making, etc. **loa'my,** *a.*

loan, *n.* thing lent; sum to be returned with or without interest. *v. t.* grant loan of.

loath, lŏth, *a.* unwilling, reluctant.

loathe (-dh), *v. t.* regard with disgust, detest. **loa'thing,** *n.* **loath'some,** *a.* repulsive, offensive, odious.

lob, *v. t.* (p.t. *lobbed*), send (ball) with slow or high-pitched motion. *n.* ball bowled under-hand at cricket or sent high in air at lawn--tennis.

lobb'y, *n.* porch, entrance-hall; anteroom or corridor; (in legislative building) hall open to public. **lobb'ying,** *n.* frequenting of par-liamentary lobby to influence votes.

lōbe, *n.* rounded projection of body or plant organ; lower hanging part of outer ear. **lōbed** (-bd), *a.* having lobes.

lobē'lia, *n.* garden flower used esp. as edging.

lob'ster, *n.* long-tailed edible shell-fish with pair of pincer-like claws. **lobster pot,** trap, usu. of wicker, for lobsters.

lō'cal, *a.* of place or district; of a part, not of the whole. **local anaesthetic,** anaesthetic affecting only limited part of body. **local col-our,** (esp.) details of place or time inserted in story, etc., to make it more realistic. **local government,** administration of town, etc., by elected inhabitants (*local authority*). **local time,** time measured from sun's position over place. **local'ity,** *n.* thing's position; site or scene of something. **lō'calize,** *v. t.* attach or restrict to particular place. **lōcaliză'tion,** *n.*

locale' (-ahl), *n.* scene or locality of operation or events.

locāte', *v.* discover exact place of; establish in place. **locā'tion,** *n.* (esp.) place other than studio where (part of) film is shot.

loch (-*ch*), *n.* Scottish lake or arm of sea.

lock[1], *n.* one of portions into which hair natu-rally groups itself; tuft of wool; (pl.) the hair.

lock[2], *n.* fastening for door, lid, etc.; mechan-ism by which gun is fired; section of river or canal confined within sluiced gates for shift-ing boats from one level to another. *v.* fasten with lock; bring or come into rigidly fixed position; jam or catch. *lock up*, store inacces-sibly; confine in prison, etc.; shut up (house, etc.) by locking outer doors. **lock'jaw,** tetanus in which jaws remain rigidly closed. **lock-keeper,** keeper of canal or river lock. **lock'smith,** maker and mender of locks. **lock-up,** (time of) locking up school, etc., for night; room, etc., for detention of prison-ers.

lock'er, *n.* (esp.) small cupboard, esp. one reserved for individual's use.

lock'ĕt, *n.* small gold or silver case for por-trait, etc., hung from neck.

lŏcomō'tion, *n.* going from one place to another; power of doing this. **lŏcomō'tive,** *a.* of or effecting locomotion. *n.* (esp.) engine for drawing train along rails.

lō'cum (ten'ens), (-z), deputy acting for doc-tor, clergyman, etc., in his absence.

lō'cust, *n.* winged insect flying in great swarms and destroying crops; (fruit of) any of various trees.

locū'tion, *n.* style of speech; phrase, idiom.

lōde, *n.* vein of ore. **lōde'star,** *n.* star that is steered by, esp. pole star; (fig.) guiding prin-ciple. **lodestone:** see **loadstone.**

lodge, *n.* gatekeeper's cottage or porter's room; (of freemasons, etc.) members of branch, place where they meet; beaver's or otter's lair. *v.* provide with sleeping quarters; reside as lodger; fix in; place; deposit (valu-ables, etc.) for security, (papers, etc.) for attention. **lodg'er,** *n.* person paying for accommodation in another's house. **lodg'-ing,** *n.* place where one lodges. **lodging--house,** house in which lodgings are let.

lodge'ment (-jm-), *n.* position or foothold gained.

loft, *n.* attic; room or (storage-)space imme-diately under roof of house, stable, barn, etc.; gallery in church or hall.

lof'ty, *a.* of imposing height; haughty, high--flown; exalted, sublime.

log[1], *n.* unhewn piece of felled tree; any large rough piece of wood; apparatus for measur-ing ship's speed; detailed record of ship's voyage, aircraft's flight, etc. *v. t.* (esp.) enter in log; (of ship, etc.) make (distance). **log--book,** book in which record of voyage, etc., is made.

log[2], *abbrev.* logarithm.

lō'ganberry, *n.* hybrid between raspberry and American blackberry.

log'arithm (-dhm), *n.* (abbrev. *log*) one of series of numbers arranged in form of tables for simplifying calculation. **logarith'mic,** *a.*

logg'erhead (-gerhed), *n.* *at loggerheads*, dis-agreeing or disputing (*with*).

logg'ia (-ja), *n.* open-sided gallery or arcade.

lo'gic, *n.* science of reasoning; chain of reasoning, arguments. **lo'gical,** *a.* in accor-dance with principles of logic; capable of correct reasoning. **logi'cian** (-shn), *n.* person skilled in logic.

loin, *n.* (pl.) back of vertebrate between hip--bones and ribs; (sing.) joint of meat includ-ing vertebrae of loins. **loin-cloth,** cloth worn round loins as garment.

loi'ter, *v. i.* linger on the way; stand about. **loi'terer,** *n.*

loll, *v.* recline or stand in lazy attitude; (of tongue) hang *out*.

loll'ipop, *n.* large boiled sweet on stick.

Lon'doner (lu-), *n.* native or inhabitant of London.

lōne, *a.* having no companion; solitary; unfrequented. **lōne′some,** a. lonely.

lōne′ly (-nl-), a. solitary, isolated; unfrequented; dejected by feeling alone. **lōne′- liness,** n.

long[1], a. (*longer, longest,* pr. -ngg-), measuring much from end to end in space or time; of specified length; lengthy, tedious; slow. n. long interval or period. adv. for or by a long time; throughout specified time. **long′boat,** sailing-ship's largest boat. **long-bow,** bow drawn by hand and discharging long arrow. **long′hand,** ordinary writing (opp. *shorthand*). **long′shore,** found or employed on or frequenting the shore. **long sight,** vision that sees (only) distant objects clearly. **long- -sighted,** having long sight. **long-suffering,** not easily provoked; patient. **long-winded,** tedious, lengthy. **long′ways, long′wise** (-z), advv. lengthwise.

long[2], v.i. wish earnestly and intently (*for, to* do). **long′ing,** n. & a. **long′ingly,** adv.

longev′ity (-j-), n. long life.

lon′gitŭde (-j-; or -ngg-), n. distance, measured in degrees, that point on earth's surface is E. or W. of prime meridian (O°). *line of longitude,* meridian. **longitŭ′dinal,** a. of or in length; lying lengthways; of longitude.

lōō′fah (-a), n. fibrous pod of plant used as sponge or skin-brush.

look, v. use or direct one's eyes; make effort to see; make search (*for*); express by eyes; have specified appearance or aspect; face or be turned in some direction. *look after,* attend to, have charge of. *look forward to,* anticipate (with pleasure). *look into,* investigate. *look on,* watch, observe; regard (*as*). n. gaze or glance; expression of the eyes; (esp. pl.) personal appearance. **looker-on** (pl. *lookers-on*), one who observes or watches, spectator. **look′ing-glass,** mirror. **look-out,** watch; post of observation; man stationed to watch.

lōōm[1], n. apparatus for weaving fabrics.

lōōm[2], v.i. appear dimly; be seen in vague magnified or threatening shape.

lōōp, n. figure made by curve crossing itself; similarly shaped part of cord, etc., so crossed or meeting. v. make loop(s) in; form loop; fasten with loop. *loop the loop,* (cause aircraft to) describe vertical loop in air. **loop- -line,** railway or telegraph line that leaves main line and joins it again.

lōōp′-hōle, n. narrow vertical slit in wall; (fig.) means of evading rule, etc.

lōōse, a. released from bonds or restraint; not compact or fixed or tight; not close-fitting; not exact or literal; careless; wanton. v.t. set free, untie; detach from moorings. **loose- -box,** stall in which horse can move about. **loose-leaf,** (of notebook, etc.) with leaves separate and detachable. **lōōse′ly,** adv.

lōō′sen, v. make or become loose or looser. *loosen up,* relax, limber up.

lōōse′strīfe (-s-s-), n. tall flowering plant growing in moist places.

lōōt, n. goods plundered or stolen; illicit gains. v. take loot from; carry off loot.

lop[1], v.t. (p.t. *lopped*), cut away branches or twigs (of tree); cut off.

lop[2], v.i. (p.t. *lopped*), hang loosely or limply. **lop-eared,** (of animal) having drooping ears. **lop-sī′ded,** a. with one side lower, smaller, etc.

lōpe, n. & v.i. (run with) long bounding stride.

loquā′cious (-shus), a. talkative. **loqua′city,** n.

lord, n. feudal superior, master, ruler, chief (chiefly Poet. or Hist.); God or Christ; nobleman; (prefixed to name of) peer; honorary title (e.g. of bishops, Lord Mayors, judges of supreme court). v.i. (esp.) *lord it over,* domineer. **House of Lords,** upper house of Parliament. **Lord Mayor,** mayor of London, York, and other cities. **Lord's day,** Sunday. **Lord's prayer,** prayer beginning 'Our Father' taught by Christ to his disciples. **Lord's Supper,** Eucharist. **lord′ly,** a. haughty, imperious; grand; of or fit for a lord. **lord′ship,** n. rule, ownership *of, over; estate, domain; your (his) lordship,* used when speaking to (of) peers, bishops, judges.

lore, n. body of traditional facts or beliefs relating to subject, people, place, etc.

lorgnette (lornyet′), n. pair of eyeglasses held in hand, usu. by long handle.

lo′rry, n. strong, usu. flat open, truck for carrying heavy goods by road.

lose (lōōz), v. (p.t. & p.p. *lost*), be deprived of; cease to possess or have; let pass from one's control; be defeated in; be the worse off (*by*). (p.p.) vanished, not to be found; deprived of help or salvation, astray. **los′er,** n.

loss, n. losing; what is lost; disadvantage resulting from losing. *at a loss,* (esp.) puzzled.

lost: see **lose.**

lot, n. one of set of objects used to secure chance selection; this method of deciding, share or office given by it; share, destiny; appointed task; allotment of land; item at auction; (*informal*) considerable number or amount. *draw lots,* select by drawing slip, etc., from receptacle.

loth: see **loath.**

lō′tion, n. liquid medicinal or cosmetic preparation applied externally to skin, ètc.

lott′ery, n. arrangement for distributing prizes by chance among holders of purchased tickets.

lott′ō, n. game of chance with numbers drawn at random.

lō′tus, n. legendary plant whose fruit, when eaten, induced state of dreamy forgetfulness; Egyptian or Asian water-lily.

loud, a. strongly audible, sonorous; noisy; (of

colour, etc.) conspicuous, flashy. *adv.* loudly. **loud-speaker,** (esp. Radio) device for converting electrical impulses into sounds loud enough to be heard at a distance.

lough (lo*ch*), *n.* Irish loch.

lounge (-nj), *v.i.* loll, recline; stand about lazily; idle. *n.* spell of, place for, lounging; sitting-room in hotel, etc. **lounge suit,** man's suit for day wear.

lour, low'er² *v.i.* frown, look sullen; (of sky, etc.) look dark and threatening.

louse, *n.* (pl. *lĭce*), blood-sucking insect parasitic on mammals; biting insect parasitic on birds and mammals. **lous'y** (-z-), *a.* infested with lice; (*slang*) very bad; swarming *with.*

lout, *n.* hulking or rough-mannered fellow. **lout'ish,** *a.*

lo'vable (lu-), *a.* inspiring affection.

love (luv), *n.* fondness, warm affection; sexual passion or desire; loved person or object; (in games) no score, nil. *in love* (*with*), having love and desire (for). *make love,* pay amorous attentions (*to*); engage in sexual intercourse. *v.* be in love (with); feel affection for; be fond of; delight in; admire. **love affair,** temporary or illicit relationship between persons in love. **love-bird,** small parrot. **love-letter,** letter from lover to beloved. **love'sick,** languishing with love. **love'less** (luvl-), *a.* unloving; unloved.

lovely (luv'li), *a.* very beautiful; (*informal*) delightful.

lo'ver (lu-), *n.* suitor or sweetheart; partner in irregular or illicit sexual relationship; admirer or devotee (*of*); (pl.) pair in love.

lo'ving (lu-), *a.* kind, affectionate. **loving--cup,** large drinking-vessel passed round at banquet. **loving-kindness,** affectionate and tender consideration.

low¹ (lō), *v.i. & n.* (utter) sound made by cows, moo.

low² (lō), *a.* not placed high; not high or tall; of humble rank; lacking in vigour; mean, vulgar; no longer full or abundant; not shrill or loud. *adv.* in or to low place; in low voice. **low'brow,** (person) not highly intellectual or cultured. **lower deck,** petty officers and men of Navy or of ship. **lower orders,** people of inferior social position. **low tide, low water,** level of ebbed sea; time of extreme ebb.

lower¹ (lō'er), *v.* let or haul down; make or become lower; be degrading to; reduce bodily condition of.

lower²: see **lour.**

low'land (lō-), *a.* of lowlands. **low'lander,** *n.* inhabitant of lowlands, esp. of Scotland. **low'lands** (-z-), *n.pl.* low-lying country, esp. (*Lowlands*) less mountainous part of Scotland.

low'ly (lō-), *a.* humble.

loy'al, *a.* faithful; true to allegiance; devoted to sovereign, mother country, etc. **loy'alist,** *a. & n.* (person) remaining loyal to ruler, government, etc. **loy'alty,** *n.*

loz'enge (-nj), *n.* diamond-shaped figure, rhombus; small tablet, usu. of medicated or flavoured sugar, to be dissolved in mouth.

lubb'er, *n.* clumsy fellow, lout. **lubb'erly,** *a.* awkward, unskilful.

lu'bricant (lōō- *or* lū-), *a. & n.* lubricating (substance). **lu'bricāte,** *v.t.* apply oil or grease to (machinery, etc.) in order to minimize friction. **lubrică'tion,** *n.*

lucerne' (lōō-), *n.* clover-like plant grown for fodder, alfalfa.

lu'cid (lōō- *or* lū-), *a.* clear; clearly expressed or arranged. **lucid'ity,** *n.*

Lu'cifer (lōō-), *n.* Satan; the planet Venus as morning star.

luck, *n.* good or ill fortune. **luck'less,** *a.* unfortunate; unhappy.

luck'y, *a.* favoured by fortune; enjoying good luck; due to luck rather than skill or merit; bringing, etc., good luck.

lu'crative (lōō-), *a.* very profitable.

lucre (lōōk'er), *n.* money, profit, regarded as discreditable motive.

lu'dicrous (lōō- *or* lū-), *a.* absurd; laughable.

luff, *v.i.* (Naut.) bring ship's head nearer wind.

lug, *v.* (p.t. *lugged*), drag with effort or violence; pull hard *at. n.* hard pull.

lugg'age, *n.* (bags, trunks, etc. for) property traveller takes with him on a journey.

lugg'er (-g-), *n.* small ship with four-cornered sails set fore-and-aft.

lugu'brious (lōōgōō-), *a.* doleful, mournful.

lukewarm (lōōk'worm), *a.* (of liquid, etc.) neither hot nor cold, tepid; half-hearted.

lull, *v.* send to sleep; allay, quiet; (of storm or noise) lessen, fall quiet. *n.* pause in storm, noise, etc.

lull'abȳ, *n.* soothing song to lull child to sleep.

lumbā'gō, *n.* painful, usu. inflammatory, affection of muscles of loins.

lum'bar, *a.* of the loins.

lum'ber¹, *n.* disused articles of furniture, etc.; useless or cumbersome material; roughly prepared timber. *v.* hamper or obstruct; cut and prepare forest timber. **lum'berjack,** man who fells (and transports) trees.

lum'ber², *v.i.* move in blundering noisy way.

lu'minary (lōō- *or* lū-), *n.* shedder of light, esp. sun or moon.

lu'minous (lōō- *or* lū-), *a.* emitting or full of light, shining; glowing in the dark. **luminos'ity,** *n.*

lump, *n.* compact shapeless mass; whole taken together; swelling or protuberance; (*informal*) heavy or dull person. *v.* class or mass *together.* **lump sugar,** loaf sugar. **lump sum,** sum including number of items or paid down all at once.

lum'pish, *a.* heavy; clumsy; dull.

lum'py, *a.* full of or covered with lumps; (of water) choppy.

lu'nacy (lōō-), *n.* insanity, folly.

lu'nar (lŏŏ-), *a.* of, depending on, caused by, the moon. **lunar month,** interval between new moons, about 29½ days; four weeks.

lu'natic (lŏŏ-), *a.* insane; outrageously foolish. *n.* lunatic person.

lunch, *n.* midday meal. *v.i.* take lunch.

lun'cheon (-shn), *n.* formal midday meal; lunch.

lung, *n.* either of pair of breathing-organs in man and many other vertebrates.

lunge (-nj), *n.* thrust with sword, etc.; sudden forward movement, plunge. *v.* make lunge; drive (weapon, etc.) violently.

lu'pin (lŏŏ-), *n.* cultivated leguminous plant with long tapering flower-spikes.

lurch[1], *n.* *leave in the lurch*, desert (friend, ally) in difficulties.

lurch[2], *n.* sudden shifting of the weight to one side, stagger. *v.i.* make lurch(es), stagger.

lur'cher, *n.* cross-bred dog between collie and greyhound.

lūre, *n.* falconer's apparatus (usu. bunch of feathers) for recalling hawk; something used to entice; enticing quality. *v.t.* recall with lure; entice.

lūr'id, *a.* ghastly or glaring in colour, etc.; sensational.

lurk, *v.i.* keep oneself out of sight; be hidden; be latent or elusive.

lu'scious (-shus), *a.* richly sweet in taste or smell; appealing to senses; cloying.

lush, *a.* luxuriant, succulent.

lust, *n.* strong sexual desire; intense desire. *v.i.* have lust (*for*, *after*). **lust'ful,** *a.* full of (esp. sexual) lust.

lus'tre (-ter), *n.* quality of shining by reflected light; gloss; brilliance, splendour. **lus'trous,** *a.* shining.

lus'ty, *a.* healthy and strong; vigorous. **lus'tily,** *adv.*

lute (-ŏŏ- *or* -ū-), *n.* plucked stringed instrument resembling guitar but with body shaped like halved pear. **lu'tanist, lu'tenist,** *n.* lute-player.

Lu'theran (lŏŏ-), *a.* of Protestant reformer Martin Luther or the Lutheran Church. *n.* member of Lutheran Church. **Lu'theranism,** *n.*

luxūr'iant (*or* -gz-), *a.* profuse in growth; (of style) florid. **luxūr'iance,** *n.* **luxūr'iâte,** *v.i.* feel keen delight in; grow profusely; take one's ease.

luxūr'ious (*or* -gz-), *a.* full of luxury, very comfortable; voluptuous; self-indulgent.

lux'ury (-ksher-), *n.* use of, indulgence in, what is choice or costly; intense enjoyment; something desirable but not essential.

lycée (lē'sā), *n.* State secondary school in France. (French)

lych'-gâte, *n.* roofed gateway of churchyard.

lying: see **lie**[1],[2].

lymph, *n.* colourless fluid from tissues or organs of body; (*vaccine lymph*) preparation used in vaccination against smallpox. **lymphat'ic,** *a.* of or secreting lymph. **lymph'oid,** resembling lymph or tissue of lymphatic glands.

lynch, *v.t.* execute by mob action without lawful trial.

lynx, *n.* short-tailed tufted-eared wild animal of cat family. **lynx-eyed,** keen-sighted.

lȳre, *n.* obsolete harp-like U-shaped instrument. **lyre-bird,** Australian bird with lyre-shaped tail.

ly'ric, *a.* of or like song; (of poem, etc.) expressing writer's own sentiments, etc., and usu. short. *n.* lyric poem; (often pl.) words of song. **ly'rical,** *a.* resembling, using language appropriate to, lyric poetry. **ly'ricism,** *n.*

M

M, m, as Roman numeral, 1,000.

ma'am (mam, mahm), *n.* madam (esp. in addressing queen or royal princess).

mac, *n.* (*informal*) macintosh.

maca'bre (-ahbr), *a.* gruesome.

macad'am, *n.* road surface made by compacting stone broken small. **macad'amize,** *v.t.*

macarō'ni, *n.* dried wheaten paste formed into long slender tubes.

macarōōn', *n.* biscuit or small cake of ground almonds, etc.

mâce[1], *n.* ornamented staff carried before certain officials as symbol of authority.

mâce[2], *n.* nutmeg-husks dried and used as spice.

ma'cerâte, *v.* make or become soft by soaking; become emaciated by fasting.

mach (num'ber) (mahk), ratio of velocity of body to velocity of sound in some fluid medium.

mach'ete (-it; *or* machā'ti), *n.* broad heavy

knife used as implement and weapon in Central America and W. Indies.

Machiavell'ian (-ki-), *a.* unscrupulous, scheming, crafty.

machinā'tion (-ki-), *n.* (usu. in pl.) intrigue; scheme, plot.

machine' (-shēn), *n.* apparatus in which action of several parts is combined for applying mechanical force; controlling organization in politics, etc. *v.t.* sew, print, make, etc., with machine. **machine-gun,** mechanically operated continuous-firing gun. **machi'nist** (-shē-), *n.* operator of machine.

machi'nery (-shē-), *n.* machines; organization.

mack'erel, *n.* edible sea-fish.

mac'intosh, mack'intosh, *n.* cloth waterproofed with rubber; coat of this or of plastic or nylon material.

mac'rocosm, *n.* the universe; any great whole.

mad, *a.* (*madder, maddest*), of disordered mind, insane; wildly foolish; (*informal,* esp. U.S.) angry, annoyed. **mad'cap,** wildly reckless person. **mad'house,** (Hist.) mental hospital. **mad'man, mad'woman** (-woo-), *nn.* **mad'ness,** *n.*

mad'am, *n.* polite form of address to woman.

madame' (-ahm), *n.* (pl. *mesdames,* pr. mādahm') French form of madam and (*Madame*) Mrs.

madd'en, *v.t.* make mad; irritate.

Madeir'a (-ēra), *n.* fortified wine from Madeira. **madeira cake,** rich cake without fruit.

mademoiselle (madmwazel'), *n.* (pl. *mesdemoiselles,* pr. mād-), French form of miss and (*Mademoiselle*) Miss.

Madonn'a, *n.* (picture or statue of) Virgin Mary.

mad'rigal, *n.* part song for several voices, usu. unaccompanied.

mael'strom (māl-), *n.* whirlpool.

magazine' (-zēn), *n.* store for arms or explosives; chamber for cartridges of repeating firearm, or for camera-film, projector-slides, etc.; periodical publication containing articles, etc., by different writers.

magen'ta, *n.* (colour of) brilliant crimson aniline dye.

magg'ot, *n.* grub or larva, esp. of bluebottle.

Mā'gī, *n.pl.* the 'wise men from the East' who visited the infant Jesus; priests of ancient Persia.

ma'gic, *a.* & *n.* (of) pretended art of influencing events by occult control of nature or spirits; mysterious agency or power; conjuring tricks. **magic lantern,** early form of projector for glass slides. **ma'gical,** *a.* **magi'cian** (-shn), *n.* one skilled in magic; wizard.

magistēr'ial, *a.* of magistrate; authoritative.

ma'gistrāte, *n.* civil officer administering law (in England and Wales either *Justice of the Peace* or *stipendiary magistrate*). **magis-**

trates' court, court of justice for minor cases. **ma'gistracy, ma'gistrature,** *nn.*

magnan'imous, *a.* having, showing, generosity of spirit. **magnanim'ity,** *n.*

mag'nāte, *n.* man of wealth, authority, etc.

magnē'sia (-sha), magnesium oxide. **magnē'sian,** *a.*

magnē'sium (-z-), *n.* silvery-white metallic element burning with bright white light.

mag'net, *n.* piece of iron or other magnetic material having property of attracting iron and of pointing north; thing that attracts. **magnet'ic,** *a.* of or like or acting as magnet. **magnetic north,** point (about 6° W. of true N.) to which compass needle points.

mag'nētism, *n.* (science of) magnetic phenomena or properties; attraction, personal charm.

mag'nētize, *v.t.* make into magnet; attract like magnet. **magnētizā'tion,** *n.*

magnē'to, *n.* (pl. *magnetos*), (esp.) ignition apparatus of internal-combustion engine.

magnif'icent, *a.* splendid; imposing; excellent. **magnif'icence,** *n.*

mag'nifȳ, *v.t.* increase apparent size of with lens, etc.; exaggerate; (*archaic*) extol. **magnificā'tion,** *n.*

magnil'oquence, *n.* pompous words or style. **magnil'oquent,** *a.*

mag'nitūde, *n.* greatness; size; importance.

magnō'lia, *n.* flowering tree.

mag'num, *n.* two-quart bottle.

mag'pīe, *n.* black and white chattering bird.

Mag'yar, *n.* & *a.* (member, language) of race predominant in Hungary. **mag'yar,** *a.* (of sleeve) cut in one with bodice.

maharaja(h) (mah-harah'ja), *n.* title of some Indian princes. **mahara'nee,** *n.* maharaja's wife.

mahat'ma (ma-h-), *n.* (in India, etc.) person revered as having more than natural powers.

mahog'any (ma-h-), *n.* (tropical American tree with) reddish-brown wood used for furniture, etc. *a.* colour of mahogany.

Mahometan: see **Muhammadan.**

mahout (ma-howt'), *n.* driver of elephant.

maid, *n.* female servant; (*archaic*) girl.

mai'den, *n.* (Poet.) girl, young unmarried woman. *a.* unmarried; untried; with blank record. **mai'denhair,** fern with delicate fronds. **mai'denhead,** virginity; hymen. **maiden name,** woman's surname before marriage. **maiden speech,** M.P.'s first speech in Parliament. **mai'denhood,** *n.* **mai'denly,** *a.*

mail¹, *n.* armour of metal rings or plates. **mailed fist,** physical force.

mail², *n.* letters, etc., conveyed by post; the post. *v.t.* send by post. **mail order,** order for goods to be sent by post.

maim, *v.t.* cripple, mutilate.

main, *a.* chief, principal. *n.* chief part; high seas; main pipe, wire, etc., for water, electricity, etc. *in the main,* for the most part.

with might and main, with all one's strength.
main'land, country or continent without adjacent islands. **main'mast,** principal mast.
main'sail (-sl), sail set on mainmast. **main'-spring,** chief spring of watch or clock.
main'stay, chief support. **main'ly,** *adv.* chiefly; in the main.
maintain', *v.t.* carry on, continue; keep in repair; support; assert as true. **main'tenance,** *n.* maintaining; subsistence.
maisonette' (-z-), *n.* (esp.) part of house let or used separately, not all on same floor.
maize, *n.* (edible seed of) American cereal plant.
maj'esty, *n.* stateliness of aspect, language, etc.; title used in speaking to or of sovereign. **majes'tic,** *a.*
mā'jor, *a.* greater, larger; senior; (Mus., of scale) having two full tones between keynote and third note. *n.* army officer; person who has reached age of majority.
majo'rity, *n.* the greater number; (*age of*) *majority,* age of legal responsibility (18, formerly 21).
māke, *v.* (p.t. *māde*), create, manufacture; cause to exist, bring about; cause to be, render; amount to, constitute; earn; perform, execute. *make for,* go in direction of. *make good,* fulfil (promise, etc.), pay for or repair (damage, etc.). *make out,* write out (list, etc.), represent as, understand. *make over,* transfer. *make up,* supply deficiency, complete, compensate (*for*), apply cosmetics (to). **māke,** *n.* way thing is made; brand. **make-believe,** pretence. **make'shift,** method, tool, etc., used when nothing better is available. **make-up,** way actor is made up; cosmetics; fundamental qualities of character.
mā'ker, *n.* one who makes; (*Maker*) God.
mā'king, *n.* (esp., pl.) essential qualities.
mal-, *pref.* bad(ly); not.
maladjus'ted, *a.* unable to adjust oneself to environment, etc. **maladjust'ment,** *n.*
maladministrā'tion, *n.* faulty administration.
mal'adroit, *a.* bungling, tactless.
mal'ady, *n.* ailment, disease.
mal'apropism, *n.* ludicrous misuse of words (e.g. *allegory* for *alligator*).
malapropos' (-pō), *adv.* & *a.* (done, said, etc.) inopportunely.
malā'ria, *n.* fever transmitted by bites of certain mosquitoes. **malā'rial,** *a.*
māle, *a.* of the sex which begets offspring or reproduces by fertilizing the female; of men; (Mechanics, etc.) adapted to fit into corresponding or female part. *n.* male person, animal, or plant.
malĕdic'tion, *n.* curse.
mal'ĕfactor, *n.* criminal, evil-doer.
malev'olent, *a.* wishing ill to others; spiteful. **malev'olence,** *n.*
mal'formed (-md), *a.* badly formed or shaped. **malformā'tion,** *n.*

mal'ice, *n.* ill will; desire to do harm. **mali'cious** (-shus), *a.*
malign' (-īn), *a.* injurious. *v.t.* slander, misrepresent.
malig'nant, *a.* feeling or showing intense ill will; (of disease, etc.) tending to be dangerous or fatal. **malig'nancy,** *n.*
malig'nity, *n.* malignant character or feeling.
maling'er (-ngg-), *v.i.* pretend illness to escape duty.
mall'ěable, *n.* that can be shaped by hammering; pliable. **mallěabil'ity,** *n.*
mall'ět, *n.* hammer, usu. of wood; implement for striking croquet or polo ball.
malnūtri'tion, *n.* insufficiency or lack of (the right kind of) food.
malŏ'dorous, *a.* stinking.
malt (-o- *or* -aw-), *n.* barley or other grain prepared for brewing, etc. *v.t.* convert (grain) into malt.
Maltese (mawltēz'), *a.* & *n.* (native, language) of Malta. **Maltese Cross,** cross with four equal limbs broadened at ends.
maltreat', *v.t.* ill-treat. **maltreat'ment,** *n.*
mam(m)a' (-ah), *n.* mother.
mamm'al, *n.* member of class of animals having milk-secreting organs and suckling their young. **mammā'lian,** *a.*
mamm'ary, *a.* of the breasts.
mamm'on, *n.* wealth regarded as idol or evil influence.
mamm'oth, *n.* large extinct elephant. *a.* huge.
mamm'y, *n.* child's word for mother; (U.S.) white children's Negro nurse.
man, *n.* (pl. *men*), human being; human race; male and usu. adult person; husband; piece in chess, draughts, etc. *v.t.* (p.t. *manned*), supply with men; guard. **man-at-arms,** soldier, esp. medieval. **man-of-war,** warship. **man-power,** number of men available for State or other service.
man'acle, *n.* (usu. in pl.) & *v.t.* fetter, handcuff.
man'age, *v.t.* conduct working of; control; cajole, contrive. **man'ageable,** *a.*
man'agement (-ijm-), *n.* managing or being managed; administration; manager(s).
man'ager (-ij-), *n.* person conducting business, etc.; one skilled in managing money, etc. **man'ageress,** *n.fem.* **managēr'ial,** *a.*
man'darin, *n.* Chinese official; small orange.
man'dāte, *n.* authoritative command; commission to act for another; authority given to representative by voters. **man'datary,** *n.* receiver of a mandate. **man'datory,** *a.* (esp.) obligatory.
man'dible, *n.* lower jaw-bone; either part of bird's beak; either half of crushing organ in mouth-parts of insects, etc.
man'dolin, *n.* musical instrument resembling lute, played with a plectrum.
māne, *n.* long hair on horse's or lion's neck.
man'ful, *a.* brave, resolute. **man'fully,** *adv.*
mang'anese (-ngganēz), *n.* grey brittle metal-

lic element; black dioxide of this.

mānge (-nj), *n.* skin disease of dogs, etc.

mang'el-wurzel (-ngg-), *n.* large kind of beet used as cattle-food.

mān'ger (-j-), *n.* trough in stable for horses or cattle to eat from.

mang'le[1] (-nggl), *n.* machine for rolling and pressing washed clothes. *v.t.* put through mangle.

mang'le[2] (-nggl), *v.t.* hack, mutilate; spoil.

mang'o (-nggō), *n.* (pl. *mangoes*), (fleshy fruit of) tropical tree.

man'grōve, *n.* tropical sea-shore tree with interlacing roots above ground.

mān'gy (-j-), *a.* having mange; squalid, shabby.

man'handle, *v.t.* move by men's strength alone; handle roughly.

man'hōle, *n.* opening in floor, sewer, etc., for man to pass through.

man'hood, *n.* state of being a man; manliness.

mā'nia, *n.* mental derangement marked by great excitement and (often) violence; craze (*for*). **mā'niac**, *n. & a.* (person) affected with mania. **mani'acal**, *a.*

man'icūre, *n.* cosmetic care and treatment of hands, esp. finger-nails. *v.t.* apply manicure to. **man'icūrist**, *n.*

man'ifest, *a.* clear to sight or mind; indubitable. *v.t.* show plainly. **manifestā'tion**, *n.*

manifes'tō, *n.* (pl. *manifestos*), declaration of policy.

man'ifold, *a.* of various forms, functions, etc.; many and diverse.

mani(l)l'a, *n.* plant fibre used for ropes, etc. **manilla envelope**, strong envelope. **manilla paper**, strong brown wrapping-paper.

man'ioc, *n.* cassava.

manip'ūlāte, *v.t.* handle with skill. **manipūlā'tion**, *n.* **manip'ūlative**, *a.* **manip'ūlātor**, *n.*

mankīnd', *n.* human species.

man'līke, *a.* of or like a man.

man'ly, *a.* having qualities or bearing of, befitting, a man. **man'liness**, *n.*

mann'a, *n.* (Bibl.) food miraculously supplied to Israelites in wilderness.

mann'équin (-kin), *n.* person employed to wear and show off clothes, model.

mann'er, *n.* way thing is done or happens; sort or kind; style; (pl.) social behaviour. **mann'erism**, *n.* trick of style or behaviour. **mann'erly**, *a.* having good manners, polite.

mann'ish, *a.* characteristic of man as opp. to woman.

manoeu'vre (-ōover), *n.* planned movement (of armed forces); (pl.) series of such movements (esp. as training exercise); skilful or crafty plan. *v.* perform manoeuvre(s); manipulate. **manoeu'vrable**, *a.*

man'or, *n.* unit of land under feudal system; (country estate with) substantial house. **man-or'ial**, *a.*

manse, *n.* (esp. Sc. Presbyterian) minister's house.

man'sion (-shn), *n.* large dwelling-house.

man'slaughter (-awter), *n.* killing of a person unlawfully but without intending to do so.

man'telpiece, *n.* structure around, esp. shelf above, fireplace.

mantill'a, *n.* Spanish woman's lace veil worn over head and shoulders.

man'tle, *n.* loose sleeveless cloak; (fig.) covering; fragile hood round gas jet to give incandescent light; region lying below earth's crust.

manū-, *pref.* hand-.

man'ūal, *a.* of or done with hands. *n.* handbook, textbook; organ keyboard.

manūfac'ture (-cher), *n.* making of articles or material, esp. in large quantities. *v.t.* produce by labour, esp. on large scale; invent, fabricate.

manūre', *n.* dung or other substance used for making soil fertile. *v.t.* treat with manure.

man'ūscript, *a. & n.* (book) written by hand; author's copy for printer.

ma'ny (me-), *a.* numerous. *n.* a great number.

Maori (mow'ri), *n. & a.* (member, language) of aboriginal New Zealand race.

map, *n.* flat representation of (part of) earth or of (part of) heavens. *v.t.* (p.t. *mapped*), make map of. *map out*, plan, arrange in detail.

mā'ple, *n.* any of various trees grown for shade, ornament, wood, or sugar.

mar, *v.t.* (p.t. *marred*), impair, spoil.

ma'rathon, *n.* foot-race of great length.

maraud' (ma-r-), *v.i.* make raid, pillage. **marau'der**, *n.*

mar'ble, *n.* hard limestone used in sculpture and architecture; (pl.) collection of sculpture; small ball of glass, etc., used in child's game. *v.t.* give veined or mottled appearance to.

March[1], *n.* third month of year.

march[2], *v.* (cause to) walk in military manner or with regular paces; progress steadily. *n.* action or piece of marching; progress; piece of music suitable for marching to.

march[3], *n.* (usu. pl.) boundary. *v.i.* have common boundary (*with*).

mar'chioness (-shon-), *n.* wife of marquis.

māre, *n.* female of horse or other equine animal.

mar'garine (-g- *or* -j-; *or* -ēn'), *n.* edible fat resembling butter, made from animal or vegetable fats.

mar'gin, *n.* blank space round printed or written matter on page; border or edge; amount (of time, money, etc.) above what is necessary. **mar'ginal**, *a.*

marguerite' (-gerēt; *or* mar'-), *n.* large daisy.

ma'rigōld, *n.* any of various yellow-flowered plants.

marijua'na (ma-rihwah'na), *n.* dried leaves of common hemp used, esp. in cigarettes, as narcotic.

mari'na (ma-rē'-), *n.* dock or basin with

moorings for yachts or other small craft.

marināde' (ma-r-), *n.* mixture of wine or vinegar with herbs, etc., in which meat or fish is steeped before cooking. *v.t.* steep in marinade. **ma'rināte,** *v.t.* marinade.

marine' (ma-rēn'), *a.* of, from, or beside the sea; of shipping. *n.* shipping; soldier serving on board ship. **ma'riner,** *n.* sailor.

marionette' (ma-r-), *n.* puppet worked with strings.

ma'rital, *a.* of or between husband and wife.

ma'ritime, *a.* situated, dwelling, or found near the sea; connected with seafaring.

mar'joram, *n.* aromatic herb used in cooking.

mark[1], *n.* principal unit of money of Germany.

mark[2], *n.* visible trace, sign, stain, spot or dent; target; normal standard; unit in estimating merit of work. *v.* make mark on; distinguish with mark; assign mark to; notice; observe. *mark off,* separate by line or boundary. *mark out,* make lines to show limits of. **marked** (-kt), *a.* (esp.) noticeable, conspicuous. **mar'kĕdly,** *adv.* **mar'ker,** *n.*

mar'kĕt, *n.* gathering for sale of commodities or livestock; building or space used for it; place of, facilities for, trade. *v.* send to or sell in market; buy goods in market. **market cross,** cross in market-place. **market garden,** garden where vegetables are grown for sale. **market-place,** open space where market is held. **mar'kĕtable,** *a.* fit for sale; in demand.

mar'king, *n.* (esp.) colouring of feathers, skin, etc. **marking-ink,** indelible ink for marking linen, clothes, etc.

marks'man, *n.* (pl. *-men*), one skilled in shooting, esp. with rifle. **marks'manship,** *n.*

mar'malāde, *n.* jam made with peel, pulp, and juice of (usu. bitter) oranges, etc.

marmor'ĕal, *a.* of marble; white or cold or polished as marble.

mar'moset (-z- *or* -s-), *n.* small monkey.

mar'mot, *n.* burrowing rodent of squirrel family.

ma'rocain, *n.* fine dress-fabric.

maroōn'[1] (ma-r-), *n.* brownish-crimson colour; firework exploding with loud report. *a.* maroon-coloured.

maroōn'[2] (ma-r-), *v.t.* put and leave ashore on desert island or coast; leave stranded.

marquee' (-kē), *n.* large tent.

mar'quetry (-kit-), *n.* decoration of flat surface with shaped pieces of wood, etc., fitted together.

mar'quis, mar'quess, *n.* peer ranking between duke and earl or count.

ma'rriage (-rij), *n.* act, ceremony, or procedure by which a man and a woman are legally united for the purpose of living together; union. **marriage lines,** certificate of marriage. **ma'rriageable,** *a.* old enough or fit for marriage.

ma'rrow (-ō), *n.* fatty substance in cavity of bones; (*vegetable*) *marrow,* large fleshy fruit of plant of gourd family, used as vegetable.

ma'rry, *v.* take husband or wife; unite or give in marriage.

Mars (-z), *n.* (Rom. myth.) god of war; a planet.

Marseillaise (marselāz'), *n.* national anthem of France.

marsh, *n.* piece of low watery ground. **marsh marigold,** marigold growing in moist meadows. **mar'shy,** *a.*

mar'shal[1], *n.* official of royal household, etc., directing ceremonies; officer of high or highest rank.

mar'shal[2], *v.t.* (p.t. *marshalled*), arrange in proper order; conduct. **marshalling yard,** *n.* railway yard in which goods trains, etc., are assembled.

marsū'pial, *a.* of class of mammals that carry their young in a pouch. *n.* marsupial animal.

mart, *n.* market.

martell'ō tow'er, small circular fort for coast defence.

mar'ten, *n.* weasel-like animal with valuable fur.

mar'tial (-shl), *a.* warlike.

Mar'tian (-shn), *a.* of Mars. *n.* supposed inhabitant of Mars.

mar'tin, *n.* bird of swallow family.

martinet', *n.* strict disciplinarian.

Mar'tinmas, *n.* St. Martin's day, 11th November.

mar'tyr (-ter), *n.* person undergoing death or suffering for any great cause. *v.t.* make a martyr of. **mar'tyrdom,** *n.* martyr's death or suffering.

mar'vel, *n.* wonderful thing; wonderful example *of. v.i.* (p.t. *marvelled*), feel surprise, wonder. **mar'vellous,** *a.* astonishing, extraordinary, wonderful.

Marx'ist, Marx'ian, *aa.* & *nn.* (supporter) of doctrine of Karl Marx, German economist and socialist (1818-83).

marzipan', *n.* sweet confection of ground almonds.

mascar'a, *n.* cosmetic preparation for darkening eyelashes, etc.

mas'cot, *n.* person,, thing, or animal which is believed to bring luck.

mas'cūline, *a.* (Gram.) of male gender; male; manly; vigorous, mannish. *n.* masculine gender, noun, etc. **masculin'ity,** *n.*

mā'ser (-z-), *n.* device for amplifying microwaves.

mash, *n.* malt, grain, bran, etc., mixed with hot water; (*slang*) mashed potatoes. *v.t.* make into mash; crush or pound to pulp.

mash'ie, *n.* kind of golf-club.

mask (mah-), *n.* hollow figure of face or head; covering for concealing or protecting (part of) face; face or head of fox; (fig.) disguise. *v.t.* cover with mask; disguise, hide.

mas'ochism (-k-), *n.* unnatural pleasure in suffering abuse or cruelty. **mas'ochist,** *n.*

masochis′tic, *a.*

mā′son, *n.* worker in stone; freemason. **mason′ic,** *a.* of freemasons. **mā′sonry,** *n.* stonework; freemasonry.

masque (mahsk), *n.* poetic drama with pageantry, common in 16th-17th centuries.

masqueráde′ (mahsker-), *n.* masked ball; false show, pretence. *v.i.* appear in disguise.

Mass¹, *n.* (esp. R.C.) celebration of Eucharist; (music for) liturgy used in this.

mass², *n.* body of matter of irregular shape; dense aggregation, large number, (*of*); (Phys.) quantity of matter a body contains corresponding to its inertia. *the masses,* great body of ordinary working people. *v.* gather into mass. **mass medium,** (usu.in pl., *mass media*) means of communication (radio, television, newspapers, etc.) reaching large number of people. **mass production,** production of (standardized articles) in large quantities by mechanical means. **mass-produced** (*a.*).

mass′acre (-ker), *n.* cruel killing of large numbers of (esp. defenceless) people. *v.t.* perform massacre of.

mass′age (-ahzh), *n.* kneading and rubbing of muscles, usu. with hands. *v.t.* treat thus. **masseur′** (-er), *n.* **masseuse′** (-erz), *n.fem.* one who practises massage.

mass′if (-ēf), *n.* mountain heights forming compact group.

massive, *a.* large and heavy; substantial.

mast¹ (-ah-), *n.* fruit of beech, oak, etc., esp. as food for pigs.

mast² (-ah-), *n.* long upright pole to which ship's yards and sails are attached; tall pole, etc., supporting flag, aerial, etc. **mast-head,** highest part of ship's mast.

ma′ster (mah-), *n.* person having control; ship's captain; male head of household; male teacher; employer; skilled workman; great artist; holder of university degree above bachelor (*Master of Arts,* etc.). *v.t.* acquire complete knowledge of; overcome. **master-key,** key opening a set of different locks. **mas′terpiece,** excellent piece of workmanship, best work. **ma′sterful,** *a.* domineering. **ma′sterly,** *a.* worthy of master, skilful. **ma′stery,** *n.* authority, control; masterly knowledge or skill.

mas′ticāte, *v.t.* chew. **masticā′tion,** *n.*

mas′tiff (*or* mah-), *n.* dog of large strong breed.

mas′todon, *n.* large extinct elephant-like mammal.

mas′turbāte, *v.* produce orgasm by stimulation of the genitals, not by sexual intercourse. **masturbā′tion,** *n.*

mat¹, *n.* coarse fabric of plaited fibre, etc.; piece of material laid on floor, table, etc., to protect surface; tangled mass. *v.* (p.t. *matted*), bring or come into thickly tangled state.

mat²: see **matt.**

mat′ador, *n.* man whose task is to kill bull in bullfight.

match¹, *n.* slip of wood (*match-stick*) with head that ignites when rubbed on rough surface or on prepared side of container (*match-box*).

match², *n.* person or thing equal to or nearly resembling or corresponding to another; marriage; contest, game. *v.* find or be match for; be equal, correspond. **match′board,** board with tongue along one edge and groove along other, for fitting into others. **match′less,** *a.* without equal, peerless.

māte¹, *n.* one of pair of birds or animals; partner in marriage; fellow-worker; subordinate officer on merchant ship. *v.* (of animals or birds) come or bring together for breeding.

māte², *n. & v.t.* checkmate in chess.

matē′rial, *n.* that from which thing is or can be made; stuff, fabric. *a.* composed of or connected with matter; not spiritual; important, essential.

matē′rialism, *n.* belief that only matter is real or important; rejection of spiritual values, etc. **matē′rialist,** *n.* **matērialis′tic,** *a.*

matē′rialīze, *v.* (cause to) appear in bodily form; become fact.

mater′nal, *a.* of or like mother; motherly; related on mother's side.

mater′nity, *n.* motherhood.

mathemat′ics, *n.* abstract science of numbers, quantities, and spatial relationships. **mathemat′ical,** *a.* of mathematics, rigorously precise. **mathemati′cian** (-shn), *n.* **maths,** *n.* (*informal*) mathematics.

mat′inée (-inā), *n.* theatrical, etc., performance in afternoon. **matinée coat,** baby's short knitted coat.

mat′ins (-z), *n.* service of morning prayer.

mā′triarch (-k), *n.* woman head of family or tribe. **mā′triarchy,** *n.* social organization in which woman is head of family. **mā′triarchal,** *a.*

mat′ricīde, *n.* killing, killer, of own mother.

matric′ūlāte, *v.* admit, be admitted, as student in university. **matricūlā′tion,** *n.*

mat′rimony, *n.* marriage. **matrimō′nial,** *a.*

mā′trix (*or* mat-), *n.* (pl. *matricēs, matrixes*), mould in which type, etc., is cast or shaped; mass of rock enclosing fossils, gems, etc.; place in which thing is developed; (Math.) rectangular arrangement of quantities.

mā′tron, *n.* married woman; woman in charge of nursing in hospital; housekeeper in school or institution; nurse in boarding-school. **mā′tronly,** *a.*

matt, mat², *a.* without lustre, dull.

matt′er, *n.* anything that occupies space and has mass; material substance; thing(s); material; affair, concern; importance; pus. *v.i.* be of importance. **matter-of-fact,** *a.* unimaginative, keeping to facts.

matt′ing, *n.* fabric of hemp, etc., for mats, etc.

matt′ock, *n.* tool like pickaxe.

matt'ress, *n.* case stuffed with soft material or containing springs and usu. supported on bedstead, for sleeping on; framework of springs, wires, etc., as part of bedstead.

matūre', *a.* complete in natural development or growth; ripe; adult. *v.* bring to or reach mature state. **matūr'ity,** *n.*

matū'tinal (*or* -tī'-), *a.* of or in the morning.

maud'lin, *a.* tearfully sentimental.

maul, *n.* heavy hammer, usu. of wood. *v.t.* injure by rough or brutal handling.

maun'der, *v.i.* talk ramblingly.

maun'dy mon'ey (muni), silver coins minted for royal almsgiving on **Maundy Thursday** (Thursday before Easter).

mausolē'um, *n.* (pl. *-s* or *mausolea*), magnificent tomb.

mauve (mōv), *n.* & *a.* pale purple.

mav'erick, *n.* (U.S.) unbranded calf, etc.; unorthodox or independent person.

mā'vis, *n.* song thrush.

maw, *n.* stomach of animal.

maw'kish, *a.* feebly sentimental.

max'im, *n.* general truth of science or experience; principle or rule of conduct.

max'imum, *n.* (pl. *maxima*), highest possible degree or magnitude or quantity. *a.* greatest.

may[1], *v.aux.* (3rd. sing. *may*; p.t. *might* pr. mīt), expressing possibility, permission, request, wish, etc.

May[2], *n.* fifth month of year; (*may*), hawthorn blossom. **May Day,** May 1st. **may-fly,** ephemeral insect. **may'pole,** flower-decked pole danced round on May Day. **may-tree,** hawthorn. **may'ing,** *n.* celebration of May Day festivities.

may'bē, *adv.* perhaps.

may'day, word (from French *m'aider*) used as international radio-telephone distress signal.

mayonnaise' (-z), *n.* (dish with) creamy dressing of oil, egg-yolk, vinegar, etc.

mayor (mār), *n.* head of town corporation. **mayoralty** (mār'alti), *n.* mayor's (period of) office. **mayoress** (mār'es), *n.* mayor's wife or lady fulfilling her ceremonial duties.

māze, *n.* complex and baffling network of paths, lines, etc.; tangle, confusion.

mazur'ka, *n.* (music for) lively Polish dance in triple time.

mē, *pron.* objective case of **I.**

mead[1], *n.* alcoholic drink made from fermented honey and water.

mead[2], *n.* (Poet.) meadow.

meadow (med'ō), *n.* piece of grassland, esp. one used for hay; low-lying ground, esp. near river. **meadow-sweet,** meadow plant with fragrant flowers.

mea'gre (-ger), *a.* lean, poor, scanty.

meal[1], *n.* coarsely ground edible part of grain or pulse.

meal[2], *n.* (occasion of taking) food.

mea'lie, *n.* (usu. pl.) (S. Afr.) maize.

mea'ly, *a.* of, like, meal; dry and powdery. **mealy-mouthed,** not outspoken.

mean[1], *a.* of poor quality, inferior; ignoble; ungenerous, stingy.

mean[2], *v.* (p.t. *meant*, pr. ment), intend; be resolved; intend to convey or indicate; signify. **mea'ning,** *n.* what is meant; sense, significance. *a.* expressive, significant. **mea'ningful, mea'ningless,** *aa.*

mean[3], *a.* equally distant from two extremes; intermediate; average. *n.* mean degree, state or course. **means** (-z), *n.pl.* method, process, by which result is obtained; resources; money. **means test,** inquiry into financial resources of applicant for assistance, etc. **mean'tīme, mean'whīle,** *nn.* & *advv.* (in) intervening time.

mèan'der, *v.i.* wind about; wander at random. *n.pl.* windings of river, path, etc.

meaning: see **mean**[2].

mea'sles (-zlz), *n.* acute infectious disease with red rash. **mea'sly** (-z-), *a.* of, having, measles; (*slang*) scanty, worthless.

measure (mezh'er), *v.t.* find out extent or quantity of by comparison with fixed standard; be of specified length, etc. *measure out,* give measured quantity of, mark out. *n.* size or quantity found by measuring; vessel, rod, tape, etc., for measuring; rhythm, metre, musical time; suitable action; legislative enactment. **meas'urable,** *a.* **meas'ure-ment,** *n.*

meat, *n.* flesh of animals as food. **mea'ty,** *a.* (esp., fig.) full of substance.

mèchan'ic (-k-), *n.* skilled workman, esp. one making, repairing, or using machinery.

mèchan'ical (-k-), *a.* of, working, or produced by machinery; machine-like, automatic. **mèchan'ically,** *adv.*

mèchan'ics (-k-), *n.* science of motion; mechanism, functioning; science of machinery.

mech'anism (-k-), *n.* way machine works; structure, technique; piece of machinery.

mech'anize (-k-), *v.t.* make mechanical; substitute mechanical power for man-power or horse-power in (army, etc.). **mechani-zā'tion,** *n.*

med'al, *n.* piece of metal, usu. coin-shaped, commemorating event, etc., or awarded as distinction. **med'allist,** *n.* winner of prize-medal.

medall'ion, *n.* large medal; circular picture.

medd'le, *v.i.* busy oneself unduly *with;* interfere *in.* **medd'lesome,** *a.*

mediaeval: see **medieval.**

mē'dial, *a.* in the middle; average.

mē'dian, *a.* in the middle. *n.* line from angle of triangle to middle of opposite side.

mē'diāte, *v.i.* act as go-between or peace-maker. **mēdiā'tion,** *n.* **mē'diātor,** *n.*

med'ical, *a.* of medicine; of medical (opp. *surgical*) treatment. *n.* (*informal*) medical examination for fitness.

mèdic'ament (*or* med'-), *n.* substance used in medical treatment.

med'icăte, *v.t.* impregnate with medicinal substance; treat medically.

mèdi'cinal, *a.* healing; curative.

medicine (med'sn), *n.* science and art of restoring and preserving health; remedial substance, esp. taken internally. **medicine-man,** witch-doctor.

mediè'val, mediae'val, *a.* of the Middle Ages. **mediè'valism,** *n.*

mē'diŏcre (-ker), *a.* middling; second-rate. **mēdioc'rity,** *n.*

med'ităte, *v.* think about; consider; exercise mind in serious thought. **meditā'tion,** *n.* **med'itative,** *a.*

Mediterrā'nean, *a.* & *n.* (of, living near) inland sea between S. Europe and N. Africa.

mē'dium, *n.* (pl. *mediums, media*), middle quality, degree, etc.; means or agency; person through whom spirits of the dead are alleged to communicate with living persons. *a.* intermediate; average.

med'lar, *n.* (tree with) fruit like small brown apple, palatable when half-rotten.

med'ley, *n.* mixture of diverse elements.

meed, *n.* (Poet.) reward; merited portion.

meek, *a.* submissive; gentle.

meer'schaum (-shm), *n.* creamy clay used esp. for tobacco-pipe bowls.

meet¹, *a.* (*archaic*) fitting, proper.

meet², *v.* (p.t. *met*), come together or face to face (with); become acquainted (with); go to receive on arrival; become perceptible to; satisfy (need, etc.); experience. *n.* assembly for hunting, etc.

mee'ting, *n.* assembly, encounter. **meeting--house,** (esp.) Friends' place of worship.

mega-, *pref.* great, large; a million times.

meg'alith, *n.* huge prehistoric stone.

megalomā'nia, *n.* insanely exaggerated idea of one's own importance.

meg'aphône, *n.* speaking-trumpet for magnifying sound of voice.

melanchŏ'lia (-k-), *n.* depression. **melanchol'ic,** *a.*

mel'ancholy (-k-), *a.* sad, depressed; depressing. *n.* sadness; depression.

mêlée (mel'ā), *n.* confused fight, skirmish.

mellif'luous (-loo-), *a.* sweet-sounding.

mell'ow (-ō), *a.* soft and rich in flavour, colour, or sound; softened by age, etc.; genial. *v.* make or become mellow; ripen.

melod'ic, *a.* of melody.

melŏ'dious, *a.* full of melody.

mel'odrama (-rah-), *n.* drama marked by crude appeals to emotion. **melodramat'ic,** *a.*

mel'ody, *n.* sweet music; arrangement of notes in musically expressive succession; principal part in harmonized music.

mel'on, *n.* (large juicy edible fruit of) any of various gourds.

melt, *v.* (p.p. *melted*; also *mŏlten*), (cause to) become liquefied by heat; soften, be softened; disintegrate, vanish (*away*).

mem'ber, *n.* limb or other bodily organ; distinct part of complex structure; person belonging to society, order, etc. **Member of Parliament** (abbrev. *M.P.*), person elected to House of Commons. **mem'bership,** *n.* being member; (number of) members.

mem'brāne, *n.* layer of connective tissue round organ, lining cavity, etc., in living organism. **membrā'nèous, mem'branous,** *aa.*

memen'tŏ, *n.* (pl. *mementos* or *-oes*), object serving as reminder or kept as memorial.

mem'ŏ, *n.* (pl. *memos*), (*informal*) memorandum.

mem'oir (-war), *n.* brief biography; essay on learned subject; (pl.) account of one's life or experiences.

mem'orable, *a.* likely or worthy to be remembered.

memoran'dum, *n.* note or record for future use (pl. *memoranda*); informal (business) letter without signature (pl. *memorandums*).

memor'ial, *n.* monument, object, custom, etc., to keep alive memory of person or event; written statement as basis of petition, etc. *a.* commemorative.

mem'orīze, *v.t.* learn by heart.

mem'ory, *n.* faculty by which things are recalled to or kept in mind; what is remembered; reputation after one is dead.

mem'-sah'ib, *n.* (in India, etc.) European married woman.

men, *pl.* of **man.**

men'ace, *n.* threat. *v.t.* threaten. **men'acing,** *a.*

ménage (mā'nahzh), *n.* household. (French)

mèna'gerie, *n.* collection of wild animals in captivity.

mend, *v.* repair, patch; put right; improve. *n.* mended hole, tear, etc. *on the mend,* improving.

mendā'cious (-shus), *a.* untruthful; often telling lies. **menda'city,** *n.*

men'dicant, *n.* beggar. *a.* begging.

men'hir (-hēr), *n.* prehistoric tall upright stone.

mē'nial, *n.* household servant. *a.* fit for a servant; lowly, degrading.

meningī'tis (-j-), *n.* inflammation of membranes enveloping brain and spinal cord.

men'opause (-z), *n.* period of woman's life when menstruation ceases.

men'sēs (-z), *n.pl.* monthly discharge of blood and tissue debris from womb.

men'strual (-oo-al), *a.* of menses. **men'struăte,** *v.i.* discharge menses. **menstruā'tion,** *n.*

mensūrā'tion, *n.* measuring; mathematical rules for reckoning length, area, etc.

men'tal, *a.* of or in the mind; (*slang*) feeble--minded. **mental age,** stage of development normally reached at specified age. **mental defective,** person whose mind is arrested or incomplete in development. **mental hospital,** hospital for care of mentally ill persons.

mental'ity, *n.* intellectual power; mind, character. **men'tally,** *adv.*

men'thol, *n.* crystalline camphor-like substance obtained from mint-oils.

men'tion, *v.t.* speak of, refer to. *n.* mentioning.

men'tor, *n.* trusted adviser, counsellor.

men'ū, *n.* list of dishes to be served or available.

mer'cantile, *a.* trading; of trade or merchants.

mer'cènary, *a.* working merely for money. *n.* hired soldier in foreign service.

mer'cer, *n.* dealer in textile fabrics, esp. silks. **mer'cery,** *n.*

mer'cerized, *a.* (of cotton) treated with caustic alkali to give silky lustre.

merch'andise, *n.* goods for sale.

mer'chant, *n.* wholesale trader esp. with foreign countries; dealer. **merchant navy, service,** ships employed in commerce, their officers and men.

mer'ciful, *a.* having or showing mercy.

mer'ciless, *a.* cruel, pitiless.

mercūr'ial, *a.* of lively temperament; of or containing mercury.

mer'cūry, *n.* heavy lustrous silver-white metallic element, normally liquid. **mercūr'ic,** *a.*

Mer'cūry, *n.* (Rom. myth.) god of eloquence, etc., and messenger of the gods; a planet.

mer'cy, *n.* abstention from infliction of suffering or punishment; compassion; blessing. *at the mercy of,* in the power of.

mēre¹, *n.* lake.

mēre², *a.* barely or only what it is said to be, nothing more than. **mēre'ly,** *adv.* only.

merètri'cious (me-; -shus), *a.* attractive in a showy way; flashy.

merge, *v.* (cause to) lose character or identity in something else; join or blend (*into, with*). **mer'ger,** *n.* (esp.) combination of firms, etc., into one.

mèrid'ian, *n.* sun's position at noon; star's highest altitude; (semi-)circle passing through the N. and S. poles and any point on earth's surface. *prime meridian,* meridian passing through Greenwich.

mèrid'ional, *a.* of the south.

meringue' (-rang), *n.* confection of sugar and beaten white of egg, baked crisp.

meri'nō (-rē-), *n.* (pl. *merinos*), kind of sheep; fine yarn or soft fabric made from its wool.

me'rit, *n.* commendable quality; goodness; (pl.) deserts; (pl.) rights and wrongs (*of* case, etc.). *v.t.* deserve. **meritor'ious,** *a.* praiseworthy.

mer'maid, *n.fem.,* **mer'man,** *n.* (pl. *-men*), fabled woman, man, of sea, with fish's tail.

me'rriment, *n.* fun; mirth.

me'rry, *a.* laughing, full of fun; slightly tipsy. **merry-go-round,** revolving machine carrying wooden horses, cars, etc., for riding in or on. **me'rrymaking,** festivity. **me'rrythought,** (*archaic*) wish-bone.

mesh, *n.* one of spaces between threads of net; net, network; openwork fabric. *v.* catch in a net; (of gear-wheels, etc.) engage.

mes'merism (mez-) *n.* hypnotism. **mesme'ric,** *a.* **mes'merize,** *v.t.* hypnotize.

mess, *n.* spilt liquid, etc.; dirty or untidy state; portion of food (*archaic*); company (esp. in army, navy, etc.) feeding together; its meal or mess-room. *v.* make dirty or untidy; take meals, potter *about. mess up,* bungle. **mess-mate,** member of same mess, esp. on ship. **mess'y,** *a.* untidy, dirty.

mess'age, *n.* communication sent; inspired communication of prophet, writer, etc.

mess'enger (-j-), *n.* bearer of message.

Messi'ah, *n.* deliverer expected by Jews; Christ in that character. **Messian'ic,** *a.*

Mess'rs. (-erz), *abbrev.* pl. of **Mr.,** prefixed as title to name of firm, etc., or introducing list of men's names.

meta- *pref.* (*met-* before vowel) with, after; involving change.

mètab'olism, *n.* process by which an organism builds up its food into living matter and obtains energy. **metabol'ic,** *a.*

met'al, *n.* any of a class of substances, typically lustrous in appearance and good conductors of heat and electricity (e.g. gold, silver, iron, etc.); broken stone for road-making; (pl.) rails of railway. *v.t.* (p.t. *metalled*), fit with metal; make (road) with metal. **metall'ic,** *a.* of, like, or yielding metal.

met'allurgy (*or* mital'-), *n.* science of extraction, working, and properties of metals and alloys. **metallur'gical,** *a.* **met'allurgist,** *n.*

metamor'phic, *a.* (Geol., of rocks) changed after formation by heat or pressure. **metamor'phism,** *n.*

metamor'phōse (-z), *v.t.* change in form. **metamor'phosis,** *n.* (pl. *metamorphosēs*), change of form; change of character, conditions, etc; (Zool.) change between immature form and adult.

met'aphor, *n.* application of name or descriptive term to object to which it is not literally applicable (e.g. a *biting* wind). **metapho'rical,** *a.*

metaphys'ics (-z-), *n.* branch of philosophy concerned with nature of being, truth, etc. **metaphys'ical,** *a.*

mēte, *v.t.* mete out, portion out, allôt.

mē'tèor, *n.* small particle moving round sun, becoming luminous and destroying itself on entering earth's atmosphere, shooting star. **mētèo'ric,** *a.* of meteors; (fig.) dazzling, rapid. **mē'tèorīte,** *n.* fragment of rock or nickel iron which has fallen to earth's surface from space.

mētèorol'ogy, *n.* study of atmospheric phenomena, esp. as determining weather. **mētèorolo'gical,** *a.* **mētèorol'ogist,** *n.*

mē'ter, *n.* apparatus registering amount of water, gas, electricity, etc., passing through, time elapsed, etc. *v.* count or measure by meter.

mĕthinks', v. impers. (archaic) it seems to me.

meth'od, n. way of doing something, system; orderliness. **mĕthod'ical**, a.

Meth'odism, n. beliefs, worship, etc., of religious denomination following the teaching of John Wesley and others. **Meth'odist**, n.

meth'ylāte, v.t. mix (alcohol, etc.) with methyl alcohol (wood alcohol), usu. to make it unfit for drinking (as methylated spirit).

metic'ūlous, a. excessively accurate or correct or proper.

mĕ'tre¹ (-ter), n. any form of verse-rhythm.

mĕ'tre² (-ter), n. basic unit of length in metric system (39·37 in.).

met'ric, a. of metric system. **metric system**, decimal measuring system. **metric ton**, see **ton.**

met'rical, a. of or in metre; involving measurement.

metricā'tion, n. conversion to metric system.

met'ronōme, n. (musician's) instrument marking time by means of inverted pendulum, etc.

metrop'olis, n. chief city of country, capital. **metropol'itan**, a.

mett'le, n. quality of endurance and courage; (esp. of horse) spirit. **mett'lesome**, a. high-spirited.

mew¹, n. sea-gull.

mew², n. & v.i. (utter) cat's cry.

mews (-z), n. series of stables round yard or along sides of lane (now usu. garages, flats, etc.)

mezzo (met'sō), adv. (Mus.) moderately. **mezzo-soprano**, (person with) voice between soprano and contralto.

mezz'anine (-ēn), a. & n. (low storey) between two others, esp. ground and first floors.

mīas'ma, (-z-), n. (pl. miasmata), unwholesome exhalation from marshes, putrid matter, etc.

mi'ca, n. any of group of minerals found as small glittering scales in granite, etc., or as crystals.

mice, pl. of **mouse.**

Mich'aelmas (-klm-), n. feast of St. Michael, 29th September.

micro-, pref. small, minute; millionth part of. **microbiol'ogy**, n. study of micro-organisms. **mi'crocosm** (-z-), n. little world, epitome (of). **mi'crofilm**, (photographic reproduction on) very small film. **micro-or'ganism**, n. organism not visible to unaided eye. **mi'crophōne**, n. device converting sound waves into electrical energy, used in transmitting or recording speech, etc. **mi'croscōpe**, n. lens or combination of lenses making minute objects visible. **microscop'ic**, a. too small to be seen clearly without microscope. **mi'cros'copy**, n. **mi'crowāve**, n. radio wave of wavelength less than 30 cm.

mi'crōbe, n. micro-organism, esp. bacterium causing disease (not in scientific use).

mid, a. middle of; intermediate. **mid'day**, noon or about noon.

midd'en, n. dunghill; rubbish-heap.

midd'le, a. equally distant from extremities; intermediate in rank, quality, etc. n. middle point or position. **middle age**, period between youth and old age. **Middle Ages**, about A.D. 500 - 1450. **midd'leman** (pl. -men), trader intermediate between producer and consumer.

midd'ling, a. moderately good; fairly well in health. adv. fairly or moderately.

midge, n. gnat, small fly.

midg'ĕt, n. & a. very small (person); dwarf.

mid'land, a. remote from sea or borders. **Mid'lands**, midland counties of England.

mid'night (-nīt), n. twelve o'clock at night. a. of, at dark as, midnight.

mid'riff, n. diaphragm.

mid'shipman, n. (pl. -men), (Hist.) junior naval officer between cadet and sub-lieutenant.

midst, n. middle. prep. amidst.

mid'summer, n. period of summer solstice, about 21st June. **Mid'summer Day**, 24th June.

mid'wīfe, n. (pl. midwives), woman who assists others in childbirth. **mid'wifery** (-wifri), n. work of midwife; obstetrics.

mien (mēn), n. person's bearing or look.

might¹, p.t. of **may¹.**

might² (mīt), n. great power or strength or resources. **might'y**, a. powerful, great.

mignonette' (minyo-), n. plant with fragrant greyish-green flowers.

mi'graine (or mē-), n. recurrent severe headache, often accompanied by nausea.

mi'grant, a. & n. (bird, etc.) that migrates.

migrāte', v.i. move from one place to another; (of birds, etc.) come and go with the seasons. **migrā'tion**, n. **mi'gratory**, n.

Mika'dō (-kah-), n. (pl. Mikados), an emperor of Japan.

milch, a. giving, kept for, milk.

mīld, a. gentle; not severe or harsh; not bitter. **mīld'ness**, n.

mil'dew, n. growth of minute fungi on plants, or on leather, cloth, etc., exposed to damp. v. taint, be tainted, with mildew.

mile, n. measure of length (1,760 yds.). **mile'stone**, roadside pillar marking miles; stage (in career, etc.). **mī'l(e)age**, n. distance in miles; travelling allowance at fixed rate per mile.

mil'itant, a. engaged in warfare; aggressive. n. militant person. **mil'itancy**, n.

mil'itarism, n. exaltation of or reliance on military force or methods. **mil'itarist**, n.

mil'itary, a. of or for soldiers, the army, or land warfare. n. soldiery.

mil'itāte, v.i. serve as argument or influence against.

mili'tia (-sha), *n.* military force, esp. of trained civilians not in regular army. **mili'tiaman,** *n.* (pl. *-men*).

milk, *n.* opaque white fluid secreted by female mammals for feeding young; cow's milk as food. *v.t.* draw milk from. **milk'maid,** woman milking cows or working in dairy. **milk'man,** man who sells or delivers milk. **milk'sop,** unmanly fellow. **milk-teeth,** temporary first teeth in young mammals. **mil'ky,** *a.* of or like or mixed with milk; cloudy. **Milky Way,** luminous band of countless stars in night sky, Galaxy.

mill, *n.* building or apparatus for grinding corn; grinding machine; factory. *v.* grind or treat in mill; produce grooves, etc., in (metal, edge of coin); (of cattle, etc.) move round and round in mass. **mill-pond,** water retained by dam for driving water-mill. **mill'stone,** one of two circular stones between which corn is ground.

millenn'ium, *n.* (pl. *-s* or *millennia*), period of 1,000 years; hoped-for time of happiness on earth.

mill'épède, *n.* small crawling animal with many double pairs of legs.

mill'er, *n.* one whose business is to grind corn.

mill'ét, *n.* (very small seeds of) a cereal plant.

milli-, *pref.* one thousandth of. **mill'igram(me),** *n.* thousandth of gram. **mill'isecond,** *n.* thousandth of second. **mill'imetre** (-ter), *n.* thousandth of metre.

mill'iard, *n.* a thousand millions.

mill'iner, *n.* one who makes or sells women's hats. **mill'inery,** *n.*

mill'ion (-yon), *n.* a thousand thousand. **millionaire',** *n.* possessor of a million pounds or dollars. **mill'ionth,** *a.* & *n.*

mime, *n.* simple drama acted with gestures, usu. without words. *v.* act with gestures and without words.

mimet'ic (*or* mī-), *a.* of or showing imitation or mimicry.

mim'ic, *v.t.* (p.t. *mimicked*), copy speech or gestures of, esp. to amuse others; imitate, or resemble closely. *n.* person who mimics. *a.* pretended, esp. to amuse; sham; imitative. **mim'icry,** *n.* mimicking; resemblance of animal, etc., in colour, etc., to environment or other animal.

mimō'sa (-z-), *n.* kind of acacia with clusters of sweet-smelling, ball-shaped, yellow flowers.

min'aret, *n.* tall slender tower or turret of mosque.

min'atory, *a.* threatening.

mince, *v.* cut (meat, etc.) very small; walk with affectedly short steps. *n.* minced meat. **mince'meat,** mixture of minced apples, currants, spices, suet, etc. **mince-pie,** small pie filled with mincemeat.

mind, *n.* seat of consciousness, thought, will, and feeling; intellectual powers; memory; opinion. *v.t.* bear in mind; heed; have charge of; object (to). **mind'ed,** *a.* inclined. **mind'ful,** *a.* not forgetful (*of*).

mine¹, *possessive pron.* the one(s) belonging to me. *a.* belonging to me.

mine², *n.* excavation from which minerals are extracted; explosive charge placed in or on sea, dropped from aircraft, or buried, during war. *v.* dig for minerals; burrow; lay mines. **mine'layer,** vessel for laying mines. **mine'sweeper,** ship for clearing away mines. **mi'ner,** *n.* worker in mine, esp. coal-mine.

min'eral, *n.* substance obtained by mining; inorganic natural substance; substance neither animal nor vegetable; mineral water. *a.* of or belonging to minerals. **mineral water,** water naturally containing (esp. medicinal) mineral(s); effervescent drink.

mineral'ogy, *n.* science of minerals. **mineralo'gical,** *a.* **mineral'ogist,** *n.*

ming'le (-nggl), *v.* (cause to) mix; blend; unite *with.*

mini-, *pref.* miniature, (very) small. **min'i-(car),** small car. **min'iskirt,** very short skirt.

min'iature (-cher), *n.* small painted portrait; small-scale model. *a.* small-scale. **min'iaturist,** *n.* painter of miniatures.

min'im, *n.* (Mus.) open-headed note with stem, equal to half semibreve.

min'imize, *v.t.* reduce to, estimate at, smallest possible amount or degree.

min'imum, *n.* (pl. *minima*), least possible or least recorded amount, degree, etc.

min'ion, *n.* favourite; servile agent.

min'ister, *n.* person in charge of department of State; diplomatic representative, esp. ranking below ambassador; (esp. Non-conformist) clergyman. *v.i.* give help or service (*to*). **ministe̅'rial,** *a.*

min'istrant, *a.* & *n.* ministering (person).

ministrā'tion, *n.* (act of) ministering.

min'istry, *n.* priestly office; ministers of a church; office or building or department of minister of State; ministers forming government.

mink, *n.* small semi-aquatic stoat-like animal; its valuable fur.

minn'ow (-ō), *n.* very small freshwater fish.

mi'nor, *a.* lesser of two units or sets; of lesser kind, importance, etc.; (Mus., of scale) having three semitones between keynote and third note. *n.* person under age of majority (18, formerly 21).

mino'rity (*or* mī-), *n.* smaller number or part; state or period of being a minor.

min'ster, *n.* large church, cathedral.

min'strel, *n.* medieval singer or musician; poet; (pl.) band of entertainers with blacked faces, etc.

mint¹, *n.* aromatic herb used in cooking; peppermint.

mint², *n.* place where money is coined. *v.t.* coin (money); invent.

minūet', *n.* (music for) slow stately dance in

triple time; (Mus.) piece or movement in style of minuet.

mi′nus, *prep.* less, with deduction of. *n.* minus sign (−).

min′ute[1] (-nit), *n.* sixtieth part of hour or angular degree; short time; memorandum, summary, (pl.) official record of proceedings. *v.t.* draft; make minute of.

minūte′[2], *a.* very small; exact, going into details.

minū′tia (-shia), *n.* (pl. *minutiae*, pr. -shi-i), trivial point; small detail.

minx, *n.* sly girl, hussy.

mi′racle, *n.* event due to supernatural agency; remarkable event or object. **miracle plays,** medieval dramas based on Bible stories or legends of saints. **mirac′ūlous,** *a.* supernatural; wonderful.

mirage (mi′rahzh), *n.* unreal image produced by atmospheric conditions; illusion.

mīre, *n.* swampy ground; mud. *v.* sink in, bespatter with, mud.

mi′rror, *n.* smooth surface, esp. of glass backed with mercury, etc., reflecting images; model, faithful reflection. *v.t.* reflect as in mirror. **mirror image,** image (as) reflected in mirror, with right and left sides transposed.

mirth, *n.* merriment; laughter. **mirth′ful, mirth′less,** *aa.*

mīr′y, *a.* muddy, swampy.

mis-, *pref.* badly, wrongly, unfavourably.

misadven′ture, *n.* unlucky accident.

misalli′ance, *n.* unsuitable marriage.

mis′anthrōpe (*or* -z-), *n.* hater of all mankind. **misanthrop′ic,** *a.* **misan′thropy,** *n.*

misapply′, *v.t.* apply or use wrongly.

misapprehend′, *v.t.* misunderstand. **misapprehen′sion** (-shn), *n.*

misapprō′priāte, *v.t.* take or keep dishonestly for one's own use. **misappropriā′tion,** *n.*

misbĕgott′en, *a.* illegitimate.

misbehāve′, *v.i. & refl.* behave badly. **misbehá′viour** (-yer), *n.*

miscal′cūlāte, *v.t.* calculate wrongly. **miscalcūlā′tion,** *n.*

miscall′ (-awl), *v.t.* call by wrong name.

misca′rriage (-rij), *n.* miscarrying; abortion, esp. spontaneous. *miscarriage of justice,* legal decision resulting in injustice.

misca′rry, *v.i.* (of plan, effort, etc.) fail; (of woman) have miscarriage.

miscĕgĕnā′tion, *n.* interbreeding between races.

miscellā′nĕous, *a.* of mixed composition or character; of various kinds. **miscell′any,** *n.* miscellaneous collection.

mischance′ (-ahns), *n.* unlucky accident.

mis′chief (-chif), *n.* harm, injury, done intentionally; discord; childish pranks; playful malice. **mis′chievous** (-chiv-), *a.* causing trouble; full of mischief.

misconceive′ (-sĕv), *v.* have wrong idea of; misunderstand. **misconcep′tion,** *n.*

miscon′duct, *n.* improper conduct, esp. adultery. **misconduct′,** *v.t. & refl.*

misconstrue′ (-ōō), *v.t.* interpret wrongly (person's words, actions, etc.). **misconstruc′tion,** *n.*

mis′count, *n.* wrong count, esp. of votes. **miscount′,** *v.t.* count wrongly.

mis′crèant, *n.* villain.

misdāte′, *v.t.* date wrongly.

misdeal′, *v.* make mistake in dealing cards. *n.* wrong deal.

misdeed′, *n.* wrongful act.

misdĕmea′nour (-ner), *n.* unlawful act; misdeed.

misdīrect′ (*or* -di-), *v.t.* direct wrongly. **misdirec′tion,** *n.*

misdo′ing (-dōō-), *n.* (often in pl.) misdeed.

mi′ser (-z-), *n.* person living frugally in order to hoard money. **mi′serly,** *a.*

mis′erable (-z-), *a.* wretchedly unhappy, poor, or uncomfortable; pitiable; mean. **mis′erably,** *adv.*

mis′ery (-z-), *n.* acute unhappiness; distressing poverty.

misfīre′, *v.i.* (of gun) fail to fire; (of internal-combustion engine) fail to ignite; (fig.) fail to produce intended result. *n.* such failure.

mis′fit, *n.* garment, etc., that does not fit; person ill-adapted to surroundings, etc.

misfor′tūne (*or* -choon), *n.* bad luck; calamity.

misgiv′ing, *n.* feeling of mistrust or apprehension; uneasy doubt.

misguī′ded (-gī-), *a.* wrong, erring.

mishan′dle (-s-h-), *v.t.* handle roughly or improperly.

mishap′ (-s-h-), *n.* unlucky accident.

misinform′, *v.t.* give wrong information to. **misinformā′tion,** *n.*

misinter′prèt, *v.t.* interpret wrongly. **misinterprĕtā′tion,** *n.*

misjudge′, *v.t.* judge wrongly.

mislay′, *v.t.* (p.t. *mislaid*), so place (thing) as to be unable to find it.

mislead′ (-lĕd), *v.t.* (p.t. *misled*), lead astray; give wrong impression to.

misman′age, *v.t.* manage badly or wrongly. **misman′agement,** *n.*

misnō′mer, *n.* (use of) wrongly applied name or term.

misog′yny (-j- *or* -g-; *or* mi-), *n.* hatred of women. **misog′ynist,** *n.*

misplāce′, *v.t.* put in wrong place; bestow (affections, etc.) on ill-chosen object. **misplāce′ment,** *n.*

mis′print, *n.* error in printing. **misprint′,** *v.t.* print wrongly.

mispronounce′, *v.t.* pronounce wrongly. **mispronunciā′tion,** *n.*

misquōte′, *v.t.* quote wrongly. **misquōtā′tion,** *n.*

misread′, *v.t.* (p.t. *misread*, pr. -red), read or interpret wrongly.

misreprèsent′ (-z-), *v.t.* give false account of.

misreprèsentā'tion, *n.*

misrule' (-rōōl), *v.t.* rule badly; *n.* bad government.

miss[1], *v.* fail to hit, reach, meet, find, catch, or perceive; regret absence of; fail. *n.* failure to hit or attain.

miss[2], *n.* (title of) unmarried woman or girl.

miss'al, *n.* (R.C. Ch.) Mass-book.

miss'el(-thrush), *n.* large thrush.

mis-shā'pen, *a.* deformed.

miss'īle, *n.* object or weapon capable of being thrown or projected.

miss'ing, *a.* not present, not found.

mi'ssion (-shn), *n.* persons sent out as envoys or evangelists; missionary post, organization, etc.; errand of mission; vocation; (U.S.) operational sortie by spacecraft.

mi'ssionary (-sho-), *a.* of religious missions. *n.* person doing missionary work.

miss'ive, *n.* letter.

mis-spell', *v.t.* (p.t. *mis-spelt* or *-spelled*, pr. -spelt; p.p. *mis-spelt*), spell wrongly.

mis-spend', *v.t.* (p.t. *mis-spent*), spend amiss or wastefully.

mis-stāte', *v.t.* state wrongly. mis-stāte'-ment, *n.*

mist, *n.* water-vapour in drops smaller than rain; dimness, blurring, caused by tears in eyes, etc.

mistāke', *v.* (p.t. *mistook*; p.p. *mistāken*), misinterpret; erroneously take (person or thing) *for* another; (*p.p.*) due to error, ill--judged. *n.* error, blunder; mistaken opinion or act.

mis'ter, *n.* title prefixed to surname of man (always written Mr.).

mistīme', *v.t.* say, do, (thing) at wrong time.

mis'tletoe (-sltō), *n.* plant with whitish sticky berries, parasitic on trees.

mistranslāte', *v.t.* translate incorrectly. mis-translā'tion, *n.*

mis'tress, *n.* woman having authority over servants or control of household; female teacher; woman who has a continuing sexual relationship with a man to whom she is not married.

mistrust', *v.t.* feel no confidence in. *n.* lack of confidence; uneasy doubts.

mis'ty, *a.* of, in, or like mist; of dim outline; obscure. mis'tily, *adv.*

misunderstand', *v.* (p.t. *misunderstood*), not understand rightly. misunderstan'ding, *n.*

misūse' (-z), *v.t.* put to wrong use; ill-treat. misūse' (-s), *n.* wrong use.

mīte, *n.* coin of very small value (Bibl.); small child or person; small arachnid.

mit'igāte, *v.t.* alleviate; reduce severity of. mitigā'tion, *n.*

mī'tre[1] (-ter), *n.* bishop's tall pointed head--dress. mī'tred, *a.* wearing a mitre.

mī'tre[2] (-ter), *n.* joint in which line of junction bisects angle between joined pieces. *v.t.* join thus.

mitt, *n.* mitten.

mitt'en, *n.* glove leaving fingers and thumb--tip bare, or covering four fingers together and thumb separately.

mix, *v.* unite or blend into one mass; compound together; become united, mingle (*with*). *mix up*, confuse. mixed (-kst), *a.* of diverse qualities or elements; of or for both sexes. *mixed up*, confused. mix'er, *n.* (esp.) apparatus for mixing or beating ingredients in cookery.

mix'ture, *n.* mixing; what is mixed, esp. medicinal preparation.

miz(z)'en-mast (-mah-), *n.* mast nearest stern of three-masted ship.

mnemon'ic (n-), *a. & n.* (verse, etc.) designed to help the memory. *n.pl.* mnemonic art or system.

moan, *n.* low inarticulate sound expressing pain or grief. *v.* utter moan; lament, complain.

moat, *n.* wide, usu. water-filled, ditch round castle, town, etc. moa'ted, *a.* surrounded with moat.

mob, *n.* riotous crowd; rabble; gang. *v.t.* (p.t. *mobbed*), attack in mob; crowd round and molest.

mob'-cap, *n.* (Hist.) woman's indoor cap.

mō'bile, *a.* moving, able to be moved, easily; of changing expression. *n.* sculpture, etc., with parts that move in currents of air. mobil'ity, *n.*

mō'bilize, *v.t.* call up, assemble, prepare, for warfare, etc. mōbilizā'tion, *n.*

mocc'asin, *n.* Amer. Indian soft shoe of deer-skin, etc.

mock, *v.* ridicule, mimic; scoff *at*. *a.* (not *pred.a.*) sham, mimic, counterfeit. mock orange, shrub with white scented flowers, syringa. mock-up, full-sized model. mock'ery, *n.* derision; laughing-stock; travesty.

mōde, *n.* way in which thing is done; current fashion.

mod'el, *n.* representation of designed or actual object; design, pattern; object of imitation; person employed to pose for artist, show off clothes, etc. *v.* (p.t. *modelled*), fashion, shape; act as model, wear for display.

mod'erate, *a.* avoiding extremes, temperate; fairly large or good; not excessive. mod'-erāte, *v.* make or become less violent or excessive. moderā'tion, *n.* mod'erātor, *n.* president of Presbyterian assembly.

mod'ern, *a.* of present and recent times; new--fashioned; not concerned with classics. moder'nity, *n.*

mod'ernīze, *v.t.* make modern; adapt to modern ideas, taste, etc. modernizā'tion, *n.*

mod'est, *a.* not overrating one's own merit; unassuming; not excessive; decorous. mod'esty, *n.*

mod'icum, *n.* (sing. only) small quantity.

mod'ify, *v.t.* tone down, qualify; make less severe; make some changes in. modificā'-

modish

tion, *n.*

mo′dish, *a.* fashionable.

mod′ūlăte, *v.* vary or regulate tone or pitch of; (Mus.) pass from one key to another. **modŭlā′tion**, *n.*

mod′ūle, *n.* standardized unit of measurement used in building, etc.; independent unit forming section of spacecraft.

mo′hair, *n.* hair of Angora goat; yarn or fabric of it.

Mohammedan: see Muhammadan.

moi′ĕty, *n.* half (esp. in legal use).

moist, *a.* slightly wet, damp. **moi′sten** (-sn), *v.* make or become moist. **mois′ture** (-cher), *n.* liquid diffused through air or condensed on surface.

mōke, *n.* (*slang*) donkey.

mō′lar, *a.* & *n.* grinding (tooth).

molass′es (-z), *n.* treacle-like syrup drained from raw sugar.

mōle¹, *n.* pigmented spot on human skin.

mōle², *n.* small burrowing mammal with dark velvety fur. **mole′hill,** mound of soil thrown up by mole.

mōle³, *n.* massive structure, esp. of stone, extending into water as pier or causeway.

mol′ĕcūle, *n.* smallest particle (usu. group of atoms) that can exist without losing its chemical identity. **molec′ūlar,** *a.*

molest′, *v.t.* trouble or annoy intentionally. **molestā′tion**, *n.*

moll′ifȳ, *v.t.* calm down, appease. **mollificā′tion**, *n.*

moll′usc, *n.* one of class of invertebrates with soft body and (usu.) hard shell, as snail, limpet, mussel, oyster, etc.

moll′ycoddle, *n.* person who is coddled. *v.t.* coddle.

mōl′ten, *a.* (alternative p.p. of **melt**) liquefied by great heat.

mō′ment, *n.* point or brief space of time; importance. **mō′mentary**, *a.* lasting only a moment. **momen′tous**, *a.* of great importance.

momen′tum, *n.* (pl. *momenta*), quantity of motion of moving body; force of motion gained by a moving body.

mon′arch (-k), *n.* sovereign with title of king, emperor, etc.; supreme ruler. **monar′chical,** *a.* **mon′archy**, *n.* (State under) monarchical government.

mon′astery, *n.* residence of community of monks. **monas′tic**, *a.* of monks or monasteries.

Mon′day (mun-), *n.* second day of week.

mon′ĕtary (mun-), *a.* of coinage or money.

mon′ey (mun-), *n.* (pl. *moneys*), coin or banknotes. **moneyed** (mun′id), *a.* wealthy. **money-lender,** person who lends money at interest. **money order,** order for payment of money through post office, bought by sender and cashed by recipient.

Mong′ol, Mongō′lian (-ngg-), *n.* & *a.* (member) of race inhabiting Mongolia or of yellow-skinned type of mankind; (*mongol*), (mental defective) of type physically resembling Mongols (i.e. having broad heads and slanting eyes). **mong′olism**, *n.* this type of mental deficiency. **Mong′oloid**, *a.* & *n.* Mongolian, (*m-*) mongol.

mong′ōōse (-ngg-), *n.* (pl. *mongooses*), small tropical carnivorous mammal.

mong′rel (mungg-), *a.* & *n.* (animal, esp. dog) of no definable breed or type, resulting from various crossings; hybrid.

mon′itor, *n.* pupil with disciplinary, etc., duties in school; one who listens to and reports on foreign broadcasts, etc; apparatus for testing transmission of broadcast, etc. *v.t.* act as monitor of (broadcast, etc.).

monk (mu-), *n.* man living as member of a community under religious vows. **monk′ish,** *a.* of or like monks.

monk′ey (mu-), *n.* (pl. *monkeys*), any of various (long-)tailed mammals of order of primates, related to and resembling man. *v.i.* play tricks (*with*). **monkey-nut,** peanut. **monkey-puzzle,** tree with prickly spines.

mon′ō, *n.* & *a.* monophonic (sound, etc.).

mono-, *pref.* alone, sole, single.

mon′ochrōme (-k-), *n.* & *a.* (picture, etc.) having only one colour. **monochromat′ic,** *a.*

mon′ocle, *n.* single eyeglass.

monog′amy, *n.* custom of being married to only one person at a time. **monog′amous**, *a.*

mon′ogram, *n.* two or more letters, esp. person's initials, interwoven in one design.

mon′olith, *n.* single block of stone as pillar, monument, etc. **monolith′ic,** *a.*

mon′ologue (-g), *n.* soliloquy; dramatic composition for one speaker.

monomā′nia, *n.* obsession of mind by single idea or intent. **monomā′niac,** *n.*

monophon′ic, *a.* (of sound) transmitted, etc., on single channel, not stereophonic.

mon′oplāne, *n.* aircraft with one pair of wings.

monop′olist, *n.* holder or supporter of monopoly.

monop′olīze, *v.t.* secure monopoly of. **monopolīzā′tion**, *n.*

monop′oly, *n.* exclusive trading privilege; sole possession or control of.

mon′orail, *n.* railway with cars running on single rail.

mon′osyllable, *n.* word of one syllable. **monosyllab′ic,** *a.*

mon′othēism, *n.* doctrine that there is only one God. **mon′othēist,** *n.* **monothēis′tic,** *a.*

mon′otōne, *n.* sound continuing or repeated on one note or without change of tone.

monot′onous, *a.* unvarying in tone; always the same, without variety. **monot′ony,** *n.* lack of change or variety.

monox′īde, *n.* oxide containing one oxygen atom.

Monsieur (mosyer′), *n.* (pl. *Messieurs*, pr. māsyer′), French form of Mr. and Sir.

(French)

monsoon', *n.* seasonal wind prevailing in S. Asia; rainy season accompanying SW. monsoon.

mon'ster, *n.* abnormally mis-shapen creature; large or unnatural person or thing; inhumanly cruel or wicked person.

monstros'ity, *n.* monstrousness; mis-shapen creature; outrageous thing.

mon'strous, *a.* like monster; huge; outrageous. **mon'strously**, *adv.*

month (mu-), *n.* period of moon's revolution (*lunar month*); any of twelve divisions of year (*calendar month*). **month'ly**, *a.* recurring, payable, etc., once a month. *n.* monthly magazine, etc. *adv.* once a month.

mon'ument, *n.* anything designed or serving to commemorate person, event, etc. **monūmen'tal**, *a.* of or serving as monument; colossal, stupendous.

moo, *v.i. & n.* (make) lowing sound.

mood¹, *n.* (Gram.) group of forms in conjugation of verb serving to indicate function, as indicative, subjunctive, etc.

mood², *n.* state of mind or feeling. **moo'dy**, *a.* subject to changes of mood; gloomy, sullen.

moon, *n.* heavenly body revolving round earth and reflecting light from sun. *v.i.* go dreamily or listlessly (*about*). **moon'beam**, ray of light from moon. **moon'light**, light of moon. **moon'shine**, foolish ideas or talk. **moon'stone**, kind of precious stone of pearly appearance. **moon'struck**, mad. **moo'ny**, *a.* dreamy.

moor¹, *n.* tract of uncultivated and often heather-covered ground. **moor'hen**, *n.* red-billed water-bird. **moor'land**, *n. & a.* (of) moors.

moor², *v.t.* attach (boat, etc.) by rope, etc., to shore or something fixed. **moor'age**, *n.* place, charge, for mooring. **moor'ings** (-z), *n.pl.* place, anchors and chains, etc., for mooring.

Moor³, *n.* one of a Muslim race inhabiting NW. Africa. **Moor'ish**, *a.*

moose, *n.* (pl. same), N. American elk.

moot, *n.* (Hist.) meeting, esp. legislative or judicial. *a.* that can be argued, debatable. *v.t.* raise (question, etc.) for discussion.

mop, *n.* bundle of yarn, etc., fixed to stick for use in cleaning. *v.* (p.t. *mopped*), clean or wipe (as) with mop; wipe *up* (as) with mop.

mope, *v.i.* be dejected and spiritless.

mo'ped, *n.* motorized bicycle.

moraine', *n.* debris deposited by glacier.

mo'ral, *a.* concerned with character, etc., or with right and wrong; good, virtuous. *n.* moral teaching; (pl.) habits or conduct from moral point of view. **mo'rally**, *adv.*

morale' (-ahl), *n.* discipline and spirit pervading army or group of people.

mo'ralist, *n.* one who points out morals; one who teaches morality. **moralis'tic**, *a.*

moral'ity, *n.* moral principles or rules; moral conduct. **mo'rality play,** medieval moralizing drama.

mo'ralize, *v.* talk or write on moral aspect of things; interpret morally.

morass', *n.* wet swampy area, bog.

mor'bid, *a.* not natural and healthy; of, indicating, disease. **morbid'ity**, *n.*

mor'dant, *a.* biting, stinging; (of acids) corrosive.

more, *a. & pron.* greater or additional quantity or number or degree (of). *adv.* to greater degree or extent or amount. **moreō'ver**, *adv.* besides, further.

morganat'ic, *a. morganatic marriage,* one between man of high rank and woman of lower rank who remains in her former station and whose children have no claim to property, title, etc.

morgue (-g), *n.* mortuary.

mo'ribund, *a.* in dying state.

Mor'mon, *n. & a.* (member) of U.S. religious sect. **Mor'monism**, *n.*

morn, *n.* (Poet.) morning.

mor'ning, *n.* day from dawn till noon or midday meal.

morocc'o, *n.* fine flexible leather of goatskin specially treated.

mor'on, *n.* feeble-minded person. **moron'ic**, *a.*

morōse', *a.* sullen and bad-tempered.

mor'phia, **mor'phine** (-ēn), *nn.* substance made from opium and used to lessen pain.

mo'rris (dance), English traditional dance performed by men.

mo'rrow (-ō), *n.* next day.

Morse (cōde), system of short or long signals (dots and dashes) representing letters of alphabet, signalled by lamp, radio, etc.

mor'sel, *n.* mouthful, bit; small quantity.

mor'tal, *a.* that must die, that cannot live forever; causing death. *n.* human being. **mor'tally**, *adv.* so as to cause death; extremely, exceedingly.

mortal'ity, *n.* being mortal; loss of life on large scale; death-rate.

mor'tar, *n.* vessel in which drugs, etc., are pounded with a pestle; short gun throwing shells, etc., at high angles; mixture of lime, sand, and water used to make joints between bricks, etc. **mortar board,** board on which building mortar is held for use; college cap with flat square top.

mortgage (mor'gij), *n.* transference of right to property in return for loan of money, until this loan is repaid. *v.t.* make over by mortgage; pledge in advance. **mortgagee'**, *n.* holder of mortgage. **mortgagor'** (-jor), *n.* person who pledges property in mortgage.

mor'tify, *v.* bring under control by discipline and self-control; humiliate, distress; (of flesh) be affected with gangrene. **mortificā'tion**, *n.*

mor'tise, *n.* hole into which end (*tenon*) of another part of framework, etc., is fitted. *v.t.*

make mortise in; join by mortise.

mor'tuary, *n.* building or room for temporary reception of corpses. *a.* of or for burial.

mosā'ic[1] (-z-), *n.* picture or pattern made with small coloured pieces of stone, glass, etc. *a.* of or like such work.

Mosā'ic[2] (-z-), *a.* of Moses.

Moslem: see **Muslim**.

mosque (-k), *n.* Muslim place of worship.

mosqui'tō (-kē-), *n.* (pl. *mosquitoes*), two--winged insect, of which females are blood--sucking and some carry disease (e.g. malaria). **mosquito-net**, net for keeping mosquitoes from bed, room, etc.

moss, *n.* any of various small flowerless plants growing on moist surfaces. **moss'y**, *a.* overgrown with moss.

mōst, *a. &* n. greatest number, quantity, or degree (of). *adv.* in great or greatest degree. **mōst'ly**, *adv.* predominantly, for the most part.

mōte, *n.* particle of dust.

mōtel', *n.* roadside hotel for motorists.

moth, *n.* any of various (usu. nocturnal) winged insects resembling butterflies; (also *clothes-moth*), small insect with larvae feeding on wool, fur, etc. **moth-eaten**, *a.* destroyed or damaged by moths; antiquated.

mo'ther (mudh-), *n.* female parent; head of convent, etc. *v.t.* (esp.) act like mother to. **mother country**, native land; country in relation to its colonies. **mother-in-law**, wife's or husband's mother. **mother of pearl**, iridescent lining of oyster and other shells. **mother tongue**, one's native language. **mo'therhood**, *n.* **mo'therless**, *a.* **mo'therly**, *a.*

mōtif' (-ēf), *n.* distinctive feature or dominant idea of design, composition, etc.

mō'tion, *n.* moving; gesture; proposition formally made in deliberative assembly; evacuation of bowels; faeces. *v.* make gesture, esp. to direct or guide person. **motion picture**, series of moving pictures produced by rapid projection on screen of succession of photographs taken by cinecamera. **mō'tionless**, *a.*

mō'tivāte, *v.t.* supply motive or inducement to. **mōtivā'tion**, *n.*

mō'tive, *n.* what causes person to take action. *a.* productive of motion or action.

mot'ley, *a.* parti-coloured; composed of diverse elements. *n.* fool's motley garb.

mō'tor, *n.* apparatus or engine supplying motive power for vehicle or machinery, esp. internal-combustion engine; motor car. *a.* giving, imparting, or producing motion; driven by motor. *v.* go or convey by motor car. **motor car**, motor-driven, usu. four--wheeled, passenger road vehicle. **motor cycle**, two-wheeled motor-driven road vehicle. **mō'torway**, fast highway for motor vehicles. **mō'torist**, *n.* driver of motor car. **mō'torīze**, *v.t.* equip or supply with motor

transport or engine.

motte, *n.* (Hist.) mound as site of castle or keep.

mott'le, *v.t.* mark or cover with spots or blotches. **mott'led**, *a.*

mott'ō, *n.* (pl. *mottoes*), (esp. heraldic) inscription expressing appropriate sentiment; maxim used as guiding rule of conduct.

mould[1] (mōld), *n.* loose earth; soil rich in organic matter.

mould[2] (mōld), *n.* fungous growth on damp surface.

mould[3] (mōld), *n.* hollow vessel in which fluid or plastic material is shaped or cast; pudding, etc., shaped in mould; form or character. *v.t.* shape (as) in mould; model.

moul'der (mōl-), *v.i.* decay to dust; crumble away.

moul'ding (mōl-), *n.* (esp.) ornamental moulded strip applied to building, etc.

moul'dy (mōl-), *a.* covered with mould; decaying.

moult (mōlt), *v.* (of birds) shed feathers; (of animals) shed hair. *n.* moulting.

mound, *n.* heap or bank of earth.

mount[1], *n.* mountain or hill.

mount[2], *v.* ascend, go upwards; climb on to; put on, provide with, animal for riding; provide with or fix on or in support(s), setting, etc. **mount up**, increase in amount. *n.* card, etc., forming surround to picture, etc.; setting; horse, etc., for riding.

moun'tain (-tin), *n.* natural elevation of earth's surface rising notably above surrounding level; large heap or pile. **mountain ash**, scarlet-berried tree. **mountaineer'**, *n.* (esp. skilled) mountain-climber. *v.i.* climb mountains. **moun'tainous**, *a.* having many mountains; huge.

moun'tèbank, *n.* impudent trickster; (*archaic*) itinerant quack.

mourn (morn), *v.* be sorrowful or distressed; grieve for the loss of. **mour'ner**, *n.* one who mourns; person attending funeral. **mourn'ful**, *a.* **mour'ning**, *n.* grief; (wearing of) black clothes as sign of bereavement.

mouse, *n.* (pl. *mice*), small rodent; shy or timid person. *v.t.* (-z), hunt for or catch mice.

moustache (mustahsh'), *n.* hair on upper lip.

mouth, *n.* (pl. pr. mowdhz), opening in the face used in speaking and eating; opening or entrance of anything; outfall of river. *v.i.* make grimaces in speaking. **mouth-organ**, small reed musical instrument played by ɔlowing and sucking. **mouth'piece**, *n.* part of musical instrument or tobacco-pipe placed before or between lips; part of telephone, etc., spoken into; person speaking for others. **mouth'ful**, *n.* (pl. *mouthfuls*).

mō'vable (mōōv-), *a.* that can be moved or removed; (of property) personal. *n.* (pl.) personal property.

move (mōōv), *v.* change position, posture,

place, or residence; stir or rouse; affect with emotion; propose as resolution. *n.* moving, esp. of piece at chess, etc.; step or action.

move'ment (mōovm-), *n.* moving; moving mechanism, esp. of watch; division, usu. complete in itself, of a musical work; (group organized for) combined action or endeavour *for* some purpose.

mo'ver (mōō-), *n.* (esp.) proposer of motion.

mo'vie (mōō-), *n.* (*informal*) motion picture.

mo'ving (mōō-), *a.* (esp.) touching, affecting. **moving staircase,** escalator.

mow (mō), *v.* (p.p. *mown,* pr. mōn), cut grass, etc., with scythe or machine. **mō'wer,** (-ōer), *n.* (esp.) mowing machine.

Mr.: see **mister.**

Mrs. (mis'iz), title prefixed to surname of married woman.

much, *a.* & *pron.* great quantity or amount (of). *adv.* in great degree; by a great deal. *much of a muchness,* very nearly the same.

mū'cilage, *n.* viscous substance obtained from plants; adhesive substance.

muck, *n.* manure; dirt, filth; rubbish. *v. muck out,* clean out (stable, etc.). *muck about,* (*slang*) potter. *muck up,* (*slang*) bungle, make mess of. **muck'y,** *a.*

mū'cous, *a.* secreting, covered by, mucus. **mucous membrane,** inner surface-lining of hollow organs of body. **mū'cus,** *n.* sticky substance secreted by and usu. protecting mucous membrane.

mud, *n.* soft mixture of earth and water. **mud'guard** (-gard), *n.* guard over wheels as protection against mud.

mudd'le, *v.* bewilder, confuse; mix *up;* be unmethodical. *n.* muddled condition.

mudd'y, *a.* covered with mud; thick, turbid. *v.t.* make muddy.

muezz'in (moo-ez-), *n.* official of mosque proclaiming hours of prayer from minaret.

muff[1], *n.* cover of fur, etc., for hands.

muff[2], *n.* stupid or awkward person. *v.t.* fail in, bungle; miss (catch, etc.).

muff'in, *n.* light round tea-cake toasted and eaten hot with butter.

muff'le, *v.t.* wrap *up* for warmth; wrap up to deaden sound. **muff'ler,** *n.* warm scarf.

muf'ti, *n.* plain clothes worn by official normally wearing uniform.

mug, *n.* drinking-vessel, usu. cylindrical; (*slang*) stupid person. *v.t.* (p.t. *mugged*), (*informal*) rob (person in street), esp. using violence.

mugg'y (-g-), *a.* (of weather) warm, damp, and oppressive.

Muhamm'adan, Mohamm'ēdan, Mahom'-ētan, *a.* of the prophet Muhammad or the religion of Islam revealed through him.

mūlatt'ō, *n.* (pl. *mulattos*), person of mixed Negro and white blood.

mul'berry, *n.* (tree bearing) dark-red oval edible fruit.

mulch, *n.* straw, leaves, etc., spread on ground above plants' roots. *v.* cover or spread with mulch.

mulct, *v.t.* punish by a fine; deprive *of.*

mūle[1], *n.* offspring of mare and he-ass; kind of spinning-machine. **mūlèteer',** *n.* mule-driver. **mū'lish,** *a.* obstinate, intractable.

mūle[2], *n.* kind of slipper.

mull, *v.t.* heat and spice (wine, beer).

mull'ėt, *n.* an edible sea-fish.

mulligataw'ny, *n.* highly seasoned curry-flavoured soup.

mull'ion, *n.* vertical shaft, usu. of stone, separating lights of divided window. **mull'ioned** (-nd), *a.*

multi-, *pref.* many. **multifār'ious,** *a.* of many kinds. **mul'tiform,** *a.* of many forms. **multi-lat'eral,** *a.* many-sided; (of treaty, etc.) involving more than two parties. **multi-millionaire',** *n.* person with fortune of several millions.

mul'tiple, *a.* of many parts, components, branches, kinds, etc. *n.* quantity exactly divisible by another.

multiplicand', *n.* quantity to be multiplied.

multiplicā'tion, *n.* multiplying.

multipli'city, *n.* manifold variety; great number *of.*

mul'tiplier, *n.* (esp.) quantity by which another is multiplied.

mul'tiplÿ, *v.* make or become many; find the quantity produced if a quantity is added to itself a given number of times.

mul'titūde, *n.* great number; crowd of people. **multitū'dinous,** *a.*

mum[1], *n.* (*informal*) mother.

mum[2], *int.* enjoining silence or secrecy (esp. in phr. *mum's the word*). *a.* silent.

mum'ble, *v.* speak or pronounce indistinctly. *n.* indistinct talk.

mum'bō-jum'bō, *n.* meaningless ritual; mystification, obscurity of language, etc.

mumm'er, *n.* actor in traditional dumb show. **mumm'ery,** *n.* ridiculous ceremonial.

mumm'ifÿ, *v.t.* make into a mummy.

mumm'ÿ[1], *n.* dead body preserved by embalming, esp. by ancient Egyptians.

mumm'ÿ[2], *n.* (*informal*) mother.

mumps, *n.* acute infectious disease with painful swelling of neck and face.

munch, *v.* chew steadily.

mun'dāne, *a.* of this world, ordinary.

mū̆ni'cipal, *a.* of or carried on by a municipality. **mū̆nicipal'ity,** *n.* town with local self-government; its governing body.

mū̆nif'icent, *a.* splendidly generous. **mū̆-nif'icence,** *n.*

mū̆ni'tions (-z-), *n.pl.* military weapons, ammunition, equipment, and stores.

mūr'al, *a.* of, in, on, wall. *n.* mural painting, etc.

mur'der, *n.* unlawful and intentional killing of human being. *v.t.* kill (human being) unlawfully and intentionally. **mur'derer,** *n.* **mur'deress,** *n.fem.* **mur'derous,** *a.*

mur'ky, *a.* dark, gloomy; (of darkness, atmosphere) thick, dense.

mur'mur (-er), *n.* low continuous sound; subdued grumble; hushed speech. *v.* produce, say, or speak in murmur; grumble.

mus'cat, *n.* kind of grape. **muscatel'**, *n.* muscat; kind of raisin or strong sweet wine made from muscats.

mu'scle (-sl), *n.* fibrous band or bundle in animal body that can be contracted or extended to produce movement. **mus'cūlar**, *a.* of, in, the muscles; having well-developed muscles. **musculā'rity**, *n.*

mūse¹ (-z), *v.i.* ponder; meditate.

Mūse² (-z), *n.* (Gk. myth.) one of nine sister goddesses presiding over arts and sciences; poet's inspiration or genius.

mūsē'um (-z-), *n.* building or place where objects illustrating antiquities, the arts, science, etc., are exhibited. **museum-piece**, object fit for museum; something very old-fashioned.

mush, *n.* soft pulp; (U.S.) maize porridge. **mush'y**, *a.* soft; (*slang*) weakly sentimental.

mush'room, *n.* edible fungus noted for rapidity of growth. *v.i.* gather mushrooms; spread or grow rapidly.

mū'sic (-z-), *n.* art of combining sounds for reproduction by voice or instrument(s) in rhythmic, melodic, and harmonic form; sounds so produced; score of these; any pleasant sound. **music-hall**, variety theatre. **mū'sical**, *a.* of, fond of, skilled in, set to, music; sweet-sounding. *n.* play, film, etc., of which (esp. light) music is essential part. **mūsi'cian** (-shn), *n.* person skilled in music. **mūsi'cianship**, *n.*

musk, *n.* substance obtained from male musk-deer and used as basis of perfumes. **musk-deer**, small hornless ruminant of Central Asia. **musk-ox**, shaggy-coated ruminant of Arctic America. **musk-rat**, large N. Amer. aquatic rodent. **musk-rose**, rose with fragrant white flowers. **mus'ky**, *a.*

mus'kėt, *n.* (Hist.) infantry soldier's hand-gun. **muskėteer'**, *n.* (Hist.) soldier armed with musket. **mus'kėtry**, *n.* (instruction in) rifle-shooting.

Mus'lim (moos-; *or* -z-), **Mos'lem** (*or* -z-), *n.* one who believes in or professes the religion of Islam. *a.* of Muslims.

mus'lin (-z-), *n.* fine gauzy cotton fabric.

mus'quash (-osh), *n.* (fur of) musk-rat.

muss'el, *n.* a bivalve mollusc.

Muss'ulman, *a.* & *n.* (*pl. -mans*), Muslim.

must¹, *n.* grape-juice before or during fermentation; new wine.

must², *v.aux.* be obliged to; be certain to. *n.* something imperative.

mus'tang, *n.* small wild or half-wild horse of Mexico, California, etc.

mus'tard, *n.* (hot pungent seeds of) yellow-flowered plant; condiment made from its ground seeds.

mus'ter, *n.* assembling of men for inspection, etc. *pass muster*, be considered satisfactory. *v.* bring or come together, collect.

mus'ty, *a.* mouldy; stale.

mū'table, *a.* liable to change; fickle. **mūtabil'ity**, *n.*

mutā'tion, *n.* change; (organism arising from) change in gene structure of reproductive cell.

mūte, *a.* silent; without speech, dumb; soundless. *n.* dumb person; appliance for restricting tone of musical instrument.

mū'tilāte, *v.t.* injure, make imperfect, by removing a part. **mūtilā'tion**, *n.*

mūtineer', *n.* person who mutinies. **mū'tinous**, *a.* rebellious.

mū'tiny, *n.* open revolt against authority, esp. refusal of members of armed forces to obey orders. *v.i.* engage in mutiny.

mutt'er, *v.* speak, utter, in low tone; grumble. *n.* muttering.

mutt'on, *n.* flesh of sheep as food.

mū'tūal, *a.* felt or done by each to other; standing in the same relation to each other. **mū'tūally**, *adv.*

muzz'le, *n.* animal's snout; open end of gun-barrel; cage, etc., put over animal's snout to prevent it from biting. *v.t.* put muzzle on; force silence upon.

muzz'y, *a.* confused in mind.

mȳ, *possessive a.* of, belonging to, me.

myŏ'pia, *n.* short sight. **myŏp'ic**, *a.*

my'riad, *n.* & *a.* vast number (of).

myr'midon (mer-), *n.* faithful follower; ruthless servant, hired ruffian.

myrrh (mer), *n.* gum-resin used in medicine, perfumes, etc.

myr'tle (mer-), *n.* evergreen shrub with shiny leaves and fragrant white flowers.

mȳself', *pron.* emphatic and reflexive form of **I**.

mystēr'ious, *a.* full of, wrapped in, mystery; delighting in mystery.

mys'tery, *n.* revealed religious truth, esp. one beyond human understanding; anything obscure or inexplicable; miracle play; (pl.) secret religious rites (of ancient Greece, Rome, etc.).

mys'tic, *a.* spiritually symbolic; esoteric; enigmatical. *n.* person who claims to obtain insight into religious mysteries, esp. when in a state of spiritual ecstacy. **myst'ical**, *a.* **mys'ticism**, *n.*

mys'tifȳ, *v.t.* puzzle, bewilder. **mystificā'tion**, *n.*

mystique' (-tēk), *n.* atmosphere of mystery surrounding some doctrines, arts, etc.

myth, *n.* fictitious tale embodying (esp. ancient) popular belief or idea; fictitious person or thing. **myth'ical**, *a.*

mythol'ogy, *n.* stories of the fabulous history of the gods and heroes of antiquity; study of myths. **mytholo'gical**, *a.*

myxomatŏ'sis, *n.* infectious fatal disease of rabbits, caused by a virus.

N

nab, v.t. (p.t. *nabbed*), (*slang*) catch, arrest.

nā′bob, n. ostentatiously rich person.

nā′cre (-ker), n. mother of pearl.

nā′dir, n. point in celestial sphere opposite zenith; (fig.) lowest point.

nag¹, n. (*informal*) horse.

nag², v. (p.t. *nagged*), find fault (with) or scold persistently (*at*). **nagg′ing** (-g-), a. (esp. of pain, etc.) gnawing, persistent.

nai′ad (nī-), n. (pl. *naiads* or *naiadēs*), water nymph.

nail, n. horny growth on tip of human finger or toe; bird's or beast's claw; small, usu. pointed and broad-headed, metal spike. v.t. fasten with nail(s); secure.

nain′sook, n. fine soft cotton fabric.

naïve (nah-ēv′), a. natural and innocent in speech and behaviour, unsophisticated. **naïve′té** (-vtā), **naïv′ěty,** n.

nā′kėd, a. unclothed, nude; defenceless; bare, uncovered; plain; (of flame, etc.) unprotected; (of eye) unaided.

nam′by-pam′by, a. feebly sentimental; insipid.

nāme, n. word by which individual person, animal, place, or thing is spoken of or to; family, clan; reputation, fame. v.t. give name to; appoint; mention. **nāme′sāke,** n. person or thing of same name. **nāme′less,** a. obscure; left unnamed; unmentionable. **nāme′ly,** adv. that is to say.

nankeen′, n. yellowish-buff cotton cloth.

nann′y, n. child's nurse.

nann′y-goat, n. female goat.

nap¹, v.i. & n. (take) short sleep, esp. by day. *catch napping,* find asleep; catch unawares (in error, etc.).

nap², n. soft or downy surface on cloth. v.t. raise nap on (cloth).

nap³, n. card-game.

nā′palm (-ahm), n. jellied petrol for use as incendiary.

nāpe, n. back of neck.

nā′pery, n. table-linen.

naph′tha, n. inflammable oil distilled from coal, etc. **naph′thalēne,** n. white crystalline compound used for dyes, to protect clothes against moth, etc.

nap′kin, n. piece of linen, etc., for wiping lips, etc., at table; piece of folded material wrapped round waist and between legs of baby.

narciss′ism, n. morbid self-love or self-admiration. **narciss′ist,** n. **narcissis′tic,** a.

narciss′us, n. (pl. *narcissuses, narcissi*), kind of flowering bulbous plant.

narcō′sis, n. unconsciousness induced by narcotic drug(s).

narcot′ic, a. inducing drowsiness, sleep, stupor, or insensibility. n. narcotic drug.

narrāte′ (na-r-), v.t. give continuous account of, recount, relate. **narrā′tion,** n. **narrā′tor,** n. **na′rrative,** n. spoken or written recital of connected events. a. of, in, by, narration.

na′rrow (-ō), a. of small width in proportion to length; restricted; with little margin; intolerant, prejudiced. n. (usu. pl.) narrow part of river, strait, etc. v. make or become narrower; lessen, contract. **na′rrow-mīnd′ed,** a. **na′rrowly,** adv. (esp.) closely.

nā′sal (-z-), a. of nose; sounded through nose. **nā′salīze,** v.t. utter with nasal sound. **nāsalīzā′tion,** n.

nā′scent (-snt), a. in process of birth; just beginning to be.

nastur′tium (-shm), n. trailing plant with red, orange, or yellow flowers.

nas′ty (nah-), a. repulsively dirty; obscene; ill-natured, spiteful; unpleasant; disagreeable. **nas′tily,** adv.

nā′tal, a. of or connected with one's birth.

nātator′ial, nā′tatory (*or* na-), aa. of swimming, adapted for swimming.

nā′tion, n. people having common descent, language, history, etc.; society united under one government in political State. **nā′tionhood,** n. state or fact of being a nation.

na′tional (-shon-), a. of nation; common to or characteristic of whole nation. n. member of specified State. **national anthem,** official song or hymn of a nation. **na′tionalism,** n. patriotic feeling, etc.; policy of national independence. **na′tionalist,** n. **nationalis′tic,** a. **national′ity,** n. (esp.) status as member of nation.

na′tionalize (-shon-), v.t. (esp.) transfer (land, industry, etc.) from private ownership and control to that of State. **nationalizā′tion,** n.

nā′tive, a. inborn; by virtue or reason of

(place of) one's birth; occurring naturally; born in specified place, indigenous; of natives. *n.* native person; indigenous animal or plant.

nativ'ity, *n.* birth, esp. (*Nativity*) of Christ.

natt'y, *a.* spruce, trim.

na'tural (-cher-), *a.* of, according to, or provided by, nature; physically existing; not artificial or conventional; (Mus., of note) not flat or sharp; illegitimate. *n.* half-witted person; person naturally endowed (*for*); (Mus.) (sign ♮, indicating) natural note. **natural history,** (esp. popular or unscientific) study of animal and plant life. **natural selection,** process by which organisms most suited to environment tend to survive.

na'turalist (-cher-), *n.* student of animals or plants.

na'turalize (-cher-), *v.t.* admit (alien) to citizenship; adopt (foreign word, etc.); introduce (plant, etc.) into new environment. **naturaliza'tion,** *n.*

na'turally (-cher-), *adv.* in a natural way; by nature; of course.

na'ture (-cher), *n.* thing's essential qualities; person's innate character; kind, sort, class; (physical power causing) phenomena of material world. *state of nature,* uncultured, uncultivated, or undomesticated state, nakedness.

naught (nawt), *n.* nothing.

naught'y (nawt-), *a.* badly behaved; disobedient.

nau'sea (*or* -z-), *n.* feeling of sickness; feeling of disgust. **nau'seate,** *v.t.* affect with nausea.

nau'seous, *a.* causing nausea; nasty; disgusting, loathsome.

nau'tical, *a.* of sailors or navigation; maritime. **nautical mile,** 6,080 ft.

na'val, *a.* of navy; of ships, esp. warships.

nave, *n.* body of church apart from chancel and aisles.

na'vel, *n.* depression on belly left by severance of umbilical cord.

nav'igable, *a.* that can give passage to ships; (of ship, etc.) that can be navigated.

nav'igate, *v.* control or direct course of (ship, aircraft, etc.); sail over, on, through, (sea, river, etc.). **naviga'tion,** *n.* (esp.) methods of determining position and course of ship, aircraft, etc. **nav'igator,** *n.*

navv'y, *n.* labourer excavating for canals, roads, etc.

na'vy, *n.* warships with their crews and organization; officers and men of navy; fleet.

nay, *adv.* no (*archaic*); or rather, and even. *n.* refusal.

Nazi (nah'tsi), *n. & a.* (Hist.) (member) of German National Socialist Party.

neap(-tide), *n.* tide with high-water level at its lowest.

Neapol'itan, *a. & n.* (inhabitant) of Naples. **Neapolitan ice,** ice-cream in layers of various colours and flavours.

near, *adv.* in(to) proximity in space or time; nearly; closely. *prep.* near to in space, time, condition, or semblance. *a.* closely related; close (to); (of way) direct, short; with little difference; left-hand. *v.* draw near (to).

near-sighted, short-sighted. **near'ly,** *adv.* almost; closely.

neat[1], *n.* (*archaic*) ox, cow; cattle. **neat'herd,** cowherd.

neat[2], *a.* nicely made or proportioned; tidy, methodical; cleverly done, phrased, etc.; deft, dextrous; (of liquor, esp. alcoholic) undiluted.

neb'ula, *n.* (pl. *nebulae*), cloudy luminous patch in night-sky. **neb'ular,** *a.*

neb'ulous, *a.* cloud-like; hazy, vague. **nebulos'ity,** *n.*

ne'cessary, *a.* indispensable; that must be done; inevitable. *n.* thing without which life cannot be maintained; desirable thing not regarded as luxury.

necess'itate, *v.t.* make necessary; involve as condition, result, etc.

necess'itous, *a.* poor, needy.

necess'ity, *n.* constraint or compulsion regarded as law governing (all) human action; imperative need (*for*); indispensable thing; want, poverty.

neck, *n.* part of body connecting head with shoulders; contracted or narrow part of anything between wider parts. *neck-and-neck,* (of race, etc.) close. **neck'lace,** ornament round neck. **neck'tie,** band of material placed round neck and tied in front. **neck'let,** *n.* ornament, small fur, etc., worn round neck.

nec'romancy, *n.* pretended art of predicting future by means of communication with the dead; magic, sorcery. **nec'romancer,** *n.*

necrop'olis, *n.* cemetery.

nec'tar, *n.* (Gk. Myth.) drink of the gods; sweet fluid yielded by plants. **nec'tary,** *n.* plant's nectar-secreting organ.

nec'tarine (*or* -ēn), *n.* kind of peach with thin smooth skin.

née (nā), *a.* (before married woman's maiden name) born (e.g. *Mrs. J. Smith, née Brown*). (French)

need, *n.* want, requirement; necessity (*of*); time of difficulty; destitution, poverty. *v.* be in need of, require; be under necessity *to* do. **need'ful,** *a.* necessary, requisite. **need'less,** *a.* unnecessary.

nee'dle, *n.* pointed slender instrument pierced with eye for thread, etc.; knitting-needle; magnetized bar of mariner's compass; indicator on dial, etc.; pointed instrument used in etching, surgery, etc.; obelisk; sharp rock, peak; leaf of fir or pine. **nee'dlewoman,** woman skilled in needlework. **nee'dlework,** sewing, embroidery, etc.

needs (-z), *adv. needs must,* of necessity.

need'y, *a.* poor; in want.

ne'er (nār), *adv.* (Poet.) never. **ne'er-do-well,**

useless or good-for-nothing person.

nefār'ious, *a.* wicked.

negā'tion, *n.* denying; negative statement, etc.; contradiction; negative or unreal thing.

neg'ative, *a.* expressing or implying denial or refusal; lacking positive attributes; opposite to positive; (Electr.) of type of electricity (opp. *positive*) carried by particles (*electrons*) that make up electric current. *n.* negative statement, word, quality, quantity, etc.; (Photog.) image with reversed lights and shadows, from which positive prints are made. *v.t.* veto; serve to disprove; contradict; neutralize.

neglect', *v.t.* leave uncared for; disregard; leave undone. *n.* neglecting or being neglected; careless treatment; negligence. **neglect'ful,** *a.*

négligé (neg'lizhā), *n.* incomplete or informal attire; woman's loose dressing-gown.

neg'ligence, *n.* lack of proper care or attention; carelessness. **neg'ligent,** *a.*

neg'ligible, *a.* so small or unimportant that it need not be considered.

negō'tiable (-shi-), *a.* that can be negotiated.

negō'tiāte (-shi-), *v.* talk together to try to reach agreement or compromise; get or give money-value for (bill, cheque); deal successfully with. **negōtiā'tion,** *n.* **negō'tiātor,** *n.*

Nē'gress, *n.* female Negro.

Nē'grō, *n.* (pl. *Negroes*), member of black-skinned African race. *a.* of this race. **nē'groid,** *a.* & *n.* (person) with some Negro characteristics.

neigh (nā), *v.i.* & *n.* (utter) cry of horse.

neighbour (nā'ber), *n.* person living next door, near, in same district, or in adjacent country; person or thing near or next another. **neigh'bourhood,** *n.* adjacent district. **neigh'bouring,** *a.* near or next. **neigh'bourly,** *a.* like good neighbour, friendly, helpful.

neith'er (n¯dh-; *or* nēdh-), *adv.* not either. *conj.* nor; nor yet. *a.* & *pron.* not the one or the other.

nem'ĕsis, *n.* just punishment for wrong-doing.

nē'o-, *pref.* new. **nēolith'ic,** *a.* of later stone age, with polished stone implements.

nēol'ogism, *n.* coining or use of new words; new word or expression.

nē'on, *n.* colourless inert atmospheric gas. *a.* of or using or characterized by bright coloured light from tube containing neon.

nē'ophȳte, *n.* new convert; religious novice; beginner, tiro.

ne'phew (-v- *or* -f-), *n.* brother's or sister's son.

nep'otism, *n.* favouritism to relatives, esp. in conferring offices, etc.

Nep'tūne, *n.* (Rom. myth.) god of the sea; a planet.

nerve, *n.* fibre or bundle of fibres conveying impulses of sensation and motion between brain or spinal cord, and some part of the body; coolness in danger; self-assurance; boldness; (pl.) exaggerated sensitiveness, nervousness. *v.t.* give strength or courage to.

nerve'less (-vl-), *a.* lacking vigour or spirit.

ner'vous, *a.* of the nerves; excitable, highly strung; agitated, tense; timid. **nervous breakdown,** loss of emotional and mental stability. **nervous system,** system of nerves in animal body.

ner'vy, *a.* (*informal*) nervous, apprehensive.

nes'ciĕnt, *a.* ignorant. **nes'ciĕnce,** *n.*

nest, *n.* structure or place made or chosen by bird for laying eggs and sheltering young; breeding-place or lair; snug retreat; shelter, bed, haunt; number of like things fitting one inside the other. *v.i.* make or have nest. **nest-egg,** money saved up as reserve. **nes'tling** (-sl-), *n.* bird too young to leave nest.

nes'tle (-sl), *v.* settle oneself, be settled, comfortably; press close to.

net¹, *n.* openwork fabric of cord, thread, wire, etc.; piece of this used for catching fish, etc., or for covering, dividing, protecting, etc. *v.* (p.t. *netted*), cover, confine, catch, with net; make net.

net², **nett,** *a.* free from deduction; remaining after necessary deductions. *net price,* price off which discount is not allowed. *net profit,* profit left after expenses are deducted. *net weight,* weight of contents only. *v.t.* (p.t. *netted*), yield (sum) as net profit.

net'ball, *n.* team game in which ball is thrown so as to fall through net hanging from horizontal ring on tall post.

neth'er (-dh-), *a.* lower. **neth'ermōst,** *a.*

nett: see **net².**

nett'ing, *n.* fabric of netted string, etc.

nett'le, *n.* plant having stinging hairs on leaves, etc. *v.t.* irritate, provoke. **nett'le-rash,** skin eruption like that caused by nettle-stings.

net'work (-werk), *n.* arrangement or pattern of intersecting lines; complex system *of;* system of interlinked radio, etc., stations.

neural'gia (nūr-; -ja), *n.* pain in nerves, esp. of face and head.

neurasthē'nia (nūr-), *n.* nervous debility. **neurasthen'ic,** *a.*

neurī'tis (nūr-), *n.* inflammation of nerve(s).

neurō'sis (nūr-), *n.* (pl. *neurōsēs*), nervous illness with (usu.) intense anxiety and sometimes physical symptoms. **neurot'ic,** *a.* & *n.* (person) suffering from neurosis.

neut'er (nū-), *a.* (Gram.) neither masculine nor feminine; neither male nor female. *n.* neuter word, etc.; neutered animal. *v.t.* castrate.

neut'ral (nū-), *a.* not favouring either side, impartial; neither acid nor alkaline; neither positive nor negative; vague, indeterminate. *n.* neutral State or person; position of gear mechanism in which no power is transmitted. **neutral'ity,** *n.* **neu'tralīze,** *v.t.* make neutral; counterbalance; render ineffective. **neut-**

ralīzā'tion, *n.*

neu'tron (nŭ-), *n.* neutral elementary particle of almost same mass as proton.

nev'er, *adv.* at no time, not ever; not at all. *never mind,* it does not matter, do not worry. **nevermore',** never again. **nevertheless',** notwithstanding, all the same, yet.

new, *a.* now first introduced or discovered; fresh, additional; different, changed; recent, not worn. **new-born,** just born. **new'comer,** newly arrived person. **newfang'led,** (-nggld), different from good old fashion. **new-laid,** (of eggs) recently laid. **new penny,** see **penny.** **New Testament,** part of Bible dealing with Christ and his followers. **New Year's Day,** 1st January.

new'el, *n.* centre pillar of winding stair; corner- or end-post of stair-rail.

new'ly, *adv.* recently; in a new way.

news (-z), *n.* report or account of what has recently happened; piece of information. **news'agent,** dealer in newspapers, etc. **news-flash,** brief item of (esp. broadcast) news. **news'paper,** periodical publication with news, etc. **news'print,** paper for newspapers. **news-reel,** cinema film of recent news. **news'y,** *a.* (*informal*) full of news.

newt, *n.* small amphibian with tail.

new'ton, *n.* (Phys.) unit of force.

next, *a.* nearest; immediately following or preceding. *adv.* in next place or degree, on next occasion. *prep.* in or into next place or degree to. *n.* next person or thing. **next-of-kin,** nearest relative.

nex'us, *n.* (pl. *nexuses*), bond, link; connected group or series.

nib, *n.* writing-point of pen.

nibb'le, *v.* take small bites at; bite gently or cautiously. *n.* nibbling.

nib'lick, *n.* kind of golf-club.

nice, *a.* pleasant; agreeable; good; kind, friendly, considerate; punctilious, subtle, fine. **nice'ly,** *adv.*

ni'cĕty, *n.* precision; minute distinction, unimportant detail; (pl.) minutiae. *to a nicety,* without error or misjudgement.

niche, *n.* shallow recess in wall for statue, vase, etc.; suitable place or position.

nick, *n.* notch or groove serving as mark, record, etc. *in the nick of time,* only just in time. *v.t.* make nick(s) in; (*slang*) steal.

nick'el, *n.* silver-white metallic element used esp. in alloys and as plating; (U.S.) (coin worth) five cents.

nick'nāme, *n.* name added to, or substituted for, real name. *v.t.* give nickname to.

nic'otine (-tēn), *n.* poisonous alkaloid present in tobacco.

niece, *n.* brother's or sister's daughter.

nif'ty, *a.* (*slang*) neat, smart, clever.

nigg'ard, *n.* one who gives grudgingly. **nigg'ardly,** *a.* stingy; meanly small.

nigg'er (-g-), *n.* offensive word for Negro or other dark-skinned person.

nigg'le, *v.i.* give too much time or attention to unimportant details. **nigg'ling,** *a.*

nigh (nī), *adv. & prep.* near (chiefly Poet.).

night (nīt), *n.* time from sunset to sunrise; (period of) darkness. **night-cap,** (esp.) drink before going to bed. **night-club,** club open late at night. **night'dress, night'gown,** loose garment worn by woman or girl in bed. **night'fall,** end of daylight. **night'jar,** nocturnal bird with harsh cry. **night'mare,** horrible dream. **night'shade,** see **deadly nightshade.** **night-watch,** (person or party keeping) watch by night. **night-watchman,** man employed to guard building, etc., at night. **night'ly,** *a.* happening, done, etc. in night; recurring every night. *adv.* every night.

night'ingále (n'tingg-), *n.* small bird with melodious song heard at night as well as by day.

night'y (nīt-), *n.* (*informal*) nightdress.

nil, *n.* nothing.

nim'ble, *a.* agile, swift; (of mind, etc.) quick, clever.

nim'bus, *n.* (pl. *nimbī, nimbuses*), halo; rain-cloud.

nim'iny-pim'iny, *a.* affected, prim.

nin'compōop, *n.* simpleton, ninny.

nine, *a. & n.* one more than eight (9, IX). **nine'pins,** kind of skittles.

nine'teen' (-nt-), *a. & n.* one more than eighteen (19, XIX). **nine'teenth',** *a. & n.*

nine'ty (-nt-), *a. & n.* nine times ten (90, XC). **nine'tiĕth,** *a. & n.*

ninn'y, *n.* person of weak character or mind.

ninth, *a. & adv.* next after eighth.

nip[1], *v.* (p.t. *nipped*), squeeze sharply, pinch, bite; check growth of; (*slang*) go nimbly. *nip in the bud,* stop at very beginning. *n.* pinch, sharp squeeze, bite; biting cold.

nip[2], *n.* small quantity of spirits, etc.

nipp'er, *n.* boy (*slang*); great claw of crab, etc.; (pl.) implement with jaws for gripping or cutting.

nipp'le, *n.* point of mammal's breast or udder in which mammary ducts terminate; nipple-like protuberance or projection.

nit, *n.* egg of louse or other parasite.

ni'trāte, *n.* salt of nitric acid.

ni'tre (-ter), *n.* saltpetre. **ni'tric,** *a.*

ni'trogĕn, *n.* colourless odourless gas forming largest part of atmosphere. **nitro'gĕnous,** *a.* of or containing nitrogen.

nitrogly'cerine (-ēn), *n.* violently explosive oily liquid.

ni'trous, *a.* of, like, or impregnated with nitre; of or containing nitrogen. **nitrous oxide,** colourless sweet-smelling gas used as mild anaesthetic.

nit'wit, *n.* (*slang*) fool, idiot.

nō, particle used to express negative reply to question, request, etc. *a.* not any, not one, not a. *adv.* not; by no amount, not at all. *n.* (pl. *noes*), word *no,* denial or refusal; (pl.) voters against motion. **no one,** no person.

Nō'ah (-a), *n.* Old Testament patriarch. **Noah's ark**, child's toy model of ark, with Noah, his family, and animals.

nob¹, *n.* (*slang*) head.

nob², *n.* (*slang*) member of upper classes.

nobil'ity, *n.* class of nobles; noble character or rank.

nō'ble, *a.* illustrious by rank, title, or birth; of high character or ideals; of imposing appearance. *n.* nobleman. nō'bleman, *n.* (pl. -*men*), peer.

noblesse' oblige' (-lēzh), privilege imposes responsibility. (French)

nō'body, *n.* no person; person of no importance.

noctur'nal, *a.* of, in, active in, the night.

noc'turne, *n.* musical composition suggesting romantic beauty of night; picture of night--scene.

nod, *v.* (p.t. *nodded*), incline head slightly and quickly; let head droop, be drowsy; (of flowers, etc.) dance. *n.* nodding of head, esp. in assent.

nōde, *n.* knob; swelling; (Bot.) point at which leaves spring from stem. nō'dal, *a.*

nod'ūle, *n.* small rounded lump. nod'ūlar, nod'ūlāted, *aa.*

nogg'in (-g-), *n.* small mug; small measure of liquor.

noise (-z), *n.* loud or confused sound; any sound. noise'less, *a.*

noi'some, *a.* injurious to health; nasty--smelling; offensive.

noi'sy (-z-), *a.* loud; full of or making much noise; rowdy. noi'sily, *adv.*

nō'mad, *a.* & *n.* (member of tribe) roaming from place to place for pasture. nomad'ic, *a.*

nomen'clature (*or* nō'-), *n.* system of names or naming; terminology.

nom'inal, *a.* existing in name or word only; not real or substantial; (of fee, rent, etc.) inconsiderable, very low.

nom'inăte, *v.t.* appoint, propose for election, to office. nominā'tion, *n.* nom'inător, *n.* nominee', *n.* one who is nominated.

nom'inative, *a.* & *n.* (Gram.) (case) used as subject; (word) in this case.

non-, *pref.* not. non-appear'ance, *n.* failure to appear, esp. in court of law. non-belli'-gerent, *a.* & *n.* (State) not taking active or open part in war. non-collē'giate, *a.* not belonging to college; not having collegiate system. non-com'batant, *a.* & *n.* (person, esp. member of armed forces) not taking part in fighting. non-commi'ssioned (-nd), *a.* not holding commission (esp. of Army officers below lieutenant). non-committ'al, *a.* not committing oneself to opinion, course of action, etc. non-conduc'tor, *n.* substance that does not conduct heat or electricity. non-confor'mist, *n.* & *a.* (person, esp. Protestant) refusing to conform to doctrines of established church. nonconfor'mity, *n.* non-flamm'able, *a.* non-inflammable. non--inflamm'able, *a.* not easily set on fire. non--interven'tion, *n.* (esp.) policy of not interfering in affairs of other States. non-smō'ker, *n.* person who does not smoke; railway carriage, etc., where smoking is not permitted. non-stop, *a.* not stopping, esp. at intermediate stations, etc.; *adv.* without a pause. non-ū'nion, *a.* not belonging to a trade union.

nōn'age, *n.* state of being under age of majority (see **age**).

nōnagenā̄r'ian, *n.* person between 90 and 100 years old.

nonce, *n.* for the nonce, for the present occasion only.

non'chalant (-sh-), *a.* cool, indifferent; unenthusiastic; unmoved. non'chalance, *n.*

non'dĕscript, *a.* not easily classified; not striking in any way.

none (nun), *pron.* not any (*of*); no person(s). *adv.* by no amount, not at all. *none the less*, nevertheless.

nonen'tity, *n.* non-existence; person of no importance.

nonesuch: see **nonsuch**.

nonpareil' (-rel), *a.* unrivalled, unique. *n.* unrivalled person or thing.

nonplus', *v.t.* (p.t. *nonplussed*), bring to state of perplexity.

non'sense, *n.* absurd or meaningless words or ideas. nonsen'sical, *a.*

non'such, none'such (nuns-), *n.* unrivalled person or thing; paragon.

nōō'dle¹, *n.* simpleton.

nōō'dle², *n.* (usu.pl.) strip of dough made with flour, eggs, etc., served in soups, etc.

nook, *n.* secluded corner, recess.

nōōn, *n.* twelve o'clock in the day. nōōn'day, nōōn'tīde, *nn.* midday.

nōōse, *n.* loop with running knot; snare. *v.t.* catch with or enclose in noose.

nor, *conj.* and not, neither, and no more, and not either.

Nor'dic, *a.* of tall blond racial type of N. Europe, esp. Scandinavia.

norm, *n.* standard, type.

nor'mal, *a.* conforming to standard, usual, regular, ordinary. *n.* usual state, level, etc.; normal temperature of human body (about 98·4 °F, 37 °C). nor'malcy, *n.* normal'ity, *n.* nor'malize, *v.t.* make normal.

Nor'man, *n.* native or inhabitant of Normandy. *a.* of Normans or Normandy.

Norse, *a.* of (language of) ancient Scandinavia, esp. Norway.

north, *adv.*, *n.* & *a.* (towards, at, near, blowing from) point of horizon lying to left of person facing due east; (towards, in) northern part of world, country, town, etc. north--east, north-west, regions half-way between north and east, north and west. north-easter, north-wester, north-east, north-west, wind. north-eastern, north-eastward(s), north--eastwardly, north-western, north-

-westward(s), **north-westwardly,** in or towards north-east, north-west. **north pole:** see pole². **north star,** pole-star. **north-west,** etc., see **north-east,** etc. **nor'therly** (-dh-), *a. & adv.* towards, blowing from, north or thereabouts. **north'ward,** *a., adv., & n.* **north'wards,** *adv.*

nor'thern (-dh-), *a.* living or situated in, coming from, characteristic of, north, esp. of England, Europe, or U.S.A. **northern lights,** aurora borealis. **nor'therner,** *n.* inhabitant of north.

nōse (-z), *n.* part of face or head above mouth, serving as organ of smell; sense of smell; open end of nozzle of pipe, etc.; projecting part. *v.* smell *out*; pry or search; push one's way with nose (esp. of ship). **nose-bag,** fodder-bag hung to horse's head. **nose-dive,** (make) aircraft's steep downward plunge. **nose'gay,** bunch of flowers.

nō's(e)y (-z-), *a.* (*slang*) inquisitive.

nostal'gia (-ja), *n.* homesickness; wistful or regretful remembrance of what is past. **nostal'gic,** *a.*

nos'tril, *n.* either opening in nose, admitting air to lungs, etc.

nos'trum, *n.* quack remedy, patent medicine; favourite remedy or scheme.

not, *adv.* expressing negation, refusal, or denial.

nōtabil'ity, *n.* prominent person; being notable.

nō'table, *a.* worthy of note, striking, eminent. *n.* eminent person.

nō'tary pub'lic, (pl. *notaries public*) person authorized to draw up deeds and perform other formal duties.

notā'tion, *n.* representing of numbers, quantities, musical notes, etc., by symbols; set of symbols used for this.

notch, *n.* V-shaped indentation on edge or across surface. *v.t.* make notches in; mark, record, etc., by notches.

nōte, *n.* written sign representing pitch and duration of musical sound; single tone of definite pitch made by instrument, voice, etc.; sign, characteristic; brief record of fact, etc.; comment on passage in book; short letter; banknote; distinction, eminence. *v.t.* observe, notice; set down as thing to be remembered. **note'book,** book for memoranda, etc. **note'paper,** writing-paper. **nō'ted,** *a.* celebrated, well known *for.*

nōte'worthy (-twerdhi), *a.* worthy of note or attention; remarkable.

no'thing (nu-), *n.* no thing, not anything, nought; no amount; thing of no importance. *adv.* not at all; in no way. **no'thingness,** *n.* (esp.) non-existence; what does not exist.

nō'tice, *n.* notification; heed, attention; warning of forthcoming termination of agreement (esp. between landlord and tenant, or employer and employee); review or comment in newspaper, etc. *v.t.* perceive, observe;

remark upon. **no'tice-board,** board for posting notices on. **nō'ticeable** (-sabl), *a.*

nō'tify, *v.t.* make known; announce; give notice of; inform. **nō'tifiable,** *a.* that must be notified. **nōtificā'tion,** *n.*

nō'tion, *n.* concept; idea; view, opinion.

nōtōr'ious, *a.* known and talked of; known to deserve (esp. bad) name. **nōtōrī'ĕty,** *n.*

notwithstan'ding, *prep.* in spite of. *adv.* nevertheless, still, yet.

nougat (nōō'gah), *n.* sweet made of sugar, white of egg, nuts, etc.

nought (nawt), *n.* the figure 0; nothing.

noun, *n.* (Gram.) word used as name of person, place or thing, substantive.

nou'rish (nu-), *v.t.* sustain with food; cherish (hope, feeling). **nou'rishment,** *n.* sustenance, food, nutrition.

nous, *n.* (*informal*) common sense, gumption.

nov'el¹, *n.* fictitious prose tale of considerable length. **novelette',** *n.* short romantic novel without literary merit. **nov'elist,** *n.* writer of novels.

nov'el², *a.* of new kind, strange, hitherto unknown. **nov'ĕlty,** *n.*

Nōvem'ber, *n.* eleventh month of year.

nov'ice, *n.* person received into religious order on probation before taking vows; beginner. **novi'ciate, novi'tiate** (-shi-), *n.* period of being novice; novices' quarters.

now, *adv.* at the present time; in the immediate past; *n.* this time; the present. **now'adays** (-z), *adv.* in our time; as things are now. *n.* this time, the present.

nō'where (-ār) *adv.* in, at, to, no place.

nō'wise (-z), *adv.* in no manner or degree.

no'xious (-kshus), *a.* harmful, unwholesome. **no'xiously,** *a.* **no'xiousness,** *n.*

nozz'le, *n.* vent or spout of bellows, hose-pipe, etc.

nuance (nū'ahns), *n.* delicate difference in shade of meaning, colour, etc.

nū'clēar, *a.* (esp.) of atomic nuclei, atomic. **nuclear fission,** splitting of certain large nuclei into parts, with enormous release of energy. **nuclear reactor: see reactor.**

nū'clēus, *n.* (pl. *nūclēi*) central part or thing round which others collect; kernel of aggregate or mass; central part of living cell; positively charged internal core of atom. **nūclē'ic,** *a.*

nūde, *a.* naked, unclothed. **nū'dist,** *n.* one who advocates or practises going unclothed. *a.* of nudists. **nū'dity,** *n.*

nudge, *v.t. & n.* push or touch with elbow, esp. to draw attention privately.

nū'gatory, *a.* trivial; inoperative.

nugg'ĕt (-g-), *n.* rough lump of gold, etc.

nui'sance (nūs-), *n.* source of annoyance; annoying or obnoxious act, circumstance, thing, or person.

null, *a.* not valid. *null and void,* (Law) void.

null'ify, *v.t.* cancel, annul; neutralize; make null and void. **nullificā'tion,** *n.*

null'ity, *n.* being null and void; invalidity.

numb (-m), *a.* lacking or deprived of the ability to feel or move. *v.t.* make numb. **numb'ness,** *n.*

num'ber, *n.* sum, count, total, of units, persons, things, etc.; word or symbol stating how many, numeral; numbered person or thing, esp. single issue of magazine, etc.; item. *v.t.* count; mark or distinguish with number; have or amount to specified number. **num'ber-plate,** plate bearing motor vehicle's registration number. **num'bered** (-erd), *a.* (esp.) restricted or few in number. **num'berless,** *a.* countless.

nu'merable, *a.* that can be counted.

nu'meral, *a.* of number; denoting number. *n.* word, figure(s), or letter(s) denoting number.

nu'merate, *a.* & *n.* (person) familiar with basic principles of mathematics or science. **nu'meracy,** *n.*

numerā'tion, *n.* numbering.

nu'merātor, *n.* number above line in vulgar fraction.

nume'rical, *a.* of, in, denoting, etc., number.

nu'merous, *a.* comprising many units; many.

numismat'ic (-z-), *a.* of coins or medals. **numismat'ics,** *n.* study of coins and medals. **numis'matist,** *n.*

num'skull, *n.* stupid person.

nun, *n.* woman living in convent under religious vow. **nun's veiling,** thin woollen fabric. **nunn'ery,** *n.* convent, community of nuns.

nup'tial (-shl), *a.* of marriage or wedding. **nup'tials** (-z), *n. pl.* wedding.

nurse, *n.* person trained for care of the sick; woman or girl (*nursemaid*) who has charge of child(ren); wet-nurse. *v.* act as nurse to, be nurse; suckle; cherish. **nurs(e)'ling,** *n.*

infant, esp. in relation to its nurse. **nur'sing,** *a.* & *n.* **nur'sing home,** (usu. privately run) house for care of sick, etc.

nur'sery, *n.* room assigned to children; (*day nursery*) institution taking charge of young children during day. **nursery garden,** plot of ground where young plants, vegetables, etc., are grown, esp. for sale. **nursery rhyme,** traditional verse for young children. **nursery school,** school for children under official school age.

nur'ture (-cher), *n.* bringing up, fostering, care; nourishment. *v.t.* bring up, rear.

nut, *n.* (kernel of) fruit consisting of hard shell enclosing edible kernel; piece of metal screwed on to end of bolt to secure it. *v.i.* go **nutting,** look for, gather, nuts. **nut'crackers,** instrument for cracking nuts open. **nut'shell,** hard outer covering of nut. *in a nutshell,* in fewest possible words. **nut-tree,** (esp.) hazel.

nut'meg, *n.* hard aromatic seed of E. Indian tree used as spice, etc.

nu'trient, *a.* & *n.* (thing) serving as or providing nourishment. **nu'triment,** *n.* nourishing food. **nūtri'tious** (-shus), *a.* efficient as food, nourishing. **nu'tritive,** *a.* serving as food; of nutrition.

nutt'y, *a.* (esp.) of rich mellow flavour.

nuzz'le, *v.* burrow, press, rub, or sniff with nose; nose; nestle, lie snug.

ny'lon, *n.* synthetic plastic of great strength and durability, made into fibre, textile fabric, moulded objects, etc.; (pl., esp.) stockings made of nylon.

nymph, *n.* mythological semi-divine maiden of mountains, waters, woods, etc.; immature form of some insects.

O

O, oh (ō), *int.* expressing various emotions, or prefixed to name in speaking to person.

oaf, *n.* (pl. *oafs*), awkward lout. **oaf'ish,** *a.*

oak, *n.* forest tree with hard wood, acorns, and lobed leaves; its wood. *a.* made of oak. *oak-apple,* round growth on oak caused by insect. **oak'en,** *a.* made of oak.

oak'um, *n.* fibre for caulking, obtained by picking old rope to pieces.

oar (or), *n.* long stout shaft with blade, used to row boat. **oars'man** (-z-), *n.* (pl. *-men*), rower. **oars'manship,** *n.* skill in rowing.

ōā'sis, *n.* (pl. *ōāsēs*), fertile place in desert, with water and trees, etc.

oast, *n.* kiln for drying hops. **oast-house,** building containing oast.

oat, *n.* (pl.) (grain of) cereal grown as food for man and horses. **oat-cake,** thin unleavened cake of oatmeal. **oat'meal,** oats ground to meal. **oat'en,** *a.* made of oats (chiefly Poet.).

oath, *n.* (pl. pr. ōdhz), appeal to God, etc., in witness of truth of statement, binding character of promise, etc.; profanity.

ob-, *pref.* (becoming *oc-* before *c*, *of-* before *f*, *op-* before *p*), expressing openness, meeting, opposition or hostility, hindrance, completeness, or (in modern scientific words) inversion, contrary direction.

obbliga'tŏ (-gah-), *a.* & *n.* (Mus.) (part, accompaniment) forming essential part of composition.

ob'dūrate, *a.* stubborn. **ob'dūracy**, *n.*

obē'diénce, *n.* obeying; submission; complying.

obē'diént, *a.* doing what one is told to do; submissive, dutiful.

obei'sance (-bā-), *n.* gesture expressing submission, respect, etc.; homage.

ob'ĕlisk, *n.* tall tapering stone pillar of square or rectangular section.

obēse', *a.* fat, corpulent. **obē'sity**, *n.*

obey' (-bā), *v.* perform the bidding of, be obedient (to); carry out (command).

obit'ūary, *n.* notice of death; brief biography of person who has died. *a.* recording death; concerning deceased person.

ob'ject, *n.* material thing; person or thing to which action or feeling is directed; (Gram.) word governed by transitive verb or preposition. **object'**, *v.* announce opposition (to); feel dislike or reluctance (to); give as reason against. **objec'tor**, *n.*

objec'tion, *n.* objecting; adverse reason or statement; expression of disapproval or dislike. **objec'tionable**, *a.* disagreeable, offensive.

objec'tive, *a.* external to the mind; actually existing; dealing with outward things, not thoughts or feelings; (Gram.) constructed as, or appropriate to, object. *n.* objective case; object or purpose aimed at. **objec'tivism**, *n.* **objectiv'ity**, *n.*

objurgā'tion, *n.* chiding, scolding.

oblā'tion, *n.* thing offered to God; pious donation. **oblā'tional**, *a.*

obligā'tion, *n.* binding agreement, esp. written contract or bond; duty; indebtedness for service or benefit. **oblig'atory**, *a.* binding; not optional.

oblīge', *v.t.* constrain, compel, require; be binding on; confer favour on; (pass.) be bound (*to*) by gratitude. **oblī'ging**, *a.* ready to help others; accommodating.

oblique' (-lēk), *a.* slanting; diverging from straight line or course; inclined at other than a right angle, greater or less than a right angle; indirect. **oblique'ly**, *adv.* **obli'quity**, (-ikw-), *n.*

oblit'ĕrāte, *v.t.* blot out, erase, efface. **obliterā'tion**, *n.*

obliv'ion, *n.* state of having forgotten or being forgotten. **obliv'ious**, *a.* forgetful (*of*), unaware (*of*).

ob'long, *a.* & *n.* (figure, object) greater in length than breadth; (rectangle) with adjacent sides unequal.

ob'loquy, *n.* (pl. *obloquies*), abuse, detraction; bad repute.

obno'xious (-kshus), *a.* offensive, objectionable; disliked.

ō'bŏe, *n.* double-reed wood-wind instrument of treble range, with penetrating sweet tone.

obscēne', *a.* indecent, esp. grossly or repulsively so; lewd; abominable, disgusting; (Law, of publications, etc.) tending to deprave and corrupt.

obscū'ran'tism, *n.* opposition to inquiry, enlightenment, and reform. **obscūran'tist**, *a.* & *n.*

obscūrā'tion, *n.* darkening, being darkened; eclipse.

obscūre', *a.* dark, indistinct; hidden, undistinguished; not clear. *v.t.* make obscure or invisible. **obscūr'ity**, *n.*

ob'sēquies (-iz), *n.pl.* funeral rites; funeral.

obsē'quious, *a.* showing excessive eagerness to serve, obey, or respect.

obser'vable (-z-), *a.* that can be seen or noticed.

obser'vance (-z-), *n.* keeping or observing (of law, occasion, etc.); rite, ceremonial act.

obser'vant (-z-), *a.* quick to notice things.

observā'tion (-z-), *n.* observing or being observed; comment, remark, statement.

obser'vatory (-z-), *n.* building for astronomical observation.

observe' (-z-), *v.* keep, follow, adhere to; perceive, watch, take notice of; say, esp. as comment. **obser'ver**, *n.* one who observes; one who keeps watch.

obsess', *v.t.* (of fear, false or fixed idea, etc.) fill mind of, continually distress. **obse'ssion** (-shn), *n.* **obse'ssional, obsess'ive**, *aa.*

obsoles'cent, *a.* becoming obsolete. **obsoles'cence**, *n.*

ob'solēte, *a.* no longer used; out of date.

ob'stacle, *n.* hindrance; something that stands in the way.

obstet'ric, obstet'rical, *aa.* of childbirth or midwifery. **obstet'rics**, *n.* childbirth studied as branch of medicine.

ob'stinate, *a.* resisting argument or persuasion; not easily overcome. **ob'stinacy**, *n.*

obstrep'erous, *a.* unruly; noisily resisting control.

obstruct', *v.* block up; make impassable or difficult to pass; slow up or stop progress of.

obstruc'tion, *n.* obstructing, being obstructed; obstacle. **obstruc'tionism**, *n.* **obstruc'tionist**, *n.* & *a.*

obstruc'tive, *a.* causing or designed to cause obstruction.

obtain', *v.* acquire; get; be prevalent or established. **obtain'able**, *a.*

obtrude' (-ōōd), *v.* push or thrust forward. **obtru'sion** (-ōōzhn), *n.* **obtru'sive**, *a.*

obtūse', *a.* blunt, not sharp or pointed; greater than one right angle (90°) and less than two (180°); dull.

ob'verse, *n.* side of coin or medal that bears the head or principal design; front or top side; counterpart or complement of statement, etc.

ob'viăte, *v.t.* clear away, get rid of (difficulty, danger, etc.); prevent.

ob'vious, *a.* seen or realized at first glance; evident. **ob'viously,** *adv.*

oc-, *pref.*: see **ob-.**

ocari'na (-rē-), *n.* small egg-shaped musical wind-instrument with finger-holes.

occā'sion (-zhn), *n.* (time marked by) particular occurrence; suitable time, opportunity; reason. *v.t.* be occasion or cause of. **occā'sional,** *a.* not regular or frequent; made or meant for special occasion, purpose, etc. **occā'sionally,** *adv.* sometimes.

Oc'cident (oks-), *n. the Occident,* the West. **occiden'tal,** *a.*

occlude' (-ōōd), *v.t.* close, obstruct; (Chem.) absorb (gases). **occlu'sion** (-ōōzhn), *n.*

occult', *a.* kept secret; mysterious; mystical, magical; hidden.

occ'ŭpant, *n.* person holding property or office; one who resides or is in a place. **occ'ŭpancy,** *n.*

occŭpā'tion, *n.* (period of) occupying or being occupied; calling or employment. **occŭpā'tional,** *a.* (esp.) arising from or connected with one's occupation. **occupational therapy,** treatment of patients by encouraging them to work at handicrafts, etc.

occ'ŭpier, *n.* occupant of land, house, etc.

occ'ŭpў, *v.t.* take military possession of; reside in; hold (office); take up, fill (space, time, attention, the mind).

occur', *v.i.* (p.t. *occurred*), be met with or found in some place or conditions; come about, present itself, happen; come into one's mind. **occu'rrence,** *n.* happening; incident.

ocean (ō'shn), *n.* (one of main divisions of) great body of water surrounding land of the earth; the sea; immense expanse or quantity. **ōcĕan'ic** (*or* -shi-), *a.* **ōceanog'rapher,** **ōceanog'raphy** (ōshn-), *nn.*

o'cĕlot, *n.* S. Amer. feline mammal resembling leopard.

ochre (ō'ker), *n.* mineral used as pigment; (esp.) pale brownish-yellow colour.

o'clock', *adv.* by the clock.

oct-, *pref.*: see **octo.**

octa-, *pref.* eight.

oc'tagon, *n.* plane figure with eight angles and sides; octagonal building. **octag'onal,** *a.* eight-sided.

oc'tave, *n.* (Mus.) note eight diatonic degrees above or below a given note (both notes being counted); interval between them.

octā'vō, *n.* (pl. *octavos*), (size of) book with sheets of paper folded into eight leaves or sixteen pages.

octet(te)', *n.* (musical composition for) eight singers or players; group of eight.

octo-, oct-, *pref.* (*oct-* before vowel), eight.

Octō'ber, *n.* tenth month of year.

octogĕnār'ian, *a.* & *n.* (person) between 80 and 90 years old.

oc'topus, *n.* (pl. *octopuses*), marine cephalopod with eight 'arms', provided with suckers, surrounding mouth.

octosyll'able, *n.* metrical line of eight syllables. **octosyllab'ic,** *a.*

oc'ŭlar, *a.* of, for, by, with, the eyes or sight, visual. **oc'ŭlist,** *n.* specialist in diseases and defects of the eye.

odd, *a.* not even, not divisible by two; additional; casual; extraordinary, strange. **odd jobs,** casual unconnected pieces of work. **odd'ly,** *adv.* **odd'ness,** *n.*

odd'ity, *n.* strangeness, oddness; peculiar trait; peculiar person or thing.

odd'ment, *n.* remnant, stray fragment.

odds (-z), *n.pl.* difference; variance, strife; ratio between amounts staked by parties to a bet; chances in favour of some result. **odds and ends,** small articles, bits and pieces, of various sorts.

ōde, *n.* lyric poem of exalted style and tone.

ō'dious, *a.* hateful, repulsive.

ō'dium, *n.* general dislike or disapproval.

odontol'ogy, *n.* scientific study of teeth.

ōdorif'erous, *a.* diffusing (usu. pleasant) odours.

ō'dour (-der), *n.* pleasant or unpleasant smell; fragrance. **ō'dorous,** *a.*

od'yssey, *n.* (account of) long adventurous journey.

oecumenical: see **ecumenical.**

o'er (or), *adv.* & *prep.* (Poet.) over.

oesoph'agus (ēs-), *n.* canal leading from mouth to stomach, gullet.

oes'trus (ēs-), *n.* period of sexual activity in most female mammals.

of (ov), *prep.* from; concerning; out of; among; relating to.

of-, *pref.*: see **ob-.**

off, *adv.* away, at or to a distance; out of position; loose, separate, gone; discontinued, stopped. *prep.* from; no longer upon. *a.* further; far; (of horses, vehicles, etc.) on the right. **off and on,** occasionally, intermittently. **off-hand,** casual, curt; without preparation. **off-peak,** not at or of (time of) greatest use, intensity, etc. **off'scourings,** worthless part, dregs. **off shore,** a short way out to sea. **off-shore,** (*a.*). **offside',** (Footb., etc., of player) in position where he may not kick, handle, or hit ball.

off-, *pref.* off.

off'al, *n.* waste stuff, refuse; animal's liver, heart, kidneys, etc., as food; carrion.

offence', *n.* illegal act, misdeed, sin; aggressive action; wounded feeling, resentment; wounding of feelings.

offend', *v.* do wrong, transgress; hurt feelings of; outrage. **offen'der,** *n.*

offen'sive, *a.* aggressive; causing offence to mind or senses; disgusting, repulsive. *n.* attack.

off'er, *v.* hold out, put forward, for acceptance or refusal; present as sacrifice; express readiness or show intention (*to* do); present itself, occur; attempt. *n.* expression of readiness to do or give or sell; proposal, esp. of marriage; bid. **off'ering,** *n.* thing offered or presented. **off'ertory,** *n.* collection of money at religious service.

off'ice, *n.* room or building used as place of business or for administrative or clerical work; duty, task, function; tenure of official position; authorized form of worship; (pl.) kitchen, bathroom, etc., of house. *in office,* holding official position.

off'icer, *n.* holder of public, civil, or church office; holder of authority in armed services, merchant navy, etc., esp. one with commission in armed forces; president, treasurer, etc., of society, etc.

offi'cial (-shl), *a.* of office or its tenure; holding office; properly authorized. *n.* person holding public office or engaged in official duties. **offi'cialdom,** *n.* officials collectively; official routine. **offi'cialism,** *n.* (excessive) official routine. **officialēse'** (-z), *n.* language of official documents.

offi'ciāte (-shi-), *v.i.* perform, celebrate, religious service or ceremony; act in official capacity.

offi'cious (-shus), *a.* too ready or eager to help, etc., meddlesome.

off'ing, *n.* part of visible sea distant from shore. *in the offing,* at hand, ready or likely to happen, etc.

off'set, *n.* short prostrate side-shoot of plant, rooting and becoming new plant; counterbalance, compensation; method of printing by transferring ink from plate, etc., to rubber roller and thence to paper. *v.t.* (p.t. *offset*), set off; counterbalance, compensate for.

off'shoot, *n.* side shoot or branch.

off'spring, *n.* (pl. same), child(ren) or young; progeny, issue.

oft, *adv.* (Poet.) often. **oft-times,** *adv.* (*archaic*) often.

often (o'fn), *adv.* many times; in a large proportion of instances; at short intervals.

ō'gle, *v.* look amorously (at), make eyes (at). *n.* amorous glance.

ō'gre (-ger), *n.* (in folklore and fairy-tales) man-eating giant.

oh: see **O.**

ohm (ōm), *n.* unit of electrical resistance.

oil, *n.* one of group of smooth, often thick, liquid substances of vegetable, animal, or mineral origin; oil-colour (usu. pl.). *v.t.* apply oil to, lubricate; treat with oil. **oil-cake,** compressed linseed, etc., as cattle-food or manure. **oil-colour,** paint or pigment ground in oil. **oil-field,** tract of oil-bearing strata. **oil-painting,** use of, picture in, oil-colours. **oil rig,** rig for drilling in search of oil. **oil'skin,** cloth waterproofed with oil; garment or (pl.) suit of it. **oil-well,**

well yielding mineral oil. **oil'y,** *a.* of, like, covered, or soaked with, oil; (of manner or speech) smooth, unctuous.

oint'ment, *n.* soft oily preparation used to heal or beautify the skin.

O.K. (ō kā), *a.* **ōkay',** *a. & adv.* all right. *n.* approval, sanction. *v.t.* sanction.

ōld, *a.* advanced in age; not young or near its beginning; dating from far back; long-established; former. *of old,* of old time, long since. **old age,** latter part of life. **old country,** mother country. **old-fashioned,** antiquated, not up-to-date in tastes, ideas, etc. **old maid,** elderly spinster. **Old Testament,** part of Bible dealing with pre-christian times. **old-time,** of the past.

ōl'den, *a.* (*archaic*) old-time.

ōlēa'ginous, *a.* having properties of or producing oil; oily, greasy.

ōlèan'der, *n.* evergreen poisonous flowering shrub growing in warm regions.

olfac'tory, *a.* concerned with smelling.

ol'igarchy (-ki), *n.* government by few persons; State governed by few persons.

ol'ive, *n.* oval hard-stoned fruit yielding oil; tree bearing it; olive-colour. *a.* dull yellowish green; (of complexion, etc.) light brownish yellow. **olive-branch,** branch of olive-tree as symbol of peace. **olive oil,** clear pale-yellow non-drying oil obtained from olives.

Olym'pian, *a.* of Olympus (Greek mountain, home of the gods in Gk. myth.); (of manners, etc.) magnificent, condescending; aloof.

olym'piad, *n.* period of four years between ancient-greek Olympic Games; modern celebration of Olympic Games.

Olym'pic Gãmes (-mz), four-yearly athletic contest in ancient Greece, revived in modern times as international event.

om'budsman (-boodz-), *n.* (pl. *ombudsmen*), official appointed to investigate individuals' complaints of injustice caused by maladministration by government departments; (in U.K.) Parliamentary Commissioner.

ō'mēga, *n.* last letter of Greek alphabet; last of series, etc.

om'elèt(te) (-ml-), *n.* dish of beaten eggs cooked in butter in shallow pan.

ō'men, *n.* (thing or event regarded as) sign of good or evil to come. **om'inous,** *a.* of evil omen, threatening.

omi'ssion (-shn), *n.* (instance of) omitting or being omitted.

omit', *v.t.* (p.t. *omitted*), leave out, not include; leave undone, neglect.

omni-, *pref.* all.

om'nibus, *n.* (pl. *omnibuses*), bus. *a.* serving several purposes at once; comprising several items.

omnip'otent, *a.* having infinite power. **omnip'otence,** *n.*

omnipres'ent (-z-), *a.* present everywhere. **omnipres'ence,** *n.*

omni'sciènt, *a.* knowing everything. **omni'science,** *n.*

omniv'orous, *a.* feeding on all kinds of food; (fig.) reading anything that is available.

on, *prep.* (so as to be) supported by, covering, attached to, etc.; (so as to be) close to, in direction of; at, near; concerning, about; added to. *adv.* (so as to be) on something; in some direction, forward; in advance; in(to) movement or operation or activity. **on to, on'to** (-too), *prep.* to position on.

on-, *pref.* on.

once (wuns), *adv.* for one time or on one occasion only; at some time in the past. *at once,* without delay. *once (and) for all,* once as final act, definitively. *conj.* as soon as. *n.* one time, performance, etc.

on'coming (-n-ku-), *n.* approach. *a.* approaching.

one (wun), *a.* lowest cardinal number; single and integral; only; identical, same. *n.* number or figure 1 (I), unit, unity; single thing, person, or example. *pron.* any person; the speaker. *one another,* each other. **one-sided,** lopsided; partial, unfair. **one-track,** (of mind) fixed on one line of thought or action. **one-way,** (of street, etc.) along which traffic is permitted in one direction only. **one'ness,** *n.* singleness; singularity; agreement; sameness.

on'erous, *a.* requiring effort, burdensome.

oneself' (wun-), *pron.* emphatic and reflexive form of **one.**

onion (un'yon), *n.* edible bulb with strong smell and flavour.

on'looker, *n.* looker-on, spectator.

ŏ'nly, *a.* that is, or are, the one or all the specimen(s) of the class; sole. *adv.* solely, merely, exclusively. *conj.* but then; with the exception that.

onomatopoe'ia (-pēa), *n.* formation of words by imitation of sound(s) associated with object or action to be named (e.g. *cuckoo, hiss*). **onomatopoe'ic,** *a.*

on'rush, *n.* onward rush; rapid advance.

on'set, *n.* attack; beginning.

on'slaught (-awt), *n.* fierce attack.

onto: see **on.**

ŏ'nus, *n.* responsibility for, or burden of, doing something.

on'ward, on'wards (-z), *advv.* farther on; towards the front; with advancing motion. **on'ward,** *a.* directed onward.

on'yx, *n.* semi-precious stone with different colours in layers.

ōōze, *n.* wet mud, slime; sluggish flow; exudation. *v.* pass slowly through pores, etc.; exude; leak *out* or *away.*

op-, *pref.:* see **ob-.**

opa'city, *n.* opaqueness.

ŏ'pal, *n.* milk-white or bluish precious stone with iridescent reflections. **ōpales'cence,** *n.* changing of colour as in opal. **ōpales'cent,** *a.* **ŏ'paline,** *a.* like opal.

opāque' (-k), *a.* not allowing light to pass through; not transparent; dull.

ŏ'pen, *a.* not closed; unlocked; unconfined, uncovered; exposed, manifest; public; not exclusive; spread out; unfolded; clear; communicative, frank. *v.* make or become open; unclose, unlock; begin, make start. *n.* open space, open competition, etc. **open air,** outdoors. **open-handed,** generous, liberal. **open mind,** willingness to accept new ideas; unprejudiced or undecided state. **open question,** matter on which opinions differ. **o'penwork,** (pattern) with insterstices in material. **ŏ'pener** (-pn-), *n.* (esp.) implement for opening bottles, tins, etc.

ŏ'pening (-pn-), *n.* (esp.) gap, aperture; commencement; preliminary statement; opportunity. *a.* (esp.) initial, first.

ŏ'penly, *adv.* publicly, frankly.

op'era, *n.* (branch of art concerned with) dramatic composition or performance of which music is essential part. **opera-glass(es),** small binoculars for use in theatre, etc. **opera hat,** man's collapsible top hat. **opera house,** theatre for operas.

op'erable, *a.* (Med.) that can be treated by operation.

op'erăte, *v.* be in action, produce effect; perform or carry on operation(s); work (machine, etc.). **operating theatre,** room in hospital, etc., for surgical operations.

operat'ic, *a.* of or like opera.

opera'tion, *n.* action, working; financial transaction; piece of surgery; military action. **operā'tional,** *a.*

op'erative, *a.* in operation; practical; of surgical operations. *n.* worker, esp. in factory.

op'erător, *n.* (esp.) one who works machine, etc. (esp. telephone switchboard).

operett'a, *n.* short light opera.

ophthal'mia (of-th-), *n.* inflammation of the eye. **ophthal'mic,** *a.* of or for the eye; affected with ophthalmia. **ophthalmol'ogy,** study of (diseases of) the eye. **ophthal'moscōpe,** *n.* instrument for examining the eye.

ŏ'piate, *n.* drug for easing pain or inducing sleep. *a.* inducing drowsiness.

opīne', *v.t.* express or hold the opinion (*that*).

opin'ion (-yon), *n.* belief based on grounds which do not provide proof; what one thinks about something; professional advice. **opinion poll,** see **poll[1]. opin'ionāted,** *a.* unduly confident in one's opinion; stubborn.

ŏ'pium, *n.* drug made from poppy and used as narcotic, intoxicant, etc.

oposs'um, *n.* small Amer. marsupial; possum.

oppo'nent, *n.* person against whom one fights, plays game, argues, etc.; one who opposes.

opp'ortūne, *a.* (of time) suitable, favourable, well-selected; done, coming, at favourable time. **opp'ortūnism,** *n.* adaptation of policy or method to circumstances; acting in accordance with self-interest, not principles. **opp'ortūnist,** *n.*

opportū'nity, *n.* favourable juncture, good chance, opening.

oppōse' (-z), *v.t.* place in opposition or contrast (*to*); set oneself against; resist. **oppōs'able,** *a.* (of digit, esp. thumb) that can be moved so as to meet another digit.

opp'osite (-z-), *a.* facing, front to front or back to back with; diametrically different; *the opposite,* the other (of contrasted pair). *n.* opposite thing or term. *adv.* in opposite position or direction. *prep.* opposite to. **opposite number,** person in corresponding position in another set, etc.

opposi'tion (-z-), *n.* antagonism, resistance; (chief) political party opposed to that in office; contrast; diametrically opposite position. *a.* (esp.) of Parliamentary opposition.

oppress', *v.t.* govern tyrannically; treat with cruelty or injustice; weigh down. **oppre'ssion** (-shn), *n.* **oppress'or,** *n.* **oppress'ive,** *a.* oppressing; (of weather, etc.) sultry, close.

opprō'brious, *a.* abusive, vituperative; infamous, disgraceful. **opprō'brium,** *n.* disgrace, infamy; expression of this.

op'tative (*or* optā'-), *a. & n.* (Gram.) (mood) expressing wish.

op'tic, *a.* of eye or sight. **op'tical,** *a.* visual; aiding sight; of optics. **opti'cian** (-shn), *n.* maker or seller of optical instruments, esp. eye-glasses. **op'tics,** *n.* science of sight and of properties of light.

op'timism, *n.* belief that all will come right; habitually hopeful disposition. **op'timist,** *n.* **optimis'tic,** *a.*

op'timum, *n.* most favourable conditions; best amount. *a.* best.

op'tion, *n.* choice, choosing; thing that is or may be chosen; right to choose. **op'tional,** *a.* depending on choice or preference; not obligatory.

op'ülent, *a.* rich, wealthy; abundant. **op'ülence,** *n.*

or, *conj.* introducing second of two alternatives.

o'racle, *n.* place at which ancient Greeks consulted gods for advice or prophecy; response received there; divine revelation; person or thing serving as infallible guide. **orac'ūlar,** *a.* (esp.) dogmatic; obscure in meaning.

or'al, *a.* spoken, verbal; of, by, or for the mouth. *n.* spoken examination. **or'ally,** *adv.*

o'range (-rinj), *n.* globular reddish-yellow citrous fruit, tree bearing it; its colour. *a.* orange-coloured. **orange-stick,** small stick of orange-wood for manicuring nails. **orangeâde',** *n.* drink made from or flavoured like oranges. **o'rangery,** *n.* (part of) building for protection of orange trees.

O'range (-rinj), *n.* (*attrib. & as pref.*) of Irish ultra-protestant party.

o'rang-u'tan (-ōōt-), **orang'-outang'** (-oot-),

n. large long-armed anthropoid ape.

orā'tion, *n.* speech, esp. of ceremonial kind.

o'rator, *n.* maker of speech; eloquent public speaker.

orator'iŏ (o-r-), *n.* (pl. *oratorios*), musical composition for chorus, soloists, and orchestra, etc., usu. on sacred theme.

o'ratory[1], *n.* (art of making) speeches; rhetoric; eloquent language. **orato'rical,** *a.*

o'ratory[2], *n.* small chapel.

orb, *n.* sphere, globe; globe surmounted by cross as part of regalia.

or'bit, *n.* curved course of planet, comet, satellite, etc., complete circuit of this; range, sphere; eye-socket. *in orbit,* travelling in an orbit round (esp. earth). *v.* (cause to) travel in orbit (round). **or'bital,** *a.*

or'chard, *n.* piece of ground, usu. enclosed, for cultivation of fruit-trees.

or'chestra (-k-), *n.* body of instrumental players, combination of stringed, wind, and percussion instruments; place in theatre, etc., for orchestra. **orches'tral,** *a.* **or'chestrāte,** *v.t.* arrange or score for orchestra. **orchestrā'tion,** *n.*

or'chid (-k-), *n.* (flower of) any of various plants, some having brilliantly coloured or grotesquely shaped flowers. **orchidā'ceous** (-shus), *a.*

or'chis (-k-), *n.* (esp. wild) orchid.

ordain', *v.t.* appoint or admit ceremonially to Christian ministry; destine; decree.

ordeal' (*or* or'-), *n.* trying experience, severe test of character or endurance.

or'der, *n.* manner in which things are placed or events occur in relation to one another; tidiness; efficient state; law-abiding state; authoritative direction or instruction; social class or rank; grade of Christian ministry; religious fraternity; company to which distinguished persons are admitted as honour or reward; (Biol.) classificatory group. *in order to do,* for the purpose of doing. *v.t.* put in order; ordain; command, prescribe; direct tradesman, etc., to supply.

or'derly, *a.* methodically arranged; tidy; not unruly; (Mil.) of or for orders or administrative business. *n.* soldier in attendance on officer; hospital attendant.

or'dinal, *a.* of or defining place in series. *n.* ordinal number. **ordinal numbers,** first, second, third, etc.

or'dinance, *n.* authoritative command; religious rite.

or'dinand, *n.* candidate for ordination.

or'dinary, *a.* normal; not exceptional; commonplace; usual, customary. *n.* ordinary condition, course, etc. **or'dinarily,** *adv.*

ordinā'tion, *n.* ordaining or being ordained.

ord'nance, *n.* mounted guns; department for military stores, etc. **ordnance survey,** official survey (for construction of maps) of U.K.

or'dūre (*or*-dyer), *n.* excreme it; filth.

ore, *n.* mineral yielding metal.

or'gan, *n.* musical instrument from which sounds are produced by air forced through pipes, played by keys and pedals; part of body serving some vital function; voice; medium of opinion, esp. newspaper. organ- -builder, maker of organs. organ-grinder, player of barrel-organ. organ-stop, (device bringing into action) set of organ-pipes of similar tone-quality.

organ'die (*or* or'-), *n.* fine stiffish muslin.

organ'ic, *a.* of or affecting bodily organ(s); structural; organized; produced by, or occurring naturally in, organisms; (Chem.) containing carbon.

or'ganism, *n.* living animal or plant; anything capable of growth and reproduction; whole with interdependent parts.

or'ganist, *n.* player of organ.

organīzā'tion, *n.* (esp.) organized body or system.

or'ganize, *v.* give orderly structure to; bring into working order; make arrangements for. or'ganizer, *n.*

or'gasm (-z-), *n.* climax of sexual excitement.

or'gy (-ji), *n.* drunken or licentious revel; revelry, excessive indulgence. orgias'tic, *a.*

or'iel, *n.* projecting part of upper storey containing window; (also *oriel window*) such window.

Or'iènt, *n.* the East. or'iènt, *a.* (of sun, etc.) rising; oriental. *v.t.* orientate.

orien'tal (ori-en-), *a.* of Eastern or Asian world or its civilization. *n.* native of East. orien'talist, *n.* expert in oriental languages, cultures, etc.

or'iëntāte, *v.t.* settle or find (compass) bearings of; (place so as to) face east. *orientate oneself*, take one's bearings, become accustomed to new situation.

orienteer'ing, *n.* (competitive sport of) finding one's way across country, esp. on foot, with aid of map(s) and compass.

o'rifice, *n.* mouth of cavity, aperture.

o'rigin, *n.* beginning or rising from something; source; extraction; starting-point.

ori'ginal (o-r-), *a.* existent from the first; primitive; earliest; not imitative or derived; creative, inventive. *n.* thing from which another is copied; archetype; eccentric person. ori'ginally, *adv.* original'ity, *n.*

ori'ginăte, *v.* give origin to, cause to arise or begin; spring, be derived, (*from, in, with*). originā'tion, *n.* ori'ginător, *n.*

or'iōle, *n.* (esp.) *golden oriole*, migratory bird.

o'rison (-zn), *n.* (*archaic*) prayer.

or'molu (-lōō), *n.* gilded bronze; gold- -coloured alloy; articles made of or decorated with these.

or'nament, *n.* thing that adds beauty to something; person whose presence confers grace or honour; decorative work. ornament', *v.t.* adorn, beautify. ornamen'tal, *a.* ornamen-
tā'tion, *n.*

ornāte', *a.* elaborately adorned.

ornithol'ogy, *n.* scientific study of birds. ornitholo'gical, *a.* ornithol'ogist, *n.*

or'phan, *n.* & *a.* (child) who has lost parent(s) through death. *v.t.* bereave of parent(s). or'phanage, *n.* institution for orphans.

o'rrery, *n.* clockwork model of the planetary system.

ortho-, *pref.* straight, right, correct.

or'thodox, *a.* holding correct or accepted views; not heretical. or'thodoxy, *n.*

orthog'raphy, *n.* (correct or conventional) spelling. orthograph'ic(al), *aa.*

orthopae'dic (-pē-), *a.* of orthopaedics. orthopae'dics, *n.* cure or treatment of abnormalities and injuries of limbs, spine, etc.

os'cillāte (osi-), *v.* swing like pendulum, move to and fro, vibrate; vacillate. oscillā'- tion, *n.* os'cillātor, *n.* os'cillātory, *a.*

os'cūlāte (oskū-), *v.* kiss. oscūlā'tion, *n.*

ō'sier (-z-; *or* -zher), *n.* (shoot of) willow used in basket-work.

os'prey, *n.* (pl. *ospreys*), large bird that preys on fish; egret plume.

oss'èous, *a.* bony, having bones.

oss'ify, *v.* turn into bone; harden; make or become rigid. ossificā'tion, *n.*

osten'sible, *a.* professed, apparent; (of reason) used to conceal real reason. osten'- sibly, *adv.*

ostentā'tion, *n.* pretentious display (of wealth, learning, etc.); showing off. osten- tā'tious (-shus), *a.*

osteo-, *pref.* bone.

ostēol'ogy, *n.* scientific study of bones.

ostēop'athy, *n.* treatment of disease by manipulation of the bones. os'tèopath, *n.* practitioner of osteopathy. ostèopath'ic, *a.*

os'tler (-sl-), *n.* (Hist.) man looking after horses at inn.

os'tracize, *v.t.* exclude from society; refuse to associate with. os'tracism, *n.*

os'trich, *n.* large flightless swift-running bird valued for its feathers.

oth'er (udh-), *a.* not the same; separate in identity, distinct in kind; alternative, additional. *every other*, each alternate. *the other day*, a few days ago. *other than*, distinct from, besides. *pron.* other person, thing, specimen, etc. *adv.* otherwise. oth'erwise (-z), *adv.* in different way, state, circumstances, or respects; or else.

ōtiōse' (*or* -shi-), *a.* not required, serving no practical purpose.

ott'er, *n.* aquatic fur-bearing fish-eating mammal.

ott'oman, *n.* (pl. *ottomans*), cushioned seat without back or arms (often a box with cushioned lid).

oubliette' (ōō-;-i-et), *n.* secret dungeon with entrance only by trapdoor above.

ought (awt), *v.aux.* expressing duty, rightness, probability, etc.

ounce, *n.* (abbrev. *oz.*) unit of weight, $\frac{1}{16}$ lb. avoirdupois, $\frac{1}{12}$ lb. troy. *fluid ounce*, measure of capacity, $\frac{1}{20}$ pint.

our (ower), *pron.* & *a.* possessive case of **we**, with absolute form **ours**.

ourself' (ower-), *pron.* I, myself (used with royal or editiorial *we*).

ourselves' (owerselvz), *pron.* emphatic and reflexive form of **we**.

ousel, ouzel (ōō'zl), *n.* *ring ousel*, bird related to blackbird, with white patch on throat.

oust, *v.t.* put out of possession; eject; seize place of.

out, *adv.* away from or not in a place or correct position, etc.; not at home; not burning; in(to) open, sight, notice, etc.; to or at an end, completely. *out of*, without; beyond; by the use of, from; because of. *out of date*, old-fashioned, obsolete, (*out-of-date*, *a.*). *out of doors*, outside house, in(to) open air. *out of the way*, inaccessible, unusual.

out-, *pref.* out of, external, not at centre, to excess, so as to defeat or excel, etc.

out'back, *n.* remote inland areas of Australia.

outbal'ance, *v.t.* outweigh.

outbid', *v.t.* (p.t. *outbade*, pr.-bad, *outbid*; p.p. *outbidden, outbid*), bid higher than.

out'board (-ord), *a.* (esp., of motor-boat) with engine, etc., attached outside at stern; (of motor) so attached.

out'break (-āk), *n.* breaking out of emotion, war, disease, fire, etc.

out'building (-bi-), *n.* building subordinate to and separate from main building; outhouse.

out'burst, *n.* bursting out, esp. of emotion in vehement words.

out'cast (-ah-), *a.* & *n.* (person) cast out from home and friends.

out'come (-kum), *n.* result, issue.

out'crop, *n.* rock, etc., emerging at surface; breaking out.

out'crȳ, *n.* clamour, uproar; public protest (*against*).

outdā'ted, *a.* made out of date (by passing of time).

outdis'tance, *v.t.* get far ahead of.

outdo' (-ōō), *v.t.* (p.t. *outdid*; p.p. *outdone*, pr. -dun), surpass, excel.

out'door (-dor), *a.* existing, done, etc., out of doors. **outdoors'** (-z), *adv.* out of doors.

out'er, *a.* farther from centre or inside; on outside. **out'ermōst**, *a.*

outfāce', *v.t.* disconcert by staring at (person); brave, defy.

out'fall (-awl), *n.* mouth of river, etc.

out'fit, *n.* all clothing, etc., required for a purpose. *v.t.* (p.t. *outfitted*), supply with outfit. **out'fitter**, *n.* supplier of equipment; retailer of men's clothes.

outflank', *v.t.* get round flank of.

out'flow (-ō), *n.* what flows out.

out'gōings (-z), *n.pl.* expenditure, outlay.

outgrow' (-ō), *v.t.* (p.t. *outgrew*; p.p. *outgrown*), grow faster or get taller than; get rid

of (habit, etc.) as one grows older; get too big for (clothes, etc.).

out'growth (-ōth), *n.* that which grows out of something; offshoot.

out'house, *n.* shed or other building near or adjoining main house.

out'ing, *n.* pleasure-trip.

outland'ish, *a.* looking or sounding foreign; unfamiliar, bizarre.

outlast' (-ah-), *v.t.* last longer than.

out'law, *n.* person deprived of protection of the law. *v.t.* declare outlaw. **out'lawry**, *n.*

out'lay, *n.* expenses.

out'lèt, *n.* means of exit; vent.

out'line, *n.* line(s) enclosing visible object; external boundary; contour; rough draft, summary. *v.t.* draw or describe in outline; mark outline of.

outlive', *v.t.* live longer than; live beyond (specified time); get over effect of.

out'look, *n.* view, prospect; what seems likely to happen.

out'lȳing, *a.* far from centre; remote.

outmanoeu'vre (-nōōver), *v.t.* overcome, get the better of, by superior strategy.

outmatch', *v.t.* be more than a match for, excel.

outmō'ded, *a.* out of date, old-fashioned.

outnum'ber, *v.t.* exceed in number.

outpāce', *v.t.* move faster than.

out'pātient (-shnt), *n.* person attending hospital for treatment but not lodged there.

out'pōst, *n.* detachment on guard at some distance from army; outlying settlement, etc.

out'pouring (-por-), *n.* lengthy verbal or literary expression of emotion.

out'put (-poot), *n.* what is produced; amount produced.

out'rāge, *n.* forcible violation of others' rights, feelings, etc.; gross offence or indignity. *v.t.* inflict outrage upon; insult; infringe violently. **outrā'geous** (-jus), *a.* excessive; violent, furious; grossly cruel, offensive, etc. **outrā'geously**, *adv.*

out'rider, *n.* mounted attendant, motor-cyclist, riding before, behind, or beside carriage, car, procession, etc.

out'rigger (-g-), *n.* iron bracket supporting rowlock beyond boat's side; long float attached by beam(s) to boat's side. **outrigger (canoe)**, canoe having such float(s).

outright' (-rīt), *adv.* completely; once for all; without reservation. **out'right**, *a.* not qualified or limited, thorough.

outrun', *v.t.* (p.t. *outran*; p.p. *outrun*), outstrip; pass limit of.

out'set, *n.* start, beginning.

outshine', *v.t.* (p.t. *outshone*), be more brilliant than.

out'side', *n.* external surface, outer parts; external appearance; position without; highest reckoning. *a.* of, on, or nearer outside. **outside'**, *adv.* on or to outside; not within. *prep.* at or to outer side of; beyond limits of.

outsī'der, *n.* non-member of circle, party, etc.; horse, competitor, thought to have little chance of winning race, etc.

out'size, *n.* & *a.* (person or thing) larger than normal or than standard size.

out'skirts, *n.pl.* outer border, fringe, of city, etc.

outspō'ken, *a.* frank, unreserved.

out'spread' (-ed), *a.* spread out.

outstand'ing, *a.* prominent, notable, conspicuous; still unsettled. **outstand'ingly**, *adv.*

outstay', *v.t.* stay longer than; stay beyond limits of.

out'stretched (-cht), *a.* stretched out, extended.

outstrip', *v.t.* (p.t. *outstripped*), pass in running, etc.; surpass.

outvōte', *v.t.* outnumber in voting; defeat by a majority of votes.

out'ward, *a.* directed towards outside; going away from home; physical; external, superficial. *adv.* outwards. **out'wardly**, *adv.* in outward appearance; on the surface. **out'wards** (-z), *adv.* in outward direction.

outweigh' (-wā), *v.t.* exceed in weight, value, importance, or influence.

outwit', *v.t.* (p.t. *outwitted*), prove too clever for, defeat by cunning.

out'work (-erk), *n.* advanced or detached part of fortress, etc.

outworn', *a.* worn out; exhausted.

ouzel: see **ousel.**

ō'val, *a.* approximately egg-shaped; having outline of egg or elongated circle. *n.* oval closed curve; thing with oval outline.

ō'vary, *n.* ovum-producing organ in female; seed-vessel in plant. **ovār'ian**, *a.*

ovā'tion, *n.* enthusiastic reception; general applause.

oven (u'vn), *n.* receptacle heated for baking or cooking in; small furnace or kiln.

ō'ver, *adv.* outward and downward from brink or erect position, etc.; above; more than; covering whole surface; from one side, end, etc., to other; from beginning to end; remaining; at an end. *n.* (Cricket) number of balls bowled from one end of pitch before change is made to other. *prep.* above; concerning; across; on or to other side, end, etc.

ōver-, *pref.* over, too, excessive, too much.

overact', *v.* act, or act part, in exaggerated way.

ō'verall (-awl), *n.* garment worn over others as protection against dirt, etc.; (pl.) protective trousers or suit. **ō'ver-all**, *a.* taking everything into account, inclusive.

ō'verarm, *a.* & *adv.* with arm raised above shoulder in bowling, etc.; with arm(s) lifted out of water in swimming.

overawe', *v.t.* restrain or repress by awe.

overbal'ance, *v.* (cause to) lose balance and fall; outweigh.

overbear' (-ār), *v.t.* (p.t. *overbore*; p.p. *over-*

borne), overcome by weight or force; repress; outweigh. **ōverbear'ing**, *a.* domineering, masterful.

ōverblown' (-ōn), *a.* (of flower) too fully open, past its prime.

ō'verboard (-bord), *adv.* from within ship into water. *throw overboard*, abandon, discard.

ōverbur'den, *v.t.* burden too much.

ō'vercast (-ah-), *a.* (of sky) covered with clouds; dark, gloomy. **ōvercast'**, *v.t.* (p.t. *overcast*), sew over raw edges of.

ōvercharge', *v.* charge too much; fill or load too heavily. **ō'vercharge**, *n.* excessive charge.

ō'vercoat, *n.* large coat worn over ordinary clothing, esp. in cold weather.

ōvercome' (-kum), *v.* (p.t. *overcame*; p.p. *overcome*), gain mastery over, conquer; be victorious. *a.* exhausted, deprived of self--possession.

ōverdo' (-dōō), *v.t.* (p.t. *overdid*; p.p. *overdone*, pr. -dun), do to excess; cook too long. *overdo it*, overtax one's strength.

ō'verdōse, *n.* excessive dose.

ō'verdraft (-ah-), *n.* overdrawing; amount by which bank account is overdrawn.

ōverdraw', *v.* (p.t. *overdrew*, pr. -ōō; p.p. *overdrawn*), draw money from bank in excess of one's credit balance.

ōverdress', *v.* dress with too much display and ornament.

ōverdūe', *a.* beyond due date or time.

ōveres'timāte, *v.t.* estimate too highly. **ōveres'timate**, *n.* too high an estimate.

ōverflow' (-ō), *v.* flow over, flood; extend beyond limits or capacity of. **ō'verflow**, *n.* what overflows or is superfluous.

ōvergrow' (-ō), *v.* (chiefly in p.p. *overgrown*), cover with growth; grow too large. **ō'vergrowth**, *n.*

ō'verhand, *a.* & *adv.* overarm.

ōverhang', *v.* (p.t. *overhung*), jut out (over); threaten. **ō'verhang**, *n.* overhanging part.

ōverhaul', *v.t.* examine thoroughly in order to ascertain condition of; overtake. **ō'verhaul**, *n.* examination for purpose of repairing, cleaning, etc.

ōverhead' (-hed), *adv.* above one's head; in sky; above. **ō'verhead**, *a.* placed overhead; (of charges, etc.) due to office expenses, etc. **ō'verheads** (-z), *n.pl.* overhead expenses.

ōverhear', *v.t.* (p.t. *overheard*, pr. -herd), hear as unperceived or unintended listener.

overjoyed' (-oid), *a.* greatly delighted.

overlā'den, *a.* too heavily loaded.

ō'verland', *adv.* by land and not by sea. **ō'verland**, *a.* entirely or partly by land.

overlap', *v.* (p.t. *overlapped*), partly cover; cover and extend beyond; partly coincide.

overlay', *v.t.* (p.t. *overlaid*), cover surface of *with* coating, etc. **ō'verlay**, *n.* thing laid over something.

overlie', *v.t.* (p.t. *overlay*; p.p. *overlain*), lie on top of; smother thus.

ōverlook', *v.t.* have view of from above; fail to see or notice; let pass without punishment; superintend.

ō'verlord, *n.* supreme lord; feudal superior.

ō'vermantel, *n.* ornamental carving, mirror, etc., over mantelpiece.

ōvermuch', *a. & adv.* too much.

ōvernight' (-nīt), *adv.* on preceding evening; through night. *a.* done, etc., overnight; for the night.

ō'verpass (-ahs), *n.* fly-over.

ōverpow'er, *v.t.* overcome with superior power, subdue; overwhelm, be too intense or violent for.

ōverprodūce', *v.t.* produce in excess of demand. **ōverproduc'tion**, *n.*

ōverrāte', *v.t.* have too high an opinion of; assess too high.

ōverreach', *v.* outwit. *overreach oneself*, strain oneself by reaching too far.

ōverride', *v.t.* (p.t. *overrode*; p.p. *overridden*), have or claim superior authority to; set aside.

ōverrule' (-ōōl), *v.t.* set aside by superior authority.

ōverrun', *v.t.* (p.t. *overran*; p.p. *overrun*), harry and destroy (enemy's country); swarm or spread over; exceed (limit).

ōverseas' (-z), **ōversea'**, *adv. & a.* across or beyond the sea.

ōversee', *v.t.* (p.t. *oversaw*; p.p. *overseen*), superintend, supervise. **ō'verseer**, *n.*

ōvershad'ow (-ō), *v.t.* cast shadow over; (fig.) be more conspicuous than, outshine.

ō'vershoe (-ōō), *n.* shoe of rubber, felt, etc., worn outside another.

ōvershōōt', *v.t.* (p.t. *overshot*), go, send missile, beyond (mark, etc.).

ō'vershot, *a.* (of wheel) turned by water falling on it from above.

ō'versight (-sīt), *n.* failure to notice; mistake due to inadvertence; supervision.

ōversleep', *v. refl. & i.* (p.t. *overslept*), miss intended time for rising by sleeping too long.

ō'verspill, *n.* (esp.) excess population of town, etc., accommodated elsewhere.

ōverstāte', *v.t.* state too strongly, exaggerate. **ōverstāte'ment**, *n.*

ōverstrain', *v.t.* damage by exertion; stretch too far. **ō'verstrain**, *n.*

ōverstrung', *a.* (of piano) with strings in sets crossing each other obliquely; (of person or nerves) intensely strained.

ō'vert (*or* overt'), *a.* done openly; unconcealed. **ō'vertly** (*or* overt'-), *adv.*

ōvertāke', *v.t.* (p.t. *overtook*; p.p. *overtaken*), catch up; draw level with and pass; (of misfortune, etc.) come suddenly upon.

ōvertax', *v.t.* make excessive demand on; burden with excessive taxes.

ōverthrow' (-ō), *v.t.* (p.t. *overthrew*; p.p. *overthrown*), cast out from power; put an end to; vanquish; knock down, demolish. **ō'verthrow**, *n.*

ō'vertīme, *adv.* beyond regular hours of work. *n.* (payment for) extra time worked.

ōvertop', *v.t.* (p.t. *overtopped*), be or become higher than; surpass.

ō'vertūre, *n.* orchestral piece beginning opera, oratorio, etc., or played as concert item; (often pl.) opening of negotiations.

ōverturn', *v.* (cause to) fall down or over; upset; overthrow.

ōverween'ing, *a.* arrogant, conceited.

ō'verweight (-wāt), *n.* excessive weight. *a.* beyond weight allowed or desirable. **ōverweight'ed**, *a.* overburdened, overloaded.

ōverwhelm', *v.t.* bury, submerge utterly; crush, bring to sudden ruin; overpower with emotion, etc. **ōverwhel'ming**, *a.* **ōverwhel'mingly**, *adv.*

ōverwind', *v.t.* (p.t. *overwound*), damage (watch, etc.) by winding too far.

ōverwork' (-erk), *v.* work too hard; weary or exhaust with work. *n.* excessive work.

ōverwrought' (-rawt), *a.* over-excited; suffering reaction from excitement; (of style, etc.) too elaborate.

ō'vīne, *a.* of or like sheep.

ovi'parous, *a.* (Zool.) producing young by means of eggs which hatch outside the body.

ōv'oid, *a.* egg-shaped.

ovūlā'tion, *n.* development and discharge of ovum from ovary.

ōv'ūle, *n.* female germ-cell of flowering plant, developing into seed when fertilized.

ōv'um, *n.* (pl. *ova*), female germ-cell of animals, capable of developing into new individual when fertilized by male sperm; egg.

owe (ō), *v.* be under obligation to (re)pay or render; be in debt to. **ow'ing**, *pred. a.* yet to be paid, due. *owing to*, caused by; because of.

owl, *n.* night-flying bird of prey. **owl'ėt**, *n.* young owl. **owl'ish**, *a.* like owl.

own (ōn), *a.* (following possessive adj. or case) in full ownership, individual, and not another's; (abs.) own property, kindred, etc. *v.* have as property, possess; acknowledge authorship or paternity of; admit as valid, true, etc. *own up*, (informal) confess. **own'er**, *n.* possessor. **own'ership**, *n.* **own'erless**, *a.*

ox, *n.* (pl. *oxen*), large ruminant quadruped; castrated male of domestic kind, used as draught animal or reared for food.

Ox'bridge, *n.* universities of Oxford and Cambridge. *a.* of Oxford or Cambridge University.

oxidation: see **oxidize**.

ox'īde, *n.* compound of oxygen with another element.

ox'idīze, *v.* (cause to) combine with oxygen; rust; cover with coating of oxide. **oxidā'tion**, *n.*

Oxō'nian, *a. & n.* (member) of Oxford University; (citizen) of Oxford.

oxy-acet'ylēne, *a.* of, using, or welding with,

mixture of oxygen and acetylene.

ox′ygen, *n.* colourless odourless gas, essential to life and to combustion, comprising about one fifth of the atmosphere. **ox′ygenāte, ox′ygenīze,** *vv.t.* supply, treat, or mix with oxygen; oxidize.

ōyez′, *int.* 'Listen!', uttered, usu. thrice, by town crier or court officer.

oy′ster, *n.* edible bivalve shell-fish.

ō′zōne, *n.* form of oxygen with pungent smell, used as bleaching agent, etc.; invigorating seaside air.

P

pāce, *n.* (space covered by) single step in walking or running; gait; rate of progression. *v.* walk, esp. with slow or regular step; measure by pacing; test speed of; set pace for. **pace-maker,** one who sets pace.

pach′yderm (-k-), *n.* large thick-skinned mammal, esp. elephant or rhinoceros. **pachyder′matous,** *a.*

pacif′ic, *a.* making or loving peace; peaceful.

pa′cifism, *n.* (support of) policy of avoiding or abolishing war. **pa′cifist,** *n.* believer in pacifism.

pa′cify, *v.t.* calm, appease; bring to state of peace or quiet. **pacificā′tion,** *n.*

pack, *n.* bundle of things wrapped or tied together for carrying; method of packing of merchandise; set; number of hounds kept for hunting or of wild animals naturally associating; set of playing-cards. *v.* put (things) together into bundle, box, bag, etc., for transport or storing; make (*up*) into parcel or package; crowd together, cram, fill. *pack off,* send away. *send packing,* dismiss quickly without formality. **pack-horse,** horse used for carrying packs. **pack-ice,** mass of large pieces of floating ice. **packing-case,** box or crate for packing goods.

pack′age, *n.* parcel; box in which goods are packed. **package tour,** inclusive holiday (esp. abroad) at fixed price.

pack′et, *n.* small package; mail-boat.

pact, *n.* binding agreement, compact.

pad, *n.* cushioning of soft stuff used to give protection, raise surface, improve shape, etc.; leg-guard in games; sheets of writing or drawing paper fastened together at edge(s); paw of fox, hare, etc.; launching pad. *v.t.* put pad(s) on or in; fill out (sentence, etc.) with superfluous words. **padd′ing,** *n.*

padd′le, *n.* short oar with broad blade at one or each end; striking-board in paddle-wheel. *v.* propel with paddle; row gently; walk with bare feet in shallow water. **paddle-wheel,** wheel with boards at right angles to circum-

ference, for propelling ship.

padd′ock, *n.* small field (usu. for horses); (Austral., N.Z.) field.

padd′y, *n.* rice that is growing or in the husk. **padd′y-field,** *n.*

pad′lock, *n.* detachable lock hanging by hinged or pivoted hoop. *v.t.* secure with padlock.

padre (pah′drā), *n.* (*informal*) chaplain, clergyman.

paeʹan (pē-), *n.* song of thanksgiving or praise; shout or song of triumph or joy.

paediat′rics, pēdiat′rics, *n.* branch of medicine concerned with diseases of children. **p(a)ediat′ric,** *a.* **p(a)ediatri′cian** (-shn), *n.* specialist in paediatrics.

pā′gan, *n.* & *a.* heathen. **pā′ganism,** *n.*

pāge¹, *n.* (also *page-boy*) boy employed as liveried servant or personal attendant.

pāge², *n.* (one side of) leaf of book, etc.

pa′geant (-jnt), *n.* spectacular performance, usu. illustrative of historical events; any brilliant show. **pa′geantry,** *n.* splendid display.

pagō′da, *n.* temple, esp. sacred tower of several storeys, in Eastern countries.

paid, *p.t.* & *p.p.* of **pay.**

pail, *n.* bucket.

pain, *n.* sensation experienced when (part of) body is injured or afflicted by certain diseases; distress of mind; (pl.) trouble taken. *v.t.* inflict pain on. **pain-killer,** substance or medicine that lessens or removes pain. **pain′ful, pain′less,** *aa.* **pains′tāking** (-z-) *a.* careful, industrious.

paint, *n.* colouring-matter prepared for applying to surface. *v.* coat or adorn with paint; portray, make pictures, in colours; (fig.) depict in words. **pain′ter¹,** *n.* **pain′ting,** *n.*

painter², *n.* rope at bow of boat for attaching it to ship, pier, etc.

pair, *n.* set of two; thing with two corresponding parts always joined; engaged or married couple; mated couple of birds, etc. *v.* arrange or unite as pair or in pairs; mate. *pair off,* form into pairs, go off in twos.

pal, *n.* (*slang*) comrade, friend.

pal′ace, *n.* official residence of sovereign, archbishop, or bishop; stately mansion.

palaeo- (palēo-; *or* pă-), *pref.* ancient. **pa-laeog′raphy,** *n.* study of ancient writing and inscriptions. **palaeolith′ic,** *a.* of earlier stone age, with primitive stone implements. **palaeontol′ogy,** *n.* study of extinct animals and plants. **palaeontol′ogist,** *n.* **palaeozō′ic,** *a.* of, containing, ancient forms of life.

palanquin′ (-kēn), *n.* covered litter used in some Eastern countries.

pal′atable, *a.* pleasant to taste; agreeable to the mind.

pal′ate, *n.* bony and fleshy structure separating cavity of mouth from that of nose; (sense of) taste, liking. **pal′atal,** *a.* of palate.

palā′tial (-shl), *a.* like palace; magnificent.

palat′inate, *n.* (Hist.) territory of count or earl ruling as king.

pala′ver (-lah-), *n.* conference; profuse or useless talk. *v.* talk profusely; cajole.

păle¹, *n.* stake, etc., as part of fence; boundary, limit.

păle², *a.* (of complexion, etc.) whitish, not ruddy; faintly coloured; faint, dim. *v.* grow or make pale. **păle′ly** (-l-li), *adv.*

pal′ette, *n.* thin board (with hole for thumb) on which artist mixes colours. **palette-knife,** knife with round-ended flexible blade.

pal′frey (pawl-), *n.* (*archaic*) horse for riding.

pal′indrŏme, *n.* word, verse, etc., that reads the same backwards as forwards (e.g. *madam*).

pā′ling, *n.* (fence of) pales.

palisāde′, *n.* fence of pales; row of pointed stakes fixed in ground as defence.

pall¹ (pawl), *n.* cloth spread over coffin, etc.; (fig.) cloak, mantle. **pall-bearer,** person helping to carry coffin at funeral.

pall² (pawl), *v.i.* become uninteresting.

pall′et, *n.* bed or mattress filled with straw; small mean bed or couch.

pall′iasse, *n.* straw mattress.

pall′iāte, *v.t.* relieve (pain, etc.) without curing; excuse, extenuate. **pall′iative,** *a.* & *n.* (thing) serving to palliate.

pall′id, *a.* pale, wan.

pall′or, *n.* paleness.

palm¹ (pahm), *n.* inner surface of hand between wrist and fingers. *v.* conceal (coin, etc.) in hand when performing trick, etc. *palm off,* impose (thing *on* person), esp. by trickery or fraud.

palm² (pahm), *n.* any of various (chiefly tropical) trees with usu. unbranched stem and crown of large leaves; (prize for) supreme excellence. **Palm Sunday,** Sunday before Easter. **palm′er,** *n.* (Hist.) pilgrim returned from Holy Land with palm branch or leaf.

palm′ist (pahm-), *n.* one practising art of telling character or fortune by examining lines, etc., on palm of hand. **palm′istry,** *n.*

palm′y (pahm-), *a.* flourishing, prosperous.

pal′pable, *a.* that can be touched or felt; readily perceived, obvious.

pal′pitāte, *v.i.* pulsate rapidly, throb; tremble. **palpitā′tion,** *n.* palpitating; (Med.) sensation of quickened beating of heart.

palsy (pawl′zi), *n.* paralysis. *cerebral palsy,* congenital condition of weakness, imperfect control of movement, and spasms.

pal′ter (pawl-), *v.i.* deal insincerely *with*; equivocate, prevaricate.

pal′try (pawl-), *a.* petty, contemptible.

pam′pas, *n.pl.* vast treeless plains of S. America. **pampas grass,** gigantic ornamental grass.

pam′per, *v.t.* spoil by over-indulgence.

pam′phlet, *n.* small unbound treatise. **pamphleteer′,** *n.* (Hist.) writer of controversial pamphlets.

pan¹, *n.* shallow vessel used in cooking, etc.; shallow receptacle or tray; pan-shaped depression or concavity. **pan′cake,** thin flat batter-cake, usu. fried. **pancake landing,** landing of aircraft without use of undercarriage.

Pan², *n.* (Gk. myth.) god of flocks and shepherds, represented with goat's horns, ears, and legs. **pan-pipe(s),** primitive musical instrument of graduated series of reeds or pipes.

pan-, *pref.* of or for all. **pan-African,** *a.* of, for, all Africans. **pan-American,** *a.* of all States of N. and S. America.

panacē′a, *n.* universal remedy.

panache′ (-ash *or* -ahsh), *n.* plume of feathers on (knight's) helmet; display, swagger.

panama′ (-ah; *or* pan′-), *n. panama* (*hat*), hat of fine pliant straw-like material.

pancake: see **pan¹.**

pan′crĕas, *n.* gland near stomach supplying secretion that aids digestion. **pancrĕat′ic,** *a.*

pan′da, *n.* raccoon-like Himalayan animal; (*giant*) *panda,* large bear-like black-and-white mammal of Tibet, etc.

pandĕmō′nium, *n.* (scene of) utter confusion and uproar.

pan′der, *v.i. pander to,* encourage, minister to (weaknesses or vices, or person in respect of these).

pāne, *n.* single sheet of glass in (division of) window.

panĕgy′ric, *n.* speech or piece of writing in praise of person, thing, or achievement.

pan′el, *n.* distinct part of surface, esp. of door or wall; (long) narrow rectangular board; list of jurors, jury; group of people for special purpose. **pan′elled** (-ld), *a.* furnished or adorned with panels. **pan′elling,** *n.*

pang, *n.* brief keen spasm of pain; sudden sharp feeling of remorse, etc.

pan′ic, *n.* sudden and excessive feeling of fright; infectious alarm. *a.* (of fear, etc.) unreasoning, excessive. *v.* (p.t. *panicked*), affect, be affected, with panic. **panic-**

-stricken, panic-struck, stricken with panic. **pan'icky,** *a.*

pann'ier, *n.* one of pair of baskets or bags slung over back of donkey, mule, etc., or back wheel of bicycle, etc.

pann'ikin, *n.* small metal drinking-cup.

pan'oply, *n.* complete suit of armour (Hist.); complete equipment, splendid array. **pan'-oplied,** *a.*

panora'ma (-rah-), *n.* (representation of) landscape, prospect, continuous series of scenes, etc., spread out before or (partly) surrounding spectator. **panoram'ic,** *a.*

pan'sy (-z-), *n.* wild or cultivated plant of violet family, with variously coloured flowers.

pant, *v.* take short quick breaths; gasp; throb; yearn. *n.* gasp; throb.

pantaloon', *n.* (in pantomime, etc.) foolish old man, esp. clown's butt; (pl., Hist.) tight trousers strapped under insteps.

pantech'nicon (-kn-), *n.* large van for transporting furniture.

pan'theism, *n.* doctrine that God is everything and everything is God; heathen worship of all gods. **pan'theist,** *n.* **panthéis'tic,** *a.*

pan'theon, *n.* temple of all the gods; building with memorials of illustrious dead.

pan'ther, *n.* leopard; (U.S.) puma.

pan'ties (-iz), *n.pl.* (*informal*) short-legged knickers.

pan'tile, *n.* curved roof-tile.

panto-, *pref.* all.

pan'tograph (-ahf), *n.* instrument for copying plan, drawing, etc., on any scale.

pan'tomime, *n.* dumb show; dramatic, usu. Christmas, entertainment based on traditional fairy-tale.

pan'try, *n.* room in which provisions, etc., are kept.

pants, *n.pl.* men's two-legged undergarment; (*informal*) knickers; (U.S.) trousers.

pap¹, (*archaic*) nipple of breast.

pap², *n.* soft or semi-liquid food.

papa' (-ah), *n.* father.

pā'pacy, *n.* position of, authority of, Pope; papal system. **pā'pal,** *a.* of Pope or his office.

pā'per, *n.* substance in form of thin flexible sheets, manufactured from fibres of wood, rags, etc.; newspaper; set of examination questions; essay. *v.t.* paste paper on (wall, etc.). **pa'perback,** book bound in paper cover. **paper-chase,** cross-country run following trail of torn paper. **paper-hanger,** one who decorates rooms with wallpaper. **paper money,** banknotes.

papier-mâché (pap'yā mah'shā), *n.* moulded paper pulp made into solid objects.

pā'pist, *n.* Roman Catholic (usu. in hostile sense). **papis'tical,** *a.*

papoōse', *n.* N. Amer. Indian young child.

pap'rika, *n.* red pepper made from dried pods of two kinds of capsicum.

papȳr'us, *n.* (pl. *papȳri*), water plant of sedge family; writing-material made by ancient Egyptians from its stem; manuscript written on this.

par, *n.* equality, equal footing; average or normal amount, degree, etc.; face value.

para-¹ *pref.* (usu. par- before vowel), beside, beyond, wrong, irregular.

para-², *pref.* protection against.

pa'rable, *n.* simple story used to teach moral or spiritual truth.

parab'ola (pa-), *n.* open plane curve formed by intersection of cone with plane parallel to its side, resembling path of object thrown into the air.

pa'rachute (-shōot), *n.* umbrella-shaped apparatus of nylon, etc., allowing person or object to descend safely from a height, esp. from an aircraft. *v.* convey or descend by parachute. **pa'rachutist,** *n.*

parāde', *n.* display, ostentation; assembly of troops for inspection, etc.; public promenade. *v.* assemble for parade; display ostentatiously; march with display.

pa'radigm (-īm), *n.* example, pattern, esp. of inflexion of word.

pa'radīse, *n.* garden of Eden; heaven; region or state of supreme bliss.

pa'radox, *n.* statement, etc., that seems self--contradictory but is possibly true. **paradox'ical,** *a.* **paradox'ically,** *adv.*

pa'raffin, *n.* inflammable oily or waxy substance obtained by distillation of petroleum, shale, etc.

pa'ragon, *n.* model of excellence; excellent person or thing.

pa'ragraph (-ahf), *n.* distinct passage in book, etc., usually marked by indentation of first line; detached item of news in newspaper.

pa'rakeet, *n.* small parrot with long pointed tail.

pa'rallel, *a.* (of lines) continuously equidistant from each other; (of one line, etc.) having this relation (*to, with*); exactly similar, analogous, or corresponding. *n.* imaginary line on earth's surface, line on map, marking degree of latitude; comparison; analogy. *v.t.* (p.t. *paralleled*), compare; correspond to. **pa'rallelism,** *n.*

parallelep'iped (pa-; *or* -ipī'pid), *n.* solid figure whose six sides are parallelograms.

parallel'ogram (pa-), *n.* four-sided plane figure whose opposite sides are parallel.

pa'ralȳse (-z), *v.t.* affect with paralysis; make helpless or ineffectual.

paral'ysis (pa-), *n.* (partial) incapacity to move or feel; powerless or immobile state. **paralyt'ic,** *a.* causing, affected with, paralysis. *n.* person affected with paralysis.

pa'ramount, *a.* supreme; pre-eminent.

pa'ramour (-oor), *n.* (*archaic*) illicit lover of married man or woman.

pa'rapet, *n.* low wall at edge of roof, bridge,

etc.; mound along front of trench.

paraphernā'lia (pa-), *n.pl.* personal belongings; accessories, odds and ends of equipment.

pa'raphrāse (-z), *n.* restatement of sense of a passage in other words. *v.t.* express meaning of in other words.

paraplē'gia (pa-), *n.* paralysis of lower part of body. **paraplē'gic,** *a. & n.*

pa'rasīte, *n.* animal or plant living in or on another; person living at another's expense. **parasit'ic(al),** *aa.*

parasol' (pa-; *or* pa'-), *n.* light umbrella used to give protection from sun.

pa'ratrŏŏps, *n.pl.* airborne troops trained to land by parachute. **pa'ratrŏŏper,** *n.*

par'boil, *v.t.* boil (food) until partially cooked; make uncomfortably hot.

par'cel, *n.* thing, goods, wrapped up for carrying, posting, etc.; piece of land. *part and parcel,* essential part. *v.t.* (p.t. *parcelled*), divide (*out*) into portions; make (*up*) into parcel(s).

parch, *v.* make or become hot and dry; roast slightly.

parch'ment, *n.* skin of sheep, goat, etc., prepared for writing, etc.; manuscript on this. **parchment(-paper),** kind of toughened paper.

par'don, *n.* forgiveness; remission of punishment; courteous forbearance. *v.t.* forgive; excuse. **par'donable,** *a.* that can be excused. **par'doner,** *n.* (Hist.) licensed seller of papal indulgences.

pāre, *v.t.* trim or reduce by cutting away edge or surface of. **pār'ing,** *n.* (esp.) strip of rind.

pār'ent, *n.* person or animal that begets or gives birth to offspring; father or mother; source, origin. **pār'entage,** *n.* descent from parents, lineage. **paren'tal,** *a.* of parent(s).

paren'thĕsis, *n.* (pl. *parenthĕsēs*), word, clause, or sentence inserted into sentence but not grammatically essential to it; (sing. or pl.) round brackets ( ) used for this. **paren-thet'ic,** *a.* **parenthet'ically,** *adv.*

parī'ah (-a; *or* pa'ria), *n.* (in S.India) person of low caste or of no caste; outcast from society.

pa'rish, *n.* division of diocese having its own church and clergy(man); local government district, esp. (Hist.) for poor-law administration. **pari'shioner** (-shon-), *n.* inhabitant of parish.

pa'rity, *n.* being on a par or at par; equivalence.

park, *n.* large enclosed piece of land attached to country house, or laid out or preserved for public use; place where vehicles may be left. *v.t.* leave in park or other place until required. **parking-meter,** mechanical device for collecting parking-fee, esp. in street.

par'lance, *n.* way of speaking.

par'ley, *n.* (pl. *parleys*), meeting between representatives of opposed forces to discuss terms. *v.i.* hold discussion on terms.

par'liament (-la-), *n.* deliberative body consisting of House of Commons and House of Lords and forming, with sovereign, legislature of United Kingdom; legislative assembly in other countries. **parliamentār'ian,** *n.* skilled parliamentary debater. **parliamen'tary,** *a.* of, in, concerning, parliament. **Parliamentary Commissioner (for Administration),** title of ombudsman in United Kingdom.

par'lour (-ler), *n.* sitting-room; room in convent, inn etc., for private conversation. **parlour-maid,** maid who waits at table.

par'lous, *a.* dangerous, precarious.

Parmĕsan' (-z-), *n.* hard cheese of kind made at Parma in Italy.

Parnass'us, *n.* Greek mountain, in ancient Greece sacred to Apollo and the Muses.

parŏ'chial (-k-), *a.* of parish; of narrow range, merely local. **parŏ'chialism,** *n.*

pa'rody, *n.* (piece of) writing in which an author's characteristics are ridiculed by imitation; feeble imitation, travesty. *v.t.* make parody of.

parōle', *n.* word of honour, esp. prisoner's promise not to attempt escape.

pa'roxysm, *n.* fit (*of* pain, rage, laughter, etc.).

par'quet (-ki *or* -kā), *n.* flooring of wooden blocks arranged in a pattern.

pa'rricide, *n.* killing, killer, of own father.

pa'rrot, *n.* any of various (mainly tropical) birds with hooked bill and (usu.) brilliant plumage, some of which can imitate speech.

pa'rry, *v.t.* ward off, turn aside (blow, etc.). *n.* parrying.

parse' (-z), *v.t.* describe (word), analyse (sentence), in terms of grammar.

par'simony, *n.* carefulness in use of money or resources; stinginess. **parsimō'nious,** *a.*

pars'ley, *n.* herb with divided and curled leaves, used for seasoning and garnishing.

par'snip, *n.* (plant with) sweet fleshy root used as vegetable.

par'son, *n.* rector; vicar; (*informal*) any clergyman. **par'sonage,** *n.* parson's house. **parson'ic(al),** *aa.*

part, *n.* some but not all; share, portion, section; region; assigned role; side in dispute, etc.; (Mus.) line of notes assigned to particular instrument or voice. *part of speech,* (Gram.) each of classes of words, as noun, verb, adjective, etc. **part,** *adv.* partly, in part. *v.* divide into parts; separate; quit one another's company. *part with,* give up, say good-bye to. **part-song,** song for two or more voice-parts. **part-time,** employed for, taking up, only part of working-day, etc.

partāke', *v.i.* (p.t. *partook,* p.p. *partāken*), take share (*in, of, with*); eat or drink some *of.*

par'tial (-shl), *a.* favouring one side, unfair; not total or complete. **partial'ity** (-shi-), *n.* favouritism, bias; fondness (*for*). **par'tially,**

adv.

parti'cipant, *n.* one who participates.

parti'cipāte, *v. i.* have share, take part, (*in*). **participātion,** *n.*

par'ticiple, *n.* adjective formed from verb (*past participle, present participle*). **particip'ial,** *a.*

par'ticle, *n.* very small piece of matter; smallest possible quantity; minor (esp. indeclinable) part of speech, e.g. conjunction, preposition, etc.; prefix or suffix having distinct meaning.

par'ticoloured (-kulerd), *a.* partly of one colour, partly of another; variegated in colour.

partic'ular, *a.* relating to one as distinguished from others; special; scrupulously exact; fastidious. *n.* detail, item; (pl.) detailed account. **particula'rity,** *n.* **partic'ularly,** *adv.* very; to special extent; in detail.

partic'ularīze, *v.* mention one by one; go into particulars. **particŭlarīzā'tion,** *n.*

par'ting, *n.* leave-taking; dividing-line of combed hair; place or point of separation.

partisan' (-z-), *n.* adherent of (political, etc.) party, side, or cause; guerilla. **partisan'ship,** *n.*

parti'tion, *n.* division into parts; structure separating such parts; compartment. *v. t.* divide into parts. *partition off,* separate by means of partition.

par'titive, *a.* & *n.* (Gram.) (word) denoting part of collective whole (e.g. *some, any*).

part'ly, *adv.* with respect to a part; in some degree; not wholly.

part'ner, *n.* person associated with another or others in business, etc.; either of pair in marriage or dancing or game. *v. t.* be partner of; make partner(s). **part'nership,** *n.*

part'ridge, *n.* kind of game-bird.

par'ty, *n.* body of persons united in cause or in opposition to another body; body of persons travelling or working together; social reception; person taking part in or approving of action, etc.; either side in lawsuit, contract, etc. **party line,** shared telephone line; set policy of political party.

par'venŭ, *n.* person who has risen from obscurity; upstart.

pash'a (*or* pah-), *n.* (Hist.) title of Turkish or Egyptian officer of high rank.

pass (-ah-), *v.* (p.p. *passed,* or as adj. *past*), move onward, proceed; cause to go; change; die; go by; come to end; percolate; be accepted as adequate; be sanctioned; satisfy examiner(s); happen; outstrip, surpass; spend (time, etc.); hand on; utter. *n.* passing, esp. of examination; state, critical position; written permission or ticket or order; thrust in fencing; (Footb., etc.) passing of ball from one player to another; narrow passage through mountains, etc. **pass-book,** book recording customer's transactions with bank. **pass-key,** master-key. **pass'word,** selected word or phrase enabling friend to be distin-

guished from enemy.

pass'able (pah-), *a.* that can pass muster; fairly good; (of road, bridge, etc.) that can be passed over or crossed.

pass'age, *n.* passing, transit; journey, voyage from port to port; way through; corridor; part of speech or of literary or musical work.

pass'enger (-j-), *n.* traveller in public conveyance; traveller in car, etc., who is not driving; ineffective member of team, etc.

passer-by' (pah-), *n.* one who passes, esp. by chance.

pass'erine, *a.* of order of birds which have feet adapted for perching; of sparrow kind.

pass'ing (pah-), *a.* (esp.) transient, fleeting. *adv.* (*archaic*) very. *in passing,* incidentally.

passe-partout (pahspartōō'), *n.* adhesive tape or paper fastening edges of glass to mount of photograph or small picture to form frame; master-key.

pa'ssion (-shn), *n.* strong emotion; anger; sexual love; strong enthusiasm (*for*); (*Passion*) sufferings of Christ during his last days and at his crucifixion; (musical setting of) Gospel narrative of this.

pa'ssionate (-shon-), *a.* easily moved to anger or other strong emotion; filled with, showing, passion. **pa'ssionately,** *adv.*

pass'ive, *a.* acted upon, not acting; not offering active resistance, submissive; of or in passive voice. *n.* passive form or voice. *passive voice,* (Gram., opp. *active*) form of verb used when subject undergoes action of the verb. **passiv'ity,** *n.*

Pass'ōver (pah-), *n.* Jewish religious festival commemorating deliverance from bondage in Egypt.

pass'port (pah-), *n.* official document showing identity, nationality, etc., of traveller abroad.

past (pah-), *a.* gone by; just over; (Gram.) expressing past action or state. *n.* past time; person's past life or career. *prep.* beyond. *adv.* so as to pass. **past master,** thorough master, expert.

pas'ta (*or* pah-) *n.* (dish of) kind of Italian food-paste used to make macaroni, etc.

pāste, *n.* flour kneaded with lard, butter, suet, etc., and water as material for pastry; substance used as adhesive; relish of pounded fish, meat, etc.; any soft plastic mixture; material of imitation gems. *v. t.* fasten with paste; cover (as) by pasting; (*slang*) beat, thrash. **paste'board,** stiff substance made by pasting together sheets of paper.

pas'tel, *n.* stick of powdered colouring-matter bound with gum, used for drawing; drawing made with pastels. *a.* (of colour) soft, pale.

pas'tern, *n.* part of horse's foot between fetlock and hoof.

pas'teurīze (-ter-), *v. t.* destroy harmful bacteria in (milk, etc.) by special process of heating. **pasteurīzā'tion,** *n.*

pas'tille (*or* -ēl'), *n.* kind of small, esp. medicated, sweet.

pas'time (pah-), *n.* recreation; sport or game.

pas'tor (pah-), *n.* minister in charge of a congregation.

pas'toral (pah-), *a.* of shepherds; of country life; of pastor. *n.* pastoral poem or picture. **pastoral (letter)**, letter from bishop to clergy and people. **pastoral staff**, crosier.

pā'stry, *n.* baked paste of flour, lard, etc.; food made (partly) of this.

pas'turage (pahs'cher-), *n.* pasturing; pasture, pasture-land.

pas'ture (pahs'cher), *n.* growing herbs, esp. grass, eaten by cattle, etc.; land or field under such crop.

pas'ty[1] (*or* pah-), *n.* pie of meat, etc., encased in pastry and baked without dish.

pā'sty[2], *a.* of or like paste; of pale complexion.

pat, *v.t.* (p.t. *patted*), strike gently with open hand or other flat surface. *n.* patting touch or sound; small mass, esp. of butter, made (as) by patting. *adv. & a.* to the point, opportunely; promptly.

patch, *n.* piece put on to mend hole, etc.; protective covering for injured eye; large or irregular spot on surface; distinct area or period; small plot of ground. *v.t.* mend with patch(es). *patch up*, repair, esp. hastily; settle (quarrel, etc.). **patch'work**, piece of material made of small pieces of different colours, etc., sewn together. **patch'y**, *a.* (esp.) irregular, uneven.

pāte, *n.* (*informal*) head.

pâté (pah'tā), *n.* smooth paste of minced meat, etc.; patty.

patell'a, *n.* (pl. *patellae*, *patellas*), knee-cap.

pat'en, *n.* shallow dish for bread at Eucharist.

pā'tent (*or* pa-), *a.* obvious, unconcealed; patented; *letters patent*, open letter from sovereign, etc. conferring (esp. sole) right to make, use, or sell invention. *n.* letters patent; grant of sole right to make or sell, invention protected by this. *v.t.* obtain patent for (invention). **patent leather**, leather with glossy varnished surface. **patentee'**, *n.* holder of patent.

pater'nal, *a.* of father, fatherly; related through father, on father's side. **pater'nalism**, *n.* (esp.) government, etc., (as) by father. **paternalis'tic**, *a.* **pater'nity**, *n.* fatherhood; one's paternal origin.

pā'ter, *n.* (*slang*) father.

pat'ernos'ter, *n.* Lord's prayer, esp. in Latin.

path (pahth, *pl.* pr. pahdhz), *n.* foot-way; track; line along which person or thing moves.

pathet'ic, *a.* arousing pity or sadness. **pathet'ically**, *adv.*

pathol'ogy, *n.* systematic study of bodily diseases. **patholog'ical**, *a.* **pathol'ogist**, *n.*

pā'thos, *n.* pathetic quality.

pā'tience (-shns), *n.* endurance of pain or provocation; forbearance; calm and quiet waiting; card-game (esp. for one).

pā'tient (-shnt), *a.* having or showing patience. *n.* person receiving, or on doctor's list for, medical treatment.

pat'iō (*or* pah-), *n.* (pl. *patios*), roofless inner courtyard; paved area near house.

pat'ois (-twah), *n.* (pl. same), regional dialect; jargon.

pā'triarch (-k), *n.* father and ruler of family or tribe; venerable old man. **pātriarch'al**, *a.* **pā'triarchy**, *n.*

patri'cian (-shn), *n. & a.* (person) of noble birth, esp. in ancient Rome; aristocrat(ic).

pat'ricide, *n.* parricide.

pat'rimony, *n.* property inherited from father or ancestors.

pā'triot (*or* pa-), *n.* one who loves his country and is ready to defend its freedom or rights. **patriot'ic**, *a.* **pā'triotism**, *n.*

patrōl', *n.* going round, traversing, (camp, streets, etc.) for purpose of watching, guarding, etc.; man, party, ship(s), etc., doing this; unit of six to eight Scouts or Guides. *v.* (p.t. *patrolled*), act as patrol; go round (camp, town, etc.) as patrol.

pā'tron (*or* pa-), *n.* one who encourages or gives financial support to (interests of person(s), cause, art); (esp. regular) customer of shop, etc; (often *patron saint*) guardian saint; person having right of appointing to benefice. **patrō'nal**, *a.* of patron saint. **pa'troness**, *n. fem.*

pat'ronage (*or* pā-), *n.* patron's help; customer's support; right of appointing to benefice or office; patronizing manner.

pat'ronīze, *v.t.* act as patron to; support and encourage; treat condescendingly.

patronym'ic, *a. & n.* (name) derived from that of father or ancestor.

patt'en, *n.* wooden sole mounted on iron ring formerly worn to raise shoe above mud, etc.

patt'er[1], *v.* talk rapidly and mechanically. *n.* rapid talk introduced into a song, etc; lingo, jargon.

patt'er[2], *v.i.* (of rain, etc.) make tapping sound; run with quick short steps. *n.* sound of pattering.

patt'ern, *n.* excellent example; model, design, from which something can be made; sample, esp. of cloth, etc.; design, esp. on surface. *v.t.* decorate with pattern.

patt'y, *n.* small pie or pasty.

pau'city, *n.* smallness of number or quantity.

paunch, *n.* belly, stomach.

pau'per, *n.* person with no means of livelihood, esp. (Hist.) one receiving poor-law relief. **pau'perism**, *n.*

pause (-z), *n.* interval of inaction or silence; break made in speaking or reading; (Mus.) mark (⌢) denoting lengthening of note or rest. *v.i.* make a pause; wait.

pāve, *v.t.* cover (ground, floor) with layer of flat stones, tiles, asphalt, etc. *pave the way*, prepare, make the way easy, (*for*, *to*).

pave′ment (-vm-), *n.* paved foot-way at side of street; paved surface.

pavil′ion, *n.* building for players or spectators of outdoor game; light ornamental building for concerts, etc.; large tent.

paw, *n.* foot of beast having claws or nails. *v.* touch with paw; (of horse) strike ground with hoof; (*informal*) handle awkwardly or rudely.

paw′ky, *a.* (Sc.) sly, shrewd; drily humorous.

pawn¹, *n.* chessman of smallest value and size; (fig.) mere tool.

pawn², *n.* thing handed over as pledge or security; state of being pledged. *v.t.* deposit as security for money lent. **pawn′brōker**, *n.* keeper of shop (**pawn′shop**) where money is lent on security of pawned goods. **pawn-ticket**, receipt for object pawned.

pay, *v.* (p.t. *paid*), give as due; discharge debt to; bear cost; suffer penalty *for*; give, render (compliment, attention, etc.); yield adequate return; let *out* (rope) by slackening it. *pay back*, repay; retaliate. *pay out*, take revenge on. **pay-as-you-earn**, collection of income tax by deduction from earnings. **pay′able**, *a.* (esp.) that must be paid, due. **payee′**, *n.* person to whom payment is (to be) made. **pay′ment**, *n.* paying; amount paid.

pea, *n.* plant bearing round seeds in pods and cultivated for food; one of the seeds.

peace, *n.* freedom from, or cessation of, war; civil order; quiet, calm; harmonious relationship. **peace-māker**, one who helps to bring about peace or reconciliation. **peace-offering**, gift offered to show willingness to make peace. **peace′able**, *a.* not quarrelsome; quiet. **peace′ful**, *a.* full of, marked by, peace. **peace′fully**, *adv.* **peace′fulness**, *n.*

peach, *n.* (tree bearing) round stone-fruit with downy skin. **peach(-coloured)**, *a.* of soft yellowish-pink colour of ripe peach.

pea′cock, *n.* male bird having splendid plumage and able to make fanlike display with elongated tail coverts. **peacock blue**, bright lustrous blue of peacock's neck-feathers. **pea′fowl**, *n.* peacock or peahen. **pea′hen**, *n.* female of peacock.

peak¹, *n.* pointed top, esp. of mountain; highest point in curve or record of fluctuations (in traffic intensity, electricity consumption, etc.); projecting part of cap. **peaked¹** (-kt), *a.* having peak.

peak², *v.i.* (*archaic*) waste away. **peaked²**, (-kt), *a.* sharp-featured, pinched. **pea′ky**, *a.* sickly, puny.

peal, *n.* loud ringing of bell(s); set of bells; outburst of sound. *v.* sound forth, ring (bells), in peal.

pea′nut, *n.* (fruit of) plant with pod ripening underground, containing two seeds valued as food and for their oil.

pear (pār), *n.* (tree bearing) fleshy edible fruit tapering towards stalk. **pear-shaped**, *a.*

pearl (perl), *n.* hard lustrous, usu. white and spherical, body formed in oyster and other shells and prized as gem. *v.* fish for pearls; (of moisture) form drops (on). **pearl button**, button of (imitation) mother of pearl. **pearl′y**, *a.*

peas′ant (pez-), *n.* countryman, worker on land. **peas′antry**, *n.* peasants collectively.

pease pu′dding (-z-poo-), pudding made of split dried peas, etc.

peat, *n.* vegetable matter decomposed by water and partly carbonized; piece of this as fuel.

pebb′le, *n.* small stone worn and rounded by action of water. **pebb′ly**, *a.*

peccadill′ō, *n.* (pl. *peccadilloes*), trivial misdeed.

pecc′ary, *n.* (skin of) small wild pig of Central and S. America.

peck¹, *n.* measure of capacity (2 gallons) for dry goods.

peck², *v.* strike (*at*), pick up (food), make (hole), with beak. *peck at one's food*, (*informal*) nibble without appetite. *n.* act of pecking with beak, mark made by it; hurried unemotional kiss.

pec′tin, *n.* gelatinous substance in ripe fruits, etc., causing jam to set.

pec′toral, *a.* of, for, breast or chest.

pec′ūlāte, *v.* embezzle. **pecūlā′tion**, *n.*

pecū′liar, *a.* belonging exclusively (*to*); particular, special; odd, strange. **pecūlia′rity**, *n.* being peculiar; characteristic; oddity.

pecū′niary, *a.* of money.

ped′agogue (-gog), *n.* schoolmaster; pedant. **ped′agogy** (-gi; *or* -ji), *n.* science of teaching. **pedago′gical**, *a.*

ped′al, *n.* lever worked by foot in piano, bicycle, etc.; (wooden) key of organ played with foot. *v.* (p.t. *pedalled*), work pedals of bicycle, etc.; work bicycle, etc., thus.

ped′ant, *n.* one who overrates or parades learning or knowledge or insists on strict adherence to formal rules. **pēdan′tic**, *a.* **ped′antry**, *n.*

pedd′le, *v.* be a pedlar; trade or deal as pedlar.

ped′estal, *n.* base of column; block on which something stands; either support of knee-hole desk.

pedes′trian, *a.* going or performed on foot; of walking; for those on foot; dull, uninspired. *n.* walker, traveller on foot. **pedestrian crossing**, street-crossing for pedestrians. **pedes′trianism**, *n.*

ped′igree, *n.* genealogical table; line of descent; ancient descent. *a.* having a recorded line of descent.

ped′iment, *n.* low-pitched gable over front of building.

ped′lar, *n.* travelling seller of small goods.

pēdom′ēter, *n.* instrument for estimating distance walked.

peek, *n. & v.i.* peep, glance.

peel¹, *v.* strip peel, rind, bark, etc., from (fruit, vegetable, tree, etc.); take *off* (skin,

bark, etc.); shed bark, skin, paint, etc. *n.*
outer layer, rind, of fruit, etc. **peel'ings** (-z),
n.pl. what is peeled off.
peel², **pēle**, *n.* (Hist.) small square fortified
tower near Scottish border.
peep¹, *v.i.* look through narrow opening; look
quickly or furtively; come cautiously or
partly into view. *n.* (esp. stealthy) glance;
first light (*of dawn, day*). **peep-hole**, small
hole to peep through.
peep², *n. & v.i.* cheep, squeak.
peer¹, *v.i.* look closely (*at, into*).
peer², *n.* person's equal in rank or merit;
duke, earl, marquis, viscount, or baron.
peer'age, *n.* peers; rank of peer. **peer'ess**, *n.*
peer's wife; female holder of peerage.
peer'less, *a.* unequalled.
peeved (-vd), *a.* (*slang*) irritated.
peev'ish, *a.* complaining, irritable.
peewit: see **pewit.**
peg, *n.* pin or bolt of wood, metal, etc., for
holding together parts of framework, hanging
things on, holding tent-ropes, adjusting tension of strings of violin, etc.; clip, etc., for
fastening washed clothes to line. *v.* (p.t.
pegged), fix with peg(s).
pē'jorative (*or* pijo'-), *a. & n.* depreciatory
(word).
Pēkin(g)ēse' (-z), *n.* small breed of dog with
long silky coat and flat face.
pele: see **peel².**
pel'ican, *n.* water-bird with large bill from
which is suspended a pouch for storing fish.
pell'ét, *n.* small ball of paper, etc.; pill; small
shot.
pell-mell', *adv.* in disorder; headlong.
pēllū'cid (*or* -ōō-), *a.* transparent, clear.
pel'mét, *n.* narrow board or short curtain concealing curtain-rod(s) above window, etc.
pelt¹, *v.* attack with missiles; (of rain, etc.)
come down hard; run rapidly. *n.* (*at*) *full
pelt*, at utmost speed.
pelt², *n.* animal's skin, esp. with the fur, hair,
or wool on it.
pel'vis, *n.* basin-shaped cavity formed in most
vertebrates by hip-bones and lower part of
backbone. **pel'vic**, *a.*
pemm'ican, *n.* preparation of dried and
pounded meat, etc.
pen¹, *n.* implement for writing with ink; writing or literary style. *v.t.* (p.t. *penned*), compose and write (letter, etc.). **pen-friend**, correspondent one has not met. **pen'knife**, small
pocket-knife. **pen'manship**, skill in, style
of, handwriting. **pen-name**, literary
pseudonym.
pen², *n.* small enclosure for cattle, sheep,
poultry, etc. *v.t.* (p.t. *penned*), put or keep in
confined space.
pen³, *n.* female swan.
pē'nal, *a.* of or involving punishment; punishable; punitive. **penal servitude**, (Hist.)
imprisonment with hard labour. **pē'nalize**,
v.t. make punishable; give penalty to, place

at disadvantáge.
pen'alty, *n.* fine or other punishment; (Footb.,
etc.) disadvantage imposed for breaking rule,
etc.
pen'ance, *n.* act performed as expression of
penitence. *do penance*, perform such act.
pence: see **penny.**
pen'cil, *n.* implement for drawing or writing,
esp. (*lead pencil*) of graphite enclosed in
wooden cylinder or metal case with tapering
end. *v.t.* (p.t. *pencilled*), draw, mark, or
write with lead pencil.
pen'dant, *n.* ornament hung from necklace,
etc.
pen'dent, *a.* hanging, overhanging; still to be
decided, pending.
pen'ding, *a.* awaiting decision or settlement.
prep. during, until.
pen'dūlous, *a.* hanging, swinging.
pen'dūlum, *n.* weight, rod, etc., suspended so
as to be free to swing, esp. in clock.
pen'étrable, *a.* that can be penetrated.
pen'étrāte, *v.* find access or pass into or
through; permeate; find out, discern. **pen'-
étrāting**, *a.* discerning, gifted with insight;
(of voice, etc.) easily heard through or above
other sounds. **penétrā'tion**, *n.* **pen'étrative**,
a.
peng'uin (-nggw-), *n.* flightless sea-bird with
flipper-like wings used for swimming.
penicill'in, *n.* antibiotic obtained from mould,
effective against many micro-organisms of
disease.
penin'sūla, *n.* piece of land almost surrounded
by water or projecting far into sea, etc.
penin'sūlar, *a.*
pē'nis, *n.* organ of urination and copulation in
male mammals.
pen'itent, *a.* feeling or showing sorrow and
regret for sin or wrongdoing. *n.* penitent person; person doing penance. **pen'itence**, *n.*
peniten'tiary (-sha-), *a.* of penance or reformatory treatment. *n.* (Hist.) reformatory prison; (U.S.) prison.
penn'ant, *n.* tapering flag, esp. that flown at
mast-head of ship in commission.
penn'iless, *a.* having no money, destitute.
penn'on, *n.* long narrow triangular or
swallow-tailed flag.
penn'y, *n.* (pl. *pence, pennies*), (coin worth)
one-twelfth of shilling (abbrev. *d.*, Hist.);
(*new*) *penny*, (coin worth) one hundredth of
pound sterling (abbrev. *p.*).
pen'sion (-shn), *n.* periodical payment made
in consideration of past service, old age,
widowhood, etc. *v.t.* grant pension to. *pension off*, dismiss with pension. **pen'sionable**,
a. (esp.) entitled to pension. **pen'sioner**, *n.*
person receiving a pension.
pen'sive, *a.* plunged in thought, meditative.
pent, *a.* closely confined, shut *in* or *up.*
penta-, *pref.* five. **pen'tagon**, *n.* five-sided
plane figure. **pentag'onal**, *a.* **pentam'éter**,
n. verse line of five metrical feet. **Pen'-**

tateuch (-ūk), n. first five books of Old Testament. **pentath'lon,** n. athletic contest in which each competitor takes part in five events.

Pen'tĕcost, n. Jewish harvest festival fifty days after Passover; Whit Sunday.

pent'house (-t-h-), n. structure with sloping roof attached to wall of main building; separate flat, house, etc., on roof of building.

pĕnul'timate, a. last but one.

pĕnum'bra, n. partly lighted shadow around total shadow of opaque body (esp. moon or earth in eclipse); partial shadow.

pĕnūr'ious, a. poor; mean, stingy.

pen'ūry, n. destitution, poverty.

pĕ'ony, n. garden plant with large handsome globular flowers.

people (pē'pl), n. (collective, with pl. verb) persons in general; subjects; parents or other relatives; (sing., with pl. peoples) race, tribe, nation. v.t. fill with people; populate.

pep, n. (slang) vigour, energy, spirit. **pep-talk,** talk meant to inspire hearers to exceptional effort, etc.

pepp'er, n. hot-tasting dried berries (usu. ground into powder) of certain plants, used for seasoning; (fruit of) capsicum. v.t. sprinkle or flavour with pepper; sprinkle; pelt with missiles. **pepper-and-salt,** (cloth) of dark and light wool, etc., interwoven. **pepp'ercorn,** dried pepper berry; (fig.) this as nominal rent. **pepp'ermint,** (kind of mint grown for) essential oil with strong aromatic flavour; sweet flavoured with it. **pepp'ery,** a. like pepper; hot-tempered.

per, prep. by, through, by means of; for each. **per annum,** (so much) for each year, yearly. **per cent,** for, in, to, every hundred (symbol %).

per-, pref. through, all over; completely; very; away entirely, to destruction.

peradven'ture (-cher), adv. (archaic) perhaps; by chance.

peram'bŭlāte, v. walk through, over, or about. **perambŭlā'tion,** n. **peram'bŭlātor,** n. (esp.) pram.

perceive' (-sēv), v.t. become aware of through one of the senses, esp. sight; grasp with the mind, understand.

percen'tage, n. rate or proportion per cent (see **per**); proportion, share.

percep'tible, a. that can be perceived. **percep'tibly,** adv. **perceptibil'ity,** n.

percep'tion, n. act of perceiving; ability to perceive. **percep'tive,** a. of, concerned with, perception; having insight. **perceptiv'ity,** n.

perch[1], n. bird's resting place; elevated position; measure of length (5½ yds.). v. alight or rest on perch; put (as) on perch.

perch[2], n. common freshwater fish.

perchance' (-ahns), adv. by chance (archaic); possibly, perhaps.

per'cŏlāte, v. (of liquid) pass slowly (through); filter (through). **percŏlā'tion,** n.

per'cŏlātor, n. (esp.) apparatus for making coffee by percolation.

percu'ssion (-shn), n. forcible striking of one (usu. solid) body against another; sound so made; (Mus.) instruments struck with stick or hand or struck together in pairs.

perdi'tion, n. damnation.

perĕgrinā'tion, n. journey; travelling about.

pe'rĕgrine, n. kind of falcon.

pe'rĕmptory (or peremp'-), a. imperious, dictatorial; urgent.

perenn'ial, a. not coming to an end; (of plant) coming up year after year. n. perennial plant.

per'fect, a. complete, not deficient; faultless; thoroughly learned or skilled or trained; exact, precise; entire; (Gram., of tense) expressing completed action. n. perfect tense. **perfect',** v.t. make perfect. **perfec'tible,** a. **perfectibil'ity,** n.

perfec'tion, n. being or making perfect; perfect state; perfect person, specimen, etc.; highest standard attainable. **perfec'tionist,** n. (informal) one who is satisfied with nothing less than perfection.

per'fectly, adv. quite, quite well; in perfect manner.

per'fidy, n. breach of faith; treachery. **perfid'ious,** a.

per'fŏrāte, v. pierce; make hole(s), esp. row(s) of holes, through. **perfŏrā'tion,** n.

perforce', adv. of necessity, unavoidably.

perfor'mance, n. carrying out, doing; performing, esp. of play, etc.; notable feat.

perform', v. carry out (command, task, etc.); do, act, play, (public function, drama, piece of music, etc.); (of animals) do tricks. **perfor'mer,** n. **perfor'ming,** a.

per'fūme, n. (sweet) smell; scent; fragrance. **perfūme'** (or per'fūm), v.t. give fragrance to. **perfū'mer,** n. maker or seller of perfumes. **perfū'mery,** n.

perfunc'tory, a. done with least possible effort; superficial. **perfunc'torily,** adv.

per'gola, n. arbour or covered walk formed of growing plants trained over framework.

perhaps', (per-h-), adv. it may be, possibly.

pēr'i, n. fairy of Persian mythology.

peri-, pref. round, about.

pe'rigee, n. point nearest to earth in orbit of moon, planet, or artificial satellite.

pe'ril, n. danger, risk. **pe'rilous,** a.

perim'ĕter, n. line or set of lines bounding closed figure; boundary, outer edge or limits.

pēr'iod, n. definite portion or length of time; indefinite portion of history, life, etc.; occurrence of menstruation; full stop. **pēriod'ic,** a. recurring at (regular) intervals.

pēriod'ical, a. periodic; published at regular intervals. n. periodical magazine, etc.

peripatet'ic (pe-), a. going from place to place on one's business, itinerant.

periph'ery, n. bounding line, esp. of figure enclosed by curved lines; boundary, surrounding surface, area, etc.

pe′riscōpe, *n*. apparatus of tube and mirrors for viewing objects above surface or eye-level, beyond obstruction, etc.

pe′rish, *v*. suffer destruction, lose life. *perished with cold*, very cold. **pe′rishable**, *a*. that will not last long. **pe′rishables** (-lz), *n. pl.* perishable goods.

peritonē′um (pe-), *n*. membrane lining abdominal cavity. **peritoni′tis**, *n*. inflammation of peritoneum.

pe′riwig, *n*. (Hist.) wig.

pe′riwinkle[1], *n*. trailing plant with blue starry flowers.

pe′riwinkle[2], *n*. edible salt-water shell-fish like small snail.

per′jure (-jer), *v. refl. perjure oneself*, swear falsely; make untrue statement while on oath to speak the truth. **per′jured**, *a*. guilty of perjury. **per′jurer**, *n*. **per′jury**, *n*. swearing to statement known to be false; false evidence given under oath; breach of oath.

perk[1], *v*. lift or prick *up* self-assertively or jauntily; cheer or brighten or smarten *up*. **per′ky**, *a*. self-assertive, jaunty.

perk[2], *n*. (*slang*, usu. in pl.) perquisite.

perm, *n*. (*informal*) permanent wave. *v. t.* give permanent wave to.

per′manence, *n*. being permanent. **per′manency**, *n*. permanence; permanent thing, employment, etc.

per′manent, *a*. lasting or meant to last indefinitely. **permanent wave**, artificial wave in the hair, intended to last for some months.

per′mëable, *a*. that can be permeated by fluid, etc.

per′mëate, *v*. penetrate, pervade, saturate; diffuse itself (*through, among*).

permiss′ible, *a*. that may be permitted.

permi′ssion (-shn), *n*. consent; liberty or licence (*to* do). **permiss′ive**, *a*. giving permission; not forbidding or hindering.

permit′, *v*. (p.t. *permitted*), give leave or consent or opportunity (for or *to*); allow doing or occurrence (of). **per′mit**, *n*. written order giving permission.

permūtā′tion, *n*. change in order in which set of things is arranged.

permūte′, *v.t.* change arrangement of, esp. in all possible ways.

perni′cious (-shus), *a*. destructive, injurious.

pernick′ety, *a*. (*informal*) fastidious, (too) precise.

perorā′tion (pe-), *n*. lengthy speech; summing up and conclusion of speech, etc.

perox′īde, *n*. compound of oxygen containing maximum proportion of oxygen; peroxide of hydrogen used as bleach, antiseptic, etc.

perpendic′ūlar, *a*. at right angles to plane of horizon or to given line, etc.; upright; very steep. *n*. perpendicular line, etc.

per′pētrāte, *v.t.* perform, commit (crime, blunder, etc.). **perpētrā′tion**, *n*. **per′pētrātor**, *n*.

perpet′ūal, *a*. eternal; held or holding for life;

continuous. **perpet′ūally**, *adv*.

perpet′ūāte, *v. t.* make perpetual; not allow to go out of use or memory. **perpet′ūā′tion**, *n*.

perpetū′ity, *n*. perpetual continuance or possession. *in perpetuity*, for ever.

perplex′, *v.t.* bewilder, puzzle; complicate, tangle. **perplex′ity**, *n*.

per′quisite (-z-), *n*. casual profit in money or goods, attached to employment beyond wages or salary.

pe′rry, *n*. fermented drink made from pears.

per′sécūte, *v. t.* treat cruelly, oppress, esp. because of religious beliefs; harass, worry. **persécū′tion**, *n*. **per′sécūtor**, *n*.

persévēre′, *v. i.* continue steadfastly, persist (*in, with*). **persévēr′ance**, *n*.

Per′sian (-shn), *a*. & *n*. (native, language) of Persia (Iran). **Persian lamb**, silky curly fur of young of Asian breed of sheep.

per′siflage (-ahzh), *n*. banter; frivolous manner of treating any subject.

persist′, *v. t.* continue firmly or obstinately (*in* course, opinion, etc.); survive. **persis′tence**, *n*. **persis′tency**, *n*. **persis′tent**, *a*.

per′son, *n*. individual human being; man, woman, or child; one's body or bodily presence; character in play; one of three divine beings in the Trinity; (Gram.) one of three classes of pronouns and corresponding verb forms indicating persons as follows: *1st person*, person(s) speaking; *2nd person*, person(s) spoken to; *3rd person*, (person(s) spoken of. *in person*, oneself.

per′sonable, *a*. good-looking.

per′sonage, *n*. person of rank or importance; character in play, etc.

persō′na grā′ta (-ahta), acceptable person. **persona non grata**, unacceptable person. (Latin)

per′sonal, *a*. one's own; individual, private; referring to an individual; (Gram.) of or denoting one of the three persons (esp. in *personal pronoun*). **per′sonally**, *adv*. in person; for one's own part.

personal′ity, *n*. personal existence or identity; distinctive personal character; (esp. well-known) person.

per′sonalty, *n*. personal property.

per′sonāte, *v. t.* pretend to be (another person), esp. for purpose of fraud. **personā′tion**, *n*.

person′ifỹ, *v. t.* regard or represent (thing, idea) as a person; symbolize (quality, etc.) by human figure; be typical example of. **personificā′tion**, *n*.

personnel′, *n*. body of employees; persons engaged in particular service, profession, etc.

perspec′tive, *n*. art of drawing so as to give effect of solidity and relative position and size; relation between visible objects, parts of subject, etc.; view, prospect. *in perspective*, according to rules of perspective, in proportion.

per'spex, *n.* light transparent plastic substitute for glass. **P.**

perspica'cious (-shus), *a.* having mental penetration or discernment. **perspica'city,** *n.*

perspic'uous, *a.* clearly expressed; stating things clearly. **perspicu'ity,** *n.*

perspire', *v.* sweat. **perspira'tion,** *n.* sweat, sweating.

persuade' (-sw-), *v.t.* convince; influence by reasoning. **persua'dable,** *a.* **persua'sion** (-zhn), *n.* persuading; conviction; religious belief or sect. **persua'sive,** *a.* able to persuade, winning.

pert, *a.* forward, saucy.

pertain', *v.i.* belong or relate *to.*

pertina'cious (-shus), *a.* persistent, obstinate. **pertina'city,** *n.*

per'tinent, *a.* to the point; pertaining; relevant. **per'tinence,** *n.*

perturb', *v.t.* disquiet; throw into agitation. **perturba'tion,** *n.*

peruke' (-ook), *n.* (Hist.) wig.

peruse' (-ooz), *v.t.* read through carefully. **peru'sal,** *n.*

pervade', *v.t.* spread through, permeate, saturate. **perva'sive,** *a.*

perverse', *a.* obstinately or wilfully in the wrong; wayward; peevish. **perver'sity,** *n.*

perver'sion (-shn), *n.* perverting or being perverted; change from proper or normal practice, etc. **perver'sive,** *a.* tending to pervert.

pervert', *v.t.* turn or lead aside from proper or normal use, practice, religious belief, etc.; interpret wrongly; lead astray. **per'vert,** *n.* perverted person.

per'vious, *a.* allowing passage or access (*to*); open (*to* influence, etc.).

pess'imism, *n.* tendency to believe that things will go badly. **pess'imist,** *n.* **pessimis'tic,** *a.*

pest, *n.* troublesome or destructive animal, thing, or person; (*archaic*) pestilence.

pes'ter, *v.t.* trouble, annoy, esp. with repeated requests or questions.

pestif'erous, *a.* spreading disease; morally harmful.

pes'tilence, *n.* fatal epidemic disease, esp. bubonic plague. **pes'tilent,** *a.* deadly or pestiferous; troublesome; obnoxious. **pestilen'tial** (-shl), *a.* pestilent.

pe'stle (-sl), *n.* club-shaped implement for pounding substances in a mortar.

pet[1], *n.* animal kept as companion or treated with affection; darling, favourite. **pet-name,** name expressing fondness or familiarity. *v.t.* (p.t. *petted*) treat as pet; fondle, caress.

pet[2], *n.* fit of bad temper, peevishness.

pet'al, *n.* each division of flower corolla.

petard', *n.* (Hist.) small explosive device for blowing in door, etc.

pe'ter, *v.i. peter out,* come (gradually) to an end.

pe'tersham, *n.* thick ribbed or corded ribbon used for waist-bands, hat-bands, etc.

petite' (-tet), *a. fem.* of small dainty build.

peti'tion, *n.* request, supplication, esp. written. *v.* make petition (to); ask humbly. **peti'tioner,** *n.* (esp.) plaintiff in divorce suit.

pet'rel, *n.* any of various sea-birds. **storm petrel,** small petrel with white rump.

petrifac'tion, *n.* petrifying, being petrified; petrified mass.

pet'rify, *v.* turn into stone; paralyse or stupefy with terror, astonishment, etc.

pet'rol, *n.* refined petroleum used as fuel in internal-combustion engine. **petrol station,** filling-station.

petro'leum, *n.* mineral oil found in upper strata of earth.

pett'icoat, *n.* woman's undergarment worn immediately beneath dress.

pett'ifogger (-g-), *n.* inferior or rascally lawyer. **pett'ifogging,** *a.* dishonest, quibbling; petty.

pett'ish, *a.* fretful, peevish.

pett'y, *a.* unimportant, trivial; mean; minor, inferior. **petty cash,** (cash kept for) small items of expenditure. **petty officer,** non-commissioned officer in navy.

pet'ulant, *a.* peevishly impatient or irritable. **pet'ulance,** *n.*

petu'nia, *n.* plant with vivid funnel-shaped flowers.

pew, *n.* fixed bench with back, in church.

pe'wit, **pee'wit,** *n.* kind of plover named from its cry, lapwing.

pew'ter, *n.* grey alloy of tin with small proportion of lead or other metal(s).

pha'eton (*or* fat-), *n.* light four-wheeled horse-drawn carriage.

phal'anx, *n.* (pl. *phalanxes,* or *phalanges* pr. -jez), (Gk. antiquity) body of infantry in close formation; united or organized body or company; bone of finger or toe.

phan'tasm (-azm), *n.* illusion; supposed vision of absent or dead person.

phantasmagor'ia (-z-), *n.* crowd or succession of dim or doubtfully real persons.

phantasy: see **fantasy.**

phan'tom, *n.* apparition, ghost; (attrib.) unreal.

Pharaoh (far'o), *n.* title of ruler of ancient Egypt.

Pha'risee, *n.* member of ancient-jewish sect noted for strict observance of law; (*pharisee*), self-righteous person. **pharisa'ic(al),** *aa.*

pharmaceu'tical (-su-), *a.* of pharmacy; of use or sale of medicinal drugs.

phar'macist, *n.* person qualified to practise pharmacy.

pharmacol'ogy, *n.* science of the nature and action of drugs. **pharmacol'ogist,** *n.*

pharmacopoe'ia (-pea), *n.* book (esp. officially published) containing list of drugs with directions for their use; stock of drugs.

phar'macy, *n.* (shop, etc. for) preparation and dispensing of drugs.

pharyn'geal (-j-), *a.* of the pharynx. **pharyn-**

gī'tis (-j-), *n.* inflammation of membranes of pharynx. **pha'rynx**, *n.* cavity behind mouth and nose.

phāse (-z), *n.* state or stage of change or development or recurring sequence; aspect of moon according to extent of illumination. *v.t.* divide into or carry out by phases.

pheas'ant (fez-), *n.* long-tailed game-bird, the cock having bright plumage.

phĕnom'ĕnal, *a.* of or concerned with phenomena; remarkable, prodigious. **phĕnom'-ĕnally**, *adv.*

phĕnom'ĕnon, *n.* (pl. *phenomena*), observed or apparent object or fact or occurrence; remarkable person or thing, wonder.

phi'al, *n.* small bottle.

phil-, *pref.*: see **philo-**.

philan'der, *v.i.* make love, esp. without serious intentions; flirt with women. **philan'-derer**, *n.*

philanthrop'ic, *a.* loving one's fellow men; of, engaged in, promotion of human well-being. **philanthrop'ically**, *adv.*

philan'thropy, *n.* love, practical benevolence, towards mankind. **philan'thropist**, *n.*

philat'ĕly, *n.* study and collection of postage-stamps. **philat'ĕlic**, *a.* **philat'ĕlist**, *n.*

philharmon'ic (-lar-), *a.* (in names of societies, orchestras, etc.) devoted to music.

philipp'ic, *n.* bitter criticism, invective.

Phil'istīne, *n.* member of ancient warlike people constantly harassing Israelites. *n. & a.* uncultured, materialistic, (person).

philo-, *pref.* (**phil-** before vowel or *h*), fond of; lover of.

philol'ogy, *n.* science of language. **philolog'ical**, *a.* **philol'ogist**, *n.*

philos'opher, *n.* student of philosophy; one who shows philosophic calmness in trying circumstances.

philosoph'ic(al), *aa.* of or consistent with philosophy; accepting the inevitable calmly.

philos'ophize, *v.i.* theorize; moralize.

philos'ophy, *n.* study of wisdom or knowledge, esp. of ultimate reality or of general causes and principles; philosophical system; system for conduct of life; serenity, resignation.

phil'tre (-ter), *n.* potion supposed to be capable of arousing love.

phlĕbī'tis, *n.* inflammation of walls of a vein.

phlegm (flem), *n.* bronchial mucus ejected by coughing; coolness of character or temperament; impassivity. **phleg'matic** (fleg-), *a.* not easily agitated; sluggish.

phlox, *n.* plant with clusters of white or coloured flowers.

phō'bia, *n.* very strong fear or aversion.

Phoe'bus (fē-), *n.* (Gk. myth.) sun-god (*Phoebus Apollo*); (Poet.) sun.

phoenix (fē-), *n.* mythical bird fabled to burn itself and rise renewed from its ashes.

phon, *n.* unit for measuring loudness of sound.

phōne, *n. & v.* (*informal*) telephone.

phonet'ic, *a.* of or representing vocal sound; of sounds of spoken language. **phonet'ics**, *n.* (study of) phonetic phenomena of a language.

phō'n(e)y, *a.* (*slang*) sham, not genuine.

phon'ic (*or* -ō-), *a.* acoustic; phonetic.

phō'nograph (-ahf), *n.* (U.S.) gramophone.

phonol'ogy, *n.* science of vocal sounds; system of sounds in a language. **phŏnolo'gical**, *a.*

phos'phate, *n.* salt of phosphoric acid.

phosphores'cence, *n.* faint luminosity without (perceptible) heat. **phosphores'cent**, *a.*

phos'phorus, *n.* non-metallic wax-like element appearing luminous in dark. **phospho'ric**, **phos'phorous**, *aa.* containing phosphorus.

phō'tō, *n.* (pl. *photos*), (*informal*) photograph. **pho'tocopy**, (make) photographic copy of document, etc. **photo-finish**, close finish of race in which winner is identified by photography.

photo-, *pref.* light. **phō'to-ĕlec'tric**, *a.* of or utilizing interaction between light and electricity.

phōtogen'ic, *a.* producing light; photographing well.

phō'tograph (-ahf), *n.* picture taken by means of chemical action of light on sensitive film. *v.* take photograph of. *photograph well* or *badly*, look well or badly in photograph. **photog'rapher**, *n.* **photog'raphy**, *n.* **photograph'ic**, *a.*

photom'ĕter, *n.* instrument for measuring intensity of light. **photom'ĕtry**, *n.* **phōtomet'ric**, *a.*

phrāse (-z), *n.* small group of words, usu. without predicate; short pithy expression; (Mus.) short sequence of notes. *v.t.* express in words; (Mus.) group in phrases.

phrāsĕol'ogy (-z-), *n.* choice or arrangement of words.

phrĕnol'ogy, *n.* study of external contours of bones of skull, as supposed indication of mental faculties, etc. **phrĕnol'ogist**, *n.*

phys'ic (-z-), *n.* (*informal*) medicine. *v.t.* (p.t. *physicked*), (*informal*) dose.

phys'ical (-z-), *a.* of matter, material (not mental, moral, or spiritual); of the body; of, according to laws of, nature; of physics.

physi'cian (-zishn), *n.* doctor; doctor specializing in medical (opp. *surgical*) diagnosis and treatment.

phys'icist (-z-), *n.* person learned in physics.

phys'ics (-z-), *n.* science of properties, nature, and interaction of matter and energy.

physiogn'omy (-zion-), *n.* face as indication of character; art of judging character from face or form; characteristic aspect.

physiol'ogy (-z-), *n.* science of functioning of living organisms. **physiolo'gical**, *a.* **physiol'ogist**, *n.*

physiothe′rapy (-z-), *n.* treatment of disease by exercise, heat, or other physical agencies. **physiothe′rapist,** *n.*

physique′ (-zēk), *n.* bodily structure and development.

pī, *n.* (Math.) Gk. letter *p* (written *π*) as symbol of ratio of circumference to diameter of circle (3·14159).

pianiss′imŏ, *adv.* & *a.* (Mus.) very soft(ly).

pi′anist (pē-), *n.* player of piano.

pian′ŏ¹, *adv.* & *a.* (Mus.) soft(ly).

pian′ŏ² (pl. *pianos*), **pianŏfor′tê,** *nn.* musical instrument played by keys which cause hammers to strike metal strings.

pibroch (pē′bro*ch*), *n.* series of variations for Scottish bagpipe.

pic′ador, *n.* horseman who provokes bull with lance in bullfight.

picaresque′ (-esk), *a.* (of fiction) dealing with adventures of rogues.

piccalill′i, *n.* pickle of chopped vegetables, mustard, and spices.

picc′aninny, *n.* Negro child.

picc′olŏ, *n.* (pl. *piccolos*), small flute, an octave higher in pitch than ordinary flute.

pick¹, *n.* tool with sharp-pointed iron cross--bar for breaking up ground, etc.

pick², *v.* pluck, gather; select carefully; break (ground, etc.), make (hole), (as) with pick; probe (teeth, etc.) with pointed instrument; open (lock) with skeleton key, etc.; clear (bone, etc.) of flesh. *pick up,* take hold of and lift; take into vehicle as passenger or cargo; acquire; recover health. *n.* picking; selection; *the* best. **pick′pocket,** one who steals from pockets.

pick′-a-back, *adv., a.* & *n.* (ride) on person′s shoulders or back like a bundle.

pick′axe, *n.* pick. *v.* break, work, with pickaxe.

pick′ĕt, *n.* pointed stake driven into ground; small body of men on military police duty; man or party stationed to deter would-be workers during strike, etc. *v.t.* set with stakes; tether; post or act as picket; beset with pickets.

pick′le, *n.* brine or other liquor for preserving food, etc.; (usu. pl.) vegetables, etc., preserved in vinegar, etc.; (fig.) predicament; young rascal. *v.t.* preserve in pickle.

pic′nic, *n.* pleasure party including meal out of doors. *v.i.* (p.t. *picnicked*), take part in picnic. **pic′nicker,** *n.*

Pict, *n.* one of ancient race formerly inhabiting parts of northern Britain. **Pict′ish,** *a.*

pictor′ial, *a.* of, in, by, or with painting or pictures.

pic′ture (-cher), *n.* painting or drawing of object(s), esp. as work of art; portrait; photograph; beautiful object; scene; mental image; cinema film. *v.t.* represent in picture; describe graphically; imagine.

picturesque′ (pikcheresk), *a.* (of place, scene, etc.) charming or striking in appearance; (of language, etc.) vivid, graphic.

pidg′in, **pi′geon²** (-jn), *n.* (*informal*) business, concern. **pidgin English,** jargon, used esp. in dealings with Chinese.

pie, *n.* dish of meat or fruit encased in or covered with pastry. **pie′crust,** pastry encasing or covering pie.

piebald (pī′bawld), *a.* & *n.* (horse, etc.) having dark and light (esp. black and white) patches of irregular shape.

piece, *n.* distinct part of composite whole; fragment; separate instance or example; unit, quantity, portion; coin; artistic, literary, or musical composition; drama. *v.t.* put together, mend. **piece-goods,** textile fabrics woven in recognized lengths. **piece-work,** work paid for according to amount done.

piece′meal (-sm-), *adv.* & *a.* (done, etc.) piece by piece, part at a time.

pied (pīd), *a.* of black and white or of mixed colours.

pier (pēr), *n.* structure built out into sea, etc., as protection for harbour, or as promenade or landing-stage; pillar supporting span of bridge; solid masonry between windows, etc.

pierce (pērs), *v.* go through or into like spear, needle, etc.; penetrate; bore.

pierrot (pēr′ŏ), *n.* entertainer with whitened face and loose white fancy dress.

pi′ĕty, *n.* quality of being pious.

pig, *n.* non-ruminant hoofed quadruped esp. common domesticated kind reared for its flesh; (*informal*) greedy, dirty, obstinate, or annoying person; oblong mass of smelted iron or other metal. *v.i.* (p.t. *pigged*), *pig it,* (*informal*) live in dirty untidy way. **pig--headed,** obstinate. **pig-iron,** iron in pigs or rough bars. **pig′skin,** leather made of pig′s skin. **pig-sticking,** hunting of wild boar with spears. **pig-sty,** enclosure for keeping pigs in; dirty hovel. **pig′tail,** plait of hair hanging from back of head. **pigg′ery,** *n.* pig-breeding establishment; pig-sty. **pigg′ish,** *a.* **pig′lĕt,** **pig′ling,** *nn.* young pig.

pi′geon¹ (-jn), *n.* bird with many varieties, wild and tame; dove. **pigeon-hole,** (*n.*) one of set of compartments in desk, etc., for papers, etc.; (*v.t.*) put in pigeon-hole.

pigeon²: see **pidgin.**

pig′ment, *n.* colouring-matter. *v.t.* colour (tissue) with natural pigment. **pigmentā′tion,** *n.* natural coloration.

pigmy: see **pygmy.**

pike, *n.* spear formerly used by infantry; peaked top of hill; large voracious freshwater fish. **pike′staff,** wooden shaft of pike. *plain as a pikestaff,* quite clear, obvious.

pil′chard, *n.* small edible sea-fish related to herring.

pile¹, *n.* heap, esp. of flat things laid on one another; pyre; imposing building; (*atomic*) *pile,* nuclear reactor (see **reactor**). *v.t.* lay or throw in pile; load.

pīle², *n.* heavy beam or column of wood, concrete, etc., driven vertically into ground, river-bed, etc., as support for heavy structure.

pile³, *n.* nap of velvet, carpet, etc.

pile⁴, *n.* (usu. in pl.) haemorrhoid.

pil'fer, *v.* steal or thieve in petty way.

pil'grim, *n.* person who journeys to sacred place for religious reasons. **pil'grimage,** *n.* pilgrim's journey.

pill, *n.* small ball of medicinal substance to be swallowed whole. **pill-box,** small round box for pills; (Mil.) small round concrete fortification.

pill'age, *n.* & *v.* plunder.

pill'ar, *n.* slender upright structure of stone, wood, etc., used as support or standing alone as monument, etc.; column. **pillar-box,** official letter-box in form of hollow cylinder.

pill'ion, *n.* seat for passenger behind saddle of motor cycle, etc.

pill'ory, *n.* (Hist.) frame with holes for head and hands in which offender was secured. *v.t.* set in pillory (Hist.); expose to ridicule.

pill'ow (-ō), *n.* cushion as support for head, esp. in bed; pillow-shaped thing. *v.t.* serve as pillow to. **pillow-case, -slip,** washable cover for pillow.

pi'lot, *n.* person qualified to take charge of ships entering or leaving harbour, etc.; person operating flying controls of aircraft; guide. *v.t.* act as pilot to; guide course of. *a.* preliminary, experimental, small-scale.

pimen'tó, *n.* (pl. *pimentos*), (W. Indian tree yielding) allspice.

pim'pernel, *n.* plant with small scarlet (or blue or white) flowers closing in dull weather.

pim'ple, *n.* small round swelling on skin, usu. inflamed. **pim'ply,** *a.*

pin, *n.* piece of thin stiff wire with point and head used for fastening; wooden or metal peg, rivet, etc.; skittle. *v.t.* (p.t. *pinned*), fasten with pin(s); seize and hold fast. **pin down, bind** (*to* statement, promise, etc.). **pin-money,** allowance to woman for small personal expenses; very small sum. **pin'prick,** petty irritation.

pin'afore, *n.* (esp. child's) overall. **pinafore (dress),** sleeveless dress worn over jersey or blouse.

pince-nez (paṅs'nā), *n.* pair of eyeglasses held on nose by spring.

pin'cers (-z), *n.pl.* (*pair of*) *pincers*, gripping tool; pincer-shaped claw in crustaceans, etc. **pin'cer,** *a.* (of attacking movement) converging.

pinch, *v.* nip, esp. with finger and thumb; hurt by squeezing; stint, be stingy; (of cold) nip, shrivel; (*slang*) steal, arrest. *n.* nip, squeeze; stress of want, etc.; very small quantity. *at a pinch,* in emergency, if absolutely necessary.

pine¹, *v.i.* languish, lose strength, through grief, want, etc.; long (*for*).

pine², *n.* (wood of) any of various evergreen

coniferous trees with needles growing in clusters. **pine-cone,** fruit of pine.

pine'apple (-na-), *n.* large juicy tropical fruit resembling pine-cone in shape.

ping, *n.* abrupt high-pitched ringing sound. *v.i.* make ping.

ping'-pong, *n.* table-tennis.

pin'ion¹, *n.* outer joint of bird's wing; (Poet.) wing. *v.t.* cut off pinion(s) to prevent flight; restrain (person) by binding arms.

pin'ion², *n.* small cog-wheel engaging with larger.

pink¹, *n.* pale-red colour; garden plant with sweet-smelling flowers; fox-hunter's red coat; point of perfection, most excellent condition. *a.* pink-coloured.

pink², *v.t.* pierce or prick with sword, etc.; ornament with perforations or with zigzag edge.

pink³, *v.i.* (of imperfectly running motor engine) make slight high-pitched metallic sound.

pinn'ace, *n.* warship's boat, formerly with two tiers of oars; ship's boat.

pinn'acle, *n.* small pointed turret crowning buttress, roof, etc.; high slender mountain-peak; highest point.

pint, *n.* measure of capacity, ⅛ gallon or 20 fluid ounces.

pioneer', *n.* original explorer or settler; beginner of any enterprise, etc.; (Mil.) member of advance corps preparing way for troops. *v.* act as pioneer (in).

pi'ous, *a.* earnestly religious, devout; (*archaic*) dutiful.

pip¹, *n.* seed of apple, pear, orange, etc.

pip², *n.* spot on domino, die, or playing-card; star on army-officer's shoulder. *v.t.* (*informal*) defeat, beat; fail in examination.

pip³, *n.* high-pitched momentary sound, esp. as time-signal.

pipe, *n.* tube of metal, etc., esp. for conveying water, gas, etc.; wind-instrument of single tube with holes; each of tubes in organ; boatswain's whistle; (pl.) bagpipes; tubular organ in body; tube with bowl at one end for smoking tobacco. *v.* play on pipe; (of bird) sing; convey through pipes; trim with piping. **pipe-clay,** fine white clay used for whitening belts, etc., and (formerly) for making tobacco-pipes. **pipe-dream,** impossible wish. **pipe-line,** line of pipes for conveying petroleum, etc., across country; channel of supply, etc. **pi'per,** *n.* (esp.) bagpiper. *pay the piper,* bear the cost. **pi'ping,** *n.* (esp.) cord-like ornamentation. *a.* shrill, *piping hot,* very hot.

pipette', *n.* small glass tube used in laboratories, usu. filled by suction.

pip'it, *n.* small bird related to wagtail.

pipp'in, *n.* type of apple.

piquant (pē'knt), *a.* pungent, sharp, appetizing, stimulating. **pi'quancy,** *n.*

pique (pēk), *v.t.* wound pride of; stir curiosity

of; pride *oneself* (*on*). *n.* resentment.

piqué (pē'kā), *n.* stiff ribbed cotton fabric.

piquet' (-ket), *n.* card-game for two.

pir'ate, *n.* (ship used by) sea-robber; one who infringes copyright or regulations. *v.t.* publish regardless of copyright. **pir'acy**, *n.* **pir-at'ical**, *a.*

pirouette' (pi-roo-), *n.* & *v.i.* (ballet-dancer's) spin round on one foot.

piscator'ial, *a.* of fishing.

Pisces (pi'sēz; *or* pī-), *n.* the Fishes, constellation and twelfth sign of the zodiac.

pista'chio (-shiō; *or* -tah-), *n.* (pl. *pistachios*), nut with green edible kernel.

pis'til, *n.* female or ovule-bearing organ of flower.

pis'tol, *n.* small firearm used with one hand.

pis'ton, *n.* short cylinder fitting bore of hollow cylinder in which it moves to and fro.

pit, *n.* (deep) hole in ground; hole made in digging for mineral, etc.; depression in skin or any surface; (seats on) floor of theatre behind stalls. *v.t.* (p.t. *pitted*) make pit(s) in; store in pit; match *against*. **pit'fall**, covered pit as trap; unsuspected danger. **pit'man**, *n.* (pl. -*men*), coal-miner.

pit'-(a-)pat, *adv.* & *n.* (with) sound as of light quick steps.

pitch[1], *n.* dark resinous tarry substance. *v.t.* coat, smear, etc. with pitch. *pitch black, dark*, etc., intensely dark. **pitch'blende**, mineral containing uranium oxide, source of radium, etc. **pitch-pine**, pine with resinous wood.

pitch[2], *v.* set up (tent, camp, wickets, etc.); give chosen height, gradient, intensity, etc., to; throw, fling, fall; incline, dip. *n.* pitching; height, degree, intensity, gradient; (Mus.) degree of highness or lowness of tone; part of cricket-ground where wickets are pitched; football, hockey, etc., ground; part of street, etc., where trader, performer, etc., is stationed. **pitch'fork**, (*n.*) two--pronged fork for pitching hay, etc.; (*v.t.*) (esp.) thrust forcibly *into* (office, position, etc.). **pitch'er**[1], *n.* (esp.) baseball player who delivers ball.

pitch'er[2], *n.* large jug.

pit'eous, *a.* arousing or deserving pity; deplorable.

pith, *n.* spongy cellular tissue in stems of plants or lining rind of orange, etc.; essential part, gist. **pith'y**, *a.* of, like, full of, pith; concise, terse.

pit'iable, *a.* deserving of pity or contempt.

pit'iful, *a.* arousing pity; contemptible.

pit'iless, *a.* showing no pity.

pitt'ance, *n.* scanty allowance, small amount.

pit'y, *n.* sorrow for another's suffering; cause for regret or compassion. *v.t.* feel pity for. **pit'ying**, *a.* **pit'yingly**, *adv.*

piv'ot, *n.* shaft or pin on which something turns; central point. *v.* turn (as) on pivot; hinge, depend, (*on*). **piv'otal**, *a.*

pix'ie, pix'y, *n.* small fairy.

pizzicato (pitsikah'tō), *adv.* & *a.* (Mus.) (played) by plucking string of violin, etc., with finger.

plac'able, *a.* easily appeased; mild-tempered.

plac'ard, *n.* paper with announcement for posting on board, etc. *v.t.* post placards on; advertise by placards.

placate', *v.t.* conciliate, pacify. **placa'tory**, *a.*

place, *n.* particular part of space; space or room of or for person or thing; town, village, residence, building; rank, station, position. *in place of*, instead of. *out of place*, unsuitable, inappropriate. *v.t.* put in place; find place for; assign rank, order, class, etc., to; give (order for goods etc.).

placen'ta, *n.* (pl. *placentae*), spongy organ nourishing foetus in mammals. **placen'tal**, *a.*

pla'cid, *a.* not easily disturbed or irritated; calm, peaceful. **placid'ity**, *n.*

plack'et, *n.* opening in woman's skirt, etc., for ease in putting on or off.

pla'giarize, *v.* take and use another's (writings, etc.) as one's own. **pla'giarism**, *n.* **pla'giarist**, *n.*

plague (-g), *n.* fatal epidemic disease, esp. bubonic plague; infestation *of* pest. *v.t.* pester, bother.

plaice, *n.* edible flat-fish.

plaid (*or* plad), *n.* long piece of woollen cloth as part of Highland costume; tartan cloth.

plain, *a.* clear, evident; straightforward; ordinary; not decorated or luxurious; not good--looking. *adv.* clearly. *n.* level tract of country. *plain sailing*, simple course of action. **plain'song**, traditional church music sung in unison and in free rhythm.

plain'tiff, *n.* person bringing action into court of law.

plain'tive, *a.* mournful-sounding.

plait (plat), *n.* length of three or more interlaced tresses of hair or strands of straw, etc. *v.t.* form into plait.

plan, *n.* drawing showing relative position and size of parts of building, etc.; diagram, map; project, design. *v.* (p.t. *planned*), make plan of; design; arrange beforehand, scheme.

plane[1], *n.* tall spreading broad-leaved tree.

plane[2], *n.* level surface; (wing or supporting part of) aeroplane; level (*of* attainment, etc.). *a.* flat, level. *v.i.* glide (*down*).

plane[3], *n.* tool for smoothing (esp. wooden) surface by paring shavings from it. *v.t.* smooth, pare (*away*, etc.) with plane.

plan'et, *n.* celestial body revolving round sun or another planet. **planetar'ium**, *n.* model or structure representing solar system, etc. **plan'etary**, *a.* of planets.

plank, *n.* long flat piece of sawn timber. *v.t.* cover, lay, with planks.

plant (-ah-), *n.* living organism without power of locomotion or special organs of digestion, etc.; kind of this smaller than tree or shrub; equipment for manufacturing process.

v. t. place (seed, etc.) in ground to grow; fix firmly, establish. **plant-louse,** kind of aphis.

plan'tain[1] (-tn), *n.* herb yielding seed used as food for cage-birds.

plan'tain[2] (-tn), *n.* (tree-like tropical herbaceous plant bearing) fruit like banana.

plantā'tion, *n.* number of trees, etc., planted together; estate for cultivation of cotton, tobacco, etc.

plan'ter (-ah-), *n.* (esp.) occupier of (esp. tropical or sub-tropical) plantation.

plaque (plahk), *n.* tablet of metal or porcelain fixed to wall as ornament or memorial.

plash[1], *n. & v.* splash.

plash[2]**, pleach,** *vv. t.* bend and interweave (growing stems, branches) to make or renew hedge.

plas'ma (-z-), *n.* (*blood*) *plasma,* liquid in which blood cells are suspended.

pla'ster (-ah-), *n.* soft plastic mixture of lime, sand, etc., spread on ceilings, walls, etc., and hardening to smooth surface; fabric spread with medicinal substance, etc., for application to body; sticking-plaster; preparation of gypsum used to make moulds, etc. *v. t.* cover with plaster; coat, smear. **plaster of Paris,** white powder of gypsum, setting hard when mixed with water. **plaster cast,** mould, cast, of plaster of Paris; mould of gauze and plaster of Paris for immobilizing limb, etc. **pla'sterer,** *n.* person skilled in plastering ceilings, etc.

plas'tic, *a.* easily moulded; made of (esp. synthetic) plastic. *n.* natural or synthetic substance that can be moulded by heat or pressure. **plastic surgery,** (Med.) repair or restoration of lost or damaged tissue, etc. **plasti'city,** *n.*

plāte, *n.* shallow, usu. circular, vessel from which food is eaten; sheet of metal, glass, etc.; (Biol., etc.) thin flat organic formation; engraved piece of metal; illustration printed from engraved plate, etc.; table-utensils of gold or silver; part of denture fitting to mouth and holding teeth. *v.* cover (esp. ship) with plates of metal; cover with thin coating of silver, gold, etc.

pla'teau (-tō), *n.* (pl. *plateaux* or *plateaus,* pr. -z), expanse of level land high above sea-level.

plat'form, *n.* flat structure raised above floor-or ground-level; area, esp. raised surface, along side of line at railway station.

plat'inum, *n.* silvery-white heavy valuable metal.

plat'itūde, *n.* commonplace statement. **platitū'dinous,** *a.*

Platon'ic, *a.* of Plato or his doctrines; (of love, etc.) free from sexual desire.

platōōn', *n.* subdivision of an infantry company.

platt'er, *n.* (*archaic*) (wooden) plate or dish.

plat'ypus, *n.* (also *duckbill, duck-billed platypus*) primitive Australian aquatic furred egg-laying mammal.

plaud'it, *n.* (usu. pl.) round of applause.

plau'sible (-z-), *a.* (deceptively) seeming reasonable or probable; apparently honest, true, etc. **plausibil'ity,** *n.*

play, *v.* amuse oneself; engage in games, gambling, acting, etc.; perform on musical instrument; take part in (game); move piece, produce card, strike ball, etc., in game; act, act as; move about in lively way; have free movement. *play at,* take part in (game, pursuit) in light-hearted way. *play back,* reproduce (newly recorded music, etc.). *play fair,* play or act fairly. *play the game,* play fair. *play with,* amuse oneself with, trifle with. *n.* recreation; playing of game, ball, etc.; dramatic piece; gambling; fitful or light movement; freedom of movement. *play* (*up*)*on words,* pun. **play-act,** play a part, pose. **play-bill,** theatre poster. **play'fellow,** companion in childhood. **play'ground,** school recreation ground. **play'house,** (*archaic*) theatre. **play'mate,** playfellow. **play'thing,** toy. **play'wright,** writer of plays, dramatist. **play'er,** *n.* person taking part in game, performing on musical instrument, acting in play, etc. **play'ful,** *a.* frolicsome, humorous. **playing-card,** *n.* one of pack or set of cards used for games. **playing-field,** *n.* ground for such games as football, cricket, etc.

plea, *n.* pleading, earnest request; excuse; defendant's or prisoner's statement.

pleach: see **plash**[2].

plead, *v.* address lawcourt as advocate or party; allege formally as plea. *plead guilty, not guilty,* admit, deny, liability or guilt. *plead* (*with*), make earnest appeal (to). **plead'ing,** *n.* formal statement of charge or defence.

pleas'ance (plez-), *n.* (*archaic*) pleasure-ground.

pleas'ant (plez-), *a.* agreeable; giving pleasure. **pleas'antry,** *n.* jest.

please (-z), *v.* be agreeable, give joy or gratification, (to); choose, be willing, like. *int.* or *adv.* used as courteous qualification to request, etc. **pleased,** *a.* **plea'sing,** *a.*

pleasure (plezh'er), *n.* feeling of satisfaction; enjoyment; sensuous gratification; will, desire. **plea'surable,** *a.* giving pleasure.

pleat, *n.* flattened fold made by doubling cloth upon itself. *v. t.* make pleat(s) in.

plēbei'an (-bē-), *n.* commoner; one of the common people in ancient Rome. *a.* of low birth; of the common people.

pleb'iscite (*or* -sīt), *n.* (expression of community's opinion by) direct voting of all electors.

plec'trum, *n.* (pl. *plectra*), small implement of horn, metal, etc., for plucking strings of zither, etc.

pledge, *n.* thing handed over as security; thing pawned; token; solemn promise. *v. t.* hand over as pledge; pawn; drink to, toast. *pledge* *oneself*, *one's word*, etc., promise, undertake.

ple'nary, *a.* (of powers, authority) absolute, unqualified; (of assembly) attended by all members.

plenipoten'tiary (-sha-), *n. & a.* (ambassador, etc.) having full powers.

plen'itude, *n.* completeness; abundance.

plen'teous, *a.* (chiefly Poet.) plentiful.

plen'tiful, *a.* present or existing in large quantities or numbers.

plen'ty, *n.* as much as, or more than, is needed or desired; large number or quantity (*of*).

pleth'ora, *n.* excessive amount.

pleur'isy (ploor-), *n.* inflammation of membrane enclosing lungs.

pli'able, pli'ant, *aa.* easily bent or influenced; supple, yielding; accommodating. **pliabil'ity, pli'ancy**, *nn.*

pli'ers (-z), *n.pl.* (*pair of*) *pliers*, pincers with flat grip for bending wire, etc.

plight[1] (plīt), *v.t.* (*archaic*) pledge. **plight'ed**, *p.p.* engaged (*to* person).

plight[2] (plīt), *n.* condition, state, esp. unfortunate one.

Plim'soll line, mark, line on hull of ship marking how far it may legally go down in water when loaded.

plim'solls (-z), *n.pl.* rubber-soled canvas shoes.

plinth, *n.* slab or course between ground and pillar, wall, pedestal, etc.; base of statue, vase, etc.

plod, *v.i.* (p.t. *plodded*), walk or work persistently and laboriously. **plodd'er**, *n.* **plodd'ing**, *a.*

plot, *n.* small piece of land; plan, story, of play, novel, etc.; secret scheme, conspiracy. *v.* (p.t. *plotted*), devise secretly; hatch secret plans; make chart or graph of. **plott'er**, *n.*

plough (plow), *n.* implement for furrowing and turning up soil. *v.* turn up (earth) with plough; use plough; advance laboriously (*through*). **plough back**, (fig.) reinvest (profits) in business. **plough'man**, (pl. *-men*), guider of plough. **plough'share**, blade of plough making horizontal cut.

plo'ver (-uv-), *n.* any of various birds nesting on ground in open country, often near water; (*green plover*) lapwing, pewit.

ploy, *n.* (*informal*) manoeuvre, move; (north.) undertaking, occupation.

pluck, *v.* strip (bird) of feathers; pick or gather; pull at, twitch; sound (string of guitar, etc.) thus. *pluck up courage*, summon up one's courage. *n.* animal's heart, liver, and lungs as food; courage. **pluck'y**, *a.* brave, spirited.

plug, *n.* something fitting into and stopping a hole; pin, etc., for making electrical contacts; (piece of) tobacco pressed into cake or stick. *v.* (p.t. *plugged*), stop with plug; put plug into; (*informal*) make known by fre-

quent repetition or commendation.

plum, *n.* (tree bearing) fleshy stone-fruit. **plum cake, plum pudding**, cake, pudding, containing raisins, currants, etc.

plu'mage (-oo-), *n.* bird's feathers.

plumb (-m), *n.* ball of lead (*plumb-bob*) attached to line for testing whether wall, etc., is perpendicular; sounding-lead. *a.* vertical; level. *adv.* vertically; exactly. *v.* sound (water); measure (depth); get to bottom of; make vertical; work as plumber. **plumb-line**, cord with plumb attached.

plumbā'gō, *n.* graphite; herbaceous plant with spikes of (esp. blue) flowers.

plumb'er (-mer), *n.* man skilled at fitting and repairing pipes, cisterns, etc. **plumb'ing**, *n.* work of plumber; system of water and drainage pipes in building, etc.

plume (-oo-), *n.* feather, esp. large and showy; feathery ornament on hat, etc.; feather-like formation, esp. of smoke. *v.t.* trim with plume(s); pride *oneself* (*on*); preen (feathers).

plumm'et, *n.* plumb, plumb-line; sounding-lead. *v.i.* plunge.

plump[1], *a.* of full and rounded form. *v.* make or become plump, fatten *up*, swell *out*. **plump'ness**, *n.*

plump[2], *v.* drop or plunge abruptly. *plump for*, (*informal*) choose unhesitatingly. *adv.* abruptly; bluntly.

plun'der, *v.* rob forcibly, esp. as in war; rob, steal, embezzle. *n.* goods acquired violently or dishonestly; spoils.

plunge (-nj), *v.* immerse completely; put suddenly, throw oneself, dive, (*into*); (of horse) start violently forward. *n.* plunging, dive.

pluper'fect (-oo-), *a. & n.* (tense) expressing action completed before past point of time.

plur'al (-oor-), *a.* more than one in number. *n.* plural number, word, or form. **plural'ity**, *n.* being plural; large number; majority (*of*).

plus, *prep.* with the addition of; or more. *a.* additional, extra; positive. *n.* symbol (+) of addition or positive quantity or charge; additional or positive quantity.

plush, *n.* fabric resembling velvet, but with longer and less dense pile. **plush'y**, *a.*

Plu'tō (-loo-), *n.* (Gk. & Rom. myth.) god of infernal regions; a planet.

plutoc'racy (-loo-), *n.* State in which power belongs to the rich; wealthy class. **plu'tocrat**, *n.* rich person. **plutocrat'ic**, *a.*

plu'vial (-oo-), *a.* of or caused by rain.

ply[1], *n.* thickness; strand. *two-, three-ply*, etc., having two, three, etc., thicknesses or strands. **ply'wood**, strong board made by gluing together thin layers of wood.

ply[2], *v.* wield vigorously; work at; supply persistently (*with*); (of ship, vehicle, etc.) go regularly to and fro; (of taxi-driver, etc.) seek custom.

pneumat'ic (nū-), *a.* of, acting by, containing, filled with, (compressed) air.

pneumō'nia (nū-), *n.* acute inflammation of the lungs. **pneumon'ic**, *a.*

poach[1], *v.t.* cook (esp. egg without shell) by simmering.

poach[2], *v.* take (game, fish) illegally; encroach or trespass (*on*), esp. for this purpose. **poa'cher**, *n.*

pock, *n.* eruptive spot in smallpox, etc. **pock--marked**, scarred or pitted, esp. after smallpox.

pock'ėt, *n.* small bag or pouch attached to garment; money resources; pouch of billiard--table; cavity in earth, rock, etc. **in pocket**, having gained money. **out of pocket**, having lost money by some transaction. *a.* suitable for carrying in pocket; very small. *v.* put into pocket; appropriate for oneself; submit to (insult, etc.), conceal (feelings). **pocket--book**, small case for banknotes, etc.; (U.S.) woman's handbag. **pocket-knife**, small folding knife. **pocket-money**, money for small expenses, esp. allowance to children.

pod, *n.* long seed-vessel of pea, bean and other leguminous plants. *v.* (p.t. *podded*), form pods; take from pods, shell, hull.

podg'y, *a.* short, thick, and fat.

pŏ'ėm, *n.* composition in verse; piece of poetry.

pŏ'ėt, *n.* writer in verse, composer of poetry. **poet laureate**, see **laureate**. **pŏėtas'ter**, *n.* inferior poet. **pŏ'ėtess**, *n.fem.*

pŏet'ic, pŏet'ical, *aa.* of poets or poetry; suitable to, having qualities of, poetry. **poetic justice**, ideal distribution of reward and punishment. **poetic licence**, see **licence**.

pŏ'ėtry, *n.* poet's art or work; expression, esp. in verse, of elevated thought or feeling; poems; quality calling for poetical expression.

pŏ'gŏ-stick, *n.* short pole with cross-piece for feet and strong spring, enabling user to progress by series of jumps.

pog'rom (*or* pogrom'), *n.* organized massacre (originally that of Jews in Russia).

poignant (poi'nyant; *or* -nant), *a.* distressing to feelings; moving, vivid; keen, sharp; pungent. **poign'ancy**, *n.*

point, *n.* dot; particular place or spot; exact moment; unit of measurement, value, scoring, etc.; item, detail; salient feature; sharp end, tip; promontory; (pl.) tapering movable rails for directing train, etc., from one line to another. *to the point*, relevant(ly). *v.* sharpen, provide with point; fill joints of (brickwork, etc.) with mortar or cement; direct attention (as) by extending finger; direct (finger, weapon, etc., *at*); (of dog) stand rigid, facing towards game. *point out*, show, call attention to. **point-blank**, with aim or weapon level, at short range. **point-duty**, duty of policeman, etc., stationed at particular point to regulate traffic. **point of view**, way of looking at question, etc., opinion. **poin'tėd**, *a.* (esp.) cutting, emphatic; made

evident. **poin'tėdly**, *adv.* **point'less**, *a.* without point, meaningless, useless.

poin'ter, *n.* rod used to point to things on screen, etc.; indicator on dial, etc.; breed of dog trained to point towards game; (*informal*) hint, indication.

poise (-z), *v.* be or keep in balanced or steady position; carry (one's head, etc.) in specified way; hover in air. *n.* balance; bearing, carriage; ease of manner, assurance.

poi'son (-zn), *n.* substance that, when absorbed by living organism, kills or injures it; harmful influence, etc. *v.t.* administer poison to; kill, harm, with poison; corrupt, spoil. **poison gas**, noxious gas used in war. **poison pen**, anonymous writer of libellous or scurrilous letters. **poi'soner**, *n.* **poi'soning**, *n.* **poi'sonous**, *a.*

pŏke, *v.* push with (end of) finger, stick, etc.; stir (fire); make thrusts (*at*, etc.) with stick, etc.; thrust forward. *n.* poking; thrust, nudge. **poke-bonnet**, bonnet with projecting brim or front. **pŏ'ker**[1], *n.* metal rod for poking fire.

pŏ'ker[2], *n.* card-game for two or more players. **poker-face**, (person with) impassive face.

pŏ'ky, *a.* (of room, etc.) small, mean.

pŏ'lar, *a.* of or near either pole of earth; having polarity; directly opposite. **polar bear**, white bear of Arctic regions. **pŏla'rity**, *n.* tendency to point to magnetic poles; possession of negative and positive poles; direction towards single point. **pŏ'larize**, *v.t.* confine vibrations of (esp. light-waves) to single direction or plane; give polarity to. **pŏlarīzā'tion**, *n.*

pŏle[1], *n.* long slender rounded piece of wood, metal, etc., esp. as support for scaffolding, tent, etc.; measure of length (5½ yds.). *v.t.* push, move, with pole. **pole-jump, -vault**, jump with aid of pole held in hands.

pŏle[2], *n.* either extremity of earth's axis, or either of two points in sky about which stars appear to rotate (*North pole, South Pole*); each of two points in magnet which attract or repel magnetic bodies; positive or negative terminal of electric cell, etc.; each of two opposed principles, etc. **pole star**, star (*Polaris*) near N. celestial pole.

Pŏle[3], *n.* Polish person.

pŏle'-axe (-lax), *n.* (Hist.) battle-axe; (Hist.) naval weapon and implement; cattle--slaughtering implement. *v.t.* fell with pole--axe.

pole'cat (pōlk-), *n.* fetid weasel-like animal.

polem'ic, *a.* controversial. *n.* controversial discussion; (pl.) practice of this. **polem'ical**, *a.*

police' (-ēs), *n.* (*collective*) (members of) organized body responsible for maintaining public order or employed to enforce regulations, etc. *v.t.* control, provide with, police; act as police in. **police'man, police'woman**, (pl. -*men*), member of police force. **police--station,** office of local police force.

pol'icy[1], *n.* course of action adopted and pursued by government, party, etc.; prudent conduct.

pol'icy[2], *n.* (*insurance*) *policy,* document containing contract of insurance.

pō'liō (*informal*), **pōliōmȳ̈elī'tis,** *nn.* infectious disease of central nervous system with temporary or permanent paralysis.

pol'ish, *v.* make or become smooth or glossy by friction; make elegant or cultured; finish *off* quickly. *n.* smoothness, glossiness; substance used to produce polished surface; refinement.

polite', *a.* having, showing, good manners; cultured, refined. **polite'ness,** *n.*

pol'itic, *a.* (of actions, etc.) well-judged, expedient; (of persons) wise, prudent. **body politic,** see **body.**

polit'ical, *a.* of State or its government; of public affairs; of politics. **political economy,** economics.

politi'cian (-shn), *n.* person engaged in politics.

pol'itics, *n.* science and art of government; (pl.) political affairs, principles, etc.

pol'ity, *n.* form of civil administration; organized society, State.

pol'ka, *n.* (music for) lively dance in duple time. **polka dot(s),** pattern of regularly arranged dots.

pōll[1], *n.* head; counting of voters, voting, number of votes; (*opinion*) *poll,* questioning of sample of population to estimate trend of public opinion. *v.* crop hair of; cut off top of (tree, etc.) or horns of (beast); take votes of, vote, receive votes of. **poll-tax,** tax levied on every person.

Poll[2], *n.* parrot. **poll-parrot,** parrot.

poll'ard, *n.* tree made by polling to produce close head of young shoots; hornless animal. *v.t.* make pollard of (tree). **poll'arded,** *a.*

poll'en, *n.* powder produced in flower's anther, containing male cells for fertilizing ovules.

poll'ināte, *v.t.* fertilize with pollen. **pollinā'tion,** *n.*

pollute' (*or* -ōōt), *v.t.* destroy purity of; make (atmosphere, water, etc.) foul or filthy. **pollu'tion,** *n.*

pō'lō, *n.* game somewhat resembling hockey, played on horseback. **water polo,** ball-game with goals, played by swimmers. **polo-neck, -necked,** (having) close-fitting rolled collar.

polonaise' (-z), *n.* (music for) slow dance in triple time, of Polish origin.

poltroon', *n.* coward. **poltroon'ery,** *n.*

pol'tergeist (-gīst), *n.* spirit supposedly announcing its presence by noises.

poly-, *pref.* many.

polyan'dry, *n.* having more than one, or several, husbands. **polyan'drous,** *a.*

polyan'thus, *n.* cultivated kind of primula.

polyg'amy, *n.* having more than one, or several, wives or husbands. **polyg'amous,** *a.*

pol'ygon, *n.* figure (usu. plane, straight-sided) with many angles and sides. **polyg'onal,** *a.*

pol'yglot, *a.* speaking or writing several languages; of, written in, several languages. *n.* polyglot person.

polyhed'ron (*or* -hē-), *n.* solid figure with many (usu. more than six) sides. **polyhed'ral,** *a.*

pol'ymer, *n.* compound formed by combination of large number of identical molecules. **polym'erize,** *v.* combine to form polymer. **polymerīzā'tion.** *n.*

pol'ysyllable, *n.* word having many syllables. **polysyllab'ic,** *a.*

polytech'nic (-k-), *n.* school or college giving instruction in various technical subjects.

pol'ythēism, *n.* belief in more than one god. **pol'ythēist,** *n.* **polythēis'tic,** *a.*

pol'ythēne, *n.* synthetic plastic material used for insulating, packaging, etc.

pomāde' (*or* -ahd), *n.* scented ointment for the hair. *v.t.* apply pomade to.

pom'egranate, *n.* large many-seeded fruit with tough rind.

Pomerā'nian, *n.* dog of small breed with long silky hair and pointed snout.

pomm'el (pu-), *n.* knob of sword-hilt; upward projecting front part of saddle. *v.t.* (p.t. *pommelled*), pummel.

pomp, *n.* splendid display; splendour.

pom'pom, pom'pon, *nn.* tuft of silk threads, etc., on shoe, etc.; kind of dahlia or chrysanthemum with small globular flower-heads.

pom'pous, *a.* showing self-importance or exaggerated dignity; (of language) exaggeratedly dignified. **pompos'ity,** *n.*

pond, *n.* small area of still water, artificially formed; natural pool or small lake.

pon'der, *v.* think (over), muse.

pon'derable, *a.* & *n.* (thing) that can be weighed or estimated. **ponderabil'ity,** *n.*

pon'derous, *a.* heavy; unwieldy; laborious; laboured.

pon'iard, *n.* dagger.

pon'tiff, *n.* pope; bishop; chief priest.

pontif'ical, *a.* of or befitting a pontiff; solemnly dogmatic. **pontif'icate,** *n.* (period of) office of bishop or pope. **pontif'icāte,** *v.i.* officiate as bishop; speak or act pompously or dogmatically.

pontōōn', *n.* flat-bottomed boat, etc., used with others as support for temporary bridge (*pontoon bridge*).

pō'ny, *n.* horse of any small breed. **pony-tail,** hair tied at back of head and hanging like horse's tail.

pōōd'le, *n.* breed of dog with long curling hair, often clipped in elaborate style.

pōōh (*or* poo-), *int.* of contempt. **pooh-pooh',** *v.t.* express contempt for.

pōōl[1], *n.* small area of still water; puddle; deep still place in river.

pool², *n.* collective stake in cards or betting; (usu. pl.) organized gambling (esp. by post) on football-match results; combination of manufacturers, etc.; common fund. *v.t.* place in common fund; merge; share.

poop, *n.* (raised deck at) stern of ship.

poor, *a.* having little money or means; deficient (in); (of soil) unproductive; inadequate; despicable, insignificant; deserving pity. **Poor Law**, (Hist.) law relating to support of paupers. **poor'ly**, *adv.* in a poor way; scantily, defectively. *a.* unwell. **poor'ness**, *n.* defectiveness; deficiency. ·

pop¹, *n.* small abrupt explosive sound. *v.* (p.t. *popped*), make pop; put (*in, out, down, etc.*) quickly or suddenly; come, go (*in*, etc.) thus. *adv.* with sound of pop; suddenly. **pop'corn**, sweetened parched maize. **pop'gun**, toy gun making popping sound.

pop², *a.* (of music, etc.) popular.

pope, *n.* bishop of Rome as head of R. C. Church. **po'pery**, *n.* (in hostile sense) papal system, Roman Catholicism. **po'pish**, *a.* of popery.

pop'-eyed (-īd), *a.* having bulging eyes.

pop'injay, *n.* conceited person, fop.

pop'lar, *n.* large rapidly-growing tree.

pop'lin, *n.* closely woven ribbed fabric.

popp'et, *n.* darling.

popp'y, *n.* wild or cultivated plant with bright flowers. **poppy(-red)**, bright scarlet.

pop'ulace, *n.* the common people.

pop'ular, *a.* of the people; generally liked or admired. **popula'rity**, *n.* being generally liked. **pop'ularize**, *v.t.* make popular. **popularizā'tion**, *n.* **pop'ularly**, *adv.*

pop'ulāte, *v.t.* form population of; supply with inhabitants. **populā'tion**, *n.* (number of) inhabitants; people of a country, etc. **pop'ulous**, *a.* thickly populated.

porcelain (por'slin), *n.* (articles made of) finest kind of earthenware. *a.* of porcelain.

porch, *n.* covered approach to entrance of building; (U.S.) veranda.

por'cine, *a.* of or like pigs.

por'cupine, *n.* rodent having body and tail covered with long erectile spines.

pore¹, *n.* very small opening in skin, membrane, etc., for sweating, transpiration, etc.

pore², *v.i.* pore over, have eyes or mind intent on.

pork, *n.* flesh of pig as food. **por'ker**, *n.* young fattened hog.

pornog'raphy, *n.* explicit description or exhibition of obscene subjects in literature, films, etc., to arouse erotic feelings. **pornograph'ic**, *a.*

por'ous, *n.* allowing liquid to pass through, permeable; having pores.

por'phyry, *n.* rock with large crystals in fine-grained ground mass.

por'poise (-pus), *n.* sea mammal related to whale, with blunt rounded snout.

po'rridge, *n.* oatmeal or other meal boiled in water (or milk).

po'rringer (-j-), *n.* small bowl from which porridge, etc., is eaten.

port¹, *n.* harbour; town or place possessing harbour.

port², *n.* opening in ship's side for entrance, loading, etc. **port-hole**, opening in ship's side to admit light and air.

port³, *v.t.* hold (rifle, sword) diagonally across and close to body.

port⁴, *n.* left-hand side of ship, etc., looking forward (opp. *starboard*).

port⁵, *n.* strong sweet (esp. dark red) wine.

por'table, *a.* that can be carried about, movable. **portabil'ity**, *n.*

por'tage, *n.* (cost of) transport of goods; carrying necessary between two rivers, etc.

por'tal, *n.* door(way), gate(way).

portcull'is, *n.* grating raised and lowered in grooves as defence of gateway of castle, etc.

portend', *v.t.* foreshadow; be omen of.

por'tent, *n.* omen, significant sign. **porten'tous**, *a.* of or like portent; extraordinary; solemn.

por'ter¹, *n.* gate-keeper, door-keeper, esp. of large building.

por'ter², *n.* person employed to carry loads, esp. passengers' luggage.

por'ter³, *n.* dark-brown bitter beer.

portfo'lio, *n.* (pl. *portfolios*), case for loose drawings, papers, etc.; securities held by investor, etc.; office of minister of State.

por'tico, *n.* (pl. *porticos*), roof supported by pillars, serving as porch to building.

por'tion, *n.* part allotted, share; amount of food served for one person; dowry (*archaic*); destiny, lot; part, some (*of*). *v.t.* divide into portions, share *out*.

port'ly, *n.* stout, corpulent; stately.

portman'teau (-tō), *n.* (pl. *portmanteaus, portmanteaux*, pr. -z), travelling-bag opening into two equal parts. **portmanteau word**, word formed by blending two others (e.g. *motel* from *motor* and *hotel*).

por'trait (-trit), *n.* painting, drawing, photograph, of person or animal; description. **por'traiture**, *n.* portraying; portrait(s).

portray', *v.t.* make picture of; describe; act part of. **portray'al**, *n.* portraying; description.

pose (-z), *v.* put (question), propound (problem); arrange (artist's model, etc.) in, assume, a certain attitude; behave in affected manner. *pose as*, pretend to be.

po'ser (-z-), *n.* puzzling question or problem.

posh, *a.* (*slang*) smart, stylish; high-class.

posi'tion (-z-), *n.* way thing is placed; state of affairs; mental attitude; rank or status; proper place; office, post; strategic point. *v.t.* place in position. **posi'tional**, *a.*

pos'itive (-z-), *a.* definite; sure; unquestionable; absolute; confident in opinion; not negative; (Gram., of degree of adj., etc.) expressing simple quality without comparison; (Electr.) of type of electricity (opp. *negative*) produced by rubbing glass with silk; (Photog.) showing lights and shades as in nature. **pos'itively,** *adv.*

pos'itron (-z-), *n.* positive counterpart of electron.

poss'e, *n.* body *of* police, or of men summoned to aid sheriff.

possess' (-zes), *v.t.* hold as property; have, own; (of demon, etc.) occupy, dominate, (person); have mastery of; seize.

posse'ssion (-zeshn), *n.* possessing or being possessed; occupancy; thing possessed; (pl.) property.

possess'ive (-zes-), *a.* of or indicating possession; eager to own, unwilling to share. *n.* (Gram.) possessive case or word.

possess'or (-zes-), *n.* one who possesses, owner.

poss'et, *n.* (*archaic*) drink of hot milk curdled with ale, wine, etc., often spiced.

possibil'ity, *n.* state or fact of being possible; thing that may exist or happen.

poss'ible, *a.* that can exist, be done, or happen; that may be or become; tolerable, reasonable, intelligible. **poss'ibly,** *adv.*

poss'um, *n.* small Australian marsupial; (*informal*) opossum. *play possum,* pretend to be ill or dead.

post[1], *n.* stake, stout pole, fixed upright in ground, etc. *v.t.* display (notice, etc.) on post, notice-board, wall, etc.

post[2], *n.* official conveying of letters and parcels; single collection, delivery, etc., of letters, etc.; post office, letter-box. *v.* put (letter, etc.) into letter-box, take (letter, etc.) to post office, for transmission; travel with relays of horses (Hist.); hurry; supply with latest information. *adv.* with post-horses; express, in haste. **post'card,** card conveying message by post. **post-chaise,** (Hist.) chaise hired from stage to stage. **post-haste,** with all possible speed. **post-horses,** horses formerly kept at inns, etc., for travellers, etc. **post'man,** (pl. *-men*), man who collects or delivers post. **post'mark,** official mark stamped on letters, etc. **post'master, post'mistress,** official in charge of post office. **post office,** building or room in which postal business is carried on.

post[3], *n.* place where soldier, etc., is stationed; place of duty; appointment, job; trading-post. *last post,* (Mil., etc.) last bugle-call of day. *v.t.* assign post or duty to; send or appoint to office, command, etc.

post-, *pref.* after, behind. **post-date,** *v.t.* affix or assign later than actual date to (cheque, event, etc.). **postgrad'uate,** (*n.*) person carrying on studies after graduation; (*a.*) of such studies. **post-war,** *a.* of period after war, esp. of 1914-18 or 1939-45.

pos'tage, *n.* charge for carriage by post. **postage-stamp,** stamp affixed to envelope, etc.

pos'tal, *a.* of, carried by, post. **postal order,** kind of money order.

pos'ter, *n.* placard for posting in public place.

poste res'tante (-tahnt), post-office department to which letters may be addressed, to be kept till applied for.

poster'ior, *a.* at back; later in time or order. *n.* buttocks.

poste'rity, *n.* person's descendants; all succeeding generations.

pos'tern (*or* pō-), *n.* back or side entrance, esp. to castle.

post'humous (-tū-), *a.* born after father's death; published after author's death.

postil'ion, *n.* man riding one of horses drawing carriage.

post merid'iem, after noon (abbrev. *p.m.*, e.g. *1 p.m.*, etc.). (Latin)

post-mor'tem, *a.* after death. *n.* examination (by dissection) of dead body to ascertain cause of death.

postpone', *v.t.* cause to take place at a later time. **postpone'ment,** *n.*

post'script, *n.* additional sentence(s), esp. at end of letter after signature (abbrev. *P.S.*).

pos'tulant, *n.* candidate, esp. for admission to religious order.

pos'tulate, *v.t.* claim, assume as basis of reasoning, etc. **pos'tulate,** *n.* thing postulated, prerequisite.

pos'ture (-cher), *n.* attitude of body or mind. *v.i.* pose.

po'sy (-z-), *n.* small bunch of flowers.

pot, *n.* vessel, usu. round, of earthenware, metal, etc.; chamber-pot; (*slang,* esp. in pl.) large sum; (*slang*) marijuana. *v.t.* (p.t. *potted*), put in pot; plant in flower-pot.

pot'ash, *n.* crude potassium carbonate.

potass'ium, *n.* light soft silvery-white metallic element.

pota'to, *n.* (pl. *potatoes*), plant with tubers used as food; its tuber.

poteen', *n.* Irish whiskey from illicit still.

po'tent, *a.* powerful; strong; convincing. **po'tency,** *n.* **po'tentate,** *n.* ruler, monarch.

poten'tial (-shl), *a.* that can or may come into existence or action; possible. *n.* potential resources or energy. **potential'ity** (-shi-), *n.*

poth'er (-dh-), *n.* fuss, disturbance; din.

pot'-hole, *n.* deep hole or pit in ground, etc.; depression in road surface. **pot'-holer, pot'-holing,** *nn.* explorer, exploring, of pot-holes.

pot'-hook, *n.* hook for hanging pots over fire, etc.

po'tion, *n.* dose of liquid medicine or poison; drink, draught.

pot-pourri (pō'poori; *or* -ē'), *n.* scented mixture of dried petals and spices; musical or literary medley.

pot'sherd, *n.* piece of broken pottery (esp. in archaeology).

pott'er[1], *v.i.* move (*about*, etc.), work, in feeble or aimless or unmethodical manner.

pott'er², *n.* maker of earthenware pots, etc.
pott'ery, *n.* earthenware; potter's work or workshop.
pott'y, *a.* (*slang*) insignificant; crazy.
pouch, *n.* small bag carried in pocket, attached to belt, etc.; bag-like receptacle, esp. that in which marsupials carry their young. *v.* put into pouch; hang like pouch.
pouffe (poōf), *n.* low stuffed seat or cushion.
poul'terer (pōl-), *n.* dealer in poultry.
poul'tice (pōl-), *n.* soft, usu. hot, dressing applied to sore or inflamed part of skin. *v.t.* apply poultice to.
poul'try (pōl-), *n.* (*collective*) domestic fowls (e.g. hens, geese, turkeys, etc.).
pounce, *v.i.* swoop, come suddenly down (*on*). *n.* pouncing, sudden swoop.
pound¹, *v.* crush, bruise, (as) with pestle; thump, pummel; walk, run, etc., heavily.
pound², *n.* enclosure where stray cattle, etc., may be detained; police enclosure for vehicles officially removed.
pound³, *n.* measure of weight (abbrev. *lb.*), 16 oz. avoirdupois, 12 oz. troy; unit of money (symbol £, written before figure), 100 new pence (formerly 20 shillings). **poun'dage**, *n.* charge for postal order, etc.
pour (por), *v.* (cause to) flow in continuous stream; discharge copiously; (of rain) descend heavily.
pout, *v.* protrude lips, (of lips) protrude, esp. pettishly, etc. *n.* pouting. **pout'er**, *n.* (esp.) pigeon with great power of inflating crop.
pov'erty, *n.* state of being poor, esp. having little or no money; want. **poverty-stricken**, *a.* extremely poor, destitute.
pow'der, *n.* mass of fine dry particles; cosmetic or medicine in this form; gunpowder. *v.* reduce to powder; sprinkle with powder; apply powder to. **pow'dery**, *a.*
pow'er, *n.* ability to do or act; vigour, energy, influence, control; authority; State with international influence; (Phys., etc.) rate of doing work or consuming energy; (Math.) product of number mutiplied by itself (e.g. 2^4, or the 4th power of 2, $=16$). **power--station**, building for generating and distributing electric power. **pow'ered** (-erd), *a.* equipped with mechanical power.
pow'erful, *a.* having great power. **pow'-erfully**, *adv.* **pow'erless**, *a.* without power; wholly unable (*to*).
pow'wow, *n.* N.Amer. Indian conference or council; (*informal*) conference, palaver.
pox, *n.* (*archaic*) syphilis.
prac'ticable, *a.* that can be done, used, etc. **practicabil'ity**, *n.*
prac'tical, *a.* of, concerned with, shown in, action or practice; likely to take action; useful; virtual. **practical'ity**, *n.*
prac'tically, *adv.* (esp.) almost, virtually.
prac'tice, *n.* action as opposed to theory; habitual action; established method; exercise to improve skill; professional business of doc-

tor, lawyer, etc. *general practice*, practice of doctor who treats all kinds of diseases (opp. *specialist*). **practi'cian** (-shn), *n.* practitioner.
prac'tise, *v.* do habitually, carry out in action; be a professional worker in (medicine, law, etc.); exercise oneself in. **prac'tised** (-ist), *a.* experienced, expert.
practi'tioner, *n.* professional worker, esp. in medicine, law, etc. *general practitioner* (abbrev. *G.P.*), doctor in general practice.
pragmat'ic, *a.* treating facts of history with reference to their practical lessons; practical.
prag'matism, *n.* matter-of-fact treatment of things; philosophical doctrine estimating value of ideas, etc., by practical considerations.
prair'ie, *n.* large treeless tract of (esp. N.Amer.) grassland.
praise (-z), *v.t.* express favourable opinion of; commend; ascribe glory and honour to (God, deity). *n.* praising, commendation. **praise'-worthy** (-werdhi), *a.* commendable, worthy of praise.
pram, *n.* hand-pushed carriage for baby, perambulator.
prance (-ah-), *v.i.* (of horse) spring from hind--legs; walk, move, in elated or arrogant manner. *n.* spring, caper.
pran'dial, *a.* of or at dinner.
prank, *n.* frolic, practical joke.
prate, *v.i.* talk foolishly; talk too much.
pratt'le, *v.i.* talk in childish or artless way. *n.* prattling talk.
prawn, *n.* crustacean resembling large shrimp.
pray, *v.* offer prayers, make supplication; ask earnestly (*for, that*).
prayer (prār), *n.* (form of words used in) address of thanksgiving, entreaty, etc., to God; praying; entreaty. **prayer-book**, book of forms of prayer. **prayer'ful**, *a.*
pre-, *pref.* before (in time, place, order, or importance).
preach, *v.* give a sermon; talk like preacher of sermon; give moral advice; advocate, exhort. **preach'er**, *n.*
prēam'ble, *n.* part of document, speech, etc., serving as introduction.
prē-arrānge' (-nj), *v.* arrange beforehand.
preb'endary, *n.* (in some cathedrals) canon.
prēcār'ious, *a.* uncertain; unstable; perilous.
prēcau'tion, *n.* thing done beforehand to avoid evil or ensure good result. **prēcau'-tionary**, *a.*
prēcēde', *v.* come or go before in place or time. **pre'cēdence** (*or* prisē'-), *n.* priority; right of preceding others; superiority, higher position. **pre'cēdent**, *n.* previous case, decision, etc., taken as example; rule, etc.
prēcen'tor, *n.* clergyman in control of music of cathedral; leader of singing of congregation.
prē'cept, *n.* rule for action or conduct; writ,

warrant.

prĕcep'tor, *n.* teacher, instructor.

prē'cinct, *n.* space enclosed by boundaries of particular place or building; (partly) traffic--free area in town, etc.; (pl.) environs.

pre'cious (-shus), *a.* of great value, valuable, highly valued; affectedly refined.

pre'cipice, *n.* vertical or very steep face of rock, cliff, mountain, etc.

precipitance, precipitancy: see **precipitate.**

prĕcip'itāte, *v.t.* hurl down; cause to happen suddenly or hurriedly; (Chem.) cause (solid in solution) to be deposited; condense (vapour) into drops. **prĕcip'itate,** *a.* hasty, rash; done too soon. *n.* (Chem.) solid matter precipitated. **prĕcip'itance, prĕcip'itancy,** *nn.* (esp.) rash haste. **prĕcipitā'tion,** *n.* (esp.) fall of rain, sleet, snow, etc.

prĕcip'itous, *a.* of or like a precipice; very steep.

prĕcis (prā'sē), *n.* (pl. same pr. -z), summary.

prĕcīse', *a.* accurately worded; definite, exact; particular. **prĕcīse'ly,** *a.* (esp.) exactly. **prĕci'sion** (-zhn), *n.* accuracy. *a.* (of tool, etc.) designed for exact work.

prĕclude' (-ōōd), *v.t.* exclude, prevent; make impracticable. **prĕclu'sion** (-zhn), *n.* **prĕclu'sive,** *a.*

prĕcō'cious (-shus), *a.* that has developed remarkably early. **prĕcō'ciousness, prĕco'city,** *nn.*

prĕconceive' (-sēv), *v.t.* form (opinion, etc.) beforehand. **prĕconcep'tion,** *n.* preconceived idea; prejudice.

prĕcur'sor, *n.* forerunner. **prĕcur'sory,** *a.* preceding, foreshadowing.

pred'ator, *n.* predatory animal.

pred'atory, *a.* plundering; (of animal) preying on others.

prĕdĕcease', *v.t.* die before (another). *n.* death before another's.

prē'dĕcessor, *n.* former holder of office or position; thing to which another thing has succeeded.

prĕdestinā'tion, *n.* (esp.) doctrine of God's foreordaining of part of mankind to salvation and eternal life. **prēdes'tine,** *v.t.* appoint or decree beforehand.

prĕdēter'mine, *v.t.* determine beforehand.

prĕdic'ament, *n.* unpleasant, trying, or dangerous situation.

pred'icate¹, *n.* (Gram.) what is said about the subject, including copula. **predic'ative,** *a.* (of a. & n., opp. *attributive*) forming (part of) predicate.

pred'icate², *v.t.* assert as true (*of*).

predict', *v.* forecast; prophesy. **predic'table,** *a.* **predic'tion,** *n.* **predic'tive,** *a.*

prĕdilec'tion, *n.* mental preference, partiality, (*for*).

prĕdispōse' (-z), *v.t.* render liable, subject, or willing (*to*) beforehand. **prĕdisposi'tion,** *n.* state favourable (*to*).

prĕdom'inate, *v.i.* be superior in number,

power, or influence. **prĕdom'inance,** *n.* **prĕdom'inant,** *a.*

prĕ-em'inent, *a.* excelling all others; distinguished beyond others. **prĕ-em'inence,** *n.*

preen, *v.t.* (of bird) trim (feathers) with beak; (of person) smarten *oneself*, show pride in *oneself*.

prē-exist' (-igz-), *v.i.* exist earlier, esp. in previous life. **prē-exis'tence,** *n.*

prē'fab', *n.* (*informal*) prefabricated house. **prēfab'ricāte,** *v.t.* make in sections for assembly on site. **prēfabricā'tion,** *n.*

pref'ace, *n.* introductory remarks prefixed to book, etc.; preamble of speech, etc. *v.t.* introduce or begin (as) with preface. **pref'atory,** *a.*

prē'fect, *n.* senior pupil with disciplinary duties in school; title of various civil or military officers in ancient Rome. **prēfector'ial,** *a.*

prefer', *v.t.* (p.t. *preferred*), choose rather, like better; bring forward (claim, etc.); promote *to* office. **pref'erable,** *a.* **pref'erably,** *adv.* **pref'erence,** *n.* preferring, thing preferred; prior right. *preference shares,* shares on which dividend is paid before any on ordinary shares. **preferen'tial** (-shl), *a.* of, giving, receiving, preference.

prefer'ment, *n.* advancement, promotion.

prē'fix, *n.* particle, preposition, adverb, or combining form of word placed at beginning of word to qualify meaning; title, etc., prefixed to name. *v.t.* add or join at beginning.

preg'nant, *a.* having developing child or young in womb; (of words, etc.) full of meaning, suggestive. **preg'nancy,** *n.*

prĕhen'sile (*or* -il), *a.* (of tail, foot, etc.) capable of grasping.

prēhisto'ric, *a.* before period recorded in history. **prēhis'tory,** *n.*

prējudge', *v.t.* pass judgement on before trial or proper inquiry. **prējudge'ment,** *n.*

prej'udice (-joo-), *n.* preconceived opinion, favourable or unfavourable bias. *v.t.* damage validity or prospects of; inspire with prejudice. **prejudi'cial** (-shl), *a.* causing prejudice or harm to.

prel'ate, *n.* church dignitary of high rank.

prēlim'inary, *a.* preceding and leading up to main business, etc.; introductory. *n.* preliminary step or arrangement.

prel'ŭde, *n.* performance, event, etc., serving as introduction (*to*); (Mus.) introductory movement or piece. *v.t.* serve as prelude to; introduce.

prem'atūre, *a.* occurring or done before right or usual time; hasty. **prem'atūrity,** *n.*

prĕmed'itāte (*or* prē-), *v.t.* think out or design beforehand. **premeditā'tion,** *n.*

prem'ier, *a.* first in position, importance, or order. *n.* prime minister. **prem'iership,** *n.*

première' (-myār), *n.* first performance of play, etc.

prem'ise, *n.* premiss; (pl.) house or building

with grounds, outhouses, etc.

prem′iss, *n.* proposition from which inference is drawn.

prē′mium, *n.* amount or instalment payable for insurance policy; fee for instruction in profession, etc.; bonus. *at a premium,* at more than nominal value. **Premium (Savings) Bond,** Government bond providing periodical chance of cash prize instead of interest.

prēmoni′tion, *n.* forewarning; presentiment, foreboding. **prēmon′itory,** *a.*

prēoccūpā′tion, *n.* mental absorption, engrossing of person's whole attention. **prēocc′ūpȳ,** *v.t.* engross (mind), prevent from attending to other things. **prēocc′ūpied** (-pĭd), *a.*

prep, *n.* (*informal*) school preparation. **prep school,** preparatory school.

preparā′tion, *n.* preparing; (usu. pl.) thing(s) done to make ready; (time spent in) preparation of school lessons, homework; substance prepared for special use, etc.

prēpa′ratory, *a.* serving to prepare; introductory (*to*). **preparatory school,** school preparing for higher, esp. public, school.

prēpāre′, *v.* make ready; put or get in order or proper state; make preparations (*for*).

prēpay′, *v.t.* (p.t. *prepaid*), pay in advance.

prēpon′derāte, *v.i.* be heavier; be superior in influence, quantity, or number. **prēpon′derance, prēpon′derant,** *a.*

preposi′tion (-z-), *n.* indeclinable word used to show relation between noun or pronoun it governs and another word. **preposi′tional,** *a.*

prēpossess′ing (-zes-), *a.* making a favourable impression, pleasing.

prēpos′terous, *a.* utterly absurd; contrary to reason or common sense.

prē′pūce, *n.* foreskin.

prēre′quisite (-z-), *a. & n.* (thing) required as previous condition.

prērog′ative, *n.* right of the sovereign (*Royal prerogative*); special right or privilege.

pres′age, *n.* omen; presentiment. **presāge′,** *v.t.* foreshadow, foretell.

Presbytēr′ian, *a.* (of Church) governed by elders (*presbyters*). *n.* member of Presbyterian Church, e.g. Church of Scotland. **pres′bytery,** *n.* court of ministers and elders of Presbyterian Church; (R.C.Ch.) priest's house.

prē′scient (-shi-), *a.* having foreknowledge or foresight. **prē′science** (-shi-), *n.*

prēscrībe′, *v.* order, direct, authoritatively; advise use of; suggest remedy (*for*). **prēscrip′tion,** *n.* prescribing; doctor's (usu. written) direction for composition and use of medicine. **prēscrip′tive,** *a.* prescribing; based on custom or usage.

pres′ence (-z-), *n.* being present, being there; person's bearing or aspect. *presence of mind,* calmness, or quickness of thought and action, in emergency.

pres′ent¹ (-z-), *a.* in place in question, here; now existing, occurring, being dealt with, etc.; (Gram.) expressing present action, etc. *n.* present tense; *the* present time. *at present,* now. *for the present,* just now, until later.

pres′ent² (-z-), *n.* gift.

prēsent′³ (-z-), *v.t.* set in conspicuous position; introduce; exhibit; offer, give. *present arms,* hold rifle, etc., in saluting position. **prēsent′able,** *a.* of decent appearance; fit to be shown. **presentā′tion,** *n.* presenting, esp. formally; gift.

prēsen′timent (-z-), *n.* mental impression of some future event; vague expectation (esp. of coming evil).

pres′ently (-z-), *adv.* soon; (U.S.) now.

preservā′tion (-z-), *n.* preserving, being preserved. **prēser′vative** (-z-), *a. & n.* (substance) tending to preserve.

prēserve′ (-z-), *v.t.* keep safe (*from* harm, etc.); maintain, retain; keep from decay; treat (food, etc.) to prevent decomposition or fermentation; keep (game, river, etc.) undisturbed for private use. *n.* jam; place where game, etc., is preserved.

prēsīde′ (-z-), *v.i.* have or take position of control or authority.

pres′idency (-z-), *n.* (period of) office of president. **pres′ident** (-z-), *n.* person presiding over meetings or proceedings of society, etc.; head of college, council, company, etc.; elected head of a republic. **presiden′tial** (-shl), *a.*

press¹, *v.* subject to steady push or squeeze; flatten, smooth (esp. clothes), etc., thus; exert pressure; be urgent; crowd; force (offer, etc.) *on. n.* crowding, crowd; instrument for compressing, etc.; machine for printing, printing establishment; large cupboard with shelves; *the* press, newspapers generally. **press′man,** journalist, reporter. **press-stud,** fastener closing by pressure. **press′ing,** *a.* urgent; persistent.

press², *v.t.* (Hist.) force to serve in army or navy. **press-gang,** (Hist.) body of men employed to press men.

pre′ssure (-sher), *n.* exertion of continuous force, (amount of) force so exerted; urgency; compelling influence. **pressure-cooker,** vessel for cooking in steam at high pressure. **pre′ssurized** (-zd), *a.* designed for maintenance of normal air-pressure at high altitudes.

prestige′ (-tēzh), *n.* influence or reputation derived from past achievements, success, etc.

pres′tō, *a., adv., & n.* (pl. *prestos*), (Mus.) quick (movement, passage).

prēsūme′ (-z-), *v.* take for granted; venture (*to*); be presumptuous. **prēsū′mably,** *adv.* as may be presumed, probably.

prēsump′tion (-z-), *n.* supposition; balance of probability; arrogance, effrontery.

prēsump′tive (-z-), *a.* giving ground for presumption. *heir presumptive*: see **heir**.

prèsump'tùous (-z-), *a.* unduly confident, arrogant, forward.

prèsuppóse' (-z), *v.t.* assume beforehand; involve; imply. **prèsupposi'tion**, *n.*

prétence', *n.* pretending; pretext.

prétend', *v.* make oneself appear (*to* be or do); profess falsely; lay claim. **prèten'der**, *n.* claimant (*to* title, etc.).

prèten'sion (-shn), *n.* (assertion of) claim; pretentiousness. **prèten'tious** (-shus), *a.* claiming great merit or importance; ostentatious. **prèten'tiousness**, *n.*

preter-, *pref.* past, beyond.

pret'erite, *a. & n.* (Gram.) (past) tense.

prèterna'tural (-cher-), *a.* supernatural.

prè'text, *n.* false reason; excuse.

prètt'y, *a.* attractive to eye or ear. *adv.* fairly, moderately. **prètt'ily**, *adv.* **prètt'iness**, *n.*

prèvail', *v.i.* be victorious (*against, over*); attain one's object; predominate; be usual or current. *prevail on*, persuade.

prev'alent, *a.* current, common, widespread. **prev'alence**, *n.*

prèva'ricāte, *v.i.* make evasive or misleading statements. **prèvarica'tion**, *n.*

prèvent', *v.t.* stop, keep (*from* doing something); stop, hinder (occurrence). **prèven'table, prèven'tible**, *aa.* **prèven'tion**, *n.* **prèven'tative, prèven'tive**, *aa. & nn.* (agent, drug, etc.) serving to prevent (e.g. disease).

prè'vious, *a.* coming before in time or order; prior (*to*). **prè'viously**, *adv.*

prey (prā), *n.* animal hunted or killed by carnivorous animal for food; victim. *v.i.* prey (*up*)*on*, seek or take as prey; exert harmful or destructive influence on.

price, *n.* money for which thing is bought or sold; what must be given, done, etc., to obtain thing. *v.t.* fix or inquire price of; estimate value of. **price'less**, *a.* too valuable to be priced.

prick, *v.* pierce slightly, make tiny hole in; pain sharply; spur, goad; erect (ears) alertly. *prick up one's ears*, listen intently. *n.* pricking, mark of it.

prick'le, *n.* thorn-like outgrowth; hard-pointed spine of hedgehog, etc. *v.i.* feel sensation as of prick(s). **prick'ly**, *a.*

pride, *n.* unduly high opinion of oneself; arrogance; (proper) sense of one's own worth, position, etc.; group (of lions). *v. refl. pride oneself* (*up*)*on*, be proud of.

priest, *n.* clergyman, esp. one above deacon and below bishop; official of non-christian religion (fem. *priestess*). **priest'hood**, *n.* office of priest; priests. **priest'ly**, *a.*

prig, *n.* boringly, affectedly, or primly moral, cultured, or learned person. **prigg'ish**, *a.*

prim, *a.* consciously or affectedly precise, formal; prudish. **prim'ly**, *adv.* **prim'ness**, *n.*

pri'macy, *n.* office of primate; pre-eminence.

pri'ma donn'a (prē-), principal female singer

in opera.

pri'mary, *a.* original; holding first place in time, importance, or development. **primary colour**, colour not obtained by mixing others. **primary school**, school for first stage of education. **pri'marily**, *adv.*

pri'mate, *n.* archbishop; (Zool., pr. -māt) member of highest order of mammals (including man, apes, monkeys, lemurs, etc.).

prime, *a.* chief, most important; primary, fundamental; first-rate. *n.* first or best part of something; state of highest perfection; prime number. *v.t.* put water into (pump) to make it start working; supply (*with* information, etc.); cover (wood) with under-coat, etc., before painting. **prime minister**, head of Government. **prime number**, integer with no factors.

pri'mer (*or* pri-), *n.* elementary school-book; manual.

primē'val, *a.* of the first age of the world; ancient, primitive.

prim'itive, *a.* of early or old-fashioned kind; ancient; simple, rude, rough; original.

primor'dial, *a.* existing at or from the beginning; original, primitive, fundamental.

prim'rōse (-z), *n.* (plant bearing) pale-yellow early spring flower; pale yellow.

prim'ūla, *n.* genus of flowering plants including primrose.

pri'mus (**stōve**), cooking-stove burning vaporized oil. **P.**

prince, *n.* sovereign; ruler of small State; male member of royal family. **prince'ly**, *a.* (worthy) of a prince; sumptuous, splendid.

prin'cess (*or* -ses'), *n.* prince's wife; female member of royal family.

prin'cipal, *a.* most important; chief, leading. *n.* head of college, school, etc.; original sum lent or invested. **prin'cipally**, *adv.* chiefly.

principal'ity, *n.* State ruled by prince; *the Principality*, Wales.

prin'ciple, *n.* fundamental truth; law of nature; general law; rule by which conduct may be guided.

prink, *v.* smarten, dress up.

print, *n.* mark left on surface by pressure; impression left on paper by inked type, etc.; reading-matter produced from type, etc.; engraving, photograph; printed fabric. *in print*, (of book) printed and on sale. *out of print*, (of book) sold out. *v.t.* stamp or impress; produce by means of printing-type, etc.; write in imitation of printing; stamp (fabric) in colours. **prin'ter**, *n.* (esp.) one who prints books, etc.

pri'or', *n.* head of religious house or order. **pri'oress**, *n. fem.*

pri'or², *a.* earlier; antecedent. *adv. prior to*, before. **priō'rity**, *n.* precedence in time, order, rank, etc.; (thing having) claim to early or earliest consideration, action, etc.

pri'ory, *n.* religious house governed by prior

or prioress.

prise (-z), *v.t.* force (*open*, *up*, etc.) by leverage.

prism (-zm), *n.* solid figure whose two ends are similar, equal, and parallel rectilineal figures and whose sides are parallelograms; transparent body of this form which splits light into rainbow-like spectrum. **prismat'ic**, *a.* of or like prism; (of colours) brilliant, varied.

pris'on (-zn), *n.* place of captivity or confinement, esp. for law-breakers.

pris'oner (-z-), *n.* person kept in prison; member of enemy's forces captured in war; captive.

pris'tine (*or* -ēn), *a.* unspoilt, original.

prith'ee (-dhi), *int.* (*archaic*) please.

priv'acy (*or* prī-), *n.* being private; freedom from publicity or observation.

prī'vate, *a.* not public or official; individual, personal; secret, confidential; secluded. *n.* private soldier. *in private*, privately, not in public. **private soldier**, soldier not holding commissioned or non-commissioned rank. **prī'vately**, *a.*

privateer', *n.* (Hist.) armed privately-owned ship authorized by government to attack (esp. merchant) shipping of hostile State.

privā'tion, *n.* lack of food and comforts; hardship.

priv'et, *n.* white-flowered evergreen shrub much used for hedges.

priv'ilege, *n.* right, advantage, or immunity belonging to person, class, or office. **priv'ileged**, *a.* having privilege(s).

priv'y, *a.* secret, private, confidential. *privy to*, in the secret of. *n.* (*archaic*) private place for defecation or urination. **Privy Council**, body of advisers chosen by sovereign. **privy purse**, allowance from public revenue for monarch's private expenses.

prize[1], *n.* reward given as symbol of victory or superiority; thing (to be) striven for. *v.t.* value highly.

prize[2], *n.* ship or property captured in naval warfare.

prize[3], *v.t.* prise.

prō, *n.* (*informal*) professional.

pro-, *pref.* before, for, on behalf of; favouring or siding with.

prō and con, for and against. **pros and cons**, reasons for and against.

probabil'ity, *n.* being probable; (most) probable event; likelihood.

prob'able, *a.* that may be expected to happen or prove true or correct; likely. **prob'ably**, *adv.* most likely.

prō'bate (*or* -āt), *n.* official proving of will.

probā'tion, *n.* testing of person's conduct or character; system of supervising offenders who would otherwise be sent to prison. **probation officer**, official supervising offender on probation. **probā'tionary**, *a.* **probā'tioner**, *n.* person on probation; nurse at early stage of training.

prōbe, *n.* blunt-ended surgical instrument for exploring wound, etc.; probing, investigation. *v.* explore with probe; examine closely.

prō'bity, *n.* honesty, uprightness.

prob'lem, *n.* doubtful or difficult question; thing hard to understand or deal with. **problemat'ic(al)**, *aa.* doubtful, questionable.

probos'cis, *n.* (pl. *proboscises*), elephant's trunk; long flexible snout; elongated part of mouth of some insects.

procē'dure (-dyer), *n.* way of conducting (esp. parliamentary, etc., or legal) business; particular action or mode of action.

proceed', *v.i.* go on; continue or resume; issue, originate; take legal action (*against*).

procee'ding, *n.* (esp.) action; (pl.) business done at meeting; legal steps or action. **prō'ceeds** (-z), *n.pl.* result, profit.

prō'cess, *n.* state of going on or being carried on; method of operation in manufacture, etc.; (Zool., etc.) outgrowth, protuberance.

proce'ssion (-shn), *n.* body of persons going along in fixed order. **proce'ssional**, *a.*

proclaim', *v.t.* announce publicly and officially; tell or declare openly. **proclamā'tion**, *n.*

procliv'ity, *n.* natural inclination or tendency (*to*, *towards*).

procras'tināte, *v.i.* delay action, put off doing things. **procrastinā'tion**, *n.*

prō'crēate, *v.* bring into existence by natural process of reproduction. **prōcrēā'tion**, *n.*

proc'tor, *n.* university official with disciplinary powers. **proctor'ial**, *a.*

procūr'able, *a.* that can be procured.

proc'ūrātor-fiscal, *n.* (in Scotland) law officer of a district.

procūre', *v.t.* succeed in getting; bring about. **procūre'ment**, *n.*

prod, *v.t.* (p.t. *prodded*), poke with stick, etc., esp. to arouse or urge on. *n.* prodding touch.

prod'igal, *a.* wasteful, lavish (*of*); *n.* spendthrift. **prodigal'ity**, *n.* wasteful or lavish spending.

prodi'gious (-jus), *a.* marvellous; enormous.

prod'igy, *n.* wonderful person, esp. precocious child; marvellous thing.

prodūce', *v.t.* bring forward for inspection, etc.; yield, give birth to; cause or bring about; make or manufacture; bring (play, etc.) before public. **prod'ūce**, *n.* amount produced, yield; agricultural or garden products.

prodū'cer, *n.* (esp.) person producing articles for consumers; person directing production of play, etc. **prodū'cible**, *a.*

prod'uct, *n.* thing produced by natural process or manufacture; (Math.) quantity obtained by multiplying quantities together.

produc'tion, *n.* producing; thing(s) produced; literary or artistic work.

produc'tive, *a.* producing, esp. abundantly. **productiv'ity**, *n.* (esp.) efficiency in industrial production.

profana'tion, *n.* profaning.

profane', *a.* secular (not sacred); heathen, unhallowed; irreverent, blasphemous. *v.t.* treat with irreverence; pollute. **profan'ity**, *n.* blasphemy; profane speech or behaviour.

profess', *v.t.* declare that one has (belief, feeling, quality, etc.); declare oneself, pretend, to be or do; have as one's profession. **profess'edly**, *adv.* (esp.) by one's own account.

profe'ssion (-shn), *n.* occupation, calling, esp. of learned, scientific, or artistic kind; declaration, avowal. **profe'ssional**, *a.* of or belonging to a profession, following occupation as means of livelihood; played, etc., by professionals; not amateurish. *n.* professional worker, player, etc.

profess'or, *n.* university teacher of highest rank in faculty or branch of learning. **professor'ial**, *a.*

proff'er, *v.t.* & *n.* offer.

profi'cient (-shnt), *a.* & *n.* expert, adept. **profi'ciency**, *n.*

prō'file, *n.* side view, side outline, esp. of human face; journalistic biographical sketch.

prof'it, *n.* advantage, benefit; money gain, excess of returns over outlay. *v.* be of advantage (to); be benefited. **prof'itable**, *a.* useful; yielding profit. **profiteer'**, *v.i.* make large profits on scarce or necessary goods, esp. in war-time. *n.* one who profiteers.

prof'ligate, *a.* & *n.* debauched, dissolute, or recklessly extravagant (person). **prof'ligacy**, *n.*

profound', *a.* deep; of great insight or knowledge; hard to penetrate or unravel; intense, unqualified. **profun'dity**, *n.*

profūse', *a.* lavish, extravagant, copious, excessive. **profū'sion** (-zhn), *n.*

progen'itor, *n.* ancestor.

pro'gĕny, *n.* offspring; descendants.

prognō'sis, *n.* (pl. *prognosēs*), forecast of course of disease.

prognos'tic, *n.* omen (*of*); prediction. *a.* foretelling, predictive (*of*). **prognos'ticāte**, *v.t.* foretell; betoken. **prognosticā'tion**, *n.*

prō'gramme, prō'gram, *n.* plan of what is to be done; descriptive notice or list of series of events, items, etc.; broadcast production; (usu. *program*) set of coded instructions enabling computer to perform task. *v.t.* (usu. *program*, p.t. *programmed*), express (problem) in this way, feed program into (computer).

prō'gress, *n.* forward movement; advance; development; improvement. **progress'**, *v.i.* make progress.

progre'ssion (-shn), *n.* progress; advance from stage to stage. **progre'ssional**, *n.*

progress'ive, *a.* moving forward; proceeding step by step; advancing in social conditions, character, etc.; favouring progress or reform; (of disease) continuously increasing in sever-

ity, etc. **progress'ively**, *adv.*

prohib'it, *v.t.* forbid, debar, prevent. **prohibi'tion**, *n.* forbidding; order that forbids something; forbidding by law of making or selling of alcoholic drinks. **prohib'itive**, *a.* prohibiting; (of price) so high that it prevents purchase. **prohib'itory**, *a.* prohibiting.

project', *v.* make plans for; throw, impel; cause (light, image, etc.) to appear on a surface; jut out, protrude. **proj'ect**, *n.* thing planned to be carried out; plan, scheme.

projec'tile, *n.* missile. *a.* impelling forward; that can be projected by force.

projec'tion, *n.* projecting; part that juts out; orderly system of representing earth, etc., on plane surface, e.g. map.

projec'tor, *n.* (esp.) apparatus for projecting picture(s) on screen.

prōlētār'ian, *n.* & *a.* (member) of proletariat. **prōlētār'iat**, *n.* lowest class of community, wage-earners; lowest class in ancient Rome.

prolif'erāte, *v.* increase rapidly, multiply; (Biol.) reproduce, or grow, by cell-division, etc. **proliferā'tion**, *n.*

prolif'ic, *a.* producing (numerous) offspring; abundantly productive.

prō'lix, *a.* wordy, tedious. **prolix'ity**, *n.*

prō'logue (-g), *n.* poem or speech introducing play; act, event, serving as introduction (*to*).

prolong', *v.t.* make longer; cause to continue. **prōlongā'tion**, *n.*

prom, *n.* (*informal*) promenade concert; promenade.

prom'ĕnade' (-ahd), *n.* leisurely walk; place made or used for this. *v.i.* take promenade. **promenade concert**, concert at which (part of) audience is not provided with seats.

prom'inence, *n.* being prominent; protuberance. **prom'inent**, *a.* projecting; conspicuous; distinguished.

promis'cūous, *a.* indiscriminate, (esp.) having sexual intercourse with many persons. **promiscū'ity**, *n.*

prom'ise, *n.* definite undertaking to do or not to do something; thing promised; favourable indications. *v.* make promise (to) to give, do, etc.; seem likely (*to*); offer good, etc., prospect. **prom'ising**, *a.* likely to turn out well; full of promise.

prom'issory, *a.* containing or implying a promise.

prom'ontory, *n.* headland.

promōte', *v.t.* move up to higher office or position; help forward or initiate process or formation of; encourage. **promō'ter**, *n.* **promō'tion**, *n.* **promō'tional**, *a.*

prompt, *a.* acting, done, sent, given, etc., at once or without delay. *adv.* promptly. *v.t.* incite, prime, inspire; help (actor, etc.) by supplying words. **promp'ter**, *n.* (esp.) person prompting actors. **promp'titūde**, *n.* promptness.

prom'ulgāte, *v.t.* publish as coming into force or having authority. **promulgā'tion**, *n.*

prŏne, *a.* lying face or front downwards; (loosely) lying flat; inclined, disposed (*to*).

prong, *n.* spike of fork. **pronged** (-ngd), *a.* having prongs.

prŏnom'inal, *a.* of (nature of) pronoun.

prŏ'noun, *n.* word serving as substitute for noun.

pronounce', *v.* utter formally; give (as) one's opinion; articulate, esp. with reference to mode of pronouncing. **pronounced'**, *a.* (esp.) strongly marked; decided. **pronounce'ment**, *n.* authoritative or formal declaration of opinion, etc.

pronunciā'tion, *n.* way in which word is pronounced; person's way of pronouncing words.

prŏŏf, *n.* fact, evidence, or reasoning that proves truth or existence of something; test, trial; impression from type, etc., that can be corrected before final printing. *proof against*, impenetrable by; able to resist. *v.t.* make proof against (water, bullets, etc.). **proof reader**, person employed in correcting printer's proofs.

prop, *n.* thing used to support something or keep it upright. *v.t.* (p.t. *propped*), support (as) by prop, hold *up* thus.

propagan'da, *n.* (means of) spreading doctrine, information, etc.; (esp. misleading) information so spread.

prop'agăte, *v.* multiply or reproduce by sowing, grafting, breeding, etc.; spread, disseminate. **propagā'tion**, *n.*

propel', *v.t.* (p.t. *propelled*), drive or push forward; give onward motion to. *a. & n.* (thing, esp. explosive) that propels. **propell'er**, *n.* revolving shaft with blades for propelling ship, aircraft, etc.

propen'sity, *n.* inclination, tendency.

prop'er, *a.* right, correct; fitting, suitable; decent, decorous; real; own (*archaic*); thorough (*informal*). *proper name, noun*, noun beginning with capital, denoting individual person, place, etc. **prop'erly**, *adv.*

prop'erty, *n.* thing or things owned; land and buildings, real estate; attribute or quality; portable thing used on stage.

proph'ecy, *n.* prophesying; foretelling of future events; prophetic utterance.

proph'esȳ, *v.* speak as prophet; foretell future events; predict.

proph'ĕt, *n.* inspired teacher, revealer or interpreter of divine will; spokesman, advocate (*of*); one who predicts. **proph'etess**, *n. fem.* **prophet'ic(al)**, *aa.* of prophet; predicting.

prophylac'tic, *a. & n.* (medicine, measure) tending to prevent disease. **prophylax'is**, *n.*

propin'quity, *n.* nearness; close kinship.

propi'tiăte (-shi-), *v.t.* gain forgiveness or favour of; appease. **propitiā'tion**, *n.* **propi'tiatory**, *a.*

propi'tious (-shus), *a.* favourable; favourably disposed.

propor'tion, *n.* comparative part; part bearing definite relation to whole; comparative relation, ratio; symmetry; correct relation between things or parts of thing; (pl.) dimensions. *v.t.* make proportionate. **propor'tional**, *a.* in proper proportion, corresponding in degree or amount. **propor'tionally**, *adv.* **propor'tionate**, *a.* that is in proportion (*to*).

propŏ'sal (-z-), *n.* act of proposing; offer of marriage; scheme of action, etc., proposed.

propŏse' (-z), *v.* put forward as plan, object, problem, candidate, toast, etc.; offer marriage (*to*); intend.

proposi'tion (-z-), *n.* statement; proposal, scheme proposed; (Math.) formal statement of theorem or problem.

propound', *v.t.* put forward for consideration or solution.

proprī'etary, *a.* of proprietor; owning property; held in private ownership; of which manufacture or sale is restricted by patent, etc.

proprī'etor, *n.* owner. **proprī'etress**, *n. fem.*

proprī'ety, *n.* correctness of behaviour or morals; fitness, rightness; (pl.) conventions of polite behaviour.

propul'sion (-shn), *n.* (means of) propelling; impelling influence. **propul'sive**, *a.*

prorogue (pro-rŏg'), *v.* discontinue meetings of (British Parliament, etc.) without dissolving it; be prorogued. **prŏrogā'tion**, *n.*

prosā'ic (-z-), *a.* unpoetical; commonplace.

proscē'nium, *n.* part of theatre stage in front of curtain, esp. with enclosing arch.

proscrībe', *v.t.* outlaw; banish; exile; forbid by law. **proscrip'tion**, *n.*

prŏse (-z), *n.* ordinary non-metrical form of language, not verse.

pros'ĕcūte, *v.t.* start legal proceedings against; continue (studies, etc.), carry on (trade, etc.). **prosĕcū'tion**, *n.* prosecuting; prosecuting party. **pros'ĕcūtor**, *n.* one who prosecutes, esp. in criminal court.

pros'ĕlȳte, *n.* convert from one faith, opinion, or party to another. **pros'ĕlytize**, *v.t.* make proselyte of.

pros'ody, *n.* science of versification.

pros'pect, *n.* extensive view; mental scene; expectation. **prospect'**, *v.* explore (*for* gold, etc.). **prospec'tor**, *n.*

prospec'tive, *a.* concerned with, applying to, the future; expected, future.

prospec'tus, *n.* booklet, etc., describing chief features of school, commercial company, etc.

pros'per, *v.* be successful, flourish, increase in wealth; make successful. **prospe'rity**, *n.* prospering; wealth. **pros'perous**, *a.* successful, flourishing; wealthy.

pros'titūte, *n.* woman offering her body for sexual intercourse for payment. *v.t.* put to unworthy or immoral use. **prostitū'tion**, *n.*

pros'trăte, *a.* lying with face to ground, esp.

in submission or humility; lying at full length; overthrown; exhausted. **prostrāte'**, *v.t.* throw or lay flat on ground; overcome; reduce to extreme physical weakness. **prosträ'tion**, *n.*

prō'sy (-z-), *a.* tedious, dull.

protag'onist, *n.* chief person in drama, etc.; advocate or champion of a cause.

protect', *v.t.* keep safe, defend, guard (*from*, *against*). **protec'tion**, *n.* protecting or being protected; thing that protects. **protec'tive**, *a.* serving to protect; showing desire to protect. **protec'tor**, *n.* person who, or thing that, protects. **protec'torate**, *n.* protectorship or control of State or territory by stronger State; such State or territory. **protec'torship**, *n.*

prot'égé (-āzhā), *n.* (fem. *protégée*), person under protection or patronage of another.

prō'tein, *n.* any of class of organic compounds forming important part of all living organisms and essential constituents of food of animals.

prō'test, *n.* formal statement of dissent or disapproval; solemn declaration. **protest'**, *v.* make protest (*against*); affirm strongly.

Prot'estant, *n.* member of any of western Christian Churches or bodies that separated from the Roman Catholic Church in the Reformation, or their later branches. *a.* of Protestants or Protestantism. **Prot'estantism**, *n.*

protestā'tion, *n.* solemn affirmation; protest.

prōto-, *pref.* first.

prō'tocol, *n.* draft of diplomatic document, esp. of agreed terms of treaty; (rigid observance of) rules of diplomatic etiquette.

prō'ton, *n.* positively charged particle forming part (or in hydrogen whole) of nucleus of atom.

prō'toplasm, *n.* essential matter of living organisms, viscid translucent substance of which cells principally consist.

prō'totype, *n.* original type or model in relation to any copy, later specimen, improved form, etc. **prō'totȳpal, prōtotyp'ical**, *aa.*

protract', *v.t.* lengthen time taken by, prolong; extend. **protrac'tion**, *n.* **protrac'tor**, *n.* instrument for measuring angles.

protrude' (-ōōd), *v.* stick out, project; thrust out. **protru'sion** (-zhn), *n.* **protru'sive**, *a.*

protū'berance, *n.* bulging; bulge, swelling. **protū'berant**, *a.* bulging out; prominent.

proud, *a.* valuing oneself (too) highly; arrogant; feeling or showing (proper) pride; feeling greatly honoured; splendid. **proud'ly**, *adv.*

prove (prōōv), *v.* (p.p. *proved*, archaic *proven*), establish as true; demonstrate truth of; ascertain by experience; establish genuineness and validity of (will); turn out (*to* be); test. **prov'able**, *a.*

prov'énder, *n.* fodder.

prov'erb, *n.* short wise saying in general use. **prover'bial**, *a.* of proverbs; widely known,

constantly spoken of.

provīde', *v.* give, supply (thing needed); make proper preparation (*for*, *against*); stipulate. *provide for*, (esp.) secure maintenance of. **provī'ded, provī'ding**, *conjj.* on condition or understanding (*that*).

prov'idence, *n.* prudent foresight; beneficent care of God or nature; (*Providence*), God. **prov'ident**, *a.* having or showing foresight, thrifty. **providen'tial** (-shl), *a.* of or by divine providence; extremely lucky.

prov'ince, *n.* large administrative division of a country; sphere of action; concern; (pl.) whole of country outside capital. **provin'cial** (-shl), *a.* of province; (having manners, speech, narrow views, etc.) of provinces. *n.* inhabitant of provinces.

provi'sion (-zhn), *n.* providing; what is provided; (pl.) food and drink; proviso. **provi'sional**, *a.* temporary, subject to revision. **provi'sionally**, *adv.*

provī'so (-zō), *n.* (pl. *provisos*), stipulation. **provī'sory**, *a.* conditional; making provision.

provocā'tion, *n.* provoking; thing that provokes. **provoc'ative**, *a.* provoking, stimulating interest; intentionally arousing sexual desire, anger, etc.

provōke', *v.t.* irritate, make angry; arouse (feeling, etc.); incite (*to*); cause. **provō'king**, *a.* (esp., *informal*) annoying.

prov'ost, *n.* head of Scottish municipal corporation or burgh, corresponding to mayor in England and Wales; head of certain colleges.

prow, *n.* fore-part of ship or boat.

prow'ess, *n.* bravery, daring; great skill in fighting, etc.

prowl, *v.* go about stealthily in search of prey or plunder; pace restlessly; traverse (streets, etc.). *n.* prowling. **prow'ler**, *n.*

prox'imate, *a.* nearest, next before or after. **proxim'ity**, *n.* nearness in space, time, or kinship. **prox'imō**, *a.* of next month (abbrev. *prox.*).

prox'y, *n.* person authorized to act for another; authorization to act for another, esp. in voting; vote so given. *a.* done, given, etc., by proxy.

prude (prōōd), *n.* person of extreme or exaggerated propriety.

pru'dence (-ōō-), *n.* being prudent; practical wisdom, discretion. **pru'dent**, *a.* acting only after careful thought; wise, discreet. **pruden'tial** (-shl), *a.* of or involving prudence.

pru'dery (-ōō-), *n.* conduct or notions of prudes. **pru'dish**, *a.*

prune¹ (prōōn), *n.* dried plum.

prune² (prōōn), *v.t.* trim (tree, etc.) by cutting away unnecessary branches, shoots, etc.; rid of unnecessary parts.

prur'ient (-oor-), *a.* lewd. **prur'ience**, *n.*

Prus'sian blue (-shn), deep greenish-blue pigment.

prȳ, *v.i.* look, inquire, etc., inquisitively

(*into*).

psalm (sahm), *n.* one of the songs in the Book of Psalms in the Bible; sacred song, hymn. **psalm'ist**, *n.* author of psalms. **psal'ter** (sawl-), *n.* (version, copy, of) Book of Psalms.

psal'tery (sawl-), *n.* ancient and medieval plucked stringed instrument.

pseudo- (psū- *or* sū-), *pref.* false(ly), seeming(ly), professed(ly) but not real(ly).

pseu'donym (sū-), *n.* fictitious name, esp. one assumed by author.

pshaw (*or* sh-), *int.* expressing contempt, disbelief, or impatience.

psychèdel'ic (sīk-; *or* -dē-), *a.* (of drug) hallucinatory, giving illusion of freedom from limitations of reality; suggesting experience or effect of such drugs.

psychï'atry (sīk-), *n.* study and treatment of mental diseases. **psȳchiat'ric(al)**, *aa.* **psȳchï'atrist**, *n.*

psy'chic (sīk-), *a.* psychical; sensitive to psychical or occult influences. **psȳ'chical**, *a.* of soul or mind; of phenomena, etc., apparently outside sphere of physical law.

psychō- (sīk-), *pref.* soul, mind, mental(ly).

psychō-anal'ysis (sīk-), *n.* branch of psychology dealing with the unconscious mind; therapeutic method based on this. **psȳchō-an'alȳse** (-z-), *v.t.* **psȳchō-an'alyst**, *n.*

psychol'ogy (sīk-), *n.* science of the nature, functions, and phenomena of the mind; mind, psychological characteristics. **psȳcholo'gical**, of psychology or mind. **psȳchol'ogist**, *n.*

psy'chōpath (sīk-), *n.* mentally deranged or emotionally unstable person. **psȳchōpath'ic**, *a.*

psychō'sis (sīk-), *n.* (pl. *psychosēs*), severe mental illness. **psychot'ic**, *a. & n.* (person) suffering from or liable to suffer from psychosis.

psychōsomat'ic (sīk-), *a.* of or resulting from interaction of mind and body.

psychōthe'rapy (sīk-), *n.* therapy by psychological means. **psȳchōthe'rapist**, *n.*

ptar'migan (t-), *n.* bird of grouse family.

pub, *n.* (*informal*) public house.

pū'berty, *n.* state of having become capable of begetting or bearing offspring.

pub'lic, *a.* of or concerning the community as a whole; open to, shared by, people in general; done, etc., in public. *n.* (members of, section of,) community as a whole. *in public*, in state open to public view or access. **public house**, house licensed to sell alcoholic drinks. **public school**, large, usu. endowed, private secondary school (usu. boarding-school).

pub'lican, *n.* keeper of public house; (Bibl.) tax-collector.

publicā'tion, *n.* publishing; published book, periodical, etc.

publi'city, *n.* being or making public, esp.

(business of) advertising or making publicly known.

pub'licīze, *v.t.* make publicly known.

pub'licly, *adv.* in public; openly.

pub'lish, *v.t.* make generally known; formally announce; prepare and issue copies of (book, etc.) for sale to public. **pub'lisher**, *n.* person whose trade is publishing books, etc.

pūce, *a. & n.* brownish purple.

Puck, puck[1], *n.* mischievous goblin.

puck[2], *n.* rubber disc used in ice-hockey.

puck'er, *v.* contract or gather (*up*) into wrinkles or folds. *n.* wrinkle, fold, bulge.

pu'dding (poo-), *n.* dish made of ingredients mixed in soft mass; sweet course of meal.

pudd'le, *n.* small dirty pool; rough cement of kneaded clay. *v.i.* work (clay) into puddle; stir (molten iron); dabble in water or mud.

pū'erīle, *a.* childish; trivial. **pūeril'ity**, *n.*

puff, *n.* short quick blow of breath or wind; amount of smoke or vapour sent out at one time; soft pad for applying powder to skin; laudatory review or advertisement. *v.* emit puff or puffs; smoke in puffs; pant; inflate, become inflated; praise excessively. *puffed up*, proud, conceited. **puff pastry**, light flaky pastry. **puff'y**, *a.* short-winded; inflated, swollen.

puff'in, *n.* sea-bird with large bill.

pug, *n.* small snub-nosed breed of dog.

pū'gilism, *n.* boxing. **pū'gilist**, *n.* boxer. **pūgilis'tic**, *a.*

pugnā'cious (-shus), *a.* fond of, or in the habit of, fighting. **pugna'city**, *n.*

pūke, *v.* vomit.

pūle, *v.i.* cry querulously, whine.

pull (pool), *v.* cause to move towards oneself by exertion of force; exert pulling force; pluck. *pull a face*, make a grimace. *pull down*, demolish, lower in health, etc. *pull* (something, it) *off*, be successful. *pull round*, (help to) recover. *pull through*, get safely through. *pull up*, stop. **pull**, *n.* pulling, tug; means of exerting influence; draught of liquor; handle for pulling.

pu'llèt (poo-), *n.* young domestic hen.

pu'lley (poo-), *n.* grooved wheel(s) for cord, etc., to run over, mounted in block and used to lift weight, etc.

Pull'man (coach) (poo-), railway-coach arranged as comfortable saloon.

pull'ōver (poo-), *n.* (esp. knitted) garment pulled on over head.

pul'monary, *a.* of the lungs.

pulp, *n.* fleshy part of fruit, animal body, etc.; soft formless mass, esp. of materials for paper-making. *v.* reduce to pulp; become pulpy. **pul'py**, *a.*

pu'lpit (poo-), *n.* raised enclosed structure in church, etc., for preacher.

pul'sar, *n.* (Astron.) source of pulsating radio waves.

pulsāte' (*or* pul'-), *v.i.* expand and contract rhythmically; beat, vibrate. **pulsā'tion**, *n.*

pulse¹, *n.* rhythmical pulsation of arteries as blood is pumped into them by the heart, as felt at wrist, etc.; rhythmical beat. *v.i.* pulsate.

pulse², *n.* (*collective*) edible seeds of peas, beans, lentils, etc.; (with pl.) any kind of these.

pul'verīze, *v.* reduce, crumble, to powder or dust; demolish, crush, smash. **pulverizā'tion,** *n.*

pū'ma, *n.* large tawny American carnivore of cat family, cougar.

pum'ice, *n.* (also *pumice-stone*), light kind of porous lava used for rubbing off stains, polishing, etc.

pumm'el, *v.t.* (p.t. *pummelled*), strike repeatedly, esp. with fists.

pump¹, *n.* machine used for raising water; machine for raising or moving liquids, compressing gas, etc. *v.* work pump; remove, raise, compress, inflate, etc., (as) by pumping. *pump up,* inflate (tyre, etc.). **pump-room,** room at spa where medicinal water is sold.

pump², *n.* light shoe for dancing, etc.

pump'kin, *n.* large round fleshy edible fruit of trailing plant of gourd family.

pun, *n.* humorous use of word to suggest different meanings, or of words of same sound with different meanings. *v.i.* (p.t. *punned*), make pun(s).

punch¹, *v.* strike with fist; bore or perforate (as) with punch. *n.* blow with fist; tool for cutting holes in leather, paper, metal, etc.; tool for impressing design on surface. *punch-drunk,* stupefied with repeated punches.

punch², *n.* mixture of spirits or wine with (hot) water, lemon, spice, etc. **punch-bowl,** bowl in which punch is mixed; deep round hollow in hill(s).

Punch³, *n.* humpbacked figure in puppet-show called *Punch and Judy.*

punctil'ious, *a.* attentive to points of conduct, ceremony, or honour; careful about detail.

punc'tual, *a.* coming, etc., at the appointed time; not late. **punctual'ity,** *n.*

punc'tūate, *v.t.* mark or divide with stops, commas, etc. (*punctuation marks*). **punctūā'tion,** *n.* practice or art of punctuating.

punc'ture (-cher), *n.* pricking; hole made by it, esp. one made accidentally in pneumatic tyre. *v.* make puncture in; suffer puncture.

pun'dit, *n.* learned Hindu; learned person, expert.

pun'gent (-j-), *a.* having strong sharp taste or smell; stinging, caustic, biting. **pun'gency,** *n.*

pun'ish, *v.t.* cause to suffer for offence; inflict penalty on; (*informal*) handle or test severely. **pun'ishable,** *a.* **pun'ishment,** *n.*

pū'nitive, *a.* inflicting punishment, retributive.

punn'et, *n.* small basket of thin strips of wood for fruit, etc.

punt, *n.* flat-bottomed boat with square ends, propelled by pole. *v.* propel with, use, punt-pole; convey, go, in punt.

pū'ny, *a.* undersized, feeble.

pup, *n.* puppy. *v.* (p.t. *pupped*), bear pups, litter.

pū'pa, *n.* (pl. *pupae*), insect in inactive pre-adult form, after larva but before imago.

pū'pil, *n.* person being taught; opening in centre of iris of eye, regulating passage of light to retina.

pupp'et, *n.* figure of person, etc., with jointed limbs moved by strings, etc.; person whose acts are controlled by another. **puppet-play, -show,** play, etc., with puppets as characters.

pupp'y, *n.* young dog.

pur'blind, *a.* partly or nearly blind; (fig.) lacking discernment, dull.

pur'chase, *n.* buying; thing bought; leverage, fulcrum; grip, hold. *v.t.* buy.

pur'dah (-da), *n.* (in India, etc.) curtain screening women from strangers; system of secluding women.

pūre, *a.* unmixed, free from admixture or adulteration; clear; chaste, innocent (*archaic*); mere. **pūre'ly,** *adv.*

purée (pūr'ā), *n.* vegetables, fruit, etc., (boiled to pulp and) passed through sieve.

pur'gative, *a.* purging; purifying. *n.* medicine that purges.

pur'gatory, *n.* condition or place of spiritual purging; place of temporary suffering or expiation.

purge, *v.t.* make physically or spiritually clean; clear (bowels) by evacuation; rid of objectionable or alien elements, members, etc. *n.* purging; purgative.

pūrificā'tion, *n.* purifying; ritual cleansing.

pūr'ifȳ, *v.t.* make pure, cleanse; clear of extraneous elements.

pūr'ist, *n.* person who insists on purity or correctness, esp. in language or style.

pūr'itan, *n.* person of extreme strictness in religion or morals; (Hist., *Puritan*) member of extreme English Protestant party regarding Reformation as incomplete. **pūritan'ical,** *a.*

pūr'ity, *n.* pureness, cleanness, freedom from physical or moral pollution.

purl¹, *v.i.* (of stream, etc.) flow with whirling motion and babbling sound.

purl², *n.* inverted stitch in knitting (opp. *plain*). *v.* knit using purl stitch.

pur'lieus (-lūz), *n.pl.* outskirts, outlying region.

purloin', *v.t.* steal, pilfer.

pur'ple, *n.* colour obtained by mixing red and blue; crimson (Hist.); *the purple,* imperial, royal, etc., rank, power, or office. *a.* of purple.

pur'port, *n.* meaning, implication, of document or speech. **purport',** *v.t.* have as its purport; profess, be intended to seem (*to* do).

pur'pose (-us), *n.* object, thing intended; fact, faculty, of resolving on something. *on pur-*

pose, deliberately, not by accident. *to good, little, no*, etc., *purpose*, with good, little, etc., effect or result. *v.t.* intend. **pur'poseful**, *a.* having a purpose, meaningful. **pur'posely**, *adv.* on purpose.

purr, *n.* low continuous vibratory sound with which cat expresses pleasure; sound resembling this. *v.* make, utter with, purr.

purse, *n.* small pouch for carrying money in; funds. *v.* contract (esp. lips) in wrinkles; become wrinkled. **pur'ser**, *n.* ship's officer keeping accounts and superintending comfort, etc., of passengers.

pursu'ance, *n.* carrying out, pursuing, (*of* plan, object, etc.).

pursue', *v.* follow in order to overtake, capture, etc.; harass; seek; proceed along; continue; follow (profession, etc.). **pursuit'** (-ūt), *n.* pursuing; profession, employment, recreation.

pūr'ulent (-ool-), *a.* of, containing, or discharging pus. **pūr'ulence**, *n.*

purvey' (-vā), *v.* procure and supply (provisions); act as purveyor. **purvey'or**, *n.* person whose business it is to supply provisions, etc., esp. on large scale.

pur'view (-vū), *n.* range of physical or mental vision.

pus, *n.* yellowish fluid containing white blood cells, cell debris, and (often) bacteria, formed as result of inflammation of body tissues.

push (poosh), *v.* cause to move (away) by exertion of force; make one's way forcibly or persistently; propel, impel, urge. *n.* act of pushing; application of propelling force; vigorous effort; enterprise, self-assertion. **push-chair**, child's carriage like chair on wheels. **push'ful**, **push'ing**, *aa.* (esp.) thrusting, self-asserting.

pūsillan'imous, *a.* lacking in courage or strength of mind. **pūsillanim'ity**, *n.*

puss (poos), *n.* (word used to call) cat.

pu'ssy (-oo-), *n.* (pet-name for) cat. **pussy-willow**, kind of willow with silky catkins.

pus'tūle, *n.* pimple containing pus.

put (poot), *v.t.* (*p.t. put*; pres.p. *putting*), transfer to particular place; set in particular position; cause to be in some state or condition; express in words; (Athletics) hurl

(*weight*, etc.). *put down*, stop by force, suppress. *put off*, postpone (action, holding of event, etc.); dissuade. *put on*, assume, simulate. *put out*, (esp.) extinguish. *put through*, connect by telephone. *put up*, propose; lodge and entertain. *put up with*, submit to, tolerate.

pū'tative, *a.* supposed, reputed.

pū'trēfy̆, *v.* become putrid, go bad, rot. **pūtrēfac'tion**, *n.* **pū'trēfactive**, *a.*

pū'trid, *a.* decomposed, rotten; stinking.

putt, *v.* (Golf) strike ball gently to roll it towards or into hole. *n.* putting stroke. **putt'er**, *n.* club for putting. **putting-green**, *n.* smooth area of turf around hole.

putt'ee (-i), *n.* long strip of cloth wound spirally round leg and serving as gaiter.

putt'y̆, *n.* paste of whiting, linseed oil, etc., for fixing panes of glass, etc. *v.t.* fix, fill, etc., with putty.

puzz'le, *n.* difficult question or problem; problem or toy designed to test knowledge, skill, etc. *v.* perplex, be perplexed (*over*). *puzzle out*, understand, solve, by exercising ingenuity, etc. **puzz'lement**, *n.* **puzz'ling**, *a.*

pyg'my̆, **pig'my̆**, *n.* member of race of small people of equatorial Africa; very small person or thing. *a.* of pygmies; dwarf; diminutive.

pyja'mas (-ahmaz), *n.pl.* loose-fitting jacket and trousers for sleeping in.

py̆'lon, *n.* tall (metal) structure, esp. supporting overhead electric cables; gateway, esp. of Egyptian temple.

py̆orrhoe'a (-rēa), *n.* disease of tooth-sockets.

py'ramid, *n.* solid figure with triangular, square, or polygonal base and sloping sides meeting at apex; monumental (esp. ancient Egyptian) stone structure of this shape. **pyram'idal**, *a.*

py̆re, *n.* pile of wood, etc., esp. for burning a corpse.

py̆rotech'nic(al) (-tek-), *aa.* of or like fireworks. **py̆rotech'nics**, *n.* art of making fireworks; display of fireworks.

Py'rrhic vic'tory (-rik), victory won at too great a cost.

py̆'thon, *n.* large non-venomous snake that kills its prey by squeezing it.

pyx, *n.* vessel in which Host is reserved.

Q

quack[1] *n.* harsh cry of ducks. *v.i.* utter quack(s).

quack[2], *n.* ignorant person claiming knowledge and skill, esp. in medicine. **quack'ery**, *n.*

quad (-od), *n.* (*informal*) quadrangle; quadruplet.

quadr-, *pref.*: see **quadri-**.

quadrangle (kwod′ranggl), *n.* four-sided figure, esp. square or rectangle; four-sided court (partly) surrounded by building(s) of college, etc. **quadrang′ular**, *a.*

quad′rant (-od-), *n.* quarter of a circle or of its circumference; instrument for taking angular measurements.

quadrat′ic (-od-), *a.* involving second and no higher power of unknown quantity or variable. *n.* quadratic equation.

quadrenn′ial (-od-), *a.* occurring every four years; lasting four years.

quadri- (-od-), *pref.* (*quadr-* before vowel; sometimes *quadru-* before *p*), four.

quadrilat′eral (-od-), *a.* four-sided. *n.* four-sided plane figure or area.

quadrille′, *n.* (music for) a square dance.

quad′ruped (-odroo-), *n.* four-footed animal, esp. four-footed mammal. *a.* four-footed.

quad′ruple (-odroo-), *a.* of four parts or parties; four times greater than; (Mus., of time) with four beats in bar. *n.* number or amount four times greater than another. *v.* multiply by four. **quadru′plicate** (-rōō-), *a.* four times repeated or copied.

quad′ruplet (-odroo-), *n.* one of four children born at one birth.

quaff (kwoff), *v.* drink in long draught(s).

quag′mīre (*or* -og-), *n.* piece of wet swampy ground; quaking bog; marsh.

quail[1], *n.* bird related to partridge.

quail[2], *v.i.* flinch, show fear.

quaint, *a.* unfamiliar or old-fashioned; odd in a pleasing way.

quāke, *v.i.* tremble; shake. *n.* quaking; earthquake.

Quā′ker, *n.* member of religious Society of Friends founded by George Fox in 17th c., Friend. **Quā′kerism**, *n.*

qualifica′tion (-ol-), *n.* qualifying; thing that qualifies; modification. **qualifica′tory**, *a.*

qual′ify (-ol-), *v.* make or become competent, fit, eligible, etc. (*for*, *to*); describe as; modify, limit; moderate, lessen severity of.

qual′itative (-ol-), *a.* of, concerned with, quality.

qual′ity (-ol-), *n.* degree of excellence, relative nature or kind or character; (characteristic) feature; attribute; (*archaic*) high social position.

qualm (-ahm), *n.* scruple of conscience; misgiving; momentary faint or sick feeling.

quan′dary (-on-), *n.* state of doubt or perplexity; dilemma.

quan′titative (-on-), *a.* of or measured or measurable by quantity.

quan′tity (-on-), *n.* amount; specified or considerable amount; (figure or symbol representing) thing having quantity; length or shortness of sound or syllable.

quan′tum (-on-), *n.* required, desired, or allowed amount; (Phys.) discrete quantity of energy, etc.

quarantine (kwo′rantēn), *n.* (period of) isolation imposed on ship, person, or animal that may carry infection. *v.t.* put in quarantine.

quark (*or* -ork), *n.* (Phys.) hypothetical component of known elementary particles.

qua′rrel (kwo-), *n.* violent disagreement or argument; rupture of friendly relationship; occasion of complaint. *v.i.* contend violently, have dispute, (*with*); find fault *with*. **qua′rrelsome**, *a.*

qua′rry[1] (kwo-), *n.* hunted animal, intended prey; thing eagerly sought after.

qua′rry[2] (kwo-), *n.* place from which stone, slate, etc., is extracted for building, etc. *v.* extract from quarry; form quarry.

quart (kwort), *n.* quarter of gallon, two pints.

quar′ter (kwor-), *n.* fourth part; one of four equal or corresponding parts; quarter of hundredweight (28 lb.); fourth part of year, esp. as divided by quarter-days; point of compass, direction; locality; mercy shown to enemy in battle; (pl.) lodgings, esp. place where troops are stationed. *v.t.* divide into quarters; put (esp. troops) into quarters. **quarter-day,** one of four days in year on which quarterly payments are due. **quarter-deck,** part of ship's upper deck towards stern. **quar′termaster,** (Naut.) petty officer in charge of steering, signals, hold-stowing, etc.; (Mil.) officer in charge of quartering, rations, etc.

quar′terly (kwor-). *a.* occurring, due, every quarter of year *n.* quarterly magazine. *adv.* once every quarter.

quartet(te)′ (kwor-), *n.* musical composition for four instruments or voices; group of players or singers rendering this; set of four.

quar′tō (kwor-), *n.* (pl. *quartos*), (size of) book with sheets of paper folded into four leaves or eight pages.

quartz (-or-), *n.* widely distributed mineral consisting of silica.

quā′sar (*or* -z-), *n.* (Astron.) very remote, very luminous source of strong radio waves.

quash (kwosh), *v.t.* annul; reject as not valid.

quāsi- (*or* kwahzi-), *pref.* (used, hyphenated, with n. or adj.) seeming(ly), not real(ly); almost (e.g. *a quasi-official position*).

quat′er-centē′nary, *n.* 400th anniversary.

quatrain (kwot′rin), *n.* four-line stanza.

quā′ver, *v.* (of voice) shake, tremble; utter or sing in trembling tones. *n.* quavering sound; (Mus.) black-headed note with tailed stem, equal to half crotchet.

quay (kē), *n.* landing-place, usu. of stone, etc., for loading and unloading ships.

quea′sy (-z-), *a.* feeling sick, easily upset; liable to qualms or scruples.

queen, *n.* king's wife; female sovereign of kingdom; perfect female of bee, wasp, etc.; court-card between king and knave; piece in chess. *v.i. queen it,* act like queen. **queen mother,** king's widow who is mother of king or queen. **Queen's Counsel** (abbrev. *Q.C.*), barrister appointed as counsel to the Crown.

queen'ly, *a.*

queer, *a.* strange, odd, eccentric; shady, suspect; dizzy, faint.

quell, *v. t.* suppress, crush.

quench, *v. t.* satisfy (thirst); extinguish (fire, flame). **quench'less,** *a.* unquenchable.

quern, *n.* hand-mill for grinding corn, etc.

que'rulous (-roo-), *a.* complaining.

quer'y, *n.* question, question-mark, esp. indicating doubt of correctness of statement, etc. *v. t.* question accuracy of.

quest, *n.* seeking; thing sought; inquiry, search. *v. i.* go *about* in search of something.

ques'tion (-chn), *n.* sentence requesting information or requiring an answer; problem, concern, matter; subject under discussion; doubt. *call in question,* throw doubt on. *in question,* under consideration. *v. t.* ask question of; throw doubt on. **question-mark,** punctuation mark (?) used at end of question. **ques'tionable,** *a.* doubtful; not clearly consistent with honesty or wisdom.

questionnaire' (*or* ke-), *n.* series of questions for obtaining information on special points.

queue (kū), *n.* line of persons, vehicles, etc., awaiting turn to buy, proceed, etc.; pigtail. *v. i.* (pres. p. *queuing*), *queue* (*up*), form a queue.

quibb'le, *n.* equivocation, evasion, argument depending on ambiguity of word. *v. i.* use quibbles.

quick, *a.* moving rapidly, swift; done, traversed, etc., in a short time, prompt; lively, intelligent; hasty; (*archaic*) living. *n.* sensitive flesh below nails or skin; (fig.) feelings. *adv.* quickly. **quick'sand,** unslaked lime. **quick'sand,** loose wet sand readily swallowing up heavy objects. **quick'set,** (of hedge) formed of living plants. **quick'silver,** mercury. **quick'ly,** *adv.* **quick'ness,** *n.*

quick'en, *v.* make or become quicker; (cause to) become (more) lively, vigorous, or active.

quid, *n.* (pl. same), (*slang*) a pound.

quid prō quō, one thing or action in return for another, tit for tat. (Latin)

quies'cent, *a.* motionless, inert, silent, dormant. **quies'cence,** *n.*

qui'ĕt, *a.* with little or no sound or motion; of gentle disposition; (of colour, etc.) not showy or conspicuous; tranquil. *n.* undisturbed state; tranquillity, repose; calm, silence. *v.* soothe, calm, reduce to quiet; become quiet. **qui'ĕten,** *v.* quiet. **qui'ĕtŭde,** *n.* quietness.

quiff, *n.* flat curl on forehead; lock of hair brushed upwards in front.

quill, *n.* large feather of wing or tail; hollow stem of feather; pen, plectrum, etc., made of quill; porcupine's spine.

quilt, *n.* cover, esp. of quilted material, lying over other bed-clothes; bedspread. *v. t.* make

or line with padding kept in place between two layers of material by lines of stitching.

quin, *n.* (*informal*) quintuplet.

quince, *n.* (tree bearing) hard, acid, yellowish pear-shaped fruit.

quincentē'nary, *n.* 500th anniversary.

quinine' (-ēn), *n.* bitter drug obtained from bark of tropical tree, used esp. in treatment of malaria.

quinque-, *pref.* five.

quinquenn'ial, *a.* occurring every five years; lasting five years. **quinquenn'ium,** *n.* period of five years.

quin'sy (-z-), *n.* abscess forming round tonsil.

quintess'ence, *n.* purest or most perfect form or example of some quality, etc.; highly refined extract.

quintet(te)', *n.* musical composition for five instruments or voices; group of players or singers rendering this; set of five.

quintŭ'plet, *n.* one of five children born at one birth.

quip, *n.* witty and sarcastic remark.

quire[1], *n.* 24 sheets of writing-paper.

quire[2], *n.* (*archaic*) choir.

quirk, *n.* trick of action or behaviour.

quis'ling (-z-), *n.* person collaborating with invading or occupying enemy forces.

quit, *v.* (p.t. *quitted* or *quit*), depart from; give up, abandon; (U.S.) stop. *pred. a.* rid *of.*

quitch, *n.* couch-grass.

quite, *adv.* completely, altogether, absolutely; rather, somewhat.

quits, *pred. a.* on even terms, by repayment or retaliation.

quiv'er[1], *n.* case for arrows.

quiv'er[2], *v. i.* tremble or vibrate with slight rapid motion. *n.* quivering.

quixot'ic, *a.* idealistic but impracticable, absurdly generous, chivalrous, etc. **quix'otry,** *n.*

quiz, *v. t.* (p.t. *quizzed*), examine, put series of questions to. *n.* (pl. *quizzes*), series of questions, esp. as entertainment or competition. **quizz'ical,** *a.* mocking, gently amused.

quoit (koit), *n.* ring of iron or (in *deck-quoits*) rope, thrown in attempt to encircle peg in game of *quoits.*

quor'um, *n.* number of persons that must be present to constitute a valid meeting.

quō'ta, *n.* share to be contributed to or received from total by one of parties concerned; limited amount or number.

quotā'tion, *n.* quoting; passage or price quoted. **quotation marks,** punctuation marks (' ' *or* " ") used at beginning and end of quoted words.

quōte, *v.* cite as example, authority, etc.; repeat or copy out passage(s), statement(s), etc., (of); state price (of).

quŏth, *v. t.* p.t. 1st & 3rd pers. (*archaic*) said.

quotid'ian, *a.* daily; everyday.

quō'tient (-shnt), *n.* result given by dividing one quantity by another.

R

rabb'et, *n.* groove or slot cut along edge or face of wood to receive another piece of wood, etc.

rabb'ī, *n.* appointed Jewish religious leader; (title of respect for) Jewish scholar or teacher of Jewish law.

rabb'it, *n.* gregarious burrowing mammal related to hare. *v. i.* hunt rabbits.

rabb'le, *n.* disorderly crowd, mob; *the rabble*, (contempt.) the lowest classes.

rab'id, *a.* furious, violent, unreasoning; affected with rabies. **rabid'ity**, *n.*

rā'bies (-ēz), *n.* canine madness, acute virus disease of (esp.) dogs, etc., communicable to man by bite of infected animal.

rac(c)oon', *n.* bushy-tailed N. American nocturnal flesh-eating mammal.

rāce[1], *n.* contest of speed, (pl.) series of these for horses, etc.; strong current in sea, etc.; channel of stream; (fig.) course of life. *v.* (make) go at full speed; compete in speed (with). **race-card**, programme of races. **race-course**, ground for horse-racing. **race--horse**, horse bred for racing. **race-meeting**, horse-racing fixture.

rāce[2], *n.* group of persons (regarded as) of common ancestry; great division of living creatures; descent, kindred; distinct ethnical stock.

ra'cēme (*or* -ēm'), *n.* inflorescence with flowers attached by short stalks along central stem. **ra'cēmōse**, *a.*

rā'cial (-shl), *a.* of race. **rā'cialism**, *n.* encouragement of antagonism between human races. **rā'cialist**, *n. & a.* **rā'cism**, *n.* belief in unchanging fundamental differences between races. **rā'cist**, *n. & a.*

rack[1], *n.* framework with bars, pegs, or shelves, etc., for holding fodder or for keeping articles on or in; cogged or indented rail or bar gearing with wheel, pinion, etc.; (Hist.) instrument of torture for stretching victim's joints. *v. t.* torture on rack (Hist.); inflict torture or strain on.

rack[2], *n.* destruction (chiefly in phr. *go to rack and ruin*).

rack'ĕt[1], **rac'quet** (-kit), *n.* network of catgut, nylon, etc., stretched across elliptical frame with handle, used to strike ball in tennis, etc.; (pl.) ball-game played with rackets in four-walled court.

rack'ĕt[2], *n.* uproar, din; ordeal; (*slang*) way of making money, etc., by dubious or illegal means. *v. i.* live gay life. **rackĕteer'**, *n.* person engaged in illegal racket. **rack'ĕty**, *a.* noisy; dissipated.

rā'cy, *a.* vigorous; lively, piquant.

rā'dar, *n.* system, apparatus, for determining direction and range of objects by reflection of radio waves.

radd'le, *n.* red ochre. *v. t.* paint with raddle; plaster with rouge.

rā'dial, *a.* of, in, or like rays or radii; having, lying or moving along, spokes or radiating lines; of radius of arm. **rā'dially**, *adv.*

rā'diance, *n.* brilliant light; radiant look.

rā'diant, *a.* sending out rays; issuing or operating radially; beaming with joy, etc.; bright.

rā'diāte, *v.* diverge or emit from centre; emit rays of light, heat, etc.; transmit by radio; be arranged like spokes; spread, disseminate. **rādiā'tion**, *n.* radiating; (esp.) (emission of) rays and particles characteristic of radioactive substances. **radiation sickness**, effects of exposure to radioactivity. **rā'diātor**, *n.* apparatus for radiating warmth, cooling motor-engine, etc.

rad'ical, *a.* of, from, or going to root(s); fundamental, inherent, essential; thorough; (Politics) advocating great reforms. *n.* person holding radical political opinions; (Math.) quantity expressed as root of another.

rā'diō, *n.* transmission and reception of messages, etc., by means of electromagnetic waves of certain frequency (*radio frequency*); broadcasting; radio receiving set; wireless. *a.* of, operated by, radio. *v.* transmit by radio. **radio wave**, electromagnetic wave of radio frequency.

rā'diō-, *pref.* of rays or radiation; of radio; of radium or radioactivity; radioactive. **rādiō-activ'ity**, *n.* emission of rays capable of penetrating opaque bodies, etc.; property of emitting these. **rādiōac'tive**, *a.* **rādiō--astron'omy**, *n.* branch of astronomy dealing with study of celestial bodies by means of radio waves reflected or emitted by them.

ră'diŏgram, *n.* radio receiver and gramophone combined. **ră'diŏgraph,** *n.* X-ray photograph. **rădiog'raphy,** *n.* photography or examination by means of X-rays. **rădio'grapher,** *n.* **rădiol'ogy,** *n.* scientific study of X-rays, radioactivity, etc., and (esp.) use of X-rays, etc., in medicine. **rădiol'ogist,** *n.* **rădiŏteleg'raphy, rădiŏteleph'ony,** *nn.* telegraphy, telephony, by radio. **ră'diŏsonde,** *n.* sonde with radio for transmitting information to observers on ground. **rădiŏ-tel'ĕscŏpe,** *n.* apparatus for collecting radio waves from space, used in radio--astronomy. **rădiŏthe'rapy,** *n.* treatment of disease by X-rays or other forms of radiation.

rad'ish, *n.* (plant with) crisp hot-tasting root eaten raw.

ră'dium, *n.* radioactive metallic element.

ră'dius, *n.* (pl. *rădiī*), straight line from centre to circumference of circle or sphere; spoke; circular area as measured by its radius; thicker and shorter bone of forearm.

raff'ia, *n.* kind of palm-tree; soft fibre from its leaves.

raff'ish, *a.* of disreputable appearance.

raff'le, *n.* sale of article by lottery. *v.t.* sell by raffle.

raft (-ah-), *n.* flat floating structure of timber, esp. as substitute for boat in emergencies; logs, etc., fastened together for transportation by water. *v.* transport, travel, by raft.

raf'ter (rah-), *n.* one of sloping beams forming framework of roof.

rag¹, *n.* torn or frayed piece of cloth; odd piece of cloth; (pl.) tattered clothes. *glad rags,* fine clothes. *rag, tag, and bobtail,* see **bobtail. rag'time,** music with much syncopation. **rag'wort,** yellow-flowered wild plant.

rag², *v.* (p.t. *ragged*), (*slang*) indulge in horseplay; tease, play practical jokes on. *n.* ragging; students' procession, etc., with horseplay.

rag'amuffin, *n.* ragged dirty boy or man.

răge, *n.* (fit of) violent anger; object of widespread temporary popularity. *v.i.* rave, storm; be violent; be full of anger.

ragg'ĕd (-g-), *a.* torn or frayed; having rough or irregular edge or outline or surface; wearing rags. **ragged robin,** crimson-flowered wild plant.

rag'lan, *a.* (of sleeve) cut so that top of sleeve continues to neck of garment.

raid, *n.* sudden attack to secure military advantage, booty, etc.; air raid; surprise visit by police. *v.* make raid (upon).

rail¹, *n.* level or sloping bar as part of fence, gate, etc.; iron bar forming part of track of railway or tram-lines; railway. *v.t.* furnish or enclose with rails. **rail'road,** (esp. U.S.) railway. **rail'way,** way laid with rails for

passage of trains; company, organization, etc., required for working of this.

rail², *v.i.* use abusive language (*at, against*).

rail'ing, *n.* (esp.) (often in pl.) structure of rails, etc., as barrier or fence.

raill'ery, *n.* banter.

railroad, railway: see **rail¹.**

rai'ment, *n.* (*archaic*) clothing, apparel.

rain, *n.* condensed moisture of atmosphere falling visibly in separate drops; fall of these; (rain-like descent of) falling objects, etc. *v.* fall or send down (like) rain. *it rains, it is raining,* rain falls, there is a rain of. **rain'bow,** arch of prismatic colours formed in rain or spray by sun's rays. **rain'coat,** waterproof coat. **rain'fall,** total amount of rain falling within given area in given time. **rain'y,** *a.*

raise (-z), *v.t.* set upright; put or take into higher position; cause to rise; rouse; rear, bring up (esp. U.S.); breed; cause to grow; increase amount or heighten level of; levy, collect; end (seige, blockade).

rai'sin (-zn), *n.* dried grape.

raja(h) (rah'ja), *n.* Indian king or prince.

răke¹, *n.* pole with comb-like cross-bar for drawing hay, etc., together, smoothing loose soil, etc.; any of various implements resembling rake. *v.* use rake; collect, draw together, (as) with rake; search (*through,* etc.); sweep with eyes, shot, etc.

răke², *n.* dissipated or immoral man.

răke³, *v.* (of ship) project beyond keel at upper part of bow or stern; (of mast, funnel, etc.) incline towards stern; give backward inclination to. *n.* amount to which thing rakes; raking position or build.

ră'kish, *a.* of dissolute appearance or manners; (of ship) smart, seeming built for speed.

rallentan'dŏ, (as musical direction, abbrev. *rall.*) gradually slower.

rall'y, *v.* bring or come together (again) for united effort; revive by effort of will; recover partly or temporarily. *n.* act of rallying; recovery of energy or spirit; mass meeting; motorists' or motor-cyclists' competitive event; (Tennis, etc.) series of strokes between service and winning of point.

ram, *n.* uncastrated male sheep; battering--ram; (part of) pile-driving or hydraulic or pumping machine. *v.* (p.t. *rammed*), strike and push heavily; beat firm; force home; impress by repetition. **ram'rod,** (Hist.) rod for ramming home charge of firearm.

ram'ble, *v.i.* walk without definite route; talk in disconnected way. *n.* rambling walk. **ram'bler,** *n.* freely climbing rose. **ram'bling,** *a.* (esp.) disconnected; irregularly planned or arranged.

ram'ifў, *v.* form branches or subdivisions; develop into complicated system. **ramificā'tion,** *n.*

ramp¹, *n.* sloping way from one level to another. *v.* be rampant; furnish or construct with ramp.

ramp², *n.* (*slang*) swindle; charging of exorbitant prices.

rampage', *v.i.* rage, storm, rush about. *n. be* (*go*) *on the rampage*, be (go) rampaging.

ram'pant, *a.* (Herald., esp. of lion) standing on hind legs with fore-paws in air; extravagant, unrestrained, rank, luxuriant. **ram'pancy**, *n.*

ram'part, *n.* defensive mound of earth; (fig.) defence, protection.

ram'shackle, *a.* rickety, tumbledown.

ran, *p.t.* of **run**.

ranch, *n.* large N.Amer. farm or estate, esp. one where cattle, horses, etc., are bred and reared. *v.i.* conduct ranch.

ran'cid, *a.* smelling or tasting like rank stale fat. **rancid'ity**, *n.*

ran'cour (-ker), *n.* bitter, lasting hatred; spitefulness. **ran'corous**, *a.*

rand, *n.* (in S.Africa) highlands on either side of river valley; S.Afr. unit of money.

ran'dom, *n. at random*, without aim, purpose, or principle; haphazard. *a.* made, done, etc., at random.

ra'nee (rah-), *n.* Indian queen or princess.

rang, *p.t.* of **ring**.

range (-nj), *n.* row, line, or series of things, esp. buildings or mountains; ground with targets for shooting at; freedom or opportunity to range; sphere; scope; compass; distance attainable by gun, etc., or between gun, etc., and target; fireplace with oven, etc., for cooking. *v.* place or arrange in row, ranks, etc.; extend, reach; vary between limits; rove, wander. **range-finder**, instrument for estimating range of target, etc.

ran'ger (-j-), *n.* (esp.) keeper of royal or other park; (*Ranger*), senior Guide.

rank¹, *n.* row, line; soldiers in single line abreast; distinct social class; grade in armed forces, etc.; relative position; (pl.) ordinary soldiers. *rank and file*, ordinary soldiers, ordinary or undistinguished people. *v.* arrange in rank; assign rank to; have rank or place. **rank'er**, *n.* (officer who has been) soldier in the ranks.

rank², *a.* too luxuriant, and usu. coarse, in growth; offensive, foul-smelling; flagrant, gross.

rank'le, *v.i.* continue to cause bitter feelings.

ran'sack, *v.t.* search thoroughly; search and rob.

ran'som, *n.* sum of money, etc., paid or demanded for release of captive; ransoming. *v.t.* buy freedom or restoration of; redeem.

rant, *v.* use pompous or exaggerated language; declaim or preach noisily and theatrically.

ranun'culus, *n.* (pl. *ranunculuses*, *ranunculi*), genus of flowering plants including buttercup.

rap¹, *n.* smart light blow or stroke; sound of this, esp. on door. *v.* (p.t. *rapped*), strike

smartly; make sound of rap.

rap², *n.* (*not*) the least bit.

rapa'cious (-shus), *a.* grasping, greedy, esp. for money; predatory. **rapa'city**, *n.*

rāpe¹, *n.* act of having sexual intercourse with woman without her consent; seizing, taking, by force. *v.t.* commit rape upon.

rāpe², *n.* plant grown as food for sheep and for its oil-yielding seed.

rap'id, *a.* moving, done, etc., with great speed. *n.* (often pl.) steep descent in river-bed causing swift current. **rapid'ity**, *n.*

rā'pier, *n.* light slender sword.

rapscall'ion, *n.* rascal.

rapt, *a.* engrossed, entranced.

rap'ture (-cher), *n.* (expression of) intense delight. **rap'turous**, *a.*

rāre¹, *a.* scarce, uncommon, unusual; remarkably good; thin, not dense.

rāre², *a.* (esp. of steak) underdone.

rare'bit (rārb-; *or* rab-), *n.* melted or toasted cheese, etc., served on toast (esp. *Welsh rarebit* or *rabbit*).

rār'efy, *v.* lessen density or solidity of; refine; become less dense. **rārefac'tion**, *n.*

rare'ly (-āǐl-), *adv.* seldom, not often; uncommonly.

rār'ity, *n.* rareness; rare thing.

ra'scal (rah-), *n.* dishonest, unprincipled person; mischievous child, scamp. **ra'scally**, *a.*

rase: see **raze**.

rash¹, *n.* eruption of spots or red patches on the skin.

rash², *a.* acting, done, without enough consideration of the consequences; hasty, impetuous.

rash'er, *n.* thin slice of bacon or ham.

rasp (-ah-), *n.* coarse file; grating sound or effect. *v.* scrape with rasp; scrape roughly; grate upon; make grating sound.

ra'spberry (rahzb-), *n.* (shrub bearing) edible juicy, usu. red, fruit. **raspberry cane**, raspberry plant.

rat, *n.* rodent resembling mouse, but larger. *v.i.* (p.t. *ratted*), hunt or kill rats; desert one's party, side, etc.; betray one's friends. **rat-race**, ruthless competitive struggle.

ratafi'a (-fēa), *n.* liqueur or biscuit flavoured with almonds, fruit-kernels, etc.

ratch'et, *n.* set of inclined teeth on bar or wheel (*ratchet-wheel*), with catch preventing reversed motion.

rāte¹, *n.* statement of numerical proportion between two sets of things; standard or way of reckoning; (measure of) value, tariff charge, cost, (relative) speed; tax levied by local authority on assessed value of property. *v.* estimate worth or value of; regard as; rank or be rated *as*. **rāte'able**, *a.* liable to, or assessed for, payment of local rates. **rāte'payer**, *n.*

rāte², *v.t.* scold angrily.

ra'ther (-ahdh-), *adv.* more willingly, for preference; sooner (*than*); more correctly;

somewhat; (*informal*, as answer) most certainly.

rat'ify, *v.t.* confirm or accept by signature or other formality. **ratificā'tion**, *n.*

rā'ting¹, *n.* (esp.) position or class in warship's crew; non-commissioned member of ship's company.

rā'ting², *n.* angry scolding.

rā'tiō (-shi-), *n.* (pl. *ratios*), relation between two quantities determined by number of times one contains the other.

ra'tion, *n.* fixed allowance or share of food, etc. *v.t.* put on ration; share (*out*) in fixed quantities.

ra'tional (-shon-), *a.* able to reason; sensible; sane; of or based on reason. **rational'ity**, *n.*

ra'tionalize (-shon-), *v.* bring into conformity with reason; reorganize scientifically; find plausible or reasonable motive(s), reason(s), etc., (for). **rationalizā'tion**, *n.*

rattan', *n.* palm with long thin many-jointed stems; cane of this.

ratt'le, *v.* give short sharp sounds in rapid succession; cause such sounds by shaking something; say or recite rapidly. *n.* toy or instrument made to rattle; rattling sound. **ratt'lesnake**, venomous snake with horny rings at end of tail making rattling sound. **ratt'ling**, *a. & adv.* remarkably (good, fast, etc.).

rau'cous, *a.* harsh-sounding; hoarse.

rav'age, *v.* lay waste, plunder; make havoc. *n.* devastation; (pl.) destructive effects *of*.

rāve, *v.* talk wildly or deliriously; (of sea, wind, etc.) roar, rage; speak with rapturous admiration (*about, of*).

rav'el, *v.* (p.t. *ravelled*), make or become tangled; confuse, complicate; separate into threads, fray.

rā'ven, *n.* large black raucous-voiced bird of crow family. *a.* of glossy black.

rav'enous, *a.* very hungry; voracious.

ravine' (-ēn), *n.* deep narrow gorge.

rav'ish, *v.t.* enrapture, fill with delight; commit rape upon.

raw, *a.* uncooked; in natural or unwrought state; crude, inexperienced, unskilled; stripped of skin; sore, sensitive to touch; (of weather) damp and cold. *n.* sensitive spot; raw state. **raw deal**, unfair treatment.

ray¹, *n.* single line or narrow beam of light or other radiant energy; any of set of radiating lines, parts, or things. *v.* issue, come *out*, etc., in rays.

ray², *n.* flat-fish related to skate.

ray'on, *n.* synthetic fabric made (esp.) from cellulose.

rāze, rāse (-z), *v.t.* destroy (town, etc.) completely (esp. in phr. *raze to the ground*).

rā'zor, *n.* sharp-edged instrument for shaving. **rā'zorbill**, sea-bird of auk family.

rē, *prep.* in the matter of, concerning.

re-, *pref.* again, anew, afresh, repeated; back.

reach, *v.* stretch *out*, extend; get as far as, attain, arrive at; pass or take with outstretched hand. *n.* range of hand, etc.; compass, scope; continuous stretch of river, etc.

react', *v.i.* produce mutual or responsive effect; respond to stimulus; move or tend in reverse direction; undergo (esp. chemical) change.

reac'tion, *n.* return of previous condition after a period of the opposite; response to stimulus; retrograde tendency in politics, etc.; (Chem.) interaction of substances resulting in chemical change. **reac'tionary**, *a. & n.* (person) inclined or favourable to reaction.

reac'tive, *a.* tending to react.

reac'tor, *n.* (esp.) (*nuclear*) *reactor*, large apparatus for initiating and controlling chain reaction, used esp. for production of atomic energy.

read, *v.* (p.t. *read*, pr. red), look at and (be able to) convert into intended meaning printed or written words, etc.; reproduce mentally or vocally printed or written words; study by reading; interpret in certain sense; read and mark (printer's *proof*) for correction. **read'able**, *a.* (esp.) interestingly written.

rea'der, *n.* person employed by publisher to read and report on manuscripts; proof-reader; senior university lecturer; reading textbook.

read'ily (red-), *adv.* willingly; easily.

read'iness (red-), *n.* willingness; quickness; ready or prepared state.

rea'ding, *n.* interpretation, view taken; literary knowledge; figure, etc., shown by instrument, dial, etc.

read'y (red-), *a.* with preparations complete; in a fit state; willing; quick; within reach; fit for immediate use or action. **ready-made**, (of clothes) made in standard sizes.

rēā'gent, *n.* substance used to produce chemical reaction.

rē'al, *a.* actually existing or occurring; not supposed or pretended or artificial; genuine; consisting of immovable property such as land and houses.

rē'alism, *n.* regarding and dealing with things as they really are; (in art, etc.) fidelity of representation. **rē'alist**, *n. & a.* **rēalis'tic**, *a.*

real'ity, *n.* being real; real existence; existent thing; what is real.

rē'alize, *v.t.* understand clearly; convert (hope, plan) into fact; convert (shares, property) into money; fetch as price. **rēalizā'tion**, *n.*

rē'ally, *adv.* in fact, in reality; positively. *really?* is that so?

realm (relm), *n.* kingdom; (fig.) sphere.

ream, *n.* twenty quires of paper.

rēan'imāte, *v.t.* impart fresh vigour to.

reap, *v.* cut grain, etc., with sickle or machine; gather in as harvest or (fig.) reward. **rea'per**, *n.* (esp.) machine for reaping.

rear¹, *v.* bring up, breed, cultivate; raise; (esp. of horse) rise on hind legs.

rear², *n.* back part of anything; space or position at back. *a.* back, hinder. **rear-admiral,** naval officer below vice-admiral. **rear'-guard,** troops protecting rear of army, esp. in retreat. **rear'ward,** *a.*, *adv.*, & *n.* **rear'-wards** (-z), *adv.*

rea'son (-z-), *n.* (fact put forward or serving as) argument, motive, cause, or justification; power of the mind to think and reach conclusions from facts, etc.; sense, sanity; moderation. *v.* use argument *with* in order to persuade; form or try to reach conclusions by connected thought; think *out*. **rea'sonable,** *a.* having sound judgement; moderate; tolerable, fair.

reassure' (-ashoor), *v.t.* remove fears or doubts, restore confidence, of (person).

re'bāte, *n.* deduction from sum to be paid, discount.

reb'el, *n.* person who rises in arms against or refuses allegiance to established government; person who resists authority or control; (attrib.) of rebels, rebellious. **rebel',** *v.i.* (p.t. *rebelled*), act as rebel (*against*); resist authority.

rebell'ion, *n.* open, esp. armed, resistance to established government or any authority.

rebell'ious, *a.* in rebellion; disposed to rebel, insubordinate, unmanageable.

rebound', *v.i.* spring back after impact; recoil. **re'bound,** *n.* rebounding, recoil; reaction after emotion.

rebuff', *n.* & *v.t.* check, snub, repulse.

rebūke', *v.t.* find fault with, speak severely to. *n.* rebuking, being rebuked; reproof.

rebut', *v.t.* force back; disprove. **rebutt'al,** *n.*

recal'citrant, *a.* obstinately disobedient or refractory. **recal'citrance,** *n.*

recall' (-awl), *v.t.* summon back; bring back *to* memory; (cause to) remember; revive, resuscitate; revoke, annul. *n.* recalling, being recalled.

recant', *v.* withdraw and renounce (statement, belief, etc.) as erroneous or heretical. **recantā'tion,** *n.*

re'cap, *v.* (p.t. *recapped*), (*informal*) recapitulate. *n.* recapitulation.

recapit'ūlāte, *v.* summarize, restate briefly. **recapitūlā'tion,** *n.*

recap'ture (-cher), *v.t.* capture again; recover.

recēde', *v.i.* go or shrink back; slope backwards; withdraw, retreat.

receipt' (-sēt), *n.* receiving or being received; amount of money received (usu. pl.); written acknowledgement or receipt of payment, etc.; (*archaic*) recipe. *v.t.* write or give receipt on or for.

receive' (-sēv), *v.* accept, take, get, (something offered, sent, etc.); admit, welcome; entertain as guest; accept or buy (stolen goods) from thief. **received',** *a.* widely accepted as true or correct. **recei'vable,** *a.* **recei'ver,** *n.* (esp.) person appointed to

administer debtor's or disputed property; one who receives stolen goods; earpiece of telephone; apparatus for transforming radio waves into audible sound, radio (*receiving set*).

re'cent, *a.* not long past, that happened or existed lately; not long established, modern. **re'cently,** *adv.*

recep'tacle, *n.* that which receives and holds something; containing vessel, space, or place.

recep'tion, *n.* receiving or being received; (ceremonious) welcome; occasion of receiving guests. **reception-room,** room available or suitable for receiving guests; living-room.

recep'tionist, *n.* person appointed to receive clients, etc.

recep'tive, *a.* able or quick to receive impressions, ideas, etc. **receptiv'ity,** *n.*

recess'ive, *a.* tending to recede.

recess', *n.* temporary stopping of work, etc.; part of room, etc., where wall is set back from main part; inner place. *v.t.* set back; provide with recess(es).

reces'sion (-shn), *n.* receding, withdrawal; temporary decline in activity or prosperity. **reces'sional,** *n.* hymn sung while clergy and choir withdraw after service.

re'cipe, *n.* statement of ingredients and procedure for preparing or cooking dish, etc.

recip'ient, *n.* one who receives (something).

recip'rocal, *a.* in return; mutual; inversely correspondent. *n.* (Math.) function or expression so related to another that their product is unity.

recip'rocāte, *v.* interchange; give in return, make return (*with*); go with alternate backward and forward motion. **reciprocā'tion,** *n.*

recipro'city, *n.* reciprocal condition; mutual action; give-and-take, esp. between States.

recī'tal, *n.* programme of music by one or two persons; detailed account of facts, etc.

recitā'tion, *n.* reciting; piece recited.

recitative' (-ēv), *n.* style of sung speech, used in narrative and dialogue parts of oratorio and opera; passage (to be) sung thus.

recīte', *v.* repeat aloud, declaim, from memory; mention in order, enumerate.

reck'less, *a.* rash; heedless.

reck'on, *v.* ascertain number or amount (of) by working with numbers; count; calculate; rely or base plans (*up*)on. **reckon with,** take into consideration. **reck'oning,** *n.* (esp.) bill. *day of reckoning,* time of atonement, punishment, etc.

reclaim', *v.t.* bring (land) under cultivation from sea or from waste state; reform (person). **reclamā'tion,** *n.*

reclīne', *v.* assume or be in horizontal or recumbent position; lie or lean back or on one side.

reclūse' (-ōōs), *n.* person who lives in solitude and seclusion.

recogni'tion, *n.* recognizing, being recognized; acknowledgement.

rec'ognize, *v.t.* know again, identify as known before; accord notice or consideration to; acknowledge or realize validity, quality, character, claims, etc., of. **recogni'zable,** *a.*

recoil', *v.i.* start back or shrink in horror, disgust, or fear; rebound; (of gun) spring back by force of discharge. *n.* recoiling.

recollect', *v.t.* succeed in remembering, remember. **recollec'tion,** *n.* thing remembered; (extent of) person's memory.

recommend', *v.t.* speak favourably of, suggest, as fit for employment, etc.; advise; entrust *to* care of. **recommenda'tion,** *n.*

rec'ompense, *v.t.* reward, requite; make amends to; compensate. *n.* reward; requital; compensation.

rec'oncile, *v.t.* make friendly again after quarrel or estrangement; make resigned; harmonize; make compatible. **reconci'lable,** *a.* **reconcilia'tion,** *n.*

rec'ondite (*or* rikon'-), *a.* obscure, little known.

recondi'tion, *v.t.* restore to proper, habitable, or usable condition.

reconn'aissance (-nis-), *n.* reconnoitring survey or party.

reconnoi'tre (-ter), *v.* (pres. p. *reconnoitring*), approach and try to learn position and condition or strategic features of (enemy, district, etc.).

recon'stitute, *v.t.* constitute again; reconstruct. **reconstitu'tion,** *n.*

reconstruct', *v.t.* construct again, repair, restore to former condition or appearance. **reconstruc'tion,** *n.* (esp.) model, etc., of something lost or damaged.

record', *v.* register, set down for remembrance or reference; represent in permanent form, esp. for reproduction. **rec'ord,** *n.* being recorded, recorded state; (document, etc., preserving) recorded evidence, information, etc.; disc bearing trace from which music, etc., can be reproduced; facts known about person's past; best performance, etc., of its kind. *a.* best, etc., recorded. **record-player,** apparatus for reproducing sound of record.

recor'der, *n.* person or thing that records; senior barrister or solicitor appointed to act as judge; any of 'a series of end-blown flutes varying in range.

recount'¹, *v.t.* narrate; tell in detail.

recount'², *v.t.* count again. **re'count,** *n.* recounting, esp. of votes.

recoup' (-ōōp), *v.t.* compensate for (loss); repay, refund.

recourse' (-ors), *n.* resorting *to* possible source of help; thing resorted to.

reco'ver (-ku-), *v.* regain possession or use or control of; reclaim; regain health or normal state or position. **reco'very,** *n.*

rec'reant, *a.* cowardly, unfaithful. *n.* coward, apostate, deserter.

recrea'tion, *n.* refreshment of mind or body; pleasurable exercise or occupation.

recrim'inate, *v.i.* make counter-charge(s) against one's accuser. **recrimina'tion,** *n.*

recrudes'cence (-ōō-; *or* rē-), *n.* fresh outbreak (of disease, etc.).

recruit' (-ōōt), *n.* newly enlisted soldier, etc. *v.* enlist recruits (for), enlist (person); replenish, reinvigorate. **recruit'ment,** *n.*

rec'tangle (-nggl), *n.* plane figure bounded by four straight lines and having four right angles. **rectang'ular,** *a.*

rec'tify, *v.t.* put right, correct; exchange for what is right. **rectifica'tion,** *n.*

rectilin'eal, *a.* recitilinear.

rectilin'ear, *a.* in or forming straight line; bounded or characterized by straight lines.

rec'titude, *n.* moral uprightness.

rec'tor, *n.* clergyman in charge of parish; head of some educational or religious institutions. **rec'tory,** *n.* parish rector's house.

rec'tum, *n.* final section of alimentary canal, terminating at anus. **rec'tal,** *a.*

recum'bent, *a.* lying, reclining.

recu'perate, *v.* restore, recover, from exhaustion, illness, loss, etc. **recupera'tion,** *n.* **recu'perative,** *a.*

recur', *v.i.* (p.t. *recurred*), occur again, be repeated; return to mind. **recu'rrence,** *n.* **recu'rrent,** *a.* occurring again, often, or periodically.

red, *a.* (*redder, reddest*), of colour ranging from crimson to orange; having to do with revolution; communist. *n.* red colour; debtor side of account; radical or (esp.) communist. **red'breast,** robin. **red'brick,** (of university) of modern foundation. **red cross,** St. George's Cross, emblem of England. **Red Cross,** (emblem of) international societies for care of wounded, etc., in war and for relief of suffering in disasters. **red deer,** large reddish-brown kind of deer. **red ensign,** flag of British merchant ships. **red-handed,** in act of crime. **red herring,** (esp.) subject raised to divert attention. **Red Indian,** N. American Indian. **red-letter day,** joyfully memorable day. **red tape,** excessive attention to forms, etc., in official transactions. **redd'en,** *v.* **redd'ish,** *a.*

redeem', *v.t.* buy back; recover by expenditure of effort; perform (promise); save, rescue; deliver from sin; compensate for. **redee'mer,** *n.* one who ransoms or redeems, esp. Christ. **redemp'tion,** *n.* **redemp'tive,** *a.*

red'olent, *a.* smelling strongly, strongly suggestive, *of.* **red'olence,** *n.*

redoub'le¹ (-dubl), *v.* intensify, increase.

redoub'le² (-dubl), *v.t.* double again.

redoubt' (-owt), *n.* detached outwork without flanking defences.

redoubt'able (-owt-), *a.* formidable.

redound', *v.i.* result in contributing greatly *to* advantage, credit, etc.

rĕdress', *v.t.* put right again; remedy, make up for. *n.* redressing; reparation.

rĕdūce', *v.* bring down; lower; weaken; diminish; subdue; bring, come, convert, *to* other form, etc. **rĕdŭ'cible**, *a.* **rĕduc'tion**, *n.*

rĕdun'dant, *a.* superfluous, excessive; dispensed with, dismissed, as no longer needed. **rĕdun'dancy**, *n.*

rĕdŭ'plicâte, *v.t.* make double, repeat.

rē-ech'ō (-k-), *v.* echo; go on echoing.

reed, *n.* (tall straight stalk of) firm-stemmed water or marsh plant; vibrating part (of thin cane or metal) of some wood-wind or other musical instruments.

reef¹, *n.* one of strips along top or bottom of sail that can be taken in or rolled up. *v.* take in reef(s). **reef-knot**, symmetrical double knot. **ree'fer¹**, *n.* (esp.) close-fitting double-breasted jacket.

reef², *n.* ridge of rock, shingle, or sand at or just above or below surface of water.

ree'fer², *n.* marijuana cigarette.

reek, *n.* foul or stale smell; smoke, vapour. *v.i.* smell unpleasantly (*of*); emit smoke.

reel¹, *n.* winding-apparatus; cylinder for holding wound cotton, etc.; quantity of cinema film, etc., on one reel. *v.* wind on, take *off*, reel; rattle *off* without pause or effort.

reel², *v.i.* be giddy; sway, stagger; be shaken.

reel³, *n.* (music for) lively Scottish dance.

reeve, *n.* (Hist.) chief magistrate of town or district.

rĕfec'tory, *n.* room for meals in monastery, etc.

rĕfer', *v.* (p.t. *referred*), send on or direct *to* some authority; turn or go *to* (for information, etc.); make allusion *to*; point *to* as source or cause.

referee', *n.* arbitrator, person chosen to decide between opposing parties; umpire; person prepared to vouch for another's character, etc.

ref'erence, *n.* referring of matter to some authority; allusion *to*; direction *to* page, book, etc. for information; (written testimonial of) referee. **reference book**, encyclopedia, dictionary, etc. **reference library**, library of books that may be consulted but not taken away.

referen'dum, *n.* referring of (political) question to electorate for direct decision by vote.

rĕfîne', *v.* free from impurities or defects; purify; make elegant or cultured; improve (*up*)*on* by subtlety or ingenuity. **rĕfîne'ment**, *n.*

rĕfî'nery, *n.* place where oil, sugar, etc., is refined.

rē'fill, *n.* what serves to refill something. **rĕfill'**, *v.t.* fill again.

rĕfit', *v.* (p.t. *refitted*), restore (ship, etc.) to serviceable condition; fit again; undergo refitting. **rē'fit**, *n.* process of refitting.

rēflā'tion, *n.* restoration of economy to previous condition after deflation.

rĕflect', *v.* throw back (light, heat, sound); (of mirror, etc.) show image (of); bring credit, discredit, etc., *on*; mediate, consider. **rĕflec'tion**, *n.* reflected light, image, etc.; thing bringing discredit *on*; thought; reconsideration. **rĕflec'tive**, *a.* (esp.) thoughtful, given to meditation. **rĕflec'tor**, *n.* body or surface reflecting rays (of light, heat, etc.), esp. in required direction.

rē'flex, *n.* reflected light or image; reflex action. *a.* (esp.) of, connected with, reflex action. **reflex action**, involuntary action of muscle, etc., as automatic response to stimulus of sensory nerve (e.g. sneezing).

rĕflex'ive, *a.* & *n.* (Gram.) (verb) indicating identity of subject and object (e.g. *he absented himself*); (pronoun) referring to subject (e.g. Mary hurt *herself*); (word, form) implying agent's action on himself (e.g. *self*-control).

rĕform', *v.* make or become better; abolish or cure abuses, etc. *n.* removal of abuse(s), esp. in politics; amendment; improvement. **rĕfor'mative**, *a.*

reformā'tion, *n.* reforming, being reformed, esp. radical change for the better in political, religious, or social affairs. *The Reformation*, 16th-c. movement for reform of Church of Rome ending in establishment of Reformed or Protestant Churches.

refor'matory, *a.* reformative. *n.* (Hist.) institution for reform of (esp. juvenile) offenders.

rĕfract', *v.t.* (of water, glass, etc.) deflect (light) at certain angle at point of passage from medium of different density. **rĕfrac'tion**, *n.*

rĕfrac'tory, *a.* stubborn, unmanageable; rebellious; resistant to heat, treatment, etc.

rĕfrain'¹, *n.* recurring phrase or line, esp. at end of stanzas.

rĕfrain'², *v.* hold back, keep oneself from some act, etc., or *from* indulgence, action, etc.

rĕfresh', *v.t.* make feel fresher; provide with refreshment; revive (memory, etc.). **rĕfresh'ment**, *n.* (esp., usu. pl.) light meal, food and drink.

rĕfri'gerâte, *v.t.* make cool or cold; expose (food, etc.) to low temperature, esp. to preserve it. **rĕfrigerā'tion**, *n.* **rĕfri'gerâtor**, *n.* cabinet, room, or apparatus for refrigerating.

rēfū'el, *v.* (p.t. *refuelled*), fuel again.

ref'ūge, *n.* shelter from pursuit, danger, or trouble; person, thing, etc., giving shelter or resorted to in difficulties. **refūgee'**, *n.* person escaped, esp. abroad, from persecution, war, etc.

rĕful'gent, *a.* shining, gloriously bright.

rĕfund', *v.t.* repay. **rē'fund**, *n.* money, etc., repaid.

rĕfū'sal (-z-), *n.* refusing; chance of taking thing before it is offered to others.

rĕfūse'¹ (-z), *v.* say or convey by action that

one will not accept, give, grant, do, or consent.

ref'ūse², *n.* what is rejected as worthless or left over after use, etc.

rèfūte', *v.t.* prove falsity or error of; rebut by argument. **refūtā'tion**, *n.*

règain', *v.t.* get back possession of; reach (place, etc.) again.

rē'gal, *a.* of or by kings; magnificent.

rēgale', *v.* entertain sumptuously (*with*); give delight to.

rēgā'lia, *n.pl.* insignia of royalty (crown, sceptre, etc.) used at coronation; emblems, decorations, etc., of an order, etc.

règard', *v.* gaze at; pay attention to; take into account; look on *as*, consider; concern, have relation to. *n.* look; attention, heed, care, concern; esteem; (pl.) friendly feelings. *with regard to, regarding,* concerning, with reference to. **règard'less**, *a.* taking no account *of.*

règatt'a, *n.* meeting for boat or yacht races.

rē'gency, *n.* (period of) office of regent.

règen'erāte, *v.* reform spiritually or morally; give new strength or life to; (Biol., etc.) be restored or renewed. **règen'erate**, *a.* regenerated. **règenerā'tion**, *n.* **règen'erative**, *a.*

rē'gent, *n.* person appointed to rule kingdom during minority, absence, or illness of monarch.

re'gicide, *n.* killing or killer of a king.

régime, regime (rāzhēm'), *n.* method of government; prevailing system of things; regimen.

re'gimen, *n.* prescribed course of treatment, way of life, or (esp.) diet.

re'giment, *n.* permanent unit of army consisting of several battalions; large number (*of*). *v.t.* organize in groups or according to system. **regimen'tal**, *a.* **regimen'tals** (-z), *n.pl.* military uniform, regimental dress. **regimentā'tion**, *n.* regimenting, organizing.

rē'gion (-jn), *n.* tract of land; area or district of more or less definitely marked boundaries or characteristics; sphere or realm *of.* **rē'gional**, *a.*

re'gister, *n.* book in which items are recorded for reference; official list; range of voice or musical instrument; mechanical recording device. *v.* record; enter, cause to be entered, in register; record automatically, indicate; show (emotion, etc.) in face, etc. **register office,** place where registers of births, deaths, and marriages are kept, and marriages may be performed. **registered letter,** letter handed in at post office with fee for insurance against loss. **registrar'**, *n.* person charged with keeping register or records; hospital doctor. **registrā'tion**, *n.* **re'gistry,** *n.* place where registers are kept. **registry office,** (esp.) register office.

règress', *v.i.* move backwards. **règre'ssion** (-shn), *n.* backward movement; reversion. **règress'ive**, *a.*

règret', *v.t.* (p.t. *regretted*), be sorry for loss

of; remember with distress or longing; grieve at. *n.* sorrow for loss or for something done or left undone, etc. **règret'ful**, *a.* **règrett'able**, *a.*

reg'ūlar, *a.* following or exhibiting a principle; consistent; systematic; habitual; orderly; not casual; not defective or amateur. *n.* soldier of regular or standing army (usu. in pl.). **regūla'rity**, *n.* **reg'ūlarīze**, *v.t.*

reg'ūlāte, *v.t.* control by rule, subject to restrictions; adjust (watch, etc.) to work accurately. **reg'ūlātor**, *n.* (esp.) device for regulating.

regūlā'tion, *n.* regulating; prescribed rule, authoritative direction; (attrib.) according to rules, usual, formal.

rēgur'gitāte, *v.* gush back; pour or cast out again. **rēgurgitā'tion**, *n.*

rēhabil'itāte, *v.t.* restore to rights, reinstate; restore to previous condition; train (disabled person) to overcome the handicap of his disabilty. **rēhabilitā'tion**, *n.*

rēhearse' ('-hers), *v.* practise before performing in public; recite, repeat; give list of, enumerate. **rēhear'sal**, *n.*

reign (rān), *n.* (period of) sovereignty, rule. *v.i.* be king or queen, rule; prevail.

rēimburse', *v.t.* repay (person, money expended). **rēimburse'ment**, *n.*

rein (rān), *n.* long narrow strap used to guide and check horse (often pl.); means of control. *v.t.* check with reins; control.

rēincarnā'tion, *n.* (religious doctrine of) re-birth of soul in another body.

rein'deer (rān-), *n.* deer of cold climates.

rēinforce', *v.t.* support or strengthen by additional men or material. **rēinforce'ment**, *n.* (esp., often pl.) additional men, ships, etc.

rēinstāte', *v.t.* re-establish *in* former position, condition, etc. **rēinstāte'ment**, *n.*

rēit'erāte, *v.t.* repeat over again or several times. **rēiterā'tion**, *n.*

rèject', *v.t.* put aside or discard as not to be accepted, believed, used, etc. **rē'ject**, *n.* rejected thing or person. **rèjec'tion**, *n.*

rèjoice', *v.* feel joy, be glad; make glad; engage in festivities. **rèjoi'cing**, *n.* (esp., pl.) festivities.

rèjoin', *v.* say in answer; retort; join again. **rèjoin'der**, *n.* retort, reply.

rèju'venāte (-ōō-), *v.* make or grow young again. **rèjuvenā'tion**, *n.*

rèlapse', *v.i.* fall back into worse state after improvement. *n.* relapsing.

rèlāte', *v.* narrate, recount; bring into relation; have reference or stand in some relation *to.* **rèlā'ted**, *a.* connected; of same family or lineage by blood or marriage.

rèlā'tion, *n.* way in which one thing is thought of in connection with another; any connection between persons or things; relative; narration. **rèlā'tionship**, *n.* being related; connection; kinship.

rel'ative, *a.* in relation or proportion to something else; having application or reference *to*; (Gram.) referring to antecedent, attached to antecedent by relative word. *n.* person related by blood or marriage; (Gram.) relative term or word, esp. pronoun.

rĕlax′, *v.* (cause or allow to) be come loose or slack or limp; make or grow less severe, rigid, tense, etc. **rĕlaxā′tion,** *n.* relaxing; recreation. **rĕlax′ing,** *a.*

rĕlay′ (*or* rē′-), *n.* fresh set of men, horses, etc., to replace others in performance of task, etc.; relaying; radio programme, etc., relayed. *v.t.* provide with, replace by, relays; pass on or re-broadcast (message, radio programme, etc.) received from another source. **rē′lay race,** race between teams of which each member does part of distance.

rĕlease′, *v.t.* set free, liberate, allow to go; unfasten; allow (news) to be published; allow (film) to be exhibited generally or for first time. *n.* liberation from confinement, fixed position, trouble, etc.; releasing of film.

rel′ĕgāte, *v.t.* send or dismiss *to* (usu.) inferior position, sphere, etc.; (esp.) transfer (Footb., etc., team) to lower division of league. **rĕlĕgā′tion,** *n.*

rĕlent′, *v.i.* become less severe; abandon harsh intention; yield to pity. **rĕlent′less,** *a.* not relenting, pitiless.

rel′ĕvant, *a.* connected with, relating *to*, the matter being discussed or considered. **rel′ĕvance,** *n.*

rĕli′able, *a.* that may be relied or depended upon. **rĕliabil′ity,** *n.*

rĕli′ance, *n.* trust, confidence. **rĕli′ant,** *a.*

rel′ic, *n.* part of holy person's body or belongings kept as object of reverence; surviving trace or memorial *of* past period, etc.; (pl.) dead body, remains, of person.

rel′ict, *n.* widow.

rĕlief′[1], *n.* lessening of or deliverance from pain, distress, etc.; assistance given to victims of disaster, etc.; freeing *of* place from siege; (replacing by) person(s) appointed to take turn of duty.

rĕlief′[2], *n.* carving, etc., in which design stands out from surface; effect of relief given by colour, shading, etc.; distinctness of outline.

rĕlieve′, *v.t.* bring, give, be, relief to; bring into relief, make stand out. *relieve of*, free from (task, burden).

rĕli′gion (-jn), *n.* system of faith and worship; human recognition of God or gods; monastic state, being monk or nun. **rĕli′gious** (-jus), *a.* of religion; imbued with religion; paying serious attention to observances of religion. *n.* person bound by monastic vows.

rĕlin′quish, *v.t.* give up, let go, surrender.

rel′ish, *n.* distinctive flavour or taste *of*; enjoyment of food or other things; zest; savoury sauce, etc. *v.* get pleasure out of, be pleased with; taste, smack, *of*.

rĕluc′tant, *a.* unwilling, disinclined. **rĕluc′-**

tance, *n.*

rĕlȳ′, *v.i.* depend (*up*)*on* with full trust or confidence.

rĕmain′, *v.i.* be left over; stay in same place or condition; be left behind; continue to be. **rĕmain′der,** *n.* residue; remaining persons or things; number left after subtraction or division. **rĕmains′** (-z), *n.pl.* what is left over; relics of antiquity, etc.; dead body.

rĕmand′ (-ah-), *v.t.* order (accused person) to be kept in custody while further evidence is sought. *n.* remanding or being remanded.

rĕmark′, *v.* say as observation or comment; notice. *n.* thing said, comment; noticing, notice. **remar′kable,** *a.* worth notice; exceptional, striking.

rem′ĕdy, *n.* cure for disease or any evil; healing medicine or treatment; redress. *v.t.* put right, make good. **rĕmē′dial,** *a.*

rĕmem′ber, *v.t.* keep in, recall to, memory; not forget; make present to, tip; convey greetings from. **rĕmem′brance,** *n.* memory; keepsake. **Remembrance Sunday,** Sunday nearest 11th Nov., as day of remembrance of those who died in wars of 1914-18 and 1939-45.

rĕmind′, *v.t.* cause to remember. **rĕmin′der,** *n.* thing that reminds.

reminis′cence, *n.* remembering; remembered fact or incident; (pl.) collection of memories in literary form. **reminis′cent,** *a.* recalling past things; reminding or suggestive *of*.

rĕmiss′, *a.* careless of duty; negligent.

rĕmi′ssion (-shn), *n.* forgiveness of sins, etc.; remittance of debt, etc.; lessening (of pain, effort, etc.).

rĕmit′, *v.* (p.t. *remitted*), pardon (sins, etc.); refrain from exacting or inflicting (payment, punishment, etc.); abate; send (esp. money); send back (lawsuit, etc.) to lower court. **rĕmitt′ance,** *n.* sending of money, money sent.

rem′nant, *n.* small remaining quantity, piece, or number.

rĕmon′strance, *n.* remonstrating; protest.

rem′onstrāte (*or* rimon′-), *v.* make protest, argue in protest (*with, against*).

rĕmorse′, *n.* bitter regret and repentance; compunction. **rĕmorse′ful,** *a.* **rĕmorse′less,** *a.*

rĕmōte′, *a.* far apart; far away in place or time; distant *from*; secluded; slight.

rĕmount′, *v.* mount again.

rĕmo′vable (-mōō-), *a.* that can be removed. **removabil′ity,** *n.*

rĕmo′val (-mōō-), *n.* removing, being removed.

rĕmove′ (-ōōv), *v.* take off or away from place occupied; convey to another place; change one's residence; dismiss. *n.* stage, degree. **rĕmoved** (-ōōvd), *a.* distant or remote (*from*).

rĕmū′nerāte, *v.t.* pay for service rendered. **rĕmūnerā′tion,** *n.* pay. **rĕmū′nerative,** *a.*

profitable.

Rènaiss'ance, *n.* great revival of art and literature in 14th-16th centuries; (*renaissance*), any similar revival.

rē'nal, *a.* of the kidneys.

rènas'cence, *n.* re-birth; renaissance. **rènas'cent,** *a.* springing up anew; being reborn.

rend, *v.* (p.t. *rent*), (*archaic*) tear; split.

ren'der, *v.t.* give in return; pay as due; present, submit; portray; translate; melt (fat) *down*. **ren'dering,** *n.* (esp.) translation; interpretation, performance.

rendezvous (ron'dāvōō), *n.* (pl. same, pr. -ōōz), place appointed for meeting; meeting by appointment. *v.i.* meet at rendezvous.

ren'ègàde, *n.* one who deserts party or principles, turncoat; apostate.

rènew', *v.* make (as good as) new; patch, fill up, replace; begin, make, say, etc., anew. **rènew'al,** *n.*

renn'ēt, *n.* curdled milk from calf's stomach used in curdling milk for cheese, junket, etc.; artificial preparation used similarly.

rènounce', *v.t.* consent formally to abandon; repudiate; surrender, give up; discontinue.

ren'ovàte, *v.t.* restore to good condition or vigour; repair. **renovā'tion,** *n.*

rènown', *n.* fame, high distinction; being celebrated. **rènowned'** (-nd), *a.* famous.

rent¹, *p.t. & p.p.* of **rend.**

rent², *n.* tear in garment, etc.; gap, cleft, fissure, split.

rent³, *n.* periodical payment for use of land, house, room, etc. *v.* take, occupy, or use at a rent; let or hire for rent. **ren'tal,** *n.* sum payable as rent.

rènunciā'tion, *n.* renouncing; self-denial, giving up of things.

rep, repp, *n.* ribbed upholstery fabric.

rèpair'¹, *v.i.* go (*to*).

rèpair'², *v.t.* restore to good condition by replacing or refixing part(s), etc.; remedy; make amends for. *n.* restoring to good condition; condition for working or using.

rep'arable, *a.* that can be repaired or made good. **reparā'tion,** *n.* recompense for injury; compensation, esp. (pl.) that paid by defeated country for damage done in war.

repartee', *n.* witty retort(s).

rèpast' (-ah-), *n.* a meal.

rèpat'riàte (*or* -pā-), *v.t.* send or bring back (person) to own country. **rèpatriā'tion,** *n.*

rèpay', *v.* (p.t. *repaid*), give back money spent; make recompense or return for. **rèpay'ment,** *n.*

rèpeal', *v.t.* withdraw, revoke, cancel. *n.* repealing, revocation.

rèpeat', *v.* say or do over again; recite, rehearse; reproduce; recur. *n.* repeating, thing repeated. **rèpea'tedly,** *adv.* several times.

rèpel', *v.t.* (p.t. *repelled*), drive back; ward off; affect (person) with distaste or aversion.

rèpell'ent, *a.* repelling; distasteful.

rèpent', *v.* feel regret, contrition, etc., for what one has done or left undone; think with regret or contrition *of*. **rèpen'tance,** *n.* **rèpen'tant,** *a.*

rèpercu'ssion (-shn), *n.* recoil after impact; indirect effect or reaction (*of*).

rep'ertoire (-twar), *n.* stock of plays, pieces, etc., that company or performer is accustomed or prepared to give.

rep'ertory, *n.* repertoire. **repertory company, theatre,** one having repertoire of plays, or presenting different play each week, etc.

rèpeti'tion, *n.* repeating or being repeated; recitation; copy, replica. **rèpet'itive,** *a.*

rèpīne', *v.i.* fret, be discontented.

rèplàce', *v.t.* put back in place; take or fill up place of, provide substitute for. **rèplàce'able,** *a.* **rèplàce'ment,** *n.*

rèplēte', *a.* filled, sated. **rèplē'tion,** *n.*

rep'lica, *n.* duplicate made by original artist; exact copy, facsimile.

rèplý', *v.* make spoken or written answer; respond. *n.* replying; what is replied.

rèport', *v.* bring back account of; tell as news; take down, write description of, etc., for publication; give account of. *n.* description or account; statement; rumour; reputation; sound of explosion. **rèpor'ter,** *n.* (esp.) person reporting for newspaper.

rèpōse'¹ (-z), *v.t.* place (trust, etc.) *in.*

rèpōse'² (-z), *v.* rest; lay (one's head, etc.) to rest; give rest to; lie. *n.* rest; sleep; peaceful state, tranquillity.

rèpos'itory (-z-), *n.* place where things are stored; receptacle.

repp: see **rep.**

rèprèhend', *v.t.* rebuke, blame. **rèprèhen'sible,** *a.* blameworthy. **rèprèhen'sion** (-shn), *n.*

rèprèsent' (-z-), *v.t.* place likeness of before mind or senses; explain, point out; describe or depict as; play, perform, act part of; symbolize, stand for; be entitled to speak for; be substitute or deputy for. **rèprèsentā'tion,** *n.*

rèprèsen'tative (-z-), *a.* serving to represent, esp. typical of class or group; (of government, etc.) based on representation of (esp. all the) people by elected deputies. *n.* sample, specimen; agent; person representing another or others.

rèpress', *v.t.* check, restrain, put down, keep under. **rèpre'ssion** (-shn), *n.*

rèprieve', *v.t.* suspend or cancel execution of; give respite to. *n.* remission or commuting of sentence of death; respite.

rep'rimand (-ah-), *n.* official rebuke. *v.t.* rebuke officially.

rèprint', *v.t.* print again. **rē'print,** *n.* new impression of book, etc., esp. without alterations.

rèprī'sal (-zl), *n.* act of retaliation (often pl.).

rèproach', *v.t.* speak disapprovingly to (person) about his discreditable action. *n.* reproof, censure; thing that brings discredit. **reproach'ful,** *a.*

rep'robāte, *v.t.* express or feel disapproval of, condemn. **rep'robate** (or -āt), *a.* & *n.* (person) of immoral character or behaviour.

rĕprodūce', *v.* produce again; produce copy or representation of; carry on (species, etc.) by breeding or propagation. **rĕprodū'cible,** *a.* **rĕproduc'tion,** *n.* (esp.) breeding or propagation; copy.

rĕproof', *n.* (expression of) blame or disapproval. **rĕprove'** (-ōov), *v.t.* blame, rebuke.

rep'tile, *n.* crawling or creeping animal, esp. member of cold-blooded lung-breathing class of vertebrates including snakes. **reptil'ian,** *a.*

rĕpub'lic, *n.* State in which supreme power rests in the people and their elected representatives. **rĕpub'lican,** *a.* of republic(s). *a.* & *n.* (person) advocating or supporting republican government.

rĕpū'diāte, *v.* disown, deny knowledge of; refuse to recognize (authority, debt, etc.). **repūdiā'tion,** *n.*

rĕpug'nance, *n.* strong dislike, distaste, or aversion. **repug'nant,** *a.* distasteful, objectionable.

rĕpulse', *v.t.* drive back; rebuff, reject. *n.* defeat, rebuff. **rĕpul'sion** (-shn), *n.* aversion; (Phys.) tendency of bodies to repel each other. **rĕpul'sive,** *a.* arousing repulsion; loathsome, disgusting.

rep'ūtable, *a.* of good repute.

repūtā'tion, *n.* what is generally said or believed about character of person or thing; credit, respectability, good fame.

rĕpūte', *n.* what is generally thought or supposed; reputation. **repū'tĕd,** *a.* generally considered (to be); supposed.

rĕquest', *n.* expression of desire for something; thing asked for. *in request,* sought after. *v.t.* ask to be given, favoured with, etc.; ask.

re'quiem (-kwi-em), *n.* Mass for the dead; musical setting for this.

rĕquīre', *v.t.* demand, order; insist on as a right or by authority; need. **rĕquīre'ment,** *n.*

re'quisite (-z-), *a.* needed, required. *n.* what is needed or necessary.

requisi'tion (-z-), *n.* formal demand, usu. in writing; order to furnish supplies for army, etc. *v.t.* demand supply or use of; press into service.

rĕquīte', *v.t.* make return for; reward or avenge. **rĕquī'tal,** *n.*

rĕscind', *v.t.* cancel, revoke. **rĕsci'ssion** (-zhn), *n.*

res'cūe, *v.t.* deliver, free, or save from attack, imprisonment, danger, or harm. *n.* rescuing, being rescued.

·ĕsearch' (-ser-), *n.* careful search or inquiry; scientific study or investigation to discover facts. *v.* engage in research (*into*).

rĕsem'ble (-z-), *v.t.* be like; be similar to. **rĕsem'blance,** *n.*

rĕsent' (-z-), *v.t.* feel or show indignation at; feel injured or insulted by. **rĕsent'ful,** *a.* **rĕsent'ment,** *n.*

reservā'tion (-z-), *n.* reserving; limitation or exception; engaging of seats, room, etc., in advance; tract of land for special use.

rĕserve' (-z-), *v.t.* postpone use or enjoyment of; defer (decision, etc.); retain; set apart (*for*); engage (seat, etc.) in advance. *n.* something reserved for future use; tract of land reserved for special use; troops held in reserve; forces outside regular army, etc., liable to be called out in emergency; limitation; reticence, lack of cordiality. **rĕserved',** *a.* reticent, uncommunicative.

res'ervoir (-zervwar), *n.* place (often artificial lake) where large quantity of water is stored; place where anything is kept in store.

rĕshuff'le, *v.t.* shuffle again; re-arrange (posts in Cabinet, etc.) without altering membership, etc. *n.* instance of reshuffling.

rĕsīde' (-z-), *v.i.* have one's home, live; (of rights, etc.) rest, be vested, *in.* **res'idence,** *n.* residing; place where one resides, house. **res'ident,** *a.* residing. *n.* permanent inhabitant. **residen'tial** (-shl), *a.* of private houses.

rĕs'idūe (-z-), *n.* what is left over, remainder. **resid'ūal,** *a.* remaining, left over. **resid'ūary,** *a.* of residue of (deceased person's) estate. **resid'ūum,** *n.* (pl. *residua*), what remains, esp. (Chem.) after combustion or evaporation.

rĕsign' (-zīn), *v.* give up (office, membership, etc.); relinquish; retire. *resign oneself* (*to*), be ready to accept or endure without protest. **resignā'tion** (-zig-), *n.* resigning of office, etc.; uncomplaining endurance. **rĕsigned'** (-zīnd), *a.* having resigned oneself; content to endure; submissive.

rĕsil'iĕnce (-z-), *n.* power of resuming original form after compression, etc.; elasticity; buoyancy, power of recovery. **rĕsil'iĕnt,** *a.*

res'in (-z-), *n.* sticky substance, hardening in air, secreted by and exuding from certain plants; any of various synthetic substances resembling this. **res'inous,** *a.*

rĕsist' (-zi-), *v.* stop course of, withstand action or effect of; strive against, oppose; offer resistance. **rĕsis'tance,** *n.* resisting; power of resisting. **rĕsis'tible,** *a.* **rĕsis'ter,** *n.* **rĕsis'tor,** *n.* (Electr.).

res'olūte (-z-; *or* -ōot), *a.* determined, having fixed resolve; constant, firm.

resolū'tion (-z-; *or* -ōo-), *n.* resolute character, temper, or conduct; thing resolved on; formal expression of opinion of meeting; solving *of* question, etc.; resolving or being resolved.

rĕsolve' (-z-), *v.* disintegrate, break up into parts; convert or be converted *into*; (Mus.) convert (discord), be converted, into concord; solve, settle; decide upon. *n.* mental resolution; steadfastness.

res'onant (-z-), *a.* echoing, resounding; reinforcing or prolonging sound, esp. by vibration. **res'onance,** *n.*

res'onâte (-z-), *v.i.* produce or show resonance. **res'onâtor,** *n.*

rèsort' (-z-), *v.i.* turn for aid, etc., *to*; go often or in numbers *to. n.* thing turned to for aid, expedient; recourse; place frequented for holidays, etc. *in the last resort,* as a last expedient.

rèsound' (-z-), *v.i.* ring or echo; go on sounding, fill place with sound.

rèsource' (-sors), *n.* (pl.) means of supplying want, stock that can be drawn on; (sing.) expedient, device; means of passing time. **resource'ful,** *a.* good at devising expedients.

rèspect', *n.* deferential esteem; (pl.) message or attention conveying this; heed or regard *to*; reference or relation (*to*); detail, aspect. *v.t.* treat or regard with deference, esteem, or honour; treat with consideration, spare.

rèspec'table, *a.* of fair social standing, honest, decent; of some amount or size or merit. **rèspectabil'ity,** *n.*

rèspect'ful, *a.* showing deference.

rèspec'tive, *a.* of, connected with, each of those in question; separate, particular. **respec'tively,** *adv.*

rèspire, *v.* breathe; take breath. **res'pirable,** *a.* **res'piratory,** *a.* **respirâ'tion,** *n.* breathing, single act of breathing in and out. **res'pirâtor,** *n.* apparatus worn over mouth and nose to warm or filter inhaled air; gas-mask; device for maintaining respiration artifically.

res'pite (*or* -ît), *n.* interval of rest or relief; delay permitted in discharge of obligation or suffering of penalty.

rèsplen'dent, *a.* brilliant, splendid. **rèsplen'dence,** *n.*

rèspond', *v.i.* answer; act, etc., in response (*to*). **rèspon'dent,** *a.* responding. *n.* defendant in divorce suit; one who answers.

rèsponse', *n.* answer; action, feeling, etc., aroused by stimulus, etc.

rèsponsibil'ity, *n.* being responsible; charge, trust.

rèspon'sible, *a.* liable to answer or account for conduct, etc.; morally accountable for actions; trustworthy; involving responsibility.

rèspon'sive, *a.* responding readily; answering.

rest[1], *v.* be still; cease from exertion or action; lie in sleep or death; be tranquil; give relief or repose to; place, lie, lean, rely, etc., (*up*)*on. n.* repose or sleep; resting; prop, support, etc.; (Mus.) interval of silence (of part or parts).

rest[2], *v.i.* remain in specified state. *n. the rest,* the remainder; the others.

res'taurant (-tor-; *or* -ahn), *n.* place where meals may be bought and eaten.

rest'ful, *a.* quiet, soothing.

restitū'tion, *n.* restoring of property, etc., to its owner; reparation.

res'tive, *a.* restless, resisting control.

rest'less, *a.* finding or affording no rest; uneasy, agitated, fidgety.

restorâ'tion, *n.* action or process of restoring; representation of original form of ruined building, extinct animal, etc.

rèstor'ative, *a. & n.* (medicine, etc.) tending to restore health or strength.

rèstore', *v.t.* give back, make restitution of; replace; repair, alter, so as to bring back as nearly as possible to original form, state, etc.; bring back *to* dignity, etc., or to health, into use, etc.

rèstrain', *v.t.* check or hold in (from); keep under control; repress; confine. **rèstrain'èdly,** *adv.* with restraint.

rèstraint', *n.* restraining or being strained; check; confinement; self-control; avoidance of exaggeration; reserve.

rèstrict', *v.t.* confine, bound, limit. **rèstric'tion,** *n.* **rèstric'tive,** *a.*

rèsult' (-z-), *v.i.* arise as consequence, effect, or conclusion (*from*); end *in. n.* what results; consequence; outcome; quantity, etc., obtained by calculation. **rèsul'tant,** *a.* resulting.

rèsūme' (-z-), *v.* take again; take back; begin again. **rèsump'tion,** *n.*

résumé (rā'zūmā), *n.* summary.

rèsur'gent, *a.* rising again after defeat, destruction, etc. **rèsur'gence,** *n.*

resurrect' (-z-), *v.t.* bring back to life; revive practice or memory of.

resurrec'tion (-z-), *n.* rising again after death; revival from disuse, decay, etc. *the Resurrection,* rising of Christ from the tomb.

rèsus'citâte, *v.* revive, return or restore to life, consciousness, vigour, fashion, etc. **rèsuscitâ'tion,** *n.*

rē'tail, *n.* sale of goods in small quantities. *adv.* by retail. **rètail',** *v.* sell by retail; be retailed; recount, relate. **rètai'ler** (*or* rē'-), *n.*

rètain', *v.t.* keep in place, hold fixed; continue to have; keep in mind; secure services of (esp. barrister), by preliminary fee. **rètai'ner,** *n.* preliminary fee paid to barrister, etc.; (Hist.) dependent of nobleman, etc.; servant.

rètal'iâte, *v.* repay in kind; make return (esp. of injury, insult, etc.). **rètaliâ'tion,** *n.*

rètard', *v.t.* make slow or late; delay progress, accomplishment, etc., of. **rètardâ'tion,** *n.* **rètar'ded,** *a.* (esp. of child) behind what is normal in mental or physical development.

rètch, *v.i.* make motion of vomiting.

rèten'tion, *n.* retaining. **rèten'tive,** *a.* having power of retaining or remembering.

ret'icent, *a.* disinclined to speak freely, saying little. **ret'icence,** *n.*

rètic'ūlate, *a.* reticulated. **rètic'ūlâted,** *a.* divided, arranged, marked, in(to) network.

ret′icŭle, *n.* (*archaic*) small handbag.
ret′ina, *n.* (pl. *retinas* or *retinae*), layer or coating at back of eyeball, sensitive to light. **ret′inal**, *a.*
ret′inŭe, *n.* great person's suite of attendants.
rětīre′, *v.* withdraw from place or company; (cause or compel to) give up occupation, etc.; go to bed. **rětīred′**, *a.* having retired from occupation, etc.; secluded. **rětīre′-ment**, *n.* state of having retired from work; seclusion. **retirement pension,** weekly State payment to person of specified age. **rětīr′-ing**, *a.* shy; avoiding company.
rětort′¹, *v.* answer sharply or with counter-charge, or counter-argument; retaliate. *n.* sharp answer; countercharge; retaliation.
rětort′², *n.* cylinder in which coal is car-bonized; furnace in which iron is heated to produce steel; (glass) vessel with long downward-bent neck, for distilling liquids.
rětouch′ (-tuch), *v.t.* amend or improve (esp. photograph) by additional touches.
rětrāce′, *v.t.* trace back to source or begin-ning; go back over (one's steps, way, etc.).
rětract′, *v.* withdraw (promise, statement); recant; (of part of body or machine) draw, be drawn or be capable of being drawn, back or in. **rětrac′table, rětrac′tile**, *aa.* **rětrac′tion**, *n.*
rětreat′, *v.* go back, withdraw, relinquish a position (esp. of army, etc.); recede. *n.* act of or military signal for retreating; place of seclusion or shelter.
rětrench′, *v.* reduce amount of, cut down; economize. **rětrench′ment**, *n.*
retribū′tion, *n.* recompense for evil done; vengeance. **rětrib′ūtive**, *a.*
rětrieve′, *v.* regain possession of; rescue *from* bad state, etc., restore to good state; (of dog) find and bring in game. **rětrie′val**, *n.* retriev-ing. **rětrie′ver**, *n.* dog of breed specially adapted for retrieving game.
retro-, *pref.* backwards, back.
ret′rogrăde, *a.* directed backwards; reversing progress; reverting, esp. to inferior state; declining.
retrogress′, *v.i.* move backwards; deteriorate. **retrogre′ssion** (-shn), *n.* **retrogress′ive**, *a.*
ret′rospect, *n.* view or survey of past time or events. **retrospec′tion**, *n.* looking back; meditation on the past. **retrospec′tive**, *a.* of, in, etc., retrospection; having application to the past.
rěturn′, *v.* come or go back; revert; give, send, pay, lead, etc., back; elect as member of Parliament. *n.* returning or being returned; what is returned; (coming in of) proceeds or profit; report. *in return* (*for*), as repayment (for). **return (ticket),** ticket for journey to place and back again.
rěŭ′nion, *n.* reuniting, being reunited; social gathering.
rěŭnīte′, *v.* bring or come together again.
rěveal′, *v.t.* disclose, betray; show, let

appear; make known by supernatural means.
rěveill′e (-veli *or* -vali), *n.* military waking--signal sounded on bugle.
rev′el, *v.i.* (p.t. *revelled*), be riotously festive, make merry; take keen delight *in*. *n.* revel-ling, occasion of noisy festivity.
revelā′tion, *n.* revealing; striking disclosure; knowledge disclosed by divine or super-natural agency, esp. (*the Revelation of St. John the Divine*) last book of N.T.
rev′elry, *n.* revelling, merrymaking.
rěvenge′ (-nj), *v.t.* inflict injury, etc., for wrong done; avenge (*oneself* or another). *n.* desire for vengeance; act that satisfies this. **rěvenge′ful**, *a.*
rev′enŭe, *n.* annual income, esp. of State; department collecting State revenue.
rěver′berāte, *v.* echo or throw back or reflect (esp.) sound. **rěverberā′tion**, *n.* (esp.) echo, rolling sound.
rěvēre′, *v.t.* regard with deep and affectionate or religious respect.
rev′erence, *n.* revering or being revered; deep respect. *v.t.* revere.
rev′erend, *a.* deserving reverence; *the Reverend* (abbrev. *Rev.*), esp. as prefix to clergyman's name.
rev′erent, *a.* feeling or showing reverence. **reveren′tial** (-shl), *a.* of or showing rever-ence.
rev′erie, *n.* musing; day-dream.
rěvers′ (-vēr), *n.* (pl. same, pr. -vērz), turned--back front edge of coat, etc.
rěver′sal, *n.* reversing or being reversed.
rěverse′, *a.* contrary, inverted, upside down. *v.* turn the other way round or up, or inside out; invert; transpose; revoke; (cause to) move or turn in opposite direction. *n. the* contrary (*of*); misfortune, defeat; back of coin, etc. **reverse (gear),** gear permitting vehicle to be driven backwards. **rěver′sible**, *a.* able to be reversed.
rěver′sion (-shn), *n.* reverting, return to former condition or habit.
rěvert′, *v.i.* come or go back *to* former condi-tion, primitive state, etc.; come or go back to in talk or thought.
rěview′ (-vū), *n.* survey, inspection; retro-spect; published account or criticism of book, play, etc.; periodical. *v.* survey, look back on; hold review of (troops, etc.); write review of (book, etc.).
rěvile′, *v.t.* call bad names, abuse.
rěvise′ (-z), *v.t.* re-read carefully; examine, esp. in order to correct or improve. **rěvi′sion** (-zhn), *n.* revising; revised edition or form.
rěvi′val, *n.* reviving or being revived; reawakening of religious fervour.
rěvive′, *v.* come or bring back to conscious-ness, life, vigour, notice, or fashion.
rev′ocable, *a.* that may be revoked. **revo-cā′tion**, *n.* (instance of) revoking.
rěvōke′, *v.* cancel, withdraw; (in card-games) fail to follow suit though able to.

rĕvōlt′, v. rise against rulers or authority, rebel; feel revulsion; affect with disgust. n. insurrection; sense of loathing. **rĕvōl′ting**, a. disgusting, horrible.

revolu′tion (-lōō- or -ŭ-), n. revolving; single complete turning of wheel, etc.; complete change; forcible substitution of new government or ruler for old. **revolu′tionary**, a. involving great change; of political revolution. n. supporter, etc., of political revolution. **revolu′tionize**, v.t. (esp.) change completely or fundamentally.

revolve′, v. turn round or round and round; rotate. **revol′ver**, n. (esp.) pistol that will fire several shots without reloading.

rĕvūe′, n. light entertainment with variety of scenes, songs, etc., reviewing or satirizing current events, etc.

rĕvul′sion (-shn), n. sudden violent change of feeling (esp. to aversion or disgust).

rĕward′ (-ord), n. something given or received in return for service or merit; sum offered for detection of criminal, restoration of lost thing, etc.; requital for good or evil. v.t. give reward to, recompense.

rhap′sody, n. elaborate enthusiastic utterance or composition. **rhap′sodīze**, v.

rhē′sus, n. small monkey of N. India. **rhesus factor**, complex substance or antigen normally present in human red blood cells.

rhet′oric, n. art of speaking or writing effectively; elaborate or exaggerated language. **rheto′rical**, a. (esp. of question) asked not for information but to produce effect.

rheumat′ic (-ōō-), a. of, suffering from, or caused by, rheumatism. n. rheumatic patient. **rheu′matism**, n. disease marked by inflammation and pain in joints. **rheu′matoid**, a. of, like, rheumatism.

rhīno′ceros, n. large mammal with horn or two horns on nose and thick folded skin.

rhī′zōme, n. (Bot.) horizontal, usu. underground, stem sending out roots from lower surface and shoots from upper surface.

rhōdoden′dron, n. evergreen shrub with large flowers.

rhomb, rhom′bus, nn. plane equilateral figure with opposite angles equal and acute or obtuse; lozenge- or diamond-shaped object, marking, etc.

rhu′barb (rōō-), n. plant with fleshy leaf-stalks cooked and eaten as fruit.

rhȳme, n. sameness of sound in endings of words or verse-lines; word rhyming with another; rhymed verse; poem, poetry. v. (of words, etc.) end in rhymes; be, use as, rhyme (to, with); write rhymes.

rhythm (-dhm), n. measured flow or pattern produced in verse, music, or motion, by relation in quantity, stress, duration, or energy, between successive syllables, words, notes, or movements. **rhyth′mic(al)**, aa.

rib, n. one of curved bones round upper part of body; ridge along surface serving to support, strengthen, etc.; hinged rod of umbrella frame; ridged effect in knitting or weaving. v.t. (p.t. ribbed), provide with ribs; mark with ridges.

rib′ald (-awld), a. impolitely or coarsely humorous. **rib′aldry**, n. ribald talk.

rib′and, n. (archaic) ribbon.

ribb′on, n. (piece or length of) silk, etc., woven into narrow band; long narrow strip.

rībonŭclē′ic a′cid, (abbrev. RNA), substance present in living cells and participating in synthesis of proteins.

rice, n. (white seeds, used as food, of) annual cereal plant grown in marshy ground in warm climates. **rice-paper**, edible paper used in baking, etc.; thin paper made from rice-straw; Chinese painting-paper.

rich, a. wealthy, having much money; fertile, abounding in; (of dress, etc.) splendid; (of food) containing much fat, sugar, etc.; highly amusing; abundant. **rich′es** (-iz), n. wealth; valuable possessions. **rich′ly**, adv. (esp.) fully.

rick[1], n. stack of hay, straw, etc.

rick[2], n. & v.t. wrench, sprain.

rick′ĕts, n. disease of children marked by softening and distortion of bones, caused by deficiency of vitamin D. **rick′ĕty**, a. of, having, rickets; shaky, insecure.

rick′shaw, n. light two-wheeled hooded vehicle drawn by man on foot or bicycle.

ric′ochet (-shā), n. rebounding of projectile, etc., from object it strikes; hit made after this. v.i. (p.t. ricocheted, pr. -shād), glance or skip with rebounds.

rid, v.t. (p.t. rid or ridded; p.p. rid), make free or relieve (of). **get rid of**, get free of, throw away, discard. **ridd′ance**, n.

ridd′le[1], n. question intentionally worded in puzzling manner for amusement; puzzling fact, thing, or person.

ridd′le[2], n. coarse sieve. v.t. sift; fill with holes (esp. by firing at).

ride, v. (p.t. rōde; p.t. ridden), sit on and be carried by horse, etc.; go on horseback, bicycle, train, etc.; manage horse; lie at anchor; float buoyantly. n. spell of riding; journey in vehicle; road, esp. through wood, for riding on. **rī′dable**, a. **rī′der**, n. one who rides; clause added to document; opinion, etc., added to verdict. **rī′ding**[1], n.

ridge, n. line in which two upward sloping surfaces meet; long narrow hill-top; mountain range; any narrow raised strip. v. form or break up into ridges; mark with ridges.

rid′icūle, v.t. make (person, thing) object of fun or mocking laughter, deride, laugh at. n. derision, mockery. **ridic′ūlous**, a. deserving to be laughed at, absurd.

rī′ding[2], n. former administrative division of Yorkshire.

rife, pred. a. occurring frequently; prevailing, current, numerous.

riff′-raff, n. rabble; disreputable people.

ri'fle, *v.t.* search and rob; make spiral grooves in (gun, etc.). *n.* gun with rifled barrel.

rift, *n.* fissure, cleft, chasm, split.

rig[1], *v.t.* (p.t. *rigged*), provide (ship) with spars, ropes, etc.; fit (*out, up*) with clothes or equipment; set *up* hastily or as makeshift. *n.* way ship's masts, sails, etc., are arranged; outfit; apparatus, plant. **rigg'ing** (-g-), *n.* (esp.) ropes, etc., used to support masts, set sails, etc.

rig[2], *v.t.* (p.t. *rigged*), manage or conduct fraudulently.

right (rīt), *a.* morally good, just; proper, correct, true; of or on side of body which has, in most persons, the more easily and skilfully used hand (opp. *left*), having corresponding relation to front of any object; in good or normal condition; not mistaken. *v.t.* restore to proper position; make amends for; correct, set in order. *n.* what is just; fair treatment; fair claim; what one is entitled to; right-hand region, part, or direction; (pl.) right condition; (Politics) more conservative or traditional party, etc. *adv.* all the way (*round, to,* etc.), completely; justly, correctly, truly; to right hand. **right angle**, angle of 90°. **right--hand**, *a.* of, on, right side.

righteous (rī'chus), *a.* virtuous, upright, just, honest. **right'eousness**, *n.*

right'ful (rīt-), *a.* according to law or justice; that one is entitled to.

right'ly (rīt-), *adv.* justly; correctly; justifiably.

ri'gid, *a.* stiff, unyielding, not flexible; strict, harsh. **rigid'ity**, *n.*

rig'marōle, *n.* rambling meaningless talk or tale.

rig'our (-ger), *n.* severity, strictness, harshness; hardship, great distress. **rig'orous**, *a.*

rīle, *v.t.* (*informal*) anger, irritate.

rill, *a.* tiny stream.

rille, *n.* (Astron.) long narrow trench or valley on moon's surface.

rim, *n.* outer ring of wheel's framework; outer frame; (esp. raised) edge or border. *v.t.* (p.t. *rimmed*), provide with rim, serve as rim to.

rīme[1], *n. & v.* (*archaic*) rhyme.

rīme[2], *n.* hoar-frost. **rī'my**, *a.*

rīnd, *n.* peel of fruit, etc.; skin of bacon, etc.; outer crust of cheese.

ring[1], *n.* circlet of gold, etc., worn esp. on finger; circular object, appliance, arrangement, etc.; enclosure for circus-riding, boxing, etc. *v.t.* (p.t. *ringed*), surround; hem in; fit with ring. **ring'leader**, leader in mutiny, riot, etc. **ring-master**, manager of circus performance. **ring'worm**, skin-disease in circular patches.

ring[2], *v.* (p.t. *rang*; p.p. *rung*), give out clear resonant sound; (of place) resound, re-echo; cause bell to ring; signal or summon by sound of bell. *ring off,* end telephone call. *ring up,* make telephone call to. *n.* ringing sound; act of ringing bell; set of (church) bells.

ring'lĕt, *n.* (esp. hanging) curl of hair.

rink, *n.* stretch of ice used for skating or curling; floor for roller-skating.

rinse, *v.t.* pour water into and out of to remove dirt, etc.; put through clean water to remove soap; pour liquid over. *n.* rinsing; liquid for rinsing, esp. for tinting hair.

rī'ot, *n.* violent disturbance of the peace by crowd; tumult; loud revelry. *v.i.* make or engage in riot. **rī'oter**, *n.* **rī'otous**, *a.*

rip[1], *v.* (p.t. *ripped*), cut or tear or split, esp. with single quick motion; strip *off,* open *up,* etc.; thus; (of material) be ripped; rush along. *n.* long tear or cut.

rip[2], *n.* dissolute person, rake.

ripār'ian, *a.* of or on river-bank.

rīpe, *a.* ready to be reaped, gathered, used, etc.; mature, fully developed. **rī'pen**, *v.* mature, make or grow ripe.

ripōste', *n.* quick return thrust in fencing; retort. *v.i.* deliver riposte.

ripp'le, *n.* ruffling of water's surface; small wave(s); gentle lively sound rising and falling. *v.* form or flow in ripples; sound like ripples; make ripples in.

rise (-z), *v.i.* (p.t. *rōse*; p.p. *risen*), get up from lying or sitting or kneeling; get out of bed; revolt; ascend, soar; increase; swell upwards; come to surface; have origin, begin to flow. *n.* upward slope; increase in rank, price, amount, wages, etc. **rī'sing**, *n.* (esp.) insurrection.

risk, *n.* possibility or chance of danger or loss or harm. *v.t.* expose to risk; venture on, take chances of. **ris'ky**, *a.* full of risk; risqué.

ris'qué (-kā), *a.* suggestive of indecency.

riss'ōle, *n.* fried ball of minced meat, etc.

ritardan'dō,[0] (as musical direction, abbrev. *rit.*) gradually slower.

rīte, *n.* religious or solemn ceremony or observance. **rit'ūal,** *a.* of or with rites. *n.* performance of ritual acts; prescribed order for performing religious service.

rī'val, *n.* person or thing competing with another. *a.* in position of rival(s). *v.t.* (p.t. *rivalled*), vie with, be comparable to. **rī'-valry,** *n.*

rīve, *v.* (chiefly Poet. except in p.p. *riven*) strike or rend asunder; split.

riv'er, *n.* large natural stream of water flowing in channel.

riv'ĕt, *n.* nail or bolt for holding together metal plates, etc. *v.t.* join or fasten with rivets; clinch; fix or concentrate (eyes, attention) on; engross attention (of). **riv'ĕter**, *n.*

riv'ūlĕt, *n.* small stream.

roach, *n.* small freshwater fish.

road, *n.* way, esp. with prepared surface, for foot passengers, riders, and vehicles; way of getting *to*; route; (usu. pl.) stretch of water near shore where ships can ride at anchor. **road'side**, (at) border of road. **road'stead,** sea-roads. **road'way**, (esp.) part of road, bridge, etc., used by vehicles. **road'worthy,** (of vehicle) fit to be used on road.

roam, v. ramble, rove, wander (about).

roan, a. & n. (animal, esp. horse or cow) with coat of which prevailing colour is mixed with white or grey.

roar (ror), n. loud deep hoarse sound (as) of lion, thunder, or voice(s) in pain, rage, etc. v. utter or emit roar; say, sing, etc., in or with roar. **roar'ing,** a. (esp.) boisterous, noisy; (of trade) brisk.

roast, v. cook by exposure to open fire or in oven; undergo roasting. a. roasted. n. roast meat.

rob, v. (p.t. robbed), steal from; plunder with violence; deprive (of). **robb'er,** n. **robb'ery,** n.

robe, n. long loose garment; (often pl.) such garment as indication of rank, office, etc. v. put robe(s) on (person); put on one's robe(s).

rob'in, n. small brown red-breasted bird.

rō'bot, n. machine designed to work and look like a man; automaton; machine-like person. a. automatically controlled.

robust', a. strong and healthy; vigorous; sensible, straightforward.

roc, n. gigantic bird of Eastern legends.

rock[1], n. solid mass of mineral material forming part of earth's crust; mass of this forming cliff, crag, etc.; large detached piece of this, boulder. **rock crystal,** crystallized quartz. **rock-garden,** rockery. **rock-plant,** plant growing among rocks or suitable for rockery. **rock salmon,** dogfish. **rock'ery,** n. artificial heap of rough stones and soil for growing rock-plants.

rock[2], v. (cause to) move gently to and fro or from side to side (as) in cradle; shake; oscillate. **rock'er,** n. (esp.) one of curved bars on which cradle, etc., rocks. **rocking-chair, -horse,** chair, child's wooden horse, mounted on rockers.

rock'ĕt, n. cylindrical case that can be projected to height or distance by reaction of gases when contents are ignited; shell or bomb projected, spacecraft, etc., driven, by rocket propulsion. v.t. fly straight upwards, fly fast and high; (of prices) rise rapidly. **rocket propulsion,** propulsion by reaction of gases expelled backwards at high speed. **rock'ětry,** n. science or practice of rocket propulsion.

rock'y[1], a. full of rocks, hard as rock.

rock'y[2], a. unsteady, tottering.

rocò'cō, a. & n. (of) elaborate style of decoration with much scroll work, shell motifs, etc.

rod, n. slender straight round stick or metal bar; cane or birch for punishment; measure of length (5¼ yds.).

rode, p.t. of **ride.**

rō'dent, n. & a. (mammal) of order including mice, rats, squirrels, beavers, etc., with strong incisors for gnawing.

rōde'ō (-dā-), n. round-up of cattle for branding, etc.; exhibition of cowboys' skill.

rōe[1], n. (also roe-deer) small kind of deer. **rōe'buck,** n. male roe.

rōe[2], n. mass of eggs, esp. in fish's ovarian membrane.

rogā'tion, n. (usu. pl.) prayers (esp. for harvest) chanted or said on the three days (Rogation days) preceding Ascension Day.

rōgue (-g), n. rascal, swindler; mischievous child; arch or sly person. **rō'guery,** n. **rō'guish,** a. (esp.) playfully mischievous.

roi'ster, v.i. revel noisily, be uproarious. **roi'sterer,** n. **roi'stering,** n. & a.

rōle, n. actor's part; one's task or function.

rōll, n. cylinder formed by turning paper, cloth, etc., over and over on itself without folding; register, list; more or less cylindrical mass of something; (very) small loaf of bread; rolling motion or gait; continuous sound of thunder, drums, etc.. v. move or send or go in some direction by turning over and over on axis; wallow; sway or rock; flatten with roller; make into or from roll. **roll--call,** calling over of list of persons. **rō'ller,** n. (esp.) cylinder used alone or as part of machine for smoothing, crushing, etc.; long swelling wave. **roller skate,** device with small wheels, attached beneath boot-sole, for gliding over smooth surface. **rō'lling,** n. & a. **rolling-pin,** roller for pastry, etc. **rolling-stock,** railway locomotives, wagons, etc.

roll'icking, a. extremely gay, boisterous.

rō'ly-pō'ly, n. pudding of paste covered with jam, rolled up and boiled.

Rō'man, a. of ancient or modern city of Rome; of Christian Church of Rome. n. member of ancient-roman State; inhabitant of Rome; roman type. **Roman Catholic,** (member) of Church of Rome. **Roman numerals,** numerals expressed in letters of Roman alphabet (I, V, X, etc.). **roman type,** ordinary upright type (opp. italic).

romance', n. medieval tale of chivalry; love story; love affair; exaggeration, picturesque falsehood. v.i. tell exaggerated or invented stories, lie.

roman'tic, a. enjoying or suggestive of romance; fanciful and unpractical; imaginative in style. **roman'ticism,** n.

Rom'any, n. gipsy; the gipsy language. a. of gipsies or gipsy language.

romp, v.i. play in lively or boisterous manner; (informal) move quickly and easily. n. romping.

ron'deau (-dō), n. (pl. rondeaux, pr. -dōz), **ron'del,** n. poem with two rhymes only, and with opening words used twice as refrain.

ron'dō, n. (pl. rondos), (Mus.) movement or piece in which principal theme recurs twice or oftener.

rōōd, n. crucifix (esp. on rood-screen, separating nave and choir); measure of land (usu. ¼ acre).

roof, *n.* upper covering of house or building; top of covered vehicle, tent, etc. *roof of the mouth*, palate. *v.t.* cover with roof; be roof of. **roof-tree**, horizontal beam along ridge of roof. **roo͞o'fing**, *n.* material used for roofs.

rook[1], *n.* large gregarious bird of crow family. *v.t.* defraud by cheating, esp. at cards; charge extortionately. **rook'ery**, *n.* collection of rooks' nests in group of trees.

rook[2], *n.* castle-shaped piece in chess.

room, *n.* space occupied or that might be occupied by something; scope, opportunity; part of house, etc., enclosed by walls; (pl.) apartments or lodgings. **room'ful**, *n.* **roo͞o'my**, *a.* large, of ample dimensions.

roost, *n.* bird's resting-place. *v.t.* settle for sleep; be perched or lodged for the night. **roos'ter**, *n.* domestic cock.

root, *n.* part of plant that fixes it to earth, etc., and conveys nourishment to it from soil; embedded part of bodily organ or structure; source, means of growth, basis; (Math.) factor of quantity which multiplied by itself gives that quantity; ultimate unanalysable element of word; (Mus.) fundamental note of chord. *v.* (cause to) take root; establish firmly; pull *up* by root; turn up ground in search of food; rout (*out*).

rope, *n.* stout cord made by twisting together strands of hemp, manila, etc.; string *of* pearls, etc.; stringy formation in beer or other liquid. *know the ropes*, be familiar with conditions in some sphere of action. *v.t.* fasten or connect with rope; enclose or mark *off* with rope. **rope-dancer**, performer on tight-rope. **ro͞o'py**, *a.*

ro͞o'sary (-z-), *n.* (R.C. Ch.) set series of prayers, string of beads for keeping count of these; rose-garden.

rose[1] (-z), *n.* (prickly shrub bearing) beautiful and usu. fragrant flower; rose-shaped design or object; nozzle of watering-can; warm pink. *a.* of warm pink. **rose'bud**, bud of rose. **rose-water**, perfume distilled from roses. **rose window**, circular window, usu. with spoke-like tracery. **rose'wood**, hard fragrant wood used in cabinet-making.

rose[2], *p.t.* of **rise**.

ro͞o'sèate (-z-), *a.* rose-coloured.

rose'mary (-zm-), *n.* evergreen shrub with fragrant leaves.

rosette' (-z-), *n.* rose-shaped ornament made of ribbons, etc., or carved in stone, etc.

ros'in (-z-), *n.* resin, esp. in solid form. *v.t.* rub (esp. bow of violin, etc.) with rosin.

ro͞o'ster (*or* ro-), *n.* list showing turns of duty, etc.

ros'trum, *n.* (pl. *rostrums, rostra*), platform for public speaking; pulpit.

ro͞o'sy (-z-), *a.* rose-coloured, warmly pink; promising, hopeful.

rot, *v.* (p.t. *rotted*), (cause to) become rotten. *n.* decay, rottenness; (*slang*) nonsense.

ro͞o'ta, *n.* list of persons acting, or duties to be done, in rotation.

ro͞o'tary, *a.* rotating, acting by rotation.

rotâte', *v.* move round axis or centre, revolve; arrange or take in rotation. **rotâ'tion**, *n.* rotating; recurrent series or period; regular succession. **ro͞o'tatory**, *a.* **rotâ'tional**, *a.*

rôte, *n.* *by rote*, in mechanical manner, by exercise of memory without understanding.

ro͞o'tor, *n.* rotatory part of machine; rotating system of helicopter.

rott'en, *a.* decomposed, putrid; falling to pieces from age or use; corrupt; worthless.

rotund', *a.* rounded, plump. **rotun'da**, *n.* circular building, esp. with dome. **rotun'dity**, *n.*

rou'ble (roo-), *n.* Russian unit of money.

rouge (roozh), *n.* red powder or other cosmetic for colouring cheeks. *v.t.* colour with rouge.

rough (ruf), *a.* of uneven or irregular surface; not smooth or level; shaggy; coarse in texture; violent; stormy; riotous; harsh, unfeeling; deficient in finish; incomplete; approximate. *n.* rough ground; hard part of life; rowdy, hooligan. *v.t.* make rough; plan *out*, sketch *in*, roughly. *rough it*, do without ordinary comforts. **rough-and-ready**, roughly efficient or effective. **rough'cast**, (coat, coated with) plaster of lime and gravel. **rough-hew**, shape or carve out roughly. **rough'shod**, (of horse) having shoes with nail-heads projecting. *ride roughshod, domineer over.* **rough'age**, *n.* indigestible fibrous matter or cellulose in foodstuffs. **rough'en**, *v.* make or become rough.

roulette' (roo-), *n.* gambling game played on table with revolving centre over which ball runs.

round, *a.* spherical, circular, or cylindrical; entire, continuous, full; plain, genuine, candid. *n.* round object; slice of bread; circular movement; recurring succession or series (of events, duties, etc.); customary course, walk, etc.; (ammunition for) single discharge of gun; bout or spell of game, etc.; canon for voices at same pitch or at octave. *adv.* circularly; with rotation; with return to starting-point; to, at, etc., all points or sides of. *prep.* so as to encircle or enclose; about. *v.* give round shape to, assume round shape; pass round. *round up*, gather (cattle, etc.) by riding, etc., round. **round'about**, (*a.*) circuitous; (*n.*) merry-go-round; road-junction where traffic must follow circular course. **Round'head**, member of Parliamentary party in 17th-c. civil war. **round numbers**, numbers stated without odd units, etc. **rounds'man**, tradesman's employee going round with goods. **round-up**, rounding up.

roun'dèlay, *n.* short song with refrain.

roun'ders (-z), *n.* team-game with bat and ball.

round'ly, *adv.* outspokenly; thoroughly.

rouse (-z), *v.* wake, or stir up, from sleep,

inactivity, complacency, etc.; evoke (feelings); cease to sleep; become active.

rout¹, *n.* disorderly retreat of defeated troops; utter defeat. *v. t.* defeat utterly.

rout², *v. t.* search *out*, force or fetch *out*.

route (rōot; (Mil.) rowt), *n.* way taken in getting from starting-point to destination. *v. t.* (pres. p. *routeing*), send, etc., along particular route. **route-march**, (Mil.) training march.

routine (rōotēn'), *n.* regular procedure, fixed way of doing certain things. *a.* performed habitually or by rule.

rōve, *v.* wander (over or through); move from place to place; (of eyes) look from place to place. **rō'ver**, *n.* wanderer.

row¹ (rō), *n.* number of persons or things in more or less straight line.

row² (rō), *v.* propel boat with oars; convey in boat. *n.* spell of rowing. **rowing-boat**, *n.* boat propelled with oars.

row³, *n.* (*informal*) disturbance, noise; dispute. *v.* reprimand; engage in dispute (*with*).

row'an (*or* rō-), *n.* mountain-ash; its scarlet berry.

row'dy, *a.* rough, noisy, and disorderly. *n.* rowdy person. **row'dyism**, *n.*

row'el, *n.* spiked revolving disc at end of spur.

row'lock (rul- *or* rol-), *n.* device serving as point of support for oar.

roy'al, *a.* of or belonging to king or queen or their family; splendid. **royal standard**, square flag bearing royal arms. **roy'ally**, *adv.* **roy'alist**, *n.* supporter of monarchy. **roy'alty**, *n.* being royal; royal person(s); royal licence to work minerals; payment by lessee of mine to landowner; payment to patentee for use of patent, or to author or composer for each copy of work sold or for each public performance.

rub, *v.* (p.t. *rubbed*), move (one thing) over or up and down on surface of (another); polish, clean, abrade, chafe, make dry, make sore, by rubbing; take (mark, etc.) *out*; get frayed or worn by friction. *n.* spell of rubbing; impediment or difficulty.

rubb'er¹, *n.* tough elastic substance made from milky juice (*latex*) of certain plants; indiarubber; person or thing employed to rub. **rubb'erize**, *v.t.* treat or coat with rubber. **rubb'ery**, *a.*

rubb'er², *n.* three successive games between same persons at bridge, whist, etc.; winning of two games in rubber.

rubb'ish, *n.* waste or worthless matter, refuse, litter; nonsense. **rubb'ishy**, *a.*

rubb'le, *n.* waste fragments of stone, brick, etc.

ru'bicund (rōo-), *a.* ruddy, red-faced.

ru'bric (rōo-), *n.* heading or passage printed in red or in special lettering.

ru'by (rōo-), *n.* crimson or rose-coloured precious stone; glowing red colour. *a.* ruby-coloured.

ruche (rōosh), *n.* frill or pleated strip of lace, etc. **ru'ching**, *n.* parallel rows of gathering.

ruck, *v.* & *n.* crease, wrinkle.

ruck'sack (roo- *or* ru-), *n.* walker's or climber's bag for necessaries, slung from shoulders and resting on back.

ruc'tion, *n.* (usu. pl., *informal*) dispute, row.

rudd'er, *n.* broad flat piece of wood, metal, etc., hinged to stern of ship or boat for steering with. **rudd'erless**, *a.*

rudd'y, *a.* healthily red; reddish.

rude (rōod), *a.* impolite, unmannerly; insolent, offensive; primitive; in natural state; uncivilized, uneducated; roughly made; startling, violent; vigorous.

ru'diment (rōo-), *n.* (pl.) first principles (*of* knowledge or some subject); (pl.) germ of something undeveloped; (sing.) part or organ imperfectly developed. **rudimen'tary**, *a.*

rue¹ (rōo), *n.* evergreen shrub with bitter strong-scented leaves.

rue² (rōo), *v.t.* (pres. p. *rueing*), repent of; wish something had not been done or taken place. **rue'ful**, *a.* dejected, downcast.

ruff¹, *n.* projecting starched and goffered neck-frill; band of feathers, hair, or colour round bird's or animal's neck.

ruff², *n.* & *v.* trump(ing) at whist, etc.

ruff'ian, *n.* brutal, violent, lawless person. **ruff'ianism**, *n.* **ruff'ianly**, *a.*

ruff'le, *v.t.* disturb smoothness or tranquillity of. *n.* frill of lace, etc.; ripple.

rug, *n.* large, esp. woollen, wrap or bed-cover; floor-mat.

Rug'by, *n.* (also *Rugby football*), form of football in which ball may be carried.

rugg'ed (-g-), *a.* of rough uneven surface; harsh; austere.

rugg'er (-g-), *n.* (*informal*) Rugby football.

ru'in (rōo-), *n.* (cause of) destruction, downfall, decay; fallen or wrecked state; (often pl.) remains of building. etc., fallen into total disrepair. *v.t.* cause ruin of; reduce to ruins; destroy, bankrupt. **ruinā'tion**, *n.* **ru'inous**, *a.* in ruins; bringing ruin.

rule (rōol), *n.* principle or regulation to which action or procedure conforms or is bound or intended to conform; dominant custom, standard, normal state of things; sway, government; graduated, often jointed, strip of metal, etc., for measuring. *v.* have sway or influence over; keep under control; govern; make line(s) with ruler. **ru'ler**, *n.* person (esp. sovereign) who rules; strip of wood, etc., for drawing straight lines. **ru'ling**, *n.* (esp.) authoritative pronouncement, judicial decision.

rum, *n.* spirit distilled from products of sugar-cane.

rum'ble, *v.i.* & *n.* (make) sound as of distant thunder, heavy vehicle, etc.

ru'minant (rōo-), *n.* mammal that chews the cud (e.g. cow, deer, etc.). *a.* of ruminants; ruminating. **ru'mināte**, *v.i.* chew the cud;

meditate, ponder. **ruminā′tion,** *n.* **ru′-minative,** *a.*

rumm′age, *v.* ransack, make search (in). *n.* rummaging search; odds and ends.

rumm′y, *n.* card-game with object of collecting sets or groups of cards.

rumour (rōō′mer), *n.* general talk, report, or hearsay, of doubtful accuracy. *v.t.* (chiefly in passive) report by way of rumour.

rump, *n.* tail-end of animal or bird.

rum′ple, *v.t.* crease, tousle.

rum′pus, *n.* (*slang*) row, uproar.

run, *v.* (p.t. *ran*; p.p. *run*; pres. p. *running*), go or pass with speed, smooth motion, or regularity; compete in race, etc.; spread rapidly; flow; work or be in action; (of bus, etc.) ply; be current, operative, or valid; be worded; control; smuggle. *n.* act or spell of running; (Cricket) point scored by running between wickets, etc.; way things tend to move; (Mus.) rapid scale-passage; continuous stretch, spell, or course; general demand; enclosure for fowls, etc.; freedom to make use of; ladder in stocking, etc.

run′away, *n.* fugitive; bolting horse. *a.* fugitive; bolting; out of control.

rune (rōōn), *n.* letter of earliest Germanic alphabet; similar mysterious mark. **ru′nic,** *a.*

rung[1], *n.* cross-bar forming step of ladder.

rung[2], *p.p.* of **ring**[2].

runn′el, *n.* brook; gutter.

runn′er, *n.* racer; messenger; creeping stem capable of rooting itself; sliding ring on rod, etc.; part on which something slides; long strip of cloth, carpet, etc. **runner (bean),** any of various climbing beans (esp. *scarlet runner*). **runner-up,** competitor taking second place.

runn′ing, *a.* consecutive; successive; flowing; discharging (pus); (of loop, etc.) made with knot that slides along rope, etc.

runt, *n.* undersized animal, esp. smallest pig of litter.

run′way, *n.* specially prepared section of airfield for taking off and landing of aircraft.

ru′pee′ (rōō-), *n.* unit of money of India and Pakistan.

rup′ture (-cher), *n.* breaking, breach; quarrel; abdominal hernia. *v.* burst, break; sever; affect with hernia; suffer rupture.

rur′al (roor-), *a.* in, of, or suggesting the country; pastoral, agricultural. **rural dean,** see **dean.**

ruse (rōōz), *n.* stratagem, trick, dodge.

rush[1], *n.* marsh plant with slender pithy stem; its stem. **rush′light,** candle made by dipping pith of rush in tallow.

rush[2], *v.* impel or carry along violently or rapidly; run with haste or great speed; go or act or do without proper consideration; take by sudden assault. *n.* act of rushing; violent or tumultuous movement or advance; spurt; sudden migration of large numbers. **rush hour,** time when traffic, etc., is heaviest.

rusk, *n.* piece of bread rebaked.

russ′et, *a.* of soft reddish-brown. *n.* russet colour; apple with rough russet skin.

Ru′ssian (-shn), *n.* & *a.* (native, language) of Russia (U.S.S.R.).

rust, *n.* reddish-brown coating formed on iron by oxidation, esp. as effect of moisture, and corroding it; colour of this; disease of plants. *v.* affect, become affected, with rust.

rus′tic, *a.* rural; of or like country people or peasants; uncouth; of roughly trimmed branches, with rough surface. *n.* countryman. **rusti′city,** *n.*

rus′ticate, *v.* retire to or live in the country; send away temporarily from university as punishment. **rusticā′tion,** *n.*

rus′tle (-sl), *n.* succession of light crisp sounds, as of dry leaves blown. *v.* (cause to) make rustle; go with rustle.

rus′ty, *a.* rusted, affected with rust; (of accomplishment, etc.) weakened by lack of practice.

rut[1], *n.* track sunk by passage of wheels; settled routine, groove. **rutt′ed,** *a.*

rut[2], *n.* period of sexual excitement in some male mammals (e.g. deer, seal).

ruth′less (rōō-), *a.* without pity or compassion. **ruth′lessly,** *adv.* **ruth′lessness,** *n.*

rȳe, *n.* (grain of) cereal used as fodder or for bread, etc.

S

sabbatār′ian, *a.* sabbath-keeping; keeping Sunday as sabbath. *n.* sabbatarian person.

sabb′ath, *n.* rest-day appointed for Jews on seventh day of week (Saturday); Sunday, esp. as day of obligatory abstinence from work and play.

sa'ble, *n.* small dark-furred carnivorous mammal of cold climates; its fur. *a.* (Poet.) black.

sab'ot (-ō), *n.* wooden shoe.

sab'otage (-ahzh), *n.* deliberate damage to machinery, etc., esp. by enemy agents in war-time or dissatisfied workmen. *v. t.* commit sabotage on; wilfully damage or destroy. **saboteur'** (-er), *n.*

sa'bre (-er), *n.* cavalry sword with curved blade.

sac, *n.* bag-like membrane enclosing cavity or forming envelope of cyst, etc.

sacch'arin(e) (-k-; *or* -ēn) white, intensely sweet, crystalline substance used as sugar--substitute. **sacch'arīne** (*or*-ēn), *a.* sugary.

sacerdō'tal, *a.* of priest(s), priestly.

sa'chet (-shā), *n.* small perfumed bag, esp. bag of dried lavender, etc.

sack¹, *n.* large bag, esp. of coarse flax, hemp, etc.; loose dress or gown; *the sack,* (*informal*) dismissal. **sack'cloth,** *n.* sacking. **sack'ing,** *n.* coarse stuff for making sacks.

sack², *v. t.* plunder (captured town, etc.). *n.* sacking of captured place.

sack³, *n.* (Hist.) white wine from Spain, etc. **sack'but,** *n.* former name of trombone.

sac'rament, *n.* symbolic religious ceremony (e.g. baptism, Eucharist, etc.); thing of mysterious and sacred significance. **sacramen'-tal,** *a.*

sā'crēd, *a.* holy; consecrated *to* deity; dedicated to some person or purpose; hallowed by religious association; sacrosanct. **sā'-crēdness,** *n.*

sac'rifice, *n.* slaughter of victim, presenting of gift, or doing of act, to gain favour of a god; such victim, gift, or act; giving up of thing for sake of something more estimable, important, or urgent. *v.* offer (as) sacrifice (*to*); give up as of inferior importance (*to*). **sacrifi'cial** (-shl), *a.*

sac'rilege (-ij), *n.* violation of what is sacred. **sacrile'gious** (-ijus *or*-ējus), *a.*

sac'ristan, *n.* official in charge of sacred vessels, vestments, etc., of a church.

sac'rosanct, *a.* secured by religious sanction against outrage or violation.

sad, *a.* feeling sorrow or grief; showing or causing sorrow; (of bread, etc.) heavy. **sadd'en,** *v.* **sad'ness,** *n.*

sadd'le, *n.* rider's seat on back of horse, etc., or on bicycle, etc.; saddle-shaped thing; joint of mutton or venison. *v. t.* put saddle on; burden *with* task, etc. **saddle-bag,** one of pair of bags slung across horse, etc. **sadd'ler,** *n.* maker of saddles, harness, etc. **sadd'lery,** *n.*

sā'dism (*or* sad- *or*sah-), *n.* taking pleasure in cruelty to others. **sad'ist,** *n.* **sadis'tic,** *a.*

safar'i, *n.* (E. Afr., etc.) expedition for observation of wild life or for hunting.

safe, *a.* out of or not exposed to danger; not dangerous; cautious; reliable; sure. **safe--conduct,** immunity from arrest or harm; document granting this.

safe'guard (-fgard), *n.* condition, circumstance, etc., giving protection against foreseen risks. *v. t.* protect.

safe'ty (-ft-), *n.* being safe; freedom from danger or risks. **safety belt,** strap(s) securing occupant to seat of aircraft, vehicle, etc. **safety curtain,** fireproof theatre-stage curtain. **safety lamp,** miner's lamp so constructed as not to ignite firedamp. **safety match,** match igniting only on specially prepared surface. **safety-valve,** vent opening automatically to relieve excessive pressure of steam; (fig.) harmless outlet for excitement, etc.

saff'ron, *n.* & *a.* (colour of) orange-yellow.

sag, *v. i.* (p.t. *sagged*), sink or curve downwards under weight or pressure; hang sideways or droop in centre. *n.* sagging.

sa'ga (sah-), *n.* medieval Icelandic or Norwegian prose tale; lengthy narrative or story.

sagā'cious (-shus), *n.* having or showing insight and practical wisdom. **saga'city,** *n.*

sāge¹, *a.* aromatic herb with greyish-green leaves used in cookery.

sage², *a.* wise, judicious, experienced. *n.* profoundly wise person.

Sagittā'rius, *n.* the Archer, constellation and ninth sign of the zodiac.

sā'gō, *n.* starch prepared from palm-pith and used for puddings, etc.

sah'ib, *n.* (in India, etc.) (respectful title of address for) man of rank or authority.

said, *p. t.* & *p. p.* of **say.**

sail, *n.* piece of canvas, etc., extended on rigging to catch wind and propel vessel; wind--catching apparatus attached to arm of windmill; spell of sailing. *v.* progress on water by use of sail(s) or engine-power; start on voyage; navigate ship; glide, move smoothly or easily. **sail-cloth,** canvas for sails; kind of coarse linen. **sai'ling,** *n.* **sailing-ship,** vessel propelled by sails.

sai'lor, *n.* seaman; member of ship's crew.

saint, *n.* person canonized or officially recognized by Church as having won by exceptional holiness high place in heaven (abbrev. *St.*, *S.*); one of blessed dead or other member of company of heaven; saintly person. **saint'ly,** *a.*

sāke, *n. for the sake of, for my,* etc., *sake,* out of consideration for; in the interest of; in order to please, get, etc.

salaam' (-lahm), *n.* oriental greeting (meaning 'Peace'); low bow. *v. i.* make low bow.

salā'cious (-shus), *a.* indecent, lewd.

sal'ad, *n.* cold dish of usu. uncooked vegetables; vegetable, esp. lettuce, used for salad.

sal'amander, *n.* amphibian with tail, related to newts; mythical lizard-like animal supposed to live in fire.

sal'ary, *n.* fixed periodical payment made to person, esp. for other than manual or mechanical work. **sal'aried,** *a.* paid by salary.

sāle, *n.* selling; amount sold; public auction; special selling of goods at low prices. **sā'-leable** (-labl), **sā'lable,** *a.* fit for sale; finding purchasers. **sāleabil'ity,** *n.* **sāles'man** (-lzm-), *n.* (pl. *-men*), shop assistant; middleman between producer and retailer. **sāles'manship,** *n.* skill in selling. **sāles'woman,** *n. fem.* (pl. *-women*).

sā'liėnt, *a.* prominent, conspicuous; standing out. *n.* projecting section of battle line, etc.

sā'line, *a.* containing salt; of or like salt.

sali'va, *n.* liquid secreted by salivary glands and mucous glands of the mouth. **sal'ivary,** *a.* of, or secreting, saliva.

sall'ow (-ō), *a.* (having complexion) of sickly yellow or yellowish brown.

sall'y, *n.* sudden rush from besieged place to attack enemy; witty remark. *v.i.* make military sally; go *forth* or *out* for walk, etc.

salmon (sam'on), *n.* large fish with orange--pink flesh, much prized for food and sport. *a.* of colour of salmon.

salon (sal'awn), *n.* (gathering of distinguished persons in) great lady's drawing-room (chiefly Hist.); hairdresser's establishment.

saloon', *n.* large public room; large cabin in liner, etc.; motor car with closed body.

salt (-o- *or* -aw-), *n.* sodium chloride (*common salt*) obtained from sea-water by evaporation or from earth by mining, used to season or preserve food and in manufacturing processes; substance formed when (part of) hydrogen of acid is replaced by a metal or base; piquancy, pungency, wit; experienced sailor. *a.* containing, tasting of, or preserved with salt. *v.t.* preserve or season with salt. **salt--cellar,** vessel holding salt for table use. **salt--pan,** hollow near sea for getting salt by evaporation.

saltpetre (soltpē'ter; *or* saw-), *n.* white crystalline substance used in making gunpowder, preserving meat, etc.

sal'ty (so- *or* saw-), *a.* full of salt, tasting of salt; witty.

salū'brious (*or* -ōō-), *a.* healthy. **salu'brity,** *n.*

sal'ūtary, *a.* producing good effect, beneficial.

salūtā'tion, *n.* friendly or respectful greeting; words or gesture used in this.

salute' (-ōōt), *n.* gesture expressing respect, courteous recognition, etc.; (Mil., etc.) prescribed movement, use of flags, or discharge of gun(s) as sign of respect. *v.* make salute or salutation (to); greet.

sal'vage, *n.* (payment for) saving of ship or its cargo from loss at sea, or of property from fire; saving and utilization of waste materials; salvaged property. *v.t.* save from wreck, fire, etc.

salvā'tion, *n.* saving of the soul, deliverance from sin or its consequences; preservation from loss, calamity, etc. **Salvation Army,**

organization engaging in world-wide evangelical and charitable work.

salve, *n.* healing ointment; something that soothes. *v.t.* soothe (pride, conscience, etc.).

sal'ver, *n.* tray, often of silver, etc., for handing refreshments, etc.

sal'vō, *n.* (pl. *salvoes*), simultaneous firing of guns, etc.; round of loud applause.

sal volat'ilė, *n.* aromatic solution of ammonium carbonate used as smelling-salts.

sāme, *a.* not different; identical; unchanged; uniform, unvarying; previously referred to. *the same,* the same thing; in the same manner. *all the same,* nevertheless, in spite of that. **sāme'ness** (-mn-), *n.*

sam'ite, *n.* rich medieval silk dress-fabric.

sam'ovar, *n.* Russian tea-urn.

sam'pan, *n.* small river or coastal boat of China, Japan, etc.

sa'mple (sah), *n.* part or piece taken to show quality of whole; specimen or pattern. *v.t.* try qualities of.

sa'mpler (sah-), *n.* piece of embroidery worked by girl as specimen of proficiency.

sanator'ium, *n.* (pl. *-s* or *sanatoria*), residential establishment for invalids, convalescents, etc.; room or building for the sick in school or college.

sanc'tify, *v.t.* make holy. **sanctificā'tion,** *n.*

sanctimō'nious, *a.* making a show of sanctity or piety. **sanc'timony,** *n.*

sanc'tion, *n.* authoritative permission; penalty imposed for non-compliance with international law, etc.; consideration causing any rule to be obeyed. *v.t.* authorize, permit (action, etc.).

sanc'tity, *n.* saintliness; sacredness, inviolability.

sanc'tüary, *n.* place recognized as holy or inviolable; part of church within altar rails; place of refuge; (Hist.) (sacred) place where fugitive was immune from arrest or violence.

sanc'tum, *n.* holy place; person's private room. ·

sand, *n.* tiny fragments resulting from wearing down of rocks; (pl.) expanse of sand. *v.t.* sprinkle, mix, or polish with sand. **sand'bag,** bag filled with sand, used for fortification, protection, ballast, etc. **sand-dune,** dune. **sand'paper,** (polish or smooth with) paper with layer of sand on surface. **sand'pit,** unroofed enclosure filled with sand for children to play in. **sand'stone,** rock composed of consolidated grains, usu. of quartz.

san'dal, *n.* sole attached to foot by thongs or straps. **san'dalled** (-ld), *a.* wearing sandals.

san'dalwood, *n.* fragrant wood obtained from various trees.

sand'wich, *n.* two (or more) slices of bread, etc., with meat, cheese, etc., between; cake of two layers with jam, etc., between. *v.t.* insert between or among other things, etc. **sand'wich man,** (pl. *-men*), man carrying advertisement boards (*sandwich-boards*) hung one before and one behind.

san′dy, *a.* covered with sand; (of hair) yellowish-red; having sandy hair.

sāne, *a.* mentally healthy, not mad; sensible, rational.

sang, *p.t.* of **sing**.

sang-froid (sahṅfrwah′), *n.* coolness in danger or difficulty.

sang′uinary (-nggwi-), *a.* bloody; blood-thirsty.

sang′uine (-nggwin), *a.* habitually hopeful, confident; optimistic; ruddy, florid.

san′hedrin (-ni-), *n.* supreme council and court of justice in ancient Jerusalem.

san′itary, *a.* of conditions that affect health, esp. with regard to cleanliness and precautions against infection; free from, protecting against, influences harmful to health; of sanitation; used during menstruation. **sanitā′-tion**, *n.* (esp.) drainage and disposal of sewage.

san′ity, *n.* being sane.

sank, *p.t.* of **sink**.

San′skrit, *n.* & *a.* (of) ancient and sacred language of Hindus in India.

San′ta Claus (-z), legendary personage supposed to bring presents to children at Christmas.

sap¹, *n.* vital juice of plants; vitality. *v.t.* (p.t. *sapped*), drain of sap; weaken.

sap², *n.* tunnel or trench dug to get nearer to enemy, etc. *v.* (p.t. *sapped*), make sap; undermine (wall, etc.); destroy (faith, etc.) insidiously. **sapp′er**, *n.* (esp.) private of Royal Engineers.

sā′pience, *n.* wisdom (often used ironically). **sā′pient**, *a.* would-be wise.

sap′ling, *n.* young tree.

sapph′īre, *n.* blue precious stone; its colour, azure. *a.* of sapphire blue.

sa′raband, *n.* (music for) slow Spanish dance in triple time.

Sa′racen, *n.* Arab or Muslim of time of Crusades.

sar′casm, *n.* bitter or wounding, esp. ironic, remark; use of sarcasm(s). **sarcas′tic**, *a.*

sarcoph′agus, *n.* (pl. *sarcophagi*, pr.-gī or -jī), stone coffin.

sardine′ (-ēn), *n.* small fish of herring kind usu. tinned in oil.

sardon′ic, *a.* mocking, scornful, bitter.

sa′ri (sah-), *n.* length of material wrapped round body, worn as main garment by Hindu women.

sarong′, *n.* long piece of cloth worn by Malays, etc., tucked round waist as skirt.

sartor′ial, *a.* of tailors or clothes.

sash¹, *n.* long strip of material worn over one shoulder or round waist.

sash², *n.* frame holding window-glass, usu. made to slide up and down in grooves.

Sass′enach (-*ch*), *n.* (Sc. & Ir.) Englishman.

sat, *p.t.* & *p.p.* of **sit**.

Sā′tan, *n.* the Devil. **satan′ic**, *a.* of or like Satan; diabolical.

satch′el, *n.* bag, esp. for school-books, often with strap to sling over shoulder(s).

sāte, *v.t.* satiate.

sateen′, *n.* cotton fabric, shiny on one side.

sat′ellīte, *n.* planet revolving round larger one; artificial body launched from earth and orbiting it or other planet, etc.; follower, underling; State nominally independent but dominated by another.

sā′tiāte (-shi-), *v.t.* satisfy fully; cloy, surfeit. **sati′ety**, *n.* state of being glutted or satiated.

sat′in, *n.* silk fabric, shiny on one side.

sat′inwood, *n.* fine wood of a tropical tree.

sat′īre, *n.* literary composition in which vice or folly is ridiculed; use of ridicule, sarcasm or irony to expose folly. **sati′ric**, *a.* of or containing satire. **sati′rical**, *a.* **sat′irist**, *n.* writer of satires. **sat′irīze**, *v.t.* attack with satire(s); describe satirically.

satisfac′tion, *n.* satisfying or being satisfied; thing that satisfies desire or gratifies feeling; payment of debt; amends for injury. **satisfac′tory**, *a.* causing satisfaction; adequate.

sat′isfy̆, *v.t.* meet expectations or wishes of; be accepted by (person, etc.) as adequate; pay, fulfil, comply with; still cravings of; convince; be sufficient for. **sat′isfied** (-īd), *a.* **sat′isfy̆ing**, *a.*

sat′urāte (-cher-), *v.t.* fill with moisture, soak, steep; cause to take in as much as possible of something. **sat′urāted**, *a.* (of solution) containing maximum possible quantity of dissolved substance. **saturā′tion**, *n.*

Sat′urday, *n.* seventh day of week.

Sat′urn, *n.* (Rom. myth.) god of agriculture; a large planet.

Saturnā′lia, *n.pl.* (Rom. antiquity) festival of Saturn; (*s-*), scene or time of wild revelry.

sat′urnīne, *a.* sullen, gloomy.

sat′yr (-er), *n.* (Gk. & Rom. myth.) woodland god, partly human and partly bestial in form; lustful man.

sauce, *n.* liquid or soft preparation taken as relish with food; (*informal*) sauciness. **sauce′boat**, vessel in which sauce is served. **sauce′pan**, pan, usu. of metal and with long handle, for boiling, stewing, etc.

sau′cer, *n.* small shallow, usu. round, vessel placed under cup, etc.; round shallow depression in ground.

sau′cy, *a.* impudent, cheeky.

sau′na (sow- or saw-), *n.* steam bath or bath-house, of Finnish origin.

saun′ter, *v.i.* walk in leisurely way. *n.* leisurely ramble or gait.

saus′age (sos-), *n.* minced and seasoned meat stuffed into cylindrical case of animal tissue, etc.

sav′age, *a.* uncivilized, in primitive state; fierce, cruel. *n.* member of savage tribe; brutal or barbarous person. *v.t.* (of animal) attack and bite or trample. **sav′agery**, *n.*

savann′a, savann′ah, *n.* wide treeless grassy

plain, esp. in tropical America.

sav'ant (-ahṅ), *n.* man of learning, scholar.

sāve, *v.* rescue or preserve from danger or harm; bring about spiritual salvation of; keep for future use; put money, etc., by; economize (in); prevent loss of. *save up*, accumulate by economy. *prep.* except, but. **sā'ving**, *a.* (esp.) that redeems or compensates. *n.* (esp.) something saved; (pl.) amount of money put by. **savings-bank,** bank that receives deposits and pays interest.

sā'viour (-vyer), *n.* deliverer, redeemer; person who saves another or others.

sa'voir faire' (-vwar), quickness to see and do the right thing; social tact. (French)

sā'vour (-ver), *n.* characteristic taste, flavour; tinge or hint *of. v.* appreciate flavour of, enjoy; suggest presence *of.* **sā'voury,** *a.* with appetizing taste or smell; of salt or piquant flavour, not sweet. *n.* savoury dish, esp. at end of dinner.

savoy', *n.* rough-leaved winter cabbage.

saw¹, *p.t.* of **see².**

saw², *n.* proverbial saying, maxim.

saw³, *n.* implement with toothed edge for cutting wood, etc. *v.* (p.p. *sawn* or *sawed*), cut or make with, use, saw; make to-and-fro motion as of saw or sawing. **saw'dust,** fine wood fragments made in sawing. **saw'mill,** mill for mechanical sawing of wood into planks, etc. **saw'yer,** *n.* workman who saws timber.

saxe, *n.* slightly greenish blue colour.

sax'horn, *n.* any of a set of brass wind instruments with valves.

sax'ifrage (-ij), *n.* any of various Alpine or rock plants.

Sax'on, *n.* & *a.* (member, language) of Germanic people who conquered and occupied parts of Britain in 5th-6th centuries.

sax'ony, *n.* a fine woollen fabric.

sax'ophône, *n.* wind-instrument made of brass but with keys and having a reed like that of clarinet.

say, *v.* (3rd. sing. pres. (*says*) pr. sez; p.t. *said,* pr. sed), utter or recite in speaking voice; state, speak, tell, express; repeat. *n.* (opportunity of saying) what one has to say; share in decision. **say'ing,** *n.* (esp.) remark commonly made; maxim.

scab, *n.* crust formed over sore in healing; skin-disease, esp. of sheep; plant-disease. **scabb'y,** *a.*

scabb'ard, *n.* sheath of sword, dagger, etc.

scā'bies (-z), *n.* (also called *the itch*), contagious skin-disease caused by tiny parasite.

scā'bious, *n.* any of various wild or cultivated flowering herbaceous plants.

scab'rous, *a.* rough-surfaced; (of subject, situation, etc.) hard to handle with decency.

scaff'old, *n.* platform on which criminal is executed. **scaff'olding,** *n.* structure of poles and planks providing builders, etc., with platform(s) to stand on while working.

scald (-aw-), *v.t.* injure or pain with hot liquid or vapour; cleanse with boiling water; heat (liquid, esp. milk) to near boiling-point. *n.* injury to skin by scalding.

scāle¹, *n.* one of thin horny or bony overlapping plates protecting skin of fishes, reptiles, etc.; thin plate or flake or film; scab; tartar on teeth. *v.* remove scales or scale from; form, come off in, scales. **scā'ly,** *a.*

scāle², *n.* pan of balance; (pl.) weighing instrument, esp. (*pair of scales*) beam pivoted at middle with pan, etc., suspended at either end, balance.

scāle³, *n.* series of degrees; graduated arrangement, system, etc.; (Mus.) definite series of sounds ascending or descending by fixed intervals; relative dimensions (of plan, map, etc.); tool or instrument marked for measuring; system of numeration or numerical notation in which value of figure depends on its place in order. *v.* climb up; represent in true relative proportions.

scā'lēne, *a.* (of triangle) with no two sides equal.

scall'op (*or* sko-), *n.* bivalve mollusc with shell edged with small semicircular lobes; one of series of rounded projections at edge of garment. **scallop(-shell),** one valve of scallop, esp. as utensil in which savoury dish is cooked and served. *v.t.* ornament with scallops.

scall'ywag, *n.* (*slang*) scamp, scapegrace.

scalp, *n.* skin and hair of upper part of head; (Hist.) this taken as trophy by N. Amer. Indians. *v.t.* take scalp of.

scal'pel, *n.* surgeon's small knife.

scamp¹, *n.* rascal.

scamp², *v.t.* do (work, etc.) quickly and inadequately.

scam'per, *v.i.* run nimbly, like startled animal or playing child. *n.* scampering run.

scam'pi, *n. pl.* large prawns.

scan, *v.* (p.t. *scanned*), test metre of (verse) by dividing into feet; be metrically correct; look at all parts successively of; (Television) resolve (picture) into elements of light and shade for transmission; traverse systematically with radar beam, etc.

scan'dal, *n.* (thing causing) general feeling of outrage or indignation, esp. as expressed in talk; malicious gossip. **scan'dalize,** *v.t.* horrify, shock. **scan'dalmonger** (-ungg-), *n.* one who invents or spreads scandals. **scan'dalous,** *a.*

Scandinā'vian, *a.* & *n.* (native) of Scandinavia (Norway, Sweden, Denmark, Iceland).

scan'sion (-shn), *n.* scanning of verse.

scant, *a.* barely sufficient; very little, less than enough. **scan'ty,** *a.* barely sufficient; of small extent or amount.

scāpe'goat (-pg-), *n.* person blamed or punished for wrongdoing or faults of others.

scāpe'grāce (-pg-), *n.* scamp; person who is frequently in trouble.

scap'ŭla, *n.* (pl. *scapulae*), shoulder-blade.

scar[1], *n.* mark left on skin, etc., by wound, etc. *v.* (p.t. *scarred*), mark with scar(s); form scar(s).

scar[2], *n.* precipitous craggy part of mountain--side.

sca'rab, *n.* sacred beetle of ancient Egypt; ancient gem cut in form of beetle.

scarce, *a.* not plentiful; rare. *make oneself scarce,* go away.

scarce'ly (-sli), *adv.* hardly, barely; surely not.

scar'city, *n.* being scarce; scanty supply (*of*).

scare, *v.t.* strike with sudden terror, frighten (*away, off,* etc.). *n.* sudden fright or alarm. **scare'crow,** figure of man dressed in old clothes, set up to scare birds away from crops; oddly dressed or grotesque person.

scarf, *n.* (pl. *scarves* or *scarfs*), long strip of material worn round neck, shoulders, or head.

sca'rifỹ, *v.t.* make slight surgical incisions in (Med.); scratch. **scarificā'tion,** *n.*

scarlati'na (-tē-), *n.* scarlet fever.

scar'lĕt, *n.* & *a.* (of) brilliant orange-red colour. **scarlet fever,** infectious fever with sore throat and scarlet rash. **scarlet runner,** scarlet-flowered climbing bean.

scā'thing (-dh-), *a.* (of criticism, etc.) severe, withering.

scatt'er, *v.* throw or put here and there; sprinkle; diffuse by reflection from particles (Phys.); separate and disperse in flight, etc. *n.* scattering. **scatter-brain,** careless forgetful person. **scatt'ered,** *a.* (esp.) not situated together, wide apart; sporadic.

scav'enge (-nj), *v.* be or act as scavenger. **scav'enger,** *n.* person employed to keep streets clean (Hist.); animal feeding on carrion, rubbish, etc.

scēne, *n.* place where events occur in fact or in fiction; piece of continuous action forming part of play, etc.; stormy action or encounter or outburst, esp. with display of temper; painted canvas, properties, etc., representing scene of action, stage set with these. *behind the scenes,* out of view of audience; (fig.) out of sight, hearing, or knowledge of general public. **scene-shifter,** one who changes scenes in theatre. **scē'nery,** *n.* stage scenes; (general appearance of) natural features of a district. **scē'nic,** *a.* of the stage; picturesque.

scent, *v.t.* discern by smell; detect; make fragrant, perfume. *n.* characteristic odour of something; fragrance; odour of animal, etc., enabling hound, etc. to track it; liquid perfume.

scep'tic (sk-), *n.* person who doubts truth of religious doctrines; sceptical person. **scep'tical,** *a.* critical, doubtful, incredulous, hard to convince. **scep'ticism,** *n.*

scep'tre (-ter), *n.* staff borne in hand as symbol of regal or imperial authority; (fig.) sovereignty. **scep'tred** (-terd), *a.* having sceptre.

sched'ūle (sh-; U.S. sk-), *n.* tabulated statement of details, inventory, list, etc.; time--table. *on schedule,* at time appointed. *v.t.* make schedule of; include in schedule.

schēme (sk-), *n.* systematic arrangement; outline; plan of action; artful or underhand plan or plot. *v.* make plans; plan, esp. in secret or underhand way. **schē'mer,** *n.* **schē'ming,** *a.*

scherzo (skār'tsō), *n.* (pl. *scherzos*), (Mus.) vigorous and lively movement or composition.

schism (sizm), *n.* splitting of a Church into two factions.

schist (sh-), *n.* fine-grained metamorphic rock splitting in thin irregular plates.

schiz'oid (skits-), *a.* of or resembling schizophrenia. **schizophrē'nia** (skitso-), *n.* mental illness marked by disconnection between thoughts, feelings, and actions. **schizophren'ic,** *a.* & *n.*

schol'ar (sk-), *n.* learned person; holder of scholarship; (*archaic*) child at school. **schol'arly,** *a.* learned; of or befitting learned person. **schol'arship,** *n.* learning; sum allowed to student from funds of school, college, State, etc., usu. after competitive examination.

scholas'tic (sk-), *a.* of schools or education; academic, pedantic.

school[1] (sk-), *n.* institution for educating children or giving instruction; its buildings; its pupils; group of artists, philosophers, etc., following or holding similar principles, opinions, etc. *v.t.* discipline, bring under control, train or accustom *to.* **school'boy, school'girl,** pupil at school. **school'master, school'mistress,** teacher in school. **school'ing,** *n.*

school[2] (sk-), *n.* shoal of fish, whales, porpoises, etc.

schoo'ner (sk-), *n.* small sea-going fore--and-aft rigged sailing-ship.

schottische (shotēsh'), *n.* dance like slow polka.

sciat'ic, *a.* of hip or sciatic nerve; of sciatica. **sciatic nerve,** large nerve passing down back of thigh to foot. **sciat'ica,** *n.* inflammation of, or pain in, sciatic nerve.

sci'ence, *n.* (pursuit of) systematic and formulated knowledge; branch of knowledge, esp. one of *natural* sciences dealing with material phenomena and based on observation, experiment, and induction (chemistry, biology, physics, etc.); such sciences as a whole; trained skill in sport, etc. **scientif'ic,** *a.* according to principles of science; of science or natural sciences. **sci'entist,** *n.* person learned in natural science(s).

scim'itar, *n.* short curved Oriental sword.

scin'tillāte, *v.i.* sparkle, twinkle; display brilliant wit, etc. **scintillā'tion,** *n.*

sci'on, *n.* shoot cut for grafting; young member of (esp. old or noble) family.

sciss'ors (-zerz), *n. pl.* (*pair of*) *scissors*, cutting implement of two blades pivoted together.

scoff, *v. i.* speak with scorn or derision; mock or jeer *at. n.* mocking words; taunt.

scold, *v.* blame angrily; find fault noisily. *n.* scolding or nagging woman. **scōl'ding**, *n.*

sconce, *n.* bracket candlestick for fastening to wall, etc.; socket holding candle.

scone (-on *or* -ōn), *n.* soft flat cake of flour, etc., baked quickly.

scoōp, *n.* short-handled deep shovel for grain, flour, etc.; long-handled ladle; gouge-like instrument; scooping; (*informal*) obtaining and publishing of news before and to exclusion of competitors. *v.* lift (*up*), hollow (*out*), (as) with scoop; (*informal*) gain advantage over (rival) by obtaining scoop.

scoōt, *v. i.* (*slang*) dart, shoot along; hurry off.

scoō'ter, *n.* child's toy vehicle of foot-board on wheels, propelled by pushes of one foot on ground; light small-wheeled motor cycle.

scope, *n.* sphere or extent of action or observation, range; opportunity, outlet.

scorch, *v.* burn surface of so as to discolour, shrivel, pain, etc.; become discoloured, slightly burned, etc., with heat; be very hot. *n.* mark of scorching. **scor'ching**, *a.* (esp.) extremely hot.

score, *n.* notch cut; line cut or drawn; reckoning; number of points made by player or side in game; copy of music showing all instrumental or vocal parts; (set of) twenty; category. *v.* mark with or make notches, incisions, or lines; furrow; record or keep score; make point(s) in game, etc.; have good luck; orchestrate, arrange (*for* instrument, etc.). **scor'er**, *n.* (esp.) keeper of score at cricket, etc.

scorn, *n.* contempt, disdain, derision; object of contempt. *v. t.* feel or show contempt for; abstain from, refuse *to* do, as unworthy. **scorn'ful**, *a.* full of scorn, contemptuous.

Scor'piŏ, *n.* the Scorpion, constellation and eighth sign of the zodiac.

scor'pion, *n.* lobster-like arachnid with jointed stinging tail.

scot[1], *n.* (Hist.) tax or rate. **scot-free**, *a.* unharmed, unpunished.

Scot[2], *n.* native of Scotland.

scotch[1], *v. t.* wound without killing; put an end to (a rumour, etc.).

Scotch[2], *a.* made, grown, etc., in Scotland; Scottish. *n.* (*informal*) Scotch whisky. **Scotch terrier**, small rough-coated short-legged terrier. **Scots**, *a.* Scottish. *n.* dialect(s) of English spoken in (esp. Lowlands of) Scotland. **Scots'man**, **Scots'woman**, *nn.*, (pl. -*men*). **Scott'ish**, *a.* of Scotland or its people or dialect(s).

scoun'drel, *n.* wicked unscrupulous person; rogue. **scoun'drelly**, *a.*

scour[1] (-ower), *v. t.* rub clean or bright; clean out. *n.* act of scouring.

scour[2] (-ower), *v.* hasten over or along, esp. in search of something or someone.

scourge (skerj), *n.* whip (*archaic*); cause of suffering. *v. t.* cause great misery to; (*archaic*) whip.

scout[1], *n.* man sent out to reconnoitre; (*Scout*, formerly *Boy Scout*), member of boys' organization for practising open-air skills and developing character. *v. i.* act as scout.

scout[2], *v. t.* reject with scorn.

scow, *n.* large flat-bottomed boat.

scowl, *n.* bad-tempered frown. *v. i.* wear scowl, frown (*at*, etc.).

scrabb'le, *v. i.* scratch or grope busily (*about*).

scrag, *n.* bony part, esp. of neck of mutton or lamb. **scragg'y**, *n.* thin and bony.

scram'ble, *v.* make one's way by clambering, etc.; struggle with competitors to secure share of something; cook (eggs) by stirring in heated pan with butter; alter frequency of sound in telephoning, etc., to make message unintelligible without special receiver; go rapidly or hastily. *n.* climb or rough walk; motor cycle race over rough ground; eager struggle (*for*).

scrap[1], *n.* small detached piece; fragment, shred; (pl.) leavings; waste material, esp. old iron (*scrap-iron*), collected for re-working; cutting from newspaper, etc. *v. t.* (*p. t. scrapped*), discard; condemn as past use. **scrap-book**, book in which cuttings, etc., are pasted. **scrap-heap**, pile of scrap metal or waste material.

scrap[2], *n. & v. i.* (p.t. *scrapped*), (engage in) scrimmage, fight, or quarrel.

scrape, *v.* clean or smooth by drawing something sharp over surface; draw along with, or produce, scraping sound; pass along so as (almost) to graze or be grazed; amass by scraping, with difficulty, etc.; practise economy. *scrape through*, get through so as just to escape failure. *n.* act or sound of scraping; awkward predicament. **scra'per**, *n.*

scratch, *v.* score or wound on surface with claw or nail or something pointed; rub with the nails to relieve itching; make *hole*, strike *out*, etc., by scratching; withdraw from list of competitors, etc. *n.* wound, mark, or sound made by scratching; slight cut; starting-line for race. *start from scratch*, start without any advantages, preparations, etc. *a.* gathered together hastily; improvised.

scrawl, *v.* write or draw in hurried sprawling untidy way. *n.* something scrawled; hurried illegible handwriting.

scraw'ny, *a.* lean, scraggy.

scream, *v.* utter piercing cry (of terror, pain, mirth, etc.); utter in or with this noise. *n.* screaming cry or sound.

scree, *n.* loose stones covering steep mountain-side and sliding when trodden on.

screech, *n.* loud shrill harsh cry or sound. *v.* make, or utter with, screech.

screed, *n.* long, usu. tedious, letter.

screen, *n.* partition partly shutting off part of room, etc., esp. that between nave and choir of church; movable piece of furniture designed to shelter from observation, draughts, etc.; anything used for or serving as shelter or concealment; upright surface on which films, slides, etc., are projected; part of television or radar receiver on which pictures, etc., appear; large sieve. *v.t.* shelter; hide; show on screen; sift, grade; investigate (person's life and character), esp. to establish reliability.

screw (-ōō), *n.* cylinder with slotted head and spiral ridge (*thread*) running round outside, for holding pieces of wood, etc., together; thing turned like screw and used for exerting pressure, tightening, etc.; propeller; sideways curling motion; miser. *put the screw(s) on,* (fig.) put pressure on, coerce. *v.* fasten or tighten with screw; extort *out of. screw up,* tighten by screwing; contract, twist up. **screw'driver,** tool for turning screw by its slot.

scribb'le, *v.* write hurriedly or carelessly; scrawl; (*informal*) be a writer. *n.* thing scribbled; scrawl.

scribe, *n.* (Hist.) copyist, esp. of manuscripts; (Hist.) clerk, secretary; writer; (*Scribe,* Bibl.) ancient-jewish keeper of records and interpreter of the Law.

scrimm'age, *n.* tussle, confused struggle. *v.i.* engage in scrimmage.

scrimp, *v.* skimp.

scrip, *n.* (Hist.) wallet, satchel.

script, *n.* handwriting; printing-type imitating handwriting; handwriting resembling printing; written examination answers; typescript or text of play, film, broadcast, etc.

scrip'ture (-cher), *n.* sacred writings, the Bible; (*attrib.*) taken from, or relating to, the Bible. **scrip'tural,** *a.*

scroll, *n.* roll of parchment or paper, esp. written on; ornament, etc., resembling scroll; flowing or curling lines, etc.

scro'tum, *n.* (pl. *scrota*), pouch enclosing testes.

scrounge (-nj), *v.* (*informal*) obtain by foraging; cadge. **scroun'ger** (-j-), *n.*

scrub[1], *v.* (p.t. *scrubbed*), rub hard, esp. with hard-bristled brush (*scrubbing-brush*); use such brush. *n.* scrubbing.

scrub[2], *n.* (ground covered with) shrubs, brushwood, or stunted trees. **scrubb'y,** *a.*

scruff, *n.* back (of the neck).

scruff'y, *a.* untidy, shabby, dirty.

scrum, *n.* scrummage; (*informal*) dense crowd.

scrumm'age, *n.* (Rugby footb.) formation of forwards of both teams packed together with ball on ground between them; scuffle.

scrump'tious (-shus), *a.* (*slang*) delicious, delightful.

scrunch, *n. & v.* crunch.

scru'ple (-ōō-), *n.* doubt or hesitation in

regard to right and wrong, duty, etc. *v.t.* hesitate owing to scruples *to* do. **scru'pulous,** *a.* conscientious even in small matters; (over-)attentive to details, esp. to small points of conscience. **scru'pulously,** *adv.*

scrutineer' (-ōō-), *n.* official conducting scrutiny of votes.

scru'tinize (-ōō-), *v.t.* look closely at; examine critically or in detail.

scru'tiny (-ōō-), *n.* critical gaze; close or detailed examination; official examination of votes cast at election.

scud, *v.i.* (p.t. *scudded*), run, fly, straight and fast; skim along; (Naut.) run before the wind.

scuff'le, *n.* confused struggle. *v.i.* engage in scuffle.

scull, *n.* one of pair of small light oars used by single rower; oar used to propel boat by working it over stern. *v.* row, propel, with scull(s). **scull'er,** *n.* one who sculls; boat for rowing with sculls.

scull'ery, *n.* back kitchen for washing dishes, etc.

scull'ion, *n.* (*archaic*) menial servant.

sculp'tor, *n.* one who practises sculpture. **sculp'tress,** *n. fem.*

sculp'ture (-cher), *n.* art of forming representations by chiselling, carving, casting, or modelling; work(s) of sculpture. *v.* represent in, form by, adorn with, or practise, sculpture. **sculp'tural,** *a.*

scum, *n.* impurities that rise to surface of liquid; (fig.) worst or worthless part (*of*). **scumm'y,** *a.*

scupp'er, *n.* opening in ship's side to allow water to drain off deck.

scurf, *n.* flakes of dead skin, esp. on head, cast off as new skin develops below; scaly matter on a surface. **scur'fy,** *a.*

scu'rrilous, *a.* coarsely abusive. **scurril'ity,** *n.* scurrilous talk or remark.

scu'rry, *v.i.* run hurriedly, scamper. *n.* scurrying; bustle; flurry (*of* snow, etc.).

scur'vy, *n.* disease resulting from deficiency of vitamin C. *a.* (*archaic*) contemptible.

scut, *n.* short tail, esp. of rabbit, hare, or deer.

scutch'eon (-chon), *n.* escutcheon.

scutt'er, *v.i.* scurry.

scutt'le[1], *n.* coal-scuttle.

scutt'le[2], *n.* lidded opening in ship's deck or side. *v.t.* sink (ship) by making or opening holes in it.

scutt'le[3], *v.i.* scurry; run away.

scythe (-dh), *n.* mowing and reaping implement wielded with both hands with long sweeping stroke. *v.t.* cut with scythe.

se-, *pref.* apart, without.

sea, *n.* expanse of salt water; ocean; swell, great billow; vast quantity or expanse *of. at sea,* away from land, aboard ship; (fig.) bewildered. *put to sea,* leave port or land. **sea-anchor,** floating, usu. canvas, anchor. **sea-anemone,** primitive plant-like marine animal. **sea'board,** coastal region. **sea-dog,** old sailor. **sea'faring,** (*a.*) occupied in sea voyages; (*n.*) such occupation. **sea front,** part of town, etc., facing sea. **sea-going,** designed for sailing on sea. **sea-gull,** gull. **sea-horse,** small fish with fore part of body shaped like horse's head and neck. **sea-level,** mean level of sea between high and low tides used as standard in measuring heights and depths. **sea-lion,** large seal with ears. **sea'-man** (pl. *-men*), person expert in navigating ship, etc.; naval rating. **sea'manship,** skill of good seaman. **sea mew,** gull. **sea-pink,** thrift (plant). **sea'plane,** aircraft able to take off from and alight on water. **sea'port,** coastal town with harbour. **sea rover,** pirate. **sea'-scape,** picture of scene at sea. **sea-shell,** shell of salt-water mollusc. **sea'shore,** land close to sea; foreshore. **sea'sick,** suffering sickness caused by motion of ship, etc. **sea'-side,** place(s) close to sea as residence or resort. **sea-urchin,** marine animal covered with spines. **sea'weed,** plant growing in sea, esp. marine alga. **sea'worthy,** *a.* (of ship, etc.) in fit state to put to sea.

seal[1], *n.* piece of wax, etc., stamped with design, etc., attached to document as evidence of authenticity, or to envelope, receptacle, or door so that it cannot be opened without breaking seal; stamp, etc., used in making seal; this as mark of office; act, etc., regarded as confirmation or guarantee of; substance used to close aperture, etc. *v.t.* affix seal to; stamp, fasten, or certify as correct, with seal; ratify; close securely or hermetically; stop or shut *up*; set significant mark on. **sealing-wax,** composition, softening when heated, used for sealing letters, etc.

seal[2], *n.* amphibious marine mammal with limbs developed into flippers. *v.i.* hunt seals. **seal'skin,** fur of some kinds of seal.

seam, *n.* line where two edges join, esp. those of two pieces of cloth, etc., sewn together; line, groove, etc., formed by two abutting edges, mark resembling this; thin layer or stratum between two thicker strata. *v.t.* join, mark, or score, with seam(s). **seam'less,** *a.* **seam'stress** (sem-), **semp'stress,** *nn.* sewing-woman. **sea'my,** *a.* showing seams. *seamy side,* (esp., fig.) worst or roughest aspect, esp. of life.

séance (sā'ahns; *or* -ans), *n.* meeting, esp. one at which spiritualist medium attempts to communicate with spirits.

sear, *v.t.* scorch surface of, esp. by application of hot iron; (fig.) make callous.

search (ser-), *v.* examine thoroughly, esp. in order to find something; make search or investigation (*for*). *n.* act of searching, investigation, quest. **search'light,** (light from) lamp designed to throw strong beam of light in any desired direction. **sear'ching,** *a.* thorough; probing.

sea'son (-zn), *n.* each of four periods into which year is divided by earth's changing position in relation to sun; proper, suitable, or favourable time; period of indefinite or various length. *v.* bring or be brought into efficient or sound condition by exposure, use, etc., acclimatize; flavour or make piquant. **sea'sonable,** *a.* suitable to season; opportune. **sea'sonal,** *a.* depending on or varying with seasons. **sea'soning,** *n.* flavouring added to food to make it palatable, piquant, etc.; condiments.

seat, *n.* thing made or used for sitting on; right to sit as member of council, committee, etc.; site or location; country house. *v.t.* make sit; provide sitting accommodation for. *seat oneself,* sit down. *be seated,* sit. *two-seater, four-seater,* etc., (vehicle) with seats for two, four, etc., persons. **seat belt,** safety belt.

se'cant (*or* se-), *a.* cutting, intersecting. *n.* (Trig., abbrev. *sec*) reciprocal of cosine.

secateurs (sek'aterz), *n.pl.* small shears with curved crossed blades for pruning, etc.

secēde', *v.i.* withdraw formally from membership of Church or other body. **sece'ssion** (-shn), *n.* seceding; body of seceders.

seclude (-ōōd), *v.t.* keep remote or away from company of others. **seclu'sion** (-ōōzhn), *n.* secluding, being secluded; retirement, privacy; secluded place.

sec'ond[1], *a.* next after first in time, order, position, rank, etc.; other, another; of subordinate importance, value, etc.; inferior. *n.* second person, class, etc.; supporter, helper, esp. of boxer or duellist; sixtieth part of minute of time or angular degree; (pl.) goods of second quality. *adv.* as second in succession. *v.t.* give one's support to. **second cousin,** child of one's parent's cousin. **second--hand,** not new, not original; bought after use by another. **second-rate,** of inferior quality. **second sight,** power of seeing future or distant occurrences as if present. **second string,** person or thing kept in reserve. **second thoughts,** (decision, etc., after) reconsideration. **second wind,** recovered breath after exhaustion during exertion. **sec'onder,** *n.* (esp.) person speaking in support of resolution, etc. **sec'ondly,** *adv.* (in enumerating) second.

second'[2], *v.t.* transfer temporarily (officer or official) to another appointment, department, etc. **second'ment,** *n.*

sec'ondary, *a.* of less importance; subsidiary; not original or primary; (of education, school) between primary school and higher or university education.

se'crecy, *n.* being secret.

se'cret, *a.* kept from general view or knowledge; not (to be) made known; confidential; working, etc., in secret. *n.* thing (to be) kept secret. *in secret,* in private, secretly. **secret service,** service to government of undisclosed nature; (*popularly*) espionage. **se'-**

crĕtly, *adv.*

secrētar̃'iat, *n.* department of secretaries.

sec'rĕtary, *n.* person appointed to deal with correspondence, keep records, make business arrangements, etc., for another or for an organization; minister in charge of State department (*Secretary of State*). secrētar̃'ial, *a.* sec'rĕtaryship, *n.*

sĕcrēte'¹, *v.t.* hide, conceal.

sĕcrēte'², *v.t.* produce by secretion. sĕcrē'tion, *n.* process by which certain substances in living organisms are extracted (from blood, sap, etc.) and (usu.) elaborated for use or for excretion; substance so produced. sĕcrē'tory, *a.*

sĕ'crĕtive (*or* sikrē'-), *a.* having secrets; uncommunicative, needlessly reserved.

sect, *n.* group of persons holding religious doctrines different from those of established or orthodox Church; religious denomination. sectār̃'ian, *a.* & *n.* sectār̃'ianism, *n.*

sec'tion, *n.* part cut off; one of parts into which something is divided; part of community with separate interests or characteristics; thin slice cut off for microscopic examination; (figure resulting from) cutting of solid by plane; (Surg.) cutting. sec'tional, *a.* (esp.) made up of sections that may be fitted together.

sec'tor, *n.* plane figure contained by two radii and arc of circle; (Mil.) subdivision of defensive position or system; branch (of industry, etc.).

sec'ūlar, *a.* concerned with affairs of this world, not of the Church or religion; not monastic; not sacred. sec'ūlarize, *v.t.*

sĕcūre', *a.* safe from danger, free from anxiety; impregnable; safe, reliable; firmly fastened or established, etc. *v.t.* make secure; make fast; obtain. sĕcūr'ity, *n.* secure state or feeling; thing serving as guarantee or pledge (to fulfil undertaking, pay loan or other sum of money, etc.); guarantor, surety; certificate of stock, etc.; safety of State from foreign interference or espionage.

sĕdan', *n.* (also *sedan-chair*) 17th-18th-c. covered-in chair carried on poles by two men; (U.S.) saloon motor car.

sĕdāte', *a.* collected, composed, not hurried or agitated. sĕdāte'ness (-tn-), *n.*

sĕdā'tion, *n.* (Med.) treatment by sedatives.

sed'ative, *a.* soothing, calming. *n.* sedative drug, etc.

sed'entary, *a.* sitting; involving much sitting.

sedge, *n.* grass-like plant growing in marshes or by water; mass of such plants.

sed'iment, *n.* matter that settles to bottom of liquid, dregs; water- or wind-deposited material which consolidates to make rock. sedimen'tary, *a.* sedimentā'tion, *n.*

sĕdi'tion, *n.* conduct or language inciting to rebellion. sĕdi'tious (-shus), *a.*

sĕdūce', *v.t.* induce to have sexual intercourse with one; lead astray, tempt into sin or crime.

sĕdūc'tion, *n.* seducing or being seduced; something that seduces or allures. sĕdūc'tive, *a.* (esp.) alluring, enticing, attractive.

sed'ūlous, *a.* assiduous, persistent.

see¹, *n.* office, position, or jurisdiction of bishop.

see², *v.* (p.t. *saw*; p.p. *seen*), have or use power of perceiving with eye(s); observe, look at; understand; grant interview to; escort (*home*, etc.). *see about*, attend to. *see to*, attend to, take care of or about.

seed, *n.* (one of) germs of plants, esp. as used for sowing; seed-like fruit; semen; (Bibl.) descendants; germ or latent beginning *of*; thing resembling seed; seeded player. *v.* produce or let fall seed; remove seeds from; arrange (players in tournament, etc.) so that certain players do not meet in early rounds. seeds'man, dealer in seeds. seed-vessel, pod or capsule containing seeds. seed'ling, *n.* young plant raised from seed. see'dy, *a.* full of seed; shabby; unwell.

see'ing, *pres.p.* of see², used as *conj.* considering the fact *that*; since, because.

seek, *v.* (p.t. *sought*, pr. sawt), go in search of, look for; try to obtain or bring about, try *to* do; ask for, request. *sought after*, much in demand.

seem, *v.i.* have air or appearance of being; appear or be apparently perceived or discovered *to* be or do. see'ming, *a.* apparent but perhaps not real. see'mingly, *adv.*

seem'ly, *a.* decorous, decent, proper.

seen, *p.p.* of see².

seep, *v.i.* ooze, percolate. seep'age, *n.*

seer, *n.* prophet, divinely inspired person.

seer'sucker, *n.* thin fabric of cotton, nylon, etc., with puckered surface.

see'saw, *a.* & *adv.* with backward--and-forward or up-and-down motion. *n.* (game on) long board supported in middle so that ends on which children, etc., sit move alternately up and down. *v.i.* play at see-saw; move up and down or to and fro; vacillate.

seethe (-dh), *v.* boil, bubble; be agitated.

seg'ment, *n.* part cut off or separable from other parts; part of circle or sphere cut off by straight line or plane. *v.* divide into segments. segmentā'tion, *n.*

seg'rĕgāte, *v.* set apart, isolate; separate from the rest; subject to racial segregation. segrĕgā'tion, *n.* segregating; enforced separation of racial groups within community or institution.

seignior (sā'nyor), *n.* (Hist.) feudal lord.

seine (sān), *n.* large vertical fishing-net.

seis'mic (sīz-), *a.* of earthquake(s). seis'mograph, *n.* instrument for recording tremors of earthquakes. seismol'ogy, *n.* scientific study of earthquakes.

seize (sēz), *v.* take or take hold of forcibly; suddenly or eagerly; snatch; take possession of by warrant or legal right; understand quickly or clearly. sei'zure (-zher), *n.* (esp.)

sudden attack of illness, e.g. apoplexy.

sel′dom, *adv.* rarely; not often.

sèlect′, *a.* chosen for excellence; picked, choice; exclusive. *v.t.* choose as best or most suitable. **sèlec′tion,** *n.* selecting; what is selected; number of things from which to select; (Biol.) natural selection (see **natural**).

self, *n.* (pl. *selves*) person's or thing's own individuality or essence; (concentration on) one's own nature, state, interests, or pleasure.

self-, *pref.* expressing reflexive action, automatic or independent action, or sameness. **self-ac′ting,** *a.* automatic. **self-asser′tion,** *n.* insistence on one's own claims, individuality, etc. **self-asser′tive,** *a.* **self-cen′tred,** *a.* preoccupied with oneself or one's own affairs. **self-co′loured,** *a.* of same colour as main part. **self-command′,** *n.* power of controlling one's emotions. **self-con′fidence,** *n.* confidence in one's own abilities. **self-con′scious,** *a.* embarrassed because unable to forget oneself. **self-contained′,** *a.* (esp., of flat, etc.) complete in itself. **self-control′,** *n.* control of oneself, one's emotions, etc. **self-dèni′al,** *n.* voluntary abstention from pleasurable things. **self-impor′tant,** *a.* having exaggerated idea of one's own importance. **self-in′terest,** *n.* regard for one's own interests or advantage only. **self-possessed′,** calm, confident. **self-posse′ssion,** *n.* **self-rèli′ant,** *a.* relying one one's own efforts. **self-rèspect,** *n.* proper regard for one's dignity, standard of conduct, etc. **self-righ′teous,** *a.* laying stress on one's own virtue. **self-sac′rifice,** *n.* giving up of one's interest or desires for the sake of others. **self′sáme,** *a.* (the) very same. **self-sat′isfied,** *a.* conceited. **self-see′king,** *a.* seeking one's own advantage only. **self-ser′vice,** *a.* in or at which customers help themselves and pay cashier afterwards. **self-styled′,** *a.* having taken name or description without justification. **self-suffi′cient,** *a.* requiring nothing from outside, independent. **self-willed′** (-ld), *a.* determined to do as one wishes, obstinate.

sel′fish, *a.* lacking in consideration for others; acting in, actuated by, self-interest. **sel′fishly,** *adv.* **sel′fishness,** *n.* **self′less,** *a.* without thought of one's own interests.

sell, *v.* (p.t. *sôld*), hand over or dispose of in exchange for money; deal in, keep stock of for sale; (of goods) be sold; betray for money, etc. *sell off,* sell remainder of at reduced prices. *sell out,* sell (all) one's shares in company; sell whole stock of something. **sell′er,** *n.*

sell′otápe, *n. & v.t.* (seal with) adhesive, usu. transparent, cellulose tape. **P.**

sel′vage, sel′vèdge, *n.* edge of cloth so woven that it cannot unravel.

sem′aphore, *n.* post with movable arms as signalling apparatus; signalling by person holding flag in each hand.

sem′blance, *n.* outward appearance, show.

sē′men, *n.* whitish fluid secreted by male animal, containing spermatozoa.

semi-, *pref.* half-, partly-, to some extent; partial(ly), imperfect(ly). **sem′ibrēve,** *n.* (Mus.) longest note in general use, equal to half breve. **sem′icircle,** *n.* half of circle or its circumference. **semicir′cŭlar,** *a.* **semicō′lon,** *n.* punctuation-mark (;). **semi-conduc′tor,** *n.* substance which is partial conductor of electricity in certain conditions. **semi-dètached′,** *a.* (of house) joined to another on one side only. **semi-fī′nal,** *n.* match or round preceding final. **semi-pre′cious,** *a.* (of gem) of less value than those called precious. **sem′iquâver,** *n.* (Mus.) note equal to half quaver. **sem′itône,** *n.* (Mus.) smallest interval used in European music.

sem′inal, *a.* of seed or semen.

sem′inary, *n.* school or college for training R.C. priests; (*archaic*) school.

Sē′mite, *n.* member of any of races supposed to be descended from Shem (including Jews, Arabs, etc.). **Semit′ic,** *a.* of Semites or their language(s).

semoli′na (-lē-), *n.* hard round grains of wheat used for puddings, etc.

sempstress: see **seamstress.**

sen′ate, *n.* State council of ancient Rome; upper house of legislature in some countries; governing body of some universities. **sen′ator,** *n.* member of senate.

send, *v.* (p.t. *sent*), cause to be conveyed, cause to go, to destination; drive, cause to go (*to*, etc.); send message; (of deity) grant, inflict. *send down,* send away from university. *send for,* summon, cause to be brought. **sen′der,** *n.*

sen′eschal (-shl), *n.* steward of medieval great house.

sē′níle, *a.* of, or characteristic of, old age; having (esp. mental) feebleness of old age. **senil′ity,** *n.*

sē′nior, *a.* older in age or superior in standing. *n.* person senior by age, length of service, etc.; one's elder or superior. **sênio′rity,** *n.*

senn′a, *n.* purgative prepared from dried pods or leaves of certain plants.

sensá′tion, *n.* consciousness of perceiving or seeming to perceive some state or condition of one's body, senses, or mind; (event or person arousing) excited or violent feeling, esp. *in* community. **sensá′tional,** *a.*

sense, *n.* any of special bodily faculties (*of* sight, hearing, smell, taste, touch) by which sensation is roused; feeling, consciousness; ability to perceive or feel; practical wisdom; meaning; (pl.) normal state of mind, sanity. **sense′less,** *a.* unconscious; wildly foolish; meaningless, purposeless.

sensibil′ity, *n.* capacity to feel; sensitiveness (*to*); delicacy of feeling.

sen′sible, *a.* having or showing good sense;

reasonable, judicious; aware, *of*; perceptible by the senses.

sen′sitive, *a.* very open *to* or acutely affected by external impressions; easily hurt or offended; responsive to or recording slight changes of condition; readily affected by or susceptible *to* (light, etc.). **sensitiv′ity,** *n.*

sen′sitize, *v.t.* make or render sensitive.

sen′sory, *a.* of sensation or the senses; conveying sensation.

sen′sual (*or* -shoo-), *a.* dependent on the senses only; gratifying the senses; excessively fond of such gratification.

sen′suous, *a.* of, derived from, affecting, appealing to, the senses.

sent, *p.t.* & *p.p.* of **send.**

sen′tence, *n.* series of words grammatically complete in itself; (judicial declaration of) punishment allotted. *v.t.* pronounce judicial sentence on; condemn *to* (a punishment).

senten′tious (-shus), *a.* affectedly or pompously moralizing.

sen′tient (-shi-), *a.* capable of feeling, having the power of perception by the senses.

sen′timent, *n.* mental attitude; opinion; emotional thought expressed in words; feeble or insincere tenderness. **sentimen′tal,** *a.* swayed or influenced by shallow emotion; designed to arouse or gratify the softer emotions. **sentimental′ity,** *n.*

sen′tinel, *n.* sentry.

sen′try, *n.* soldier, etc., posted to keep guard. **sentry-box,** hut large enough to hold sentry standing. **sentry-go,** duty of pacing up and down as sentry.

sep′al, *n.* leaf or division of calyx.

sep′arable, *a.* that can be separated.

sep′arate, *a.* divided or withdrawn from others; not joined or united, distinct, individual. **sep′arāte,** *v.t.* make separate, sever; part, withdraw *from*, go different ways; remove (*from* mixture, etc.). **separā′tion,** *n.*

sē′pia, *n.* (rich brown colour of) pigment made from inky secretion of cuttlefish.

sē′poy, *n.* (Hist.) Indian soldier in British-indian army.

sep′sis, *n.* poisoning of tissues or blood-stream by harmful bacteria.

sept-, *pref.* seven.

septet(te)′, *n.* (musical composition for) seven singers or players; group of seven.

Septem′ber, *n.* ninth month of year.

sep′tic, *a.* caused by or in a state of sepsis; putrefying. **septic tank,** tank in which organic matter in sewage is rapidly decomposed.

septicae′mia (-sēm-), *n.* blood-poisoning.

septŭagēnār′ian, *a.* & *n.* (person) between 70 and 80 years old.

sep′ulchre (-ker), *n.* tomb, burial vault or cave. **sēpul′chral** (-k-), *a.* of sepulchre(s); suggestive of tomb, gloomy, dismal.

sē′quel, *n.* what follows (event, etc.); continuation or resumption of story, etc.; result.

sē′quence, *n.* order of succession; coming after or next; chain of events; unbroken series; set of things belonging next each other; episode in film.

sèques′ter, *v.t.* set apart, isolate; confiscate (temporarily). **sèques′tered** (-erd), *a.* (esp.) secluded, sheltered, retired.

sèques′trāte (*or* sē′kwis-), *v.t.* seize temporarily (property, income) until legal claims are met. **sèquèstrā′tion,** *n.*

sē′quin, *n.* small glittering disc of metal, etc., sewn to dress, etc.

se′raph, *n.* (pl. *seraphs*, *seraphim*), angel of highest rank. **seraph′ic,** *a.* angelic.

sēre, *a.* (Poet.) dry, withered.

serenāde′ (se-), *n.* (composition suitable for) performance of music in open at night, esp. by lover under lady's window. *v.t.* entertain with serenade.

serendip′ity (se-), *n.* faculty of making happy discoveries by accident.

sērēne′, *a.* calm, peaceful; untroubled, placid. **sèren′ity,** *n.*

serf, *n.* labourer performing feudal services, attached to his overlord's estate and transferred with it (Hist.); oppressed person, drudge. **serf′dom,** *n.*

serge, *n.* durable twilled worsted fabric.

sergeant (sar′jant), *n.* non-commissioned officer above corporal and below sergeant-major; police officer above constable and below inspector. **sergeant-major,** non-commissioned officer of highest grade.

sēr′ial, *a.* of, in, or forming, series; (of story, etc.) issued, broadcast, etc., in instalments. *n.* serial story, etc.

sēr′ies (-z), *n.* (pl. same), succession, sequence, or set of similar or similarly related things, etc.

sēr′ious, *a.* thoughtful, not frivolous or joking; important, esp. because of possible danger; requiring earnest thought or application; sincere.

ser′mon, *n.* discourse on religious or moral subject, esp. delivered from pulpit; admonition. **ser′monize,** *v.* talk like a preacher.

ser′pent, *n.* snake, esp. large snake; (fig.) treacherous person.

ser′pentine, *a.* of or like serpent; winding, tortuous, sinuous.

serrā′ted (se-), *a.* having notched edge.

se′rried (-rid), *a.* pressed close together, in close order, crowded.

sēr′um, *n.* (pl. -*s* or *sera*), watery part of the blood; watery fluid in animal body.

ser′vant, *n.* person employed to work in a household; devoted follower, person who serves another. *public servant*, State official.

serve, *v.* be servant (to); do service or be useful (to); be obedient to; meet needs (of), suffice; do what is required for; distribute, hand food or goods; treat; set ball in play at tennis, etc. *n.* (turn for) serving ball. **ser′ver,** *n.*

ser′vice, *n.* being servant; position as servant;

department of royal or public employment, esp. (pl.) armed forces; work done for, benefit conferred on, another; maintenance and repair work; provision or supply of what is necessary; supply of gas, water, etc., to house, etc.; use, assistance; meeting of congregation for worship; set of dishes, etc., for serving meal; (Tennis, etc.) act or turn of serving. *v. t.* maintain or repair (car, etc.).

ser'viceable (-sabl), *a.* useful; durable.

serviette' (-i-et), *n.* table-napkin.

ser'vile, *a.* of slaves; like slave; cringing, mean-spirited, slavish. **servil'ity,** *n.*

ser'vitūde, *n.* slavery, subjection, bondage.

se'ssion (-shn), *n.* sitting, series of sittings, of legislative or administrative body, lawcourt, etc.; academic year in some universities, etc.

set¹, *v.* (p.t. *set*; pres. p. *setting*), place or cause to be in certain position, condition, relation, etc.; cause to stand; place ready; fix in position; cause to work; apply oneself *to* work, etc.; arrange (type) for printing; provide (song, words) with music; insert (gem, etc.) in gold, etc.; solidify, harden; (of sun, etc.) sink below horizon; clench (teeth). *set about*, begin. *set back*, impede. *set in*, arise, become established. *set off*, be adornment or foil to; start. *set out*, (esp.) begin journey. *set sail*, (esp.) start on voyage. *set up*, start; establish in some capacity; prepare (machine) for operation. **set¹,** *n.* direction of current or wind; fit or hang (of garment); setting of hair in desired style; posture; slip or shoot for planting; badger's burrow; stage setting. **set-back,** check or relapse. **set square,** draughtsman's appliance for drawing lines at certain angles.

set², *n.* number of things or persons that belong or consort together; series, collection, group; group of games in tennis, etc.; receiving apparatus for radio, etc.

settee', *n.* long seat with back and (usu.) arms, for more than one person.

sett'er, *n.* breed of dog trained to stand rigid when it scents game.

sett'ing, *n.* music to which words are set; frame in which gem, etc., is set; surroundings; place or period as background for action of play, novel, etc.

sett'le¹, *n.* wooden bench with high back and arms.

sett'le², *v.* establish or become established in dwelling or place or way of life; cease from wandering; determine, agree upon, decide; colonize (country); subside, sink; (of bird, etc.) come to rest (*on*); deal effectually with; pay (bill); bestow legally for life *on*.

sett'lement, *n.* terms on which disagreement ends; legal settling of property on person; centre established by social workers in poor or crowded district; newly settled tract of country.

sett'ler, *n.* (esp.) one who settles in newly developed (tract of) country. **sett'lor,** *n.*

(Law) one who makes settlement of property.

sev'en, *a. & n.* one more than six (7, VII). **sev'enth,** *a. & n.*

seventeen', *a. & n.* one more than sixteen (17, XVII). **sev'enteenth',** *a. & n.*

sev'enty, *a. & n.* seven times ten (70, LXX). **sev'entiĕth,** *a. & n.*

sev'er, *v.* separate, divide; cut or break off. **sev'erance,** *n.*

sev'eral, *a. & n.* more than two or three but not very many; separate, diverse, distinct; individual, respective. **sev'erally,** *adv.*

sĕvēre', *a.* austere, strict; harsh; violent or extreme; arduous, exacting; unadorned, plain. **sĕve'rity,** *n.*

sew (sō), *v.* (p.p. *sewn, sewed*, pr. sōn, sōd), use needle and thread or sewing-machine to make stitches in fabric; fasten, join, or make, by sewing. **sew'ing,** *n.* **sewing-machine,** apparatus in which needle is worked mechanically.

sew'age, *n.* liquid waste matter of community.

sew'er, *n.* (usu. underground) pipe or conduit for conveying sewage for disposal. **sew'erage,** *n.* (draining by) sewers.

sewing, sewn: see **sew.**

sex, *n.* being male or female; males or females collectively; sexual instincts, desires, etc.; coitus. **sex'less,** *n.*

sex-, *pref.* six.

sex'tant, *n.* instrument for measuring altitude of sun, used in navigation.

sextet(te)', *n.* (musical composition for) six singers or players; group of six.

sex'ton, *n.* person in charge of a church building and its contents, often with duties of bell-ringing and grave-digging.

sex'ūal, *a.* of or connected with sex or the sexes. **sexual intercourse,** coitus. **sex'ūally,** *adv.* **sexūal'ity,** *n.*

shabb'y, *a.* faded, worn, dilapidated; shabbily dressed; mean, contemptible. **shabb'ily,** *adv.* **shabb'iness,** *n.*

shack, *n.* roughly built hut or shanty.

shack'le, *n.* metal loop or staple, coupling link; (pl.) fetters, handcuffs, restraint. *v. t.* fasten or couple with shackle; fetter, impede.

shāde, *n.* comparative darkness, esp. area sheltered from direct rays of sun, etc.; comparative obscurity; darker part of picture; slight difference, small amount; unreal thing, ghost; screen excluding or moderating light, etc. *v.* screen from light; make dark(er); pass by degrees into another shade of colour, opinion, etc.

shad'ow (-ō), *n.* (patch of) shade; dark figure projected on ground, etc., by body intercepting rays of light; inseparable companion; unreal thing, phantom; obscurity; shelter or protection. *v. t.* (esp.) follow closely, persistently, and (usu.) secretly. **shadow cabinet,** prospective cabinet ministers of Parliamentary opposition. **shad'owy,** *a.* (esp.) like shadow, indistinct.

shā′dy, *a.* giving or situated in shade; of doubtful honesty, disreputable.

shaft (-ah-), *n.* rod of spear, arrow, etc.; long straight part connecting or supporting other parts, etc.; stem, stalk; arrow; ray *of* light; one of bars between which horse, etc., is harnessed to vehicle; long narrow (usu. vertical) opening for giving access to mine, containing lift, etc.

shag, *n.* rough mass of hair; strong cut tobacco; sea-bird like small cormorant.

shagg′y, *a.* hairy, rough-haired; rough, tangled.

shagreen′, *n.* untanned leather with rough granular surface, usu. dyed green.

shah, *n.* king of Persia (Iran).

shāke, *v.* (p.t. *shook*; p.p. *shāken*), move irregularly and quickly up and down or to and fro; (cause to) tremble or rock or vibrate; jolt or jar; brandish; weaken or make less stable; shock, disturb; *shake hands,* give (person) handshake. *n.* shaking, jolt, shock; crack in growing timber. **shake′down,** improvised bed. **shā′ky,** *a.* unsteady, trembling, unsound, wavering; unreliable.

shāle, *n.* fine-grained sedimentary rock splitting easily into thin layers.

shall, *v. aux.* (p.t. & conditional *should,* pr. shood), forming compound tenses or moods expressing futurity, command, obligation, intention, etc.

shallot′, *n.* kind of small onion.

shall′ow (-ō), *a.* of little depth; superficial, trivial. *n.* shallow place.

shalt, (*archaic*) 2nd pers. sing. pres. of **shall.**

sham, *n.* imposture, pretence; person pretending to be what he is not; counterfeit thing. *a.* pretended, counterfeit. *v.* (p.t. *shammed*), pretend.

sham′ble, *v. i.* walk or run in shuffling or ungainly way. *n.* shambling gait.

sham′bles (-blz), *n.* scene of slaughter; scene of chaotic confusion; (Hist.) slaughter--house.

shāme, *n.* feeling of mental discomfort aroused by consciousness of guilt, being ridiculous, offending against modesty, etc.; state of disgrace or discredit; (*informal*) regrettable or unlucky thing. *v.t.* make ashamed, bring disgrace on; force by shame *into, out of,* etc. **shāme′fāced,** *a.* bashful; ashamed, abashed. **shāme′ful,** *a.* **shāme′less,** *a.*

shampoo′, *v.t.* wash (hair); wash (carpet, etc.) without removing from position. *n.* shampooing; shampooing agent.

sham′rock, *n.* kind of trefoil, national emblem of Ireland.

shank, *n.* leg; lower part of leg from knee to ankle; stem or shaft.

shantung′, *n.* soft Chinese silk, usu. undyed.

shan′t (-ah-), informal contraction of *shall not.*

shan′ty¹, *n.* hut, cabin; mean, roughly constructed dwelling.

shan′ty², chan′ty (-ah-), *n.* sailors' song, with chorus, sung esp. while heaving, etc.

shāpe, *n.* total effect produced by thing's outlines, outer form; external appearance, guise; orderly arrangement, proper condition; pattern or mould. *v.* give desired or definite shape to; plan; develop (*into*). **shāpe′ly,** *a.* well-formed; of pleasing shape. **shāpe′less,** *a.*

shard, sherd, *n.* potsherd.

shāre¹, *n.* part that falls to individual out of common stock or burden or achievement; one of equal parts into which company's capital is divided. *v.* apportion; give, get, have, share of; possess, use, endure, jointly with others. *share out,* distribute. **share′holder,** owner of shares in a company.

shāre², *n.* ploughshare.

shark, *n.* large voracious sea-fish; extortioner, swindler.

sharp, *a.* well adapted for cutting or piercing, with fine edge or point; peaked, pointed; abrupt, angular, steep; keen, pungent; biting; harsh; severe, painful; acute; clever, quick; unscrupulous; speedy; (Mus.) above pitch. *n.* (Mus.) note raised by semitone, sign (♯) indicating this. *v. i.* cheat, esp. at cards. **sharp′shooter,** *n.* skilled shot. **shar′pen,** *v.* make or become sharp.

shatt′er, *v.* break suddenly and violently in pieces; wreck, utterly destroy.

shāve, *v.* remove (hair), free chin, etc., of hair, with razor; pare; pass close to without touching. *n.* shaving, being shaved; narrow miss, escape, or failure (*close, narrow, shave*). **shā′ven,** *a.* shaved. **shā′ver,** *n.* (esp.) electrical appliance for shaving face, etc. **shā′ving,** *n.* (esp.) thin slice taken from surface of wood with plane.

shawl, *n.* rectangular piece of fabric, often folded into triangle, worn over shoulders or head, etc., or wrapped round baby.

shē, *pron.* subjective case of 3rd personal pron. (pl. *they;* objective *her,* pl. *them*), female person or animal previously referred to. *n.* female, woman. *a.* female.

sheaf, *n.* (pl. *sheaves*), bundle of corn plants tied together after reaping; bundle of arrows, papers, etc., laid lengthwise together.

shear, *v.t.* (p.t. *sheared*; p.p. *shorn* or *sheared*), clip, cut, with shears; clip wool from. *shorn of,* deprived of. **shear′ling,** *n.* sheep shorn once. **shears** (-z), *n. pl.* (*pair of*) *shears,* cutting implement like large scissors.

sheath, *n.* (pl. pr. -dhz), close-fitting cover, esp. for blade or tool. **sheathe** (-dh), *v.t.* put into sheath; protect with casing, etc.

shed¹, *v.t.* (p.t. *shed*), let fall off, drop, part with; let or make flow (tears, blood); diffuse or radiate.

shed², *n.* roofed structure for shelter, storage, etc., sometimes with open front or sides.

sheen, *n.* brightness, lustre.

sheep, *n.* (pl. same), timid woolly ruminant

mammal bred and kept in flocks for flesh and wool. **sheep′dog,** dog trained to herd and guard sheep. **sheep′shank,** knot for shortening rope without cutting it. **sheep′skin,** sheep's skin with wool on it, used for garments, etc. **sheep′walk,** pasture-land for sheep. **sheep′ish,** *a.* bashful or embarrassed in manner.

sheer[1], *a.* mere, absolute; thin, transparent; very steep. *adv.* perpendicularly; directly; clean.

sheer[2], *v.i.* deviate from course.

sheet, *n.* large rectangular piece of linen, cotton, etc., used in pairs for sleeping between; broad thin flat piece of glass, paper, etc.; complete piece of paper as made; expanse of water, flame, etc.; rope at lower corner of sail, used to extend it, etc. *v.t.* secure (sail) with sheet. **sheet anchor,** large anchor used only in emergencies; best or only refuge.

sheik(h) (-āk *or* -ēk), *n.* Arab chief.

shek′el, *n.* ancient Hebrew, etc., weight or coin.

shel′drake, *n.* large wild duck frequenting sandy coasts. **shel′duck,** *n.fem.*

shelf, *n.* (pl. *shelves*), horizontal board projecting from wall or forming one tier of book-case or cupboard; ledge on cliff-face, etc.; reef or sand-bank.

shell, *n.* hard outer case enclosing birds' eggs, nuts, some seeds and fruits, some molluscs and crustaceans, etc.; walls of unfinished or gutted building; explosive artillery projectile. *v.t.* remove shell or pod from; fire shells at. **shell′fish,** aquatic mollusc or crustacean with shell.

shellac′ (*or* shel′-), *n.* purified lac, esp. in thin plates, used in varnishes, etc.

shel′ter, *n.* shield or protection against exposure to danger, cold, wind, etc.; thing, place, giving shelter. *v.* act or serve as shelter to; take shelter.

shelve[1], *v.t.* fit with shelves; put aside (plan, etc.) for a time; defer consideration of.

shelve[2], *v.i.* slope gently.

shep′herd (-perd), *n.* man who tends sheep. *v.t.* tend or drive sheep; marshal, guide, like sheep. **shep′herdess,** *n.fem.*

sher′bet, *n.* Eastern cooling drink of fruit-juice, etc.; effervescing drink, powder from which it is made.

sherd: see **shard.**

she′riff, *n.* chief executive officer of county, charged with keeping the peace, etc.

she′rry, *n.* Spanish, usu. fortified, wine; similar wine made elsewhere.

shew, (*archaic*) variant of **show** *v.*

shibb′oleth, *n.* belief or behaviour once considered essential but now generally abandoned; catchword.

shield, *n.* piece of defensive armour carried, usu. on arm, to ward off blows; escutcheon; shield-shaped thing; protective plate, etc., in machinery, etc.; person or thing serving as

protection. *v.t.* protect, screen.

shie′ling, *n.* (Sc.) rough hut; shelter.

shift, *v.* change or move from one position to another. *shift for oneself,* manage to make a living by one's own efforts. *n.* change of place, character, etc.; expedient; relay or change of workers. **shift′less,** *a.* lacking in resource; lazy. **shif′ty,** *a.* evasive, deceitful.

shille′lagh (-ā′la), *n.* Irish cudgel.

shill′ing, *n.* (Hist.) (coin worth) twelve pence or one-twentieth of pound sterling (abbrev. *s.*).

shill′y-shall′y, *v.i.* waver, be irresolute.

shimm′er, *n.* & *v.i.* (shine with) tremulous and faint light. **shimm′ery,** *a.*

shin, *n.* bony front of lower leg. *v.i.* (p.t. *shinned*), climb (*up*) by using arms and legs.

shine, *v.* (p.t. *shone*), emit or reflect light, glow; be brilliant, excel; (*informal*, p.t. *shined*) polish (shoes, etc.). *n.* light, brightness; lustre. **shi′ny,** *a.* having bright or glistening surface.

shing′le[1] (-nggl), *n.* thin piece of wood used as roof-tile, etc. *v.t.* cover, roof, with shingles; cut (woman's) hair short and tapering from back of head to nape of neck.

shing′le[2] (-nggl), *n.* small rounded pebbles on seashore. **shing′ly,** *a.*

shing′les (-ngglz), *n.* painful virus infection of nerves, with outbreaks of small blisters.

shiny: see **shine.**

ship, *n.* large sea-going vessel. *v.* (p.t. *shipped*), put, take, send away, etc., on ship; embark; lay (oars) inside boat; have (water) coming in over side of vessel. **ship′shape,** in good order. **ship′wreck,** (cause, suffer) sinking or destruction of ship; ruin. **ship′wright,** ship-builder. **ship′yard,** ship-building establishment. **ship′ment,** *n.* putting of goods, etc., on board; goods shipped. **shipp′er,** *n.* exporter or importer. **shipp′ing,** *n.* (esp.) ships (of country, port, etc.).

shire, *n.* county.

shirk, *v.* avoid meanly, evade, (duty, responsibility). **shir′ker,** *n.*

shirr, *v.t.* gather with several parallel threads.

shirt, *n.* man's (or woman's) garment for upper part of body, usu. with long sleeves. *in shirt sleeves,* without coat. **shirt′waister,** woman's dress with bodice like shirt.

shiv′er[1], *v.i.* tremble, quiver, esp. with cold or fear. *n.* quivering or trembing, tremor. **shiv′ery,** *a.*

shiv′er[2], *v.* shatter into small fragments or splinters. *n.* small fragment or splinter.

shoal[1], *n.* large number of fish, etc., swimming together; crowd. *v.i.* form shoals.

shoal[2], *n.* shallow place in water; submerged sand-bank. *v.i.* grow shallow(er).

shock[1], *n.* stook of corn-sheaves.

shock[2], *n.* thick or shaggy mass (of hair).

shock[3], *n.* violent concussion or impact; violent shake or tremor of earth's crust as part of earthquake; sudden and disturbing physical or mental impression; sudden passage of electric current through body; state of prostration following accident, wound, etc. *v.t.* affect with horror or disgust; appear improper or outrageous to; cause to suffer shock. **shock'ing,** *a.* (esp.) scandalous; improper; very bad.

shod, *p.t.* & *p.p.* of **shoe.**

shodd'y, *n.* (cloth of) woollen yarn made from shreds of old fabric. *a.* of poor quality.

shoe (-ōō), *n.* outer covering of leather, etc., for foot; thing like shoe in shape or use; horseshoe. *v.* (p.t. *shod*; pres. p. *shoeing*), fit with shoe(s). **shoe'horn,** curved piece of metal, etc., for easing heel into shoe. **shoe-lace, -string,** cord, etc., for lacing shoe. **shoe'maker,** person who makes shoes and boots. **shoe'making,** *n.* trade of shoemaker. **shoe-tree,** shaped piece of wood, etc., for keeping shoe in shape.

shone, *p.t.* & *p.p.* of **shine.**

shoo, *int.* used to frighten birds, etc., away. *v.* utter shoo; drive *away* thus.

shook, *p.t.* of **shake.**

shoot, *v.* (p.t. *shot*), come or go swiftly or suddenly; discharge or propel (gun, bullet, etc.); wound or kill with missile from gun, etc.; sprout; jut *out* or rise *up* sharply; (Footb., etc.) aim ball at goal; photograph with cine-camera. *n.* bud or young branch, etc.; shooting-party; land where game is shot. **shoot'ing,** *n.* (esp.) right of shooting over estate, etc. **shoo'ting-brake,** estate car. **shooting-gallery,** place for indoor shooting at targets. **shooting star,** meteor. **shooting-stick,** spiked walking-stick convertible into seat.

shop, *n.* building or room for retail sale of goods; workshop or place of manufacture; (talk dealing with) one's profession, business, etc. *v.i.* (p.t. *shopped*), go to shop(s) to make purchases. **shop'keeper,** keeper of retail shop. **shop'lifter,** pretended customer who steals goods from shop. **shop-soiled,** soiled or faded by being shown in shop. **shop-steward,** person elected by fellow workmen as their spokesman. **shop'walker,** attendant in large shop directing customers. **shopp'er,** *n.* person who shops; shopping-bag. **shopp'ing,** *n.* (esp.) goods bought in shop(s).

shore¹, *n.* land that skirts sea or other large body of water.

shore², *n.* beam set obliquely against wall, etc., to support it. *v.t.* prop *up*, support, with shores.

shorn, *p.p.* of **shear.**

short, *a.* not long in space or time; not tall; soon traversed or finished; of less than named amount; failing to reach measure or quality *of*; concise; angrily curt; (of pastry, etc.) crumbling easily. *adv.* abruptly; before reaching the end. *n.* (Cinema) short film; (*informal*) short circuit; (pl.) trousers reaching to point above knee. *v.t.* (*informal*) short-circuit. **short'bread,** kind of rich sweet biscuit. **short circuit,** (esp. accidental) electric circuit through smaller resistance than in normal circuit; anything causing this. **short-circuit,** (*v.*). **short'coming,** failure to reach standard or perform duty; defect. **short commons,** scanty allowance of food. **short'hand,** method of writing enabling writer to keep pace with speaker. **short-handed,** not having full number of workers required. **short sight,** ability to see clearly only objects that are near. **short-sighted,** having short sight; lacking in foresight. **short-tempered,** easily angered. **short-winded,** easily becoming out of breath. **shor'tage,** *n.* (amount of) deficiency. **shor'ten,** *v.* make or become short(er). **short'ly,** *adv.* (esp.) before long; a short time *before* or *after*.

shot¹, *p.t.* & *p.p.* of **shoot.** *a.* (of fabric) woven so that colour changes with position of viewer.

shot², *n.* attempt to hit something by shooting, throwing, or striking, or to attain end or solve question; discharging of gun, etc.; person of specified skill in shooting; small lead pellet(s) in cartridge, etc.; injection of drug, etc.; photograph.

should: see **shall.**

shoul'der (shōl-), *n.* part of body at which arm or foreleg or wing is attached; projection or expansion comparable to human shoulder; (pl.) upper part of back. *v.* push with shoulder, jostle; hoist on to one's shoulders; assume (responsibility, etc.). **shoulder-blade,** either flat bone of back jointed with upper arm-bone. **shoulder-strap,** band over shoulder supporting garment; band on shoulder of uniform, etc.

shout, *n.* loud cry. *v.* utter shout; speak or say loudly, call out.

shove (-uv), *v.* & *n.* push.

sho'vel (shu-), *n.* spade-like scoop for shifting earth, coal, etc. *v.t.* (p.t. *shovelled*), shift with shovel.

show (-ō), *v.* (p.p. *shown*, rarely *showed*), allow or cause to be seen; display, exhibit; offer for inspection; demonstrate, make understand. *show off,* display in favourable way; act or talk for show, display skill, etc., ostentatiously. *show up,* expose (fraud, impostor); appear. *n.* showing; outward appearance; ostentation; display, exhibition; entertainment, spectacle. **show-down,** final test, disclosure of achievements or possibilities. **show'man,** exhibitor or proprietor of show. **show-room,** room in which goods are exhibited for sale.

show'er, *n.* brief fall of rain, hail, etc.; great number of missiles, gifts, questions, etc.; shower-bath. *v.* descend, send, give, in shower; take shower-bath. **shower-bath,** bath in which water is sprayed from above. **show'ery,** *a.* rainy.

show'y (-ŏi), *a.* striking, making good display; tastelessly brilliant. **show'ily,** *adv.*

shrank, *p.t.* of **shrink.**

shrap'nel, *n.* (pieces scattered by) shell scattering bullets, pieces of metal, etc., on explosion.

shred, *n.* small torn, broken, or cut piece; fragment; least amount. *v.* (p.t. *shredded*), cut, tear, fray, etc., to shreds.

shrew (-ōō), *n.* small mouse-like insectivorous mammal with long snout; scolding woman. **shrew'ish,** *a.* ill-tempered.

shrewd (-ōōd), *a.* sagacious, penetrating, astute.

shriek, *v.* & *n.* (utter, make) loud shrill scream.

shrike, *n.* bird with strong curved beak.

shrill, *a.* piercing and high-pitched.

shrimp, *n.* small edible ten-footed marine crustacean. *v.i.* go catching shrimps.

shrine, *n.* tomb or casket holding sacred relics; sacred place.

shrink, *v.* (p.t. *shrank*; p.p. *shrunk*), become or make smaller; (cause to) become smaller when wetted; recoil or flinch (*from*). **shrink'age,** *n.* (amount of) shrinking of textile fabric, etc.

shrive, *v.t.* (p.t. *shrōve*; p.p. *shriven*), (*archaic*) hear confession of and give absolution to.

shriv'el, *v.* (p.t. *shrivelled*), contract into wrinkled, contorted, or dried-up state.

shroud, *n.* garment for corpse, winding-sheet; (pl.) set of ropes supporting mast. *v.t.* clothe for burial; cover or disguise.

shrōve, *p.t.* of **shrive. Shrove Tuesday,** day before Ash Wednesday.

shrub, *n.* woody plant smaller than tree and usu. branching from near ground. **shrubb'ery,** *n.* plantation of shrubs. **shrubb'y,** *a.*

shrug, *v.* (p.t. *shrugged*), draw up shoulders momentarily as gesture of indifference, etc. *n.* shrugging.

shrunk, *p.p.* of **shrink.**

shudd'er, *n.* sudden shivering due to horror, cold, etc. *v.i.* shiver thus.

shuff'le, *v.* move by dragging or scraping feet along ground; manipulate (cards in pack, etc.) so that relative positions are changed; re-arrange, intermingle, confuse; keep shifting one's position; prevaricate. *n.* shuffling; general change of relative positions.

shun, *v.t.* (p.t. *shunned*), avoid, keep away from.

shunt, *v.* move (train, etc.) on to side track or different line.

shut, *v.* (p.t. *shut*), move (door, lid, etc.) into position to stop an opening; bring (one's lips) together; become shut; be able to be shut; fold up (pocket-knife, book, etc.).

shutt'er, *n.* movable screen of wood, iron, etc., inside or outside window; device for opening and closing aperture of camera.

shutt'le, *n.* boat-shaped weaving implement

on which weft-thread is carried backwards and forwards across and through warp-threads. *v.* (cause to) move to and fro.

shutt'lecock (-lk-), *n.* small piece of weighted and feathered cork, etc., struck to and fro with battledore or badminton racket.

shȳ¹, *v.* & *n.* (*informal*) throw, fling.

shȳ², *a.* avoiding observation, timid, bashful, uneasy in company; wary. *v.i.* start aside in alarm (*at*). *n.* shying. **shȳ'ly,** *adv.* **shȳ'ness,** *n.*

Sīamēse' (-z), *a.* of Siam (now Thailand). **Siamese cat,** cream-coloured cat with chocolate markings. **Siamese twins,** twins born joined together.

sib'ilant, *a.* hissing, sounding like hiss. *n.* sibilant speech sound (*s, z, x,* etc.). **sib'-ilance,** *n.*

sib'ling, *n.* any of two or more children having one or both parents in common.

sib'yl, *n.* (in ancient times) woman uttering prophecies and oracles as mouthpiece of god.

sic, spelt or used thus. (Latin)

sick, *a.* vomiting or inclined to vomit; ill, unwell; tired *of.* **sick-bed,** bed of person who is ill. **sick'en,** *v.* begin to be ill; cause to feel nausea or loathing. **sick'ening,** *a.* (esp.) annoying, disgusting.

sick'le, *n.* implement with semicircular blade for reaping, lopping, etc. *a.* sickle-shaped.

sick'ly, *a.* apt to be ill, chronically ailing; causing or suggesting sickness; weakly sentimental.

sick'ness, *n.* being ill; disease; vomiting.

side, *n.* one of more or less flat inner or outer surfaces of object; one of these as distinct from top and bottom, front and back; one of lines bounding geometric figure; either surface of thing regarded as having only two; part of body, part, position, aspect, etc., to right or left; either of two opposing parties; (*slang*) swaggering conduct. *a.* of, on, from, or to, side; oblique, indirect; subordinate, subsidiary. *v.i.* **side with,** support (in dispute, etc.). **side'board,** table or chest against dining-room wall. **side'car,** car for passenger attachable to side of motor cycle. **side'light,** (esp., fig.) incidental light *on* subject, etc. **side'long,** oblique(ly), not direct(ly). **side-road,** minor road; road diverging from main road. **side-saddle,** saddle for rider seated with both legs same side of horse. **sides'-man,** (pl. *-men*), assistant to churchwarden. **side-track,** (esp., fig.) divert from course, purpose, etc. **side'ways** (-z), *adv.* & *a.* to, from, or on, side.

sidēr'eal, *a.* of, measured by, stars.

si'ding, *n.* short track by side of railway for shunting, etc.

si'dle, *v.i.* walk in a shy or nervous manner.

siege, *n.* besieging or being besieged.

sienn'a (si-e-), *n.* brownish-yellow or reddish-brown colouring-matter.

sie'rra (si-e-), *n.* mountain-range with serrated outline (esp. in Spain and S. America).

sies'ta (si-e-), *n.* afternoon rest in hot countries.

sieve (siv), *n.* utensil with meshed or perforated bottom through which liquids or fine particles can pass. *v.t.* put through, sift with, sieve.

sift, *v.* put through, separate or get *out* with, sieve; use sieve; closely examine details of; sprinkle. **sif'ter,** *n.*

sigh (sī), *n.* prolonged audible breath expressive of dejection, longing, relief, etc. *v.* utter, or utter with, sigh; yearn *for.*

sight (sīt), *n.* faculty of seeing; seeing or being seen; range or field of vision; scene or spectacle; appliance attached to gun, etc., for aiming precisely. *at (first) sight,* on first seeing. *v.t.* get sight of. **sight-reading,** reading music at sight. **sight'seer, sight'seeing,** (person) going to see places of special interest. **sight'ed,** *a.* (esp.) not blind. **sight'less,** *a.* blind.

sign (sīn), *n.* significant gesture; mark or device with special meaning, symbol; token, indication, trace (*of*); omen; (board with) name, design, etc., in front of inn, shop, etc. *v.* write one's name or initials on; make sign (*to*). **sign'post,** post at crossroads, etc., indicating direction of place(s).

sig'nal[1], *a.* remarkable, striking.

sig'nal[2], *n.* sign, sound, movement, etc., conveying information or direction, esp. from a distance; message made up of such signs; message sent out by radio, etc. *v.* (p.t. *signalled*), make signal(s) to; transmit, announce, by signal. **sig'nal-box,** cabin on railway from which signals are worked. **sig'nalman,** *n.* (pl. *-men*), one who works railway signals. **sig'naller,** *n.* **sig'nalīze,** *v.t.* distinguish, make remarkable.

sig'natory, *n.* (party) whose signature is on a document, esp. a treaty.

sig'nature (-cher), *n.* person's name in his own handwriting; (Mus.) sign indicating time or key. **signature tune,** tune used to identify performer, broadcast series, etc.

sig'nèt, *n.* small seal, esp. one set in finger-ring (*signet-ring*).

signif'icance, *n.* being significant; meaning; consequence, importance.

signif'icant, *a.* having or conveying a meaning; full of meaning; important.

significā'tion, *n.* (esp.) exact meaning.

sig'nifȳ, *v.* be sign or symbol of; represent, mean, denote; announce; be important, matter.

Sikh (sēk), *n.* member of religious sect founded in N. India in 16th century.

sī'lage, *n.* preservation of green crops in silo; crops preserved thus.

sī'lence, *n.* being silent; abstinence from speech or noise; absence of sound. *v.t.* reduce to silence; repress.

sī'lent, *a.* not speaking; not uttering, making,

or accompanied by, sound; (of letter) not pronounced; speaking little.

silhouette' (-loo-), *n.* portrait in profile, esp. in solid black on white; dark outline, shadow, of object seen against light.

sil'ica, *n.* silicon dioxide, a hard mineral occurring as quartz and sand, etc.

sil'icon, *n.* non-metallic element occurring only in combination. **sil'icōne,** *n.* any of group of silicon compounds used in polishes, lubricants, etc.

silk, *n.* strong soft lustrous fibre produced by silkworms; thread or textile fabric made from this; (*attrib.*) made of silk. **silk'worm,** mulberry-feeding moth caterpillar spinning cocoon of silk. **sil'ken,** *a.* made of silk; soft or lustrous as silk. **sil'ky,** *a.* like silk.

sill, *n.* shelf or slab of wood or stone at base of window or door.

sill'y, *a.* foolish, thoughtless; weak of intellect. *n.* (*informal*) silly person. **sill'iness,** *n.*

sī'lō, *n.* (pl. *silos*), pit or tall airtight structure for preserving green crops (*silage*) for animals in winter.

silt, *n.* sediment of fine soil left by moving water. *v.* choke, be choked, (*up*) with silt.

silvan: see **sylvan.**

sil'ver, *n.* white shining precious metal; coins made of it or a substitute; vessels or implements made of it. *a.* of silver; silvery. *v.t.* coat or plate with silver. **silver-gilt,** of silver gilded over. **silver paper,** tinfoil. **sil'versmith,** smith working in silver. **silver wedding,** 25th wedding anniversary. **sil'very,** *a.* like silver in whiteness and lustre; having clear soft ringing sound.

sim'ian, *a.* & *n.* (of) ape, esp. anthropoid ape; ape(-like), monkey(-like).

sim'ilar, *a.* like, having resemblance (*to*); of same kind; (Geom.) having same shape. **sim'ilarly,** *adv.* **simila'rity,** *n.*

sim'ilė, *n.* comparison made by writer or speaker as illustration or ornament (e.g. *he is as strong as a horse*).

simil'itūde, *n.* likeness; outward appearance; comparison.

simm'er, *v.* be or keep just below boiling-point. *n.* simmering state.

sī'mony, *n.* offence of offering or accepting money for ecclesiastical appointment.

sim'per, *v.* smile in silly affected way. *n.* affected and self-conscious smile.

sim'ple, *a.* not compound or complex; not complicated or elaborate or adorned; artless, natural; humble; foolish, half-witted; easily solved or understood or done; (of interest) reckoned on principal only.

sim'pleton (-plt-), *n.* foolish, half-witted, or gullible person.

simpli'city, *n.* being simple.

sim'plifȳ, *v.t.* make simple, make easy to do or understand. **simplificā'tion,** *n.*

sim'ūlāte, *v.t.* pretend to be; pretend to have or feel. **simūlā'tion,** *n.*

simultă′neous, *a.* existing, occurring, operating, at same time (*with*). **simultanĕ′ity**, *n.*

sin[1], *n.* breaking of commandments of God; offence against morality, good taste, etc. *v.i.* (p.t. *sinned*), commit sin; offend *against*.

sin[2], *abbrev.* sine.

since, *prep.* from (specified time) till now, within period between (specified past time) and now. *conj.* from time that; seeing that, because. *adv.* from that time till now; later; before now.

sincēre′, *a.* without pretence or deceit, genuine; honest, frank. **sincēre′ly**, *adv.* yours sincerely, polite way of ending letter. **since′rity**, *n.*

sīne, *n.* (Trig., abbrev. *sin*) (of angle) ratio between hypotenuse of right-angled triangle and side opposite angle concerned.

sin′ěcūre (*or* sī-), *n.* office of honour or with payment, without duties attached.

sin′ew, *n.* (piece of) tough fibrous animal tissue uniting muscle to bone; (pl.) muscles, strength. **sin′ewy**, *a.*

sin′ful, *a.* guilty of sin; wicked.

sing, *v.* (p.t. *sang*; p.p. *sung*), utter words or sounds in tuneful succession, esp. in set tune; produce vocal melody; make humming, etc., sounds; celebrate in verse. **sing′er**, *n.*

singe (-nj), *v.* (pres. p. *singeing*), burn superficially or slightly, burn ends or edges (of); undergo singeing. *n.* superficial burn.

sing′le (singgl), *a.* one only; individual; of or for one person or thing; solitary, unaided; unmarried; (of journey, etc.) not return; (of game) with one person on each side. **single file**, line of persons, etc., going one behind another. **single-handed**, unaided. **single-minded**, keeping one purpose in view.

sing′lĕt (-ngg-), *n.* undershirt, vest.

sing′song, *n. & a.* (in, recited with) monotonous rhythm or cadence; impromptu vocal concert.

sing′ūlar (-ngg-), *a.* extraordinary, uncommon, surprising; strange, peculiar; (Gram.) denoting or expressing one person or thing. *n.* (Gram.) singular form, singular word. **singūla′rity**, *n.* (esp.) eccentricity, peculiarity.

sin′ister, *a.* of evil omen; harmful; wicked, corrupt, evil; villainous.

sink, *v.* (p.t. *sank*; p.p. *sunk*), become wholly or partly submerged in water, etc.; fall or move slowly downwards; pass out of sight or below horizon; decline, subside; gradually lose strength, etc.; send below surface of liquid or ground; make (well, etc.) by excavating; send (ship, etc.) to bottom; ruin, finish. *n.* large fixed receptacle with outflow pipe and water supply.

sinn′er, *n.* sinful person.

sin′ūous, *a.* with many curves; tortuous, undulating.

sī′nus, *n.* cavity, esp. one of cavities in bone of skull communicating with nostrils. **sinus-ī′tis**, *n.* inflammation of sinus.

sip, *v.* (p.t. *sipped*), drink by small mouthfuls. *n.* one such mouthful.

sī′phon, *n.* bent tube for drawing off liquids by atmospheric pressure; bottle with inserted tube through which soda-water is forced by pressure of gas.

sir, *n.* title of honour (*Sir*) placed before name of knight or baronet; used (without name) in addressing man, esp. superior in rank, age, etc.

sīre, *n.* father or male ancestor; male parent of beast, (esp.) stallion; (*archaic*) title of address to king, etc. *v.t.* beget.

sīr′en, *n.* (Gk. myth., pl.) fabulous creatures living on rocky isle and luring seafarers by their singing; dangerously fascinating woman; apparatus producing loud wailing sound, used as warning or signal.

Si′rius, *n.* brightest star in sky, dog-star.

sir′loin, *n.* best part of loin of beef.

sirocc′o, *n.* (pl. *siroccos*), hot moist oppressive wind reaching Italy from Africa.

si′rrah, *n.* (*archaic*, contempt.) sir.

si′sal, *n.* (plant yielding) strong white fibre used for ropes, etc.

sis′ter, *n.* daughter of same parents as another person; member of religious sisterhood, nun; hospital nurse in authority over others. **sister-in-law**, one's husband's or wife's sister; one's brother's wife. **sis′terhood**, *n.* (esp.) society of women bound by monastic vows or devoting themselves to charitable work. **sis′terly**, *a.*

sit, *v.* (p.t. *sat*), take, be in, position in which weight of body rests on the buttocks; occupy seat as judge, member of legislative assembly, etc.; take examination; (of assembly) hold session; (of bird) remain on nest to hatch eggs. **sitt′ing**, *n.* (esp.) time during which assembly, etc., sits. **sitting-room**, room used for sitting in. **sitt′ing**, *a.* (esp.) holding office, position, etc.; in possession or occupancy.

sit′ar (*or* -ar′), *n.* plucked stringed instrument with long neck, used in Indian music.

sīte, *n.* ground on which town, building, etc., stands, stood, or is to stand. *v.t.* locate, place, provide with site.

sit′ūāted, *a.* in specified situation.

situā′tion, *n.* place, with its surroundings, occupied by something; set of circumstances, position of affairs, critical point or complication; position, esp. as domestic servant.

six, *a. & n.* one more than five (6, VI). **six′-pence**, (silver or cupro-nickel coin worth) 6d. or 2½p.

sixteen′, *a. & n.* one more than fifteen (16, XVI). **sixteenth′**, *a. & n.*

sixth, *a.* next after fifth. *n.* sixth part; sixth form. **sixth form**, highest form in secondary school.

six′ty, *a. & n.* six times ten (60, LX). **six′-tieth**, *a. & n.*

sīze[1], *n.* dimensions, degree of largeness or

smallness; one of, usu. numbered, classes into which things are divided by size. *v.t.* group or sort in sizes or by size.

size², *n.* glutinous substance used for glazing paper, stiffening textiles, etc. *v.t.* treat with size.

size'able (-zabl), *a.* of fairly large size.

sizz'le, *n.* & *v.i.* (make) spluttering or hissing noise, esp. in cooking.

skāte¹, *n.* large edible flat-fish.

skāte², *n.* one of pair of steel blades attached beneath boots and enabling wearer to glide over ice; roller-skate. *v.i.* move, glide, on skates; pass lightly *over*.

skein (-ān), *n.* quantity of yarn, etc., coiled and usu. loosely twisted; flight of wild geese, etc.

skel'éton, *n.* hard framework of bones, shell, woody fibre, etc., supporting or containing animal or vegetable body; dried bones of body fastened together in same relative positions as in life; (mere) outlines, elements, etc., *of.* **skel'étal**, *a.*

sketch, *n.* preliminary, rough, or merely outlined drawing or painting; brief account or narrative, general outline; short play, usu. of single scene. *v.* make or give sketch of; make sketches. **sketch'y**, *a.* resembling sketch, hurried, rough.

skew, *a.* turned to one side, slanting; not straight.

skew'bald (-awld), *a.* & *n.* (horse, etc.) having irregular patches of white and some colour.

skew'er, *n.* pin of wood or metal for holding meat together, etc. *v.t.* pierce with skewer.

ski (skē, shē), *n.* one of pair of long slender pieces of wood, etc., strapped to feet for gliding over snow. *v.i.* go on skis. **ski'er**, *n.* **ski'ing**, *n.*

skid, *n.* act of skidding; braking-device placed under wheel of vehicle; runner as part of landing-gear of aircraft. *v.i.* (p.t. *skidded*), (of wheel, etc.) slide without revolving; (of vehicle, etc.) slide sideways.

skiff, *n.* small light (esp. rowing-)boat.

skil'ful, *a.* having or showing skill, expert.

skill, *n.* ability gained by practice; craft, art, etc., requiring skill. **skilled** (-ld), *a.* properly trained or experienced; requiring skill.

skim, *v.* (p.t. *skimmed*), take scum, cream, etc., from surface of liquid; glide or pass over lightly; read superficially, glance over. **skim milk**, milk with cream removed.

skimp, *v.* supply meagrely, use too little of; be parsimonious. **skim'py**, *a.* meagre, inadequate, too small or tight.

skin, *n.* tough flexible natural outer covering of animal body; peel or rind; hide of skinned animal; complexion. *v.t.* (p.t. *skinned*), strip the skin from; peel. **skin-deep**, not deep or lasting. **skin-diving**, underwater sport for which swimmer wears mask and flippers and uses aqualung. **skin'flint**, niggard, miser.

skinn'y, *a.* lean, thin.

skip¹, *v.* (p.t. *skipped*), jump about lightly, caper; spring or leap over rope revolved over head and under feet; omit parts in reading, etc. *n.* skipping movement.

skip², *n.* captain of side at bowls or curling.

skip³, *n.* cage, etc., in which men or materials are lowered or raised in mines, etc.

skipp'er, *n.* captain of ship, aircraft, etc.

skirl, *n.* & *v.i.* (make) sound of bagpipes.

skir'mish, *n.* & *v.i.* (engage in) irregular or unimportant fighting or contest.

skirt, *n.* woman's garment hanging from waist, or this part of dress, coat, etc.; border or outlying part. *v.* go or lie along or round edge or border of. **skirting-board**, narrow board along bottom of wall of room.

skit, *n.* light piece of satire, burlesque.

skitt'ish, *a.* playful; frivolous; lively.

skitt'le, *n.* one of wooden pins set up to be knocked down with bowls in game of *skittles*.

skulk, *v.i.* lurk, conceal oneself, move stealthily, esp. in cowardly or sinister way.

skull, *n.* bony case of brain; bony framework of head. *skull and crossbones*, figure of skull and two thigh-bones crossed, as emblem of death. **skull-cap**, brimless cap for top of head.

skunk, *n.* N. Amer. black-and-white mammal sending out offensive smell when attacked.

skȳ, *n.* apparent arch or vault formed by region of atmosphere overhead. *v.t.* hit (ball) high into air. **sky-blue**, colour of clear summer sky. **sky'lark**, common lark, soaring towards sky while singing. **sky'light**, window in roof or ceiling. **sky'scraper**, very high building of many storeys.

slab, *n.* flat broad thickish piece of solid material.

slack, *a.* lazy, remiss; sluggish; not busy; relaxed; loose. *n.* slack part of rope; small coal; (pl.) trousers for casual wear. *v.* be idle or remiss or careless; fall off in vigour, speed, etc. **slack'en**, *v.* make or become slack. **slack'er**, *n.* shirker; idler.

slag, *n.* refuse separated from metal in smelting; clinkers.

slain, *p.p.* of **slay**.

slāke, *v.t.* quench, allay, (thirst); cause (lime) to heat and crumble by action of water.

slam¹, *v.* (p.t. *slammed*), shut, throw or put *down* violently, with bang. *n.* sound (as) of slammed door.

slam², *n.* winning of all tricks (*grand slam*) or all but one (*little slam*) at bridge, etc.

sla'nder (-ah-), *n.* false report uttered to damage person's character. *v.t.* utter slander about, defame falsely. **sla'nderous**, *a.*

slang, *n.* words or meanings of words in common colloquial use but not regarded as standard English; special language of some class or profession. *v.t.* (*slang*) use abusive language to. **slang'y**, *a.*

slant (-ah-), *v.* be or put in sloping or oblique position. *n.* slope.

slap, *v.t.* (p.t. *slapped*), hit with palm of hand; smack. *n.* smart blow, esp. with palm of hand or something flat. **slap'dash,** (*a.*) careless, happy-go-lucky; (*adv.*) in slapdash manner. **slap'stick,** (of) boisterous type of comedy.

slash, *v.* cut with sweep of sharp weapon or implement; make gashes in, slit; lash with whip; reduce (prices) drastically. *n.* (wound or slit made by) slashing cut.

slat, *n.* long narrow strip of wood.

slāte, *n.* fine-grained rock easily split into thin smooth plates; trimmed plate of this used esp. in roofing or for writing on. *v.t.* roof with slates; scold. **slā'ty,** *a.*

slatt'ern, *n.* untidy or slovenly woman. **slatt'ernly,** *a.*

slaught'er (-awt-), *n.* killing of animal(s) for food; slaying, esp. of many persons or animals at once. *v.t.* kill ruthlessly or in great numbers. **slaughter-house,** place for killing animals for food. **slaught'erous,** *a.*

Slav (-ahv), *a.* & *n.* (member) of any of the peoples of East and Central Europe speaking a Slavonic language.

slāve, *n.* person who is the property of another; human chattel; helpless victim *to* or *of* some influence; devoted servant; drudge. **slave-driver,** overseer of slaves at work; hard taskmaster. **slave trade,** traffic in slaves, esp. former transportation of African Negroes to America. **slā'ver¹,** *n.* (Hist.) ship or person engaged in slave trade. **slā'very,** *n.* condition of slave; slave-holding; drudgery.

sla'ver², *v.i.* let saliva run from mouth, dribble. *n.* saliva running from mouth.

slā'vish, *a.* servile; servilely imitative.

Slavon'ic, *a.* & *n.* (language) of the Slavs. *Slavonic languages,* group of languages including Russian, Polish, Czech, etc.

slay, *v.t.* (p.t. *slew*, pr. -ōō; p.p. *slain*), kill.

sled, *n.* sledge.

sledge¹, *n.* vehicle on runners instead of wheels, for use esp. on snow. *v.i.* go, travel, in sledge.

sledge², sledge'-hammer, *nn.* large heavy hammer usu. wielded with both hands.

sleek, *a.* soft, smooth, and glossy; of well-fed appearance. *v.t.* make sleek.

sleep, *n.* condition in which eyes are closed and nervous system is inactive; spell of this. *v.i.* (p.t. *slept*), be or fall asleep; be dormant or inactive. **sleeping-car,** railway coach with berths or beds. **sleep-walker,** somnambulist. **slee'per,** *n.* sleeping person; one of wooden, etc., beams on which rails rest; sleeping-car. **sleep'less,** *a.* unable to sleep. **sleep'lessness,** *n.* **slee'py,** *a.* feeling need of sleep, drowsy; without stir or bustle.

sleet, *n.* snow falling in half-melted state. **slee'ty,** *a.*

sleeve, *n.* part of garment covering arm; tube fitting over rod, spindle, etc.; cover for gramophone record. **sleeved,** *a.* **sleeve'less,** *a.*

sleigh (slā), *n.* sledge, esp. as passenger-vehicle drawn by horse(s).

sleight (slīt), *n.* **sleight-of-hand,** trick(s) displaying great dexterity, conjuring; clever deception.

slen'der, *a.* of small girth or breadth; slim, scanty, slight, meagre.

slept, *p.t.* & *p.p.* of **sleep.**

sleuth (slōō-), *n.* sleuth-hound; detective. *v.i.* play the detective. **sleuth-hound,** bloodhound.

slew¹, slue (slōō), *v.* turn or swing round on axis.

slew², *p.t.* of **slay.**

slīce, *n.* thin broad piece cut from esp. meat, bread, or cake; portion, share; slicing cut or motion; cook's utensil with wide flat blade. *v.* cut into slices, cut *off.*

slick, *a.* sleek; adroit; smooth, plausible. *n.* patch or film of oil on water.

slide, *v.* (p.t. *slid*), progress smoothly over surface; glide over ice without skates; (cause to) go smoothly or imperceptibly. *n.* sliding; track, etc., for people, goods, part of machine, etc., to slide on; slip of glass, etc., with object for microscope or picture for projector.

slight (-īt), *a.* slender, slim; not good or substantial; scanty; unimportant. *v.t.* treat with indifference or discourtesy, disdain, ignore. *n.* instance of slighting or being slighted. **slight'ly,** *adv.* in (only) slight degree, etc.

slim, *a.* slender; not stout or thickset. *v.* (p.t. *slimmed*), make or become slim, esp. by dieting.

slime, *n.* soft sticky semi-fluid substance. **sli'my,** *a.* of, like, covered with, slime; disgusting; repulsively meek or flattering.

sling, *n.* band, etc., passed round object to support or suspend it; strap, etc., for hurling stones. *v.t.* (p.t. *slung*), throw, hurl; hang or suspend.

slink, *v.i.* (p.t. *slunk*), go stealthily or with sneaking air.

slip¹, *n.* cutting from a plant; slim girl or boy; (narrow) piece (*of* paper, etc.).

slip², *v.* (p.t. *slipped*), slide momentarily by accident; lose footing or balance thus; make casual mistake; go unobserved or quietly; (make) go easily; cease to check or hold; escape from. *n.* act of slipping; accidental or casual mistake, etc.; inclined plane on which ships are built or repaired; petticoat; pillow-case. **slip'stream,** current of air driven astern by propulsion unit of aircraft. **slip'way,** slip from which ships are launched.

slipp'er, *n.* light comfortable indoor shoe.

slipp'ery, *a.* with smooth, oily, or icy surface, making foothold insecure or object difficult to grasp or hold; elusive, shifty.

slip'shod, *a.* slovenly, careless, unsystematic.

slit, v. (p.t. *slit*), cut or tear lengthwise; make slit in; cut in strips. *n.* long cut; long narrow opening.

slith′er (-dh-), v.i. slide unsteadily.

sliv′er, n. splinter of wood; small narrow slice or piece.

slobb′er, v.i. & n. slaver.

slōe, n. (small bluish-black fruit of) black-thorn.

slog, v. (p.t. *slogged*), hit hard and (usu.) wildly; work or walk doggedly.

slō′gan, n. short catchy phrase used by adver-tiser, political group, etc.; rallying-cry, war--cry.

slōōp, n. small one-masted sailing-ship.

slop, v. (p.t. *slopped*), spill; (allow to) flow over edge of vessel; splash. *n.* (pl.) dirty or waste water of kitchen, etc.; (pl.) liquid or semi-liquid food. **slopp′y**, a. wet; careless; excessively sentimental.

slōpe, n. stretch of rising or falling ground; inclined surface or way; deviation from hori-zontal or perpendicular, inclination. *v.* have or show slope; slant.

slot[1], n. groove, slit, etc., provided in machine, etc., to receive other part, coin, etc. v.t. (p.t. *slotted*), provide with slot(s). **slot machine**, machine, esp. automatic retailer of small wares, operated by coin placed in slot.

slot[2], n. track of deer, etc.

slōth, n. laziness, indolence; slow-moving arboreal mammal of tropical America. **slōth′ful**, a. lazy, indolent.

slouch, n. ungainly or stooping carriage of body. *v.* move, walk, or sit, with slouch; droop. **slouch hat**, soft hat with flexible brim.

slough[1] (-ow), n. swamp; miry place.

slough[2] (sluf), n. skin periodically cast by snake, etc. *v.* drop off as, cast, slough.

slo′ven (slu-), n. person who has careless, untidy, or dirty habits. **slo′venly**, a. untidy, careless.

slow (-ō), a. not quick; taking long time to do, traverse, etc.; dull-witted; tedious; gradual; (of clock, etc.) behind correct time. *adv.* slowly. *v.* (usu with *up* or *down*) (cause to) reduce speed (of). **slow′ly**, adv.

slow-worm (slō′werm), n. small legless lizard.

sludge, n. thick greasy mud; sewage; sedi-ment.

slue: see **slew**[1].

slug, n. slimy shell-less mollusc.

slugg′ard, n. lazy sluggish person. **slugg′ish**, a. inactive, slow-moving.

sluice (-ōōs), n. (sliding gate in) dam, etc., with contrivance for controlling volume or flow of water; water-channel. *v.* flood or scour with flow of water.

slum, n. dirty squalid overcrowded district, street, etc.

slum′ber, n. & v.i. sleep. **slum′b(e)rous**, a.

slump, n. heavy, sudden, or continued fall in prices, demand, etc. v.i. undergo slump; flop down heavily and slackly.

slung, p.t. & p.p. of **sling**.

slunk, p.t. & p.p. of **slink**.

slur, v. (p.t. *slurred*), pronounce indistinctly, with sounds running into one another; pass *over* lightly; (Mus.) join (notes) smoothly. *n.* discredit, slight; (Mus.) curved lines over or under notes to be slurred.

slush, n. thawing snow; mud; silly sentiment. **slush′y**, a.

slut, n. slovenly woman. **slutt′ish**, a.

slȳ, a. skilful in deceit, wily; secretive; under-hand; knowing, insinuating.

smack[1], n. flavour; trace, suggestion, *of.* v.i. taste *of*; suggest presence *of*.

smack[2], n. small single-masted sailing-vessel, used esp. for fishing.

smack[3], n. sharp slight sound as of slap; slap, loud kiss. *v.* strike with palm or something flat; part lips noisily.

small (-awl), a. not large; comparatively little in size, importance, number, etc.; petty, mean, paltry. *n. the* small or narrow part (esp. *of* back). *adv.* into small pieces, on small scale, etc. **small-holding**, agricultural holding smaller than farm. **small′pox**, acute contagious disease with skin eruption and subsequent scarring.

smar′my, a. fulsomely flattering, toadying.

smart, a. of fresh or well-dressed or fashion-able appearance; severe, sharp; brisk; clever, ingenious. *n.* stinging pain. v.i. feel, be felt as, stinging pain. **smar′ten**, v. make or become smart; brighten *up*.

smash, v. break to pieces; bring or come to disaster; defeat utterly; bring or drive violently *down, into*, etc. *n.* (sound of) breaking to pieces; collision; sudden disas-ter. *adv.* with a smash.

smatt′ering, n. slight knowledge *of*.

smear, v. daub, stain, (with grease, ink, etc.); blur, smudge; discredit publicly. *n.* (mark, stain made by) smearing. **smear′y**, a.

smell, n. sense by which odours are perceived and of which the nose is the organ; property perceived by this; smelling, sniff; bad odour, stench. *v.* (p.t. *smelt*), perceive or detect by smell; have or emit smell; stink. **smelling--salts**, sharp-smelling substance sniffed as cure for faintness, etc.

smelt[1], p.t. of **smell**.

smelt[2], v.t. fuse or melt (ore) to extract metal; obtain (metal) thus.

smelt[3], n. small edible fish.

smile, v. express pleasure, amusement, etc., with parting of lips, upward curving of cor-ners of mouth, etc.; look pleasant, have bright or propitious aspect. *n.* (act of) smi-ling.

smirch, v.t. & n. stain, smear.

smirk, n. affected, self-satisfied, or silly smile. v.i. smile thus.

smite, v. (p.t. *smōte*; p.p. *smitten*), strike, hit; afflict.

smith, n. worker in iron or other metal. **smith'y** (-dh-), n. blacksmith's workshop, forge.

smithereens' (-dh-;-z), n.pl. (*informal*) small fragments.

smitten, p.p. of **smite**.

smock, n. loose-fitting long-sleeved garment, often with gathered or smocked upper part. v.t. adorn with gathers worked in honeycomb design.

smog, n. dense smoky fog.

smōke, n. visible gas-like product given off by burning substance; act of smoking tobacco. v. emit smoke or visible vapour; stain, dim, preserve, drive *out*, etc., with smoke. **smoke-stack,** chimney or funnel. **smō'ker,** n. (esp.) one who smokes tobacco. **smō'ky,** a.

smōōth (-dh), a. of even surface; free from projections, roughness, or difficulties; not harsh; pliable. v. make or become smooth.

smote, p.t. & p.p. of **smite**.

smoth'er (-udh-), v.t. cause death of by stopping breath of; cover entirely; suppress. n. dense or suffocating smoke, dust, etc.

smoul'der (smōl-), v.i. burn and smoke without flame.

smudge, n. dirty mark, blur, smear. v. make smudge; smear, blur; become blurred or smeared. **smudg'y,** a.

smug, a. consciously virtuous, respectable, etc.; self-satisfied.

smugg'le, v. convey goods secretly, esp. to evade payment of customs duties. **smugg'-ler,** n.

smut, n. (black mark made by) flake of soot; indecent talk; disease of cereals and other plants. v.t. (p.t. *smutted*), mark with smut(s); infect with smut. **smutt'y,** a.

snack, n. light hasty meal. **snack-bar,** counter where sandwiches, etc., may be obtained.

snaff'le, n. simple jointed bridle-bit.

snag, n. sharp projecting point, stump, etc.; (unexpected) drawback.

snail, n. aquatic or terrestrial mollusc with shell capable of covering whole body.

snāke, n. scaly limbless, often poisonous, reptile; treacherous person. **snā'ky,** a.

snap, v. (p.t. *snapped*), make quick or sudden bite; speak with sudden irritation; break sharply; produce from or emit sudden sharp sound; take snapshot (of). n. act, fact, sound, of snapping; brief spell of cold or frost; simple card-game. **snap'dragon,** plant with flowers that can be made to gape. **snap-fastener,** press-stud. **snap'shot,** rapidly taken photograph. **snapp'ish,** a. peevish, malicious. **snapp'y,** snappish; quick, lively.

snāre, n. trap, esp. of running-noose kind. v.t. catch with snare.

snarl, v. (of dog, etc.) bare teeth and make

angry sound; (of person) speak, say, ill-temperedly. n. act or sound of snarling.

snatch, v. seize, catch *at*, quickly or eagerly. n. hasty or sudden grab.

sneak, v.i. go furtively; (*slang*) tell tales. n. mean underhand person; tell-tale.

sneer, v. (usu. with *at*) smile scornfully; utter scornful words. n. sneering smile or remark.

sneeze, n. sudden involuntary noisy breathing-out through nose. v.i. make sneeze.

snick, v.t. make slight notch or cut in. n. slight notch or cut.

snick'er, v.i. & n. neigh, whinny.

snide, a. (*slang*) slyly scornful; counterfeit, bogus.

sniff, v. draw up air audibly through nose; draw (*up*) (air, scent, etc.) into nose. n. act or sound of sniffing.

snigg'er (-g-), n. & v.i. (utter) half-suppressed secretive laugh.

snip, v. (p.t. *snipped*), cut with scissors, etc., esp. in small strokes. n. act of snipping; piece snipped off.

snipe, n. marsh game-bird with long straight bill. v. shoot snipe; shoot (*at*) person(s) from hiding-place. **sni'per,** n.

snipp'et, n. small piece cut off; scrap.

sniv'el, v.i. (p.t. *snivelled*), snuffle; weep or pretend to weep weakly.

snob, n. person who admires and seeks to associate with those of superior social position, intellect, etc., disdaining those he considers inferior. **snobb'ery,** n. **snobb'ish,** a.

snōōd, n. band or net for woman's hair.

snōōze, v.i. & n. (take) nap.

snore, n. & v. (make) harsh or noisy respiration through mouth (and nose) during sleep.

snor'kel, n. (also *snorkel-tube*) breathing-tube used for swimming with face down in water on or near surface.

snort, n. loud sound made by driving breath violently out through nose. v. make snorting sound; utter with snort(s).

snout, n. projecting part, including nose and mouth, of animal's head; nozzle.

snow (-ō), n. frozen atmospheric vapour falling to earth in light white flakes (*snow-flakes*). v. let fall as or like snow, shower down. *it is snowing,* snow is falling. *snow under,* submerge, overwhelm. *snowed up,* blocked, imprisoned, by fallen snow. **snow'ball,** snow pressed into hard ball; anything growing or increasing rapidly. **snow'-drift,** snow piled up by wind. **snow'drop,** early-flowering bulbous plant. **snow-line,** level above which snow lies all year round. **snow-plough,** device for clearing snow from road, railway-line, etc. **snow-shoe,** one of pair of strung frames attachable to feet for walking on snow. **snow-white,** pure white. **snow'y,** a.

snub¹, v.t. (p.t. *snubbed*), check, humiliate, in sharp or cold manner. n. snubbing, rebuff.

snub², a. (of nose) short and turned up.

snuff[1], *v.t.* put out, trim wick of, candle.

snuff[2], *n.* powdered tobacco for sniffing up into nostrils.

snuff'le, *v.i.* sniff, esp. audibly or noisily; speak like person with a cold. *n.* sniff; snuffling sound or speech.

snug, *a.* sheltered, cosy; comfortable; neat.

snugg'le, *v.* move or lie close *up to* for warmth, etc.; hug, cuddle.

sō, *adv. & conj.* to the extent, in the manner, with the result, described or indicated; of the kind, in the condition, indicated; by that name or designation; for that reason, consequently, accordingly; indeed, in fact, also.

soak, *v.* place, leave, lie, in liquid for saturation; make or be saturated; take *up,* suck *in,* (liquid). *n.* soaking.

soap, *n.* substance consisting of fat or oil combined with alkali, used in washing. *v.* rub, smear, lather, etc., with soap. soap'suds, froth of soapy water. soap'y, *a.*

soar (sor), *v.i.* mount to, or fly at, a great height; hover in air without flapping of wings or without motor power.

sob, *n.* convulsive drawing-in of breath, esp. in weeping. *v.* (p.t. *sobbed*), weep, breathe, or speak with sobs.

sō'ber, *a.* not drunk; moderate; serious; quiet. *v.* make or become sober. sobrī'ĕty, *n.*

sob'riquet (-kā), sou'briquet (sōō-), *n.* nickname.

socc'er (-k-), *n.* (*informal*) Association football.

sō'ciable (-sha-), *a.* fitted or inclined for companionship or conversation; friendly, showing friendship. sōciabil'ity, *n.*

sō'cial (-shl), *a.* living in communities; concerned with society, mutual relationships, or welfare of people; of society. *n.* social gathering or party. social security, provision by the State out of taxation, etc., for the adequate economic and social welfare of all members of the community.

sō'cialism (-sha-), *n.* principle that community as a whole should have ownership and control of all means of production and distribution; policy aiming at this. sō'cialist, *n.*

soci'ĕty, *n.* state of living in association with other individuals; (customs and organization of) social community; upper classes, people of fashion; company or companionship; association, club.

sōciol'ogy, *n.* scientific study of human, esp. civilized, society. sōciol'ogist, *n.*

sock[1], *n.* short stocking not reaching knee; removable inner shoe-sole.

sock[2], *n.* (*slang*) hard blow. *v.t.* hit hard.

sock'ĕt, *n.* hollow part for thing to fit into, etc.; cavity holding eye, tooth, etc.

sod, *n.* (piece of) turf.

sō'da, *n.* sodium carbonate or bicarbonate; soda-water. soda-water, water made effervescent by being charged under pressure with carbon dioxide.

sodd'en, *a.* saturated with moisture.

sō'dium, *n.* soft silver-white metallic element. sodium bicarbonate, see bicarbonate. sodium carbonate, washing-soda. sodium chloride, common salt.

sō'fa, *n.* long upholstered seat with raised end(s) and back.

soft, *a.* not hard; yielding to pressure; of yielding texture, smooth to feel; mild; not loud; gentle, quiet; easily touched, compassionate; easy; feeble, silly; (of water) not hard; (of drink) non-alcoholic; (of letters *c, g*) pronounced *s, j. adv.* softly. soften (so'-fn), *v.* make or become soft(er). soft'ly, *adv.*

sogg'y (-g-), *a.* sodden; swampy.

soil[1], *v.* smear or stain with dirt, etc.; sully, defile; become (easily) soiled. *n.* dirty mark; refuse, sewage.

soil[2], *n.* ground, upper layer of earth in which plants grow.

soirée (swah'rā), *n.* evening party.

soj'ourn (-ern), *n. & v.i.* (make) temporary stay. soj'ourner, *n.*

sol'ace, *n. & v.t.* comfort in distress or disappointment.

sō'lar, *a.* of or reckoned by the sun. solar plexus, complex of nerves in abdomen behind stomach. solar system, sun with planets, etc., revolving round it.

sold, *p.t. & p.p.* of sell.

sōl'der (*or* sol-), *n.* fusible metal or alloy used for joining metal surfaces or parts. *v.t.* join with solder. soldering iron, tool used for soldering.

sōl'dier (-jer), *n.* member of army, esp. private or non-commissioned officer. *v.i.* serve as soldier. sōl'dierly, *a.* sōl'diery, *n.* soldiers of a State, in a district, etc.

sōle[1], *n.* edible flat-fish.

sōle[2], *n.* under-surface of foot (often excluding heel), part of shoe or stocking below this. *v.t.* provide with (new) sole.

sōle[3], *a.* only; exclusive. sōle'ly, *adv.*

sol'ecism, *n.* error of grammar or syntax; offence against good manners or etiquette.

sol'emn (-m), *a.* accompanied or performed with ceremony; serious; impressive. solem'nity, *n.* sol'emnize, *v.t.* celebrate (festival); perform (esp. marriage ceremony). solemnizā'tion, *n.*

sol-fa: see tonic sol-fa.

soli'cit, *v.t.* ask repeatedly and urgently; request, invite (vote, custom, etc.).

soli'citor, *n.* lawyer qualified to advise clients, brief barristers, etc.

soli'citous, *a.* anxious, concerned; extremely careful or attentive. soli'citūde, *n.* being solicitous; anxiety, concern.

sol'id, *a.* of stable shape, not liquid or fluid; rigid, hard and compact; of three dimensions; without cavities, spaces, etc., not hollow; alike all through; substantial, real. *n.* solid substance or body; body or magnitude of three dimensions. solid'ity, *n.* solid'ifỹ, *v.*

solida'rity, n. unity resulting from common interests, sympathies, etc.

solil'oquy, n. (pl. *soliloquies*), (instance of) speaking one's thoughts aloud without addressing any person. **solil'oquize,** v. i.

solitaire' (*or* sol'-), n. diamond, etc., set by itself; game for one person, with marbles or pegs on a board.

sol'itary, a. alone, living alone; without companions; single; secluded, lonely. **sol'itūde,** n. being solitary; secluded or lonely place.

sō'lō, n. (pl. *solos*), music, dance, etc., performed by single player, singer, dancer, etc. a. & adv. alone, without companion or partner. **sō'lōist,** n.

sol'stice, n. time, point in ecliptic, at which sun is farthest N. or S. of equator (*summer solstice,* about 22 June; *winter solstice,* about 22 December).

sol'ūble, a. that can be dissolved; that can be solved. **solūbil'ity,** n.

solu'tion (-lōō-), n. solving or being solved; answer, explanation; dissolving or being dissolved; fluid substance produced by dissolving.

solve, v. t. find answer to (problem, etc.).

sol'vency, n. being financially solvent. **sol'vent,** a. able to pay all debts; that dissolves or can dissolve. n. liquid capable of or used for dissolving something.

som'bre (-ber), a. gloomy; dark-coloured.

sombrer'o (-ā́rō), n. (pl. *sombreros*), broad-brimmed hat, usu. of felt.

some (sum), a. & pron. particular but unknown or unspecified (person or thing); certain quantity or number of (something); considerable quantity or number (of). **some'body,** n. & pron. some person; person of importance. **some'how,** adv. in some indefinite way, by some means or other. **some'one,** pron. somebody. **some'thing,** n. some thing, esp. of unknown or indefinite kind. **some'time,** a. (*archaic*) former. **some'times** (-mz), adv. at some times. **some'what,** adv. in some degree. **some'where,** adv. in, at, to, some place.

so'mersault (su-), n. spring in the air, forward or backward roll on the ground, in which person turns heels over head. v. i. turn somersault.

somnam'būlism, n. walking or performing other action during sleep. **somnam'būlist,** n.

som'nolent, a. sleepy, drowsy; inducing drowsiness. **som'nolence,** n.

son (sun), n. male child in relation to his parents; male descendant; offspring, native. **son-in-law,** daughter's husband.

sō'nar, n. echo-sounding device for detecting objects under water, asdic.

sona'ta (-nah-), n. musical composition in several movements for one or two instruments.

sonde, n. device for obtaining information on atmospheric conditions at high altitudes.

song, n. singing, vocal music; set of words for singing; poetry, poem. **song-bird,** bird with musical song. **song'ster,** n. song-bird.

son'ic, a. of, using, etc., sound or sound-waves. **sonic boom,** explosive noise produced by aircraft flying faster than speed of sound.

sonn'ĕt, n. poem of fourteen lines with rhymes arranged in definite scheme.

sonor'ous (*or* son'-), a. resonant, giving out rich or powerful sound.

sōon, adv. not long after present time or time in question; early; willingly.

soot, n. black powdery substance rising in and deposited by smoke of coal, wood, etc.

sōoth, n. (*archaic*) truth. **sōoth'sayer,** n. one claiming power of foretelling future events.

sōothe (-dh), v. t. calm; reduce force or intensity of. **sōo'thing,** a.

soot'y, a. of or like soot; black with soot.

sop, n. piece of bread dipped in soup, milk, etc.; something given to pacify or bribe. v. (p.t. *sopped*), soak. *sopping* (*wet*), soaked through. **sopp'y,** a. wet; weakly sentimental.

soph'ism, n. plausible but false or misleading argument. **soph'ist,** n. **soph'istry,** n.

sophis'ticāted, a. having lost simplicity or naturalness, worldly-wise; (of mechanism) very complicated. **sophisticā'tion,** n.

soporif'ic, a. & n. (drug, etc.) causing sleep.

soppy: see **sop.**

sopra'nō (-ah-), n. (pl. *sopranos*), (singer having) highest singing voice in women or boys.

sor'cerer, n. user of magic arts, magician, wizard. **sor'ceress,** n. *fem.* **sor'cery,** n.

sor'did, a. dirty, mean, squalid; contemptible, ignoble; greedy, mercenary.

sore, a. painful, hurting when touched or used; irritated, annoyed. n. sore place on skin, etc.

so'rrel[1], n. sour-leaved herb.

so'rrel[2], a. & n. bright reddish-brown (horse).

so'rrow (-ō), n. distress of mind caused by loss, suffering, disappointment, etc.; occasion or cause of this. v. i. feel sorrow; mourn. **so'rrowful,** a. **so'rrowfully,** adv.

so'rry, a. sad or regretful because of something; feeling pity; wretched, shabby.

sort, n. kind, species, variety, class. v. t. separate into sorts or classes; take *out* (certain sorts from others).

sor'tie, n. sally, esp. of besieged party; flight made by aircraft on military operation.

S.O.S. (es'ōes'), international signal of extreme distress, sent out in Morse code; (*informal*) urgent appeal for help.

sot, n. person stupefied by habitual drunkenness. **sott'ish,** a.

sott'ō vō'ce (-chi), in an undertone. (Italian)

soufflé (sōo'flā), n. spongy dish made light with beaten white of egg.

sough (sow, suf), n. & v. i. (make) sighing or rustling sound as of wind in trees.

sought, *p.t.* & *p.p.* of **seek.**

soul (sōl), *n.* spiritual part of man; moral and emotional part of man; human being; departed and disembodied spirit. **soul'ful,** *a.* expressing or appealing to emotions. **soul'less,** *a.* (esp.) inhuman, unfeeling.

sound[1], *n.* sensation produced in ear(s) when surrounding air vibrates; vibrations causing this; what is or may be heard. *v.* (cause to) emit sound; convey specified impression; pronounce; (Med.) examine (chest, heart) with stethoscope or by tapping chest. **sound barrier,** excessive resistance of air to object moving at speed near that of sound. **sound-track,** part of film, etc., carrying record of sound.

sound[2], *a.* healthy, free from disease or defects or corruption or heresy; dependable; (of sleep) deep, unbroken. *adv.* soundly (*asleep*).

sound[3], *n.* strait.

sound[4], *v.* test depth or quality of bottom of (sea, etc.) with sounding-lead; question cautiously. **sounding-lead,** lump of lead attached to line for sounding.

soup (sōōp), *n.* liquid food made by stewing bones, meat, vegetables, etc.

sour (sowr), *a.* tasting sharp or acid like unripe fruit or vinegar; (of smell) suggesting fermentation; bad-tempered, embittered. *v.* turn sour.

source (sors), *n.* place from which stream issues; origin, cause, (*of*); document, etc., supplying original information, evidence, etc.

souse, *v.* put in pickle; plunge (*into* liquid), soak (*in*), drench.

south, *adv.*, *n.*, & *a.* (towards, at, near, blowing from) point of horizon directly opposite north; (towards, in) southern part of world, country, town, etc. **south-east, south-west,** regions half-way between south and east, south and west. **south-easter, south-wester,** south-east, south-west, wind. **south'erly** (sudh-), *a.* & *adv.* towards, blowing from, south. **south'ward,** *a.*, *adv.*, & *n.* **south'wards** (-z), *adv.*

south'ern (sudh-), *a.* of, in, facing, south. **south'erner,** *n.* inhabitant of south.

souvenir (sōō'venēr), *n.* thing given, bought, kept, etc., as reminder of person, place, etc.

sou'wes'ter, *n.* south-west wind; waterproof hat with broad flap behind to protect neck.

sov'ereign (-vrin), *a.* supreme; excellent. *n.* supreme ruler, esp. monarch; (Hist.) English gold coin worth £1. **sov'ereignty,** *n.* supreme power.

Sov'iet (*or* sō-), *n.* council of district, republic, etc., or (*Supreme Soviet*) whole, of U.S.S.R. (Russia). *a.* of Soviets or Soviet Union. **Soviet Union,** U.S.S.R.

sow[1] (sō), *v.* (p.p. *sowed* or *sown*), scatter seed on or in earth, plant *with* seed. **sow'er** (sō'er), *n.*

sow[2], *n.* adult female pig.

soy'a(-bean), *n.* (seed of) Asian leguminous plant yielding meal, oil, etc.

spa (-ah), *n.* spring(s) of mineral water; place having such spring(s).

space, *n.* immeasurable expanse in which solar and stellar systems, etc., are situated; region beyond earth's atmosphere; interval between points or objects; interval of time; (sufficient) extent, area, room. *v.* set (*out*) at intervals, put spaces between. **space'craft, space-ship,** craft designed for travelling in space.

spa'cious (-shus), *a.* having ample space, roomy.

spade, *n.* tool for digging, etc., with broad blade and long handle. **spade-work,** hard work, esp. at start of project.

spaghett'i (-get-), *n.* dried wheaten paste in long rods thinner than macaroni.

spake: see **speak.**

span[1], *n.* distance between tips of thumb and little finger of extended hand; nine inches; period of time; distance between piers of bridge, tips of wings, etc.; arch of bridge. *v.t.* (p.t. *spanned*), extend, form arch, across.

span[2], *p.t.* of **spin.**

spangle (spang'gl), *n.* small disc of glittering metal sewn to garment; any small sparkling object. *v.t.* cover (as) with spangles.

Span'iard, *n.* native of Spain. **Span'ish** *a.* & *n.* (language) of Spain or Spaniards.

span'iel (-yel), *n.* dog of various breeds with long hair and large drooping ears.

spank[1], *v.i.* move (*along*) quickly or dashingly.

spank[2], *v.t.* & *n.* slap or smack with open hand, esp. on buttocks.

spann'er, *n.* tool, usu. steel bar with jaw, socket, etc., at end(s), for turning nut of bolt, etc.

spar[1], *n.* stout pole, esp. of kind used for ship's masts, etc.

spar[2], *v.i.* (p.t. *sparred*), make motions of boxing; practise boxing; argue.

spare, *v.* refrain from hurting, punishing, etc., refrain from taking (life); dispense with, do without; use frugally; part with, give. *a.* that can be spared; kept in reserve; frugal, lean. *n.* spare part. **spare part,** substitute part for machine, etc. **spar'ing,** *a.* (esp.) economical, frugal, grudging.

spark[1], *n.* fiery particle thrown off from burning substance or produced by striking flint, etc.; flash of light accompanying electrical discharge; (pl., *informal*) radio operator. *v.* emit spark(s). **sparking-plug,** device for firing explosive mixture in internal-combustion engine.

spark[2], *n.* gay young man.

spark'le, *v.i.* (seem to) send out sparks; glitter, flash, scintillate. *n.* sparkling; spark, glitter. **spark'ling,** *a.* (esp., of wine, etc.)

effervescing.

spa'rrow (-ō), *n.* small brownish-grey bird, esp. common house-sparrow. **sparrow--hawk,** small hawk.

sparse, *a.* thinly scattered. **sparse'ness,** *n.*

Spar'tan, *a.* of ancient Sparta, in Greece; (*spartan*), austere, hardy, unflinching. *n.* native of Sparta; (*spartan*), person of courage and endurance.

spasm, *n.* convulsive muscular contraction. **spasmod'ic,** *a.* sudden and violent; occurring at intervals.

spas'tic, *a.* caused by, subject to, spasms; suffering from cerebral palsy. *n.* person suffering from cerebral palsy. **spas'ticism,** *n.*

spat[1], *n.* short gaiter.

spat[2], *p.t. & p.p.* of **spit**[2].

spāte, *n.* river-flood, esp. sudden.

spāthe (-dh), *n.* large bract enclosing flower(s).

spā'tial (-shl), *a.* of, in, or relating to, space.

spatt'er, *v.* fly, send (mud, etc.) flying, in drops; splash. *n.* spattering; pattering.

spat'ula, *n.* implement with broad flat blade for spreading ointments, mixing pigments, etc. **spat'ulate,** *a.* having broad rounded end.

spawn, *n.* eggs of fish, frogs, etc.; mass of thread-like tubes from which mushrooms, etc., grow. *v.* cast spawn; produce or generate as spawn.

spay, *v.t.* remove ovaries of (female animal).

speak, *v.* (p.t. *spōke,* archaic *spāke*; p.p. *spōken*), utter words; say; pronounce; make a speech. **spea'ker,** *n.* (esp.) person of specified skill in speech-making; loud-speaker; (*Speaker*), official president of House of Commons.

spear, *n.* thrusting or hurling weapon with long shaft and sharp-pointed head. *v.t.* pierce or strike (as) with spear. **spear'mint,** common garden mint.

spe'cial (-shl), *a.* of particular or restricted kind; of or for particular person, occasion, or thing; not general; exceptional. **spe'cialist,** *n.* one who devotes himself to particular branch of profession, etc., esp. medicine; expert. **special'ity** (-shi-), **spe'cialty,** *nn.* special feature or characteristic; special skill, product, etc. **spe'cially,** *adv.* in special manner, to special degree or extent; oɳ purpose, particularly. **spe'cialize,** *v.i.* be or become specialist. **specializā'tion,** *n.*

spē'cies (-shēz), *n.* (pl. same), group of organisms having common characteristic(s) not shared by other groups, subdivision of genus; kind, sort.

specif'ic, *a.* definite, distinctly formulated; of species; of, for, particular disease, condition, etc. *n.* specific remedy. **specific gravity,** ratio of weight of substance to that of equal volume of water, hydrogen, etc., taken as standard. **specif'ically,** *adv.*

spe'cifỹ, *v.t.* name specifically, mention definitely. **specificā'tion,** *n.* specified detail, esp. detailed description of work undertaken, invention, patent, etc.

spe'cimen, *n.* part or piece or individual as example of class or whole, esp. serving for investigation, scientific study, etc.

spē'cious (-shus), *a.* deceptively fair; plausible.

speck, *n.* small spot or stain or particle. *v.t.* mark with specks. **speck'less,** *a.*

speck'le, *n.* small spot, stain, or (esp. natural) coloured marking. **speck'led,** *a.*

spec'tacle, *n.* public show, display; noteworthy scene. (*pair of*) *spectacles,* pair of eyeglasses in frame. **spec'tacled,** wearing spectacles.

spectac'ular, *a.* of or like spectacle or show; striking, flamboyant.

spectā'tor, *n.* looker-on; person present at performance, etc.

spec'tral, *a.* ghost-like, unreal; of the spectrum.

spec'tre (-ter), *n.* ghost, apparition.

spec'trum, *n.* (pl. *spectra*), band of colours (*red, orange, yellow, green, blue, indigo, violet*) into which beam of light is decomposed by prism, etc.

spec'ūlāte, *v.i.* conjecture, guess; buy shares or goods in hope of selling them later at profit. **speculā'tion,** *n.* **spec'ūlātor,** *n.* **spec'ūlative,** *a.*

sped, *p.t. & p.p.* of **speed.**

speech, *n.* act, faculty, or manner of speaking; talk, discourse, delivered to audience; language, dialect. **speech'ifỹ,** *v.i.* make speeches; speak lengthily. **speech'less,** *a.* unable to speak because of emotion.

speed, *n.* rate of time at which something moves, travels, or operates; rapidity. *v.* (p.t. *sped*), go fast; (*archaic*) be or make prosperous or successful. *speed up* (p.t. *speeded up*), (cause to) increase speed. **speed-boat,** fast motor boat. **speed-limit,** maximum speed permitted on road, etc. **speed'way,** racing track for motor cycles, etc. **speedom'eter,** *n.* instrument for registering speed of motor vehicle. **spee'dy,** *a.* rapid, swift; prompt.

speed'well, *n.* small blue-flowered plant.

spēl(a)eol'ogy, *n.* scientific study of caves. **spēl(a)eol'ogist,** *n.*

spell[1], *n.* words used as a charm; fascination. **spell'bound,** *a.* held (as) by spell, fascinated, entranced.

spell[2], *n.* turn or period of work, activity, etc.; (short) period of time.

spell[3], *v.* (p.t. *spelt* or *spelled,* pr. spelt), name or write in order letters of word, etc.; form words, etc. thus. *spell out,* spell aloud, explain in detail. **spell'ing,** *n.*

spen'cer, *n.* woman's short woollen bodice worn under dress, etc.

spend, *v.* (p.t. *spent*), pay out (money, for purchase, etc.); use, use up, exhaust; live or stay through (period of time). **spend'thrift,** extravagant or wasteful person.

sperm, *n.* semen; spermatozoon. **sperm- -whale,** large whale yielding soft scaly substance used for ointments, etc., and in perfumery.

spermatozŏ'on, *n.* (pl. *spermatozŏa*), very small active fertilizing cell of male organism.

spew, *v.* vomit.

sphag'num, *n.* genus of mosses growing in boggy and swampy places.

sphere, *n.* figure or body having all points of its surface equidistant from point within called *centre*; ball, globe; field of action, influence, or existence. **sphe'rical,** *a.* sphere-shaped. **spher'oid,** *a.* almost spherical.

sphinx, *n.* (Gk. myth.) winged monster with woman's head and lion's body; ancient- -egyptian figure of recumbent lion with head of man, ram, etc.; person who keeps his thoughts and intentions secret.

spice, *n.* aromatic or pungent vegetable substance used as flavouring; thing that adds zest, excitement, etc. *v.t.* flavour with spice(s).

spick and span, *adj. phr.* smart, trim, new- -looking.

spi'cy, *a.* of, like, flavoured with, spice; sensational, slightly improper.

spi'der, *n.* eight-legged animal, of which many kinds spin webs for capture of insects as food. **spi'dery,** *a.*

spig'ot, *n.* wooden plug stopping up hole of cask.

spike, *n.* sharp projecting point; large stout nail; long cluster of flowers growing directly from single stem. *v.t.* furnish with spike(s); fix with spike(s); plug vent of (gun) with spike. *spike guns of,* spoil plans of. **spi'ky,** *a.*

spike'nard (-kn-), *n.* (Eastern plant yielding) ancient costly aromatic substance.

spill¹, *n.* strip of wood, folded paper, etc., for lighting candle, pipe, etc., from flame.

spill², *v.* (p.t. *spilt* or *spilled*), (allow liquid, etc., to) fall or run out from vessel; shed (blood). *n.* fall, esp. from horse or vehicle; tumble.

spin, *v.* (p.t. *span* or *spun*; p.p. *spun*; pres. p. *spinning*), make yarn by drawing out and twisting together fibres of wool, cotton, etc.; (of spider or insect) make (web, etc.) by producing fine thread-like substance; (cause to) revolve like top, etc.; fish with spinning bait. *spin a yarn,* tell a story. *spin out,* prolong, last. *n.* spinning motion, esp. of aircraft in diving descent, ball struck aslant or bowled in certain manner, etc.; brisk or short drive, etc. **spin-drier,** machine for drying clothes, etc., in rotating drum. **spinning-wheel,** spinning apparatus with spindle driven by wheel worked by hand or foot.

spin'ach (-nij), *n.* (plant with) succulent leaves used as vegetable.

spi'nal, *a.* of spine. **spinal column,** spine. **spinal cord,** rope-like mass of nerve-cells, etc., enclosed within and protected by spine.

spin'dle, *n.* slender rod used to twist and wind thread in spinning; rod serving as axis on which something revolves. **spind'ly,** *a.* slender, thin.

spin'drift, *n.* spray blown along surface of sea.

spine, *n.* articulated series of vertebrae extending from skull to coccyx, backbone; sharp-pointed process, thorn, prickle. **spine'less,** *a.* (esp.) lacking backbone or character.

spin'et (*or* -et'), *n.* small keyboard instrument of harpsichord kind.

spinn'aker, *n.* large three-cornered extra sail of racing-yacht.

spinn'eret, *n.* spinning organ in spider, silk- -worm, etc.

spinn'ey, *n.* (pl. *spinneys*), small wood.

spinning: see **spin.**

spin'ster, *n.* unmarried woman.

spi'ny, *a.* full of spines, prickly.

spir'al, *a.* coiled in cylindrical or conical manner; curving continuously round fixed point at steadily increasing distance from it. *n.* spiral curve or course; progressive rise or fall. *v.i.* (p.t. *spiralled*), wind, move, ascend, descend, in spiral path or course.

spire, *n.* tapering structure rising above tower, esp. of church.

spir'it, *n.* animating or vital principle, immaterial part, of man; mental or moral nature or qualities; disembodied soul; supernatural being; courage; (often pl.) distilled alcoholic liquor. *high spirits,* cheerful mood. *low spirits,* depressed mood. *v.t.* convey mysteriously *away,* etc. **spi'rited,** *a.* lively; courageous. **spi'ritless,** *a.* lacking in courage, energy,etc.

spi'ritual, *a.* of, concerned with, or proceeding from spirit, soul, or God; of sacred or religious things; ecclesiastical. *n.* characteristic religious song of American Negroes. **spiritual'ity,** *n.*

spi'ritualism, *n.* belief that spirits of the dead can communicate with the living, esp. through a medium. **spi'ritualist,** *a. & n.* **spiritualis'tic,** *a.*

spi'rituous, *a.* containing much alcohol.

spit¹, *n.* pointed rod thrust into meat, etc., so that it can be revolved while roasting; point of land projecting into sea, etc. *v.t.* (p.t. *spitted*), pierce (as) with spit.

spit², *v.* (p.t. *spat*), eject saliva, etc., (*out*) from mouth; (of cat, etc.) make spitting noise as sign of hostility, etc. *n.* spittle. **spit'fire,** *n.* fiery-tempered person.

spit³, *n.* spade's depth in digging.

spite, *n.* ill-will, malice. *in spite of,* not being, not to be, prevented by. *v.t.* humiliate or annoy intentionally. **spite'ful,** *a.* full of or showing spite.

spitt'le, *n.* saliva.

spittōōn', *n.* receptacle for spittle.

spiv, *n.* (flashily-dressed) person who lives by his wits, esp. by activities only just within the law.

splash, *v.* cause (liquid, etc.) to fly about in drops; (of liquid) fly about in drops; wet or soil by splashing; step, fall, *into, through,* etc., with splashing; mottle. *n.* splashing, sound or mark made by it; irregular patch of colour, etc. **splash-down,** landing of space-craft on sea.

splay, *v.* construct (aperture) with diverging sides; be so shaped or set. *a.* spread or turned outwards.

spleen, *n.* abdominal organ concerned with formation of antibodies, etc.; bad temper.

splen'did, *a.* magnificent, admirable, glorious, excellent. **splen'dour** (-der), *n.* great brightness; magnificence, pomp, brilliance.

splice, *n.* joining of two ends of rope, etc., by untwisting and interweaving; overlapping join of two pieces of wood, etc. *v.t.* join by splice.

splint, *n.* appliance of rigid material holding broken bone, etc., in position. *v.t.* put into, secure with, splint(s).

splin'ter, *n.* rough, usu. sharp and thin, fragment broken or split off from some hard material. *v.* break into splinters, come *off* as splinter.

split, *v.* (p.t. *split*), break into parts, esp. along grain or length; divide into shares, factions, etc. *n.* splitting; fissure, rent.

splutt'er, *v.* utter, talk, hastily and indistinctly; sputter. *n.* spluttering noise.

spoil, (p.t. *spoilt* or *spoiled*), destroy or impair good or effective qualities of; prevent enjoyment of; injure character of by over-indulgence; cosset; deteriorate, go bad; (*archaic*) plunder, deprive *of* by force or stealth. *n.* (usu. pl. or *collective*), goods taken from enemy or acquired by violence, etc.; (pl.) public offices, etc., distributed among supporters of successful political party. **spoil'sport,** person who spoils sport or enjoyment of others.

spōke¹, *n.* any of radiating bars connecting hub and rim of wheel.

spoke², spoken, *p.t.* & *p.p.* of **speak.**

spōkes'man (-ks-), *n.* (pl. *-men*), person who speaks for others; representative.

spōliā'tion, *n.* spoiling, plundering.

spon'dee, *n.* metrical foot of two long (or stressed) syllables. **spondā'ic,** *a.*

sponge (-unj), *n.* any of various simple aquatic (chiefly marine) animals; soft light porous skeleton of sponge used as absorbent in bathing, cleaning, etc.; pad of porous rubber, etc., used similarly; sponge-cake. *v.* wipe, etc., with sponge; be meanly dependent *on.* **sponge-cake,** light sweet cake of flour, eggs, and sugar. **spon'ger,** *n.* (esp.) one who

sponges for money, etc., parasite. **spon'gy,** *a.* (esp.) porous, compressible, absorbent, light, etc., as sponge.

spon'sor, *n.* godfather or godmother; person making himself responsible for another; advertiser paying cost of broadcast programme, etc. *v.t.* act as sponsor for; support. **spon'sorship,** *n.*

spontā'nèous, *a.* resulting from natural impulse; not forced, suggested, or caused from outside; not deliberate or laboured. **spontanē'ity,** *n.*

spōōk, *n.* ghost. **spōō'ky,** *a.*

spōōl, *n.* reel for thread, photographic film, etc.

spōōn, *n.* utensil consisting of shallow, usu. oval, bowl and handle, used for conveying food to mouth, cooking, etc. *v.t.* take, lift, (*up, out,* etc.) with spoon. **spōōn'ful,** *n.* (pl. *spoonfuls*).

spōō'nerism, *n.* accidental interchange of initial letters of two or more words (e.g. *blushing crow* for *crushing blow*).

spoor, *n.* track, esp. of wild animal.

sporad'ic, *a.* occurring in isolated instances or very small numbers; scattered; occasional. **sporad'ically,** *adv.*

spore, *n.* very small reproductive body in ferns, fungi, etc.

spo'rran, *n.* pouch worn in front of kilt.

sport, *n.* amusement, diversion; pastime(s), game(s), esp. of outdoor or athletic kind; (pl.) (meeting for competition in) athletic pastimes; (*slang*) good fellow. *v.* gambol; wear. **sports car,** open low-built fast car. **sports'man, sports'woman,** person fond of sports; person fair to opponents, cheerful in defeat, etc. **spor'ting,** *a.* (esp.) sportsman-like. *sporting chance,* chance involving some risk. **spor'tive,** *a.* playful.

spot, *n.* small, esp. roundish, mark or stain; pimple; moral blemish; particular place; (*informal*) small amount (*of*). *v.* (p.t. *spotted*), mark with spot(s); (*informal*) detect or pick out. **spot'light,** beam of light thrown on one spot, esp. of stage. **spot'less,** *a.* (esp.) absolutely clean, unblemished. **spott'y,** *a.*

spouse (*or* -z), *n.* husband or wife.

spout, *n.* projecting tube or lip through which rain-water is carried from roof, or liquid is poured or issues; gush or jet of liquid. *v.i.* gush or pour out in jet; speechify.

sprain, *v.t.* wrench (joint) so as to cause pain and swelling. *n.* such injury.

sprang, *p.t.* of **spring.**

sprat, *n.* small European herring or similar fish.

sprawl, *v.* fall, lie, etc., with limbs spread out in careless or ungainly way; straggle. *n.* sprawling attitude or movement.

spray¹, *n.* liquid dispersed in small mist-like drops; instrument for spraying. *v.* scatter, diffuse, as spray; sprinkle (as) with spray.

spray², *n.* graceful branch or twig with flow-

ers, etc.; jewel or other ornament in form of
spray.

spread (-ed), *v.* (p.t. *spread*), extend surface
of by unfolding, flattening, etc.; cover surface of; stretch or open *out*; diffuse, be diffused. *n.* spreading, being spread. **spread
eagle,** figure of eagle with wings and legs
spread. **spread-eagle,** (*v.*) extend, fix, etc.,
in form of spread eagle.

spree, *n.* spell of lively enjoyment.

sprig, *n.* small branch, twig, spray; small
headless nail.

spright'ly (-rīt-), *a.* vivacious, lively.

spring, *v.* (p.t. *sprang*; p.p. *sprung*), move
rapidly or suddenly (upwards), esp. from rest
or (as) by action of spring; arise; originate;
sprout; develop, produce, suddenly or unexpectedly. *n.* act of springing up; (piece of
coiled metal, etc., giving) elasticity; place
where water wells up from earth; flow of
water rising from earth; source, origin;
season between summer and winter, in which
vegetation begins. **spring-board,** board giving impetus to diver or jumper. **spring-bok,**
S. Afr. gazelle. **spring tide,** highest tide,
occurring after new and full moon. **spring'-
time,** season of spring. **spring'y** (-ngi), *a.*

sprink'le, *v.* scatter in or with small drops or
particles. **sprink'ling,** *n.* (esp.) a few here
and there.

sprint, *v.i.* run, etc., at top speed, esp. for
short distance. *n.* short fast race, etc.

sprite, *n.* fairy, elf.

sprock'et, *n.* projection on rim of wheel
engaging with links of chain.

sprout, *v.* begin to grow, put forth shoots;
produce by sprouting. *n.* shoot, new growth;
(pl.) Brussels sprouts.

spruce[1] (-ōōs), *a.* of trim smart appearance. *v.*
smarten (*up*), make spruce.

spruce[2] (-ōōs), *n.* (wood of) kind of fir.

sprung, p.p. of **spring.**

spry, *a.* active, nimble, lively.

spume, *n.* & *v.i.* froth, foam.

spun, *p.t.* & *p.p.* of **spin.**

spunk, *n.* (*informal*) courage, pluck.

spur, *n.* pricking instrument worn on horseman's heel; incentive, stimulus; projection
on back of cock's leg or at base of flower;
ridge, etc., projecting from mountain range.
v. (p.t. *spurred*), urge on (as) with spurs; ride
hard.

spur'ious, *a.* not genuine or authentic.

spurn, *v.t.* reject with contempt.

spurt, *v.* gush out in jet or stream; make spurt.
n. sudden gushing out; short sudden violent
effort, increase of speed, etc.

sput'nik (-oo-), *n.* Russian artificial satellite.

sputt'er, *v.* emit with, make, spitting sound;
speak, utter, rapidly or confusedly. *n.* sputtering.

spy, *n.* person secretly collecting and reporting information, esp. relating to another
country, rival firm, etc. *v.* act as spy (*on*);

notice, discern. **spy-glass,** small telescope.

squabb'le (-o-), *n.* & *v.i.* (engage in) petty or
noisy quarrel.

squad (-od), *n.* small group of persons working or being trained together.

squad'ron (-od-), *n.* division of fleet or
air-force, or of cavalry regiment.
squadron-leader, R.A.F. officer below
wing-commander.

squal'id (-ol-), *a.* dirty, mean, wretched.

squall (-awl), *n.* sudden violent gust or storm;
scream. *v.* scream loudly. **squall'y,** *a.*

squal'or (-ol-), *n.* filth, dirt; wretched poverty
and neglect.

squan'der, (-o-), *v.t.* spend wastefully.

square, *n.* plane rectangle with four equal
sides; object of (roughly) this shape; open
space, esp. enclosed by houses, etc.; instrument for testing or obtaining right angles;
product of quantity multiplied by itself. *a.* of
(approximate) shape of square; rectangular;
angular, not round; honest, fair; even, equal,
level. *adv.* squarely. *v.* make square; multiply number, etc., by itself; make or be consistent (*with*). **square dance,** dance in which
four couples face inwards. **square-rigged,**
having sails on horizontal yards slung to mast
by middle. **square root,** (Math.) root producing given quantity when multiplied by
itself once.

squash (-o-), *v.* squeeze, be squeezed, flat or
into pulp; force into small space; snub,
suppress; crowd. *n.* crowded state; crowd;
drink made of juice of crushed fruit. **squash
(rackets),** game like rackets, played in
smaller court.

squat (-ot), *v.i.* (p.t. *squatted*), sit with knees
drawn up and heels touching hams; crouch;
settle on or in unoccupied or unused land,
building, etc. *a.* dumpy. **squatt'er,** *n.* person
squatting on land or in house, esp. without
title or payment of rent.

squaw, *n.* Amer. Indian woman or wife.

squawk, *n.* & *v.i.* (utter) harsh cry.

squeak, *n.* short shrill cry or sound. **narrow
squeak,** narrow escape. *v.* emit, utter with,
squeak(s). **squea'ky,** *a.*

squeal, *v.* utter (with), emit, (long) shrill cry
or sound. *n.* sharp shrill sound.

squea'mish, *a.* easily made (to feel) sick;
easily disgusted; over-scrupulous.

squeeze, *v.* exert pressure on so as to crush,
drain liquid from, etc.; force by pressure;
extort money, etc., (from) by pressure; force
one's way. *n.* squeezing; crowd, crush.

squelch, *v.* walk or tread heavily on wet
ground; make sound as of foot lifted out of
mud; crush, squash.

squib, *n.* small hissing firework.

squid, *n.* kind of cuttlefish.

squigg'le, *n.* curly mark.

squint, *v.i.* have eyes turned in different directions; look sidelong or through small aperture. *n.* squinting position of the eyeballs.

squire, *n.* country gentleman, esp. chief landed proprietor in district; (Hist.) attendant on knight. *v.t.* escort (woman) on social outing, etc.

squirm, *v.i.* twist the body, wriggle, (from discomfort, shame, or embarrassment). *n.* squirming movement.

squi′rrel, *n.* small bushy-tailed rodent, often living in trees.

squirt, *v.* eject, be ejected, (as) from syringe. *n.* syringe; small jet or spray.

squitch, *n.* couch-grass.

stab, *n.* thrust or wound with sharp pointed weapon or implement; sudden acute pain or attack. *v.* (p.t. *stabbed*), pierce or wound with something pointed.

stabil′ity, *n.* being stable, **stā′bilīze**, *v.* make stable, steady. **stābilīzā′tion**, *n.*

stā′ble¹, *a.* firmly fixed or established, not fluctuating or changing; steady.

stā′ble², *n.* building in which horses are kept; establishment for training race-horses. *v.t.* put or keep in stable. **stā′bling**, *n.* stable-accommodation.

stacca′tō (-kah-), *a.* & *adv.* (Mus.) (to be played) with each note short and separate.

stack, *n.* (orderly) pile of hay, sheaves, wood, etc.; group of chimneys. *v.t.* pile in stack(s).

stā′dium, *n.* (pl. *stadia* or *stadiums*), enclosed ground for athletic sports, games, etc., with tiers of seats for spectators.

staff (-ahf), *n.* (pl. *-s* or *stāves*), stick or pole as weapon or support or as symbol of office; group of officers under commanding officer; group of persons working under central direction in business, educational institution, etc.; (Mus., pl. *staves*) stave. *v.t.* provide with staff of officers, teachers etc.

stag, *n.* male of (esp. red) deer.

stāge, *n.* platform, esp. in theatre, where actors, etc., perform; acting profession; scene of action; division of journey, process, development, etc.; point reached; stopping-place. *v.t.* put (play, etc.) on stage; arrange so as to give dramatic effect. **stage-coach**, (Hist.) coach running by stages between two places. **stā′ging**, *n.0*(esp.) scaffolding, shelving. **stā′gy**, *a.* theatrical in style.

stagg′er (-g-), *v.* go unsteadily as if about to fall; (cause to) totter, reel, be shocked, etc.; arrange in zigzag or alternate order; arrange (hours of work, etc.) so that they do not coincide with those of others. *n.* act or amount of staggering.

stag′nant, *a.* (of water, pool, etc.) without current or tide; still and stale; unchanging, inactive. **stag′nancy**, *n.* **stagnāte′**, *v.i.* be stagnant. **stagnā′tion**, *n.*

staid, *a.* sober, steady, sedate.

stain, *v.* discolour, soil; colour with pigment that penetrates; colour (glass) wih transparent colours. *n.* dirty mark, patch, etc., one not easily removable; dye, etc., for staining; blot, blemish. **stain′less**, *a.* (esp., of steel)

not liable to rust or tarnish.

stair, *n.* each of a series of steps, esp. indoors; (pl.) set or flight of these. **stair′case**, flight or series of flights of stairs, with supporting structure, banisters, etc.

stāke, *n.* stick or post pointed for driving into ground; post to which person was bound for burning alive (Hist.); amount risked in wager, match etc. *at stake*, risked, dependent upon an issue. *v.t.* mark *off*, *out*, secure, with stake(s); risk.

stal′actīte, *n.* deposit of carbonate of lime hanging like icicle from roof of cavern, etc. **stalactit′ic**, *a.*

stal′agmīte, *n.* deposit of carbonate of lime, etc., rising like spike from floor of cavern, etc. **stalagmit′ic**, *a.*

stāle, *a.* lacking freshness; musty or otherwise the worse for age; lacking novelty; having lost vigour through too much training, practice, etc. **stāle′māte**, *n.* (Chess) position in which player can make no move without putting his king in check; deadlock, inconclusive position.

stalk¹ (-awk), *n.* main stem of herbaceous plant; attachment or support of leaf, flower, etc.

stalk² (-awk), *v.* steal up to game, etc., under cover or unperceived; stride in stately or imposing manner.

stall (-awl), *n.* (division for one animal in) stable or cow-house; fixed seat in church, etc.; seat in part of theatre nearest stage; stand, booth, etc., in market, etc.; stalling of engine, aircraft, etc. *v.* put or keep in stall; (of motor engine) stop accidentally; (of aircraft) (cause to) be out of control owing to loss of speed.

stall′ion, *n.* uncastrated male horse.

stal′wart (-awl-, -ol-), *a.* sturdy, strong; courageous, resolute.

stā′men, *n.* male or pollen-bearing organ of flowering plants.

stam′ina, *n.* staying-power, power of endurance.

stamm′er, *v.* speak haltingly, esp. with rapid involuntary repetition of certain sounds in word, etc.; utter with stammer. *n.* stammering speech; tendency to stammer.

stamp, *v.* bring foot down heavily on ground, etc.; crush (ore, etc.); impress pattern or mark on with die, etc.; affix postage stamp to; characterize. *n.* (sound of) stamping; stamped impress; mark or adhesive label on document, letter, etc., to show that duty, postage, etc., has been paid; characteristic mark; character, kind.

stampēde′, *n.* rush of horses, cattle, or people under sudden common impulse, esp. panic. *v.* (cause to) take part in stampede.

stance, *n.* player's position for making stroke; pose, attitude.

stanch (-ah-), *v.t.* check flow of (esp. blood); check flow from (esp. wound).

stan'chion (-ahnshn), *n.* upright bar, stay, or support. *v.t.* provide, strengthen, with stanchion(s).

stand, *v.* (p.t. **stood**), be in stationary upright position; rise up; assume stationary position; be set or situated; remain firm, valid, etc.; offer oneself for election, etc.; put up with; provide at one's expense. *stand for,* represent, signify. *stand out,* be prominent or conspicuous. *stand up,* rise to, maintain, standing position. *n.* stationary condition or position; resistance to attack, etc.; pedestal, rack, etc., on which things may be put; raised structure for spectators to sit or stand on. **stand'point,** point of view. **stand'still,** stop, pause.

stan'dard, *n.* distinctive flag; required degree of some quality, measurement, etc.; type, model; average quality; upright support for lamp, etc.; shrub or tree trained on erect stem. *a.* of recognized or average merit, authority, measurement, etc. **stan'dardize,** *v.t.* make according to fixed standards; make uniform. **standardiza'tion,** *n.*

stan'ding, *a.* established and permanent; upright (on one's feet). *n.* established reputation or position; duration.

stank, *p.t.* of **stink.**

stan'za, *n.* group of lines forming division of song or poem.

stā'ple[1], *n.* U-shaped piece of metal for driving into wood, etc.; similar contrivance, esp. bent wire for fastening sheets of paper together. *v.t.* provide, fasten, with staple(s).

stā'ple[2], *n.* important or principal product or article of commerce; textile fibre with respect to its quality or length. *a.* principal.

star, *n.* celestial body appearing as point of light; rayed figure or object representing star as ornament, etc.; brilliant or prominent person, esp. chief actor or actress. *v.* (p.t. **starred**), mark, adorn, with star(s) or asterisk; present, perform, as star. **star'fish,** star-shaped marine animal. **star'light,** light of stars. **Stars and Stripes,** national flag of U.S.A.

star'board (-berd), *n.* right-hand side of ship, etc., looking forward (opp. *port*).

starch, *n.* white carbohydrate forming important constituent of human food; preparation of this for stiffening linen, etc. *v.t.* stiffen with starch. **starch-reduced,** having smaller than normal proportion of starch. **star'chy,** *a.* of or like starch; stiff and formal in manner.

stāre, *v.* gaze fixedly with eyes wide open; (of eyes) be wide open; be conspicuous. *n.* staring gaze.

stark, *a.* stiff, rigid; bare, barren; sheer, absolute. *adv.* completely, utterly.

star'ling, *n.* common, noisy, mimicking bird, living in flocks in town or country.

starr'y, *a.* set with stars; bright as star; star-like.

start, *v.* make sudden involuntary movement; move suddenly; begin journey, operations, etc.; set going. *n.* sudden involuntary movement; beginning of journey, race, action, etc., starting-place; (amount of) advantage gained or allowed in starting.

star'tle, *v.t.* cause to start with surprise or fright; frighten, surprise. **star'tling,** *a.*

starve, *v.* (cause to) die or suffer acutely from lack or shortage of food; deprive *of;* force *into, out,* etc., by starvation. **starvā'tion,** *n.* **star'veling** (-vl-), *n.* starving person.

stāte, *n.* position or condition; stage of process, work, etc.; ceremonial pomp; organized political community, nation (also attrib.). *v.t.* express, esp. fully or clearly, in speech or writing; specify (number, etc.). **state-room,** room for ceremonial occasions; passenger's private cabin on ship. **stāte'ly** (-tli), *a.* dignified; imposing; grand. **stāte'ment** (-tm-), *n.* stating; thing stated; formal account of facts, financial position, etc. **stātes'man** (-tsm-), *n.* (pl. *-men*), person skilled or taking leading part in management of State affairs. **stātes'manlīke,** *a.* **stātes'manship,** *n.*

stat'ic, *a.* of or concerning statics; not changing or moving. **stat'ics,** *n.* branch of mechanics dealing with bodies at rest and forces in equilibrium.

stā'tion, *n.* place in which person or thing stands or is placed, esp. habitually or for definite purpose, etc.; stopping-place on railway, etc., with buildings; position in life. *v.t.* assign position to. **station-master,** official controlling railway station.

stā'tionary (-shon-), *a.* remaining in one place, not moving or movable; not changing.

stā'tioner (-shon-), *n.* dealer in stationery. **stā'tionery,** *n.* writing materials (e.g. pens, ink, paper, etc.).

statis'tics, *n.* branch of study concerned with collection and classification of numerical facts; facts so collected, numerical data. **statis'tical,** *a.* **statisti'cian** (-shn), *n.*

stat'ūary, *a.* of statues, sculptured. *n.* sculpture, statues.

stat'ūe, *n.* sculptured, usu. (nearly) life-sized, figure of person, etc. **statūesque'** (-k), *a.* like statue, esp. in beauty or dignity. **statūette',** *n.* small statue.

stat'ure (-yer), *n.* bodily height (often fig.).

stā'tus, *n.* social or legal position or condition; rank, prestige.

stā'tus quō, unchanged position, previous position, of affairs. (Latin)

stat'ūte, *n.* written law of legislative body; permanent ordinance of corporation, etc. **stat'ūtory,** *a.* enacted, required, imposed, by statute.

staunch, *a.* constant to obligations or purpose; untiring in service or loyalty. *v.t.* stanch.

stāve, *n.* one of narrow strips of wood forming sides of cask; (Mus.) set of five parallel horizontal lines on and between which notes are placed to indicate pitch; stanza. *v.t.* (p.t. *stōve* or *stāved*), break hole *in. stave off*, ward off, delay.

stay[1], *n.* large rope supporting mast, etc.; rope supporting flagstaff, etc.; prop, support; (pl.) corset.

stay[2], *v.* check, stop; remain, dwell temporarily; show powers of endurance. *n.* period of staying; (Law) postponement.

stead (sted), *n. in his stead*, instead of him; *stand in good stead*, be of advantage or service to.

stead'fast (sted-), *a.* constant, firm, unwavering. **stead'fastly**, *adv.* **stead'fastness**, *n.*

stead'y, (sted-), *a.* stable, firm, not faltering or shaking or rocking; resolute; settled; regular. *v.* make or become steady. *adv.* steadily. **stead'ily**, *adv.* **stead'iness**, *n.*

steak (stāk), *n.* thick slice of beef or fish.

steal, *v.* (p.t. *stōle*; p.p. *stōlen*), take dishonestly and esp. secretly what is another's; move secretly or silently.

stealth (stel-), *n.* secrecy; secret or underhand procedure. **steal'thy**, *a.* **steal'thily**, *adv.*

steam, *n.* invisible vapour into which water is converted by heat, esp. as motive power; steam mixed with air, etc., in form of white cloud or mist; (attrib.) worked, etc., by steam. *v.* cook, soften, etc., by action of steam; emit, exhale, steam or vapour; cover, be covered, with condensed vapour; travel, move, by steam-power. **steam-engine**, locomotive or stationary engine worked by steam. **steam-roller**, heavy locomotive engine with roller and wide wheels, used in road-making. **steam'ship**, ship propelled by steam. **stea'mer**, *n.* steamship; vessel in which food is cooked by steam. **stea'my**, *a.*

steed, *n.* (chiefly Poet.) horse.

steel, *n.* hard alloy of iron with carbon, etc.; steel rod for sharpening knives on. *v.t.* nerve (*oneself to* do), fortify (*oneself against*). **steel wool**, fine shavings of steel massed together, used for scouring, smoothing, etc. **stee'ly**, *a.* of steel; hard as steel.

steep[1], *v.* soak, be soaked, in liquid; (fig.) permeate, pervade with. *n.* steeping.

steep[2], *a.* sloping sharply; having almost perpendicular face or slope. **stee'pen**, *v.* make or become steep or steeper.

stee'ple, *n.* lofty structure, esp. church-tower with spire. **stee'plechase**, horse-race across country. **stee'plejack**, man who climbs steeples, tall chimneys, etc., to do repairs, etc.

steer[1], *n.* young, esp. castrated, male ox.

steer[2], *v.* guide vessel, etc., by rudder, helm, etc., or by mechanical means; direct one's course. **steering-wheel**, wheel for steering car, ship, etc. **steers'man** (-z-), *n.* (pl. -*men*), person steering ship, etc. **steer'age**, *n.* (esp.) part of ship allotted to passengers travelling at cheapest rate.

stell'ar, *a.* of stars; star-shaped.

stem[1], *n.* main body above ground of tree, etc.; stalk of leaf, flower, or fruit; stem--shaped part; part of word to which suffix is added; stock, ancestry; main upright timber at bow of ship. *v.* (p.t. *stemmed*), remove stem of; make headway against (tide, etc.). *stem from*, originate in.

stem[2], *v.t.* (p.t. *stemmed*), check flow of, dam up.

stench, *n.* bad smell.

sten'cil, *n.* plate of metal, etc., in which pattern, etc., is cut out; pattern, etc., reproduced by colouring paper, etc., through stencil. *v.t.* produce, copy, etc., by use of stencil(s).

stėnog'raphy, *n.* writing in shorthand. **stėnog'rapher**, *n.*

stentor'ian, *a.* (of voice) extremely loud.

step, *v.* (p.t. *stepped*), lift and set down foot or alternate feet in walking, etc.; go short distance, progress, by stepping; pace. *n.* movement or manner of stepping; distance covered by stepping; footfall; action towards result, (pl.) measures taken; flat-topped structure for placing foot on in ascending and descending; (pl.) step-ladder. **step-ladder**, portable short ladder with flat steps. **stepping-stone**, stone set in stream, etc., as help in crossing.

step-, *pref.* related by remarriage of parent. **step'child**, **step'daughter**, **step'son**, child by previous marriage of one's wife or husband (so **step'brother**, **step'father**, **step'-mother**, **step'sister**.).

steppe, *n.* vast treeless plain, esp. in Russia.

stēr'ėō, *n.* & *a.* stereophonic (sound, etc.).

stēr'ėo-, *pref.* solid; three-dimensional; stereoscopic. **stēr'ėophon'ic**, *a.* of system of recording and reproducing sound by use of separate microphones and loud-speakers to give realistic effect. **stēr'ėoscōpe**, *n.* instrument for combining pictures of object, etc., from two slightly different points of view, to give three-dimensional effect. **stēr'ėoscop'ic**, *a.* **stēr'ėotȳpe**, *n.* printing-plate cast from mould of set-up type. **stēr'ėotȳped**, *a.* fixed in form, conventional.

stē'rīle, *a.* barren; not producing, not capable of producing, fruit or offspring; free from living micro-organisms. **steril'ity**, *n.*

stē'rilize, *v.t.* make incapable of producing offspring; free from living micro-organisms by treating with heat, antiseptic, etc. **sterilizā'tion**, *n.*

ster'ling, *n.* money of United Kingdom. *a.* of sterling; genuine, of standard value or purity; solidly excellent.

stern[1], *a.* severe, strict; hard, harsh.

stern[2], *n.* rear end of ship, etc.

ster'torous, *a.* (of breathing, etc.) producing snoring or rasping sound. **ster'torously**, *adv.*

steth'oscope, *n.* doctors' instrument for listening to sound made by heart, lungs, etc.

stē'vėdore, *n.* man employed in loading and

stowing ships' cargoes.

stew, *v.* cook by long simmering in closed vessel with liquid. *n.* dish of stewed meat, etc.

stew′ard, *n.* person paid to manage another's estate or house, or to cater for college, club, etc.; attendant on passengers in ship or aircraft (fem. *stewardess*); official managing race-meeting, show, etc.

stick, *v.* (p.t. *stuck*), thrust pointed thing *in*(*to*) or *through*; fix, be fixed, (as) by point or (as) by adhesion of surfaces with glue, etc.; become jammed or unable to continue; (*slang*) bear, endure. *stick out, up*, (cause to) project or protrude. *n.* (small) slender piece of wood; small rod-like piece of chocolate, chalk, etc. **sticking-plaster,** sticky material for covering cut or injury.

stick′leback (-lb-), *n.* small spiny-finned fish.

stick′ler, *n.* (with *for*) person who insists on (trivial points of) accuracy, etiquette, etc.

stick′y, *a.* tending to stick.

stiff, *a.* not easily bent or changed in shape; not working freely, sticking; difficult; reserved or formal in manner. **stiff-necked,** obstinate. **stiff′en,** *v.* make or become stiff.

sti′fle, *v.* smother; (cause to) feel oppressed or unable to breathe; suppress.

stig′ma, *n.* (pl. *stigmas, stigmata*), mark of disgrace, stain on one's good name; (Bot.) part of flower to which pollen grains adhere; (pl., *stigmata*) marks resembling wounds on crucified body of Christ. **stig′matize,** *v.t.* (esp., fig.) describe in terms of disgrace or condemnation.

stile, *n.* set of steps, bars, etc., to enable persons to pass over fence, wall, etc.

stilett′ō, *n.* (pl. *stilettos*), short dagger; pointed implement for making eyelets, etc.

still¹, *n.* apparatus for distilling liquids (esp. for making alcoholic spirits). **still-room,** housekeeper's store-room in large house.

still², *a.* (almost) without motion or sound; tranquil; (of wine, etc.) not effervescing. *n.* deep silence; photograph, esp. single shot from motion film. *v.* quiet, calm, appease, make or grow still. *adv.* now as formerly, then as before; nevertheless; even, yet. **still-born,** born dead. **still life,** representation in painting, etc., of fruit, furniture, or other inanimate things. **still′y,** *a.* (Poet.) still, quiet.

stilt, *n.* one of pair of poles with foot-rests enabling user to walk with feet some distance above ground. **stil′ted,** *a.* (of style, manner, etc.) stiff, pompous.

stim′ulant, *a.* producing temporary increase of activity or energy. *n.* stimulant drug, drink, etc.

stim′ulate, *v.t.* animate, excite, make more vigorous or active. **stimūlā′tion,** *n.*

stim′ulus, *n.* (pl. *stimuli*), thing that rouses to activity or energy; rousing effect.

sting, *n.* sharp-pointed organ in some insects, etc., sharp-pointed hair in some plants, capable of giving painful, irritable, or dangerous wound, rash, etc.; wound or pain caused by sting; (fig.) acute bodily or mental pain. *v.* (p.t. *stung*), wound with sting; feel or cause acute pain; be able to sting.

stin′gy (-ji), *a.* mean, niggardly, not generous.

stink, *v.* (p.t. *stank* or *stunk*; p.p. *stunk*), have bad or offensive smell; drive *out* by stink, fumes, etc. *n.* bad or offensive smell.

stint, *v.t.* keep on short allowance, supply or give in niggardly or grudging way. *n.* limitation of supply, etc.; fixed or allotted amount of work, etc.

sti′pend, *n.* salary. **stipen′diary,** *a.* receiving stipend. *n.* stipendiary magistrate. **stipendiary magistrate,** paid legally qualified magistrate.

stipp′le, *v.* paint or draw by using dots rather than lines, etc.

stip′ūlāte, *v.* require or insist upon, make express demand *for*, as essential condition. **stipūlā′tion,** *n.*

stir, *v.* (p.t. *stirred*), set, keep, (begin to) be, in motion; agitate soft or liquid mass with circular motion; rouse, touch emotions of. *stir up,* incite, rouse; cause (trouble, etc.). *n.* (slight sound of) movement; stirring; commotion, excitement.

sti′rrup, *n.* support, usu. of metal, suspended by strap from saddle for rider's foot.

stitch, *n.* (loop of thread, etc., made or left by) each movement of threaded needle in and out of fabric in sewing, or single movement of needle, hook, etc., in knitting, crochet, etc.; method of making stitch, kind of work produced; acute pain in side of body. *v.* sew.

stoat, *n.* animal of weasel kind, esp. ermine in its brown summer coat.

stock, *n.* store of goods, etc., ready to draw on; equipment for carrying on business, etc.; animals of a farm; growing plant into which graft is inserted; base or handle of implement, rifle, etc.; (source of) family or breed; money loaned to form State fund or capital of company; liquor made by stewing meat, bones, etc.; wide band for neck; fragrant flowering-plant; (pl.) timbers on which ship rests while building; (pl., Hist.) wooden framework set up in public in which offenders' ankles were secured. *v.t.* provide (shop, farm) with goods, livestock, etc.; keep (goods) in stock. **stock′broker,** person who buys and sells stocks and shares for clients. **stock exchange,** market, building, for buying and selling of stocks and shares. **stock′man,** (pl. -*men*), man employed to look after cattle, etc. **stock-still,** quite motionless.

stockāde′, *n.* & *v.t.* (fortify or enclose with) line of upright stakes as defence, etc.

stock′inet (*or* -et′), *n.* fine knitted textile material.

stock'ing, *n.* close-fitting, usu. knitted, covering for foot and leg up to or above knee.

stock'ist, *n.* person who stocks specified goods for sale.

stock'y, *a.* short and strongly built, sturdy.

stodg'y, *a.* heavy, solid; dull.

stō'ic, *n.* person of great fortitude and self--control. **stō'ical,** *a.* **stō'icism,** *n.*

stōke, *v.* feed or tend fire or furnace (of). **stō'ker,** *n.* one who stokes furnace, esp. of ship or locomotive.

stōle¹, *n.* long narrow band worn by officiating clergyman round neck, with ends hanging down in front; woman's shoulder-wrap.

stole², stolen, *p.t. & p.p.* of **steal.**

stol'id, *a.* slow to feel or show feeling; not easily moved; dull. **stolid'ity,** *n.*

stomach (stum'ak), *n.* cavity into which food passes for digestion; desire or courage *for.* *v.t.* endure, tolerate.

stōne, *n.* piece of rock, esp. of small or moderate size; stones or rock as substance or material; (hard wood-like case of) kernel in stone-fruit; unit of weight (14 lb.). *v.t.* pelt with stones; take stones out of (fruit). *stone--blind, -cold, -dead, -deaf,* etc., quite blind, etc. **stone-fruit,** fruit with seed enclosed in hard shell surrounded by pulp. **stō'ny,** *a.* abounding in stones; hard or unfeeling.

stood, *p.t. & p.p.* of **stand.**

stook, *n.* group of corn-sheaves propped together in field. *v.t.* arrange in stooks.

stōol, *n.* seat without arms or back; footstool; faeces discharged from bowels.

stōop, *v.* bend down; carry head and shoulders bowed forward; lower oneself, condescend, (*to*). *n.* stooping carriage of body.

stop, *v.* (p.t. *stopped*), bring (motion) to an end; check progress, motion, or operation of; hinder or prevent; cease (from), discontinue; close or fill aperture, cavity, etc.; forbid or block passage through; (*informal*) remain, stay. *n.* stopping, being stopped; pause, halt; place at which bus, etc., stops; (full stop; organ-stop. **stop'cock,** valve stopping or regulating flow of liquid through pipe. **stop'gap,** makeshift, temporary substitute. **stop-press,** (news) inserted in paper after printing has begun. **stop-watch,** watch that may be started and stopped at will for timing races, etc. **stopp'age,** *n.* action of stopping; being stopped. **stopp'er,** *n.* (esp.) plug for closing bottle, etc.

stor'age, *n.* (space for, charge for) storing of goods. **storage heater,** electric radiator storing heat accumulated in off-peak periods.

store, *n.* quantity or supply of something accumulated for use as needed; large shop selling goods of many different kinds; (U.S.) shop. *in store,* in reserve, to come, waiting for. *v.t.* keep for future use; deposit or keep in warehouse. **store'house,** place where things are stored. **store-room,** room for storing supplies.

stor'ey, *n.* (pl. *storeys*), each stage or portion into which building is divided horizontally.

stork, *n.* large long-legged wading bird with long stout bill.

storm, *n.* violent disturbance of the atmosphere, with high winds, rain, thunder, etc.; heavy fal' of rain, etc.; disturbance in human affairs, tumult, agitation; assault on fortified place. *take by storm,* take by assault (often fig.). *v.* take by storm; rush violently; rage; shout angrily (*at*). **storm'bound,** unable to continue voyage, etc., because of storm(s). **stor'my,** *a.* like, characteristic of, marked by, associated or connected with, storm(s).

stor'y, *n.* narrative of past or imaginary events or of course of life of person, institution, etc.; plot of novel, play, or film; (*informal*) lie, fib.

stout, *a.* of considerable thickness or strength; corpulent; undaunted, resolute. *n.* heavy dark type of beer.

stove¹, *p.t. & p.p.* of **stave.**

stove², *n.* closed apparatus designed to contain burning fuel or consume gas, electricity, etc., for heating, cooking, etc.

stow (-ō), *v.t.* pack (*away*), esp. closely or compactly. **stow'away,** person hiding on ship or aircraft, esp. to avoid paying fare. **stow'age,** *n.* stowing; room or space for stowing.

stradd'le, *v.* spread legs wide apart; stand or sit across with straddled legs.

stragg'le, *v.i.* lag behind or stray from main body, be dispersed or scattered, grow irregularly or loosely. **stragg'ler,** *n.*

straight (-āt), *a.* extending uniformly in same direction, without curve or bend; not oblique; correctly placed; in proper order; going direct to mark; without delay; upright, honest, candid. *adv.* in straight line; direct. **straight away,** immediately. **straightfor'ward,** honest, open; not complicated. **straight'en,** *v.* make or become straight.

strain¹, *n.* breed, stock.

strain², *v.* stretch tightly; stretch beyond normal degree, force to extreme effort, exert to utmost; injure by over-use, etc.; strive intensely; clear liquid of solid matter by passing through sieve, etc. *n.* (injury or damage due to) straining or being strained; tension; (part of) melody; tone, style, character. **strained** (-nd), *a.* (esp., of feelings and behaviour) produced by effort, artificial; dangerously tense. **strai'ner,** *n.* (esp.) utensil for straining or filtering.

strait, *a.* (*archaic*) narrow. *n.* narrow passage of water connecting two larger bodies of water; (pl.) difficult position, need. **strait jacket,** strong garment used to restrain violent persons. **strait-laced,** severely virtuous, strict in morals. **strai'ten,** *v.t.* reduce to poverty. **straitened circumstances,** inadequate means of living, poverty.

strand¹, *n.* land bordering sea, river, etc. *v.*

run aground. **stran'ded,** *a.* left without adequate resources or means of transport.

strand², *n.* one of threads, strings, etc., twisted together to form rope, etc.; thread, string of beads, filament or lock of hair.

strānge (-nj), *a.* not previously known, met with, or experienced; foreign; not one's own; queer, surprising, unexpected; unaccustomed *to,* bewildered.

strân'ger (-j-), *n.* person in place, company, etc., he does not belong to; person strange to someone or something.

strang'le (-nggl), *v.t.* kill by external compression of throat; hinder breathing of; suppress.

strang'ŭlāte (-ngg-), *v.t.* constrict so as to prevent circulation or passage of fluid. **strangŭlā'tion,** *n.* strangling, being strangled; strangulating.

strap, *n.* flat strip of leather, etc., esp. with buckle, etc., for holding things together. *v.t.* (p.t. *strapped*), supply, fasten, with strap; apply strapping to; thrash with strap. **strapp'ing,** *a.* tall and strong. *n.* (esp.) strip(s) of sticking-plaster; thrashing.

strata: see **stratum.**

strat'agèm, *n.* device(s) for deceiving enemy; trick.

stratē'gic, *a.* of, by, or serving purpose of, strategy; advantageous. **stratē'gical,** *a.* **stratē'gically,** *adv.*

strat'ègy, *n.* art of war; planning and conduct of campaign or war. **strat'ègist,** *n.*

strathspey' (-pā), *n.* (music for) Scottish dance.

strat'ifȳ, *v.* form or divide into, arrange in, strata or layers. **stratificā'tion,** *n.*

strat'osphēre, *n.* region of atmosphere above troposphere, in which temperature does not decrease with increasing height.

strā'tum (-ah- *or* -ā-), *n.* (pl. *strata*), layer of sedimentary rock; level or grade in social position, etc.

straw, *n.* dry cut stalks of various cereals; single stalk of this; insignificant trifle.

straw'berry, *n.* (trailing plant bearing) juicy edible pulpy, usu. red, fruit.

stray, *v.i.* turn aside or get separated from right way, companions, home, etc.; wander, go aimlessly. *a.* strayed; isolated, occasional. *n.* strayed animal; homeless or friendless person.

streak, *n.* irregular line or band of different colour or substance from rest of surface, material, etc.; trace, trait. *v.* mark with streaks; go very fast. **strea'ky,** *a.*

stream, *n.* (esp. small) body of running water; current or flow. *v.* flow or move as or in stream; run with liquid; float or wave in wind, current of water, etc. **strea'mer,** *n.* ribbon, etc., attached at one end and floating or waving at the other. **stream'lèt,** *n.* small stream, brook.

stream'līne, *v.t.* shape (esp. aircraft, car, etc.)

so as to give minimum of resistance to air, etc. **stream'līned,** *a.*

street, *n.* road in town or village with houses or shops on one side or both.

strength, *n.* being strong; degree in which person or thing is strong; number of persons present or available. *on the strength of,* relying on, arguing from. **streng'then,** *v.* make or become stronger.

stren'ūous, *a.* making or requiring great exertion.

stress, *n.* pressure, tension, strain; (Mech.) force exerted between contiguous bodies or parts; emphasis; greater force used in uttering syllable, etc., playing musical note, etc. *v.t.* lay stress on; emphasize; subject to mechanical stress.

stretch, *v.* draw, be drawn, or be able to be drawn out into greater length, size, etc.; make taut; tighten, straighten; extend; strain; exaggerate; be of specified length or extent. *stretch out,* extend hand, etc. *n.* stretching, being stretched; continuous expanse, tract, or spell. *a.* (of fabric, etc.) elastic. **stretch'er,** *n.* (esp.) oblong frame with handles at each end for carrying sick or injured person. **stretch'y,** *a.* liable to stretch.

strew (-ōō), *v.t.* (p.t. *strewed*; p.p. *strewed* or *strewn*), scatter over surface; cover (surface, etc.) with small objects scattered.

striā'ted, *a.* marked with lines, slight ridges or furrows, etc. **striā'tion,** *n.*

strick'en, *a.* afflicted with disease, grief, etc.

strict, *a.* (of discipline, obedience, etc.) permitting no relaxation or indulgence; stern; exact, precise, accurately defined or limited.

stric'ture (-cher), *n.* (usu. in pl.) criticism or blame, critical remark.

strīde, *v.* (p.t. *strōde*; p.p. *stridden*), walk with long steps; pass *over, across,* etc., with one step. *n.* single step in walking or running.

strī'dent, *a.* loud and harsh, grating.

strīfe, *n.* conflict, struggle, dispute.

strīke, *v.* (p.t. *struck*; p.p. *struck* or occasionally *stricken*), deliver blow(s) or stroke(s) (on), hit; afflict, attack suddenly; make (coin) by stamping; touch (string or key of musical instrument); (of clock) sound hour; reach oil, etc., by drilling; produce fire, spark, etc., by friction; arrest attention of, occur to mind of, produce impression on; assume (attitude); cease work, esp. by common agreement, to obtain better conditions, pay, etc. *strike off,* erase, cancel. *n.* concerted refusal to go on working; sudden discovery of oil, ore, etc. *on strike,* taking part in strike. **strī'ker,** *n.* (esp.) worker on strike. **strī'king,** *a.* (esp.) noticeable, impressive.

string, *n.* fine cord, twine; length of this or some other material serving to tie, attach, lace, etc.; catgut, wire, etc., yielding tone(s) in musical instruments; tough fibre; things threaded together; succession of things. *v.*

(p.t. *strung*), supply, fit, tie, with string(s); thread on string. **stringed** (-ngd), *a.* (of musical instrument) having strings. **string'y** (-ngi), *a.* fibrous; like string.

strin'gent (-j-), *a.* strict, binding. **strin'gency,** *a.*

strip[1], *n.* long narrow piece or tract; strip cartoon. **strip cartoon,** set or line of drawings telling story; comic strip.

strip[2], *v.* (p.t. *stripped*), make naked or bare; deprive *of* covering, property, etc.; undress; pull or tear off.

stripe[1], *n.* long narrow band differing in colour or texture from surface on either side; piece of braid, etc., sewn on, esp. chevron indicating non-commissioned rank. **striped,** *a.* marked, ornamented, with stripes.

stripe[2], *n.* (*archaic*) stroke or lash with whip, etc.

strip'ling, *n.* youth approaching manhood.

strive, *v.i.* (p.t. *strōve*; p.p. *striven*), try hard; engage in strife *with*; contend *against*.

strode, *p.t.* of **stride.**

strōke[1], *n.* act of striking, blow; sudden favourable piece *of* luck; apoplectic seizure; movement of a recurrent or regulated kind; sound made by a striking clock; (mark made by) movement of pen, pencil, brush, etc.; oarsman rowing nearest stern and setting rate of rowing. *v.t.* act as stroke to (boat, crew).

strōke[2], *v.t.* pass hand gently over.

strōll, *v.i.* walk in leisurely manner. *n.* leisurely walk.

strong, *a.* (*stronger, strongest,* pr. -ngg-), physically, morally, or mentally powerful, vigorous, or robust; powerful in numbers, equipment, etc.; difficult to capture, escape from, etc.; not easily broken, damaged, etc.; powerfully affecting senses or mind; (of drink) with large proportion of alcohol, flavouring ingredient, etc.; (of verbs) forming inflexions by vowel change in root syllable. **strong'hold,** fortress, citadel. **strong point,** (esp.) thing in which person excels. **strong'ly,** *adv.*

strop, *n.* strip of leather, etc., for sharpening razor. *v.t.* (p.t. *stropped*), sharpen on strop.

strove, *p.t.* of **strive.**

struck, *p.t.* & *p.p.* of **strike.**

struc'ture (-cher), *n.* way in which building, etc., is constructed; supporting framework or essential parts; thing constructed; complex whole; building; (Biol.) component part of organism. **struc'tural,** *a.*

strugg'le, *v.i.* fight, grapple; throw limbs about in violent effort to get free; make one's way with difficulty; strive hard. *n.* struggling; effort under difficulties; hard contest.

strum, *v.* (p.t. *strummed*), play unskilfully or monotonously on piano, etc. *n.* strumming sound.

strum'pêt, *n.* (*archaic*) prostitute.

strung, *p.t.* & *p.p.* of **string.**

strut, *n.* bar inserted in framework to resist pressure or thrust in direction of its length; strutting gait. *v.* (p.t. *strutted*), walk in pompous way; brace with struts.

strych'nine (-knēn), *n.* highly poisonous alkaloid.

stub, *n.* stump of tree, tooth, etc.; short remnant of cigarette, pencil, etc. *v.t.* (p.t. *stubbed*), rid (ground) of stubs, dig up (root, etc.); bump (toe) painfully (*on*); put *out* (cigarette) by pressing lighted end against something.

stubb'le, *n.* short grain-stalks left in ground after reaping; stubble-like growth of hair, esp. on unshaven face. **stubb'ly,** *a.*

stubb'orn, *a.* obstinate, unyielding; difficult to manage.

stucc'ō, *n.* fine plaster for ceilings, cornices, etc.; coarse plaster or cement for coating exterior of walls. *v.t.* coat or ornament with stucco.

stuck, *p.t.* & *p.p.* of **stick.**

stud[1], *n.* projecting nail-head or knob on surface; kind of two-headed button for use with two eyelets or button-holes. *v.t.* (p.t. *studded*), set with studs. **studd'ed,** *a.* thickly set or strewn *with*.

stud[2], *n.* number of horses kept for breeding, racing, etc.

stū'dent, *n.* person undergoing instruction in university, college, etc.; person engaged in or devoted to study.

stū'diō, *n.* (pl. *studios*), work-room of sculptor, painter, photographer, etc.; room or premises used for transmission of broadcasts, making films or recordings, etc.

stū'dious, *a.* having habit of studying, devoted to learning; painstaking.

stud'y, *n.* devotion of time and thought to acquiring information, esp. from books; pursuit of some branch of knowledge; (Mus.) composition designed to develop player's skill; room used for literary, etc., work. *v.* make a study of; give time and thought to understanding subject, etc.; scrutinize. **stud'ied,** *a.* deliberate, intentional.

stuff, *n.* material for making garments; woollen fabric; substance or things of uncertain kind or inferior quality; (*informal*) nonsense. *v.* fill tightly (*with*); fill out skin to restore original shape of (bird, beast, etc.); fill with stuffing. **stuff'ing,** *n.* mixture of chopped seasoned meat, bread-crumbs, herbs, etc., used to stuff fowl, etc., before cooking; padding for furniture. **stuff'y,** *a.* lacking ventilation, close, oppressive.

stul'tifÿ, *v.t.* render worthless or useless; reduce to foolishness or absurdity.

stum'ble, *v.i.* lurch forward, have partial fall, from catching foot, etc.; make blunder(s) in speaking, etc.; come accidentally (*up*)*on*. *n.* act of stumbling. **stumbling-block,** circumstance causing difficulty or hesitation.

stump, *n.* part of felled or fallen tree that remains projecting from ground; part remaining of broken branch or tooth, amputated limb, etc.; (Cricket) one of three uprights of wicket. *v.* walk stiffly, clumsily, and noisily; (of wicket-keeper) end innings of (batsman out of his ground) by touching stumps with ball; (*informal*) bewilder, baffle. **stum'py,** *a.* short and thick.

stun, *v.t.* (p.t. *stunned*), knock senseless; daze or stupefy with strong emotion, etc.

stung, *p.t. & p.p.* of **sting.**

stunk, *p.t. & p.p.* of **stink.**

stunt¹, *v.t.* check growth or development of, dwarf. **stun'ted,** *a.* undersized.

stunt², *n.* (*informal*) spectacular or daring feat; advertising device.

stū'pėfȳ, *v.t.* make stupid or torpid, dull wits or senses of. **stūpėfac'tion,** *n.*

stūpen'dous, *a.* amazing; of vast size or importance.

stū'pid, *a.* dull by nature, slow-witted, unintelligent; in state of stupor; uninteresting. **stūpid'ity,** *n.*

stū'por, *n.* dazed or almost unconscious state; helpless amazement.

stur'dy, *a.* robust, vigorous, solidly built.

stur'geon (-jn), *n.* large edible fish.

stutt'er, *v. & n.* stammer.

stȳ¹, *n.* (pl. *stīes*), pig-sty (see **pig**).

stȳ² (pl. *stīes*), **stȳe** (pl. *stȳes*), *nn.* inflamed swelling on edge of eyelid.

Sty'gian, *a.* of Styx or Hades; dark, gloomy.

stȳle, *n.* manner of writing, speaking, or doing; manner characteristic of artist, writer, period, etc.; title, mode of address; kind, pattern, type; fashion; noticeably superior quality or manner; stylus (ancient writing-implement); (Bot.) slender part of pistil supporting stigma. **stȳ'lish,** *a.* having good style, fashionable. **stȳlis'tic,** *a.* of literary or artistic style.

stȳ'lus, *n.* fine point (of diamond or sapphire) used in making or playing gramophone records; pointed rod with which the ancients wrote on wax-covered tablets.

styp'tic, *a. & n.* (substance) that checks bleeding.

Styx, *n.* (Gk. myth.) river of Hades over which shades of the dead were ferried.

suave (swahv), *a.* blandly polite; smooth in manner.

sub-, *pref.* (often assimilated to *suc-* before *c, suf-* before *f, sug-* before *g, sup-* before *p, sus-* before *c, p, t*; sometimes to *sum-* before *m, sur-* before *r*) under, below; subordinate(ly), subsidiary, secondary; next below or after, near or close (to); further.

sub'altern, *n.* (Mil.) commissioned officer below rank of captain.

subcon'scious (-shus), *a. & n.* (of) those mental activities of which one is not (fully) aware.

subcon'tinent, *n.* land-mass of great extent not classed as continent.

subcūtā'nėous, *a.* under the skin.

subdivīde', *v.* divide further. **subdivi'sion** (-zhn), *n.*

subdūe', *v.t.* conquer, bring into subjection, overcome; soften, tone down.

sub-ed'it, *v.t.* act as assistant editor of; prepare (copy) for editor to supervise. **sub-ed'itor,** *n.* assistant editor.

subhū'man, *a.* less than human; characteristic of animals other than human beings.

sub'ject, *a.* under government; politically dependent; owing obedience *to*; liable or exposed or prone *to*. *subject to*, conditional(ly) upon. *n.* person subject to political rule; member of State or of subject State; thinking or feeling entity, conscious self; person of specified characteristics; theme of discussion; department of study; (Gram.) thing about which something is predicated; (Mus.) principal phrase or melody of movement or composition. **subject'**, *v.t.* subdue, make subject. *subject to*, expose or make liable to, cause to undergo or experience. **subjec'tion,** *n.*

subjec'tive, *a.* having its source in the mind; concerned with thoughts or feelings; personal, individual; (Gram.) of subject, nominative.

subjoin', *v.t.* add at end.

sub ju'dicė (joō-), (Law) under judicial consideration, not yet decided. (Latin)

sub'jugāte (-joo-), *v.t.* bring into subjection, conquer. **subjugā'tion,** *n.*

subjunc'tive, *a.* (Gram., of verbal mood) expressing wish, or conditional or hypothetical events, etc. *n.* subjunctive mood.

sublet', *v.t.* (p.t. *sublet*), let (property of which one is tenant) to subtenant.

sub'limate, *n.* (Chem.) product of sublimation. **sub'limāte,** *v.t.* convert into something nobler, more refined, etc. **sublimā'tion,** *n.* sublimating; (Chem.) conversion of substance by heat to vapour which on cooling is deposited in solid form.

sublime', *a.* of most exalted kind; inspiring awe and wonder by beauty, vastness, grandeur, etc. **sublim'ity,** *n.*

sublim'inal, *a.* below threshold of consciousness, too faint or rapid to be recognized.

sub'marine (-ēn; *or* -ēn'), *a.* existing, lying, operating, etc., under surface of sea. *n.* vessel, esp. warship, which can be submerged and navigated under water.

submerge', *v.* (cause to) sink or plunge under water; cover with water, inundate. **submer'gence,** *n.*

submersed' (-st), *a.* submerged; (Bot.) growing under water. **submer'sible,** *a.* **submersibil'ity,** *n.* **submer'sion** (-shn), *n.*

submi'ssion (-shn), *n.* submitting, being submitted; submissive attitude, conduct, etc. **submiss'ive,** *a.* inclined to submit, humble, obedient.

submit', *v.* (p.t. *submitted*), surrender oneself, become subject, yield (*to*); put forward for consideration, decision, etc.

subnor'mal, *a.* below normal.

subor'dinate, *a.* of inferior importance or rank. *n.* person under control or orders of another. **subor'dinate,** *v.t.* make subordinate; treat or regard as of minor importance. **subordina'tion,** *n.*

suborn', *v.t.* bribe or induce to commit perjury or other unlawful act.

sub-plot, *n.* secondary plot of play, etc.

subpoe'na (-pēn-), *n.* writ commanding person's attendance in court of justice. *v.t.* serve subpoena on.

subscribe', *v.* make contribution *to* common fund, society, etc.; express one's agreement, acquiescence, etc., *to*; sign (one's name). **subscri'ber,** *n.* **subscrip'tion,** *n.*

sub'sequent, *a.* following in order, time, or succession, esp. coming immediately after. **sub'sequently,** *adv.*

subser'vience, *n.* (esp.) subservient behaviour, attitude or conduct, obsequiousness.

subser'vient, *a.* slavishly submissive, obsequious; subordinate, subject (*to*); serving as means to further end or purpose.

subside', *v.i.* sink down, sink to low(er), esp. normal, level; (of swelling, etc.) go down; abate, die away. **sub'sidence** (*or* -ī-), *n.*

subsid'iary, *a.* subordinate and serving to assist or supplement; secondary.

sub'sidize, *v.t.* pay subsidy to; support by subsidies.

sub'sidy, *n.* financial aid from government or organization towards expenses of an undertaking, etc., or to keep prices down.

subsist', *v.t.* (continue to) exist; maintain or support oneself. **subsis'tence,** *n.* subsisting; means of supporting life.

sub'soil, *n.* soil immediately under surface soil.

subson'ic, *a.* having speed less than speed of sound.

sub'stance, *n.* particular kind or species of matter; material; reality; essence or most important part of anything; general meaning, gist; (*archaic*) possessions, wealth.

sub-stan'dard, *a.* inferior, of lower than average standard.

substan'tial (-shl), *a.* of solid material or structure; of considerable amount or importance; real, actually existing; well-to-do; sound. **substantial'ity** (-shi-), *n.*

substan'tiate (-shi-), *v.t.* demonstrate or verify by proof or evidence. **substantia'tion,** *n.*

sub'stantive, *a.* having separate and independent existence. *n.* noun.

sub'stitute, *n.* person or thing acting or serving in place of another. *v.* put in place of another; act as substitute. **substitu'tion,** *n.*

substra'tum (-ah- *or* -ā-), *n.* (pl. *substrata*), lower layer; basis.

subten'ant, *n.* person who rents property from a tenant. **subten'ancy,** *n.*

subtend', *v.t.* (Geom., of line, etc.) be opposite to (angle, arc).

subter-, *pref.* under; secretly.

sub'terfuge, *n.* trick or excuse, esp. one adopted to escape or avoid blame, difficulty, etc.

subterra'nean, *a.* underground.

sub'-title, *n.* subordinate or additional title of book, etc.; film caption. *v.t.* add sub-titles to.

subtle (sut'l), *a.* difficult to perceive or analyse because of fineness and delicacy; making fine distinctions; ingenious, clever; crafty, cunning. **subtlety** (sut'lti), *n.*

subtract', *v.t.* take away (part, quantity, number) from whole, quantity, or number, esp. in arithmetic, etc. **subtrac'tion,** *n.*

subtrop'ical, *a.* (characteristic of regions) bordering on the tropics.

sub'urb, *n.* residential district lying on or near outskirts of town. **subur'ban,** *a.* **subur'bia,** *n.* suburbs; their inhabitants.

subver'sion (-shn), *n.* subverting, being subverted. **subver'sive,** *a.* tending to subvert.

subvert', *v.t.* overthrow, bring about destruction or ruin of (religion, government, etc.).

sub'way, *n.* underground passage, esp. for pedestrians to cross below road(s), etc.; (U.S.) underground railway.

suc-, *pref.*: see **sub-.**

succeed' (-ks-), *v.* come next after and take place of; come next (to), follow; come by inheritance or in course of time to title, office, etc.; be successful; accomplish one's purpose.

success' (-ks-), *n.* favourable outcome; attainment of object, wealth, fame, etc.; person or thing that succeeds. **success'ful,** *a.* **success'fully,** *adv.*

succe'ssion (-kseshn), *n.* following in order; series of things one after another; (right of) succeeding to throne. **success'ive,** *a.* coming one after another in uninterrupted sequence. **success'or,** *n.* person or thing succeeding another.

succinct' (-ks-), *a.* brief, concise, terse.

succ'our (-ker), *v.t.* come to assistance of. *n.* help given in time of need.

succ'ulent, *a.* juicy; (Bot.) having fleshy or juicy tissues. *n.* succulent plant. **succ'ulence,** *n.*

succumb' (-m), *v.i.* be conquered; give way *to*; die.

such, *a.* of kind, degree, or extent described, referred to, or implied; so great, so eminent, etc. *pron.* that; the action, etc., referred to; other such thing(s).

suck, *v.* draw (liquid) into mouth by contracting muscles of lips, tongue, and cheeks; draw liquid or nourishment from; perform sucking action, make sucking sound. *n.* sucking. *give suck,* suckle.

suck'er, *n.* animal organ adapted for sucking,

or for adhering by suction to surfaces; shoot springing from root of plant; person, thing, etc., that sucks; (*slang*) person easily deceived or tricked.

suck'le, *v.t.* feed (young) at breast or udder.

suck'ling, *n.* child or animal that has not been weaned.

sū'crōse, *n.* kind of sugar obtained from sugar-cane, sugar-beet, etc.

suc'tion, *n.* sucking; production of vacuum so that external atmospheric pressure forces fluid into vacant space or causes adhesion of surfaces.

sudd'en, *a.* coming, happening, performed, etc., unexpectedly or without warning; abrupt, sharp. **sudd'enly,** *adv.* **sudd'enness** (-n-n-), *n.*

suds (-z), *n.pl.* mass of bubbles in soapy water; lather.

sūe, *v.* institute legal proceedings, bring civil action, (against); plead, appeal (*for*).

suede (swād), *n.* kid-skin or other leather with flesh side rubbed into nap.

sū'ĕt, *n.* hard fat surrounding kidneys of cattle and sheep, used in cooking.

suf-, *pref.*: see **sub-**.

suff'er, *v.* undergo or be subjected to pain, loss, punishment, grief, etc.; permit (*to*), tolerate. **suff'erance,** *n.* tacit permission or toleration. **suff'ering,** *n.* (esp.) pain, etc., suffered.

suffice', *v.* be enough; meet needs of.

suffi'cient (-shnt), *a.* sufficing; adequate, esp. in amount or number; enough. **suffi'ciency,** *n.* (esp.) sufficient supply, adequate provision.

suff'ix, *n.* syllable(s), particle, etc., attached to end of word in inflexion or to make another word.

suff'ocāte, *v.* kill, stifle, choke, by stopping respiration; (cause to) feel suffocated. **suffocā'tion,** *n.*

suff'ragan, *a.* & *n.* (bishop) appointed to assist diocesan bishop in particular part of diocese.

suff'rage, *n.* right of voting, esp. in political elections. **suffragette',** *n.* (Hist.) woman campaigning for women's suffrage.

suffūse' (-z), *v.t.* (of colour, light, tears, etc.) spread, become diffused, over. **suffū'sion** (-zhn), *n.*

sug-, *pref.*: see **sub-**.

su'gar (shoo-), *n.* sweet crystalline substance obtained from juices, esp. of sugar-cane and sugar-beet; (Chem.) any of group of soluble sweet carbohydrates. *v.t.* sweeten or coat with sugar; make agreeable or palatable. **sugar-beet,** white beet yielding sugar. **sugar-cane,** tall tropical and subtropical grass yielding sugar. **sugar-loaf,** conical mass of refined sugar. **su'gary,** *a.* like sugar; containing much sugar; cloying, sentimental.

suggest' (suj-), *v.t.* propose for acceptance; cause (idea) to be present to mind; give hint

or inkling of. **sugges'tible,** *a.* (esp.) capable of being influenced by suggestion. **suggestibil'ity,** *n.* **sugges'tion,** *n.* suggesting; theory, plan, thought, etc., suggested. **sugges'tive,** *a.* (esp.) having an indecent meaning.

sū'icīde, *n.* intentional killing of oneself; person who kills himself intentionally; action destructive to one's own interests, etc. **sūicī'dal,** *a.*

suit (sūt *or* sōōt), *n.* set of garments (esp. coat and trousers or skirt); any of four sets of playing-cards in pack; suing; lawsuit; courting of woman, courtship. *v.t.* adapt or make appropriate *to*; meet requirements of; be convenient to; go well with; be becoming to. **suit-case,** case for carrying clothes, etc., usu. with flat hinged lid and one handle. **suit'able,** *a.* suited *to* or *for*; well fitted for purpose; appropriate to occasion. **suitabil'ity,** *n.*

suite (swēt), *n.* set of attendants, retinue; set of rooms or furniture; (Mus.) set of instrumental compositions.

suit'or (sūt-), *n.* man courting a woman; plaintiff or petitioner in lawsuit.

sulk, *v.i.* be sulky. *n.* (usu. in pl.) sulky fit or state. **sul'ky,** *a.* silent, inactive, or unsociable from resentment or bad temper; sullen.

sull'en, *a.* silently bad-tempered or resentful; gloomy, dismal.

sull'y, *v.t.* soil, tarnish; (fig.) be stain on, discredit.

sul'phāte, *n.* salt of sulphuric acid. **sul'phīde,** *n.* compound of sulphur with another element.

sul'phur (-er), *n.* pale-yellow non-metallic element burning with blue flame and stifling smell. **sulphūr'ēous,** *a.* of or like sulphur; having qualities associated with (burning) sulphur. **sulphūr'ic,** *a.* of, containing, sulphur. **sulphuric acid,** dense, highly corrosive, oily acid. **sul'phūrous,** *a.* sulphureous; (pr. -fūr'-) (Chem.) containing sulphur of lower valency than sulphuric compounds.

sul'tan, *n.* sovereign of Muslim country, esp. (Hist.) of Turkey. **sul'tanate,** *n.*

sulta'na (-tah-), *n.* small light-coloured seedless raisin; sultan's wife.

sul'try, *a.* oppressively hot.

sum, *n.* total resulting from addition of items; amount of money; arithmetical problem. *v.* (p.t. *summed*), *sum up*, give total of; summarize; (of judge, etc.) recapitulate evidence, etc.

sum-, *pref.*: see **sub-**.

summ'arize, *v.t.* make or be summary of.

summ'ary, *a.* giving essential points, brief; done quickly and without formality. *n.* summary account or statement, abridgement.

summ'er, *n.* warmest season of year. *v.* pass summer; pasture (cattle). **summer-house,** light building in garden, etc.

summ'it, _n._ highest point, top, apex; highest degree. **summit conference**, meeting of heads of States.

summon, _v.t._ call together, require presence or attendance of; order by authority to appear before court or judge. **summon up**, call up (courage, etc.) to one's aid. **summ'ons** (-z), _n._ (pl. _summonses_), authoritative order, esp. (Law) to appear in court, answer charge, etc. _v.t._ take out summons against.

sump, _n._ oil-reservoir at bottom of internal--combustion engine; pit for collecting water, etc.

sump'tuous, _a._ costly, magnificent.

sun, _n._ celestial body forming centre of system of worlds or planets, esp. central body of solar system; light or warmth of sun. _v._ (p.t. _sunned_), expose to sun. _sun oneself_, bask in sun. **sun-bath**, exposure of skin to sun. **sun--bathe**, take sun-bath. **sun'beam**, beam of sunlight. **sun'burn**, tanning or superficial inflammation of skin from exposure to sun. **sun'dial**, contrivance for showing time by shadow cast by sun on marked surface. **sun'down**, sunset. **sun'downer**, (Austral.) tramp arriving at sheep-farm, etc., at sunset. **sun'flower**, composite plant with large yellow flower-heads. **sun'light**, light of sun. **sun'rise**, (time of) sun's rising. **sun'set**, (time of) sun's setting. **sun'shade**, parasol. **sun'shine**, sunlight, area illuminated by it; cheerfulness, bright influence. **sun'spot**, one of dark patches sometimes observed on sun's surface. **sun'stroke**, illness caused by excessive exposure to heat of sun. **sun'less**, _a._ **sunn'y**, _a._ bright with sunlight; cheerful.

sun'dae (-dā), _n._ confection of ice cream with fruit, nuts, etc.

Sun'day, _n._ first day of week, observed by Christians as day of rest and worship.

sun'der, _v.t._ (_archaic_ & Poet.) separate.

sun'dry, _a._ various, several. **sun'dries** (-iz), _n.pl._ oddments, small items.

sung, _p.p._ of **sing**.

sunk, _p.p._ of **sink**.

sunk'en, _a._ (of eyes, cheeks, etc.) hollow, fallen in.

sunny: see **sun**.

sup, _v._ (p.t. _supped_), take supper.

sup-, _pref._: see **sub-**.

super- (_or_ sōō-), _pref._ over, above, on top (of); beyond, besides; exceeding, transcending; of higher kind; more than usually.

superabun'dant, _a._ very or too abundant.

superann'uate, _v.t._ cause to retire with pension, esp. after reaching certain age; dismiss or discard as too old or out of date. **superannuā'tion**, _n._

superb' (_or_ sooo-), _a._ of most excellent or impressive kind, magnificent, majestic.

supercil'ious, _a._ haughtily contemptuous, disdainful, or superior.

superfi'cial (-shl), _a._ of or on the surface; without depth. **superficial'ity** (-shi-), _n._

su'perfine, _a._ extremely fine in quality.

superflu'ity (-floo-), _n._ superfluous amount.

super'fluous (-floo-), _a._ more than enough, excessive; needless, uncalled-for.

superhu'man, _a._ beyond normal human capacity; higher or greater than (that of) man.

superimpôse' (-z), _v.t._ place on something else.

superintend', _v._ have or exercise charge or direction (of), supervise. **superinten'dence**, _n._ **superinten'dent**, _n._ officer or official having control, oversight, or direction of institution, etc.; police officer ranking above inspector.

super'ior (_or_ soo-), _a._ higher in place, upper; higher in rank, degree, quality, etc.; having or showing consciousness of having above average qualities. _n._ person of higher rank, authority, etc.; head of monastery or convent (_Father Superior, Mother Superior_). **superio'rity**, _n._

super'lative (_or_ soo-), _a._ surpassing all others; of highest degree; (Gram., of adj., etc.) expressing highest degree of quality, etc., denoted by simple form. _n._ superlative degree or form.

su'perman, _n._ (pl. _supermen_), ideal superior man of future; man of superhuman powers or achievement.

su'permarket, _n._ self-service store selling food and household goods of all kinds.

superna'tural (-cher-), _a._ due to, manifesting, some agency above forces of nature; outside ordinary operation of cause and effect.

supernu'merary, _a. & n._ (person or thing) in excess of the normal number.

superpôse' (-z), _v.t._ place above or on something else, esp. so as to coincide. **superpô'sable**, _a._

su'perscribe, _v.t._ write or inscribe over, at top of, or outside something. **superscrip'tion**, _n._

supersēde', _v.t._ take the place of; be adopted or accepted instead of.

superson'ic, _a._ having speed greater than that of sound.

supersti'tion, _n._ (habit or belief based on) irrational fear of the unknown; belief in magic, supernatural powers, etc. **supersti'tious** (-shus), _a._

su'perstructure (-cher), _n._ structure resting on something else as a foundation; parts of ship, etc., above main deck.

supervēne', _v.i._ occur as an interruption or as bringing about a change. **superven'tion**, _n._

su'pervise (-z; _or_ -īz'), _v.t._ superintend performance, movements, work, etc., of; oversee. **supervi'sion** (-zhn), _n._ **su'pervisor**, _n._ **supervi'sory**, _a._

su'pine, _a._ lying face upwards; indolent, lethargic, inert.

supp'er, _n._ meal taken at end of day, esp. evening meal less formal and substantial than dinner. **supp'erless**, _a._

supplant' (-ah-), *v.t.* seize the place of, esp. by dishonourable or treacherous means.

supp'le, *a.* easily bent, pliant, flexible. *v.t.* make supple.

supp'lément, *n.* thing added to supply deficiency, give more information, etc.; addition to complete literary work, etc.; special part or number of periodical. **supplèment',** *v.t.* make additions to. **supplèmen'tary,** *a.*

supp'liant, *n.* humble petitioner. *a.* supplicating.

supp'licáte, *v.* make humble request to or for. **supplicá'tion,** *n.* **supplicá'tory,** *a.*

suppli'er, *n.* person or firm supplying goods, etc.

supply', *v.t.* furnish or provide (with) thing needed; make up for (deficiency, etc.). *n.* provision of what is needed; stock, store; (pl.) necessaries; person, esp. teacher, acting as temporary substitute for another.

support', *v.t.* bear (part of) weight of; keep from falling; give strength or assistance to, encourage; supply with home, food, clothing, etc.; substantiate; be in favour of; endure; be supporting or being supported; person or thing that supports. **suppor'ter,** *n.*

suppóse' (-z), *v.t.* assume to be true, take as fact; be inclined to think, accept as probable. *be supposed,* be required or expected *to* do. **suppó'sedly,** *adv.* **supposi'tion,** *n.* what is supposed or assumed.

suppress', *v.t.* put down, quell, put an end to existence or activity of; keep secret or unexpressed. **suppre'ssion** (-shn), *n.* **suppress'or,** *n.* (esp.) device to suppress electrical interference with radio or TV reception.

supp'úráte, *v.i.* form pus. **suppúrá'tion,** *n.*

súpra-, *pref.* super-.

súprem'acy (*or* soo-), *n.* being supreme; position of supreme authority or power.

súprême', (*or* soo-), *a.* highest in authority or rank; of highest quality, degree, or amount.

sur-, *pref.*: see **sub-.**

sur'charge, *n.* extra charge; extra or excessive load. **surcharge',** *v.t.* charge additional amount; overload.

sure (shoor), *a.* certain, confident, convinced (of); having no doubt; certain *to* do or be; reliable; faithful. *adv.* undoubtedly, certainly. **sure'ly,** *adv.* with certainty or safety; assuredly. **sure'ty,** *n.* security; person undertaking to be liable (i.e. pay specified sum, etc.) for another's failure to appear in court, or pay debts, etc.

surf, *n.* mass or line of white foamy water caused by swell of sea breaking on rock or (esp. shallow) shore.

sur'face, *n.* outermost or uppermost boundary of material body, water, soil, etc.; outward aspect or appearance of immaterial thing; (Geom.) continuous extent with two dimensions only. *v.* put special surface on; rise to surface of water, etc. *a.* of or on surface;

travelling, etc., on surface of land or water.

sur'feit (-fit), *n.* excess, esp. in eating or drinking; satiety. *v.t.* overfeed; satiate *with.*

surge, *v.t.* rise and fall, move to and fro (as) in waves or billows. *n.* surging motion; waves.

sur'geon (-jn), *n.* doctor specializing in surgical (opp. *medical*) treatment. **sur'gery,** *n.* treatment of disorders or injuries of the body by operating with instruments or by manipulation; consulting room of medical practioner, dentist, etc. **sur'gical,** *a.* of surgery or surgeons.

sur'ly, *a.* sullen, bad-tempered, rude.

surmise' (-z), *n.* conjecture, idea formed on slight evidence. *v.* infer doubtfully or conjecturally; guess.

surmount', *v.t.* overcome, prevail over; be on top of. **surmount'able,** *a.*

sur'náme, *n.* name following Christian or first name(s), common to all members of family.

surpass' (-ahs), *v.t.* do better than, excel. **surpa'ssing,** *a.* greatly exceeding or excelling others.

sur'plice, *n.* loose wide-sleeved white vestment worn by clergy, choristers, etc.

sur'plus, *n.* amount left over after needs have been met. *a.* that is in excess of what is taken, used, or needed.

surprise' (-z), *n.* catching person(s) unprepared; emotion aroused by the unexpected; thing, event, causing this. *v.t.* attack or come upon suddenly and without warning; astonish, be surprise to. **surpri'sing,** *a.* causing surprise, astonishing.

surré'alism (su-), *n.* movement in art and literature seeking to express subconscious activities of mind by representing phenomena of dreams, etc. **surré'alist,** *n.* & *a.*

surren'der, *v.* give up possession, control, etc., of, esp. upon compulsion or demand; yield to enemy; give oneself up. *n.* surrendering, being surrendered.

surrepti'tious (su-; -shus), *a.* done secretly or stealthily. **surrepti'tiously,** *adv.*

su'rrogate, *n.* deputy, esp. of bishop.

surround', *v.t.* come, lie, or be all round or on all sides; enclose, encompass, encircle. **surroun'dings** (-z), *n.pl.* surrounding objects or circumstances, environs, environment.

sur'tax, *n.* tax levied in addition to income-tax on incomes above certain level.

surveill'ance (servál-), *n.* supervision; close watch, esp. on suspected person.

survey' (-vá), *v.t.* take general view of; scan; examine condition of (building, etc.); take linear and angular measurements of (tract of ground, etc.), esp. to construct map, etc. **sur'vey** (-vá), *n.* general view; act or action of surveying (building, land); report or map showing result of this. **survey'or** (-vá-), *n.* person professionally engaged in surveying.

survi'val, *n.* surviving; relic of earlier time.

survíve', *v.* outlive, continue to live after

death or end of, or after occurrence of (disaster); remain alive or existent. **survi'vor,** *n.*

sus-, *pref.*: see **sub.**

suscep'tible, *a.* readily affected by or moved to emotion, impressionable; accessible or sensitive *to*; admitting *of.* **susceptibil'ity,** *n.*

suspect', *v.t.* have suspicions or doubts about; imagine something (wrong) about; think guilty (*of*); think possible or likely. **sus'pect,** *pred. a.* regarded with distrust; suspected. *n.* suspected person.

suspend', *v.t.* deprive (temporarily) of office, etc.; put (temporary) stop to; defer; hang up; hold, cause to be held, in suspension. **suspen'der,** *n.* (esp.) attachment holding up sock or stocking; (pl., U.S.) braces.

suspense', *n.* state of anxious uncertainty, expectation, or waiting for information; undetermined state.

suspen'sion (-shn), *n.* suspending, being suspended; diffusion as particles through fluid medium. **suspension bridge,** bridge suspended from steel cables, etc., extended between towers or other supports.

suspi'cion (-shn), *n.* suspecting, being suspected; partial or unconfirmed belief, esp. that something is wrong or that person is guilty; slight trace, very small amount, *of.* **suspi'cious** (-shus), *a.* feeling, indicating, deserving of, or arousing, suspicion; distrustful.

sustain', *v.t.* keep from falling or giving way; support, bear weight of; keep up, keep going; give strength to; undergo, suffer, (injury, loss, etc.); uphold.

sus'tenance, *n.* livelihood; means of sustaining life, food.

su'ture (-cher), *n.* surgical stitching of edges of wound, etc.; catgut, etc., used for this.

su'zerain, *n.* sovereign or State having political control over another; (Hist.) feudal overlord. **su'zerainty,** *n.*

svelte, *a.* slim, slender, willowy.

swab (-ob), *n.* mop, esp. for cleaning deck; pad of cotton wool, etc., for medical use. *v.t.* (p.t. *swabbed*), clean or wipe (as) with swab.

swadd'le, (-od-), *v.t.* wrap in swaddling-clothes. **swadd'ling-clothes,** narrow strips of cloth wrapped round new-born child to prevent free movement (now chiefly fig.).

swagg'er (-ger), *v.i.* walk or behave in superior or blustering manner. *n.* swaggering gait or manner.

swain, *n.* suitor; (*archaic*) country lad.

swall'ow[1] (-olō), *v.t.* cause to pass down one's throat; take in, exhaust, cause to disappear (often with *up*); accept (statement, etc.) credulously; recant (words); repress (emotion). *n.* act of swallowing.

swall'ow[2] (-olō), *n.* migratory insect-eating bird with long pointed wings and forked tail.

swam, *p.t.* of **swim.**

swamp (-o-), *n.* piece of wet spongy ground, marsh. *v.t.* submerge, inundate, soak, with

water; overwhelm with numbers or quantity of anything. **swam'py,** *a.*

swan (-on), *n.* large, long-necked, usu. white, swimming bird. **swans'down,** swan's down or fine soft feathers. **swan-song,** last production or achievement. **swann'ery,** *n.*

swap (-op), **swop,** *v.* (p.t. *swapped*), (*slang*) exchange. *n.* act of swapping.

sward (-ord), *n.* (expanse of) turf.

swarm[1] (-orm), *n.* cluster of bees leaving hive, etc., with queen bee to establish new hive; large or dense group, multitude, of insects, persons, etc., esp. flying or moving about. *v.i.* move in or like swarm, congregate; be overrun or crowded; (of bees) leave hive in swarm.

swarm[2] (-orm), *v.* climb (*up*) clasping or clinging with arms and legs.

swar'thy (-ordhi), *a.* having dark complexion.

swash (-o-), *v. & n.* (make) sound of water beating against something. **swash'buckler,** swaggering ruffian.

swas'tika (swos-), *n.* cross with equal arms, each arm with limb of same length at right angles to its end.

swat (-ot), *v.t.* (p.t. *swatted*), crush (fly, etc.) with blow.

swath (-aw-), *n.* (pl. pr. -dhs), row or line of grass, corn, etc., as it falls when cut; space left clear by sweep of scythe, etc.

swāthe (-dh), *v.t.* wrap up or round, envelop, like bandage or (as) with wrapping.

sway, *v.* have unsteady swinging motion; waver; give swaying motion to; have influence over; rule over. *n.* swaying motion; rule, government.

swear (swār), *v.* (p.t. *swore*; p.p. *sworn*), take oath; state or promise on oath; use profane oaths. **swear-word,** profane oath or word.

sweat (-et), *n.* moisture exuded through pores of skin, perspiration; condition or fit of sweating. *v.* (cause to) exude sweat; (cause to) form drops like sweat; work hard, toil; employ for long hours at low wages. **sweat'er,** *n.* (esp.) woollen pullover. **sweat'y,** *a.*

Swēde, *n.* native of Sweden; (*swede*), yellow variety of turnip. **Swē'dish,** *a. & n.* (language) of Sweden.

sweep, *v.* (p.t. *swept*), glide swiftly; go majestically; extend in continuous curve, line, or slope; carry (*along, off,* etc.) in impetuous course; clear everything from; clear of dust, soot, litter, with broom, etc.; gather *up,* collect, (as) with broom. *n.* sweeping; chimney-sweep; sweepstake. **sweep'stake,** form of gambling in which stakes go to drawer(s) of winning or placed horse(s), etc. **swee'ping,** *a.* (esp., of statement, etc.) extreme, unqualified, careless of accuracy.

sweet, *a.* tasting like sugar, honey, etc.; pleasing to sense of smell, fragrant; melodious; fresh; not sour or bitter; dear, beloved; amiable; (*informal*) pretty. *n.* sweet-tasting morsel made of sugar, chocolate, etc., with fruit or other flavouring, filling, etc.; sweet dish, pudding; (pl.) delights. **sweet′bread,** pancreas of animal, esp. calf, as food. **sweet--brier,** single-flowered fragrant-leaved rose. **sweet chestnut,** Spanish or edible chestnut. **sweet corn,** sweet-flavoured kind of maize. **sweet′heart,** darling; either of pair of people in love. **sweet′meat,** sweet, candy, crystallized fruit, etc. **sweet pea,** garden annual with many-coloured sweet-smelling flowers. **sweet pepper,** fruit of kind of capsicum. **sweet′ly,** adv. **sweet′ness,** n. **swee′ten,** v. make or become sweet. **swee′tening,** n.

swell, v. (p.p. swōllen, occasionally swelled), (cause to) grow bigger or louder; dilate, expand; rise or raise up; bulge out; increase in volume, force, or intensity. n. (esp.) (gentle rising of sea with) long, esp. unbroken, waves. **swell′ing,** n. (esp.) distension of injured or diseased part of body.

swel′ter, v.i. be oppressively hot; be oppressed with heat. **swel′tering,** a.

swept, p.t. & p.p. of sweep. **swept-back,** (of aircraft wing) with axis running backwards at acute angle to that of fuselage.

swerve, v. turn aside, deviate from straight or direct course. n. swerving motion; divergence from course.

swift, a. rapid, speedy, quick, prompt. adv. swiftly. n. swift-flying long-winged insectivorous bird.

swill, v. rinse, pour water over or through; drink greedily. n. swilling; liquid or partly liquid food given to pigs.

swim, v. (p.t. swam; p.p. swum; pres. p. swimming), progress at or below surface of water by working limbs, fins, tail, etc.; traverse thus; be flooded with moisture; have dizzy effect or sensation. n. spell of swimming; main current of affairs. **swim-suit,** bathing-suit. **swimm′er,** n. **swimm′ing,** n. **swimming-bath, -pool,** pool for swimming in. **swimm′er,** n. **swimm′ingly,** adv. (esp.) with easy unobstructed progress.

swin′dle, v. cheat; defraud. n. piece of swindling; fraud. **swin′dler,** n.

swine, n. (pl. same), pig. **swi′nish,** a. beastly.

swing, v. (p.t. swung), move with to-and-fro or curving motion of object having fixed end, point, or side but otherwise free; oscillate. n. act of swinging; oscillation; seat slung by ropes or chains for swinging in. **swing-wing,** (of aircraft) having wings that can be swung back to aid streamlining.

swin′geing (-jing), a. forcible; (informal) huge.

swipe, v. hit hard and recklessly; (slang) steal by snatching. n. reckless hard hit.

swirl, n. eddying or whirling motion; twist, convolution; eddy. v. carry, be carried, or flow, with swirling motion.

swish, n. hissing sound of cane, etc., moved rapidly through air; swishing movement. v.

make, move with, swish.

Swiss, a. & n. (native) of Switzerland. **Swiss roll,** thin oblong sponge cake spread with jam, etc., and rolled up.

switch, n. any of various devices for making or breaking contact or altering connections in electric circuit; mechanism for moving points on railway; slender flexible twig, stick, etc.; act of switching, change, change-over. v. switch on, off, etc., change connection (over) with switch; change. **switch′back,** fun-fair railway with alternate steep ascents and descents. **switch′board,** apparatus with set of switches for varying connections between electric circuits, esp. of telephones.

swiv′el, n. ring and pivot or other device connecting two parts, etc., so that one can turn without the other. v. (p.t. swivelled), turn (as) on swivel.

swollen, p.p. of swell.

swoon, v.i. & n. faint.

swoop, v.i. come down with rush like bird of prey; make sudden attack. n. act of swooping; sudden pounce.

sword (sord), n. weapon with long blade for cutting or thrusting. cross swords, engage in dispute (with). **sword′fish,** large sea-fish with upper jaw elongated into sword-like point. **sword-play,** plying or wielding a sword briskly. **swords′man** (-z-), n. (pl. -men), one skilled in use of sword.

swore, sworn, p.t. & p.p. of swear.

swot, v. (p.t. swotted), (slang) work hard, esp. at learning. n. (slang) one who swots.

swum, p.p. of swim.

swung, p.t. & p.p. of swing.

syb′arite, n. person devoted to luxury and pleasure. **sybarit′ic,** a.

syc′amore, n. large species of maple.

syc′ophant, n. flatterer, toady. **syc′ophancy,** n. **sycophan′tic,** a.

syllab′ic, a. of or in syllables.

syll′able, n. whole word or part of word containing one vowel sound.

syll′abus, n. (pl. syllabuses, syllabi), concise statement of subjects of lectures, course of study, etc.

syll′ogism, n. form of reasoning consisting of two premisses from which conclusion is drawn.

sylph, n. imaginary spirit of the air; slender graceful woman. **sylph′like,** a. slender and graceful.

syl′van, sil′van, a. of wood(s); consisting of, abounding in, woods or trees.

sym′bol, n. thing standing for or representing something else, esp. material thing taken to represent immaterial or abstract thing; written character conventionally standing for object, process, etc. **symbol′ic(al),** aa. **sym′bolism,** n. **sym′bolize,** v.t. be symbol of; represent by symbol.

symm′etry, n. such structure as allows object to be divided into two (or more) parts exactly similar in size, shape, or relative position; quality of having correct proportions; balance, harmony. **symmet′rical,** *a.*

sympathet′ic, *a.* full of, expressing, or feeling, sympathy; capable of evoking sympathy; approving, not antagonistic. **sym′pathize,** *v. i.* feel or express sympathy (*with*).

sym′pathy, *n.* sharing of another's feelings, etc.; mental participation in another's trouble; favourable attitude of mind.

sym′phony, *n.* musical composition in several movements for full orchestra. **symphon′ic,** *a.* of or like symphony.

sympō′sium (-z-), *n.* (pl. *symposia*), meeting or conference for discussion of subject; collection of articles contributed by number of persons on special topic.

symp′tom, *n.* change in body or its functions indicating presence of disease; sign of existence of something. **symptomat′ic,** *a.*

syn-, *pref.* with, together, alike.

syn′agogue (-og), *n.* (building for) regular assembly of Jews for religious instruction and worship.

syn′chronize (-k-), *v.* be simultaneous (*with*); (cause to) keep time (*with*), go at same rate, etc. **synchronizā′tion,** *n.*

syn′copāte, *v. t.* (Mus.) displace beat or normal accent in bar. **syncopā′tion,** *n.*

syn′dicate, *n.* combination of financiers, firms, etc., for promotion of financial or commercial undertaking. *v.* (-āt), form into syndicate; publish simultaneously in several periodicals.

syn′drōme, *n.* (Med.) set of concurrent symptoms.

syn′od, *n.* assembly of clergy (and laity) of Church for discussing and deciding ecclesiastical affairs; council. **syn′odal, synod′ical,** *aa.*

syn′onym, *n.* word having same meaning as another in same language. **synon′ymous,** *a.*

synop′sis, *n.* (pl. *synopsēs*), summary, brief general survey. **synop′tic,** *a.*

syn′tax, *n.* (branch of grammar dealing with) arrangement of words in sentence. **syntac′tical,** *a.*

syn′thesis, *n.* (pl. *synthesēs*), putting together of parts or elements to make up complex whole; (Chem.) formation of compounds, esp. artificial production of naturally occurring compounds. **synthet′ic,** *a.* produced by synthesis; artificial.

syph′ilis, *n.* a venereal disease.

syring′a (-ngg-), *n.* popular name of mock orange (see **mock**); (*Syringa*), generic name of lilac.

sy′ringe (-j), *n.* cylindrical instrument drawing in liquid by suction and ejecting it in stream or jet. *v. t.* sluice, spray, with syringe.

sy′rup, *n.* thick sweet liquid, esp. fruit juice, etc., containing much sugar; condensed sugar-cane juice. **sy′rupy,** *a.*

sys′tem, *n.* set, organized body, of connected things or parts forming complex whole;. *the* animal body as organized whole; set of principles, etc.; orderly method or arrangement. **systèmat′ic,** *a.* methodical; arranged, conducted, according to system. **sys′tèmatize,** *v. t.* arrange according to system.

T

tab, *n.* short broad strap, flat loop, or projecting part by which thing can be taken hold of, fastened, identified, etc.

tab′ard, *n.* herald's tunic-like coat emblazoned with royal arms.

tabb′y, *n.* brownish or grey cat with darker stripes (also *tabby- cat*); she-cat.

tab′ernacle, *n.* tent used as sanctuary by Jews during wanderings in the wilderness; place of worship; canopied niche; receptacle for pyx.

tā′ble, *n.* piece of furniture with flat top supported on legs, etc., esp. one on which meals are laid, work is done, games are played, etc.; flat, usu. rectangular, surface; flat elevated tract of land; orderly arrangement of facts, numerical data, etc. *at table,* at meal(s). *v. t.* (esp.) bring forward for discussion. **tableland,** extensive elevated region with level surface. **table linen,** table-cloths, napkins, etc. **ta′blespoon,** large spoon for serving food. **table tennis,** game played on table with bats and small hollow celluloid or plastic ball.

tab′leau (-lō), *n.* (pl. *tableaux,* pr. -ōz), presentation, esp. group of persons, etc., producing picturesque effect.

table d′hôte (tahbl-dōt′), meal in restaurant, etc., served at fixed price and stated hours.

tab′lèt, *n.* small slab with inscription, carving, etc.; small compressed mass of drug, etc.;

cake of soap; (Hist.) small thin flat piece of ivory, wood, etc., for writing on.

tab′loid, *n.* small-sized newspaper giving news in concentrated and simplified form.

taboo′, *a.* set apart as sacred or accursed; not to be mentioned, touched, used, etc. *n.* (pl. *taboos*), (practice or state of) setting or be'ng set apart as taboo; ban, prohibition. *v.t.* put under taboo.

tā′bor, *n.* (Hist.) small drum.

tab′ūlar, *a.* of, arranged in, tables or columns. **tab′ūlāte,** *v.t.* arrange, summarize, exhibit, in form of tables. **tabūlā′tion,** *n.* **tab′ūlātor,** *n.* (esp.) typewriter attachment for tabulating.

ta′cit, *a.* implied or understood but not expressed; saying nothing, silent.

ta′citurn, *a.* (in the habit of) saying very little; uncommunicative. **tacitur′nity,** *n.*

tack, *n.* small sharp, usu. broad-headed, nail; long stitch used in sewing materials temporarily together; zigzag course of sailing-ship, etc., to take advantage of wind; course of action or policy. *v.* attach with tacks; stitch lightly together; add, append (*to, on to*); sail in zigzag course obliquely against wind.

tack′le, *n.* gear or appliances, esp. for fishing or other sport; rope(s) and pulley(s) used in working sails, hoisting weights, etc.; (Footb., etc.) tackling. *v.t.* attack, try to deal with (task, difficulty, etc.); (Footb., etc.) obstruct or intercept (opponent with ball).

tack′y, *a.* slightly sticky or adhesive.

tact, *n.* ability to avoid causing hurt feelings or embarrassment; skill in dealing with persons or circumstances. **tact′ful,** *a.* **tact′less,** *a.*

tac′tics, *n.* (as sing. or pl.) art of deploying and manoeuvring air, military, or naval forces, esp. when in contact with enemy; procedure, device(s) for achieving purpose. **tac′tical,** *a.* **tacti′cian** (-shn), *n.*

tac′tile, *a.* of, perceived by, or connected with, sense of touch.

tad′pōle, *n.* larva of frog or toad, esp. when it seems to consist simply of round head with a tail.

taff′ēta, *n.* fine plain-woven lustrous fabric of silk (or other material).

taff′rail, *n.* rail round ship's stern.

tag, *n.* label for tying on; metal point of shoe-lace, etc.; loose or ragged end; hackneyed quotation, etc. *v.t.* (p.t. *tagged*), furnish with tag(s); fasten *on*, etc.; trail behind.

tail, *n.* hindmost part of animal, esp. when prolonged beyond rest of body; slender prolongation or appendage; rear end or part; reverse of coin; (pl.) dress-coat. *v.* tail (*after*), follow close behind. *tail off*, diminish and cease. **tail-lamp,-light,** red light carried at rear of train, vehicle, etc. **tailed** (-ld), *a.* having tail. **tail′less,** *a.*

tai′lor, *n.* maker of men's outer garments, or of similar clothes for women. *v.* be, work as, tailor; make by tailor's methods; adapt, fit, *to* requirements, etc. **tai′loring,** *n.*

taint, *n.* spot or trace of decay, corruption, or disease; corrupt condition, infection. *v.* introduce corruption or disease into, infect, be infected.

tāke, *v.* (p.t. *took*; p.p. *taken*), get hold of, seize; capture, catch; appropriate, steal; receive into body or mind; accept, obtain; convey or conduct; have; need; write *down*; captivate; win; secure photograph (of). *take away*, remove, deduct, subtract. *take fire*, begin to burn. *take-in*, (*informal*) deceive. *take* (*one's*) *leave*, say goodbye. *take off*, (of aircraft, etc.) become airborne. **take-off,** (*n.*). *take over*, acquire possession or control of. *take part*, assist, participate, (*in*). *take place*, occur, esp. by arrangement. **tā′king,** *a.* attractive. **tā′kings** (-z), *n.pl.* money received, receipts.

talc, *n.* soft mineral with soapy feel. **tal′cum,** *n.* talc. *talcum* (*powder*), (usu. perfumed) powdered talc for dusting body after bath, etc.

tāle, *n.* story; narrative of events; idle or mischievous gossip; lie.

tal′ent, *n.* special aptitude, gift (*for*); high mental or artistic ability; ancient weight and unit of money. **tal′ented,** *a.* having talent.

tal′isman (-z-), *n.* charm, amulet; thing believed to bring good luck or protect from harm.

talk (tawk), *v.* convey or exchange ideas, information, etc., by speech; have or use faculty of speech. *n.* conversation; short conversational address or lecture; rumour, (theme of) gossip. **talk′ative,** *a.* fond of talking.

tall (tawl), *a.* of more than average stature or height; high, lofty. **tall′boy,** tall chest of drawers.

tall′ow (-ō), *n.* fat, esp. of sheep, ox, etc., melted down for making soap, candles, etc.

tall′y, *n.* piece of wood scored with notches for items of account and split into halves of which each party kept one (Hist.); account, score; distinguishing mark, ticket, label. *v.i.* agree, correspond, (*with*).

tally-hō′, *int.* & *n.* (pl. *tally-hos*), huntsman's cry to hounds on catching sight of fox.

tal′on, *n.* claw, esp. of bird of prey.

tam′arisk, *n.* feathery-leaved evergreen shrub or small tree growing in sandy places.

tambourine′ (-borēn), *n.* musical instrument resembling shallow drum with one end open and pairs of small cymbals round circumference.

tāme, *a.* (of animals) brought under control and care of man, domesticated; not wild; lacking spirit; uninteresting. *v.t.* make tame; subdue, curb.

tam-o′-shan′ter, *n.* round Scottish cap with wide flat baggy top.

tamp, *v.t.* plug (hole containing blasting charge) with clay, etc.; block up; ram down.

tam′per, *v.i.* meddle or interfere *with.*

tam′pon, *n.* plug inserted in wound, etc., to stop bleeding, absorb secretions, etc.

tan[1], *n.* bark of oak, etc., used for tanning; yellowish-brown of tanned leather; bronzed colour of skin exposed to sun. *a.* yellowish--brown. *v.* (p.t. *tanned*), convert (hide) into leather by steeping in infusion of oak-bark, etc.; make or become brown by exposure to sun; (*slang*) thrash.

tan[2], *abbrev.* tangent.

tan′dem, *n.* bicycle with two or more seats and sets of pedals, one behind another. *adv.* one behind another.

tang, *n.* strong or penetrating taste or smell; characteristic quality; trace or touch *of.*

tan′gent (-j-), *n.* (Geom.) straight line touching but not intersecting curve; (Trig.) ratio of side of right-angled triangle opposite one acute angle to that opposite the other (abbrev. *tan).*

tangerine′ (-jerēn), *n.* kind of small orange.

tan′gible (-j-), *a.* that can be touched; real, definite. **tangibil′ity,** *n.*

tang′le (-nggl), *v.* intertwine, become twisted or involved, in confused mass; entangle; complicate. *n.* tangled condition or mass.

tang′ō (-ngg-), *n.* (pl. *tangos*), (music for) slow S.American dance.

tank, *n.* (large) container for liquid, gas, etc.; armoured motor vehicle equipped with guns and moving by means of caterpillar tracks.

tank′ard, *n.* large one-handled drinking--vessel of pewter, silver, etc., often with lid.

tank′er, *n.* ship or motor vehicle carrying mineral oil, etc., in bulk.

tann′er, *n.* one who tans hides. **tann′ery,** *n.* place where hides are tanned.

tann′in, *n.* substance obtained from tree--barks, etc., used in tanning, dyeing, medicine, etc. **tann′ic,** *a.* of or like, derived from, tannin.

tan′sy (-zi), *n.* a yellow-flowered herb.

tan′talize, *v.t.* torment, tease, by sight or promise of something desired that is out of reach or withheld. **tan′talizing,** *a.*

tan′tamount, *pred. a.* equivalent *to.*

tan′trum, *n.* outburst or display of bad temper.

tap[1], *n.* appliance for controlling flow of liquid or gas from pipe, cask, etc. *on tap,* ready for immediate consumption or use. *v.t.* (p.t. *tapped*), insert tap into (cask, etc.); draw off fluid from; draw supplies or information from. **tap-root,** long tapering main root.

tap[2], *v.* (p.t. *tapped*), strike (with) light or gentle blow; rap. *n.* (sound of) light blow or rap; (pl., U.S.) last bugle-call of day. **tap--dancing,** stage-dancing with elaborate rhythmical tapping of feet.

tāpe, *n.* narrow woven strip of cotton, etc., used for tying, and in dressmaking, etc.; strip of paper, fabric, flexible metal, electromag-

netic material, etc. *v.t.* provide, fasten, join, with tape(s); record on electromagnetic tape. **tape-measure,** tape marked for use as measure. **tape-recorder,** machine for recording sounds on electromagnetic tape and reproducing them. **tape′worm,** long flat worm parasitic in intestines of vertebrates.

tā′per, *n.* long wick coated with wax, for lighting lamp, etc. *v.* make, become, gradually smaller towards one end.

tap′estry, *n.* thick fabric in which pictorial design is woven into canvas in (esp.) wool, silk, etc.; wall-hanging of this; machine--woven fabric imitating tapestry.

tapiō′ca, *n.* starchy granular foodstuff prepared from cassava.

tā′pir, *n.* mammal of tropical America and Malaya, with flexible snout.

tar, *n.* thick inflammable black or dark--coloured liquid obtained from coal, wood, etc. *v.t.* (p.t. *tarred*), cover, smear, with tar. **tar′mac (P.),** tarmacad′am, road-making material of crushed stone, tar, etc.; road, runway, etc., of this.

tarantell′a (ta-), *n.* (music for) rapid whirling dance of S.Italian peasants.

taran′tūla (ta-), *n.* large black S.European spider with slightly poisonous bite.

tar′bōōsh, *n.* cap like a fez.

tar′dy, *a.* slow to act, come, or happen; behind time, late.

tāre, *n.* kind of vetch; (Bibl., usu. pl.) darnel (weed growing among corn).

tar′gèt (-g-), *n.* mark for shooting at, esp. with concentric circles round central ring or spot; anything aimed at.

ta′riff, *n.* (list of) customs duties; duty on goods; list or scale of charges.

tar′latan, *n.* thin stiff muslin.

tarmac, tarmacadam: see **tar.**

tarn, *n.* small mountain lake.

tar′nish, *v.* dull lustre of, discolour by oxidation, etc.; lose lustre; (fig.) sully, stain. *n.* tarnished state; blemish, stain.

tarpau′lin, *n.* (sheet or covering of) canvas coated with tar, or other waterproof cloth.

tarr′y[1] (tahr-), *a.* of, like, smeared with, tar.

ta′rry[2], *v.i.* delay, be late; linger.

tart[1], *a.* sharp-tasting, acid; cutting, biting.

tart[2], *n.* piece of pastry, usu. circular, with jam, fruit, etc., on top; pie containing fruit. **tart′lèt,** *n.* small tart.

tart[3], *n.* (*slang*) girl or woman, esp. of immoral character, prostitute.

tar′tan, *n.* (cloth woven in) distinctive pattern of Highland clan, with stripes of various colours crossing at right angles; any similar pattern.

tar′tar[1], *n.* substance deposited in wine-cask during fermentation of grape-juice; hard crust forming on the teeth.

tar′tar[2], *n.* intractable or violent-tempered person.

tartlet: see **tart**[2].

task (tah-), *n.* piece of work to be done. *v.t.* put strain upon, tax. **task'master,** one who imposes heavy burden or labour.

tass'el, *n.* tuft of loosely hanging threads, etc., as ornament; tassel-like head of some plants. **tass'elled** (-ld), *a.* having tassel(s).

tåste, *n.* sensation aroused when tongue is in contact with some substances, flavour; sense by which this is perceived; small portion (*of* food, etc.); liking (*for*); discernment and enjoyment of what is excellent, beautiful, fitting, etc. *v.* perceive or learn flavour of; eat small portion of, sample; have taste (*of*). **tåste'ful,** *a.* showing, having, or done in, good taste. **tåste'less,** *a.* insipid, without taste; lacking good taste. **tä'ster,** *n.* (esp.) person who selects teas, wines, etc., by tasting. **tä'sty,** *a.* of pleasing flavour.

tat, *v.* (p.t. *tatted*), do, make by, tatting.

tatt'er, *n.* (usu. in pl.) rag, irregularly torn piece, esp. hanging loose. **tatt'ered** (-erd), *a.*

tatt'ing, *n.* (art or process of making) kind of knotted lace.

tatt'le, *v.i.* & *n.* (engage in) gossip or idle talk.

tattōō'[1], *n.* evening signal summoning soldiers to quarters; music, marching of troops, etc., as entertainment, esp. by artificial light; drumming; drum-beat.

tattōō'[2], *v.t.* mark skin indelibly by pricking it and inserting pigment; make (design) thus. *n.* tattooed mark or design.

taught, *p.t.* & *p.p.* of **teach.**

taunt, *n.* insulting or provoking remark. *v.t.* reproach, mock at, insultingly or contemptuously.

Taur'us, *n.* the Bull, constellation and second sign of the zodiac.

taut, *a.* drawn tight; stiff, tense. **tau'ten,** *v.* make or become taut.

tautol'ogy, *n.* repetition of same statement, idea, etc., in different words; instance of this. **tautolo'gical,** *a.*

tav'ern, *n.* inn, public house.

taw'dry, *a.* showy or gaudy without real value. **taw'driness,** *n.*

taw'ny, *a.* & *n.* (of) yellowish-brown colour.

tax, *n.* contribution levied on person, property, etc., for support of State; strain, heavy demand, (*up*)*on.* *v.t.* impose tax on, subject to taxation; make demands on, burden. **tax'able,** *a.* **taxā'tion,** *n.* taxes or the imposition of taxes.

tax'i, *n.* motor vehicle, esp. with taximeter, plying for hire. *v.* go, convey, in taxi; (of aircraft) run along surface before taking off or after landing.

tax'idermy, *n.* art of preparing and stuffing skins of animals so as to produce lifelike effect. **tax'idermist,** *n.*

tax'imĕter, *n.* automatic device fitted to taxi, indicating fare due.

tea, *n.* dried leaves of shrub grown in China, India, etc.; infusion of them as drink; meal at which this is served. **tea'cake,** light flat bun. **tea-leaf,** (esp., pl.) leaves of tea after infusion. **tea'pot,** vessel with lid, handle, and spout, for making and pouring tea. **tea-room,** room where light refreshments, tea, etc., may be bought and consumed. **tea'spoon,** small spoon for stirring tea, etc.

teach, *v.* (p.t. *taught,* pr. tawt), impart knowledge or skill (to); give instruction or lessons to; instil, inspire with. **teach-in,** (*informal*) meeting for sharing information on subject of topical interest. **teach'able,** *a.* (esp.) easy to teach, docile. **tea'cher,** *n.* one who teaches, esp. in school. **tea'ching,** *n.* profession of teacher; doctrine.

teak, *n.* (heavy durable timber of) large tropical tree.

teal, *n.* (pl. same) small freshwater duck.

team, *n.* two or more oxen, horses, etc., harnessed together (with vehicle they draw); set of players forming side in game or sport; set of persons working together. *v.* team (*up*), join, put together (*with*). **team-work,** combined effort, organized co-operation. **team'ster,** *n.* driver of team.

tear[1] (tār), *v.* (p.t. *tore;* p.p. *torn*), pull apart or to pieces by force; make rent or tear in; be torn; move at great speed, rush. *n.* tearing; rent in cloth, etc.

tear[2], *n.* drop of salty water appearing in or flowing from eye; something resembling tear. **tear-gas,** vapour causing tears, used to disable opponents. **tear'ful,** *a.* shedding tears; sad.

tease (-z), *v.* annoy playfully or maliciously; vex; separate fibres of (wool, etc.); comb (fabric) into nap with teasels, etc. *n.* person fond of teasing others.

tea'sel (-zl-), **tea'zle,** *n.* (plant having) flower-heads with hooked prickles, used for teasing fabric into nap; contrivance used similarly.

teat, *n.* nipple of breast or udder, from which milk is sucked by young; artificial nipple of feeding-bottle.

tech'nical (tek-), *a.* of, in, or peculiar to particular art, science, profession, etc.; of, in, or for mechanical and applied sciences generally. **technical'ity,** *n.* technical term, detail, point, etc. **techni'cian** (-shn), *n.* one skilled in technique of particular art or subject; expert in practical application of science.

technique (teknēk'), *n.* manner of execution or performance in painting, music, etc.; mechanical part of art, craft, etc.

technol'ogy (-k-), *n.* (study of) practical uses of scientific knowledge; applied sciences collectively. **technolo'gical,** *a.* **technol'ogist,** *n.*

tedd'y-bear (bār), *n.* soft toy bear.

Tĕ Dĕ'um, ancient Latin hymn beginning *Te Deum laudamus,* 'We praise thee O God'.

tĕ'dious, *a.* tiresomely long, wearisome. **tĕ'dium,** *n.* tediousness, boredom.

tee, *n*. (Golf) place from which players drive ball at beginning of each hole; small pile of sand or peg of wood, etc., on which ball is placed for driving off.

teem[1], *v.i.* swarm *with*; be abundant.

teen-âge, *a*. in the teens; of or for teenagers.

teen'âger, *n*. person in the teens. **teens**, *n.pl.* years of one's age from 13 to 19.

tee'ter, *v*. move unsteadily; waver.

teeth, *pl.* of **tooth**.

teethe (-dh), *v.i.* (of baby) develop teeth and have them appear through gums.

teetŏ'tal, *a*. abstaining entirely from alcoholic drinks. **teetŏ'talism**, *n*. **teetŏ'taller**, *n*.

teg'ûment, *n*. natural covering of (part of) animal body.

tele-, *pref.* far, at a distance; of or by television.

telĕcommûnicâ'tions (-z), *n*. (study of) means of communication over a distance.

tel'ĕgram, *n*. message sent by telegraph.

tel'ĕgraph (-ahf), *n*. (apparatus for) instantaneous conveyance of messages to any distance by transmission of electrical impulses along wires. *v*. send message by telegraph. **telĕgraph'ic**, *a*. **telĕg'raphy**, *n*. communication by telegraph. **telĕg'raphist**, *n*.

telĕp'athy, *n*. communication of thoughts or ideas from mind to mind without the aid of the senses. **telĕpath'ic**, *a*.

tel'ĕphône, *n*. instrument for transmitting speech, etc., to a distance. *v*. send message, speak, by telephone. **telephone exchange, switchboard**, see these words. **telĕphon'ic**, *a*. **telĕph'onist**, *n*. telephone operator.

tel'ĕprinter, *n*. system by which messages typed on keyboard of special apparatus are transmitted by telegraph to similar distant apparatus which retypes them.

tel'ĕscôpe, *n*. optical instrument of tube(s) with arrangement of lenses for making distant objects appear nearer and larger. *v*. force or drive, be forced, one into another like tubes of hand-telescope; close, slide together, in this way. **telĕscop'ic**, *a*. **telĕs'copy**, *n*.

tel'ĕvision (-zhn), *n*. transmission and simultaneous visual reproduction of scenes, etc., over a distance; apparatus for reception of televised images. **tel'ĕvise** (-z), *v.t.* transmit by television.

tell, *v*. (p.t. *tŏld*), state, express, in words; relate or narrate; inform, give information, *of*, etc.; reveal; betray secret; ascertain, distinguish; produce marked effect (*on*); (*archaic*) count. **tell-tale**, person who reveals secrets, informs against others, etc. **tell'er**, *n*. (esp.) person appointed to count (esp. votes in House of Commons).

tème'rity, *n*. audacity, rashness.

tem'per, *v.t.* toughen and harden (esp. metal) by heating, sudden cooling, and reheating; modify, lessen severity of. *n*. degree of hardness, etc., of metal, etc.; habitual or tempo-rary disposition of mind; fit of anger.

tem'perament, *n*. nature or character of person as it affects his way of feeling, thinking, and acting. **temperamen'tal**, *a*. of, relating to, temperament; liable to sudden changes of mood.

tem'perance, *n*. moderation; moderation in use of, or total abstinence from, alcoholic drinks.

tem'perate, *a*. moderate, avoiding excesses or extremes; (of climate) neither extremely hot nor extremely cold.

tem'perature, *n*. degree or intensity of warmth or coldness of body or atmosphere, esp. as shown by thermometer; abnormally high warmth of body in illness.

tem'pĕst, *n*. violent storm. **tempes'tûous**, *a*.

tem'ple[1], *n*. building dedicated to a god; religious edifice of Jews in ancient Jerusalem; place of Christian worship.

tem'ple[2], *n*. flat part of side of head between forehead and ear.

tem'pŏ, *n*. (pl. *tempos, tempi*), (Mus.) speed at which passage is (to be) played.

tem'poral, *a*. of this life only, secular, lay; of, existing in, time; of the temples on side of head.

tem'porary, *a*. lasting only for a time; held or occupied during limited time only, not permanent. **tem'porarily**, *a*.

tem'porīze, *v.i.* delay making decision, giving answer, etc., act so as to gain time.

tempt, *v.t.* entice, incite; allure, attract. **temptâ'tion**, *n*. tempting or being tempted; thing that attracts. **temp'ter**, *n*. **temp'tress**, *n. fem.* **temp'ting**, *a*. alluring, attractive.

ten, *a. & n.* one more than nine (10, X). *Ten Commandments*, see **decalogue**. **tenth**, *a. & n.* **tenth'ly**, *adv*.

ten'able, *a*. that can be defended against argument; that can be held *for* period, *by* person, etc.

tēnâ'cious (-shus), *a*. holding fast; clinging tightly; retentive. **tēna'city**, *n*.

ten'ancy, *n*. (period of) holding property as tenant.

ten'ant, *n*. person who rents land, house, etc., from landlord. *v.t.* occupy as tenant. **ten'antry**, *n*. tenants.

tench, *n*. freshwater fish of carp family.

tend[1], *v.i.* move, be directed, in certain direction; be apt or inclined (*to*).

tend[2], *v.t.* take care of, look after.

ten'dency, *n*. fact or quality of tending or inclining (*to, towards*, thing, *to* do).

tenden'tious (-shus), *a*. written, etc., with an underlying purpose.

ten'der[1], *v*. offer, hand in, or present; offer as payment; make tender (*for*). *n*. offer, esp. to do work or supply goods at fixed price. *legal tender*, currency legally recognized as acceptable in payment of debt.

ten'der[2], *n*. (esp.) vessel attending larger one to supply stores, convey orders, etc.; truck attached to locomotive and carrying fuel and water.

ten'der³, *a*. not tough or hard; easily touched or wounded; delicate, fragile; solicitous; loving. **ten'derly**, *adv*. **ten'derness**, *n*.

ten'don, *n*. tough fibrous tissue connecting muscle to bone etc.

ten'dril, *n*. thread-like, often spiral, organ of some climbing plants, that attaches itself to a support.

ten'ement, *n*. rented flat or room in tenement--house. **tenement-house**, large building divided into tenements.

ten'et, *n*. belief, doctrine, principle.

tenn'is, *n*. lawn tennis; ball-game played with rackets in walled court with net.

ten'on, *n*. shaped end or side of piece of wood, etc., fitting into mortise.

ten'or, *n*. general course or direction; meaning, drift; (Mus.) (part for, singer having,) male voice between baritone and alto; (*attrib*.) (of instrument, etc.) of which range is approximately that of tenor voice.

tense¹, *n*. any of forms of verb indicating time of action or state denoted by it (as *present, past, future*, etc., *tense*).

tense², *a*. stretched taut; strained, showing mental or emotional strain.

ten'sile, *a*. of tension; capable of being drawn out or stretched.

ten'sion (-shn), *n*. stretching, being stretched; tenseness; strained state; effect produced by forces pulling against each other.

tent, *n*. portable shelter or dwelling of canvas, etc.

ten'tacle, *n*. slender flexible process in (esp. invertebrate) animals, serving as organ of touch or attachment.

ten'tative, *a*. done by way of trial, experimental. **ten'tatively**, *adv*.

ten'terhooks, *n. pl*. hooks or bent nails for fastening cloth on framework for drying. *on tenterhooks*, in state of anxious suspense or uncertainty.

ten'uous, *a*. thin, slender; subtle.

ten'ure (-yer), *n*. (conditions or period of) holding *of* property or office.

te'pee, *n*. N. American Indian conical tent.

tep'id, *a*. slightly warm, lukewarm. **tepid'ity**, *n*.

tercente'nary, *a*. of 300 years. *n*. 300th anniversary.

term, *n*. limited period; each period appointed for sitting of lawcourts, or for instruction in school, university, etc.; word or phrase considered as name or symbol of something; (Math.) each of quantities joined by signs of addition, subtraction, etc.; (pl.) conditions, stipulations, payment offered or asked; footing, mutual relationship between parties. *v.t.* name, call.

ter'magant, *n*. abusive or scolding woman.

ter'minable, *a*. that may be terminated.

ter'minal, *a*. of or forming limit, terminus,

end, or extremity; of, lasting for, occurring in each, term. *n*. terminating thing, extremity, esp. each of free ends of open electric circuit; terminus.

ter'minate, *v*. bring or come to an end; end *at, in*, etc. **termina'tion**, *n*. (esp.) final syllable or letter(s) of word; ending, suffix.

terminol'ogy, *n*. system of terms in science or subject; technical terms collectively.

ter'minus, *n*. (pl. *termini, terminuses*), (station at) end of railway line, bus-route, etc.

ter'mite, *n*. (chiefly tropical) social insect destructive to timber.

tern, *n*. sea-bird with long pointed wings and forked tail.

te'rrace, *n*. raised level place, natural or artificial; row of houses built in one block. **te'rraced** (-st), *a*. having terrace(s); built in form of terrace(s).

terracott'a (te-), *n*. (brownish-red colour of) fine hard unglazed pottery. *a*. of terracotta.

te'rra fir'ma, dry land.

terrain' (te-), *n*. tract of country considered with regard to its natural features or (Mil.) tactical advantages.

te'rrapin, *n*. edible tortoise of N. America.

terres'trial, *a*. of the earth, of this world; of land as opposed to water.

te'rrible, *a*. arousing terror; grievous; (*informal*) very great or bad. **te'rribly**, *adv*. (*informal*) extremely.

te'rrier, *n*. active hardy, usu. small, dog of various breeds, often pursuing quarry into burrow or earth.

terrif'ic, *a*. terrifying, of tremendous intensity; (*informal*) very great, excessive. **terrif'ically**, *adv*.

te'rrify, *v. t*. fill with terror, frighten severely.

territor'ial (te-), *a*. of territory; of particular territory or locality.

te'rritory, *n*. land under jurisdiction of sovereign, State, etc.; tract of land, region; area defended, claimed or dominated, by animal(s), side in game, etc.

te'rror, *n*. extreme fear; terrifying person or thing; (*informal*) tiresome or troublesome person, esp. child. **te'rrorism**, *n*. policy of ruling or coercing by violence and intimidation. **te'rrorist**, *n*. & *a*. **te'rrorize**, *v*. fill with terror; rule by terrorism. **terroriza'tion**, *n*.

te'rry, *n*. & *a*. (pile-fabric) with loops forming pile left uncut.

terse, *a*. concise, curt; brief and forcible in style.

tess'ellated, *a*. paved with small coloured blocks of marble, etc., arranged in pattern.

test, *n*. critical examination or trial of qualities or nature of person or thing; standard for comparison or trial; examination on limited subject. *v. t*. subject to test, make trial of; try severely, tax.

tes'tament, *n*. will (esp. in phr. *last will and testament*). *Old Testament, New Testament*, main divisions of Bible.

tes'tāte, *a.* having left valid will.

testā'tor, testā'trix, *nn.* man, woman, who makes a will or has died leaving a will.

tes'ticle, *n.* testis, esp. in man and most other mammals.

tes'tifȳ, *v.* give evidence; affirm, declare; be evidence of.

testimō'nial, *n.* formal statement of character, conduct, or qualifications; gift presented as mark of esteem, in acknowledgement of services, etc.

tes'timony, *n.* evidence, esp. (Law) statement made under oath or affirmation.

tes'tis, *n.* (pl. *testēs*), male organ in which sperms are produced; in man and most other mammals, each of two such organs enclosed in scrotum.

tes'ty, *a.* easily angered, touchy.

tet'anus, *n.* disease with spasms and rigidity of muscles, usu. caused by entry of harmful bacteria through wound.

tête-à-tête (tāt'ätät'), *n.* private conversation or interview between two persons. *adv.* in private, without presence of third person.

teth'er (-dh-), *n.* rope, etc., by which grazing animal is confined. *end of one's tether*, extreme limit of one's strength, patience, etc. *v.t.* fasten with tether.

tetra-, *pref.* four.

tetrahē'dron, *n.* (pl. *tetrahedra, tetrahedrons*), solid figure bounded by four plane triangles; triangular pyramid. **tetrahē'dral,** *a.*

tet'rarch (-k), *n.* (in Rom. Empire) governor of fourth part of country or province, subordinate ruler. **tet'rarchy,** *n.*

Teuton'ic, *a.* of Germans or ancient Teutons.

text, *n.* wording of anything written or printed, esp. as opposed to translation, commentary, etc.; short passage, esp. of Scripture, chosen as subject of sermon, etc. **text'book,** book giving instruction in any branch of study; work recognized as authority. **tex'tūal,** *a.* of or in text.

tex'tile, *a.* of weaving; woven. *n.* woven material, fabric.

tex'ture (-cher), *n.* character of textile fabric resulting from way it is woven; structure, constitution. **tex'tural,** *a.*

thalid'omīde, *n.* sedative drug, taking of which by pregnant women was followed, *c.* 1960, by birth of malformed babies.

than (dhan), *conj.* introducing second part of a comparison.

thāne, *n.* (Hist.) one holding land in return for military service, with rank below that of hereditary nobles, or (Sc.) with rank of earl's son.

thank, *v.t.* express gratitude to. *thank you*, polite formula of gratitude, etc. **thanks,** *n.pl.* (expression of) gratitude. *thanks to*, as result of. **thank-offering,** gift made as expression of gratitude, esp. to God. **thanks'giving,**

expression of gratitude, esp. to God. **Thanksgiving (Day),** U.S. annual festival and legal holiday on 4th Thursday of November. **thank'ful,** *a.* **thank'fully,** *adv.* **thank'-less,** *a.* (esp.) not likely to win thanks, unprofitable.

that (dh-), *demonstrative a. & pron.* (pl. *thōse*, pr. -z), the (person, thing); the person or thing referred to, pointed to, observed, understood, etc., esp. the farther, less obvious, etc., of two. *that is* (*to say*), in other words. *conj.* introducing clause, esp. expressing result or consequence.

thatch, *n.* roof-covering of straw, reeds, etc. *v.t.* roof or cover with thatch.

thaw, *v.* (cause to) become unfrozen, (cause to) become liquid or flexible, by raising or rise of temperature; (fig.) become genial. *n.* thawing; melting of ice and snow after frost.

the (*before vowel* and emphatically, dhē; *before consonant* dhi), *a.* (definite article), applied to person(s) or thing(s) already mentioned, existent, unique, etc.; used with sing. nouns as representing class, etc., or with adjectives used as nouns; used emphatically with best known person or thing. *adv.* *the...the*, by how much... by so much (e.g. *the sooner he comes the better*).

thē'atre (-ter), *n.* building for dramatic performances; room or hall for lectures, etc., with seats in tiers; scene of action; operating theatre; dramatic literature or art. **thēat'-rical,** *a.* of or for acting; showy, affected. **thēat'ricals** (-z), *n.pl.* (esp. amateur) theatrical performances.

thee (dh-), *pron.* objective case of **thou.**

theft, *n.* stealing.

their (dhār), *pron. & a.* possessive case of **they,** and corresponding adjective with absolute form **theirs.**

thē'ism, *n.* belief in god(s), esp. in one God as creator and supreme ruler of the universe. **thē'ist,** *n.* **thēis'tic(al),** *aa.*

them (dh-), *pron.* objective case of **they.**

thēme, *n.* subject of discussion, composition, etc.; (Mus.) subject developed in composition; melody, etc., on which variations are constructed. **thēmat'ic,** *a.*

themselves' (dh-; -vz), *pron.* emphatic and reflexive form of **they.**

then (dh-), *adv.* at that time; after that, next; accordingly. *n.* that time.

thence (dh-), *adv.* from there; from that. **thenceforth', thencefor'ward,** *advv.* from that time forward.

thēoc'racy, *n.* government, State governed, by laws believed to be those of God, or by a priestly class.

thēod'olīte, *n.* surveying instrument for measuring angles.

thēol'ogy, *n.* science of religion, study of God or god(s). **thēolō'gian,** *n.* **thēolo'gical,** *a.*

thē'orem, *n.* (Math.) proposition demonstrable by chain of reasoning.

thĕoret′ic, thĕoret′ical, *aa.* of or relating to theory; based on theory, not on practice or experience.

thĕ′ory, *n.* scheme or system of ideas held to explain observed facts; (knowledge of) principles of art, technical subject, etc., opp. *practice*; individual opinion or view. **thĕ′orist,** *n.* **thĕ′orīze,** *v.*

thĕos′ophy, *n.* philosophy professing to attain to knowledge of God by direct intuition, spiritual ecstasy, etc. **thĕosoph′ical,** *a.* **thĕos′ophist,** *n.*

therapeu′tic (the-) *a.* of treatment of disease, curative. **therapeu′tics,** *n.* branch of medicine concerned with remedial treatment of disease. **the′rapy,** *n.* curative treatment. **the′rapist,** *n.*

there (dhār), *adv.* in or at that place; to that place or point; yonder. *n.* that place or point. *int.* drawing attention to anything. **there′about(s),** *adv.* near that place or amount or time. **thereaf′ter,** *adv.* thenceforward. **there′bў,** *adv.* by that means or agency. **there′fore,** *adv.* for that reason; accordingly. **there′in,** *adv.* in it or them. **thereof′** (-v), *adv.* of that, of it. **there′upon′,** *adv.* after or in consequence of that.

therm, *n.* British unit of heat energy, used esp. as basis of charge for gas supplied.

ther′mal, *a.* of heat; determined, measured, operated, by heat. **thermal springs,** hot springs.

ther′mion, *n.* electrically charged particle emitted from incandescent body. **thermion′ic,** *a.* **thermionic valve,** vacuum tube in which electrons are emitted from heated electrodes.

thermo-, *pref.* heat-, thermo-electric.

ther′modўnam′ics, *n.* science dealing with relationship between heat and all other forms of energy. **ther′modўnam′ic,** *a.*

ther′mo-electri′city, *n.* electricity produced by action of heat at junction of two different metals. **ther′mo-elec′tric,** *a.*

ther′monŭ′clèar, *a.* of nuclear fusion, which requires high temperatures, such as those generated by nuclear fission, for its inception. **thermonuclear bomb,** hydrogen bomb.

thermom′ĕter, *n.* instrument for measuring temperature, usu. by expansion and contraction of mercury, alcohol, etc., in sealed and graduated glass tube. **ther′momet′ric(al),** *aa.*

ther′mos, *n.* (also *thermos flask, jar, jug*) brand of vacuum flask, etc. **P.**

ther′mostat, *n.* device for automatically maintaining constant temperature. **thermostat′ic,** *a.*

these: see **this.**

thĕ′sis, *n.* (pl. *thĕsĕs,* pr. -z), statement put forward to be discussed and defended, esp. treatise submitted by candidate for university degree.

thews (-z), *n.pl.* muscles; vigour.

they (dhā), *pron.* (objective *them*; possessive *their*), serving as plural of **he, she, it.**

thick, *a.* of considerable or specified depth between opposite surfaces; (of line, etc.) broad, not fine; made of thick material; closely set; dense; viscid, stiff; muddy, cloudy, not clear; (*informal*) close in friendship. *n.* thick or crowded part of anything, esp. fight, etc. **thick-headed,** stupid. **thick′set,·** growing close together; stocky, sturdy. **thick-skinned,** not sensitive to criticism. **thick′en,** *v.* make or become thicker. **thick′ness,** *n.* depth (as dimension other than length and breadth); being thick; layer.

thick′ĕt, *n.* group of small trees, shrubs, etc., growing closely together.

thief, *n.* (pl. *thieves*), one who steals. **thieve,** *v.* be thief, steal. **thie′very,** *n.* **thie′vish,** *a.*

thigh (thī), *n.* upper part of leg, from hip to knee.

thim′ble, *n.* cap of metal, etc., worn on end of finger for pushing needle in sewing.

thin, *a.* of little thickness; of small diameter; slender; lean; sparse; lacking fullness, volume, or substance. *v.* (p.t. *thinned*), make or become thin; reduce, be reduced, in bulk or number. **thin′ness,** *n.*

thīne (dh-), *possessive pron.* the one(s) belonging to **thee.**

thing, *n.* what is or may be the object of perception, knowledge, or thought; inanimate object; what is (to be) done, deed, occurrence; what is said; possession; (pl.) clothes; (pl.) implements, utensils; (pl.) affairs, matters.

think, *v.* (p.t. *thought*, pr. -awt), consider, be of opinion; exercise mind in active way, form connected ideas; reflect; contemplate. *think out,* consider carefully and make plan, etc., for. **think′er,** *n.* **think′ing,** *a.*

third, *a.* next after second. *n.* one of three equal divisions of whole. *third party,* (Law) party in case other than the two principals. **third′ly,** *adv.*

thirst, *n.* sensation caused by need or desire to drink; ardent desire, craving, (*for*). **thirs′ty,** *a.* feeling thirst; parched; arid; (*informal*) causing thirst.

thirteen′, *a. & n.* one more than twelve (13, XIII). **thirteenth′,** *a. & n.*

thir′ty, *a. & n.* three times ten (30, XXX). **thir′tiĕth,** *a. & n.*

this (dh-), *demonstrative a. & pron.* (pl. *thĕse,* pr. -z), the (person or thing) near, present, or just mentioned.

thi′ther (dhidh-), *adv.* (*archaic*) to that place.

thōle, *n.* each of two pins in gunwhale of boat between which oar is worked.

thong, *n.* narrow strip of leather used as lace, lash, etc. *v.t.* furnish with thong.

thor′ax, *n.* part of trunk between neck and abdomen. **thora′cic,** *a.*

thorn, *n.* stiff sharp-pointed process on plant;

thorny plant, esp. hawthorn. **thor'ny,** *a.* prickly; difficult, troublesome.

thorough (thu'ro), *a.* done, acting, etc., with attention to every part or detail; complete, unqualified. **tho'roughbred,** (animal, esp. horse) of pure breed. **tho'roughfare,** public way open at both ends, esp. main road. **tho'roughgoing,** extreme, thorough. **tho'roughly,** *adv.* **tho'roughness,** *n.*

those: see **that.**

thou (dh-), *pron.* (*archaic* or Poet.) subjective case of 2nd personal pronoun singular (objective *thee*).

though (dhō), *conj.* in spite of the fact that; but, all the same; even if. *adv.* (*informal*) nevertheless, however.

thought¹, *p.t.* & *p.p.* of **think.**

thought² (thawt), *n.* process, power, act, of thinking; what one thinks, idea, notion; consideration, heed; meditation; intention. **thought'ful,** *a.* engaged in, characterized by, meditation; considerate. **thought'less,** *a.* unthinking, heedless, imprudent; inconsiderate.

thous'and (-z-), *a.* & *n.* ten hundred (1000, M). **thous'andth,** *a.*

thrall (-awl), *n.* slave; bondage. **thral'dom,** *n.*

thrash, *v.t.* beat, esp. with stick or whip; conquer; thresh. **thrash out,** (fig.) discuss exhaustively.

thread (-ed), *n.* length of spun and usu. twisted fibres of flax, cotton, silk, etc.; thread-shaped or thread-like thing; that which connects successive points in narrative, argument, etc.; spiral ridge of screw. *v.t.* pass thread through; pick one's way through. **thread'bare,** with nap worn off and threads showing; shabby; commonplace, hackneyed.

threat (-et), *n.* declaration or indication of intention to punish or hurt; indication of coming evil. **threat'en,** *v.* use threat(s) to; be source of danger to; give sign or warning of.

three, *a.* & *n.* one more than two (3, III). **three-cornered,** having 3 angles or corners; (of contest, etc.) between 3 persons. **three-dimensional,** (producing illusion of) having length, breadth, and depth. **three'fold,** of 3 parts or kinds, triple. **three'pence** (threp-), sum of 3 pence. **three'penny** (threp-), costing 3 pence.

thren'ody, *n.* song of lamentation.

thresh, *v.* beat out or separate grain from husks of corn, etc.

thresh'old, *n.* plank or stone forming bottom of doorway; entrance; start, beginning.

threw, *p.t.* of **throw.**

thrice, *adv.* three times.

thrift, *n.* economical management, frugality; plant of coasts and mountains, with pink flower-heads. **thrif'ty,** *a.* practising thrift, economical.

thrill, *n.* wave of excitement or intense emo-

tion. *v.* (cause to) experience thrill. **thrill'er,** *n.* (esp.) sensational play, novel, etc.

thrive, *v.i.* (p.t. *thrōve*; p.p. *thriven*), prosper; grow vigorously.

throat, *n.* front of neck, region containing gullet and windpipe; narrow passage or entrance. **throa'ty,** *a.* guttural, hoarse.

throb, *v.i.* (p.t. *throbbed*), (of heart, etc.) beat strongly; pulsate, vibrate. *n.* (sound of) throbbing.

thrōe, *n.* (usu. in pl.) violent pang(s); desperate or agonizing struggle, anguish.

thrombō'sis, *n.* (pl. *thrombōsēs*), formation of blood clot in heart or blood-vessel.

thrōne, *n.* chair of state for sovereign, bishop, etc.; sovereign power.

throng, *n.* crowd, multitude. *v.* come, go, press, in crowds; fill (as) with crowd.

thro'stle (-sl), *n.* song-thrush.

thrott'le, *v.t.* strangle, choke; check flow of steam, fuel, etc., in engine. *throttle down,* slow down (engine). *n.* valve controlling flow of steam, fuel, etc., in engine.

through (-rōō), *prep.* from end to end or side to side of; between sides, walls, parts, etc., of; from beginning to end of; by means of; by reason of. *adv.* in one end, etc., and out the other; from end to end; to the end. *a.* going through; (of travel, train, etc.) all the way. **throughout',** *adv.* in every part or respect. *prep.* from end to end of; in every part of.

throw (-ō), *v.* (p.t. *threw,* pr. -ōō; p.p. *thrown,* pr. -ōn), launch (object) into air with some force; use as missile; (of horse, etc.) cause (rider) to fall to ground; put carelessly or hastily *on, off,* etc.; shape (pottery) on wheel. *n.* throwing; cast of dice.

thrum, *v.* (p.t. *thrummed*), strum; sound monotonously. *n.* sound of thrumming.

thrush¹, *n.* any of various song-birds, esp. song-thrush and missel-thrush.

thrush², *n.* disease causing whitish spots in the mouth; disease affecting frog of horse's foot.

thrust, *v.* (p.t. *thrust*), push, drive, exert force of impact on or against; make sudden push with pointed weapon; push oneself forward; force (*upon*). *n.* stab or lunge; driving force of engine, etc.

thud, *n.* & *v.i.* (p.t. *thudded*), (make, fall with) low dull sound as of blow on something soft.

thug, *n.* ruffian, cut-throat. **thugg'ery** (-g-), *n.*

thumb (-um), *n.* short thick inner digit, opposable to fingers, of human hand; similar digit in other animals. *v.t.* soil, wear, (pages, etc.) with thumb. **thumb'screw,** (Hist.) instrument of torture squeezing the thumb.

thump, *n.* (sound of) heavy blow, bang. *v.* beat heavily, esp. with fist.

thun'der, *n.* loud noise accompanying lightning; any loud rumbling noise. *v.* give forth thunder (usu. *it thunders*, etc.); sound like thunder; utter in loud or impressive manner; fulminate. **thun′derbolt,** lightning-flash regarded as destroying power; unexpected and terrible event, etc. **thun′derstruck,** amazed, terrified, confounded. **thun′derous,** *a.* loud as thunder. **thun′dery,** *a.* (of weather) oppressive.

Thurs′day (-z-), *n.* fifth day of week.

thus (dh-), *adv.* in this way, like this; accordingly, and so; to this extent.

thwack, *n.* & *v.t.* whack.

thwart (-ort), *v.t.* frustrate. *n.* seat across boat for rower.

thy (dhī), *possessive a.* of, belonging to, **thee.**

thyme (tīm), *n.* herb with aromatic leaves, used in cooking.

thȳ′roid, *n.* ductless gland lying near larynx. *a.* of, connected with, thyroid.

thȳself′ (dh-), *pron.* reflexive and emphatic form of **thou, thee.**

tiar′a, *n.* Pope's head-dress of triple crown; woman's jewelled coronet.

tib′ia, *n.* (pl. *tibiae*), inner and (usu.) larger bone of lower leg, shin-bone.

tic, *n.* habitual involuntary twitching of muscles, esp. of face.

tick[1]**,** *n.* quick light distinct recurring sound, esp. of watch or clock; moment (*informal*); small mark (√) made against items in list, etc., in checking. *v.* (of clock, etc.) make ticks; mark (*off*) with tick. *tick over,* (of motor engine) run slowly and quietly with gears disconnected.

tick[2]**,** *n.* any of various parasitic arachnids or insects.

tick[3]**,** *n.* case of mattress, etc.; ticking.

tick[4]**,** *n.* (*informal*) credit.

tick′et, *n.* card or paper securing admission, etc., or serving as label or notice. *v.t.* put ticket on, label. **ticket-collector,** railway official taking or checking passengers' tickets.

tick′ing, *n.* strong linen or cotton cloth for covering mattresses, pillows, etc.

tick′le, *n.* act, sensation, of tickling. *v.* touch lightly so as to excite nerves and (usu.) produce laughter; cause, feel, this sensation; amuse. **tick′lish,** *a.* sensitive to tickling; difficult, needing careful handling.

ti′dal, *a.* of, due to, or resembling, tide(s).

tidd′lywinks, *n.* game of flipping small counters into receptacle.

tide, *n.* rising and falling of sea, due to attraction of moon (and sun); something like tide in ebbing and flowing, turning, etc.; (*archaic*) season.

ti′dings (-z), *n.pl.* news.

ti′dy, *a.* orderly, neat; (*informal*) considerable, fairly large. *n.* receptacle for odds and ends. *v.t.* make tidy; put in order. **ti′dily,** *adv.* **ti′diness,** *n.*

tie, *v.* (pres. p. *tying*), bind, fasten, secure, with cord, etc.; form into knot or bow; re-

strict; be equal in contest; (Mus.) connect notes by tie. *n.* necktie; uniting or connecting element or part; draw, equal score; (Mus.) slur connecting two notes of same pitch, to be performed as one.

tier (tēr), *n.* row, rank, esp. one of several placed one above another. *v.t.* arrange in tiers.

tiff, *n.* slight quarrel.

ti′ger (-g-), *n.* large carnivore of cat family, tawny-yellow with blackish transverse stripes. **ti′gress,** *n.* female tiger.

tight (tīt), *a.* closely held, drawn, fastened, fitting, etc.; taut, stretched so as to leave no slack; closely or firmly constructed, impervious to fluid, etc.; (of money) not easily obtainable; (*slang*) drunk. **tight′rope,** tightly stretched rope, etc., on which acrobats, etc., perform. **tight′en,** *v.* make or become tight. **tights,** *n.pl.* close-fitting garment covering legs and lower part of body.

tile, *n.* thin piece of baked clay for covering roof, paving floor, etc. *v.t.* cover, pave, etc., with tiles.

till[1]**,** *prep.* up to, as late as. *conj.* up to the time when; to the degree that.

till[2]**,** *n.* drawer, box, etc., for money in shop, bank, etc.

till[3]**,** *v.t.* cultivate (land). **till′age,** *n.* tilling; tilled land. **till′er**[1]**,** *n.*

till′er[2]**,** *n.* lever by which rudder is turned.

tilt, *v.* (cause to) assume sloping or slanting position; (Hist.) engage in tilt; thrust, run, *at,* with weapon. *n.* sloping or slanting position; (Hist.) combat between two horsemen armed with lances. (*at*) *full tilt,* at full speed, with full force.

tim′ber, *n.* wood as material for building or carpentry; beam. *standing timber,* trees, woods. **tim′bered** (-erd), *a.* made (partly) of wood; wooded.

timbre (tam′ber), *n.* characteristic quality of musical sound depending on voice or instrument producing it.

tim′brel, *n.* (Bibl.) tambourine.

time, *n.* indefinite continuous duration regarded as dimension; finite duration as distinct from eternity; portion or measure of this; point of time; season; occasion; rhythm or measure of musical composition; (pl., preceded by numeral, etc.) expressing multiplication. *v.t.* choose (right) time for; take or record time of. **time-honoured,** respected on account of antiquity. **time-keeper,** watch, clock, etc.; one who takes or records time. **time′piece,** watch or clock. **time-server,** selfish opportunist. **time-signature,** (Mus.) figures resembling fraction, showing value of beat and number of beats in bar. **time-table,** list or schedule of times of classes, arrival and departure of trains, etc. **time′less,** *a.* unending, eternal; not subject to time. **time′ly,** *a.* seasonable, opportune.

tim′id, *a.* easily alarmed; shy. **timid′ity,** *n.*

tim′orous, *a.* timid.

tim′pani, *n. pl.* (sing. *timpano*), kettledrums of orchestra. **tim′panist,** *n.*

tin, *n.* silvery-white, easily worked, light metal; vessel or box of tin or tinplate. *v.t.* (p.t. *tinned*), cover, coat, with tin; can (fruit, etc.). *a.* of tin. **tin′foil,** tin hammered or rolled into thin sheets for wrapping, etc. **tin′plate,** sheet-iron coated with tin. **tinn′y,** *a.*

tinc′ture (-cher), *n.* solution of medicinal substance; tinge, smattering, slight flavour. *v.t.* colour slightly; tinge, flavour; affect slightly.

tin′der, *n.* dry inflammable substance readily taking fire from a spark. **tin′dery,** *a.*

tinge (-nj), *v.t.* (pres. p. *tingeing*), colour slightly (*with*); qualify, modify, affect slightly. *n.* tint, slight colouring; trace, smack, (*of*).

ting′le (-nggl), *n. & v.i.* (feel) slight pricking or stinging sensation.

tink′er, *n.* (esp. travelling) mender of kettles, pans, etc.; (Sc. & Ir.) gipsy. *v.i.* work unskilfully or clumsily *at, with.*

tink′le, *n. & v.* (make, cause to make) succession of short light ringing sounds (as) of small bell.

tin′sel, *n.* threads or strips of shining metallic material, used to give sparkling effect; tawdry brilliance; flashiness. **tin′selled** (-ld), **tin′selly,** *aa.*

tint, *n.* (usu. slight or delicate) colour, esp. one of several tones of same colour. *v.t.* apply tint to, colour.

tintinnabūlā′tion, *n.* (sound of) ringing of bells.

tī′ny, *a.* very small.

tip¹, *n.* extremity, esp. of small or tapering thing; small piece or part attached to tip. *v.t.* (p.t. *tipped*), furnish with tip. **tip′toe,** (*n. & adv.*) (on) tips of toes; with heels raised from ground; (*v.i.*) walk on tiptoe.

tip², *v.* (p.t. *tipped*), (cause to) lean or slant, topple, overturn; discharge (contents of jug, wagon, etc.) thus; strike or touch lightly; give tip to. *n.* (usu. small) present of money given, esp. to waiter, servant, etc.; piece of useful information, advice, etc.; place where refuse is tipped. **tip′staff,** sheriff's officer.

tipp′et, *n.* small cape or collar of fur, etc.

tipp′le, *v.i.* be habitual drinker of alcoholic liquor. *n.* alcoholic drink.

tip′sy, *a.* (partly) intoxicated.

tīrāde′ (*or* ti-), *n.* long vehement speech, esp. of denunciation or abuse.

tīre¹, *v.* make, grow, weary. *tire out,* weary greatly. **tīred,** *a.* weary. *tired of,* having experienced as much as one is willing to bear; bored with. **tīre′less,** *a.* of inexhaustible energy. **tīre′some,** *a.* trying, annoying; tedious.

tire²: see **tyre.**

tīr′ō, tȳr′ō, *n.* (pl. -*s*), beginner.

tiss′ūe (*or* -shōō), *n.* (esp. rich or fine) woven fabric; network (*of* lies, etc.); substance of (part of) animal or plant body; piece of soft absorbent paper. **tissue-paper,** thin soft paper for wrapping, etc.

tit¹, *n.* (also *titmouse,* pl. -*mīce*), any of various small active birds (*blue tit, great tit, coal tit,* etc.).

tit², *n. tit for tat,* equivalent given in return, blow for blow, retaliation.

Tī′tan, *n.* (Gk. myth.) member of family of gigantic gods; person of superhuman strength, size, etc. **titan′ic,** *a.* gigantic, colossal.

tit′bit, *n.* choice or delicate morsel or item.

tīthe (-dh), *n.* (Hist.) tenth part of annual agricultural produce payable for support of clergy, church, etc. **tithe-barn,** barn built to hold corn paid as tithes.

tit′illāte, *v.t.* tickle; excite pleasantly. **titillā′-tion,** *n.*

tit′ivāte, *v.* adorn, smarten, (oneself); put finishing touches to appearance (of).

tī′tle, *n.* name of book, work of art, etc.; heading of chapter; word(s) indicating person's status, rank, office, etc.; legal right to possession of (esp. real) property; just or recognized claim (*to*). **title-deed,** document constituting evidence of ownership. **title-page,** page at beginning of book bearing title, name of author, etc. **tī′tled** (-ld), *a.* having title of nobility.

titmouse: see **tit¹.**

titt′er, *v.i. & n.* giggle.

titt′le, *n.* (*archaic*) particle, very small bit.

titt′le-tattle, *n. & v.i.* gossip, tattle.

titt′up, *v.i.* go mincingly; prance.

tit′ūlar, *a.* existing in name only, nominal.

T-junc′tion, *n.* junction, esp. of two roads, in shape of T.

to (tōō, too), *prep.* in direction of; as far as; also expressing comparison, ratio, reference, etc., introducing indirect object of verb, etc., as sign of or substitute for infinitive, expressing purpose, consequence, etc. *adv.* to or in normal or required position, esp. to a standstill. *to and fro,* backwards and forwards, up and down.

toad, *n.* frog-like amphibian breeding in water but living chiefly on land. **toad′stool,** fungus with round disc-like top and slender stalk. **toa′dy,** *n.* servile flatterer. *v.i.* flatter in hope of gain or advantage.

toast, *n.* bread sliced and browned at fire or other heat; person or thing drunk to. *v.* make brown, warm, by exposure to heat; drink to health or in honour of by raising glass and taking sip of wine. **toa′ster,** *n.* (esp.) electrical device for toasting bread.

tobacc′ō, *n.* (pl. *tobaccos*), plant of American origin; its leaves dried and prepared for smoking, etc. **tobacc′onist,** *n.* dealer in tobacco, cigarettes, etc.

tobogg′an, *n. & v.i.* (ride on) long light narrow sledge, used esp. for coasting down snow-covered slopes.

toc′sin, *n.* (bell rung as) alarm or signal.

today′, *adv.* & *n.* (on) this day; nowadays, (in) modern times.

todd′le, *v. i.* go with small unsteady steps (as) of young child. **todd′ler**, *n.* (esp.) child who has just learned to walk.

todd′y, *n.* sweetened drink of whisky or other spirits, hot water, etc.; fresh or fermented sap of certain palms as beverage.

to-do′ (-ōō), *n.* commotion, fuss.

tōe, *n.* each digit of foot, forepart of foot. *v. t.* touch or reach with toes.

toff′ee (-fi), *n.* sweet made of boiled butter, sugar, etc.

tō′ga, *n.* ancient-roman citizen's outer garment of single piece of stuff covering whole body except right arm.

togeth′er (-dh-), *adv.* in(to) company, conjunction, union, etc.; simultaneously; in uninterrupted succession.

togg′le, *n.* short pin, peg, etc., passed through loop of rope, etc., as fastening.

toil, *v. i.* work long or arduously (*at*). *n.* labour, drudgery. **toi′ler**, *n.* **toil′some**, *a.* involving toil, tiring. **toil′worn**, *a.* worn by, showing marks of, toil.

toi′lèt, *n.* process of washing, dressing, etc.; lavatory. **toi′lètries** (-z), *n.pl.* articles for use in washing, dressing, etc.

toilette (twahlet′), *n.* (style of) dress. (French).

toils (-z), *n.pl.* net, snare.

toilsome, toilworn: see **toil.**

tō′ken, *n.* sign, symbol (*of*); evidence; keepsake; anything used to represent something else, esp. money; gift coupon.

told, *p. t.* & *p. p.* of **tell.**

tol′erable, *a.* that can be endured; fairly good.

tol′erance, *n.* willingness or capacity to tolerate. **tol′erant**, *a.*

tol′erāte, *v. t.* endure; permit; allow to exist, be practised, etc., without interference or molestation; not judge harshly. **tolerā′tion,** *n.*

tōll¹, *n.* fee charged for passage along road, over bridge, etc.; cost, esp. in suffering, loss, etc. **toll-bar, toll-gate,** barriers preventing passage without payment of toll.

tōll², *v.* cause (bell) to ring, (of bell) ring, with slow succession of strokes, esp. for death or funeral; announce, give out, thus. *n.* tolling sound.

tom, *n.* tomcat.

tom′ahawk (-a-h-), *n.* light axe of N. Amer. Indians, used as weapon and tool.

toma′tō (-ah-), *n.* (pl. *tomatoes*), (plant bearing) glossy red (or yellow) fleshy edible fruit.

tomb (tōōm), *n.* grave; burial-vault; sepulchral monument. **tomb′stone,** memorial stone over grave.

tom′boy, *n.* spirited romping girl.

tom′cat, *n.* male cat.

tōme, *n.* volume, esp. large heavy one.

tomfōōl′ery, *n.* foolish behaviour, silliness.

tomo′rrow (-ō), *adv.* & *n.* (on) the day after today; (in) the future.

tom′tom, *n.* drum of India, Africa, etc., usu. beaten with hands.

ton (tun), *n.* measure of weight, 20 cwt. or 2240 lb., or (U.S., also *short ton*) 2000 lb., avoirdupois; unit of internal capacity of ship (100 cu. ft.). *metric ton,* 1000 kilograms. **tonn′age,** *n.* carrying capacity of ship expressed in tons; total tonnage of shipping; charge per ton on cargo.

tōne, *n.* sound, esp. with reference to pitch, quality, and strength; quality, pitch, modulation, etc., of voice or spoken sound; musical interval equal to two semitones; tint or shade of colour; firmness or tension proper to healthy bodily organs or tissues; prevailing character of morals, sentiments, etc. *v.* give tone or quality to; harmonize. *tone down,* make or become less emphatic, violent, etc.

tongs (-z), *n.pl.* (*pair of*) *tongs,* implement for grasping and lifting objects.

tongue (tung), *n.* movable fleshy organ in mouth, used in tasting, speaking, swallowing, etc.; language; manner of speaking; tongue-like piece or part. **tongue-tied,** speechless from embarrassment, shyness, etc.; (almost) unable to speak because of defect of tongue. **tongue-twister,** word(s) difficult to articulate. **tongued** (-ngd), *a.* having tongue.

ton′ic, *a.* of, maintaining, restoring, bodily tone; bracing; (Mus.) of, founded upon, tonic or keynote. *n.* tonic medicine; invigorating influence; (Mus.) keynote. **tonic sol-fa,** system of singing at sight from syllabic notation in which tonic of all major keys is *doh.*

tonight′ (-nīt), *adv.* & *n.* (on) present night, (on) night of today.

tonnage: see **ton.**

tonne (tun), *n.* metric ton (see **ton**).

ton′sil, *n.* either of pair of small organs of lymphatic tissue at sides of root of tongue. **tonsilli′tis,** *n.* inflammation of tonsils.

ton′sure (-sher), *n.* shaving of head or of circular patch on crown, esp. on admission to priesthood or monastic order; part of head thus shaved. *v.* give tonsure to.

tōō, *adv.* in addition, besides, also; in excess; more than is right or fitting; very.

took, *p. t.* of **take.**

tōōl, *n.* implement used in working upon something; person used to help forward another's purpose. *v.* work with tool; ornament (leather, etc.) with tool.

tōōt, *n.* sound of horn, etc. *v.* emit toot; sound (horn, etc.).

tōōth, *n.* (pl. *teeth*), any of hard processes with points or edges, rooted in jaws and used for biting or chewing food, etc., or as weapons; projecting part, point, etc., resembling tooth. *cut a tooth,* have new tooth appear through gum. *v.* provide with teeth; interlock. **tooth'ache,** ache in tooth or teeth. **tŏŏth'some,** *a.* pleasant to eat.

tŏŏ'tle, *v.* toot gently.

top[1], *n.* summit, upper part, surface, of something; highest place, rank, etc.; part or piece forming upper part or covering of something. *on top,* supreme, dominant. *a.* highest; that is at or on top. *v.t.* (p.t. *topped*), provide with top or cap; remove top of; exceed in height. **top-boot,** high boot with wide band of lighter colour round top. **top-coat,** overcoat. **top hat,** man's tall stiff cylindrical hat. **top-heavy,** overweighted at top. **top'knot,** bow, tuft, crest, etc., worn or growing on top of head. **top'sail** (-sl), square sail set next above lowest. **top secret,** most secret, extremely secret. **top'less,** *a.* **top'môst,** *a.* uppermost.

top[2], *n.* toy rotating on its point when set in motion by hand, spring, string, etc.

tŏ'paz, *n.* semi-precious stone of various colours, esp. yellow.

tŏ'per, *n.* habitual drunkard.

tŏ'piary *a.* & *n.* (of) art of clipping shrubs or trees into ornamental shapes.

top'ic, *a.* subject of conversation, discourse, argument, etc. **top'ical,** having reference to current events. **topical'ity,** *n.*

topog'raphy, *n.* (description or delineation of) physical features of place or locality. **topog'rapher,** *n.* **topograph'ic(al),** *aa.*

topp'le, *v.* (cause to) tumble or fall headlong, as if top-heavy.

top'sy-tur'vy, *adv.* & *a.* upside down; in(to) utter confusion.

tŏque (-k), *n.* woman's small, usu. swathed, brimless hat.

tor, *n.* craggy or rocky hill or hill-top, esp. in Devon and Cornwall.

torch, *n.* burning piece of resinous wood, etc., as light for carrying in hand; small portable electric lamp. **torch'light,** *n.* & *a.*

tore, p.t. of **tear**[1].

to'rĕador, *n.* mounted bullfighter (term still current in English but not in modern Spanish).

torer'o (-ārŏ), *n.* (pl. *toreros*), bullfighter. (Spanish)

tor'ment, *n.* (cause of) severe bodily or mental suffering. **torment',** *v.t.* subject to torment; tease, annoy.

torn, *p.p.* of **tear**[1].

tornā'dŏ, *n.* (pl. *tornadoes*), very violent storm; destructive rotatory storm advancing in narrow path for many miles.

torpē'dŏ, *n.* (pl. *torpedoes*), flat-fish capable of inflicting electric shocks; self-propelled dirigible explosive underwater missile. *v.t.* attack, damage, destroy, (as) with torpedo. **torpedo-boat,** small fast armoured vessel carrying torpedoes.

tor'pid, *a.* benumbed, dormant; sluggish. **torpid'ity,** *n.* **torpor,** *n.*

to'rrent, *n.* swift, violent, rushing stream of water, etc.; downpour of rain; violent flow (of words, etc.). **torren'tial** (-shl), *a.*

to'rrid, *a.* intensely hot. **torrid zone,** tropics.

tor'sion (-shn), *n.* twisting, twist. **tor'sional,** *a.*

tor'sŏ, *n.* (pl. *torsos*), statue lacking head and limbs; trunk of human body.

tor'toise (-tus), *n.* slow-moving four-footed reptile with body encased in shell. **tortoise-shell,** mottled brown and yellow shell of marine turtle, used for ornamental articles.

tor'tŭous, *a.* full of twists or turns; circuitous, not straightforward. **tor'tŭousness, tortŭos'ity,** *nn.*

tor'ture (-cher), *n.* infliction of severe bodily pain, esp. to extort something from victim; severe physical or mental pain. *v.t.* subject to torture; distort, strain, wrench.

Tor'y, *n.* & *a.* (member) of Conservative Party.

toss, *v.* throw, esp. lightly, carelessly, or easily; (of bull, etc.) fling up with horns; throw (*up*) coin to decide choice, etc., by whichever side falls uppermost; throw back *head*; throw or roll about from side to side. *toss off,* drink in one draught; dispatch (work, etc.) rapidly and easily. *n.* tossing. **toss-up,** doubtful question, even chance.

tot[1], *n.* small child; small quantity (*of* drink, esp. alcoholic spirits).

tot[2], *v.* (p.t. *totted*), add (*up*), mount *up* (*to*).

tŏ'tal, *a.* complete; comprising or involving whole; utter, unqualified. *n.* sum of all items; total amount. *v.* (*p.t. totalled*), amount to, mount *up to*; reckon total of. **total'ity,** *n.* **tŏ'tally,** *adv.* **tŏ'talīze,** *v.*

tŏtalitār'ian, *a.* of regime permitting no rival loyalties or parties.

tŏtalīzā'tor, tōte, *nn.* device registering number and amount of bets staked, amount due to winners, etc.

tŏ'tem, *n.* (image of) natural, esp. animal, object assumed as emblem of family or clan. **totem pole,** post with carved and painted totem(s), esp. in front of N. Amer. Indian dwelling.

tott'er, *v.i.* walk, stand, unsteadily or shakily; rock or shake as if about to fall. *n.* tottering gait.

touch (tuch), *v.* put hand, etc., on something so as to feel it; come or be in contact with; strike lightly; tint slightly *with*; concern; stir sympathy or other emotion in; effect slightly; reach, approach. *n.* act or fact of touching; sense of feeling; light stroke with pencil, brush, etc.; manner of touching keys or strings of musical instrument; communication, contact. *touch-and-go,* of uncertain result, risky. **touch-down,** contact with ground on landing of aircraft. **touch'stone,** black quartz used for testing alloys of gold, etc.; (fig.) standard, criterion. **touch'wood,** wood in soft rotten state, usable as tinder.

touch′ing, *a.* affecting, pathetic. *prep.* as regards. **touch′y,** *a.* easily taking offence, over-sensitive.

tough (tuf), *a.* of close tenacious substance or great endurance; hard to chew; not easily injured or broken; hard to tackle or overcome; hardy. *n.* street ruffian, tough person. **tough′en,** *v.* make or become tough.

tou′pee (tōō-), *n.* false hair worn to cover bald patch.

tour (toor), *n.* journey through (part of) country from place to place; visit to, walk round, exhibition, institution, etc. *v.* make tour (of). **tour′ism,** *n.* organized touring. **tour′ist,** *n.* one who travels for pleasure.

tour de force (toor), feat of strength or (esp.) great skill. (French)

tour′nament (toor-), *n.* medieval sport of mounted combat with blunted weapons; contest of skill between a number of competitors.

tourniquet (toor′nikǎ), *n.* bandage tightened by twisting rigid bar put through it, for stopping bleeding by compression.

tou′sle (-zl), *v.t.* pull about, handle roughly, make (esp. hair) untidy.

tout, *v.i.* pester possible customers for orders. *n.* one who touts.

tow¹ (tō), *n.* (coarse and broken) fibres of flax, etc., prepared for spinning.

tow² (tō), *v.t.* draw along through water by rope or chain; pull along behind one. *n.* towing, being towed. *in tow,* being towed. **towing-path, tow′path,** path beside canal or river for use in towing.

towards, toward (tord(z), tooword(z)′), *prep.* in direction of; near, approaching; as contribution or help to.

tow′el, *n.* absorbent cloth, etc., for drying or wiping after washing, etc. *v.t.* rub or dry with towel. **tow′elling,** *n.* material for towels.

tow′er, *n.* tall structure, often forming part of church or other large building; fortress, etc., having tower. *v.i.* rise, reach, high (*above* surroundings); (of eagle, etc.) soar. **tow′ering,** *a.* high, lofty; (of rage, etc.) violent.

town, *n.* inhabited place larger than village; inhabitants, business or shopping area, of town. **town crier,** (chiefly Hist.) officer making public announcements in streets, etc. **town hall,** large building used for transaction of public business of town, etc. **town planning,** construction of plans for regulation of growth, provision and siting of amenities, etc., of town(s). **towns′people,** people of a town.

tox′ic, *a.* of, caused by, or acting as poison. **toxi′city,** *n.* **toxicol′ogy,** *n.* study of poisons. **toxicol′ogist,** *n.*

tox′in, *n.* poisonous substance of animal or vegetable origin, esp. one produced by micro-organisms.

toy, *n.* thing designed to be played with, esp.

by child; small or trifling thing. *v.i.* play, amuse oneself, (*with*).

trāce¹, *n.* track or mark left behind; indication of existence or occurrence of something; slight amount (*of*). *v.t.* copy (drawing, etc.) by marking its lines on tracing-paper, etc.; follow, discover, etc., by observing marks, tracks, evidence, etc. **trā′cing,** *n.* (esp.) copy made by tracing. **tracing-paper,** semi-transparent paper placed′ over drawings, etc., to be traced.

trāce², *n.* either of pair of straps, chains, etc., by which vehicle is pulled by horse, etc.

trā′cery, *n.* (pattern, etc., resembling) decorative stone openwork.

trachē′a (-k-), *n.* windpipe. **trachēot′omy,** *n.* surgical incision of trachea.

track, *n.* mark, series of marks, left by vehicle, person, animal, etc., in passing; path, esp. one beaten by use; prepared course for racing, etc.; railway line; band round wheels of tank, etc. *v.* follow track of; pursue, follow up. **tracker dog,** dog used to track fugitives by scent. **track′less,** *a.* pathless.

tract¹, *n.* area, stretch, expanse, (*of* land, etc.); system of related parts in animal body.

tract², *n.* short treatise, pamphlet, esp. on religious subject.

trac′table, *a.* easily managed; docile.

trac′tion, *n.* pulling; drawing of vehicles or loads along road or track. **traction engine,** steam or diesel engine for drawing loads on road, etc.

trac′tor, *n.* motor vehicle for drawing heavy loads, used esp. on farms.

trāde, *n.* dealing in goods for profit; particular branch of this; business, calling, skilled handicraft. *v.* engage in trade, buy and sell; have business transactions *with. trade in,* hand over (used article) in part payment (*for*). *trade on,* take (esp. unscrupulous) advantage of. **trade mark,** manufacturer's registered device or name to distinguish his goods. **trades′man,** (pl. -*men*), person engaged in trade, esp. shopkeeper. **trade union,** organized association of employees to protect and further common interests. **trade wind,** constant wind blowing towards equator from NE. and SE. **trā′der,** *n.* person engaged in trading. **trā′ding,** *n.* **trading-post,** establishment in remote part of country for trading in goods. **trading-stamp,** coupon offered by retailer.

tradi′tion, *n.* handing down of beliefs, customs, etc., from one generation to another; tale, belief, custom, etc., thus handed down. **tradi′tional,** *a.* **tradi′tionally,** *adv.*

tradūce′, *v.t.* slander, misrepresent.

traff′ic, *n.* coming and going of persons, goods, or esp. vehicles or vessels, along road, canal, etc.; transport of persons or goods; dealing or bargaining, esp. in something which should not be subject of trade. *v.*

(p.t. *trafficked*; pres. p. *trafficking*), trade (*in*), esp. illegally or reprehensibly. **traffic warden,** official supervising and regulating traffic and (esp.) parking.

tragĕ'dian, *n.* author of, actor in, tragedies.

tragĕdienne' (-i-en), *n.* tragic actress.

tra'gĕdy, *n.* drama, etc., of serious character, with fatal or disastrous conclusion; tragic event, calamity. **tra'gic,** *a.* of, in style of, tragedy; sad, calamitous, distressing. **tra'gically,** *adv.*

trail, *v.* draw or be drawn along behind something, esp. on ground; walk wearily; lag behind; hang loosely; (of plant) grow along ground, etc., creep; track, shadow. *n.* track, scent, or other sign of passage left by moving object; beaten path, esp. through wild region. **trai'ler,** *n.* trailing plant; vehicle, esp. caravan, drawn by another; extracts from film exhibited in advance as advertisement.

train, *v.* bring to desired standard of efficiency, obedience, etc., by instruction and practice; make physically fit for contest, etc.; cause (plant) to grow in desired shape; point, aim, (gun, etc.). *n.* part of robe or gown trailing behind; retinue; succession of events; locomotive with the coaches or wagons it draws; railway travel; line of gunpowder laid as explosive charge. **train-bearer,** person holding up train of another's robe. **trainee',** *n.* person being trained (for occupation). **trai'ner,** *n.* **trai'ning,** *n.*

train'-oil, *n.* whale-blubber oil.

traipse, trāpes, *v. i.* trudge wearily.

trait (trā), *n.* feature, distinguishing quality.

trai'tor, *n.* one who betrays a trust or acts disloyally (*to* his country, cause, etc.). **trai'torous,** *a.*

trajec'tory, *n.* path of body moving under given forces, esp. of projectile in flight through air.

tram, *n.* (also *tram-car*) passenger car, usu. electrically driven, running on tram-lines on public road. **tram-lines,** parallel metal rails laid flush with road surface.

tramm'el, *n.* kind of fishing-net; shackle; (usu. pl.) hampering influence, restraint. *v.t.* (p.t. *trammelled*), hamper.

tramp, *v.* walk with firm heavy tread; walk, traverse, on foot; be tramp. *n.* sound (as) of troops marching; long walk or march; person who tramps roads, esp. as vagrant; cargo-vessel running on no regular line.

tramp'le, *v.* tread heavily and (esp.) injuriously (on); crush or destroy thus (often fig.).

tram'poline, *n.* contrivance of strong canvas attached by springs to horizontal frame, used for gymnastic and acrobatic leaping.

trance (-ah-), *n.* sleep-like state; dreamy state; absorption, ecstasy.

tran'quil, *a.* free from agitation or disturbance, quiet; serene, calm. **tranquill'ity,** *n.*

trans-, *pref.* across, beyond, over, to or on

farther side of.

transact' (-z- *or* -s-), *v.t.* do, carry on, (action, business, etc.). **transac'tion,** *n.* transacting, being transacted; piece of business; (pl.) records of learned society's proceedings.

transatlan'tic (-z-), *a.* across, on or from other side of, Atlantic; crossing the Atlantic.

transcend', *v.t.* go beyond, exceed, limits of; rise above, surpass, excel. **transcen'dence,** *n.*

transcen'dent, *a.* transcending ordinary limits, supreme, pre-eminent; outside or beyond experience. **transcen'dency,** *n.* **transcenden'tal,** *a.* not derived from experience; obscure, visionary.

transcontinen'tal (-z-), *a.* extending or passing across a continent.

transcrībe', *v.t.* copy out; reproduce in ordinary writing; (Mus.) adapt for other than original instrument, etc. **tran'script,** *n.* written copy; (Law) copy of legal record. **transcrip'tion,** *n.* transcribing, being transcribed; something transcribed.

tran'sept, *n.* (either arm of) transverse part of cross-shaped church.

transfer', *v.* (p.t. *transferred*), convey, transmit, hand over, etc., from one person, place, etc., to another; (Law) convey by legal process; convey (design, etc.) from one surface to another; change from one train, bus, line, etc., to another. **trans'fer,** *n.* transferring, being transferred; transferred thing; design or picture on prepared paper for transferring. **trans'ferable,** *a.* that can be transferred. **trans'ference,** *n.* act or process of transferring.

transfig'ure (-ger), *v.t.* alter form or appearance of, esp. change so as to elevate or idealize. **transfigurā'tion,** *n.*

transfix', *v.t.* pierce with, impale on, sharp-pointed instrument; render motionless (with horror, grief, etc.).

transform', *v.t.* change form, appearance, condition, function, etc., of. **transformā'tion,** *n.* transforming, being transformed. **transfor'mer,** *n.* (esp., Electr.) apparatus for changing voltage of alternating current.

transfūse' (-z), *v.t.* cause (fluid, etc.) to pass from one vessel, etc., to another; transfer (blood of one person) into veins of another. **transfū'sion** (-zhn), *n.*

transgress' (-z- *or* -s-), *v.* break (law, etc.); go beyond (limit, bound); sin. **transgre'ssion** (-shn), *n.* **transgress'or,** *n.*

tranship', trans-ship', *v.* transfer, change, from one ship to another. **tranship'ment,** *n.*

tran'siènt (-z-), *a.* lasting for a short time only; fleeting; brief. **tran'siènce,** *n.*

transis'tor, *n.* very small electronic device capable of replacing thermionic valve; radio receiver using transistors. **transis'torīze,** *v.t.* provide with transistors.

tran'sit (-z-), *n.* passing or passage across,

over, or through.

transi'tion, *n.* passage from one state, subject, set of circumstances, etc., to another; period of this. **transi'tional,** *a.*

trans'itive, *a.* (of verb) requiring a direct object to complete the sense.

tran'sitory, *a.* not lasting; momentary, brief, fleeting.

translăte', *v.t.* change (word, book, etc.) from one language into another; interpret; remove (bishop) to another see; (Bibl.) convey to heaven without death. **translă'table,** *a.* **translā'tion,** *n.* **translā'tor,** *n.*

translit'erăte (-z-), *v.t.* re-write (word, passage) in letters of a different alphabet or language. **transliterā'tion,** *n.*

translu'cent (-zlōō-), *a.* allowing passage of light, but diffusing it. **translu'cence,** *n.*

trans'migrăte (-z-), *v.i.* (of soul) pass after death into another body; migrate. **transmigrā'tion,** *n.*

transmi'ssion (-zmishn), *n.* transmitting, being transmitted; radio or television programme transmitted; mechanism transmitting power from engine to axle in motor vehicle, etc.

transmit' (-z-), *v.t.* (p.t. *transmitted*), send, pass on, to another person, place, or thing; communicate (heat, electricity, emotion, etc.). **transmiss'ible, transmitt'able,** *aa.* **transmitt'er,** *n.* (esp.) (part of) radio, etc., station or set for sending out radio waves.

transmūte' (-z-), *v.t.* change form, nature, or substance of; convert (one substance, species, etc.) into another. **transmūtā'tion,** *n.*

tran'som, *n.* horizontal bar across window or separating door from window above it.

transpa'rent (*or* -pār'-), *a.* allowing light to pass through so that objects beyond are clearly visible; easily seen through, obvious; candid, open. **transpa'rence,** *n.* being transparent. **transpa'rency,** *n.* transparence; picture on glass or other transparent substance, to be viewed by light shining through it.

transpīre', *v.* emit, be emitted, as vapour or liquid through skin, tissue, etc.; come to be known. **transpirā'tion,** *n.*

transplant' (-lah-), *v.t.* remove and replant or establish elsewhere; (Med.) transfer (living tissue) from one part of body to another, or (tissue or organ) from one person or animal to another; bear transplanting. **trans'plant,** *n.* **transplantā'tion,** *n.*

transport', *v.t.* carry, convey, from one place to another; (Hist.) deport (convict) to penal colony; (usu. passive) carry away by strong emotion. **trans'port,** *n.* transporting of goods or passengers; means of conveyance, vehicles; troop-ship, troop-carrier; very strong emotion. **transportā'tion,** *n.* (esp.) deportation to penal settlement.

transpōse (-z-), *v.t.* change order or place of; (Mus.) put into different key. **transposi'tion,** *n.*

trans-ship: see **tranship.**

transubstan'tiăte (-shi-), *v.t.* change into different substance. **transubstantiā'tion,** *n.* (esp., Theol.) doctrine that bread and wine of Eucharist are converted into body and blood of Christ.

transverse', *a.* situated, lying, or set across or athwart.

transves'tism, *n.* practice of dressing in clothes of opposite sex. **transves'tīte,** *n.*

trap¹, *n.* device for catching or ensnaring animal(s), etc.; scheme, plan, for detecting, enticing, or deceiving; light, esp. two--wheeled, horse-carriage; U-shaped section of drain-pipe, etc. *v.t.* (p.t. *trapped*), catch (as) in trap; set traps for game, etc. **trap'-door,** hinged or sliding door in ceiling, floor, etc. **trapp'er,** *n.* (esp.) one who traps wild animals for their fur, etc.

trap², *v.t.* (p.t. *trapped*), adorn with trappings.

trapēze', *n.* horizontal cross-bar suspended by ropes as apparatus for acrobats, etc.

trapē'zium, *n.* (pl. *-s* or *trapezia*), quadrilateral with (only) two sides parallel; (U.S.) trapezoid. **trap'ezoid,** *n.* quadrilateral with no sides parallel; (U.S.) trapezium.

trapper: see **trap¹.**

trapp'ings (-z), *n.pl.* ornamental cloth covering for horse, etc.; adornments, ornamental accessories.

traps, *n.pl.* (*informal*) belongings, luggage.

trapse: see **traipse.**

trash, *n.* waste or worthless stuff; nonsense; worthless people. **trash'y,** *a.*

trau'ma, *n.* (pl. *traumata, traumas*), injury, wound; (Psychol.) emotional shock. **traumat'ic,** *a.*

trav'ail, *n.* & *v.i.* (*archaic*) (suffer) pains of childbirth; (*archaic*) (make) laborious effort.

trav'el, *v.* (p.t. *travelled*), make journey(s), esp. of some length or to foreign countries; act as commercial traveller; move, be capable of moving, along fixed course. *n.* travelling. **trav'eller,** *n.* person who travels or is travelling; commercial traveller. **trav'elling,** *a.* used, designed for use, by traveller(s).

trav'elogue (-g), *n.* illustrated narrative of travel; documentary film on travel.

trav'erse, *v.* travel or lie across; swivel, turn as on pivot. *n.* thing, esp. structure, that crosses another; horizontal crossing of face of precipice in climbing.

trav'esty, *n.* gross parody, ridiculous imitation. *v.t.* make or be travesty of.

trawl, *n.* large wide-mouthed net dragged by boat along bottom of sea, etc. *v.* fish with trawl. **traw'ler,** *n.* boat used in trawling.

tray, *n.* flat piece of wood, metal, etc., usu. with raised rim, for carrying or holding light articles, etc.

treach'erous (-ech-), *a.* breaking faith or betraying trust; not to be relied on, deceptive. **treach'ery,** *n.* being treacherous;

treacherous act(s).

trea'cle, *n.* uncrystallized syrup produced in process of refining sugar. **trea'cly,** *a.*

tread (-ed), *v.* (p.t. *trod*; p.p. *trodden*), set one's foot down; (of foot) be set down; traverse on foot; step, trample, *on. n.* manner or sound of walking; (piece of rubber, etc., placed on) top surface of step in a stair; part of tyre coming in contact with ground.

tread'le (-ed-), *n.* lever moved by foot and imparting motion to sewing-machine, lathe, etc.

tread'mill (-ed-), *n.* appliance for producing motion by treading on steps fixed to revolving cylinder; (fig.) monotonous routine.

trea'son (-z-), *n.* violation by subject of allegiance to sovereign or State; breach of faith, disloyalty. **trea'sonable, trea'sonous,** *aa.* involving treason.

trea'sure (-ezher), *n.* wealth or riches stored up, esp. hoard of precious metals, gems, etc.; highly valued thing or person. *v.t.* value highly; hoard. **treasure trove,** gold, silver, etc., found hidden in ground, etc., owner of which is unknown. **trea'surer,** *n.* person responsible for funds of institution, society, etc.

trea'sury (-zheri), *n.* place where precious and valuable objects are kept (often fig.); funds or revenue of State, corporation, etc.; (*Treasury*) State department advising Chancellor of the Exchequer, administering expenditure of public revenue, etc.

treat, *v.* act or behave towards in specified way; deal with, apply process to; deal with disease, etc., in order to relieve or cure; pay for food, drink, or entertainment of; negotiate (*with*). *n.* entertainment, esp. given free; great pleasure, delight, or gratification.

trea'tise, *n.* book or writing dealing methodically with a particular subject.

treat'ment, *n.* (particular way of) dealing with or behaving towards person or thing; (method of) treating patient or disease.

trea'ty, *n.* formal signed agreement between States relating to peace, alliance, commerce, etc.

treb'le, *a.* & *n.* threefold, triple (sum, quantity); soprano (part, voice, singer, esp. boy); high-pitched, shrill (sound, etc). *v.* multiply, be multiplied, by three.

tree, *n.* perennial plant with woody main stem (usu. developing branches at some distance from ground); boot- or shoe-tree; family tree.

tre'foil (*or* -ē-), *n.* any of various plants with compound leaves of three leaflets (e.g. clover, shamrock).

trek, *v.* (p.t. *trekked*), travel, migrate, esp. by ox-wagon; make arduous journey, esp. on foot. *n.* trekking; (stage of) long and arduous journey.

trell'is, *n.* structure of light bars of wood, etc., crossing each other, used as support for climbing plants. *v.t.* furnish with trellis.

trellis-work, trellis.

trem'ble, *v.i.* shake involuntarily with fear or other emotion, weakness, etc.; be affected with fear, agitation, suspense, etc. *n.* trembling, quiver, tremor.

trêmen'dous, *a.* awe-inspiring, terrible; (*informal*) extraordinarily great, immense. **tremen'dously,** *adv.*

trem'or, *n.* tremulous or vibratory movement or sound, vibration, shaking; quiver; thrill of fear or other emotion.

trem'ulous, *a.* trembling, quivering; timid; tremblingly sensitive or responsive.

trench, *n.* deep ditch, esp. one dug by troops as shelter from enemy's fire. *v.* make trench(es) or ditch(es) in, dig trench(es); make series of trenches so as to bring lower soil to surface.

trench'ant, *a.* sharp, keen; cutting, decisive. **trench'ancy,** *n.*

trench'er, *n.* (esp.) wooden platter for cutting bread on.

trend, *v.i.* have specified direction, course, or general tendency. *n.* general direction, course, tendency. **tren'dy,** *a.* (*informal*) following latest trends of fashion, etc.

trêpan', *n.* & *v.t.* (p.t. *trepanned*), (*archaic*) trephine.

trêphine' (-ēn), *n.* surgeon's cylindrical saw for cutting out circular disc from skull. *v.t.* operate on with trephine.

trepidā'tion, *n.* agitation, alarm, anxiety.

tres'pass, *v.i.* enter unlawfully on another's land or property; encroach, make unwarrantable claim, *on*; (*archaic*) sin. *n.* act of trespassing; (*archaic*) sin. **tres'passer,** *n.*

tress, *n.* lock or braid of hair; (pl., Poet.) (esp. long) hair.

tre'stle (-sl), *n.* supporting structure, usu. of wood, for table-top, etc. **trestle-table,** table of board(s) laid across trestles.

trews (-ōōz), *n.pl.* tartan trousers.

tri-, *pref.* three, three times.

trī'al, *n.* (instance of) judicial trying or being tried; testing, investigation by experience; test of qualities, skill, efficiency, etc.; affliction, hardship.

trī'angle (-nggl), *n.* figure bounded by three straight lines; three-cornered object, space, etc.; (Mus.) percussion instrument of steel rod bent into triangle. **trïang'ūlar,** *a.* triangle-shaped, three-cornered.

tribe, *n.* group of (esp. primitive) families with common ancestor, living under recognized chief(s). **trī'bal,** *a.* **trī'balism,** *n.* **tribes'man** (-bz-), *n.* (pl.-*men*).

tribol'ogy (*or* trī-), *n.* study of friction, wear, and lubrication.

tribūlā'tion, *n.* great affliction.

trībū'nal (*or* -i-), *n.* board or committee appointed to inquire into or adjudicate on particular question, etc.; court of justice.

trib'ūne[1], *n.* platform, rostrum.

trib'ūne[2], *n.* (Rom. hist.) officer protecting

interests and rights of plebeians.

trib'ūtary, *a.* & *n.* (stream or river) flowing into another; (person or State) paying tribute.

trib'ūte, *n.* periodical payment exacted by one ruler or State from another; thing said, done, or given as mark of esteem or affection.

trice¹, *n.* instant, moment.

trice², *v.t.* (Naut.) haul *up* and secure with rope or lashing.

trick, *n.* crafty or deceitful, esp. mean, act or scheme; hoax, joke; feat of skill, knack; mannerism, habit; (winning of) one round in card-game. *v.t.* deceive by trick, cheat; dress, deck (*out*). **trick'ery**, *n.* deceitful conduct, stratagem.

trick'le, *v.* (cause to) flow in drops or scantily and haltingly. *n.* trickling flow.

trick'ster, *n.* deceiver, rogue.

trick'y, *a.* requiring cautious or adroit handling; skilful, adroit.

tric'olour (-uler), *a.* & *n.* three-coloured (flag, esp. French national flag of three vertical bands of blue, white, and red).

tri'cycle, *n.* three-wheeled pedal- or motor--driven vehicle.

tri'dent, *n.* three-pronged fish-spear borne as sceptre by Neptune and Britannia; three--pronged weapon used in Roman gladiatorial combats.

trienn'ial, *a.* occurring every three years; lasting three years.

tri'fle, *n.* thing, fact, circumstance, of slight value or importance; small amount or article; sweet dish of sponge-cake, jam, fruit, whipped cream, etc. *v.i.* toy, play, *with*; act or speak idly or frivolously. **tri'fling**, *a.* (esp.) of small importance or value.

trigg'er (-g-), *n.* lever pulled to release spring or catch, esp. of firing mechanism of gun, etc. *v.* set *off* reaction, process, etc.

trigonom'ètry, *n.* branch of mathematics dealing with calculation of sides and angles of triangles, and with certain functions of angles. **trigonomet'ric(al)**, *aa.*

trilat'eral, *a.* three-sided.

tril'by, *n.* man's soft felt hat.

trill, *n.* (Mus.) rapid alternation of two notes a tone or a semitone apart; rapidly vibrating sound. *v.* produce trill(s); warble.

trill'ion, *n.* a million million millions; (U.S. and Canada) a million millions.

tril'ogy, *n.* set of three related dramatic or other literary works.

trim, *a.* neat, tidy; in good order. *v.* (p.t. *trimmed*), make trim, esp. by cutting away irregular or unsightly parts of; ornament; adjust balance of (ship, aircraft); arrange (sails) to suit wind. *n.* state or degree of readiness, fitness, adjustment, etc.; trimming, being trimmed. **trimm'ing**, *n.* (esp.) ornamental addition to dress, hat, etc.; (pl.) accessories, usual accompaniments.

trī'maran, *n.* boat with three hulls side by side.

trin'ity, *n.* being three; group of three. **Trin'-ity**, *n.* (Christian theology) existence of God in three persons (Father, Son, and Holy Spirit).

trink'èt, *n.* small fancy article; ornament or jewel of small value.

trīnō'mial, *a.* & *n.* (algebraic expression) consisting of three terms.

tri'o (-ēō), *n.* (pl. *trios*), group or set of three, esp. (Mus.) performers; musical composition for three instruments or voices; middle division of minuet or scherzo.

trī'olèt, *n.* verse-form with eight lines and two rhymes, in which first line is repeated as fourth and seventh, and second line as eighth.

trip, *v.* (p.t. *tripped*), go lightly and quickly along; catch one's foot and stumble; commit blunder or fault. *trip up*, (cause to) stumble; detect in error, inconsistency, etc. *n.* excursion for pleasure; (short) journey; stumble.

trīpar'tīte, *a.* engaged in, concluded, between three parties; divided into three parts.

trīpe, *n.* first or second stomach of ox or other ruminant prepared as food.

trip'le, *a.* three times as much or as many; of three parts; (Mus., of time) having three beats in bar. *v.* make, become, three times as great or as many; treble.

trip'lèt, *n.* set of three; three successive lines of verse rhyming together; each of three children born at one birth; (Mus.) group of three notes performed in time of two of same value.

trip'licate, *a.* threefold, forming three exactly corresponding copies. *n. in triplicate*, in three exactly corresponding copies.

trī'pod, *n.* three-legged or three-footed stand, support, seat, etc.

tripp'er, *n.* person who goes on an excursion, esp. for a day.

trip'tych (-k), *n.* altar-piece, etc., of three, usu. folding, panels.

trī'rēme, *n.* ancient Greek or Roman warship with three tiers of oars.

trīsect', *v.t.* divide into three, esp. equal, parts.

trīte, *a.* made stale by constant use or repetition; commonplace.

trī'umph, *n.* triumphing; (glory of) victory; rejoicing in success; (Rom. hist.) solemn processional entry into Rome of victorious general. *v.i.* be victorious, prevail (*over*); rejoice in victory, exult (*over*). **trium'phal**, *a.* of, celebrating, commemorating, triumph or victory. **trium'phant**, *a.* victorious, successful; triumphing, exultant.

trīum'vir, *n.* one of group of three jointly exercising power. **trīum'virate**, *n.* office or function of triumvir; set of triumvirs.

triv'èt, *n.* stand, esp. tripod, for pot, kettle, etc., placed over fire.

triv'ial, *a.* of small value or importance, trifling, slight. **trivial'ity**, *n.*

trŏ'chee (-k), *n.* metrical foot of one long (or stressed) syllable and one short (or unstressed) syllable. **trochă'ic,** *a.*

trod, trodden, *p.t.* & *p.p.* of **tread.**

trog'lodўte, *n.* cave-dweller, caveman.

troi'ka, *n.* (Russian vehicle drawn by) three horses abreast.

Trŏ'jan, *a.* & *n.* (inhabitant) of ancient Troy.

trŏll¹, *v.* sing (*out*) in carefree manner; fish by drawing bait along in water.

trŏll², *n.* (Scandinavian myth.) supernatural being.

troll'ey, *n.* (pl. *trolleys*), low truck, esp. running along rails; small table on wheels or castors; light hand-cart; wheel running along overhead electric wire, usu. on pole down which current is conveyed to vehicle. **trolley-bus,** bus with motive power derived from trolley.

troll'op, *n.* slatternly or disreputable woman.

trom'bŏne, *n.* large brass wind-instrument with sliding tube. **trombŏ'nist,** *n.*

trŏŏp, *n.* body of soldiers; (pl.) armed forces; (Mil.) unit of cavalry or artillery; unit of Scouts; number of persons, animals, etc., collected together, company, herd. *v.* assemble, move, come or go, etc., in large numbers. **troop-carrier, troop-ship,** aircraft, ship, for transporting troops. **trŏŏ'per,** *n.* horse-soldier; troop-ship.

trŏ'phy, *n.* arms, etc., taken from enemy and displayed as memorial of victory; anything taken in war, hunting, etc.; prize, memento of success or victory.

trop'ic, *n.* parallel of approx. latitude 23½° N. (*tropic of Cancer*) or S. (*tropic of Capricorn*) of the equator; (pl.) region lying between these parallels, torrid zone. **trop'ical,** *a.* of, occurring in, etc., the tropics; very hot, ardent, or luxuriant.

trop'osphēre, *n.* layer of atmosphere extending from earth's surface to stratosphere, within which temperature falls as height increases.

trot, *n.* quadruped's gait between walk and gallop; gait between walking and running; spell of trotting. *v.* (p.t. *trotted*), (make) go at trot; cover (distance) by trotting. *trot out,* produce, bring forward.

trŏth, *n.* (*archaic*) faith, loyalty; solemn promise.

troubadour (trŏŏ'badoor), *n.* medieval lyric poet and singer, of S. France, N. Italy, etc.

troub'le (trub-), *n.* (cause of) affliction, grief, bother, inconvenience, difficulty, etc.; discontent, public unrest; exertion. *v.* disturb, agitate; distress, grieve; subject, be subjected to, inconvenience or exertion. **trouble-maker,** one who stirs up trouble. **trouble-shooter,** person employed to trace and remove cause of defective working, etc. **troub'lesome,** *a.* causing trouble. **troub'lous,** *a.* (*archaic*) disturbed; unsettled.

trough (-of), *n.* long narrow box-like receptacle for liquid, etc., to stand in; hollow comparable to this; region of lower barometric pressure between two of higher.

trounce, *v.t.* beat; defeat heavily; scold.

troupe (-ŏŏ-), *n.* company, esp. of actors, etc. **trou'per,** *n.* (esp.) theatrical performer.

trou'sers (-zerz), *n.pl.* (*pair of*) trousers, two-legged garment, usu. from waist to ankles.

trou'sseau (-ŏŏsŏ), *n.* (pl. *-s* or *trousseaux*, pr. *-z*), bride's outfit of clothes, etc.

trout, *n.* small freshwater fish of salmon kind, fished for sport and valued as food.

trove: see **treasure trove.**

trow (-ŏ), *v.t.* (*archaic*) think, believe.

trow'el, *n.* flat-bladed tool for spreading mortar, etc.; gardener's short-handled tool with hollow scoop-like blade.

troy, *n.* system of weights used for precious metals, etc.

tru'ant (-ŏŏ-), *n.* one who absents himself from duty, etc., esp. pupil who stays away from school without leave. **tru'ancy,** *n.*

truce (-ŏŏ-), *n.* (agreement for) temporary stopping of fighting; respite.

truck¹, *n.* barter; dealings.

truck², *n.* strong vehicle for heavy goods; open railway-wagon; barrow for moving luggage, etc.

truck'le-bed, *n.* low bed on wheels that can be pushed under another.

truc'ŭlent, *a.* (of person) aggressive; (of criticism, etc.) harsh. **truc'ŭlence,** *n.*

trudge, *v.i.* walk laboriously or wearily but persistently. *n.* laborious and tiring walk.

true (-ŏŏ), *a.* in accordance with fact or reality; genuine, real, correct, proper; accurately placed, fitted, or shaped; loyal, faithful, (*to*). *v.t.* make accurate, straight, level, etc.

truff'le, *n.* richly-flavoured underground fungus valued as delicacy.

trug, *n.* shallow, usu. wooden, gardeners' basket.

tru'ism (-ŏŏ-), *n.* obvious or hackneyed truth.

tru'ly (-ŏŏ-), *adv.* with truth; sincerely; loyally; accurately.

trump¹, *n.* playing-card of suit ranking above others for one game. *v.t.* defeat, take, with trump. *trump up,* (*informal*) fabricate, invent.

trump², *n.* (*archaic*) (sound of) trumpet.

trum'pery, *a.* showy but worthless, trashy; trumped-up.

trum'pĕt, *n.* brass wind instrument of bright ringing tone, with narrow tube (usu. bent on itself) flared at end, and (usu.) valves; trumpet-shaped thing. *v.* proclaim (as) by sound of trumpet; extol, celebrate; (of elephant) make loud sound. **trum'pĕter,** *n.* player of trumpet, esp. cavalry-soldier giving signals with trumpet.

truncāte', *v.t.* cut off top or end of; cut short.

trun'cheon (-chn), *n.* short thick staff or club, esp. that carried by policeman. *v.t.* strike or beat with truncheon.

trun'dle, v. (cause to) roll along; draw, be drawn, along on wheels or in wheeled vehicle.

trunk, n. main stem of tree; body without head or limbs; elephant's long flexible nose; large box with hinged lid for carrying clothes, etc., while travelling; (pl.) brief close-fitting shorts worn by swimmers, etc. **trunk call,** telephone call to exchange at some distance. **trunk-line,** main line of railway, telephone system, etc. **trunk road,** important main road.

truss, n. bundle of hay or straw; supporting structure of roof, bridge, etc.; surgical appliance for support in cases of hernia. v.t. make into trusses; support with truss(es); tie (up), bind; tie up (fowl) compactly for cooking.

trust, n. confidence in or reliance on quality of person or thing, truth of statement, future state or happening, etc.; credit; being trusted; responsibility, charge; trusteeship; property committed to trustee(s); combination of commercial firms to reduce competition, etc. v. put trust in; treat as reliable; commit to care of; hope. **trust'ful, trus'ting,** aa. full of trust, confiding. **trust'worthy,** a. worthy of trust, reliable. **trus'ty,** a. (archaic) trustworthy.

trustee', n. person to whom property is entrusted for benefit of another; one of a number of persons appointed to manage affairs of institution. **trustee'ship,** n. position of trustee.

truth (-ōō-), n. (pl. pr. -dhz), being true; what is true, true statement, account, belief, etc.; reality, fact. **truth'ful,** a. habitually speaking the truth; true. **truth'fully,** adv. **truth'fulness,** n.

trȳ, v. test; make severe demands on; make attempt (at); investigate and decide (case), determine guilt or non-guilt of (person), judicially. n. attempt. **trȳ'ing,** a. (esp.) exhausting; exasperating; difficult to bear.

tryst (or -ī-), n. (archaic) appointed meeting.

tsar (or zar), n. (Hist.) emperor of Russia. **tsari'na** (-ēn-), **tsarit'sa,** nn. empress of Russia.

tset'sè, n. (also tsetse-fly) African fly transmitting disease to men and animals.

T-shirt, n. short-sleeved collarless shirt.

T-square, n. T-shaped instrument for obtaining or testing right angles.

tub, n. open, usu. round, wooden vessel used for washing and other purposes; (informal) bath-tub, bath; slow clumsy ship; short broad boat, esp. for rowing practice. v. (p.t. tubbed), bathe in tub; plant, pack, in tub. **tub-thumper,** ranting preacher or orator.

tū'ba, n. large low-pitched brass wind--instrument with valves.

tubb'y, a. tub-shaped; short and fat.

tūbe, n. long hollow cylinder, esp. for conveying or holding liquids, gases, etc.; main body of wind-instrument; short cylinder of flexible metal, etc., for holding semi-liquid material; inner tube containing air in pneumatic tyre; underground railway.

tū'ber, n. short thick rounded root or underground stem of plant.

tū'bercle, n. small rounded swelling in part or organ of body, esp. mass of granulation-cells characteristic of tuberculosis. **tuber'cular, tūber'cūlous,** aa. **tūbercūlō'sis,** n. infectious disease characterized by formation of tubercles, esp. in lungs.

tūber'cūlin, n. preparation from cultures of tubercle bacillus, used for diagnosis of tuberculosis. **tuberculin-tested,** (of milk) from cows free of tuberculosis.

tū'berous, a. of, like, tuber; bearing tubers.

tū'bing, n. (esp.) tubes; length or piece of tube; material for tubes.

tū'būlar, a. tube-shaped; having or consisting of tubes.

tuck, n. flattened fold sewn in garment, etc.; (slang) eatables. v. put tuck(s) in; stow away; thrust or turn (in, up), ends or edges of anything; settle (person) in bed by tucking in bedclothes. **tuck in,** (slang) eat heartily.

Tū'dor, a. of Tudor sovereigns (Henry VII to Elizabeth I) of England; of domestic architecture of their period.

Tūe'sday (-ūz-), n. third day of week.

tuft, n. number of feathers, threads, hairs, grass-blades, etc., growing or joined together in cluster or knot. v.t. furnish with tuft(s).

tug, v. (p.t. tugged), pull hard or violently (at); tow with tug. n. tugging, violent pull; small powerful steamer for towing other vessels. **tug-of-war,** athletic contest between two teams hauling on rope from opposite ends.

tūi'tion, n. giving of lessons; instruction.

tū'lip, n. (showy cup-shaped or inverted bell--shaped flower of) bulbous spring-flowering plant.

tulle (tūl), n. thin soft fine silk net.

tum'ble, v. (cause to) fall, esp. helplessly or violently; roll, toss; rumple; perform acrobatic feats, esp. somersaults. tumble to, grasp, understand, realize. n. fall; tumbled condition, confused heap. **tum'bledown,** in ruinous state.

tum'bler, n. (esp.) acrobat; stemless drinking--glass; pigeon that turns over and over in flight.

tum'brel, tum'bril, n. tipping cart, esp. for manure; cart in which condemned persons were conveyed to guillotine in French Revolution.

tū'mid, a. swollen; inflated, pompous.

tumm'y, n. (informal) stomach.

tū'mour (-mer), n. swelling, esp. morbid mass of new tissue.

tū'mult, n. commotion of a crowd, esp. with confused cries and uproar; agitation, disturbance; confused and violent emotion.

tŭmul'tŭous, *a.*

tŭ'mŭlus, *n.* (pl. *tŭmŭlĭ*), ancient burial-mound, barrow.

tun, *n.* large cask or barrel.

tŭ'na, *n.* tunny, esp. of Californian coast.

tun'dra, *n.* vast level treeless region with arctic climate and vegetation.

tŭne, *n.* rhythmical succession of musical tones forming melody or air; correct intonation in singing or instrumental music; accordance, harmony. *v.* adjust tones of (musical instrument) to standard of pitch; bring into accord, harmony, proper or desirable condition. *tune in,* adjust (radio set) to receive signal. **tuning-fork,** small two-pronged steel instrument giving musical note of constant pitch when struck. **tŭne'ful,** *a.* melodious. **tŭ'ner,** *n.* (esp.) person whose occupation is tuning pianos, etc.

tung'sten, *n.* heavy steel-grey metallic element.

tŭ'nic, *n.* ancient Greek and Roman garment reaching to about knees; woman's similar garment worn over skirt or trousers; (close-fitting) short coat of police or military uniform; gym-tunic.

tunn'el, *n.* artificial underground passage through hill, under river, etc.; burrowing animal's underground passage. *v.* (p.t. *tunnelled*), make tunnel (through).

tunn'y, *n.* large sea-fish fished for sport and valued as food.

tup, *n.* male sheep, ram.

tur'ban, *n.* man's oriental head-dress made by winding cloth round head.

tur'bid, *a.* muddy, thick, not clear; (fig.) confused, disordered. **turbid'ity,** *n.*

tur'bine (*or* -in), *n.* rotary motor driven by water, steam, gas, etc.

tur'bō-jet', *a.* & *n.* (jet engine) in which gas-turbine drives air-compressor.

tur'bot, *n.* large edible flat-fish.

tur'bŭlent, *a.* in commotion, troubled, stormy; disturbed by, causing, turbulence; unruly, violent. **tur'bŭlence,** *n.* (esp.) eddying or sinuous motion of air, etc.

tŭreen', *n.* deep covered dish for serving soup.

turf, *n.* (pl. *-s* or *turves*), short grass with surface earth bound together by its roots; sod; piece of peat. *the Turf,* horse-racing. *v.t.* lay (ground) with turf.

tur'gid, *a.* (of language) bombastic, pompous. **turgid'ity,** *n.*

tur'key, *n.* (pl. *turkeys*), large domestic bird valued as food.

Tur'kish, *a.* & *n.* (language) of Turks or Turkey. **Turkish bath,** hot-air or steam bath followed by massage, etc. **Turkish delight,** sugar-coated sweet of flavoured jelly. **Turkish towel,** rough towel of terry cloth.

tur'moil, *n.* agitation, commotion.

turn, *v.* move on or as on axis; give rotary motion to, have rotary motion; change from one side to another, invert, reverse; give new direction to, take new direction; adapt, be adapted; go round (corner); cause to go, send, put; change in nature, form, or condition; shape in lathe. *turn down,* fold down, place face downwards; reduce flame, etc., of, esp. by turning tap; (*slang*) reject. *turn in,* (esp., *informal*) go to bed. *turn out,* drive out, expel; be found to be; result. *turn over,* (esp.) do business to amount of. *turn turtle,* capsize. *turn up,* (esp.) appear, happen. **turn,** *n.* turning; rotation, esp. single revolution of wheel, etc.; change of direction, course, colour, or condition; angle, bend; turning back (esp. of tide); opportunity or obligation coming in rotation; act of good or ill will; item in entertainment. *in turn,* in succession. **turn'coat,** person who changes principles or party. **turn'key,** person in charge of keys of prison. **turn'out,** carriage, horses, and attendants; assemblage; equipment, outfit. **turn'over,** kind of pie; amount turned over in trade. **turn'pike,** (Hist.) toll-gate; road with gates, etc., for collecting tolls. **turn'stile,** revolving barrier allowing people to pass one by one. **turn'table,** circular revolving platform, esp. for reversing railway vehicles, etc., or for playing gramophone records. **tur'ner,** *n.* (esp.) one who works with lathe. **tur'nery,** *n.* **tur'ning,** *n.* place where road, etc., turns or turns off from another; road, etc., turning off. **tur'ning-point,** point at which decisive change takes place.

tur'nip, *n.* plant with fleshy root used as vegetable and for feeding cattle and sheep.

tur'pentine, *n.* resin obtained from various coniferous trees; inflammable oil distilled from this and used in mixing paints, etc.

tur'pitŭde, *n.* baseness, wickedness.

tur'quoise (-kwoiz, -kwahz), *n.* (blue-green colour of) opaque precious stone.

tu'rret, *n.* small tower, esp. rounded addition to angle of building; towerlike (usu. revolving) armoured structure in which guns are mounted or housed. **tu'rrĕted,** *a.* having turret(s).

tur'tle¹, *n.* (usu. *turtle-dove*), wild dove noted for soft cooing and affection for mate.

tur'tle², *n.* marine tortoise, esp. any of various edible kinds.

tusk, *n.* long pointed tooth projecting beyond mouth in elephant, wild boar, walrus, etc. **tus'ker,** *n.* elephant, wild boar, with developed tusks.

tuss'le, *n.* & *v.i.* struggle, scuffle.

tuss'ock, *n.* tuft, clump, of grass, etc.

tuss'ore, *n.* strong coarse brownish silk.

tut, tut-tut', *ints.* of impatience or rebuke.

tŭ'tèlage, *n.* (being under) guardianship; instruction, tuition. **tŭ'tèlary,** *a.* of guardian, protective.

tŭ'tor, *n.* private teacher; university teacher directing studies of undergraduates; instruction book. *v.* act as tutor (to); subject to discipline. **tútor′ial,** *a.* of tutor. *n.* period of instruction given to single student or small group.

tuxé′dŏ, *n.* (pl. *tuxedos*), (U.S.) dinner-jacket.

twadd′le (-od-), *n.* nonsensical talk.

twain, *a.* & *n.* (*archaic*) two.

twang, *n.* sharp ringing sound (as) of plucking of tense string, wire, etc.; nasal intonation; peculiarity of pronunciation. *v.* (cause to) make twang; play by plucking strings (of).

tweak, *n.* twitch, sharp pull, pinch. *v.t.* seize and pull sharply with twisting movement.

tweed, *n.* twilled woollen, usu. rough-surfaced, cloth; (pl.) tweed clothes.

twee′zers (-z), *n.pl.* (*pair of*) *tweezers*, small pincer-like instrument for picking up small objects, plucking out hairs, etc.

twelfth, *a.* & *n.* next after eleventh; (that is) one of twelve equal parts. **Twelfth Night,** (evening of) Epiphany (Jan. 6th) formerly last day of Christmas festivities.

twelve, *a.* & *n.* one more than eleven (12, XII). **twelve′month,** year.

twen′ty, *a.* & *n.* twice ten (20, XX). **twen′-tiĕth,** *a.* & *n.*

twice, *adv.* two times; on two occasions; double.

twidd′le, *v.t.* turn or twist idly about. *n.* slight twirl, quick twist.

twig¹, *n.* small shoot or branch of tree or shrub; divining-rod.

twig², *v.* (p.t. *twigged*), (*slang*) observe, notice; catch meaning (of).

twī′light (-īt), *n.* (period of) half light between sunset and dark or (less usu.) daybreak and sunrise; faint light.

twill, *n.* (textile fabric with) surface of parallel diagonal ribs. *v.t.* weave with twill.

twin, *n.* each of two children or young born at one birth; each of closely related pair; counterpart. *a.* born as (one of) twins; consisting of two similar parts or things. *v.* (p.t. *twinned*), bear twins; join or match closely, pair.

twīne, *n.* thread or string of thickness used for tying small parcels, sewing coarse materials, etc. *v.* twist; entwine; wreathe; coil, wind.

twinge (-nj), *n.* sharp darting pain.

twink′le, *v.i.* shine with light that comes and goes rapidly; sparkle; move to and fro, in and out, etc., rapidly; flicker. *n.* twinkling; sparkle.

twirl, *v.* spin, swing, or twist, quickly and lightly round; turn round and round idly. *n.* twirling, whirling; flourish of pen, etc.

twist, *v.* wind (strands, etc.) one round the other; give spiral form to; bend, curl; wrench out of natural shape, distort. *n.* twisting, being twisted; manner or degree of twisting; peculiar tendency of mind, character, etc.; distortion; twisted thing. **twis′ter,** *n.* (esp.) dishonest person, crook.

twit, *v.t.* (p.t. *twitted*), tease, taunt (*with*).

twitch, *v.* pull with light jerk, pull at; quiver or jerk spasmodically. *n.* twitching.

twitt′er, *v.* (of bird) utter succession of light tremulous notes, chirp continuously (often fig., of person). *n.* twittering; state of agitation.

two (tŏŏ), *a.* & *n.* one more than one (2, II). **two-edged,** having two cutting edges; (fig.) ambiguous. **two′fold,** double, doubly. **two-handed,** wielded with both hands; worked by two persons; (of card-game, etc.) for two players. **twopence** (tup′ens), sum of two pence. **twopenny** (tup′eni), costing twopence; paltry. **two-way,** (esp.) moving, allowing movement, etc., in either of two directions; reciprocal.

týcŏŏn′, *n.* business magnate.

tym′pani, *n.pl.* timpani. **tym′panist,** *n.* timpanist.

tym′panum, *n.* (pl. *tympana, tympanums*), ear-drum.

týpe, *n.* person, thing, event, or model serving as illustration, symbol, or characteristic specimen; general form, character, etc., distinguishing class or group; kind; small block with raised letter, figure, etc., for use in printing; set, supply, or kind of these. *v.* determine type of, classify according to type; write with typewriter. **type′script,** typewritten document or copy. **type′setter,** one who sets type by hand or machine, compositor. **type′writer,** machine with keyboard enabling user to produce printed characters instead of writing.

týphoid, *n.* (also *typhoid fever*), infectious disease with fever and inflammation of intestines, caused by bacillus in contaminated water, food, etc.

týphoŏn′, *n.* violent cyclonic storm, esp. of China seas, etc. **týphon′ic,** *a.*

tý′phus, *n.* acute contagious fever transmitted to man by infected parasites. **tý′phous,** *a.*

typ′ical, *a.* serving as type; characteristic, distinctive.

typ′ifÿ, *v.t.* serve as type or example of; represent by type or symbol.

tý′pist, *n.* (esp. skilled) user of typewriter.

týpog′raphy, *n.* art or practice of printing from types; style, appearance, of printed matter. **týpog′rapher,** *n.* **týpograph′ic(al),** *aa.*

tyrann′ical (ti- or tī-), *a.* acting like, characteristic of, tyrant; despotic, cruel.

ty′rannīze, *v.i.* rule despotically or cruelly (*over*).

ty′rannous, *a.* tyrannical.

ty′ranny, *n.* oppressive or despotic government, arbitrary or cruel use of power; State ruled by tyrant.

tyr′ant, *n.* oppressive, unjust, or cruel ruler; person using power or authority arbitrarily or cruelly.

tȳre, tīre[2], *n.* circular band of solid rubber, tubular rubber filled with air, or reinforced rubber covering pneumatic inner tube, fitted on rim of wheel; metal hoop round wheel (of wagon, etc.).

tyro: see **tiro.**

U

ūbi′quity, *n.* being everywhere or in many places at the same time. ūbi′quitous, *a.*

U-boat (ū-), *n.* German submarine.

udd′er, *n.* baggy milk-secreting organ in female cow, goat, etc., provided with teats.

ugh (u(h) *or* oo(h)), *int.* expressing disgust, etc.

ug′ly, *a.* unpleasant or repulsive to look at or to listen to; vile; threatening.

ūkule′le (-lāli), *n.* small four-stringed guitar.

ul′cer, *n.* open sore on external or internal surface of body; corroding or corrupting influence. ul′cerous, *a.* ul′cerāte, *v.*

ul′na, *n.* (pl. *ulnae*), inner bone of forearm. ul′nar, *a.*

ul′ster, *n.* long loose overcoat.

ultē̄r′ior, *a.* further; more remote; beyond what is seen or admitted.

ul′timate, *a.* last, final; fundamental.

ultimā′tum, *n.* (pl. *-s* or *ultimata*), final offer of terms, rejection of which may lead to rupture, declaration of war, etc.

ul′timô, *a.* of last month (abbrev. *ult.*).

ultra-, *pref.* lying beyond; going beyond, surpassing; having quality, etc., in extreme or excessive degree. ultramīcroscop′ic, *a.* too small to be seen with microscope. ultrason′ic, *a.* beyond range of human hearing. ultra-vī′olet, *a.* (of light rays) lying beyond violet end of visible spectrum.

ultramarine′ (-ēn), *a. & n.* (of colour of) brilliant deep-blue pigment.

ul′ūlāte, *v. i.* howl, wail. ūlūlā′tion, *n.*

um′ber, *n.* brown earth used as pigment. *burnt umber*, reddish-brown preparation of this.

um′brage, *n.* feeling of slight or resentment, offence.

umbrell′a, *n.* portable folding protection against rain, etc., of fabric stretched on slender ribs attached radially to a stick.

um′pīre, *n.* person chosen to decide between contending parties, or enforce rules of game or contest, etc. *v.* act as umpire (in).

un-, *pref.* freely used before adjectives, adverbs, and nouns to express negation; freely used before verbs, verbal derivatives, etc., to express contrary or reverse action, deprivation or removal of quality, etc.

(N.B.: many words with this prefix of which the meaning is obvious are not listed here.)

unaccom′panied (-um-), *a.* not attended or escorted; (Mus.) without accompaniment.

unaccoun′table, *a.* strange, inexplicable.

unaccus′tomed (-md), *a.* not accustomed (*to*); not usual.

unadop′ted, *a.* (of road) not maintained by local authority.

unadul′terāted, *a.* not mixed with inferior ingredients, pure.

unai′ded, *a.* without help.

unalloyed′ (-oid), *a.* unmixed, pure.

ūnan′imous, *a.* being in complete agreement; given, etc., with general agreement or consent. ūnanim′ity, *n.*

unan′swerable (-ahnser-), *a.* that cannot be refuted.

unassū′ming, *a.* modest, unpretentious.

unavai′ling, *a.* ineffectual, useless.

unavoi′dable, *a.* inevitable, that cannot be avoided. unavoi′dably, *adv.*

unawāre′, *a.* not aware (*of*). unawāres′ (-z), *adv.* by surprise; unexpectedly; unconsciously.

unbal′anced (-st), *a.* (esp.) mentally unstable or deranged.

unbear′able (-bār-), *a.* that cannot be endured. unbear′ably, *adv.*

unbēcom′ing (-um-), *a.* not suiting, not looking well on; not appropriate or befitting.

unbēlief′, *n.* disbelief, incredulity; lack of belief in God. unbēlie′vable, *a.* impossible to believe. unbēlie′ver, *n.* (esp.) one who does not believe in God. unbēlie′ving, *a.* unbēlie′vingly, *adv.*

unbend′, *v.* relax; straighten.

unben′ding, *a.* inflexible, unyielding.

unbidd′en, *a.* not asked, not invited.

unbo′som (-booz-), *v.t.* disclose. *unbosom oneself*, disclose one's thoughts, feelings, etc.

unbrī′dled (-ld), *a.* unrestrained, uncontrolled.

unbrō′ken, *a.* (esp.) uninterrupted, continuous; not subdued; (of record) not surpassed.

unbur′den, *v.t.* relieve (one's mind, conscience, etc.) by confession, etc.

uncalled'-for (-kawld-), *a.* not required or requested; impertinent, unprovoked.

uncann'y, *a.* mysterious, uncomfortably strange or unfamiliar. **uncann'ily,** *adv.*

uncerémö'nious (-se-r-), *a.* informal; abrupt.

uncer'tain, *a.* not certain; not to be depended on; changeable. **uncer'tainty,** *n.*

uncha'ritable, *a.* severe in judging others.

unchris'tian (-kr-), *a.* not in accordance with Christian principles.

unciv'il, *a.* impolite, rude.

unciv'ilized (-zd), *a.* not civilized; uncivil.

unc'le, *n.* father's or mother's brother or brother-in-law.

unclean', *a.* (esp.) ceremonially impure.

uncom'fortable (-ku-), *a.* feeling discomfort; uneasy; causing discomfort.

uncomm'on, *a.* unusual.

uncommü'nicative, *a.* reticent, reserved.

uncom'promising (-z-), *a.* refusing compromise; unyielding, firm.

unconcerned' (-nd), *a.* free from anxiety; not caring; not concerned (*in*, *with*).

uncondi'tional, *a.* without conditions; absolute.

uncon'scionable (-sho-), *a.* unscrupulous; unreasonable, excessive.

uncon'scious (-shus), *a.* not conscious; not aware (*of*); done, etc., without conscious action. *n.* unconscious mind. **uncon'-sciousness,** *n.*

unconsid'ered (-erd), *a.* not considered; not worth consideration, disregarded.

unconven'tional, *a.* disregarding, not in accordance with, accepted custom.

uncoup'le (-ku-), *v.t.* release, disconnect.

uncouth' (-ōō-), *a.* awkward, clumsy, uncultured.

unco'ver (-ku-), *v.* remove covering from; disclose, reveal.

unc'tion, *n.* anointing with oil as religious rite or symbol; affected enthusiasm. **unc'tüous,** *a.* oily, greasy; affectedly bland, smug, self--satisfied.

uncul'tured (-cherd), *a.* not refined or well--educated.

undéceive', *v.t.* free from deception or mistake.

undéci'ded, *a.* not settled; not having reached a decision, hesitating.

undémon'strative, *a.* reserved, not characterized by open expression of feelings.

undéni'able, *a.* that cannot be denied; undoubtedly true. **undéni'ably,** *adv.*

undénominä'tional, *a.* not confined to or connected with any particular religious denomination.

un'der, *prep.* in or to position lower than, below; inferior to, less than; subjected to, undergoing, liable to; governed, controlled, or bound by; in accordance with; in the time, reign, etc., of. *a.* lower. *under age*, under age of majority.

under-, *pref.* below; beneath, lower than; insufficient(ly), incomplete(ly); subordinate.

un'derarm, *a.* & *adv.* with arm lower than shoulder in bowling, etc.

underbid', *v.* (p.t. *underbid*), bid less than; bid too little on.

un'dercarriage (-karij), *n.* landing-wheels of aircraft.

un'derclothes (-ōdhz *or* -ōz), *n.pl.* clothes worn under outer garments, esp. next to skin.

un'dercover (-kuv-), *a.* acting, or done, surreptitiously or secretly.

un'dercurrent (-ku-), *n.* current flowing below surface; suppressed or underlying activity, force, tendency, etc.

undercut', *v.t.* (p.t. *undercut*; pres. p. *undercutting*), supplant by working for lower payment, selling at lower prices, etc.

un'derdog, *n.* loser in fight, etc.; person in state of subjection or inferiority.

underdone' (-dun), *a.* incompletely or insufficiently cooked.

underes'timäte, *v.* form or make too low an estimate (of).

undergö', *v.t.* (p.t. *underwent*; p.p. *undergone*), be subjected to, suffer, endure.

undergrad'üate, *n.* member of university who has not yet taken degree.

underground', *adv.* below surface of ground; in(to) secrecy or concealment. *a.* & *n.* (un'-), (railway) situated underground; (political movement, etc.) conducted or existing in secret.

un'dergrowth (-ōth), *n.* plants or shrubs growing under trees, etc.

un'derhand, *a.* secret, deceitful; underarm. *adv.* underarm.

un'derlay, *n.* (esp.) felt, etc., laid under carpet.

underlie', *v.t.* (p.t. *underlay*; p.p. *underlain*), lie, be situated, under; be basis of, lie beneath surface aspect of. **un'derlÿing,** *a.*

underlïne', *v.t.* draw line(s) under (words, etc.) for emphasis; emphasize, stress.

un'derling, *n.* (usu. contempt.) subordinate.

undermanned' (-nd), *a.* supplied with too few workers, crew, etc; short-handed.

undermïne', *v.t.* make excavation, tunnel, etc., under; wear away base or foundation of; weaken insidiously, secretly, or imperceptibly.

un'dermöst, *a.* in lowest place or position.

underneath', *adv.* & *prep.* at or to lower place (than), below. *a.* & *n.* lower (surface, part).

un'derpass (-ahs), *n.* (junction with) road, etc., passing under another.

underpin', *v.t.* (p.t. *underpinned*), support or strengthen (esp. building) from beneath.

underpriv'ileged (-ijd) *a.* relatively poor, not enjoying normal living standard or rights and privileges of civilized society.

underrâte', *v.t.* underestimate.

undersell', *v.t.* (p.t. *undersold*), sell at lower

price than.

undersigned' (-īnd), *a. the undersigned*, person(s) whose signature(s) appear(s) below.

un'dersized' (-zd), *a.* of less than normal size.

understand', *v.* (p.t. *understood*), grasp mentally, perceive meaning of; know how to deal with; infer, esp. from information received; take for granted. **understan'ding**, *n.* intelligence, intellect, insight; agreement; stipulation. *a.* having understanding; sympathetic, tolerant.

understate'ment (-tm-), *n.* incomplete or excessively restrained statement of facts or truth.

un'derstudy, *n.* actor who studies part in order to play it at short notice in absence of usual performer. *v.t.* act as understudy to.

undertake', *v.* (p.t. *undertook*; p.p. *undertaken*), bind oneself to perform; engage in, start on; promise; guarantee. **un'dertaker**, *n.* (esp.) one who carries out arrangements for funerals. **un'dertaking**, *n.* work, etc., undertaken, enterprise; business of funeral undertaker.

un'dertone, *n.* low or subdued tone; underlying or subordinate tone.

un'dertow (-ō), *n.* current below sea-surface moving in contrary direction to surface motion of breaking waves, etc.

un'derwater (-waw-), *a.* placed, situated, carried on, etc., under surface of water; (Naut.) below water-line.

un'derwear (-wār), *n.* underclothes.

un'derworld (-wer-), *n.* (esp.) abode of spirits of the dead (Myth.); lowest or criminal stratum of society.

underwrite' (-rīt), *v.* (p.t. *underwrōte*; p.p. *underwritten*), (esp.) undertake (esp. marine) insurance. **un'derwriter**, *n.*

undesīr'able (-z-), *a.* objectionable. *n.* undesirable person.

undig'nified (-īd), *a.* lacking, inconsistent with, dignity.

undisgui'sedly (-gīz-), *adv.* openly.

undo' (-ōō), *v.t.* (p.t. *undid*; p.p. *undone*, pr. -un), annul, cancel; reduce to condition of not having been done, etc.; unfasten and open; ruin.

undoubt'edly (-owt-), *adv.* without doubt.

undress', *v.* take off clothes (of). **un'dress**, *n.* (esp. Mil., etc.) uniform for ordinary occasions (often attrib.).

undūe', *a.* excessive.

un'dūlāte, *v.* move in or like waves; rise and fall, have wavy surface or outline. **un'dūlant**, *a.* undulating. **undūlā'tion**, *n.* wavy motion or form, gentle rise and fall. **un'dūlātory**, *a.*

undū'ly, *adv.* improperly; excessively.

undȳ'ing, *a.* that does not die; everlasting, never-ending.

unearth' (-er-), *v.t.* dig up; bring to light, find by searching.

unearth'ly (-er-), *a.* not of this world; super-

natural, ghostly; (*informal*) absurdly early or inconvenient.

unea'sy (-zi), *a.* restless; troubled, anxious, uncomfortable in mind. **unea'siness**, *n.*

unemploy'able, *a.* unfitted or unsuitable for paid employment. **unemployed'**, (-oid), *a.* out of work; not being used. **unemploy'ment**, *n.* state of being unemployed; prevalence or extent of this state.

unen'ding, *a.* not coming to an end; perpetual.

unē'qual, *a.* not equal; variable or uneven in quality; not equal or adequate *to* (task, etc.).

unēquiv'ocal, *a.* of unmistakable meaning, not ambiguous. **unēquiv'ocally**, *adv.*

unerr'ing, *a.* accurate, sure; making no error. **unerr'ingly**, *adv.*

unē'ven, *a.* not level or smooth; irregular; not uniform.

unexam'pled (-igzahm'pld), *a.* without precedent.

unexcep'tionable, *a.* with which no fault can be found.

unexpec'ted, *a.* not expected or foreseen.

unfai'ling, *a.* unceasing, constant; certain, reliable. **unfai'lingly**, *adv.*

unfair', *a.* not just or equitable; not impartial. **unfair'ly**, *adv.* **unfair'ness**, *n.*

unfaith'ful, *a.* not faithful; adulterous. **unfaith'fulness**, *n.*

unfamil'iar, *a.* strange; not well known *to*.

unfath'omable (-dh-), *a.* that cannot be fathomed or measured; impossible to understand.

unfee'ling, *a.* lacking sensibility, without feeling; harsh; cruel. **unfee'lingly**, *adv.*

unfeign'ēdly (-fān-), *adv.* sincerely.

unfit', *a.* not fit, unsuitable; in poor health. **unfitt'ed**, *a.* not fitted or suitable (*for*).

unföld', *v.* open out; reveal; develop.

unforeseen' (-fors-), *a.* not foreseen; unexpected.

unfor'tūnate (*or* -choon-), *a.* unlucky; unhappy; ill-advised. *n.* unfortunate person. **unfor'tūnately**, *adv.*

unfoun'ded, *a.* groundless, not based on facts.

unfrock', *v.t.* dismiss from priesthood.

unfurl', *v.* unroll, spread out.

ungain'ly, *a.* awkward, clumsy, ungraceful.

ungen'tlemanly (-tlm-), *a.* not gentlemanly.

ungod'ly, *a.* impious, wicked.

ungo'vernable (-gu-), *a.* that cannot be controlled.

ungrā'cious (-shus), *a.* not polite; unmannerly.

ungrammat'ical, *a.* breaking or offending against rules of grammar.

unguar'ded (-gar-), *a.* not guarded; careless, indiscreet. **unguar'dedly**, *adv.*

ung'uent (-nggw-), *n.* ointment.

ung'ūlate (-ngg-), *a. & n.* hoofed (mammal).

unhall'owed (-ōd), *a.* unconsecrated; unholy.

unhand', *v.t.* (*archaic*) let go, take one's

hands off (person).

unhapp'y, *a.* not happy. **unhapp'ily**, *adv.* **unhapp'iness**, *n.*

unheal'thy (-hel-), *a.* sickly; diseased; damaging to health; unwholesome.

unhinge' (-nj), *v.t.* remove from its hinges; derange, disorder (mind).

unhō'ly, *a.* profane, wicked; (*informal*) awful, dreadful.

ūni-, *pref.* one-; having, composed or consisting of, one.

ū'nicorn, *n.* (heraldic representation of) fabulous animal with horse's body and single horn projecting from forehead.

ū'niform, *a.* unvarying; plain, unbroken; conforming to one standard, rule, etc. *n.* distinctive dress of same style, cut, colour, etc., worn by members of military or other organization, etc. **ūnifor'mity**, *n.* sameness, consistency, conformity.

ū'nifȳ, *v.t.* unite, make uniform. **ūnificā'tion**, *n.*

ūnilat'eral, *a.* of, on, affecting, done by, or binding on, one side only.

unimpea'chable, *a.* that cannot be questioned, doubted, or discredited.

uninformed' (-md), *a.* not having, made without, adequate information; not enlightened.

uninhab'itable, *a.* not suitable or fit to be lived in.

unintell'igible, *a.* that cannot be understood.

uninvī'ting, *a.* not attractive.

ū'nion, *n.* uniting, being united; coalition; marriage; concord, agreement; whole resulting from combination of parts or members; trade union; (premises of) general club and debating society for members of university; coupling for pipes, etc. **Union Jack,** national flag of United Kingdom.

ū'nionist, *n.* member of trade union, advocate of trade unions. **ū'nionism**, *n.*

ūnique' (-ēk), *a.* of which there is only one; having no like, equal, or parallel.

ū'nison, *n.* coincidence in pitch; combination of voices or instruments at same pitch or in octaves; (fig.) concord, agreement.

ū'nit, *n.* the number one (1); determinate quantity, magnitude, etc., as basis of standard of measurement; individual thing, person, or group. *a.* of, being, or forming, a unit; individual. **ū'nitary**, *a.*

Unitār'ian (ū-), *n.* member of a Christian denomination maintaining that God exists in one person, not a Trinity. *a.* of Unitarians or their doctrine. **Unitār'ianism**, *n.*

ūnīte', *v.* join together; make or become one, combine; consolidate; agree, co-operate (*in*). **United Kingdom** (abbrev. *U.K.*), Great Britain and Ireland (1801-1922); Great Britain and N. Ireland (from 1922). **United States (of America)** (abbrev. *U.S.(A.)*), republic of N. America consisting of 50 States.

ū'nity, *n.* oneness, being one or single or individual; (thing showing) interconnection and coherence of parts, (thing forming) complex whole; numeral 1 as basis of number (Math.); agreement, harmony.

ūniver'sal, *a.* of, belonging to, or done by, all; applicable to all cases; of the universe. **ūniversal'ity**, *n.*

ū'niverse, *n.* all existing things; all creation; world or earth; cosmos; all mankind.

ūniver'sity, *n.* (colleges, buildings, etc., of) corporate institution providing instruction in higher branches of learning, and having power of conferring degrees.

unjust', *a.* not observing, not in accordance with, justice or fairness.

unkempt', *a.* dishevelled, untidy, neglected--looking.

unkind', *a.* not kind; harsh, cruel. **unkind'ness**, *n.*

unknown' (un-nōn), *a.* not known; not identified. *n. the unknown*, that which is not known.

unlaw'ful, *a.* not permitted by law, illegal.

unleash', *v.t.* free from leash or restraint.

unlea'vened (-levnd), *a.* not leavened, made without yeast.

unless', *conj.* if ... not; except when.

unlike', *a. & prep.* not like, different (from).

unlike'ly (-klī), *a.* improbable.

unlim'ited, *a.* not limited; very numerous.

unload', *v.* remove cargo, load, etc., (from); remove charge from (gun).

unlock', *v.t.* undo lock of.

unlooked'-for (-kt-), *a.* not expected.

unlōōse', *v.t.* loose; untie.

unluck'y, *a.* not lucky; unsuccessful; ill--fated.

unman', *v.t.* (p.t. *unmanned*), deprive of courage, strength, firmness, etc.

unman'ageable (-ja-), *a.* unruly; difficult to control, handle, etc.

unmann'erly, *a.* lacking good manners; impolite.

unmask', *v.* remove mask (from); disclose true character or intentions of.

unmen'tionable (-shn-), *a.* not fit to be mentioned; unspeakable.

unmistā'kable, *a.* that cannot be mistaken or doubted. **unmistā'kably**, *adv.*

unmit'igāted, *a.* unqualified, absolute.

unmoved' (-ōōvd), *a.* unaffected by emotion; steadfast; calm.

unna'tural (un-nacher-), *a.* contrary to nature; lacking natural feelings; artificial.

unne'cèssary (un-n-), *a.* not necessary, needless.

unnerve' (un-n-), *v.t.* deprive of nerve, courage, self-control, etc. **unner'ving, a.**

unnum'bered (un-n-; -erd), *a.* countless; not marked, etc., with number.

unobserved' (-zervd), *a.* not seen, not noticed.

unobtru'sive (-ōōs-), *a.* not prominent or conspicuous; modest.

unoffen'ding, *a.* harmless.

unoffi′cial (-shl), *a.* not authorized or authoritative. **unoffi′cially,** *adv.*

unpack′, *v.t.* open and take out contents of (trunk, box, etc.).

unpa′ralleled (-eld), *a.* having no parallel or equal.

unparliamen′tary (-lam-), *a.* contrary to parliamentary usage.

unpick′, *v.t.* undo stitches of (anything sewn or knitted).

unpleas′ant (-lez-), *a.* not pleasant, disagreeable. **unpleas′antness,** *n.* disagreeable situation, etc.; hostility, quarrel.

unpop′ular, *a.* disliked. **unpopula′rity,** *n.*

unprac′tised (-st), *a.* inexperienced, inexpert.

unpre′cedented, *a.* for which there is no precedent.

unprej′udiced (-joo-; -st), *a.* impartial.

unpremed′itāted, *a.* not deliberately planned.

unprēpossess′ing (-zes-), *a.* not making a favourable impression.

unpresen′table (-z-), *a.* not fit to be presented to company; not fit to be seen.

unprēten′ding, unprēten′tious (-shus), *aa.* modest, not pretentious.

unprin′cipled (-ld), *a.* not having, not based on, sound or honest principles of conduct; unscrupulous.

unprofe′ssional (-sho-), *a.* not professional; not worthy of member of profession.

unprof′itable, *a.* not yielding profit; useless.

unprovōked′ (-kt), *a.* without provocation.

unqual′ified (-olif′d-), *a.* not qualified; not modified or limited.

unques′tionable (-chon-), *a.* that cannot be questioned or doubted. **unques′tionably,** *adv.*

unques′tioned (-chond), *a.* not disputed.

unqui′ĕt, *a.* restless; agitated.

unrav′el, *v.* (p.t. *unravelled*), undo, become undone, from tangled or woven state; free from intricacy or obscurity.

unrē′al, *a.* imaginary, visionary, not real.

unrea′sonable (-z-), *a.* not in accordance with reason or good sense; excessive.

unrea′soning (-z-), *a.* not reasoning; not guided by reason.

unrēhearsed′ (-herst), *a.* not practised or prepared; spontaneous.

unrēli′able, *a.* that cannot be relied or depended upon. **unrēliabil′ity,** *n.*

unrēlieved′ (-vd), *a.* (esp.) monotonous, not varied (*by*).

unrēmitt′ing, *a.* incessant.

unrēqui′ted, *a.* not returned or rewarded.

unrēser′vĕdly (-z-), *adv.* without reservation or restriction; frankly.

unrest′, *n.* disturbance, turmoil, trouble.

unrīpe′, *a.* (of fruit, etc.) not ripe.

unri′valled (-ld), *a.* having no equal; incomparable.

unrōll′, *v.* open out from rolled-up state; extend, spread out to view.

unru′ly (-ōō-), *a.* not amenable to rule or discipline; turbulent.

unsā′voury (-veri), *a.* disagreeable, offensive; disgusting.

unscâthed′ (-dhd), *a.* uninjured, unharmed.

unscientif′ic, *a.* not in accordance with scientific principles.

unscrip′ted, *a.* not made, read, etc., from prepared script.

unscrū′pūlous (-ōōp-), *a.* without scruples; unprincipled.

unsea′sonable (-ēz-), *a.* not suited to or in accordance with season of year; ill-timed.

unseat′, *v.t.* throw from saddle; dislodge, deprive of seat, esp. in House of Commons.

unseem′ly, *a.* (of behaviour, etc.) not suitable or proper.

unseen′, *a.* not seen; invisible. *n.* passage to be translated without previous preparation.

unsel′fish, *a.* not selfish or self-interested; generous.

unsett′le, *v.t.* disturb; make restless. **unsett′led** (-ld), *a.* restless, disturbed, anxious; liable to change; (of bill, etc.) not paid.

unshā′keable (-kabl), *a.* (esp.) firm, resolute, steadfast.

unshā′ken, *a.* (esp.) firm, unyielding.

unsight′ly (-ī′t-), *a.* not pleasing to the eye, ugly.

unskilled′ (-ld), *a.* not trained, experienced, or skilled; not involving or requiring skill.

unsoli′cited, *a.* not asked for; given or done voluntarily.

unsophis′ticāted, *a.* natural, simple, inexperienced.

unsound′, *a.* not sound; diseased; rotten; erroneous; unreliable.

unspea′kable, *a.* inexpressible, unutterable; indescribably repulsive, objectionable, etc. **unspea′kably,** *adv.*

unspār′ing, *a.* liberal, lavish; merciless.

unstā′ble, *a.* not steady in position; changeable, variable; liable to emotional instability.

unstead′y (-edi), *a.* not steady or firm; shaking, reeling; changeable; not regular. **unstead′ily,** *adv.*

unstressed′ (-st), *a.* not bearing stress, not emphasized.

unstuck′, *a.* *come unstuck,* cease to stick; (*informal*) fail, go wrong.

unstud′ied, *a.* easy, natural, spontaneous.

unsuit′ed (-sū- *or* -sōō-), *a.* lacking the qualities required (*to, for*).

unthink′able, *a.* that cannot even be imagined; not to be considered as a possibility.

unthink′ing, *a.* not thinking; done, said, etc., without thought of the effect. **unthink′ingly,** *adv.*

unti′dy, *a.* not neat or orderly. **unti′dily,** *adv.* **unti′diness,** *n.*

until′, *prep. & conj.* till.

unti′mely (-mli), *a. & adv.* (occurring) at a wrong or unsuitable time, or too soon.

un′to (-oo), *prep.* (*archaic*) to.

untōld′, *a.* (esp.) too many, too much, or too

great to be counted, measured, etc.

untouch'able (-tu-), *n*. Hindu of lowest caste or no caste.

untō'ward (*or* -tooword'), *a*. (*archaic*) perverse; awkward; unlucky.

untroub'led (-trubld), *a*. calm, not disturbed or agitated.

untrue' (-ōō), *a*. false; not faithful (*to*); not straight, level, exact, etc.

un'truth (-rōō-), *n*. lie, falsehood. **untruth'-ful**, *a*. **untruth'fully**, *adv*. **untruth'fulness**, *n*.

untū'tored (-terd), *a*. untaught; ignorant.

unū'sual (-zhoo-), *a*. not usual; remarkable. **unū'sually**, *adv*.

unutt'erable, *a*. beyond description.

unvar'nished (-sht), a. not varnished; not embellished; (of statements, etc.) plain, straightforward.

unvār'ying (-i-ing), *a*. not changing; not differing or deviating.

unveil' (-vāl), *v.t*. remove covering from; reveal.

unwa'rrantable (-wo-), *a*. not justifiable; indefensible.

unwār'y, *a*. incautious, heedless.

unwā'vering, *a*. resolute, not wavering.

unwell', *a*. not in good health, ill.

unwept', *a*. not wept for, not lamented.

unwholesome (-hōl'sum), *a*. not favourable to or promoting physical or mental health; harmful, noxious, corrupting.

unwiel'dy, *a*. awkward to handle or control by reason of size, shape, or weight.

unwill'ing, *a*. not willing; reluctant.

unwind', *v*. (p.t. *unwound*), undo (what is wound); uncoil; (*informal*) relax.

unwise' (-z), *a*. imprudent; foolish.

unwitt'ing, *a*. not knowing, unaware; unintentional. **unwitt'ingly**, *adv*.

unwor'thy (-werdhi), *a*. not worthy, not befitting the character, (*of*); discreditable.

unwritt'en (unrit-), *a*. not written (down); oral; traditional.

unwrought' (-rawt), *a*. (of materials) not fashioned or worked on.

unyield'ing, *a*. firm; obstinate.

unzip', *v*. (p.t. *unzipped*), undo zip-fastener of; be able to be unzipped.

up, *adv*. to or in high or higher place, amount, value, etc.; to or in capital, university, place further north, etc.; to or in erect or vertical position; (after verbs, usu.) expressing complete or effectual result, etc.; (*informal*) amiss, wrong. *up and down*, to and fro along. *prep*. to, at, or in a higher point of. *n*. upward slope or movement. *ups and downs*, rises and falls, alternations of fortune, etc.

up-, *pref*. up.

upbraid', *v.t*. chide, reproach.

up'bringing, *n*. bringing up, early rearing and training.

up-coun'try (-kun-), *n*., *a*., & *adv*. (to, in, of) inland part of country.

up-dāte', *v.t*. advance date of; bring up to date.

up'-grāde, *n*. upward slope. *on the up-grade*, ascending, improving. **up-grāde'**, *v.t*. raise to higher grade, promote.

uphea'val (-p-h-), *n*. sudden and violent heaving up, esp. of part of earth's crust; sudden radical change or disturbance.

up'hill (-p-h-), *a*. sloping upwards; arduous, difficult, laborious. **uphill'**, *adv*. with upward slope, upwards on hill.

uphold' (-p-h-), *v.t*. (p.t. *upheld*), give support to; maintain, confirm.

uphōl'ster (-p-h-), *v.t*. provide (chair, etc.) with padding, textile covering, etc. **uphōl'-sterer**, *n*. **uphōl'stery**, *n*.

up'keep, *n*. (cost of) maintenance in good condition or repair.

up'land, *a*. situated, living, etc., on high ground. **up'lands** (-z), *n.pl*. piece of high ground, hilly or mountainous country.

uplift', *v.t*. raise up; elevate; edify. **up'lift**, *n*. (*informal*) elevating or edifying effect, moral inspiration.

upon', *prep*. on. *take upon oneself*, assume responsibility for; venture, presume.

upp'er, *a*. higher in place; superior in rank, dignity, etc. *n*. upper part of shoe or boot. *upper hand*, mastery, control, advantage. **upp'ermōst**, *a*. highest in rank or place. *adv*. on or to the top. **upp'ish**, *a*. self-assertive; pert.

up'right (-rī't), *a*. standing up, erect, vertical; (of piano) with vertical frame; righteous, strictly honourable or honest. *n*. upright piano; post or rod fixed upright. **up'-rightness**, *n*.

upri'sing (-z-), *n*. (esp.) insurrection.

up'roar (-ror), *n*. tumult, violent disturbance, clamour. **uproar'ious**, *a*.

uprōōt', *v.t*. tear up by the roots.

upset', *v*. (p.t. *upset*; pres. p. *upsetting*), overturn, be overturned; disturb temper, digestion, composure, peace, etc., of. *n*. upsetting, being upset.

up'shot, *n*. final issue, conclusion.

up'side-down', *adv*. & *a*. with top where bottom should be, inverted; in(to) total disorder.

upstāge', *adv*. away from footlights or front of stage. *a*. (*slang*) supercilious, haughty.

upstairs' (-z), *adv*. **up'stair(s)**, *a*. to or on an upper storey. **up'stairs**, *n*. upper part of house.

upstan'ding, *a*. strong and healthy; standing up.

up'start, *n*. person who has newly or suddenly risen in importance, position, etc.

upstream', *adv*. **up'stream**, *a*. (situated) higher up river, etc.; (moving, done, etc.) against the current.

up'tāke, *n*. *quick in the uptake*, (*informal*) quick to understand.

upturned' (-nd), *a*. turned upside-down.

up'ward, *a*. directed or moving towards

higher place, status, etc. **up'ward(s),** *adv.* in upward direction. *upwards of,* (rather) more than.

ūrā'nium, *n.* heavy greyish radioactive metallic element capable of nuclear fission.

Urā'nus (ūr-), *n.* a planet.

ur'ban, *a.* of, living in, city or town. **ur'-banīze,** *v.t.* render urban; deprive of rural character. **urbanīzā'tion,** *n.*

urbāne', *a.* courteous; suave. **urban'ity,** *n.*

ur'chin, *n.* (roguish or shabbily clothed) boy.

ūrē'thra, *n.* duct through which urine is discharged from bladder.

urge, *v.t.* drive forcibly; entreat, exhort, earnestly or persistently; advocate pressingly. *n.* impelling motive, force, or pressure, esp. from within. **ur'gent,** *a.* pressing, calling for immediate action or attention. **ur'gency,** *n.*

ūr'inal, *n.* vessel, etc., for receiving urine; building, etc., for urinating. **ūr'ināte,** *v.i.* pass urine. **ūrinā'tion,** *n.*

ūr'ine, *n.* fluid excreted by kidneys and discharged from bladder. **ūr'inary,** *a.*

urn, *n.* vase with base, esp. as used for storing ashes of the dead; large vessel with tap in which water is kept hot or tea, etc., is made.

ur'sīne, *a.* of, like, bear(s).

us, *pron.* objective case of **we.**

ū'sage (-z-), *n.* manner of using, treatment; habitual or customary practice; established use (esp. of word).

ūse (-z), *v.* employ for purpose or as instrument or material; avail oneself of; treat in specified manner. *use up,* use whole of, exhaust. **ūse** (-s), *n.* (right or power of) using; employment; purpose for which thing can be used. **ū'sable** (-z-), *a.* **used**[1] (ūst), *p.t.* was or were accustomed, had as constant or frequent practice. *p.p.* accustomed. **used**[2] (ūzd), *a.* that has been used; second-hand. **ūse'ful** (-sf-), *a.* of use, serviceable; advantageous, profitable. **ūse'less,** *a.* serving no useful purpose; having no effect; inefficient. **ū'ser** (-z-), *n.* one who uses anything.

ush'er, *n.* official acting as door-keeper, showing persons to seats, or walking before person of rank; (chiefly Hist.) assistant schoolmaster. *v.t.* act as usher; precede, announce. **usherette',** *n.* woman showing people to seats in cinema, etc.

U.S.S.R., *abbrev.* Union of Soviet Socialist Republics (Russia).

ū'sual (-zhoo-), *a.* commonly or habitually observed, practised, happening, etc.; ordinary, customary. **ū'sually,** *adv.*

ū'surer (-zhu-), *n.* one who practises usury.

ūsurp' (-z-), *v.* seize or assume (throne, power, etc.) wrongfully. **ūsurpā'tion,** *n.*

ū'sury (-zhu-), *n.* lending of money at exorbitant interest. **ūsūr'ious** (-z-), *a.*

ūten'sil, *n.* instrument, implement, vessel, esp. in common or domestic use.

ū'terus, *n.* (pl. *ūteri*), womb. **ū'terīne.** *a.*

ūtilitār'ian, *a.* of, consisting in, based on, utility; regarding greatest good of greatest number as chief consideration of morality. *n.* holder or supporter of utilitarian views. **ūtilitār'ianism,** *n.* utilitarian principles, doctrine, etc.

ūtil'ity, *n.* usefulness; useful thing. (*public*) *utilities,* (organizations supplying) gas, water, electricity, etc., provided for community.

ū'tilize, *v.t.* make use of, use. **ūtilīzā'tion,** *n.*

ut'mōst, *a.* farthest, extreme; that is such in highest degree. *n.* utmost point, degree, limit, etc.; best of one's ability, power, etc.

Utō'pia (ū-), *n.* imaginary perfect social and political system. **Utō'pian** (ū-), *a.* & *n.*

utt'er[1], *a.* extreme, complete, total, unqualified. **utt'erly,** *adv.* **utt'ermōst,** *a.* most complete; farthest.

utt'er[2], *v.t.* emit audibly; express in words; put (false money, etc.) into circulation. **utt'erance,** *n.* uttering; spoken words.

ū'vūla, *n.* (pl. *uvulae*), conical fleshy prolongation hanging from margin of soft palate. **ū'vūlar,** *a.*

uxor'ious, *a.* excessively fond of one's wife.

V

V,v, as Roman numeral, 5.

vac, *n.* (*informal*) vacation.

vā'cancy, *n.* being vacant; vacant place or space; not occupied post, office, etc.; lack of intelligence, inanity.

vā'cant, *a.* empty; without occupant or contents; unoccupied with thought; without intelligence.

vacāte', *v.t.* give up possession or occupancy of; leave vacant.

vaca′tion, *n.* time during which lawcourts, universities, etc., are closed; holiday; vacating.

vac′cinate (-ks-), *v.t.* inoculate, esp. with vaccine lymph against smallpox. **vaccina′tion,** *n.* **vac′cine** (-ksĕn), *n.* preparation of cowpox virus used for vaccination against smallpox (usu. *vaccine lymph*); any preparation used for inoculation.

va′cillate, *v.i.* waver between different opinions, etc. **vacilla′tion,** *n.*

vacu′ity, *n.* emptiness; lack of intelligence. **vac′uous,** *a.* vacant, unintelligent.

vac′uum, *n.* (pl. *vacuums* or *vacua*), space entirely empty of matter; space, vessel, from which air has been withdrawn. **vacuum cleaner,** apparatus for removing dust, etc., by suction. **vacuum flask, jar, jug,** etc., vessel with double wall enclosing vacuum, for keeping liquids, etc., hot or cold.

vag′abond, *a.* wandering, having no settled habitation or home. *n.* wanderer; vagrant.

vā′gary (*or* vagār′i), *n.* capricious, odd, or absurd action, idea, etc.

vagi′na, *n.* membranous canal leading from vulva to uterus in female mammals.

vā′grant, *n.* person without settled home or regular work, wandering from place to place; (Law) idle and disorderly person. *a.* of vagrant; wandering. **vā′grancy,** *n.*

vague (-g), *a.* not clearly expressed or perceived; indefinite; indistinct; not clear-thinking, uncertain.

vain, *a.* worthless, meaningless; unavailing; having too high an opinion of one's looks, attainments, etc. *in vain,* without effect or success, uselessly. **vainglor′y,** *n.* boastfulness, extreme vanity. **vainglor′ious,** *a.*

val′ance, *n.* short curtain, esp. round frame or canopy of bedstead.

vāle, *n.* valley.

valedic′tion, *n.* (words used in) saying farewell. **valedic′tory,** *a. & n.* (speech, etc.) saying farewell.

vā′lency, vā′lence, *nn.* (Chem.) combining power of an atom as compared with that of a hydrogen atom.

val′entine, *n.* sentimental or comic letter or card sent, usu. anonymously, to person of opposite sex on St. Valentine's Day (14th February); sweetheart chosen on St. Valentine's Day.

val′et (*or* -lā), *n.* man's personal male servant. *v.* wait on, act, as valet.

valetūdinār′ian, *n. & a.* invalid; (person) excessively concerned about health.

Valhall′a, *n.* (Norse myth.) hall of heroes slain in battle.

val′iant, *a.* brave, courageous.

val′id, *a.* sound, well-founded; having legal force. **valid′ity,** *n.*

val′idate, *v.t.* make valid, confirm. **validā′tion,** *n.*

valise′ (-ēs *or* -ēz), *n.* (U.S.) travelling-bag, suitcase.

vall′ey, *n.* (pl. *valleys*), long depression or hollow between hills, usu. having river or stream flowing along bottom.

val′our (-ler), *n.* (*archaic* or Poet.) courage, esp. in battle. **val′orous,** *a.*

valse (vahls), *n.* waltz. (French)

val′uable, *a.* of great value or worth; very useful or helpful. *n.* (usu. in pl.) valuable thing, esp. small article.

valuā′tion, *n.* estimation (esp. by professional valuer) of thing's worth; estimated value.

val′ue, *n.* amount of commodity, money, etc., considered equivalent for something else; material or monetary worth of thing; worth, desirability, utility; number, quality, duration, etc., represented by figure, note, etc. *v.t.* estimate value of; have high opinion of. **val′ueless,** *a.* having no value. **val′uer,** *n.* (esp.) one who estimates or assesses values professionally.

valve, *n.* device for controlling flow of fluid, etc., or escape of air, etc., usu. acting by yielding to pressure in one direction only; (Mus.) device for altering pitch by varying length of tube in trumpet, etc.; thermionic valve used in radio, etc.; (Zool.) each half of hinged shell. **val′vular,** *a.*

vamp[1], *n.* upper front part of boot or shoe. *v.* repair, make *up*, produce, (as) by patching; (Mus.) improvise (accompaniment, etc.).

vamp[2], *n.* woman who uses her attractiveness to exploit men. *v.t.* allure, exploit, (man).

vam′pire, *n.* corpse superstitiously supposed to leave grave at night and suck blood of sleeping persons; person who preys on others.

van[1], *n.* vanguard, forefront.

van[2], *n.* covered vehicle, closed railway-truck, for conveyance of goods, etc.

van′dal, *n.* wilful or ignorant destroyer of anything beautiful, worthy of preservation, etc. **van′dalism,** *n.*

vāne, *n.* weather-vane; sail of windmill, blade of propeller, etc.

van′guard (-gard), *n.* front part, foremost division, of army, fleet, etc., moving forward or onward; leaders of movement, etc.

vanill′a, *n.* (podlike capsules of) tropical climbing plant; aromatic extract of this used as flavouring.

van′ish, *v.i.* disappear from sight, esp. suddenly and mysteriously; fade away; cease to exist. *vanishing point,* (in perspective) point at which receding parallel lines appear to meet.

van′ity, *n.* fact, quality, of being vain; vain and worthless thing; futility. **vanity-bag, -case,** woman's handbag or case containing mirror, cosmetics, etc.

van′quish, *v.t.* conquer, overcome.

vap′id, *a.* insipid, flat, dull.

vā′porize, *v.* convert, be converted, into

vapour. **văporĭzā′tion,** *n.*

vă′pour (-per), *n.* matter diffused or suspended in air, esp. gaseous form of a liquid (or solid) present above it and into which it is entirely converted when heated above boiling-point. **vă′porous,** *a.*

văr′iable, *a.* apt or liable to vary, capable of variation; shifting, inconstant. *n.* variable thing or quantity.

văr′iance, *n.* disagreement, lack of harmony, discrepancy. *at variance,* disagreeing, out of harmony, (*with*). **văr′iant,** *a.* differing from something or from standard, etc. *n.* variant form, spelling, etc.

vărĭā′tion, *n.* (extent of) varying, esp. from normal condition or standard or type; (Mus.) each of series of repetitions of theme with changes which do not disguise its identity.

va′ricōse, *a.* (of vein) having abnormal local enlargement. **varicos′ity,** *n.*

văr′iĕgāted, *a.* varied in colour, marked with patches or spots of different colours.

vari′ĕty, *n.* diversity; absence of monotony or uniformity; collection of different things; different form, kind, sort, (*of*); subdivision of species; variety entertainment. **variety entertainment, show,** etc., entertainment consisting of a number of different independent turns. **variety theatre,** theatre where variety entertainment is given.

văr′ious, *a.* of several kinds; diverse; several.

var′lĕt, *n.* (*archaic*) menial, rascal.

var′nish, *n.* resinous solution or other preparation applied to surface to produce transparent, usu. glossy, protective coating. *v.t.* coat with varnish; (fig.) gloss over, disguise.

var′sity, *n.* (*informal*) university.

văr′y, *v.* change, make or become different, modify, diversify; be different or of different kinds.

vas′cŭlar, *a.* (Biol., etc.) of, containing, supplied with, tubular vessels.

vase (vahz), *n.* vessel, usu. of greater height than width, used as ornament, for holding cut flowers, etc.

vas′ĕline (-ēn), *n.* ointment and lubricant obtained from petroleum. **P.**

vass′al, *n.* (Hist.) holder of land from feudal lord in return for certain services; humble servant or subordinate, slave. **vass′alage,** *n.*

vast (vah-), *a.* immense, huge, very great.

vat, *n.* large tub, cask, or other vessel, used esp. in brewing, dyeing, etc.

Vat′ican, *n.* Pope's palace and official residence in Rome; the papal government.

vau′deville (vōdv-), *n.* variety entertainment.

vault[1], *n.* arched structure of masonry serving as roof or carrying other parts of building; cellar, tomb, etc., esp. one covered by vault; any arched vault-like surface, esp. apparently concave surface of sky. *v.t.* construct with, cover (as) with, vault.

vault[2], *v.* leap, spring, (over), esp. with the hand(s) resting on something or with help of pole. *n.* leap or spring performed by vaulting.

vaunt, *v. & n.* (*archaic* and Poet., etc.) boast.

veal, *n.* flesh of calf as food.

vec′tor, *n.* (Math.) (representation of) quantity having both magnitude and direction.

veer, *v.i.* (of wind) change direction; (fig.) change (opinion, etc.) esp. gradually.

ve′gĕtable, *a.* of, derived from, concerned with, or comprising, plants. *n.* plant, esp. (edible part of) herbaceous plant cultivated for food. **vegetable marrow,** see **marrow.**

vegĕtār′ian, *n.* person who eats no animal food, or none obtained by destruction of animal life. *a.* of vegetarians; living on, consisting of, vegetables. **vegĕtār′ianism,** *n.*

ve′gĕtāte, *v.i.* grow as or like plants; lead dull monotonous life. **vegĕtā′tion,** *n.* vegetating; plants collectively. **ve′gĕtative,** *a.*

ve′hement (vē′im-), *a.* intense, violent; showing, caused by, strong feeling or excitement. **ve′hemence,** *n.*

vehicle (vē′ikl), *n.* conveyance for persons or goods, esp. by land; liquid, etc., used as medium for applying or administering pigment, drug, etc.; thing, person, as channel or instrument of expression, communication, etc. **vehic′ūlar,** *a.*

veil (vāl), *n.* piece of light material worn to hide or protect face; piece of linen, etc., draping head and shoulders as part of nun's head-dress; curtain; disguise. *take the veil,* become nun. *v.t.* cover (as) with veil; conceal, disguise, mask.

vein (vān), *n.* one of tubular vessels carrying blood from all parts of body back to heart; one of slender bundles of tissue forming framework of leaf, etc.; anything resembling vein; fissure in rock containing metallic ore; mood, state of mind.

veld, veldt (-lt), *n.* fenced or unfenced grassland in South Africa.

vell′um, *n.* calfskin dressed and prepared for writing, etc.; smooth-surfaced writing-paper.

vĕlo′city, *n.* rapidity of motion, operation, or action; speed of motion in a particular direction.

vĕlour(s) (-oor), *n.* woven fabric with thick smooth pile; (hat of) felt with similar surface.

vel′vĕt, *n.* textile fabric, esp. of silk or nylon, with dense smooth pile on one side. *a.* of, soft as, velvet. **velvĕteen′,** *n. & a.* (of) cotton fabric resembling velvet. **vel′vĕty,** *a.*

vē′nal, *a.* willing to accept bribes; mercenary, unprincipled. **vēnal′ity,** *n.*

vend, *v.t.* sell. **ven′ding machine,** slot machine. **ven′dor,** *n.* seller.

vendett′a, *n.* feud involving bloodshed.

vĕneer′, *v.t.* cover (wood, etc.) with thin layer of finer wood. *n.* thin sheet of fine wood; superficial show or appearance.

ven′erable, *a.* entitled to veneration. **venerabil′ity,** *n.* **ven′erāte,** *v.t.* regard with respect and reverence; consider as sacred.

venerā'tion, *n.*

vĕnēr'ĕal, *a.* (of disease) communicated by sexual intercourse with infected person.

Vēnē'tian (-shn), *a.* & *n.* (inhabitant) of Venice. **Venetian blind,** window-blind of horizontal slats that may be turned to admit or exclude light.

ven'geance (-jns), *n.* infliction of injury or punishment for wrong done; revenge. *with a vengeance,* in extreme degree, thoroughly, violently. **venge'ful** (-jf-), *a.* seeking vengeance; vindictive.

vē'nial, *a.* pardonable, excusable.

ven'ison (-z-), *n.* flesh of deer as food.

ven'om, *n.* poisonous fluid secreted by certain snakes, etc., and injected by biting or stinging; (fig.) bitter or malignant feeling, language, etc. **ven'omous,** *a.*

vent[1], *n.* small outlet or inlet for air, smoke, etc.; (fig.) outlet for feelings. *v.t.* give vent or free expression to.

vent[2], *n.* opening in garment, esp. at lower edge of skirt, sleeve, etc.

ven'tilāte, *v.t.* cause air to circulate in (room, etc.); expose to fresh air; make public, discuss freely. **ventilā'tion,** *n.* **ven'tilātor,** *n.* (esp.) contrivance or opening for ventilating.

ven'tral, *a.* of or on abdomen. **ven'trally,** *adv.*

ven'tricle, *n.* cavity of body, esp. either of two cavities of heart from which blood is pumped into arteries.

ventril'oquism, *n.* act or art of producing vocal sounds without visible movement of the lips, so that voice appears to come from some other person or object. **ventril'oquist,** *n.*

ven'ture, *n.* undertaking in which there is some risk. *v.* dare; not be afraid *to* do, hazard. **Venture Scout,** senior Scout. **ven'turesome,** *a.* bold, daring.

Vē'nus, *n.* (Rom. myth.) goddess of beauty and love; a planet.

verā'cious (-shus), *a.* truthful; true. **vera'city,** *n.*

veran'da, *n.* open roofed portico or gallery along side of house.

verb, *n.* part of speech which expresses action, occurrence, or being. **ver'bal,** *a.* of or concerned with words; oral; word for word; of, derived from, verb. **ver'bally,** *adv.*

verbā'tim, *adv.* & *a.* word for word.

verbē'na, *n.* any of various, chiefly American, herbaceous plants.

ver'biage, *n.* needless abundance of words.

verbōse', *a.* wordy. **verbos'ity,** *n.*

ver'dant, *a.* abounding in green foliage; green.

ver'dict, *n.* decision of jury; decision, judgement.

ver'digris (-ēs), *n.* green or greenish-blue deposit forming on copper or brass.

ver'dure (-dyer), *n.* (colour of) fresh green vegetation.

verge, *n.* extreme edge, brink, border; grass edging of road, flower-bed, etc.; point at which something begins. *v.i.* border *on.*

ver'ger, *n.* church caretaker and attendant; official carrying rod, etc., before dignitaries.

ve'rify, *v.t.* (examine in order to) establish truth or correctness of. **ve'rifiable,** *a.* **verificā'tion,** *n.*

ve'rily, *adv.* (*archaic*) truly.

verisimil'itūde, *n.* appearance of truth or reality; probability; apparent truth.

ve'ritable, *a.* real, rightly so called.

ve'rity, *n.* truth; true statement.

vermicell'i, *n.* pasta in long slender threads.

vermic'ūlar, *a.* of worms; worm-like.

ver'miform, *a.* worm-shaped. **vermiform appendix,** see **appendix.**

vermil'ion, *n.* (brilliant scarlet colour of) crystalline mercuric sulphide. *a.* of this colour.

ver'min, *n.* (collective) mammals and birds injurious to game, crops, etc.; harmful or offensive creeping or wingless, esp. parasitic, insects, etc. **ver'minous,** *a.* (esp.) infested with vermin.

vernac'ūlar, *a.* (of language, idiom, etc.) of one's own country, native, not literary or foreign. *n.* vernacular language or dialect.

ver'nal, *a.* of or in the season of spring.

veron'ica, *n.* any of various flowering shrubs or herbaceous plants.

ver'satile, *a.* turning easily from one subject, occupation, etc., to another; showing facility in varied subjects, skills, etc. **versatil'ity,** *n.*

verse, *n.* literary composition in metre, poetry; metrical line; stanza, short poem; numbered subdivision of Bible chapter. **versed** (-st), *a.* experienced or skilled *in.*

ver'sify, *v.* turn into or relate in verse; make verses. **versificā'tion,** *n.*

ver'sion (-shn), *n.* particular translation of work, etc., into another language; particular form of narrative, statement, etc.

ver'sus, *prep.* (esp. Law, Sport) against.

ver'tĕbra, *n.* (pl. *vertebrae*), each of the bony segments comprising the spine. **ver'tĕbral,** *a.*

ver'tĕbrate, *a.* & *n.* (animal) having cranium and spine.

ver'tex, *n.* (pl. *verticēs*), top, highest part or point; (Math.) point opposite base of figure, point where axis meets curve or surface, or where lines forming angle meet.

ver'tical, *a.* placed or moving at right angles to plane of horizon; perpendicular, upright; of or at vertex or zenith. **ver'tically,** *a.*

verti'ginous, *a.* of vertigo; causing or tending to cause giddiness. **ver'tigō** (*or* vertī'-), *n.* (esp. Med.) giddiness, dizziness.

verve, *n.* enthusiasm, energy, vigour.

ve'ry, *adv.* in high degree, to great extent, extremely. *very well,* formula of consent. **ve'ry,** *a.* real, true.

ves'pers (-z), *n.* church service in the evening.

vess'el, *n.* hollow receptacle for liquid, etc.;

ship or boat; duct or canal holding or circulating blood, sap, etc.

vest¹, *n.* garment worn next to skin; (chiefly U.S.) waistcoat.

vest², *v.* invest *with* power, authority, etc.; place or secure *in* full or legal possession of person, etc.

ves'tal, *a.* chaste, virgin. **Vestal virgin,** priestess, vowed to chastity, of Vesta, ancient-roman goddess of hearth and household.

ves'tibŭle, *n.* antechamber, lobby; entrance-hall.

ves'tige, *n.* trace, evidence (of something no longer existing or present). **vesti'gial,** *a.*

vest'ment, *n.* official garment worn by priest, etc., during divine service; ceremonial robe.

ves'try, *n.* room or part of church for keeping of vestments, robing of clergy, parish meetings, etc.

vet, *n.* (*informal*) veterinary surgeon. *v.t.* (p.t. *vetted*), examine, treat, (animal, person) medically.

vetch, *n.* any of various leguminous plants, many of which are valuable for fodder.

vet'eran, *a.* grown old in service, esp. in armed forces; experienced by long practice. *n.* veteran person, esp. soldier; (U.S.) ex-serviceman. **veteran car,** motor car of date before 1904.

vet'erinary, *a.* of or for (treatment of) diseases and injuries of domestic and other animals. **veterinary surgeon,** person professionally qualified to treat diseases, etc., of animals.

vē'tō, *n.* (pl. *vetoes*), (excercise of) constitutional right to prohibit passing or putting into force of an enactment or measure; prohibition. *v.t.* exercise veto against.

vex, *v.t.* anger by petty annoyance or slight; irritate. **vexā'tion,** *n.* being vexed; annoying thing. **vexā'tious** (-shus), *a.* **vexed** (-kst), *a.* (of question, etc.) much discussed or contested.

vī'a, *prep.* by way of, through (specified place).

vī'able, *a.* capable of living or surviving; workable.

vī'aduct, *n.* bridge-like structure carrying railway or road over valley, river, etc.

vī'al, *n.* small glass bottle.

vī'ands (-z), *n.pl.* articles of food; victuals.

vībrāte', *v.* (cause to) move periodically (and rapidly) to and fro, oscillate, quiver; (of sound) have quivering or pulsating effect. **vībrā'tion,** *n.* vibrating; (Phys.) to-and-fro motion of particles of elastic body or medium, caused by disturbance of its equilibrium. **vī'bratory,** *a.*

vic'ar, *n.* clergyman in charge of parish. **vic'arage,** *n.* vicar's house.

vicār'ious, *a.* acting, done, undergone, by one person in place of another; deputed, delegated. **vicār'iously,** *adv.*

vīce¹, *n.* evil, esp. grossly immoral, habit or conduct; serious fault; fault, bad trick (of horse, etc.).

vīce², *n.* appliance with two jaws in which things may be gripped and held steady.

vī'cè³, *prep.* in place of, in succession to.

vice-, *pref.* acting or qualified to act in place of, or as assistant and next in rank to. **vice--chan'cellor** (-ah-), *n.* (esp.) acting representative of university Chancellor, performing administrative duties. **vīcerē'gal,** *a.* of viceroy. **vice'roy,** *n.* person governing in name of and by authority of supreme ruler.

vīce ver'sa, the other way round, conversely.

vicin'ity, *n.* surrounding district; nearness in place; *in the vicinity* (*of*), in the neighbourhood (of).

vī'cious (-shus), *a.* of the nature of vice; addicted to vice; evil; depraved; bad-tempered, spiteful.

viciss'itŭde (*or* vī-), *n.* change of circumstances, esp. of condition or fortune.

vic'tim, *n.* living creature sacrificed to deity, etc.; person killed or made to suffer by cruelty or oppression; one who suffers injury, hardship, etc. **vic'timīze,** *v.t.* treat unjustly or with undue harshness; make victim of cruelty, swindle, spite, etc. **victimīzā'tion,** *n.*

vic'tor, *n.* conqueror; winner of contest.

victor'ia, *n.* light four-wheeled horse-drawn carriage with collapsible hood. **Victoria Cross** (abbrev. *V.C.*), decoration for conspicuous bravery of member of armed forces. **Victor'ian,** *a.* & *n.* (person) of reign of Queen Victoria.

vic'tory, *n.* winning of battle, war, or contest. **victor'ious,** *a.* conquering, triumphant.

victual (vit'l), *n.* (usu. in pl.) food, provisions. *v.* supply with victuals; lay in supply of victuals. **victualler** (vit'ler), *n.* purveyor of victuals, esp. (*licensed victualler*) licensee of public-house.

vid'éō, *a.* & *n.* (U.S.) television. **video recording, tape,** recording, record on magnetic tape, of television programme, etc.

vīe, *v.i.* (pres. p. *vȳing*), contend or compete (with) for superiority.

view (vū), *n.* what is seen, scene, prospect; range of vision; visual inspection; mental survey; mental attitude, opinion; intention, purpose. *in view of,* having regard to, considering. *with a view to,* for the purpose of, as a step towards. *v.t.* look at, survey mentally; regard, consider. **view-point,** point from which something is viewed, point of view.

vi'gil, *n.* watching, keeping awake; (devotional watch kept on) eve of festival. **vi'gilance,** *n.* watchfulness, caution, circumspection. **vi'gilant,** *a.* watchful.

vignette (vēnyet'), *n.* decorative design in book, photograph, with edges shaded off into background; word-sketch (of incident or person).

vig'our (-ger), *n.* activity and strength of body

or mind. **vig'orous**, *a.* active; forcible.

Vi'king, *n.* & *a.* (one) of Scandinavian sea-adventurers, traders, pirates, etc., of 8th--11th centuries.

vile, *a.* despicable on moral grounds; depraved, base; worthless; disgusting; shameful.

vil'ify, *v.t.* speak evil of, defame. **vilifica'tion**, *n.*

vill'a, *n.* detached or semi-detached small house in suburban or residential district; country residence in Italy, southern France, etc.

vill'age, *n.* collection of houses, etc., in country district, smaller than town and usu. having church. **vill'ager**, *n.* dweller in village; rustic.

vill'ain (-an), *n.* person guilty or capable of great wickedness; character in play, novel, etc., with evil motives or actions. **vill'ainous**, *a.* vile, wicked. **vill'ainy**, *n.*

vill'ein (-in), *n.* feudal serf. **vill'einage**, *n.*

vin'dicate, *v.t.* show or prove truth, justice, merits, etc. of; justify. **vindica'tion**, *n.*

vindic'tive, *a.* revengeful, avenging; punitive.

vine, *n.* trailing or climbing woody-stemmed plant that bears grapes; any trailing or climbing plant. **vi'nery**, *n.* greenhouse for grape-vine(s).

vin'egar, *n.* sour liquid produced by fermentation of wine, malt liquors, etc. **vin'egary**, *a.* sour, acid.

vineyard (vin'yard), *n.* plantation of grape-vines, esp. for wine-making.

vin'tage, *n.* (season of) grape-harvest; wine from grapes of particular district (in particular year); date of wine as indication of quality. **vintage car**, motor car of date between 1904 and 1931.

vint'ner, *n.* wine-merchant.

vi'ol, *n.* medieval musical instrument, making and playing of which has been revived, resembling violin but usu. having six strings.

vi'ola[1], *n.* garden plant of violet family.

vio'la[2], *n.* musical instrument of violin family, lower in pitch and slightly larger than violin.

vi'olate, *v.t.* break (law, terms of treaty, etc.); break in upon; desecrate; commit rape upon. **viola'tion**, *n.*

vi'olence, *n.* violent conduct or treatment; unlawful exercise of physical force. **vi'olent**, *a.* marked or caused by, acting with, great physical force; intense, passionate, furious. **vi'olently**, *adv.*

vi'olet, *n.* wild or cultivated plant with (usu. sweet-scented) violet or white flowers; purplish-blue colour at opposite end of spectrum from red. *a.* of this colour.

violin', *n.* four-stringed musical instrument played with bow; violinist. **violin family**, group of instruments comprising violin, viola, violoncello, and double-bass. **violin'ist**, *n.* player of violin.

violoncell'o (-che-), *n.* (pl. *violoncellos*),

(more usu. *cello*) large bass instrument of violin family, supported on floor between player's knees. **violoncell'ist**, *n.* (more usu. *cellist*).

vi'per, *n.* adder; malignant or treacherous person. **vi'perish**, **vi'perous**, *aa.*

vira'go (*or* -ah-), *n.* (pl. *viragos*), fierce or abusive woman.

vir'gin, *n.* person, esp. woman, who has had no sexual intercourse. *the (Blessed) Virgin Mary*, the mother of Christ. **vir'gin**, *a.* that is a virgin; of or befitting a virgin; undefiled, not previously touched, used, etc. **virgin'ity**, *a.*

vir'ginal, *a.* being, befitting, belonging to, a virgin. *n.* (often pl.) keyboard musical instrument, earliest form of harpsichord, usu. without legs.

Virgin'ia cree'per, ornamental climbing plant whose leaves turn scarlet in autumn.

Vir'go, *n.* the Virgin, constellation and sixth sign of the zodiac.

vi'rile, *a.* manly, masculine; capable of begetting offspring; vigorous, strong. **viril'ity**, *n.*

virol'ogy, *n.* science or study of viruses. **virol'ogist**, *n.*

vir'tual, *a.* that is so in essence or effect, although not formally or actually. **vir'tually**, *adv.*

vir'tue, *n.* moral goodness; particular moral excellence; chastity, esp. of women; efficacy. *by, in, virtue of*, on the strength of.

virtuo'so (*or* -z-), *n.* (pl. *virtuosi*), person skilled in technique of an art, esp. of performance on musical instrument. **virtuos'ity**, *n.*

vir'tuous, *a.* morally upright; chaste.

vi'rulent (*or* -roo-), *a.* poisonous; spiteful, malignant, bitter; (of disease) extremely violent. **vi'rulence**, *n.*

vir'us, *n.* ultramicrosopic disease-producing organism capable of growth and multiplication only within living cells.

visa (ve'za), *n.* stamp, etc., on passport permitting holder to enter particular country.

vis'age (-z-), *n.* face.

vis-à-vis (vezave'), *prep.* & *adv.* in comparison with; facing, face-to-face (with). (French)

vis'cera, *n.pl.* internal organs of principal cavities of animal body. **vis'ceral**, *a.*

vis'cid, *a.* glutinous, sticky. **viscid'ity**, *n.*

viscos'ity, *n.* quality or degree of being viscous.

vi'scount (vik-), *n.* peer ranking between earl and baron; courtesy title of earl's eldest son. **vi'scountcy, vi'scounty**, *nn.* **vi'scountess**, *n. fem.*

vis'cous, *a.* glutinous, sticky; intermediate between solid and fluid.

vis'ible (-z-), *a.* capable of being seen; that can be seen; in sight; apparent, open, obvious. **visibil'ity**, *n.* (esp.) conditions of light, atmosphere, etc., when distinguishing objects by sight.

vi'sion (-zhn), *n*. act or faculty of seeing; power of discerning future conditions, etc.; thing, person, etc., seen in dream or trance; supernatural apparition; sight of unusual beauty. **vi'sionary**, *a*. dreamy, having fanciful ideas; existing only in imagination; unreal, unpractical. *n*. visionary person.

vis'it (-z-), *v*. go or come to see (person, place, etc.); stay with or at. *n*. call on person or at place; temporary residence; doctor's professional call. **vis'itant**, *n*. (esp.) migratory bird.

visitā'tion, *n*. official visit; affliction regarded as divine punishment.

vis'itor (-z-), *n*. one who visits.

vi'sor (-z-), *n*. movable front part of helmet, protecting face; (U.S.) peak of cap; movable shield fixed above windscreen of car to protect eyes from glare of sun, etc.

vis'ta, *n*. view, prospect, esp. through avenue of trees or other long narrow opening.

vis'ual (-z- *or* -zh-), *a*. of or concerned with seeing; received through sight. **vis'ualize**, *v. t*. form mental vision or image of.

vi'tal, *a*. of, concerned with, or essential to organic life; essential to existence, success, etc.; fatal. **vital statistics**, statistics relating to births, deaths, health, disease, etc. **vital'ity**, *n*. vital power; hold on life; persistent energy, animation, liveliness. **vi'talize**, *v. t*. put life or animation into, infuse with vitality. **vi'tals** (-z), *n. pl*. vital parts of body.

vit'amin (*or* vī-), *n*. any of a number of substances occurring in foodstuffs and essential to health, normal growth, etc. **vit'aminize**, *v. t*. introduce extra vitamin(s) into (food).

vi'tiāte (-shi-), *v. t*. damage or weaken quality of; corrupt, debase, spoil.

vit'reous, *a*. of glass; like glass in composition, brittleness, hardness, lustre, etc. **vit'rify**, *v*. convert, be converted, into glass or glass-like substance. **vitrifac'tion**, *n*.

vit'riol, *n*. sulphuric acid. **vitriol'ic**, *a*. (esp.) caustic, scathing, malignant, bitter.

vitū'perāte (*or* vī-), *v. t*. revile, abuse. **vitūperā'tion**, *n*. **vitū'perative**, *a*.

vi'va, *n*. (*informal*) viva voce.

vivā'cious (-shus), *a*. lively, animated. **viva'city**, *n*.

vī'va vō'cē, oral(ly); oral examination.

viv'id, *a*. bright; intense; lively; incisive, clear. **viv'idly**, *adv*. **viv'idness**, *n*.

viv'ifȳ, *v. t*. enliven, animate.

vivip'arous, *a*. (Zool.) bearing young in developed state, not hatching from egg.

vivisec'tion, *n*. performance of surgical experiments on living animals.

vix'en, *n*. she-fox; spiteful woman. **vix'enish**, *a*.

vizier' (-ēr), *n*. (chiefly Hist.) high administrative official in some Muslim countries.

vocab'ūlary, *n*. list of words with their meanings; (sum of) words used in a language, or by particular person, class, profession, etc.

vō'cal, *a*. of, with, or for, voice; uttered by voice; expressive, eloquent. **vocal cords**, voice-producing organs, two strap-like membranes stretched across larynx. **vō'calist**, *n*. singer.

vocā'tion, *n*. divine call to, sense of fitness for, career or occupation; occupation, calling. **vocā'tional**, *a*.

voc'ative, *a*. & *n*. (Gram.) (case) used in addressing (person) or invoking (deity, etc.).

vocif'erāte, *v*. shout, clamour, bawl. **vocif'erous**, *a*. clamorous, making loud demands.

vod'ka, *n*. alcoholic spirit distilled esp. in Russia from rye, etc.

vōgue (-g), *n*. popular favour, general acceptance or currency; prevailing fashion.

voice, *n*. sound uttered by mouth, esp. human utterance; use of voice, expression in words; opinion, etc., expressed, vote; sound uttered with vibration or resonance of vocal cords; (quality of) singing voice; (Gram.) set of forms of verb showing relation of subject to action. *v. t*. give voice to; utter with voice.

void, *a*. empty, vacant; having no legal validity. *n*. empty space. *v. t*. invalidate; discharge, excrete.

voile, *n*. thin semi-transparent dress material.

vol'atīle, *a*. readily evaporating at ordinary temperatures; changeable, lively; transient. **volatil'ity**, *n*.

volcā'nō, *n*. (pl. *volcanoes*), mountain or hill with opening(s) through which ashes, gases, (molten) rocks, etc., are or have been periodically ejected. **volcan'ic**, *a*. of, produced by, volcano; characterized by volcanoes.

vōle, *n*. any of various small rodents with short ears and (usu.) short tail.

voli'tion, *n*. act or power of willing or resolving; exercise of will. **voli'tional**, *a*.

voll'ey, *n*. (pl. *volleys*), simultaneous discharge of guns, missiles, etc.; (Tennis, etc.) return-stroke at ball before it touches ground. *v*. discharge, return, hit, etc., in volley(s).

vōlt, *n*. unit of electro-motive force. **vōl'tage**, *n*. electro-motive force expressed in volts.

volte-face' (-tfahs), *n*. complete change of attitude or opinion.

vol'uble, *a*. fluent; speaking or spoken with great fluency. **volūbil'ity**, *n*.

vol'ūme, *n*. book, esp. one of set of books; bulk, mass; space occupied, esp. as measured in cubic units; size, amount, (*of*); quantity, power, fullness, of tone or sound.

volū'minous, *a*. of great volume, bulky, ample; of many volumes; copious.

vol'untary, *a*. acting, done, given, of one's own free will; (of work, etc.) done without compulsion and (usu.) without payment; (of institution) maintained by voluntary contributions; (of bodily action, etc.) controlled by will. *n*. organist's solo, esp. before or after church service. **vol'untarily**, *adv*.

volunteer', *n*. person who voluntarily offers services or enrols himself for enterprise, esp.

for service in armed forces. *v.* undertake, offer voluntarily; make voluntary offer of one's services.

volup'tŭary, *n.* person given up to indulgence in luxury and sensuous pleasures. **volup'tŭous**, *a.* of, addicted to, or promising or suggesting, gratification of the senses.

vom'it, *v.* eject contents of stomach through mouth; bring up, eject, (as) by vomiting, belch forth. *n.* matter vomited.

vorā'cious (-shus), *a.* greedy in eating; ravenous; insatiable. **vorac'ity**, *n.*

vor'tex, *n.* (pl. *vortexes* or *vortices*), whirlpool; whirlwind; anything comparable to these, esp. in rush or excitement, absorbing or engulfing effect, etc.

vō'tary, *n.* person bound by vow(s), esp. to religious life; devotee, ardent follower, (*of*).

vŏte, *n.* expression of preference, acceptance, rejection, etc., signified by ballot, show of hands, etc.; right to vote; opinion expressed, resolution or decision carried, by voting. *v.* give vote; decide by majority of votes. **vō'ter**, *n.* (esp.) person entitled to vote.

vō'tive, *a.* given in fulfilment of vow.

vouch, *v.i.* answer, be surety, *for.*

vou'cher, *n.* document confirming payment of money, correctness of accounts, etc.; coupon.

vouchsāfe', *v.t.* give, grant, etc., in condescending or gracious manner; deign *to* do.

vow, *n.* solemn promise or undertaking, esp. to deity or saint. *v.t.* promise or undertake solemnly.

vow'el, *n.* (letter representing) speech sound produced by vibration of vocal cords but without audible friction (e.g. *a, e, i, o, u*).

voy'age, *n.* & *v.i.* journey or travel, esp. to some distance, by water.

vul'canite, *n.* ebonite. **vul'canīze**, *v.t.* harden (rubber, etc.), esp. by combining it with sulphur at high or at ordinary temperatures. **vulcanīzā'tion**, *n.*

vul'gar, *a.* offending against good taste, coarse, low; of the common people; in common use, generally prevalent. **vulgar fraction**, fraction represented by number above line for numerator and below for denominator. **vulgā̄r'ian**, *n.* (esp. rich) person with vulgar taste and manners. **vulga'rity**, *n.* **vul'garīze**, *v.t.* make commonplace or ordinary. **vulgarīzā'tion**, *n.*

vul'nerable, *a.* that can be wounded; open to or not proof against attack, injury, criticism, etc. **vulnerabil'ity**, *n.*

vul'pīne, *a.* of or like fox; cunning.

vul'ture, *n.* large bird of prey feeding on carrion; rapacious person. **vul'turīne**, *a.*

vul'va, *n.* external female genital organs, esp. external opening of vagina.

W

wad (wod), *n.* small compressed mass of soft material used as pad, plug, etc.; (U.S.) tight roll, esp. of banknotes. *v.t.* (p.t. *wadded*), pad with wadding; plug with wad. **wadd'ing** (wo-), *n.* loose soft fibrous material for padding, packing, etc.

wadd'le (wo-), *v.i.* walk with short steps and swaying motion, as duck or goose.

wāde, *v.* walk through water, mud, etc.; progress slowly or with difficulty (*through*). **wā'der**, *n.* (esp.) long-legged bird that wades in shallow water; (pl.) high waterproof boots worn by anglers, etc.

wa'di (wah- *or* wo-), *n.* in N. Africa, etc., rocky watercourse, dry except in rainy season.

wā'fer, *n.* very thin light crisp biscuit; thin disc of unleavened bread used at Eucharist. **waff'le** (wo-), *n.* small flat crisp batter cake. **waffle-iron**, utensil for baking waffles.

waft (wo- *or* wah-), *v.* convey, float, smoothly and lightly along (as) through air or over water. *n.* whiff of perfume, etc.

wag[1], *v.* (p.t. *wagged*), shake or move briskly to and fro. *n.* single wagging motion.

wag[2], *n.* habitual joker, wit.

wāge[1], *n.* (often pl.) amount paid periodically, esp. by week, for work of employee; (usu. pl.) requital, reward.

wāge[2], *v.t.* carry on (war, etc.).

wā'ger, *n.* & *v.t.* bet.

wagg'ish (-g-), *a.* of or like a wag.

wagg'le, *v.* move (something held or fixed at one end) to and fro. *n.* act of waggling.

wag'on, wagg'on, *n.* four-wheeled vehicle for heavy loads; open railway-truck. **wag(g)'oner**, *n.* driver of horse-drawn wagon. **wag(g)onette'**, *n.* four-wheeled open horse-drawn carriage with facing side-seats.

wag'tail, *n.* small long-tailed bird.

waif, *n.* homeless or helpless person, esp. abandoned child; animal found ownerless.

wail, *n.* prolonged plaintive cry; lamentation. *v.* utter wail(s).

wain, *n.* (*archaic* and Poet.) wagon.

wain'scot, *n.* wooden panelling on room wall. **wain'scoting**, *n.* (wood for) wainscot.

waist, *n.* part of human body between ribs and hips; middle narrower part of anything. **waist'coat** (*or* wes'kot), *n.* usu. sleeveless and collarless garment worn under jacket. **wai'sted**, *a.* narrowed or close-fitting at waist.

wait, *v.* defer action until expected event occurs; pause; be expectant or on the watch (*for*); act as attendant on; serve food and drink, etc., at table. *wait upon*, (*archaic*) pay respectful visit to. *n.* act or time of waiting; (pl.) street singers of Christmas carols. **wai'-ter**, *n.* **wai'tress**, *n. fem.* man, woman, serving at table in restaurant, etc. **wai'ting**, *n. in waiting*, (esp.) in official attendance at court.

waive, *v.t.* give up, not insist on, (right, claim, etc.). **wai'ver**, *n.* (Law) waiving.

wăke[1], *n.* track left by ship, etc., on water. *in the wake of*, following, after.

wăke[2], *v.* (p.t. *wŏke*, *wāked*; p.p. *wŏken*, *wāked*), cease to sleep, rouse from sleep; cease, rouse, from inactivity, etc.; arouse, excite. *n.* (chiefly in Ireland) watch by corpse before burial; (pl.) annual holiday in (industrial) north of England. **wăke'ful**, *a.* unable to sleep; vigilant; sleepless. **wā'ken**, *v.* cause to be, become, awake.

walk (wawk), *v.* progress by alternate movement of legs so that one foot is always on ground; (of quadruped) go at gait in which two feet are always on ground; travel, go, on foot. *n.* walking gait or pace; journey on foot; avenue, footpath, etc. **walking-stick**, stick carried for support or display when walking. **walk-over**, easy victory.

wall (wawl), *n.* structure of stone, etc., of some height serving as rampart, defensive enclosure, or to enclose or divide off house, room, field, etc.; something resembling wall in appearance or function. *v.t.* provide or protect with wall; shut *in*, *off*, block *up*, with wall(s). **wall'flower**, fragrant garden plant; (*informal*) woman sitting at side of room during dancing, for lack of partner. **wall'paper**, paper for covering walls of room, etc.

wa'llaby (wo-), *n.* any of various small species of kangaroo.

wa'llèt (wo-), *n.* small, usu. leather, folding case for banknotes, etc.; (Hist.) travelling--bag.

wa'llop (wo-), *n.* & *v.t.* (*slang*) whack.

wallow (wol'ō), *v.i.* roll about in mud, water, etc.; take gross delight *in*.

wal'nut (wawl-), *n.* (tree bearing) edible nut in spheroid shell; wood of walnut-tree, used in cabinet-making.

wal'rus (wawl-), *n.* large carnivorous amphi-bious mammal with long tusks.

waltz (wawls *or* wols), *n.* (music in triple time for) dance for couples who gyrate smoothly. *v.i.* dance waltz.

wan (won), *a.* unusally or unhealthily pale; colourless.

wand (-o-), *n.* slender rod or staff; fairy's or magician's magic rod.

wan'der (won-), *v.* move about, go from place to place, without settled route or destination; wind, meander; be inattentive or delirious. **wan'derer**, **wan'dering**, *nn.* **wan'derlust**, *n.* strong or irresistible desire to travel.

wāne, *v.i.* decrease in brilliance, size, etc., lose vigour, importance, etc.; (of moon) show a gradually decreasing bright area (opp. *wax*). *n.* (period of) waning, decline.

wang'le (-nggl), *v.t.* (*informal*) get, bring about, by scheming or contrivance. *n.* act of wangling.

want (wo-), *a.* lack, absence, need, (*of*); destitution; need; something needed or desired. *v.* require; desire, wish for possession or presence of. *want for*, lack; be without. **wan'ted**, *a.* (esp.) sought for by police. **wan'ting**, *a.* (esp.) lacking *in*; lacking, without.

wan'ton (wo-), *a.* playful, capricious; luxuriant; licentious, unchaste; unprovoked, reckless. *n.* unchaste woman.

war (wor), *n.* armed conflict, usu. between nations; (fig.) hostility between persons; organized effort against some evil, etc. *civil war*, see **civil**. *v.i.* (p.t. *warred*), be at war. **war-cry**, phrase or name formerly shouted in battle; party catchword. **war-head**, explosive head of torpedo, rocket, etc. **war-paint**, paint applied to face and body by N. Amer. Indians before battle; (*informal*) one's best clothes and finery. **war-path**, (route taken by) warlike expedition of N. Amer.Indians. **war'ship**, ship armed and manned for war. **war'fāre**, *n.* state of war; being engaged in war; conflict. **war'līke**, *a.* skilled in, fond of, war; of, used in, war.

war'ble (wor-), *v.* sing in continuous trilling manner. *n.* warbling sound. **war'bler**, *n.* small song-bird.

ward (-or-), *n.* person, esp. minor, under care of guardian; guardianship; division of hospital; administrative division of borough, city, etc. *v.t. ward off*, prevent occurrence of, parry (blow, etc.).

war'den (wor-), *n.* person having control or authority; president; governor (*of* certain colleges, schools, etc.).

war'der (wor-), *n.* official in charge of prisoners in gaol. **ward'ress**, *n. fem.*

ward'rōbe (wor-), *n.* place, esp. large cupboard, where clothes are kept; person's stock of clothes.

ward'-rōom (wor-), *n.* mess-room, etc., of naval officers below commanding officer.

wāre[1], *n.* articles made for sale (esp. in com-

pounds, as *hardware, silverware,* etc.);
(esp.) vessels of earthenware; (pl.) goods
person has for sale.

wāre², *v.t.* (usu. in imperative) look out for,
beware of.

ware'house (wār-h-), *n.* building for storage
of goods for sale; large store house; bonded
warehouse. *v.t.* store in warehouse.

warfare, warlike: see **war.**

war'lock (wor-), *n.* (*archaic*) wizard.

warm (-or-), *a.* of or at rather high temperature, moderately hot; (of clothes, etc.) serving to keep wearer warm; (of feelings, etc.)
affectionate, sympathetic, hearty, excited;
(of colour) suggesting warmth. *v.* make
warm; become warm, animated, or sympathetic. **warm-hearted,** generous, affectionate, sympathetic. **warmth,** *n.*

warn (-or-), *v.t.* give timely notice of impending danger or misfortune; give cautionary
notice or advice. **war'ning,** *n.* thing that
serves to warn; notice of, caution against,
danger, etc.

warp (-or-), *n.* threads stretched lengthwise in
loom to be crossed by weft; rope used in
towing or warping (ship); distortion in timber; mental twist. *v.* make or become distorted or twisted; move ship, etc., by hauling
on rope attached to fixed point.

wa'rrant (wo-), *n.* justification or authority;
document authorizing payment of money, or
conveying authority to arrest, search, etc.
v.t. serve as warrant for, justify, guarantee.
wa'rranty, *n.* guarantee; authorization, justification.

wa'rren (wo-), *n.* piece of land where rabbits
breed and abound.

wa'rrior (wo-), *n.* distinguished or veteran
soldier; fighting man of past ages or primitive peoples.

wart (-or-), *n.* small round dry growth on
skin. **war'ty,** *a.*

wār'y, *a.* habitually vigilant, cautious.

was: see **be.**

wash (wo-), *v.* cleanse with liquid; wash
oneself; wash clothes; (of water) flow past,
beat upon, (shore, walls, etc.); brush watery
colour over. *wash one's hands of,* decline
responsibility for. *wash up,* wash (table utensils, etc.) after use. *n.* washing, being
washed; waves caused by passage of vessel;
lotion. **wash'er¹,** *n.* person or thing that
washes. **wash'erwoman,** woman whose
occupation is washing clothes. **wash'ing,** *n.*
(esp.) clothes (to be) washed. **washing-
-machine,** (esp. electric) machine for washing clothes. **washing-soda,** crystalline
sodium carbonate used for cleansing purposes. **wash'y,** *a.* dilute, weak; pale; feeble.

wa'sher² (wo-), *n.* perforated disc or flattened
ring of metal, leather, rubber, etc., for making joint, nut, etc., tight.

wasp (wo-), *n.* winged stinging insect with
black and yellow barred body. **wasp'ish,** *a.*

irritable, spiteful, snappish.

wassail (wo'sl, wa'sl; *or* -āl'), *n.* (*archaic*)
spiced ale drunk at Christmas, etc. *v.i.* make
merry; carouse and drink healths.

wast (wo-), (*archaic*) 2nd pers. sing. p.t. of
be.

wā'stage, *n.* loss or diminution by use, wear,
decay, etc.; amount wasted.

wāste, *a.* (of land) desert, barren, not inhabited or cultivated; left over after use,
rejected, worthless. *lay waste,* ruin, destroy,
(land, buildings, etc.). *v.* squander, use
extravagantly; lose substance or volume by
gradual loss, decay, etc., dwindle. *n.* waste
region; loss or diminution from use, etc.;
squandering; waste matter. *run to waste,* be
expended uselessly. **waste-pipe,** pipe carrying off used water, etc. **wā'steful** (-tf-), *a.*
extravagant; not economical. **wā'ster,** *n.*
(esp., *informal*) ne'er-do-well. **wā'strel,** *n.*
waster; spendthrift.

watch (wo-), *v.* keep eyes fixed on, follow
observantly; be on the alert *for;* exercise
protecting care *over;* remain awake for devotional or other purpose. *n.* watching; spell of
duty (4 or 2 hours) on board ship; small
clock-like instrument worn or carried on person; (Hist.) man or men patrolling streets at
night. **watch-dog,** dog kept to guard house,
property, etc. **watch'maker,** one who
makes, sells, and repairs watches. **watch'-
man,** man employed to guard building, etc.
watch'word, military password (Hist.);
word or phrase expressing guiding principle
or rule of action. **watch'ful,** *a.* watching,
vigilant, showing vigilance.

wa'ter (waw-), *n.* transparent colourless
tasteless liquid compound of hydrogen and
oxygen, forming seas, rivers, etc., falling as
rain, etc.; liquid resembling, and usu. containing, water; solution, etc., of substance in
water; body of water; (often pl.) water of
mineral spring(s); transparency and lustre of
diamond and pearl. *v.* sprinkle or adulterate
or dilute with water; provide (horse, plant,
etc.) with water; (of mouth, eyes) secrete or
run with water. **water-closet,** place for urination and defecation, with water-supply for
flushing pan. **water-colour,** (picture painted,
art of painting with) artists' paint of pigment
mixed with gum and diluted with water.
wa'tercourse, (bed or channel of) stream of
water. **wa'tercress,** cress with pungent
leaves growing in springs and running
streams. **wa'terfall,** more or less vertical fall
of water of stream or river over ledge of rock
or precipice. **wa'terfowl,** bird(s) frequenting
water. **water-hen,** moorhen. **watering-can,**
portable vessel with long tubular spout for
watering plants. **watering-place,** spa; seaside holiday or health resort. **water-lily,**
plant growing in water, with broad floating
leaves and showy flowers. **water-line,** line
along which surface of water touches ship's

side, esp. proper line of flotation when ship is fully loaded. **wa′terlogged,** saturated with water; (of boat, etc.) so full of water that it will scarcely float. **wa′terman,** (pl. -*men*), boatman. **wa′termark,** distinguishing design, etc., in paper visible when it is held up against light. **water-melon,** oval smooth-skinned melon with watery juice. **water polo,** see **polo. water-power,** mechanical force derived from weight or motion of water. **wa′terproof,** (garment, material) that does not let water through; (*v.t.*) make waterproof. **water-rat,** water-vole. **wa′tershed,** summit or boundary-line separating river-basins. **wa′terspout,** (esp.) gyrating column of water or spray produced by action of whirlwind on sea and clouds above it. **water-table,** level below which ground is saturated with water. **wa′tertight,** so closely constructed or fitted that water cannot leak through; (of argument, etc.) unassailable. **water-vole,** aquatic kind of vole. **wa′terway,** navigable channel. **wa′terworks,** machinery, building, etc., for supplying water through pipes. **wa′tery,** *a.* covered or running with, containing too much, water; pale, diluted, vapid, insipid.

watt (wo-), *n.* unit of (esp. electric) power. **watt′age,** *n.* electric power expressed in watts.

watt′le[1] (wo-), *n.* rods interlaced with twigs or branches, used for fences, roofs, etc.; this plastered with clay or mud for building huts, etc. (usu. *wattle and daub*); Australian acacia with fragrant yellow flowers, adopted as national emblem; (Austral.) wattle bark.

watt′le[2] (wo-), *n.* fleshy piece hanging from neck or throat of turkey, etc.

wāve, *n.* moving ridge of water between two troughs, one of such ridges successively breaking on shore; something resembling this in shape or motion; vibration or disturbance propagated from place to place, conveying light, sound, etc.; act or gesture of waving. *v.* (cause to) move to and fro, shake, sway; move in waves, undulate; wave one's hand; make or be wavy. **wave′length,** distance between successive points of equal phase in direction of propagation of wave. **wā′vy,** *a.* undulating; having wave-like curves.

wā′ver, *v.i.* be undecided or irresolute; flicker, fluctuate, vary; falter. **wā′vering,** *a.*

wavy: see **wave.**

wax[1], *v.i.* (of moon) show a gradually increasing bright area (opp. *wane*); (*archaic*) grow, increase; become.

wax[2], *n.* sticky yellowish substance (*beeswax*) secreted by bees as material for honeycomb; this used, bleached and purified, for candles, etc.; any of various substances resembling beeswax; (*attrib.*) made of wax. **wax′work** (-erk), *n.* figure modelled in wax; (pl.) exhibition of such figures. **wax′en,** *a.* made of wax; resembling wax. **wax′y,** *a.*

way, *n.* road, track, path, street; place of passage; course, route; direction; distance (to be) travelled; method; manner of behaving, habit, custom. *by way of,* via, in capacity or function of. *give way,* see **give.** *under way,* (of ship, etc.) having begun to move through water; in progress. **way′farer,** *n.* traveller, esp. on foot. **waylay′,** *v.t.* (p.t. *waylaid*), wait for and speak to (person). **way′side,** *n.* (land bordering) side of road or path.

way′ward, *a.* childishly self-willed; capricious, erratic, perverse.

wē, *pron.* (objective *us*; possessive *our*), subjective plural of *I*; used by sovereign, newspaper editor, etc., instead of *I*.

weak, *a.* lacking in strength, power, or number; fragile; feeble; unsound; (Gram., of verb) forming past tense by addition of suffix. **weak-kneed,** (esp.) lacking in resolution or determination. **wea′ken,** *v.* make or become weaker. **weak′ling,** *n.* weak or feeble person or animal. **weak′ly**[1], *adv.* **weak′ly**[2], *a.* not robust, sickly. **weak′ness,** *n.* (esp.) weak point, failing; special or foolish liking *for.*

weal[1], *n.* ridge or mark raised on flesh by stroke of cane, lash, etc.

weal[2], *n.* (*archaic*) welfare, well-being.

weald, *n.* tract of formerly wooded country in SE. England.

wealth (wel-), *n.* abundance of possessions; riches, being rich; large amount or number *of.* **weal′thy,** *a.*

wean, *v.t.* accustom (child or other young mammal) to food other than mother's milk; detach, free, gradually *from* (habit, etc.).

weap′on (wep-), *n.* thing designed for or used in fighting; means of attack or defence.

wear (wār), *v.* (p.t. *wore*; p.p. *worn*), be dressed in, have on; carry or exhibit on one's person; damage, deteriorate, by use, friction, etc.; exhaust, tire; have lasting quality. *wear out,* use or be used until unfit for further use; tire out. *n.* things to wear; capacity to endure use; damage caused by ordinary use. **wear′-able,** *a.* **wear′er,** *n.*

wear′y, *a.* feeling need of rest after continued exertion, etc.; tired *of;* dispirited; tiring, toilsome. *v.* make or grow weary. **wear′iness,** *n.* **wear′isome,** *a.* causing weariness, monotonous.

wea′sel (-zl), *n.* small slender-bodied reddish-brown carnivorous mammal.

weath′er (wedh-), *n.* atmospheric conditions prevailing at specified time or place with respect to heat, cold, sunshine, fog, wind, etc.; rain, frost, wind, etc., as harmful or destructive agents. *v.* wear away, discolour, etc., by exposure to weather; come safely through (storm, etc.). **weath′erbeaten,** worn, bronzed, etc., by exposure to weather. **weath′ercock,** weather-vane in shape of cock. **weather-vane,** plate of metal on vertical spindle, turning readily with wind to show direction from which it is blowing.

weave, v. (p.t. *wōve*; p.p. *wōven*), form fabric by interlacing threads; form fabric out of (threads), esp. in loom; make (basket, etc.) by interlacing osiers, etc.; put together, compose (story, plot, etc.). n. style, method, of weaving.

web, n. cobweb, gossamer; tissue or membrane connecting toes of aquatic bird or animal; woven fabric. **web-footed, web-toed,** having toes connected by membrane, etc. **webb'ing,** n. (esp.) strong closely-woven material in form of narrow bands.

wed, v. (p.t. & p.p. *wedded* or *wed*), marry. *wedded to,* obstinately attached to (pursuit, etc.). **wedd'ing,** n. marriage ceremony with its attendant festivities.

wedge, n. piece of wood, metal, etc., thick at one end and tapering to thin edge at other, used for splitting stone, etc., forcing things apart, fixing them immovably, etc.; wedge--shaped thing. v.t. fix firmly with wedge; pack or crowd (*in*) tightly.

wed'lock, n. married state. *born in, out of, wedlock,* legitimate, illegitimate.

Wednesday (wenz'dā), n. fourth day of week.

wee, a. (chiefly Sc.) very small, tiny.

weed, n. herbaceous plant not valued for use or beauty, growing wild and rank in cultivated ground; (*informal*) tobacco; lanky and weakly person or horse. v. remove, clear ground or crop of, weeds. **wee'dy,** a. full of weeds; weak and lanky.

weeds (-z), n.pl. mourning worn by widow.

week, n. period of seven days beginning with Sunday; any period of seven days; the six days other than Sunday; working hours during a seven-day period. **week'day,** day other than Sunday. **week-end,** holiday period at end of week, esp. Saturday and Sunday. **week'ly,** a. occurring, done, etc., once a week; of, for, lasting, a week. adv. once a week, every week. n. weekly periodical.

ween, v.t. (*archaic*) think, suppose.

weep, v. (p.t. *wept*), shed tears. **wee'ping,** n. (esp., of willow, birch, etc.) having long slender drooping branches. **wee'py,** a. inclined to weep.

wee'vil, n. small beetle or any insect damaging stored grain, etc.

weft, n. threads crossing from side to side of loom and interwoven with warp.

weigh (wā), v. find weight of; estimate relative value or importance of; be of specified weight or importance. *weigh anchor,* heave up anchor before sailing. *weigh down,* bend or force down by pressure of weight; (fig.) burden, depress. **weigh-bridge,** platform scale flush with road for weighing vehicles, etc.

weight (wāt), n. force with which body is attracted to earth (or other celestial body); amount thing, etc., weighs; piece of metal, etc., of known weight for use in weighing;

heavy body; load or burden; influence; importance. v.t. attach weight to; impede or burden with load. **weight'less,** a. **weight'-lessness,** n. **weigh'ty,** a. heavy; important; worthy of consideration; influential.

weir (wēr), n. dam or barrier across river, etc., to retain water and regulate its flow.

weird (wērd), a. uncanny; (*informal*) fantastic.

wel'come, int. of greeting. n. kind or glad reception. v.t. give welcome to, receive gladly; greet. a. gladly received; acceptable as visitor; ungrudgingly permitted *to* use or accept.

weld, v. unite (pieces of, esp. heated, metal, etc.) into solid mass by hammering or pressure; (fig.) unite to form compact whole. n. joint made by welding. **wel'der,** n.

wel'fare, n. health, freedom from want, happiness. **Welfare State,** State having highly developed social services controlled or financed by government.

well¹, n. (usu. circular) pit or shaft sunk in ground to obtain water, oil, etc.; enclosed space resembling well-shaft. v.i. spring *up, out,* etc., (as) from fountain.

well², adv. (*better, best*), in good manner or style, satisfactorily, rightly; thoroughly, carefully, completely; to considerable distance, degree, or extent. *as well,* with equal reason; in addition, also. *as well as,* in addition to. a. (chiefly *pred.* a.) in good health, satisfactory. int. expressing astonishment, resignation, etc.

well-, *pref.* well. **well-advised'** (-zd), a. (esp.) prudent, wise. **well-appoin'ted,** a. properly equipped. **well-bal'anced** (-st), a. sensible, sane. **well-behāved'** (-vd) a. having or showing good manners. **well'-bēing,** n. happy, healthy, or prosperous condition; moral or physical welfare. **well-bred',** a. having or displaying good breeding or manners. **well--connec'ted,** a. (esp.) of good family. **well--disposed'** (-zd), a. having kind feelings (*towards*). **well-informed'** (-md), a. having wide knowledge, or access to reliable information. **well-knit',** a. strongly and compactly built. **well-mea'ning,** a. having or showing good intentions. **well'nigh** (-nī), adv. almost. **well-off',** a. fortunately situated; fairly or sufficiently rich. **well-read'** (-red), a. well-informed as result of wide reading. **well-spō'ken,** a. refined in speech. **well-to-do'** (-ōō), a. prosperous. **well'--wisher,** n. one who wishes well to another, a cause, etc. **well'-worn,** a. (esp.) trite, hackneyed.

well'ingtons (-z), n.pl. waterproof rubber boots reaching to knee.

Welsh¹, a. & n. (people, Celtic language) of Wales. *Welsh rarebit,* see **rarebit.**

welsh², v. (of bookmaker) leave race-course secretly without paying (winner(s) of bets).

welt, n. strip of leather sewn between edge of

sole and turned-in edge of upper of shoe, etc.; ribbed border of knitted garment. *v.t.* provide with welt.

wel'ter, *v.i.* wallow; be tossed about. *n.* turmoil, upheaval; surging or confused mass.

wen, *n.* benign swelling on scalp, etc.

wench, *n.* (*archaic*) girl or young woman.

wend, *v.* direct (one's *way*); (*archaic*) go.

went, *p.t.* of **go.**

wept, *p.t.* & *p.p.* of **weep.**

were: see **be.**

wert, (*archaic*) 2nd pers. sing. p.t. of **be.**

wer(e)wolf (wēr'woolf), *n.* (in folklore) human being who changes into a wolf.

Wes'leyan (*or* -z-), *a.* & *n.* (follower) of John Wesley, founder of Methodism.

west, *adv.*, *n.*, & *a.* (towards, at, near, blowing from) point of horizon where sun sets (opp. *east*); (towards, in) western part of world, country, region, etc. **wes'terly,** *a.* & *adv.* towards, coming from, west. **west'-ward,** *adv.*, *a.*, & *n.* **west'wards** (-z), *adv.*

wes'tern, *a.* of, in, coming from, west; of Western (i.e. W. European and American) countries or races. *n.* film, etc., dealing with frontier life, cowboys, etc., in American West. **wes'ternize,** *v.t.* make (more) Western in institutions, ideas, etc. **westernizā'-tion,** *n.*

wet, *a.* (*wetter, wettest*), soaked, covered or supplied with, employing, etc., water or other liquid; rainy. *v.t.* (p.t. *wet or wetted*), make wet; moisten. *n.* rainy weather. **wet-nurse,** woman employed to suckle another's child.

weth'er (-dh-), *n.* castrated ram.

whack, *n.* heavy resounding blow, esp. with stick. *v.t.* beat or strike vigorously.

whāle, *n.* very large fish-like marine mammal. *v.i.* hunt whales. **whale'bone,** elastic horny substance in upper jaw of some whales. **whale-oil,** oil obtained from whale's blubber. **whā'ler,** *n.* ship, man, engaged in whaling.

wharf (-orf), *n.* (pl. *wharves* or *wharfs*), structure at water's edge for loading or unloading vessels lying alongside. **whar'fage,** *n.* wharf accommodation or dues. **whar'finger** (-j-), *n.* owner or keeper of wharf.

what (-ot), *a.* (*interrog.*) asking for selection from indefinite number, or for specification of amount, kind, etc.; (*exclamation*) how great, how remarkable, etc. *pron.* (*interrog.*) what thing; (*relative*) that thing which. *what not*, anything. **whatev'er,** *pron.* & *a.* any-(thing) at all (that); no matter what. **what-sōev'er,** *pron.* & *a.* (more emphatic for) whatever.

wheat, *n.* a cereal plant; its grain providing chief bread-stuff in temperate countries. **whea'ten,** *a.* of (grain or flour of) wheat.

whee'dle, *v.t.* cajole, persuade, by flattery or coaxing; get *out of* by wheedling.

wheel, *n.* disc or circular spoked frame revol-

ving on axle; wheel-like structure or thing. *v.* push or pull (bicycle, pram, etc.); turn (as if) on axis or pivot, (cause to) move in circle. **wheel'barrow,** shallow box with shafts and one wheel for shifting small loads. **wheel-chair,** invalid's chair on wheels. **wheel'-wright** (-rīt), *n.* maker and repairer of (wooden) wheels. **wheeled** (-ld), *a.* provided with wheels.

wheeze, *v.* breathe with audible whistling sound. *n.* sound of wheezing. **whee'zy,** *a.*

whelk, *n.* spiral-shelled marine mollusc.

whelp, *n.* puppy; (*archaic*) cub. *v.i.* pup.

when, *adv.* & *conj.* at what time, on what occasion; at the time, on the occasion, etc., that; and (just) then; considering that; whereas. **whenev'er,** *adv.* & *conj.* at whatever time, on whatever occasion; every time that.

whence, *adv.* & *conj.* (*archaic*) from where, from what place or source; from which.

where (-ār), *adv.* & *conj.* at or in what place, position, or circumstances; in what respect, from what source, etc.; to what place; in, at, or to which; and there. *n.* place, locality. **whereabouts',** *adv.* in or near what place. **where'abouts,** *n.* (approximate) position or situation. **whereas'** (-z), *conj.* considering the fact that; in contrast with the fact that. **whereby',** *adv.* (*archaic*) by which. **wherev'er,** *adv.* at or to whatever place. **where'fore,** *adv.* for what; why; and therefore; (*archaic*) because of, in consequence of, which. **wherein',** **whereof** (-v), **whereon',** **wherewith'** (-dh), *advv.* (*archaic* or formal) in, of, on, or with what or which. **wheresōev'er,** *adv.* (*archaic*) wherever. **whereupon',** *adv.* (esp.) after which, and thereupon. **where'withal** (-dhawl), *n.* (*informal*) means, esp. money (for or *to* do).

whe'rry, *n.* (large) light boat.

whet, *v.t.* (p.t. *whetted*), sharpen; make (more) acute. **whet'stone,** stone for sharpening tools.

wheth'er (-dh-), *conj.* introducing dependent question, etc., and expressing doubt, choice, etc., between alternatives. *pron.* (*archaic*) which of the two.

whey (-ā), *n.* watery liquid left after separation of curds from milk.

which, *a.* & *pron.* (*interrog.*) what one(s) of stated or implied set of persons, things, or alternatives; (*relative*) and that, it, they, etc.; that. **whichev'er,** *a.* & *pron.* any or either that; no matter which.

whiff, *n.* puff or breath of air, smoke, odour, etc. *v.* blow or puff lightly.

whiff'le, *v.* blow in puffs; veer or shift *about*; make light whistling sound.

Whig, *n.* & *a.* (member) of political party that preceded Liberal Party.

while, *n.* space of time; time spent in doing something. *all the while*, during the whole time (that). *worth* (one's) *while*, worth doing. *adv. & conj.* during the time that; for as long as; although; besides that. *v.t.* pass (time, etc.) *away* in leisurely manner. **whilst,** *adv. & conj.* while.

whim, *n.* sudden fanciful desire or notion.

whim′per, *v.i.* cry with feeble whining broken sound. *n.* such sound.

whim′sical (-z-), *a.* capricious, fantastic, characterized by whims. **whimsical′ity,** *n.*

whim′sy (-zi), *n.* whim, fad.

whin, *n.* gorse, furze.

whine, *n.* prolonged complaining cry (as) of dog; sound resembling this; complaining tone; undignified complaint. *v.* utter whine(s); complain.

whinn′y, *n.* gentle or joyful neigh. *v.* utter whinny.

whip, *n.* instrument, usu. stick with lash attached, for urging on horse, etc., or for flogging or beating; hunt-official managing hounds; official maintaining discipline of political party in House of Parliament; whip's written notice requesting members' attendance. *v.* (p.t. *whipped*), apply whip to; make (eggs, cream, etc.) light and frothy by stirring vigorously; bind round closely with twine, etc.; sew over and over, overcast; move suddenly or briskly, dart; snatch. **whipping-boy,** (Hist.) boy educated with young prince and punished in his stead. **whipp′y,** *a.* flexible, springy.

whipp′er-snapper, *n.* young and insignificant but impertinent person.

whipp′et, *n.* small dog like greyhound.

whipp′oorwill, *n.* American nightjar named from its call.

whirl, *v.* swing round and round, revolve rapidly; move swiftly, rush along; (of brain, senses) seem to spin round. *n.* whirling, swift, or violent movement; rush; dizzy state. **whirl′pool,** place in sea, river, etc., where there is constant circular movement. **whirl′wind,** whirling mass or column of air moving over land or water. **whir′ligig** (-g-), *n.* spinning toy.

whirr, *n. & v.i.* (make) continuous vibratory sound (as) of swiftly turning wheel, etc.

whisk, *n.* bunch of hair, bristles, etc., for brushing, dusting, etc.; implement for whipping eggs, cream, etc.; rapid sweeping movement. *v.* move, go, convey, brush, (*off, away*) lightly and rapidly; whip (eggs, etc.).

whis′ker, *n.* (usu. in pl.) hair on cheeks or sides of face of adult man; one of projecting hairs or bristles growing near mouth of cat, etc. **whis′kered** (-erd), **whis′kery,** *aa.*

whis′key, *n.* Irish whisky.

whis′ky, *n.* alcoholic spirit distilled from malted barley, rye, etc.

whis′per, *n.* (remark made in) speech without vibration of vocal cords; soft rustling sound; insinuation, rumour, hint. *v.* make, utter in, whisper; communicate, etc., confidentially.

whist, *n.* card-game, usu. for two pairs of opponents.

whi′stle (-sl), *n.* clear shrill sound made by forcing breath through lips contracted to narrow opening; similar sound made by bird, wind, or missile, or produced by pipe, etc.; instrument constructed to produce whistle. *v.* emit whistle; summon, give signal, etc., thus; produce (tune) thus.

whit, *n.* particle, jot.

Whit, Whit′sun, *aa.* of or following **Whit Sunday,** seventh Sunday after Easter, commemorating descent of Holy Spirit.

white, *a.* of colour of snow or milk; pale; innocent, unstained. *n.* white part of anything; (nearly) white colour; white pigment, clothes, material, etc.; viscid fluid surrounding yolk of egg; white man, butterfly, etc. **white ant,** termite. **white′bait,** small silvery-white fry of various fishes. **white coffee,** coffee with milk. **white elephant,** burdensome or useless possession. **white ensign,** flag of British Navy, etc. **white feather,** symbol or emblem of cowardice. **white frost,** hoar-frost. **white man,** member of race with light-coloured skin. **white′wash,** liquid composition of lime or whiting and water, etc., for whitening ceilings, walls, etc. *v.* apply whitewash to; gloss over, clear of blame, etc. **white wine,** wine of (pale) yellow colour. **whi′ten,** *v.* make, become, white. **whi′ting**[1], *n.* preparation of finely powdered chalk. **whi′tish,** *a.*

whith′er (-dh-), *adv. & pron.* (*archaic*) to where or which.

whi′ting[2], *n.* common edible sea-fish.

whit′low (-ō), *n.* inflamed swelling, usu. with suppuration, esp. under or near nail.

Whitsun, etc.: see **Whit.**

whitt′le, *v.* pare or shape (wood) with knife; pare *down*, take *away*, by degrees.

whiz(z), *n.* buzzing or hissing sound made by body rushing through air. *v.* (cause to) move swiftly (as) with whizz.

who (hōō), *pron.* (objective *whom*, pr. hōōm; possessive *whose*, pr. hōōz), (*interrog.*) what or which person(s); (*relative*) person(s) that; and or but he (she, they). **whoev′er,** *pron.* whatever person(s), any (one) who; no matter who. **whosoev′er,** *pron.* (*archaic,* emphatic) whoever.

whole (hōl), *a.* in uninjured, intact, undiminished, or undivided state; all, all of. *n.* full, complete, or total amount (*of*); complete thing; complex system, total made up of parts. **whole-hearted,** thoroughly heartfelt, sincere. **whole′meal,** meal or flour made from whole grain of wheat. **wholly** (hōl′-li), *adv.* entirely, to the full extent, altogether.

whole′sale (hōls-), *n.* selling in large quantities, esp. for retail by others. *a.* selling wholesale; (fig.) unlimited, indiscriminate. *adv.* in large quantities; at wholesale price; in abundance, indiscriminately.

wholesome (hōl′sum), *a.* healthy; promoting

or favourable to physical or moral health or well-being.

wholly: see **whole.**

whom: see **who.**

whoop (h-), *n.* cry of excitement, exultation, etc.; characteristic drawing-in of breath after cough in **whooping-cough,** infectious disease with violent convulsive cough.

whore (hor), *n.* prostitute.

whorl, *n.* ring of leaves, etc., round stem; one turn of coil, spiral, etc.

whor'tleberry (wer-), *n.* bilberry.

whose (hōōz), *pron.* possessive case of **who** (and occasionally of **which**).

whŷ, *adv.* (*interrog.*) for what reason or purpose; (*relative*) on account of which. *int.* expressing mild or slight surprise, etc.

wick, *n.* strip of loosely woven or twisted cotton, etc., drawing up oil or grease to maintain flame of oil-lamp, candle, etc.

wick'ĕd, *a.* sinful, vicious, morally depraved; (*informal*) very bad, malicious, mischievous.

wick'er, *n.* pliant twigs or osiers plaited or woven together to make baskets, chairs, etc. **wick'erwork,** things made, craft of making things, of wicker.

wick'ĕt, *n.* small gate or door, esp. beside or in larger one; (Cricket) set of three uprights (*stumps*) surmounted by two bails; ground between and about wickets. **wicket-keeper,** fieldsman stationed behind wicket.

wide, *a.* measuring much, having specified measurement, from side to side; broad; extending far, embracing much; open to full extent. *wide of,* far from (point, mark). *adv.* at or to many points; with wide interval or opening; so as to miss mark or way. *wide awake,* fully awake. **wide'spread,** found, distributed, over large area. **wide'ly,** *adv.* over wide area or range; far apart. **wi'den,** *v.* make or become wider.

widgeon (wij'on), *n.* kind of wild duck.

wid'ow (-ō), *n.* woman whose husband is dead and who has not married again. *widow's weeds,* see **weeds. wid'owed** (-ōd), *a.* bereaved of one's husband (or wife). **wid'ower** (-ōer), *n.* man whose wife has died.

width, *n.* distance or measurement from side to side; large extent.

wield, *v.t.* hold and use; exercise (authority, power, etc.).

wife, *n.* (pl. *wives*), married woman, esp. in relation to her husband. **wife'ly,** *a.*

wig, *n.* artificial head-covering of hair.

wigg'ing (-g-), *n.* (*informal*) severe scolding.

wigg'le, *v.* (*informal*) move rapidly, jerk, shake, from side to side or up and down.

wight (wīt), *n.* (*archaic*) person.

wig'wam, *n.* N. Amer. Indian round or oval dwelling made of bark.

wīld, *a.* in original natural state; not domesticated, tame, or cultivated; uncivilized; tempestuous; lawless; out of control; violently agitated or excited; rash, random. *n.* wild or

waste place. **wild'fowl,** wild birds, esp. wild game. *wild goose chase,* foolish, fruitless, or hopeless quest.

wil'dèbeest (*or* vil'dibāst), *n.* African quadruped of antelope family but resembling ox or buffalo.

wil'derness, *n.* wild uncultivated waste land; desolate expanse.

wile, *n.* trick, stratagem. *v.t.* entice, lure.

wil'ful, *a.* deliberate, intentional; obstinately self-willed; wayward.

will[1], *v. aux.* (p.t. & conditional *would,* pr. wood), forming future or conditional statement or question. *v.t.* wish, choose, consent, to; be likely, be observed from time to time, to.

will[2], *n.* mental faculty directed to conscious and intentional action; act of willing; intention, determination; desire, wish; formal written statement of person's intention as to disposal of his property, etc., after his death. *at will,* as one pleases. *v.* exercise the will; (try to) induce (*to* do) by exercise of will; direct by will or testament, bequeath. **will--power,** (strength of) will, esp. power to control one's own actions, etc.

will'ing, *a.* ready to be of use or service; done, given, etc., readily, cheerfully, or eagerly. **will'ingly,** *adv.* **will'ingness,** *n.*

will-o'-the-wisp', *n.* phosphorescent light seen on marshy ground; elusive or delusive person or thing.

will'ow (-ō), *n.* tree with pliant branches, usu. growing by water. **will'owy,** *a.* (esp.) lithe and slender.

willynill'y, *adv.* whether one likes it or not.

wilt[1], (*archaic*) 2nd pers. sing. pres. of **will**[1].

wilt[2], *v.* (cause to) fade, droop, become limp.

wi'ly, *a.* full of wiles, cunning.

wim'ple, *n.* head-dress covering neck and sides of face, worn by nuns.

win, *v.* (p.t. *won,* pr. wun), be victorious in (game, battle, race, etc.), gain victory; get or gain as result of fight, contest, bet, etc.; gain affection or allegiance of. *n.* victory in game or contest. **winn'er,** *n.* **winn'ing,** **win'some,** *aa.* attractive. **winn'ings** (-z), *n.pl.* money won by gambling, betting, etc.

wince, *v.i.* & *n.* (make, give) start or involuntary shrinking movement of pain, etc.

win'cey, *n.* durable fabric of wool and (usu.) cotton. **winceyette',** *n.* similar fabric of cotton.

winch, *n.* hoisting or hauling apparatus of rope, etc., attached to revolving cylinder turned by crank, or mechanically; crank of wheel, etc. *v.t.* hoist or draw *up* with winch.

wīnd[1], *v.* (p.t. *wound*), move, go, in curved or sinuous course; coil, wrap closely round something or upon itself; draw *up* with winch, etc.; tighten *up* coiled spring of clock, etc. *wind up,* bring or come to an end. **winding sheet,** linen in which corpse is wrapped. **wīn'der,** *n.*

wind², *n.* current of air occurring naturally in atmosphere; breath as needed in exertion, for sounding musical instrument, etc.; gas in stomach or intestines; wind-instruments of orchestra. *v. t.* detect presence of by scent; deprive of breath. **wind′bag,** bag for reserve of air in bagpipes; wordy talker. **wind′fall,** fruit blown down by wind; piece of unexpected good fortune, esp. legacy. **wind-instrument,** musical instrument in which sound is produced by current of air. **wind′-mill,** mill worked by action of wind on sails. **wind-pipe,** air passage between throat and lungs. **wind′screen,** (esp.) sheet of glass in front of driver of motor car, etc. **wind′-shield,** (U.S.) windscreen. **wind-sock,** open-ended cone of canvas, etc., flown from mast-head or tall pole, to show aircraft, etc., direction of wind. **wind′ward,** *a.*, *adv.*, & *n.* (region) lying in direction from which wind blows, facing the wind. **win′dy,** *a.* exposed to or stormy with wind; in which wind is frequent or prevalent.

wind′lass, *n.* hoisting or hauling apparatus, winch.

win′dow (-ō), *n.* opening, usu. filled with glass, in wall, etc., to admit light and air; window space of shop, etc., used for display of goods, etc.; opening resembling window in form or function.

wine, *n.* alcoholic drink made of fermented grape-juice; fermented drink resembling it made from other fruits, etc.; purplish red colour.

wing, *n.* one of limbs or organs of flight in birds, insects, etc.; thing resembling wing in form or function, esp. one of main supporting surfaces of aircraft; mudguard of motor vehicle; side extension of something, esp. building, army in battle formation, etc.; division of air force. *v.* equip with wings; travel, traverse, on wings; wound in wing or arm. **wing-commander,** R.A.F. officer next below group-captain. **winged** (-ngd), **wing′-less,** *aa.*

wink, *v.* close one eye momentarily; blink; (cause to) flicker like eyelid, twinkle; convey (hint, etc.) by winking. **wink at,** pretend not to notice, connive at. *n.* act of winking.

wink′le, *n.* edible sea-snail, periwinkle. *v. t.* **winkle out,** extract, prise out.

winner, winning, winsome: see **win.**

win′ter, *n.* coldest season of year, between autumn and spring. *v.* spend the winter *at, in,* etc.; keep, feed, during winter. *a.* of, occurring or used in, winter. **winter sports,** skiing, skating, etc. **win′try,** *a.* cold, windy, cheerless.

wipe, *v.* clean or dry surface by rubbing with something soft; get rid of (tears), clean (container) *out,* make *clean,* etc., by wiping. *n.* act of wiping. **wi′per,** *n.* (esp.) *windscreen wiper,* device for keeping windscreen clear.

wire, *n.* (piece of) metal drawn out into slender flexible rod or thread; (*informal*) telegram. *v.* support, stiffen, secure, with wires; (*informal*) telegraph. **wire netting,** netting made of wire. **wi′ry,** *a.* like wire; tough, sinewy, untiring.

wire′less (-īrl-), *a.* having no wire(s), radio. *n.* & *v.* radio.

wis′dom (-z-), *n.* being wise; soundness of judgement in matters relating to life and conduct; knowledge, learning. **wisdom tooth,** hindmost molar, usu. cut at age of about 20.

wise¹ (-z), *a.* having, showing, sound judgement resulting from experience and knowledge; prudent, sensible; having knowledge.

wise² (-z), *n.* (*archaic*) way, manner.

wi′seacre (-zāker), *n.* dull bore who thinks himself wise.

wish, *n.* (expression of) desire; thing desired; request; (*pl.*) expression of desire for another's happiness, success, etc. *v.* have or express wish (*for*); want or demand; hope or desire. **wish-bone,** forked bone between neck and breast of cooked fowl. **wish′ful,** *a.* wishing, desirous. *wishful thinking,* belief founded on hopes rather than facts.

wish′y-washy (-wo-), *a.* washy.

wisp, *n.* small bundle or twist of hay, straw, etc.; slight piece or scrap (of). **wis′py,** *a.*

wist, *p. t.* of **wit².**

wistar′ia, wister′ia, *n.* climbing shrub with hanging racemes of (usu.) pale purple flowers.

wist′ful, *a.* yearningly or mournfully expectant or wishful. **wist′fully,** *adv.*

wit¹, *n.* (sing. or pl.) intelligence, understanding; (sing.) amusing ingenuity of speech, ideas, etc.; person noted for this. **wit′ted,** *a.* having wits or understanding of specified quality (e.g. *quick-witted, slow-witted*).

wit², *v.* (*archaic;* pres. *wot;* p.t. *wist*), know. *to wit,* that is to say.

witch, *n.* woman supposed to have dealings with devil or evil spirits. **witch′craft,** *n.* use of magic. **witch′-doctor,** *n.* sorcerer of primitive people.

witch′-hazel, *n.* N. American shrub; astringent extract of its bark and leaves.

with (-dh), *prep.* in company of, among, beside; having; by means of; on the side of; in care or charge of; in same way, at same time, as; in regard to; despite; so as to be separated from.

withal′ (-dhawl), *adv.* (*archaic*) moreover.

withdraw′ (-dh-), *v.* (p.t. *withdrew,* pr.-ōō; p.p. *withdrawn*), pull or draw back; take away, remove; take back (statement, offer, etc.); go away or apart. **withdraw′al,** *n.*

withe (-dh; *or* with), **with′y** (-dhi), *n.* tough flexible branch, esp. of willow.

with′er (-dh-), *v.* make or become dry or shrivelled; deprive of or lose vigour, freshness, etc.; (fig.) paralyse (*with* look of scorn, etc.).

with′ers (-dherz), *n. pl.* ridge between

shoulder-blades of horse, etc.

withhold' (-dh-h-), *v.t.* (p.t. *withheld*), refuse to grant; keep back.

within' (-dh-), *adv.* inside; indoors. *prep.* inside; not out of or beyond; not exceeding.

without' (-dh-), *prep.* not having or feeling or showing; in want of; free from; in absence of. *adv.* (*archaic*) outside.

withstand', *v.t.* (p.t. *withstood*), resist, oppose (successfully).

withy: see **withe.**

wit'less, *a.* foolish, unintelligent.

wit'ness, *n.* person present at event; person giving sworn testimony; person attesting another's signature to document; person or thing whose existence, position, etc., is testimony *to* or proof *of*. *bear witness* (*to*), give or be evidence (*of*), be confirmation (*of*). *v.* sign (document) as witness; see, be spectator of; bear witness. **witness-box,** enclosed space from which witness gives evidence.

witted: see **wit¹.**

witt'icism, *n.* witty remark.

witt'ingly, *adv.* consciously, intentionally.

witt'y, *a.* full of wit.

wiz'ard, *n.* magician, sorcerer; male witch. **wiz'ardry**, *n.*

wiz'ened (-nd), *a.* of shrivelled or dried-up appearance.

woad, *n.* (plant yielding) blue dye, used by ancient-britons to stain their bodies.

wobb'le, *v.i.* move unsteadily from side to side; rock, quiver, shake; hesitate, waver. **wobb'ly**, *a.*

woe, *n.* affliction, bitter grief; (pl.) troubles. **woe'begone**, *a.* dismal-looking. **woe'ful**, *a.* **woe'fully**, *adv.*

woke, woken, *p.t.* & *p.p.* of **wake¹.**

wold, *n.* undulating uplands.

wolf (woo-), *n.* (pl. *wolves*), largish wild mammal related to dog. *v.t.* (*slang*) devour greedily. **wolf-hound**, dog of kind kept for hunting wolves. **wolf'ish**, *a.* of, like, wolf.

wo'man (woo-), *n.* (pl. *women*, pr. wim'in), adult human female; (*attrib.*) female. **wo'mankind**, women in general. **wo'menfolk, wo'menkind,** women; women of one's family. **women's rights**, rights of equal privileges and opportunities with men. **wo'manhood**, *n.* being a (grown) woman; womanly character. **wo'manish**, *a.* effeminate, unmanly. **wo'manly**, *a.* having qualities befitting (grown) woman; not masculine or girlish.

womb (woom), *n.* organ in female mammal in which developing child or young is carried and nourished until birth, uterus.

wom'bat, *n.* burrowing beaver-like Australian marsupial.

women: see **woman.**

won, *p.t.* & *p.p.* of **win.**

won'der (wu-), *n.* strange or remarkable thing, event, etc.; miracle; prodigy; emotion aroused by novel or unexpected thing; aston-

ishment. *v.* be affected with wonder; feel doubt or curiosity, be desirous to know or learn. **won'derful**, *a.* marvellous, suprising; surprisingly fine, excellent, etc. **won'derfully**, *adv.* **won'drous**, *a.* & *adv.* (Poet.) wonderful(ly).

wont, *a.* (*archaic*) accustomed, used, (*to* do). *n.* custom; habit. **won'ted**, *a.* habitual.

won't, informal contraction of *will not.*

woo, *v.t.* court, esp. with view to marriage; seek to win, invite. **woo'er**, *n.*

wood, *n.* growing trees covering piece of ground; hard fibrous substance of tree, whether growing or cut for timber or fuel; something made of wood, esp. *the* cask in which wine, etc., is stored, bowl in game of bowls, etc. *out of the wood*, clear of danger, difficulty, etc. **wood alcohol**, alcohol got by distillation of wood. **wood'bine**, honeysuckle; (U.S.) Virgina creeper. **wood'cut**, print from design cut on wood block. **wood'land**, wooded country. **wood-louse** (pl., -*lice*), small terrestrial crustacean. **wood'man**, forester. **wood-nymph**, nymph of tree or woods. **wood'pecker**, bird pecking tree-trunks, etc., in search of insects. **wood-pulp**, wood fibre prepared as material for paper. **wood-wind**, wind-instruments of the orchestra (usu. or formerly) made of wood. **wood'work**, work done in wood, carpentry. **wood'worm**, larva of common furniture beetle, destructive to wood. **woo'ded**, *a.* covered with growing trees; abounding in woods. **woo'den**, *a.* of or resembling wood; dull, stiff, inexpressive. **woo'dy**, *a.* wooded; of or resembling wood.

woof, *n.* (*archaic*) weft.

wool, *n.* fine wavy hair forming fleecy coat of domesticated sheep, etc.; woollen yarn or cloth or garments. **wool-gathering**, day-dreaming. **wool'sack**, Lord Chancellor's seat in House of Lords. **woo'llen**, *a.* & *n.* (fabric) made of wool. **woo'lly**, *a.* bearing or covered with wool; of or suggesting wool; confused, vague.

word (werd), *n.* (written or printed symbol(s) representing) sound(s) having meaning and constituting smallest possible element of language; (usu. pl.) thing(s) said, speech, text of song, actor's part, etc.; (pl.) altercation; password; tidings; command; promise, assurance. *word for word*, exact(ly). *word of honour*, solemn promise. *v.t.* put into words; select words to express. **wor'ding**, *n.* (esp.) form of words used, phrasing. **wor'dy**, *a.* using or containing (too) many words.

wore, *p.t.* of **wear.**

work (werk), *n.* action involving effort or exertion, esp. as means of livelihood; (Phys.) operation of force in producing movement, etc.; something to do or be done; thing done or made; book, picture, or other product of art; (pl.) operative parts of machine; (pl.) factory, etc. *at work*, working. *in* (*out of*) *work*, having (not having) paid employment. *v.* engage, be engaged in, bodily or mental work; make efforts; (cause to) operate, act; effect, bring about; knead, hammer, fashion, into shape, etc. *work out*, find or solve by calculation. *work up*, bring to efficient or desired state; excite. **work′aday,** ordinary. **work′basket, work′box,** receptacles for sewing-materials. **work′house,** (Hist.) public institution for maintenance of paupers. **work′man,** (pl. *-men*), man hired to do work or (usu.) manual labour. **work′manlike,** showing practised skill. **work′manship,** degree of skill in workman or of finish in his product. **work′shop,** room or building in which manufacture, manual work, etc., is carried on. **work′shȳ,** disinclined for work, lazy. **work′able,** *a.* (esp.) that can be worked or will work. **work′er,** *n.*

world (wer-), *n.* human existence, *this* present life; earth; planet or other heavenly body; universe; everything, all people; human society; sphere of interest, action, or thought; vast amount or extent. **world′wide,** known or found everywhere; universal. **world′ly,** *a.* temporal, earthly; devoted to affairs of this life, esp. to pursuit of wealth or pleasure.

worm (werm), *n.* slender limbless creeping invertebrate anim , esp. earthworm; internal parasite; larva, n ggot, grub; spiral part of screw, etc. *v.* pro ress with crawling or wriggling motion; m ke one's way insidiously; draw *out* (secret, tc.) by craft.

worm′wood (wer-), *n.* woody herb with bitter taste; (cause of) b tter humiliation.

worn, *p.p.* of **wear.**

wo′rry (wu-), *n.* cause of) anxiety or concern; (pl.) cares, troubles. *v.* be trouble or anxiety to; vex, ster, importune; make or be anxious or un y; (of dog, etc.) shake or pull about with t .

worse (wers), *a.* adv., used as compar. of *bad, evil, badly* l, or as opp. of *better*; in worse condition anner, etc.; less good or well. *n.* worse ing(s); worse condition. **wor′sen,** *v.* mak or become worse.

wor′ship (wer-), *n.* reverent homage paid to being or power regarded as divine; acts or ceremonies displaying this; adoration, devotion; title of respect for mayor, etc. *v.* (p.t. *worshipped*), adore; honour with religious rites; idolize; attend public worship. **wor′-shipful,** *a.* honourable. **wor′shipper,** *n.*

worst (wer-), *a.* & *adv.* used as superl. of *bad*(*ly*), *evil, ill*; least good or well. *n.* worst part, state, result, etc. *v.t.* defeat, outdo.

wors′tëd (woos-), *n.* (fabric made from) fine woollen yarn. *a.* made of worsted.

worth (wer-), *a.* of value of (specified amount, sum, etc.), equivalent to or good return for; having property amounting to. *n.* value; merit. *worth while,* worth the time or effort spent. **worth′less,** *a.* lacking worth.

worthy (werdhi), *a.* estimable, deserving respect; deserving *of*; of sufficient worth, merit, etc. *n.* person of some distinction. **wor′thiness,** *n.*

wot: see **wit**[2].

would (wood): see **will**[1]. **would′-bē,** *a.* desiring or professing to be.

wound[1] (wōō-), *n.* injury caused by cut, stab, blow, bullet, etc. *v.t.* inflict wound on; hurt (person's feelings, etc.), pain.

wound[2], *p.t.* & *p.p.* of **wind**[1].

wove, woven, *p.t.* & *p.p.* of **weave.**

wrack (r-), *n.* seaweed cast up on shore.

wraith (r-), *n.* ghost, apparition.

wrangle (rang′gl), *n.* & *v.i.* (engage in) noisy argument or dispute.

wrap (r-), *v.* (p.t. *wrapped*), envelop, pack, swathe, (*up*) in garment or folded or soft covering material. *n.* shawl, rug, etc. **wrapp′er,** *n.* cover; loose robe or gown.

wrath (raw- *or* ro-), *n.* anger, indignation. **wrath′ful,** *a.* **wrath′fully,** *adv.*

wreak (r-), *v.t.* give expression to (anger, etc.); inflict (vengeance) *up*(*on*).

wreath (r-), *n.* (pl. *-s*, pr. -dhz), flowers, leaves, etc., wound or woven together into ring; curl or ring of smoke, cloud, etc.

wreathe (rēdh), *v.* encircle as, or (as) with, wreath; (of smoke, etc.) move in wreaths.

wreck (r-), *n.* destruction or disablement, esp. of ship; ship that has suffered wreck; greatly damaged building, motor car, etc. *v.t.* cause wreck of; ruin. **wreck′age,** *n.* remnants of wreck. **wreck′er,** *n.* (esp.) one who tries from shore to bring about shipwreck in order to plunder wreckage.

wren (r-), *n.* small, usu. brown, song-bird.

wrench (r-), *n.* violent twist, pull, or turn; tool for gripping and turning nuts, etc.; (fig.) pain caused by parting, etc. *v.t.* twist, turn; pull (*away, off,* etc.) violently or with effort; injure by straining or stretching.

wrest (r-), *v.t.* force, wrench away, (*from*).

wrestle (re′sl), *v.* strive with strength and skill to throw opponent to ground by grappling with him; struggle *with* or *against*. *n.* wrestling-match; hard struggle.

wretch (r-), *n.* very unfortunate or miserable person; vile or contemptible person. **wretch′ëd,** *a.* miserable, afflicted; of poor quality; contemptible; causing discontent, discomfort, or nuisance.

wrigg′le (r-) *v.* twist or turn body about with short writhing movements; move (*out, along,* etc.) by wriggling. *n.* wriggling movement.

wring (r-), *v.t.* (p.t. *wrung*), squeeze, twist, esp. so as to force out moisture; get, extort, *out of* or *from* by pressure; clasp (person's hand) forcibly or with emotion. *wring one's hands,* twist hands together in distress, etc. *n.* squeeze, act of wringing.

wrink′le (r-), *n.* crease or furrow of skin or other flexible surface. *v.t.* make wrinkles in;

become wrinkled. **wrink'ly,** *a.*

wrist (r-), *n.* joint connecting hand and forearm. **wrist'band,** band of sleeve covering wrist. **wrist-watch,** watch worn on wrist. **wrist'lèt,** *n.* band, bracelet, etc., worn round wrist.

writ (r-), *n.* formal written court order to do or refrain from doing specified act. *Holy Writ,* the Bible.

write (r-), *v.* (p.t. *wrŏte*; p.p. *written*), form symbol(s) representing letter(s) or word(s) with pen, pencil, brush, etc., esp. on paper, parchment, etc.; set down, express, in writing; write letter (to); be author or writer. *write off,* cancel debt, etc.; reckon as lost. **wri'ter,** *n.* one who writes books, articles, etc.; clerk. **wri'ting,** *n.* handwriting; (piece of) literary work. **wri'ting-paper,** paper for writing letters on.

writhe (rīdh), *v.* twist or roll oneself about (as) in pain; squirm.

wrong (r-), *a.* not morally right or equitable; not correct or proper; not true, mistaken; in error; not in good order; not what is required, intended, or expected. *n.* what is morally wrong; wrong action; injustice; being wrong. *v.t.* treat unjustly, do injustice to. **wrong'-doer,** offender. **wrong'doing,** transgression. **wrong'ful,** *a.* lacking justification; unlawful. **wrong'fully,** *adv.*

wroth (rō- *or* ro-), *a.* (*archaic*) angry.

wrought (rawt), *a.* worked, manufactured; (of metals) beaten out or shaped with hammer, etc., not cast. **wrought-up,** excited or agitated.

wrung, *p.t. & p.p.* of **wring.**

wrŷ (r-), *a.* distorted, turned to one side; contorted in disgust, etc.

X

X, x, as Roman numeral, 10.

xenophŏ'bia (z-), *n.* strong dislike of foreigners. **xen'ophŏbe,** *n.*

Xēr'ox (z-; *or* zār-), *n.* photo-electric copying process; copy thus produced. *v.t.* copy by Xerox. **P.**

X-ray (eks-), *n.* (pl.) electromagnetic radiations of very short wavelength capable of passing through extensive thickness of any body; (sing.) X-ray photograph. *v.t.* photograph, examine, treat, with X-rays. **X-ray photograph,** shadow-photograph, esp. of bodies impervious to light, made with X--rays.

xŷ'lophŏne (z-), *n.* musical instrument of graduated series of flat wooden bars played by striking with small wooden hammers.

Y

yacht (yot), *n.* light sailing vessel for racing; vessel used for private pleasure outings, cruising, etc. *v.i.* race or cruise in yacht. **yachts'man,** *n.* (pl. -*men*), one who yachts.

yak, *n.* large humped bovine animal of Tibet, etc.

yam, *n.* (edible starchy tuberous root of) any of various tropical twining plants.

yank, *n. & v.* (*slang*) (pull with) sudden sharp tug or jerk.

Yank'ee, *n.* (*informal*) native or inhabitant of (esp. northern) U.S.A.

yap, *n.* short shrill bark. *v.i.* (p.t. *yapped*), (esp. of small dog) utter yaps.

yard[1], *n.* unit of long measure (3 ft. or 36 in.); cubic yard of gravel, etc.; spar slung from mast to support and extend sail. **yard'stick,** stick as yard-measure; (fig.) standard of comparison. **yar'dage,** *n.* number of yards of material, etc.

yard[2], *n.* piece of (partly) enclosed ground, esp. attached to building(s); (U.S., etc.) garden.

yarn, *n.* fibre spun and prepared for weaving,

knitting, etc.; (*informal*) story, tale. *v.i.* tell yarns.

ya'rrow (-ō), *n.* common wild plant with flat clusters of composite flowers.

yash'mak, *n.* Muslim woman's veil concealing face below eyes.

yaw, *v.i.* (of ship or aircraft) deviate from straight course. *n.* yawing.

yawl, *n.* kind of sailing-boat; kind of fishing--boat; kind of ship's boat.

yawn, *v.i.* breathe in involuntarily with mouth wide open, as from drowsiness, boredom, etc.; gape, have wide opening. *n.* act of yawning.

yĕ, *pron.* (*archaic*) you.

yea (yā), *adv. & n.* (*archaic*) yes.

year (yer) *n.* time occupied by one revolution of earth round sun (about 365¼ days); period from January 1 to December 31 inclusive, any period of twelve months; (pl.) age (of person); (pl.) a very long time. **year'ling,** *n. & a.* (animal) a year old. **year'ly,** *a. & adv.* (occurring, done, etc.) once a year or every year, annual(ly).

yearn (yern), *v.i.* long; be moved with compassion or tenderness. **year'ning,** *n.* longing.

yeast, *n.* substance obtained esp. from fermenting malt liquors, and used as fermenting agent, in raising bread, etc. **yeas'ty,** *a.*

yell, *n.* sharp loud cry of strong and sudden emotion; shout of pain, anger, laughter, etc. *v.* make, utter with, yell(s).

yell'ow (-ō), *a.* of colour of gold, lemons, buttercups, etc.; (of newspaper, etc.) sensational; cowardly. *n.* yellow colour. *v.* turn yellow.

yelp, *n. & v.i.* (utter) shrill bark or cry (as) of dog in excitement, pain, etc.

yen¹, *n.* (pl. same) principal monetary unit of Japan.

yen², *n.* (U.S. *slang*) intense longing.

yeo'man (yō-), *n.* (pl. -*men*), (also *yeoman farmer*) man owning and farming small estate. *Yeomen of the Guard,* bodyguard of British sovereign, now acting chiefly as warders of Tower of London. *yeoman service,* long and efficient service. **yeo'manry,** *n.* (Hist.) volunteer cavalry force in British army.

yes, *adv.* particle expressing affirmative reply to question, request, etc. *n.* word, answer, *yes.*

yes'terday, *n. & adv.* (on) the day immediately preceding today. **yes'teryear,** *n.* (chiefly Poet.) last year, the recent past.

yet, *adv.* up to this or that time; at some time in the future; in addition; (with compar.) even, still. *as yet,* hitherto. *nor yet,* and also not. *not yet,* still not. *conj.* in spite of that, nevertheless.

yet'i, *n.* unidentified animal alleged to have been seen and to have left tracks in snow on high slopes of Himalayas, 'abominable snowman'

yew, *n.* dark-leaved evergreen coniferous tree or its wood.

Yidd'ish, *n.* form of German used by Jews in Europe and America.

yield, *v.* produce as fruit, profit, or result; surrender or submit (*to*); give way *to* persuasion, entreaty, etc., give consent; give way (*to*). *n.* amount yielded or produced.

yŏ'del, *v.* (p.t. *yodelled*), sing or warble with interchange of ordinary and falsetto voice in manner of mountain-dwellers of Switzerland, etc. *n.* yodelling cry.

Yō'ga, *n.* Hindu system of meditation, asceticism, etc., as means of attaining union with the universal spirit. **yō'gi** (-gi), *n.* devotee of Yoga.

yog(h)'urt (-gert), *n.* semi-solid food made from fermented milk.

yŏke, *n.* wooden neck-piece for coupling pair of draught oxen, etc.; pair *of* oxen, etc.; sway, dominion, servitude; wooden shoulder-piece for carrying pair of pails; upper part of garment from which the rest hangs. *v.t.* put yoke upon; couple, link (*together*).

yŏ'kel, *n.* (contempt.) country bumpkin.

yolk (yōk), *n.* yellow(ish) part of (esp. bird's) egg, serving as nourishment for young before hatching; corresponding part in ovum of other animals.

yon, *a.* (Sc. & north.) yonder.

yon'der, *adv. & a.* (situated) over there; at some distance (but within sight).

yore, *n. of yore,* in or of time long past.

York'shire pu'dding (-erpoo-), baked batter eaten with or before meat, esp. roast beef.

you (yōō, yoo), *pron.* (objective same), subjective case of 2nd pers. sing. (with pl. verb) and 2nd pers. pl. pronoun; the person(s) addressed; (in general statements) one, a person.

young (yu-), *a.* (*younger, youngest,* pr. -ngg-), that has lived, existed, etc., a relatively short time; recent, new; youthful. *n.* (*collective*) young ones of animals; young people. *with young,* pregnant. **young'ster,** *n.* young person, esp. young man; child, esp. boy.

your (ūr, yor), *pron. & a.* possessive case of **you** and corresponding adjective, with absolute form **yours. yourself', yourselves'** (-vz), *prons.* emphatic and reflexive forms of **you.**

youth (yōō-), *n.* (pl. pr. -dhz), being young; early part of life, esp. adolescence; young person, esp. young man; (*collective*) young people. **youth hostel,** place where young holiday-makers, etc., can stay the night. **youth'ful,** *a.*

yŏ'-yŏ, *n.* (pl. *yo-yos*), small thick double disc made to fall and rise as its weight causes unwinding and rewinding of string attached to its short axle.

yule (yōōl), *n.* (also *yule-tide*) festival of Christmas.

Z

zā'ny, *n.* buffoon, simpleton.

zeal, *n.* ardour, eagerness, in pursuit of an end or in favour of a person or cause. **zeal'ous** (zel-), *a.*

zeal'ot (zel-), *n.* fanatical enthusiast.

zē'bra (*or* ze-), *n.* African striped horse-like quadruped. **zebra crossing,** street-crossing with black and white stripes, on which pedestrians have precedence over traffic.

zē'bū, *n.* humped ox domesticated in India, etc.

zeitgeist (tsīt'gīst), *n.* spirit of the times, characteristic trend of thought, culture, etc., of a period. (German)

zena'na (-nah-), *n.* part of dwelling-house in which women of family are or were secluded in India, etc.

zen'ith, *n.* point of heavens directly overhead; highest point or state, culmination, acme.

zeph'yr (-er), *n.* west wind, esp. personified; mild gentle wind or breeze.

zepp'elin, *n.* (Hist.) large German airship.

zēr'ō, *n.* (pl. *zeros*), figure 0, nought, nil; point marked 0 on graduated scale, esp. in thermometer, etc.; lowest point, bottom of scale; nullity, nonentity. **zero-hour,** hour at which planned, esp. military, operation is timed to begin; crucial or decisive moment.

zest, *n.* piquancy; keen interest or enjoyment, relish, gusto.

Zeus (zūs), *n.* (Gk. myth.) chief of the gods, corresponding to Roman Jupiter.

zig'zag, *n.* line, course, etc., having abrupt turns to right and left alternately. *a.* having form of zigzag; turning abruptly in alternate directions. *adv.* in zigzag manner or course. *v.i.* (p.t. *zigzagged*), move in zigzag course.

zinc, *n.* hard bluish-white metal.

zinn'ia, *n.* composite garden plant with showy flowers.

Zī'on, *n.* hill in Jerusalem which became the centre of Jewish life and worship; the Jewish religion; the Christian Church; the Kingdom of Heaven. **Zī'onism,** *n.* movement resulting in re-establishment of a Jewish nation in Israel. **Zī'onist,** *n.* & *a.*

zip, *n.* light sharp sound as of tearing canvas, flying bullet, etc.; energy, force, impetus; zip-fastener. *v.* (p.t. *zipped*), close or fasten (*up*) with zip-fastener; move or go with sound of zip or with great rapidity. **zip-fastener,** fastening device of two flexible interlocking toothed strips and sliding clip pulled between them. **zipp'er,** *n.* zip-fastener.

zith'er, *n.* stringed musical instrument with flat box-like body, placed horizontally and plucked with plectrum and fingers.

zō'diac, *n.* belt of sky including all apparent positions of sun and planets as known to ancient astronomers, and divided into 12 equal parts (*signs of the zodiac*) named after 12 constellations formerly contained in them.

zōne, *n.* tract, region, part of town, etc., esp. one marked off from other parts for particular use or purpose; each of five encircling regions into which surface of earth is divided by tropics and polar circles. *v.t.* mark, encircle, with zone; divide into zones, esp. in town planning, etc. **zō'nal,** *a.*

zōo, *n.* zoological gardens.

zōolo'gical, *a.* of zoology. **zoological gardens,** park where wild animals are kept for exhibition.

zōol'ogy, *n.* scientific study of animals. **zōol'ogist,** *n.*

zōom, *v.* make, move with, loud low-pitched buzzing sound; make (aircraft) mount at high speed and steep angle; (of camera lens) make object appear progressively closer. *n.* act or action of zooming.

zō'ophyte, *n.* animal resembling plant or flower in form. **zōophyt'ic,** *a.*

Zulu (zōō'lōō), *n.* member, language, of a S. African Bantu people.

zȳ'gōte, *n.* (Biol.) fertilized ovum, cell arising from union of two gametes.

PREFIXES AND SUFFIXES

PREFIXES

A prefix is placed at the beginning of a word to alter its meaning or to form a new word. The following prefixes have entries in their alphabetical places in the dictionary:

a-, ab-, abs, ac-, ad-, aero-, af-, afore-, ag-, al-, ambi-, amphi-, an-, ana-, Anglo-, ante-, anti-, ap-, apo-, ar-, arch-, at-, audio-, auto-, be-, bene-, bi-, bio-, cat-, cata-, cath-, centi-, circum-, co-, col-, com-, con-, contra-, cor-, counter-, cryo-, de-, deca-, deci-, demi-, di-, dia-, dif-, dis-, dys-, e-, ef-, electro-, em-, en-, epi-, equi-, eu-, ex-, extra-, for-, fore-, geo-, haemo-, hecto-, helio-, hemi-, hemo-, hepta-, hetero-, hexa-, hippo-, homo-, hydro-, hyper-, hypo-, il-, im-, in-, infra-, inter-, intra-, intro-, kilo-, mal-, manu-, mega-, met(a)-, micro-, milli-, mini-, mis-, mono-, multi-, neo-, non-, ob-, oc-, oct-, octa-, octo-, of-, off-, omni-, on-, op-, ortho- osteo-, out-, over-, palaeo-, pan-, panto-, para-, penta-, per-, peri-, philo-, photo-, poly-, post-, pre-, preter-, pro-, proto, pseudo-, psycho-, quadr(i)-, quasi-, quinque-, radio-, re-, retro-, se-, self-, semi-, sept-, sex-, step-, stereo-, sub-, subter-, suc-, suf-, sug-, sum-, sup-, super-, supra-, sur-, sus-, syn-, tele-, tetra-, thermo-, trans-, tri-, ultra-, under-, uni-, up-, vice-, well-.

SUFFIXES

A suffix is placed at the end of a word to form a new word or to form the plural, past tense, comparative, etc.

-ability, forming nouns from adjectives in **-able.**

-able, -ible, -ble, (-uble), forming adjectives: that can, may, must, be —*d*; that can be made the subject of; that is relevant to or in accordance with.

-aceous, forming adjectives: of the nature of.

-acious, forming adjectives: full of, inclined to.

-acity, forming nouns corresponding to adjectives in **-acious.**

-acy, forming nouns of quality, state, or condition.

-ade, forming nouns: action done; body concerned; product of material or action.

-age, forming nouns: aggregate of; function, condition; action; charge for (using); product of action.

-al, forming adjectives (some also used as nouns): of the kind of; relating to; also forming nouns of action.

-an, forming adjectives (often used as nouns): of or belonging to.

-ana, forming plural nouns: anecdotes, publications, or other items concerning (person, place, period, etc.).

-ance, -ence, forming nouns of quality, state, or action.

-ancy, -ency, forming nouns of quality or state.

-ane, forming adjectives (often showing differentiation of meaning when a similar adjective exists in **-an).**

-aneous, forming adjectives: belonging to.

-ant, -ent, forming nouns denoting agent, thing producing effect; also forming adjectives.

-ar, forming adjectives: belonging to, of the nature of; also forming nouns denoting agent.

-ard, (-art), forming nouns, often implying disapproval or blame.

-arian, forming nouns and adjectives denoting age, membership of sect, etc.

-ary, forming adjectives: of or relating to; of the nature of; also forming nouns.

-ate^1, forming nouns: office; state or function; group; product; also in Chem. use.

-ate^2, forming adjectives (some also used as nouns): acted upon (in such way); brought into, being in, (such state); also forming adjectives: having, provided with.

-ate^3, forming verbs: act, act upon, (in such way); cause to be affected by; cause to become; provide with.

-atic, forming adjectives and nouns.

-ation, forming nouns: action of verb; instance of this; resulting state; resulting thing.

-ative, forming adjectives (some also used as nouns): of the nature of; connected with; tending to.

-bility, forming nouns from adjectives in **-ble.**

-ble: see **-able.**

-cide

363

-logical

-cide, forming nouns: killing of, killer of.

-cle: see **-cule.**

-cracy, forming nouns: rule of, ruling body or class of.

-craft, forming nouns: art or skill of.

-crat, forming nouns: member of —**cracy.**

-cule, -cle, forming diminutives.

-cy, forming nouns denoting action, function, state, condition.

-dom, forming nouns denoting rank, office, domain, condition, state.

-ed, forming p.t. and p.p. of weak verbs; also forming adjectives: having, possessed of.

-ee, forming nouns denoting person affected by action of verb.

-eer, forming nouns: person concerned with or dealing with.

-el, forming diminutives.

-en¹, forming adjectives: made of.

-en², forming verbs: cause to be or to have; become.

-ence, -ency: see **-ance, -ancy.**

-ent: see **-ant.**

-er¹, forming nouns denoting agent.

-er², forming comparatives of adjectives and adverbs.

-ery, -ry, forming nouns: condition; occupation; place of work; class of goods.

-esce, forming verbs denoting beginning of action.

-escent, forming adjectives: beginning, beginning to be; slightly.

-ese, forming adjectives: of or belonging to; also forming nouns: inhabitant; language.

-esque, forming adjectives: in the style of.

-ess, forming feminine nouns.

-est, forming superlatives of adjectives and adverbs.

-ette, forming diminutives.

-faction, forming nouns of action related to verbs ending in **-fy.**

-ferous, forming adjectives: bearing, having.

-fic, forming adjectives: making, causing.

-fication, forming nouns of action from verbs in **-fy.**

-fold, forming adjectives and adverbs: multiplied by.

-ful, forming adjectives: full of; having qualities of; also forming nouns: amount required to fill.

-fy, forming verbs: make; bring into (such) state.

-gen, forming nouns in scientific use: that which produces; something produced.

-gon, forming nouns: having (so many) angles (and sides).

-gram, forming nouns: something written.

-graph, forming nouns: something that records; something written or recorded.

-graphy, forming nouns: descriptive science; style of graphic representation.

-hood, forming nouns of condition, state, or quality.

-ian, forming adjectives and nouns; esp. forming adjectives (often used as nouns) from proper names.

-ibility, forming nouns from adjectives in **-ible.**

-ible: see **able.**

-ic, forming adjectives (some also used as nouns): of or relating to, of the nature of, in the style of; also forming Chem. adjectives; also forming nouns denoting arts, systems of thought, etc., and (usu. in pl. **-ics,** but often taking sing. verb) sciences.

-ical, forming adjectives from nouns in **-ic;** also forming adjectives parallel to adjectives in **-ic,** often with wider or different meaning.

-ice, forming abstract nouns.

-ician, forming nouns: person skilled in.

-icity, forming abstract nouns from adjectives in **-ic.**

-ide, forming Chem. nouns.

-ie: see **-y³.**

-ine, forming adjectives: of or relating to; of the nature of; also forming nouns (including some Chem. terms).

-ing¹, forming nouns, esp. of action, from verbs.

-ing², forming pres. participles (also participial adjectives) of verbs.

-ion, -tion, -sion, (-xion), forming nouns of condition and action.

-ious, forming adjectives: characterized by; full of.

-ise¹: see **-ize.**

-ise², forming nouns.

-ish, forming adjectives: somewhat; belonging to, of the nature of.

-ism, forming abstract nouns denoting action, conduct, system or principle, or condition.

-ist, forming nouns denoting agent, adherent of creed, practiser of profession, art, etc.

-ite, forming adjectives and nouns: (member) of; forming names of minerals, etc.; also in Chem. use.

-ition, forming nouns of action and condition.

-itious, forming adjectives: characterized by; full of.

-itis, forming nouns: inflammation of.

-ive, forming adjectives: tending to; having the nature of.

-ize, -ise, forming verbs: bring or come into (such state); make; treat like; charge, treat, or affect with.

-kin, forming diminutives.

-less, forming adjectives: devoid of, free from; unable to.

-let, forming diminutives.

-like, forming adjectives: having the characteristics of.

-ling, forming nouns: person concerned with; also forming diminutives (sometimes in unfavourable sense).

-lite, forming names of minerals; also in Chem. use.

-logical, forming adjectives from nouns in **-logy.**

-logist, forming nouns: expert in, student of.

-logy, forming nouns denoting names of sciences or departments of study.

-ly¹, forming adverbs from adjectives, denoting manner.

-ly², forming adjectives: having the qualities of; also denoting recurrence.

-ment, forming nouns expressing result or means of verbal action.

-most, forming superlative adjectives.

-ness, forming nouns from adjectives, participles, etc., expressing state, condition, or degree.

-oid, forming adjectives and nouns: (thing) having the form of, resembling.

-ol, forming Chem. nouns.

-or, forming nouns denoting agent.

-ory, forming adjectives: of the nature of; serving as.

-ose, forming adjectives: full of.

-osis, forming nouns of process or condition.

-osity, forming nouns from adjectives in **-ose** (or **-ous**).

-ous, forming adjectives: abounding in; characterized by; of the nature of; also forming Chem. adjectives.

-pathy, forming nouns: suffering, feeling; also with sense of curative treatment.

-phil, forming nouns and adjectives: (person who is) fond of.

-phobe, forming nouns and adjectives: (person) fearing or disliking.

-phobia, forming nouns: fear or strong dislike of.

-ry: see **-ery.**

-ship, forming nouns denoting state or condition, status, (tenure of) office, skill.

-sion: see **-ion.**

-some, forming adjectives denoting quality, condition, or tendency.

-t, variant of **-ed** in p.t. and p.p. of some verbs.

-teen, inflected form of ten added to (combining forms of) 3-9 to form 13-19.

-th¹, forming nouns of action or state, quality or condition.

-th², forming ordinal numerals.

-tion: see **-ion.**

-tomy, forming nouns: cutting.

-tude, forming nouns denoting quality or state.

-ty¹, forming nouns of quality, condition, or degree.

-ty², forming numerals: tens.

-uble, rare form of **-ble.**

-ule, forming diminutives.

-ure, forming nouns: (result of) action or process; function, rank; collective body.

-vore, forming nouns: eater of, feeder on.

-vorous, forming adjectives: feeding on, eating.

-ward, forming adverbs and adjectives denoting direction.

-wards, forming adverbs denoting direction.

-ways, forming adverbs denoting direction or manner.

-wise, forming adverbs: in (such) manner, way, or respect; in (such) direction.

-xion: see **-ion.**

-y¹, *a.* forming adjectives: having the character of; full of; covered with; resembling; tending towards.

-y², forming nouns: state, condition, quality; (result of) an activity; body, group, etc.

-y³, -ie, forming diminutives, pet-names, etc.

APPENDIX II

ADJECTIVES RELATING TO SOME GEOGRAPHICAL AND OTHER PROPER NOUNS

Aberdō′nian, of Aberdeen.
Abyssin′ian, of Abyssinia (now *Ethiopia*).
Af′ghan (-gan), of Afghanistan.
African: see the dictionary.
Albā′nian, of Albania.
Algēr′ian, of Algeria.
Alsā′tian (-shn), of Alsace.
American: see the dictionary.
Ando′rran, of Andorra.
Angolese (anggolĕz′), of Angola.
Arab, Arabian, Arabic: see the dictionary.
Argentin′ian, of the Argentine (*Argentina*).
Asian, Asiatic: see the dictionary.
Athē′nian, of ancient or modern Athens.
Atlan′tic, of the Atlantic Ocean.
Australian: see the dictionary.
Aus′trian, of Austria.

Baha′mian (-hah- *or* -hā-), of the Bahama Islands.
Balinese′ (bah-; -z), of Bali.
Bal′kan (bawl- *or* bol-) of the Balkans.
Bal′tic (bawl- *or* bol-), of the Baltic Sea.
Barbā′dian, of Barbados.
Bel′gian (-jn), of Belgium.
Bengali (benggaw′li), of Bengal.
Bermū′dian, of Bermuda.
Bhutanese (bōōtanĕz′), of Bhutan.
Boliv′ian, of Bolivia.
Brazil′ian, of Brazil.
Bret′on, of Brittany.
British: see the dictionary.
Bulgār′ian, of Bulgaria.
Burmēse′ (-z), of Burma.
Burun′dian (boo-roo-), of Burundi.

Cambō′dian, of Cambodia.
Cameroo′nian, of Cameroon.
Canadian: see the dictionary.
Cantabrigian: see the dictionary.
Caribbē′an (ka-), of the southern West Indian islands or the Caribbean Sea.
Chad′ian, of Chad.
Chil′ĕan, of Chile.
Chinese: see the dictionary.
Colom′bian, of Colombia.
Congolēse′ (-z), of the Congo.
Cor′nish, of Cornwall.
Cos′ta Ri′can (-rĕ-), of Costa Rica.
Crē′tan, of Crete.
Crimē′an, of the Crimea.
Cū′ban, of Cuba.
Cyp′rian, Cyp′riot, of Cyprus.
Czech (chek), **Czechoslō′vak, Czecho-slova′kian** (-vah-), of Czechoslovakia.

Danish: see the dictionary.
Domin′ican, of the Dominican Republic.
Dutch: see the dictionary.

Ecuador′ian (ekwa-), of Ecuador.
Edwardian: see the dictionary.
Egyptian: see the dictionary.
English: see the dictionary.
Estō′nian, of Estonia.
Ethiō′pian (ē-), of Ethiopia (formerly *Abyssinia*).
European: see the dictionary.

Fārōēse′ (-z), of the Faroe Islands.
Fijian (fējē′an), of Fiji.
Filipi′nō (-pē-), of the Filipinos or the Philippines.
Finn′ish, of Finland.
Flemish: see the dictionary.
Flo′rentine, of Florence.
Formō′san (-z-), of Formosa (*Taiwan*).
French: see the dictionary.

Gabonēse (-z), of Gaboon (*Gabon*).
Gam′bian, of the **Gambia.**
Georgian: see the dictionary.
German: see the dictionary.
Ghanaian (gahnā′an), of Ghana.
Gibraltār′ian (-awl- *or* -ol-), of Gibraltar.
Glaswē′gian (-jn), of Glasgow.
Greek: see the dictionary.
Guatama′lan (gwahtamah-), of Guatamala.
Guin′ĕan (gin-), of Guinea.
Guyanēse (gīanĕz′), of Guyana.

Hai′tian (-shn; *or* hī-), of Haiti.
Hawai′ian (-wī′an), of Hawaii.
Hebridē′an, of the Hebrides.
Hebraic, Hebrew: see the dictionary.
Helvē′tian (-shn), Swiss.
Himalay′an (*or* himah′-), of the Himalayas.
Hondūr′an, Hondūr′ĕan, of Honduras.
Hungār′ian, of Hungary.

Icelan′dic (īsl-), of Iceland.
Indian: see the dictionary.
Indonē′sian (i-; -zian *or* -zhn), of Indonesia.
Irā′nian (i-), of Iran (*Persia*).
Iraqi (i-rah′ki), of Iraq.
Irish: see the dictionary.
Israeli, Israelite: see the dictionary.
Italian: see the dictionary.

Jamai′can, of Jamaica.
Japanese: see the dictionary.
Javanēse′ (jah-; -z), of Java.

Johnsō'nian (jon-), of Dr. Samuel Johnson.
Jordā'nian, of Jordan.

Kashmir'i (-mēr'i), of Kashmir (*Jammu and Kashmir*).
Ken'tish, of Kent.
Ken'yan (*or* kē-), of Kenya.
Korē'an, of Korea.
Kuwai'ti (-wī-), of Kuwait.

Laotian (low'shn), of Laos.
Lat'vian, of Latvia.
Lebanēse' (-z), of the Lebanon.
Levantine: see the dictionary.
Lībēr'ian, of Liberia.
Lib'yan, of Libya.
Lithūā'nian, of Lithuania.
Liverpud'lian, of Liverpool.

Malagas'y, of Madagascar (*Malagasy Republic*).
Malay', Malay'an, of the Malays or their language.
Malay'sian (-zi-; *or* -shn), of Malaysia.
Maltēse' (-awl- *or* -ol-; -z), of Malta.
Mancū'nian, of Manchester.
Manx, of the Isle of Man.
Mauri'tian (mori'shn), of Mauritius.
Mediterranean: see the dictionary.
Mex'ican, of Mexico.
Monegasque' (-sk), of Monaco.
Mongolian: see the dictionary.
Morocc'an, of Morocco.

Napōlēon'ic, of Napoleon Bonaparte.
Nepalēse' (-z), of Nepal.
Neth'erlands (-dh-; -z), of the Netherlands (*Holland*), Dutch.
Nicarag'ūan, of Nicaragua.
Nigēr'ian, of Nigeria.
Norman: see the dictionary.
Norwē'gian (-jn), of Norway.
Nōvōcas'trian, of Newcastle upon Tyne.

Oma'ni (-mah-), of Oman.
Orcā'dian, of the Orkney Islands.
Oxonian: see the dictionary.

Pacif'ic, of the Pacific Ocean.
Pakistani (pahkistah'ni), of Pakistan.
Palestin'ian, of Palestine.
Panamā'nian, of Panama.
Pap'ūan, of Papua New Guinea.
Paraguày'an (pa-; -gwai- *or* -gwī-), of Paraguay.
Paris'ian (pa-; -z-), of Paris.
Persian: see the dictionary.
Peru'vian (-roō-), of Peru.
Phil'ippīne, of the Philippines, Filipino.
Pō'lish, of Poland.
Portūguēse' (-gēz), of Portugal.
Puer'tō Ri'can (pwer-; rē-), of Puerto Rico.

Rhodē'sian (rō-; -zhn *or* -shn) of Rhodesia.
Roman: see the dictionary.
Rumā'nian (roō-), **Romā'nian,** of Rumania.

Russian: see the dictionary.

Sahar'an (sa-), of the Sahara.
Salvador'ēan, of El Salvador.
Samō'an, of Samoa.
Sau'di Arā'bian (sa-oō'di a-r-), of Saudi Arabia.
Scandinavian: see the dictionary.
Scillō'nian, of the Isles of Scilly.
Scotch, Scots, Scottish: see the dictionary.
Senēgalēse' (-z), of Senegal.
Shākespear'ian (-kspēr-), of William Shakespeare.
Shā'vian, of George Bernard Shaw.
Siamese: see the dictionary.
Sibēr'ian, of Siberia.
Sicil'ian, of Sicily.
Sie'rra Lēō'nèan (si-e-), of Sierra Leone.
Singapor'ēan (-ngg-), of Singapore.
Sinhalēse' (-z), of Sri Lanka (formerly *Ceylon*).
Sino-Japanēse' (-z), of China and Japan.
Soma li (-ah-), of Somalia.
South Af'rican, of the Republic of South Africa.
Soviet: see the dictionary.
Spanish: see the dictionary.
Spartan: see the dictionary.
Sudanēse' (soō-; -z), of the Sudan.
Swa'zi (swah-), of Swaziland.
Swedish: see the dictionary.
Swiss: see the dictionary.
Sy'rian, of Syria.

Tahi'tian (-hē'shn), of Tahiti.
Taiwanese (tīwanēz'), of Taiwan.
Tanzani'an (-nē-; *or* -zā'nian), of Tanzania.
Tasmā'nian (-z-), of Tasmania.
Thai (tī), of Thailand (formerly *Siam*).
Tibet'an, of Tibet.
Tōgolēse' (-z), of Togo.
Tong'an (-ngg-), of Tonga (the *Tongan* or *Friendly Islands*).
Trinidā'dian, of Trinidad (*Trinidad and Tobago*).
Tūnis'ian (-z-), of Tunisia.
Turkish: see the dictionary.
Tyrolē'an, Tyrolēse' (ti-;-z), of the Tyrol.

Ugan'dan (ū-), of Uganda.
Ukrai'nian (ū-), of the Ukraine.
Uruguayan (ūroogwī'an), of Uruguay.

Venetian: see the dictionary.
Venèzue'lan (-zwä-), of Venezuela.
Victorian: see the dictionary.
Vietnamēse' (vi-et-; -z), of Vietnam.

Welsh: see the dictionary.
West In'dian, of the West Indies.

Yem'éni, Yem'énite, of Yemen.
Yugoslav' (-slahv), **Yugosla'vian,** of Yugoslavia.

Zaï'rian (zah-ēī'-), of Zaïre.
Zam'bian, of Zambia.

SOME ABBREVIATIONS IN GENERAL USE

A list of *Abbreviations used in the Dictionary* is on pages viii and ix.

In this Appendix foreign words are printed in italics, and the English meaning follows.

Many of the abbreviations given here with the full stop are also used without it.

A., Associate of; answer; ampere(s); Advanced (level of G.C.E.).

A.A., Automobile Association; anti-aircraft; Alcoholics Anonymous.

A.A.A., Amateur Athletic Association.

A.B., able rating or seaman.

A.B.M., anti-ballistic-missile missile.

A.C., a.c., alternating current.

a/c, account.

A.D.: see **Anno Domini** in the dictionary.

A.D.C., aide-de-camp.

A.F.C., Air Force Cross.

A.F.M., Air Force Medal.

a.m., *ante meridiem* (Latin), before noon.

A.S.A., Amateur Swimming Association.

Asdic, Anti-submarine Detection Investigation Committee: see **asdic** in the dictionary.

Assoc., Association.

Asst., Assistant.

A.V., Authorized Version (of the Bible).

Ave., Avenue.

A.W.O.L., absent without leave.

B., Bachelor; *Beatus*, *Beata* (Latin), Blessed; black (of pencil lead).

b., born; bowled by; bye.

B.A., Bachelor of Arts; British Academy.

B.A.O.R., British Army of the Rhine.

Bart., Baronet.

B.B.C., British Broadcasting Corporation.

B.C., before Christ.

B.Ch.: see **Ch.B.**

B.D., Bachelor of Divinity.

B.Ed., Bachelor of Education.

B.E.M., British Empire Medal.

bk., book.

B.M., Bachelor of Medicine; British Museum.

B.M.A., British Medical Association.

B.Mus., Bachelor of Music.

B.O., body odour.

B.P., boiling-point; British Pharmacopoeia.

Bp., Bishop.

B.R., British Rail.

B.R.C.S., British Red Cross Society.

B.S., Bachelor of Surgery.

B.Sc., Bachelor of Science.

B.S.I., British Standards Institution.

B.S.T., British Standard Time; British Summer Time.

Bt., Baronet.

B.V.M., Blessed Virgin Mary.

C., Celsius, Centigrade; Conservative.

c., caught by; century; cubic; *circa* (Latin), about.

ca., *circa* (Latin), about.

C.A.B., Citizens' Advice Bureau.

Cantab., Cantabrigian: see the dictionary.

CAT, College of Advanced Technology.

C.B., Companion of (the Order of) the Bath.

C.B.E., Commander of (the Order of) the British Empire.

C.B.I., Confederation of British Industry.

C.C., County Council.

c.c., cubic centimetre(s).

C.C.F., Combined Cadet Force.

cent., century.

C.E.N.T.O., Cento, Central Treaty Organization.

cf., *confer* (Latin), compare.

C.G.M., Conspicuous Gallantry Medal.

C.G.S., Chief of General Staff; (usu. **c.g.s.**) centimetre-gram-second.

C.H., Companion of Honour.

ch., chapter.

Ch.B., B.Ch., *Chirurgiae Baccalaureus* (Latin), Bachelor of Surgery.

C.I.D., Criminal Investigation Department.

C.-in-c., Commander-in-chief.

cl., centilitre(s); class.

cm., centimetre(s).

C.M.G., Companion of (the Order of) St. Michael and St. George.

C.N.D., Campaign for Nuclear Disarmament.

C.O., Commanding Officer; conscientious objector.

Co., Company; County.

c/o, care of.

C.O.D., cash on delivery; Concise Oxford Dictionary.

C. of E., Church of England.

C.P.R.E., Council for the Protection of Rural England.

Cr., creditor.

C.S.E., Certificate of Secondary Education.

cu., cubic.

C.U.P., Cambridge University Press.

C.V.O., Commander of the Royal Victorian Order.

d., daughter; died; *denarius, denarii* (Latin) (old) penny, pence.

D.B.E., Dame Commander of (the Order of) the British Empire.

D.C., d.c., direct current.

D.C.B., Dame Commander of (the Order of) the Bath.

D.C.L., Doctor of Civil Law.

D.C.M., Distinguished Conduct Medal.

D.C.M.G., Dame Commander of (the Order of) St. Michael and St. George.

D.C.V.O., Dame Commander of the Royal Victorian Order.

D.D., Doctor of Divinity.

D.D.T., dichlor-diphenyl-trichlorethane (insecticide).

D.F.C., Distinguished Flying Cross.

D.F.M., Distinguished Flying Medal.

D.G., *Dei gratia* (Latin), by the grace of God.

D.I.Y., do-it-yourself.

dl., decilitre(s).

D.Litt., *Doctor Litterarum* (Latin), Doctor of Letters.

D.M., Doctor of Medicine.

D.Mus., Doctor of Music.

DNA, deoxyribonucleic acid.

D.N.B., Dictionary of National Biography.

Do., do., ditto.

D.O.E., Department of the Environment.

D.P.H. Diploma in Public Health.

D.Phil., Doctor of Philosophy.

D.P.M., Diploma in Psychological Medicine.

Dr., debtor; Doctor.

D.Sc., Doctor of Science.

D.S.C., Distinguished Service Cross.

D.S.M., Distinguished Service Medal.

D.S.O., Distinguished Service Order.

D.V., *Deo volente* (Latin), God willing.

E., East; engineering.

Econ., Economics.

E.C.S.C., European Coal and Steel Community.

E.E.C., European Economic Community (the Common Market).

E.F.T.A., European Free Trade Association.

e.m.f., electromotive force.

E.N.T., Ear, Nose, and Throat.

E.P.N.S., electroplated nickel silver.

E.R., *Elizabetha Regina* (Latin), Queen Elizabeth.

E.S.N., educationally subnormal.

E.S.P., extrasensory perception.

Esq., Esquire.

E.T.A., e.t.a., estimated time of arrival.

et seq., *et sequentia* (Latin), and what follows.

EURATOM, Euratom, European Atomic Energy Community.

F., Fahrenheit; Fellow of.

f., female; feminine; from; *forte* (Italian), loud(ly).

F.A., Football Association.

F.A.O., Food and Agriculture Organization (of the United Nations).

F.B.A., Fellow of the British Academy.

F.D., *Fidei Defensor* (Latin), Defender of the Faith.

ff, *fortissimo* (Italian), very loud(ly).

fl., *floruit* (Latin), flourished.

F.M., f.m., frequency modulation.

F.P., freezing-point.

F.R.S., Fellow of the Royal Society.

g., gram(s); (acceleration due to) gravity.

GATT, General Agreement on Tariffs and Trade.

G.B. Great Britain.

G.B.E., Dame *or* Knight Grand Cross of (the Order of) the British Empire.

G.C., George Cross.

G.C.B., Dame *or* Knight Grand Cross of (the Order of) the Bath.

G.C.E., General Certificate of Education.

G.C.M.G., Dame *or* Knight Grand Cross of (the Order of) St. Michael and St. George.

G.C.V.O., Dame *or* Knight Grand Cross of the Royal Victorian Order.

G.H.Q., General Headquarters.

G.I., (U.S.) government (*or* general) issue: see also the dictionary.

G.L.C., Greater London Council.

G.M., George Medal.

G.M.C., General Medical Council.

G.M.T., Greenwich Mean Time.

G.N.P., gross national product.

G.O.C., General Officer Commanding.

G.P., general practitioner.

H., hard (of pencil lead); hospital.

h., hour(s).

h. and c., hot and cold (water).

HB, hard and black (of pencil lead).

H.C.F., highest common factor.

H.E., His Excellency; His Eminence; high explosive.

H.F., h.f., high frequency.

H.M., Her (His) Majesty('s).

H.M.I.(S.), Her (His) Majesty's Inspector (of Schools).

H.M.S., Her (His) Majesty's ship.

H.M.S.O., Her (His) Majesty's Stationery Office.

H.N.C., Higher National Certificate.

H.N.D., Higher National Diploma.

Hon., honorary; Honourable.

h.p., hire purchase; horsepower.

H.Q., headquarters.

H.R.H., His (Her) Royal Highness.

H.T., h.t., high tension.

Hz, hertz.

I., Island(s); Isle.

I.A.T.A., International Air Transport Association.

ib., ibid., *ibidem* (Latin), in the same book, passage, etc.

I.B.A., Independent Broadcasting Authority.
I.C.B.M., intercontinental ballistic missile.
id., *idem* (Latin), the same author, etc.
IHS, (abbrev. of Greek word for) Jesus.
I.L.O., International Labour Organization.
I.M.F., International Monetary Fund.
Ind., Independent; India(n).
inst., instant: see the dictionary.
IOU, I owe you: see the dictionary.
I.Q., intelligence quotient.
I.R.A, Irish Republican Army.
I.S.O., Imperial Service Order.
i.t.a., initial teaching alphabet.
I.T.V., independent television.

J.P., Justice of the Peace.
Jr., Jun., Junr., junior.

K.B.E., K.C.B., K.C.M.G., K.C.V.O., Knight Commander of (the Order of) the British Empire, the Bath, St. Michael and St. George, of the Royal Victorian Order.
kg., kilogram(s).
km., kilometre(s).
K.O., knock-out.
Kt., Knight.

L., Latin; learner; left; Linnaeus; Liberal; Licentiate in.
l., left; line; litre(s).
£, *libra(e)* (Latin), pound(s) (in money).
Lab., Labour.
Lat., Latin.
lat., latitude.
lb., *libra(e)* (Latin), pound(s) (in weight).
l.b.w., leg before wicket.
L.C.M., lowest common multiple.
L.D.S., Licentiate in Dental Surgery.
L.E.A., Local Education Authority.
Lib., Liberal.
Litt.D., Doctor of Letters.
ll., lines.
Ll.B., Ll.D., Bachelor, Doctor, of Laws.
log., logarithm.
long., longitude.
L.P., long-playing (of gramophone record, etc.).
LSD, lysergic acid diethylamide (hallucinogenic drug).
L.S.D., £. s. d., (Hist.) pounds, shillings, and pence.
L.T., l.t., low tension.
L.T.A., Lawn Tennis Association.
Ltd., Limited.
LV, luncheon voucher.

M., motorway; member of; *Monsieur* (French), Mr.
m., male; masculine; married; metre(s); mile(s); minute(s); million(s).
M.A., Master of Arts.
M.B., Bachelor of Medicine.
M.B.E., Member (of the Order) of the British Empire.

M.C., Military Cross; Master of Ceremonies.
M.C.C., Marylebone Cricket Club.
M.D., Doctor of Medicine; mentally deficient.
M.F.H., Master of Foxhounds.
mg., milligram(s).
ml., millilitre(s).
Mlle., *Mademoiselle* (French), Miss.
MM., *Messieurs* (French), Messrs.
M.M., Military Medal.
mm., millimetre(s).
Mme., *Madame* (French), Mrs.
M.O., Medical Officer.
M.O.H., Medical Officer of Health.
M.P., Member of Parliament; Military Police.
m.p.g., miles per gallon.
m.p.h., miles per hour.
M.P.S., Member of the Pharmaceutical Society.
MS., manuscript.
M.Sc., Master of Science.
MSS., manuscripts.
M.T.B., motor torpedo-boat.
Mus. B(ac)., Bachelor of Music.
Mus. D(oc)., Doctor of Music.
M.V., motor vessel.

N., North.
NAAFI, Naafi, Navy, Army, and Air Force Institutes.
NASA, (U.S.) National Aeronautics and Space Administration.
NATO, Nato, North Atlantic Treaty Organization.
N.B., *nota bene* (Latin), note well.
N.C.B., National Coal Board.
N.C.O., non-commissioned officer.
N.E.B., New English Bible.
N.H.S., National Health Service.
N.I., National Insurance.
No., Nos., number, numbers.
nr., near.
N.S.B., National Savings Bank.
N.S.P.C.C., National Society for the Prevention of Cruelty to Children.
N.T., New Testament.
N.U.S., National Union of Students.
N.Y., New York.
N.Z., New Zealand.

O., ordinary (level of G.C.E.)
O.B.E., Officer of (the Order of) the British Empire.
O.C., Officer Commanding.
OCTU, Octu, Officer Cadets Training Unit.
O.E.D., Oxford English Dictionary.
O.H.M.S., On Her (His) Majesty's Service.
O.M., (member of the) Order of Merit.
O.N.C., Ordinary National Certificate.
O.N.D., Ordinary National Diploma.
O.T., Old Testament; occupational therapy.
O.U.P., Oxford University Press.
Oxfam, Oxford Committee for Famine Relief.

Oxon., Oxford University; Oxfordshire.

P., parking(-place).

p., pence, penny; page; participle; past; *piano* (Italian), soft(ly).

p. and p., postage and packing.

P.A.Y.E., Pay-as-you-earn.

P.C., Police Constable; postcard.

p.c., per cent; postcard.

P.D.S.A., People's Dispensary for Sick Animals.

P.E., physical education.

P.E.N., (International Association of) Poets, Playwrights, Editors, Essayists, and Novelists.

per pro., *per procurationem* (Latin), by proxy.

P.G., paying guest.

Ph.D., Doctor of Philosophy.

P.M., Prime Minister.

p.m., *post meridiem* (Latin) after noon; post--mortem.

P.N.E.U., Parents' National Educational Union.

P.O., Post Office; postal order.

P.O.P., Post Office preferred (envelope size).

P.O.W., prisoner of war.

pp., pages; *pianissimo* (Italian), very soft(ly).

P.P.S., *post-postscriptum* (Latin), further postscript.

prox., proximo: see the dictionary.

P.S., postscript.

P.T.O., please turn over.

Q., question.

Q.C., Queen's Counsel.

Q.E.D., *quod erat demonstrandum* (Latin), which was to be proved.

q.v., *quod vide* (Latin), which see.

R., *Regina, Rex* (Latin), Queen, King; right; River; Railway.

r., right.

R.A., Royal Academician; Royal Academy; Royal Artillery.

R.A.C., Royal Automobile Club.

R.A.D.A., Royal Academy of Dramatic Art.

R.A.F., Royal Air Force.

R.A.M., Royal Academy of Music.

R.B.A., **R.B.S.**, Royal Society of British Artists, of British Sculptors.

R.C., Roman Catholic; Red Cross.

R.C.A., Royal College of Art.

R.C.M., Royal College of Music.

R.C.O., Royal College of Organists.

R.C.O.G., Royal College of Obstetricians and Gynaecologists.

R.C.P., Royal College of Physicians.

R.C.S., Royal College of Surgeons.

Rd., Road.

ref., reference.

ret., **retd.**, retired.

Revd., Reverend.

R.G.S., Royal Geographical Society.

R.H.S., Royal Horticultural Society.

R.I.B.A., Royal Institute of British Architects.

R.I.P., *requiesca(n)t in pace* (Latin), may he, she, (they), rest in peace.

R.M., Royal Marines; Royal Mail.

R.N., Royal Navy.

RNA, ribonucleic acid.

R.N.L.I., Royal National Lifeboat Institution.

r.p.m., revolutions per minute.

R.R.C., (Lady of the) Royal Red Cross.

R.S.A., Royal Scottish Academician, Academy; Royal Society of Arts.

R.S.P.C.A., Royal Society for the Prevention of Cruelty to Animals.

R.S.V.P., *répondez s'il vous plaît* (French), please answer.

Rt. Hon., Right Honourable.

Rt. Revd., Right Reverend.

R.V., Revised Version (of the Bible).

S., Saint; South.

s., second(s); singular; son; shilling.

S.A., Salvation Army; South Africa.

s.a.e., stamped addressed envelope.

S.A.Y.E., Save-as-you-earn.

Sc.D., Doctor of Science.

S.C.F., Save the Children Fund.

S.C.M., State Certified Midwife; Student Christian Movement.

S.E.A.T.O., **Seato**, South-east Asia Treaty Organization.

Sec., secretary.

sec., second.

S.O.S.: see the dictionary.

sq., square.

S.R.N., State Registered Nurse.

SS., Saints.

S.S., steamship.

S.S.A.F.A., Soldiers', Sailors', and Airmen's Families Association.

St., Saint; Street.

st., stone(s) (in weight).

STD, subscriber trunk dialling.

s.v., *sub voce* (Latin), under the word.

t., ton(s).

T. & A.V.R., Territorial and Army Volunteer Reserve.

T.B., tuberculosis.

T.N.T., trinitrotoluene (high explosive).

T.O., turn over.

T.R.H., Their Royal Highnesses.

T.T., teetotal(ler); Tourist Trophy; tuberculin-tested.

T.U., Trade Union.

T.U.C., Trades Union Congress.

TV, T.V., television.

U.D.I., Unilateral Declaration of Independence.

U.F.O., unidentified flying object.

U.K., United Kingdom.

ult., ultimo: see the dictionary.
U.N., United Nations.
UNESCO, Unesco, United Nations Educational, Scientific, and Cultural Organization.
U.N.I.C.E.F., Unicef, United Nations International Children's Emergency Fund.
U.P.U., Universal Postal Union.
U.S., United States (of America).
U.S.A., United States of America.
U.S.S.R.: see the dictionary.

V, volt(s).
v., verb; verse; versus; volt(s).
V.A.T., Value Added Tax.
V. & A., Victoria and Albert Museum.
V.C., Victoria Cross.
V.D., venereal disease.
V.H.F., very high frequency.
V.I.P., very important person.
V.O., (Royal) Victorian Order.
vol., volume.

V.S.O., Voluntary Service Overseas.

W., West; watt(s).
w., wife; with; watt(s).
W.C., w.c., water-closet.
W.E.A., Workers' Educational Association.
W.H.O., World Health Organization.
W.I., West Indies; Women's Institute.
W.P., weather permitting.
W.R.A.C., Women's Royal Army Corps.
W.R.A.F., Women's Royal Air Force.
W.R.N.S., Women's Royal Naval Service.
W.R.V.S., Women's Royal Voluntary Service.

Y.H.A., Youth Hostels Association.
Y.M.C.A., Young Men's Christian Association.
yr., yrs., year, years; your, yours.
Y.W.C.A., Young Women's Christian Association.